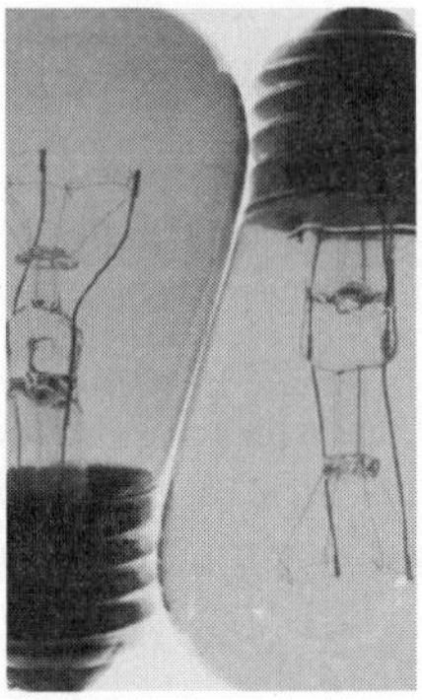

Data Structures & Problem Solving Using Java

third edition

mark allen weiss
florida international university

PEARSON
Addison Wesley

Boston San Francisco New York
London Toronto Sydney Tokyo Singapore Madrid
Mexico City Munich Paris Cape Town Hong Kong Montreal

Senior Acquisitions Editor	Michael Hirsch
Production Supervisor	Marilyn Lloyd
Production and Editorial Services	Gillian Hall and Juliet Silveri
Copyeditor	Penelope Hull
Proofreader	Holly McLean-Aldis
Marketing Manager	Michelle Brown
Marketing Assistant	Jake Zavracky
Cover Design Supervisor	Joyce Cosentino Wells
Cover Design	Night & Day Design
Prepress Buyer	Caroline Fell
Cover Image	© 2004 Photodisc

Access the latest information about Addison-Wesley titles from our World Wide Web site: http://www.aw-bc.com/computing

Library of Congress Cataloging-in-Publication Data

Weiss, Mark Allen.

Data structures and problem solving using Java / Mark Allen Weiss.-- 3rd ed.

p. cm.

Includes bibliographical references and index.

ISBN 0-321-32213-4

1. Java (Computer program language) 2. Data structures (Computer science)
3. Problem solving--Data processing. I. Title.

QA76.73.J38W45 2005
005.13'3--dc22

2004031048

12345678910- HT-070605

To the love of my life, Jill.

preface

This book is designed for a two-semester sequence in computer science, beginning with what is typically known as Data Structures and continuing with advanced data structures and algorithm analysis. It is appropriate for the courses from both the two-course and three-course sequences in "B.1 Introductory Tracks," as outlined in the final report of the Computing Curricula 2001 project (CC2001)—a joint undertaking of the ACM and the IEEE.

The content of the Data Structures course has been evolving for some time. Although there is some general consensus concerning topic coverage, considerable disagreement still exists over the details. One uniformly accepted topic is principles of software development, most notably the concepts of encapsulation and information hiding. Algorithmically, all Data Structures courses tend to include an introduction to running-time analysis, recursion, basic sorting algorithms, and elementary data structures. Many universities offer an advanced course that covers topics in data structures, algorithms, and running-time analysis at a higher level. The material in this text has been designed for use in both levels of courses, thus eliminating the need to purchase a second textbook.

Although the most passionate debates in Data Structures revolve around the choice of a programming language, other fundamental choices need to be made:

- Whether to introduce object-oriented design or object-based design early
- The level of mathematical rigor

- The appropriate balance between the implementation of data structures and their use
- Programming details related to the language chosen (for instance, should GUIs be used early)

My goal in writing this text was to provide a practical introduction to data structures and algorithms from the viewpoint of abstract thinking and problem solving. I tried to cover all the important details concerning the data structures, their analyses, and their Java implementations, while staying away from data structures that are theoretically interesting but not widely used. It is impossible to cover all the different data structures, including their uses and the analysis, described in this text in a single course. So I designed the textbook to allow instructors flexibility in topic coverage. The instructor will need to decide on an appropriate balance between practice and theory and then choose the topics that best fit the course. As I discuss later in this Preface, I organized the text to minimize dependencies among the various chapters.

a unique approach

My basic premise is that software development tools in all languages come with large libraries, and many data structures are part of these libraries. I envision an eventual shift in emphasis of data structures courses from implementation to use. In this book I take a unique approach by separating the data structures into their specification and subsequent implementation and taking advantage of an already existing data structures library, the Java Collections API.

A subset of the Collections API suitable for most applications is discussed in a single chapter (Chapter 6) in Part Two. Part Two also covers basic analysis techniques, recursion, and sorting. Part Three contains a host of applications that use the Collections API's data structures. Implementation of the Collections API is not shown until Part Four, once the data structures have already been used. Because the Collections API is part of Java students can design large projects early on, using existing software components.

Despite the central use of the Collections API in this text, it is neither a book on the Collections API nor a primer on implementing the Collections API specifically; it remains a book that emphasizes data structures and basic problem-solving techniques. Of course, the general techniques used in the design of data structures are applicable to the implementation of the Collections API, so several chapters in Part Four include Collections API implementations. However, instructors can choose the simpler implementations in Part Four that do not discuss the Collections API protocol. Chapter 6, which presents the Collections API, is essential to understanding the code in Part Three. I attempted to use only the basic parts of the Collections API.

Many instructors will prefer a more traditional approach in which each data structure is defined, implemented, and then used. Because there is no dependency between material in Parts Three and Four, a traditional course can easily be taught from this book.

prerequisites

Students using this book should have knowledge of either an object-oriented or procedural programming language. Knowledge of basic features, including primitive data types, operators, control structures, functions (methods), and input and output (but not necessarily arrays and classes) is assumed.

Students who have taken a first course using C++ or Java may find the first four chapters "light" reading in some places. However, other parts are definitely "heavy" with Java details that may not have been covered in introductory courses.

Students who have had a first course in another language should begin at Chapter 1 and proceed slowly. If a student would like to use a Java reference book as well, some recommendations are given in Chapter 1, pages 3–25.

Knowledge of discrete math is helpful but is not an absolute prerequisite. Several mathematical proofs are presented, but the more complex proofs are preceded by a brief math review. Chapters 7 and 19–24 require some degree of mathematical sophistication. The instructor may easily elect to skip mathematical aspects of the proofs by presenting only the results. All proofs in the text are clearly marked and are separate from the body of the text.

summary of changes in the third edition

1. The code was completely rewritten to use generics, which were introduced in Java 5. The code also makes significant use of the enhanced `for` loop and autoboxing.
2. In Java 5, the priority queue is now part of the standard Collections API. This change is reflected in the discussion in Chapter 21 and in some of the code in Part Three.

3. Chapter 4 contains new material discussing covariant arrays (and newly added covariant return types), as well as a primer on writing generic classes.

java

This textbook presents material using the Java programming language. Java is a relatively new language that is often examined in comparison with C++. Java offers many benefits, and programmers often view Java as a safer, more portable, and easier-to-use language than C++.

The use of Java requires that some decisions be made when writing a textbook. Some of the decisions made are as follows:

1. *The minimum required compiler is Java 5.* Please make sure you are using a compiler that is Java 5-compatible.
2. *GUIs are not emphasized.* Although GUIs are a nice feature in Java, they seem to be an implementation detail rather than a core Data Structures topic. We do not use Swing in the text, but because many instructors may prefer to do so, a brief introduction to Swing is provided in Appendix B.
3. *Applets are not emphasized.* Applets use GUIs. Further, the focus of the course is on data structures, rather than language features. Instructors who would like to discuss applets will need to supplement this text with a Java reference.
4. *Inner classes are used.* Inner classes are used primarily in the implementation of the Collections API, and can be avoided by instructors who prefer to do so.
5. *The concept of a pointer is discussed when reference variables are introduced.* Java does not have a pointer type. Instead, it has a reference type. However, pointers have traditionally been an important Data Structures topic that needs to be introduced. I illustrate the concept of pointers in other languages when discussing reference variables.
6. *Threads are not discussed.* Some members of the CS community argue that multithreaded computing should become a core topic in the introductory programming sequence. Although it is possible that this will happen in the future, few introductory programming courses discuss this difficult topic.

Java 5 adds some features that we have opted not to use. Some of these features include

- Static imports, not used because in my opinion it actually makes the code harder to read.
- Enumerated types, not used because there were few places to declare public enumerated types that would be usable by clients. In the few possible places, it did not seem to help the code's readability.
- Simplified I/O, not used because I view the standard I/O structure as a teaching opportunity for discussing the decorator pattern.

text organization

In this text I introduce Java and object-oriented programming (particularly abstraction) in Part One. I discuss primitive types, reference types, and some of the predefined classes and exceptions before proceeding to the design of classes and inheritance.

In Part Two, I discuss Big-Oh and algorithmic paradigms, including recursion and randomization. An entire chapter is devoted to sorting, and a separate chapter contains a description of basic data structures. I use the Collections API to present the interfaces and running times of the data structures. At this point in the text, the instructor may take several approaches to present the remaining material, including the following two.

1. Discuss the corresponding implementations (either the Collections API versions or the simpler versions) in Part Four as each data structure is described. The instructor can ask students to extend the classes in various ways, as suggested in the exercises.
2. Show how each Collections API class is used and cover implementation at a later point in the course. The case studies in Part Three can be used to support this approach. As complete implementations are available on every modern Java compiler, the instructor can use the Collections API in programming projects. Details on using this approach are given shortly.

Part Five describes advanced data structures such as splay trees, pairing heaps, and the disjoint set data structure, which can be covered if time permits or, more likely, in a follow-up course.

chapter-by-chapter text organization

Part One consists of four chapters that describe the basics of Java used throughout the text. Chapter 1 describes primitive types and illustrates how to write basic programs in Java. Chapter 2 discusses reference types and illustrates the general concept of a pointer—even though Java does not have pointers—so that students learn this important Data Structures topic. Several of the basic reference types (strings, arrays, files, and string tokenizers) are illustrated, and the use of exceptions is discussed. Chapter 3 continues this discussion by describing how a class is implemented. Chapter 4 illustrates the use of inheritance in designing hierarchies (including exception classes and I/O) and generic components. Material on design patterns, including the wrapper, adapter, decorator patterns can be found in Part One.

Part Two focuses on the basic algorithms and building blocks. In Chapter 5 a complete discussion of time complexity and Big-Oh notation is provided. Binary search is also discussed and analyzed. Chapter 6 is crucial because it covers the Collections API and argues intuitively what the running time of the supported operations should be for each data structure. (The implementation of these data structures, in both Collections API-style and a simplified version, is not provided until Part Four). This chapter also introduces the iterator pattern as well as nested, local, and anonymous classes. Inner classes are deferred until Part Four, where they are discussed as an implementation technique. Chapter 7 describes recursion by first introducing the notion of proof by induction. It also discusses divide-and-conquer, dynamic programming, and backtracking. A section describes several recursive numerical algorithms that are used to implement the RSA cryptosystem. For many students, the material in the second half of Chapter 7 is more suitable for a follow-up course. Chapter 8 describes, codes, and analyzes several basic sorting algorithms, including the insertion sort, Shellsort, mergesort, and quicksort, as well as indirect sorting. It also proves the classic lower bound for sorting and discusses the related problems of selection. Finally, Chapter 9 is a short chapter that discusses random numbers, including their generation and use in randomized algorithms.

Part Three provides several case studies, and each chapter is organized around a general theme. Chapter 10 illustrates several important techniques by examining games. Chapter 11 discusses the use of stacks in computer languages by examining an algorithm to check for balanced symbols and the classic operator precedence parsing algorithm. Complete implementations with code are provided for both algorithms. Chapter 12 discusses the basic utilities of file compression and cross-reference generation, and provides a complete implementation of both. Chapter 13 broadly examines simulation by looking at one problem that can be viewed as a simulation and then at the more classic event-driven simulation. Finally, Chapter 14 illustrates how data structures are used to implement several shortest path algorithms efficiently for graphs.

Part Four presents the data structure implementations. Chapter 15 discusses inner classes as an implementation technique and illustrates their use in the `ArrayList` implementation. In the remaining chapters of Part Four, implementations that use simple protocols (`insert`, `find`, `remove` variations) are provided. In some cases, Collections API implementations that tend to use more complicated Java syntax (in addition to being complex because of their large set of required operations) are presented. Some mathematics is used in this part, especially in Chapters 19–21, and can be skipped at the discretion of the instructor. Chapter 16 provides implementations for both stacks and queues. First these data structures are implemented using an expanding array, then they are implemented using linked lists. The Collections API versions are discussed at the end of the chapter. General linked lists are described in Chapter 17. Singly linked lists are illustrated with a simple protocol, and the more complex Collections API version that uses doubly linked lists is provided at the end of the chapter. Chapter 18 describes trees and illustrates the basic traversal schemes. Chapter 19 is a detailed chapter that provides several implementations of binary search trees. Initially, the basic binary search tree is shown, and then a binary search tree that supports order statistics is derived. AVL trees are discussed but not implemented, but the more practical red–black trees and AA-trees are implemented. Then the Collections API `TreeSet` and `TreeMap` are implemented. Finally, the B-tree is examined. Chapter 20 discusses hash tables and implements the quadratic probing scheme as part of `HashSet` and `HashMap`, after examination of a simpler alternative. Chapter 21 describes the binary heap and examines heapsort and external sorting. There is now a priority queue in the Java 5 Collections API, so we implement the standard version.

Part Five contains material suitable for use in a more advanced course or for general reference. The algorithms are accessible even at the first-year level. However, for completeness, sophisticated mathematical analyses that are almost certainly beyond the reach of a first-year student were included. Chapter 22 describes the splay tree, which is a binary search tree that seems to perform extremely well in practice and is competitive with the binary heap in some applications that require priority queues. Chapter 23 describes priority queues that support merging operations and provides an implementation of the pairing heap. Finally, Chapter 24 examines the classic disjoint set data structure.

The appendices contain additional Java reference material. Appendix A lists the operators and their precedence. Appendix B has material on Swing, and Appendix C describes the bitwise operators used in Chapter 12.

chapter dependencies

Generally speaking, most chapters are independent of each other. However, the following are some of the notable dependencies.

- *Part One* (*Tour of Java*)*:* The first four chapters should be covered in their entirety in sequence first, prior to continuing on to the rest of the text.
- *Chapter 5* (*Algorithm Analysis*): This chapter should be covered prior to Chapters 6 and 8. Recursion (Chapter 7) can be covered prior to this chapter, but the instructor will have to gloss over some details about avoiding inefficient recursion.
- *Chapter 6* (*The Collections API*): This chapter can be covered prior to or in conjunction with material in Part Three or Four.
- *Chapter 7* (*Recursion*): The material in Sections 7.1–7.3 should be covered prior to discussing recursive sorting algorithms, trees, the Tic-Tac-Toe case study, and shortest-path algorithms. Material such as the RSA cryptosystem, dynamic programming, and backtracking (unless Tic-Tac-Toe is discussed) is otherwise optional.
- *Chapter 8* (*Sorting Algorithms*): This chapter should follow Chapters 5 and 7. However, it is possible to cover Shellsort without Chapters 5 and 7. Shellsort is not recursive (hence there is no need for Chapter 7), and a rigorous analysis of its running time is too complex and is not covered in the book (hence there is little need for Chapter 5).
- *Chapter 15* (*Inner Classes and Implementations of ArrayLists*): This material should precede the discussion of the Collections API implementations.
- *Chapters 16 and 17* (*Stacks and Queues/Linked Lists*): These chapters may be covered in either order. However, I prefer to cover Chapter 16 first because I believe that it presents a simpler example of linked lists.
- *Chapters 18 and 19* (*Trees/ Binary Search Trees*): These chapters can be covered in either order or simultaneously.

separate entities

The other chapters have little or no dependencies:

- *Chapter 9* (*Randomization*): The material on random numbers can be covered at any point as needed.
- *Part Three* (*Applications*): Chapters 10–14 can be covered in conjunction with or after the Collections API (in Chapter 6) and in roughly any order. There are a few references to earlier chapters. These include Section 10.2 (Tic-Tac-Toe), which refers to a discussion in Section 7.7, and Section 12.2 (cross-reference generation), which refers to similar lexical analysis code in Section 11.1 (balanced symbol checking).
- *Chapters 20 and 21* (*Hash Tables/A Priority Queue*): These chapters can be covered at any point.
- *Part Five* (*Advanced Data Structures*): The material in Chapters 22–24 is self-contained and is typically covered in a follow-up course.

mathematics

I have attempted to provide mathematical rigor for use in Data Structures courses that emphasize theory and for follow-up courses that require more analysis. However, this material stands out from the main text in the form of separate theorems and, in some cases, separate sections or subsections. Thus it can be skipped by instructors in courses that deemphasize theory.

In all cases, the proof of a theorem is not necessary to the understanding of the theorem's meaning. This is another illustration of the separation of an interface (the theorem statement) from its implementation (the proof). Some inherently mathematical material, such as Section 7.4 (*Numerical Applications of Recursion*), can be skipped without affecting comprehension of the rest of the chapter.

course organization

A crucial issue in teaching the course is deciding how the materials in Parts Two–Four are to be used. The material in Part One should be covered in depth, and the student should write one or two programs that illustrate the design, implementation, testing of classes and generic classes, and perhaps object-oriented design, using inheritance. Chapter 5 discusses Big-Oh notation. An exercise in which the student writes a short program and compares the running time with an analysis can be given to test comprehension.

In the separation approach, the key concept of Chapter 6 is that different data structures support different access schemes with different efficiency. Any case study (except the Tic-Tac-Toe example that uses recursion) can be used to illustrate the applications of the data structures. In this way, the student can see the data structure and how it is used but not how it is efficiently implemented. This is truly a separation. Viewing things this way will greatly enhance the ability of students to think abstractly. Students can also provide simple implementations of some of the Collections API components (some suggestions are given in the exercises in Chapter 6) and see the difference between efficient data structure implementations in the existing Collections API and inefficient data structure implementations that they will write. Students can also be asked to extend the case study, but again, they are not required to know any of the details of the data structures.

Efficient implementation of the data structures can be discussed afterward, and recursion can be introduced whenever the instructor feels it is appropriate, provided it is prior to binary search trees. The details of sorting can be discussed at any time after recursion. At this point, the course can continue by using the same case studies and experimenting with modifications to the implementations of the data structures. For instance, the student can experiment with various forms of balanced binary search trees.

Instructors who opt for a more traditional approach can simply discuss a case study in Part Three after discussing a data structure implementation in Part Four. Again, the book's chapters are designed to be as independent of each other as possible.

exercises

Exercises come in various flavors; I have provided four varieties. The basic *In Short* exercise asks a simple question or requires hand-drawn simulations of an algorithm described in the text. The *In Theory* section asks questions that either require mathematical analysis or asks for theoretically interesting solutions to problems. The *In Practice* section contains simple programming questions, including questions about syntax or particularly tricky lines of code. Finally, the *Programming Projects* section contains ideas for extended assignments.

pedagogical features

- Margin notes are used to highlight important topics.

- The *Key Concepts* section lists important terms along with definitions and page references.

- The *Common Errors* section at the end of each chapter provides a list of commonly made errors.
- References for further reading are provided at the end of most chapters.

supplements

A variety of supplemental materials are available for this text. The following resources are available at `http://www.aw-bc.com/cssupport` for all readers of this textbook:

- *Source code files* from the book. (The *On the Internet* section at the end of each chapter lists the filenames for the chapter's code.)

- *PowerPoint slides* of all figures in the book.

In addition, the following supplements are available to qualified instructors. To access them, visit `http://www.aw-bc.com/computing` and search our catalog by title for *Data Structures and Problem Solving Using Java*. Once on the catalog page for this book, select the link to Instructor Resources.

- *Instructor's Guide* that illustrates several approaches to the material. It includes samples of test questions, assignments, and syllabi. Answers to select exercises are also provided.

acknowledgments

Many, many people have helped me in the preparation of this book. Many have already been acknowledged in the prior edition and the related C++ version. Others, too numerous to list, have sent e-mail messages and pointed out errors or inconsistencies in explanations that I have tried to fix in this edition.

For this edition, I would like to thank all of the folks at Addison-Wesley: my editor Michael Hirsch, project editors Juliet Silveri and Gillian Hall, and

Michelle Brown in marketing. Thanks also go to the copyeditor Penelope Hull, to the proofreader Holly McLean-Aldis, and to Joyce Wells for an outstanding cover design.

Some of the material in this text is adapted from my textbook *Efficient C Programming: A Practical Approach* (Prentice Hall, 1995) and is used with permission of the publisher. I have included end-of-chapter references where appropriate.

My World Wide Web page, `http://www.cs.fiu.edu/~weiss`, will contain updated source code, an errata list, and a link for receiving bug reports.

M. A. W.
Miami, Florida

contents

part one Tour of Java

part two Algorithms and Building Blocks

part three Applications

part four Implementations

part five **Advanced Data Structures**

part one

Tour of Java

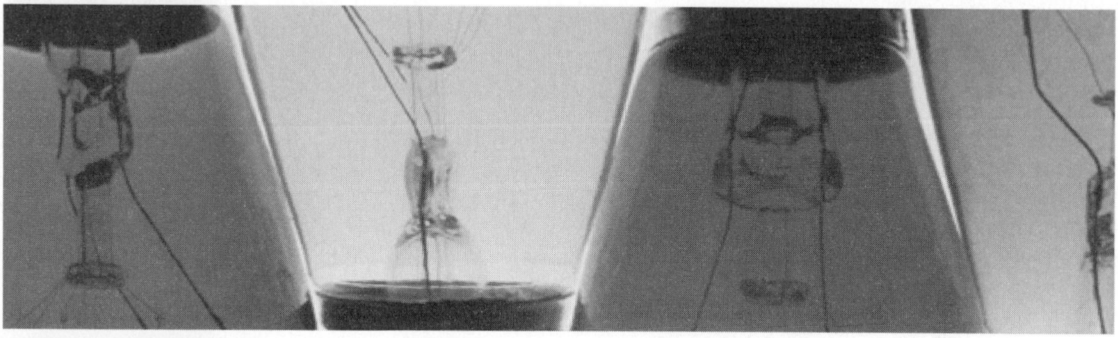

chapter 1

primitive java

The primary focus of this book is problem-solving techniques that allow the construction of sophisticated, time-efficient programs. Nearly all of the material discussed is applicable in any programming language. Some would argue that a broad pseudocode description of these techniques could suffice to demonstrate concepts. However, we believe that working with live code is vitally important.

There is no shortage of programming languages available. This text uses Java, which is popular both academically and commercially. In the first four chapters, we discuss the features of Java that are used throughout the book. Unused features and technicalities are not covered. Those looking for deeper Java information will find it in the many Java books that are available.

We begin by discussing the part of the language that mirrors a 1970s programming language such as Pascal or C. This includes primitive types, basic operations, conditional and looping constructs, and the Java equivalent of functions.

In this chapter, we will see

- Some of the basics of Java, including simple lexical elements
- The Java primitive types, including some of the operations that primitive-typed variables can perform

- How conditional statements and loop constructs are implemented in Java
- An introduction to the *static method*—the Java equivalent of the function and procedure that is used in non-object-oriented languages

1.1 the general environment

How are Java application programs entered, compiled, and run? The answer, of course, depends on the particular platform that hosts the Java compiler.

javac compiles `.java` files and generates `.class` files containing *bytecode. java* invokes the Java interpreter (which is also known as the *Virtual Machine*).

Java source code resides in files whose names end with the `.java` suffix. The local compiler, *javac*, compiles the program and generates `.class` files, which contain bytecode. Java *bytecodes* represent the portable intermediate language that is interpreted by running the Java interpreter, *java*. The interpreter is also known as the *Virtual Machine*.

For Java programs, input can come from one of many places:

- The terminal, whose input is denoted as *standard input*
- Additional parameters in the invocation of the Virtual Machine—*command-line arguments*
- A GUI component
- A file

Command-line arguments are particularly important for specifying program options. They are discussed in Section 2.4.5. Java provides mechanisms to read and write files. This is discussed briefly in Section 2.6.3 and in more detail in Section 4.5.3 as an example of the *decorator pattern*. Many operating systems provide an alternative known as *file redirection*, in which the operating system arranges to take input from (or send output to) a file in a manner that is transparent to the running program. On Unix (and also from an MS/DOS window), for instance, the command

```
java Program < inputfile > outputfile
```

automatically arranges things so that any terminal reads are redirected to come from `inputfile` and terminal writes are redirected to go to `outputfile`.

1.2 the first program

Let us begin by examining the simple Java program shown in Figure 1.1. This program prints a short phrase to the terminal. Note the line numbers shown on the left of the code *are not part of the program*. They are supplied for easy reference.

Place the program in the source file `FirstProgram.java` and then compile and run it. Note that the name of the source file must match the name of the class (shown on line 4), including case conventions. If you are using the JDK, the commands are[1]

```
javac FirstProgram.java
java FirstProgram
```

1.2.1 comments

Java has three forms of comments. The first form, which is inherited from C, begins with the token /* and ends with */. Here is an example:

```
/* This is a
   two-line comment */
```

Comments do not nest.

Comments make code easier for humans to read. Java has three forms of comments.

The second form, which is inherited from C++, begins with the token //. There is no ending token. Rather, the comment extends to the end of the line. This is shown on lines 1 and 2 in Figure 1.1.

The third form begins with /** instead of /*. This form can be used to provide information to the *javadoc* utility, which will generate documentation from comments. This form is discussed in Section 3.3.

figure 1.1

A simple first program

```
 1 // First program
 2 // MW, 5/1/05
 3
 4 public class FirstProgram
 5 {
 6     public static void main( String [ ] args )
 7     {
 8         System.out.println( "Is there anybody out there?" );
 9     }
10 }
```

1. If you are using Sun's JDK, *javac* and *java* are used directly. Otherwise, in a typical interactive development environment (IDE), such as JCreator, these commands are executed behind the scenes on your behalf.

Comments exist to make code easier for humans to read. These humans include other programmers who may have to modify or use your code, as well as yourself. A well-commented program is a sign of a good programmer.

1.2.2 `main`

When the program is run, the special method `main` is invoked.

A Java program consists of a collection of interacting classes, which contain methods. The Java equivalent of the function or procedure is the *static method*, which is described in Section 1.6. When any program is run, the special static method `main` is invoked. Line 6 of Figure 1.1 shows that the static method `main` is invoked, possibly with command-line arguments. The parameter types of `main` and the `void` return type shown are required.

1.2.3 terminal output

`println` is used to perform output.

The program in Figure 1.1 consists of a single statement, shown on line 8. `println` is the primary output mechanism in Java. Here, a constant string is placed on the standard output stream `System.out` by applying a `println` method. Input and output is discussed in more detail in Section 2.6. For now we mention only that the same syntax is used to perform output for any entity, whether that entity is an integer, floating point, string, or some other type.

1.3 primitive types

Java defines eight *primitive types*. It also allows the programmer great flexibility to define new types of objects, called *classes*. However, primitive types and user-defined types have important differences in Java. In this section, we examine the primitive types and the basic operations that can be performed on them.

1.3.1 the primitive types

Java's primitive types are integer, floating-point, Boolean, and character.

The Unicode standard contains over 30,000 distinct coded characters covering the principal written languages.

Java has eight primitive types, shown in Figure 1.2. The most common is the integer, which is specified by the keyword `int`. Unlike with many other languages, the range of integers is not machine-dependent. Rather, it is the same in any Java implementation, regardless of the underlying computer architecture. Java also allows entities of types `byte`, `short`, and `long`. These are known as *integral types*. Floating-point numbers are represented by the types `float` and `double`. `double` has more significant digits, so use of it is recommended over use of `float`. The `char` type is used to represent single characters. A `char` occupies 16 bits to represent the Unicode standard. The Unicode standard contains over 30,000 distinct coded characters covering the principal written

Primitive Type	What It Stores	Range
`byte`	8-bit integer	–128 to 127
`short`	16-bit integer	–32,768 to 32,767
`int`	32-bit integer	–2,147,483,648 to 2,147,483,647
`long`	64-bit integer	-2^{63} to $2^{63}-1$
`float`	32-bit floating-point	6 significant digits (10^{-46}, 10^{38})
`double`	64-bit floating-point	15 significant digits (10^{-324}, 10^{308})
`char`	Unicode character	
`boolean`	Boolean variable	`false` and `true`

figure 1.2

The eight primitive types in Java

languages. The low end of Unicode is identical to ASCII. The final primitive type is `boolean`, which is either `true` or `false`.

1.3.2 constants

Integer constants can be represented in either decimal, octal, or hexadecimal notation. Octal notation is indicated by a leading `0`; hexadecimal is indicated by a leading `0x` or `0X`. The following are all equivalent ways of representing the integer 37: `37`, `045`, `0x25`. Octal integers are not used in this text. However, we must be aware of them so that we use leading `0`s only when we intend to. We use hexadecimals in only one place (Section 12.1), and we will revisit them at that point.

Integer constants can be represented in either *decimal*, *octal*, or *hexadecimal* notation.

A *character constant* is enclosed with a pair of single quotation marks, as in `'a'`. Internally, this character sequence is interpreted as a small number. The output routines later interpret that small number as the corresponding character. A *string constant* consists of a sequence of characters enclosed within double quotation marks, as in `"Hello"`. There are some special sequences, known as *escape sequences*, that are used (for instance, how does one represent a single quotation mark?). In this text we use `'\n'`, `'\\'`, `'\''`, and `'\"'`, which mean, respectively, the newline character, backslash character, single quotation mark, and double quotation mark.

A *string* `constant` consists of a sequence of characters enclosed by double quotes.

Escape sequences are used to represent certain character constants.

1.3.3 declaration and initialization of primitive types

Any variable, including those of a primitive type, is declared by providing its name, its type, and optionally, its initial value. The name must be an *identifier*. An identifier may consist of any combination of letters, digits, and the underscore character; it may not start with a digit, however. Reserved words, such

A variable is named by using an *identifier*.

as `int`, are not allowed. Although it is legal to do so, you should not reuse identifier names that are already visibly used (for example, do not use `main` as the name of an entity).

Java is case-sensitive.

Java is *case-sensitive*, meaning that `Age` and `age` are different identifiers. This text uses the following convention for naming variables: All variables start with a lowercase letter and new words start with an uppercase letter. An example is the identifier `minimumWage`.

Here are some examples of declarations:

```
int num3;                      // Default initialization
double minimumWage = 4.50;     // Standard initialization
int x = 0, num1 = 0;           // Two entities are declared
int num2 = num1;
```

A variable should be declared near its first use. As will be shown, the placement of a declaration determines its scope and meaning.

1.3.4 terminal input and output

Basic formatted terminal I/O is accomplished by `readLine` and `println`. The standard input stream is `System.in`, and the standard output stream is `System.out`.

The basic mechanism for formatted I/O uses the `String` type, which is discussed in Section 2.3. For output, `+` combines two `String`s. If the second argument is not a `String`, a temporary `String` is created for it if it is a primitive type. These conversions to `String` can also be defined for objects (Section 3.4.3). For input, things are complicated: we must associate a `BufferedReader` object with `System.in`. Then a `String` is read and can be parsed. A more detailed discussion of I/O, including a treatment of formatted files, is in Section 2.6.

1.4 basic operators

This section describes some of the operators available in Java. These operators are used to form *expressions*. A constant or entity by itself is an expression, as are combinations of constants and variables with operators. An expression followed by a semicolon is a simple statement. In Section 1.5, we examine other types of statements, which introduce additional operators.

1.4.1 assignment operators

A simple Java program that illustrates a few operators is shown in Figure 1.3. The basic *assignment operator* is the equals sign. For example, on line 16 the variable a is assigned the value of the variable c (which at that point is 6). Subsequent changes to the value of c do not affect a. Assignment operators can be chained, as in z=y=x=0.

Another assignment operator is the +=, whose use is illustrated on line 18 of the figure. The += operator adds the value on the right-hand side (of the += operator) to the variable on the left-hand side. Thus, in the figure, c is incremented from its value of 6 before line 18, to a value of 14.

Java provides a host of *assignment operators*, including =, +=, -=, *=, and /=.

Java provides various other assignment operators, such as -=, *=, and /=, which alter the variable on the left-hand side of the operator via subtraction, multiplication, and division, respectively.

```
 1 public class OperatorTest
 2 {
 3     // Program to illustrate basic operators
 4     // The output is as follows:
 5     // 12 8 6
 6     // 6 8 6
 7     // 6 8 14
 8     // 22 8 14
 9     // 24 10 33
10
11     public static void main( String [ ] args )
12     {
13         int a = 12, b = 8, c = 6;
14
15         System.out.println( a + " " + b + " " + c );
16         a = c;
17         System.out.println( a + " " + b + " " + c );
18         c += b;
19         System.out.println( a + " " + b + " " + c );
20         a = b + c;
21         System.out.println( a + " " + b + " " + c );
22         a++;
23         ++b;
24         c = a++ + ++b;
25         System.out.println( a + " " + b + " " + c );
26     }
27 }
```

figure 1.3

Program that illustrates operators

1.4.2 binary arithmetic operators

Java provides several *binary arithmetic operators*, including +, -, *, /, and %.

Line 20 in Figure 1.3 illustrates one of the *binary arithmetic operators* that are typical of all programming languages: the addition operator (+). The + operator causes the values of b and c to be added together; b and c remain unchanged. The resulting value is assigned to a. Other arithmetic operators typically used in Java are -, *, /, and %, which are used, respectively, for subtraction, multiplication, division, and remainder. Integer division returns only the integral part and discards any remainder.

As is typical, addition and subtraction have the same precedence, and this precedence is lower than the precedence of the group consisting of the multiplication, division, and mod operators; thus 1+2*3 evaluates to 7. All of these operators associate from left to right (so 3-2-2 evaluates to –1). All operators have precedence and associativity. The complete table of operators is in Appendix .

1.4.3 unary operators

Several *unary operators* are defined, including -.

In addition to binary arithmetic operators, which require two operands, Java provides *unary operators*, which require only one operand. The most familiar of these is the unary minus, which evaluates to the negative of its operand. Thus -x returns the negative of x.

Autoincrement and *autodecrement* add 1 and subtract 1, respectively. The operators for doing this are ++ and --. There are two forms of incrementing and decrementing: prefix and postfix.

Java also provides the autoincrement operator to add 1 to a variable—denoted by ++—and the autodecrement operator to subtract 1 from a variable—denoted by --. The most benign use of this feature is shown on lines 22 and 23 of Figure 1.3. In both lines, the *autoincrement operator* ++ adds 1 to the value of the variable. In Java, however, an operator applied to an expression yields an expression that has a value. Although it is guaranteed that the variable will be incremented before the execution of the next statement, the question arises: What is the value of the autoincrement expression if it is used in a larger expression?

In this case, the placement of the ++ is crucial. The semantics of ++x is that the value of the expression is the new value of x. This is called the *prefix increment*. In contrast, x++ means the value of the expression is the original value of x. This is called the *postfix increment*. This feature is shown in line 24 of Figure 1.3. a and b are both incremented by 1, and c is obtained by adding the *original* value of a to the *incremented* value of b.

1.4.4 type conversions

The *type conversion operator* is used to generate a temporary entity of a new type.

The *type conversion operator* is used to generate a temporary entity of a new type. Consider, for instance,

```
double quotient;
int x = 6;
int y = 10;
quotient = x / y;    // Probably wrong!
```

The first operation is the division, and since x and y are both integers, the result is integer division, and we obtain 0. Integer 0 is then implicitly converted to a double so that it can be assigned to quotient. But we had intended quotient to be assigned 0.6. The solution is to generate a temporary variable for either x or y so that the division is performed using the rules for double. This would be done as follows:

```
quotient = ( double ) x / y;
```

Note that neither x nor y are changed. An unnamed temporary is created, and its value is used for the division. The type conversion operator has higher precedence than division does, so x is type-converted and then the division is performed (rather than the conversion coming after the division of two ints being performed).

1.5 conditional statements

This section examines statements that affect the flow of control: conditional statements and loops. As a consequence, new operators are introduced.

1.5.1 relational and equality operators

The basic test that we can perform on primitive types is the comparison. This is done using the equality and inequality operators, as well as the relational operators (less than, greater than, and so on).

In Java, the *equality operators* are == and !=. For example,

In Java, the *equality operators* are == and !=.

```
leftExpr==rightExpr
```

evaluates to true if leftExpr and rightExpr are equal; otherwise, it evaluates to false. Similarly,

```
leftExpr!=rightExpr
```

evaluates to true if leftExpr and rightExpr are not equal and to false otherwise.

The *relational operators* are <, <=, >, and >=. These have natural meanings for the built-in types. The relational operators have higher precedence than the equality operators. Both have lower precedence than the arithmetic operators

The *relational operators* are <, <=, >, and >=.

but higher precedence than the assignment operators, so the use of parentheses is frequently unnecessary. All of these operators associate from left to right, but this fact is useless: In the expression `a<b<6`, for example, the first `<` generates a `boolean` and the second is illegal because `<` is not defined for `booleans`. The next section describes the correct way to perform this test.

1.5.2 logical operators

Java provides *logical operators* that are used to simulate the Boolean algebra concepts of AND, OR, and NOT. The corresponding operators are `&&`, `||`, and `!`.

Java provides *logical operators* that are used to simulate the Boolean algebra concepts of AND, OR, and NOT. These are sometimes known as *conjunction*, *disjunction*, and *negation*, respectively, whose corresponding operators are `&&`, `||`, and `!`. The test in the previous section is properly implemented as `a<b && b<6`. The precedence of conjunction and disjunction is sufficiently low that parentheses are not needed. `&&` has higher precedence than `||`, while `!` is grouped with other unary operators (and is thus highest of the three). The operands and results for the logical operators are `boolean`. Figure 1.4 shows the result of applying the logical operators for all possible inputs.

Short-circuit evaluation means that if the result of a logical operator can be determined by examining the first expression, then the second expression is not evaluated.

One important rule is that `&&` and `||` are short-circuit evaluation operations. *Short-circuit evaluation* means that if the result can be determined by examining the first expression, then the second expression is not evaluated. For instance, in

```
x != 0 && 1/x != 3
```

if `x` is 0, then the first half is `false`. Automatically the result of the AND must be `false`, so the second half is not evaluated. This is a good thing because division-by-zero would give erroneous behavior. Short-circuit evaluation allows us to not have to worry about dividing by zero.[2]

figure 1.4

Result of logical operators

x	y	x && y	x || y	!x
false	false	false	false	true
false	true	false	true	true
true	false	false	true	false
true	true	true	true	false

2. There are (extremely) rare cases in which it is preferable to not short-circuit. In such cases, the `&` and `|` operators with `boolean` arguments guarantee that both arguments are evaluated, even if the result of the operation can be determined from the first argument.

1.5.3 the `if` statement

The `if` statement is the fundamental decision maker. Its basic form is

The `if` statement is the fundamental decision maker.

```
if( expression )
    statement
next statement
```

If `expression` evaluates to `true`, then `statement` is executed; otherwise, it is not. When the `if` statement is completed (without an unhandled error), control passes to the next statement.

Optionally, we can use an `if-else` statement, as follows:

```
if( expression )
    statement1
else
    statement2
next statement
```

In this case, if `expression` evaluates to `true`, then `statement1` is executed; otherwise, `statement2` is executed. In either case, control then passes to the next statement, as in

```
System.out.print( "1/x is " );
if( x != 0 )
    System.out.print( 1 / x );
else
    System.out.print( "Undefined" );
System.out.println( );
```

Remember that each of the `if` and `else` clauses contains at most one statement, no matter how you indent. Here are two mistakes:

```
if( x == 0 );     // ; is null statement (and counts)
    System.out.println( "x is zero " );
else
    System.out.print( "x is " );
    System.out.println( x ); // Two statements
```

The first mistake is the inclusion of the ; at the end of the first `if`. This semicolon by itself counts as the *null statement*; consequently, this fragment won't compile (the `else` is no longer associated with an `if`). Once that mistake is fixed, we have a logic error: that is, the last line is not part of the `else`, even though the indentation suggests it is. To fix this problem, we have to use a *block*, in which we enclose a sequence of statements by a pair of braces:

A semicolon by itself is the *null statement.*

A *block* is a sequence of statements within braces.

```
if( x == 0 )
    System.out.println( "x is zero" );
else
{
    System.out.print( "x is " );
    System.out.println( x );
}
```

The `if` statement can itself be the target of an `if` or `else` clause, as can other control statements discussed later in this section. In the case of nested `if-else` statements, an `else` matches the innermost dangling `if`. It may be necessary to add braces if that is not the intended meaning.

1.5.4 the `while` statement

The `while` statement is one of three basic forms of looping.

Java provides three basic forms of looping: the `while` statement, `for` statement, and `do` statement. The syntax for the `while` statement is

```
while( expression )
    statement
next statement
```

Note that like the `if` statement, there is no semicolon in the syntax. If one is present, it will be taken as the null statement.

While `expression` is `true`, `statement` is executed; then `expression` is reevaluated. If `expression` is initially `false`, then `statement` will never be executed. Generally, `statement` does something that can potentially alter the value of `expression`; otherwise, the loop could be infinite. When the `while` loop terminates (normally), control resumes at the next statement.

1.5.5 the `for` statement

The `for` statement is a looping construct that is used primarily for simple iteration.

The `while` statement is sufficient to express all repetition. Even so, Java provides two other forms of looping: the `for` statement and the `do` statement. The `for` statement is used primarily for iteration. Its syntax is

```
for( initialization; test; update )
    statement
next statement
```

Here, `initialization`, `test`, and `update` are all expressions, and all three are optional. If `test` is not provided, it defaults to `true`. There is no semicolon after the closing parenthesis.

The `for` statement is executed by first performing the `initialization`. Then, while `test` is `true`, the following two actions occur: `statement` is performed, and then `update` is performed. If `initialization` and `update` are omitted, then the `for` statement behaves exactly like a `while` statement. The advantage of a `for` statement is clarity in that for variables that count (or iterate), the `for` statement makes it much easier to see what the range of the counter is. The following fragment prints the first 100 positive integers:

```
for( int i = 1; i <= 100; i++ )
    System.out.println( i );
```

This fragment illustrates the common technique of declaring a counter in the initialization portion of the loop. This counter's scope extends only inside the loop.

Both `initialization` and `update` may use a comma to allow multiple expressions. The following fragment illustrates this idiom:

```
for( i = 0, sum = 0; i <= n; i++, sum += n )
    System.out.println( i + "\t" + sum );
```

Loops nest in the same way as `if` statements. For instance, we can find all pairs of small numbers whose sum equals their product (such as 2 and 2, whose sum and product are both 4):

```
for( int i = 1; i <= 10; i++ )
    for( int j = 1; j <= 10; j++ )
        if( i + j == i * j )
            System.out.println( i + ", " + j );
```

As we will see, however, when we nest loops we can easily create programs whose running times grow quickly.

Java 5 adds an "enhanced" `for` loop. We discuss this addition in Section 2.4 and Chapter 6.

1.5.6 the `do` statement

The `while` statement repeatedly performs a test. If the test is `true`, it then executes an embedded statement. However, if the initial test is `false`, the embedded statement is never executed. In some cases, however, we would like to guarantee that the embedded statement is executed at least once. This is done using the `do` statement. The `do` statement is identical to the `while` statement, except that the test is performed after the embedded statement. The syntax is

> The `do` statement is a looping construct that guarantees the loop is executed at least once.

```
do
    statement
while( expression );
next statement
```

Notice that the do statement includes a semicolon. A typical use of the do statement is shown in the following pseudocode fragment:

```
do
{
    Prompt user;
    Read value;
} while( value is no good );
```

The do statement is by far the least frequently used of the three looping constructs. However, when we have to do something at least once, and for some reason a for loop is inappropriate, then the do statement is the method of choice.

1.5.7 break and continue

The for and while statements provide for termination before the start of a repeated statement. The do statement allows termination after execution of a repeated statement. Occasionally, we would like to terminate execution in the middle of a repeated (compound) statement. The break statement, which is the keyword break followed by a semicolon, can be used to achieve this. Typically, an if statement would precede the break, as in

```
while( ... )
{
    ...
    if( something )
        break;
    ...
}
```

The break statement exits the innermost loop or switch statement. The labeled break statement exits from a nested loop.

The break statement exits the innermost loop only (it is also used in conjunction with the switch statement, described in the next section). If there are several loops that need exiting, the break will not work, and most likely you have poorly designed code. Even so, Java provides a labeled break statement. In the labeled break statement, a loop is labeled, and then a break statement can be applied to the loop, regardless of how many other loops are nested. Here is an example:

```
 outer:
    while( ... )
    {
        while( ... )
            if( disaster )
                break outer; // Go to after outer
    }
    // Control passes here after outer loop is exited
```

Occasionally, we want to give up on the current iteration of a loop and go on to the next iteration. This can be handled by using a `continue` statement. Like the `break` statement, the `continue` statement includes a semicolon and applies to the innermost loop only. The following fragment prints the first 100 integers, with the exception of those divisible by 10:

The `continue` statement goes to the next iteration of the innermost loop.

```
for( int i = 1; i <= 100; i++ )
{
    if( i % 10 == 0 )
        continue;
    System.out.println( i );
}
```

Of course, in this example, there are alternatives to the `continue` statement. However, `continue` is commonly used to avoid complicated `if-else` patterns inside loops.

1.5.8 the `switch` statement

The `switch` statement is used to select among several small integer (or character) values. It consists of an expression and a block. The block contains a sequence of statements and a collection of labels, which represent possible values of the expression. All the labels must be distinct compile-time constants. An optional default label, if present, matches any unrepresented label. If there is no applicable case for the `switch` expression, the `switch` statement is over; otherwise, control passes to the appropriate label and all statements from that point on are executed. A `break` statement may be used to force early termination of the `switch` and is almost always used to separate logically distinct cases. An example of the typical structure is shown in Figure 1.5.

The `switch` statement is used to select among several small integer (or character) values.

1.5.9 the conditional operator

The *conditional operator* `?:` is used as a shorthand for simple `if-else` statements. The general form is

The *conditional operator* `?:` is used as a shorthand for simple `if-else` statements.

```
testExpr ? yesExpr : noExpr
```

`testExpr` is evaluated first, followed by either `yesExpr` or `noExpr`, producing the result of the entire expression. `yesExpr` is evaluated if `testExpr` is `true`; otherwise, `noExpr` is evaluated. The precedence of the conditional operator is just above that of the assignment operators. This allows us to avoid using parentheses when assigning the result of the conditional operator to a variable. As an example, the minimum of `x` and `y` is assigned to `minVal` as follows:

```
minVal = x <= y ? x : y;
```

figure 1.5

Layout of a switch statement

```
switch( someCharacter )
{
  case '(':
  case '[':
  case '{':
    // Code to process opening symbols
    break;

  case ')':
  case ']':
  case '}':
    // Code to process closing symbols
    break;

  case '\n':
    // Code to handle newline character
    break;

  default:
    // Code to handle other cases
    break;
}
```

1.6 methods

A *method* is similar to a function in other languages. The *method header* consists of the name, return type, and parameter list. The *method declaration* includes the body.

A `public static` method is the equivalent of a "C-style" global function.

In *call-by-value*, the actual arguments are copied into the formal parameters. Variables are passed using call-by-value.

What is known as a function or procedure in other languages is called a *method* in Java. A more complete treatment of methods is provided in Chapter 3. This section presents some of the basics for writing functions, such as `main`, in a non-object-oriented manner (as would be encountered in a language such as C) so that we can write some simple programs.

A *method header* consists of a name, a (possibly empty) list of parameters, and a return type. The actual code to implement the method, sometimes called the *method body*, is formally a *block*. A *method declaration* consists of a header plus the body. An example of a method declaration and a `main` routine that uses it is shown in Figure 1.6.

By prefacing each method with the words `public static`, we can mimic the C-style global function. Although declaring a method as `static` is a useful technique in some instances, it should not be overused, since in general we do not want to use Java to write "C-style" code. We will discuss the more typical use of `static` in Section 3.5.

The method name is an identifier. The parameter list consists of zero or more *formal parameters*, each with a specified type. When a method is called, the *actual arguments* are sent into the formal parameters using normal assign-

```java
public class MinTest
{
    public static void main( String [ ] args )
    {
        int a = 3;
        int b = 7;

        System.out.println( min( a, b ) );
    }

    // Method declaration
    public static int min( int x, int y )
    {
        return x < y ? x : y;
    }
}
```

figure 1.6

Illustration of method declaration and calls

ment. This means primitive types are passed using *call-by-value* parameter passing only. The actual arguments cannot be altered by the function. As with most modern programming languages, method declarations may be arranged in any order.

The `return` statement is used to return a value to the caller. If the return type is `void`, then no value is returned, and `return;` should be used.

The `return` statement is used to return a value to the caller.

1.6.1 overloading of method names

Suppose we need to write a routine that returns the maximum of three `int`s. A reasonable method header would be

```java
int max( int a, int b, int c )
```

In some languages, this may be unacceptable if `max` is already declared. For instance, we may also have

```java
int max( int a, int b )
```

Java allows the *overloading* of method names. This means that several methods may have the same name and be declared in the same class scope as long as their *signatures* (that is, their parameter list types) differ. When a call to `max` is made, the compiler can deduce which of the intended meanings should be applied based on the actual argument types. Two signatures may have the same number of parameters, as long as at least one of the parameter list types differs.

Overloading of a method name means that several methods may have the same name as long as their parameter list types differ.

Note that the return type is not included in the signature. This means it is illegal to have two methods in the same class scope whose only difference is the return type. Methods in different class scopes may have the same names, signatures, and even return types; this is discussed in Chapter 3.

1.6.2 storage classes

Entities that are declared inside the body of a method are local variables and can be accessed by name only within the method body. These entities are created when the method body is executed and disappear when the method body terminates.

`static final` variables are constants.

A variable declared outside the body of a method is global to the class. It is similar to global variables in other languages if the word `static` is used (which is likely to be required so as to make the entity accessible by static methods). If both `static` and `final` are used, they are global symbolic constants. As an example,

```
static final double PI = 3.1415926535897932;
```

Note the use of the common convention of naming symbolic constants entirely in uppercase. If several words form the identifier name, they are separated by the underscore character, as in `MAX_INT_VALUE`.

If the word `static` is omitted, then the variable (or constant) has a different meaning, which is discussed in Section 3.4.6.

summary

This chapter discussed the primitive features of Java, such as primitive types, operators, conditional and looping statements, and methods that are found in almost any language.

Any nontrivial program will require the use of nonprimitive types, called *reference types*, which are discussed in the next chapter.

key concepts

assignment operators In Java, used to alter the value of a variable. These operators include `=`, `+=`, `-=`, `*=`, and `/=`. (9)

autoincrement (++) and **autodecrement (--) operators** Operators that add and subtract 1, respectively. There are two forms of incrementing and decrementing prefix and postfix. (10)

binary arithmetic operators Used to perform basic arithmetic. Java provides several, including +, -, *, /, and %. (10)

block A sequence of statements within braces. (13)

break statement A statement that exits the innermost loop or switch statement. (16)

bytecode Portable intermediate code generated by the Java compiler. (4)

call-by-value The Java parameter-passing mechanism whereby the actual argument is copied into the formal parameter. (18)

comments Make code easier for humans to read but have no semantic meaning. Java has three forms of comments. (5)

conditional operator (?:) An operator that is used in an expression as a shorthand for simple if-else statements. (17)

continue statement A statement that goes to the next iteration of the innermost loop. (17)

do statement A looping construct that guarantees the loop is executed at least once. (15)

equality operators In Java, == and != are used to compare two values; they return either true or false (as appropriate). (11)

escape sequence Used to represent certain character constants. (7)

for statement A looping construct used primarily for simple iteration. (14)

identifier Used to name a variable or method. (7)

if statement The fundamental decision maker. (13)

integral types byte, char, short, int, and long. (6)

java The Java interpreter, which processes bytecodes. (4)

javac The Java compiler; generates bytecodes. (4)

labeled break statement A break statement used to exit from nested loops. (16)

logical operators &&, ||, and !, used to simulate the Boolean algebra concepts of AND, OR, and NOT. (12)

main The special method that is invoked when the program is run. (6)

method The Java equivalent of a function. (18)

method declaration Consists of the method header and body. (18)

method header Consists of the name, return type, and parameter list. (18)

null statement A statement that consists of a semicolon by itself. (13)

octal and hexadecimal integer constants Integer constants can be represented in either decimal, octal, or hexadecimal notation. Octal notation is indicated by a leading 0; hexadecimal is indicated by a leading 0x or 0X. (7)

overloading of a method name The action of allowing several methods to have the same name as long as their parameter list types differ. (19)

primitive types In Java, integer, floating-point, Boolean, and character. (6)

relational operators In Java, <, <=, >, and >= are used to decide which of two values is smaller or larger; they return `true` or `false`. (11)

`return` statement A statement used to return information to the caller. (19)

short-circuit evaluation The process whereby if the result of a logical operator can be determined by examining the first expression, then the second expression is not evaluated. (12)

signature The combination of the method name and the parameter list types. The return type is not part of the signature. (18)

standard input The terminal, unless redirected. There are also streams for standard output and standard error. (4)

`static final` entity A global constant. (20)

`static` method Occasionally used to mimic C-style functions; discussed more fully in Section 3.5. (18)

string constant A constant that consists of a sequence of characters enclosed by double quotes. (7)

`switch` statement A statement used to select among several small integral values. (17)

type conversion operator An operator used to generate an unnamed temporary variable of a new type. (10)

unary operators Require one operand. Several unary operators are defined, including unary minus (`-`) and the autoincrement and autodecrement operators (`++` and `--`). (10)

Unicode International character set that contains over 30,000 distinct characters covering the principle written languages. (6)

`while` statement The most basic form of looping. (14)

Virtual Machine The bytecode interpreter. (4)

common errors

1. Adding unnecessary semicolons gives logical errors because the semicolon by itself is the null statement. This means that an unintended semicolon immediately following a `for`, `while`, or `if` statement is very likely to go undetected and will break your program.
2. At compile time, the Java compiler is required to detect all instances in which a method that is supposed to return a value fails to do so. Occasionally, it provides a false alarm, and you have to rearrange code.
3. A leading `0` makes an integer constant octal when seen as a token in source code. So `037` is equivalent to decimal `31`.

4. Use && and || for logical operations; & and | do not short-circuit.
5. The `else` clause matches the closest dangling `if`. It is common to forget to include the braces needed to match the `else` to a distant dangling `if`.
6. When a `switch` statement is used, it is common to forget the `break` statement between logical cases. If it is forgotten, control passes through to the next case; generally, this is not the desired behavior.
7. Escape sequences begin with the backslash \, not the forward slash /.
8. Mismatched braces may give misleading answers. Use `Balance`, described in Section 11.1, to check if this is the cause of a compiler error message.
9. The name of the Java source file must match the name of the class being compiled.

on the internet

Following are the available files for this chapter. Everything is self-contained, and nothing is used later in the text.

FirstProgram.java	The first program, as shown in Figure 1.1.
OperatorTest.java	Demonstration of various operators, as shown in Figure 1.3.
MinTest.java	Illustration of methods, as shown in Figure 1.6.

exercises

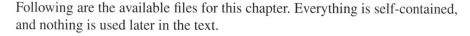

IN SHORT

1.1 What extensions are used for Java source and compiled files?

1.2 Describe the three kinds of comments used in Java programs.

1.3 What are the eight primitive types in Java?

1.4 What is the difference between the * and *= operators?

1.5 Explain the difference between the prefix and postfix increment operators.

1.6 Describe the three types of loops in Java.

1.7 Describe all the uses of a `break` statement. What is a labeled `break` statement?

1.8 What does the `continue` statement do?

1.9 What is method overloading?

1.10 Describe call-by-value.

IN THEORY

1.11 Let b have the value of 5 and c have the value of 8. What is the value of a, b, and c after each line of the following program fragment:

```
a = b++ + c++;
a = b++ + ++c;
a = ++b + c++;
a = ++b + ++c;
```

1.12 What is the result of `true && false || true`?

1.13 For the following, give an example in which the `for` loop on the left is not equivalent to the `while` loop on the right:

```
                                   init;
for( init; test; update )          while( test )
{                                  {
    statements                         statements
                                       update;
}                                  }
```

1.14 For the following program, what are the possible outputs?

```
public class WhatIsX
{
    public static void f( int x )
      { /* body unknown */ }

    public static void main( String [ ] args )
    {
        int x = 0;
        f( x );
        System.out.println( x );
    }
}
```

IN PRACTICE

1.15 Write a `while` statement that is equivalent to the following `for` fragment. Why would this be useful?

```
for( ; ; )
    statement
```

1.16 Write a program to generate the addition and multiplication tables for single-digit numbers (the table that elementary school students are accustomed to seeing).

1.17 Write two static methods. The first should return the maximum of three integers, and the second should return the maximum of four integers.

1.18 Write a static method that takes a year as a parameter and returns `true` if the year is a leap year, and `false` otherwise.

PROGRAMMING PROJECTS

1.19 Write a program to determine all pairs of positive integers, (a, b), such that $a < b < 1000$ and $(a^2 + b^2 + 1)/(ab)$ is an integer.

1.20 Write a method that prints the representation of its integer parameter as a Roman numeral. Thus, if the parameter is `1998`, the output is `MCMXCVIII`.

1.21 Suppose you want to print out numbers in brackets, formatted as follows: `[1][2][3]`, and so on. Write a method that takes two parameters: `howMany` and `lineLength`. The method should print out line numbers from 1 to `howMany` in the previous format, but it should not output more than `lineLength` characters on any one line. It should not start a `[` unless it can fit the corresponding `]`.

1.22 In the following decimal arithmetic puzzle, each of the ten different letters is assigned a digit. Write a program that finds all possible solutions (one of which is shown).

```
  MARK     A=1 W=2 N=3 R=4 E=5       9147
+ ALLEN    L=6 K=7 I=8 M=9 S=0     + 16653
  -----                              -----
  WEISS                              25800
```

references

Some of the C-style material in this chapter is taken from [5]. The complete Java language specification may be found in [2]. Introductory Java books include [1], [3] and [4].

1. G. Cornell and C. S. Horstmann, *Core Java 2 Volumes 1 and 2*, 7th ed., Prentice Hall, Upper Saddle River, NJ, 2005.
2. J. Gosling, B. Joy, and G. Steele, *The Java Language Specification*, 2nd ed., Addison-Wesley, Reading, MA, 2000.
3. J. Lewis and W. Loftus, *Java Software Solutions: Java 1.4 Edition*, Addison-Wesley, Boston, MA, 2005.
4. W. Savitch, *Java: An Introduction to Computer Science & Programming*, 3rd ed., Prentice Hall, Upper Saddle River, NJ, 2004.
5. M. A. Weiss, *Efficient C Programming: A Practical Approach*, Prentice Hall, Upper Saddle River, NJ, 1995.

chapter 2

reference types

Chapter 1 examined the Java primitive types. All types that are not one of the eight primitive types are *reference types*, including important entities such as strings, arrays, and file streams.

In this chapter, we will see

- What a reference type and value is
- How reference types differ from primitive types
- Examples of reference types, including strings, arrays, and streams
- How exceptions are used to signal erroneous behavior

2.1 what is a reference?

Chapter 1 described the eight primitive types, along with some of the operations that these types can perform. All other types in Java are reference types, including strings, arrays, and file streams. So what is a reference? A *reference variable* (often abbreviated as simply *reference*) in Java is a variable that somehow stores the memory address where an object resides.

As an example, in Figure 2.1 are two objects of type `Point`. It happens, by chance, that these objects are stored in memory locations 1000 and 1024, respectively. For these two objects, there are three references: `point1`, `point2`, and `point3`. `point1` and `point3` both reference the object stored at memory location 1000; `point2` references the object stored at memory location 1024. Both `point1` and `point3` store the value 1000, while `point2` stores the value 1024. Note that the actual locations, such as 1000 and 1024, are assigned by the runtime system at its discretion (when it finds available memory). Thus these values are not useful externally as numbers. However, the fact that `point1` and `point3` store identical values is useful: It means they are referencing the same object.

A reference will always store the memory address where some object is residing, unless it is not currently referencing any object. In this case, it will store the *null reference*, `null`. Java does not allow references to primitive variables.

There are two broad categories of operations that can be applied to reference variables. One allows us to examine or manipulate the reference value. For instance, if we change the stored value of `point1` (which is 1000), we could have it reference another object. We can also compare `point1` and `point3` and determine if they are referencing the same object. The other category of operations applies to the object being referenced; perhaps we could examine or change the internal state of one of the `Point` objects. For instance, we could examine some of `Point`'s *x* and *y* coordinates.

Before we describe what can be done with references, let us see what is not allowed. Consider the expression `point1*point2`. Since the stored values of `point1` and `point2` are 1000 and 1024, respectively, their product would be 1024000. However, this is a meaningless calculation that could not have any possible use. Reference variables store addresses, and there is no logical meaning that can be associated with multiplying two addresses.

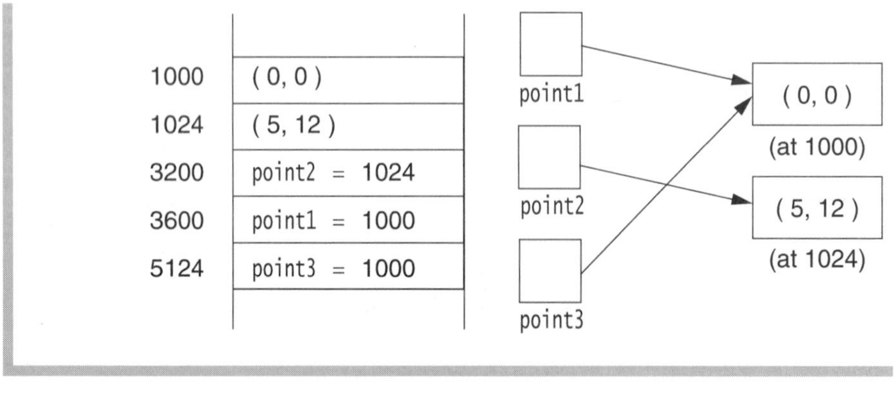

figure 2.1

An illustration of a reference. The `Point` object stored at memory location 1000 is referenced by both `point1` and `point3`. The `Point` object stored at memory location 1024 is referenced by `point2`. The memory locations where the variables are stored are arbitrary.

Similarly, `point1++` has no Java meaning; it suggests that `point1`—1000—should be increased to 1001, but in that case it might not be referencing a valid `Point` object. Many languages (e.g., C++) define the *pointer*, which behaves like a reference variable. However, pointers in C++ are much more dangerous because arithmetic on stored addresses is allowed. Thus, in C++, `point1++` has a meaning. Because C++ allows pointers to primitive types, one must be careful to distinguish between arithmetic on addresses and arithmetic on the objects being referenced. This is done by explicitly *dereferencing* the pointer. In practice, C++'s unsafe pointers tend to cause numerous programming errors.

Some operations are performed on references themselves, while other operations are performed on the objects being referenced. In Java, the only operators that are allowed for reference types (with one exception made for `String`s) are assignment via `=` and equality comparison via `==` or `!=`.

Figure 2.2 illustrates the assignment operator for reference variables. By assigning `point3` the stored value of `point2`, we have `point3` reference the same object that `point2` was referencing. Now, `point2==point3` is `true` because `point2` and `point3` both store 1024 and thus reference the same object. `point1!=point2` is also `true` because `point1` and `point2` reference different objects.

The other category of operations deals with the object that is being referenced. There are only three basic actions that can be done:

1. Apply a type conversion (Section 1.4.4).
2. Access an internal field or call a method via the dot operator (`.`) (Section 2.2.1).
3. Use the `instanceof` operator to verify that the stored object is of a certain type (Section 3.5.3).

The next section illustrates in more detail the common reference operations.

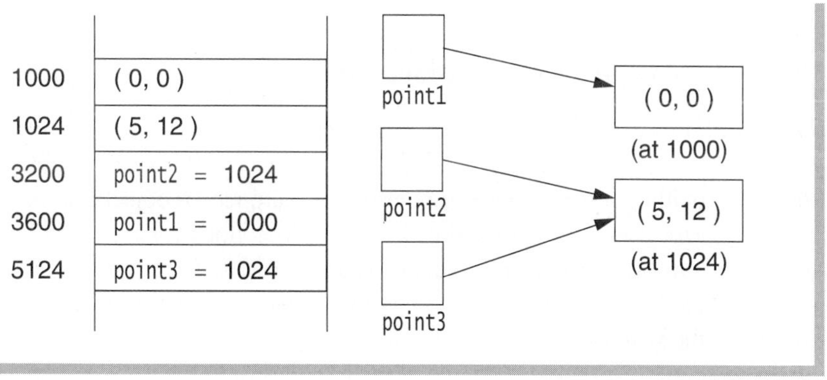

figure 2.2

The result of `point3=point2`: `point3` now references the same object as `point2`.

2.2 basics of objects and references

In Java, an *object* is an instance of any of the nonprimitive types.

In Java, an *object* is an instance of any of the nonprimitive types. Objects are treated differently from primitive types. Primitive types, as already shown, are handled by *value*, meaning that the values assumed by the primitive variables are stored in those variables and copied from primitive variable to primitive variable during assignments. As shown in Section 2.1, reference variables store references to objects. The actual object is stored somewhere in memory, and the reference variable stores the object's memory address. Thus a reference variable simply represents a name for that part of memory. This means that primitive variables and reference variables behave differently. This section examines these differences in more detail and illustrates the operations that are allowed for reference variables.

2.2.1 the dot operator (.)

The dot operator (`.`) is used to select a method that is applied to an object. For instance, suppose we have an object of type `Circle` that defines an `area` method. If `theCircle` references a `Circle`, then we can compute the area of the referenced `Circle` (and save it to a variable of type `double`) by doing this:

```
double theArea = theCircle.area( );
```

It is possible that `theCircle` stores the `null` reference. In this case, applying the dot operator will generate a `NullPointerException` when the program runs. Generally, this will cause abnormal termination.

The dot operator can also be used to access individual components of an object, provided arrangements have been made to allow internal components to be viewable. Chapter 3 discusses how these arrangements are made. Chapter 3 also explains why it is generally preferable to not allow direct access of individual components.

2.2.2 declaration of objects

We have already seen the syntax for declaring primitive variables. For objects, there is an important difference. When we declare a reference variable, we are simply providing a name that can be used to reference an object that is stored in memory. However, the declaration by itself does not provide that object. For example, suppose there is an object of type `Button` that we want to add into an existing `Panel p`, using the method `add` (all this is provided in the Java library). Consider the statements

```
Button b;              // b may reference a Button object
b.setLabel( "No" );    // Label the button b refers to "No"
p.add( b );            // and add it to Panel p
```

All seems well with these statements until we remember that `b` is the name of some `Button` object but no `Button` has been created yet. As a result, after the declaration of `b` the value stored by the reference variable `b` is `null`, meaning `b` is not yet referring to a valid `Button` object. Consequently, the second line is illegal because we are attempting to alter an object that does not exist. In this scenario, the compiler will probably detect the error, stating that "b is uninitialized." In other cases, the compiler will not notice, and a run-time error will result in the cryptic `NullPointerException` error message.

When a reference type is declared, no object is allocated. At that point, the reference is to `null`. To create the object, use `new`.

The (only common) way to allocate an object is to use the `new` keyword. `new` is used to construct an object. One way to do this is as follows:

The `new` keyword is used to *construct* an object.

```
Button b;              // b may reference a Button object
b = new Button( );     // Now b refers to an allocated object
b.setLabel( "No" );    // Label the Button b refers to "No"
p.add( b );            // and add it to Panel p
```

Note that parentheses are required after the object name.

Parentheses are required when `new` is used.

It is also possible to combine the declaration and object construction, as in

```
Button b = new Button( );
b.setLabel( "No" );    // Label the Button b refers to "No"
p.add( b );            // and add it to Panel p
```

Many objects can also be constructed with initial values. For instance, it happens that the `Button` can be constructed with a `String` that specifies the label:

The construction can specify an initial state of the object.

```
Button b = new Button( "No" );
p.add( b );            // Add it to Panel p
```

2.2.3 garbage collection

Since all objects must be constructed, we might expect that when they are no longer needed, we must explicitly destroy them. In Java, when a constructed object is no longer referenced by any object variable, the memory it consumes will automatically be reclaimed and therefore be made available. This technique is known as *garbage collection*.

Java uses *garbage collection*. With garbage collection, unreferenced memory is automatically reclaimed.

The runtime system (i.e., the Java Virtual Machine) guarantees that as long as it is possible to access an object by a reference, or a chain of references, the object will never be reclaimed. Once the object is unreachable by a chain of references, it can be reclaimed at the discretion of the runtime system if memory is low. It is possible that if memory does not run low, the virtual machine will not attempt to reclaim these objects.

2.2.4 the meaning of =

`lhs` and `rhs` stand for *left-hand side* and *right-hand side*, respectively.

Suppose we have two primitive variables `lhs` and `rhs` where `lhs` and `rhs` stand for *left-hand side* and *right-hand side*, respectively. Then the assignment statement

```
lhs = rhs;
```

has a simple meaning: The value stored in `rhs` is copied to the primitive variable `lhs`. Subsequent changes to either `lhs` or `rhs` do not affect the other.

For objects, = is a reference assignment, rather than an object copy.

For objects, the meaning of = is the same: Stored values are copied. If `lhs` and `rhs` are references (of compatible types), then after the assignment statement, `lhs` will refer to the same object that `rhs` does. Here, what is being copied is an address. The object that `lhs` used to refer to is no longer referred to by `lhs`. If `lhs` was the only reference to that object, then that object is now unreferenced and subject to garbage collection. Note that the objects are not copied.

Here are some examples. First, suppose we want two `Button` objects. Then suppose we try to obtain them first by creating `noButton`. Then we attempt to create `yesButton` by modifying `noButton` as follows:

```
Button noButton = new Button( "No" );
Button yesButton = noButton;
yesButton.setLabel( "Yes" );
p.add( noButton );
p.add( yesButton );
```

This does not work because only one `Button` object has been constructed. Thus the second statement simply states that `yesButton` is now another name for the constructed `Button` at line 1. That constructed `Button` is now known by two names. On line 3, the constructed `Button` has its label changed to `Yes`, but this means that the single `Button` object, known by two names, is now labeled `Yes`. The last two lines add that `Button` object to the `Panel p` twice.

The fact that `yesButton` never referred to its own object is immaterial in this example. The problem is the assignment. Consider

```
Button noButton = new Button( "No" );
Button yesButton = new Button( );
yesButton = noButton;
yesButton.setLabel( "Yes" );
p.add( noButton );
p.add( yesButton );
```

The consequences are the same. Here, there are two Button objects that have been constructed. At the end of the sequence, the first object is being referenced by both noButton and yesButton, while the second object is unreferenced.

At first glance, the fact that objects cannot be copied seems like a severe limitation. Actually, it is not, although this does take a little getting used to. (Some objects do need to be copied. For those, if a clone method is available, it should be used. However, clone is not used in this text.)

2.2.5 parameter passing

Because of call-by-value, the actual arguments are sent into the formal parameters using normal assignment. If the parameter is a reference type, then we know that normal assignment means that the formal parameter now references the same object as does the actual argument. Any method applied to the formal parameter is thus also being applied to the actual argument. In other languages, this is known as *call-by-reference parameter passing*. Using this terminology for Java would be somewhat misleading because it implies that the parameter passing is different. In reality, the parameter passing has not changed; rather, it is the parameters that have changed, from nonreference types to reference types.

Call-by-value means that for reference types, the formal parameter references the same object as does the actual argument.

As an example, suppose we pass yesButton as a parameter to the clearButton routine that is defined as follows:

```
public static void clearButton( Button b )
{
    b.setLabel( "No" );
    b = null;
}
```

Then, as Figure 2.3 shows, b references the same object as yesButton, and changes made to the state of this object by methods invoked through b will be seen when clearButton returns. Changes to the value of b (i.e., which object it references) will not have any affect on yesButton.

2.2.6 the meaning of ==

For primitive types, == is true if the stored values are identical. For reference types, its meaning is different but is perfectly consistent with the previous discussion.

For reference types, == is true only if the two references reference the *same object*.

Two reference types are equal via == if they refer to the same stored object (or they are both null). Consider, for example, the following:

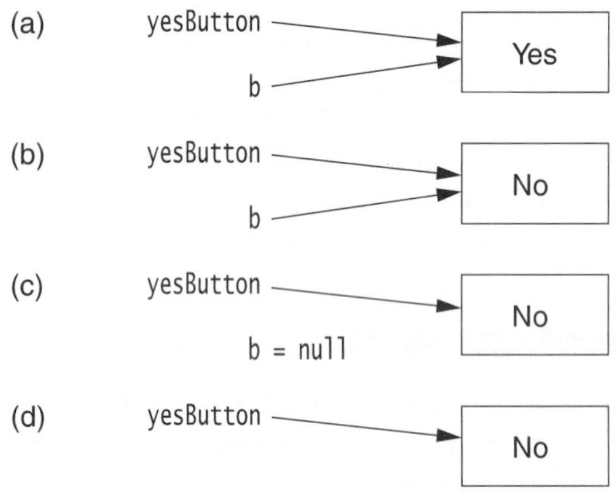

figure 2.3

The result of call-by-value. (a) b is a copy of yesButton; (b) after b.setLabel("No"): changes to the state of the object referenced by b are reflected in the object referenced by yesButton because these are the same object; (c) after b=null: change to the value of b does not affect the value of yesButton; (d) after the method returns, b is out of scope.

```
Button a = new Button( "Yes" );
Button b = new Button( "Yes" );
Button c = b;
```

Here, we have two objects. The first is known by the name a, and the second is known by two names: b and c. b==c is true. However, even though a and b are referencing objects that seem to have the same value, a==b is false, since they reference different objects. Similar rules apply for !=.

The equals method can be used to test whether two references reference objects that have identical states.

Sometimes it is important to know if the states of the objects being referenced are identical. All objects can be compared by using equals, but for many objects (including Button) equals returns false unless the two references are referencing the same object (in other words, for some objects equals is no more than the == test). We will see an example of where equals is useful when the String type is discussed in Section 2.3.

2.2.7 no operator overloading for objects

Except for the single exception described in the next section, new operators, such as +, -, *, and / cannot be defined to work for objects. Thus there is no < operator available for any object. Instead, a named method, such as lessThan, must be defined for this task.

2.3 strings

Strings in Java are handled with the `String` reference type. The language does make it appear that the `String` type is a primitive type because it provides the `+` and `+=` operators for concatenation. However, this is the only reference type for which any operator overloading is allowed. Otherwise, the `String` behaves like any other reference type.

The `String` behaves like a reference type.

2.3.1 basics of string manipulation

There are two fundamental rules about a `String` object. First, with the exception of the concatenation operators, it behaves like an object. Second, the `String` is *immutable*. This means that once a `String` object is constructed, its contents may not be changed.

Strings are *immutable*; that is, a `String` object will not be changed.

Because a `String` is immutable, it is always safe to use the `=` operator with it. Thus a `String` may be declared as follows:

```
String empty   = "";
String message = "Hello";
String repeat  = message;
```

After these declarations, there are two `String` objects. The first is the empty string, which is referenced by `empty`. The second is the `String` `"Hello"` which is referenced by both `message` and `repeat`. For most objects, being referenced by both `message` and `repeat` could be a problem. However, because `Strings` are immutable, the sharing of `String` objects is safe, as well as efficient. The only way to change the value that the string `repeat` refers to is to construct a new `String` and have `repeat` reference it. This has no effect on the `String` that `message` references.

2.3.2 string concatenation

Java does not allow operator overloading for reference types. However, a special language exemption is granted for string concatenation.

The operator `+`, when at least one operand is a `String`, performs concatenation. The result is a reference to a newly constructed `String` object. For example,

String concatenation is performed with + (and +=).

```
"this" + " that"      // Generates "this that"
"abc" + 5             // Generates "abc5"
5 + "abc"             // Generates "5abc"
"a" + "b" + "c"       // Generates "abc"
```

Single-character strings should not be replaced with character constants; Exercise 2.6 asks you to show why. Note that operator `+` is left-associative, and thus

```
"a" + 1 + 2          // Generates "a12"
1 + 2 + "a"          // Generates "3a"
1 + ( 2 + "a" )      // Generates "12a"
```

Also, operator `+=` is provided for the `String`. The effect of `str+=exp` is the same as `str=str+exp`. Specifically, this means that `str` will reference the newly constructed `String` generated by `str+exp`.

2.3.3 comparing strings

> Use `equals` and `compareTo` to perform string comparison.

Since the basic assignment operator works for `Strings`, it is tempting to assume that the relational and equality operators also work. This is not true.

In accordance with the ban on operator overloading, relational operators (`<`, `>`, `<=`, and `>=`) are not defined for the `String` type. Further, `==` and `!=` have the typical meaning for reference variables. For two `String` objects `lhs` and `rhs`, for example, `lhs==rhs` is `true` only if `lhs` and `rhs` refer to the same `String` object. Thus, if they refer to different objects that have identical contents, `lhs==rhs` is `false`. Similar logic applies for `!=`.

To compare two `String` objects for equality, we use the `equals` method. `lhs.equals(rhs)` is `true` if `lhs` and `rhs` reference `Strings` that store identical values.

A more general test can be performed with the `compareTo` method. `lhs.compareTo(rhs)` compares two `String` objects, `lhs` and `rhs`. It returns a negative number, zero, or a positive number, depending on whether `lhs` is lexicographically less than, equal to, or greater than `rhs`, respectively.

2.3.4 other `String` methods

> Use `length`, `charAt`, and `substring` to compute string length, get a single character, and get a substring, respectively.

The length of a `String` object (an empty string has length zero) can be obtained with the method `length`. Since `length` is a method, parentheses are required.

Two methods are defined to access individual characters in a `String`. The method `charAt` gets a single character by specifying a position (the first position is position 0). The method `substring` returns a reference to a newly constructed `String`. The call is made by specifying the starting point and the first nonincluded position.

Here is an example of these three methods:

```
String greeting = "hello";
int len    = greeting.length( );           // len is 5
char ch    = greeting.charAt( 1 );         // ch  is 'e'
String sub = greeting.substring( 2, 4 );  // sub is "ll"
```

2.3.5 converting other types to strings

String concatenation provides a lazy way to convert any primitive to a `String`. For instance, `""+45.3` returns the newly constructed `String` `"45.3"`. There are also methods to do this directly.

`toString` converts primitive types (and objects) to `Strings`.

The method `toString` can be used to convert any primitive type to a `String`. As an example, `Integer.toString(45)` returns a reference to the newly constructed `String` `"45"`. All reference types also provide an implementation of `toString` of varying quality. In fact, when operator `+` has only one `String` argument, the non`String` argument is converted to a `String` by automatically applying an appropriate `toString`. For the integer types, an alternative form of `Integer.toString` allows the specification of a radix. Thus

```
System.out.println( "55 in base 2: " + Integer.toString( 55, 2 ) );
```

prints out the binary representation of 55.

The `int` value that is represented by a `String` can be obtained by calling the method `Integer.parseInt`. This method generates an exception if the `String` does not represent an `int`. Exceptions are discussed in Section 2.5. Similar ideas work for a `doubles`. Here are some examples:

```
int    x = Integer.parseInt( "75" );
double y = Double.parseDouble( "3.14" );
```

2.4 arrays

An *aggregate* is a collection of entities stored in one unit. An *array* is the basic mechanism for storing a collection of identically typed entities. In Java the array is not a primitive type. Instead, it behaves very much like an object. Thus many of the rules for objects also apply to arrays.

An *array* stores a collection of identically typed entities.

Each entity in the array can be accessed via the *array indexing operator* `[]`. We say that the `[]` operator *indexes* the array, meaning that it specifies which object is to be accessed. Unlike C and C++, bounds-checking is performed automatically.

The *array indexing operator* `[]` provides access to any object in the array.

In Java, arrays are always indexed starting at zero. Thus an array `a` of three items stores `a[0]`, `a[1]`, and `a[2]`. The number of items that can be stored

Arrays are indexed starting at zero. The number of items stored in the array is obtained by the `length` field. No parentheses are used.

in an array a can always be obtained by `a.length`. Note that there are no parentheses. A typical array loop would use

```
for( int i = 0; i < a.length; i++ )
```

2.4.1 declaration, assignment, and methods

An array is an object, so when the array declaration

```
int [ ] array1;
```

To allocate an array, use `new`.

is given, no memory is yet allocated to store the array. `array1` is simply a name (reference) for an array, and at this point is `null`. To have 100 `int`s, for example, we use `new`:

```
array1 = new int [ 100 ];
```

Now `array1` references an array of 100 `int`s.

There are other ways to declare arrays. For instance, in some contexts

```
int [ ] array2 = new int [ 100 ];
```

is acceptable. Also, initializer lists can be used, as in C or C++, to specify initial values. In the next example, an array of four `int`s is allocated and then referenced by `array3`.

```
int [ ] array3 = { 3, 4, 10, 6 };
```

The brackets can go either before or after the array name. Placing them before makes it easier to see that the name is an array type, so that is the style used here. Declaring an array of reference types (rather than primitive types) uses the same syntax. Note, however, that when we allocate an array of reference types, each reference initially stores a `null` reference. Each also must be set to reference a constructed object. For instance, an array of five buttons is constructed as

```
Button [ ] arrayOfButtons;
arrayOfButtons = new Button [ 5 ];
for( int i = 0; i < arrayOfButtons.length; i++ )
    arrayOfButtons[ i ] = new Button( );
```

Figure 2.4 illustrates the use of arrays in Java. The program in Figure 2.4 repeatedly chooses numbers between 1 and 100, inclusive. The output is the number of times that each number has occurred. The `import` directive at line 1 will be discussed in Section 3.6.1.

```
 1 import java.util.Random;
 2 
 3 public class RandomNumbers
 4 {
 5     // Generate random numbers (from 1-100)
 6     // Print number of occurrences of each number
 7 
 8     public static final int DIFF_NUMBERS     =     100;
 9     public static final int TOTAL_NUMBERS    = 1000000;
10 
11     public static void main( String [ ] args )
12     {
13         // Create array; initialize to 0s
14         int [ ] numbers = new int [ DIFF_NUMBERS + 1 ];
15         for( int i = 0; i < numbers.length; i++ )
16             numbers[ i ] = 0;
17 
18         Random r = new Random( );
19 
20         // Generate the numbers
21         for( int i = 0; i < TOTAL_NUMBERS; i++ )
22             numbers[ r.nextInt( DIFF_NUMBERS ) + 1 ]++;
23 
24         // Output the summary
25         for( int i = 1; i <= DIFF_NUMBERS; i++ )
26             System.out.println( i + ": " + numbers[ i ] );
27     }
28 }
```

figure 2.4

Simple demonstration of arrays

Line 14 declares an array of integers that count the occurrences of each number. Because arrays are indexed starting at zero, the +1 is crucial if we want to access the item in position `DIFFERENT_NUMBERS`. Without it we would have an array whose indexible range was 0 to 99, and thus any access to index 100 would be out-of-bounds. The loop at lines 15 and 16 initializes the array entries to zero; this is actually unnecessary, since by default, array elements are initialized to zero for primitive and `null` for references.

Always be sure to declare the correct array size. Off-by-one errors are common.

The rest of the program is relatively straightforward. It uses the `Random` object defined in the `java.util` library (hence the `import` directive at line 1). The `nextInt` method repeatedly gives a (somewhat) random number in the range that includes zero but stops at one less than the parameter to `nextInt`; thus by adding `1`, we get a number in the desired range. The results are output at lines 25 and 26.

Since an array is a reference type, `=` does not copy arrays. Instead, if `lhs` and `rhs` are arrays, the effect of

```
int [ ] lhs = new int [ 100 ];
int [ ] rhs = new int [ 100 ];
   ...
lhs = rhs;
```

is that the array object that was referenced by `rhs` is now also referenced by `lhs`. Thus changing `rhs[0]` also changes `lhs[0]`. (To make `lhs` an independent copy of `rhs`, one could use the `clone` method, but often making complete copies is not really needed.)

Finally, an array can be used as a parameter to a method. The rules follow logically from our understanding that an array name is a reference. Suppose we have a method `methodCall` that accepts one array of `int` as its parameter. The caller/callee views are

```
methodCall( actualArray );              // method call
void methodCall( int [ ] formalArray ) // method declaration
```

The contents of an array are passed by reference.

In accordance with the parameter-passing conventions for Java reference types, `formalArray` references the same array object as `actualArray`. Thus `formalArray[i]` accesses `actualArray[i]`. This means that if the method modifies any element in the array, the modifications will be observable after the method execution has completed. Also note that a statement such as

```
formalArray = new int [ 20 ];
```

has no effect on `actualArray`. Finally, since array names are simply references, they can be returned.

2.4.2 dynamic array expansion

Dynamic array expansion allows us to allocate arbitrary-sized arrays and make them larger if needed.

Suppose we want to read a sequence of numbers and store them in an array for processing. The fundamental property of an array requires us to declare a size so that the compiler can allocate the correct amount of memory. Also, we must make this declaration prior to the first access of the array. If we have no idea how many items to expect, then it is difficult to make a reasonable choice for the array size. This section shows how to expand arrays if the initial size is too small. This technique is called *dynamic array expansion* and allows us to allocate arbitrary-sized arrays and make them larger or smaller as the program runs.

The allocation method for arrays that we have seen thus far is

```
int [ ] arr = new int[ 10 ];
```

Suppose that we decide, after the declarations, that we really need 12 `int`s instead of 10. In this case, we can use the following maneuver, which is illustrated in Figure 2.5:

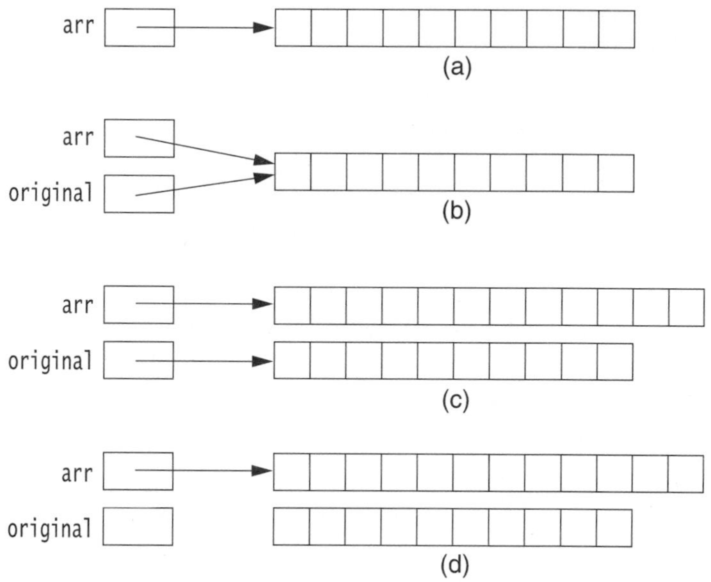

figure 2.5

Array expansion, internally: (a) At the starting point, `arr` represents 10 integers; (b) after step 1, `original` represents the same 10 integers; (c) after steps 2 and 3, `arr` represents 12 integers, the first 10 of which are copied from `original`; and (d) after step 4, the 10 integers are available for reclamation.

```
int [ ] original = arr;         // 1. Save reference to arr
arr = new int [ 12 ];           // 2. Have arr reference more memory
for( int i = 0; i < 10; i++ )  // 3. Copy the old data over
    arr[ i ] = original[ i ];
original = null;                // 4. Unreference original array
```

A moment's thought will convince you that this is an expensive operation. This is because we copy all of the elements from `original` back to `arr`. If, for instance, this array expansion is in response to reading input, it would be inefficient to reexpand every time we read a few elements. Thus when array expansion is implemented, we always make it some *multiplicative* constant times as large. For instance, we might expand it to be twice as large. In this way, when we expand the array from N items to $2N$ items, the cost of the N copies can be apportioned over the next N items that can be inserted into the array without an expansion.

Always expand the array to a size that is some multiplicative constant times as large. Doubling is a good choice.

To make things more concrete, Figures 2.6 and 2.7 show a program that reads an unlimited number of strings from the standard input and stores the result in a dynamically expanding array. An empty line is used to signal the end of input. (The minimal I/O details used here are not important for this example and are discussed in Section 2.6.) The `resize` routine performs the array expansion (or shrinking), returning a reference to the new array. Similarly, the method `getStrings` returns (a reference to) the array where it will reside.

figure 2.6

Code to read an unlimited number of `Strings` and output them (part 1)

```
1 import java.io.InputStreamReader;
2 import java.io.BufferedReader;
3 import java.io.IOException;
4
5 public class ReadStrings
6 {
7     // Read an unlimited number of Strings; return a String [ ]
8     // The minimal I/O details used here are not important for
9     // this example and are discussed in Section 2.6.
10     public static String [ ] getStrings( )
11     {
12         BufferedReader in = new BufferedReader( new
13                              InputStreamReader( System.in ) );
14         String [ ] array = new String[ 5 ];
15         String oneLine;
16         int itemsRead = 0;
17
18         System.out.println( "Enter strings, one per line; " );
19         System.out.println( "Terminate with empty line: " );
20
21         try
22         {
23             while( ( oneLine = in.readLine( ) ) != null &&
24                     !oneLine.equals( "" ) )
25             {
26                 if( itemsRead == array.length )
27                     array = resize( array, array.length * 2 );
28                 array[ itemsRead++ ] = oneLine;
29             }
30         }
31         catch( IOException e )
32         {
33             System.out.println( "Early abort of read." );
34         }
35
36         return resize( array, itemsRead );
37     }
```

At the start of `getStrings`, `itemsRead` is set to 0 and we start with an initial five-element array. We repeatedly read new items at line 23. If the array is full, as indicated by a successful test at line 26, then the array is expanded by calling `resize`. Lines 42 to 48 perform the array expansion using the exact strategy outlined previously. At line 28, the actual input item is assigned to the array and the number of items read is incremented. If an error occurs on input, we simply stop processing. Finally, at line 36 we shrink the array to match the number of items read prior to returning.

```
    // Resize a String[ ] array; return new array
    public static String [ ] resize( String [ ] array,
                                     int newSize )
    {
        String [ ] original = array;
        int numToCopy = Math.min( original.length, newSize );

        array = new String[ newSize ];
        for( int i = 0; i < numToCopy; i++ )
            array[ i ] = original[ i ];
        return array;
    }

    public static void main( String [ ] args )
    {
        String [ ] array = getStrings( );
        for( int i = 0; i < array.length; i++ )
            System.out.println( array[ i ] );
    }
}
```

figure 2.7

Code to read an unlimited number of Strings and output them (part 2)

2.4.3 ArrayList

The technique used in Section 2.4.2 is so common that the Java library contains an ArrayList type with built-in functionality to mimic it. The basic idea is that an ArrayList maintains not only a size, but also a capacity; the capacity is the amount of memory that it has reserved. The capacity of the ArrayList is really an internal detail, not something that you need worry about.

> The ArrayList is used for expanding arrays.

The add method increases the size by one, and adds a new item into the array at the appropriate position. This is a trivial operation if capacity has not been reached. If it has, the capacity is automatically expanded, using the strategy described in Section 2.4.2. The ArrayList is initialized with a size of 0.

> The add method increases the size by 1 and adds a new item to the array at the appropriate position, expanding capacity if needed.

Because indexing via [] is reserved only for primitive arrays, much as was the case for Strings, we have to use a method to access the ArrayList items. The get method returns the object at a specified index, and the set method can be used to change the value of a reference at a specified index; get thus behaves like the charAt method. We will be describing the implementation details of ArrayList at several points in the text, and eventually write our own version.

The code in Figure 2.8 shows how add is used in getStrings; it is clearly much simpler than the getStrings function in Section 2.4.2. As shown at line 23, the ArrayList specifies the type of objects that it stores. Only the specified type can be added to the ArrayList; other types will cause a compile-

```
import java.io.InputStreamReader;
import java.io.BufferedReader;
import java.io.IOException;

import java.util.ArrayList;

public class ReadStringsWithArrayList
{
    public static void main( String [ ] args )
    {
        ArrayList array = getStrings( );
        for( int i = 0; i < array.size( ); i++ )
            System.out.println( array.get( i ) );
    }

    // Read an unlimited number of Strings; return an ArrayList
    // The minimal I/O details used here are not important for
    // this example and are discussed in Section 2.6.
    public static ArrayList getStrings( )
    {
        BufferedReader in = new BufferedReader( new
                             InputStreamReader( System.in ) );
        ArrayList<String> array = new ArrayList<String>( );
        String oneLine;

        System.out.println( "Enter any number of strings, one per line; " );
        System.out.println( "Terminate with empty line: " );

        try
        {
            while( ( oneLine = in.readLine( ) ) != null &&
                    !oneLine.equals( "" ) )
                array.add( oneLine );
        }
        catch( IOException e )
        {
            System.out.println( "Early abort of read" );
        }

        System.out.println( "Done reading" );
        return array;
    }
}
```

figure 2.8

Code to read an unlimited number of `Strings` and output them, using an `ArrayList`

time error. It is important to mention, however, that only objects (which are accessed by reference variables) can be added into an `ArrayList`. The eight primitive types cannot. However, there is an easy workaround for that, which we will discuss in Section 4.6.2.

The specification of the type is a feature added in Java 5 known as *generics*. Prior to Java 5, the `ArrayList` did not specify the type of objects, and any type could be added to the `ArrayList`. For backward compatibility, failure to specify the type of objects in the `ArrayList` declaration is still allowed, but its use will generate a warning because it removes the ability of the compiler to detect type mismatches, forcing those errors to be detected much later by the Virtual Machine when the program is actually run. Sections 4.6 and 4.8 describe both the old style and the new style.

2.4.4 multidimensional arrays

Sometimes arrays need to be accessed by more than one index. A common example of this is a matrix. A *multidimensional array* is an array that is accessed by more than one index. It is allocated by specifying the size of its indices, and each element is accessed by placing each index in its own pair of brackets. As an example, the declaration

A *multidimensional array* is an array that is accessed by more than one index.

```
int [ ][ ] x = new int[ 2 ][ 3 ];
```

defines the two-dimensional array `x`, with the first index (representing the number of rows) ranging from 0 to 1 and the second index (the number of columns) ranging from 0 to 2 (for a total of six `int`s). Six memory locations are set aside for these `int`s.

In the example above, the two-dimensional array is actually an array of arrays. As such, the number of rows is `x.length`, which is 2. The number of columns is `x[0].length` or `x[1].length`, both of which are 3.

Figure 2.9 illustrates how to print the contents of a two-dimensional array. The code works not only for rectangular two-dimensional arrays, but also for *ragged two-dimensional arrays*, in which the number of columns varies from row to row. This is easily handled by using `m[i].length` at line 11 to represent the number of columns in row `i`. We also handle the possibility that a row might be `null` (which is different than length 0), with the test at line 7. The `main` routine illustrates the declaration of two-dimensional arrays for the case where initial values are known. It is simply an extension of the one-dimensional case discussed in Section 2.4.1. Array `a` is a straightforward rectangular matrix, array `b` has a `null` row, and array `c` is ragged.

figure 2.9

Printing a two-dimensional array

```
public class MatrixDemo
{
    public static void printMatrix( int [ ][ ] m )
    {
        for( int i = 0; i < m.length; i++ )
        {
            if( m[ i ] == null )
                System.out.println( "(null)" );
            else
            {
                for( int j = 0; j < m[i].length; j++ )
                    System.out.print( m[ i ][ j ] + " " );
                System.out.println( );
            }
        }
    }

    public static void main( String [ ] args )
    {
        int [ ][ ] a = { { 1, 2 }, { 3, 4 }, { 5, 6 } };
        int [ ][ ] b = { { 1, 2 }, null, { 5, 6 } };
        int [ ][ ] c = { { 1, 2 }, { 3, 4, 5 }, { 6 } };

        System.out.println( "a: " ); printMatrix( a );
        System.out.println( "b: " ); printMatrix( b );
        System.out.println( "c: " ); printMatrix( c );
    }
}
```

2.4.5 **command-line arguments**

Command-line arguments are available by examining the parameter to `main`.

Command-line arguments are available by examining the parameter to `main`. The array of strings represents the additional command-line arguments. For instance, when the program is invoked,

```
java Echo this that
```

`args[0]` references the `String` `"this"` and `args[1]` references the `String` `"that"`. Thus the program in Figure 2.10 mimics the standard *echo* command.

2.4.6 **enhanced** `for` **loop**

Java 5 adds new syntax that allows you to access each element in an array or `ArrayList`, without the need for array indexes. Its syntax is

```
public class Echo
{
    // List the command-line arguments
    public static void main( String [ ] args )
    {
        for( int i = 0; i < args.length - 1; i++ )
            System.out.print( args[ i ] + " " );
        if( args.length != 0 )
            System.out.println( args[ args.length - 1 ] );
        else
            System.out.println( "No arguments to echo" );
    }
}
```

figure 2.10
The *echo* command

```
for( type var : collection )
    statement
```

Inside `statement`, `var` represents the current element in the iteration. For instance, to print out the elements in `arr`, which has type `String[]`, we can write:

```
for( String val : arr )
    System.out.println( val );
```

The same code works unchanged if `arr` has type `ArrayList<String>`, which is a perk because without the enhanced `for` loop, the looping code must be rewritten when the type switches from an array to an `ArrayList`.

The enhanced `for` loop has some limitations. First, in many applications you must have the index, especially if making changes to the array (or `ArrayList`) values. Second, the enhanced `for` loop is useful only if you are accessing every item, in sequential order. If one item is to be excluded, you should use the standard `for` loop. Examples of loops that are not easily rewritten using an enhanced loop include

```
for( int i = 0; i < arr1.length; i++ )
    arr1[ i ] = 0;

for( int i = 0; i < args.length - 1; i++ )
    System.out.println( args[ i ] + " " );
```

In addition to allowing iteration through arrays and `ArrayList`s, the enhanced `for` loop can be used in other types of collections. This use is discussed in Chapter 6.

2.5 exception handling

Exceptions are used to handle exceptional occurrences such as errors.

Exceptions are objects that store information and are transmitted outside the normal return sequence. They are propagated back through the calling sequence until some routine *catches* the exception. At that point, the information stored in the object can be extracted to provide error handling. Such information will always include details about where the exception was created. The other important piece of information is the type of the exception object. For instance, it is clear that the basic problem is a bad index when an `ArrayIndexOutBoundsException` is propagated. Exceptions are used to signal *exceptional occurrences* such as errors.

2.5.1 processing exceptions

A `try` block encloses code that might generate an exception.

The code in Figure 2.11 illustrates the use of exceptions. Code that might result in the propagation of an exception is enclosed in a `try` block. The `try` block extends from lines 17 to 21. Immediately following the `try` block are the exception handlers. This part of the code is jumped to only if an exception is raised; at the point the exception is raised, the `try` block in which it came from is considered terminated. Each `catch` block is attempted in order until a matching handler is found. An `IOException` is generated by `readLine` if some unexpected error occurs, and a `NumberFormatException` is generated by `parseInt` if `oneLine` is not convertible to an `int`.

A `catch` block processes an exception.

The code in the `catch` block—in this case line 23 or 25—is executed if the appropriate exception is matched. Then the `catch` block and the `try/catch` sequence is considered terminated.[1] A meaningful message is printed from the exception object `e`. Alternatively, additional processing and more detailed error messages could be given.

2.5.2 the `finally` clause

The `finally` clause is always executed prior to completion of a block, regardless of exceptions.

Some objects that are created in a `try` block must be cleaned up. For instance, files that are opened in the `try` block may need to be closed prior to leaving the `try` block. One problem with this is that if an exception object is thrown during execution of the `try` block, the cleanup might be omitted because the exception will cause an immediate break from the `try` block. Although we can place the cleanup immediately after the last `catch` clause, this works only if

1. Note that both `try` and `catch` require a block and not simply a single statement. Thus braces are not optional. To save space, we often place simple `catch` clauses on a single line with their braces, indented two additional spaces, rather than use three lines. Later in the text we will use this style for one-line methods.

```java
import java.io.BufferedReader;
import java.io.InputStreamReader;
import java.io.IOException;

public class DivideByTwo
{
    public static void main( String [ ] args )
    {
            // BufferedReader is discussed in Section 2.6
        BufferedReader in = new BufferedReader( new
                              InputStreamReader( System.in ) );
        int x;
        String oneLine;

        System.out.println( "Enter an integer: " );
        try
        {
            oneLine = in.readLine( );
            x = Integer.parseInt( oneLine );
            System.out.println( "Half of x is " + ( x / 2 ) );
        }
        catch( IOException e )
          { System.out.println( e ); }
        catch( NumberFormatException e )
          { System.out.println( e ); }
    }
}
```

figure 2.11

Simple program to illustrate exceptions

the exception is caught by one of the catch clauses. And this may be difficult to guarantee.

The `finally` clause that may follow the last `catch` block (or the `try` block, if there are no `catch` blocks) is used in this situation. The `finally` clause consists of the keyword `finally` followed by the `finally` block. There are three basic scenarios.

1. If the `try` block executes without exception, control passes to the `finally` block. This is true even if the `try` block exits prior to the last statement via a `return`, `break`, or `continue`.
2. If an uncaught exception is encountered inside the `try` block, control passes to the `finally` block. Then, after executing the `finally` block, the exception propagates.
3. If a caught exception is encountered in the `try` block, control passes to the appropriate `catch` block. Then, after executing the `catch` block, the `finally` block is executed.

2.5.3 common exceptions

Runtime exceptions do not have to be handled.

There are several types of standard exceptions in Java. The *standard runtime exceptions* include events such as integer divide-by-zero and illegal array access. Since these events can happen virtually anywhere, it would be overly burdensome to require exception handlers for them. If a `catch` block is provided, these exceptions behave like any other exception. If a `catch` block is not provided for a standard exception, and a standard exception is thrown, then it propagates as usual, possibly past `main`. In this case, it causes an abnormal program termination, with an error message. Some of the common standard runtime exceptions are shown in Figure 2.12. Generally speaking, these are programming errors and should not be caught. A notable violation of this principle is `NumberFormatException`, but `NullPointerException` is more typical.

Checked exceptions must be handled or listed in a `throws` clause.

Most exceptions are of the *standard checked exception* variety. If a method is called that might either directly or indirectly throw a standard checked exception, then the programmer must either provide a `catch` block for it, or explicitly indicate that the exception is to be propagated by use of a `throws` clause in the method declaration. Note that eventually it should be handled because it is terrible style for `main` to have a `throws` clause. Some of the common standard checked exceptions are shown in Figure 2.13.

Errors are unrecoverable exceptions.

`Errors` are virtual machine problems. `OutOfMemoryError` is the most common error. Others include `InternalError` and the infamous `UnknownError`, in which the virtual machine has decided that it is in trouble, does not know why, but does not want to continue. Generally speaking, an `Error` is unrecoverable and should not be caught.

figure 2.12

Common standard runtime exceptions

Standard Runtime Exception	Meaning
`ArithmeticException`	Overflow or integer division by zero.
`NumberFormatException`	Illegal conversion of `String` to numeric type.
`IndexOutOfBoundsException`	Illegal index into an array or `String`.
`NegativeArraySizeException`	Attempt to create a negative-length array.
`NullPointerException`	Illegal attempt to use a null reference.
`SecurityException`	Run-time security violation.

Standard Checked Exception	Meaning
`java.io.EOFException`	End-of-file before completion of input.
`java.io.FileNotFoundException`	File not found to open.
`java.io.IOException`	Includes most I/O exceptions.
`InterruptedException`	Thrown by the `Thread.sleep` method.

figure 2.13
Common standard checked exceptions

2.5.4 the `throw` and `throws` clauses

The programmer can generate an exception by use of the `throw` clause. For instance, we can create and then throw an `ArithmeticException` object by

The `throw` clause is used to throw an exception.

```
throw new ArithmeticException( "Divide by zero" );
```

Since the intent is to signal to the caller that there is a problem, you should never throw an exception only to catch it a few lines later in the same scope. In other words, do not place a `throw` clause in a `try` block and then handle it immediately in the corresponding `catch` block. Instead, let it leave unhandled, and pass the exception up to the caller. Otherwise, you are using exceptions as a cheap goto statement, which is not good programming and is certainly not what an exception—signaling an exceptional occurrence—is to be used for.

Java allows programmers to create their own exception types. Details on creating and throwing user-defined exceptions are provided in Chapter 4.

As mentioned earlier, standard checked exceptions must either be caught or explicitly propagated to the calling routine, but they should, as a last resort, eventually be handled in `main`. To do the latter, the method that is unwilling to catch the exception must indicate, via a `throws` clause, which exceptions it may propagate. The `throws` clause is attached at the end of the method header. Figure 2.14 illustrates a method that propagates any `IOException`s that it encounters; these must eventually be caught in `main` (since we will not place a `throws` clause in `main`).

The `throws` clause indicates propagated exceptions.

2.6 input and output

Input and output (I/O) in Java is achieved through the use of the `java.io` package. The types in the I/O package are all prefixed with `java.io`, including, as

figure 2.14

Illustration of the throws clause

```
import java.io.IOException;

public class ThrowDemo
{
    public static void processFile( String toFile )
                                            throws IOException
    {
        // Omitted implementation propagates all
        // thrown IOExceptions back to the caller
    }

    public static void main( String [ ] args )
    {
        for( String fileName : args )
        {
            try
              { processFile( fileName ); }
            catch( IOException e )
              { System.err.println( e ); }
        }
    }
}
```

we have seen, `java.io.IOException`. The `import` directive allows you to avoid using complete names. For instance, with

```
import java.io.IOException;
```

you can use `IOException` as a shorthand for `java.io.IOException` at the top of your code. (Many common types, such as `String` and `Math`, do not require `import` directives, as they are automatically visible by the shorthands by virtue of being in `java.lang`.)

The Java library is very sophisticated and has a host of options. Here, we examine only the most basic uses, concentrating entirely on formatted I/O. In Section 4.5.3, we will discuss the design of the library.

2.6.1 basic stream operations

Like many languages, Java uses the notion of streams for I/O. To perform I/O to the terminal, a file, or over the Internet, the programmer creates an associated *stream*. Once that is done, all I/O commands are directed to that stream. A programmer defines a stream for each I/O target (for instance, each file requiring input or output).

Three streams are predefined for terminal I/O: `System.in`, the standard input; `System.out`, the standard output; and `System.err`, the standard error.

As already mentioned, the `print` and `println` methods are used for formatted output. Any type can be converted to a `String` suitable for printing by calling its `toString` method; in many cases, this is done automatically. Unlike with C and C++, which have an enormous number of formatting options, output in Java is done almost exclusively by `String` concatenation, with no built-in formatting.

> The predefined streams are `System.in`, `System.out`, and `System.err`.

A simple method for reading formatted input is to read a single line into a `String` object using `readLine`. The `readline` method reads until it encounters a line terminator or end of file. The characters that are read, minus the line terminator (if read), are returned as a newly constructed `String`. To use `readLine`, we must first construct a `BufferedReader` object from an `InputStreamReader` object that is itself constructed from `System.in`. This was illustrated in Figure 2.11 at lines 10 and 11.

> `BufferedReader` is used for line-at-a-time input.

If an immediate end of file is encountered, then `null` is returned. If a read error occurs for some reason other than end of file, then some `IOException` is generated. Note that the `IOException`, which is a standard checked exception, must eventually be caught. In many instances, the `IOException` is allowed to propagate back to a `catch` block in the `main` method; this technique was illustrated in Figure 2.14.

2.6.2 the `StringTokenizer` type

Recall that to read a single primitive type, such as an `int`, we use `readLine` to read the line as a `String` and then apply a method to generate the primitive type from the `String`. For `int`, we can use `parseInt`.

Sometimes we have several items on a line. For instance, suppose each line has two `int`s. Java provides the `StringTokenizer` type to separate a `String` into tokens. To use it by its shortened name, provide the `import` directive

> `StringTokenizer` is used to extract delimited substrings from a large string.

```
import java.util.StringTokenizer;
```

Use of the string tokenizer is illustrated in Figure 2.15. First, at line 25, we construct a `StringTokenizer` object by providing the `String` representing the line of input. The `countTokens` method, shown on line 26, will provide the number of tokens in the `String`; in this example, this should be two, or else the input is in error. Then the `nextToken` method returns the next token as a `String`. This method throws `NoSuchElementException` if there is no token, but this is a runtime exception and does not have to be caught. At lines 31 and 32, we use `nextToken` followed by `parseInt` to obtain an `int`. All errors,

figure 2.15

Program that demonstrates the string tokenizer

```
import java.io.InputStreamReader;
import java.io.BufferedReader;
import java.io.IOException;
import java.util.StringTokenizer;

public class MaxTest
{
    public static void main( String [ ] args )
    {
        BufferedReader in = new BufferedReader( new
                             InputStreamReader( System.in ) );

        String oneLine;
        StringTokenizer str;
        int x;
        int y;

        System.out.println( "Enter 2 ints on one line: " );
        try
        {
            oneLine = in.readLine( );
            if( oneLine == null )
                return;

            str = new StringTokenizer( oneLine );
            if( str.countTokens( ) != 2 )
            {
                System.out.println( "Error: need two ints" );
                return;
            }
            x = Integer.parseInt( str.nextToken( ) );
            y = Integer.parseInt( str.nextToken( ) );
            System.out.println( "Max: " + Math.max( x, y ) );
        }
        catch( IOException e )
          { System.err.println( "Unexpected IO error" ); }
        catch( NumberFormatException e )
          { System.err.println( "Error: need two ints" ); }
    }
}
```

including the failure to provide exactly two tokens, are handled in the `catch` blocks.

By default, tokens are separated by white space. The `StringTokenizer` can be constructed to recognize other characters as delimiters and to include these delimiters as tokens.

2.6.3 sequential files

One of the basic rules of Java is that what works for terminal I/O also works for files. To deal with a file, we do not construct a `BufferedReader` object from an `InputStreamReader`. Instead, we construct it from a `FileReader` object, which itself can be constructed by providing a filename.

`FileReader` is used for file input.

An example that illustrates these basic ideas is shown in Figure 2.16. Here, we have a program that will list the contents of the text files that are specified as command-line arguments. The `main` routine simply steps through the command-line arguments, passing each one to `listFile`. In `listFile`, we construct the `FileReader` object at line 24, and then use it to construct a `BufferedReader` object—`fileIn`—at line 25. At that point, reading is identical to what we have already seen.

After we are done with the file, we must close it; otherwise, we could eventually run out of streams. Note that this cannot be done at the end of the `try` block, since an exception could cause a premature exit from the block. Thus we close the file in a `finally` block, which is guaranteed to be started whether there are no exceptions, handled exceptions, or unhandled exceptions. The code to handle the `close` is complex because

1. `fileIn` must be declared outside of the `try` block in order to be visible in the `finally` block.
2. `fileIn` must be initialized to `null` to avoid compiler complaints about a possible uninitialized variable.
3. Prior to calling `close`, we must check that `fileIn` is not `null` to avoid generating a `NullPointerException` (`fileIn` would be `null` if the file was not found, resulting in an `IOException` prior to its assignment).
4. `close` might itself throw a checked exception, and it requires a `try/catch` block.

Formatted file output is similar to file input. `FileWriter`, `PrintWriter`, and `println` replace `FileReader`, `BufferedReader`, and `readLine`, respectively. Figure 2.17 illustrates a program that double-spaces files that are specified on the command line (the resulting files are placed in a file with a `.ds` extension).

`FileWriter` is used for file output.

This description of Java I/O, while enough to do basic formatted I/O, hides an interesting object-oriented design that is discussed in more detail in Section 4.5.3.

figure 2.16

Program to list contents of a file

```
import java.io.FileReader;
import java.io.BufferedReader;
import java.io.IOException;

public class ListFiles
{
    public static void main( String [ ] args )
    {
        if( args.length == 0 )
            System.out.println( "No files specified" );
        for( String fileName : args )
            listFile( fileName );
    }

    public static void listFile( String fileName )
    {
        FileReader theFile;
        BufferedReader fileIn = null;
        String oneLine;

        System.out.println( "FILE: " + fileName );
        try
        {
            theFile = new FileReader( fileName );
            fileIn  = new BufferedReader( theFile );
            while( ( oneLine = fileIn.readLine( ) ) != null )
                System.out.println( oneLine );
        }
        catch( IOException e )
          {  System.out.println( e ); }
        finally
        {
            // Close the stream
            try
            {
                if(fileIn != null )
                    fileIn.close( );
            }
            catch( IOException e )
              { }
        }
    }
}
```

```java
// Double space files specified on command line.

import java.io.FileReader;
import java.io.BufferedReader;
import java.io.FileWriter;
import java.io.PrintWriter;
import java.io.IOException;

public class DoubleSpace
{
    public static void main( String [ ] args )
    {
        for( String fileName : args )
            doubleSpace( fileName );
    }

    public static void doubleSpace( String fileName )
    {
        PrintWriter   fileOut = null;
        BufferedReader fileIn = null;

        try
        {
            fileIn  = new BufferedReader(
                           new FileReader( fileName ) );
            fileOut = new PrintWriter(
                           new FileWriter( fileName + ".ds" ) );

            String oneLine;
            while( ( oneLine = fileIn.readLine( ) ) != null )
                fileOut.println( oneLine + "\n" );
        }
        catch( IOException e )
          { e.printStackTrace( ); }

        finally
        {
            try
            {
                if( fileOut != null )
                    fileOut.close( );
                if( fileIn != null )
                    fileIn.close( );
            }
            catch( IOException e )
              { e.printStackTrace( ); }
        }
    }
}
```

figure 2.17

A program to double-space files

summary

This chapter examined reference types. A *reference* is a variable that stores either the memory address where an object resides or the special reference `null`. Only objects may be referenced; any object can be referenced by several reference variables. When two references are compared via `==`, the result is `true` if both references refer to the same object. Similarly, `=` makes a reference variable reference another object. Only a few other operations are available. The most significant is the dot operator, which allows the selection of an object's method or access of its internal data.

Because there are only eight primitive types, virtually everything of consequence in Java is an object and is accessed by a reference. This includes `String`s, arrays, exception objects, data and file streams, and a string tokenizer.

The `String` is a special reference type because `+` and `+=` can be used for concatenation. Otherwise, a `String` is like any other reference; `equals` is required to test if the contents of two `String`s are identical. An *array* is a collection of identically typed values. The array is indexed starting at 0, and index range checking is guaranteed to be performed. Arrays can be expanded dynamically by using `new` to allocate a larger amount of memory and then copying over individual elements. This process is done automatically by the `ArrayList`.

Exceptions are used to signal exceptional events. An exception is signaled by the `throw` clause; it is propagated until handled by a `catch` block that is associated with a `try` block. Except for the run-time exceptions and errors, each method must signal the exceptions that it might propagate by using a `throws` list.

`StringTokenizer`s are used to parse a `String` into other `String`s. Typically, they are used in conjunction with other input routines. Input is handled by `BufferedReader`, `InputStreamReader`, and `FileReader` objects.

The next chapter shows how to design new types by defining a *class*.

key concepts

aggregate A collection of objects stored in one unit. (37)

array Stores a collection of identically typed objects. (37)

array indexing operator `[]` Provides access to any element in the array. (37)

`ArrayList` Stores a collection of objects in array-like format, with easy expansion via the `add` method. (43)

`BufferedReader` Used for line-at-a-time input. (53)

call-by-reference In many programming languages, means that the formal parameter is a reference to the actual argument. This is the natural effect achieved in Java when call-by-value is used on reference types. (33)

catch block Used to process an exception. (48)

checked exception Must be either caught or explicitly allowed to propagate by a `throws` clause. (50)

command-line argument Accessed by a parameter to `main`. (46)

construction For objects, is performed via the `new` keyword. (31)

dot member operator (`.`) Allows access to each member of an object. (30)

dynamic array expansion Allows us to make arrays larger if needed. (40)

enhanced for loop Added in Java 5, allows iteration through a collection of items. (46)

equals Used to test if the values stored in two objects are the same. (34)

Error An unrecoverable exception. (50)

exception Used to handle exception occurrences, such as errors. (48)

FileReader Used for file input. (55)

FileWriter Used for file output. (55)

finally clause Always executed prior to exiting a `try/catch` sequence. (48)

garbage collection Automatic reclaiming of unreferenced memory. (31)

immutable Object whose state cannot change. Specifically, `Strings` are immutable. (35)

input and output (I/O) Achieved through the use of the `java.io` package. (51)

java.io Package that is used for nontrivial I/O. (51)

length field Used to determine the size of an array. (38)

length method Used to determine the length of a string. (36)

lhs and **rhs** Stand for left-hand side and right-hand side, respectively. (32)

multidimensional array An array that is accessed by more than one index. (45)

new Used to construct an object. (31)

null reference The value of an object reference that does not refer to any object. (28)

NullPointerException Generated when attempting to apply a method to a `null` reference. (31)

object A nonprimitive entity. (30)

reference type Any type that is not a primitive type. (30)

runtime exception Does not have to be handled. Examples include `ArithmeticException` and `NullPointerException`. (50)

String A special object used to store a collection of characters. (35)

string concatenation Performed with `+` and `+=` operators. (35)

StringTokenizer Used to extract delimited `Strings` from a single `String`. Found in the `java.util` package. (53)

`System.in`, `System.out`, and `System.err` The predefined I/O streams. (53)

`throw` clause Used to throw an exception. (51)

`throws` clause Indicates that a method might propagate an exception. (51)

`toString` method Converts a primitive type or object to a `String`. (37)

`try` block Encloses code that might generate an exception. (48)

common errors

1. For reference types and arrays, `=` does not make a copy of object values. Instead, it copies addresses.
2. For reference types and strings, `equals` should be used instead of `==` to test if two objects have identical states.
3. Off-by-one errors are common in all languages.
4. Reference types are initialized to `null` by default. No object is constructed without calling `new`. An "uninitialized reference variable" or `NullPointerException` indicates that you forgot to allocate the object.
5. In Java, arrays are indexed from 0 to `N-1`, where `N` is the array size. However, range checking is performed, so an out-of-bounds array access is detected at run time.
6. Two-dimensional arrays are indexed as `A[i][j]`, not `A[i,j]`.
7. Checked exceptions must either be caught or explicitly allowed to propagate with a `throws` clause.
8. Use `" "` and not `' '` for outputting a blank.

on the internet

Following are the available files for this chapter. Everything is self-contained, and nothing is used later in the text.

RandomNumbers.java Contains the code for the example in Figure 2.4.

ReadStrings.java Contains the code for the example in Figures 2.6 and 2.7.

ReadStringsWithArrayList.java Contains the code for the example in Figure 2.8.

MatrixDemo.java Contains the code for the example in Figure 2.9.

Echo.java Contains the code for the example in Figure 2.10.

ForEachDemo.java Illustrates the enhanced `for` loop.

DivideByTwo.java	Contains the code for the example in Figure 2.11.
MaxTest.java	Contains the code for the example in Figure 2.15.
ListFiles.java	Contains the code for the example in Figure 2.16.
DoubleSpace.java	Contains the code for the example in Figure 2.17.

exercises

IN SHORT

2.1 List the major differences between reference types and primitive types.

2.2 List five operations that can be applied to a reference type.

2.3 What are the differences between an array and `ArrayList`?

2.4 Describe how exceptions work in Java.

2.5 List the basic operations that can be performed on `String`s.

IN THEORY

2.6 If `x` and `y` have the values of 5 and 7, respectively, what is output by the following?

```
System.out.println( x + ' ' + y );
System.out.println( x + " " + y );
```

IN PRACTICE

2.7 A *checksum* is the 32-bit integer that is the sum of the Unicode characters in a file (we allow silent overflow, but silent overflow is unlikely if all the characters are ASCII). Two identical files have the same checksum. Write a program to compute the checksum of a file that is supplied as a command-line argument.

2.8 Modify the program in Figure 2.16 so that if no command-line arguments are given, then the standard input is used.

2.9 Write a method that returns `true` if `String str1` is a prefix of `String str2`. Do not use any of the general string searching routines except `charAt`.

2.10 Write a routine that prints the total length of the `String`s in a `String[]` passed as a parameter. Your routine must work unchanged if the parameter is changed to an `ArrayList<String>`.

2.11 What is wrong with this code?

```
public static void resize( int [ ] arr )
{
    int [ ] old = arr;
    arr = new int[ old.length * 2 + 1 ];

    for( int i = 0; i < old.length; i++ )
        arr[ i ] = old[ i ];
}
```

2.12 Implement a `split` method that returns an array of `String` containing the tokens of the `String`. The tokens are specified in the exact same way as in the `StringTokenizer` constructor. The method signature for split is

```
public static String [ ] split( String str, String tokens )
```

PROGRAMMING PROJECTS

2.13 Write a program that outputs the number of characters, words, and lines in the files that are supplied as command-line arguments.

2.14 In Java, floating-point divide-by-zero is legal and does not result in an exception (instead, it gives a representation of infinity, negative infinity, or a special not-a-number symbol).

a. Verify the above description by performing some floating-point divisions.

b. Write a static `divide` method that takes two parameters and returns their quotient. If the dividend is 0.0, throw an `ArithmeticException`. Is a `throws` clause needed?

c. Write a `main` program that calls `divide` and catches the `ArithmeticException`. In which method should the `catch` clause be placed?

2.15 Implement a text file copy program. Include a test to make sure that the source and destination files are different.

2.16 Each line of a file contains a name (as a string) and an age (as an integer).

a. Write a program that outputs the oldest person; in case of ties, output any person.

b. Write a program that outputs the oldest person; in case of ties, output all oldest people (*Hint*: Maintain the current group of oldest people in an `ArrayList`).

references

More information can be found in the references at the end of Chapter 1.

chapter 3

objects and classes

This chapter begins the discussion of *object-oriented programming*. A fundamental component of object-oriented programming is the specification, implementation, and use of objects. In Chapter 2, we saw several examples of objects, including strings and files, that are part of the mandatory Java library. We also saw that these objects have an internal state that can be manipulated by applying the dot operator to select a method. In Java, the state and functionality of an object is given by defining a *class*. An object is then an instance of a class.

In this chapter, we will see

- How Java uses the class to achieve *encapsulation* and *information hiding*
- How classes are implemented and automatically documented
- How classes are grouped into *packages*

3.1 what is object-oriented programming?

Object-oriented programming emerged as the dominant paradigm of the mid-1990s. In this section we discuss some of the things that Java provides in the way of object-oriented support and mention some of the principles of object-oriented programming.

Objects are entities that have structure and state. Each object defines operations that may access or manipulate that state.

At the heart of object-oriented programming is the *object*. An object is a data type that has structure and state. Each object defines operations that may access or manipulate that state. As we have already seen, in Java an object is distinguished from a primitive type, but this is a particular feature of Java rather than the object-oriented paradigm. In addition to performing general operations, we can do the following:

- Create new objects, possibly with initialization
- Copy or test for equality
- Perform I/O on these objects

An object is an *atomic unit*: Its parts cannot be dissected by the general users of the object.

Also, we view the object as an *atomic unit* that the user ought not to dissect. Most of us would not even think of fiddling around with the bits that represent a floating-point number, and we would find it completely ridiculous to try to increment some floating-point object by altering its internal representation ourselves.

Information hiding makes implementation details, including components of an object, inaccessible.

The atomicity principle is known as *information hiding*. The user does not get direct access to the parts of the object or their implementations; they can be accessed only indirectly by methods supplied with the object. We can view each object as coming with the warning, "Do not open—no user-serviceable parts inside." In real life, most people who try to fix things that have such a warning wind up doing more harm than good. In this respect, programming mimics the real world. The grouping of data and the operations that apply to them to form an aggregate, while hiding implementation details of the aggregate, is known as *encapsulation*.

Encapsulation is the grouping of data and the operations that apply to them to form an aggregate, while hiding the implementation of the aggregate.

An important goal of object-oriented programming is to support code reuse. Just as engineers use components over and over in their designs, programmers should be able to reuse objects rather than repeatedly reimplementing them. When we have an implementation of the exact object that we need to use, reuse is a simple matter. The challenge is to use an existing object when the object that is needed is not an exact match but is merely very similar.

Object-oriented languages provide several mechanisms to support this goal. One is the use of *generic* code. If the implementation is identical except for the basic type of the object, there is no need to completely rewrite code: Instead, we write the code generically so that it works for any type. For instance, the logic used to sort an array of objects is independent of the types of objects being sorted, so a generic algorithm could be used.

The *inheritance* mechanism allows us to extend the functionality of an object. In other words, we can create new types with restricted (or extended) properties of the original type. Inheritance goes a long way toward our goal of code reuse.

Another important object-oriented principle is *polymorphism*. A polymorphic reference type can reference objects of several different types. When methods are applied to the polymorphic type, the operation that is appropriate to the actual referenced object is automatically selected. In Java, this is implemented as part of inheritance. Polymorphism allows us to implement classes that share common logic. As is discussed in Chapter 4, this is illustrated in the Java libraries. The use of inheritance to create these hierarchies distinguishes object-oriented programming from the simpler *object-based programming*.

In Java, generic algorithms are implemented as part of inheritance. Chapter 4 discusses inheritance and polymorphism. In this chapter, we describe how Java uses classes to achieve encapsulation and information hiding.

An *object* in Java is an instance of a class. A *class* is similar to a C structure or Pascal/Ada record, except that there are two important enhancements. First, members can be both functions and data, known as *methods* and *fields*, respectively. Second, the visibility of these members can be restricted. Because methods that manipulate the object's state are members of the class, they are accessed by the dot member operator, just like the fields. In object-oriented terminology, when we make a call to a method we are passing a message to the object. Types discussed in Chapter 2, such as `String`, `ArrayList`, `StringTokenizer`, and `FileReader`, are all classes implemented in the Java library.

A *class* in Java consists of *fields* that store data and *methods* that are applied to instances of the class.

3.2 a simple example

Recall that when you are designing the class, it is important to be able to hide internal details from the class user. This is done in two ways. First, the class can define functionality as class members, called *methods*. Some of these methods describe how an instance of the structure is created and initialized, how equality tests are performed, and how output is performed. Other methods would be specific to the particular structure. The idea is that the internal data fields that represent an object's state should not be manipulated directly by the class user but instead should be manipulated only through use of the methods. This idea can be strengthened by hiding members from the user. To do this, we can specify that they be stored in a *private* section. The compiler will enforce the rule that members in the private section are inaccessible by methods that are not in the class of the object. Generally speaking, all data members should be private.

Functionality is supplied as additional members; these *methods* manipulate the object's state.

Public members are visible to nonclass routines; private members are not.

Figure 3.1 illustrates a class declaration for an `IntCell` object.[1] The declaration consists of two parts: *public* and *private*. *Public* members represent the portion that is visible to the user of the object. Since we expect to hide data, generally only methods and constants would be placed in the *public* section. In our example, we have methods that read from and write to the `IntCell` object. The *private* section contains the data; this is invisible to the user of the object. The `storedValue` member must be accessed through the publicly visible routines `read` and `write`; it cannot be accessed directly by `main`. Another way of viewing this is shown in Figure 3.2.

Members that are declared `private` are not visible to nonclass routines.

Figure 3.3 shows how `IntCell` objects are used. Since `read` and `write` are members of the `IntCell` class, they are accessed by using the dot member operator. The `storedValue` member could also be accessed by using the dot member operator, but since it is `private`, the access at line 14 would be illegal if it were not commented out.

A *field* is a member that stores data; a *method* is a member that performs an action.

Here is a summary of the terminology. The class defines *members*, which may be either *fields* (data) or *methods* (functions). The methods can act on the fields and may call other methods. The visibility modifier `public` means that the member is accessible to anyone via the dot operator. The visibility modifier `private` means that the member is accessible only by other methods of this class.

figure 3.1

A complete declaration of an `IntCell` class

```
 1 // IntCell class
 2 //  int read( )          -->  Returns the stored value
 3 //  void write( int x ) -->  x is stored
 4
 5 public class IntCell
 6 {
 7         // Public methods
 8     public int read( )          { return storedValue; }
 9     public void write( int x ) { storedValue = x; }
10
11         // Private internal data representation
12     private int storedValue;
13 }
```

figure 3.2

`IntCell` members: `read` and `write` are accessible, but `storedValue` is hidden.

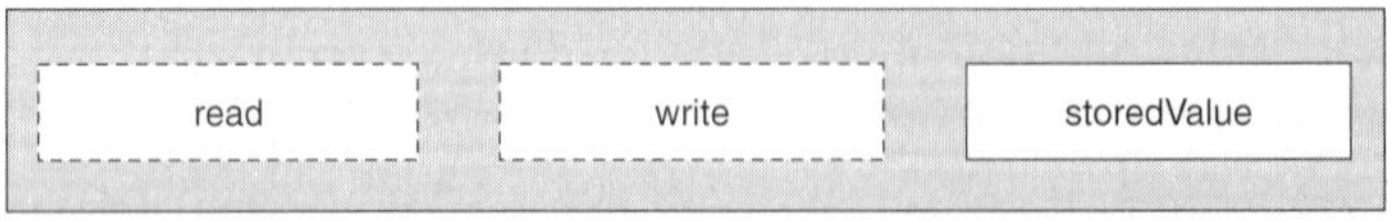

1. Public classes must be placed in files of the same name. Thus `IntCell` must be in file *IntCell.java*. We will discuss the meaning of `public` at line 5 when we talk about packages.

```java
// Exercise the IntCell class

public class TestIntCell
{
    public static void main( String [ ] args )
    {
        IntCell m = new IntCell( );

        m.write( 5 );
        System.out.println( "Cell contents: " + m.read( ) );

        // The next line would be illegal if uncommented
        // because storedValue is a private member
    //  m.storedValue = 0;
    }
}
```

figure 3.3

A simple test routine to show how `IntCell` objects are accessed

With no visibility modifier, we have package-visible access, which is discussed in Section 3.6.4. There is also a fourth modifier known as `protected`, which is discussed in Chapter 4.

3.3 *javadoc*

When designing a class, the *class specification* represents the class design and tells us what can be done to an object. The *implementation* represents the internals of how this is accomplished. As far as the class user is concerned, these internal details are not important. In many cases, the implementation represents proprietary information that the class designer may not wish to share. However, the specification must be shared; otherwise, the class is unusable.

The *class specification* describes what can be done to an object. The *implementation* represents the internals of how the specifications are met.

In many languages, the simultaneous sharing of the specification and hiding of the implementation is accomplished by placing the specification and implementation in separate source files. For instance, C++ has the class interface, which is placed in a `.h` file and a class implementation, which is in a `.cpp` file. In the `.h` file, the class interface restates the methods (by providing method headers) that are implemented by the class.

Java takes a different approach. It is easy to see that a list of the methods in a class, with signatures and return types, can be automatically documented from the implementation. Java uses this idea: The program *javadoc*, which comes with all Java systems, can be run to automatically generate documentation for classes. The output of *javadoc* is a set of HTML files that can be viewed or printed with a browser.

The *javadoc* program automatically generates documentation for classes.

The Java implementation file can also add *javadoc* comments that begin with the comment starter token /**. Those comments are automatically added in a uniform and consistent manner to the documentation produced by *javadoc*.

javadoc tags include `@author`, `@param`, `@return`, and `@throws`. They are used in *javadoc* comments.

There also are several special tags that can be included in the *javadoc* comments. Some of these are `@author`, `@param`, `@return`, and `@throws`. Figure 3.4 illustrates the use of the *javadoc* commenting features for the `IntCell` class. At line 3, the `@author` tag is used. This tag must precede the class definition. Line 10 illustrates the use of the `@return` tag, line 19 the `@param` tag. These tags must appear prior to a method declaration. The first token that follows the `@param` tag is the parameter name. The `@throws` tag is not shown, but it has the same syntax as `@param`.

Some of the output that results from running *javadoc* is shown in Figure 3.5. Run *javadoc* by supplying the name (including the `.java` extension) of the source file.

The output of *javadoc* is purely commentary except for the method headers. The compiler does not check that these comments are implemented. Nonetheless, the importance of proper documentation of classes can never be overstated. *javadoc* makes the task of generating well-formatted documentation easier.

figure 3.4

The `IntCell` declaration with *javadoc* comments

```
 1 /**
 2  * A class for simulating an integer memory cell
 3  * @author Mark A. Weiss
 4  */
 5
 6 public class IntCell
 7 {
 8     /**
 9      * Get the stored value.
10      * @return the stored value.
11      */
12     public int read( )
13     {
14         return storedValue;
15     }
16
17     /**
18      * Store a value.
19      * @param x the number to store.
20      */
21     public void write( int x )
22     {
23         storedValue = x;
24     }
25
26     private int storedValue;
27 }
```

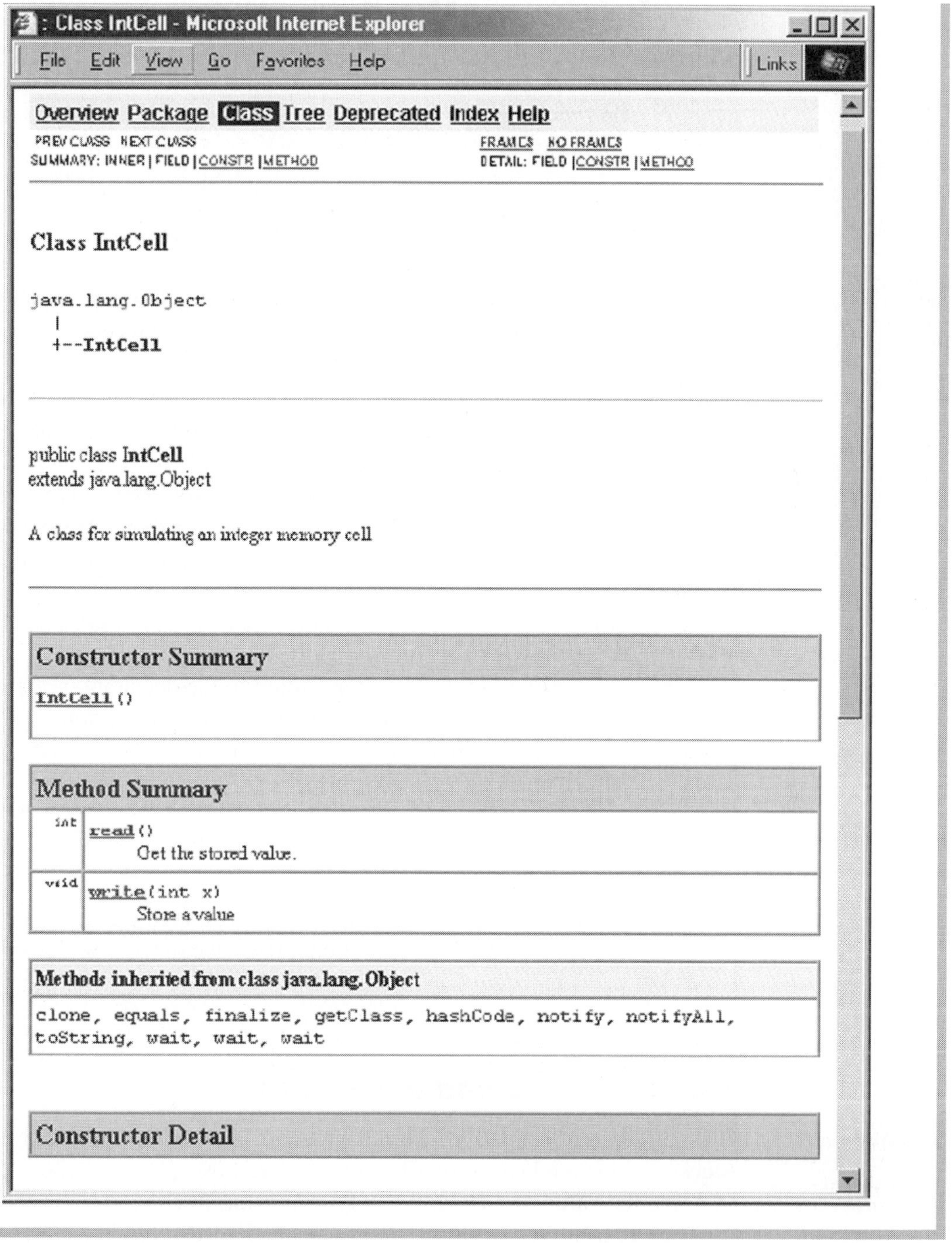

figure 3.5

javadoc output for Figure 3.4 (partial output)

3.4 basic methods

Some methods are common to all classes. This section discusses *mutators*, *accessors*, and three special methods: the constructors, `toString`, and `equals`. Also discussed is `main`.

3.4.1 constructors

A *constructor* tells how an object is declared and initialized.

As mentioned earlier, a basic property of objects is that they can be defined, possibly with initialization. In Java, the method that controls how an object is created and initialized is the *constructor*. Because of overloading, a class may define multiple constructors.

The default constructor is a member-by-member application of a default initialization.

If no constructor is provided, as in the case for the `IntCell` class in Figure 3.1, a default constructor is generated that initializes each data member using the normal defaults. This means that primitive fields are initialized to zero and reference fields are initialized to the `null` reference. (These defaults can be replaced by inline field initialization, which is executed prior to execution of constructor bodies.) Thus, in the case of `IntCell`, the `storedValue` component is 0.

To write a constructor, we provide a method that has the same name as the class and no return type (it is crucial that the return type is omitted; a common error is placing `void` as a return type, resulting in the declaration of a method that is not a constructor). In Figure 3.6, there are two constructors: one begins at line 7 and the other at line 15. Using these constructors, we can construct `Date` objects in either of the following ways:

```
Date d1 = new Date( );
Date d2 = new Date( 4, 15, 2005 );
```

Note that once a constructor is written, a default zero-parameter constructor is no longer generated. If you want one, you have to write it. Thus the constructor at line 7 is required in order to allow construction of the object that `d1` references.

3.4.2 mutators and accessors

A method that examines but does not change the state of an object is an *accessor*. A method that changes the state is a *mutator*.

Class fields are typically declared `private`. Thus they cannot be directly accessed by nonclass routines. Sometimes, however, we would like to examine the value of a field. We may even want to change it.

One alternative for doing this is to declare the fields `public`. This is typically a poor choice, however, because it violates information-hiding principles. Instead, we can provide methods to examine and change each field. A method that examines but does not change the state of an object is

```
// Minimal Date class that illustrates some Java features
// No error checks or javadoc comments

public class Date
{
        // Zero-parameter constructor
    public Date( )
    {
        month = 1;
        day = 1;
        year = 2002;
    }

        // Three-parameter constructor
    public Date( int theMonth, int theDay, int theYear )
    {
        month = theMonth;
        day   = theDay;
        year  = theYear;
    }

        // Return true if two equal values
    public boolean equals( Object rhs )
    {
        if( ! ( rhs instanceof Date ) )
            return false;
        Date rhDate = ( Date ) rhs;
        return rhDate.month == month && rhDate.day == day &&
               rhDate.year == year;
    }

        // Conversion to String
    public String toString( )
    {
        return month + "/" + day + "/" + year;
    }

        // Fields
    private int month;
    private int day;
    private int year;
}
```

figure 3.6

A minimal `Date` class that illustrates constructors and the `equals` and `toString` methods

an *accessor*. A method that changes the state is a *mutator* (because it mutates the state of the object).

Special cases of accessors and mutators examine only a single field. These accessors typically have names beginning with `get`, such as `getMonth`, while these mutators typically have names beginning with `set`, such as `setMonth`.

The advantage of using a mutator is that the mutator can ensure that changes in the state of the object are consistent. Thus a mutator that changes the `day` field in a `Date` object can make sure that only legal dates result.

3.4.3 output and `toString`

The `toString` method can be provided. It returns a `String` based on the object state.

Typically, we want to output the state of an object using `print`. This is done by writing the class method `toString`. This method returns a `String` suitable for output. As an example, Figure 3.6 shows a bare-bones implementation of the `toString` method for the `Date` class.

3.4.4 `equals`

The `equals` method can be provided to test if two references are referring to the same value.

The `equals` method is used to test if two objects represent the same value. The signature is always

```
public boolean equals( Object rhs )
```

Notice that the parameter is of reference type `Object` rather than the class type (the reason for this is discussed in Chapter 4). Typically, the `equals` method for class `ClassName` is implemented to return `true` only if `rhs` is an instance of `ClassName`, and after the conversion to `ClassName`, all the primitive fields are equal (via `==`) and all the reference fields are equal (via member-by-member application of `equals`).

The parameter to `equals` is of type `Object`.

An example of how `equals` is implemented is provided in Figure 3.6 for the `Date` class. The `instanceof` operator is discussed in Section 3.5.3.

3.4.5 `main`

When the *java* command is issued to start the interpreter, the `main` method in the class file referenced by the *java* command is called. Thus each class can have its own `main` method, without problem. This makes it easy to test the basic functionality of individual classes. However, although functionality can be tested, placing `main` in the class gives `main` more visibility than would be allowed in general. Thus calls from `main` to nonpublic methods will succeed in the test, even though they will be illegal in a more general setting.

3.4.6 static fields and methods

A *static method* is a method that does not need a controlling object.

A *static method* is a method that does not need a controlling object, and thus is typically called by supplying a class name instead of the controlling object. The most common static method is `main`. Other static methods are found in the `Integer` and `Math` classes. Examples are the methods `Integer.parseInt`,

Math.sin, and Math.max. Access to a static method uses the same visibility rules as do static fields. These methods mimic global functions found in non-object-oriented languages.

Recall from Chapter 1 that some fields of the class use the modifier static. Specifically, in conjunction with the keyword final, we have constants. Without the word final, we have *static fields*, which have another meaning, and another use of static methods, both of which are discussed in Section 3.5.5.

3.5 additional constructs

Three additional keywords are this, instanceof, and static. The keyword this has several uses in Java; two are discussed in this section. The keyword instanceof also has several general uses; it is used here to ensure that a type-conversion can succeed. Likewise, static has several uses. We have already discussed static methods. This section covers the *static field* and *static initializer.*

3.5.1 the this reference

The first use of this is as a reference to the current object. Think of the this reference as a homing device that, at any instant in time, tells you where you are. An important use of the this reference is in handling the special case of self-assignment. An example of this use is a program that copies one file to another. A normal algorithm begins by truncating the target file to zero length. If no check is performed to make sure the source and target file are indeed different, then the source file will be truncated—hardly a desirable feature. When dealing with two objects, one of which is written and one of which is read, we first should check for this special case, which is known as *aliasing*.

this is a reference to the current object. It can be used to send the current object, as a unit, to some other method.

For a second example, suppose we have a class Account that has a method finalTransfer. This method moves all the money from one account into another. In principle, this is an easy routine to write:

Aliasing is a special case that occurs when the same object appears in more than one role.

```
// Transfer all money from rhs to current account
public void finalTransfer( Account rhs )
{
    dollars += rhs.dollars;
    rhs.dollars = 0;
}
```

However, consider the result:

```
Account account1;
Account account2;
    ...
account2 = account1;
account1.finalTransfer( account2 );
```

Since we are transferring money between the same account, there should be no change in the account. However, the last statement in `finalTransfer` assures that the account will be empty. One way to avoid this is to use an alias test:

```
// Transfer all money from rhs to current account
public void finalTransfer( Account rhs )
{
    if( this == rhs )    // Alias test
        return;
    dollars += rhs.dollars;
    rhs.dollars = 0;
}
```

3.5.2 the `this` shorthand for constructors

`this` can be used to make a call to another constructor in the same class.

Many classes have multiple constructors that behave similarly. We can use `this` inside a constructor to call one of the other class constructors. An alternative to the zero-parameter `Date` constructor in Figure 3.6 would be

```
public Date( )
{
    this( 1, 1, 2005 ); // Call the 3-param constructor
}
```

More complicated uses are possible, but the call to `this` must be the first statement in the constructor; thereafter more statements may follow.

3.5.3 the `instanceof` operator

The `instanceof` operator is used to test if an expression is an instance of some class.

The `instanceof` operator performs a runtime test. The result of

```
exp instanceof ClassName
```

is `true` if `exp` is an instance of `ClassName`, and `false` otherwise. If `exp` is `null`, the result is always `false`. The `instanceof` operator is typically used prior to performing a type conversion and is `true` if the type conversion can succeed.

3.5.4 instance members versus static members

Fields and methods declared with the keyword `static` are *static members*. If they are declared without the keyword `static`, we will refer to them as *instance members*. The next subsection explains the distinction between instance and static members.

Instance members are fields or methods declared without the `static` modifier.

3.5.5 static fields and methods

Static fields are used when we have a variable that all the members of some class need to share. Typically, this is a symbolic constant, but it need not be. When a class variable is declared `static`, only one instance of the variable is ever created. It is not part of any instance of the class. Instead, it behaves like a single global variable but with the scope of the class. In other words, in the declaration

Static fields are essentially global variables with class scope.

```
public class Sample
{
    private int x;
    private static int y;
}
```

each `Sample` object stores its own `x`, but there is only one shared `y`.

A common use of a static field is as a constant. For instance, the class `Integer` defines the field `MAX_VALUE` as

```
public static final int MAX_VALUE = 2147483647;
```

If this constant was not a static field, then each instance of an `Integer` would have a data field named `MAX_VALUE`, thus wasting space and initialization time. Instead, there is only a single variable named `MAX_VALUE`. It can be accessed by any of the `Integer` methods by using the identifier `MAX_VALUE`. It can also be accessed via an `Integer` object `obj` using `obj.MAX_VALUE`, as would any field. Note that this is allowed only because `MAX_VALUE` is public. Finally, `MAX_VALUE` can be accessed by using the class name as `Integer.MAX_VALUE` (again allowable because it is public). This would not be allowed for a nonstatic field. The last form is preferable, because it communicates to the reader that the field is indeed a static field. Another example of a static field is the constant `Math.PI`.

Even without the `final` qualifier, static fields are still useful. Figure 3.7 illustrates a typical example. Here we want to construct `Ticket` objects, giving each ticket a unique serial number. In order to do this, we have to have some way of keeping track of all the previously used serial numbers; this is clearly shared data, and not part of any one `Ticket` object.

figure 3.7

The `Ticket` class: an example of static fields and methods

```
class Ticket
{
    public Ticket( )
    {
        System.out.println( "Calling constructor" );
        serialNumber = ++ticketCount;
    }

    public int getSerial( )
    {
        return serialNumber;
    }

    public String toString( )
    {
        return "Ticket #" + getSerial( );
    }

    public static int getTicketCount( )
    {
        return ticketCount;
    }

    private int serialNumber;
    private static int ticketCount = 0;
}

class TestTicket
{
    public static void main( String [ ] args )
    {
        Ticket t1;
        Ticket t2;

        System.out.println( "Ticket count is " +
                                Ticket.getTicketCount( ) );
        t1 = new Ticket( );
        t2 = new Ticket( );

        System.out.println( "Ticket count is " +
                                Ticket.getTicketCount( ) );

        System.out.println( t1.getSerial( ) );
        System.out.println( t2.getSerial( ) );
    }
}
```

Each `Ticket` object will have its instance member `serialNumber`; this is instance data because each instance of `Ticket` has its own `serialNumber` field. All `Ticket` objects will share the variable `ticketCount`, which denotes the number of `Ticket` objects that have been created. This variable is part of the class, rather than object-specific, so it is declared `static`. There is only one `ticketCount`, whether there is 1 `Ticket`, 10 `Tickets`, or even no `Ticket` objects. The last point—that the static data exists even before any instances of the class are created—is important, because it means the static data cannot be initialized in constructors. One way of doing the initialization is inline, when the field is declared. More complex initialization is described in Section 3.5.6.

A *static field* is shared by all (possibly zero) instances of the class.

In Figure 3.7, we can now see that construction of `Ticket` objects is done by using `ticketCount` as the serial number, and incrementing `ticketCount`. We also provide a static method, `getTicketCount`, that returns the number of tickets. Because it is static, it can be invoked without providing an object reference, as shown on lines 36 and 41. The call on line 41 could have been made using either `t1` or `t2`, though many argue that invoking a static method using an object reference is poor style, and we would never do so in this text. However, it is significant that the call on line 36 clearly could not be made through an object reference, since at this point there are no valid `Ticket` objects. This is why it is important for `getTicketCount` to be declared as a static method; if it was declared as an instance method, it could only be called through an object reference.

When a method is declared as a static method, there is no implicit `this` reference. As such, it cannot access instance data or call instance methods, without providing an object reference. In other words, from inside `getTicketCount`, unqualified access of `serialNumber` would imply `this.serialNumber`, but since there is no `this`, the compiler will issue an error message. Thus, a nonstatic field, which is part of each instance of the class, can be accessed by a static class method only if a controlling object is provided.

A `static` method has no implicit `this` reference, and can be invoked without an object reference.

3.5.6 **static initializers**

Static fields are initialized when the class is loaded. Occasionally, we need a complex initialization. For instance, suppose we need a static array that stores the square roots of the first 100 integers. It would be best to have these values computed automatically. One possibility is to provide a static method and require the programmer to call it prior to using the array.

An alternative is the *static initializer*. An example is shown in Figure 3.8. There, the static initializer extends from lines 5 to 9. The simplest use of the static initializer places initialization code for the static fields in a block that is preceded by the keyword `static`. The static initializer must follow the declaration of the static member.

A *static initializer* is a block of code that is used to initialize static fields.

figure 3.8

An example of a static initializer

```
public class Squares
{
    private static double [ ] squareRoots = new double[ 100 ];

    static
    {
        for( int i = 0; i < squareRoots.length; i++ )
            squareRoots[ i ] = Math.sqrt( ( double ) i );
    }
    // Rest of class
}
```

3.6 packages

A *package* is used to organize a collection of classes.

Packages are used to organize similar classes. Each package consists of a set of classes. Two classes in the same package have slightly fewer visibility restrictions among themselves than they would if they were in different packages.

Java provides several predefined packages, including `java.io`, `java.lang`, and `java.util`. The `java.lang` package includes the classes `Integer`, `Math`, `String`, and `System`, among others. Some of the classes in the `java.util` package are `Date`, `Random`, and `StringTokenizer`. Package `java.io` is used for I/O and includes the various stream classes seen in Section 2.6.

Class `C` in package `p` is specified as `p.C`. For instance, we can have a `Date` object constructed with the current time and date as an initial state using

```
java.util.Date today = new java.util.Date( );
```

Note that by including a package name, we avoid conflicts with identically named classes in other packages (such as our own `Date` class). Also, observe the typical naming convention: Class names are capitalized and package names are not.

3.6.1 the `import` directive

The `import` directive is used to provide a shorthand for a fully qualified class name.

Using a full package and class name can be burdensome. To avoid this, use the `import` directive. There are two forms of the `import` directive that allow the programmer to specify a class without prefixing it with the package name.

```
import packageName.ClassName;
import packageName.*;
```

In the first form, `ClassName` may be used as a shorthand for a fully qualified class name. In the second, all classes in a package may be abbreviated with the corresponding class name.

For example, with the `import` directives

```
import java.util.Date;
import java.io.*;
```

we may use

```
Date today = new Date( );
FileReader theFile = new FileReader( name );
```

Careless use of the `import` directive can introduce naming conflicts.

Using the `import` directive saves typing. And since the most typing is saved by using the second form, you will see that form used often. There are two disadvantages to `import` directives. First, the shorthand makes it hard to tell, by reading the code, which class is being used when there are a host of `import` directives. Also, the second form may allow shorthands for unintended classes and introduce naming conflicts that will need to be resolved by fully qualified class names.

Suppose we use

```
import java.util.*;   // Library package
import weiss.util.*;  // User-defined package
```

with the intention of importing the `java.util.Random` class and a package that we have written ourselves. Then, if we have our own `Random` class in `weiss.util`, the `import` directive will generate a conflict with `weiss.util.Random` and will need to be fully qualified. Furthermore, if we are using a class in one of these packages, by reading the code we will not know whether it originated from the library package or our own package. We would have avoided these problems if we had used the form

```
import java.util.Random;
```

and for this reason, we use the first form only in the text and avoid "wildcard" `import` directives.

`java.lang.*` is automatically imported.

The `import` directives must appear prior to the beginning of a class declaration. We saw an example of this in Figure 2.16. Also, the entire package `java.lang` is automatically imported. This is why we may use shorthands such as `Math.max`, `Integer.parseInt`, `System.out`, and so on.

In versions of Java prior to Java 5, static members such as Math.max and Integer.MAX_VALUE could not be shortened to simply max and MAX_VALUE. Programmers who made heavy use of the math library had long hoped for a generalization of the import directive that would allow methods such as sin, cos, tan to be used rather than the more verbose Math.sin, Math.cos, Math.tan. In Java 5, this feature was added to the language via the static import directive. The *static import directive* allows static members (methods and fields) to be accessed without explicitly providing the class name. The static import directive has two forms: the single member import, and the wildcard import. Thus,

```
import static java.lang.Math.*;
import static java.lang.Integer.MAX_VALUE;
```

allows the programmer to write max instead of Math.max, PI instead of Math.PI, and MAX_VALUE instead of Integer.MAX_VALUE.

3.6.2 the package statement

The package *statement* indicates that a class is part of a package. It must precede the class definition.

To indicate that a class is part of a package, we must do two things. First, we must include the package statement as the first line, prior to the class definition. Second, we must place the code in an appropriate subdirectory.

In this text, we use the two packages shown in Figure 3.9. Other programs, including test programs and the application programs in Part Three of this book, are stand-alone classes and not part of a package.

An example of how the package statement is used is shown in Figure 3.10. Here, we have the static method longPause that simply sleeps for a billion milliseconds (approximately two weeks). This method is useful because when some integrated environments run console applications from inside their environments, they close the output console as soon as the program terminates. This can make it hard to see the output. longPause keeps the console from closing in this situation.

figure 3.9

Packages defined in this text

Package	Use
weiss.util	A reimplementation of a subset of the java.util package containing various data structures.
weiss.nonstandard	Various data structures, in a simplified form, using nonstandard conventions that are different from java.util.

```java
package weiss.nonstandard;

public class Exiting
{
    // Suspend current program for a long time
    public static void longPause( )
    {
        try
          { Thread.sleep( 1000000000 ); }
        catch( InterruptedException e ) { }
    }
}
```

figure 3.10

A class `Exiting` with a single static method, which is part of the package `weiss.nonstandard`

3.6.3 the `CLASSPATH` environment variable

The `CLASSPATH` variable specifies files and directories that should be searched to find classes.

Packages are searched for in locations that are named in the `CLASSPATH` variable. What does this mean? Here are possible settings for `CLASSPATH`, first for a Windows system and second for a Unix system:

```
SET CLASSPATH=.;C:\bookcode\
setenv CLASSPATH .:$HOME/bookcode/
```

In both cases, the `CLASSPATH` variable lists directories (or jar files[2]) that contain the package's class files. For instance, if your `CLASSPATH` is corrupted, you will not be able to run even the most trivial program because the current directory will not be found.

A class in package `p` must be in a directory `p` that will be found by searching through the `CLASSPATH` list.

A class in package `p` must be in a directory `p` that will be found by searching through the `CLASSPATH` list; each `.` in the package name represents a subdirectory. Starting with Java 1.2, the current directory (directory `.`) is always scanned if `CLASSPATH` is not set at all, so if you are working from a single main directory, you can simply create subdirectories in it and not set `CLASSPATH`. Most likely, however, you'll want to create a separate Java subdirectory and then create package subdirectories in there. You would then augment the `CLASSPATH` variable to include `.` and the Java subdirectory. This was done in the previous Unix declaration when we added `$HOME/bookcode/` to the `CLASSPATH`. Inside the `bookcode` directory, you create a subdirectory named `weiss`, and in that subdirectory, `util` and `nonstandard`. In the `nonstandard` subdirectory, you place the code for the `Exiting` class.

2. A *jar* file is basically a compressed archive (like a zip file) with extra files containing Java-specific information. The *jar* tool, supplied with the JDK, can be used to create and expand jar files.

An application, written in any directory at all, can then use the `longPause` method either by issuing

```
weiss.nonstandard.Exiting.longPause( );
```

or simply using `Exiting.longPause`, if an appropriate `import` directive is provided.

3.6.4 package visibility rules

Fields with no visibility modifiers are *package visible*, meaning that they are visible only to other classes in the same package.

Non-public classes are visible only to other classes in the same package.

Packages have several important visibility rules. First, if no visibility modifier is specified for a field, then the field is *package visible*. This means that it is visible only to other classes in the same package. This is more visible than `private` (which is invisible even to other classes in the same package) but less visible than `public` (which is visible to nonpackage classes, too).

Second, only public classes of a package may be used outside the package. That is why we have often used the `public` qualifier prior to `class`. Classes may not be declared `private`.[3] Package-visible access extends to classes, too. If a class is not declared `public`, then it may be accessed by other classes in the same package only; this is a *package-visible class*. In Part IV, we will see that package-visible classes can be used without violating information-hiding principles. Thus there are some cases in which package-visible classes can be very useful.

All classes that are not part of a package but are reachable through the `CLASSPATH` variable are considered part of the same default package. As a result, package-visible applies between all of them. This is why visibility is not affected if the `public` modifier is omitted from nonpackage classes. However, this is poor use of package-visible member access. We use it only to place several classes in one file, because that tends to make examining and printing the examples easier. Since a public class must be in a file of the same name, there can be only one public class per file.

3.7 a design pattern: composite (pair)

Although software design and programming are often difficult challenges, many experienced software engineers will argue that software engineering really has only a relatively small set of basic problems. Perhaps this is an understatement, but it is true that many basic problems are seen over and over

3. This applies to top-level classes shown so far; later we will see nested and inner classes, which may be declared `private`.

in software projects. Software engineers who are familiar with these problems, and in particular, the efforts of other programmers in solving these problems, have the advantage of not needing to "reinvent the wheel."

The idea of a design pattern is to document a problem and its solution so that others can take advantage of the collective experience of the entire software engineering community. Writing a pattern is much like writing a recipe for a cookbook; many common patterns have been written and, rather than expending energy reinventing the wheel, these patterns can be used to write better programs. Thus a *design pattern* describes a problem that occurs over and over in software engineering, and then describes the solution in a sufficiently generic manner as to be applicable in a wide variety of contexts.

A *design pattern* describes a problem that occurs over and over in software engineering, and then describes the solution in a sufficiently generic manner as to be applicable in a wide variety of contexts.

Throughout the text we will discuss several problems that often arise in a design, and a typical solution that is employed to solve the problem. We start with the following simple problem.

In most languages, a function can return only a single object. What do we do if we need to return two or more things? The easiest way to do this is to combine the objects into a single object using either an array or a class. The most common situation in which multiple objects need to be returned is the case of two objects. So a common design pattern is to return the two objects as a *pair.* This is the *composite pattern.*

A common design pattern is to return two objects as a *pair.*

In addition to the situation described above, pairs are useful for implementing maps and dictionaries. In both these abstractions, we maintain key-value pairs: The pairs are added into the map or dictionary, and then we search for a key, returning its value. One common way to implement a map is to use a set. In a set, we have a collection of items, and search for a match. If the items are pairs, and the match criterion is based exclusively on the key component of the pair, then it is easy to write a class that constructs a map on the basis of a set. We will see this idea explored in more detail in Chapter 19.

Pairs are useful for implementing key-value pairs in maps and dictionaries.

summary

This chapter described the Java class and package constructs. The class is the Java mechanism that is used to create new reference types; the package is used to group related classes. For each class, we can

- Define the construction of objects
- Provide for information hiding and atomicity
- Define methods to manipulate the objects

The class consists of two parts: the specification and the implementation. The specification tells the user of the class what the class does; the implementation does it. The implementation frequently contains proprietary code and in some cases is distributed only as a `.class` file. The specification, however, is public knowledge. In Java, a specification that lists the class methods can be generated from the implementation by using *javadoc*.

Information-hiding can be enforced by using the `private` keyword. Initialization of objects is controlled by the constructors, and the components of the object can be examined and changed by accessor and mutator methods, respectively. Figure 3.11 illustrates many of these concepts, as applied to a simplified version of `ArrayList`. This class, `StringArrayList`, supports `add`, `get`, and `size`. A more complete version that includes `set`, `remove`, and `clear` is in the online code.

The features discussed in this chapter implement the fundamental aspects of object-based programming. The next chapter discusses inheritance, which is central to object-oriented programming.

key concepts

accessor A method that examines an object but does not change its state. (70)

aliasing A special case that occurs when the same object appears in more than one role. (73)

atomic unit In reference to an object, its parts cannot be dissected by the general users of the object. (64)

class Consists of fields and methods that are applied to instances of the class. (65)

class specification Describes the functionality, but not the implementation. (67)

`CLASSPATH` variable Specifies directories and files that should be searched to find classes. (81)

composite The pattern in which we store two or more objects in one entity. (83)

constructor Tells how an object is declared and initialized. The default constructor is a member-by-member default initialization, with primitive fields initialized to zero and reference fields initialized to `null`. (70)

design pattern Describes a problem that occurs over and over in software engineering, and then describes the solution in a sufficiently generic manner as to be applicable in a wide variety of contexts. (83)

encapsulation The grouping of data and the operations that apply to them to form an aggregate while hiding the implementation of the aggregate. (64)

`equals` method Can be implemented to test if two objects represent the same value. The formal parameter is always of type `Object`. (72)

field A class member that stores data. (66)

```
/**
 * The StringArrayList implements a growable array of Strings.
 * Insertions are always done at the end.
 */
public class StringArrayList
{
    /**
     * Returns the number of items in this collection.
     * @return the number of items in this collection.
     */
    public int size( )
    {
        return theSize;
    }

    /**
     * Returns the item at position idx.
     * @param idx the index to search in.
     * @throws ArrayIndexOutOfBoundsException if index is bad.
     */
    public String get( int idx )
    {
        if( idx < 0 || idx >= size( ) )
            throw new ArrayIndexOutOfBoundsException( );
        return theItems[ idx ];
    }

    /**
     * Adds an item to this collection at the end.
     * @param x any object.
     * @return true (as per java.util.ArrayList).
     */
    public boolean add( String x )
    {
        if( theItems.length == size( ) )
        {
            String [ ] old = theItems;
            theItems = new String[ theItems.length * 2 + 1 ];
            for( int i = 0; i < size( ); i++ )
                theItems[ i ] = old[ i ];
        }

        theItems[ theSize++ ] = x;
        return true;
    }

    private static final int INIT_CAPACITY = 10;

    private int         theSize = 0;
    private String [ ] theItems = new String[ INIT_CAPACITY ];
}
```

figure 3.11

Simplified StringArrayList with add, get, and size

implementation Represents the internals of how the specifications are met. As far as the class user is concerned, the implementation is not important. (67)

`import` directive Used to provide a shorthand for a fully qualified class name. Java 5 adds the static import that allows a shorthand for a static member. (78)

information hiding Makes implementation details, including components of an object, inaccessible. (64)

instance members Members declared without the static modifier. (75)

`instanceof` operator Tests if an expression is an instance of a class. (74)

javadoc Automatically generates documentation for classes. (67)

***javadoc* tag** Includes `@author`, `@param`, `@return`, and `@throws`. Used inside of *javadoc* comments. (68)

method A function supplied as a member that, if not static, operates on an instance of the class. (65)

mutator A method that changes the state of the object. (70)

object An entity that has structure and state and defines operations that may access or manipulate that state. An instance of a class. (64)

object-based programming Uses the encapsulation and information-hiding features of objects but does not use inheritance. (65)

object-oriented programming Distinguished from object-based programming by the use of inheritance to form hierarchies of classes. (63)

package Used to organize a collection of classes. (78)

package statement Indicates that a class is a member of a package. Must precede the class definition. (80)

package-visible access Members that have no visibility modifiers are only accessible to methods in classes in the same package. (82)

package-visible class A class that is not public and is accessible only to other classes in the same package. (82)

pair The composite pattern with two objects. (82)

private A member that is not visible to nonclass methods. (66)

public A member that is visible to nonclass methods. (66)

static field A field that is shared by all instances of a class. (77)

static initializer A block of code that is used to initialize static fields. (77)

static method A method that has no implicit `this` reference and thus can be invoked without a controlling object reference. (77)

`this` constructor call Used to make a call to another constructor in the same class. (74)

`this` reference A reference to the current object. It can be used to send the current object, as a unit, to some other method. (73)

`toString` method Returns a `String` based on the object state. (72)

common errors

1. Private members cannot be accessed outside of the class. Remember that, by default, class members are package visible: They are visible only within the package.
2. Use `public class` instead of `class` unless you are writing a throw-away helper class.
3. The formal parameter to `equals` must be of type `Object`. Otherwise, although the program will compile, there are cases in which a default `equals` (that simply mimics `==`) will be used instead.
4. Static methods cannot access nonstatic members without a controlling object.
5. Classes that are part of a package must be placed in an identically named directory that is reachable from the `CLASSPATH`.
6. `this` is a final reference and may not be altered.
7. Constructors do not have return types. If you write a "constructor" with return type `void`, you have actually written a method with the same name as the class, but this is *NOT* a constructor.

on the internet

Following are the files that are available:

TestIntCell.java	Contains a `main` that tests `IntCell`, shown in Figure 3.3.
IntCell.java	Contains the `IntCell` class, shown in Figure 3.4. The output of *javadoc* can also be found as **IntCell.html**.
Date.java	Contains the `Date` class, shown in Figure 3.6.
Exiting.java	Contains the `longPause` method, shown in Figure 3.10 and found in package `weiss.nonstandard`.
Ticket.java	Contains the `Ticket` static member example in Figure 3.7.
Squares.java	Contains the static initializer sample code in Figure 3.8.

StringArrayList.java Contains a more complete version of `StringArrayList` code in Figure 3.11.

ReadStringsWithStringArrayList.java Contains a test program for `StringArrayList`.

exercises

IN SHORT

3.1 What is *information hiding*? What is *encapsulation*? How does Java support these concepts?

3.2 Explain the public and private sections of the class.

3.3 Describe the role of the constructor.

3.4 If a class provides no constructor, what is the result?

3.5 Explain the uses of `this` in Java.

3.6 What is *package-visible access*?

3.7 For a class `ClassName`, how is output performed?

3.8 Give the two types of `import` directive forms that allow `longPause` to be used without providing the `weiss.util` package name.

3.9 What is a *design pattern*?

3.10 For the code in Figure 3.12, which resides entirely in one file,
  a. Line 17 is illegal, even though line 18 is legal. Explain why.
  b. Which of lines 20 to 24 are legal and which are not? Explain why.

IN THEORY

3.11 A class provides a single private constructor. Why would this be useful?

3.12 Suppose that the `main` method in Figure 3.3 was part of the `IntCell` class.
  a. Would the program still work?
  b. Could the commented-out line in `main` be uncommented without generating an error?

IN PRACTICE

3.13 A *combination lock* has the following basic properties: the combination (a sequence of three numbers) is hidden; the lock can be opened by providing the combination; and the combination can be changed,

```
class Person
{
    public static final int NO_SSN = -1;

    private int SSN = 0;
    String name = null;
}

class TestPerson
{
    private Person p = new Person( );

    public static void main( String [ ] args )
    {
        Person q = new Person( );

        System.out.println( p );              // illegal
        System.out.println( q );              // legal

        System.out.println( q.NO_SSN );       // ?
        System.out.println( q.SSN );          // ?
        System.out.println( q.name );         // ?
        System.out.println( Person.NO_SSN );  // ?
        System.out.println( Person.SSN );     // ?
    }
}
```

figure 3.12

Code for Exercise 3.10

but only by someone who knows the current combination. Design a class with public methods `open` and `changeCombo` and private data fields that store the combination. The combination should be set in the constructor.

3.14 Wildcard import directives are dangerous because ambiguities and other surprises can be introduced. Recall that both `java.awt.List` and `java.util.List` are classes. Starting with the code in Figure 3.13:

a. Compile the code; you should get an ambiguity.
b. Add an `import` directive to explicitly use `java.awt.List`. The code should now compile and run.
c. Uncomment the local `List` class and remove the `import` directive you just added. The code should compile and run.
d. Recomment the local `List`, reverting back to the situation at the start. Recompile to see the surprising result. What happens if you add the explicit `import` directive from step (b)?

figure 3.13

Code for Exercise 3.14 illustrates why wildcard imports are bad.

```
import java.util.*;
import java.awt.*;

class List  // COMMENT OUT THIS CLASS TO START EXPERIMENT
{
    public String toString( ) { return "My List!!"; }
}

class WildCardIsBad
{
    public static void main( String [ ] args )
    {
        System.out.println( new List( ) );
    }
}
```

PROGRAMMING PROJECTS

3.15 Write a class that supports rational numbers. The fields should be two `long` variables, one each that stores the numerator and denominator. Store the rational number in reduced form, with the denominator always nonnegative. Provide a reasonable set of constructors; the methods `add`, `subtract`, `multiply`, and `divide`; as well as `toString`, `equals`, and `compareTo` (that behaves like the one in the `String` class). Make sure that `toString` correctly handles the case in which the denominator is zero.

3.16 Implement a simple `Date` class. You should be able to represent any date from January 1, 1800, to December 31, 2500; subtract two dates; increment a date by a number of days; and compare two dates using both `equals` and `compareTo`. A `Date` is represented internally as the number of days since some starting time, which, here, is the start of 1800. This makes all methods except for construction and `toString` trivial.

The rule for leap years is a year is a leap year if it is divisible by 4 and not divisible by 100 unless it is also divisible by 400. Thus 1800, 1900, and 2100 are not leap years, but 2000 is. The constructor must check the validity of the date, as must `toString`. The `Date` could be bad if an increment or subtraction operator caused it to go out of range.

Once you have decided on the specifications, you can do an implementation. The difficult part is converting between the internal and external representations of a date. What follows is a possible algorithm.

Set up two arrays that are static fields. The first array, `daysTillFirstOfMonth`, will contain the number of days until the first of each month in a nonleap year. Thus it contains 0, 31, 59, 90, and so on. The second array, `daysTillJan1`, will contain the number of days until the first of each year, starting with `firstYear`. Thus it contains 0, 365, 730, 1095, 1460, 1826, and so on because 1800 is not a leap year, but 1804 is. You should have your program initialize this array once using a static initializer. You can then use the array to convert from the internal representation to the external representation.

3.17 Implement a `Complex` number class. Recall that a complex number consists of a real part and an imaginary part. Support the same operations as the `Rational` class, when meaningful (for instance, `compareTo` is not meaningful). Add accessor methods to extract the real and imaginary parts.

3.18 Implement a complete `IntType` class that supports a reasonable set of constructors, `add`, `subtract`, `multiply`, `divide`, `equals`, `compareTo`, and `toString`. Maintain an `IntType` as a sufficiently large array. For this class, the difficult operation is division, followed closely by multiplication.

references

More information on classes can be found in the references at the end of Chapter 1. The classic reference on design patterns is [1]. This book describes 23 standard patterns, some of which we will discuss later.

1. E. Gamma, R. Helm, R. Johnson, and J. Vlissides, *Elements of Reusable Object-Oriented Software*, Addison-Wesley, Reading, MA, 1995.

chapter 4

inheritance

As mentioned in Chapter 3, an important goal of object-oriented programming is code reuse. Just as engineers use components over and over in their designs, programmers should be able to reuse objects rather than repeatedly reimplement them. In an object-oriented programming language, the fundamental mechanism for code reuse is *inheritance*. Inheritance allows us to extend the functionality of an object. In other words, we can create new types with restricted (or extended) properties of the original type, in effect forming a hierarchy of classes.

Inheritance is more than simply code reuse, however. By using inheritance correctly, it enables the programmer to more easily maintain and update code, both of which are essential in large commercial applications. Understanding of the use of inheritance is essential in order to write significant Java programs, and it is also used by Java to implement generic methods and classes.

In this chapter, we will see

- General principles of inheritance, including *polymorphism*
- How inheritance is implemented in Java

- How a collection of classes can be derived from a single abstract class
- The *interface*, which is a special kind of a class
- How Java implements generic programming using inheritance
- How Java 5 implements generic programming using generic classes

4.1 what is inheritance?

In an *IS-A relationship*, we say the derived class *is a* (variation of the) base class.

Inheritance is the fundamental object-oriented principle that is used to reuse code among related classes. Inheritance models the *IS-A relationship*. In an *IS-A* relationship, we say the derived class *is a* (variation of the) base class. For example, a Circle *IS-A* Shape and a Car *IS-A* Vehicle. However, an Ellipse *IS-NOT-A* Circle. Inheritance relationships form *hierarchies*. For instance, we can extend Car to other classes, since a ForeignCar *IS-A* Car (and pays tariffs) and a DomesticCar *IS-A* Car (and does not pay tariffs), and so on.

In a *HAS-A relationship*, we say the derived class *has a* (instance of the) base class. *Composition* is used to model *HAS-A* relationships.

Another type of relationship is a *HAS-A* (or IS-COMPOSED-OF) *relationship*. This type of relationship does not possess the properties that would be natural in an inheritance hierarchy. An example of a *HAS-A* relationship is that a car *HAS-A* steering wheel. *HAS-A* relationships should not be modeled by inheritance. Instead, they should use the technique of *composition*, in which the components are simply made private data fields.

As we will see in forthcoming chapters, the Java language itself makes extensive use of inheritance in implementing its class libraries.

4.1.1 creating new classes

Our inheritance discussion will center around an example. Figure 4.1 shows a typical class. The `Person` class is used to store information about a person; in our case we have private data that includes the name, age, address, and phone number, along with some public methods that can access and perhaps change this information. We can imagine that in reality, this class is significantly more complex, storing perhaps 30 data fields with 100 methods.

Now suppose we want to have a `Student` class or an `Employee` class or both. Imagine that a `Student` is similar to a `Person`, with the addition of only a few extra data members and methods. In our simple example, imagine that the difference is that a `Student` adds a `gpa` field and a `getGPA` accessor. Similarly, imagine that the `Employee` has all of the same components as a `Person` but also has a `salary` field and methods to manipulate the salary.

```java
class Person
{
    public Person( String n, int ag, String ad, String p )
      { name = n; age = ag; address = ad; phone = p; }

    public String toString( )
      { return getName( ) + " " + getAge( ) + " "
                          + getPhoneNumber( ); }

    public String getName( )
      { return name; }

    public int getAge( )
      { return age; }

    public String getAddress( )
      { return address; }

    public String getPhoneNumber( )
      { return phone; }

    public void setAddress( String newAddress )
      { address = newAddress; }

    public void setPhoneNumber( String newPhone )
      { phone = newPhone; }

    private String name;
    private int    age;
    private String address;
    private String phone;
}
```

figure 4.1

The `Person` class stores name, age, address, and phone number.

One option in designing these classes is the classic *copy-and-paste*: We copy the `Person` class, change the name of the class and constructors, and then add the new stuff. This strategy is illustrated in Figure 4.2.

Copy-and-paste is a weak design option, fraught with significant liabilities. First, there is the problem that if you copy garbage, you wind up with more garbage. This makes it very hard to fix programming errors that are detected, especially when they are detected late.

Second is the related issue of maintenance and versioning. Suppose we decide in the second version that it is better to store names in last name, first name format, rather than as a single field. Or perhaps it is better to store addresses using a special `Address` class. In order to maintain consistency, these should be done for all classes. Using copy-and-paste, these design changes have to be done in numerous places.

figure 4.2

The `Student` class stores name, age, address, phone number, and gpa via copy-and-paste.

```
class Student
{
    public Student( String n, int ag, String ad, String p,
                    double g )
      { name = n; age = ag; address = ad; phone = p; gpa = g; }

    public String toString( )
      { return getName( ) + " " + getAge( ) + " "
             + getPhoneNumber( ) + " " + getGPA( ); }

    public String getName( )
      { return name; }

    public int getAge( )
      { return age; }

    public String getAddress( )
      { return address; }

    public String getPhoneNumber( )
      { return phone; }

    public void setAddress( String newAddress )
      { address = newAddress; }

    public void setPhoneNumber( String newPhone )
      { phone = newPhone; }

    public double getGPA( )
      { return gpa; }

    private String name;
    private int    age;
    private String address;
    private String phone;
    private double gpa
}
```

Third, and more subtle, is the fact that using copy-and-paste, `Person`, `Student`, and `Employee` are three separate entities with zero relationship between each other, in spite of their similarities. So, for instance, if we have a routine that accepted a `Person` as a parameter, we could not send in a `Student`. We would thus have to copy and paste all of those routines to make them work for these new types.

Inheritance solves all three of these problems. Using inheritance, we would say that a `Student` *IS-A* `Person`. We would then specify the changes that a `Student` has relative to `Person`. There are only three types of changes that are allowed:

1. `Student` can add new fields (e.g., `gpa`).
2. `Student` can add new methods (e.g., `getGPA`).
3. `Student` can override existing methods (e.g., `toString`).

Two changes are specifically not allowed because they would violate the notion of an *IS-A* relationship:

1. `Student` cannot remove fields.
2. `Student` cannot remove methods.

Finally, the new class must specify its own constructors; this is likely to involve some syntax that we will discuss in Section 4.1.6.

Figure 4.3 shows the `Student` class. The data layout for the `Person` and `Student` classes is shown in Figure 4.4. It illustrates that the memory footprint of any `Student` object includes all fields that would be contained in a `Person`

```
class Student extends Person
{
    public Student( String n, int ag, String ad, String p,
                    double g )
    {
      /* OOPS! Need some syntax; see Section 4.1.6 */
       gpa = g; }

    public String toString( )
      { return getName( ) + " " + getAge( ) + " "
               + getPhoneNumber( ) + " " + getGPA( ); }

    public double getGPA( )
      { return gpa; }

    private double gpa;
}
```

figure 4.3

Inheritance used to create `Student` class

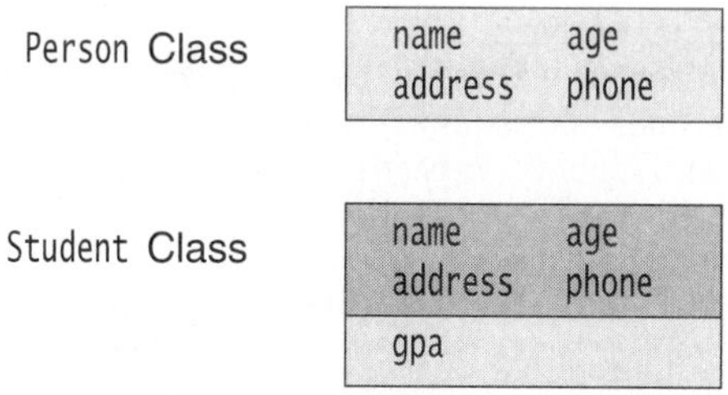

figure 4.4

Memory layout with inheritance. Light shading indicates fields that are private, and accessible only by methods of the class. Dark shading in the `Student` class indicates fields that are not accessible in the `Student` class but are nonetheless present.

object. However, because those fields are declared private by `Person`, they are not accessible by `Student` class methods. That is why the constructor is problematic at this point: We cannot touch the data fields in any `Student` method and instead can only manipulate the inherited private fields by using public `Person` methods. Of course, we could make the inherited fields public, but that would generally be a terrible design decision. It would embolden the implementors of the `Student` and `Employee` classes to access the inherited fields directly. If that was done, and modifications such as a change in the `Person`'s data representation of the name or address were made to the `Person` class, we would now have to track down all of the dependencies, which would bring us back to the copy-and-paste liabilities.

Inheritance allows us to derive classes from a *base class* without disturbing the implementation of the base class.

As we can see, except for the constructors, the code is relatively simple. We have added one data field, added one new method, and overridden an existing method. Internally, we have memory for all of the inherited fields, and we also have implementations of all original methods that have not been overridden. The amount of new code we have to write for `Student` would be roughly the same, regardless of how small or large the `Person` class was, and we have the benefit of *direct code reuse* and easy maintenance. Observe also that we have done so without disturbing the implementation of the existing class.

The `extends` clause is used to declare that a class is derived from another class.

Let us summarize the syntax so far. A derived class inherits all the properties of a base class. It can then add data members, override methods, and add new methods. Each derived class is a completely new class. A typical layout for inheritance is shown in Figure 4.5 and uses an `extends` clause. An `extends` clause declares that a class is derived from another class. A derived class *extends* a base class. Here is a brief description of a derived class:

- Generally all data is private, so we add additional data fields in the derived class by specifying them in the private section.

figure 4.5

The general layout of inheritance

```
public class Derived extends Base
{
    // Any members that are not listed are inherited unchanged
    // except for constructor.

        // public members
    // Constructor(s) if default is not acceptable
    // Base methods whose definitions are to change in Derived
    // Additional public methods

        // private members
    // Additional data fields (generally private)
    // Additional private methods
}
```

- Any base class methods that are not specified in the derived class are inherited unchanged, with the exception of the constructor. The special case of the constructor is discussed in Section 4.1.6.
- Any base class method that is declared in the derived class's public section is overridden. The new definition will be applied to objects of the derived class.
- Public base class methods may not be overridden in the private section of the derived class, because that would be tantamount to removing methods and would violate the *IS-A* relationship.
- Additional methods can be added in the derived class.

A derived class inherits all data members from the base class and may add more data members.

The derived class inherits all methods from the base class. It may accept or redefine them. It also can define new methods.

4.1.2 type compatibility

The direct code reuse described in the preceding paragraph is a significant gain. However, the more significant gain is *indirect code reuse*. This gain comes from the fact that a `Student` *IS-A* `Person` and an `Employee` *IS-A* `Person`.

Because a `Student` *IS-A* `Person`, a `Student` object can be accessed by a `Person` reference. The following code is thus legal:

Each *derived class* is a completely new class that nonetheless has some compatibility with the class from which it was derived.

```
Student s = new Student( "Joe", 26, "1 Main St",
                         "202-555-1212", 4.0 );
Person p = s;
System.out.println( "Age is " + p.getAge( ) );
```

This is legal because the static type (i.e., compile-time type) of `p` is `Person`. Thus `p` may reference any object that *IS-A* `Person`, and any method that we invoke through the `p` reference is guaranteed to make sense, since once a method is defined for `Person`, it cannot be removed by a derived class.

You might ask why this is a big deal. The reason is that this applies not only to assignment, but also to parameter passing. A method whose formal parameter is a `Person` can receive anything that *IS-A* `Person`, including `Student` and `Employee`.

So consider the following code written in *any class*:

```
public static boolean isOlder( Person p1, Person p2 )
{
    return p1.getAge( ) > p2.getAge( );
}
```

Consider the following declarations, in which constructor arguments are missing to save space:

```
Person   p = new Person( ... );
Student  s = new Student( ... );
Employee e = new Employee( ... );
```

The single `isOlder` routine can be used for all of the following calls: `isOlder(p,p)`, `isOlder(s,s)`, `isOlder(e,e)`, `isOlder(p,e)`, `isOlder(p,s)`, `isOlder(s,p)`, `isOlder(s,e)`, `isOlder(e,p)`, `isOlder(e,s)`.

All in all, we now have leveraged one non-class routine to work for nine different cases. In fact there is no limit to the amount of reuse this gets us. As soon as we use inheritance to add a fourth class into the hierarchy, we now have 4 times 4, or 16 different methods, without changing `isOlder` at all! The reuse is even more significant if a method were to take three `Person` references as parameters. And imagine the huge code reuse if a method takes an array of `Person` references.

Thus, for many people, the type compatibility of derived classes with their base classes is the most important thing about inheritance because it leads to massive *indirect code reuse*. And as `isOlder` illustrates, it also makes it very easy to add in new types that automatically work with existing methods.

4.1.3 dynamic dispatch and polymorphism

There is the issue of overriding methods: If the type of the reference and the class of the object being referenced (in the example above, these are `Person` and `Student`, respectively) disagree, and they have different implementations, whose implementation is to be used?

As an example, consider the following fragment:

```
Student s = new Student( "Joe", 26, "1 Main St",
                         "202-555-1212", 4.0 );
Employee e = new Employee( "Boss", 42, "4 Main St.",
                         "203-555-1212", 100000.0 );
Person p = null;
if( getTodaysDay( ).equals( "Tuesday" ) )
    p = s;
else
    p = e;
System.out.println( "Person is " + p.toString( ) );
```

A *polymorphic* variable can reference objects of several different types. When operations are applied to the polymorphic variable, the operation appropriate to the referenced object is automatically selected.

Here the static type of `p` is `Person`. When we run the program, the dynamic type (i.e., the type of the object actually being referenced) will be either `Student` or `Employee`. It is impossible to deduce the dynamic type until the program runs. Naturally, however, we would want the dynamic type to be used, and that is what happens in Java. When this code fragment is run, the `toString` method that is used will be the one appropriate for the dynamic type of the controlling object reference.

This is an important object-oriented principle known as *polymorphism*. A reference variable that is polymorphic can reference objects of several different types. When operations are applied to the reference, the operation that is appropriate to the actual referenced object is automatically selected.

All reference types are polymorphic in Java. This is also known as *dynamic dispatch* or *late binding* (or sometimes *dynamic binding*).

A derived class is *type-compatible* with its base class, meaning that a reference variable of the base class type may reference an object of the derived class, but not vice versa. Sibling classes (that is, classes derived from a common class) are not type-compatible.

4.1.4 inheritance hierarchies

If *X IS-A Y*, then *X* is a *subclass* of *Y* and *Y* is a *superclass* of *X*. These relationships are transitive.

As mentioned earlier, the use of inheritance typically generates a hierarchy of classes. Figure 4.6 illustrates a possible `Person` hierarchy. Notice that `Faculty` is indirectly, rather than directly, derived from `Person`—so faculty are people too! This fact is transparent to the user of the classes because *IS-A* relationships are transitive. In other words, if *X IS-A Y* and *Y IS-A Z*, then *X IS-A Z*. The `Person` hierarchy illustrates the typical design issues of factoring out commonalities into base classes and then specializing in the derived classes. In this hierarchy, we say that the derived class is a *subclass* of the base class and the base class is a *superclass* of the derived class. These relationships are transitive, and furthermore, the `instanceof` operator works with subclasses. Thus if `obj` is of type `Undergrad` (and not `null`), then `obj instanceof Person` is `true`.

4.1.5 visibility rules

We know that any member that is declared with private visibility is accessible only to methods of the class. Thus as we have seen, any private members in the base class are not accessible to the derived class.

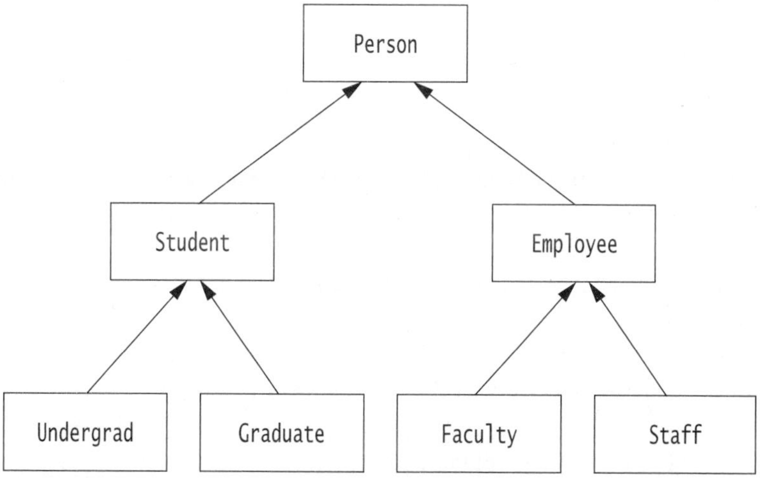

figure 4.6
The `Person` hierarchy

Occasionally we want the derived class to have access to the base class members. There are two basic options. The first is to use either public or package visible access (if the base and derived classes are in the same package), as appropriate. However, this allows access by other classes in addition to derived classes.

A *protected class member* is visible to the derived class and also classes in the same package.

If we want to restrict access to only derived classes, we can make members protected. A *protected class member* is visible to methods in a derived class and also methods in classes in the same package, but not to anyone else.[1] Declaring data members as `protected` or `public` violates the spirit of encapsulation and information hiding and is generally done only as a matter of programming expediency. Typically, a better alternative is to write accessor and mutator methods. However, if a protected declaration allows you to avoid convoluted code, then it is not unreasonable to use it. In this text, protected data members are used for precisely this reason. Protected methods are also used in this text. This allows a derived class to inherit an internal method without making it accessible outside the class hierarchy. Notice that in *toy code*, in which all classes are in the default unnamed package, protected members are visible.

4.1.6 the constructor and `super`

If no constructor is written, then a single zero-parameter default constructor is generated that calls the base class zero-parameter constructor for the inherited portion, and then applies the default initialization for any additional data fields.

Each derived class should define its constructors. If no constructor is written, then a single zero-parameter default constructor is generated. This constructor will call the base class zero-parameter constructor for the inherited portion and then apply the default initialization for any additional data fields (meaning 0 for primitive types, and `null` for reference types).

Constructing a derived class object by first constructing the inherited portion is standard practice. In fact, it is done by default, even if an explicit derived class constructor is given. This is natural because the encapsulation

---

1. The rule for protected visibility is quite complex. A protected member of class `B` is visible to all methods in any classes that are in the same package as `B`. It is also visible to methods in any class `D` that is in a different package than `B` if `D` extends `B`, but only if accessed through a reference that is type-compatible with `D` (including an implicit or explicit `this`). Specifically, it is NOT VISIBLE in class `D` if accessed through a reference of type `B`. The following example illustrates this.

```
class Demo extends java.io.FilterInputStream
{      // FilterInputStream has protected data field named in
    public void foo( )
    {
        java.io.FilterInputStream b = this;  // legal
        System.out.println( in );            // legal
        System.out.println( this.in );       // legal
        System.out.println( b.in );          // illegal
    }
}
```

viewpoint tells us that the inherited portion is a single entity, and the base class constructor tells us how to initialize this single entity.

Base class constructors can be explicitly called by using the method `super`. Thus the default constructor for a derived class is in reality

```
public Derived( )
{
    super( );
}
```

The `super` method can be called with parameters that match a base class constructor. As an example, Figure 4.7 illustrates the implementation of the `Student` constructor.

`super` is used to call the base class constructor.

The `super` method can be used only as the first line of a constructor. If it is not provided, then an automatic call to `super` with no parameters is generated.

4.1.7 `final` methods and classes

As described earlier, the derived class either overrides or accepts the base class methods. In many cases, it is clear that a particular base class method should be invariant over the hierarchy, meaning that a derived class should not override it. In this case, we can declare that the method is `final` and cannot be overridden.

A `final` method is invariant over the inheritance hierarchy and may not be overridden.

Declaring invariant methods `final` is not only good programming practice. It also can lead to more efficient code. It is good programming practice because in addition to declaring your intentions to the reader of the program and documentation, you prevent the accidental overriding of a method that should not be overridden.

```
class Student extends Person
{
    public Student( String n, int ag, String ad, String p,
                    double g )
      { super( n, ag, ad, p );  gpa = g; }

    // toString and getAge omitted

    private double gpa;
}
```

figure 4.7

A constructor for new class `Student`; uses `super`

To see why using `final` may make for more efficient code, suppose base class `Base` declares a final method `f` and suppose `Derived` extends `Base`. Consider the routine

```
void doIt( Base obj )
{
    obj.f( );
}
```

Static binding could be used when the method is invariant over the inheritance hierarchy.

Since `f` is a final method, it does not matter whether `obj` actually references a `Base` or `Derived` object; the definition of `f` is invariant, so we know what `f` does. As a result, a compile-time decision, rather than a run-time decision, could be made to resolve the method call. This is known as *static binding*. Because binding is done during compilation rather than at run time, the program should run faster. Whether this is noticeable would depend on how many times we avoid making the run-time decision while executing the program.

Static methods have no controlling object and thus are resolved at compile time using static binding.

A corollary to this observation is that if `f` is a trivial method, such as a single field accessor, and is declared `final`, the compiler could replace the call to `f` with its inline definition. Thus the method call would be replaced by a single line that accesses a data field, thereby saving time. If `f` is not declared `final`, then this is impossible, since `obj` could be referencing a derived class object, for which the definition of `f` could be different.[2] Static methods are not final methods, but have no controlling object and thus are resolved at compile time using static binding.

A *final class* may not be extended. A *leaf class* is a final class.

Similar to the final method is the *final class*. A final class cannot be extended. As a result, all of its methods are automatically final methods. As an example, the `String` class is a final class. Notice that the fact that a class has only final methods does not imply that it is a final class. Final classes are also known as *leaf classes* because in the inheritance hierarchy, which resembles a tree, final classes are at the fringes, like leaves.

In the `Person` class, the trivial accessors and mutators (those starting with `get` and `set`) are good candidates for final methods, and they are declared as such in the online code.

2. In the preceding two paragraphs, we say that static binding and inline optimizations "could be" done because although compile-time decisions would appear to make sense, Section 8.4.3.3 of the language specification makes clear that inline optimizations for trivial final methods can be done, but this optimization must be done by the virtual machine at run time, rather than the compiler at compile time. This ensures that dependent classes do not get out of sync as a result of the optimization.

4.1.8 overriding a method

Methods in the base class are overridden in the derived class by simply providing a derived class method with the same signature.[3] The derived class method must have the same return type and may not add exceptions to the throws list.[4] The derived class may not reduce visibility, as that would violate the spirit of an *IS-A* relationship. Thus you may not override a public method with a package-visible method.

The derived class method must have the same return type and signature and may not add exceptions to the throws list.

Sometimes the derived class method wants to invoke the base class method. Typically, this is known as *partial overriding*. That is, we want to do what the base class does, plus a little more, rather than doing something entirely different. Calls to a base class method can be accomplished by using super. Here is an example:

Partial overriding involves calling a base class method by using super.

```
public class Workaholic extends Worker
{
    public void doWork( )
    {
        super.doWork( );     // Work like a Worker
        drinkCoffee( );      // Take a break
        super.doWork( );     // Work like a Worker some more
    }
}
```

A more typical example is the overriding of standard methods, such as toString. Figure 4.8 illustrates this use in the Student and Employee classes.

4.1.9 type compatibility revisited

Figure 4.9 illustrates the typical use of polymorphism with arrays. At line 17, we create an array of four Person references, which will each be initialized to null. The values of these references can be set at lines 19 to 24, and we know that all the assignments are legal because of the ability of a base type reference to refer to objects of a derived type.

The printAll routine simply steps through the array and calls the toString method, using dynamic dispatch. The test at line 7 is important because, as we have seen, some of the array references could be null.

3. If a different signature is used, you simply have overloaded the method, and now there are two methods with different signatures available for the compiler to choose from.
4. Java 5 loosens this requirement and allows the return type of the derived class's method to be slightly different as long as it is "compatible." The new rule is discussed in Section 4.1.11.

figure 4.8

The complete `Student` and `Employee` classes, using both forms of `super`

```
class Student extends Person
{
    public Student( String n, int ag, String ad, String p,
                    double g )
      { super( n, ag, ad, p ); gpa = g; }

    public String toString( )
      { return super.toString( ) + getGPA( ); }

    public double getGPA( )
      { return gpa; }

    private double gpa;
}

class Employee extends Person
{
    public Employee( String n, int ag, String ad,
                     String p, double s )
      { super( n, ag, ad, p ); salary = s; }

    public String toString( )
      { return super.toString( ) + " $" + getSalary( ); }

    public double getSalary( )
      { return salary; }

    public void raise( double percentRaise )
      { salary *= ( 1 + percentRaise ); }

    private double salary;
}
```

In the example, suppose that prior to completing the printing, we want to give `p[3]`—which we know is an employee—a raise? Since `p[3]` is an `Employee`, it might seem that

```
p[3].raise( 0.04 );
```

would be legal. But it is not. The problem is that the static type of `p[3]` is a `Person`, and `raise` is not defined for `Person`. At compile time, only (visible) members of the *static type* of the reference can appear to the right of the dot operator.

We can change the static type by using a cast:

```
((Employee) p[3]).raise( 0.04 );
```

The above code makes the static type of the reference to the left of the dot operator an `Employee`. If this is impossible (for instance, `p[3]` is in a completely

```
class PersonDemo
{
    public static void printAll( Person [ ] arr )
    {
        for( int i = 0; i < arr.length; i++ )
        {
            if( arr[ i ] != null )
            {
                System.out.print( "[" + i + "] " );
                System.out.println( arr[ i ].toString( ) );
            }
        }
    }

    public static void main( String [ ] args )
    {
    Person [ ] p = new Person[ 4 ];

        p[0] = new Person( "joe", 25, "New York",
                               "212-555-1212" );
        p[1] = new Student( "jill", 27, "Chicago",
                                "312-555-1212", 4.0 );
        p[3] = new Employee( "bob", 29, "Boston",
                                "617-555-1212", 100000.0 );

        printAll( p );
    }
}
```

figure 4.9

An illustration of polymorphism with arrays

different hierarchy), the compiler will complain. If it is possible for the cast to make sense, the program will compile, and so the above code will successfully give a 4% raise to `p[3]`. This construct, in which we change the static type of an expression from a base class to a class farther down in the inheritance hierarchy is known as a *downcast*.

A *downcast* is a cast down the inheritance hierarchy. Casts are always verified at runtime by the Virtual Machine.

What if `p[3]` was not an `Employee`? For instance, what if we used the following?

```
((Employee) p[1]).raise( 0.04 ); // p[1] is a Student
```

In that case the program would compile, but the Virtual Machine would throw a `ClassCastException`, which is a run-time exception that signals a programming error. Casts are always double-checked at run time to ensure that the programmer (or a malicious hacker) is not trying to subvert Java's strong typing system. The safe way of doing these types of calls is to use `instanceof` first:

```
if( p[3] instanceof Employee )
    ((Employee) p[3]).raise( 0.04 );
```

4.1.10 compatibility of array types

One of the difficulties in language design is how to handle inheritance for aggregate types. In our example, we know that `Employee` *IS-A* `Person`. But is it true that `Employee[]` *IS-A* `Person[]`? In other words, if a routine is written to accept `Person[]` as a parameter, can we pass an `Employee[]` as an argument?

Arrays of subclasses are type-compatible with arrays of superclasses. This is known as *covariant arrays.*

At first glance, this seems like a no-brainer, and `Employee[]` should be type-compatible with `Person[]`. However, this issue is trickier than it seems. Suppose that in addition to `Employee`, `Student` *IS-A* `Person`. Suppose the `Employee[]` is type-compatible with `Person[]`. Then consider this sequence of assignments:

```
Person[] arr = new Employee[ 5 ]; // compiles: arrays are compatible
arr[ 0 ] = new Student( ... );    // compiles: Student IS-A Person
```

If an incompatible type is inserted into the array, the Virtual Machine will throw an `ArrayStoreException`.

Both assignments compile, yet `arr[0]` is actually a referencing an `Employee`, and `Student` *IS-NOT-A* `Employee`. Thus we have type confusion. The runtime system cannot throw a `ClassCastException` since there is no cast.

The easiest way to avoid this problem is to specify that the arrays are not type-compatible. However, in Java the arrays *are* type-compatible. This is known as a *covariant array type*. Each array keeps track of the type of object it is allowed to store. If an incompatible type is inserted into the array, the Virtual Machine will throw an `ArrayStoreException`.

4.1.11 covariant return types

In Java 5, the subclass method's return type only needs to be type-compatible with (i.e., it may be a subclass of) the superclass method's return type. This is known as a *covariant return type.*

Prior to Java 5, when a method was overridden, the subclass method was required to have the same return type as the superclass method. Java 5 relaxes this rule. In Java 5, the subclass method's return type only needs to be type-compatible with (i.e., it may be a subclass of) the superclass method's return type. This is known as a *covariant return type*. As an example, suppose class `Person` has a `makeCopy` method

```
public Person makeCopy( );
```

that returns a copy of the `Person`. Prior to Java 5, if class `Employee` overrode this method, the return type would have to be `Person`. In Java 5, the method may be overridden as

```
public Employee makeCopy( );
```

4.2 designing hierarchies

Suppose we have a Circle class, and for any non-null Circle c, c.area() returns the area of Circle c. Additionally, suppose we have a Rectangle class, and for any non-null Rectangle r, r.area() returns the area of Rectangle r. Possibly we have other classes such as Ellipse, Triangle, and Square, all with area methods. Suppose we have an array that contains references to these objects, and we want to compute the total area of all the objects. Since they all have an area method for all classes, polymorphism is an attractive option, yielding code such as the following:

```
public static totalArea( WhatType [ ] arr )
{
    double total = 0.0;

    for( int i = 0; i < arr.length; i++ )
        if( arr[ i ] != null )
            total += arr[ i ].area( );

    return total;
}
```

For this code to work, we need to decide the type declaration for WhatType. None of Circle, Rectangle, etc., will work, since there is no *IS-A* relationship. Thus we need to define a type, say Shape, such that Circle *IS-A* Shape, Rectangle *IS-A* Shape, etc. A possible hierarchy is illustrated in Figure 4.10. Additionally, in order for arr[i].area() to make sense, area must be a method available for Shape.

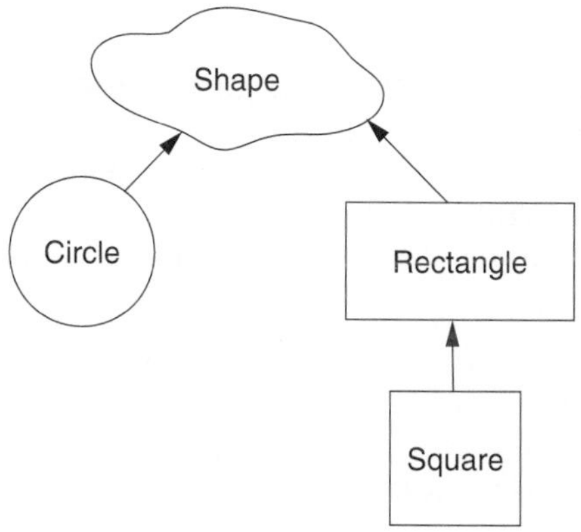

figure 4.10

The hierarchy of shapes used in an inheritance example

figure 4.11

A possible Shape class

```
public class Shape
{
    public double area( )
    {
        return -1;
    }
}
```

This suggests a class for Shape, as shown in Figure 4.11. Once we have the Shape class, we can provide others, as shown in Figure 4.12. These classes also include a perimeter method. Observe that Square reuses code inherited from Rectangle.

The code in Figure 4.12, with classes that extend the simple Shape class in Figure 4.11 that returns –1 for area, can now be used polymorphically, as shown in Figure 4.13.

Too many instanceof operators is a symptom of poor object-oriented design.

A huge benefit of this design is that we can add a new class to the hierarchy without disturbing implementations. For instance, suppose we want to add triangles into the mix. All we need to do is have Triangle extend Shape, override area appropriately, and now Triangle objects can be included in any Shape[] object. Observe that this involves the following:

- NO CHANGES to the Shape class
- NO CHANGES to the Circle, Rectangle, or Square classes
- NO CHANGES to the totalArea method

making it difficult to break existing code in the process of adding new code. Notice also the lack of any instanceof tests, which is typical of good polymorphic code.

4.2.1 abstract methods and classes

Although the code in the previous example works, improvements are possible in the Shape class written in Figure 4.11. Notice that the Shape class itself, and the area method in particular, are *placeholders*: The Shape's area method is never intended to be called directly. It is there so that the compiler and run-time system can conspire to use dynamic dispatch and call an appropriate area method. In fact, examining main, we see that Shape objects themselves are not supposed to be created either. The class exists simply as a common superclass for the others.[5]

5. Declaring a private Shape constructor DOES NOT solve the second problem: The constructor is needed by the subclasses.

```
public class Circle extends Shape
{
    public Circle( double rad )
      { radius = rad; }

    public double area( )
      { return Math.PI * radius * radius; }

    public double perimeter( )
      { return 2 * Math.PI * radius; }

    public String toString( )
      { return "Circle: " + radius; }

    private double radius;
}

public class Rectangle extends Shape
{
    public Rectangle( double len, double wid )
      { length = len; width = wid; }

    public double area( )
      { return length * width; }

    public double perimeter( )
      { return 2 * ( length + width ); }

    public String toString( )
      { return "Rectangle: " + length + " " + width; }

    public double getLength( )
      { return length; }

    public double getWidth( )
      { return width; }

    private double length;
    private double width;
}

public class Square extends Rectangle
{
    public Square( double side )
      { super( side, side ); }

    public String toString( )
      { return "Square: " + getLength( ); }
}
```

figure 4.12

Circle, Rectangle, and Square classes

figure 4.13

A sample program that uses the shape hierarchy

```
class ShapeDemo
{
    public static double totalArea( Shape [ ] arr )
    {
        double total = 0;

        for( Shape s : arr )
            if( s != null )
                total += s.area( );

        return total;
    }

    public static void printAll( Shape [ ] arr )
    {
        for( Shape s : arr )
            System.out.println( s );
    }

    public static void main( String [ ] args )
    {
        Shape [ ] a = { new Circle( 2.0 ),
                        new Rectangle( 1.0, 3.0 ),
                        null, new Square( 2.0 ) };

        System.out.println( "Total area = " + totalArea( a ) );
        printAll( a );
    }
}
```

The programmer has attempted to signal that calling `Shape`'s area is an error by returning –1, which is an obviously impossible area. But this is a value that might be ignored. Furthermore, this is a value that will be returned if, when extending `Shape`, `area` is not overridden. This failure to override could occur because of a typographical error: An `Area` function is written instead of `area`, making it difficult to track down the error at run time.

Abstract methods and classes represent placeholders.

A better solution for `area` is to throw a runtime exception (a good one is `UnsupportedOperationException`) in the `Shape` class. This is preferable to returning –1 because the exception will not be ignored.

However, even that solution resolves the problem at runtime. It would be better to have syntax that explicitly states that `area` is a placeholder and does not need any implementation at all, and that further, `Shape` is a placeholder class and cannot be constructed, even though it may declare constructors, and will have a default constructor if none are declared. If this syntax were available, then the compiler could, at compile time, declare as illegal any attempts to construct a Shape instance. It could also declare as illegal any classes, such as Triangle, for which there are attempts to construct instances, even though area has not been overridden. This exactly describes abstract methods and abstract classes.

An *abstract method* is a method that declares functionality that all derived class objects must eventually implement. In other words, it says what these objects can do. However, it does not provide a default implementation. Instead, each object must provide its own implementation.

An *abstract method* has no meaningful definition and is thus always defined in the derived class.

A class that has at least one abstract method is an *abstract class*. Java requires that all abstract classes explicitly be declared as such. When a derived class fails to override an abstract method with an implementation, the method remains abstract in the derived class. As a result, if a class that is not intended to be abstract fails to override an abstract method, the compiler will detect the inconsistency and report an error.

An example of how we can make Shape abstract is shown in Figure 4.14. No changes are required to any of the other code in Figures 4.12 and 4.13. Observe that an abstract class can have methods that are not abstract, as is the case with semiperimeter.

An abstract class can also declare both static and instance fields. Like nonabstract classes, these fields would typically be private, and the instance fields would be initialized by constructors. Although abstract classes cannot be created, these constructors will be called when the derived classes use super. In a more extensive example, the Shape class could include the coordinates of the object's extremities, which would be set by constructors, and it could provide implementation of methods, such as positionOf, that are independent of the actual type of object; positionOf would be a final method.

As mentioned earlier, the existence of at least one abstract method makes the base class abstract and disallows creation of it. Thus a Shape object cannot itself be created; only the derived objects can. However, as usual, a Shape vari-

A class with at least one abstract method must be an *abstract class.*

```
public abstract class Shape
{
    public abstract double area( );
    public abstract double perimeter( );

    public double semiperimeter( )
      { return perimeter( ) / 2; }
}
```

figure 4.14

An abstract Shape class. Figures 4.12 and 4.13 are unchanged.

able can reference any concrete derived object, such as a `Circle` or `Rectangle`. Thus

```
Shape a, b;
a = new Circle( 3.0 );          // Legal
b = new Shape( );               // Illegal
```

Before continuing, let us summarize the four types of class methods:

1. *Final methods.* The virtual machine may choose at run time to perform inline optimization, thus avoiding dynamic dispatch. We use a final method only when the method is invariant over the inheritance hierarchy (that is, when the method is never redefined).
2. *Abstract methods.* Overriding is resolved at run time. The base class provides no implementation and is abstract. The absence of a default requires either that the derived classes provide an implementation or that the classes themselves be abstract.
3. *Static methods.* Overridding is resolved at compile time because there is no controlling object.
4. *Other methods.* Overriding is resolved at run time. The base class provides a default implementation that may be either overridden by the derived classes or accepted unchanged by the derived classes.

4.3 multiple inheritance

Multiple inheritance is used to derive a class from several base classes. Java does not allow multiple inheritance.

All the inheritance examples seen so far derived one class from a single base class. In *multiple inheritance*, a class may be derived from more than one base class. For instance, we may have a `Student` class and an `Employee` class. A `StudentEmployee` could then be derived from both classes.

Although multiple inheritance sounds attractive, and some languages (including C++) support it, it is wrought with subtleties that make design difficult. For instance, the two base classes may contain two methods that have the same signature but different implementations. Alternatively, they may have two identically named fields. Which one should be used?

For example, suppose that in the previous `StudentEmployee` example, `Person` is a class with data field `name` and method `toString`. Suppose, too, that `Student` extends `Person` and overrides `toString` to include the year of graduation. Further, suppose that `Employee` extends `Person` but does not override `toString`; instead, it declares that it is `final`.

1. Since `StudentEmployee` inherits the data members from both `Student` and `Employee`, do we get two copies of `name`?
2. If `StudentEmployee` does not override `toString`, which `toString` method should be used?

When many classes are involved, the problems are even larger. It appears, however, that the typical multiple inheritance problems can be traced to conflicting implementations or conflicting data fields. As a result, Java does not allow multiple inheritance. Instead, it provides an alternative known as the *interface*.

4.4 the interface

The *interface* in Java is the ultimate abstract class. It consists of public abstract methods and public static final fields, only.

The *interface* is an abstract class that contains no implementation details.

A class is said to *implement* the interface if it provides definitions for all of the abstract methods in the interface. A class that implements the interface behaves as if it had extended an abstract class specified by the interface.

In principle, the main difference between an interface and an abstract class is that although both provide a specification of what the subclasses must do, the interface is not allowed to provide any implementation details either in the form of data fields or implemented methods. The practical effect of this is that multiple interfaces do not suffer the same potential problems as multiple inheritance because we cannot have conflicting implementations. Thus, while a class may extend only one other class, it may implement more than one interface.

4.4.1 specifying an interface

Syntactically, virtually nothing is easier than specifying an interface. The interface looks like a class declaration, except that it uses the keyword `interface`. It consists of a listing of the methods that must be implemented. An example is the `Comparable` interface, shown in Figure 4.15, which is part of the standard `java.lang` package, starting with Java 1.2. The code shown in Figure 4.15 represents the interface prior to enhancements done in Java 5. Nonetheless, code that is based on Java 1.4 and earlier versions of the `Comparable` interface will continue to compile in Java 5. We discuss the Java 5 version of `Comparable` in

figure 4.15

The Comparable interface (pre-Java 5)

```
package java.lang;

public interface Comparable
{
    int compareTo( Object other );
}
```

Section 4.7. This section discusses the simpler version of Comparable before Java 5.

The Comparable interface specifies one method that every subclass must implement: compareTo, which behaves like the String compareTo method. In fact, String implements precisely this interface. Note that we do not have to specify that these methods are public and abstract. Since these modifiers are required for interface methods, they can and usually are omitted.

4.4.2 implementing an interface

The implements clause is used to declare that a class implements an interface. The class must implement all interface methods or it remains abstract.

A class implements an interface by

1. Declaring that it implements the interface
2. Defining implementations for all the interface methods

An example is shown in Figure 4.16. Here, we complete the Shape class, which we used in Section 4.2.

Line 1 shows that when implementing an interface, we use implements instead of extends. Shape is abstract because it has abstract methods; if it did not, it would not need to be declared abstract. We can provide any methods that we want, but we must provide at least those listed in the interface. The interface is implemented at lines 6 to 17. Notice that we must implement the *exact method* specified in the interface. Thus these methods take Object as a parameter, instead of Shape or Comparable.

A class that implements an interface can be extended if it is not final. The extended class automatically implements the interface. Thus, Circle automatically implements Comparable, and it has inherited the compareTo method from Shape.

A class that implements an interface may still extend one other class. The extends clause must precede the implements clause.

```
public abstract class Shape implements Comparable
{
    public abstract double area( );
    public abstract double perimeter( );

    public int compareTo( Object rhs )
    {
        Shape other = (Shape) rhs;
        double diff = area( ) - other.area( );

        if( diff == 0 )
            return 0;
        else if( diff < 0 )
            return -1;
        else
            return 1;
    }

    public double semiperimeter( )
      { return perimeter( ) / 2; }
}
```

figure 4.16

The Shape class (final version), which implements the Comparable interface

4.4.3 multiple interfaces

As we mentioned earlier, a class may implement multiple interfaces. The syntax for doing so is simple. A class implements multiple interfaces by

1. Listing the interfaces (comma separated) that it implements
2. Defining implementations for all of the interface methods

The interface is the ultimate in abstract classes and represents an elegant solution to the multiple inheritance problem.

4.4.4 interfaces are abstract classes

Because an interface is an abstract class, all the rules of inheritance apply. Specifically,

1. The *IS-A* relationship holds. If class C implements interface I, then C *IS-A* I and is type-compatible with I. If a class C implements interfaces I_1, I_2, and I_3, then C *IS-A* I_1, C *IS-A* I_2, and C *IS-A* I_3, and is type-compatible with I_1, I_2, and I_3.

2. The `instanceof` operator can be used to determine if a reference is type-compatible with an interface.
3. When a class implements an interface method, it may not reduce visibility. Since all interface methods are public, all implementations must be public.
4. When a class implements an interface method, it may not add checked exceptions to the `throws` list. If a class implements multiple interfaces in which the same method occurs with a different `throws` list, the `throws` list of the implementation may list only checked exceptions that are in the intersection of the `throws` lists of the interface methods.
5. When a class implements an interface method, it must implement the exact signature (not including the `throws` list); otherwise, it inherits an abstract version of the interface method and has provided a non-abstract overloaded, but different, method.
6. A class may not implement two interfaces that contain a method with the same signature and incompatible return types, since it would be impossible to provide both methods in one class.
7. If a class fails to implement any methods in an interface, it must be declared abstract.
8. Interfaces can extend other interfaces (including multiple interfaces).

4.5 fundamental inheritance in java

Two important places where inheritance is used in Java are the `Object` class and the hierarchy of exceptions.

4.5.1 the `Object` class

Java specifies that if a class does not extend another class, then it implicitly extends the class `Object` (defined in `java.lang`). As a result, every class is either a direct or indirect subclass of `Object`.

The `Object` class contains several methods, and since it is not abstract, all have implementations. The most commonly used method is `toString`, which we have already seen. If `toString` is not written for a class, an implementation is provided that concatenates the name of the class, an `@`, and the class's "hash code."

Other important methods are `equals` and the `hashCode`, which we will discuss in more detail in Chapter 6, and a set of somewhat tricky methods that advanced Java programmers need to know about.

4.5.2 the hierarchy of exceptions

As described in Section 2.5, there are several types of exceptions. The root of the hierarchy, a portion of which is shown in Figure 4.17, is `Throwable`, which defines a set of `printStackTrace` methods, provides a `toString` implementation, a pair of constructors, and little else. The hierarchy is split off into `Error`, `RuntimeException`, and checked exceptions. A checked exception is any `Exception` that is not a `RuntimeException`. For the most part, each new class extends another exception class, providing only a pair of constructors. It is possible to provide more, but none of the standard exceptions bother to do so. In `weiss.util`, we implement three of the standard `java.util` exceptions. One such implementation, which shows that new exception classes typically provide little more than constructors, is shown in Figure 4.18.

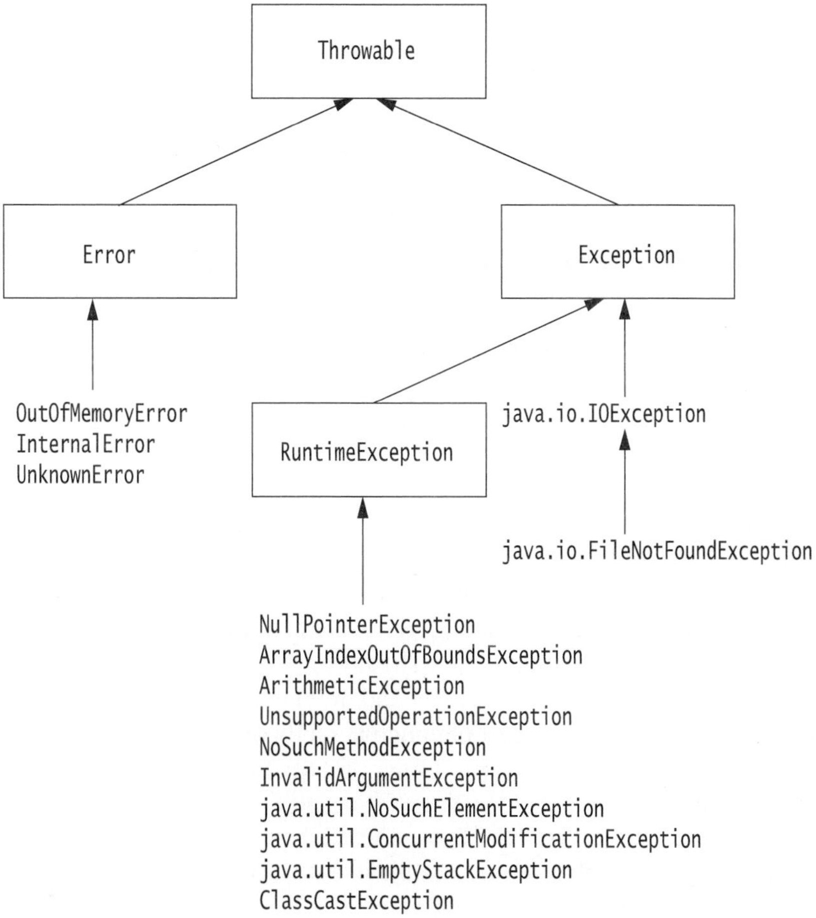

figure 4.17
The hierarchy of exceptions (partial list)

figure 4.18

`NoSuchElementException`, implemented in `weiss.util`

```
package weiss.util;

public class NoSuchElementException extends RuntimeException
{
    /**
     * Constructs a NoSuchElementException with
     * no detail message.
     */
    public NoSuchElementException( )
    {
    }

    /*
     * Constructs a NoSuchElementException with
     * a detail message.
     * @param msg the detail message.
     */
    public NoSuchElementException( String msg )
    {
        super( msg );
    }
}
```

4.5.3 i/o: the decorator pattern

I/O in Java looks fairly complex to use but works nicely for doing I/O with different sources, such as the terminal, files, and Internet sockets. Because it is designed to be extensible, there are lots of classes—over 50 in all. It is cumbersome to use for trivial tasks; for instance, reading a number from the terminal requires substantial work.

Input is done through the use of stream classes. Because Java was designed for Internet programming, most of the I/O centers around byte-oriented reading and writing.

Byte-oriented I/O is done with stream classes that extend `InputStream` or `OutputStream`. `InputStream` and `OutputStream` are abstract classes and not interfaces, so there is no such thing as a stream open for both input and output. These classes declare an abstract `read` and `write` method for single-byte I/O, respectively, and also a small set of concrete methods such as `close` and block I/O (which can be implemented in terms of calls to single-byte I/O). Examples of these classes include `FileInputStream` and `FileOutputStream`, as well as the hidden `SocketInputStream` and `SocketOutputStream`. (The socket streams are produced by methods that return an object statically typed as `InputStream` or `OutputStream`.)

Character-oriented I/O is done with classes that extend the abstract classes `Reader` and `Writer`. These also contain `read` and `write` methods. There are not as many `Reader` and `Writer` classes as `InputStream` and `OutputStream` classes.

`InputStreamReader` and `OutputStreamWriter` classes are *bridges* that allow the programmer to cross over from the `Stream` to `Reader` and `Writer` hierarchies.

However, this is not a problem, because of the `InputStreamReader` and `OutputStreamWriter` classes. These are called *bridges* because they cross over from the `Stream` to `Reader` and `Writer` hierarchies. An `InputStreamReader` is constructed with any `InputStream` and creates an object that *IS-A* `Reader`. For instance, we can create a `Reader` for files using

```
InputStream fis = new FileInputStream( "foo.txt" );
Reader fin = new InputStreamReader( fis );
```

It happens that there is a `FileReader` convenience class that does this already; Figure 4.19 provides a plausible implementation.

From a `Reader`, we can do limited I/O; the `read` method returns one character. If we want to read one line instead, we need a class called `BufferedReader`. Like other `Reader` objects, a `BufferedReader` is constructed from any other `Reader`, but it provides both buffering and a `readLine` method. Thus, continuing the previous example,

```
BufferedReader bin = new BufferedReader( fin );
```

Wrapping an `InputStream` inside an `InputStreamReader` inside a `BufferedReader` works for any `InputStream`, including `System.in` or sockets. Figure 4.20, which duplicates Figure 2.15, illustrates the use of this pattern to read two numbers from the standard input.

The wrapping idea is an example of a commonly used Java design pattern, which we will see again in Section 4.6.2.

Similar to the `BufferedReader` is the `PrintWriter`, which allows us to do `println` operations.

The `OutputStream` hierarchy includes several wrappers, such as `DataOutputStream`, `ObjectOutputStream`, and `GZIPOutputStream`.

`DataOutputStream` allows us to write primitives in binary form (rather than human-readable text form); for instance, a call to `writeInt` writes the 4 bytes

```
class FileReader extends InputStreamReader
{
    public FileReader( String name ) throws FileNotFoundException
      { super( new FileInputStream( name ) ); }
}
```

figure 4.19

The `FileReader` convenience class

figure 4.20

A program that demonstrates the wrapping of streams and readers

```
import java.io.InputStreamReader;
import java.io.BufferedReader;
import java.io.IOException;

import java.util.StringTokenizer;

public class MaxTest
{
    public static void main( String [ ] args)
    {
        BufferedReader in = new BufferedReader( new
                               InputStreamReader( System.in ) );

        String oneLine;
        StringTokenizer str;
        int x;
        int y;

        System.out.println( "Enter 2 ints on one line: " );
        try
        {
            oneLine = in.readLine( );
            if( oneLine == null )
                return;

            str = new StringTokenizer( oneLine );
            if( str.countTokens( ) != 2 )
            {
                System.out.println( "Error: need two ints" );
                return;
            }
            x = Integer.parseInt( str.nextToken( ) );
            y = Integer.parseInt( str.nextToken( ) );
            System.out.println( "Max: " + Math.max( x, y ) );
        }
        catch( IOException e )
          { System.err.println( "Unexpected IO error" ); }
        catch( NumberFormatException e )
          { System.err.println( "Error: need two ints" ); }
    }
}
```

that represent a 32-bit integer. Writing data that way avoids conversions to text form, resulting in time and (sometimes) space savings. `ObjectOutputStream` allows us to write an entire object including all its components, its component's components, etc., to a stream. The object and all its components must implement the `Serializable` interface. There are no methods in the interface; one must simply declare that a class is serializable.[6] The `GZIPOutputStream` wraps an `OutputStream` and compresses the writes prior to sending it to the `OutputStream`. In addition, there is a `BufferedOutputStream` class. Similar wrappers are found on the `InputStream` side. As an example, suppose we have an array of serializable `Person` objects. We can write the objects, as a unit, compressed as follows:

```
Person [ ] p = getPersons( );   // populate the array
FileOutputStream fout = new FileOutputStream( "people.gzip" );
BufferedOutputStream bout = new BufferedOutputStream( fout );
GZIPOutputStream gout = new GZIPOutputStream( bout );
ObjectOutputStream oout = new ObjectOutputStream( gout );
oout.writeObject( p );
oout.close( );
```

Later on, we could read everything back:

```
FileInputStream fin = new FileInputStream( "people.gzip" );
BufferedInputStream bin = new BufferedInputStream( fin );
GZIPInputStream gin = new GZIPInputStream( bin );
ObjectInputStream oin = new ObjectInputStream( gin );
Person [ ] p = (Person[ ]) oin.readObject( );
oin.close( );
```

The online code expands this example by having each `Person` store a name, a birth date, and the two `Person` objects that represent the parents.

The idea of nesting wrappers in order to add functionality is known as the *decorator pattern*. By doing this, we have numerous small classes that are combined to provide a powerful interface. Without this pattern, each different I/O source would have to have functionality for compression, serialization, character, and byte I/O, and so on. With the pattern, each source is only responsible for minimal, basic I/O, and then the extra features are added on by the decorators.

The idea of nesting wrappers in order to add functionality is known as the *decorator pattern.*

6. The reason for this is that serialization, by default, is insecure. When an object is written out in an `ObjectOutputStream`, the format is well known, so its private members can be read by a malicious user. Similarly, when an object is read back in, the data on the input stream is not checked for correctness, so it is possible to read a corrupt object. There are advanced techniques that can be used to ensure security and integrity when serialization is used, but that is beyond the scope of this text. The designers of the serialization library felt that serialization should not be the default because correct use requires knowledge of these issues, and so they placed a small roadblock in the way.

4.6 implementing generic components using inheritance

Generic programming allows us to implement type-independent logic.

Recall that an important goal of object-oriented programming is the support of code reuse. An important mechanism that supports this goal is the *generic* mechanism: If the implementation is identical except for the basic type of the object, a *generic implementation* can be used to describe the basic functionality. For instance, a method can be written to sort an array of items; the *logic* is independent of the types of objects being sorted, so a generic method could be used.

In Java, genericity is obtained by using inheritance.

Unlike many of the newer languages (such as C++, which uses templates to implement generic programming), before version 1.5 Java did not support generic implementations directly. Instead, generic programming was implemented using the basic concepts of inheritance. This section describes how generic methods and classes can be implemented in Java using the basic principles of inheritance.

Direct support for generic methods and classes was announced by Sun in June 2001 as a future language addition. Finally, in late 2004, Java 5 was released and provided support for generic methods and classes. However, using generic classes requires an understanding of the pre-Java 5 idioms for generic programming. As a result, an understanding of how inheritance is used to implement generic programs is essential, even in Java 5.

4.6.1 using `Object` for genericity

The basic idea in Java is that we can implement a generic class by using an appropriate superclass, such as `Object`.

Consider the `IntCell` class shown in Figure 3.2. Recall that the `IntCell` supports the `read` and `write` methods. We can, in principle, make this a generic `MemoryCell` class that stores any type of `Object` by replacing instances of `int` with `Object`. The resulting `MemoryCell` class is shown in Figure 4.21.

There are two details that must be considered when we use this strategy. The first is illustrated in Figure 4.22, which depicts a `main` that writes a `"37"` to a `MemoryCell` object and then reads from the `MemoryCell` object. To access a specific method of the object we must downcast to the correct type. (Of course in this example, we do not need the downcast, since we are simply invoking the `toString` method at line 9, and this can be done for any object.)

A second important detail is that primitive types cannot be used. Only reference types are compatible with `Object`. A standard workaround to this problem is discussed momentarily.

```
// MemoryCell class
//  Object read( )          -->  Returns the stored value
//  void write( Object x ) -->  x is stored

public class MemoryCell
{
        // Public methods
    public Object read( )         { return storedValue; }
    public void write( Object x ) { storedValue = x; }

        // Private internal data representation
    private Object storedValue;
}
```

figure 4.21

A generic `MemoryCell` class (pre-Java 5)

```
public class TestMemoryCell
{
    public static void main( String [ ] args )
    {
        MemoryCell m = new MemoryCell( );

        m.write( "37" );
        String val = (String) m.read( );
        System.out.println( "Contents are: " + val );
    }
}
```

figure 4.22

Using the generic `MemoryCell` class (pre-Java 5)

`MemoryCell` is a fairly small example. A larger example that is typical of generic code reuse, Figure 4.23 shows a simplified generic `ArrayList` class as it would be written before Java 5; the online code fills in some additional methods.

4.6.2 wrappers for primitive types

When we implement algorithms, often we run into a language typing problem: We have an object of one type, but the language syntax requires an object of a different type.

figure 4.23

A simplified `ArrayList`, with `add`, `get`, and `size` (pre-Java 5)

```
/**
 * The SimpleArrayList implements a growable array of Object.
 * Insertions are always done at the end.
 */
public class SimpleArrayList
{
    /**
     * Returns the number of items in this collection.
     * @return the number of items in this collection.
     */
    public int size( )
    {
        return theSize;
    }

    /**
     * Returns the item at position idx.
     * @param idx the index to search in.
     * @throws ArrayIndexOutOfBoundsException if index is bad.
     */
    public Object get( int idx )
    {
        if( idx < 0 || idx >= size( ) )
            throw new ArrayIndexOutOfBoundsException( );
        return theItems[ idx ];
    }

    /**
     * Adds an item at the end of this collection.
     * @param x any object.
     * @return true (as per java.util.ArrayList).
     */
    public boolean add( Object x )
    {
        if( theItems.length == size( ) )
        {
            Object [ ] old = theItems;
            theItems = new Object[ theItems.length * 2 + 1 ];
            for( int i = 0; i < size( ); i++ )
                theItems[ i ] = old[ i ];
        }

        theItems[ theSize++ ] = x;
        return true;
    }

    private static final int INIT_CAPACITY = 10;

    private int         theSize = 0;
    private Object [ ] theItems = new Object[ INIT_CAPACITY ];
}
```

This technique illustrates the basic theme of a *wrapper class*. One typical use is to store a primitive type, and add operations that the primitive type either does not support or does not support correctly. A second example was seen in the I/O system, in which a wrapper stores a reference to an object and forwards requests to the object, embellishing the result somehow (for instance, with buffering or compression). A similar concept is an *adapter class* (in fact, wrapper and adapter are often used interchangeably). An adapter class is typically used when the interface of a class is not exactly what is needed, and provides a wrapping effect, while changing the interface.

A *wrapper class* stores an entity (the wrapee) and adds operations that the original type does not support correctly. An *adapter class* is used when the interface of a class is not exactly what is needed.

In Java, we have already seen that although every reference type is compatible with `Object`, the eight primitive types are not. As a result, Java provides a wrapper class for each of the eight primitive types. For instance, the wrapper for the `int` type is `Integer`. Each wrapper object is *immutable* (meaning its state can never change), stores one primitive value that is set when the object is constructed, and provides a method to retrieve the value. The wrapper classes also contain a host of static utility methods.

As an example, Figure 4.24 shows how we can use the Java 5 `ArrayList` to store integers. Note carefully that we cannot use `ArrayList<int>`.

4.6.3 **autoboxing/unboxing**

The code in Figure 4.24 is annoying to write because using the wrapper class requires creation of an `Integer` object prior to the call to `add`, and then the extraction of the `int` value from the `Integer`, using the `intValue` method. Prior to Java 1.4, this is required because if an `int` is passed in a place where an `Integer` object is required, the compiler will generate an error message, and if the result of an `Integer` object is assigned to an `int`, the compiler will generate an error message. This resulting code in Figure 4.24 accurately reflects the

```
import java.util.ArrayList;

public class BoxingDemo
{
    public static void main( String [ ] args )
    {
        ArrayList<Integer> arr = new ArrayList<Integer>( );

        arr.add( new Integer( 46 ) );
        Integer wrapperVal = arr.get( 0 );
        int val = wrapperVal.intValue( );
        System.out.println( "Position 0: " + val );
    }
}
```

figure 4.24

An illustration of the `Integer` wrapper class using Java 5 generic `ArrayList` distinction between primitive types and reference types, yet, it does not cleanly express the programmer's intent of storing `int`s in the collection.

Java 5 rectifies this situation. If an `int` is passed in a place where an `Integer` is required, the compiler will insert a call to the `Integer` constructor behind the scenes. This is known as auto-boxing. And if an `Integer` is passed in a place where an `int` is required, the compiler will insert a call to the `intValue` method behind the scenes. This is known as auto-unboxing. Similar behavior occurs for the seven other primitive/wrapper pairs. Figure 4.25 illustrates the use of autoboxing and unboxing. Note that the entities referenced in the `ArrayList` are still `Integer` objects; `int` cannot be substituted for `Integer` in the `ArrayList` instantiations.

4.6.4 adapters: changing an interface

The *adapter pattern* is used to change the interface of an existing class to conform to another.

The *adapter pattern* is used to change the interface of an existing class to conform to another. Sometimes it is used to provide a simpler interface, either with fewer methods or easier-to-use methods. Other times it is used simply to change some method names. In either case, the implementation technique is similar.

We have already seen one example of an adapter: the bridge classes `InputStreamReader` and `OutputStreamWriter` that convert byte-oriented streams into character-oriented streams.

As another example, our `MemoryCell` class in Section 4.6.1 uses `read` and `write`. But what if we wanted the interface to use `get` and `put` instead? There are two reasonable alternatives. One is to cut and paste a completely new class. The other is to use *composition*, in which we design a new class that wraps the behavior of an existing class.

figure 4.25

Autoboxing and unboxing

```
import java.util.ArrayList;

public class BoxingDemo
{
    public static void main( String [ ] args )
    {
        ArrayList<Integer> arr = new ArrayList<Integer>( );

        arr.add( 46 );
        int val = arr.get( 0 );
        System.out.println( "Position 0: " + val );
    }
}
```

```
// A class for simulating a memory cell.
public class StorageCell
{
    public Object get( )
      { return m.read( ); }

    public void put( Object x )
      { m.write( x ); }

    private MemoryCell m = new MemoryCell( );
}
```

figure 4.26

An adapter class that changes the `MemoryCell` interface to use `get` and `put`

We use this technique to implement the new class, `StorageCell`, in Figure 4.26. Its methods are implemented by calls to the wrapped `MemoryCell`. It is tempting to use inheritance instead of composition, but inheritance supplements the interface (i.e., it adds additional methods, but leaves the originals). If that is the appropriate behavior, then indeed inheritance may be preferable to composition.

4.6.5 using interface types for genericity

Using `Object` as a generic type works only if the operations that are being performed can be expressed using only methods available in the `Object` class.

Consider, for example, the problem of finding the maximum item in an array of items. The basic code is type-independent, but it does require the ability to compare any two objects and decide which is larger and which is smaller. Thus we cannot simply find the maximum of an array of `Object`—we need more information. The simplest idea would be to find the maximum of an array of `Comparable`. To determine order, we can use the `compareTo` method that we know must be available for all `Comparable`s. The code to do this is shown in Figure 4.27.

It is important to mention a few caveats. First, only objects that implement the `Comparable` interface can be passed as elements of the `Comparable` array. Objects that have a `compareTo` method but do not declare that they implement `Comparable` are not `Comparable`, and do not have the requisite *IS-A* relationship.

Second, if the `Comparable` array were to have two objects that are incompatible (e.g., a `String` and a `Shape`), the `compareTo` method would throw a `ClassCastException`. This is the expected (indeed, required) behavior.

figure 4.27

A generic `findMax` routine, with demo using shapes and strings (pre-Java 5)

```
class FindMaxDemo
{
    /**
     * Return max item in a.
     * Precondition: a.length > 0
     */
    public static Comparable findMax( Comparable [ ] a )
    {
        int maxIndex = 0;

        for( int i = 1; i < a.length; i++ )
            if( a[ i ].compareTo( a[ maxIndex ] ) > 0 )
                maxIndex = i;

        return a[ maxIndex ];
    }

    /**
     * Test findMax on Shape and String objects.
     */
    public static void main( String [ ] args )
    {
        Shape [ ] sh1 = { new Circle( 2.0 ),
                          new Square( 3.0 ),
                          new Rectangle( 3.0, 4.0 ) };

        String [ ] st1 = { "Joe", "Bob", "Bill", "Zeke" };

        System.out.println( findMax( sh1 ) );
        System.out.println( findMax( st1 ) );
    }
}
```

Third, as before, primitives cannot be passed as `Comparable`s, but the wrappers work because they implement the `Comparable` interface.

Fourth, it is not required that the interface be a standard library interface.

Finally, this solution does not always work, because it might be impossible to declare that a class implements a needed interface. For instance, the class might be a library class, while the interface is a user-defined interface. And if the class is final, we can't even create a new class. Section 4.8 offers another solution for this problem, which is the *function object*. The function object uses interfaces also, and is perhaps one of the central themes encountered in the Java library.

4.7 implementing generic components using java 5 generics

We have already seen that Java 5 supports generic classes and that these classes are easy to use. However, writing generic classes requires a little more work. In this section, we illustrate the basics of how generic classes and methods are written. We do not attempt to cover all the constructs of the language, which are quite complex and sometimes tricky. Instead, we show the syntax and idioms that are used throughout this book.

4.7.1 simple generic classes and interfaces

Figure 4.28 shows a generic version of the `MemoryCell` class previously depicted in Figure 4.21. Here, we have changed the name to `GenericMemoryCell` because neither class is in a package and thus the names cannot be the same.

When a generic class is specified, the class declaration includes one or more *type parameters* enclosed in angle brackets <> after the class name. Line 1 shows that the `GenericMemoryCell` takes one type parameter. In this instance, there are no explicit restrictions on the type parameter, so the user can create types such as `GenericMemoryCell<String>` and `GenericMemoryCell<Integer>` but not `GenericMemoryCell<int>`. Inside the `GenericMemoryCell` class declaration, we can declare fields of the generic type and methods that use the generic type as a parameter or return type.

When a generic class is specified, the class declaration includes one or more *type parameters*, enclosed in angle brackets <> after the class name.

Interfaces can also be declared as generic. For example, prior to Java 5 the `Comparable` interface was not generic, and its `compareTo` method took an `Object` as the parameter. As a result, any reference variable passed to the `compareTo` method would compile, even if the variable was not a sensible type, and only

Interfaces can also be declared as generic.

```
1 public class GenericMemoryCell<AnyType>
2 {
3     public AnyType read( )
4       { return storedValue; }
5     public void write( AnyType x )
6       { storedValue = x; }
7
8     private AnyType storedValue;
9 }
```

figure 4.28

Generic implementation of the `MemoryCell` class

at runtime would the error be reported as a `ClassCastException`. In Java 5, the `Comparable` class is generic, as shown in Figure 4.29. The `String` class, for instance, now implements `Comparable<String>` and has a `compareTo` method that takes a `String` as a parameter. By making the class generic, many of the errors that were previously only reported at runtime become compile-time errors.

4.7.2 wildcards with bounds

In Figure 4.13 we saw a static method that computes the total area in an array of `Shapes`. Suppose we want to rewrite the method so that it works with a parameter that is `ArrayList<Shape>`. Because of the enhanced `for` loop, the code should be identical, and the resulting code is shown in Figure 4.30. If we pass an `ArrayList<Shape>`, the code works. However, what happens if we pass an `ArrayList<Square>`? The answer depends on whether an `ArrayList<Square>` *IS-A* `ArrayList<Shape>`. Recall from Section 4.1.10 that the technical term for this is whether we have covariance.

Generic collections are not covariant.

In Java, as we mentioned in Section 4.1.10, arrays are covariant. So `Square[]` *IS-A* `Shape[]`. On the one hand, consistency would suggest that if arrays are covariant, then collections should be covariant too. On the other hand, as we saw in Section 4.1.10, the covariance of arrays leads to code that compiles but then generates a runtime exception (an `ArrayStoreException`). Because the entire reason to have generics is to generate compiler errors rather than runtime exceptions for type mismatches, generic collections are not covariant. As a result, we cannot pass an `ArrayList<Square>` as a parameter to the method in Figure 4.30.

What we are left with is that generics (and the generic collections) are not covariant (which makes sense) but arrays are. Without additional syntax, users would tend to avoid collections because the lack of covariance makes the code less flexible.

Wildcards are used to express subclasses (or superclasses) of parameter types.

Java 5 makes up for this with *wildcards*. Wildcards are used to express subclasses (or superclasses) of parameter types. Figure 4.31 illustrates the use of wildcards with a bound to write a `totalArea` method that takes as parameter an `ArrayList<T>`, where `T` *IS-A* `Shape`. Thus, `ArrayList<Shape>` and `ArrayList<Square>` are both acceptable parameters. Wildcards can also be

figure 4.29

`Comparable` interface, Java 5 version which is generic

```
package java.lang;

public interface Comparable<AnyType>
{
    public int compareTo( AnyType other );
}
```

```java
public static double totalArea( ArrayList<Shape> arr )
{
    double total = 0;

    for( Shape s : arr )
        if( s != null )
            total += s.area( );

    return total;
}
```

figure 4.30

`totalArea` method that does not work if passed an `ArrayList<Square>`

```java
public static double totalArea( ArrayList<? extends Shape> arr )
{
    double total = 0;

    for( Shape s : arr )
        if( s != null )
            total += s.area( );

    return total;
}
```

figure 4.31

`totalArea` method revised with wildcards that works if passed an `ArrayList<Square>`

used without a bound (in which case `extends Object` is presumed) or with `super` instead of `extends` (to express superclass rather than subclass); there are also some other syntax uses that we do not discuss here.

4.7.3 generic static methods

In some sense, the `totalArea` method in Figure 4.31 is generic, since it works for different types. But there is no specific type parameter list, as was done in the `GenericMemoryCell` class declaration. Sometimes the specific type is important perhaps because one of the following reasons apply:

1. The type is used as the return type
2. The type is used in more than one parameter type
3. The type is used to declare a local variable

The generic method looks much like the generic class in that the type parameter list uses the same syntax. The type list in a generic method precedes the return type.

If so, then an explicit generic method with type parameters must be declared.

For instance, Figure 4.32 illustrates a generic static method that performs a sequential search for value `x` in array `arr`. By using a generic method instead of a nongeneric method that uses `Object` as the parameter types, we can get compile-time errors if searching for an `Apple` in an array of `Shape`s.

figure 4.32

Generic static method to search an array

```
public static <AnyType>
boolean contains( AnyType [ ] arr, AnyType x )
{
    for( AnyType val : arr )
        if( x.equals( val ) )
            return true;

    return false;
}
```

The generic method looks much like the generic class in that the type parameter list uses the same syntax. The type parameters in a generic method precede the return type.

4.7.4 type bounds

The type bound is specified inside the angle brackets <>.

Suppose we want to write a `findMax` routine. Consider the code in Figure 4.33. This code cannot work because the compiler cannot prove that the call to `compareTo` at line 6 is valid; `compareTo` is guaranteed to exist only if `AnyType` is `Comparable`. We can solve this problem by using a *type bound*. The type bound is specified inside the angle brackets <>, and it specifies properties that the parameter types must have. A naive attempt is to rewrite the signature as

```
public static <AnyType extends Comparable> ...
```

This is naive because as we know, the `Comparable` interface is now generic. Although this code would compile, a better attempt would be

```
public static <AnyType extends Comparable<AnyType>> ...
```

figure 4.33

Generic static method to find largest element in an array that does not work

```
 1 public static <AnyType> AnyType findMax( AnyType [ ] a )
 2 {
 3     int maxIndex = 0;
 4 
 5     for( int i = 1; i < a.length; i++ )
 6         if( a[ i ].compareTo( a[ maxIndex ] ) > 0 )
 7             maxIndex = i;
 8 
 9     return a[ maxIndex ];
10 }
```

However, this attempt is not satisfactory. To see the problem, suppose Shape implements Comparable<Shape>. Suppose Square extends Shape. Then all we know is that Square implements Comparable<Shape>. Thus, a Square *IS-A* Comparable<Shape>, but it *IS-NOT-A* Comparable<Square>!

As a result, what we need to say is that AnyType *IS-A* Comparable<T> where T is a superclass of AnyType. Since we do not need to know the exact type T, we can use a wildcard. The resulting signature is

```
public static <AnyType extends Comparable<? super AnyType>>
```

Figure 4.34 shows the implementation of findMax. The compiler will accept arrays of types T only such that T implements the Comparable<S> interface, where T *IS-A* S. Certainly the bounds declaration looks like a mess. Fortunately, we won't see anything more complicated than this idiom.

4.7.5 **type erasure**

Generic classes are converted by the compiler to non-generic classes by a process known as *type erasure.*

Generic types, for the most part, are constructs in the Java language but not in the Virtual Machine. Generic classes are converted by the compiler to non-generic classes by a process known as *type erasure*. The simplified version of what happens is that the compiler generates a *raw class* with the same name as the generic class with the type parameters removed. The type variables are replaced with their bounds, and when calls are made to generic methods that have an erased return type, casts are inserted automatically. If a generic class is used without a type parameter, the raw class is used.

Generics do not make the code faster. They do make the code more type-safe at compile time.

One important consequence of type erasure is that the generated code is not much different than the code that programmers have been writing before generics and in fact is not any faster. The significant benefit is that the programmer does not have to place casts in the code, and the compiler will do significant type checking.

```
public static <AnyType extends Comparable<? super AnyType>>
AnyType findMax( AnyType [ ] a )
{
    int maxIndex = 0;

    for( int i = 1; i < a.length; i++ )
        if( a[ i ].compareTo( a[ maxIndex ] ) > 0 )
            maxIndex = i;

    return a[ maxIndex ];
}
```

figure 4.34

Generic static method to find largest element in an array. Illustrates a bounds on the type parameter

4.7.6 restrictions on generics

There are numerous restrictions on generic types. Every one of the restrictions listed here is required because of type erasure.

primitive types

Primitive types cannot be used for a type parameter.

Primitive types cannot be used for a type parameter. Thus `ArrayList<int>` is illegal. You must use wrapper classes.

`instanceof` tests

`instanceof` tests and typecasts work only with the raw type.

`instanceof` tests and typecasts work only with the raw type. In the following code

```
ArrayList<Integer> list1 = new ArrayList<Integer>( );
list1.add( 4 );
Object list2 = list1;
ArrayList<String> list2 = (ArrayList<String>) list;
String s = list2.get( 0 );
```

the typecast succeeds at runtime since all types are `ArrayList`. Eventually, a runtime error results at the last line because the call to `get` tries to return a `String` but cannot. As a result, the typecast will generate a warning, and a corresponding `instanceof` test is illegal.

static contexts

Static methods and fields cannot refer to the class's type variables. Static fields are shared among the class's generic instantiations.

In a generic class, static methods and fields cannot refer to the class's type variables since after erasure, there are no type variables. Further, since there is really only one raw class, static fields are shared among the class's generic instantiations.

instantiation of generic types

It is illegal to create an instance of a generic type.

It is illegal to create an instance of a generic type. If `T` is a type variable, the statement

```
T obj = new T( );          // Right-hand side is illegal
```

is illegal. `T` is replaced by its bounds, which could be `Object` (or even an abstract class), so the call to `new` cannot make sense.

generic array objects

It is illegal to create an array of a generic type.

It is illegal to create an array of a generic type. If `T` is a type variable, the statement

```
T [ ] arr = new T[ 10 ];  // Right-hand side is illegal
```

is illegal. `T` would be replaced by its bounds, which would probably be `Object`, and then the cast (generated by type erasure) to `T[]` would fail because `Object[]` *IS-NOT-A* `T[]`. Figure 4.35 shows a generic version of `SimpleArrayList` previously seen in Figure 4.23. The only tricky part is the code at line 38. Because we cannot create arrays of generic objects, we must create an array of `Object` and then use a typecast. This typecast will generate a compiler warning about an unchecked type conversion. It is impossible to implement the generic collection classes with arrays without getting this warning. If clients want their code to compile without warnings, they should use only generic collection types, not generic array types.

arrays of parameterized types

Instantiation of arrays of parameterized types is illegal. Consider the following code:

Instantiation of arrays of parameterized types is illegal.

```
ArrayList<String> [ ] arr1 = new ArrayList<String>[ 10 ];
ArrayList<Double> lst = new ArrayList<Double>( ); lst.add( 4.5 );
Object [ ] arr2 = arr1;
arr2[ 0 ] = lst;
String s = arr1[ 0 ].get( 0 );
```

Normally, we would expect that the assignment at line 4, which has the wrong type, would generate an `ArrayStoreException`. However, after type erasure, the array type is `ArrayList[]`, and the object added to the array is `ArrayList`, so there is no `ArrayStoreException`. Thus, this code has no casts, yet it will eventually generate a `ClassCastException` at line 5, which is exactly the situation that generics are supposed to avoid.

4.8 the functor (function objects)

In Sections 4.6 and 4.7, we saw how interfaces can be used to write generic algorithms. As an example, the method in Figure 4.34 can be used to find the maximum item in an array.

However, the `findMax` method has an important limitation. That is, it works only for objects that implement the `Comparable` interface and are able to provide `compareTo` as the basis for all comparison decisions. There are many situations in which this is not feasible. As an example, consider the `SimpleRectangle` class in Figure 4.36.

The `SimpleRectangle` class does not have a `compareTo` function, and consequently cannot implement the `Comparable` interface. The main reason for this is that because there are many plausible alternatives, it is difficult to decide on a

figure 4.35

`SimpleArrayList` class using generics

```
/**
 * The GenericSimpleArrayList implements a growable array.
 * Insertions are always done at the end.
 */
public class GenericSimpleArrayList<AnyType>
{
    /**
     * Returns the number of items in this collection.
     * @return the number of items in this collection.
     */
    public int size( )
    {
        return theSize;
    }

    /**
     * Returns the item at position idx.
     * @param idx the index to search in.
     * @throws ArrayIndexOutOfBoundsException if index is bad.
     */
    public AnyType get( int idx )
    {
        if( idx < 0 || idx >= size( ) )
            throw new ArrayIndexOutOfBoundsException( );
        return theItems[ idx ];
    }

    /**
     * Adds an item at the end of this collection.
     * @param x any object.
     * @return true.
     */
    public boolean add( AnyType x )
    {
        if( theItems.length == size( ) )
        {
            AnyType [ ] old = theItems;
              theItems = (AnyType [])new Object[size( )*2 + 1];
            for( int i = 0; i < size( ); i++ )
                theItems[ i ] = old[ i ];
        }

        theItems[ theSize++ ] = x;
        return true;
    }

    private static final int INIT_CAPACITY = 10;

    private int theSize;
    private AnyType [ ] theItems;
}
```

```java
// A simple rectangle class.
public class SimpleRectangle
{
    public SimpleRectangle( int l, int w )
      { length = l; width = w; }

    public int getLength( )
      { return length; }

    public int getWidth( )
      { return width; }

    public String toString( )
      { return "Rectangle " + getLength( ) + " by "
                             + getWidth( ); }

    private int length;
    private int width;
}
```

figure 4.36

The SimpleRectangle class, which does not implement the Comparable interface

good meaning for compareTo. We could base the comparison on area, perimeter, length, width, and so on. Once we write compareTo, we are stuck with it. What if we want to have findMax work with several different comparison alternatives?

The solution to the problem is to pass the comparison function as a second parameter to findMax, and have findMax use the comparison function instead of assuming the existence of compareTo. Thus findMax will now have two parameters: an array of Object of an arbitrary type (which need not have compareTo defined), and a comparison function.

The main issue left is how to pass the comparison function. Some languages allow parameters to be functions. However, this solution often has efficiency problems and is not available in all object-oriented languages. Java does not allow functions to be passed as parameters; we can only pass primitive values and references. So we appear not to have a way of passing a function.

Functor is another name for a function object.

However, recall that an object consists of data and functions. So we can embed the function in an object and pass a reference to it. Indeed, this idea works in all object-oriented languages. The object is called a *function object*, and is sometimes also called a *functor*.

The function object class contains a method specified by the generic algorithm. An instance of the class is passed to the algorithm.

The function object often contains no data. The class simply contains a single method, with a given name, that is specified by the generic algorithm (in this case, findMax). An instance of the class is then passed to the algorithm, which in turn calls the single method of the function object. We can design different comparison functions by simply declaring new classes. Each new class contains a different implementation of the agreed-upon single method.

In Java, to implement this idiom we use inheritance, and specifically we make use of interfaces. The interface is used to declare the signature of the agreed-upon function. As an example, Figure 4.37 shows the `Comparator` interface, which is part of the standard `java.util` package. Recall that to illustrate how the Java library is implemented, we will reimplement a portion of `java.util` as `weiss.util`. Before Java 5, this class was not generic.

The interface says that any (nonabstract) class that claims to be a `Comparator` must provide an implementation of the `compare` method; thus any object that is an instance of such a class has a `compare` method that it can call.

Using this interface, we can now pass a `Comparator` as the second parameter to `findMax`. If this `Comparator` is `cmp`, we can safely make the call `cmp.compare(o1,o2)` to compare any two objects as needed. A wildcard is used in the `Comparator` parameter to indicate that the `Comparator` knows how to compare objects that are the same type or supertypes of those in the array. It is up to the caller of `findMax` to pass an appropriately implemented instance of `Comparator` as the actual argument.

An example is shown in Figure 4.38. `findMax` now takes two parameters. The second parameter is the function object. As shown on line 11, `findMax` expects that the function object implements a method named `compare`, and it must do so, since it implements the `Comparator` interface.

Once `findMax` is written, it can be called in `main`. To do so, we need to pass to `findMax` an array of `SimpleRectangle` objects and a function object that implements the `Comparator` interface. We implement `OrderRectByWidth`, a new class that contains the required `compare` method. The `compare` method returns an integer indicating if the first rectangle is less than, equal to, or greater than

figure 4.37

The `Comparator` interface, originally defined in `java.util` and rewritten for the `weiss.util` package

```
package weiss.util;

/**
 * Comparator function object interface.
 */
public interface Comparator<AnyType>
{
    /**
     * Return the result of comparing lhs and rhs.
     * @param lhs first object.
     * @param rhs second object.
     * @return < 0 if lhs is less than rhs,
     *           0 if lhs is equal to rhs,
     *         > 0 if lhs is greater than rhs.
     */
    int compare( AnyType lhs, AnyType rhs );
}
```

```java
public class Utils
{
    // Generic findMax with a function object.
    // Precondition: a.length > 0.
    public static <AnyType> AnyType
    findMax( AnyType [ ] a, Comparator<? super AnyType> cmp )
    {
        int maxIndex = 0;

        for( int i = 1; i < a.length; i++ )
            if( cmp.compare( a[ i ], a[ maxIndex ] ) > 0 )
                maxIndex = i;

        return a[ maxIndex ];
    }
}
```

figure 4.38

The generic `findMax` algorithm, using a function object

the second rectangle on the basis of widths. `main` simply passes an instance of `OrderRectByWidth` to `findMax`.[7] Both `main` and `OrderRectByWidth` are shown in Figure 4.39. Observe that the `OrderRectByWidth` object has no data members. This is usually true of function objects.

```java
class OrderRectByWidth implements Comparator<SimpleRectangle>
{
    public int compare( SimpleRectangle r1, SimpleRectangle r2 )
      { return( r1.getWidth() - r2.getWidth() ); }
}

public class CompareTest
{
    public static void main( String [ ] args )
    {
        SimpleRectangle [ ] rects = new SimpleRectangle[ 4 ];
        rects[ 0 ] = new SimpleRectangle( 1, 10 );
        rects[ 1 ] = new SimpleRectangle( 20, 1 );
        rects[ 2 ] = new SimpleRectangle( 4, 6 );
        rects[ 3 ] = new SimpleRectangle( 5, 5 );

        System.out.println( "MAX WIDTH: " +
             Utils.findMax( rects, new OrderRectByWidth( ) ) );
    }
}
```

figure 4.39

An example of a function object

7. The trick of implementing `compare` by subtracting works for `int`s as long as both are the same sign. Otherwise, there is a possibility of overflow.

The function object technique is an illustration of a pattern that we see over and over again, not just in Java, but in any language that has objects. In Java, this pattern is used over and over and over again and represents perhaps the single dominant idiomatic use of interfaces.

4.8.1 nested classes

Generally speaking, when we write a class, we expect, or at least hope, for it to be useful in many contexts, not just the particular application that is being worked on.

An annoying feature of the function object pattern, especially in Java, is the fact that because it is used so often, it results in the creation of numerous small classes, that each contain one method, that are used perhaps only once in a program, and that have limited applicability outside of the current application.

This is annoying for at least two reasons. First, we might have dozens of function object classes. If they are public, by rule they are scattered in separate files. If they are package visible, they might all be in the same file, but we still have to scroll up and down to find their definitions, which is likely to be far removed from the one or perhaps two places in the entire program where they are instantiated as function objects. It would be preferable if each function object class could be declared as close as possible to its instantiation. Second, once a name is used, it cannot be reused in the package without possibilities of name collisions. Although packages solve some namespace problems, they do not solve them all, especially when the same class name is used twice in the default package.

A *nested class* is a class declaration that is placed inside another class declaration—the outer class—using the keyword `static`.

With a nested class, we can solve some of these problems. A *nested class* is a class declaration that is placed inside another class declaration—the outer class—using the keyword `static`. A nested class is considered a member of the outer class. As a result, it can be public, private, package visible, or protected, and depending on the visibility, may or may not be accessible by methods that are not part of the outer class. Typically, it is private and thus inaccessible from outside the outer class. Also, because a nested class is a member of the outer class, its methods can access private static members of the outer class, and can access private instance members when given a reference to an outer object.

A nested class is a part of the outer class and can be declared with a visibility specifier. All outer class members are visible to the nested class's methods.

Figure 4.40 illustrates the use of a nested class in conjunction with the function object pattern. The `static` in front of the nested class declaration of `OrderRectByWidth` is essential; without it, we have an inner class, which behaves differently and is discussed later in this text (in Chapter 15).

Occasionally, a nested class is public. In Figure 4.40, if `OrderRectByWidth` was declared public, the class `CompareTestInner1.OrderRectByWidth` could be used from outside of the `CompareTestInner1` class.

```
import java.util.Comparator;

class CompareTestInner1
{
    private static class OrderRectByWidth implements Comparator<SimpleRectangle>
    {
        public int compare( SimpleRectangle r1, SimpleRectangle r2 )
          { return r1.getWidth( ) - r2.getWidth( ); }
    }

    public static void main( String [ ] args )
    {
        SimpleRectangle [ ] rects = new SimpleRectangle[ 4 ];
        rects[ 0 ] = new SimpleRectangle( 1, 10 );
        rects[ 1 ] = new SimpleRectangle( 20, 1 );
        rects[ 2 ] = new SimpleRectangle( 4, 6 );
        rects[ 3 ] = new SimpleRectangle( 5, 5 );

        System.out.println( "MAX WIDTH: " +
             Utils.findMax( rects, new OrderRectByWidth( ) ) );
    }
}
```

figure 4.40

Using a nested class to hide the `OrderRectByWidth` class declaration

4.8.2 local classes

In addition to allowing class declarations inside of classes, Java also allows class declarations inside of methods. These classes are called *local classes*. This is illustrated in Figure 4.41.

Note that when a class is declared inside a method, it cannot be declared `private` or `static`. However, the class is visible only inside of the method in which it was declared. This makes it easier to write the class right before its first (perhaps only) use and avoid pollution of namespaces.

> Java also allows class declarations inside of methods. Such classes are known as *local classes* and may not be declared with either a visibility modifier or the static modifier.

An advantage of declaring a class inside of a method is that the class's methods (in this case, `compare`) has access to local variables of the function that are declared prior to the class. This can be important in some applications. There is a technical rule: In order to access local variables, the variables must be declared `final`. We will not be using these types of classes in the text.

```
class CompareTestInner2
{
    public static void main( String [ ] args )
    {
        SimpleRectangle [ ] rects = new SimpleRectangle[ 4 ];
        rects[ 0 ] = new SimpleRectangle( 1, 10 );
        rects[ 1 ] = new SimpleRectangle( 20, 1 );
        rects[ 2 ] = new SimpleRectangle( 4, 6 );
        rects[ 3 ] = new SimpleRectangle( 5, 5 );

        class OrderRectByWidth implements Comparator<SimpleRectangle>
        {
            public int compare( SimpleRectangle r1, SimpleRectangle r2 )
              { return r1.getWidth( ) - r2.getWidth( ); }
        }

        System.out.println( "MAX WIDTH: " +
             Utils.findMax( rects, new OrderRectByWidth( ) ) );
    }
}
```

figure 4.41

Using a local class to hide the `OrderRectByWidth` class declaration further

4.8.3 anonymous classes

One might suspect that by placing a class immediately before the line of code in which it is used, we have declared the class as close as possible to its use. However, in Java, we can do even better.

An *anonymous class* is a class that has no name.

Figure 4.42 illustrates the anonymous inner class. An *anonymous class* is a class that has no name. The syntax is that instead of writing `new Inner()`, and providing the implementation of `Inner` as a named class, we write `new Interface()`, and then provide the implementation of the interface (everything from the opening to closing brace) immediately after the `new` expression. Instead of implementing an interface anonymously, it is also possible to extend a class anonymously, providing only the overridden methods.

Anonymous classes introduce significant language complications.

The syntax looks very daunting, but after a while, one gets used to it. It complicates the language significantly, because the anonymous class is a class. As an example of the complications that are introduced, since the name of a constructor is the name of a class, how does one define a constructor for an anonymous class? The answer is that you cannot do so.

Anonymous classes are often used to implement function objects.

The anonymous class is in practice very useful, and its use is often seen as part of the function object pattern in conjunction with event handling in user interfaces. In event handling, the programmer is required to specify, in a function, what happens when certain events occur.

```
class CompareTestInner3
{
    public static void main( String [ ] args )
    {
        SimpleRectangle [ ] rects = new SimpleRectangle[ 4 ];
        rects[ 0 ] = new SimpleRectangle( 1, 10 );
        rects[ 1 ] = new SimpleRectangle( 20, 1 );
        rects[ 2 ] = new SimpleRectangle( 4, 6 );
        rects[ 3 ] = new SimpleRectangle( 5, 5 );

        System.out.println( "MAX WIDTH: " +
            Utils.findMax( rects, new Comparator<SimpleRectangle>( )
            {
                public int compare( SimpleRectangle r1, SimpleRectangle r2 )
                  { return r1.getWidth( ) - r2.getWidth( ); }
            }
        ) );
    }
}
```

figure 4.42

Using an anonymous class to implement the function object

4.8.4 nested classes and generics

When a nested class is declared inside a generic class, the nested class cannot refer to the parameter types of the generic outer class. However, the nested class can itself be generic and can reuse the parameter type names of the generic outer class. Examples of syntax include the following:

```
class Outer<AnyType>
{
    public static class Inner<AnyType>
    {
    }

    public static class OtherInner
    {
        // cannot use AnyType here
    }
}

Outer.Inner<String> i1 = new Outer.Inner<String>( );
Outer.OtherInner    i2 = new Outer.OtherInner( );
```

Notice that in the declarations of `i1` and `i2`, `Outer` has no parameter types.

4.9 dynamic dispatch details

Dynamic dispatch is not important for static, final, or private methods.

A common myth is that all methods and all parameters are bound at run time. This is not true. First, there are some cases in which dynamic dispatch is never used or is not an issue:

- Static methods, regardless of how the method is invoked
- Final methods
- Private methods (since they are invoked only from inside the class and are thus implicitly final)

In other scenarios, dynamic dispatch is meaningfully used. But what exactly does dynamic dispatch mean?

In Java, the parameters to a method are always deduced statically, at compile time.

Dynamic dispatch means that the method that is appropriate for the object being operated on is the one that is used. However, it does not mean that the absolute best match is performed for all parameters. Specifically, in Java, the parameters to a method are always deduced statically, at compile time.

For a concrete example, consider the code in Figure 4.43. In the `whichFoo` method, a call is made to `foo`. But which `foo` is called? We expect the answer to depend on the run-time types of `arg1` and `arg2`.

Because parameters are always matched at compile time, it does not matter what type `arg2` is actually referencing. The `foo` that is matched will be

```
public void foo( Base x )
```

Static overloading means that the parameters to a method are always deduced statically, at compile time.

The only issue is whether the `Base` or `Derived` version is used. That is the decision that is made at run time, when the object that `arg1` references is known.

Dynamic dispatch means that once the signature of an instance method is ascertained, the class of the method can be determined at run time based on the dynamic type of the invoking object.

The precise methodology used is that the compiler deduces, at compile time, the best signature, based on the static types of the parameters and the methods that are available for the static type of the controlling reference. At that point, the signature of the method is set. This step is called *static overloading*. The only remaining issue is which class's version of that method is used. This is done by having the Virtual Machine deduce the runtime type of this object. Once the runtime type is known, the Virtual Machine walks up the inheritance hierarchy, looking for the last overridden version of the method; this is the first method of the appropriate signature that the Virtual Machine finds as it walks up toward `Object`.[8] This second step is called *dynamic dispatch*.

8. If no such method is found, perhaps because only part of the program was recompiled, then the Virtual Machine throws a `NoSuchMethodException`.

```
class Base
{
    public void foo( Base x )
      { System.out.println( "Base.Base" ); }

    public void foo( Derived x )
      { System.out.println( "Base.Derived" ); }
}

class Derived extends Base
{
    public void foo( Base x )
      { System.out.println( "Derived.Base" ); }

    public void foo( Derived x )
      { System.out.println( "Derived.Derived" ); }
}

class StaticParamsDemo
{
    public static void whichFoo( Base arg1, Base arg2 )
    {
        // It is guaranteed that we will call foo( Base )
        // Only issue is which class's version of foo( Base )
        // is called; the dynamic type of arg1 is used
        // to decide.
        arg1.foo( arg2 );
    }

    public static void main( String [] args )
    {
        Base b = new Base( );
        Derived d = new Derived( );

        whichFoo( b, b );
        whichFoo( b, d );
        whichFoo( d, b );
        whichFoo( d, d );
    }
}
```

figure 4.43

An illustration of static binding for parameters

Static overloading can lead to subtle errors when a method that is supposed to be overridden is instead overloaded. Figure 4.44 illustrates a common programming error that occurs when implementing the `equals` method.

The `equals` method is defined in class `Object` and is intended to return `true` if two objects have identical states. It takes an `Object` as a parameter, and the

figure 4.44

An illustration of overloading `equals` instead of overriding `equals`. Here, the call to the `sameVal` returns false!

```
final class SomeClass
{
    public SomeClass( int i )
      { id = i; }

    public boolean sameVal( Object other )
      { return other instanceof SomeClass && equals( other ); }

    /**
     * This is a bad implementation!
     * other has the wrong type, so this does
     * not override Object's equals.
     */
    public boolean equals( SomeClass other )
      { return other != null && id == other.id; }

    private int id;
}

class BadEqualsDemo
{
    public static void main( String [ ] args )
    {
        SomeClass obj1 = new SomeClass( 4 );
        SomeClass obj2 = new SomeClass( 4 );

        System.out.println( obj1.equals( obj2 ) );   // true
        System.out.println( obj1.sameVal( obj2 ) );  // false
    }
}
```

`Object` provides a default implementation that returns `true` only if the two objects are the same. In other words, in class `Object`, the implementation of `equals` is roughly

```
public boolean equals( Object other )
  { return this == other; }
```

When overridding `equals`, the parameter must be of type `Object`; otherwise, overloading is being done. In Figure 4.44, `equals` is not overridden; instead it is (unintentionally) overloaded. As a result, the call to `sameVal` will return `false`, which appears surprising, since the call to `equals` returns `true` and `sameVal` calls `equals`.

The problem is that the call in `sameVal` is `this.equals(other)`. The static type of `this` is `SomeClass`. In `SomeClass`, there are two versions of `equals`: the listed `equals` that takes a `SomeClass` as a parameter, and the inherited `equals` that takes an `Object`. The static type of the parameter (`other`) is `Object`, so the best match is the `equals` that takes an `Object`. At run time, the virtual machine searches for that `equals`, and finds the one in class `Object`. And since `this` and `other` are different objects, the `equals` method in class `Object` returns false.

Thus, `equals` must be written to take an `Object` as a parameter, and typically a downcast will be required after a verification that the type is appropriate. One way of doing that is to use an `instanceof` test, but that is safe only for final classes. Overriding `equals` is actually fairly tricky in the presence of inheritance, and is discussed in Section 6.7.

summary

Inheritance is a powerful feature that is an essential part of object-oriented programming and Java. It allows us to abstract functionality into abstract base classes and have derived classes implement and expand on that functionality. Several types of methods can be specified in the base class, as illustrated in Figure 4.45.

The most abstract class, in which no implementation is allowed, is the *interface*. The interface lists methods that must be implemented by a derived class. The derived class must both implement all of these methods (or itself be abstract) and specify, via the `implements` clause, that it is implementing the interface. Multiple interfaces may be implemented by a class, thus providing a simpler alternative to multiple inheritance.

Finally, inheritance allows us to easily write generic methods and classes that work for a wide range of generic types. This will typically involve using a significant amount of casting. Java 5 adds generic classes and methods that

Method	Overloading	Comments
`final`	Potentially inlined	Invariant over the inheritance hierarchy (method is never redefined).
`abstract`	Runtime	Base class provides no implementation and is abstract. Derived class must provide an implementation.
`static`	Compile time	No controlling object.
Other	Runtime	Base class provides a default implementation that may be either overridden by the derived classes or accepted unchanged by the derived classes.

figure 4.45

Four types of class methods

hide the casting. Interfaces are also widely used for generic components, and to implement the function object pattern.

This chapter concludes the first part of the text, which provided an overview of Java and object-oriented programming. We will now go on to look at algorithms and the building blocks of problem solving.

key concepts

abstract class A class that cannot be constructed but serves to specify functionality of derived classes. (113)

abstract method A method that has no meaningful definition and is thus always defined in the derived class. (113)

adapter A class that is typically used when the interface of another class is not exactly what is needed. The adapter provides a wrapping effect, while changing the interface. (127)

anonymous class A class that has no name and is useful for implementing short function objects. (144)

base class The class on which the inheritance is based. (98)

boxing Creating an instance of a wrapper class to store a primitive type. In Java 5, this is done automatically. (127)

composition Preferred mechanism to inheritance when an *IS-A* relationship does not hold. Instead, we say that an object of class B is composed of an object of class A (and other objects). (94)

covariant arrays In Java, arrays are covariant, meaning that `Derived[]` is type compatible with `Base[]`. (108)

covariant return type Overriding the return type with a subtype. This is allowed starting in Java 5. (108)

decorator pattern The pattern that involves the combining of several wrappers in order to add functionality. (123)

derived class A completely new class that nonetheless has some compatibility with the class from which it was derived. (98)

dynamic dispatch A runtime decision to apply the method corresponding to the actual referenced object. (100)

`extends` clause A clause used to declare that a new class is a subclass of another class. (98)

final class A class that may not be extended. (104)

final method A method that may not be overridden and is invariant over the inheritance hierarchy. Static binding is used for final methods. (103)

function object An object passed to a generic function with the intention of having its single method used by the generic function. (139)

functor A function object. (139)

generic classes Added in Java 5, allows classes to specify type parameters and avoid significant amounts of typecasting. (131)

generic programming Used to implement type-independent logic. (124)

***HAS-A* relationship** A relationship in which the derived class has a (instance of the) base class. (94)

`implements` clause A clause used to declare that a class implements the methods of an interface. (116)

inheritance The process whereby we may derive a class from a base class without disturbing the implementation of the base class. Also allows the design of class hierarchies, such as `Throwable` and `InputStream`. (98)

interface A special kind of abstract class that contains no implementation details. (115)

***IS-A* relationship** A relationship in which the derived class is a (variation of the) base class. (94)

leaf class A final class. (104)

local class A class inside a method, declared with no visibility modifier. (143)

multiple inheritance The process of deriving a class from several base classes. Multiple inheritance is not allowed in Java. However, the alternative, multiple interfaces, is allowed. (114)

nested class A class inside a class, declared with the `static` modifier. (142)

partial overriding The act of augmenting a base class method to perform additional, but not entirely different, tasks. (105)

polymorphism The ability of a reference variable to reference objects of several different types. When operations are applied to the variable, the operation that is appropriate to the actual referenced object is automatically selected. (100)

protected class member Accessible by the derived class and classes in the same package. (102)

raw type A class with the generic type parameters removed. (136)

static binding The decision on which class's version of a method to use is made at compile time. Is only used for static, final, or private methods. (104)

static overloading The first step for deducing the method that will be used. In this step, the static types of the parameters are used to deduce the signature of the method that will be invoked. Static overloading is always used. (146)

subclass/superclass relationships If *X* *IS-A* *Y*, then *X* is a subclass of *Y* and *Y* is a superclass of *X*. These relationships are transitive. (94)

`super` constructor call A call to the base class constructor. (103)

`super` object An object used in partial overloading to apply a base class method. (105)

type bounds Specifies properties that type parameters must satisfy. (134)

type erasure The process by which generic classes are rewritten as nongeneric classes. (135)

type parameters The parameters enclosed in angle brackets <> in a generic class or method declaration. (135)

unboxing Creating a primitive type from an instance of a wrapper class. In Java 5, this is done automatically. (127)

wildcard types A ? as a type parameter; allows any type (possibly with bounds). (134)

wrapper A class that is used to store another type, and add operations that the primitive type either does not support or does not support correctly. (127)

common errors

1. Private members of a base class are not visible in the derived class.
2. Objects of an abstract class cannot be constructed.
3. If the derived class fails to implement any inherited abstract method, then the derived class becomes abstract. If this was not intended, a compiler error will result.
4. Final methods may not be overridden. Final classes may not be extended.
5. Static methods use static binding, even if they are overridden in a derived class.
6. Java uses static overloading and always selects the signature of an overloaded method at compile time.
7. In a derived class, the inherited base class members should only be initialized as an aggregate by using the `super` method. If these members are public or protected, they may later be read or assigned to individually.
8. When you send a function object as a parameter, you must send a constructed object, and not simply the name of the class.
9. Overusing anonymous classes is a common error.
10. The `throws` list for a method in a derived class cannot be redefined to throw an exception not thrown in the base class. Return types must also match.

11. When a method is overridden, it is illegal to reduce its visibility. This is also true when implementing interface methods, which by definition are always `public`.

on the internet

All the chapter code is available online. Some of the code was presented in stages; for those classes, only one final version is provided.

PersonDemo.java	The `Person` hierarchy and test program.
Shape.java	The abstract `Shape` class.
Circle.java	The `Circle` class.
Square.java	The `Square` class.
Rectangle.java	The `Rectangle` class.
ShapeDemo.java	A test program for the `Shape` example.
NoSuchElementException.java	The exception class in Figure 4.18. This is part of `weiss.util`. **ConcurrentModificationException.java** and **EmptyStackException.java** are also online.
DecoratorDemo.java	An illustration of the decorator pattern, including buffering, compression, and serialization.
MemoryCell.java	The `MemoryCell` class in Figure 4.21.
TestMemoryCell.java	The test program for the memory cell class shown in Figure 4.22.
SimpleArrayList.java	The generic simplified `ArrayList` class in Figure 4.23, with some additional methods. A test program is provided in **ReadStringsWithSimpleArrayList.java**.
PrimitiveWrapperDemo.java	Demonstrates the use of the `Integer` class, as shown in Figure 4.24.
BoxingDemo.java	Illustrates autoboxing and unboxing, as shown in Figure 4.25.
StorageCellDemo.java	The `StorageCell` adapter as shown in Figure 4.26, and a test program.
FindMaxDemo.java	The `findMax` generic algorithm in Figure 4.27.
GenericMemoryCell.java	Illustrates the `GenericMemoryCell` class, in Figure 4.28, updated to use Java 5 generics. **TestGenericMemoryCell.java** tests the class.

GenericSimpleArrayList.java	The generic simplified `ArrayList` class in Figure 4.35, with some additional methods. A test program is provided in **ReadStrings-WithGenericSimpleArrayList.java**.
GenericFindMaxDemo.java	Illustrates the generic `findMax` method in Figure 4.34.
SimpleRectangle.java	Contains the `SimpleRectangle` class in Figure 4.36.
Comparator.java	The `Comparator` interface in Figure 4.37.
CompareTest.java	Illustrates the function object, with no nested classes, as shown in Figure 4.39.
CompareTestInner1.java	Illustrates the function object, with a nested class, as shown in Figure 4.40.
CompareTestInner2.java	Illustrates the function object, with a local class, as shown in Figure 4.41.
CompareTestInner3.java	Illustrates the function object, with an anonymous class, as shown in Figure 4.42.
StaticParamsDemo.java	The demonstration of static overloading and dynamic dispatch shown in Figure 4.43.
BadEqualsDemo.java	Illustrates the consequences of overloading instead of overriding `equals`, as shown in Figure 4.44.

exercises

IN SHORT

4.1 What members of an inherited class can be used in the derived class? What members become public for users of the derived class?

4.2 What is composition?

4.3 Explain polymorphism. Explain dynamic dispatch. When is dynamic dispatch not used?

4.4 What is autoboxing and unboxing?

4.5 What is a final method?

4.6 Consider the program to test visibility in Figure 4.46.

a. Which accesses are illegal?

b. Make `main` a method in `Base`. Which accesses are illegal?

c. Make `main` a method in `Derived`. Which accesses are illegal?

```
 1 public class Base
 2 {
 3     public    int bPublic;
 4     protected int bProtect;
 5     private   int bPrivate;
 6     // Public methods omitted
 7 }
 8
 9 public class Derived extends Base
10 {
11     public    int dPublic;
12     private   int dPrivate;
13     // Public methods omitted
14 }
15
16 public class Tester
17 {
18     public static void main( String [ ] args )
19     {
20         Base b    = new Base( );
21         Derived d = new Derived( );
22
23         System.out.println( b.bPublic + " " + b.bProtect + " "
24                           + b.bPrivate + " " + d.dPublic + " "
25                           + d.dPrivate );
26     }
27 }
```

figure 4.46

A program to test visibility

d. How do these answers change if `protected` is removed from line 4?

e. Write a three-parameter constructor for `Base`. Then write a five-parameter constructor for `Derived`.

f. The class `Derived` consists of five integers. Which are accessible to the class `Derived`?

g. A method in the class `Derived` is passed a `Base` object. Which of the `Base` object members can the `Derived` class access?

4.7 What is the difference between a final class and other classes? Why are final classes used?

4.8 What is an abstract method? What is an abstract class?

4.9 What is an interface? How does the interface differ from an abstract class? What members may be in an interface?

4.10 Explain the design of the Java I/O library. Include a class hierarchy picture for all the classes described in Section 4.5.3.

4.11 How were generic algorithms implemented in Java before Java 5? How are they implemented in Java 5?

4.12 Explain the adapter and wrapper patterns. How do they differ?

4.13 What are two common ways to implement adapters? What are the trade-offs between these implementation methods? Describe how function objects are implemented in Java.

4.14 What is a local class? What is an anonymous class?

4.15 What is type erasure? What restrictions on generic classes are a consequence of type erasure? What is a raw class?

4.16 Explain the Java rules for covariance for arrays and generic collections. What are wildcards and type bounds and how do they attempt to make the covariance rules appear the same?

IN THEORY

4.17 A local class can access local variables that are declared in that method (prior to the class). Show that if this is allowed, it is possible for an instance of the local class to access the value of the local variable, even after the method has terminated. (For this reason, the compiler will insist that these variables are marked `final`.)

4.18 This exercise explores how Java performs dynamic dispatch, and also why trivial final methods may not be inlined at compile time. Place each of the classes in Figure 4.47 in its own file.

a. Compile `Class2` and run the program. What is the output?

b. What is the exact signature (including return type) of the `getX` method that is deduced at compile time at line 14?

figure 4.47

The classes for Exercise 4.18

```
1  public class Class1
2  {
3      public static int x = 5;
4
5      public final String getX( )
6        { return "" + x + 12; }
7  }
8
9  public class Class2
10 {
11     public static void main( String [ ] args )
12     {
13         Class1 obj = new Class1( );
14         System.out.println( obj.getX( ) );
15     }
16 }
```

c. Change the getX routine at line 5 to return an int; remove the "" from the body at line 6, and recompile Class2. What is the output?

d. What is the exact signature (including return type) of the getX method that is now deduced at compile time at line 14?

e. Change Class1 back to its original, but recompile Class1 only. What is the result of running the program?

f. What would the result have been had the compiler been allowed to perform inline optimization?

4.19 In each of the following code fragments, find any errors and any unnecessary casts.

a.
```
Base [ ] arr = new Base [ 2 ];
arr[ 0 ] = arr[ 1 ] = new Derived( );

Derived x = (Derived) arr[ 0 ];
Derived y = ( (Derived[])arr )[ 0 ];
```

b.
```
Derived [ ] arr = new Derived [ 2 ];
arr[ 0 ] = arr[ 1 ] = new Derived( );

Base x = arr[ 0 ];
Base y = ( (Base[])arr )[ 0 ];
```

c.
```
Base [ ] arr = new Derived [ 2 ];
arr[ 0 ] = arr[ 1 ] = new Derived( );

Derived x = (Derived) arr[ 0 ];
Derived y = ( (Derived[])arr )[ 0 ];
```

d.
```
Base [ ] arr = new Derived [ 2 ];
arr[ 0 ] = arr[ 1 ] = new Base( );
```

IN PRACTICE

4.20 Write a generic copy routine that moves elements from one array to another identically sized and compatible array.

4.21 Write generic methods min and max, each of which accepts two parameters and returns the smaller and larger, respectively. Then use those methods on the String type.

4.22 Write generic method min, which accepts an array and returns the smallest item. Then use the method on the String type.

4.23 Write generic method max2, which accepts an array and returns an array of length two representing the two largest items in the array. The input array should be unchanged. Then use this method on the String type.

4.24 Write generic method `sort`, which accepts an array and rearranges the array in nondecreasing sorted order. Test your method on both `String` and `Shape`.

4.25 For the `Shape` example, modify the constructors in the hierarchy to throw an `InvalidArgumentException` when the parameters are negative.

4.26 Modify the `Person` class so that it can use `findMax` to obtain the alphabetically last person.

4.27 A `SingleBuffer` supports `get` and `put`: The `SingleBuffer` stores a single item and an indication whether the `SingleBuffer` is logically empty. A `put` may be applied only to an empty buffer, and it inserts an item into the buffer. A `get` may be applied only to a nonempty buffer, and it deletes and returns the contents of the buffer. Write a generic class to implement `SingleBuffer`. Define an exception to signal errors.

4.28 A `SortedArrayList` stores a collection. It is similar to `ArrayList`, except that `add` will place the item in the correct sorted order instead of at the end (however, at this point it will be difficult for you to use inheritance). Implement a separate `SortedArrayList` class that supports `add`, `get`, `remove`, and `size`.

4.29 This exercise asks you to write a generic `countMatches` method. Your method will take two parameters. The first parameter is an array of `int`. The second parameter is a function object that returns a Boolean.

a. Give a declaration for an interface that expresses the requisite function object.
b. `countMatches` returns the number of array items for which the function object returns `true`. Implement `countMatches`.
c. Test `countMatches` by writing a function object, `EqualsZero`, that implements your interface to accept one parameter and returns `true` if the parameter is equal to zero. Use an `EqualsZero` function object to test `countMatches`.

4.30 Although the function objects we have looked at store no data, this is not a requirement. Reuse the interface in Exercise 4.29(a).

a. Write a function object `EqualsK`. `EqualsK` contains one data member (`k`). `EqualsK` is constructed with a single parameter (the default is zero) that is used to initialize `k`. Its method returns `true` if the parameter is equal to `k`.
b. Use `EqualsK` to test `countMatches` in Exercise 4.29 (c).

PROGRAMMING PROJECTS

4.31 Rewrite the `Shape` hierarchy to store the area as a data member and have it computed by the `Shape` constructor. The constructors in the derived classes should compute an area and pass the result to the `super` method. Make `area` a final method that returns only the value of this data member.

4.32 Add the concept of a position to the `Shape` hierarchy by including coordinates as data members. Then add a `distance` method.

4.33 Write an abstract class for `Date` and its derived class `GregorianDate`.

4.34 Implement a tax payer hierarchy that consists of a `TaxPayer` interface and the classes `SinglePayer` and `MarriedPayer` that implement the interface.

4.35 Implement a *gzip* and *gunzip* program that performs compression and uncompression of files.

4.36 A book consists of an author, title, and ISBN number (all of which can never change once the book is created).

A library book is a book that also contains a due date and the current holder of the book, which is either a `String` representing a person who has checked the book out or `null` if the book is currently not checked out. Both the due date and holder of the book can change over time.

A library contains library books and supports the following operations:

1. Add a library book to the library.
2. Check out a library book by specifying its ISBN number and new holder and the due date.
3. Determine the current holder of a library book given its ISBN number.

a. Write two interfaces: `Book` and `LibraryBook` that abstract the functionality described above.

b. Write a library class that includes the three methods specified. In implementing the `Library` class, you should maintain the library books in an `ArrayList`. You may assume that there are never any requests to add duplicate books.

references

The following books describe the general principles of object-oriented software development:

1. G. Booch, *Object-Oriented Design and Analysis with Applications* (Second Edition), Benjamin Cummings, Redwood City, CA, 1994.
2. T. Budd, *Understanding Object-Oriented Programming With Java*, Addison-Wesley, Boston, MA, 2001.
3. D. de Champeaux, D. Lea, and P. Faure, *Object-Oriented System Development*, Addison-Wesley, Reading, MA, 1993.
4. I. Jacobson, M. Christerson, P. Jonsson, and G. Overgaard, *Object-Oriented Software Engineering: A Use Case Driven Approach* (revised fourth printing), Addison-Wesley, Reading, MA, 1992.
5. B. Meyer, *Object-Oriented Software Construction*, Prentice Hall, Englewood Cliffs, NJ, 1988.

part two

Algorithms and Building Blocks

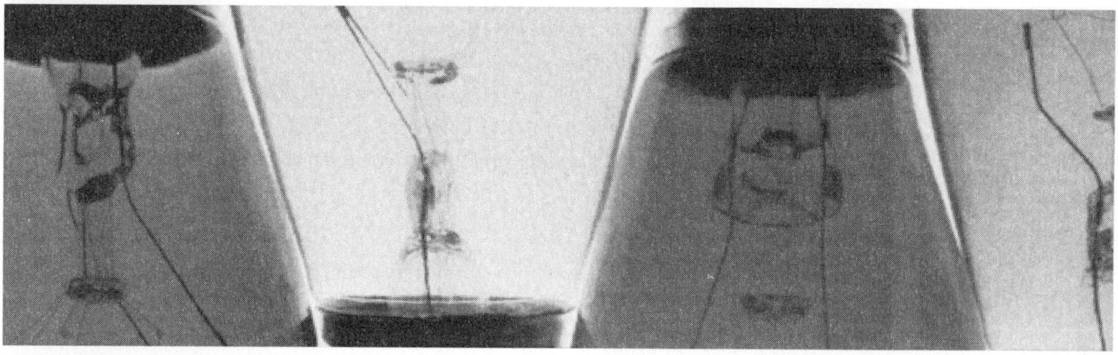

chapter 5

algorithm analysis

In Part One we examined how object-oriented programming can help in the design and implementation of large systems. We did not examine performance issues. Generally, we use a computer because we need to process a large amount of data. When we run a program on large amounts of input, we must be certain that the program terminates within a reasonable amount of time. Although the amount of running time is somewhat dependent on the programming language we use, and to a smaller extent the methodology we use (such as procedural versus object-oriented), often those factors are unchangeable constants of the design. Even so, the running time is most strongly correlated with the choice of algorithms.

An *algorithm* is a clearly specified set of instructions the computer will follow to solve a problem. Once an algorithm is given for a problem and determined to be correct, the next step is to determine the amount of resources, such as time and space, that the algorithm will require. This step is called *algorithm analysis*. An algorithm that requires several gigabytes of main memory is not useful for most current machines, even if it is completely correct.

In this chapter, we show the following:

- How to estimate the time required for an algorithm
- How to use techniques that drastically reduce the running time of an algorithm
- How to use a mathematical framework that more rigorously describes the running time of an algorithm
- How to write a simple *binary search* routine

5.1 what is algorithm analysis?

More data means that the program takes more time.

The amount of time that any algorithm takes to run almost always depends on the amount of input that it must process. We expect, for instance, that sorting 10,000 elements requires more time than sorting 10 elements. The running time of an algorithm is thus a function of the input size. The exact value of the function depends on many factors, such as the speed of the host machine, the quality of the compiler, and in some cases, the quality of the program. For a given program on a given computer, we can plot the running time function on a graph. Figure 5.1 illustrates such a plot for four programs. The curves represent four common functions encountered in algorithm analysis: linear, $O(N \log N)$, quadratic, and cubic. The input size N ranges from 1 to 100

figure 5.1

Running times for small inputs

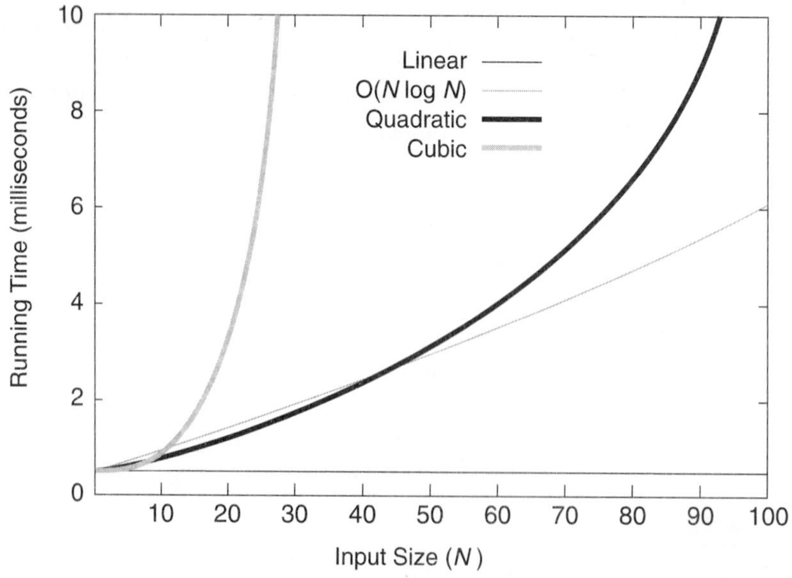

items, and the running times range from 0 to 10 milliseconds. A quick glance at Figure 5.1 and its companion, Figure 5.2, suggests that the linear, O(*N* log *N*), quadratic, and cubic curves represent running times in order of decreasing preference.

An example is the problem of downloading a file over the Internet. Suppose there is an initial 2-sec delay (to set up a connection), after which the download proceeds at 1.6 K/sec. Then if the file is *N* kilobytes, the time to download is described by the formula $T(N) = N/1.6 + 2$. This is a *linear function.* Downloading an 80K file takes approximately 52 sec, whereas downloading a file twice as large (160K) takes about 102 sec, or roughly twice as long. This property, in which time essentially is directly proportional to amount of input, is the signature of a *linear algorithm,* which is the most efficient algorithm. In contrast, as these first two graphs show, some of the nonlinear algorithms lead to large running times. For instance, the linear algorithm is much more efficient than the cubic algorithm.

Of the common functions encountered in algorithm analysis, *linear* represents the most efficient algorithm.

In this chapter we address several important questions:

- Is it always important to be on the most efficient curve?
- How much better is one curve than another?
- How do you decide which curve a particular algorithm lies on?
- How do you design algorithms that avoid being on less-efficient curves?

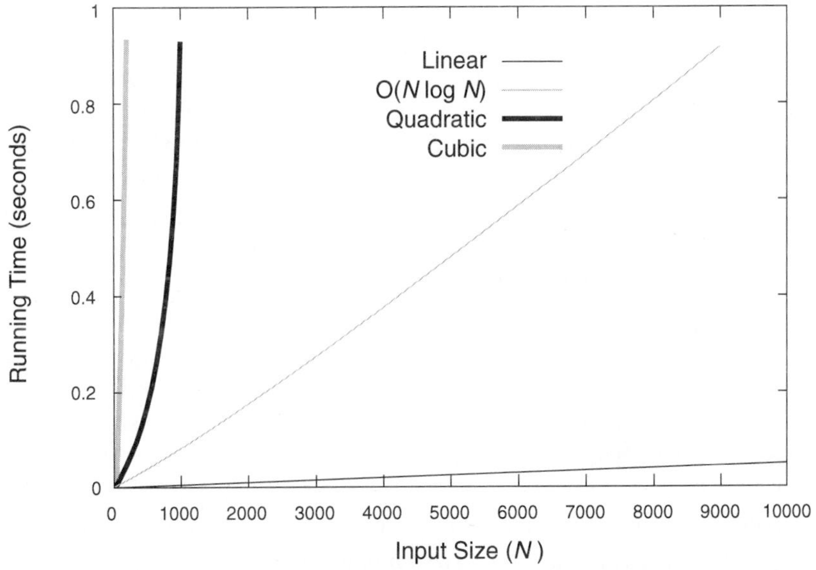

figure 5.2

Running times for moderate inputs

A *cubic function* is a function whose dominant term is some constant times N^3. As an example, $10N^3 + N^2 + 40N + 80$ is a cubic function. Similarly, a quadratic function has a dominant term that is some constant times N^2, and a linear function has a dominant term that is some constant times N. The expression $O(N \log N)$ represents a function whose dominant term is N times the logarithm of N. The logarithm is a slowly growing function; for instance, the logarithm of 1,000,000 (with the typical base 2) is only 20. The logarithm grows more slowly than a square or cube (or any) root. We discuss the logarithm in more depth in Section 5.5.

The growth rate of a function is most important when N is sufficiently large.

Either of two functions may be smaller than the other at any given point, so claiming, for instance, that $F(N) < G(N)$ does not make sense. Instead, we measure the functions' rates of growth. This is justified for three reasons. First, for cubic functions such as the one shown in Figure 5.2, when N is 1,000 the value of the cubic function is almost entirely determined by the cubic term. In the function $10N^3 + N^2 + 40N + 80$, for $N = 1{,}000$, the value of the function is 10,001,040,080, of which 10,000,000,000 is due to the $10N^3$ term. If we were to use only the cubic term to estimate the entire function, an error of about 0.01 percent would result. For sufficiently large N, the value of a function is largely determined by its dominant term (the meaning of the term *sufficiently large* varies by function).

The second reason we measure the functions' growth rates is that the exact value of the leading constant of the dominant term is not meaningful across different machines (although the relative values of the leading constant for identically growing functions might be). For instance, the quality of the compiler could have a large influence on the leading constant. The third reason is that small values of N generally are not important. For $N = 20$, Figure 5.1 shows that all algorithms terminate within 5 ms. The difference between the best and worst algorithm is less than a blink of the eye.

Big-Oh notation is used to capture the most dominant term in a function.

We use *Big-Oh* notation to capture the most dominant term in a function and to represent the growth rate. For instance, the running time of a quadratic algorithm is specified as $O(N^2)$ (pronounced "order en-squared"). Big-Oh notation also allows us to establish a relative order among functions by comparing dominant terms. We discuss Big-Oh notation more formally in Section 5.4.

For small values of N (for instance, those less than 40), Figure 5.1 shows that one curve may be initially better than another, which doesn't hold for larger values of N. For example, initially the quadratic curve is better than the $O(N \log N)$ curve, but as N gets sufficiently large, the quadratic algorithm loses its advantage. For small amounts of input, making comparisons between functions is difficult because leading constants become very significant. The function $N + 2{,}500$ is larger than N^2 when N is less than 50. Eventually, the linear function is always less than the quadratic function. Most important, for small input sizes the running times are generally inconsequential, so we need not worry about them. For instance, Figure 5.1 shows that when N is less than

25, all four algorithms run in less than 10 ms. Consequently, when input sizes are very small, a good rule of thumb is to use the simplest algorithm.

Figure 5.2 clearly demonstrates the differences between the various curves for large input sizes. A linear algorithm solves a problem of size 10,000 in a small fraction of a second. The $O(N \log N)$ algorithm uses roughly 10 times as much time. Note that the actual time differences depend on the constants involved and thus might be more or less. Depending on these constants, an $O(N \log N)$ algorithm might be faster than a linear algorithm for fairly large input sizes. For equally complex algorithms, however, linear algorithms tend to win out over $O(N \log N)$ algorithms.

This relationship is not true, however, for the quadratic and cubic algorithms. Quadratic algorithms are almost always impractical when the input size is more than a few thousand, and cubic algorithms are impractical for input sizes as small as a few hundred. For instance, it is impractical to use a naive sorting algorithm for 100,000 items, because most simple sorting algorithms (such as bubble sort and selection sort) are quadratic algorithms. The sorting algorithms discussed in Chapter 8 run in *subquadratic* time—that is, better than $O(N^2)$—thus making sorting large arrays practical.

Quadratic algorithms are impractical for input sizes exceeding a few thousand.

The most striking feature of these curves is that the quadratic and cubic algorithms are not competitive with the others for reasonably large inputs. We can code the quadratic algorithm in highly efficient machine language and do a poor job coding the linear algorithm, and the quadratic algorithm will still lose badly. Even the most clever programming tricks cannot make an inefficient algorithm fast. Thus, before we waste effort attempting to optimize code, we need to optimize the algorithm. Figure 5.3 arranges functions that commonly describe algorithm running times in order of increasing growth rate.

Cubic algorithms are impractical for input sizes as small as a few hundred.

Function	Name
c	Constant
$\log N$	Logarithmic
$\log^2 N$	Log-squared
N	Linear
$N \log N$	$N \log N$
N^2	Quadratic
N^3	Cubic
2^N	Exponential

figure 5.3

Functions in order of increasing growth rate

5.2 examples of algorithm running times

In this section we examine three problems. We also sketch possible solutions and determine what kind of running times the algorithms will exhibit, without providing detailed programs. The goal in this section is to provide you with some intuition about algorithm analysis. In Section 5.3 we provide more details on the process, and in Section 5.4 we formally approach an algorithm analysis problem.

We look at the following problems in this section:

minimum element in an array
Given an array of *N* items, find the smallest item.

closest points in the plane
Given *N* points in a plane (that is, an *x-y* coordinate system), find the pair of points that are closest together.

colinear points in the plane
Given *N* points in a plane (that is, an *x-y* coordinate system), determine if any three form a straight line.

The minimum element problem is fundamental in computer science. It can be solved as follows:

1. Maintain a variable `min` that stores the minimum element.
2. Initialize `min` to the first element.
3. Make a sequential scan through the array and update `min` as appropriate.

The running time of this algorithm will be $O(N)$, or linear, because we will repeat a fixed amount of work for each element in the array. A linear algorithm is as good as we can hope for. This is because we have to examine every element in the array, a process that requires linear time.

The closest points problem is a fundamental problem in graphics that can be solved as follows:

1. Calculate the distance between each pair of points.
2. Retain the minimum distance.

This calculation is expensive, however, because there are $N(N-1)/2$ pairs of points.[1] Thus there are roughly N^2 pairs of points. Examining all these

1. Each of N points can be paired with $N-1$ points for a total of $N(N-1)$ pairs. However, this pairing double-counts pairs A, B and B, A, so we must divide by 2.

pairs and finding the minimum distance among them takes quadratic time. A better algorithm runs in $O(N \log N)$ time and works by avoiding the computation of all distances. There is also an algorithm that is expected to take $O(N)$ time. These last two algorithms use subtle observations to provide faster results and are beyond the scope of this text.

The colinear points problem is important for many graphics algorithms. The reason is that the existence of colinear points introduces a degenerate case that requires special handling. It can be directly solved by enumerating all groups of three points. This solution is even more computationally expensive than that for the closest points problem because the number of different groups of three points is $N(N-1)(N-2)/6$ (using reasoning similar to that used for the closest points problem). This result tells us that the direct approach will yield a cubic algorithm. There is also a more clever strategy (also beyond the scope of this text) that solves the problem in quadratic time (and further improvement is an area of continuously active research).

In Section 5.3 we look at a problem that illustrates the differences among linear, quadratic, and cubic algorithms. We also show how the performance of these algorithms compares to a mathematical prediction. Finally, after discussing the basic ideas, we examine Big-Oh notation more formally.

5.3 the maximum contiguous subsequence sum problem

In this section, we consider the following problem:

> **maximum contiguous subsequence sum problem**
> Given (possibly negative) integers $A_1, A_2, \ldots, A_N$, find (and identify the sequence corresponding to) the maximum value of $\sum_{k=i}^{j} A_k$. The maximum contiguous subsequence sum is zero if all the integers are negative.

As an example, if the input is {–2, **11**, **–4**, **13**, –5, 2}, then the answer is 20, which represents the contiguous subsequence encompassing items 2 through 4 (shown in boldface type). As a second example, for the input { 1, –3, **4**, **–2**, **–1**, **6** }, the answer is 7 for the subsequence encompassing the last four items.

> Programming details are considered after the algorithm design.

In Java, arrays begin at zero, so a Java program would represent the input as a sequence A_0 to A_{N-1}. This is a programming detail and not part of the algorithm design.

> Always consider emptiness.

Before the discussion of the algorithms for this problem, we need to comment on the degenerate case in which all input integers are negative. The problem statement gives a maximum contiguous subsequence sum of 0 for this case. One might wonder why we do this, rather than just returning the largest (that is, the smallest in magnitude) negative integer in the input. The reason is that the empty subsequence, consisting of zero integers, is also a subsequence, and its sum is clearly 0. Because the empty subsequence is contiguous, there is always a contiguous subsequence whose sum is 0. This result is analogous to the empty set being a subset of any set. Be aware that emptiness is always a possibility and that in many instances it is not a special case at all.

There are lots of drastically different algorithms (in terms of efficiency) that can be used to solve the maximum contiguous subsequence sum problem.

The maximum contiguous subsequence sum problem is interesting mainly because there are so many algorithms to solve it—and the performance of these algorithms varies drastically. In this section, we discuss three such algorithms. The first is an obvious exhaustive search algorithm, but it is very inefficient. The second is an improvement on the first, which is accomplished by a simple observation. The third is a very efficient, but not obvious, algorithm. We prove that its running time is linear.

In Chapter 7 we present a fourth algorithm, which has $O(N \log N)$ running time. That algorithm is not as efficient as the linear algorithm, but it is much more efficient than the other two. It is also typical of the kinds of algorithms that result in $O(N \log N)$ running times. The graphs shown in Figures 5.1 and 5.2 are representative of these four algorithms.

5.3.1 the obvious $O(N^3)$ algorithm

A brute force algorithm is generally the least efficient but simplest method to code.

The simplest algorithm is a direct exhaustive search, or a *brute force algorithm*, as shown in Figure 5.4. Lines 9 and 10 control a pair of loops that iterate over all possible subsequences. For each possible subsequence, the value of its sum is computed at lines 12 to 15. If that sum is the best sum encountered, we update the value of `maxSum`, which is eventually returned at line 25. Two `ints`—`seqStart` and `seqEnd` (which are static class fields)—are also updated whenever a new best sequence is encountered.

The direct exhaustive search algorithm has the merit of extreme simplicity; the less complex an algorithm is, the more likely it is to be programmed correctly. However, exhaustive search algorithms are usually not as efficient as possible. In the remainder of this section we show that the running time of the algorithm is cubic. We count the number of times (as a function of the input size) the expressions in Figure 5.4 are evaluated. We require only a Big-Oh result, so once we have found a dominant term, we can ignore lower order terms and leading constants.

The running time of the algorithm is entirely dominated by the innermost `for` loop in lines 14 and 15. Four expressions there are repeatedly executed:

1. The initialization `k = i`
2. The test `k <= j`
3. The increment `thisSum += a[ k ]`
4. The adjustment `k++`

```
1  /**
2   * Cubic maximum contiguous subsequence sum algorithm.
3   * seqStart and seqEnd represent the actual best sequence.
4   */
5  public static int maxSubsequenceSum( int [ ] a )
6  {
7      int maxSum = 0;
8
9      for( int i = 0; i < a.length; i++ )
10         for( int j = i; j < a.length; j++ )
11         {
12             int thisSum = 0;
13
14             for( int k = i; k <= j; k++ )
15                 thisSum += a[ k ];
16
17             if( thisSum > maxSum )
18             {
19                 maxSum = thisSum;
20                 seqStart = i;
21                 seqEnd   = j;
22             }
23         }
24
25     return maxSum;
26 }
```

figure 5.4

A cubic maximum contiguous subsequence sum algorithm

The number of times expression 3 is executed makes it the dominant term among the four expressions. Note that each initialization is accompanied by at least one test. We are ignoring constants, so we may disregard the cost of the initializations; the initializations cannot be the single dominating cost of the algorithm. Because the test given by expression 2 is unsuccessful exactly once per loop, the number of unsuccessful tests performed by expression 2 is exactly equal to the number of initializations. Consequently, it is not dominant. The number of successful tests at expression 2, the number of increments performed by expression 3, and the number of adjustments at expression 4 are all identical. Thus the number of increments (i.e., the number of times that line 15 is executed) is a dominant measure of the work performed in the innermost loop.

A mathematical analysis is used to count the number of times that certain statements are executed.

The number of times line 15 is executed is exactly equal to the number of ordered triplets *(i, j, k)* that satisfy $1 \le i \le k \le j \le N$.[2] The reason is that the index *i* runs over the entire array, *j* runs from *i* to the end of the array, and *k* runs from *i* to *j*. A quick and dirty estimate is that the number of triplets is

2. In Java, the indices run from 0 to $N - 1$. We have used the algorithmic equivalent 1 to *N* to simplify the analysis.

somewhat less than $N \times N \times N$, or N^3, because i, j, and k can each assume one of N values. The additional restriction $i \le k \le j$ reduces this number. A precise calculation is somewhat difficult to obtain and is performed in Theorem 5.1.

The most important part of Theorem 5.1 is not the proof, but rather the result. There are two ways to evaluate the number of triplets. One is to evaluate the sum $\sum_{i=1}^{N} \sum_{j=i}^{N} \sum_{k=i}^{j} 1$. We could evaluate this sum inside out (see Exercise 5.9). Instead, we will use an alternative.

Theorem 5.1

The number of integer-ordered triplets (i, j, k) that satisfy $1 \le i \le k \le j \le N$ is $N(N+1)(N+2)/6$.

Proof

Place the following $N + 2$ balls in a box: N balls numbered 1 to N, one unnumbered red ball, and one unnumbered blue ball. Remove three balls from the box. If a red ball is drawn, number it as the lowest of the numbered balls drawn. If a blue ball is drawn, number it as the highest of the numbered balls drawn. Notice that if we draw both a red and blue ball, then the effect is to have three balls identically numbered. Order the three balls. Each such order corresponds to a triplet solution to the equation in Theorem 5.1. The number of possible orders is the number of distinct ways to draw three balls without replacement from a collection of $N + 2$ balls. This is similar to the problem of selecting three points from a group of N that we evaluated in Section 5.2, so we immediately obtain the stated result.

The result of Theorem 5.1 is that the innermost `for` loop accounts for cubic running time. The remaining work in the algorithm is inconsequential because it is done, at most, once per iteration of the inner loop. Put another way, the cost of lines 17 to 22 is inconsequential because that part of the code is done only as often as the initialization of the inner `for` loop, rather than as often as the repeated body of the inner `for` loop. Consequently, the algorithm is $O(N^3)$.

> We do not need precise calculations for a Big-Oh estimate. In many cases, we can use the simple rule of multiplying the size of all the nested loops. Note carefully that consecutive loops do not multiply.

The previous combinatorial argument allows us to obtain precise calculations on the number of iterations in the inner loop. For a Big-Oh calculation, this is not really necessary; we need to know only that the leading term is some constant times N^3. Looking at the algorithm, we see a loop that is potentially of size N inside a loop that is potentially of size N inside another loop that is potentially of size N. This configuration tells us that the triple loop has the potential for $N \times N \times N$ iterations. This potential is only about six times higher than what our precise calculation of what actually occurs. Constants are ignored anyway, so we can adopt the general rule that, when we have nested loops, we should multiply the cost of the innermost statement by the size of each loop in the nest to obtain an upper bound. In most cases, the upper bound will not be a gross overestimate.[3] Thus a program with three nested loops, each running sequentially through large portions of an array, is likely to exhibit $O(N^3)$ behavior. Note that three consecutive (nonnested) loops exhibit linear behavior; it is nesting that leads to a combinatoric explosion. Consequently, to improve the algorithm, we need to remove a loop.

5.3.2 an improved $O(N^2)$ algorithm

When we remove a nested loop from an algorithm, we generally lower the running time.

When we can remove a nested loop from the algorithm, we generally lower the running time. How do we remove a loop? Obviously, we cannot always do so. However, the previous algorithm has many unnecessary computations. The inefficiency that the improved algorithm corrects is the unduly expensive computation in the inner `for` loop in Figure 5.4. The improved algorithm makes use of the fact that $\sum_{k=i}^{j} A_k = A_j + \sum_{k=i}^{j-1} A_k$. In other words, suppose we have just calculated the sum for the subsequence $i, ..., j-1$. Then computing the sum for the subsequence $i, ..., j$ should not take long because we need only one more addition. However, the cubic algorithm throws away this information. If we use this observation, we obtain the improved algorithm shown in Figure 5.5. We have two rather than three nested loops, and the running time is $O(N^2)$.

5.3.3 a linear algorithm

If we remove another loop, we have a linear algorithm.

The algorithm is tricky. It uses a clever observation to step quickly over large numbers of subsequences that cannot be the best.

To move from a quadratic algorithm to a linear algorithm, we need to remove yet another loop. However, unlike the reduction illustrated in Figures 5.4 and 5.5, where loop removal was simple, getting rid of another loop is not so easy. The problem is that the quadratic algorithm is still an exhaustive search; that is, we are trying all possible subsequences. The only difference between the quadratic and cubic algorithms is that the cost of testing each successive subsequence is a constant $O(1)$ instead of linear $O(N)$. Because a quadratic number of subsequences are possible, the only way we can attain a subquadratic bound is to find a clever way to eliminate from consideration a large number of subsequences, without actually computing their sum and testing to see if that sum is a new maximum. This section shows how this is done.

First, we eliminate a large number of possible subsequences from consideration. Let $A_{i,j}$ be the subsequence encompassing elements from i to j, and let $S_{i,j}$ be its sum.

3. Exercise 5.16 illustrates a case in which the multiplication of loop sizes yields an overestimate in the Big-Oh result.

figure 5.5

A quadratic maximum contiguous subsequence sum algorithm

```
/**
 * Quadratic maximum contiguous subsequence sum algorithm.
 * seqStart and seqEnd represent the actual best sequence.
 */
public static int maxSubsequenceSum( int [ ] a )
{
    int maxSum = 0;

    for( int i = 0; i < a.length; i++ )
    {
        int thisSum = 0;

        for( int j = i; j < a.length; j++ )
        {
            thisSum += a[ j ];

            if( thisSum > maxSum )
            {
                maxSum = thisSum;
                seqStart = i;
                seqEnd   = j;
            }
        }
    }

    return maxSum;
}
```

Theorem 5.2

Let $A_{i,j}$ be any sequence with $S_{i,j} < 0$. If $q > j$, then $A_{i,q}$ is not the maximum contiguous subsequence.

Proof

The sum of A's elements from i to q is the sum of A's elements from i to j added to the sum of A's elements from $j + 1$ to q. Thus we have $S_{i,q} = S_{i,j} + S_{j+1,q}$. Because $S_{i,j} < 0$, we know that $S_{i,q} < S_{j+1,q}$. Thus $A_{i,q}$ is not a maximum contiguous subsequence.

An illustration of the sums generated by i, j, and q is shown on the first two lines in Figure 5.6. Theorem 5.2 demonstrates that we can avoid examining several subsequences by including an additional test: If `thisSum` is less than 0, we can `break` from the inner loop in Figure 5.5. Intuitively, if a subsequence's sum is negative, then it cannot be part of the maximum contiguous subsequence. The reason is that we can get a larger contiguous subsequence

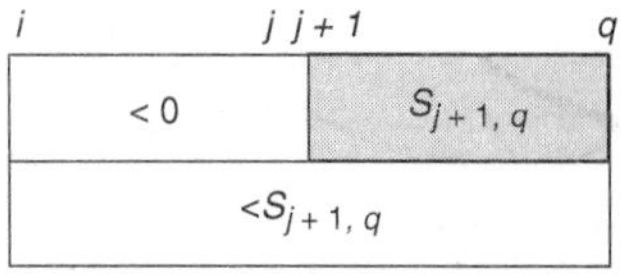

figure 5.6

The subsequences used in Theorem 5.2

by not including it. This observation by itself is not sufficient to reduce the running time below quadratic. A similar observation also holds: All contiguous subsequences that border the maximum contiguous subsequence must have negative (or 0) sums (otherwise, we would include them). This observation also does not reduce the running time to below quadratic. However, a third observation, illustrated in Figure 5.7, does, and we formalize it with Theorem 5.3.

Theorem 5.3

For any i, let $A_{i,j}$ be the first sequence, with $S_{i,j} < 0$. Then, for any $i \le p \le j$ and $p \le q$, $A_{p,q}$ either is not a maximum contiguous subsequence or is equal to an already seen maximum contiguous subsequence

Proof

If $p = i$, then Theorem 5.2 applies. Otherwise, as in Theorem 5.2, we have $S_{i,q} = S_{i,p-1} + S_{p,q}$. Since j is the lowest index for which $S_{i,j} < 0$, it follows that $S_{i,p-1} \ge 0$. Thus $S_{p,q} \le S_{i,q}$. If $q > j$ (shown on the left-hand side in Figure 5.7), then Theorem 5.2 implies that $A_{i,q}$ is not a maximum contiguous subsequence, so neither is $A_{p,q}$. Otherwise, as shown on the right-hand side in Figure 5.7, the subsequence $A_{p,q}$ has a sum equal to, at most, that of the already seen subsequence $A_{i,q}$.

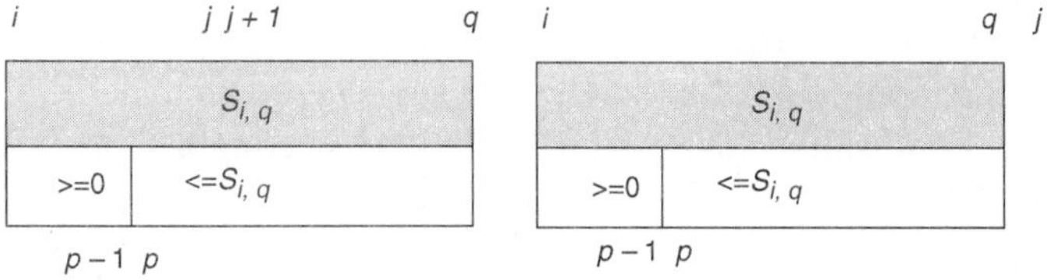

figure 5.7

The subsequences used in Theorem 5.3. The sequence from p to q has a sum that is, at most, that of the subsequence from i to q. On the left-hand side, the sequence from i to q is itself not the maximum (by Theorem 5.2). On the right-hand side, the sequence from i to q has already been seen.

figure 5.8

A linear maximum contiguous subsequence sum algorithm

```
/**
 * Linear maximum contiguous subsequence sum algorithm.
 * seqStart and seqEnd represent the actual best sequence.
 */
public static int maximumSubsequenceSum( int [ ] a )
{
    int maxSum = 0;
    int thisSum = 0;

    for( int i = 0, j = 0; j < a.length; j++ )
    {
        thisSum += a[ j ];

        if( thisSum > maxSum )
        {
            maxSum = thisSum;
            seqStart = i;
            seqEnd   = j;
        }
        else if( thisSum < 0 )
        {
            i = j + 1;
            thisSum = 0;
        }
    }

    return maxSum;
}
```

If we detect a negative sum, we can move *i* all the way past *j*.

If an algorithm is complex, a correctness proof is required.

Theorem 5.3 tells us that, when a negative subsequence is detected, not only can we `break` the inner loop, but also we can advance `i` to `j+1`. Figure 5.8 shows that we can rewrite the algorithm using only a single loop. Clearly, the running time of this algorithm is linear: At each step in the loop, we advance `j`, so the loop iterates at most N times. The correctness of this algorithm is much less obvious than for the previous algorithms, which is typical. That is, algorithms that use the structure of a problem to beat an exhaustive search generally require some sort of correctness proof. We proved that the algorithm (although not the resulting Java program) is correct using a short mathematical argument. The purpose is not to make the discussion entirely mathematical, but rather to give a flavor of the techniques that might be required in advanced work.

5.4 general big-oh rules

Now that we have the basic ideas of algorithm analysis, we can adopt a slightly more formal approach. In this section, we outline the general rules for using Big-Oh notation. Although we use Big-Oh notation almost exclusively throughout this text, we also define three other types of algorithm notation that are related to Big-Oh and used occasionally later on in the text.

> **definition:** (Big-Oh) $T(N)$ is $O(F(N))$ if there are positive constants c and N_0 such that $T(N) \le cF(N)$ when $N \ge N_0$.

> **definition:** (Big-Omega) $T(N)$ is $\Omega(F(N))$ if there are positive constants c and N_0 such that $T(N) \ge cF(N)$ when $N \ge N_0$.

> **definition:** (Big-Theta) $T(N)$ is $\Theta(F(N))$ if and only if $T(N)$ is $O(F(N))$ and $T(N)$ is $\Omega(F(N))$.

> **definition:** (Little-Oh) $T(N)$ is $o(F(N))$ if and only if $T(N)$ is $O(F(N))$ and $T(N)$ is not $\Theta(F(N))$.

The first definition, *Big-Oh* notation, states that there is a point N_0 such that for all values of N that are past this point, $T(N)$ is bounded by some multiple of $F(N)$. This is the sufficiently large N mentioned earlier. Thus, if the running time $T(N)$ of an algorithm is $O(N^2)$, then, ignoring constants, we are guaranteeing that at some point we can bound the running time by a quadratic function. Notice that if the true running time is linear, then the statement that the running time is $O(N^2)$ is technically correct because the inequality holds. However, $O(N)$ would be the more precise claim.

If we use the traditional inequality operators to compare growth rates, then the first definition says that the growth rate of $T(N)$ is less than or equal to that of $F(N)$.

Big-Oh is similar to less than or equal to, when growth rates are being considered.

The second definition, $T(N) = \Omega(F(N))$, called *Big-Omega*, says that the growth rate of $T(N)$ is greater than or equal to that of $F(N)$. For instance, we might say that any algorithm that works by examining every possible subsequence in the maximum subsequence sum problem must take $\Omega(N^2)$ time because a quadratic number of subsequences are possible. This is a lower-bound argument that is used in more advanced analysis. Later in the text, we will see one example of this argument and demonstrate that any general-purpose sorting algorithm requires $\Omega(N \log N)$ time.

Big-Omega is similar to greater than or equal to, when growth rates are being considered.

The third definition, $T(N) = \Theta(F(N))$, called *Big-Theta*, says that the growth rate of $T(N)$ equals the growth rate of $F(N)$. For instance, the maximum subsequence algorithm shown in Figure 5.5 runs in $\Theta(N^2)$ time. In other words, the running time is bounded by a quadratic function, and this

Big-Theta is similar to equal to, when growth rates are being considered.

bound cannot be improved because it is also lower-bounded by another quadratic function. When we use Big-Theta notation, we are providing not only an upper bound on an algorithm but also assurances that the analysis that leads to the upper bound is as good (tight) as possible. In spite of the additional precision offered by Big-Theta, however, Big-Oh is more commonly used, except by researchers in the algorithm analysis field.

Little-Oh is similar to less than, when growth rates are being considered.

The final definition, $T(N) = o(F(N))$, called *Little-Oh*, says that the growth rate of $T(N)$ is strictly less than the growth rate of $F(N)$. This function is different from Big-Oh because Big-Oh allows the possibility that the growth rates are the same. For instance, if the running time of an algorithm is $o(N^2)$, then it is guaranteed to be growing at a slower rate than quadratic (that is, it is a *subquadratic algorithm*). Thus a bound of $o(N^2)$ is a better bound than $\Theta(N^2)$. Figure 5.9 summarizes these four definitions.

Throw out leading constants, lower-order terms, and relational symbols when using Big-Oh.

A couple of stylistic notes are in order. First, including constants or low-order terms inside a Big-Oh is bad style. Do not say $T(N) = O(2N^2)$ or $T(N) = O(N^2 + N)$. In both cases, the correct form is $T(N) = O(N^2)$. Second, in any analysis that requires a Big-Oh answer, all sorts of shortcuts are possible. Lower-order terms, leading constants, and relational symbols are all thrown away.

Now that the mathematics have formalized, we can relate it to the analysis of algorithms. The most basic rule is that *the running time of a loop is at most the running time of the statements inside the loop (including tests) times the number of iterations*. As shown earlier, the initialization and testing of the loop condition is usually no more dominant than are the statements encompassing the body of the loop.

A *worst-case bound* is a guarantee over all inputs of some size.

The running time of statements inside a group of nested loops is the running time of the statements (including tests in the innermost loop) multiplied by the sizes of all the loops. The running time of a sequence of consecutive loops is equal to the running time of the dominant loop. The time difference between a nested loop in which both indices run from 1 to N and two consecutive loops that are not nested but

figure 5.9

Meanings of the various growth functions

Mathematical Expression	Relative Rates of Growth
$T(N) = O(F(N))$	Growth of $T(N)$ is $\le$ growth of $F(N)$.
$T(N) = \Omega(F(N))$	Growth of $T(N)$ is $\ge$ growth of $F(N)$.
$T(N) = \Theta(F(N))$	Growth of $T(N)$ is $=$ growth of $F(N)$.
$T(N) = o(F(N))$	Growth of $T(N)$ is $<$ growth of $F(N)$.

run over the same indices is the same as the space difference between a two-dimensional array and two one-dimensional arrays. The first case is quadratic. The second case is linear because $N+N$ is $2N$, which is still $O(N)$. Occasionally, this simple rule can overestimate the running time, but in most cases it does not. Even if it does, Big-Oh does not guarantee an exact asymptotic answer—just an upper bound.

The analyses we have performed thus far involved use of a *worst-case bound*, which is a guarantee over all inputs of some size. Another form of analysis is the *average-case bound*, in which the running time is measured as an average over all of the possible inputs of size N. The average might differ from the worst case if, for example, a conditional statement that depends on the particular input causes an early exit from a loop. We discuss average-case bounds in more detail in Section 5.8. For now, simply note that the fact that one algorithm has a better worst-case bound than another algorithm implies nothing about their relative average-case bounds. However, in many cases average-case and worst-case bounds are closely correlated. When they are not, the bounds are treated separately.

In an *average-case bound*, the running time is measured as an average over all of the possible inputs of size N.

The last Big-Oh item we examine is how the running time grows for each type of curve, as illustrated in Figures 5.1 and 5.2. We want a more quantitative answer to this question: If an algorithm takes $T(N)$ time to solve a problem of size N, how long does it take to solve a larger problem? For instance, how long does it take to solve a problem when there is 10 times as much input? The answers are shown in Figure 5.10. However, we want to answer the question without running the program and hope our analytical answers will agree with the observed behavior.

We begin by examining the cubic algorithm. We assume that the running time is reasonably approximated by $T(N) = cN^3$. Consequently, $T(10N) = c(10N)^3$. Mathematical manipulation yields

$$T(10N) = 1000cN^3 = 1000T(N)$$

	Figure 5.4	Figure 5.5	Figure 7.20	Figure 5.8
N	$O(N^3)$	$O(N^2)$	$O(N \log N)$	$O(N)$
10	0.000009	0.000004	0.000006	0.000003
100	0.002580	0.000109	0.000045	0.000006
1,000	2.281013	0.010203	0.000485	0.000031
10,000	NA	1.2329	0.005712	0.000317
100,000	NA	135	0.064618	0.003206

figure 5.10

Observed running times (in seconds) for various maximum contiguous subsequence sum algorithms

If the size of the input increases by a factor of f, the running time of a cubic program increases by a factor of roughly f^3.

Thus the running time of a cubic program increases by a factor of 1,000 (assuming N is sufficiently large) when the amount of input is increased by a factor of 10. This relationship is roughly confirmed by the increase in running time from $N = 100$ to 1,000 shown in Figure 5.10. Recall that we do not expect an exact answer—just a reasonable approximation. We would also expect that for $N = 10{,}000$, the running time would increase another 1,000-fold. The result would be that a cubic algorithm requires roughly 35 minutes of computation time. In general, if the amount of the input increases by a factor of f, then the cubic algorithm's running time increases by a factor of f^3.

If the size of the input increases by a factor of f, the running time of a quadratic program increases by a factor of roughly f^2.

We can perform similar calculations for quadratic and linear algorithms. For the quadratic algorithm, we assume that $T(N) = cN^2$. It follows that $T(10N) = c(10N)^2$. When we expand, we obtain

$$T(10N) = 100cN^2 = 100T(N)$$

So when the input size increases by a factor of 10, the running time of a quadratic program increases by a factor of approximately 100. This relationship is also confirmed in Figure 5.10. In general, an f-fold increase in input size yields an f^2-fold increase in running time for a quadratic algorithm.

If the size of the input increases by a factor of f, then the running time of a linear program also increases by a factor of f. This is the preferred running time for an algorithm.

Finally, for a linear algorithm, a similar calculation shows that a 10-fold increase in input size results in a 10-fold increase in running time. Again, this relationship has been confirmed experimentally in Figure 5.10. Note, however, that for a linear program, the term *sufficiently large* means a somewhat higher input size than for the other programs. The reason is the overhead of 0.000003 sec that is used in all cases. For a linear program, this term is still significant for moderate input sizes.

The analysis used here does not work when there are logarithmic terms. When an $O(N \log N)$ algorithm is presented with 10 times as much input, the running time increases by a factor slightly larger than 10. Specifically, we have $T(10N) = c(10N)\log(10N)$. When we expand, we obtain

$$T(10N) = 10cN\log(10N) = 10cN\log N + 10cN\log 10 = 10T(N) + c'N$$

Here $c' = 10c\log 10$. As N gets very large, the ratio $T(10N)/T(N)$ gets closer and closer to 10 because $c'N/T(N) \approx (10\log 10)/\log N$ gets smaller and smaller with increasing N. Consequently, if the algorithm is competitive with a linear algorithm for very large N, it is likely to remain competitive for slightly larger N.

Does all this mean that quadratic and cubic algorithms are useless? The answer is no. In some cases, the most efficient algorithms known are quadratic or cubic. In others, the most efficient algorithm is even worse (exponential). Furthermore, when the amount of input is small, any algorithm will do. Frequently the algorithms that are not asymptotically efficient are nonetheless easy to program. For small inputs, that is the way to go. Finally, a good way to test a complex linear algorithm is to compare its output with an exhaustive search algorithm. In Section 5.8 we discuss some other limitations of the Big-Oh model.

5.5 the logarithm

The list of typical growth rate functions includes several entries containing the logarithm. A *logarithm* is the exponent that indicates the power to which a number (the base) is raised to produce a given number. In this section we look in more detail at the mathematics behind the logarithm. In Section 5.6 we show its use in a simple algorithm.

We begin with the formal definition and then follow with more intuitive viewpoints.

The *logarithm* of N (to the base 2) is the value X such that 2 raised to the power of X equals N. By default, the base of the logarithm is 2.

definition: For any $B, N > 0$, $\log_B N = K$ if $B^K = N$.

In this definition, B is the base of the logarithm. In computer science, when the base is omitted, it defaults to 2, which is natural for several reasons, as we show later in the chapter. We will prove one mathematical theorem, Theorem 5.4, to show that, as far as Big-Oh notation is concerned, the base is unimportant, and also to show how relations that involve logarithms can be derived.

Theorem 5.4

The base does not matter. For any constant $B > 1$, $\log_B N = O(\log N)$.

Proof

Let $\log_B N = K$. Then $B^K = N$. Let $C = \log B$. Then $2^C = B$. Thus $B^K = (2^C)^K = N$. Hence, we have $2^{CK} = N$, which implies that $\log N = CK = C \log_B N$. Therefore $\log_B N = (\log N)/(\log B)$, thus completing the proof.

In the rest of the text, we use base 2 logarithms exclusively. An important fact about the logarithm is that it grows slowly. Because $2^{10} = 1{,}024$, $\log 1{,}024 = 10$. Additional calculations show that the logarithm of 1,000,000 is roughly 20, and the logarithm of 1,000,000,000 is only 30. Consequently, performance of an $O(N \log N)$ algorithm is much closer to a linear $O(N)$ algorithm than to a quadratic $O(N^2)$ algorithm for even moderately large amounts of input. Before we look at a realistic algorithm whose running time includes the logarithm, let us look at a few examples of how the logarithm comes into play.

bits in a binary number

How many bits are required to represent N consecutive integers?

The number of bits required to represent numbers is logarithmic.

A 16-bit `short` integer represents the 65,536 integers in the range –32,768 to 32,767. In general, B bits are sufficient to represent 2^B different integers. Thus the number of bits B required to represent N consecutive integers satisfies the equation $2^B \geq N$. Hence, we obtain $B \geq \log N$, so the minimum number of bits is $\lceil \log N \rceil$. (Here $\lceil X \rceil$ is the ceiling function and represents the smallest integer that is at least as large as X. The corresponding floor function $\lfloor X \rfloor$ represents the largest integer that is at least as small as X.)

repeated doubling

Starting from $X = 1$, how many times should X be doubled before it is at least as large as N?

The *repeated doubling principle* holds that, starting at 1, we can repeatedly double only logarithmically many times until we reach N.

Suppose we start with \$1 and double it every year. How long would it take to save a million dollars? In this case, after 1 year we would have \$2; after 2 years, \$4; after 3 years, \$8 and so on. In general, after K years we would have 2^K dollars, so we want to find the smallest K satisfying $2^K \geq N$. This is the same equation as before, so $K = \lceil \log N \rceil$. After 20 years, we would have over a million dollars. The *repeated doubling principle* holds that, starting from 1, we can repeatedly double only $\lceil \log N \rceil$ times until we reach N.

repeated halving

Starting from $X = N$, if N is repeatedly halved, how many iterations must be applied to make N smaller than or equal to 1?

The *repeated halving principle* holds that, starting at N, we can halve only logarithmically many times. This process is used to obtain logarithmic routines for searching.

If the division rounds up to the nearest integer (or is real, not integer, division), we have the same problem as with repeated doubling, except that we are going in the opposite direction. Once again the answer is $\lceil \log N \rceil$ iterations. If the division rounds down, the answer is $\lfloor \log N \rfloor$. We can show the difference by starting with $X = 3$. Two divisions are necessary, unless the division rounds down, in which case only one is needed.

Many of the algorithms examined in this text will have logarithms, introduced because of the *repeated halving principle*, which holds that, starting at N, we can halve only logarithmically many times. In other words, an algorithm is $O(\log N)$ if it takes constant ($O(1)$) time to cut the problem size by a constant fraction (which is usually $\frac{1}{2}$). This condition follows directly from the fact that there will be $O(\log N)$ iterations of the loop. Any constant fraction will do because the fraction is reflected in the base of the logarithm, and Theorem 5.4 tells us that the base does not matter.

The Nth *harmonic number* is the sum of the reciprocals of the first N positive integers. The growth rate of the harmonic number is logarithmic.

All of the remaining occurrences of logarithms are introduced (either directly or indirectly) by applying Theorem 5.5. This theorem concerns the Nth *harmonic number*, which is the sum of the reciprocals of the first N positive integers, and states that the Nth harmonic number, H_N, satisfies

$H_N = \Theta(\log N)$. The proof uses calculus, but you do not need to understand the proof to use the theorem.

Theorem 5.5

Let $H_N = \sum_{i=1}^{N} 1/i$. Then $H_N = \Theta(\log N)$. A more precise estimate is $\ln N + 0.577$.

Proof

The intuition of the proof is that a discrete sum is well approximated by the (continuous) integral. The proof uses a construction to show that the sum H_N can be bounded above and below by $\int \frac{dx}{x}$, with appropriate limits. Details are left as Exercise 5.18.

The next section shows how the repeated halving principle leads to an efficient searching algorithm.

5.6 static searching problem

An important use of computers is looking up data. If the data are not allowed to change (e.g., it is stored on a CD-ROM), we say that the data are static. A *static search* accesses data that are never altered. The static searching problem is naturally formulated as follows.

static searching problem
Given an integer X and an array A, return the position of X in A or an indication that it is not present. If X occurs more than once, return any occurrence. The array A is never altered.

An example of static searching is looking up a person in the telephone book. The efficiency of a static searching algorithm depends on whether the array being searched is sorted. In the case of the telephone book, searching by name is fast, but searching by phone number is hopeless (for humans). In this section, we examine some solutions to the static searching problem.

5.6.1 sequential search

When the input array is not sorted, we have little choice but to do a linear *sequential search*, which steps through the array sequentially until a match is found. The complexity of the algorithm is analyzed in three ways. First, we provide the cost of an unsuccessful search. Then, we give the worst-case cost of a successful search. Finally, we find the average cost of a successful search.

A *sequential search* steps through the data sequentially until a match is found.

Analyzing successful and unsuccessful searches separately is typical. Unsuccessful searches usually are more time consuming than are successful searches (just think about the last time you lost something in your house). For sequential searching, the analysis is straightforward.

A sequential search is linear.

An unsuccessful search requires the examination of every item in the array, so the time will be $O(N)$. In the worst case, a successful search, too, requires the examination of every item in the array because we might not find a match until the last item. Thus the worst-case running time for a successful search is also linear. On average, however, we search only half of the array. That is, for every successful search in position i, there is a corresponding successful search in position $N - 1 - i$ (assuming we start numbering from 0). However, $N/2$ is still $O(N)$. As mentioned earlier in the chapter, all these Big-Oh terms should correctly be Big-Theta terms. However, the use of Big-Oh is more popular.

5.6.2 binary search

If the input array is sorted, we can use the *binary search*, which we perform from the middle of the array rather than the end.

If the input array has been sorted, we have an alternative to the sequential search, the *binary search*, which is performed from the middle of the array rather than the end. We keep track of `low` and `high`, which delimit the portion of the array in which an item, if present, must reside. Initially, the range is from 0 to $N - 1$. If `low` is larger than `high`, we know that the item is not present, so we return `NOT_FOUND`. Otherwise, we let `mid` be the halfway point of the range (rounding down if the range has an even number of elements) and compare the item we are searching for with the item in position `mid`. If we find a match, we are done and can return. If the item we are searching for is less than the item in position `mid`, then it must reside in the range `low` to `mid-1`. If it is greater, then it must reside in the range `mid+1` to `high`. In Figure 5.11, lines 17 to 20 alter the possible range, essentially cutting it in half. By the repeated halving principle, we know that the number of iterations will be $O(\log N)$.

The binary search is logarithmic because the search range is halved in each iteration.

For an unsuccessful search, the number of iterations in the loop is $\lfloor \log N \rfloor + 1$. The reason is that we halve the range in each iteration (rounding down if the range has an odd number of elements); we add 1 because the final range encompasses zero elements. For a successful search, the worst case is $\lfloor \log N \rfloor$ iterations because in the worst case we get down to a range of only one element. The average case is only one iteration better because half of the elements require the worst case for their search, a quarter of the elements save one iteration, and only one in 2^i elements will save i iterations from the worst case. The mathematics involves computing the weighted average by calculating the sum of a finite series. The bottom line, however, is that the running time for each search is $O(\log N)$. In Exercise 5.20, you are asked to complete the calculation.

```
/**
 * Performs the standard binary search
 * using two comparisons per level.
 * @return index where item is found, or NOT_FOUND.
 */
public static <AnyType extends Comparable<? super AnyType>>
              int binarySearch( AnyType [ ] a, AnyType x )
{
    int low = 0;
    int high = a.length - 1;
    int mid;

    while( low <= high )
    {
        mid = ( low + high ) / 2;

        if( a[ mid ].compareTo( x ) < 0 )
            low = mid + 1;
        else if( a[ mid ].compareTo( x ) > 0 )
            high = mid - 1;
        else
            return mid;
    }

    return NOT_FOUND;     // NOT_FOUND = -1
}
```

figure 5.11

Basic binary search that uses three-way comparisons

For reasonably large values of N, the binary search outperforms the sequential search. For instance, if N is 1,000, then on average a successful sequential search requires about 500 comparisons. The average binary search, using the previous formula, requires $\lfloor \log N \rfloor - 1$, or eight iterations for a successful search. Each iteration uses 1.5 comparisons on average (sometimes 1; other times, 2), so the total is 12 comparisons for a successful search. The binary search wins by even more in the worst case or when searches are unsuccessful.

Optimizing the binary search can cut the number of comparisons roughly in half.

If we want to make the binary search even faster, we need to make the inner loop tighter. A possible strategy is to remove the (implicit) test for a successful search from that inner loop and shrink the range down to one item in all cases. Then we can use a single test outside of the loop to determine if the item is in the array or cannot be found, as shown in Figure 5.12. If the item we are searching for in Figure 5.12 is not larger than the item in the `mid` position, then it is in the range that includes the `mid` position. When we break the loop, the subrange is 1, and we can test to see whether we have a match.

figure 5.12

Binary search using two-way comparisons

```
1   /**
2    * Performs the standard binary search
3    * using one comparison per level.
4    * @return index where item is found of NOT_FOUND.
5    */
6   public static <AnyType extends Comparable<? super AnyType>>
7                 int binarySearch( AnyType [ ] a, AnyType x )
8   {
9       if( a.length == 0 )
10          return NOT_FOUND;
11
12      int low = 0;
13      int high = a.length - 1;
14      int mid;
15
16      while( low < high )
17      {
18          mid = ( low + high ) / 2;
19
20          if( a[ mid ].compareTo( x ) < 0 )
21              low = mid + 1;
22          else
23              high = mid;
24      }
25
26      if( a[ low ].compareTo( x ) == 0 )
27          return low;
28
29      return NOT_FOUND;
30  }
```

In the revised algorithm, the number of iterations is always $\lfloor \log N \rfloor$ because we always shrink the range in half, possibly by rounding down. Thus, the number of comparisons used is always $\lfloor \log N \rfloor + 1$.

Binary search is surprisingly tricky to code. Exercise 5.6 illustrates some common errors.

Notice that for small N, such as values smaller than 6, the binary search might not be worth using. It uses roughly the same number of comparisons for a typical successful search, but it has the overhead of line 18 in each iteration. Indeed, the last few iterations of the binary search progress slowly. One can adopt a hybrid strategy in which the binary search loop terminates when the range is small and applies a sequential scan to finish. Similarly, people search a phone book nonsequentially. Once they have narrowed the range to a column, they perform a sequential scan. The scan of a telephone book is not sequential, but it also is not a binary search. Instead it is more like the algorithm discussed in the next section.

5.6.3 interpolation search

The binary search is very fast at searching a sorted static array. In fact, it is so fast that we would rarely use anything else. A static searching method that is sometimes faster, however, is an *interpolation search*, which has better Big-Oh performance on average than binary search but has limited practicality and a bad worst case. For an interpolation search to be practical, two assumptions must be satisfied:

1. Each access must be very expensive compared to a typical instruction. For example, the array might be on a disk instead of in memory, and each comparison requires a disk access.
2. The data must not only be sorted, it must also be fairly uniformly distributed. For example, a phone book is fairly uniformly distributed. If the input items are {1, 2, 4, 8, 16, … }, the distribution is not uniform.

These assumptions are quite restrictive, so you might never use an interpolation search. But it is interesting to see that there is more than one way to solve a problem and that no algorithm, not even the classic binary search, is the best in all situations.

The interpolation search requires that we spend more time to make an accurate guess regarding where the item might be. The binary search always uses the midpoint. However, searching for *Hank Aaron* in the middle of the phone book would be silly; somewhere near the start clearly would be more appropriate. Thus, instead of `mid`, we use `next` to indicate the next item that we will try to access.

Here's an example of what might work well. Suppose that the range contains 1,000 items, the low item in the range is 1,000, the high item in the range is 1,000,000, and we are searching for an item of value 12,000. If the items are uniformly distributed, then we expect to find a match somewhere near the twelfth item. The applicable formula is

$$next = low + \left\lceil \frac{x - a[low]}{a[high] - a[low]} \times (high - low - 1) \right\rceil$$

The subtraction of 1 is a technical adjustment that has been shown to perform well in practice. Clearly, this calculation is more costly than the binary search calculation. It involves an extra division (the division by 2 in the binary search is really just a bit shift, just as dividing by 10 is easy for humans), multiplication, and four subtractions. These calculations need to be done using floating-point operations. One iteration may be slower than the complete binary search. However, if the cost of these calculations is insignificant when compared to the cost of accessing an item, speed is immaterial; we care only about the number of iterations.

Interpolation search has a better Big-Oh bound on average than does binary search, but has limited practicality and a bad worst case.

In the worst case, where data is not uniformly distributed, the running time could be linear and every item might be examined. In Exercise 5.19 you are asked to construct such a case. However, if we assume that the items are reasonably distributed, as with a phone book, the average number of comparisons has been shown to be $O(\log\log N)$. In other words, we apply the logarithm twice in succession. For $N = 4$ billion, $\log N$ is about 32 and $\log\log N$ is roughly 5. Of course, there are some hidden constants in the Big-Oh notation, but the extra logarithm can lower the number of iterations considerably, so long as a bad case does not crop up. Proving the result rigorously, however, is quite complicated.

5.7 checking an algorithm analysis

Once we have performed an algorithm analysis, we want to determine whether it is correct and as good as we can possibly make it. One way to do this is to code the program and see if the empirically observed running time matches the running time predicted by the analysis.

When N increases by a factor of 10, the running time goes up by a factor of 10 for linear programs, 100 for quadratic programs, and 1,000 for cubic programs. Programs that run in $O(N \log N)$ take slightly more than 10 times as long to run under the same circumstances. These increases can be hard to spot if the lower-order terms have relatively large coefficients and N is not large enough. An example is the jump from $N = 10$ to $N = 100$ in the running time for the various implementations of the maximum contiguous subsequence sum problem. Differentiating linear programs from $O(N \log N)$ programs, based purely on empirical evidence, also can be very difficult.

Another commonly used trick to verify that some program is $O(F(N))$ is to compute the values $T(N)/F(N)$ for a range of N (usually spaced out by factors of 2), where $T(N)$ is the empirically observed running time. If $F(N)$ is a tight answer for the running time, then the computed values converge to a positive constant. If $F(N)$ is an overestimate, the values converge to zero. If $F(N)$ is an underestimate, and hence wrong, the values diverge.

As an example, suppose that we write a program to perform N random searches using the binary search algorithm. Since each search is logarithmic, we expect the total running time of the program to be $O(N \log N)$. Figure 5.13 shows the actual observed running time for the routine for various input sizes on a real (but extremely slow) computer. The last column is most likely the converging column and thus confirms our analysis, whereas the increasing numbers for T/N suggest that $O(N)$ is an underestimate, and the quickly decreasing values for T/N^2 suggest that $O(N^2)$ is an overestimate.

Note in particular that we do not have definitive convergence. One problem is that the clock that we used to time the program ticks only every 10 ms. Note also that there is not a great difference between $O(N)$ and $O(N \log N)$. Certainly an $O(N \log N)$ algorithm is much closer to being linear than being quadratic.

5.8 limitations of big-oh analysis

Big-Oh analysis is a very effective tool, but it does have limitations. As already mentioned, its use is not appropriate for small amounts of input. For small amounts of input, use the simplest algorithm. Also, for a particular algorithm, the constant implied by the Big-Oh may be too large to be practical. For example, if one algorithm's running time is governed by the formula $2N \log N$ and another has a running time of $1000N$, then the first algorithm would most likely be better, even though its growth rate is larger. Large constants can come into play when an algorithm is excessively complex. They also come into play because our analysis disregards constants and thus cannot differentiate between things like memory access (which is cheap) and disk access (which typically is many thousand times more expensive). Our analysis assumes infinite memory, but in applications involving large data sets, lack of sufficient memory can be a severe problem.

Worst-case is sometimes uncommon and can be safely ignored. At other times, it is very common and cannot be ignored.

Sometimes, even when constants and lower-order terms are considered, the analysis is shown empirically to be an overestimate. In this case, the analysis needs to be tightened (usually by a clever observation). Or the average-

N	CPU Time T (milliseconds)	T/N	T/N^2	$T/(N \log N)$
10,000	100	0.01000000	0.00000100	0.00075257
20,000	200	0.01000000	0.00000050	0.00069990
40,000	440	0.01100000	0.00000027	0.00071953
80,000	930	0.01162500	0.00000015	0.00071373
160,000	1,960	0.01225000	0.00000008	0.00070860
320,000	4,170	0.01303125	0.00000004	0.00071257
640,000	8,770	0.01370313	0.00000002	0.00071046

figure 5.13

Empirical running time for N binary searches in an N-item array

case running time bound may be significantly less than the worst-case running time bound, and so no improvement in the bound is possible. For many complicated algorithms the worst-case bound is achievable by some bad input, but in practice it is usually an overestimate. Two examples are the sorting algorithms Shellsort and quicksort (both described in Chapter 8).

Average-case analysis is almost always much more difficult than worst-case analysis.

However, worst-case bounds are usually easier to obtain than their average-case counterparts. For example, a mathematical analysis of the average-case running time of Shellsort has not been obtained. Sometimes, merely defining what *average* means is difficult. We use a worst-case analysis because it is expedient and also because, in most instances, the worst-case analysis is very meaningful. In the course of performing the analysis, we frequently can tell whether it will apply to the average case.

summary

In this chapter we introduced algorithm analysis and showed that algorithmic decisions generally influence the running time of a program much more than programming tricks do. We also showed the huge difference between the running times for quadratic and linear programs and illustrated that cubic algorithms are, for the most part, unsatisfactory. We examined an algorithm that could be viewed as the basis for our first data structure. The binary search efficiently supports static operations (i.e., searching but not updating), thereby providing a logarithmic worst-case search. Later in the text we examine dynamic data structures that efficiently support updates (both insertion and deletion).

In Chapter 6 we discuss some of the data structures and algorithms included in Java's Collections API. We also look at some applications of data structures and discuss their efficiency.

key concepts

average-case bound Measurement of running time as an average over all the possible inputs of size *N*. (179)

Big-Oh The notation used to capture the most dominant term in a function; it is similar to less than or equal to when growth rates are being considered. (166)

Big-Omega The notation similar to greater than or equal to when growth rates are being considered. (177)

Big-Theta The notation similar to equal to when growth rates are being considered. (177)

binary search The search method used if the input array has been sorted and is performed from the middle rather than the end. The binary search is logarithmic because the search range is halved in each iteration. (184)

harmonic numbers The Nth harmonic number is the sum of the reciprocals of the first N positive integers. The growth rate of the harmonic numbers is logarithmic. (182)

interpolation search A static searching algorithm that has better Big-Oh performance on average than binary search but has limited practicality and a bad worst case. (188)

linear time algorithm An algorithm that causes the running time to grow as $O(N)$. If the size of the input increases by a factor of f, then the running time also increases by a factor of f. It is the preferred running time for an algorithm. (180)

Little-Oh The notation similar to less than when growth rates are being considered. (178)

logarithm The exponent that indicates the power to which a number is raised to produce a given number. For example, the logarithm of N (to the base 2) is the value X such that 2 raised to the power of X equals N. (181)

repeated-doubling principle Holds that, starting at 1, repeated doubling can occur only logarithmically many times until we reach N. (182)

repeated-halving principle Holds that, starting at N, repeated halving can occur only logarithmically many times until we reach 1. This process is used to obtain logarithmic routines for searching. (182)

sequential search A linear search method that steps through an array until a match is found. (184)

static search Accesses data that is never altered. (183)

subquadratic An algorithm whose running time is strictly slower than quadratic, which can be written as $o(N^2)$. (178)

worst-case bound A guarantee over all inputs of some size. (178)

common errors

1. For nested loops, the total time is affected by the product of the loop sizes. For consecutive loops, it is not.
2. Do not just blindly count the number of loops. A pair of nested loops that each run from 1 to N^2 accounts for $O(N^4)$ time.
3. Do not write expressions such as $O(2N^2)$ or $O(N^2 + N)$. Only the dominant term, with the leading constant removed, is needed.

4. Use equalities with Big-Oh, Big-Omega, and so on. Writing that the running time is > $O(N^2)$ makes no sense because Big-Oh is an upper bound. Do not write that the running time is < $O(N^2)$; if the intention is to say that the running time is strictly less than quadratic, use Little-Oh notation.
5. Use Big-Omega, not Big-Oh, to express a lower bound.
6. Use the logarithm to describe the running time for a problem solved by halving its size in constant time. If it takes more than constant time to halve the problem, the logarithm does not apply.
7. The base (if it is a constant) of the logarithm is irrelevant for the purposes of Big-Oh. To include it is an error.

on the internet

The three maximum contiguous subsequence sum algorithms, as well as a fourth taken from Section 7.5, are available, along with a `main` that conducts the timing tests.

MaxSumTest.java Contains four algorithms for the maximum subsequence sum problem.

BinarySearch.java Contains the binary search shown in Figure 5.11. The code in Figure 5.12 is not provided, but a similar version that is part of the Collections API and is implemented in Figure 6.15 is in **Arrays.java** as part of `weiss.util`.

exercises

IN SHORT

5.1 Balls are drawn from a box as specified in Theorem 5.1 in the combinations given in (a) – (d). What are the corresponding values of i, j, and k?

a. Red, 5, 6
b. Blue, 5, 6
c. Blue, 3, Red
d. 6, 5, Red

5.2 Why isn't an implementation based solely on Theorem 5.2 sufficient to obtain a subquadratic running time for the maximum contiguous subsequence sum problem?

5.3 Suppose $T_1(N) = O(F(N))$ and $T_2(N) = O(F(N))$. Which of the following are true?

a. $T_1(N) + T_2(N) = O(F(N))$

b. $T_1(N) - T_2(N) = O(F(N))$

c. $T_1(N) / T_2(N) = O(1)$

d. $T_1(N) = O(T_2(N))$

5.4 Group the following into equivalent Big-Oh functions:

x^2, x, $x^2 + x$, $x^2 - x$, and $(x^3 / (x - 1))$.

5.5 Programs A and B are analyzed and are found to have worst-case running times no greater than $150N \log N$ and N^2, respectively. Answer the following questions, if possible.

a. Which program has the better guarantee on the running time for large values of N ($N > 10{,}000$)?

b. Which program has the better guarantee on the running time for small values of N ($N < 100$)?

c. Which program will run faster *on average* for $N = 1{,}000$?

d. Can program B run faster than program A on *all* possible inputs?

5.6 For the binary search routine in Figure 5.11, show the consequences of the following replacement code fragments:

a. Line 13: using the test `low < high`

b. Line 15: assigning `mid = low + high / 2`

c. Line 18: assigning `low = mid`

d. Line 20: assigning `high = mid`

IN THEORY

5.7 For the typical algorithms that you use to perform calculations by hand, determine the running time to

a. Add two N-digit integers

b. Multiply two N-digit integers

c. Divide two N-digit integers

5.8 In terms of N, what is the running time of the following algorithm to compute X^N:

```
public static double power( double x, int n )
{
    double result = 1.0;

    for( int i = 0; i < n; i++ )
        result *= x;
    return result;
}
```

5.9 Directly evaluate the triple summation that precedes Theorem 5.1. Verify that the answers are identical.

5.10 For the quadratic algorithm for the maximum contiguous subsequence sum problem, determine precisely how many times the innermost statement is executed.

5.11 An algorithm takes 0.5 ms for input size 100. How long will it take for input size 500 (assuming that low-order terms are negligible) if the running time is
a. linear
b. $O(N \log N)$
c. quadratic
d. cubic

5.12 An algorithm takes 0.5 ms for input size 100. How large a problem can be solved in 1 minute (assuming that low-order terms are negligible) if the running time is
a. linear
b. $O(N \log N)$
c. quadratic
d. cubic

5.13 Complete Figure 5.10 with estimates for the running times that were too long to simulate. Interpolate the running times for all four algorithms and estimate the time required to compute the maximum contiguous subsequence sum of 10,000,000 numbers. What assumptions have you made?

5.14 Order the following functions by growth rate: N, $\sqrt{N}$, $N^{1.5}$, N^2, $N \log N$, $N \log\log N$, $N \log^2 N$, $N \log(N^2)$, $2/N$, 2^N, $2^{N/2}$, 37, N^3, and $N^2 \log N$. Indicate which functions grow at the same rate.

5.15 For each of the following program fragments, do the following:
a. Give a Big-Oh analysis of the running time.
b. Implement the code and run for several values of N.
c. Compare your analysis with the actual running times.

```
// Fragment 1
for( int i = 0; i < n; i++ )
    sum++;

// Fragment 2
for( int i = 0; i < n; i += 2 )
    sum++;
```

```
// Fragment 3
for( int i = 0; i < n; i++ )
    for( int j = 0; j < n; j++ )
        sum++;

// Fragment 4
for( int i = 0; i < n; i++ )
    sum++;
for( int j = 0; j < n; j++ )
    sum++;

// Fragment 5
for( int i = 0; i < n; i++ )
    for( int j = 0; j < n * n; j++ )
        sum++;

// Fragment 6
for( int i = 0; i < n; i++ )
    for( int j = 0; j < i; j++ )
        sum++;

// Fragment 7
for( int i = 0; i < n; i++ )
    for( int j = 0; j < n * n; j++ )
        for( int k = 0; k < j; k++ )
            sum++;

// Fragment 8
for( int i = 1; i < n; i = i * 2 )
    sum++;
```

5.16 Occasionally, multiplying the sizes of nested loops can give an overestimate for the Big-Oh running time. This result happens when an innermost loop is infrequently executed. Repeat Exercise 5.15 for the following program fragment:

```
for( int i = 1; i <= n; i++ )
    for( int j = 1; j <= i * i; j++ )
        if( j % i == 0 )
            for( int k = 0; k < j; k++ )
                sum++;
```

5.17 In a court case, a judge cited a city for contempt and ordered a fine of \$2 for the first day. Each subsequent day, until the city followed the judge's order, the fine was squared (that is, the fine progressed as follows: \$2, \$4, \$16, \$256, \$65536, . . .).

a. What would be the fine on day N?

b. How many days would it take for the fine to reach D dollars (a Big-Oh answer will do)?

5.18 Prove Theorem 5.5. *Hint*: Show that $\sum_2^N \frac{1}{i} < \int_1^N \frac{dx}{x}$. Then show a similar lower bound.

5.19 Construct an example whereby an interpolation search examines every element in the input array.

5.20 Analyze the cost of an average successful search for the binary search algorithm in Figure 5.11.

5.21 Consider the following method, whose implementation is shown:

```
// Precondition: m represents matrix with N rows, N columns
//               in each row, elements are increasing
//               in each column, elements are increasing
// Postcondition: returns true if some element in m stores val;
//                returns false otherwise
public static boolean contains( int [ ] [ ] m, int val )
{
    int N = m.length;

    for( int r = 0; r < N; r++ )
        for( int c = 0; c < N; c++ )
            if( m[ r ][ c ] == val )
                return true;
    return false;
}
```

An example of a matrix that satisfies the stated precondition is

```
int [ ] [ ] m1 = {  { 4, 6, 8 },
                    { 5, 9, 11 },
                    { 7, 11, 14 } };
```

a. What is the running time of `contains`?
b. Suppose it takes 4 seconds to run `contains` on a 100-by-100 matrix. Assuming that low-order terms are negligible, how long will it take to run `contains` on a 400-by-400 matrix?
c. Suppose `contains` is rewritten so that the algorithm performs a binary search on each row, returning true if any of the row-searches succeed, and false otherwise. What is the running time of this revised version of `contains`?

5.22 Method `hasTwoTrueValues` returns true if at least two values in an array of Booleans are true. Provide the Big-Oh running time for all three implementations proposed.

```
// Version 1
public boolean hasTwoTrueValues( boolean [ ] arr )
{
    int count = 0;

    for( int i = 0; i < arr.length; i++ )
        if( arr[ i ] )
            count++;

    return count >= 2;
}

// Version 2
public boolean hasTwoTrueValues( boolean [ ] arr )
{
    for( int i = 0; i < arr.length; i++ )
        for( int j = i + 1; j < arr.length; j++ )
            if( arr[ i ] && arr[ j ] )
                return true;

    return false;
}

// Version 3
public boolean hasTwoTrueValues( boolean [ ] arr )
{
    for( int i = 0; i < arr.length; i++ )
        if( arr[ i ] )
            for( int j = i + 1; j < arr.length; j++ )
                if( arr[ j ] )
                    return true;

    return false;
}
```

IN PRACTICE

5.23 Give an efficient algorithm to determine whether an integer i exists such that $A_i = i$ in an array of increasing integers. What is the running time of your algorithm?

5.24 A prime number has no factors besides 1 and itself. Do the following:

a. Write a program to determine if a positive integer N is prime. In terms of N, what is the worst-case running time of your program?

b. Let B equal the number of bits in the binary representation of N. What is the value of B?

c. In terms of B, what is the worst-case running time of your program?

d. Compare the running times to determine if a 20-bit number and a 40-bit number are prime.

5.25 An important problem in numerical analysis is to find a solution to the equation $F(X) = 0$ for some arbitrary F. If the function is continuous and has two points *low* and *high* such that $F(low)$ and $F(high)$ have opposite signs, then a root must exist between *low* and *high* and can be found by either a binary search or an interpolation search. Write a function that takes as parameters F, *low*, and *high* and solves for a zero. What must you do to ensure termination?

5.26 A majority element in an array A of size N is an element that appears more than $N/2$ times (thus there is at most one such element). For example, the array

3, 3, 4, 2, 4, 4, 2, 4, 4

has a majority element (4), whereas the array

3, 3, 4, 2, 4, 4, 2, 4

does not. Give an algorithm to find a majority element if one exists, or reports that one does not. What is the running time of your algorithm? (*Hint*: There is an $O(N)$ solution.)

5.27 The input is an $N \times N$ matrix of numbers that is already in memory. Each individual row is increasing from left to right. Each individual column is increasing from top to bottom. Give an $O(N)$ worst-case algorithm that decides if a number X is in the matrix.

5.28 Design efficient algorithms that take an array of positive numbers `a`, and determine

a. The maximum value of `a[j]+a[i]`, for `j` ≥ `i`
b. The maximum value of `a[j]-a[i]`, for `j` ≥ `i`
c. The maximum value of `a[j]*a[i]`, for `j` ≥ `i`
d. The maximum value of `a[j]/a[i]`, for `j` ≥ `i`

PROGRAMMING PROJECTS

5.29 The Sieve of Eratosthenes is a method used to compute all primes less than N. Begin by making a table of integers 2 to N. Find the smallest integer, i, that is not crossed out. Then print i and cross out i, $2i$, $3i$, ... When $i > \sqrt{N}$, the algorithm terminates. The running time has been shown to be $O(N \log\log N)$. Write a program to implement the Sieve and verify the running time claim. How difficult is it to differentiate the running time from $O(N)$ and $O(N \log N)$?

5.30 The equation $A^5 + B^5 + C^5 + D^5 + E^5 = F^5$ has exactly one integral solution that satisfies $0 < A \le B \le C \le D \le E \le F \le 75$. Write a program to find the solution. *Hint:* First, precompute all values of X^5

and store them in an array. Then, for each tuple (A, B, C, D, E), you only need to verify that some F exists in the array. (There are several ways to check for F, one of which is to use a binary search to check for F. Other methods might prove to be more efficient.)

5.31 Implement the maximum contiguous subsequence sum algorithms to obtain data equivalent to the data in Figure 5.10. Compile the programs with the highest optimization settings.

references

The maximum contiguous subsequence sum problem is from [5]. References [4], [5], and [6] show how to optimize programs for speed. Interpolation search was first suggested in [14] and was analyzed in [13]. References [1], [8], and [17] provide a more rigorous treatment of algorithm analysis. The three-part series [10], [11], and [12], newly updated, remains the foremost reference work on the topic. The mathematical background required for more advanced algorithm analysis is provided by [2], [3], [7], [15], and [16]. An especially good book for advanced analysis is [9].

1. A. V. Aho, J. E. Hopcroft, and J. D. Ullman, *The Design and Analysis of Computer Algorithms*, Addison-Wesley, Reading, MA, 1974.
2. M. O. Albertson and J. P. Hutchinson, *Discrete Mathematics with Algorithms*, John Wiley & Sons, New York, 1988.
3. Z. Bavel, *Math Companion for Computer Science*, Reston Publishing Company, Reston, VA, 1982.
4. J. L. Bentley, *Writing Efficient Programs*, Prentice-Hall, Englewood Cliffs, NJ, 1982.
5. J. L. Bentley, *Programming Pearls*, Addison-Wesley, Reading, MA, 1986.
6. J. L. Bentley, *More Programming Pearls*, Addison-Wesley, Reading, MA, 1988.
7. R. A. Brualdi, *Introductory Combinatorics*, North-Holland, New York, 1977.
8. T. H. Cormen, C. E. Leiserson, R. L. Rivest, and C. Stein, *Introduction to Algorithms*, 2d ed., MIT Press, Cambridge, MA, 2002.
9. R. L. Graham, D. E. Knuth, and O. Patashnik, *Concrete Mathematics*, Addison-Wesley, Reading, MA, 1989.
10. D. E. Knuth, *The Art of Computer Programming, Vol. 1: Fundamental Algorithms*, 3d ed., Addison-Wesley, Reading, MA, 1997.

11. D. E. Knuth, *The Art of Computer Programming, Vol. 2: Seminumerical Algorithms,* 3d ed., Addison-Wesley, Reading, MA, 1997.

12. D. E. Knuth, *The Art of Computer Programming, Vol. 3: Sorting and Searching*, 2d ed., Addison-Wesley, Reading, MA, 1998.

13. Y. Pearl, A. Itai, and H. Avni, "Interpolation Search – A log log *N* Search," *Communications of the ACM* **21** (1978), 550–554.

14. W. W. Peterson, "Addressing for Random Storage," *IBM Journal of Research and Development* **1** (1957), 131–132.

15. F. S. Roberts, *Applied Combinatorics*, Prentice Hall, Englewood Cliffs, NJ, 1984.

16. A. Tucker, *Applied Combinatorics*, 2d ed., John Wiley & Sons, New York, 1984.

17. M. A. Weiss, *Data Structures and Algorithm Analysis in Java*, Addison-Wesley, Reading, MA, 1999.

chapter 6

the collections api

Many algorithms require the use of a proper representation of data to achieve efficiency. This representation and the operations that are allowed for it are known as a *data structure*. Each data structure allows arbitrary insertion but differs in how it allows access to members in the group. Some data structures allow arbitrary access and deletions, whereas others impose restrictions, such as allowing access to only the most recently or least recently inserted item in the group.

As part of Java, a supporting library known as the *Collections API* is provided. Most of the Collections API resides in `java.util`. This API provides a collection of data structures. It also provides some generic algorithms, such as sorting. The Collections API makes heavy use of inheritance.

Our primary goal is to describe, in general terms, some examples and applications of data structures. Our secondary goal is to describe the basics of the Collections API, so that we can use it in Part Three. We do not discuss the theory behind an efficient Collections API implementation until Part Four, at which point we provide simplified implementations of some core Collections API components. But delaying the discussion of the Collections API's implementation until after we use it is not a problem. We do not need to know *how* something is implemented so long as we know that it *is* implemented.

In this chapter, we show

- Common data structures, their allowed operations, and their running times
- Some applications of the data structures
- The organization of the Collections API, and its integration with the rest of the language

6.1 introduction

A *data structure* is a representation of data and the operations allowed on that data.

Data structures allow us to achieve an important object-oriented programming goal: component reuse. The data structures described in this section (and implemented later, in Part Four) have recurring uses. When each data structure has been implemented once, it can be used over and over in various applications.

A *data structure* is a representation of data and the operations allowed on that data. Many, but by no means all, of the common data structures store a collection of objects and then provide methods to add a new object to, remove an existing object from, or access a contained object in the collection.

Data structures allow us to achieve component reuse.

In this chapter, we examine some of the fundamental data structures and their applications. Using a high-level protocol, we describe typical operations that are usually supported by the data structures and briefly describe their uses. When possible, we give an estimate of the cost of implementing these operations efficiently. This estimate is often based on analogy with non-computer applications of the data structure. Our high-level protocol usually supports only a core set of basic operations. Later, when describing the basics of how the data structures can be implemented (in general there are multiple competing ideas), we can more easily focus on language-independent algorithmic details if we restrict the set of operations to a minimum core set.

As an example, Figure 6.1 illustrates a generic protocol that many data structures tend to follow. We do not actually use this protocol directly in any code. However, an inheritance-based hierarchy of data structures could use this class as a starting point.

The Collections API is the one library for data structures and algorithms that is guaranteed to be available.

Then we give a description of the Collections API interface that is provided for these data structures. By no means does the Collections API represent the best way of doing things. However, it represents the one library for data structures and algorithms guaranteed to be available. Its use also illustrates some of the core issues that must be dealt with once the theory is taken care of.

We defer consideration of efficient implementation of data structures to Part IV. At that point we will provide, as part of package `weiss.nonstandard`, some com-

```
package weiss.nonstandard;

// SimpleContainer protocol
public interface SimpleContainer<AnyType>
{
    void insert( AnyType x );
    void remove( AnyType x );
    AnyType find( AnyType x );

    boolean isEmpty( );
    void makeEmpty( );
}
```

figure 6.1

A generic protocol for many data structures

peting implementations for data structures that follow the simple protocols developed in this chapter. We will also provide one implementation for the basic Collections API components described in the chapter, in package `weiss.util`. Thus we are separating the interface of the Collections API (that is, what it does, which we describe in the chapter) from its implementation (that is, how it is done, which we describe in Part Four). This approach—the separation of the interface and implementation—is part of the object-oriented paradigm. The user of the data structure needs to see only the available operations, not the implementation. Recall this is the encapsulation and information-hiding part of object-oriented programming.

The rest of this chapter is organized as follows: First, we discuss the basics of the *iterator pattern*, which is used throughout the Collections API. Then we discuss the interface for containers and iterators in the Collections API. Next we describe some Collections API algorithms, and finally, we examine some other data structures many of which are supported in the Collections API.

6.2 the iterator pattern

The Collections API makes heavy use of a common technique known as the *iterator pattern*. So before we begin our discussion of the Collections API, we examine the ideas behind the iterator pattern.

An *iterator* object controls iteration of a collection.

Consider the problem of printing the elements in a collection. Typically, the collection is an array, so assuming that the object `v` is an array, its contents are easily printed with code like the following:[1]

1. The enhanced `for` loop added in Java 5 is simply additional syntax. The compiler expands the enhanced `for` loop to obtain the code shown here.

```
for( int i = 0; i < v.length; i++ )
    System.out.println( v[ i ] );
```

In this loop, `i` is an *iterator* object, because it is the object that is used to control the iteration. However, using the integer `i` as an iterator constrains the design: We can only store the collection in an array-like structure. A more flexible alternative is to design an iterator class that encapsulates a position inside of a collection. The iterator class provides methods to step through the collection.

When we program to an interface, we write code that uses the most abstract methods. These methods will be applied to the actual concrete types.

The key is the concept of programming to an interface: We want the code that performs access of the container to be as independent of the type of the container as possible. This is done by using only methods that are common to all containers and their iterators.

There are many different possible iterator designs. If we replace `int i` with `IteratorType itr`, then the loop on page 204 expresses

```
for( itr = v.first( ); itr.isValid( ); itr.advance( ) )
    System.out.println( itr.getData( ) );
```

This suggests an iterator class that contains methods such as `isValid`, `advance`, `getData`, and so on.

We describe two designs, outside the Collections API context, that lead to the Collections API iterator design. We discuss the specifics of the Collections iterators in Section 6.3.2, deferring implementations to Part IV.

6.2.1 basic iterator design

`iterator` returns an appropriate iterator for the collection.

The first iterator design uses only three methods. The container class is required to provide an `iterator` method. `iterator` returns an appropriate iterator for the collection. The iterator class has only two methods, `hasNext` and `next`. `hasNext` returns `true` if the iteration has not yet been exhausted. `next` returns the next item in the collection (and in the process, advances the current position). This iterator interface is similar to the interface provided in the Collections API.

To illustrate the implementation of this design, we outline the collection class and provide an iterator class, `MyContainer` and `MyContainerIterator`, respectively. Their use is shown in Figure 6.2. The data members and `iterator` method for `MyContainer` are written in Figure 6.3. To simplify matters, we omit the constructors, and methods such as `add`, `size`, etc. The `ArrayList` class from earlier chapters can be reused to provide an implementation of these methods. We also avoid use of generics for now.

```java
    public static void main( String [ ] args )
    {
        MyContainer v = new MyContainer( );

        v.add( "3" );
        v.add( "2" );

        System.out.println( "Container contents: " );
        MyContainerIterator itr = v.iterator( );
        while( itr.hasNext( ) )
            System.out.println( itr.next( ) );
    }
```

figure 6.2

A `main` method, to illustrate iterator design 1

```java
package weiss.ds;

public class MyContainer
{
    Object [ ] items;
    int size;

    public MyContainerIterator iterator( )
      { return new MyContainerIterator( this ); }

    // Other methods
}
```

figure 6.3

The `MyContainer` class, design 1

The `iterator` method in class `MyContainer` simply returns a new iterator; notice that the iterator must have information about the container that it is iterating over. Thus the iterator is constructed with a reference to the `MyContainer`.

The iterator is constructed with a reference to the container that it iterates over.

Figure 6.4 shows the `MyContainerIterator`. The iterator keeps a variable (`current`) that represents the current position in the container, and a reference to the container. The implementation of the constructor and two methods is straightforward. The constructor initializes the container reference, `hasNext` simply compares the current position with the container size, and `next` uses the current position to index the array (and then advances the current position).

A limitation of this iterator design is the relatively limited interface. Observe that it is impossible to reset the iterator back to the beginning, and that the `next` method couples access of an item with advancing. The `next`, `hasNext` design is what is used in the Java Collections API; many people feel that the API should have provided a more flexible iterator. It is certainly possible to put more function-

The better design would put more functionality in the iterator.

figure 6.4

Implementation of the `MyContainerIterator`, design 1

```
// An iterator class that steps through a MyContainer.

package weiss.ds;

public class MyContainerIterator
{
    private int current = 0;
    private MyContainer container;

    MyContainerIterator( MyContainer c )
      { container = c; }

    public boolean hasNext( )
      { return current < container.size; }

    public Object next( )
      { return container.items[ current++ ]; }
}
```

ality in the iterator, while leaving the `MyContainer` class implementation completely unchanged. On the other hand, doing so illustrates no new principles.

Note that in the implementation of `MyContainer`, the data members `items` and `size` are package visible, rather than being private. This unfortunate relaxation of the usual privacy of data members is necessary because these data members need to be accessed by `MyContainerIterator`. Similarly, the `MyContainerIterator` constructor is package visible, so that it can be called by `MyContainer`.

6.2.2 inheritance-based iterators and factories

The iterator designed so far manages to abstract the concept of iteration into an iterator class. This is good, because it means that if the collection changes from an array-based collection to something else, the basic code such as lines 10 and 11 in Figure 6.2 does not need to change.

While this is a significant improvement, changes from an array-based collection to something else require that we change all the declarations of the iterator. For instance, in Figure 6.2, we would need to change line 9. We discuss an alternative in this section.

An inheritance-based iteration scheme defines an iterator interface. Clients program to this interface.

Our basic idea is to define an interface `Iterator`. Corresponding to each different kind of container is an iterator that implements the `Iterator` protocol. In our example, this gives three classes: `MyContainer`, `Iterator`, and `MyContainerIterator`. The relationship that holds is `MyContainerIterator` *IS-A* `Iterator`. The reason we do this is that each container can now create an appropriate iterator, but pass it back as an abstract `Iterator`.

Figure 6.5 shows `MyContainer`. In the revised `MyContainer`, the `iterator` method returns a reference to an `Iterator` object; the actual type turns out to be a `MyContainerIterator`. Since `MyContainerIterator` *IS-A* `Iterator`, this is safe to do.

Because `iterator` creates and returns a new `Iterator` object, whose actual type is unknown, it is commonly known as a *factory method*. The iterator interface, which serves simply to establish the protocol by which all subclasses of `Iterator` can be accessed, is shown in Figure 6.6. There are only two changes to the implementation of `MyContainerIterator`, shown in Figure 6.7 and both changes are at line 5. First, the `implements` clause has been added. Second, `MyContainerIterator` no longer needs to be a public class.

A *factory method* creates a new concrete instance but returns it using a reference to the interface type.

Figure 6.8 demonstrates how the inheritance-based iterators are used. At line 9, we see the declaration of `itr`: It is now a reference to an `Iterator`. Nowhere in `main` is there any mention of the actual `MyContainerIterator` type. The fact that a `MyContainerIterator` exists is not used by any clients of the `MyContainer` class. This is a very slick design and illustrates nicely the idea of hiding an implementation and *programming to an interface*. The implementation can be made even slicker by use of nested classes, and a Java feature known as *inner classes*. Those implementation details are deferred until Chapter 15.

Nowhere in `main` is there any mention of the actual iterator type.

```
package weiss.ds;

public class MyContainer
{
    Object [ ] items;
    int size;

    public Iterator iterator( )
      { return new MyContainerIterator( this ); }

    // Other methods not shown.
}
```

figure 6.5

The `MyContainer` class, design 2

```
package weiss.ds;

public interface Iterator
{
    boolean hasNext( );
    Object next( );
}
```

figure 6.6

The `Iterator` interface, design 2

figure 6.7

Implementation of the `MyContainerIterator`, design 2

```
// An iterator class that steps through a MyContainer.

package weiss.ds;

class MyContainerIterator implements Iterator
{
    private int current = 0;
    private MyContainer container;

    MyContainerIterator( MyContainer c )
      { container = c; }

    public boolean hasNext( )
      { return current < container.size; }

    public Object next( )
      { return container.items[ current++ ]; }
}
```

figure 6.8

A `main` method, to illustrate iterator design 2

```
    public static void main( String [ ] args )
    {
        MyContainer v = new MyContainer( );

        v.add( "3" );
        v.add( "2" );

        System.out.println( "Container contents: " );
        Iterator itr = v.iterator( );
        while( itr.hasNext( ) )
            System.out.println( itr.next( ) );
    }
```

6.3 collections api: containers and iterators

This section describes the basics of the Collections API iterators and how they interact with containers. We know that an iterator is an object that is used to traverse a collection of objects. In the Collections API such a collection is abstracted by the `Collection` interface, and the iterator is abstracted by the `Iterator` interface.

The Collections API iterators are somewhat inflexible, in that they provide few operations. These iterators use an inheritance model described in Section 6.2.2.

6.3.1 the Collection interface

The Collection interface represents a group of objects, known as its *elements*. Some implementations, such as lists, are unordered; others, such as sets and maps, may be ordered. Some implementations allow duplicates; others do not. Starting with Java 5, the Collection interface and the entire Collections API make use of generics. All containers support the following operations.

The Collection interface represents a group of objects, known as its *elements*.

boolean isEmpty( )

Returns true if the container contains no elements and false otherwise.

int size( )

Returns the number of elements in the container.

boolean add(AnyType x)

Adds item x to the container. Returns true if this operation succeeds and false otherwise (e.g., if the container does not allow duplicates and x is already in the container).

boolean contains(Object x)

Returns true if x is in the container and false otherwise.

boolean remove(Object x)

Removes item x from the container. Returns true if x was removed and false otherwise.

void clear( )

Makes the container empty.

Object [ ] toArray( )
<OtherType> OtherType [ ] toArray (OtherType [ ] arr)

Returns an array that contains references to all items in the container.

java.util.Iterator<AnyType> iterator( )

Returns an Iterator that can be used to begin traversing all locations in the container.

Because Collection is generic, it allows objects of only a specific type (AnyType) to be in the collection. Thus, the parameter to add is AnyType. The parameter to contains and remove should be AnyType also; however, for backward compatibility it is Object. Certainly, if contains or remove are called with a parameter that is not of type AnyType, the return value will be false.

The method toArray returns an array that contains references to the items that are in the collection. In some cases, it can be faster to manipulate this array than to use an iterator to manipulate the collection; however, the cost of doing so is extra space. The most common place where using the array would be useful is when the collection is being accessed several times or via nested loops. If the array is being accessed only once, sequentially, it is unlikely that using toArray will make things faster; it can make things slower while also costing extra space.

One version of toArray returns the array in a type that is Object[]. The other version allows the user to specify the exact type of the array by passing a parameter containing the array (thus avoiding the costs of casting during the subsequent manipulation). If the array is not large enough, a sufficiently large array is returned instead; however, this should never be needed. The following snippet shows how to obtain an array from a Collection<String> coll:

```
String [ ] theStrings = new String[ coll.size( ) ];
coll.toArray( theStrings );
```

At this point, the array can be manipulated via normal array indexing. The one-parameter version of toArray is generally the one that you would want to use because the runtime costs of casting are avoided.

Finally, the iterator method returns an Iterator<AnyType>, which can be used to traverse the collection.

Figure 6.9 illustrates a specification of the Collection interface. The actual Collection interface in java.util contains some additional methods, but we will be content with this subset. By convention, all implementations supply both a zero-parameter constructor that creates an empty collection and a constructor that creates a collection that refers to the same elements as another collection. This is basically a shallow-copy of a collection. However, there is no syntax in the language that forces the implementation of these constructors.

The Collection interface extends Iterable, which means that the enhanced for loop can be applied to it. Recall that the Iterable interface requires the implementation of an iterator method that returns a java.util.Iterator. The compiler will expand the enhanced for loop with appropriate calls to methods in java.util.Iterator. At line 41, we see the iterator method required by the Iterable interface. However, we remark that we are taking advantage of covariant return types (Section 4.8), because the return type for the iterator method at line 41 is actually weiss.util.Iterator, which is our own class that extends java.util.Iterator, and is shown in Section 6.3.2.

The Collections API also codifies the notion of an *optional interface method*. For instance, suppose we want an immutable collection: Once it is constructed, its state should never change. An immutable collection appears incompatible with Collection, since add and remove do not make sense for immutable collections.

```
package weiss.util;

/**
 * Collection interface; the root of all 1.5 collections.
 */
public interface Collection<AnyType> extends Iterable<AnyType>, java.io.Serializable
{
    /**
     * Returns the number of items in this collection.
     */
    int size( );

    /**
     * Tests if this collection is empty.
     */
    boolean isEmpty( );

    /**
     * Tests if some item is in this collection.
     */
    boolean contains( Object x );

    /**
     * Adds an item to this collection.
     */
    boolean add( AnyType x );

    /**
     * Removes an item from this collection.
     */
    boolean remove( Object x );

    /**
     * Change the size of this collection to zero.
     */
    void clear( );

    /**
     * Obtains an Iterator object used to traverse the collection.
     */
    Iterator<AnyType> iterator( );

    /**
     * Obtains a primitive array view of the collection.
     */
    Object [ ] toArray( );

    /**
     * Obtains a primitive array view of the collection.
     */
    <OtherType> OtherType [ ] toArray( OtherType [ ] arr );
}
```

figure 6.9

A sample specification of the `Collection` interface

However, there is an existing loophole: Although the implementor of the immutable collection must implement `add` and `remove`, there is no rule that says these methods must do anything. Instead, the implementor can simply throw a run-time `UnsupportedOperationException`. In doing so, the implementor has technically implemented the interface, while not really providing `add` and `remove`.

By convention, interface methods that document that they are *optional* can be implemented in this manner. If the implementation chooses not to implement an optional method, then it should document that fact. It is up to the client user of the API to verify that the method is implemented by consulting the documentation, and if the client ignores the documentation and calls the method anyway, the run-time `UnsupportedOperationException` is thrown, signifying a programming error.

Optional methods are somewhat controversial, but they do not represent any new language additions. They are simply a convention.

We will eventually implement all methods. The most interesting of these methods is `iterator`, which is a factory method that creates and returns an `Iterator` object. The operations that can be performed by an `Iterator` are described in Section 6.3.2.

6.3.2 `Iterator` interface

An *iterator* is an object that allows us to iterate through all objects in a collection.

As described in Section 6.2, an *iterator* is an object that allows us to iterate through all objects in a collection. The technique of using an iterator class was discussed in the context of read-only vectors in Section 6.2.

The `Iterator` interface in the Collections API is small and contains only three methods:

`boolean hasNext( )`

Returns `true` if there are more items to view in this iteration.

`AnyType next( )`

Returns a reference to the next object not yet seen by this iterator. The object becomes seen, and thus advances the iterator.

`void remove( )`

Removes the last item viewed by `next`. This can be called only once between calls to `next`.

The `Iterator` interface contains only three methods: `next`, `hasNext`, and `remove`.

Each collection defines its own implementation of the `Iterator` interface, in a class that is invisible to users of the `java.util` package.

The iterators also expect a stable container. An important problem that occurs in the design of containers and iterators is to decide what happens if the state of a container is modified while an iteration is in progress. The Collections

API takes a strict view: Any external structural modification of the container (adds, removes, and so on) will result in a `ConcurrentModificationException` by the iterator methods when one of the methods is called. In other words, if we have an iterator, and then an object is added to the container, and then we invoke the `next` method on the iterator, the iterator will detect that it is now invalid, and an exception will be thrown by `next`.

The `Iterator` methods throw an exception if its container has been structurally modified.

This means that it is impossible to remove an object from a container when we have seen it via an iterator, without invalidating the iterator. This is one reason why there is a `remove` method in the iterator class. Calling the iterator `remove` causes the last seen object to be removed from the container. It invalidates all other iterators that are viewing this container, but not the iterator that performed the `remove`. It is also likely to be more efficient than the container's `remove` method, at least for some collections. However, `remove` cannot be called twice in a row. Furthermore, `remove` preserves the semantics of `next` and `hasNext`, because the next unseen item in the iteration remains the same. This version of `remove` is listed as an optional method, so the programmer needs to check that it is implemented. The design of `remove` has been criticized as poor, but we will use it at one point in the text.

Figure 6.10 provides a sample specification of the `Iterator` interface. (Our iterator class extends the standard `java.util` version in order to allow

```
package weiss.util;

/**
 * Iterator interface.
 */
public interface Iterator<AnyType> extends java.util.Iterator<AnyType>
{
    /**
     * Tests if there are items not yet iterated over.
     */
    boolean hasNext( );

    /**
     * Obtains the next (as yet unseen) item in the collection.
     */
    AnyType next( );

    /**
     * Remove the last item returned by next.
     * Can only be called once after next.
     */
    void remove( );
}
```

figure 6.10

A sample specification of `Iterator`

figure 6.11

Print the contents of any `Collection`.

```
// Print the contents of Collection c (using iterator directly)
public static <AnyType> void printCollection( Collection<AnyType> c )
{
    Iterator<AnyType> itr = c.iterator( );
    while( itr.hasNext( ) )
        System.out.print( itr.next( ) + " " );
    System.out.println( );
}

// Print the contents of Collection c (using enhanced for loop)
public static <AnyType> void printCollection( Collection<AnyType> c )
{
    for( AnyType val : c )
        System.out.print( val + " " );
    System.out.println( );
}
```

the enhanced `for` loop to work.) As an example of using the `Iterator`, the routines in Figure 6.11 print each element in any container. If the container is an ordered set, its elements are output in sorted order. The first implementation uses an iterator directly, and the second implementation uses an enhanced `for` loop. The enhanced `for` loop is simply a compiler substitution. The compiler, in effect, generates the first version (with `java.util.Iterator`) from the second.

6.4 generic algorithms

The `Collections` class contains a set of static methods that operate on `Collection` objects.

The Collections API provides a few general purpose algorithms that operate on all of the containers. These are static methods in the `Collections` class (note that this is a different class than the `Collection` interface). There are also some static methods in the `Arrays` class that manipulate arrays (sorting, searching, etc.). Most of those methods are overloaded—a generic version, and once for each of the primitive types (except `boolean`).

We examine only a few of the algorithms, with the intention of showing the general ideas that pervade the Collections API, while documenting the specific algorithms that will be used in Part Three.

The material in Section 4.8 is an essential prerequisite to this section.

Some of the algorithms make use of function objects. Consequently, the material in Section 4.8 is an essential prerequisite to this section.

6.4.1 `Comparator` function objects

Many Collections API classes and routines require the ability to order objects. There are two ways to do this. One possibility is that the objects implement the `Comparable` interface and provide a `compareTo` method. The other possibility is that the comparison function is embedded as the `compare` method in an object that implements the `Comparator` interface. `Comparator` is defined in `java.util`; a sample implementation was shown in Figure 4.37 and is repeated in Figure 6.12.

6.4.2 the `Collections` class

Although we will not make use of the `Collections` class in this text, it has two methods that are thematic of how generic algorithms for the Collections API are written. We write these methods in the `Collections` class implementation that spans Figures 6.13 and 6.14.

Figure 6.13 begins by illustrating the common technique of declaring a private constructor in classes that contain only static methods. This prevents instantiation of the class. It continues by providing the `reverseOrder` method. This is a factory method that returns a `Comparator` that provides the reverse of the natural ordering for `Comparable` objects. The returned object, created at line 20, is an instance of the `ReverseComparator` class written in lines 23 to 29. In the `ReverseComparator` class, we use the `compareTo` method. This is an exam-

`reverseOrder` is a factory method that creates a `Comparator` representing the reverse natural order.

```
package weiss.util;

/**
 * Comparator function object interface.
 */
public interface Comparator<AnyType>
{
    /**
     * Return the result of comparing lhs and rhs.
     * @param lhs first object.
     * @param rhs second object.
     * @return < 0 if lhs is less than rhs,
     *           0 if lhs is equal to rhs,
     *         > 0 if lhs is greater than rhs.
     * @throws ClassCastException if objects cannot be compared.
     */
    int compare( AnyType lhs, AnyType rhs ) throws ClassCastException;
}
```

figure 6.12

The `Comparator` interface, originally defined in `java.util` and rewritten for the `weiss.util` package

```
package weiss.util;

/**
 * Instanceless class contains static methods that operate on collections.
 */
public class Collections
{
    private Collections( )
    {
    }

    /*
     * Returns a comparator that imposes the reverse of the
     * default ordering on a collection of objects that
     * implement the Comparable interface.
     * @return the comparator.
     */
    public static <AnyType> Comparator<AnyType> reverseOrder( )
    {
        return new ReverseComparator<AnyType>( );
    }

    private static class ReverseComparator<AnyType> implements Comparator<AnyType>
    {
        public int compare( AnyType lhs, AnyType rhs )
        {
            return - ((Comparable)lhs).compareTo( rhs );
        }
    }

    static class DefaultComparator<AnyType extends Comparable<? super AnyType>>
                implements Comparator<AnyType>
    {
        public int compare( AnyType lhs, AnyType rhs )
        {
            return lhs.compareTo( rhs );
        }
    }
```

figure 6.13

The `Collections` class (part 1): private constructor and `reverseOrder`

ple of the type of code that might be implemented with an anonymous class. We have a similar declaration for the default comparator; since the standard API does not provide a public method to return this, we declare our method to be package-visible.

Figure 6.14 illustrates the `max` method, which returns the largest element in any `Collection`. The one-parameter `max` calls the two-parameter `max`

```
    /**
     * Returns the maximum object in the collection,
     * using default ordering
     * @param coll the collection.
     * @return the maximum object.
     * @throws NoSuchElementException if coll is empty.
     * @throws ClassCastException if objects in collection
     *         cannot be compared.
     */
    public static <AnyType extends Object & Comparable<? super AnyType>>
    AnyType max( Collection<? extends AnyType> coll )
    {
        return max( coll, new DefaultComparator<AnyType>( ) );
    }

    /**
     * Returns the maximum object in the collection.
     * @param coll the collection.
     * @param cmp the comparator.
     * @return the maximum object.
     * @throws NoSuchElementException if coll is empty.
     * @throws ClassCastException if objects in collection
     *         cannot be compared.
     */
    public static <AnyType>
    AnyType max( Collection<? extends AnyType> coll, Comparator<? super AnyType> cmp )
    {
        if( coll.size( ) == 0 )
            throw new NoSuchElementException( );

        Iterator<? extends AnyType> itr = coll.iterator( );
        AnyType maxValue = itr.next( );

        while( itr.hasNext( ) );
        {
            AnyType current = itr.next( );
            if( cmp.compare( current, maxValue ) > 0 )
                maxValue = current;
        }

        return maxValue;
    }
}
```

figure 6.14

The `Collections` class (part 2): `max`

by supplying the default comparator. The funky syntax in the type parameter list is used to ensure that the type erasure of `max` generates `Object` (rather than Comparable). This is important because earlier versions of Java used Object as the return type, and we want to ensure backward compatability. The two-parameter max combines the iterator pattern with the function object pattern to step through the collection, and at line 75 uses calls to the function object to update the maximum item.

6.4.3 binary search

The Collections API implementation of the binary search is the static method Arrays.binarySearch. There are actually seven overloaded versions—one for each of the primitive types except boolean, plus two more overloaded versions that work on Objects (one works with a comparator, one uses the default comparator). We will implement the Object versions (using generics); the other seven are mindless copy-and-paste.

binarySearch uses binary search and returns the index of the matched item or a negative number if the item is not found.

As usual, for binary search the array must be sorted; if it is not, the results are undefined (verifying that the array is sorted would destroy the logarithmic time bound for the operation).

If the search for the item is successful, the index of the match is returned. If the search is unsuccessful, we determine the first position that contains a larger item, add 1 to this position, and then return the negative of the value. Thus, the return value is always negative, because it is at most -1 (which occurs if the item we are searching for is smaller than all other items) and is at least -a.length-1 (which occurs if the item we are searching for is larger than all other items).

The implementation is shown in Figure 6.15. As was the case for the max routines, the two-parameter binarySearch calls the three-parameter binarySearch (see lines 17 and 18). The three-parameter binary search routine mirrors the implementation in Figure 5.12. In Java 5, the two-parameter version does not use generics. Instead, all types are Object. But our generic implementation seems to make more sense. The three-parameter version is generic in Java 5.

We use the binarySearch method in Section 10.1.

6.4.4 sorting

The Arrays class contains a set of static methods that operate on arrays.

The Collections API provides a set of overloaded sort methods in the Arrays class. Simply pass an array of primitives, or an array of Objects that implement Comparable, or an array of Objects and a Comparator. We have not provided a sort method in our Arrays class.

```
void sort( Object [ ] arr )
```

Rearranges the elements in the array to be in sorted order, using the natural order.

```
package weiss.util;

/**
 * Instanceless class that contains static methods
 * to manipulate arrays.
 */
public class Arrays
{
    private Arrays( ) { }

    /**
     * Search sorted array arr using default comparator
     */
    public static <AnyType extends Comparable<? super AnyType>> int
    binarySearch( AnyType [ ] arr, AnyType x )
    {
        return binarySearch( arr, x,
                     new Collections.DefaultComparator<AnyType>( ) );
    }

    /**
     * Performs a search on sorted array arr using a comparator.
     * If arr is not sorted, results are undefined.
     * @param arr the array to search.
     * @param x the object to search for.
     * @param cmp the comparator.
     * @return if x is found, returns the index where it is found.
     *   otherwise, the return value is a negative number equal
     *   to -( p + 1 ), where p is the first position greater
     *   than x. This can range from -1 down to -(arr.length+1).
     * @throws ClassCastException if items are not comparable.
     */
    public static <AnyType> int
    binarySearch( AnyType [ ] arr, AnyType x, Comparator<? super AnyType> cmp )
    {
        int low = 0, mid = 0;
        int high = arr.length;

        while( low < high )
        {
            mid = ( low + high ) / 2;
            if( cmp.compare( x, arr[ mid ] ) > 0 )
                low = mid + 1;
            else
                high = mid;
        }
        if( low == arr.length || cmp.compare( x, arr[ low ] ) != 0 )
            return - ( low + 1 );
        return low;
    }
}
```

figure 6.15

Implementation of the `binarySearch` method in `Arrays` class

`void sort( Object [ ] arr, Comparator cmp )`

Rearranges the elements in the array to be in sorted order, using the order specified by the comparator.

In Java 5, these methods have been written as generic methods. The generic sorting algorithms are required to run in $O(N \log N)$ time.

6.5 the `List` interface

A *list* is a collection of items in which the items have a position.

The `List` interface extends the `Collection` interface and abstracts the notion of a position.

A *list* is a collection of items in which the items have a position. The most obvious example of a list is an array. In an array, items are placed in position 0, 1, etc.

The `List` interface extends the `Collection` interface and abstracts the notion of a position. The interface in `java.util` adds numerous methods to the `Collection` interface. We are content to add the three shown in Figure 6.16.

The first two methods are `get` and `set`, which are similar to the methods that we have already seen in `ArrayList`. The third method returns a more flexible iterator, the `ListIterator`.

figure 6.16

A sample `List` interface

```
package weiss.util;

/**
 * List interface. Contains much less than java.util
 */
public interface List<AnyType> extends Collection<AnyType>
{
    AnyType get( int idx );
    AnyType set( int idx, AnyType newVal );

    /**
     * Obtains a ListIterator object used to traverse
     * the collection bidirectionally.
     * @return an iterator positioned
     *         prior to the requested element.
     * @param pos the index to start the iterator.
     *         Use size() to do complete reverse traversal.
     *         Use 0 to do complete forward traversal.
     * @throws IndexOutOfBoundsException if pos is not
     *         between 0 and size(), inclusive.
     */
    ListIterator<AnyType> listIterator( int pos );
}
```

6.5.1 the ListIterator interface

As shown in Figure 6.17, ListIterator is just like an Iterator, except that it is bidirectional. Thus we can both advance and retreat. Because of this, the listIterator factory method that creates it must be given a value that is logically equal to the number of elements that have already been visited in the forward direction. If this value is zero, the ListIterator is initialized at the front, just like an Iterator. If this value is the size of the List, the iterator is initialized to have processed all elements in the forward direction. Thus in this state, hasNext returns false, but we can use hasPrevious and previous to traverse the list in reverse.

ListIterator is a bidirectional version of Iterator.

Figure 6.18 illustrates that we can use itr1 to traverse a list in the forward direction, and then once we reach the end, we can traverse the list backwards. It also illustrates itr2, which is positioned at the end, and simply processes the ArrayList in reverse. Finally, it shows the enhanced for loop.

```
package weiss.util;

/**
 * ListIterator interface for List interface.
 */
public interface ListIterator<AnyType> extends Iterator<AnyType>
{
    /**
     * Tests if there are more items in the collection
     * when iterating in reverse.
     * @return true if there are more items in the collection
     *  when traversing in reverse.
     */
    boolean hasPrevious( );

    /**
     * Obtains the previous item in the collection.
     * @return the previous (as yet unseen) item in the collection
     *  when traversing in reverse.
     */
    AnyType previous( );

    /**
     * Remove the last item returned by next or previous.
     * Can only be called once after next or previous.
     */
    void remove( );
}
```

figure 6.17

A sample ListIterator interface

```
import java.util.ArrayList;
import java.util.ListIterator;

class TestArrayList
{
    public static void main( String [ ] args )
    {
        ArrayList<Integer> lst = new ArrayList<Integer>( );
        lst.add( 2 ); lst.add( 4 );
        ListIterator<Integer> itr1 = lst.listIterator( 0 );
        ListIterator<Integer> itr2 = lst.listIterator( lst.size( ) );

        System.out.print( "Forward: " );
        while( itr1.hasNext( ) )
            System.out.print( itr1.next( ) + " " );
        System.out.println( );

        System.out.print( "Backward: " );
        while( itr1.hasPrevious( ) )
            System.out.print( itr1.previous( ) + " " );
        System.out.println( );

        System.out.print( "Backward: " );
        while( itr2.hasPrevious( ) )
            System.out.print( itr2.previous( ) + " " );
        System.out.println( );

        System.out.print( "Forward: ");
        for( Integer x : lst )
            System.out.print( x + " " );
        System.out.println( );
    }
}
```

figure 6.18

A sample program that illustrates bidirectional iteration

One difficulty with the `ListIterator` is that the semantics for `remove` must change slightly. The new semantics are that `remove` deletes from the `List` the last object returned as a result of calling either `next` or `previous`, and `remove` can only be called once between calls to either `next` or `previous`. To override the *javadoc* output that is generated for `remove`, `remove` is listed in the `ListIterator` interface.

6.5.2 LinkedList class

There are two basic List implementations in the Collections API. One implementation is the ArrayList, which we have already seen. The other is a LinkedList, which stores items internally in a different manner than ArrayList, yielding performance trade-offs. A third version is Vector, which is like ArrayList, but is from an older library, and is present mostly for compatibility with *legacy* (old) code. Using Vector is no longer in vogue.

The LinkedList class implements a linked list.

The ArrayList may be appropriate if insertions are performed only at the high end of the array (using add), for the reasons discussed in Section 2.4.3. The ArrayList doubles the internal array capacity if an insertion at the high end would exceed the internal capacity. Although this gives good Big-Oh performance, especially if we add a constructor that allows the caller to suggest initial capacity for the internal array, the ArrayList is a poor choice if insertions are not made at the end, because then we must move items out of the way.

The linked list is used to avoid large amounts of data movement. It stores items with an additional one reference per item overhead.

In a linked list, we store items noncontiguously rather than in the usual contiguous array. To do this, we store each object in a *node* that contains the object and a reference to the next node in the list, as shown in Figure 6.19. In this scenario, we maintain references to both the first and last node in the list.

To be more concrete, a typical node looks like this:

```
class ListNode
{
    Object   data;    // Some element
    ListNode next;
}
```

At any point, we can add a new last item x by doing this:

```
last.next = new ListNode( ); // Attach a new ListNode
last = last.next;            // Adjust last
last.data = x;               // Place x in the node
last.next = null;            // It's the last; adjust next
```

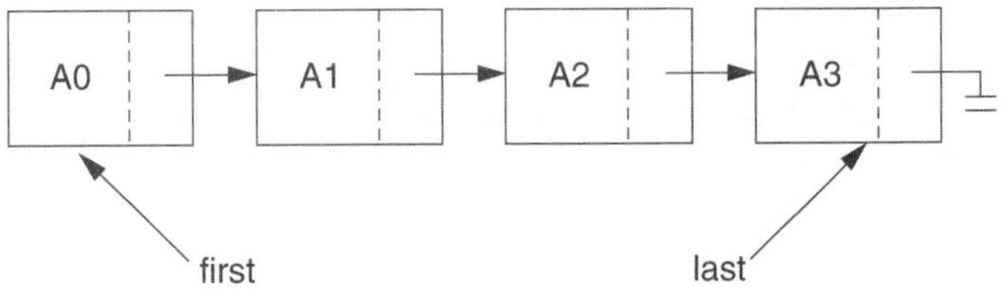

figure 6.19

A simple linked list

Now an arbitrary item can no longer be found in one access. Instead, we must scan down the list. This is similar to the difference between accessing an item on a compact disk (one access) or a tape (sequential). While this may appear to make linked lists less attractive than arrays, they still have advantages. First, an insertion into the middle of the list does not require moving all of the items that follow the insertion point. Data movement is very expensive in practice, and the linked list allows insertion with only a constant number of assignment statements.

The basic trade-off between `ArrayList` and `LinkedList` is that `get` is not efficient for `LinkedList`, while insertion and removal from the middle of a container is more efficiently supported by the `LinkedList`.

Comparing `ArrayList` and `LinkedList`, we see that insertions and deletions toward the middle of the sequence are inefficient in the `ArrayList` but may be efficient for a `LinkedList`. However, an `ArrayList` allows direct access by the index, but a `LinkedList` should not. It happens that in the Collections API, `get` and `set` are part of the `List` interface, so `LinkedList` supports these operations, but does so very slowly. Thus, the `LinkedList` can always be used unless efficient indexing is needed. The `ArrayList` may still be a better choice if insertions occur only at the end.

Access to the list is done through an iterator class.

To access items in the list, we need a reference to the corresponding node, rather than an index. The reference to the node would typically be hidden inside an iterator class.

Because `LinkedList` performs `adds` and `removes` more efficiently, it has more operations than the `ArrayList`. Some of the additional operations available for `LinkedList` are the following:

`void addLast( AnyType element )`

Appends `element` at the end of this `LinkedList`.

`void addFirst( AnyType element )`

Appends `element` to the front of this `LinkedList`.

`AnyType getFirst( )`
`AnyType element( )`

Returns the first element in this `LinkedList`. `element` was added in Java 5.

`AnyType getLast( )`

Returns the last element in this `LinkedList`.

`AnyType removeFirst( )`
`AnyType remove( )`

Removes and returns the first element from this `LinkedList`. `remove` was added in Java 5.

`AnyType removeLast( )`

Removes and returns the last element from this `LinkedList`.

We implement the `LinkedList` class in Part Four.

6.6 stacks and queues

In this section, we describe two containers: the stack and queue. In principle, both have very simple interfaces (but not in the Collections API) and very efficient implementations. Even so, as we will see, they are very useful data structures.

6.6.1 stacks

A *stack* is a data structure in which access is restricted to the most recently inserted item. It behaves very much like the common stack of bills, stack of plates, or stack of newspapers. The last item added to the stack is placed on the top and is easily accessible, whereas items that have been in the stack for a while are more difficult to access. Thus the stack is appropriate if we expect to access only the top item; all other items are inaccessible.

A *stack* restricts access to the most recently inserted item.

In a stack, the three natural operations of `insert`, `remove`, and `find` are renamed `push`, `pop`, and `top`. These basic operations are illustrated in Figure 6.20.

The interface shown in Figure 6.21 illustrates the typical protocol. It is similar to the protocol previously seen in Figure 6.1. By pushing items and then popping them, we can use the stack to reverse the order of things.

Each stack operation should take a constant amount of time, independent of the number of items in the stack. By analogy, finding today's newspaper in a stack of newspapers is fast, no matter how deep the stack is. However, arbitrary access in a stack is not efficiently supported, so we do not list it as an option in the protocol.

Stack operations take a constant amount of time.

What makes the stack useful are the many applications for which we need to access only the most recently inserted item. An important use of stacks is in compiler design.

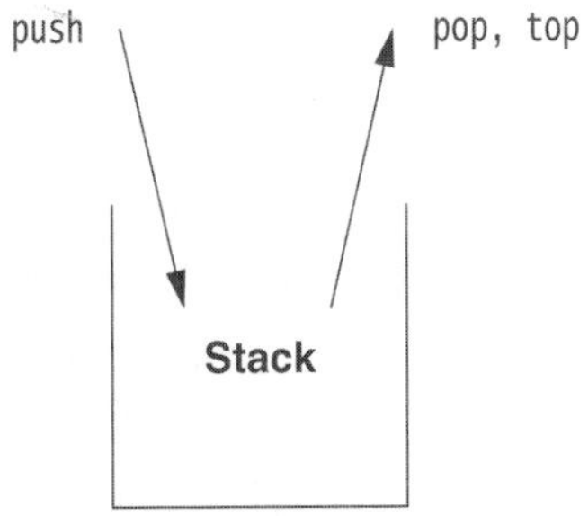

figure 6.20

The stack model: Input to a stack is by `push`, output is by `top`, and deletion is by `pop`.

figure 6.21

Protocol for the stack

```
// Stack protocol

package weiss.nonstandard;

public interface Stack<AnyType>
{
    void    push( AnyType x ); // insert
    void    pop( );            // remove
    AnyType top( );            // find
    AnyType topAndPop( );      // find + remove

    boolean isEmpty( );
    void    makeEmpty( );
}
```

6.6.2 stacks and computer languages

Compilers check your programs for syntax errors. Often, however, a lack of one symbol (e.g., a missing comment-ender */ or }) causes the compiler to spill out a hundred lines of diagnostics without identifying the real error; this is especially true when using anonymous classes.

A useful tool in this situation is a program that checks whether everything is balanced, that is, every { corresponds to a }, every [to a], and so on. The sequence [()] is legal but [(]) is not—so simply counting the numbers of each symbol is insufficient. (Assume for now that we are processing only a sequence of tokens and will not worry about problems such as the character constant '{' not needing a matching '}'.)

A stack can be used to check for unbalanced symbols.

A stack is useful for checking unbalanced symbols because we know that when a closing symbol such as) is seen, it matches the most recently seen unclosed (. Therefore, by placing opening symbols on a stack, we can easily check that a closing symbol makes sense. Specifically, we have the following algorithm.

1. Make an empty stack.
2. Read symbols until the end of the file.
   a. If the token is an opening symbol, push it onto the stack.
   b. If it is a closing symbol and if the stack is empty, report an error.
   c. Otherwise, pop the stack. If the symbol popped is not the corresponding opening symbol, report an error.
3. At the end of the file, if the stack is not empty, report an error.

In Section 11.1 we will develop this algorithm to work for (almost) all Java programs. Details include error reporting, and processing of comments, strings, and character constants, as well as escape sequences.

The algorithm to check balanced symbols suggests a way to implement method calls. The problem is that, when a call is made to a new method, all the variables local to the calling method need to be saved by the system; otherwise, the new method would overwrite the calling routine's variables. Furthermore, the current location in the calling routine must be saved so that the new method knows where to go after it is done. The reason that this problem is similar to balancing symbols is because a method call and a method return are essentially the same as an open parenthesis and a closed parenthesis, so the same ideas should apply. This indeed is the case: As discussed in Section 7.3, the stack is used to implement method calls in most programming languages.

The stack is used to implement method calls in most programming languages.

A final important application of the stack is the evaluation of expressions in computer languages. In the expression `1+2*3`, we see that at the point that the `*` is encountered, we have already read the operator `+` and the operands `1` and `2`. Does `*` operate on `2`, or `1+2`? Precedence rules tell us that `*` operates on `2`, which is the most recently seen operand. After the `3` is seen, we can evaluate `2*3` as `6` and then apply the `+` operator. This process suggests that operands and intermediate results should be saved on a stack. It also suggests that the operators be saved on the stack (since the `+` is held until the higher precedence `*` is evaluated). An algorithm that uses this strategy is *operator precedence parsing*, and is described in Section 11.2.

The *operator precedence parsing* algorithm uses a stack to evaluate expressions.

6.6.3 queues

Another simple data structure is the *queue*, which restricts access to the least recently inserted item. In many cases being able to find and/or remove the most-recently inserted item is important. But in an equal number of cases, it is not only unimportant, it is actually the wrong thing to do. In a multiprocessing system, for example, when jobs are submitted to a printer, we expect the least recent or most senior job to be printed first. This order is not only fair but it is also required to guarantee that the first job does not wait forever. Thus you can expect to find printer queues on all large systems.

The *queue* restricts access to the least recently inserted item.

The basic operations supported by queues are the following:

- `enqueue`, or insertion at the back of the line
- `dequeue`, or removal of the item from the front of the line
- `getFront`, or access of the item at the front of the line

Queue operations take a constant amount of time.

Figure 6.22 illustrates these queue operations. Historically, `dequeue` and `getFront` have been combined into one operation; we do this by having `dequeue` return a reference to the item that it has removed.

Because the queue operations and the stack operations are restricted similarly, we expect that they should also take a constant amount of time per query. This is indeed the case. All of the basic queue operations take $O(1)$ time. We will see several applications of queues in the case studies.

6.6.4 stacks and queues in the collections api

The Collections API provides a `Stack` class but no queue class. Java 5 adds a `Queue` interface.

The Collections API provides a `Stack` class but no queue class. The `Stack` methods are `push`, `pop`, and `peek`. However, the `Stack` class extends `Vector` and is slower than it needs to be; like `Vector`, its use is no longer in vogue and can be replaced with `List` operations. Before Java 1.4, the only `java.util` support for queue operations was to use a `LinkedList` (e.g., `addLast`, `removeFirst`, and `getFirst`). Java 5 adds a `Queue` interface, part of which is shown in Figure 6.23. However, we still must use `LinkedList` methods. The new methods are `add`, `remove`, and `element`.

6.7 sets

A `Set` contains no duplicates.

A `Set` is a container that contains no duplicates. It supports all of the `Collection` methods. Figure 6.24 illustrates that the interface does little more than declare a type.

The `SortedSet` is an ordered container. It allows no duplicates.

A `SortedSet` is a `Set` that maintains (internally) its items in sorted order. Objects that are added into the `SortedSet` must either be comparable, or a `Comparator` has to be provided when the container is instantiated. A `SortedSet` supports all of the `Set` methods, but its iterator is guaranteed to step through items in its sorted order. The `SortedSet` also allows us to find the smallest and largest item. The interface for our subset of `SortedSet` is shown in Figure 6.25.

figure 6.22

The queue model: Input is by `enqueue`, output is by `getFront`, and deletion is by `dequeue`.

```
package weiss.util;

/**
 * Queue interface.
 */
public interface Queue<AnyType> extends Collection<AnyType>
{
    /**
     * Returns but does not remove the item at the "front"
     * of the queue.
     * @return the front item of null if the queue is empty.
     * @throws NoSuchElementException if the queue is empty.
     */
    AnyType element( );

    /**
     * Returns and removes the item at the "front"
     * of the queue.
     * @return the front item.
     * @throws NoSuchElementException if the queue is empty.
     */
    AnyType remove( );
}
```

figure 6.23

Possible Queue interface

```
package weiss.util;

/**
 * Set interface.
 */
public interface Set<AnyType> extends Collection<AnyType>
{
}
```

figure 6.24

Possible Set implementation

6.7.1 the TreeSet class

The TreeSet is an implementation of SortedSet.

The SortedSet is implemented by a TreeSet. The underlying implementation of the TreeSet is a balanced-binary search tree and is discussed in Chapter 19.

By default, ordering uses the default comparator. An alternate ordering can be specified by providing a comparator to the constructor. As an example, Figure 6.26 illustrates how a SortedSet that stores strings is constructed. The call to printCollection will output elements in decreasing sorted order.

The SortedSet, like all Sets, does not allow duplicates. Two items are considered equal if the comparator's compare method returns 0.

figure 6.25

Possible SortedSet interface

```
package weiss.util;

/**
 * SortedSet interface.
 */
public interface SortedSet<AnyType> extends Set<AnyType>
{
    /**
     * Return the comparator used by this SortedSet.
     * @return the comparator or null if the
     * default comparator is used.
     */
    Comparator<? super AnyType> comparator( );

    /**
     * Find the smallest item in the set.
     * @return the smallest item.
     * @throws NoSuchElementException if the set is empty.
     */
    AnyType first( );

    /**
     * Find the largest item in the set.
     * @return the largest item.
     * @throws NoSuchElementException if the set is empty.
     */
    AnyType last( );
}
```

```
    public static void main( String [] args )
    {
        Set<String> s = new TreeSet<String>( Collections.reverseOrder( ) );
        s.add( "joe" );
        s.add( "bob" );
        s.add( "hal" );
        printCollection( s );    // Figure 6.11
    }
```

figure 6.26

An illustration of the TreeSet, using reverse order

In Section 5.6, we examined the static searching problem and saw that if the items are presented to us in sorted order, then we can support the find operation in logarithmic worst-case time. This is static searching because, once we are presented with the items, we cannot add or remove items. The SortedSet allows us to add and remove items.

We are hoping that the worst-case cost of the `contains`, `add`, and `remove` operations is $O(\log N)$ because that would match the bound obtained for the static binary search. Unfortunately, for the simplest implementation of the `TreeSet`, this is not the case. The average case is logarithmic, but the worst case is $O(N)$ and occurs quite frequently. However, by applying some algorithmic tricks, we can obtain a more complex structure that does indeed have $O(\log N)$ cost per operation. The Collections API `TreeSet` is guaranteed to have this performance, and in Chapter 19, we discuss how to obtain it using the *binary search tree* and its variants, and provide an implementation of the `TreeSet`, with an iterator.

We mention in closing that although we can find the smallest and largest item in a `SortedSet` in $O(\log N)$ time, finding the Kth smallest item, where K is a parameter, is not supported in the Collections API. However, it is possible to perform this operation in $O(\log N)$ time, while preserving the running time of the other operations, if we do more work.

We can also use a binary search tree to access the Kth smallest item in logarithmic time.

6.7.2 **the `HashSet` class**

In addition to the `TreeSet`, the Collections API provides a `HashSet` class that implements the `Set` interface. The `HashSet` differs from the `TreeSet` in that it cannot be used to enumerate items in sorted order, nor can it be used to obtain the smallest or largest item. Indeed, the items in the `HashSet` do not have to be comparable in any way. This means that the `HashSet` is less powerful than the `TreeSet`. If being able to enumerate the items in a `Set` in sorted order is not important, then it is often preferable to use the `HashSet` because not having to maintain sorted order allows the `HashSet` to obtain faster performance. To do so, elements placed in the `HashSet` must provide hints to the `HashSet` algorithms. This is done by having each element implement a special `hashCode` method; we describe this method later in this subsection.

The `HashSet` implements the `Set` interface. It does not require a comparator.

Figure 6.27 illustrates the use of the `HashSet`. It is guaranteed that if we iterate through the entire `HashSet`, we will see each item once, but the order

```
public static void main( String [] args )
{
    Set<String> s = new HashSet<String>( );
    s.add( "joe" );
    s.add( "bob" );
    s.add( "hal" );
    printCollection( s );    // Figure 6.11
}
```

figure 6.27

An illustration of the `HashSet`, where items are output in some order that the items are visited is unknown. It is almost certain that the order will not be the same as the order of insertion, nor will it be any kind of sorted order.

Like all Sets, the HashSet does not allow duplicates. Two items are considered equal if the equals method says so. Thus, any object that is inserted into the HashSet must have a properly overridden equals method.

Recall that in Section 4.9, we discussed that it is essential that equals is overridden (by providing a new version that takes an Object as parameter) rather than overloaded.

implementing equals and hashCode

equals must be symmetric; this is tricky when inheritance is involved.

Overriding equals is very tricky when inheritance is involved. The contract for equals states that if p and q are not null, p.equals(q) should return the same value as q.equals(p). This does not occur in Figure 6.28. In that example, clearly b.equals(c) returns true, as expected. a.equals(b) also returns true, because BaseClass's equals method is used, and that only compares the x components. However, b.equals(a) returns false, because DerivedClass's equals method is used, and the instanceof test will fail (a is not an instance of DerivedClass) at line 29.

Solution 1 is to not override equals below the base class. Solution 2 is to require identically typed objects using getClass.

There are two standard solutions to this problem. One is to make the equals method final in BaseClass. This avoids the problem of conflicting equals. The other solution is to strengthen the equals test to require that the types are identical, and not simply compatible, since the one-way compatibility is what breaks equals. In this example, a BaseClass and DerivedClass object would never be declared equal. Figure 6.29 shows a correct implementation. Line 8 contains the idiomatic test. getClass returns a special object of type Class (note the capital C) that represents information about any object's class. getClass is a final method in the Object class. If when invoked on two different objects it returns the same Class instance, then the two objects have identical types.

The hashCode method must be overridden, if equals is overridden, or the HashSet will not work.

When using a HashSet, we must also override the special hashCode method that is specified in Object; hashCode returns an int. Think of hashCode as providing a trusted hint of where the items are stored. If the hint is wrong, the item is not found, so if two objects are equal, they should provide identical hints. The contract for hashCode is that if two objects are declared equal by the equals method, then the hashCode method must return the same value for them. If this contract is violated, the HashSet will fail to find objects, even if equals declares that there is a match. If equals declares the objects are not equal, the hashCode method should return a different value for them, but this is not required. However, it is very beneficial for HashSet performance if hashCode rarely produces identical results for unequal objects. How hashCode and HashSet interact is discussed in Chapter 20.

```
class BaseClass
{
    public BaseClass( int i )
      { x = i; }

    public boolean equals( Object rhs )
    {
        // This is the wrong test (ok if final class)
        if( !( rhs instanceof BaseClass ) )
            return false;

        return x == ( (BaseClass) rhs ).x;
    }

    private int x;
}

class DerivedClass extends BaseClass
{
    public DerivedClass( int i, int j )
    {
        super( i );
        y = j;
    }

    public boolean equals( Object rhs )
    {
        // This is the wrong test.
        if( !( rhs instanceof DerivedClass ) )
            return false;

        return super.equals( rhs ) &&
               y == ( (DerivedClass) rhs ).y;
    }

    private int y;
}

public class EqualsWithInheritance
{
    public static void main( String [ ] args )
    {
        BaseClass a = new BaseClass( 5 );
        DerivedClass b = new DerivedClass( 5, 8 );
        DerivedClass c = new DerivedClass( 5, 8 );

        System.out.println( "b.equals(c): " + b.equals( c ) );
        System.out.println( "a.equals(b): " + a.equals( b ) );
        System.out.println( "b.equals(a): " + b.equals( a ) );
    }
}
```

figure 6.28

An illustration of a broken implementation of `equals`

figure 6.29

Correct implementation of `equals`

```
class BaseClass
{
    public BaseClass( int i )
      { x = i; }

    public boolean equals( Object rhs )
    {
        if( rhs == null || getClass( ) != rhs.getClass( ) )
            return false;

        return x == ( (BaseClass) rhs ).x;
    }

    private int x;
}

class DerivedClass extends BaseClass
{
    public DerivedClass( int i, int j )
    {
        super( i );
        y = j;
    }

    public boolean equals( Object rhs )
    {
          // Class test not needed; getClass() is done
          // in superclass equals
        return super.equals( rhs ) &&
               y == ( (DerivedClass) rhs ).y;
    }

    private int y;
}
```

Figure 6.30 illustrates a `SimpleStudent` class in which two `SimpleStudents` are equal if they have the same name (and are both `SimpleStudents`). This could be overridden using the techniques in Figure 6.29 as needed, or this method could be declared `final`. If it was declared `final`, then the test that is present allows only two identically typed `SimpleStudents` to be declared equal. If, with a final `equals`, we replace the test at line 40 with an `instanceof` test, then any two objects in the hierarchy can be declared equal if their names match.

The `hashCode` method at lines 47 and 48 simply uses the `hashCode` of the `name` field. Thus if two `SimpleStudent` objects have the same name (as declared by `equals`) they will have the same `hashCode`, since, presumably, the implementors of `String` honored the contract for `hashCode`.

```
/**
 * Test program for HashSet.
 */
class IteratorTest
{
    public static void main( String [ ] args )
    {
        List<SimpleStudent> stud1 = new ArrayList<SimpleStudent>( );
        stud1.add( new SimpleStudent( "Bob", 0 ) );
        stud1.add( new SimpleStudent( "Joe", 1 ) );
        stud1.add( new SimpleStudent( "Bob", 2 ) ); // duplicate

            // Will only have 2 items, if hashCode is
            // implemented. Otherwise will have 3 because
            // duplicate will not be detected.
        Set<SimpleStudent>  stud2 = new HashSet<SimpleStudent>( stud1 );

        printCollection( stud1 ); // Bob Joe Bob (unspecified order)
        printCollection( stud2 ); // Two items in unspecified order
    }
}

/**
 * Illustrates use of hashCode/equals for a user-defined class.
 * Students are ordered on basis of name only.
 */
class SimpleStudent implements Comparable<SimpleStudent>
{
    String name;
    int id;

    public SimpleStudent( String n, int i )
      { name = n; id = i; }

    public String toString( )
      { return name + " " + id; }

    public boolean equals( Object rhs )
    {
        if( rhs == null || getClass( ) != rhs.getClass( ) )
            return false;

        SimpleStudent other = (SimpleStudent) rhs;
        return name.equals( other.name );
    }

    public int hashCode( )
      { return name.hashCode( ); }
}
```

figure 6.30

Illustrates the equals and hashCode methods for use in HashSet

The accompanying test program is part of a larger test that illustrates all the basic containers. Observe that if `hashCode` is unimplemented, all three `SimpleStudent` objects will be added to the `HashSet` because the duplicate will not be detected.

It turns out that on average, the `HashSet` operations can be performed in constant time. This seems like an astounding result because it means that the cost of a single `HashSet` operation does not depend on whether the `HashSet` contains 10 items or 10,000 items. The theory behind the `HashSet` is fascinating and is described in Chapter 20.

6.8 maps

A `Map` is used to store a collection of entries that consists of *keys* and their *values*. The `Map` maps keys to values.

A `Map` is used to store a collection of entries that consists of *keys* and their *values*. The `Map` maps keys to values. Keys must be unique, but several keys can map to the same value. Thus, values need not be unique. There is a `SortedMap` interface that maintains the map logically in key-sorted order.

Not surprisingly, there are two implementations: the `HashMap` and `TreeMap`. The `HashMap` does not keep keys in sorted order, whereas the `TreeMap` does. For simplicity, we do not implement the `SortedMap` interface but we do implement `HashMap` and `TreeMap`.

The `Map` can be implemented as a `Set` instantiated with a *pair* (see Section 3.7), whose comparator or `equals/hashCode` implementation refers only to the key. The `Map` interface does not extend `Collection`; instead it exists on its own. A sample interface that contains the most important methods is shown in Figures 6.31 and 6.32.

Most of the methods have intuitive semantics. `put` is used to add a key/value pair, `remove` is used to remove a key/value pair (only the key is specified), and `get` returns the value associated with a key. `null` values are allowed, which complicates issues for `get`, because the return value from `get` will not distinguish between a failed search and a successful search that returns `null` for the value. `containsKey` can be used if `null` values are known to be in the map.

The `Map` interface does not provide an `iterator` method or class. Instead it returns a `Collection` that can be used to view the contents of the map.

The `keySet` method gives a `Collection` that contains all the keys. Since duplicate keys are not allowed, the result of `keySet` is a `Set`, for which we can obtain an iterator. If the `Map` is a `SortedMap`, the `Set` is a `SortedSet`.

Similarly, the `values` method returns a `Collection` that contains all the values. This really is a `Collection`, since duplicate values are allowed.

```java
package weiss.util;

/**
 * Map interface.
 * A map stores key/value pairs.
 * In our implementations, duplicate keys are not allowed.
 */
public interface Map<KeyType,ValueType> extends java.io.Serializable
{
    /**
     * Returns the number of keys in this map.
     */
    int size( );

    /**
     * Tests if this map is empty.
     */
    boolean isEmpty( );

    /**
     * Tests if this map contains a given key.
     */
    boolean containsKey( KeyType key );

    /**
     * Returns the value that matches the key or null
     * if the key is not found. Since null values are allowed,
     * checking if the return value is null may not be a
     * safe way to ascertain if the key is present in the map.
     */
    ValueType get( KeyType key );

    /**
     * Adds the key/value pair to the map, overriding the
     * original value if the key was already present.
     * Returns the old value associated with the key, or
     * null if the key was not present prior to this call.
     */
    ValueType put( KeyType key, ValueType value );

    /**
     * Removes the key and its value from the map.
     * Returns the previous value associated with the key,
     * or null if the key was not present prior to this call.
     */
    ValueType remove( KeyType key );
```

figure 6.31

A sample `Map` interface (part 1)

```
    /**
     * Removes all key/value pairs from the map.
     */
    void clear( );

    /**
     * Returns the keys in the map.
     */
    Set<KeyType> keySet( );

    /**
     * Returns the values in the map. There may be duplicates.
     */
    Collection<ValueType> values( );

    /**
     * Return a set of Map.Entry objects corresponding to
     * the key/value pairs in the map.
     */
    Set<Entry<KeyType,ValueType>> entrySet( );

    /**
     * Interface used to access the key/value pairs in a map.
     * From a map, use entrySet().iterator to obtain an iterator
     * over a Set of pairs. The next() method of this iterator
     * yields objects of type Map.Entry<KeyType,ValueType>.
     */
    public interface Entry<KeyType,ValueType> extends java.io.Serializable
    {
        /**
         * Returns this pair's key.
         */
        KeyType getKey( );

        /**
         * Returns this pair's value.
         */
        ValueType getValue( );

        /**
         * Change this pair's value.
         * @return the old value associated with this pair.
         */
        ValueType setValue( ValueType newValue );
    }
}
```

figure 6.32

A sample Map interface (part 2)

Finally, the `entrySet` method returns a collection of key/value pairs. Again, this is a `Set`, because the pairs must have different keys. The objects in the `Set` returned by the `entrySet` are pairs; there must be a type that represents key/value pairs. This is specified by the `Entry` interface that is nested in the `Map` interface. Thus the type of object that is in the `entrySet` is `Map.Entry`.

`Map.Entry` abstracts the notion of a pair in the map.

Figure 6.33 illustrates the use of the `Map` with a `TreeMap`. An empty map is created at line 23 and then populated with a series of `put` calls at lines 25 to 29. The last call to `put` simply replaces a value with "`unlisted`". Lines 31 and 32 print the result of a call to `get`, which is used to obtain the value for the key `"Jane Doe"`. More interesting is the `printMap` routine that spans lines 8 to 19.

In `printMap`, at line 12, we obtain a `Set` containing `Map.Entry` pairs. From the `Set`, we can use an enhanced `for` loop to view the `Map.Entrys`, and we can obtain the key and value information using `getKey` and `getValue`, as shown on lines 16 and 17.

Returning to `main`, we see that `keySet` returns a set of keys (at line 37) that can be printed at line 38 by calling `printCollection` (in Figure 6.11); similarly at lines 41 and 42, `values` returns a collection of values that can be printed. More interesting, the key set and value collection are *views* of the map, so changes to the map are immediately reflected in the key set and value collection, and removals from the key set or value set become removals from the underlying map. Thus line 44 removes not only the key from the key set but also the associated entry from the map. Similarly, line 45 removes an entry from the map. Thus the printing at line 49 reflects a map with two entries removed.

`KeySet`, `values`, and `entrySet` return views.

6.9 priority queues

Although jobs sent to a printer are generally placed on a queue, that might not always be the best thing to do. For instance, one job might be particularly important, so we might want to allow that job to be run as soon as the printer is available. Conversely, when the printer finishes a job, and several 1-page jobs and one 100-page job are waiting, it might be reasonable to print the long job last, even if it is not the last job submitted. (Unfortunately, most systems do not do this, which can be particularly annoying at times.)

The *priority queue* supports access of the minimum item only.

Similarly, in a multiuser environment the operating system scheduler must decide which of several processes to run. Generally, a process is allowed to run only for a fixed period of time. A poor algorithm for such a procedure involves use of a queue. Jobs are initially placed at the end of the queue. The scheduler repeatedly takes the first job from the queue, runs it until either it

```java
import java.util.Map;
import java.util.TreeMap;
import java.util.Set;
import java.util.Collection;

public class MapDemo
{
    public static <KeyType,ValueType>
    void printMap( String msg, Map<KeyType,ValueType> m )
    {
        System.out.println( msg + ":" );
        Set<Map.Entry<KeyType,ValueType>> entries = m.entrySet( );

        for( Map.Entry<KeyType,ValueType> thisPair : entries )
        {
            System.out.print( thisPair.getKey( ) + ": " );
            System.out.println( thisPair.getValue( ) );
        }
    }

    public static void main( String [ ] args )
    {
        Map<String,String> phone1 = new TreeMap<String,String>( );

        phone1.put( "John Doe", "212-555-1212" );
        phone1.put( "Jane Doe", "312-555-1212" );
        phone1.put( "Holly Doe", "213-555-1212" );
        phone1.put( "Susan Doe", "617-555-1212" );
        phone1.put( "Jane Doe", "unlisted" );

        System.out.println( "phone1.get(\"Jane Doe\"): " +
                            phone1.get( "Jane Doe" ) );
        System.out.println( "\nThe map is: " );
        printMap( "phone1", phone1 );

        System.out.println( "\nThe keys are: " );
        Set<String> keys = phone1.keySet( );
        printCollection( keys );

        System.out.println( "\nThe values are: " );
        Collection<String> values = phone1.values( );
        printCollection( values );

        keys.remove( "John Doe" );
        values.remove( "unlisted" );

        System.out.println( "After John Doe and 1 unlisted are removed" );
        System.out.println( "\nThe map is: " );
        printMap( "phone1", phone1 );
    }
}
```

figure 6.33

An illustration using the `Map` interface

finishes or its time limit is up, and places it at the end of the queue if it does not finish. Generally, this strategy is not appropriate because short jobs must wait and thus seem to take a long time to run. Clearly, users who are running an editor should not see a visible delay in the echoing of typed characters. Thus short jobs (that is, those using fewer resources) should have precedence over jobs that have already consumed large amounts of resources. Furthermore, some resource-intensive jobs, such as jobs run by the system administrator, might be important and should also have precedence.

If we give each job a number to measure its priority, then the smaller number (pages printed, resources used) tends to indicate greater importance. Thus we want to be able to access the smallest item in a collection of items and remove it from the collection. To do so, we use the `findMin` and `deleteMin` operations. The data structure that supports these operations is the *priority queue* and supports access of the minimum item only. Figure 6.34 illustrates the basic priority queue operations.

Although the priority queue is a fundamental data structure, before Java 5 there was no implementation of it in the Collections API. A `SortedSet` was not sufficient because it is important for a priority queue to allow duplicate items.

In Java 5, the `PriorityQueue` is a class that implements the `Queue` interface. Thus `insert`, `findMin`, and `deleteMin` are expressed via calls to `add`, `element`, and `remove`. The `PriorityQueue` can be constructed either with no parameters, a comparator, or another compatible collection. Throughout the text, we often use the terms `insert`, `findMin`, and `deleteMin` to describe the priority queue methods. Figure 6.35 illustrates the use of the priority queue.

The *binary heap* implements the priority queue in logarithmic time per operation with little extra space.

As the priority queue supports only the `deleteMin` and `findMin` operations, we might expect performance that is a compromise between the constant-time queue and the logarithmic time set. Indeed, this is the case. The basic priority queue supports all operations in logarithmic worst-case time, uses only an array, supports insertion in constant average time, is simple to implement, and is known as a *binary heap*. This structure is one of the most elegant data structures known. In Chapter 21, we provide details on the implementation of the binary heap. An alternate implementation that supports an additional

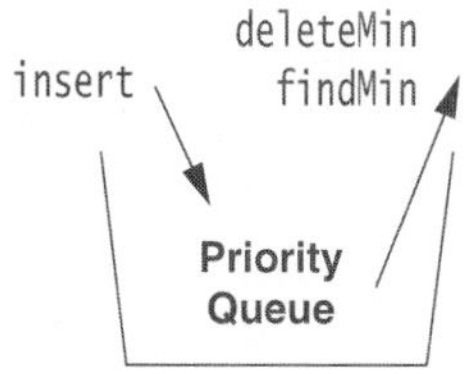

figure 6.34

The priority queue model: Only the minimum element is accessible.

figure 6.35

A routine to demonstrate the `PriorityQueue`

```
import java.util.PriorityQueue;

public class PriorityQueueDemo
{
    public static <AnyType extends Comparable<? super AnyType>>
    void dumpPQ( String msg, PriorityQueue<AnyType> pq )
    {
        System.out.println( msg + ":" );
        while( !pq.isEmpty( ) )
            System.out.println( pq.remove( ) );
    }

    // Do some inserts and removes (done in dumpPQ).
    public static void main( String [ ] args )
    {
        PriorityQueue<Integer> minPQ = new PriorityQueue<Integer>( );

        minPQ.add( 4 );
        minPQ.add( 3 );
        minPQ.add( 5 );

        dumpPQ( "minPQ", minPQ );
    }
}
```

`decreaseKey` operation is the *pairing heap*, described in Chapter 23. Because there are many efficient implementations of priority queues, it is unfortunate that the library designers did not choose to make `PriorityQueue` an interface. Nonetheless, the `PriorityQueue` implementation in Java 5 is sufficient for most priority queue applications.

An important use of priority queues is *event-driven simulation.*

An important application of the priority queue is *event-driven simulation*. Consider, for example, a system such as a bank in which customers arrive and wait in line until one of K tellers is available. Customer arrival is governed by a probability distribution function, as is the *service time* (the amount of time it takes a teller to provide complete service to one customer). We are interested in statistics such as how long on average a customer has to wait or how long a line might be.

With certain probability distributions and values of K, we can compute these statistics exactly. However, as K gets larger, the analysis becomes considerably more difficult, so the use of a computer to simulate the operation of the bank is appealing. In this way, the bank's officers can determine how many tellers are needed to ensure reasonably smooth service. An event-driven simulation consists of processing events. The two events here are (1) a customer arriving and (2) a customer departing, thus freeing up a teller. At any point we have a collection of events waiting to happen. To run the simulation, we need to determine the *next* event; this is the event whose time of occurrence is minimum. Hence, we use a priority queue that extracts the event of minimum time to process the event list efficiently. We present a complete discussion and implementation of event-driven simulation in Section 13.2.

summary

In this chapter, we examined the basic data structures that will be used throughout the book. We provided generic protocols and explained what the running time should be for each data structure. We also described the interface provided by the Collections API. In later chapters, we show how these data structures are used and eventually give an implementation of each data structure that meets the time bounds we have claimed here. Figure 6.36 summarizes the results that will be obtained for the generic `insert`, `find`, and `remove` sequence of operations.

Chapter 7 describes an important problem-solving tool known as *recursion*. Recursion allows many problems to be efficiently solved with short algorithms and is central to the efficient implementation of a sorting algorithm and several data structures.

Data Structure	Access	Comments
Stack	Most recent only, `pop`, $O(1)$	Very very fast
Queue	Least recent only, `dequeue`, $O(1)$	Very very fast
List	Any item	$O(N)$
TreeSet	Any item by name or rank, $O(\log N)$	Average case easy to do; worst case requires effort
HashSet	Any item by name, $O(1)$	Average case
Priority Queue	`findMin`, $O(1)$, `deleteMin`, $O(\log N)$	`insert` is $O(1)$ on average, $O(\log N)$ worst case

figure 6.36

A summary of some data structures

key concepts

`Arrays` Contains a set of static methods that operate on arrays. (218)

binary heap Implements the priority queue in logarithmic time per operation using an array. (241)

binary search tree A data structure that supports insertion, removal, and searching. We can also use it to access the *K*th smallest item. The cost is logarithmic average-case time for a simple implementation and logarithmic worst-case time for a more careful implementation. (231)

`Collection` An interface that represents a group of objects, known as its elements. (209)

`Collections` A class that contains a set of static methods that operate on `Collection` objects. (214)

data structure A representation of data and the operations allowed on that data, permitting component reuse. (202)

factory method A method that creates new concrete instances but returns them using a reference to an abstract class. (207)

`hashCode` A method used by `HashSet` that must be overridden for objects if the object's `equals` method is overridden. (232)

`HashMap` The Collections API implementation of a `Map` with unordered keys. (236)

`HashSet` The Collections API implementation of an (unordered) `Set`. (231)

iterator An object that allows access to elements in a container. (212)

`Iterator` The Collections API interface that specifies the protocol for a unidirectional iterator. (212)

list A collection of items in which the items have a position. (220)

`List` The Collections API interface that specifies the protocol for a list. (220)

`ListIterator` The Collections API interface that provides bidirectional iteration. (221)

linked list A data structure that is used to avoid large amounts of data movement. It uses a small amount of extra space per item. (223)

`LinkedList` The Collections API class that implements a linked list. (223)

`Map` The Collections API interface that abstracts a collection of pairs consisting of keys and their values and maps keys to values. (236)

`Map.Entry` Abstracts the idea of a pair in a map. (239)

operator precedence parsing An algorithm that uses a stack to evaluate expressions. (227)

priority queue A data structure that supports access of the minimum item only. (239)

programming to an interface The technique of using classes by writing in terms of the most abstract interface. Attempts to hide even the name of the concrete class that is being operated on. (207)

queue A data structure that restricts access to the least recently inserted item. (227)

`Set` The Collections API interface that abstracts a collection with no duplicates. (228)

`SortedSet` The Collections API interface that abstracts a sorted set with no duplicates. (228)

stack A data structure that restricts access to the most recently inserted item. (225)

`TreeMap` The Collections API implementation of a `Map` with ordered keys. (236)

`TreeSet` The Collections API implementation of a `SortedSet`. (229)

common errors

1. Do not worry about low-level optimizations until after you have concentrated on basic design and algorithmic issues.
2. When you send a function object as a parameter, you must send a constructed object, and not simply the name of the class.
3. When using a `Map`, if you are not sure if a key is in the map, you may need to use `containsKey` rather than checking the result of `get`.
4. A priority queue is not a queue. It just sounds like it is.

on the internet

There is lots of code in this chapter. Test code is in the root directory, nonstandard protocols are in package `weiss.nonstandard`, and everything else is in package `weiss.util`.

Collection.java	Contains the code in Figure 6.9.
Iterator.java	Contains the code in Figure 6.10.
Collections.java	Contains the code in Figures 6.13 and 6.14.
Arrays.java	Contains the code in Figure 6.15.
List.java	Contains the code in Figure 6.16.
ListIterator.java	Contains the code in Figure 6.17.
TestArrayList.java	Illustrates the `ArrayList`, as in Figure 6.18.

Set.java	Contains the code in Figure 6.24. The online code contains an extra method that is not part of Java 1.2.
Stack.java	Contains the nonstandard protocol in Figure 6.21.
UnderflowException.java	Contains a nonstandard exception.
Queue.java	Contains the standard interface in Figure 6.23.
SortedSet.java	Contains the code in Figure 6.25.
TreeSetDemo.java	Contains the code in Figures 6.11 and 6.26.
IteratorTest.java	Contains the code that illustrates all the iterators, including code in Figures 6.11, 6.27, and 6.30.
EqualsWithInheritance.java	Contains the code in Figures 6.28 and 6.29, combined as one.
Map.java	Contains the code in Figures 6.31 and 6.32.
MapDemo.java	Contains the code in Figure 6.33.
PriorityQueueDemo.java	Contains the code in Figure 6.35.

exercises

IN SHORT

6.1 Show the results of the following sequence: `add(4)`, `add(8)`, `add(1)`, `add(6)`, `remove()`, and `remove()` when the `add` and `remove` operations correspond to the basic operations in the following:

a. Stack
b. Queue
c. Priority queue

IN THEORY

6.2 Consider the following method, whose implementation is not shown:

```
// Precondition: Collection c represents a Collection of
//               other Collections.
//               c is not null; none of the collections are null
//               str is not null
// Postcondition: returns the number of occurrences of
//               String str in c.
public static
    int count( Collection<Collection<String>> c, String str )
```

a. Provide an implementation of `count`.
b. Assume that `Collection c` contains N collections and that each of those collections contains N objects. What is the running time of `count`, as written in part (a)?
c. Suppose it takes 2 milliseconds to run `count` when N (specified) is 100. Assuming low-order terms are negligible, how long will it take to run `count` when N is 300?

6.3 Can all of the following be supported in logarithmic time: `insert`, `deleteMin`, `deleteMax`, `findMin`, and `findMax`?

6.4 Which of the data structures in Figure 6.36 lead to sorting algorithms that could run in less than quadratic time (by inserting all items into the data structure and then removing them in order)?

6.5 Show that the following operations can be supported in constant time simultaneously: `push`, `pop`, and `findMin`. Note that `deleteMin` is not part of the repertoire. *Hint*: Maintain two stacks—one to store items and the other to store minimums as they occur.

6.6 A double-ended queue supports insertions and deletions at both the front and end of the line. What is the running time per operation?

IN PRACTICE

6.7 Write a routine that uses the Collections API to print out the items in any `Collection` in reverse order. Do not use a `ListIterator`.

6.8 Show how to implement a stack efficiently by using a `List` as a data member.

6.9 Show how to implement a queue efficiently by using a `List` as a data member.

PROGRAMMING PROJECTS

6.10 A queue can be implemented by using an array and maintaining the current size. The queue elements are stored in consecutive array positions, with the front item always in position 0. Note that this is not the most efficient method. Do the following:
a. Describe the algorithms for `getFront`, `enqueue`, and `dequeue`.
b. What is the Big-Oh running time for each of `getFront`, `enqueue`, and `dequeue` using these algorithms?
c. Write an implementation that uses these algorithms using the protocol in Figure 6.23.

6.11 The operations that are supported by the `SortedSet` can also be implemented by using an array and maintaining the current size. The array elements are stored in sorted order in consecutive array positions. Thus `contains` can be implemented by a binary search. Do the following:

a. Describe the algorithms for `add` and `remove`.
b. What is the running time for these algorithms?
c. Write an implementation that uses these algorithms, using the protocol in Figure 6.1.
d. Write an implementation that uses these algorithms, using the standard `SortedSet` protocol.

6.12 A priority queue can be implemented by using a sorted array (as in Exercise 6.11). Do the following:

a. Describe the algorithms for `findMin`, `deleteMin`, and `insert`.
b. What is the Big-Oh running time for each of `findMin`, `deleteMin`, and `insert` using these algorithms?
c. Write an implementation that uses these algorithms.

6.13 A priority queue can be implemented by storing items in an unsorted array and inserting items in the next available location. Do the following:

a. Describe the algorithms for `findMin`, `deleteMin`, and `insert`.
b. What is the Big-Oh running time for each of `findMin`, `deleteMin`, and `insert` using these algorithms?
c. Write an implementation that uses these algorithms.

6.14 By adding an extra data member to the priority queue class in Exercise 6.13, you can implement both `insert` and `findMin` in constant time. The extra data member maintains the array position where the minimum is stored. However, `deleteMin` is still expensive. Do the following:

a. Describe the algorithms for `insert`, `findMin`, and `deleteMin`.
b. What is the Big-Oh running time for `deleteMin`?
c. Write an implementation that uses these algorithms.

6.15 By maintaining the invariant that the elements in the priority queue are sorted in nonincreasing order (that is, the largest item is first, the smallest is last), you can implement both `findMin` and `deleteMin` in constant time. However, `insert` is expensive. Do the following:

a. Describe the algorithms for `insert`, `findMin`, and `deleteMin`.
b. What is the Big-Oh running time for `insert`?
c. Write an implementation that uses these algorithms.

6.16 A double-ended priority queue allows access to both the minimum and maximum elements. In other words, all of the following are supported: findMin, deleteMin, findMax, and deleteMax. Do the following:

a. Describe the algorithms for insert, findMin, deleteMin, findMax, and deleteMax.

b. What is the Big-Oh running time for each of findMin, deleteMin, findMax, deleteMax, and insert using these algorithms?

c. Write an implementation that uses these algorithms.

6.17 A median heap supports the following operations: insert, findKth, and removeKth. The last two find and remove, respectively, the *K*th smallest element (where k is a parameter). The simplest implementation maintains the data in sorted order. Do the following:

a. Describe the algorithms that can be used to support median heap operations.

b. What is the Big-Oh running time for each of the basic operations using these algorithms?

c. Write an implementation that uses these algorithms.

6.18 Write a program that reads strings from input and outputs them sorted, by length, shortest string first. If a subset of input strings has the same length, your program should output them in alphabetical order.

6.19 Collections.fill takes a List and a value, and places value in all positions in the list. Implement fill.

6.20 Collections.reverse takes a List and reverses its contents. Implement reverse.

6.21 Write a method that removes every other element in a List. Your routine should run in linear time and use constant extra space if the List is a LinkedList.

6.22 Write a method that takes a Map<String,String> as a parameter and returns a new Map<String,String> in which keys and values are swapped. Throw an exception if there are duplicate values in the map that is passed as a parameter.

references

References for the theory that underlies these data structures are provided in Part Four. The Collections API is described in most recent Java books (see the references in Chapter 1).

chapter 7

recursion

A method that is partially defined in terms of itself is called *recursive.* Like many languages, Java supports recursive methods. Recursion, which is the use of recursive methods, is a powerful programming tool that in many cases can yield both short and efficient algorithms. In this chapter we explore how recursion works, thus providing some insight into its variations, limitations, and uses. We begin our discussion of recursion by examining the mathematical principle on which it is based: *mathematical induction*. Then we give examples of simple recursive methods and prove that they generate correct answers.

In this chapter, we show

- The four basic rules of recursion
- Numerical applications of recursion, leading to implementation of an encryption algorithm
- A general technique called *divide and conquer*
- A general technique called *dynamic programming,* which is similar to recursion but uses tables instead of recursive method calls
- A general technique called *backtracking,* which amounts to a careful exhaustive search

7.1 what is recursion?

A *recursive method* is a method that directly or indirectly makes a call to itself.

A *recursive method* is a method that either directly or indirectly makes a call to itself. This action may seem to be circular logic: How can a method F solve a problem by calling itself? The key is that the method F calls itself on a different, generally simpler, instance. The following are some examples.

- Files on a computer are generally stored in directories. Users may create subdirectories that store more files and directories. Suppose that we want to examine every file in a directory D, including all files in all subdirectories (and subsubdirectories, and so on). We do so by recursively examining every file in each subdirectory and then examining all files in the directory D (discussed in Chapter 18).
- Suppose that we have a large dictionary. Words in dictionaries are defined in terms of other words. When we look up the meaning of a word, we might not always understand the definition, so we might have to look up words in the definition. Likewise, we might not understand some of those, so we might have to continue this search for a while. As the dictionary is finite, eventually either we come to a point where we understand all the words in some definition (and thus understand that definition and can retrace our path through the other definitions), we find that the definitions are circular and that we are stuck, or some word we need to understand is not defined in the dictionary. Our recursive strategy to understand words is as follows: If we know the meaning of a word, we are done; otherwise, we look the word up in the dictionary. If we understand all the words in the definition, we are done. Otherwise, we figure out what the definition means by recursively looking up the words that we do not know. This procedure terminates if the dictionary is well defined, but it can loop indefinitely if a word is circularly defined.
- Computer languages are frequently defined recursively. For instance, an arithmetic expression is an object, or a parenthesized expression, or two expressions added to each other, and so on.

Recursion is a powerful problem-solving tool. Many algorithms are most easily expressed in a recursive formulation. Furthermore, the most efficient solutions to many problems are based on this natural recursive formulation. But you must be careful not to create circular logic that would result in infinite loops.

In this chapter we discuss the general conditions that must be satisfied by recursive algorithms and give several practical examples. It shows that sometimes algorithms that are naturally expressed recursively must be rewritten without recursion.

7.2 background: proofs by mathematical induction

In this section we discuss proof by mathematical *induction*. (Throughout this chapter we omit the word *mathematical* when describing this technique.) *Induction* is commonly used to establish theorems that hold for positive integers. We start by proving a simple theorem, Theorem 7.1. This particular theorem can be easily established by using other methods, but often a proof by induction is the simplest mechanism.

Induction is an important proof technique used to establish theorems that hold for positive integers.

Theorem 7.1

For any integer $N \geq 1$, the sum of the first N integers, given by $\sum_{i=1}^{N} i = 1 + 2 + \cdots + N$, equals $N(N+1)/2$.

Obviously, the theorem is true for $N = 1$ because both the left-hand and right-hand sides evaluate to 1. Further checking shows that it is true for $2 \leq N \leq 10$. However, the fact that the theorem holds for all N that are easy to check by hand does not imply that it holds for all N. Consider, for instance, numbers of the form $2^{2^k} + 1$. The first five numbers (corresponding to $0 \leq k \leq 4$) are 3, 5, 17, 257, and 65,537. These numbers are all prime. Indeed, at one time mathematicians conjectured that all numbers of this form are prime. That is not the case. We can easily check by computer that $2^{2^5} + 1 = 641 \times 6{,}700{,}417$. In fact, no other prime of the form $2^{2^k} + 1$ is known.

A proof by induction is carried out in two steps. First, as we have just done, we show that the theorem is true for the smallest cases. We then show that if the theorem is true for the first few cases, it can be extended to include the next case. For instance, we show that a theorem that is true for all $1 \leq N \leq k$ must be true for $1 \leq N \leq k + 1$. Once we have shown how to extend the range of true cases, we have shown that it is true for all cases. The reason is that we can extend the range of true cases indefinitely. We use this technique to prove Theorem 7.1.

A proof by induction shows that the theorem is true for some simple cases and then shows how to extend the range of true cases indefinitely.

Proof of Theorem 7.1

Clearly, the theorem is true for $N = 1$. Suppose that the theorem is true for all $1 \leq N \leq k$. Then

$$\sum_{i=1}^{k+1} i = (k+1) + \sum_{i=1}^{k} i. \qquad \textbf{(7.1)}$$

(*continued on next page*)

Proof of Theorem 7.1

(continued from previous page)

By assumption, the theorem is true for k, so we may replace the sum on the right-hand side of Equation 7.1 with $k(k+1)/2$, obtaining

$$\sum_{i=1}^{k+1} i = (k+1) + (k(k+1)/2) \tag{7.2}$$

Algebraic manipulation of the right-hand side of Equation 7.2 now yields

$$\sum_{i=1}^{k+1} i = (k+1)(k+2)/2$$

This result confirms the theorem for the case $k+1$. Thus by induction, the theorem is true for all integers $N \geq 1$.

In a proof by induction, the *basis* is the easy case that can be shown by hand.

Why does this constitute a proof? First, the theorem is true for $N = 1$, which is called the *basis*. We can view it as being the basis for our belief that the theorem is true in general. In a proof by induction, the *basis* is the easy case that can be shown by hand. Once we have established the basis, we use *inductive hypothesis* to assume that the theorem is true for some arbitrary k and that, under this assumption, if the theorem is true for k, then it is true for $k + 1$. In our case, we know that the theorem is true for the basis $N = 1$, so we know that it also is true for $N = 2$. Because it is true for $N = 2$, it must be true for $N = 3$. And as it is true for $N = 3$, it must be true for $N = 4$. Extending this logic, we know that the theorem is true for every positive integer beginning with $N = 1$.

The *inductive hypothesis* assumes that the theorem is true for some arbitrary case and that, under this assumption, it is true for the next case.

Let us apply proof by induction to a second problem, which is not quite as simple as the first. First, we examine the sequence of numbers 1^2, $2^2 - 1^2$, $3^2 - 2^2 + 1^2$, $4^2 - 3^2 + 2^2 - 1^2$, $5^2 - 4^2 + 3^2 - 2^2 + 1^2$, and so on. Each member represents the sum of the first N squares, with alternating signs. The sequence evaluates to 1, 3, 6, 10, and 15. Thus, in general, the sum seems to be equal to the sum of the first N integers, which, as we know from Theorem 7.1, would be $N(N+1)/2$. Theorem 7.2 proves this result.

Theorem 7.2

The sum $\sum_{i=N}^{1} (-1)^{N-i} i^2 = N^2 - (N-1)^2 + (N-2)^2 - \cdots$ is $N(N+1)/2$.

Proof

The proof is by induction.

Basis: Clearly, the theorem is true for $N = 1$.

(continued on next page)

(*continued from previous page*)

Proof of Theorem 7.2

Inductive hypothesis: First we assume that the theorem is true for k:

$$\sum_{i=k}^{1}(-1)^{k-i}i^2 = \frac{k(k+1)}{2}.$$

Then we must show that it is true for $k+1$, namely, that

$$\sum_{i=k+1}^{1}(-1)^{k+1-i}i^2 = \frac{(k+1)(k+2)}{2}$$

We write

$$\sum_{i=k+1}^{1}(-1)^{k+1-i}i^2 = (k+1)^2 - k^2 + (k-1)^2 - \cdots \quad \textbf{(7.3)}$$

If we rewrite the right-hand side of Equation 7.3, we obtain

$$\sum_{i=k+1}^{1}(-1)^{k+1-i}i^2 = (k+1)^2 - (k^2 - (k-1)^2 + \cdots)$$

and a substitution yields

$$\sum_{i=k+1}^{1}(-1)^{k+1-i}i^2 = (k+1)^2 - (\sum_{i=k}^{1}(-1)^{k-i}i^2) \quad \textbf{(7.4)}$$

If we apply the inductive hypothesis, then we can replace the summation on the right-hand side of Equation 7.4, obtaining

$$\sum_{i=k+1}^{1}(-1)^{k+1-i}i^2 = (k+1)^2 - k(k+1)/2 \quad \textbf{(7.5)}$$

Simple algebraic manipulation of the right-hand side of Equation 7.5 then yields

$$\sum_{i=k+1}^{1}(-1)^{k+1-i}i^2 = (k+1)(k+2)/2$$

which establishes the theorem for $N = k+1$. Thus, by induction, the theorem is true for all $N \geq 1$.

7.3 basic recursion

Proofs by induction show us that, if we know that a statement is true for a smallest case and can show that one case implies the next case, then we know the statement is true for all cases.

A recursive method is defined in terms of a smaller instance of itself. There must be some base case that can be computed without recursion.

Sometimes mathematical functions are defined recursively. For instance, let $S(N)$ be the sum of the first N integers. Then $S(1) = 1$, and we can write $S(N) = S(N-1) + N$. Here we have defined the function S in terms of a smaller instance of itself. The recursive definition of $S(N)$ is virtually identical to the closed form $S(N) = N(N + 1)/2$, with the exception that the recursive definition is only defined for positive integers and is less directly computable.

Sometimes writing a formula recursively is easier than writing it in closed form. Figure 7.1 shows a straightforward implementation of the recursive function. If $N = 1$, we have the basis, for which we know that $S(1) = 1$. We take care of this case at lines 4 and 5. Otherwise, we follow the recursive definition $S(N) = S(N - 1) + N$ precisely at line 7. It is hard to imagine that we could implement the recursive method any more simply than this, so the natural question is, does it actually work?

The answer, except as noted shortly, is that this routine works. Let us examine how the call to `s(4)` is evaluated. When the call to `s(4)` is made, the test at line 4 fails. We then execute line 7, where we evaluate `s(3)`. Like any other method, this evaluation requires a call to `s`. In that call we get to line 4, where the test fails; thus we go to line 7. At this point we call `s(2)`. Again, we call `s`, and now `n` is 2. The test at line 4 still fails, so we call `s(1)` at line 7. Now we have `n` equal to 1, so `s(1)` returns 1. At this point `s(2)` can continue, adding the return value from `s(1)` to 2; thus `s(2)` returns 3. Now `s(3)` continues, adding the value of 3 returned by `s(2)` to `n`, which is 3; thus `s(3)` returns 6. This result enables completion of the call to `s(4)`, which finally returns 10.

Note that, although `s` seems to be calling itself, in reality it is calling a *clone* of itself. That clone is simply another method with different parameters. At any instant only one clone is active; the rest are pending. It is the computer's job, not yours, to handle all the bookkeeping. If there were too much bookkeeping even for the computer, then it would be time to worry. We discuss these details later in the chapter.

The *base case* is an instance that can be solved without recursion. Any recursive call must make progress toward a base case.

A *base case* is an instance that can be solved without recursion. Any recursive call must progress toward the base case in order to terminate eventually. We thus have our first two (of four) fundamental *rules of recursion*.

1. *Base case:* Always have at least one case that can be solved without using recursion.
2. *Make progress:* Any recursive call must progress toward a base case.

figure 7.1

Recursive evaluation of the sum of the first *N* integers

```
1 // Evaluate the sum of the first n integers
2 public static long s( int n )
3 {
4     if( n == 1 )
5         return 1;
6     else
7         return s( n - 1 ) + n;
8 }
```

Our recursive evaluation routine does have a few problems. One is the call `s(0)`, for which the method behaves poorly.[1] This behavior is natural because the recursive definition of $S(N)$ does not allow for $N < 1$. We can fix this problem by extending the definition of $S(N)$ to include $N = 0$. Because there are no numbers to add in this case, a natural value for $S(0)$ would be 0. This value makes sense because the recursive definition can apply for $S(1)$, as $S(0) + 1$ is 1. To implement this change, we just replace `1` with `0` on lines 4 and 5. Negative N also causes errors, but this problem can be fixed in a similar manner (and is left for you to do as Exercise 7.2).

A second problem is that if the parameter `n` is large, but not so large that the answer does not fit in an `int`, the program can crash or hang. Our system, for instance, cannot handle $N \geq 8{,}882$. The reason is that, as we have shown, the implementation of recursion requires some bookkeeping to keep track of the pending recursive calls, and for sufficiently long chains of recursion, the computer simply runs out of memory. We explain this condition in more detail later in the chapter. This routine also is somewhat more time consuming than an equivalent loop because the bookkeeping also uses some time.

Needless to say, this particular example does not demonstrate the best use of recursion because the problem is so easy to solve without recursion. Most of the good uses of recursion do not exhaust the computer's memory and are only slightly more time consuming than nonrecursive implementations. However, recursion almost always leads to more compact code.

7.3.1 printing numbers in any base

A good example of how recursion simplifies the coding of routines is number printing. Suppose that we want to print out a nonnegative number N in decimal form but that we do not have a number output function available. However, we can print out one digit at a time. Consider, for instance, how we would print the number `1369`. First we would need to print `1`, then `3`, then `6`, and then `9`. The problem is that obtaining the first digit is a bit sloppy: Given a number `n`, we need a loop to determine the first digit of `n`. In contrast is the last digit, which is immediately available as `n%10` (which is `n` for `n` less than 10).

Recursion provides a nifty solution. To print out `1369`, we print out `136`, followed by the last digit, `9`. As we have mentioned, printing out the last digit using the `%` operator is easy. Printing out all but the number represented by eliminating the last digit also is easy, because it is the same problem as printing out `n/10`. Thus, it can be done by a recursive call.

---

1. A call to `s(-1)` is made, and the program eventually crashes because there are too many pending recursive calls. The recursive calls are not progressing toward a base case.

The code shown in Figure 7.2 implements this printing routine. If `n` is smaller than 10, line 6 is not executed and only the one digit `n%10` is printed; otherwise, all but the last digit are printed recursively and then the last digit is printed.

Note how we have a base case (`n` is a one-digit integer), and because the recursive problem has one less digit, all recursive calls progress toward the base case. Thus we have satisfied the first two fundamental rules of recursion.

To make our printing routine useful, we can extend it to print in any base between 2 and 16.[2] This modification is shown in Figure 7.3.

We introduced a `String` to make the printing of a through f easier. Each digit is now output by indexing to the `DIGIT_TABLE` string. The `printInt` routine is not robust. If `base` is larger than 16, the index to `DIGIT_TABLE` could be out of bounds. If `base` is 0, an arithmetic error results when division by 0 is attempted at line 8.

Failure to progress means that the program does not work.

The most interesting error occurs when `base` is 1. Then the recursive call at line 8 fails to make progress because the two parameters to the recursive call are identical to the original call. Thus the system makes recursive calls until it eventually runs out of bookkeeping space (and exits less than gracefully).

figure 7.2

A recursive routine for printing N in decimal form

```
1  // Print n in base 10, recursively.
2  // Precondition: n >= 0.
3  public static void printDecimal( long n )
4  {
5      if( n >= 10 )
6          printDecimal( n / 10 );
7      System.out.print( (char) ('0' + ( n % 10 ) ) );
8  }
```

figure 7.3

A recursive routine for printing N in any base

```
1  private static final String DIGIT_TABLE = "0123456789abcdef";
2
3  // Print n in any base, recursively.
4  // Precondition: n >= 0, base is valid.
5  public static void printInt( long n, int base )
6  {
7      if( n >= base )
8          printInt( n / base, base );
9      System.out.print( DIGIT_TABLE.charAt( (int) ( n % base ) ) );
10 }
```

2. Java's `toString` method can take any base, but many languages do not have this built-in capability.

```
public final class PrintInt
{
    private static final String DIGIT_TABLE = "0123456789abcdef";
    private static final int    MAX_BASE    = DIGIT_TABLE.length( );

    // Print n in any base, recursively
    // Precondition: n >= 0, 2 <= base <= MAX_BASE
    private static void printIntRec( long n, int base )
    {
        if( n >= base )
            printIntRec( n / base, base );
        System.out.print( DIGIT_TABLE.charAt( (int) ( n % base ) ) );
    }

    // Driver routine
    public static void printInt( long n, int base )
    {
        if( base <= 1 || base > MAX_BASE )
            System.err.println( "Cannot print in base " + base );
        else
        {
            if( n < 0 )
            {
                n = -n;
                System.out.print( "-" );
            }
            printIntRec( n, base );
        }
    }
}
```

figure 7.4

A robust number-printing program

A *driver routine* tests the validity of the first call and then calls the recursive routine.

We can make the routine more robust by adding an explicit test for `base`. The problem with this strategy is that the test would be executed during each of the recursive calls to `printInt`, not just during the first call. Once `base` is valid in the first call, to retest it is silly because it does not change in the course of the recursion and thus must still be valid. One way to avoid this inefficiency is to set up a driver routine. A *driver routine* tests the validity of `base` and then calls the recursive routine, as shown in Figure 7.4. The use of driver routines for recursive programs is a common technique.

7.3.2 why it works

In Theorem 7.3 we show, somewhat rigorously, that the `printDecimal` algorithm works. Our goal is to verify that the algorithm is correct, so the proof is based on the assumption that we have made no syntax errors.

Theorem 7.3 The algorithm `printDecimal` shown in Figure 7.2 correctly prints `n` in base 10.

Proof Let k be the number of digits in `n`. The proof is by induction on k.

Basis: If $k = 1$, then no recursive call is made, and line 7 correctly outputs the one digit of `n`.

Inductive Hypothesis: Assume that `printDecimal` works correctly for all $k \geq 1$ digit integers. We show that this assumption implies correctness for any $k + 1$ digit integer `n`. Because $k \geq 1$, the `if` statement at line 5 is satisfied for a $k + 1$ digit integer `n`. By the inductive hypothesis, the recursive call at line 6 prints the first k digits of `n`. Then line 7 prints the final digit. Thus if any k digit integer can be printed, then so can a $k + 1$ digit integer. By induction, we conclude that `printDecimal` works for all k, and thus all `n`.

Recursive algorithms can be proven correct with mathematical induction.

The proof of Theorem 7.3 illustrates an important principle. When designing a recursive algorithm, we can always assume that the recursive calls work (if they progress toward the base case) because, when a proof is performed, this assumption is used as the inductive hypothesis.

At first glance such an assumption seems strange. However, recall that we always assume that method calls work, and thus the assumption that the recursive call works is really no different. Like any method, a recursive routine needs to combine solutions from calls to other methods to obtain a solution. However, other methods may include easier instances of the original method.

This observation leads us to the third fundamental rule of recursion.

3. *"You gotta believe":* Always assume that the recursive call works.

The third fundamental rule of recursion: Always assume that the recursive call works. Use this rule to design your algorithms.

Rule 3 tells us that when we design a recursive method, we do not have to attempt to trace the possibly long path of recursive calls. As we showed earlier, this task can be daunting and tends to make the design and verification more difficult. A good use of recursion makes such a trace almost impossible to understand. Intuitively, we are letting the computer handle the bookkeeping that, were we to do ourselves, would result in much longer code.

This principle is so important that we state it again: *Always assume that the recursive call works.*

7.3.3 how it works

Recall that the implementation of recursion requires additional bookkeeping on the part of the computer. Said another way, the implementation of any method requires bookkeeping, and a recursive call is not particularly special (except that it can overload the computer's bookkeeping limitations by calling itself too many times).

The bookkeeping in a procedural or object-oriented language is done by using a stack of *activation records*. Recursion is a natural by-product.

Java, like other languages such as C++, implements methods by using an internal stack of activation records. An *activation record* contains relevant information about the method, including, for instance, the values of the parameters and local variables. The actual contents of the activation record is system dependent.

Method calling and method return sequences are stack operations.

The stack of activation records is used because methods return in reverse order of their invocation. Recall that stacks are great for reversing the order of things. In the most popular scenario, the top of the stack stores the activation record for the currently active method. When method *G* is called, an activation record for *G* is pushed onto the stack, which makes *G* the currently active method. When a method returns, the stack is popped and the activation record that is the new top of the stack contains the restored values.

As an example, Figure 7.5 shows a stack of activation records that occurs in the course of evaluating `s(4)`. At this point, we have the calls to `main`, `s(4)`, and `s(3)` pending and we are actively processing `s(2)`.

The space overhead is the memory used to store an activation record for each currently active method. Thus, in our earlier example where `s(8883)` crashes, the system has room for roughly 8,883 activation records. (Note that `main` generates an activation record itself.) The pushing and popping of the internal stack also represents the overhead of executing a method call.

Recursion can always be removed by using a stack. This is occasionally required to save space.

The close relation between recursion and stacks tells us that recursive programs can always be implemented iteractively with an explicit stack. Presumably our stack will store items that are smaller than an activation record, so we can also reasonably expect to use less space. The result is slightly faster but longer code. Modern optimizing compilers have lessened the costs associ-

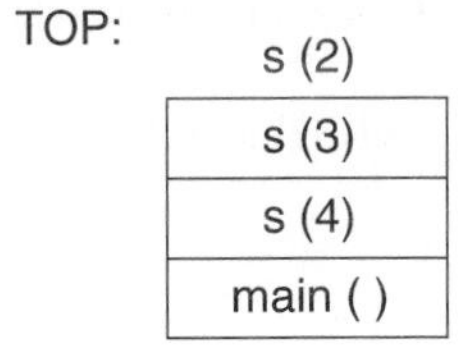

figure 7.5

A stack of activation records

ated with recursion to such a degree that, for the purposes of speed, removing recursion from an application that uses it well is rarely worthwhile.

7.3.4 too much recursion can be dangerous

Do not use recursion as a substitute for a simple loop.

In this text we give many examples of the power of recursion. However, before we look at those examples, you should recognize that recursion is not always appropriate. For instance, the use of recursion in Figure 7.1 is poor because a loop would do just as well. A practical liability is that the overhead of the recursive call takes time and limits the value of `n` for which the program is correct. A good rule of thumb is that you should never use recursion as a substitute for a simple loop.

The *i*th *Fibonacci number* is the sum of the two previous Fibonacci numbers.

A much more serious problem is illustrated by an attempt to calculate the Fibonacci numbers recursively. The *Fibonacci numbers* $F_0, F_1, \ldots, F_i$ are defined as follows: $F_0 = 0$ and $F_1 = 1$; the *i*th Fibonacci number equals the sum of the (*i*th – 1) and (*i*th – 2) Fibonacci numbers; thus $F_i = F_{i-1} + F_{i-2}$. From this definition we can determine that the series of Fibonacci numbers continues: 1, 2, 3, 5, 8, 13, 21, 34, 55, 89, … .

Do not do redundant work recursively; the program will be incredibly inefficient.

The Fibonacci numbers have an incredible number of properties, which seem always to crop up. In fact, one journal, *The Fibonacci Quarterly*, exists solely for the purpose of publishing theorems involving the Fibonacci numbers. For instance, the sum of the squares of two consecutive Fibonacci numbers is another Fibonacci number. The sum of the first *N* Fibonacci numbers is one less than F_{N+2} (see Exercise 7.9 for some other interesting identities).

Because the Fibonacci numbers are recursively defined, writing a recursive routine to determine F_N seems natural. This recursive routine, shown in Figure 7.6, works but has a serious problem. On our relatively fast machine, it takes nearly a minute to compute F_{40}, an absurd amount of time considering that the basic calculation requires only 39 additions.

The underlying problem is that this recursive routine performs redundant calculations. To compute `fib(n)`, we recursively compute `fib(n-1)`. When the recursive call returns, we compute `fib(n-2)` by using another recursive call.

figure 7.6

A recursive routine for Fibonacci numbers: A bad idea

```
// Compute the Nth Fibonacci number.
// Bad algorithm.
public static long fib( int n )
{
    if( n <= 1 )
        return n;
    else
        return fib( n - 1 ) + fib( n - 2 );
}
```

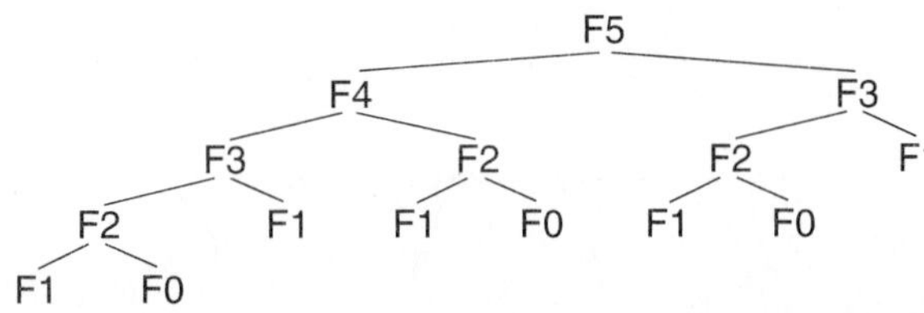

figure 7.7

A trace of the recursive calculation of the Fibonacci numbers

But we have already computed `fib(n-2)` in the process of computing `fib(n-1)`, so the call to `fib(n-2)` is a wasted, redundant calculation. In effect, we make two calls to `fib(n-2)` instead of only one.

Normally, making two method calls instead of one would only double the running time of a program. However, here it is worse than that: Each call to `fib(n-1)` and each call to `fib(n-2)` makes a call to `fib(n-3)`; thus there are actually three calls to `fib(n-3)`. In fact, it keeps getting worse: Each call to `fib(n-2)` or `fib(n-3)` results in a call to `fib(n-4)`, so there are five calls to `fib(n-4)`. Thus we get a compounding effect: Each recursive call does more and more redundant work.

The recursive routine `fib` is exponential.

Let $C(N)$ be the number of calls to `fib` made during the evaluation of `fib(n)`. Clearly $C(0) = C(1) = 1$ call. For $N \geq 2$, we call `fib(n)`, plus all the calls needed to evaluate `fib(n-1)` and `fib(n-2)` recursively and independently. Thus $C(N) = C(N-1) + C(N-2) + 1$. By induction, we can easily verify that for $N \geq 3$ the solution to this recurrence is $C(N) = F_{N+2} + F_{N-1} - 1$. Thus the number of recursive calls is larger than the Fibonacci number we are trying to compute, and it is exponential. For $N = 40$, $F_{40} = 102{,}334{,}155$, and the total number of recursive calls is more than 300,000,000. No wonder the program takes forever. The explosive growth of the number of recursive calls is illustrated in Figure 7.7.

This example illustrates the fourth and final basic rule of recursion.

The fourth fundamental rule of recursion: Never duplicate work by solving the same instance of a problem in separate recursive calls.

4. *Compound interest rule:* Never duplicate work by solving the same instance of a problem in separate recursive calls.

7.3.5 preview of trees

The *tree* is a fundamental structure in computer science. Almost all operating systems store files in trees or tree-like structures. Trees are also used in compiler design, text processing, and searching algorithms. We discuss trees in detail in Chapters 18 and 19. We also make use of trees in Sections 11.2.4 (expression trees) and 12.1 (Huffman codes).

One definition of the tree is recursive: Either a tree is empty or it consists of a root and zero or more nonempty subtrees $T_1, T_2, \ldots, T_k$, each of whose roots are connected by an edge from the root, as illustrated in Figure 7.8. In

figure 7.8

A tree viewed recursively

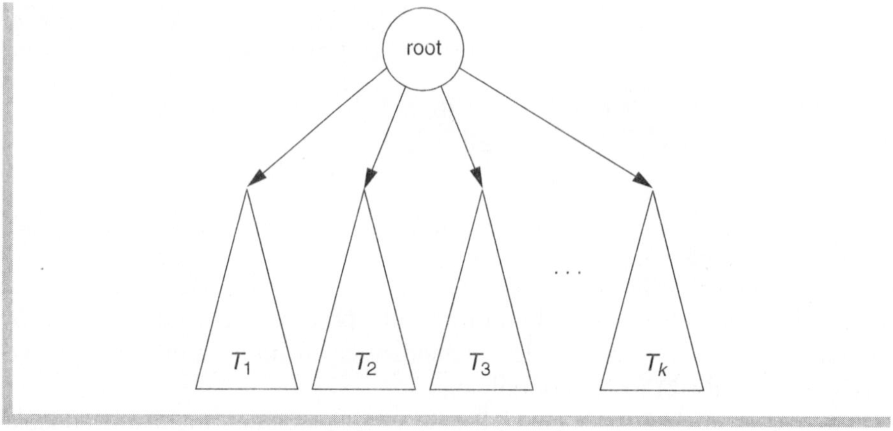

certain instances (most notably, the *binary trees* discussed in Chapter 18), we may allow some of the subtrees to be empty.

A *tree* consists of a set of nodes and a set of directed edges that connect them.

Nonrecursively, then, a *tree* consists of a set of nodes and a set of directed edges that connect pairs of nodes. Throughout this text we consider only rooted trees. A rooted tree has the following properties.

- One node is distinguished as the root.
- Every node *c*, except the root, is connected by an edge from exactly one other node *p*. Node *p* is *c*'s *parent*, and *c* is one of *p*'s *children*.
- A unique path traverses from the root to each node. The number of edges that must be followed is the *path length*.

Parents and children are naturally defined. A directed edge connects the *parent* to the *child*.

Parents and children are naturally defined. A directed edge connects the *parent* to the *child*.

A *leaf* has no children.

Figure 7.9 illustrates a tree. The root node is *A*: *A*'s children are *B, C, D,* and *E*. Because *A* is the root, it has no parent; all other nodes have parents. For instance, *B*'s parent is *A*. A node that has no children is called a *leaf.* The leaves in this tree are *C, F, G, H, I,* and *K*. The length of the path from *A* to *K* is 3 (edges); the length of the path from *A* to *A* is 0 (edges).

7.3.6 additional examples

Perhaps the best way to understand recursion is to consider examples. In this section, we look at four more examples of recursion. The first two are easily implemented nonrecursively, but the last two show off some of the power of recursion.

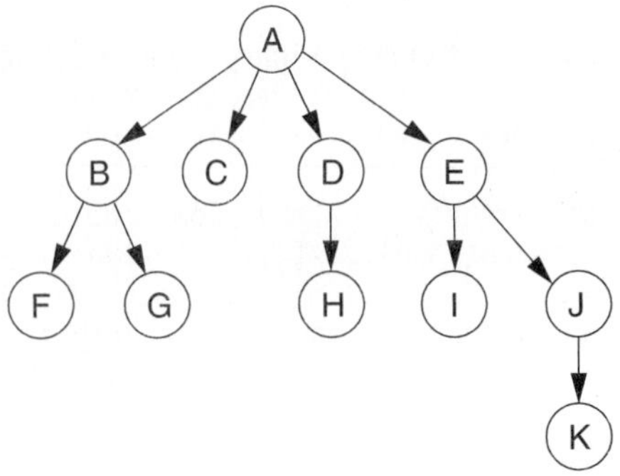

figure 7.9

A tree

factorials

Recall that $N!$ is the product of the first N integers. Thus we can express $N!$ as N times $(N-1)!$. Combined with the base case $1! = 1$, this information immediately provides all that we need for a recursive implementation. It is shown in Figure 7.10.

binary search

In Section 5.6.2 we described the binary search. Recall that in a binary search, we perform a search in a sorted array A by examining the middle element. If we have a match, we are done. Otherwise, if the item being searched for is smaller than the middle element, we search in the subarray that is to the left of the middle element. Otherwise, we search in the subarray that is to the right of the middle element. This procedure presumes that the subarray is not empty; if it is, the item is not found.

This description translates directly into the recursive method shown in Figure 7.11. The code illustrates a thematic technique in which the public driver routine makes an initial call to a recursive routine and passes on the return value. Here, the driver sets the low and high points of the subarray, namely, `0` and `a.length-1`.

In the recursive method, the base case at lines 18 and 19 handles an empty subarray. Otherwise, we follow the description given previously by making a

```
// Evaluate n!
public static long factorial( int n )
{
    if( n <= 1 )    // base case
        return 1;
    else
        return n * factorial( n - 1 );
}
```

figure 7.10

Recursive implementation of the `factorial` method

figure 7.11

A binary search routine, using recursion

```
1      /**
2       * Performs the standard binary search using two comparisons
3       * per level. This is a driver that calls the recursive method.
4       * @return index where item is found or NOT_FOUND if not found.
5       */
6      public static <AnyType extends Comparable<? super AnyType>>
7      int binarySearch( AnyType [ ] a, AnyType x )
8      {
9          return binarySearch( a, x, 0, a.length -1 );
10     }
11
12     /**
13      * Hidden recursive routine.
14      */
15     private static <AnyType extends Comparable<? super AnyType>>
16     int binarySearch( AnyType [ ] a, AnyType x, int low, int high )
17     {
18         if( low > high )
19             return NOT_FOUND;
20
21         int mid = ( low + high ) / 2;
22
23         if( a[ mid ].compareTo( x ) < 0 )
24             return binarySearch( a, x, mid + 1, high );
25         else if( a[ mid ].compareTo( x ) > 0 )
26             return binarySearch( a, x, low, mid - 1 );
27         else
28             return mid;
29     }
```

recursive call on the appropriate subarray (line 24 or 26) if a match has not been detected. When a match is detected, the matching index is returned at line 28.

Note that the running time, in terms of Big-Oh, is unchanged from the nonrecursive implementation because we are performing the same work. In practice, the running time would be expected to be slightly larger because of the hidden costs of recursion.

drawing a ruler

Figure 7.12 shows the result of running a Java program that draws ruler markings. Here, we consider the problem of marking 1 inch. In the middle is the longest mark. In Figure 7.12, to the left of the middle is a miniaturized version of the ruler and to the right of the middle is a second miniaturized version. This result suggests a recursive algorithm that first draws the middle line and then draws the left and right halves.

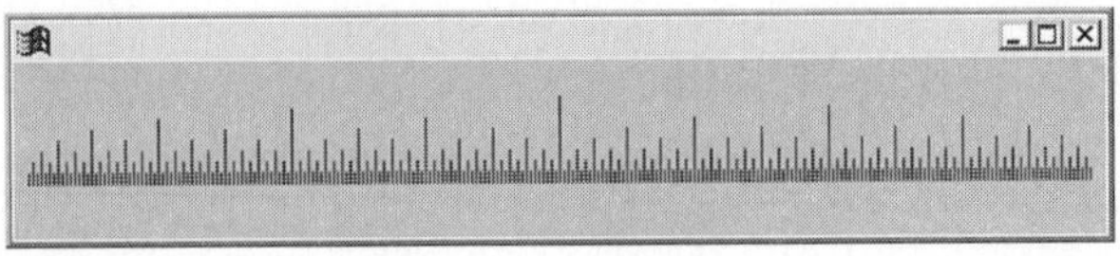

figure 7.12

A recursively drawn ruler

You do not have to understand the details of drawing lines and shapes in Java to understand this program. You simply need to know that a `Graphics` object is something that gets drawn to. The `drawRuler` method in Figure 7.13 is our recursive routine. It uses the `drawLine` method, which is part of the `Graphics` class. The method `drawLine` draws a line from one (*x*, *y*) coordinate to another (*x*, *y*) coordinate, where coordinates are offset from the top-left corner.

Our routine draws markings at `level` different heights; each recursive call is one level deeper (in Figure 7.12, there are eight levels). It first disposes of the base case at lines 4 and 5. Then the midpoint mark is drawn at line 9. Finally, the two miniatures are drawn recursively at lines 11 and 12. In the online code, we include extra code to slow down the drawing. In that way, we can see the order in which the lines are drawn by the recursive algorithm.

fractal star

Shown in Figure 7.14(a) is a seemingly complex pattern called a *fractal star*, which we can easily draw by using recursion. The entire canvas is initially gray (not shown); the pattern is formed by drawing white squares onto the gray background. The last square drawn is over the center. Figure 7.14(b) shows the drawing immediately before the last square is added. Thus prior to the last square being drawn, four miniature versions have been drawn, one in each of the four quadrants. This pattern provides the information needed to derive the recursive algorithm.

```
1   // Java code to draw Figure 7.12.
2   void drawRuler( Graphics g, int left, int right, int level )
3   {
4       if( level < 1 )
5           return;
6
7       int mid = ( left + right ) / 2;
8
9       g.drawLine( mid, 80, mid, 80 - level * 5 );
10
11      drawRuler( g, left, mid - 1, level - 1 );
12      drawRuler( g, mid + 1, right, level - 1 );
13  }
```

figure 7.13

A recursive method for drawing a ruler

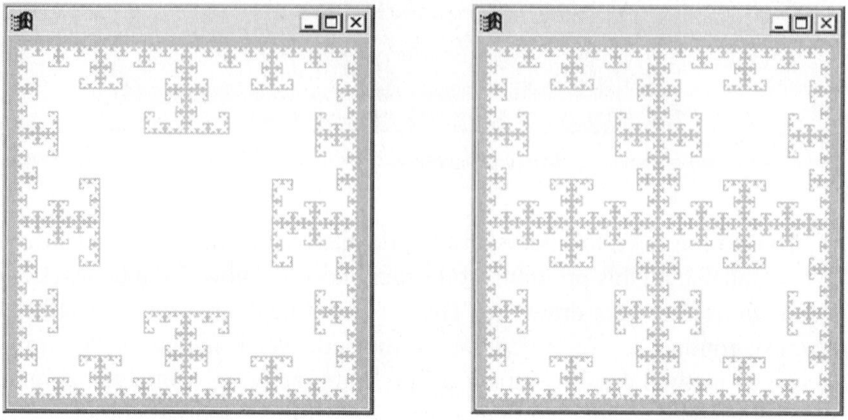

(a) (b)

figure 7.14

(a) A fractal star outline drawn by the code shown in Figure 7.15; (b) The same star immediately before the last square is added

As with the previous example, the method `drawFractal` uses a Java library routine. In this case, `fillRect` draws a rectangle; its upper left-hand corner and dimensions must be specified. The code is shown in Figure 7.15. The parameters to `drawFractal` include the center of the fractal and the overall dimension. From this, we can compute, at line 5, the size of the large central square. After

figure 7.15

Code for drawing the fractal star outline shown in Figure 7.14

```
 1  // Draw picture in Figure 7.14.
 2  void drawFractal( Graphics g, int xCenter,
 3                    int yCenter, int boundingDim )
 4  {
 5      int side = boundingDim / 2;
 6
 7      if( side < 1 )
 8          return;
 9
10          // Compute corners.
11      int left =   xCenter - side / 2;
12      int top =    yCenter - side / 2;
13      int right =  xCenter + side / 2;
14      int bottom = yCenter + side / 2;
15
16          // Recursively draw four quadrants.
17      drawFractal( g, left, top, boundingDim / 2 );
18      drawFractal( g, left, bottom, boundingDim / 2 );
19      drawFractal( g, right, top, boundingDim / 2 );
20      drawFractal( g, right, bottom, boundingDim / 2 );
21
22          // Draw central square, overlapping quadrants.
23      g.fillRect( left, top, right - left, bottom - top );
24  }
```

handling the base case at lines 7 and 8, we compute the boundaries of the central rectangle. We can then draw the four miniature fractals at lines 17 to 20. Finally, we draw the central square at line 23. Note that this square must be drawn after the recursive calls. Otherwise, we obtain a different picture (in Exercise 7.26, you are asked to describe the difference).

7.4 numerical applications

In this section we look at three problems drawn primarily from number theory. Number theory used to be considered an interesting but useless branch of mathematics. However, in the last 30 years, an important application for number theory has emerged: data security. We begin the discussion with a small amount of mathematical background and then show recursive algorithms to solve three problems. We can combine these routines in conjunction with a fourth algorithm that is more complex (described in Chapter 9), to implement an algorithm that can be used to encode and decode messages. To date, nobody has been able to show that the encryption scheme described here is not secure.

Here are the four problems we examine.

1. *Modular exponentiation:* Compute $X^N(\text{mod } P)$.
2. *Greatest common divisor:* Compute gcd(A, B).
3. *Multiplicative inverse:* Solve $AX \equiv 1(\text{mod } P)$ for X.
4. *Primality testing:* Determine whether N is prime (deferred to Chapter 9).

The integers we expect to deal with are all large, requiring at least 100 digits each. Therefore we must have a way to represent large integers, along with a complete set of algorithms for the basic operations of addition, subtraction, multiplication, division, and so on. Java provides the `BigInteger` class for this purpose. Implementing it efficiently is no trivial matter, and in fact there is extensive literature on the subject.

We use `long` numbers to simplify our code presentation. The algorithms described here work with large objects but still execute in a reasonable amount of time.

7.4.1 modular arithmetic

The problems in this section, as well as the implementation of the hash table data structure (Chapter 20), require the use of the Java `%` operator. The `%` operator, denoted as `operator%`, computes the remainder of two integral types. For example, `13%10` evaluates to 3, as does `3%10`, and `23%10`. When we compute the remainder of a division by 10, the possible results range from 0 to 9.[3] This range makes `operator%` useful for generating small integers.

If two numbers A and B give the same remainder when divided by N, we say that they are congruent modulo N, written as $A \equiv B \pmod{N}$. In this case, it must be true that N divides $A - B$. Furthermore, the converse is true: If N divides $A - B$, then $A \equiv B \pmod{N}$. Because there are only N possible remainders—0, 1, ..., $N - 1$— we say that the integers are divided into congruence classes modulo N. In other words, every integer can be placed in one of N classes, and those in the same class are congruent to each other, modulo N. We use three important theorems in our algorithms (we leave the proof of these facts as Exercise 7.10).

1. If $A \equiv B \pmod{N}$, then for any C, $A + C \equiv B + C \pmod{N}$.
2. If $A \equiv B \pmod{N}$, then for any D, $AD \equiv BD \pmod{N}$.
3. If $A \equiv B \pmod{N}$, then for any positive P, $A^P \equiv B^P \pmod{N}$.

These theorems allow certain calculations to be done with less effort. For instance, suppose that we want to know the last digit in 3333^{5555}. Because this number has more than 15,000 digits, it is expensive to compute the answer directly. However, what we want is to determine $3333^{5555} \pmod{10}$. As $3333 \equiv 3 \pmod{10}$, we need only to compute $3^{5555} \pmod{10}$. As $3^4 = 81$, we know that $3^4 \equiv 1 \pmod{10}$, and raising both sides to the power of 1388 tells us that $3^{5552} \equiv 1 \pmod{10}$. If we multiply both sides by $3^3 = 27$, we obtain $3^{5555} \equiv 27 \equiv 7 \pmod{10}$, thereby completing the calculation.

7.4.2 modular exponentiation

In this section we show how to compute $X^N \pmod{P}$ efficiently. We can do so by initializing `result` to 1 and then repeatedly multiplying `result` by X, applying the `%` operator after every multiplication. Using `operator%` in this way instead of just the last multiplication makes each multiplication easier because it keeps `result` smaller.

After N multiplications, `result` is the answer that we are looking for. However, doing N multiplications is impractical if N is a 100-digit `BigInteger`. In fact, if N is 1,000,000,000, it is impractical on all but the fastest machines.

A faster algorithm is based on the following observation. That is, if N is even, then

$$X^N = (X \cdot X)^{\lfloor N/2 \rfloor}$$

3. If `n` is negative, `n%10` ranges from 0 to –9.

and if N is odd, then

$$X^N = X \cdot X^{N-1} = X \cdot (X \cdot X)^{\lfloor N/2 \rfloor}$$

(Recall that $\lfloor X \rfloor$ is the largest integer that is smaller than or equal to X.) As before, to perform modular exponentiation, we apply a `%` after every multiplication.

The recursive algorithm shown in Figure 7.16 represents a direct implementation of this strategy. Lines 8 and 9 handle the base case: X^0 is 1, by definition.[4] At line 11, we make a recursive call based on the identity stated in the preceding paragraph. If N is even, this call computes the desired answer; if N is odd, we need to multiply by an extra X (and use `operator%`).

Exponentiation can be done in logarithmic number of multiplications.

This algorithm is faster than the simple algorithm proposed earlier. If $M(N)$ is the number of multiplications used by `power`, we have $M(N) \leq M(\lfloor N/2 \rfloor) + 2$. The reason is that if N is even, we perform one multiplication, plus those done recursively, and that if N is odd, we perform two multiplications, plus those done recursively. Because $M(0) = 0$, we can show that $M(N) < 2 \log N$. The logarithmic factor can be obtained without direct calculation by application of the halving principle (see Section 5.5), which tells us the number of recursive invocations of `power`. Moreover, an average value of $M(N)$ is $(3/2)\log N$, as in each recursive step N is equally likely to be even or odd. If N is a 100-digit number, in the worst case only about 665 multiplications (and typically only 500 on average) are needed.

```
1   /**
2    * Return x^n (mod p)
3    * Assumes x, n >= 0, p > 0, x < p, 0^0 = 1
4    * Overflow may occur if p > 31 bits.
5    */
6   public static long power( long x, long n, long p )
7   {
8       if( n == 0 )
9           return 1;
10
11      long tmp = power( ( x * x ) % p, n / 2, p );
12
13      if( n % 2 != 0 )
14          tmp = ( tmp * x ) % p;
15
16      return tmp;
17  }
```

figure 7.16
Modular exponentiation routine

4. We define $0^0 = 1$ for the purposes of this algorithm. We also assume that N is nonnegative and P is positive.

7.4.3 greatest common divisor and multiplicative inverses

The *greatest common divisor* (gcd) of two integers is the largest integer that divides both of them.

Given two nonnegative integers A and B, their greatest common divisor, gcd(A, B), is the largest integer D that divides both A and B. For instance, gcd(70, 25) is 5. In other words, the *greatest common divisor (gcd)* is the largest integer that divides two given integers.

We can easily verify that $\gcd(A, B) \equiv \gcd(A - B, B)$. If D divides both A and B, it must also divide $A - B$; and if D divides both $A - B$ and B, then it must also divide A.

This observation leads to a simple algorithm in which we repeatedly subtract B from A, transforming the problem into a smaller one. Eventually A becomes less than B, and then we can switch roles for A and B and continue from there. At some point B will become 0. Then we know that $\gcd(A, 0) \equiv A$, and as each transformation preserves the gcd of the original A and B, we have our answer. This algorithm is called *Euclid's algorithm* and was first described more than 2,000 years ago. Although correct, it is unusable for large numbers because a huge number of subtractions are likely to be required.

A computationally efficient modification is that the repeated subtractions of B from A until A is smaller than B is equivalent to the conversion of A to precisely A mod B. Thus $\gcd(A, B) \equiv \gcd(B, A \bmod B)$. This recursive definition, along with the base case in which $B = 0$, is used directly to obtain the routine shown in Figure 7.17. To visualize how it works, note that in the previous example we used the following sequence of recursive calls to deduce that the gcd of 70 and 25 is 5: $\gcd(70, 25) \Rightarrow \gcd(25, 20) \Rightarrow \gcd(20, 5) \Rightarrow \gcd(5, 0) \Rightarrow 5$.

The number of recursive calls used is proportional to the logarithm of A, which is the same order of magnitude as the other routines that we have presented in this section. The reason is that, in two recursive calls, the problem is reduced at least in half. The proof of this is left for you to do as Exercise 7.11.

figure 7.17

Computation of greatest common divisor

```
/**
 * Return the greatest common divisor.
 */
public static long gcd( long a, long b )
{
    if( b == 0 )
        return a;
    else
        return gcd( b, a % b );
}
```

The gcd algorithm is used implicitly to solve a similar mathematical problem. The solution $1 \le X < N$ to the equation $AX \equiv 1 (\text{mod } N)$ is called the *multiplicative inverse* of A, mod N. Also assume that $1 \le A < N$. For example, the inverse of 3, mod 13 is 9; that is, $3 \cdot 9$ mod 13 yields 1.

The greatest common divisor and multiplicative inverse can also be calculated in logarithmic time by using a variant of Euclid's algorithm.

The ability to compute multiplicative inverses is important because equations such as $3i \equiv 7(\text{mod } 13)$ are easily solved if we know the multiplicative inverse. These equations arise in many applications, including the encryption algorithm discussed at the end of this section. In this example, if we multiply by the inverse of 3 (namely 9), we obtain $i \equiv 63(\text{mod } 13)$, so $i = 11$ is a solution. If

$$AX \equiv 1(\text{mod } N), \quad \text{then} \quad AX + NY = 1(\text{mod } N)$$

is true for any Y. For some Y, the left-hand side must be exactly 1. Thus the equation

$$AX + NY = 1$$

is solvable if and only if A has a multiplicative inverse.

Given A and B, we show how to find X and Y satisfying

$$AX + BY = 1$$

We assume that $0 \le |B| < |A|$ and then extend the `gcd` algorithm to compute X and Y.

First, we consider the base case, $B \equiv 0$. In this case we have to solve $AX = 1$, which implies that both A and X are 1. In fact, if A is not 1, there is no multiplicative inverse. Hence A has a multiplicative inverse modulo N only if $\gcd(A, N) = 1$.

Otherwise, B is not zero. Recall that $\gcd(A, B) \equiv \gcd(B, A \text{ mod } B)$. So we let $A = BQ + R$. Here Q is the quotient and R is the remainder, and thus the recursive call is $\gcd(B, R)$. Suppose that we can recursively solve

$$BX_1 + RY_1 = 1$$

Since $R = A - BQ$, we have

$$BX_1 + (A - BQ)Y_1 = 1$$

which means that

$$AY_1 + B(X_1 - QY_1) = 1$$

Thus $X = Y_1$ and $Y = X_1 - \lfloor A/B \rfloor Y_1$ is a solution to $AX + BY = 1$. We code this observation directly as `fullGcd` in Figure 7.18. The method `inverse` just calls `fullGcd`, where *X* and *Y* are static class variables. The only detail left is that the value given for *X* may be negative. If it is, line 35 of `inverse` will make it positive. We leave a proof of that fact for you to do as Exercise 7.14. The proof can be done by induction.

figure 7.18

A routine for determining multiplicative inverse

```
1   // Internal variables for fullGcd
2   private static long x;
3   private static long y;
4
5   /**
6    * Works back through Euclid's algorithm to find
7    * x and y such that if gcd(a,b) = 1,
8    * ax + by = 1.
9    */
10  private static void fullGcd( long a, long b )
11  {
12      long x1, y1;
13
14      if( b == 0 )
15      {
16          x = 1;
17          y = 0;
18      }
19      else
20      {
21          fullGcd( b, a % b );
22          x1 = x; y1 = y;
23          x = y1;
24          y = x1 - ( a / b ) * y1;
25      }
26  }
27
28  /**
29   * Solve ax == 1 (mod n), assuming gcd( a, n ) = 1.
30   * @return x.
31   */
32  public static long inverse( long a, long n )
33  {
34      fullGcd( a, n );
35      return x > 0 ? x : x + n;
36  }
```

7.4.4 the rsa cryptosystem

For centuries, number theory was thought to be a completely impractical branch of mathematics. Recently, however, it has emerged as an important field because of its applicability to cryptography.

Number theory is used in cryptography because factoring appears to be a much harder process than multiplication.

The problem we consider has two parts. Suppose that Alice wants to send a message to Bob but that she is worried that the transmission may be compromised. For instance, if the transmission is over a phone line and the phone is tapped, somebody else may be reading the message. We assume that, even if there is eavesdropping on the phone line, there is no maliciousness (i.e., damage to the signal)—Bob gets whatever Alice sends.

A solution to this problem is to use *encryption,* an encoding scheme to transmit messages that cannot be read by other parties. Encryption consists of two parts. First, Alice *encrypts* the message and sends the result, which is no longer plainly readable. When Bob receives Alice's transmission, he *decrypts* it to obtain the original. The security of the algorithm is based on the fact that nobody else besides Bob should be able to perform the decryption, including Alice (if she did not save the original message).

Encryption is used to transmit messages so that they cannot be read by other parties.

Thus Bob must provide Alice with a method of encryption that only he knows how to reverse. This problem is extremely challenging. Many proposed algorithms can be compromised by subtle code-breaking techniques. One method, described here, is the *RSA cryptosystem* (named after the initials of its authors), an elegant implementation of an encryption strategy.

The *RSA cryptosystem* is a popular encryption method.

Here we give only a high-level overview of encryption, showing how the methods written in this section interact in a practical way. The references contain pointers to more detailed descriptions, as well as proofs of the key properties of the algorithm.

First, however, note that a message consists of a sequence of characters and that each character is just a sequence of bits. Thus a message is a sequence of bits. If we break the message into blocks of B bits, we can interpret the message as a series of very large numbers. Thus the basic problem is reduced to encrypting a large number and then decrypting the result.

computation of the rsa constants

The RSA algorithm begins by having the receiver determine some constants. First, two large primes p and q are randomly chosen. Typically, these would be at least 100 or so digits each. For the purposes of this example, suppose that $p = 127$ and $q = 211$. Note that Bob is the receiver and thus is performing these computations. Note, also, that primes are plentiful. Bob can thus keep trying random numbers until two of them pass the primality test (discussed in Chapter 9).

Next, Bob computes $N = pq$ and $N' = (p-1)(q-1)$, which for this example gives $N = 26{,}797$ and $N' = 26{,}460$. Bob continues by choosing any $e > 1$ such that $\gcd(e, N') = 1$. In mathematical terms, he chooses any e that is relatively prime to N'. Bob can keep trying different values of e by using the routine shown in Figure 7.17 until he finds one that satisfies the property. Any prime e would work, so finding e is at least as easy as finding a prime number. In this case, $e = 13{,}379$ is one of many valid choices. Next, d, the multiplicative inverse of e, mod N' is computed by using the routine shown in Figure 7.18. In this example, $d = 11{,}099$.

Once Bob has computed all these constants, he does the following. First, he destroys p, q, and N'. The security of the system is compromised if any one of these values is discovered. Bob then tells anybody who wants to send him an encrypted message the values of e and N, but he keeps d secret.

encryption and decryption algorithms

To encrypt an integer M, the sender computes $M^e (\text{mod } N)$ and sends it. In our case, if $M = 10{,}237$, the value sent is 8,422. When an encrypted integer R is received, all Bob has to do is compute $R^d (\text{mod } N)$. For $R = 8{,}422$, he gets back the original $M = 10{,}237$ (which is not accidental). Both encryption and decryption can thus be carried out by using the modular exponentiation routine given in Figure 7.16.

The algorithm works because the choices of e, d, and N guarantee (via a number theory proof beyond the scope of this text) that $M^{ed} = M (\text{mod } N)$, so long as M and N share no common factors. As the only factors of N are two 100-digit primes, it is virtually impossible for that to occur.[5] Thus decryption of the encrypted text gets the original back.

What makes the scheme seem secure is that knowledge of d is apparently required in order to decode. Now N and e uniquely determine d. For instance, if we factor N, we get p and q and can then reconstruct d. The caveat is that factoring is apparently very hard to do for large numbers. Thus the security of the RSA system is based on the belief that factoring large numbers is intrinsically very difficult. So far it has held up well.

In *public key cryptography*, each participant publishes the code others can use to send encrypted messages but keeps the decrypting code secret.

This general scheme is known as *public key cryptography*, by which anybody who wants to receive messages publishes encryption information for anybody else to use but keeps the decryption code secret. In the RSA system, e and N would be computed once by each person and listed in a publicly readable place.

The RSA algorithm is widely used to implement secure e-mail, as well as secure Internet transactions. When you access a Web page via the `https` protocol, a secure transaction is being performed via cryptography. The method

5. You are more likely to win a typical state lottery 13 weeks in a row. However, if M and N have a common factor, the system is compromised because the gcd will be a factor of N.

actually employed is more complex than described here. One problem is that the RSA algorithm is somewhat slow for sending large messages.

A faster method is called *DES*. Unlike the RSA algorithm, DES is a single-key algorithm, meaning that the same key serves both to encode and decode. It is like the typical lock on your house door. The problem with single-key algorithms is that both parties need to share the single key. How does one party ensure that the other party has the single key? That problem can be solved by using the RSA algorithm. A typical solution is that, say, Alice will randomly generate a single key for DES encryption. She then encrypts her message by using DES, which is much faster than using RSA. She transmits the encrypted message to Bob. For Bob to decode the encrypted message, he needs to get the DES key that Alice used. A DES key is relatively short, so Alice can use RSA to encrypt the DES key and then send it in a second transmission to Bob. Bob next decrypts Alice's second transmission, thus obtaining the DES key, at which point he can decode the original message. These types of protocols, with enhancements, form the basis of most practical encryption implementations.

In practice, RSA is used to encrypt the key used by a single-key encryption algorithm, such as DES.

7.5 divide-and-conquer algorithms

An important problem-solving technique that makes use of recursion is divide and conquer. A *divide-and-conquer algorithm* is an efficient recursive algorithm that consist of two parts:

- *Divide,* in which smaller problems are solved recursively (except, of course, base cases)
- *Conquer,* in which the solution to the original problem is then formed from the solutions to the subproblems

A *divide-and-conquer algorithm* is a recursive algorithm that is generally very efficient.

In *divide and conquer,* the recursion is the *divide,* and the overhead is the *conquer.*

Traditionally, routines in which the algorithm contains at least two recursive calls are called divide-and-conquer algorithms, whereas routines whose text contains only one recursive call are not. Consequently, the recursive routines presented so far in this chapter are not divide-and-conquer algorithms. Also, the subproblems usually must be disjoint (i.e., essentially nonoverlapping), so as to avoid the excessive costs seen in the sample recursive computation of the Fibonacci numbers.

In this section we give an example of the divide-and-conquer paradigm. First we show how to use recursion to solve the maximum subsequence sum problem. Then we provide an analysis to show that the running time is $O(N \log N)$. Although we have already used a linear algorithm for this problem, the solution here is thematic of others in a wide range of applications, including the sorting algorithms, such as mergesort and quicksort, discussed in Chapter 8. Consequently, learning the technique is important. Finally, we show the general form for the running time of a broad class of divide-and-conquer algorithms.

7.5.1 the maximum contiguous subsequence sum problem

In Section 5.3 we discussed the problem of finding, in a sequence of numbers, a contiguous subsequence of maximum sum. For convenience, we restate the problem here.

maximum contiguous subsequence sum problem
Given (possibly negative) integers $A_1, A_2, \ldots, A_N$, find (and identify the sequence corresponding to) the maximum value of $\sum_{k=i}^{j} A_k$. The maximum contiguous subsequence sum is zero if all the integers are negative.

The maximum contiguous subsequence sum problem can be solved with a divide-and-conquer algorithm.

We presented three algorithms of various complexity. One was a cubic algorithm based on an exhaustive search: We calculated the sum of each possible subsequence and selected the maximum. We described a quadratic improvement that takes advantage of the fact that each new subsequence can be computed in constant time from a previous subsequence. Because we have $O(N^2)$ subsequences, this bound is the best that can be achieved with an approach that directly examines all subsequences. We also gave a linear-time algorithm that works by examining only a few subsequences. However, its correctness is not obvious.

Let us consider a divide-and-conquer algorithm. Suppose that the sample input is {4, –3, 5, –2, –1, 2, 6, –2}. We divide this input into two halves, as shown in Figure 7.19. Then the maximum contiguous subsequence sum can occur in one of three ways.

- *Case 1:* It resides entirely in the first half.
- *Case 2:* It resides entirely in the second half.
- *Case 3:* It begins in the first half but ends in the second half.

We show how to find the maximums for each of these three cases more efficiently than by using an exhaustive search.

We begin by looking at case 3. We want to avoid the nested loop that results from considering all $N/2$ starting points and $N/2$ ending points independently. We can do so by replacing two nested loops by two consecutive loops. The consecutive loops, each of size $N/2$, combine to require only linear work. We can make this substitution because any contiguous subsequence that begins in the first half and ends in the second half must include both the last element of the first half and the first element of the second half.

Figure 7.19 shows that for each element in the first half, we can calculate the contiguous subsequence sum that ends at the rightmost item. We do so with a right-to-left scan, starting from the border between the two halves. Similarly, we can calculate the contiguous subsequence sum for all sequences that begin with the first element in the second half. We can then combine these two subsequences to form the maximum contiguous subsequence that spans the dividing border. In this example, the resulting sequence spans from the first element in the first half to the next-to-last element in the second half. The total sum is the sum of the two subsequences, or 4 + 7 = 11.

This analysis shows that case 3 can be solved in linear time. But what about cases 1 and 2? Because there are $N/2$ elements in each half, an exhaustive search applied to each half still requires quadratic time per half; specifically, all we have done is eliminate roughly half of the work, and half of quadratic is still quadratic. In cases 1 and 2 we can apply the same strategy—that of dividing into more halves. We can keep dividing those quarters further and further until splitting is impossible. This approach is succinctly stated as follows: *Solve cases 1 and 2 recursively.* As we demonstrate later, doing so lowers the running time below quadratic because the savings compound throughout the algorithm. The following is a summary of the main portion of the algorithm:

1. Recursively compute the maximum contiguous subsequence sum that resides entirely in the first half
2. Recursively compute the maximum contiguous subsequence sum that resides entirely in the second half
3. Compute, via two consecutive loops, the maximum contiguous subsequence sum that begins in the first half but ends in the second half
4. Choose the largest of the three sums.

First Half				Second Half				
4	−3	5	−2	−1	2	6	−2	Values
4*	0	3	−2	−1	1	7*	5	Running sums

Running sum from the center (*denotes maximum for each half).

figure 7.19

Dividing the maximum contiguous subsequence problem into halves

A recursive algorithm requires specifying a base case. When the size of the problem reaches one element, we do not use recursion. The resulting Java method is coded in Figure 7.20.

figure 7.20

A divide-and-conquer algorithm for the maximum contiguous subsequence sum problem

```
/**
 * Recursive maximum contiguous subsequence sum algorithm.
 * Finds maximum sum in subarray spanning a[left..right].
 * Does not attempt to maintain actual best sequence.
 */
private static int maxSumRec( int [ ] a, int left, int right )
{
    int maxLeftBorderSum = 0, maxRightBorderSum = 0;
    int leftBorderSum = 0, rightBorderSum = 0;
    int center = ( left + right ) / 2;

    if( left == right )  // Base case
        return a[ left ] > 0 ? a[ left ] : 0;

    int maxLeftSum  = maxSumRec( a, left, center );
    int maxRightSum = maxSumRec( a, center + 1, right );

    for( int i = center; i >= left; i-- )
    {
        leftBorderSum += a[ i ];
        if( leftBorderSum > maxLeftBorderSum )
            maxLeftBorderSum = leftBorderSum;
    }

    for( int i = center + 1; i <= right; i++ )
    {
        rightBorderSum += a[ i ];
        if( rightBorderSum > maxRightBorderSum )
            maxRightBorderSum = rightBorderSum;
    }

    return max3( maxLeftSum, maxRightSum,
                 maxLeftBorderSum + maxRightBorderSum );
}

/**
 * Driver for divide-and-conquer maximum contiguous
 * subsequence sum algorithm.
 */
public static int maxSubsequenceSum( int [ ] a )
{
    return a.length > 0 ? maxSumRec( a, 0, a.length - 1 ) : 0;
}
```

The general form for the recursive call is to pass the input array along with the left and right borders, which delimit the portion of the array being operated on. A one-line driver routine sets this action up by passing the borders 0 and $N - 1$ along with the array.

Lines 12 and 13 handle the base case. If `left==right`, there is one element, and it is the maximum contiguous subsequence if the element is nonnegative (otherwise, the empty sequence with sum 0 is maximum). Lines 15 and 16 perform the two recursive calls. These calls are always on a smaller problem than the original; thus we progress toward the base case. Lines 18 to 23 and then 25 to 30 calculate the maximum sums that touch the center border. The sum of these two values is the maximum sum that spans both halves. The routine `max3` (not shown) returns the largest of the three possibilities.

7.5.2 analysis of a basic divide-and-conquer recurrence

Intuitive analysis of the maximum contiguous subsequence sum divide-and-conquer algorithm: We spend $O(N)$ per level.

The recursive maximum contiguous subsequence sum algorithm works by performing linear work to compute a sum that spans the center border and then performing two recursive calls. These calls collectively compute a sum that spans the center border, do further recursive calls, and so on. The total work performed by the algorithm is then proportional to the scanning done over all the recursive calls.

Figure 7.21 graphically illustrates how the algorithm works for $N = 8$ elements. Each rectangle represents a call to `maxSumRec`, and the length of the rectangle is proportional to the size of the subarray (and hence the cost of the scanning of the subarray) being operated on by the invocation. The initial call is shown on the first line: The size of the subarray is N, which represents the cost of the scanning for the third case. The initial call then makes two recursive calls, yielding two subarrays of size $N/2$. The cost of each scan in case 3 is half the original cost, but as there are two such recursive calls, the combined cost of these recursive calls is also N. Each of those two recursive instances themselves make two recursive calls, yielding four subproblems that are a quarter of the original size. Thus the total of all case 3 costs is also N.

Eventually, we reach the base case. Each base case has size 1, and there are N of them. Of course, there are no case 3 costs in this instance, but we charge 1 unit for performing the check that determines whether the sole element is positive or negative. The total cost then, as illustrated in Figure 7.21, is N per level of recursion. Each level halves the size of the basic problem, so the halving principle tells us that there are approximately $\log N$ levels. In fact, the number of levels is $1 + \lceil \log N \rceil$ (which is 4 when N equals 8). Thus we expect that the total running time is $O(N \log N)$.

This analysis gives an intuitive explanation of why the running time is $O(N \log N)$. In general, however, expanding a recursive algorithm to examine behavior is a bad idea; it violates the third rule of recursion. We next consider a more formal mathematical treatment.

Note that the more formal analysis holds for all classes of algorithms that recursively solve two halves and use linear additional work.

Let $T(N)$ represent the time required to solve a maximum contiguous subsequence sum problem of size N. If $N = 1$, the program takes some constant amount of time to execute lines 12 to 13, which we call 1 unit. Thus $T(1) = 1$. Otherwise, the program must perform two recursive calls and the linear work involved in computing the maximum sum for case 3. The constant overhead is absorbed by the $O(N)$ term. How long do the two recursive calls take? Because they solve problems of size $N/2$, we know that they must each require $T(N/2)$ units of time; consequently, the total recursive work is $2T(N/2)$. This analysis gives the equations

$$T(1) = 1$$
$$T(N) = 2T(N/2) + O(N)$$

Of course, for the second equation to make sense, N must be a power of 2. Otherwise, at some point, $N/2$ will not be even. A more precise equation is

$$T(N) = T(\lfloor N/2 \rfloor) + T(\lceil N/2 \rceil) + O(N)$$

To simplify the calculations, we assume that N is a power of 2 and replace the $O(N)$ term with N. These assumptions are minor and do not affect the Big-Oh result. Consequently, we need to obtain a closed form solution for $T(N)$ from

$$T(1) = 1 \quad \text{and} \quad T(N) = 2T(N/2) + N \qquad \textbf{(7.6)}$$

This equation is illustrated in Figure 7.21, so we know that the answer will be $N \log N + N$. We can easily verify the result by examining a few values: $T(1)$, $T(2) = 4$, $T(4) = 12$, $T(8) = 32$, and $T(16) = 80$. We now prove this analysis mathematically in Theorem 7.4, using two different methods.

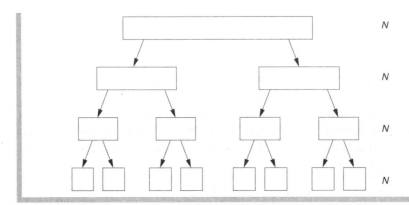

figure 7.21

Trace of recursive calls for recursive maximum contiguous subsequence sum algorithm for $N = 8$ elements

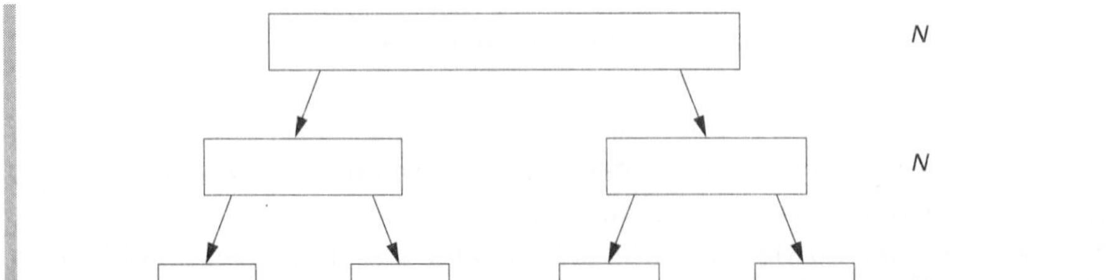

Theorem 7.4

Assuming that N is a power of 2, the solution to the equation $T(N) = 2T(N/2) + N$, with initial condition $T(1) = 1$, is $T(N) = N \log N + N$.

Proof (Method 1)

For sufficiently large N, we have $T(N/2) = 2T(N/4) + N/2$ because we can use Equation 7.6 with $N/2$ instead of N. Consequently, we have

$$2T(N/2) = 4T(N/4) + N$$

Substituting this into Equation 7.6 yields

$$T(N) = 4T(N/4) + 2N \qquad \textbf{(7.7)}$$

If we use Equation 7.6 for $N/4$ and multiply by 4, we obtain

$$4T(N/4) = 8T(N/8) + N$$

which we can substitute into the right-hand side of Equation 7.7 to obtain

$$T(N) = 8T(N/8) + 3N$$

Continuing in this manner, we obtain

$$T(N) = 2^k T(N/2^k) + kN$$

Finally, using $k = \log N$ (which makes sense, because then $2^k = N$), we obtain

$$T(N) = NT(1) + N\log N = N\log N + N$$

Although this proof method appears to work well, it can be difficult to apply in more complicated cases because it tends to give very long equations. Following is a second method that appears to be easier because it generates equations vertically that are more easily manipulated.

Proof of Theorem 7.4 (Method 2)

We divide Equation 7.6 by N, yielding a new basic equation:

$$\frac{T(N)}{N} = \frac{T(N/2)}{N/2} + 1$$

This equation is now valid for any N that is a power of 2, so we may also write the following equations:

(*continued on next page*)

Proof of Theorem 7.4 (Method 2)

(*continued from previous page*)

$$\frac{T(N)}{N} = \frac{T(N/2)}{N/2} + 1$$
$$\frac{T(N/2)}{N/2} = \frac{T(N/4)}{N/4} + 1$$
$$\frac{T(N/4)}{N/4} = \frac{T(N/8)}{N/8} + 1 \tag{7.8}$$
$$\dots$$
$$\frac{T(2)}{2} = \frac{T(1)}{1} + 1$$

A *telescoping sum* generates large numbers of canceling terms.

Now we add the collective in Equation 7.8. That is, we add all the terms on the left-hand side and set the result equal to the sum of all the terms on the right-hand side. The term $T(N/2) / (N/2)$ appears on both sides and thus cancels. In fact, virtually all the terms appear on both sides and cancel. This is called a *telescoping sum*. After everything is added, the final result is

$$\frac{T(N)}{N} = \frac{T(1)}{1} + \log N$$

because all the other terms cancel and there are $\log N$ equations. Thus all the 1s at the end of these equations sum to $\log N$. Multiplying through by N gives the final answer, as before.

Note that, if we had not divided through by N at the start of the solution, the sum would not have telescoped. Deciding on the division required to ensure a telescoping sum requires some experience and makes the method a little more difficult to apply than the first alternative. However, once you have found the correct divisor, the second alternative tends to produce scrap work that fits better on a standard sheet of paper, leading to fewer mathematical errors. In contrast, the first method is more of a brute-force approach.

Note that whenever we have a divide-and-conquer algorithm that solves two half-sized problems with linear additional work, we always have $O(N \log N)$ running time.

7.5.3 a general upper bound for divide-and-conquer running times

The general formula given in this section allows the number of subproblems, the size of the subproblems, and the amount of additional work to assume general forms. The result can be used without understanding of the proof.

The analysis in Section 7.5.2 showed that, when a problem is divided into two equal halves that are solved recursively—with $O(N)$ overhead, an $O(N \log N)$ algorithm is the result. What if we divide a problem into three half-sized problems with linear overhead, or seven half-sized problems with quadratic overhead? (See Exercise 7.17.) In this section we provide a general formula to compute the running time of a divide-and-conquer algorithm. The formula requires three parameters:

- A, which is the number of subproblems
- B, which is the relative size of the subproblems (for instance $B = 2$ represents half-sized subproblems)
- k, which is representative of the fact that the overhead is $\Theta(N^k)$

The formula and its proof is presented as Theorem 7.5. The proof of the formula requires familiarity with geometric sums. However, knowledge of the proof is not needed for you to use the formula.

Theorem 7.5

The solution to the equation $T(N) = AT(N/B) + O(N^k)$, where $A \ge 1$ and $B > 1$, is

$$T(N) = \begin{cases} O(N^{\log_B A}) & \text{for } A > B^k \\ O(N^k \log N) & \text{for } A = B^k \\ O(N^k) & \text{for } A < B^k \end{cases}$$

Before proving Theorem 7.5, let us look at some applications. For the maximum contiguous subsequence sum problem, we have two problems, two halves, and linear overhead. The applicable values are $A = 2$, $B = 2$, and $k = 1$. Hence the second case in Theorem 7.5 applies, and we get $O(N \log N)$, which agrees with our previous calculations. If we recursively solve three half-sized problems with linear overhead, we have $A = 3$, $B = 2$, and $k = 1$, and the first case applies. The result is $O(N^{\log_2 3}) = O(N^{1.59})$. Here, the overhead does not contribute to the total cost of the algorithm. Any overhead smaller than $O(N^{1.59})$ would give the same running time for the recursive algorithm. An algorithm that solved three half-sized problems but required quadratic overhead would have $O(N^2)$ running time because the third case would apply. In effect, the overhead dominates once it exceeds the $O(N^{1.59})$ threshold. At the threshold the penalty is the logarithmic factor shown in the second case. We can now prove Theorem 7.5.

Proof of Theorem 7.5

Following the second proof of Theorem 7.4, we assume that N is a power of B and let $N = B^M$. Then $N / B = B^{M-1}$ and $N^k = (B^M)^k = (B^k)^M$. We assume that $T(1) = 1$ and ignore the constant factor in $O(N^k)$. Then we have the basic equation

$$T(B^M) = AT(B^{M-1}) + (B^k)^M$$

If we divide through by A^M, we obtain the new basic equation

$$\frac{T(B^M)}{A^M} = \frac{T(B^{M-1})}{A^{M-1}} + \left(\frac{B^k}{A}\right)^M$$

Now we can write this equation for all M, obtaining

$$\begin{aligned}
\frac{T(B^M)}{A^M} &= \frac{T(B^{M-1})}{A^{M-1}} + \left(\frac{B^k}{A}\right)^M \\
\frac{T(B^{M-1})}{A^{M-1}} &= \frac{T(B^{M-2})}{A^{M-2}} + \left(\frac{B^k}{A}\right)^{M-1} \\
\frac{T(B^{M-2})}{A^{M-2}} &= \frac{T(B^{M-3})}{A^{M-3}} + \left(\frac{B^k}{A}\right)^{M-2} \\
&\cdots \\
\frac{T(B^1)}{A^1} &= \frac{T(B^0)}{A^0} + \left(\frac{B^k}{A}\right)^1
\end{aligned} \qquad \textbf{(7.9)}$$

If we add the collective denoted by Equation 7.9, once again virtually all the terms on the left-hand side cancel the leading terms on the right-hand side, yielding

$$\begin{aligned}
\frac{T(B^M)}{A^M} &= 1 + \sum_{i=1}^{M} \left(\frac{B^k}{A}\right)^i \\
&= \sum_{i=0}^{M} \left(\frac{B^k}{A}\right)^i
\end{aligned}$$

Thus

$$T(N) = T(B^M) = A^M \sum_{i=0}^{M} \left(\frac{B^k}{A}\right)^i \qquad \textbf{(7.10)}$$

If $A > B^k$, then the sum is a geometric series with a ratio smaller than 1. Because the sum of an infinite series would converge to a constant, this finite sum is also bounded by a constant. Thus we obtain

(continued on next page)

(*continued from previous page*)

Proof of Theorem 7.5

$$T(N) = O(A^M) = O(N^{\log_B A}). \quad \textbf{(7.11)}$$

If $A = B^k$, then each term in the sum in Equation 7.10 is 1. As the sum contains $1 + \log_B N$ terms and $A = B^k$ implies $A^M = N^k$,

$$T(N) = O(A^M \log_B N) = O(N^k \log_B N) = O(N^k \log N).$$

Finally, if $A < B^k$, then the terms in the geometric series are larger than 1. We can compute the sum using a standard formula, thereby obtaining

$$T(N) = A^M \frac{\left(\frac{B^k}{A}\right)^{M+1} - 1}{\frac{B^k}{A} - 1} = O\left(A^M \left(\frac{B^k}{A}\right)^M\right) = O((B^k)^M) = O(N^k)$$

proving the last case of Theorem 7.5.

7.6 dynamic programming

A problem that can be mathematically expressed recursively can also be expressed as a recursive algorithm. In many cases, doing so yields a significant performance improvement over a more naive exhaustive search. Any recursive mathematical formula could be directly translated to a recursive algorithm, but often the compiler may not do justice to the recursive algorithm and an inefficient program results. That is the case for the recursive computation of the Fibonacci numbers described in Section 7.3.4. To avoid this recursive explosion, we can use *dynamic programming* to rewrite the recursive algorithm as a nonrecursive algorithm that systematically records the answers to the subproblems in a table. We illustrate this technique with the following problem.

Dynamic programming solves subproblems nonrecursively by recording answers in a table.

change-making problem

For a currency with coins $C_1, C_2, \ldots, C_N$ (cents) what is the minimum number of coins needed to make K cents of change?

U.S. currency has coins in 1-, 5-, 10-, and 25-cent denominations (ignore the less frequently occurring 50-cent piece). We can make 63 cents by using two 25-cent pieces, one 10-cent piece, and three 1-cent pieces, for a total of six coins. Change-making in this currency is relatively simple: We repeatedly use the largest coin available to us. We can show that for U.S. currency this approach always minimizes the total number of coins used, which is an exam-

Greedy algorithms make locally optimal decisions at each step. This is the simple, but not always the correct, thing to do.

ple of so-called greedy algorithms. In a *greedy algorithm*, during each phase, a decision is made that appears to be optimal, without regard for future consequences. This "take what you can get now" strategy is the source of the name for this class of algorithms. When a problem can be solved with a greedy algorithm, we are usually quite happy: Greedy algorithms often match our intuition and make for relatively painless coding. Unfortunately, greedy algorithms do not always work. If the U.S. currency included a 21-cent piece, the greedy algorithm would still give a solution that uses six coins, but the optimal solution uses three coins (all 21-cent pieces).

The question then becomes one of how to solve the problem for an arbitrary coin set. We assume that there is always a 1-cent coin so that the solution always exists. A simple strategy to make K cents in change uses recursion as follows.

1. If we can make change using exactly one coin, that is the minimum.
2. Otherwise, for each possible value i we can compute the minimum number of coins needed to make i cents in change and $K - i$ cents in change independently. We then choose the i that minimizes this sum.

A simple recursive algorithm for change making is easily written but inefficient.

For example, let us see how we can make 63 cents in change. Clearly, one coin will not suffice. We can compute the number of coins required to make 1 cent of change and 62 cents of change independently (these are 1 and 4, respectively). We obtain these results recursively, so they must be taken as optimal (it happens that the 62 cents is given as two 21-cent pieces and two 10-cent pieces). Thus we have a method that uses five coins. If we split the problem into 2 cents and 61 cents, the recursive solutions yield 2 and 4, respectively, for a total of six coins. We continue trying all the possibilities, some of which are shown in Figure 7.22. Eventually, we see a split into 21 cents and 42 cents, which is changeable in one and two coins, respectively, thus allowing change to be made in three coins. The last split we need to try is 31 cents and 32 cents. We can change 31 cents in two coins, and we can

figure 7.22

Some of the subproblems solved recursively in Figure 7.23

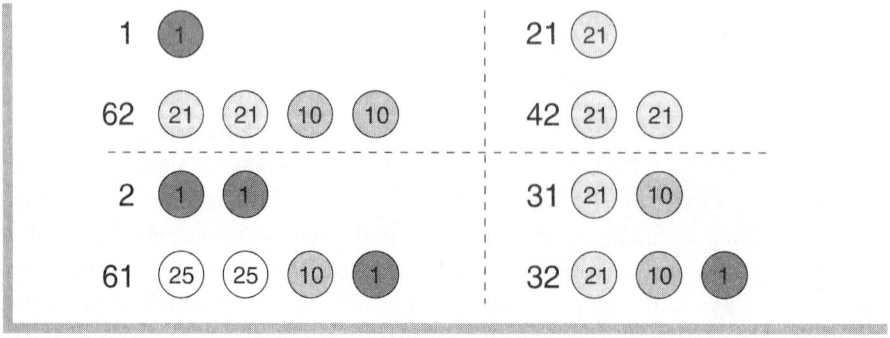

change 32 cents in three coins for a total of five coins. But the minimum remains three coins.

Again, we solve each of these subproblems recursively, which yields the natural algorithm shown in Figure 7.23. If we run the algorithm to make small change, it works perfectly. But like the Fibonacci calculations, this algorithm requires too much redundant work, and it will not terminate in a reasonable amount of time for the 63-cent case.

An alternative algorithm involves reducing the problem recursively by specifying one of the coins. For example, for 63 cents, we can give change in the following ways, as shown in Figure 7.24.

Our alternative recursive change-making algorithm is still inefficient.

- One 1-cent piece plus 62 cents recursively distributed
- One 5-cent piece plus 58 cents recursively distributed
- One 10-cent piece plus 53 cents recursively distributed
- One 21-cent piece plus 42 cents recursively distributed
- One 25-cent piece plus 38 cents recursively distributed

Instead of solving 62 recursive problems, as in Figure 7.22, we get by with only 5 recursive calls, one for each different coin. Again, a naive recursive implementation is very inefficient because it recomputes answers. For example, in the first case we are left with a problem of making 62 cents in change. In this subproblem, one of the recursive calls made chooses a 10-cent piece and recursively

```
// Return minimum number of coins to make change.
// Simple recursive algorithm that is very inefficient.
public static int makeChange( int [ ] coins, int change )
{
    int minCoins = change;

    for( int i = 0; i < coins.length; i++ )
        if( coins[ i ] == change )
            return 1;

      // No match; solve recursively.
    for( int j = 1; j <= change / 2; j++ )
    {
        int thisCoins = makeChange( coins, j )
                      + makeChange( coins, change - j );

        if( thisCoins < minCoins )
            minCoins = thisCoins;
    }

    return minCoins;
}
```

figure 7.23

A simple but inefficient recursive procedure for solving the coin-changing problem

figure 7.24

An alternative recursive algorithm for the coin-changing problem

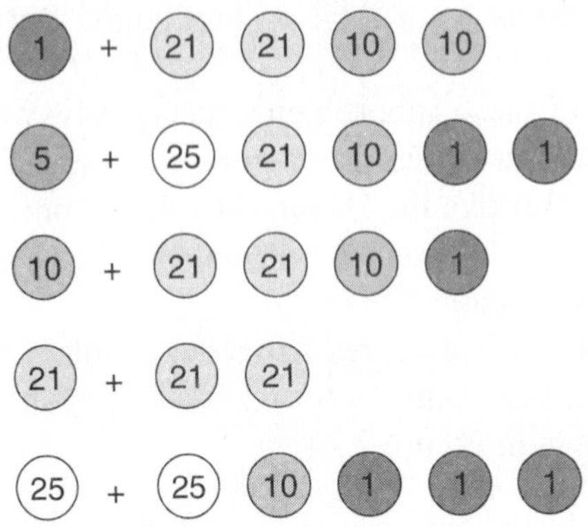

solves for 52 cents. In the third case we are left with 53 cents. One of its recursive calls removes the 1-cent piece and also recursively solves for 52 cents. This redundant work again leads to excessive running time. If we are careful, however, we can make the algorithm run reasonably fast.

The trick is to save answers to the subproblems in an array. This dynamic programming technique forms the basis of many algorithms. A large answer depends only on smaller answers, so we can compute the optimal way to change 1 cent, then 2 cents, then 3 cents, and so on. This strategy is shown in the method in Figure 7.25.

First, at line 8 we observe that 0 cents can be changed using zero coins. The `lastCoin` array is used to tell us which coin was last used to make the optimal change. Otherwise, we attempt to make `cents` worth of change, for `cents` ranging from 1 to the final `maxChange`. To make `cents` worth of change, we try each coin in succession as indicated by the `for` statement beginning at line 15. If the amount of the coin is larger than the amount of change we are trying to make, there is nothing to do. Otherwise, we test at line 19 to determine whether the number of coins used to solve the subproblem plus the one coin combine to be fewer than the minimum number of coins used thus far; if so, we perform an update at lines 21 and 22. When the loop ends for the current number of `cents`, the minimums can be inserted in the arrays, which is done at lines 26 and 27.

At the end of the algorithm, `coinsUsed[i]` represents the minimum number of coins needed to make change for `i` cents (`i==maxChange` is the particular solution that we are looking for). By tracing back through `lastCoin`, we can figure out the coins needed to achieve the solution. The running time is that of two nested `for` loops and is thus $O(NK)$, where N is the number of different denominations of coins and K is the amount of change that we are trying to make.

```java
// Dynamic programming algorithm to solve change-making problem.
// As a result, the coinsUsed array is filled with the
// minimum number of coins needed for change from 0 -> maxChange
// and lastCoin contains one of the coins needed to make the change.
public static void makeChange( int [ ] coins, int differentCoins,
            int maxChange, int [ ] coinsUsed, int [ ] lastCoin )
{
    coinsUsed[ 0 ] = 0; lastCoin[ 0 ] = 1;

    for( int cents = 1; cents <= maxChange; cents++ )
    {
        int minCoins = cents;
        int newCoin  = 1;

        for( int j = 0; j < differentCoins; j++ )
        {
            if( coins[ j ] > cents )   // Cannot use coin j
                continue;
            if( coinsUsed[ cents - coins[ j ] ] + 1 < minCoins )
            {
                minCoins = coinsUsed[ cents - coins[ j ] ] + 1;
                newCoin  = coins[ j ];
            }
        }

        coinsUsed[ cents ] = minCoins;
        lastCoin[ cents ]  = newCoin;
    }
}
```

figure 7.25

A dynamic programming algorithm for solving the change-making problem by computing optimal change for all amounts from 0 to `maxChange` and maintaining information to construct the actual coin sequence

7.7 backtracking

A *backtracking algorithm* uses recursion to try all the possibilities.

In this section we set out the last application of recursion. We show how to write a routine to have the computer select an optimal move in the game Tic-Tac-Toe. The class `Best`, shown in Figure 7.26, is used to store the optimal move that is returned by the move selection algorithm. The skeleton for a `TicTacToe` class is shown in Figure 7.27. The class has a data object `board` that represents the current game position.[6] A host of trivial methods are

6. Tic-Tac-Toe is played on a three-by-three board. Two players alternate placing their symbols on squares. The first to get three squares in a row, column, or a long diagonal wins.

figure 7.26

Class to store an evaluated move

```
final class Best
{
    int row;
    int column;
    int val;

    public Best( int v )
      { this( v, 0, 0 ); }

    public Best( int v, int r, int c )
      { val = v; row = r; column = c; }
}
```

specified, including routines to clear the board, to test whether a square is occupied, to place something on a square, and to test whether a win has been achieved. The implementation details are provided in the online code.

The challenge is to decide, for any position, what the best move is. The routine used is `chooseMove`. The general strategy involves the use of a backtracking algorithm. A *backtracking algorithm* uses recursion to try all the possibilities.

The *minimax strategy* is used for Tic-Tac-Toe. It is based on the assumption of optimal play by both sides.

The basis for making this decision is `positionValue`, which is shown in Figure 7.28. The method `positionValue` returns `HUMAN_WIN`, `DRAW`, `COMPUTER_WIN`, or `UNCLEAR`, depending on what the board represents.

The strategy used is the *minimax strategy,* which is based on the assumption of optimal play by both players. The value of a position is a `COMPUTER_WIN` if optimal play implies that the computer can force a win. If the computer can force a draw but not a win, the value is `DRAW`; if the human player can force a win, the value is `HUMAN_WIN`. We want the computer to win, so we have `HUMAN_WIN < DRAW < COMPUTER_WIN`.

For the computer, the value of the position is the maximum of all the values of the positions that can result from making a move. Suppose that one move leads to a winning position, two moves lead to a drawing position, and six moves lead to a losing position. Then the starting position is a winning position because the computer can force the win. Moreover, the move that leads to the winning position is the move to make. For the human player we use the minimum instead of the maximum.

This approach suggests a recursive algorithm to determine the value of a position. Keeping track of the best move is a matter of bookkeeping once the basic algorithm to find the value of the position has been written. If the position is a terminal position (i.e., we can see right away that Tic-Tac-Toe has been achieved or the board is full without Tic-Tac-Toe), the position's value is immediate. Otherwise, we recursively try all moves, computing the value of

```
class TicTacToe
{
    public static final int HUMAN        = 0;
    public static final int COMPUTER     = 1;
    public static final int EMPTY        = 2;

    public static final int HUMAN_WIN    = 0;
    public static final int DRAW         = 1;
    public static final int UNCLEAR      = 2;
    public static final int COMPUTER_WIN = 3;

        // Constructor
    public TicTacToe( )
      { clearBoard( ); }

        // Find optimal move
    public Best chooseMove( int side )
      { /* Implementation in Figure 7.29 */  }

        // Compute static value of current position (win, draw, etc.)
    private int positionValue( )
      {  /* Implementation in Figure 7.28 */ }

        // Play move, including checking legality
    public boolean playMove( int side, int row, int column )
      { /* Implementation in online code */ }

        // Make board empty
    public void clearBoard( )
      { /* Implementation in online code */ }

        // Return true if board is full
    public boolean boardIsFull( )
      { /* Implementation in online code */ }

        // Return true if board shows a win
    public boolean isAWin( int side )
      { /* Implementation in online code */ }

        // Play a move, possibly clearing a square
    private void place( int row, int column, int piece )
      { board[ row ][ column ] = piece; }

        // Test if a square is empty
    private boolean squareIsEmpty( int row, int column )
      { return board[ row ][ column ] == EMPTY; }

    private int [ ] [ ] board = new int[ 3 ][ 3 ];
}
```

figure 7.27

Skeleton for class `TicTacToe`

figure 7.28

Supporting routine for evaluating positions

```
    // Compute static value of current position (win, draw, etc.)
    private int positionValue( )
    {
        return isAWin( COMPUTER ) ? COMPUTER_WIN :
               isAWin( HUMAN )    ? HUMAN_WIN :
               boardIsFull( )     ? DRAW         : UNCLEAR;
    }
```

each resulting position, and choose the maximum value. The recursive call then requires that the human player evaluate the value of the position. For the human player the value is the minimum of all the possible next moves because the human player is trying to force the computer to lose. Thus the recursive method `chooseMove`, shown in Figure 7.29 takes a parameter `side`, which indicates whose turn it is to move.

Lines 12 and 13 handle the base case of the recursion. If we have an immediate answer, we can return. Otherwise, we set some values at lines 15 to 22, depending on which side is moving. The code in lines 28 to 38 is executed once for each available move. We try the move at line 28, recursively evaluate the move at line 29 (saving the value), and then undo the move at line 30. Lines 33 and 34 test to determine whether this move is the best seen so far. If so, we adjust `value` at line 36 and record the move at line 37. At line 41 we return the value of the position in a `Best` object.

Alpha–beta pruning is an improvement to the minimax algorithm.

Although the routine shown in Figure 7.29 optimally solves Tic-Tac-Toe, it performs a lot of searching. Specifically, to choose the first move on an empty board, it makes 549,946 recursive calls (this number is obtained by running the program). By using some algorithmic tricks, we can compute the same information with fewer searches. One such technique is known as *alpha–beta pruning,* which is an improvement to the minimax algorithm. We describe this technique in detail in Chapter 10. Application of alpha–beta pruning reduces the number of recursive calls to only 18,297.

summary

In this chapter we examined recursion and showed that it is a powerful problem-solving tool. Following are its fundamental rules, which you should never forget.

1. *Base cases:* Always have at least one case that can be solved without using recursion.
2. *Make progress:* Any recursive call must progress toward the base case.

```java
// Find optimal move
public Best chooseMove( int side )
{
    int opp;              // The other side
    Best reply;           // Opponent's best reply
    int dc;               // Placeholder
    int simpleEval;       // Result of an immediate evaluation
    int bestRow = 0;
    int bestColumn = 0;
    int value;

    if( ( simpleEval = positionValue( ) ) != UNCLEAR )
        return new Best( simpleEval );

    if( side == COMPUTER )
    {
        opp = HUMAN; value = HUMAN_WIN;
    }
    else
    {
        opp = COMPUTER; value = COMPUTER_WIN;
    }

    for( int row = 0; row < 3; row++ )
        for( int column = 0; column < 3; column++ )
            if( squareIsEmpty( row, column ) )
            {
                place( row, column, side );
                reply = chooseMove( opp );
                place( row, column, EMPTY );

                  // Update if side gets better position
                if( side == COMPUTER && reply.val > value
                    || side == HUMAN && reply.val < value )
                {
                    value = reply.val;
                    bestRow = row; bestColumn = column;
                }
            }

    return new Best( value, bestRow, bestColumn );
}
```

figure 7.29

A recursive routine for finding an optimal Tic-Tac-Toe move

3. *"You gotta believe":* Always assume that the recursive call works.
4. *Compound interest rule:* Never duplicate work by solving the same instance of a problem in separate recursive calls.

Recursion has many uses, some of which we discussed in this chapter. Three important algorithm design techniques that are based on recursion are divide and conquer, dynamic programming, and backtracking.

In Chapter 8 we examine sorting. The fastest known sorting algorithm is recursive.

key concepts

activation record The method by which the bookkeeping in a procedural language is done. A stack of activation records is used. (261)

alpha-beta pruning An improvement to the minimax algorithm. (294)

backtracking An algorithm that uses recursion to try all possibilities. (291)

base case An instance that can be solved without recursion. Any recursive call must progress toward a base case. (256)

basis In a proof by induction, the easy case that can be shown by hand. (254)

divide-and-conquer algorithm A type of recursive algorithm that is generally very efficient. The recursion is the *divide* part, and the combining of recursive solutions is the *conquer* part. (277)

driver routine A routine that tests the validity of the first case and then calls the recursive routine. (259)

dynamic programming A technique that avoids the recursive explosion by recording answers in a table. (287)

encryption An encoding scheme used in the transmitting of messages that cannot be read by other parties. (275)

Fibonacci numbers A sequence of numbers in which the ith number is the sum of the two previous numbers. (262)

greatest common divisor (gcd) The greatest common divisor of two integers is the largest integer that divides both of them. (272)

greedy algorithm An algorithm that makes locally optimal decisions at each step—a simple but not always correct thing to do. (287)

induction A proof technique used to establish theorems that hold for positive integers. (253)

inductive hypothesis The hypothesis that a theorem is true for some arbitrary case and that, under this assumption, it is true for the next case. (254)

leaf In a tree, a node with no children. (264)

minimax strategy A strategy used for Tic-Tac-Toe and other strategic games, which is based on the assumption of optimal play by both players. (292)

multiplicative inverse The solution $1 \le X < N$ to the equation $AX \equiv 1 (\mathrm{mod}\ N)$. (273)

public key cryptography A type of cryptography in which each participant publishes the code others can use to send the participant encrypted messages but keeps the decrypting code secret. (276)

recursive method A method that directly or indirectly makes a call to itself. (255)

RSA cryptosystem A popular encryption method. (275)

rules of recursion 1. *Base case:* Always have at least one case that can be solved without using recursion (256); 2. *Make progress:* Any recursive call must progress toward a base case (256); 3. *"You gotta believe":* Always assume that the recursive call works (260); 4. *Compound interest rule:* Never duplicate work by solving the same instance of a problem in separate recursive calls. (263)

telescoping sum A procedure that generates large numbers of canceling terms. (284)

tree A widely used data structure that consists of a set of nodes and a set of edges that connect pairs of nodes. Throughout the text, we assume the tree is rooted. (264)

common errors

1. The most common error in the use of recursion is forgetting a base case.
2. Be sure that each recursive call progresses toward a base case. Otherwise, the recursion is incorrect.
3. Overlapping recursive calls must be avoided because they tend to yield exponential algorithms.
4. Using recursion in place of a simple loop is bad style.
5. Recursive algorithms are analyzed by using a recursive formula. Do not assume that a recursive call takes linear time.

on the internet

Most of the chapter's code is provided, including a Tic-Tac-Toe program. An improved version of the Tic-Tac-Toe algorithm that uses fancier data structures is discussed in Chapter 10. The following are the filenames.

RecSum.java	The routine shown in Figure 7.1 with a simple `main`.
PrintInt.java	The routine given in Figure 7.4 for printing a number in any base, plus a `main`.

Factorial.java The routine shown in Figure 7.10, for computing factorials.

BinarySearchRecursive.java
Virtually the same as **BinarySearch.java** (in Chapter 6), but with the `binarySearch` shown in Figure 7.11.

Ruler.java The routine shown in Figure 7.13, ready to run. It contains code that forces the drawing to be slow.

FractalStar.java The routine given in Figure 7.15, ready to run. It contains code that allows the drawing to be slow.

Numerical.java The math routines presented in Section 7.4, the primality testing routine, and a `main` in **RSA.java** that illustrates the RSA computations.

MaxSumTest.java The four maximum contiguous subsequence sum routines.

MakeChange.java The routine shown in Figure 7.25, with a simple `main`.

TicTacSlow.java The Tic-Tac-Toe algorithm, with a primitive `main`. See also **Best.java**.

exercises

IN SHORT

7.1 What are the four fundamental rules of recursion?

7.2 Modify the program given in Figure 7.1 so that zero is returned for negative `n`. Make the minimum number of changes.

7.3 Following are four alternatives for line 11 of the routine `power` (in Figure 7.16). Why is each alternative wrong?

```
long tmp = power( x * x, n/2, p );
long tmp = power( power( x, 2, p ), n/2, p );
long tmp = power( power( x, n/2, p ), 2, p );
long tmp = power( x, n/2, p ) * power( x, n/2, p ) % p;
```

7.4 Show how the recursive calls are processed in the calculation $2^{63} \bmod 37$.

7.5 Compute gcd(1995, 1492).

7.6 Bob chooses p and q equal to 37 and 41, respectively. Determine acceptable values for the remaining parameters in the RSA algorithm.

7.7 Show that the greedy change-making algorithm fails if 5-cent pieces are not part of United States currency.

IN THEORY

7.8 Prove by induction the formula

$$F_N = \frac{1}{\sqrt{5}}\left(\left(\frac{(1+\sqrt{5})}{2}\right)^N - \left(\frac{1-\sqrt{5}}{2}\right)^N\right)$$

7.9 Prove the following identities relating to the Fibonacci numbers.

a. $F_1 + F_2 + \cdots + F_N = F_{N+2} - 1$

b. $F_1 + F_3 + \cdots + F_{2N-1} = F_{2N}$

c. $F_0 + F_2 + \cdots + F_{2N} = F_{2N+1} - 1$

d. $F_{N-1}F_{N+1} = (-1)^N + F_N^2$

e. $F_1F_2 + F_2F_3 + \cdots + F_{2N-1}F_{2N} = F_{2N}^2$

f. $F_1F_2 + F_2F_3 + \cdots + F_{2N}F_{2N+1} = F_{2N+1}^2 - 1$

g. $F_N^2 + F_{N+1}^2 = F_{2N+1}$

7.10 Show that if $A \equiv B(\text{mod } N)$, then for any C, D, and P, the following are true.

a. $A + C \equiv B + C(\text{mod } N)$

b. $AD \equiv BD(\text{mod } N)$

c. $A^P = B^P(\text{mod } N)$

7.11 Prove that if $A \geq B$, then $A \bmod B < A/2$. (*Hint:* Consider the cases $B \leq A/2$ and $B > A/2$ separately.) How does this result show that the running time of `gcd` is logarithmic?

7.12 Prove by induction the formula for the number of calls to the recursive method `fib` in Section 7.3.4.

7.13 Prove by induction that if $A > B \geq 0$ and the invocation `gcd(a,b)` performs $k \geq 1$ recursive calls, then $A \geq F_{k+2}$ and $B \geq F_{k+1}$.

7.14 Prove by induction that in the extended gcd algorithm, $|X| < B$ and $|Y| < A$.

7.15 Write an alternative gcd algorithm, based on the following observations (arrange that $A > B$).

a. $\gcd(A, B) = 2\gcd(A/2, B/2)$ if A and B are both even.

b. $\gcd(A, B) = \gcd(A/2, B)$ if A is even and B is odd.

c. $\gcd(A, B) = \gcd(A, B/2)$ if A is odd and B is even.

d. $\gcd(A, B) = \gcd((A+B)/2, (A-B)/2)$ if A and B are both odd.

7.16 Solve the following equation. Assume that $A \geq 1$, $B > 1$, and $P \geq 0$.

$$T(N) = AT(N/B) + O(N^k \log^P N)$$

7.17 Strassen's algorithm for matrix multiplication multiplies two $N \times N$ matrices by performing seven recursive calls to multiply two $N/2 \times N/2$ matrices. The additional overhead is quadratic. What is the running time of Strassen's algorithm?

IN PRACTICE

7.18 The `printInt` method shown in Figure 7.4 may incorrectly handle the case where $N =$ `Long.MIN_VALUE`. Explain why and fix the method.

7.19 Write a recursive method that returns the number of 1s in the binary representation of N. Use the fact that this number equals the number of 1s in the representation of $N/2$, plus 1, if N is odd.

7.20 Implement the one comparison per level binary search recursively.

7.21 The maximum contiguous subsequence sum algorithm given in Figure 7.20 gives no indication of the actual sequence. Modify it so that it fills static class fields `seqStart` and `seqEnd`, as in Section 5.3.

7.22 For the change-making problem, give an algorithm that computes the number of different ways to give exactly K cents in change.

7.23 The *subset sum problem* is as follows: Given N integers $A_1, A_2, \ldots, A_N$ and an integer K, is there a group of integers that sums exactly to K? Give an $O(NK)$ algorithm to solve this problem.

7.24 Give an $O(2^N)$ algorithm for the subset sum problem described in Exercise 7.23. (*Hint:* Use recursion.)

7.25 Write the routine with the declaration

```
public static void permute( String str );
```

that prints all the permutations of the characters in the string `str`. If `str` is `"abc"`, then the strings output are `abc`, `acb`, `bac`, `bca`, `cab`, and `cba`. Use recursion.

7.26 Explain what happens if in Figure 7.15 we draw the central square before making the recursive calls.

PROGRAMMING PROJECTS

7.27 The binomial coefficients $C(N, k)$ can be defined recursively as $C(N, 0) = 1$, $C(N, N) = 1$ and, for $0 < k < N$, $C(N, k) = C(N-1, k) + C(N-1, k-1)$. Write a method and give an analysis of the running time to compute the binomial coefficients

a. Recursively

b. By using dynamic programming

7.28 Implement the RSA cryptosystem with the library `BigInteger` class.

7.29 Improve the `TicTacToe` class by making the supporting routines more efficient.

7.30 Let A be a sequence of N distinct sorted numbers $A_1, A_2, \ldots, A_N$ with $A_1 = 0$. Let B be a sequence of $N(N-1)/2$ numbers, defined by $B_{i,j} = A_j - A_i$ $(i < j)$. Let D be the sequence obtained by sorting B. Both B and D may contain duplicates. *Example:* $A = 0, 1, 5, 8$. Then $D = 1, 3, 4, 5, 7, 8$. Do the following.

a. Write a program that constructs D from A. This part is easy.

b. Write a program that constructs some sequence A that corresponds to D. Note that A is not unique. Use a backtracking algorithm.

7.31 Consider an $N \times N$ grid in which some squares are occupied. Two squares belong to the same group if they share a common edge. In Figure 7.30 there is one group of four occupied squares, three groups of two occupied squares, and two individual occupied squares.

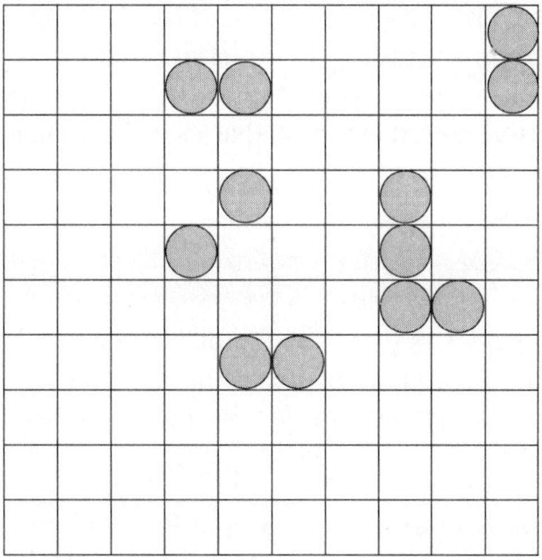

figure 7.30
Grid for Exercise 7.31

Assume that the grid is represented by a two-dimensional array. Write a program that

a. Computes the size of a group when a square in the group is given
b. Computes the number of different groups
c. Lists all groups

7.32 Write a program that expands a C++ source file's `#include` directives (recursively). Do so by replacing lines of the form

```
#include "filename"
```

with the contents of `filename`.

7.33 a. Design a recursive algorithm to find the longest increasing sequence of numbers in a rectangular grid. For example, if the grid contains

97	47	56	36
35	57	41	13
89	36	98	75
25	45	26	17

then the longest increasing sequence of numbers is the sequence of length eight consisting of 17, 26, 36, 41, 47, 56, 57, 97. Note that there are no duplicates in the increasing sequence.

b. Design an algorithm that solves the same problem but allows for nondecreasing sequences; thus there may be duplicates in the increasing sequence.

7.34 Use dynamic programming to solve the longest increasing sequence problem in Exercise 7.33 (a). *Hint*: Find the best sequence emanating from each grid element, and to do so, consider the grid elements in decreasing sorted order (so that the grid element containing 98 is considered first).

references

Much of this chapter is based on the discussion in [3]. A description of the RSA algorithm, with proof of correctness, is presented in [1], which also devotes a chapter to dynamic programming. The shape-drawing examples are adapted from [2].

1. T. H. Cormen, C. E. Leiserson, and R. L. Rivest, *Introduction to Algorithms,* MIT Press, Cambridge, MA, 1990.
2. R. Sedgewick, *Algorithms in C++*, Addison-Wesley, Reading, MA, 1992.
3. M. A. Weiss, *Efficient C Programming: A Practical Approach,* Prentice Hall, Upper Saddle River, NJ, 1995.

chapter 8

sorting algorithms

Sorting is a fundamental application for computers. Much of the output eventually produced by a computation is sorted in some way, and many computations are made efficient by invoking a sorting procedure internally. Thus sorting is perhaps the most intensively studied and important operation in computer science.

In this chapter we discuss the problem of sorting an array of elements. We describe and analyze the various sorting algorithms. The sorts in this chapter can be done entirely in main memory, so the number of elements is relatively small (less than a few million). Sorts that cannot be performed in main memory and must be done on disk or tape are also quite important. We discuss this type of sorting, called *external sorting,* in Section 21.6.

This discussion of sorting is a blend of theory and practice. We present several algorithms that perform differently and show how an analysis of an algorithm's performance properties can help us make implementation decisions that are not obvious.

In this chapter, we show

- That simple sorts run in quadratic time
- How to code Shellsort, which is a simple and efficient algorithm that runs in subquadratic time

- How to write the slightly more complicated $O(N \log N)$ mergesort and quicksort algorithms
- That $\Omega(N \log N)$ comparisons are required for any general-purpose sorting algorithm

8.1 why is sorting important?

Recall from Section 5.6 that searching a sorted array is much easier than searching an unsorted array. This is especially true for people. That is, finding a person's name in a phone book is easy, for example, but finding a phone number without knowing the person's name is virtually impossible. As a result, any significant amount of computer output is generally arranged in some sorted order so that it can be interpreted. The following are some more examples.

- Words in a dictionary are sorted (and case distinctions are ignored).
- Files in a directory are often listed in sorted order.
- The index of a book is sorted (and case distinctions are ignored).
- The card catalog in a library is sorted by both author and title.
- A listing of course offerings at a university is sorted, first by department and then by course number.
- Many banks provide statements that list checks in increasing order by check number.
- In a newspaper, the calendar of events in a schedule is generally sorted by date.
- Musical compact disks in a record store are generally sorted by recording artist.
- In the programs printed for graduation ceremonies, departments are listed in sorted order and then students in those departments are listed in sorted order.

An initial sort of the data can significantly enhance the performance of an algorithm.

Not surprisingly, much of the work in computing involves sorting. However, sorting also has indirect uses. For instance, suppose that we want to decide whether an array has any duplicates. Figure 8.1 shows a simple method that requires quadratic worst-case time. Sorting provides an alternative algorithm. That is, if we sort a copy of the array, then any duplicates will be adjacent to each other and can be detected in a single linear-time scan of the array. The cost of this algorithm is dominated by the time to sort, so if we can sort in subqua-

```
// Return true if array a has duplicates; false otherwise
public static boolean duplicates( Object [ ] a )
{
    for( int i = 0; i < a.length; i++ )
        for( int j = i + 1; j < a.length; j++ )
            if( a[ i ].equals( a[ j ] ) )
                return true;   // Duplicate found

    return false;              // No duplicates found
}
```

figure 8.1

A simple quadratic algorithm for detecting duplicates

dratic time, we have an improved algorithm. The performance of many algorithms is significantly enhanced when we initially sort the data.

The vast majority of significant programming projects use a sort somewhere, and in many cases, the sorting cost determines the running time. Thus we want to be able to implement a fast and reliable sort.

8.2 preliminaries

The algorithms we describe in this chapter are all interchangeable. Each is passed an array containing the elements, and only objects that implement the `Comparable` interface can be sorted.

The comparisons are the only operations allowed on the input data. An algorithm that makes ordering decisions only on the basis of comparisons is called a *comparison-based sorting algorithm.*[1] In this chapter, N is the number of elements being sorted.

A *comparison-based sorting algorithm* makes ordering decisions only on the basis of comparisons.

8.3 analysis of the insertion sort and other simple sorts

Insertion sort is a simple sorting algorithm that is appropriate for small inputs. It is generally considered to be a good solution if only a few elements need sorting because it is such a short algorithm and the time required to sort is not likely to be an issue. However, if we are dealing with a large amount of data, insertion sort is a poor choice because it is too time consuming. The code is shown in Figure 8.2.

An *insertion sort* is quadratic in the worst and average cases. It is fast if the input has already been sorted.

1. As shown in Section 4.8, changing the sorting interface by requiring a `Comparator` function object is straightforward.

figure 8.2

Insertion sort implementation

```
1     /**
2      * Simple insertion sort
3      */
4     public static <AnyType extends Comparable<? super AnyType>>
5     void insertionSort( AnyType [ ] a )
6     {
7         for( int p = 1; p < a.length; p++ )
8         {
9             AnyType tmp = a[ p ];
10            int j = p;
11
12            for( ; j > 0 && tmp.compareTo( a[ j - 1 ] ) < 0; j-- )
13                a[ j ] = a[ j - 1 ];
14            a[ j ] = tmp;
15        }
16    }
```

Insertion sort works as follows. In the initial state the first element, considering by itself, is sorted. In the final state all elements (assume that there are N), considered as a group, are to have been sorted. Figure 8.3 shows that the basic action of insertion sort is to sort the elements in positions `0` through `p` (where `p` ranges from 1 through $N - 1$). In each stage `p` increases by 1. That is what the outer loop at line 7 in Figure 8.2 is controlling.

When the body of the `for` loop is entered at line 12, we are guaranteed that the elements in array positions `0` through `p-1` have already been sorted and that we need to extend this to positions `0` to `p`. Figure 8.4 gives us a closer look at what has to be done, detailing only the relevant part of the array. At each step the element in boldface type needs to be added to the previously sorted part of the array. We can easily do that by placing it in a temporary variable

figure 8.3

Basic action of insertion sort (the shaded part is sorted)

Array Position	**0**	**1**	**2**	**3**	**4**	**5**
Initial State	8	5	9	2	6	3
After `a[0..1]` is sorted	5	8	9	2	6	3
After `a[0..2]` is sorted	5	8	9	2	6	3
After `a[0..3]` is sorted	2	5	8	9	6	3
After `a[0..4]` is sorted	2	5	6	8	9	3
After `a[0..5]` is sorted	2	3	5	6	8	9

Array Position	0	1	2	3	4	5
Initial State	8	5				
After a[0..1] is sorted	5	8	9			
After a[0..2] is sorted	5	8	9	2		
After a[0..3] is sorted	2	5	8	9	6	
After a[0..4] is sorted	2	5	6	8	9	3
After a[0..5] is sorted	2	3	5	6	8	9

figure 8.4

A closer look at the action of insertion sort (the dark shading indicates the sorted area; the light shading is where the new element was placed)

and sliding all the elements that are larger than it one position to the right. Then we can copy the temporary variable into the former position of the left-most relocated element (indicated by lighter shading on the following line). We keep a counter j, which is the position to which the temporary variable should be written back. Every time an element is slid, j decreases by 1. Lines 9–14 implement this process.

The *insertion sort* is quadratic in the worst and average cases. It is fast if the input has already been sorted.

Because of the nested loops, each of which can take N iterations, the insertion sort algorithm is $O(N^2)$. Furthermore, this bound is achievable because input in reverse order really does take quadratic time. A precise calculation shows that the tests at line 12 in Figure 8.2 can be executed at most $P + 1$ times for each value of P. Summing over all P gives a total time of

$$\sum_{P=1}^{N-1}(P+1) = \sum_{i=2}^{N} i = 2+3+4+\dots+N = \Theta(N^2)$$

However, if the input is presorted, the running time is $O(N)$ because the test at the top of the inner for loop always fails immediately. Indeed, if the input is almost sorted (we define *almost sorted* more rigorously shortly), the insertion sort will run quickly. Thus the running time depends not only on the amount of input, but also on the specific ordering of the input. Because of this wide variation, analyzing the average-case behavior of this algorithm is worthwhile. The average case turns out to be $\theta(N^2)$ for the insertion sort as well as a variety of other simple sorting algorithms.

An *inversion* measures unsortedness.

An *inversion* is a pair of elements that are out of order in an array. In other words, it is any ordered pair (i, j) having the property that $i < j$ but $A_i > A_j$. For example, the sequence {8, 5, 9, 2, 6, 3} has 10 inversions that correspond to the pairs (8, 5), (8, 2), (8, 6), (8, 3), (5, 2), (5, 3), (9, 2), (9, 6), (9, 3), and (6, 3). Note that the number of inversions equals the total number of times that line 13 in Figure 8.2 is executed. This condition is always true because the effect of the assignment statement is to swap the two items `a[j]` and `a[j-1]`. (We avoid the actual excessive swapping by using the temporary variable, but nonetheless it is an abstract swap.) Swapping two elements that are out of place removes exactly one inversion, and a sorted array has no inversions. Thus, if there are I inversions at the start of the algorithm, we must have I implicit swaps. As $O(N)$ other work is involved in the algorithm, the running time of the insertion sort is $O(I + N)$, where I is the number of inversions in the original array. Thus the insertion sort runs in linear time if the number of inversions is $O(N)$.

We can compute precise bounds on the average running time of the insertion sort by computing the average number of inversions in an array. However, defining *average* is difficult. We can assume that there are no duplicate elements (if we allow duplicates, it is not even clear what the average number of duplicates is). We can also assume that the input is some arrangement of the first N integers (as only relative ordering is important); these arrangements are called *permutations*. We can further assume that all these permutations are equally likely. Under these assumptions we can establish Theorem 8.1.

Theorem 8.1

The average number of inversions in an array of N distinct numbers is $N(N-1)/4$.

Proof

For any array A of numbers, consider A_r, which is the array in reverse order. For example, the reverse of array 1, 5, 4, 2, 6, 3 is 3, 6, 2, 4, 5, 1. Consider any two numbers (x, y) in the array, with $y > x$. In exactly one of A and A_r, this ordered pair represents an inversion. The total number of these pairs in an array A and its reverse A_r is $N(N-1)/2$. Thus an average array has half this amount, or $N(N-1)/4$ inversions.

Theorem 8.1 implies that insertion sort is quadratic on average. It also can be used to provide a very strong lower bound about any algorithm that exchanges adjacent elements only. This lower bound is expressed as Theorem 8.2.

Theorem 8.2

Any algorithm that sorts by exchanging adjacent elements requires $\Omega(N^2)$ time on average.

Proof

The average number of inversions is initially $N(N-1)/4$. Each swap removes only one inversion, so $\Omega(N^2)$ swaps are required.

This proof is an example of a *lower-bound proof.* It is valid not only for the insertion sort, which performs adjacent exchanges implicitly, but also for other simple algorithms such as the bubble sort and the selection sort, which we do not describe here. In fact, it is valid over an entire *class* of algorithms, including undiscovered ones, that perform only adjacent exchanges.

The *lower-bound proof* shows that quadratic performance is inherent in any algorithm that sorts by performing adjacent comparisons.

Unfortunately, any computational confirmation of a proof applying to a class of algorithms would require running all algorithms in the class. That is impossible because there are infinitely many possible algorithms. Hence any attempt at confirmation would apply only to the algorithms that are run. This restriction makes the confirmation of the validity of lower-bound proofs more difficult than the usual single-algorithm upper bounds that we are accustomed to. A computation could only *disprove* a lower-bound conjecture; it could never prove it in general.

Although this lower-bound proof is rather simple, proving lower bounds is in general much more complicated than proving upper bounds. Lower-bound arguments are much more abstract than their upper-bound counterparts.

This lower bound shows us that, for a sorting algorithm to run in subquadratic or $o(N^2)$ time, it must make comparisons and, in particular, exchanges between elements that are far apart. A sorting algorithm progresses by eliminating inversions. To run efficiently, it must eliminate more than just one inversion per exchange.

8.4 shellsort

The first algorithm to improve on the insertion sort substantially was *Shellsort,* which was discovered in 1959 by Donald Shell. Though it is not the fastest algorithm known, *Shellsort* is a subquadratic algorithm whose code is only slightly longer than the insertion sort, making it the simplest of the faster algorithms.

Shellsort is a subquadratic algorithm that works well in practice and is simple to code. The performance of Shellsort is highly dependent on the increment sequence and requires a challenging (and not completely resolved) analysis.

Shell's idea was to avoid the large amount of data movement, first by comparing elements that were far apart and then by comparing elements that were less far apart, and so on, gradually shrinking toward the basic insertion sort. Shellsort uses a sequence $h_1, h_2, \ldots, h_t$ called the *increment sequence.* Any increment sequence will do as long as $h_1 = 1$, but some choices are better than others. After a phase, using some increment h_k, we have $a[i] \le a[i + h_k]$ for every i where $i + h_k$ is a valid index; all elements spaced h_k apart are sorted. The array is then said to be h_k-sorted.

For example, Figure 8.5 shows an array after several phases of Shellsort. After a 5-sort, elements spaced five apart are guaranteed to be in correct sorted order. In the figure, elements spaced five apart are identically shaded

figure 8.5

Shellsort after each pass if the increment sequence is {1, 3, 5}

Original	81	94	11	96	12	35	17	95	28	58	41	75	15
After 5-sort	35	17	11	28	12	41	75	15	96	58	81	94	95
After 3-sort	28	12	11	35	15	41	58	17	94	75	81	96	95
After 1-sort	11	12	15	17	28	35	41	58	75	81	94	95	96

and are sorted relative to each other. Similarly, after a 3-sort, elements spaced three apart are guaranteed to be in sorted order, relative to each other. An important property of Shellsort (which we state without proof) is that an h_k-sorted array that is then h_{k-1}-sorted remains h_k-sorted. If this were not the case, the algorithm would likely be of little value because work done by early phases would be undone by later phases.

A *diminishing gap sort* is another name for Shellsort.

In general, an h_k-sort requires that, for each position i in h_k, h_{k+1}, ..., $N-1$, we place the element in the correct spot among $i, i-h_k, i-2h_k$, and so on. Although this order does not affect the implementation, careful examination shows that an h_k-sort performs an insertion sort on h_k independent subarrays (shown in different shades in Figure 8.5). Therefore, not surprisingly, in Figure 8.7, which we come to shortly, lines 9 to 17 represent a *gap insertion sort*. In a gap insertion sort, after the loop has been executed, elements separated by a distance of `gap` in the array are sorted. For instance, when `gap` is 1, the loop is identical, statement by statement, to an insertion sort.Thus Shellsort is also known as *diminishing gap sort*.

Shell's increment sequence is an improvement over the insertion sort (although better sequences are known).

As we have shown, when `gap` is 1 the inner loop is guaranteed to sort the array `a`. If `gap` is never 1, there is always some input for which the array cannot be sorted. Thus Shellsort sorts so long as `gap` eventually equals 1. The only issue remaining, then, is to choose the increment sequence.

Shell suggested starting `gap` at $N/2$ and halving it until it reaches 1, after which the program can terminate. Using these increments, Shellsort represents a substantial improvement over the insertion sort, despite the fact that it nests three `for` loops instead of two, which is usually inefficient. By altering the sequence of gaps, we can further improve the algorithm's performance. A summary of Shellsort's performance with three different choices of increment sequences is shown in Figure 8.6.

8.4.1 performance of shellsort

The running time of Shellsort depends heavily on the choice of increment sequences, and in general the proofs can be rather involved. The average-case

		Shellsort		
N	Insertion Sort	Shell's Increments	Odd Gaps Only	Dividing by 2.2
10,000	575	10	11	9
20,000	2,489	23	23	20
40,000	10,635	51	49	41
80,000	42,818	114	105	86
160,000	174,333	270	233	194
320,000	NA	665	530	451
640,000	NA	1,593	1,161	939

figure 8.6

Running time of the insertion sort and Shellsort for various increment sequences

analysis of Shellsort is a long-standing open problem except for the most trivial increment sequences.

When Shell's increments are used, the worst case is $O(N^2)$. This bound is achievable if N is an exact power of 2, all the large elements are in even-indexed array positions, and all the small elements are in odd-indexed array positions. When the final pass is reached, all the large elements will still be in the even-indexed array positions, and all the small elements will still be in the odd-indexed array positions. A calculation of the number of remaining inversions shows that the final pass will require quadratic time. The fact that this is the worst that can happen follows from the fact that an h_k-sort consists of h_k insertion sorts of roughly N/h_k elements. Thus the cost of each pass is $O(h_k(N/h_k)^2)$, or $O(N^2/h_k)$. When we sum this cost over all the passes, we obtain $O(N^2\Sigma 1/h_k)$. The increments are roughly a geometric series, so the sum is bounded by a constant. The result is a quadratic worst-case running time. We can also prove via a complex argument that when N is an exact power of 2 the average running time is $O(N^{3/2})$. Thus, on average, Shell's increments give a significant improvement over insertion sort.

In the worst case, Shell's increments give quadratic behavior.

A minor change to the increment sequence can prevent the quadratic worst case from occurring. If we divide `gap` by 2 and it becomes even, we can add 1 to make it odd. We can then prove that the worst case is not quadratic but only $O(N^{3/2})$. Although the proof is complicated, the basis for it is that in this new increment sequence, consecutive increments share no common factors (whereas in Shell's increment sequence they do). Any sequence that satisfies this property (and whose increments decrease roughly geomet-

If consecutive increments are relatively prime, the performance of Shellsort is improved.

rically) will have a worst-case running time of at most $O(N^{3/2})$.[2] The average performance of the algorithm with these new increments is unknown but seems to be $O(N^{5/4})$, based on simulations.

Dividing by 2.2 gives excellent performance in practice.

A third sequence, which performs well in practice but has no theoretical basis, is to divide by 2.2 instead of 2. This divisor appears to bring the average running time to below $O(N^{5/4})$—perhaps to $O(N^{7/6})$—but this case is completely unresolved. For 100,000 to 1,000,000 items, it typically improves performance by about 25 to 35 percent over Shell's increments, although nobody knows why. A Shellsort implementation with this increment sequence is coded in Figure 8.7. The complicated code at line 8 is necessary to avoid setting `gap` to 0. If that happens, the algorithm is broken because we never see a 1-sort. Line 8 ensures that, if `gap` is about to be set to 0, it is reset to 1.

The entries in Figure 8.6 compare the performance of insertion sort and Shellsort, with various gap sequences. We could easily conclude that Shellsort, even with the simplest gap sequence, provides a significant improvement over the insertion sort, at a cost of little additional code complexity. A simple change to the gap sequence can further improve performance. More improvement is possible (see in Exercise 8.23). Some of these improvements have theoretical backing, but no known sequence markedly improves the program shown in Figure 8.7.

```
 1    /**
 2     * Shellsort, using a sequence suggested by Gonnet.
 3     */
 4    public static <AnyType extends Comparable<? super AnyType>>
 5    void shellsort( AnyType [ ] a )
 6    {
 7        for( int gap = a.length / 2; gap > 0;
 8                     gap = gap == 2 ? 1 : (int) ( gap / 2.2 ) )
 9            for( int i = gap; i < a.length; i++ )
10            {
11                AnyType tmp = a[ i ];
12                int j = i;
13
14                for( ; j >= gap && tmp.compareTo( a[j-gap] ) < 0; j -= gap )
15                    a[ j ] = a[ j - gap ];
16                a[ j ] = tmp;
17            }
18    }
```

figure 8.7

Shellsort implementation

2. To appreciate the subtlety involved, note that subtracting 1 instead of adding 1 does not work. For instance, if N is 186, the resulting sequence is 93, 45, 21, 9, 3, 1, which all share the common factor 3.

The performance of Shellsort is quite acceptable in practice, even for N in the tens of thousands. The simplicity of the code makes it the algorithm of choice for sorting up to moderately large input. It is also a fine example of a very simple algorithm with an extremely complex analysis.

Shellsort is a good choice for moderate amounts of input.

8.5 mergesort

Recall from Section 7.5 that recursion can be used to develop subquadratic algorithms. Specifically, a divide-and-conquer algorithm in which two half-size problems are solved recursively with an $O(N)$ overhead results in the algorithm $O(N \log N)$. *Mergesort* is such an algorithm. It offers a better bound, at least theoretically, than the bounds claimed for Shellsort.

Mergesort uses divide-and-conquer to obtain an $O(N \log N)$ running time.

The mergesort algorithm involves three steps.

1. If the number of items to sort is 0 or 1, return.
2. Recursively sort the first and second halves separately.
3. Merge the two sorted halves into a sorted group.

To claim an $O(N \log N)$ algorithm, we need only to show that the merging of two sorted groups can be performed in linear time. In this section we show how to merge two input arrays, A and B, placing the result in a third array, C. We then provide a simple implementation of mergesort. The merge routine is the cornerstone of most external sorting algorithms, as demonstrated in Section 21.6.

Merging of sorted arrays can be done in linear time.

8.5.1 linear-time merging of sorted arrays

The basic merge algorithm takes two input arrays, A and B, an output array, C, and three counters, *Actr*, *Bctr*, and *Cctr*, which are initially set to the beginning of their respective arrays. The smaller of *A[Actr]* and *B[Bctr]* is copied to the next entry in C, and the appropriate counters are advanced. When either input array is exhausted, the rest of the other array is copied to C.

An example of how the merge routine works is provided for the following input:

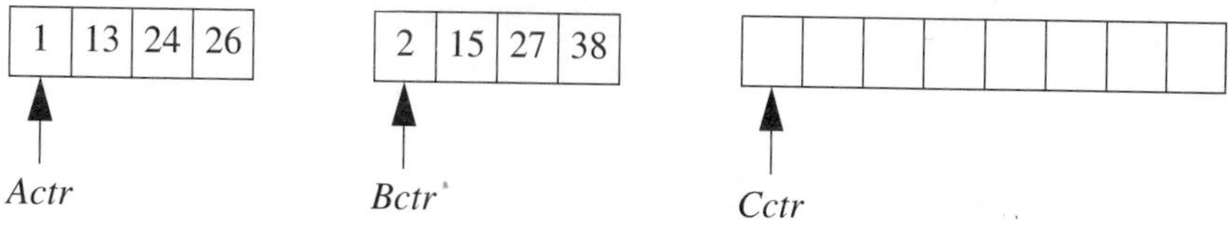

If array *A* contains 1, 13, 24, 26 and *B* contains 2, 15, 27, 38, the algorithm proceeds as follows. First, a comparison is made between 1 and 2, 1 is added to *C*, and 13 and 2 are compared:

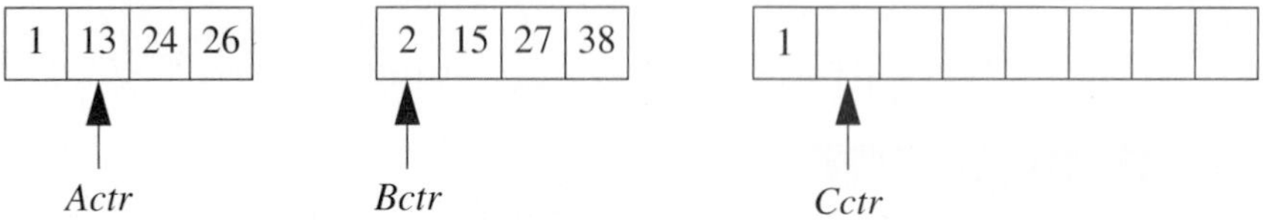

Then 2 is added to *C*, and 13 and 15 are compared:

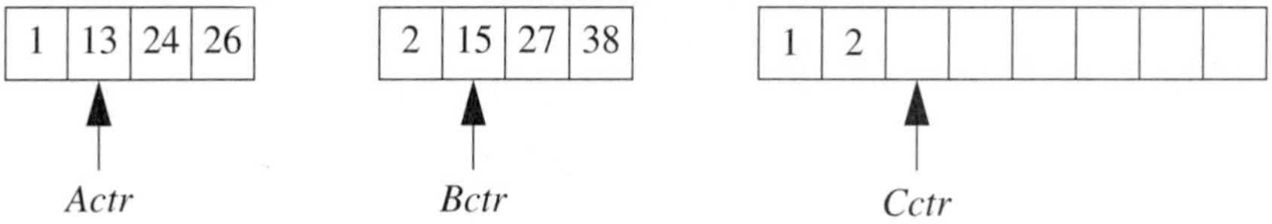

Next, 13 is added to *C*, and 24 and 15 are compared:

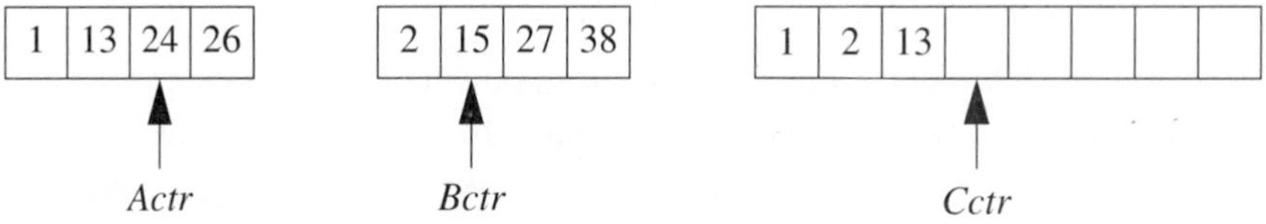

The process continues until 26 and 27 are compared:

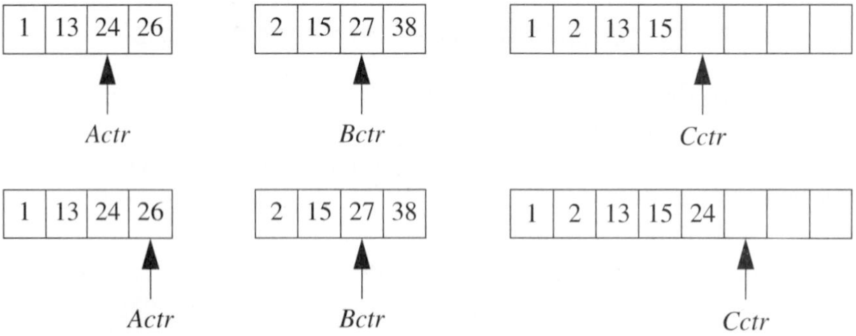

Then 26 is added to *C*, and the *A* array is exhausted:

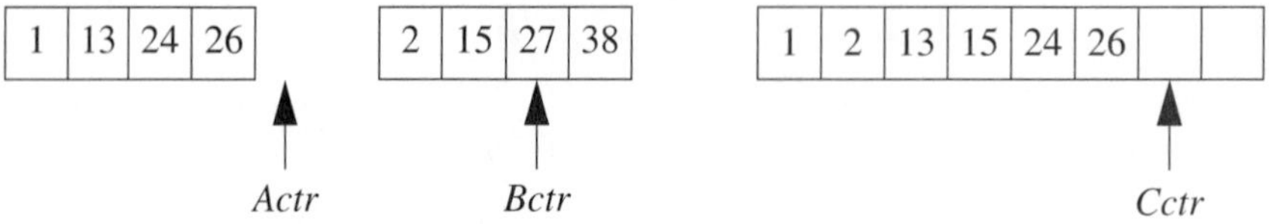

Finally, the remainder of the *B* array is copied to *C:*

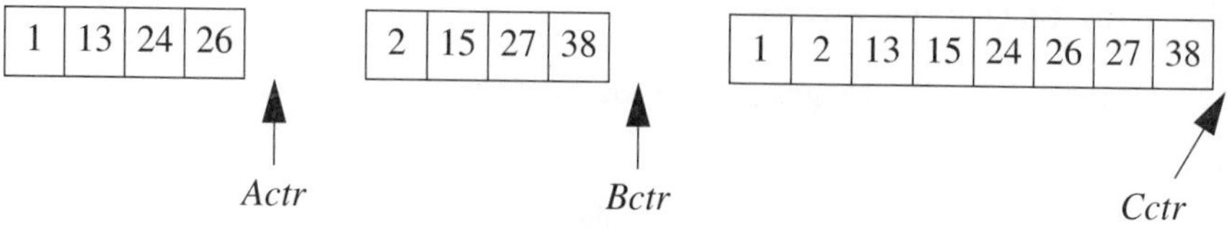

The time needed to merge two sorted arrays is linear because each comparison advances *Cctr* (thus limiting the number of comparisons). As a result, a divide-and-conquer algorithm that uses a linear merging procedure runs in $O(N \log N)$ worst-case time. This running time also represents the average-case and best-case times because the merging step is always linear.

An example of the mergesort algorithm would be sorting the 8-element array 24, 13, 26, 1, 2, 27, 38, 15. After recursively sorting the first four and last four elements, we obtain 1, 13, 24, 26, 2, 15, 27, 38. Then we merge the two halves, obtaining the final array 1, 2, 13, 15, 24, 26, 27, 38.

8.5.2 the mergesort algorithm

Mergesort uses linear extra memory, which is a practical liability.

A straightforward implementation of mergesort is shown in Figure 8.8. The one-parameter, nonrecursive `mergeSort` is a simple driver that declares a temporary array and calls recursive `mergeSort` with the boundaries of the array. The `merge` routine follows the description given in Section 8.5.1. It uses the first half of the array (indexed from `left` to `center`) as *A,* the second half (indexed from `center+1` to `right`) as *B,* and the temporary as *C*. Figure 8.9 implements the `merge` routine. The temporary is then copied back into the original array.

Excessive copying can be avoided with more work, but the linear extra memory cannot be removed without excessive time penalties.

Although mergesort's running time is $O(N \log N)$, it has the significant problem that merging two sorted lists uses linear extra memory. The additional work involved in copying to the temporary array and back, throughout the algorithm, slows the sort considerably. This copying can be avoided by judiciously switching the roles of `a` and `tmpArray` at alternate levels in the recursion. A variant of mergesort can also be implemented nonrecursively.

The running time of mergesort depends heavily on the relative costs of comparing elements and moving elements in the array (and the temporary array). In the case of sorting general objects in Java, an element comparison is expensive because in a general setting, the comparison is done by function objects. On the other hand, moving elements is inexpensive because the elements are not copied; instead, references simply change. Mergesort uses the fewest number of comparisons of all the popular sorting algorithms and thus is a good candidate for general-purpose sorting in Java. In fact, it is the algorithm used in `java.util.Arrays.sort` to sort arrays of objects. These relative

```java
/**
 * Mergesort algorithm.
 * @param a an array of Comparable items.
 */
public static <AnyType extends Comparable<? super AnyType>>
void mergeSort( AnyType [ ] a )
{
    AnyType [ ] tmpArray = (AnyType []) new Comparable[ a.length ];
    mergeSort( a, tmpArray, 0, a.length - 1 );
}

/**
 * Internal method that makes recursive calls.
 * @param a an array of Comparable items.
 * @param tmpArray an array to place the merged result.
 * @param left the left-most index of the subarray.
 * @param right the right-most index of the subarray.
 */
private static <AnyType extends Comparable<? super AnyType>>
void mergeSort( AnyType [ ] a, AnyType [ ] tmpArray,
                int left, int right )
{
    if( left < right )
    {
        int center = ( left + right ) / 2;
        mergeSort( a, tmpArray, left, center );
        mergeSort( a, tmpArray, center + 1, right );
        merge( a, tmpArray, left, center + 1, right );
    }
}
```

figure 8.8

Basic `mergeSort` routines

costs do not apply in other languages, nor do they apply for sorting primitive types in Java. An alternative algorithm is quicksort, which we describe in the next section. Quicksort is the algorithm used in C++ to sort all types, and it is used in `java.util.Arrays.sort` to sort arrays of primitive types.

8.6 quicksort

When properly implemented, *quicksort* is a fast divide-and-conquer algorithm.

As its name implies, *quicksort* is a fast divide-and-conquer algorithm. Its average running time is $O(N \log N)$. Its speed is mainly due to a very tight and highly optimized inner loop. It has quadratic worst-case performance, which can be made statistically unlikely to occur with a little effort. On the one hand, the quicksort algorithm is relatively simple to understand and prove correct because it relies

```java
/**
 * Internal method that merges two sorted halves of a subarray.
 * @param a an array of Comparable items.
 * @param tmpArray an array to place the merged result.
 * @param leftPos the left-most index of the subarray.
 * @param rightPos the index of the start of the second half.
 * @param rightEnd the right-most index of the subarray.
 */
private static <AnyType extends Comparable<? super AnyType>>
void merge( AnyType [ ] a, AnyType [ ] tmpArray,
            int leftPos, int rightPos, int rightEnd )
{
    int leftEnd = rightPos - 1;
    int tmpPos = leftPos;
    int numElements = rightEnd - leftPos + 1;

    // Main loop
    while( leftPos <= leftEnd && rightPos <= rightEnd )
        if( a[ leftPos ].compareTo( a[ rightPos ] ) <= 0 )
            tmpArray[ tmpPos++ ] = a[ leftPos++ ];
        else
            tmpArray[ tmpPos++ ] = a[ rightPos++ ];

    while( leftPos <= leftEnd )    // Copy rest of first half
        tmpArray[ tmpPos++ ] = a[ leftPos++ ];

    while( rightPos <= rightEnd )  // Copy rest of right half
        tmpArray[ tmpPos++ ] = a[ rightPos++ ];

    // Copy tmpArray back
    for( int i = 0; i < numElements; i++, rightEnd-- )
        a[ rightEnd ] = tmpArray[ rightEnd ];
}
```

figure 8.9

The merge routine

on recursion. On the other hand, it is a tricky algorithm to implement because minute changes in the code can make significant differences in running time. We first describe the algorithm in broad terms. We then provide an analysis that shows its best-, worst-, and average-case running times. We use this analysis to make decisions about how to implement certain details in Java, such as the handling of duplicate items.

The basic quicksort algorithm is recursive. Details include choosing the pivot, deciding how to partition, and dealing with duplicates. Wrong decisions give quadratic running times for a variety of common inputs.

8.6.1 the quicksort algorithm

The basic algorithm *Quicksort*(*S*) consists of the following four steps.

1. If the number of elements in *S* is 0 or 1, then return.
2. Pick *any* element *v* in *S*. It is called the *pivot*.

3. *Partition* $S - \{v\}$ (the remaining elements in *S*) into two disjoint groups: $L = \{x \in S - \{v\} | x \leq v\}$ and $R = \{x \in S - \{v\} | x \geq v\}$.
4. Return the result of *Quicksort*(*L*) followed by *v* followed by *Quicksort*(*R*).

The *pivot* divides array elements into two groups: those smaller than the pivot and those larger than the pivot.

Several points stand out when we look at these steps. First, the multibase case of the recursion includes the possibility that *S* might be an empty (multi) set. This provision is needed because the recursive calls could generate empty subsets. Second, the algorithm allows any element to be used as the pivot. The *pivot* divides array elements into two groups: elements that are smaller than the pivot and elements that are larger than the pivot. The analysis performed here shows that some choices for the pivot are better than others. Thus, when we provide an actual implementation, we do not use just any pivot. Instead we try to make an educated choice.

In the *partition* step every element except the pivot is placed in one of two groups.

In the *partition* step, every element in *S*, except for the pivot, is placed in either *L* (which stands for the left-hand part of the array) or *R* (which stands for the right-hand part of the array). The intent is that elements that are smaller than the pivot go to *L* and that elements larger than the pivot go to *R*. The description in the algorithm, however, ambiguously describes what to do with elements equal to the pivot. It allows each instance of a duplicate to go into either subset, specifying only that it must go to one or the other. Part of a good Java implementation is handling this case as efficiently as possible. Again, the analysis allows us to make an informed decision.

Figure 8.10 shows the action of quicksort on a set of numbers. The pivot is chosen (by chance) to be 65. The remaining elements in the set are partitioned into two smaller subsets. Each group is then sorted recursively. Recall that, by the third rule of recursion, we can assume that this step works. The sorted arrangement of the entire group is then trivially obtained. In a Java implementation, the items would be stored in a part of an array delimited by `low` and `high`. After the partitioning step, the pivot would wind up in some array cell `p`. The recursive calls would then be on the parts from `low` to `p-1` and then `p+1` to `high`.

Because recursion allows us to take the giant leap of faith, the correctness of the algorithm is guaranteed as follows.

- The group of small elements is sorted by virtue of the recursion.
- The largest element in the group of small elements is not larger than the pivot by virtue of the partition.
- The pivot is not larger than the smallest element in the group of large elements by virtue of the partition.
- The group of large elements is sorted by virtue of the recursion.

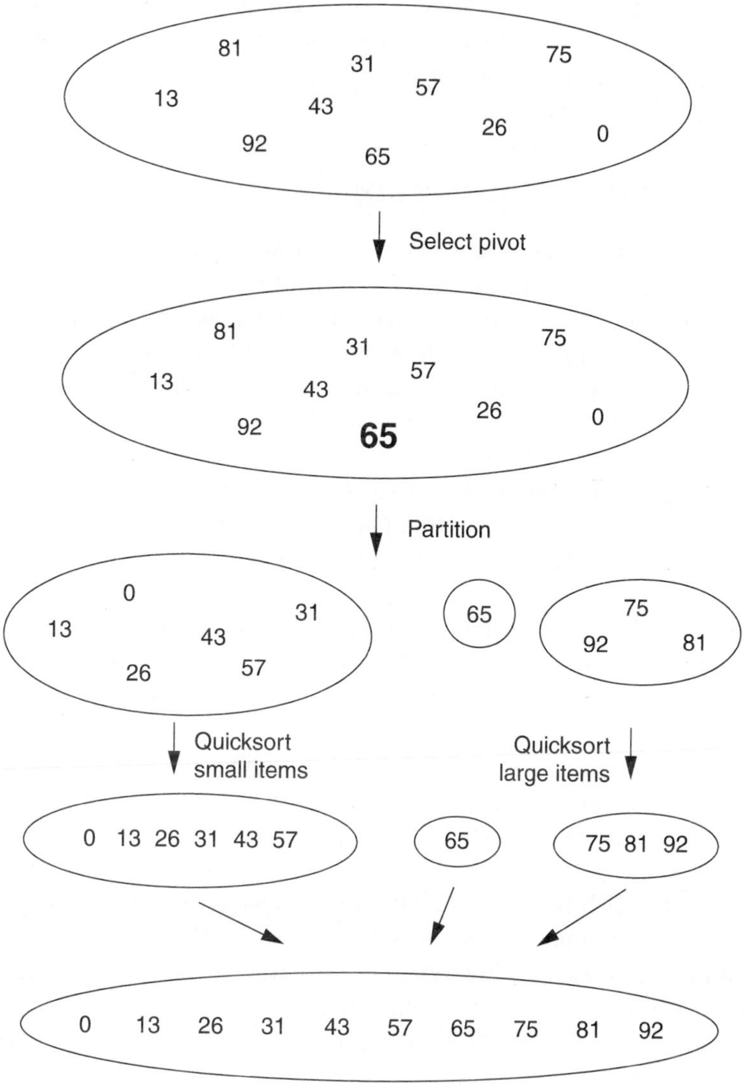

figure 8.10
The steps of quicksort

Although the correctness of the algorithm is easily established, why it is faster than mergesort is not clear. Like mergesort, it recursively solves two subproblems and requires linear additional work (in the form of the partitioning step). Unlike mergesort, however, quicksort subproblems are not guaranteed to be of equal size, which is bad for performance. However, quicksort can be faster than mergesort because the partitioning step can be performed

Quicksort is fast because the partitioning step can be performed quickly and in place.

significantly faster than the merging step can. In particular, the partitioning step can be performed without using an extra array, and the code to implement it is very compact and efficient. This advantage makes up for the lack of equally sized subproblems.

8.6.2 analysis of quicksort

The algorithm description leaves several questions unanswered: How do we choose the pivot? How do we perform the partition? What do we do if we see an element that is equal to the pivot? All these questions can dramatically affect the running time of the algorithm. We perform an analysis to help us decide how to implement the unspecified steps in quicksort.

best case

The best case occurs when the partition always splits into equal subsets. The running time is $O(N \log N)$.

The best case for quicksort is that the pivot partitions the set into two equally sized subsets and that this partitioning happens at each stage of the recursion. We then have two half-sized recursive calls plus linear overhead, which matches the performance of mergesort. The running time for this case is $O(N \log N)$. (We have not actually proved that this is the best case. Although such a proof is possible, we omit the details here.)

worst case

The worst case occurs when the partition repeatedly generates an empty subset. The running time is $O(N^2)$.

Since equally sized subsets are good for quicksort, you might expect that unequally sized subsets are bad. That indeed is the case. Let us suppose that, in each step of the recursion, the pivot happens to be the smallest element. Then the set of small elements L will be empty, and the set of large elements R will have all the elements except the pivot. We then have to recursively call quicksort on subset R. Suppose also that $T(N)$ is the running time to quicksort N elements and we assume that the time to sort 0 or 1 element is just 1 time unit. Suppose further that we charge N units to partition a set that contains N elements. Then for $N > 1$, we obtain a running time that satisfies

$$T(N) = T(N-1) + N \qquad \textbf{(8.1)}$$

In other words, Equation 8.1 states that the time required to quicksort N items equals the time to sort recursively the $N - 1$ items in the subset of larger elements plus the N units of cost to perform the partition. This assumes that in each step of the iteration we are unfortunate enough to pick the smallest element as the pivot. To simplify the analysis, we normalize by throwing out constant factors and solve this recurrence by telescoping Equation 8.1 repeatedly:

$$
\begin{aligned}
T(N) &= T(N-1) + N \\
T(N-1) &= T(N-2) + (N-1) \\
T(N-2) &= T(N-3) + (N-2) \\
&\dots \\
T(2) &= T(1) + 2
\end{aligned}
\tag{8.2}
$$

When we add everything in Equation 8.2, we obtain massive cancellations, yielding

$$T(N) = T(1) + 2 + 3 + \cdots + N = \frac{N(N+1)}{2} = O(N^2) \tag{8.3}$$

This analysis verifies the intuition that an uneven split is bad. We spend N units of time to partition and then have to make a recursive call for $N-1$ elements. Then we spend $N-1$ units to partition that group, only to have to make a recursive call for $N-2$ elements. In that call we spend $N-2$ units performing the partition, and so on. The total cost of performing all the partitions throughout the recursive calls exactly matches what is obtained in Equation 8.3. This result tells us that, when implementing the selection of the pivot and the partitioning step, we do not want to do anything that might encourage the size of the subsets to be unbalanced.

average case

The first two analyses tell us that the best and worst cases are widely different. Naturally, we want to know what happens in the average case. We would expect that, as each subproblem is half the original on average, the $O(N \log N)$ would now become an average-case bound. Such an expectation, although correct for the particular quicksort application we examine here, does not constitute a formal proof. Averages cannot be thrown around lightly. For example, suppose that we have a pivot algorithm guaranteed to select only the smallest or largest element, each with probability 1/2. Then the average size of the small group of elements is roughly $N/2$, as is the average size of the large group of elements (because each is equally likely to have 0 or $N-1$ elements). But the running time of quicksort with that pivot selection is always quadratic because we always get a poor split of elements. Thus we must carefully assign the label *average.* We can argue that the group of small elements is as likely to contain 0, 1, 2, …, or $N-1$ elements, which is also true for the group of large elements. Under this assumption we can establish that the average-case running time is indeed $O(N \log N)$.

The average case is $O(N \log N)$ Although this seems intuitive, a formal proof is required.

The average cost of a recursive call is obtained by averaging the costs of all possible subproblem sizes.

Because the cost to quicksort N items equals N units for the partitioning step plus the cost of the two recursive calls, we need to determine the average cost of each of the recursive calls. If $T(N)$ represents the average cost to quicksort N elements, the average cost of each recursive call equals the average—over all possible subproblem sizes—of the average cost of a recursive call on the subproblem:

$$T(L) = T(R) = \frac{T(0) + T(1) + T(2) + \cdots + T(N-1)}{N} \quad \textbf{(8.4)}$$

Equation 8.4 states that we are looking at the costs for each possible subset size and averaging them. As we have two recursive calls plus linear time to perform the partition, we obtain

$$T(N) = 2\left(\frac{T(0) + T(1) + T(2) + \cdots + T(N-1)}{N}\right) + N \quad \textbf{(8.5)}$$

The average running time is given by $T(N)$. We solve Equation 8.5 by removing all but the most recent recursive value of T.

To solve Equation 8.5, we begin by multiplying both sides by N, obtaining

$$NT(N) = 2(T(0) + T(1) + T(2) + \cdots + T(N-1)) + N^2 \quad \textbf{(8.6)}$$

We then write Equation 8.6 for the case $N - 1$, with the idea being that we can greatly simplify the equation by subtraction. Doing so yields

$$(N-1)T(N-1) = 2(T(0) + T(1) + \cdots + T(N-2)) + (N-1)^2 \quad \textbf{(8.7)}$$

Now, if we subtract Equation 8.7 from Equation 8.6, we obtain

$$NT(N) - (N-1)T(N-1) = 2T(N-1) + 2N - 1$$

We rearrange terms and drop the insignificant –1 on the right-hand side, obtaining

Once we have $T(N)$ in terms of $T(N-1)$ only, we attempt to telescope.

$$NT(N) = (N+1)T(N-1) + 2N \quad \textbf{(8.8)}$$

We now have a formula for $T(N)$ in terms of $T(N-1)$ only. Again the idea is to telescope, but Equation 8.8 is in the wrong form. If we divide Equation 8.8 by $N(N+1)$, we get

$$\frac{T(N)}{N+1} = \frac{T(N-1)}{N} + \frac{2}{N+1}$$

Now we can telescope:

$$\begin{aligned}
\frac{T(N)}{N+1} &= \frac{T(N-1)}{N} + \frac{2}{N+1} \\
\frac{T(N-1)}{N} &= \frac{T(N-2)}{N-1} + \frac{2}{N} \\
\frac{T(N-2)}{N-1} &= \frac{T(N-3)}{N-2} + \frac{2}{N-1} \\
&\;\;\cdots \\
\frac{T(2)}{3} &= \frac{T(1)}{2} + \frac{2}{3}
\end{aligned} \tag{8.9}$$

If we add all the equations in Equation 8.9, we have

$$\begin{aligned}
\frac{T(N)}{N+1} &= \frac{T(1)}{2} + 2\left(\frac{1}{3} + \frac{1}{4} + \cdots + \frac{1}{N} + \frac{1}{N+1}\right) \\
&= 2\left(1 + \frac{1}{2} + \frac{1}{3} + \cdots + \frac{1}{N+1}\right) - \frac{5}{2} \\
&= O(\log N)
\end{aligned} \tag{8.10}$$

The last line in Equation 8.10 follows from Theorem 5.5. When we multiply both sides by $N+1$, we obtain the final result:

We use the fact that the Nth harmonic number is $O(\log N)$.

$$T(N) = O(N \log N) \tag{8.11}$$

8.6.3 picking the pivot

Now that we have established that quicksort will run in $O(N \log N)$ time on average, our primary concern is to ensure that the worst case does not occur. By performing a complex analysis, we can compute the standard deviation of quicksort's running time. The result is that, if a single random permutation is presented, the running time used to sort it will almost certainly be close to the average. Thus we must see to it that degenerate inputs do not result in bad running times. Degenerate inputs include data that have already been sorted and data that contain only N completely identical elements. Sometimes it is the easy cases that give algorithms trouble.

Picking the pivot is crucial to good performance. Never choose the first element as pivot.

a wrong way

The popular, uninformed choice is to use the first element (i.e., the element in position `low`) as the pivot. This selection is acceptable if the input is random, but if the input has been presorted or is in reverse order, the pivot provides a poor partition because it is an extreme element. Moreover, this behavior will continue recursively. As we demonstrated earlier in the chapter, we would end up with quadratic running time to do absolutely nothing. Needless to say, that would be embarrassing. *Never* use the first element as the pivot.

Another popular alternative is to choose the larger of the first two distinct keys[3] as the pivot, but this selection has the same bad effects as choosing the first key. Stay away from any strategy that looks only at some key near the front or end of the input group.

The middle element is a reasonable but passive choice.

a safe choice

A perfectly reasonable choice for the pivot is the middle element (i.e., the element in array cell `(low+high)/2`). When the input has already been sorted, this selection gives the perfect pivot in each recursive call. Of course, we could construct an input sequence that forces quadratic behavior for this strategy (see Exercise 8.8). However, the chances of randomly running into a case that took even twice as long as the average case is extremely small.

In *median-of-three partitioning,* the median of the first, middle, and last elements is used as the pivot. This approach simplifies the partitioning stage of quicksort.

median-of-three partitioning

Choosing the middle element as the pivot avoids the degenerate cases that arise from nonrandom inputs. Note that this is a passive choice, however. That is, we do not attempt to choose a good pivot. Instead, we merely try to avoid picking a bad pivot. Median-of-three partitioning is an attempt to pick a better than average pivot. In *median-of-three partitioning,* the median of the first, middle, and last elements is used as the pivot.

The median of a group of N numbers is the $\lceil N/2 \rceil$th smallest number. The best choice for the pivot clearly is the median because it guarantees an even split of the elements. Unfortunately, the median is hard to calculate, which would slow quicksort considerably. So we want to get a good estimate of the median without spending too much time doing so. We can obtain such an estimate by *sampling*—the classic method used in opinion polls. That is, we pick a subset of these numbers and find their median. The larger the sample, the more accurate the estimate. However, the larger sample takes longer to evaluate. A sample size of 3 gives a small improvement in the average running time of quicksort and also simplifies the resulting partitioning code by elimi-

3. In a complex object, the *key* is usually the part of the object on which the comparison is based.

nating some special cases. Large sample sizes do not significantly improve performance and thus are not worth using.

The three elements used in the sample are the first, middle, and last elements. For instance, with input 8, 1, 4, 9, 6, 3, 5, 2, 7, 0, the leftmost element is 8, the rightmost element is 0, and the center element is 6; thus the pivot would be 6. Note that for already sorted items, we keep the middle element as the pivot, and in this case, the pivot is the median.

8.6.4 a partitioning strategy

There are several commonly used partitioning strategies. The one that we describe in this section gives good results. The simplest partitioning strategy consists of three steps. In Section 8.6.6 we show the improvements that occur when median-of-three pivot selection is used.

The first step in the partitioning algorithm is to get the pivot element out of the way by swapping it with the last element. The result for our sample input is shown in Figure 8.11. The pivot element is shown in the darkest shade at the end of the array.

Step 1: Swap the pivot with the element at the end.

For now we assume that all the elements are distinct and leave for later what to do in the presence of duplicates. As a limiting case, our algorithm must work properly when *all* the elements are identical.

In step 2, we use our partitioning strategy to move all the small elements to the left in the array and all the large elements to the right. *Small* and *large* are relative to the pivot. In Figures 8.11–8.16, white cells are those that we know are correctly placed. The lightly shaded cells are not necessarily correctly placed.

Step 2: Run `i` from left to right and `j` from right to left. When `i` encounters a large element, `i` stops. When `j` encounters a small element, `j` stops. If `i` and `j` have not crossed, swap their items and continue. Otherwise, stop this loop.

We search from left to right, looking for a large element, using a counter `i`, initialized at position `low`. We also search from right to left, looking for a small element, using a counter `j`, initialized to start at `high-1`. Figure 8.12 shows that the search for a large element stops at 8 and the search for a small element stops at 2. These cells have been lightly shaded. Note that, by skipping past 7, we know that 7 is not small and thus is correctly placed. Thus it is

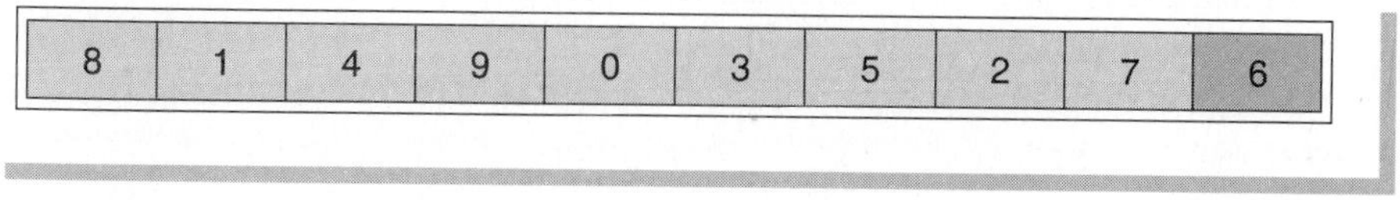

figure 8.11

Partitioning algorithm: Pivot element 6 is placed at the end.

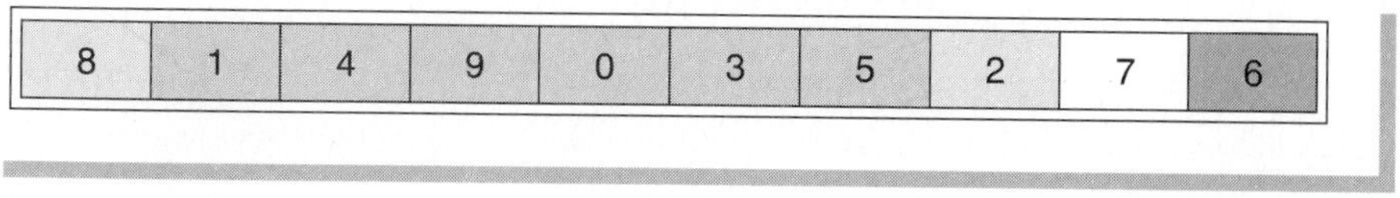

figure 8.12

Partitioning algorithm: `i` stops at large element 8; `j` stops at small element 2.

a white cell. Now, we have a large element, 8, on the left-hand side of the array and a small element, 2, on the right-hand side of the array. We must swap these two elements to place them correctly, as shown in Figure 8.13.

As the algorithm continues, `i` stops at large element 9 and `j` stops at small element 5. Once again, elements that `i` and `j` skip during the scan are guaranteed to be correctly placed. Figure 8.14 shows the result: The ends of the array (not counting the pivot) are filled with correctly placed elements.

Next, swap the elements that `i` and `j` are indexing, as shown in Figure 8.15. The scan continues, with `i` stopping at large element 9 and `j` stopping at small element 3. However, at this point `i` and `j` have crossed positions in the array. Consequently, a swap would be useless. Hence Figure 8.16 shows that the item being accessed by `j` is already correctly placed and should not move.

Step 3: Swap the element in position `i` with the pivot.

Figure 8.16 shows that all but two items are correctly placed. Wouldn't it be nice if we could just swap them and be done? Well, we can. All we need to do is swap the element in position `i` and the element in the last cell (the pivot), as shown in Figure 8.17. The element that `i` is indexing clearly is large, so moving it to the last position is fine.

figure 8.13

Partitioning algorithm: The out-of-order elements 8 and 2 are swapped.

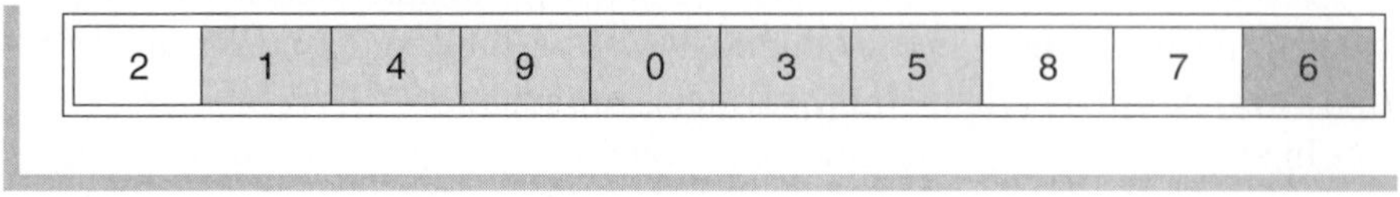

figure 8.14

Partitioning algorithm: `i` stops at large element 9; `j` stops at small element 5.

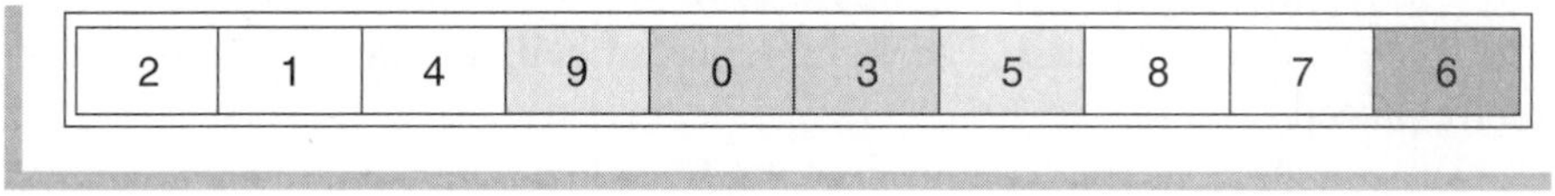

figure 8.15

Partitioning algorithm: The out-of-order elements 9 and 5 are swapped.

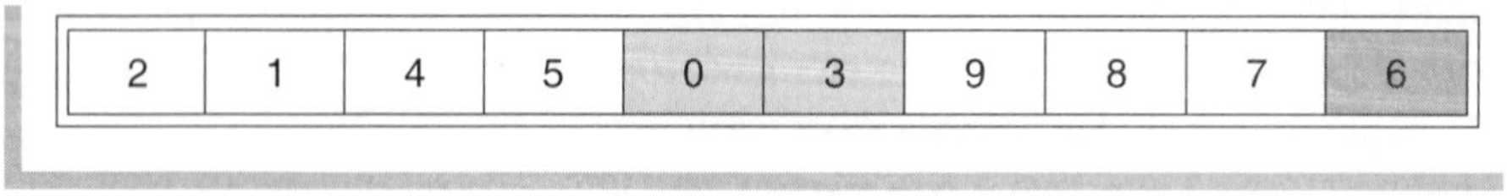

figure 8.16

Partitioning algorithm: `i` stops at large element 9; `j` stops at small element 3.

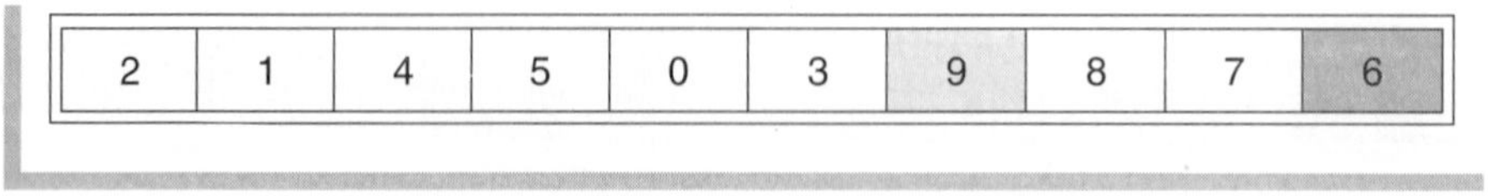

figure 8.17

Partitioning algorithm: Swap pivot and element in position `i`.

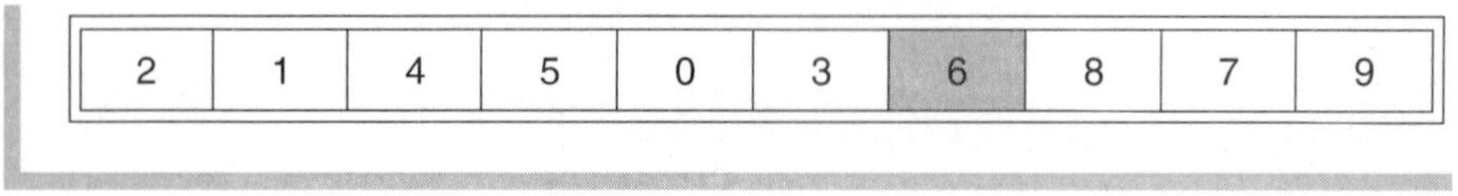

Note that the partitioning algorithm requires no extra memory and that each element is compared exactly once with the pivot. When the code is written, this approach translates to a very tight inner loop.

8.6.5 keys equal to the pivot

One important detail that we must consider is how to handle keys that are equal to the pivot. Should `i` stop when it encounters a key equal to the pivot, and should `j` stop when it encounters a key equal to the pivot? Counters `i` and `j` should do the same thing; otherwise, the partitioning step is biased. For instance, if `i` stops and `j` does not, all keys that are equal to the pivot wind up on the right-hand side.

Let us consider the case in which all elements in the array are identical. If both `i` and `j` stop, many swaps will occur between identical elements. Although these actions seem useless, the positive effect is that `i` and `j` cross in the middle, so when the pivot is replaced the partition creates two nearly equal subsets. Thus the best-case analysis applies, and the running time is $O(N \log N)$.

If neither `i` nor `j` stops, then `i` winds up at the last position (assuming of course that it does stop at the boundary), and no swaps are performed. This result seems great until we realize that the pivot is then placed as the last element because that is the last cell that `i` touches. The result is widely uneven subsets and a running time that matches the worst-case bound of $O(N^2)$. The effect is the same as using the first element as a pivot for presorted input: It takes quadratic time to do nothing.

We conclude that doing the unnecessary swaps and creating even subsets is better than risking widely uneven subsets. Therefore we have both `i` and `j` stop if they encounter an element equal to the pivot. This action turns out to be the only one of the four possibilities that does not take quadratic time for this input.

> Counters `i` and `j` must stop when they encounter an item equal to the pivot to guarantee good performance.

At first glance, worrying about an array of identical elements may seem silly. After all, why would anyone want to sort 5,000 identical elements? However, recall that quicksort is recursive. Suppose that there are 100,000 elements, of which 5,000 are identical. Eventually quicksort could make the recursive call on only the 5,000 identical elements. Then, ensuring that 5,000 identical elements can be sorted efficiently really is important.

8.6.6 median-of-three partitioning

When we do median-of-three partitioning, we can do a simple optimization that saves a few comparisons and also greatly simplifies the code. Figure 8.18 shows the original array.

Computing the median-of-three involves sorting three elements. Hence we can give the partitioning step a head start and also never worry about running off the end of the array.

Recall that median-of-three partitioning requires that we find the median of the first, middle, and last elements. The easiest way to do so is to sort them in the array. The result is shown in Figure 8.19. Note the resulting shading: The element that winds up in the first position is guaranteed to be smaller than (or equal to) the pivot, and the element in the last position is guaranteed to be larger than (or equal to) the pivot. This outcome tells us four things.

- We should not swap the pivot with the element in the last position. Instead, we should swap it with the element in the next-to-last position, as shown in Figure 8.20.
- We can start `i` at `low+1` and `j` at `high-2`.
- We are guaranteed that, whenever `i` searches for a large element, it will stop because in the worst case it will encounter the pivot (and we stop on equality).
- We are guaranteed that, whenever `j` searches for a small element, it will stop because in the worst case it will encounter the first element (and we stop on equality).

All these optimizations are incorporated into the final Java code.

8.6.7 small arrays

Sort 10 or fewer items by insertion sort. Place this test in the recursive quicksort routine.

Our final optimization concerns small arrays. Is using a high-powered routine such as quicksort worthwhile when there are only 10 elements to sort? The answer is of course not. A simple routine, such as the insertion sort, probably is faster for small arrays. The recursive nature of quicksort tells us that we

figure 8.18

Original array

8	1	4	9	6	3	5	2	7	0

figure 8.19

Result of sorting three elements (first, middle, and last)

0	1	4	9	6	3	5	2	7	8

figure 8.20

Result of swapping the pivot with the next-to-last element

0	1	4	9	7	3	5	2	6	8

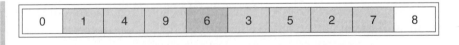

would generate many calls that have only small subsets. Thus testing the size of the subset is worthwhile. If it is smaller than some cutoff, we apply insertion sort; otherwise, we use quicksort.

A good cutoff is 10 elements, although any cutoff between 5 and 20 is likely to produce similar results. The actual best cutoff is machine dependent. Using a cutoff saves us from degenerate cases. For example, finding the median of three elements does not make much sense when there are not three elements.

In the past, many thought that an even better alternative was to leave the array slightly unsorted by doing absolutely nothing when the subset size was below the cutoff. Because the insertion sort is so efficient for nearly sorted arrays, we could show mathematically that running a final insertion sort to clean up the array was faster than running all the smaller insertion sorts. The savings were roughly the overhead of the insertion sort method calls.

Now, method calls are not as expensive as they used to be. Furthermore a second scan of the array for the insertion sort is expensive. Because of a technique called *caching,* we are better off doing the insertion sort on the small arrays. Localized memory accesses are faster than nonlocalized accesses. On many machines, touching memory twice in one scan is faster than touching memory once in each of two separate scans.

The idea of combining a second sorting algorithm when recursive calls to quicksort seem inappropriate can also be used to guarantee an $O(N \log N)$ worst case for quicksort. In Exercise 8.18 you are asked to explore combining quicksort and mergesort to get quicksort's average-case performance almost all the time with mergesort's worst-case guarantee. In practice, instead of mergesort we use another algorithm, namely *heapsort,* which we discuss in Section 21.5.

8.6.8 java quicksort routine

> We use a driver to set things up.

The actual implementation of quicksort is shown in Figure 8.21. The one-parameter `quicksort`, declared at lines 4 to 8, is merely a driver that calls the recursive `quicksort`. Thus we discuss only the implementation of the recursive `quicksort`.

At line 17 we test for small subarrays and call the insertion sort (not shown) when the problem instance is below some specified value given by the constant `CUTOFF`. Otherwise, we proceed with the recursive procedure. Lines 21 to 27 sort the low, middle, and high elements in place. In keeping with our previous discussion, we use the middle element as the pivot and swap it with the element in the next-to-last position at lines 30 and 31. We then do the partitioning phase. We initialize the counters `i` and `j` to 1 past their true initial values because the prefix increment and decrement operators will immedi-

figure 8.21

Quicksort with median-of-three partitioning and cutoff for small arrays

```
/**
 * Quicksort algorithm (driver)
 */
public static <AnyType extends Comparable<? super AnyType>>
void quicksort( AnyType [ ] a )
{
    quicksort( a, 0, a.length - 1 );
}

/**
 * Internal quicksort method that makes recursive calls.
 * Uses median-of-three partitioning and a cutoff.
 */
private static <AnyType extends Comparable<? super AnyType>>
void quicksort( AnyType [ ] a, int low, int high )
{
    if( low + CUTOFF > high )
        insertionSort( a, low, high );
    else
    {     // Sort low, middle, high
        int middle = ( low + high ) / 2;
        if( a[ middle ].compareTo( a[ low ] ) < 0 )
            swapReferences( a, low, middle );
        if( a[ high ].compareTo( a[ low ] ) < 0 )
            swapReferences( a, low, high );
        if( a[ high ].compareTo( a[ middle ] ) < 0 )
            swapReferences( a, middle, high );

            // Place pivot at position high - 1
        swapReferences( a, middle, high - 1 );
        AnyType pivot = a[ high - 1 ];

            // Begin partitioning
        int i, j;
        for( i = low, j = high - 1; ; )
        {
            while( a[ ++i ].compareTo( pivot ) < 0 )
                ;
            while( pivot.compareTo( a[ --j ] ) < 0 )
                ;
            if( i >= j )
                break;
            swapReferences( a, i, j );
        }
            // Restore pivot
        swapReferences( a, i, high - 1 );

        quicksort( a, low, i - 1 );    // Sort small elements
        quicksort( a, i + 1, high );   // Sort large elements
    }
}
```

ately adjust them before the array accesses at lines 37 and 39. When the first `while` loop at line 37 exits, `i` will be indexing an element that is greater than or possibly equal to the pivot. Likewise, when the second loop ends, `j` will be indexing an element that is less than or possibly equal to the pivot. If `i` and `j` have not crossed, these elements are swapped and we continue scanning. Otherwise, the scan is terminated and the pivot is restored at line 46. The sort is finished when the two recursive calls are made at lines 48 and 49.

The fundamental operations occur at lines 37 through 40. The scans consist of simple operations: increments, array accesses, and simple comparisons, accounting for the "quick" in quicksort. To ensure that the inner loops are tight and efficient, we want to be sure that the swap at line 43 comprises the three assignments that we expect and does not incur the overhead of a method call. Thus we declare that the `swapReferences` routine is a final static method, or in some cases, we write the three assignments explicitly (e.g., if the compiler exercises its right to not perform inline optimization).

> The inner loop of quicksort is very tight and efficient.

Although the code looks straightforward now, that is only because of the analysis we performed prior to coding. Additionally, some traps are still lurking (see Exercise 8.14). Quicksort is a classic example of using an analysis to guide a program implementation.

> Quicksort is a classic example of using an analysis to guide program implementation.

8.7 quickselect

A problem closely related to sorting is *selection,* or finding the *k*th smallest element in an array of *N* items. An important special case is finding the median, or the *N* / 2th smallest element. Obviously, we can sort the items, but as selection requests less information than sorting, we hope that selection would be a faster process. That turns out to be true. By making a small change to quicksort, we can solve the selection problem in linear time on average, giving us the algorithm quickselect. The steps for *Quickselect(S, k)* are as follows.

> *Selection* is finding the *k* th smallest element of an array.

1. If the number of elements in *S* is 1, presumably *k* is also 1, so we can return the single element in *S*.
2. Pick any element *v* in *S*. It is the pivot.
3. Partition $S - \{v\}$ into *L* and *R,* exactly as was done for quicksort.
4. If *k* is less than or equal to the number of elements in *L,* the item we are searching for must be in *L*. Call *Quickselect(L, k)* recursively. Otherwise, if *k* is exactly equal to 1 more than the number of items in *L,* the pivot is the *k*th smallest element, and we can return it as the

answer. Otherwise, the kth smallest element lies in R, and it is the $(k - |L| - 1)$th smallest element in R. Again, we can make a recursive call and return the result.

Quickselect is used to perform a selection. It is similar to quicksort but makes only one recursive call. The average running time is linear.

Quickselect makes only one recursive call compared to quicksort's two. The worst case of quickselect is identical to that of quicksort and is quadratic. It occurs when one of the recursive calls is on an empty set. In such cases quickselect does not save much. We can show that the average time is linear, however, by using an analysis similar to that used for quicksort (see Exercise 8.9).

The implementation of quickselect, shown in Figure 8.22, is simpler than our abstract description implies. Except for the extra parameter, k, and the recursive calls, the algorithm is identical to quicksort. When it terminates, the kth smallest element is in its correct position in the array. As the array begins at index 0, the fourth smallest element is in position 3. Note that the original ordering is destroyed. If this situation is undesirable, we can have the driver routine pass a copy of the array instead.

The linear worst-case algorithm is a classic result even though it is impractical.

Using median-of-three partitioning makes the chance of the worst case occurring almost negligible. By carefully choosing the pivot, we can ensure that the worst case never occurs and that the running time is linear even in the worst-case scenario. The resulting algorithm is entirely of theoretical interest, however, because the constant that the Big-Oh notation hides is much larger than the constant obtained in the normal median-of-three implementation.

8.8 a lower bound for sorting

Any comparison-based sorting algorithm must use roughly $N \log N$ comparisons on average and in the worst case.

Although we have $O(N \log N)$ algorithms for sorting, it is not clear that this is as good as we can do. In this section we prove that any algorithm for sorting that uses only comparisons requires $\Omega(N \log N)$ comparisons (and hence time) in the worst case. In other words, *any algorithm that sorts by using element comparisons must use at least roughly* $N \log N$ *comparisons for some input sequence.* We can use a similar technique to show that this condition holds on average.

The proofs are abstract; we show the worst-case lower bound.

Must every sorting algorithm work by using comparisons? The answer is no. However, algorithms that do not involve the use of general comparisons are likely to work only for restricted types, such as integers. Although we may often need to sort only integers (see Exercise 8.15), we cannot make such sweeping assumptions about the input of a general-purpose sorting algorithm.

```java
/**
 * Internal selection method that makes recursive calls.
 * Uses median-of-three partitioning and a cutoff.
 * Places the kth smallest item in a[k-1].
 * @param a an array of Comparable items.
 * @param low the left-most index of the subarray.
 * @param high the right-most index of the subarray.
 * @param k the desired rank (1 is minimum) in the entire array.
 */
private static <AnyType extends Comparable<? super AnyType>>
void quickSelect( AnyType [ ] a, int low, int high, int k )
{
    if( low + CUTOFF > high )
        insertionSort( a, low, high );
    else
    {
            // Sort low, middle, high
        int middle = ( low + high ) / 2;
        if( a[ middle ].compareTo( a[ low ] ) < 0 )
            swapReferences( a, low, middle );
        if( a[ high ].compareTo( a[ low ] ) < 0 )
            swapReferences( a, low, high );
        if( a[ high ].compareTo( a[ middle ] ) < 0 )
            swapReferences( a, middle, high );

            // Place pivot at position high - 1
        swapReferences( a, middle, high - 1 );
        AnyType pivot = a[ high - 1 ];

            // Begin partitioning
        int i, j;
        for( i = low, j = high - 1; ; )
        {
            while( a[ ++i ].compareTo( pivot ) < 0 )
                ;
            while( pivot.compareTo( a[ --j ] ) < 0 )
                ;
            if( i >= j )
                break;
            swapReferences( a, i, j );
        }
            // Restore pivot
        swapReferences( a, i, high - 1 );

            // Recurse; only this part changes
        if( k <= i )
            quickSelect( a, low, i - 1, k );
        else if( k > i + 1 )
            quickSelect( a, i + 1, high, k );
    }
}
```

figure 8.22

Quickselect with median-of-three partitioning and cutoff for small arrays

We may assume only the given—namely, that, because the items need to be sorted, any two items can be compared.

Next, we prove one of the most fundamental theorems in computer science, as Theorem 8.3. Recall first that the product of the first N positive integers is $N!$. The proof is an existence proof, which is somewhat abstract. It shows that some bad input must always exist.

Theorem 8.3 Any algorithm that sorts by using element comparisons only must use at least $\lceil \log(N!) \rceil$ comparisons for some input sequence.

Proof We may regard the possible inputs as any of the permutations of $1, 2, \ldots, N$ because only the relative order of the input items matters, not their actual values. Thus the number of possible inputs is the number of different arrangements of N items, which is exactly $N!$. Let P_i be the number of permutations that are consistent with the results after the algorithm has processed i comparisons. Let F be the number of comparisons processed when the sort terminates. We know the following: (a) $P_0 = N!$ because all permutations are possible before the first comparison; (b) $P_F = 1$ because, if more than one permutation were possible, the algorithm could not terminate with confidence that it produced the correct output; (c) there exists a permutation such that $P_i \geq P_{i-1}/2$ because, after a comparison, each permutation goes into one of two groups: the still-possible group and the no-longer-possible group. The larger of these two groups must have at least half the permutations. Furthermore, there is at least one permutation for which we can apply this logic throughout the comparison sequence. The action of a sorting algorithm is thus to go from the state P_0, in which all $N!$ permutations are possible, to the final state P_F, in which only one permutation is possible, with the restriction that there exists an input such that in each comparison only half of the permutations can be eliminated. By the halving principle, we know that at least $\lceil \log(N!) \rceil$ comparisons are required for that input.

How large is $\lceil \log(N!) \rceil$? It is approximately $N \log N - 1.44N$.

summary

For most general internal sorting applications, an insertion sort, Shellsort, mergesort, or quicksort is the method of choice. The decision regarding which to use depends on the size of the input and on the underlying environment.

Insertion sort is appropriate for very small amounts of input. Shellsort is a good choice for sorting moderate amounts of input. With a proper increment sequence, it gives excellent performance and uses only a few lines of code. Mergesort has $O(N \log N)$ worst-case performance but requires additional code to avoid some of the extra copying. Quicksort is tricky to code. Asymptotically, it has almost certain $O(N \log N)$ performance with a careful implementation, and we showed that this outcome is essentially as good as we can expect. In Section 21.5 we discuss another popular internal sort, *heapsort*.

To test and compare the merits of the various sorting algorithms, we need to be able to generate random inputs. Randomness is an important topic in general, and we discuss it in Chapter 9.

key concepts

comparison-based sorting algorithm An algorithm that makes ordering decisions only on the basis of comparisons. (305)

diminishing gap sort Another name for Shellsort. (310)

inversion A pair of elements that are out of order in an array. Used to measure unsortedness. (307)

lower-bound proof for sorting Confirms that any comparison-based sorting algorithm must use at least roughly $N \log N$ comparisons on average and in the worst case. (332)

median-of-three partitioning The median of the first, middle, and last elements is used as the pivot. This approach simplifies the partitioning stage of quicksort. (324)

mergesort A divide-and-conquer algorithm that obtains an $O(N \log N)$ sort. (313)

partition The step of quicksort that places every element except the pivot in one of two groups, one consisting of elements that are smaller than or equal to the pivot and one consisting of elements that are larger than or equal to the pivot. (318)

pivot For quicksort, an element that divides an array into two groups; one that is smaller than the pivot and one that is larger than the pivot. (318)

quickselect An algorithm used to perform a selection that is similar to quicksort but makes only one recursive call. The average running time is linear. (331)

quicksort A fast divide-and-conquer algorithm when properly implemented; in many situations it is the fastest comparison-based sorting algorithm known. (316)

selection The process of finding the kth smallest element of an array. (331)

Shellsort A subquadratic algorithm that works well in practice and is simple to code. The performance of Shellsort is highly dependent on the increment sequence and requires a challenging (and not completely resolved) analysis. (309)

common errors

1. The sorts coded in this chapter begin at array position 0, not position 1.
2. Using the wrong increment sequence for Shellsort is a common error. Be sure that the increment sequence terminates with 1 and avoid sequences that are known to give poor performance.
3. Quicksort has many traps. The most common errors deal with sorted inputs, duplicate elements, and degenerate partitions.
4. For small inputs an insertion sort is appropriate, but using it for large inputs is wrong.

on the internet

All the sorting algorithms and an implementation of quickselect are in a single file.

Duplicate.java	Contains the routine in Figure 8.1 and a test program.
Sort.java	Contains all the sorting algorithms and the selection algorithm.

exercises

IN SHORT

8.1 Sort the sequence 8, 1, 4, 1, 5, 9, 2, 6, 5 by using

a. Insertion sort
b. Shellsort for the increments {1, 3, 5}
c. Mergesort
d. Quicksort, with the middle element as pivot and no cutoff (show all steps)
e. Quicksort, with median-of-three pivot selection and a cutoff of 3

8.2 A sorting algorithm is *stable* if elements with equal keys are left in the same order as they occur in the input. Which of the sorting algorithms in this chapter are stable and which are not? Why?

8.3 Explain why the elaborate quicksort in the text is better than randomly permuting the input and choosing the middle element as pivot.

IN THEORY

8.4 When all keys are equal, what is the running time of
   a. Insertion sort
   b. Shellsort
   c. Mergesort
   d. Quicksort

8.5 When the input has been sorted, what is the running time of
   a. Insertion sort
   b. Shellsort
   c. Mergesort
   d. Quicksort

8.6 When the input has been sorted in reverse order, what is the running time of
   a. Insertion sort
   b. Shellsort
   c. Mergesort
   d. Quicksort

8.7 Suppose that we exchange elements `a[i]` and `a[i+k]`, which were originally out of order. Prove that at least 1 and at most $2k - 1$ inversions are removed.

8.8 Construct a worst-case input for quicksort with
   a. The middle element as pivot
   b. Median-of-three pivot partitioning

8.9 Show that the quickselect algorithm has linear average performance. Do so by solving Equation 8.5 with the constant 2 replaced by 1.

8.10 Using Stirling's formula, $N! \geq (N/e)^N\sqrt{2\pi N}$, derive an estimate for $\log(N!)$.

8.11 Prove that any comparison-based algorithm used to sort four elements requires at least five comparisons for some input. Then show that an algorithm that sorts four elements using at most five comparisons does indeed exist.

8.12 When implementing quicksort, if the array contains lots of duplicates, you may find it best to perform a three-way partition (into elements less than, equal to, and greater than the pivot) and make smaller recursive calls. Assume that you can use three-way comparisons.
   a. Give an algorithm that performs a three-way in-place partition of an N element subarray using only $N-1$ three-way comparisons.

If there are *d* items equal to the pivot, you may use *d* additional `Comparable` swaps, above and beyond the two-way partitioning algorithm. (*Hint:* As `i` and `j` move toward each other, maintain the five groups of elements shown.)

```
EQUAL  SMALL      UNKNOWN       LARGE        EQUAL
           i                   j
```

b. Prove that, using the algorithm in part (a), sorting an N-element array that contains only d different values takes $O(d\,N)$ time.

8.13 Suppose that both arrays A and B are sorted and contain N elements. Give an $O(\log N)$ algorithm to find the median of $A \cup B$.

IN PRACTICE

8.14 A student alters the `quicksort` routine in Figure 8.21 by making the following changes to lines 35 to 40. Is the result equivalent to the original routine?

```
35    for( i = low + 1, j = high - 2; ; )
36    {
37        while( a[ i ] < pivot )
38            i++;
39        while( pivot < a[ j ] )
40            j--;
```

8.15 If you know more information about the items being sorted, you can sort them in linear time. Show that a collection of N 16-bit integers can be sorted in $O(N)$ time. (*Hint:* Maintain an array indexed from 0 to 65,535.)

8.16 The quicksort in the text uses two recursive calls. Remove one of the calls as follows.

a. Rewrite the code so that the second recursive call is unconditionally the last line in quicksort. Do so by reversing the `if/else`, and returning after the call to `insertionSort`.

b. Remove the tail recursion by writing a `while` loop and altering `low`.

8.17 Continuing from Exercise 8.16, after part (a),

a. Perform a test so that the smaller subarray is processed by the first recursive call and the larger subarray is processed by the second recursive call.

b. Remove the tail recursion by writing a `while` loop and altering `low` or `high`, as necessary.

c. Prove that the number of recursive calls is logarithmic in the worst case.

8.18 Suppose that the recursive quicksort receives an `int` parameter, `depth`, from the driver that is initially approximately $2 \log N$.

a. Modify the recursive quicksort to call `mergeSort` on its current subarray if the level of recursion has reached `depth`. (*Hint:* Decrement `depth` as you make recursive calls; when it is 0, switch to mergesort.)

b. Prove that the worst-case running time of this algorithm is $O(N \log N)$.

c. Conduct experiments to determine how often `mergeSort` gets called.

d. Implement this technique in conjunction with tail recursion removal in Exercise 8.16.

e. Explain why the technique in Exercise 8.17 would no longer be needed.

8.19 An array contains N numbers, and you want to determine whether two of the numbers sum to a given number K. For instance, if the input is 8, 4, 1, 6 and K is 10, the answer is yes (4 and 6). A number may be used twice. Do the following.

a. Give an $O(N^2)$ algorithm to solve this problem.

b. Give an $O(N \log N)$ algorithm to solve this problem. (*Hint:* Sort the items first. After doing so, you can solve the problem in linear time.)

c. Code both solutions and compare the running times of your algorithms.

8.20 Repeat Exercise 8.19 for four numbers. Try to design an $O(N^2 \log N)$ algorithm. (*Hint:* Compute all possible sums of two elements, sort these possible sums, and then proceed as in Exercise 8.19.)

8.21 Repeat Exercise 8.19 for three numbers. Try to design an $O(N^2)$ algorithm.

8.22 In Exercise 5.30 you were asked to find the single integral solution to $A^5 + B^5 + C^5 + D^5 + E^5 = F^5$ with $0 < A \le B \le C \le D \le E \le F \le N$, where N is 75. Use the ideas explored in Exercise 8.20 to obtain a solution relatively quickly by sorting all possible values of $A^5 + B^5 + C^5$ and $F^5 - (D^5 + E^5)$, and then seeing if a number in the first group is equal to a number in the second group. In terms of N, how much space and time does the algorithm require?

PROGRAMMING PROJECTS

8.23 Compare the performance of Shellsort with various increment sequences, as follows. Obtain an average time for some input size N by generating several random sequences of N items. Use the same input for all increment sequences. In a separate test obtain the average number of `Comparable` comparisons and `Comparable` assignments. Set the number of repeated trials to be large but doable within 1 hour of CPU time. The increment sequences are

a. Shell's original sequence (repeatedly divide by 2).
b. Shell's original sequence, adding 1 if the result is nonzero but even.
c. Gonnet's sequence shown in the text, with repeated division by 2.2.
d. Hibbard's increments: 1, 3, 7, ..., $2^k - 1$.
e. Knuth's increments: 1, 4, 13, ..., $(3^k - 1)/2$.
f. Sedgewick's increments: 1, 5, 19, 41, 109, ..., with each term having the form of either $9 \cdot 4^k - 9 \cdot 2^k + 1$ or $4^k - 3 \cdot 2^k + 1$.

8.24 Code both Shellsort and quicksort and compare their running times. Use the best implementations in the text and run them on

a. Integers
b. Real numbers of type `double`
c. Strings

8.25 Write a method that removes all duplicates in an array A of N items. Return the number of items that remain in A. Your method must run in $O(N \log N)$ average time (use quicksort as a preprocessing step), and should make no use of the Collections API.

8.26 Exercise 8.2 addressed stable sorting. Write a method that performs a stable quicksort. To do so, create an array of objects; each object is to contain a data item and its initial position in the array. (This is the Composite pattern; see Section 3.7.) Then sort the array; if two objects have identical data items, use the initial position to break the tie. After the array of objects has been sorted, rearrange the original array.

8.27 Write a simple sorting utility, *sort*. The *sort* command takes a file-name as a parameter, and the file contains one item per line. By default the lines are considered strings and are sorted by normal lexicographic order (in a case-sensitive manner). Add two options: The *-c* option means that the sort should be case insensitive; the *-n* option means that the lines are to be considered integers for the purpose of the sort.

8.28 Write a program that reads N points in a plane and outputs any group of four or more colinear points (i.e., points on the same line). The obvious brute-force algorithm requires $O(N^4)$ time. However, there is a better algorithm that makes use of sorting and runs in $O(N^2 \log N)$ time.

references

The classic reference for sorting algorithms is [5]. Another reference is [3]. The Shellsort algorithm first appeared in [8]. An empirical study of its running time was done in [9]. Quicksort was discovered by Hoare [4]; that paper also includes the quickselect algorithm and details many important implementation issues. A thorough study of the quicksort algorithm, including analysis for the median-of-three variant, appears in [7]. A detailed C implementation that includes additional improvements is presented in [1]. Exercise 8.18 is based on [6]. The $\Omega(N \log N)$ lower bound for comparison-based sorting is taken from [2]. The presentation of Shellsort is adapted from [10].

1. J. L. Bentley and M. D. McElroy, "Engineering a Sort Function," *Software—Practice and Experience* **23** (1993), 1249–1265.
2. L. R. Ford and S. M. Johnson, "A Tournament Problem," *American Mathematics Monthly* **66** (1959), 387–389.
3. G. H. Gonnet and R. Baeza-Yates, *Handbook of Algorithms and Data Structures*, 2d ed., Addison-Wesley, Reading, MA, 1991.
4. C. A. R. Hoare, "Quicksort," *Computer Journal* **5** (1962), 10–15.
5. D. E. Knuth, *The Art of Computer Programming, Vol. 3: Sorting and Searching,* 2d ed., Addison-Wesley, Reading, MA, 1998.
6. D. R. Musser, "Introspective Sorting and Selection Algorithms," *Software—Practice and Experience* **27** (1997), 983–993.
7. R. Sedgewick, *Quicksort*, Garland, New York, 1978. (Originally presented as the author's Ph.D. dissertation, Stanford University, 1975.)
8. D. L. Shell, "A High-Speed Sorting Procedure," *Communications of the ACM* **2** 7 (1959), 30–32.
9. M. A. Weiss, "Empirical Results on the Running Time of Shellsort," *Computer Journal* **34** (1991), 88–91.
10. M. A. Weiss, *Efficient C Programming: A Practical Approach,* Prentice Hall, Upper Saddle River, NJ, 1995.

chapter 9

randomization

Many situations in computing require the use of random numbers. For example, modern cryptography, simulation systems, and, surprisingly, even searching and sorting algorithms rely on random number generators. Yet good random number generators are difficult to implement. In this chapter we discuss the generation and use of random numbers.

In this chapter, we show

- How random numbers are generated
- How random permutations are generated
- How random numbers allow the design of efficient algorithms, using a general technique known as the *randomized algorithm*

9.1 why do we need random numbers?

Random numbers are used in many applications. In this section we discuss a few of the most common ones.

Random numbers have many important uses, including cryptography, simulation, and program testing.

One important application of random numbers is in program testing. Suppose, for example, that we want to test whether a sorting algorithm written in Chapter 8 actually works. Of course, we could provide some small amount of input, but if we want to test the algorithms for the large data sets they were designed for, we need lots of input. Providing sorted data as input tests one case, but more convincing tests would be preferable. For instance, we would want to test the program by perhaps running 5,000 sorts for inputs of size 1,000. To do so requires writing a routine to generate the test data, which in turn requires the use of random numbers.

A *permutation* of 1, 2, ..., N is a sequence of N integers that includes each of 1, 2, ..., N exactly once.

Once we have the random number inputs, how do we know whether the sorting algorithm works? One test is to determine whether the sort arranged the array in nondecreasing order. Clearly, we can run this test in a linear-time sequential scan. But how do we know that the items present after the sort are the same as those prior to the sort? One method is to fix the items in an arrangement of 1, 2, ..., N. In other words, we start with a random permutation of the first N integers. A *permutation* of 1, 2, ..., N is a sequence of N integers that includes each of 1, 2, ..., N exactly once. Then, no matter what permutation we start with, the result of the sort will be the sequence 1, 2, ..., N, which is also easily tested.

In addition to helping us generate test data to verify program correctness, random numbers are useful in comparing the performance of various algorithms. The reason is that, once again, they can be used to provide a large number of inputs.

Another use of random numbers is in simulations. If we want to know the average time required for a service system (for example, teller service in a bank) to process a sequence of requests, we can model the system on a computer. In this computer simulation we generate the request sequence with random numbers.

Still another use of random numbers is in the general technique called the *randomized algorithm*, wherein a random number is used to determine the next step performed in the algorithm. The most common type of randomized algorithm involves selecting from among several possible alternatives that are more or less indistinguishable. For instance, in a commercial computer chess program, the computer generally chooses its first move randomly rather than playing deterministically (i.e., rather than always playing the same move). In this chapter we look at several problems that can be solved more efficiently by using a randomized algorithm.

9.2 random number generators

How are random numbers generated? True randomness is impossible to achieve on a computer, because any numbers obtained depend on the algorithm used to generate them and thus cannot possibly be random. Generally, it is sufficient to produce *pseudorandom numbers,* or numbers that *appear* to be random because they satisfy many of the properties of random numbers. Producing them is much easier said than done.

Pseudorandom numbers have many properties of random numbers. Good random number generators are hard to find.

Suppose that we need to simulate a coin flip. One way to do so is to examine the system clock. Presumably, the system clock maintains the number of seconds as part of the current time. If this number is even, we can return 0 (for heads); if it is odd, we can return 1 (for tails). The problem is that this strategy does not work well if we need a sequence of random numbers. One second is a long time, and the clock might not change at all while the program is running, generating all 0s or all 1s, which is hardly a random sequence. Even if the time were recorded in units of microseconds (or smaller) and the program were running by itself, the sequence of numbers generated would be far from random because the time between calls to the generator would be essentially identical on every program invocation.

What we really need is a *sequence* of pseudorandom numbers, that is, a sequence with the same properties as a random sequence. Suppose that we want random numbers between 0 and 999, uniformly distributed. In a *uniform distribution,* all numbers in the specified range are equally likely to occur. Other distributions are also widely used. The class skeleton shown in Figure 9.1 supports several distributions, and some of the basic methods are identical to the `java.util.Random` class. Most distributions can be derived from the uniform distribution, so that is the one we consider first. The following properties hold if the sequence 0, ..., 999 is a true uniform distribution.

In a *uniform distribution,* all numbers in the specified range are equally likely to occur.

- The first number is equally likely to be 0, 1, 2, ..., 999.
- The *i*th number is equally likely to be 0, 1, 2, ..., 999.
- The expected average of all the generated numbers is 499.5.

These properties are not particularly restrictive. For instance, we could generate the first number by examining a system clock that was accurate to 1 ms and then using the number of milliseconds. We could generate subsequent numbers by adding 1 to the preceding number, and so on. Clearly, after 1,000 numbers are generated, all the previous properties hold. However, stronger properties do not.

Typically a random sequence, rather than one random number, is required.

Two stronger properties that would hold for uniformly distributed random numbers are the following.

- The sum of two consecutive random numbers is equally likely to be even or odd.
- If 1,000 numbers are randomly generated, some will be duplicated. (Roughly 368 numbers will never appear.)

```
package weiss.util;

// Random class
//
// CONSTRUCTION: with (a) no initializer or (b) an integer
//     that specifies the initial state of the generator.
//     This random number generator is really only 31 bits,
//     so it is weaker than the one in java.util.
//
// ******************PUBLIC OPERATIONS*********************
//     Return a random number according to some distribution:
// int nextInt( )                              --> Uniform, [1 to 2^31-1]
// double nextDouble( )                        --> Uniform, (0 to 1)
// int nextInt( int high )                     --> Uniform [0..high)
// int nextInt( int low, int high )            --> Uniform [low..high]
// int nextPoisson( double expectedVal )       --> Poisson
// double nextNegExp( double expectedVal )     --> Negative exponential
// void permute( Object [ ] a )                --> Randomly permutate

/**
 * Random number class, using a 31-bit
 * linear congruential generator.
 */
public class Random
{
    public Random( )
      { /* Figure 9.2 */ }
    public Random( int initialValue )
      { /* Figure 9.2 */ }
    public int nextInt( )
      { /* Figure 9.2 */ }
    public int nextInt( int high )
      { /* Implementation in online code. */ }
    public double nextDouble( )
      { /* Implementation in online code. */ }
    public int nextInt( int low, int high )
      { /* Implementation in online code. */ }
    public int nextPoisson( double expectedValue )
      { /* Figure 9.4 */ }
    public double nextNegExp( double expectedValue )
      { /* Figure 9.5 */ }
    public static final void permute( Object [ ] a )
      { /* Figure 9.6 */ }
    private void swapReferences( Object [ ] a, int i, int j )
      { /* Implementation in online code. */ }

    private int state;
}
```

figure 9.1

Skeleton for the Random class that generates random numbers

Our numbers do not satisfy these properties. Consecutive numbers always sum to an odd number, and our sequence is duplicate-free. We say then that our simple pseudorandom number generator has failed two statistical tests. All pseudorandom number generators fail some statistical tests, but the good generators fail fewer tests than the bad ones. (See Exercise 9.14 for a common statistical test.)

In this section we describe the simplest uniform generator that passes a reasonable number of statistical tests. By no means is it the best generator. However, it is suitable for use in applications wherein a good approximation to a random sequence is acceptable. The method used is the linear congruential generator, which was first described in 1951. The *linear congruential generator* is a good algorithm for generating uniform distributions. It is a random number generator in which numbers X_1, X_2, ... are generated that satisfy

The *linear congruential generator* is a good algorithm for generating uniform distributions.

$$X_{i+1} = AX_i(\mathrm{mod}M) \qquad \textbf{(9.1)}$$

Equation 9.1 states that we can get the $(i+1)$th number by multiplying the ith number by some constant A and computing the remainder when the result is divided by M. In Java we would have

```
x[ i + 1 ] = A * x[ i ] % M
```

We specify the constants A and M shortly. Note that all generated numbers will be smaller than M. Some value X_0 must be given to start the sequence. This initial value of the random number generator is the *seed.* If $X_0 = 0$, the sequence is not random because it generates all zeros. But if A and M are carefully chosen, any other seed satisfying $1 \le X_0 < M$ is equally valid. If M is prime, X_i is never 0. For example, if $M = 11$, $A = 7$, and the seed $X_0 = 1$, the numbers generated are

The *seed* is the initial value of the random number generator.

$$7, 5, 2, 3, 10, 4, 6, 9, 8, 1, 7, 5, 2, ... \qquad \textbf{(9.2)}$$

Generating a number a second time results in a repeating sequence. In our case the sequence repeats after $M - 1 = 10$ numbers. The length of a sequence until a number is repeated is called the *period* of the sequence. The period obtained with this choice of A is clearly as good as possible because all nonzero numbers smaller than M are generated. (We must have a repeated number generated on the 11th iteration.)

The length of a sequence until a number is repeated is called its *period.* A random number generator with period P generates the same sequence of numbers after P iterations.

If M is prime, several choices of A give a full period of $M - 1$, and this type of random number generator is called a *full-period linear congruential generator.* Some choices of A do not give a full period. For instance, if $A = 5$ and $X_0 = 1$, the sequence has a short period of 5:

A *full-period linear congruential generator* has period $M - 1$.

$$5, 3, 4, 9, 1, 5, 3, 4, ... \qquad \textbf{(9.3)}$$

If we choose M to be a 31-bit prime, the period should be significantly large for most applications. The 31-bit prime $M = 2^{31} - 1 = 2{,}147{,}483{,}647$ is a common choice. For this prime, $A = 48{,}271$ is one of the many values that gives a full-period linear congruential generator. Its use has been well studied and is recommended by experts in the field. As we show later in the chapter, tinkering with random number generators usually means breaking, so you are well advised to stick with this formula until told otherwise.

Implementing this routine seems simple enough. If `state` represents the last value computed by the `nextInt` routine, the new value of `state` should be given by

```
state = ( A * state ) % M;      // Incorrect
```

Because of overflow, we must rearrange calculations.

Unfortunately, if this computation is done on 32-bit integers, the multiplication is certain to overflow. Although Java provides a 64-bit `long`, using it is computationally expensive. If we stick with the 32-bit `int`, we could argue that the result is part of the randomness. However, overflow is unacceptable because we would no longer have the guarantee of a full period. A slight reordering allows the computation to proceed without overflow. Specifically, if Q and R are the quotient and remainder of M/A, then we can rewrite Equation 9.1 as

$$X_{i+1} = A(X_i(\text{mod } Q)) - R\lfloor X_i/Q \rfloor + M\delta(X_i) \qquad \textbf{(9.4)}$$

and the following conditions hold (see Exercise 9.5).

- The first term can always be evaluated without overflow.
- The second term can be evaluated without overflow if $R < Q$.
- $\delta(X_i)$ evaluates to 0 if the result of the subtraction of the first two terms is positive; it evaluates to 1 if the result of the subtraction is negative.

Stick with these numbers until you are told otherwise.

For the values of M and A, we have $Q = 44{,}488$ and $R = 3{,}399$. Consequently, $R < Q$ and a direct application now gives an implementation of the `Random` class for generating random numbers. The resulting code is shown in Figure 9.2. The class works as long as `int` is capable of holding M. The routine `nextInt` returns the value of the state.

Several additional methods are provided in the skeleton given in Figure 9.1. One generates a random real number in the open interval from 0 to 1, and another generates a random integer in a specified closed interval (see the online code).

Finally, the `Random` class provides a generator for nonuniform random numbers when they are required. In Section 9.3 we provide the implementation for the methods `nextPoisson` and `nextNegExp`.

You might be tempted to assume that all machines have a random number generator at least as good as the one shown in Figure 9.2. Sadly, that is not the case. Many libraries have generators based on the function

$$X_{i+1} = (AX_i + C) \bmod 2^B$$

where B is chosen to match the number of bits in the machine's integer, and C is odd. These libraries, like the `nextInt` routine in Figure 9.2, also return the newly computed `state` directly, instead of (for example) a value between 0 and 1. Unfortunately, these generators always produce values of X_i that alternate between even and odd—obviously an undesirable property. Indeed, the lower k bits cycle with a period of 2^k (at best). Many other random number generators have much smaller cycles than the one we provided. These generators are not suitable for any application requiring long sequences of random numbers. The Java library has a generator of this form. However, it uses a 48-bit linear congruential generator and returns only the high 32 bits, thus avoiding the cycling problem in lower-order bits. The constants are $A = 25{,}214{,}903{,}917$, $B = 48$, and $C = 13$.

Finally, it may seem that we can get a better random number generator by adding a constant to the equation. For instance, we might conclude that

$$X_{i+1} = (48{,}271X_i + 1) \bmod (2^{31} - 1)$$

would somehow be more random. However, when we use this equation, we see that

$$(48{,}271 \cdot 179{,}424{,}105 + 1) \bmod (2^{31} - 1) = 179{,}424{,}105$$

Hence, if the seed is 179,424,105, the generator gets stuck in a cycle of period 1, illustrating how fragile these generators are.

9.3 nonuniform random numbers

Not all applications require uniformly distributed random numbers. For example, grades in a large course are generally not uniformly distributed. Instead, they satisfy the classic bell curve distribution, more formally known as the `normal` or `Gaussian distribution`. A uniform random number generator can be used to generate random numbers that satisfy other distributions.

```
    private static final int A = 48271;
    private static final int M = 2147483647;
    private static final int Q = M / A;
    private static final int R = M % A;

    /**
     * Construct this Random object with
     * initial state obtained from system clock.
     */
    public Random( )
    {
        this( (int) ( System.currentTimeMillis( ) % Integer.MAX_VALUE ) );
    }

    /**
     * Construct this Random object with
     * specified initial state.
     * @param initialValue the initial state.
     */
    public Random( int initialValue )
    {
        if( initialValue < 0 )
            initialValue += M;

        state = initialValue;
        if( state == 0 )
            state = 1;
    }

    /**
     * Return a pseudorandom int, and change the
     * internal state.
     * @return the pseudorandom int.
     */
    public int nextInt( )
    {
        int tmpState = A * ( state % Q ) - R * ( state / Q );
        if( tmpState >= 0 )
            state = tmpState;
        else
            state = tmpState + M;

        return state;
    }
```

figure 9.2

Random number generator that works if INT_MAX is at least $2^{31}-1$

An important nonuniform distribution that occurs in simulations is the *Poisson distribution,* which models the number of occurrences of a rare event. Occurrences that happen under the following circumstances satisfy the Poisson distribution.

The *Poisson distribution* models the number of occurrences of a rare event and is used in simulations.

1. The probability of one occurrence in a small region is proportional to the size of the region.
2. The probability of two occurrences in a small region is proportional to the square of the size of the region and is usually small enough to be ignored.
3. The event of getting k occurrences in one region and the event of getting j occurrences in another region disjoint from the first region are independent. (Technically this statement means that you can get the probability of both events simultaneously occurring by multiplying the probability of individual events.)
4. The mean number of occurrences in a region of some size is known.

If the mean number of occurrences is the constant a, the probability of exactly k occurrences is $a^k e^{-a}/k!$.

The Poisson distribution generally applies to events that have a low probability of a single occurrence. For example, consider the event of purchasing a winning lottery ticket, where the odds of winning the jackpot are 14,000,000 to 1. Presumably the picked numbers are more or less random and independent. If a person buys 100 tickets, the odds of winning become 140,000 to 1 (the odds improve by a factor of 100), so condition 1 holds. The odds of the person holding two winning tickets are negligible, so condition 2 holds. If someone else buys 10 tickets, that person's odds of winning are 1,400,000 to 1, and these odds are independent of the first person's, so condition 3 holds. Suppose that 28,000,000 tickets are sold. The mean number of winning tickets in this situation is 2 (the number we need for condition 4). The actual number of winning tickets is a random variable with an expected value of 2, and it satisfies the Poisson distribution. Thus the probability that exactly k winning tickets have been sold is $2^k e^{-2}/k!$, which gives the distribution shown in Figure 9.3. If the expected number of winners is the constant a, the probability of k winning tickets is $a^k e^{-a}/k!$.

Winning Tickets	0	1	2	3	4	5
Frequency	0.135	0.271	0.271	0.180	0.090	0.036

figure 9.3

Distribution of lottery winners if the expected number of winners is 2

figure 9.4

Generation of a random number according to the Poisson distribution

```
/**
 * Return an int using a Poisson distribution, and
 * change the internal state.
 * @param expectedValue the mean of the distribution.
 * @return the pseudorandom int.
 */
public int nextPoisson( double expectedValue )
{
    double limit = -expectedValue;
    double product = Math.log( nextDouble( ) );
    int count;

    for( count = 0; product > limit; count++ )
        product += Math.log( nextDouble( ) );

    return count;
}
```

To generate a random unsigned integer according to a Poisson distribution that has an expected value of a, we can adopt the following strategy (whose mathematical justification is beyond the scope of this book): Repeatedly generate uniformly distributed random numbers in the interval (0, 1) until their product is smaller than (or equal to) e^{-a}. The code shown in Figure 9.4 does just that, using a mathematically equivalent technique that is less sensitive to overflow. The code adds the logarithm of the uniform random numbers until their sum is smaller than (or equal to) $-a$.

The *negative exponential distribution* has the same mean and variance. It is used to model the time between occurrences of random events.

Another important nonuniform distribution is the *negative exponential distribution,* shown in Figure 9.5, which has the same mean and variance and is used to model the time between occurrences of random events. We use it in the simulation application shown in Section 13.2.

Many other distributions are commonly used. Our main purpose here is to show that most can be generated from the uniform distribution. Consult any book on probability and statistics to find out more about these functions.

figure 9.5

Generation of a random number according to the negative exponential distribution

```
/**
 * Return a double using a negative exponential
 * distribution, and change the internal state.
 * @param expectedValue the mean of the distribution.
 * @return the pseudorandom double.
 */
public double nextNegExp( double expectedValue )
{
    return - expectedValue * Math.log( nextDouble( ) );
}
```

9.4 generating a random permutation

Consider the problem of simulating a card game. The deck consists of 52 distinct cards, and in the course of a deal, we must generate cards from the deck, without duplicates. In effect, we need to shuffle the cards and then iterate through the deck. We want the shuffle to be fair. That is, each of the 52! possible orderings of the deck should be equally likely as a result of the shuffle.

This type of problem involves the use of a *random permutation.* In general, the problem is to generate a random permutation of 1, 2, ..., *N*, with all permutations being equally likely. The randomness of the random permutation is, of course, limited by the randomness of the pseudorandom number generator. Thus all permutations being equally likely is contingent on all the random numbers being uniformly distributed and independent. We demonstrate that random permutations can be generated in linear time, using one random number per item.

A random permutation can be generated in linear time, using one random number per item.

A routine, `permute`, to generate a random permutation is shown in Figure 9.6. In the `permute` routine the first loop initializes the permutation with 1, 2, ..., *N*. The second loop performs a random shuffling. In each iteration of the loop, we swap `a[j]` with some array element in positions `0` to `j` (it is possible to perform no swap).

Clearly, `permute` generates shuffled permutations. But are all permutations equally likely? The answer is both yes and no. The answer, based on the algorithm, is yes. There are *N*! possible permutations, and the number of different possible outcomes of the `N` – 1 calls to `nextInt` at line 11 is also *N*! The reason is that the first call produces 0 or 1, so it has two outcomes. The second call produces 0, 1, or 2, so it has three outcomes. The last call has *N* outcomes. The total number of outcomes is the product of all these possibilities because each random number is independent of the previous random numbers. All we have to show is that each sequence of random numbers corresponds to only one permutation. We can do so by working backward (see Exercise 9.6).

The correctness of `permute` is subtle.

```
1    /**
2     * Randomly rearrange an array.
3     * The random numbers used depend on the time and day.
4     * @param a the array.
5     */
6    public static final void permute( Object [ ] a )
7    {
8        Random r = new Random( );
9
10       for( int j = 1; j < a.length; j++ )
11           swapReferences( a, j, r.nextInt( 0, j ) );
12   }
```

figure 9.6

A permutation routine

However, the answer is actually no—all permutations are not equally likely. There are only $2^{31} - 2$ initial states for the random number generator, so there can be only $2^{31} - 2$ different permutations. This condition could be a problem in some situations. For instance, a program that generates 1,000,000 permutations (perhaps by splitting the work among many computers) to measure the performance of a sorting algorithm almost certainly generates some permutations twice—unfortunately. Better random number generators are needed to help the practice meet the theory.

Note that rewriting the call to `swap` with the call to `r.nextInt(0,n-1)` does not work, even for three elements. There are $3! = 6$ possible permutations, and the number of different sequences that could be computed by the three calls to `nextInt` is $3^3 = 27$. Because 6 does not divide 27 exactly, some permutations must be more likely than others.

9.5 randomized algorithms

Suppose that you are a professor who is giving weekly programming assignments. You want to ensure that the students are doing their own programs or, at the very least, that they understand the code that they are submitting. One solution is to give a quiz on the day each program is due. However, these quizzes take time from class and doing so might be practical for only roughly half the programs. Your problem is to decide when to give the quizzes.

Of course, if you announce the quizzes in advance, that could be interpreted as an implicit license to cheat for the 50 percent of the programs that will not get a quiz. You could adopt the unannounced strategy of giving quizzes on alternate programs, but students would quickly figure out that strategy. Another possibility is to give quizzes on what seem like the important programs, but that would likely lead to similar quiz patterns from semester to semester. Student grapevines being what they are, this strategy would probably be worthless after one semester.

One method that seems to eliminate these problems is to flip a coin. You make a quiz for every program (making quizzes is not nearly as time consuming as grading them), and at the start of class, you flip a coin to decide whether the quiz is to be given. This way neither you nor your students can know before class whether a quiz will be given. Also, the patterns do not repeat from semester to semester. The students can expect a quiz to occur with 50 percent probability, regardless of previous quiz patterns. The disadvantage of this strategy is that you could end up giving no quizzes during an entire semester. Assuming a large number of programming assignments, however, this is not likely to happen unless the coin is suspect. Each semester the expected number of quizzes is half the number of programs, and with high probability, the number of quizzes will not deviate much from this.

This example illustrates the *randomized algorithm,* which uses random numbers, rather than deterministic decisions, to control branching. The running time of the algorithm depends not only on the particular input, but also on the random numbers that occur.

A *randomized algorithm* uses random numbers rather than deterministic decisions to control branching.

The worst-case running time of a randomized algorithm is almost always the same as the worst-case running time of the nonrandomized algorithm. The important difference is that a good randomized algorithm has no bad inputs—only bad random numbers (relative to the particular input). This difference may seem only philosophical, but actually it is quite important, as we show in the following example.

Let us say that your boss asks you to write a program to determine the median of a group of 1,000,000 numbers. You are to submit the program and then run it on an input that the boss will choose. If the correct answer is given within a few seconds of computing time (which would be expected for a linear algorithm), your boss will be very happy, and you will get a bonus. But if your program does not work or takes too much time, your boss will fire you for incompetence. Your boss already thinks that you are overpaid and is hoping to be able to take the second option. What should you do?

The running time of a randomized algorithm depends on the random numbers that occur, as well as the particular input.

The quickselect algorithm described in Section 8.7 might seem like the way to go. Although the algorithm (see Figure 8.22) is very fast on average, recall that it has quadratic worst-case time if the pivot is continually poor. By using median-of-three partitioning, we have guaranteed that this worst case will not occur for common inputs, such as those that have been sorted or that contain a lot of duplicates. However, there is still a quadratic worst case, and as Exercise 8.8 showed, the boss will read your program, realize how you are choosing the pivot, and be able to construct the worst case. Consequently, you will be fired.

By using random numbers, you can statistically guarantee the safety of your job. You begin the quickselect algorithm by randomly shuffling the input by using lines 10 and 11 in Figure 9.6.[1] As a result, your boss essentially loses control of specifying the input sequence. When you run the quickselect algorithm, it will now be working on random input, so you expect it to take linear time. Can it still take quadratic time? The answer is yes. For any original input, the shuffling may get you to the worst case for quickselect, and thus the result would be a quadratic-time sort. If you are unfortunate enough to have this happen, you lose your job. However, this event is statistically impossible. For a million items, the chance of using even twice as much time as the average would indicate is so small that you can essentially ignore it. The computer is much more likely to break. Your job is secure.

Randomized quickselect is statistically guaranteed to work in linear time.

Instead of using a shuffling technique, you can achieve the same result by choosing the pivot randomly instead of deterministically. Take a random item

1. You need to be sure that the random number generator is sufficiently random and that its output cannot be predicted by the boss.

in the array and swap it with the item in position `low`. Take another random item and swap it with the item in position `high`. Take a third random item and swap it with the item in the middle position. Then continue as usual. As before, degenerate partitions are always possible, but they now happen as a result of bad random numbers, not bad inputs.

Let us look at the differences between randomized and nonrandomized algorithms. So far we have concentrated on nonrandomized algorithms. When calculating their average running times, we assume that all inputs are equally likely. This assumption does not hold, however, because nearly sorted input, for instance, occurs much more often than is statistically expected. This situation can cause problems for some algorithms, such as quicksort. But when we use a randomized algorithm, the particular input is no longer important. The random numbers are important, and we get an *expected* running time, in which we average over all possible random numbers for any particular input. Using quickselect with random pivots (or a shuffle preprocessing step) gives an $O(N)$ expected time algorithm. That is, *for any input*, including already sorted input, the running time is expected to be $O(N)$, based on the statistics of random numbers. On the one hand an expected time bound is somewhat stronger than an average-case time bound because the assumptions used to generate it are weaker (random numbers versus random input) but it is weaker than the corresponding worst-case time bound. On the other hand, in many instances solutions that have good worst-case bounds frequently have extra overhead built in to assure that the worst case does not occur. The $O(N)$ worst-case algorithm for selection, for example, is a marvelous theoretical result but is not practical.

Some randomized algorithms work in a fixed amount of time but randomly make mistakes (presumably with low probability). These mistakes are *false positives* or *false negatives.*

Randomized algorithms come in two basic forms. The first, as already shown, always gives a correct answer but it could take a long time, depending on the luck of the random numbers. The second type is what we examine in the remainder of this chapter. Some randomized algorithms work in a fixed amount of time but randomly make mistakes (presumably with low probability), called *false positives* or *false negatives.* This technique is commonly accepted in medicine. False positives and false negatives for most tests are actually fairly common, and some tests have surprisingly high error rates. Furthermore, for some tests the errors depend on the individual, not random numbers, so repeating the test is certain to produce another false result. In randomized algorithms we can rerun the test on the same input using different random numbers. If we run a randomized algorithm 10 times and get 10 positives—and if a single false positive is an unlikely occurrence (say, 1 chance in 100)—the probability of 10 consecutive false positives (1 chance in 100^{10} or one hundred billion billion) is essentially zero.

9.6 randomized primality testing

Recall that in Section 7.4 we described some numerical algorithms and showed how they could be used to implement the RSA encryption scheme. An important step in the RSA algorithm is to produce two prime numbers p and q. We can find a prime number by repeatedly trying successive odd numbers until we find one that is prime. Thus the issue boils down to determining whether a given number is prime.

The simplest algorithm for primality testing is *trial division*. In this algorithm, an odd number greater than 3 is prime if it is not divisible by any other odd number smaller than or equal to $\sqrt{N}$. A direct implementation of this strategy is shown in Figure 9.7.

Trial division is the simplest algorithm for primality testing. It is fast for small (32-bit) numbers but cannot be used for larger numbers.

Trial division is reasonably fast for small (32-bit) numbers, but it is unusable for larger numbers because it could require the testing of roughly $\sqrt{N}/2$ divisors, thus using $O(\sqrt{N})$ time.[2] What we need is a test whose running time is of the same order of magnitude as the `power` routine in Section 7.4.2. A well-known theorem, called *Fermat's Little Theorem,* looks promising. We state and provide a proof of it in Theorem 9.1 for completeness, but the proof is not needed for an understanding of the primality-testing algorithm.

Theorem 9.1

Fermat's Little Theorem: If P is prime and $0 < A < P$, then $A^{P-1} \equiv 1 (\text{mod } P)$.

Proof

Consider any $1 \le k < P$. Clearly, $Ak \equiv 0 (\text{mod } P)$ is impossible because P is prime and is greater than A and k. Now consider any $1 \le i < j < P$. $Ai \equiv Aj (\text{mod } P)$ would imply $A(j-i) \equiv 0 (\text{mod } P)$, which is impossible by the previous argument because $1 \le j - i < P$. Thus the sequence $A, 2A, \ldots, (P-1)A$, when considered $(\text{mod } P)$, is a permutation of $1, 2, \ldots, P-1$. The product of both sequences $(\text{mod } P)$ must be equivalent (and non-zero), yielding the equivalence $A^{P-1}(P-1)! \equiv (P-1)! \, (\text{mod } P)$ from which the theorem follows.

If the converse of Fermat's Little Theorem were true, then we would have a primality-testing algorithm that would be computationally equivalent to modular exponentiation (i.e., $O(\log N)$). Unfortunately, the converse is not true. For example, $2^{340} \equiv 1 (\text{mod } 341)$, but 341 is composite (11×31).

Fermat's Little Theorem is necessary but not sufficient to establish primality.

2. Though $\sqrt{N}$ may seem small, if N is a 100-digit number, then $\sqrt{N}$ is still a 50-digit number; tests that take $O(\sqrt{N})$ time are thus out of the question for the `BigInteger` type.

figure 9.7

Primality testing by trial division

```java
/**
 * Returns true if odd integer n is prime.
 */
public static boolean isPrime( long n )
{
    for( int i = 3; i * i <= n; i += 2 )
        if( n % i == 0 )
            return false; // not prime

    return true;          // prime
}
```

To do the primality test, we need an additional theorem, Theorem 9.2.

Theorem 9.2

If P is prime and $X^2 \equiv 1 (\mathrm{mod}\ P)$, then $X \equiv \pm 1 (\mathrm{mod}\ P)$.

Proof

Because $X^2 - 1 \equiv 0 (\mathrm{mod}\ P)$ implies $(X - 1)(X + 1) \equiv 0 (\mathrm{mod}\ P)$ and P is prime, then $X - 1$ or $X + 1 \equiv 0 (\mathrm{mod}\ P)$.

A combination of Theorems 9.1 and 9.2 is useful. Let A be any integer between 2 and $N - 2$. If we compute $A^{N-1} (\mathrm{mod}\ N)$ and the result is not 1, we know that N cannot be prime; otherwise, we would contradict Fermat's Little Theorem. As a result, A is a value that proves that N is not prime. We say then that A is a *witness to N's compositeness*. Every composite number N has some witnesses A, but for some numbers, called the *Carmichael numbers*, these witnesses are hard to find. We need to be sure that we have a high probability of finding a witness no matter what the choice of N is. To improve our chances, we use Theorem 9.1.

In the course of computing A^i, we compute $(A^{\lfloor i/2 \rfloor})^2$. So we let $X = A^{\lfloor i/2 \rfloor}$ and $Y = X^2$. Note that X and Y are computed automatically as part of the `power` routine. If Y is 1 and if X is not $\pm 1 (\mathrm{mod}\ N)$, then by Theorem 9.1, N cannot be prime. We can return 0 for the value of A^i when that condition is detected, and N will appear to have failed the test of primality implied by Fermat's Little Theorem.

The routine `witness`, shown in Figure 9.8, computes $A^i (\mathrm{mod}\ P)$, augmented to return 0 if a violation of Theorem 9.1 is detected. If `witness` does not return 1, then A is a witness to the fact that N cannot be prime. Lines 12 through 14 make a recursive call and produce X. We then compute X^2, as is

```
/**
 * Private method that implements the basic primality test.
 * If witness does not return 1, n is definitely composite.
 * Do this by computing a^i (mod n) and looking for
 * nontrivial square roots of 1 along the way.
 */
private static long witness( long a, long i, long n )
{
    if( i == 0 )
        return 1;

    long x = witness( a, i / 2, n );
    if( x == 0 )    // If n is recursively composite, stop
        return 0;

    // n is not prime if we find a nontrivial square root of 1
    long y = ( x * x ) % n;
    if( y == 1 && x != 1 && x != n - 1 )
        return 0;

    if( i % 2 != 0 )
        y = ( a * y ) % n;

    return y;
}

/**
 * The number of witnesses queried in randomized primality test.
 */
public static final int TRIALS = 5;

/**
 * Randomized primality test.
 * Adjust TRIALS to increase confidence level.
 * @param n the number to test.
 * @return if false, n is definitely not prime.
 *     If true, n is probably prime.
 */
public static boolean isPrime( long n )
{
    Random r = new Random( );

    for( int counter = 0; counter < TRIALS; counter++ )
        if( witness( r.nextInt( (int) n - 3 ) + 2, n - 1, n ) != 1 )
            return false;

    return true;
}
```

figure 9.8

A randomized test for primality

normal for the `power` computation. We check whether Theorem 9.1 is violated, returning 0 if it is. Otherwise, we complete the `power` computation.

> If the algorithm declares a number not to be prime, it is not prime with 100 percent certainty. Each random attempt has at most a 25 percent false positive rate.

The only remaining issue is correctness. If our algorithm declares that N is composite, then N *must* be composite. If N is composite, are all $2 \le A \le N-2$ witnesses? The answer, unfortunately, is no. That is, some choices of A will trick our algorithm into declaring that N is prime. In fact, if we choose A randomly, we have at most a 1/4 chance of failing to detect a composite number and thus making an error. Note that this outcome is true for *any* N. If it were obtained only by averaging over all N, we would not have a good enough routine. Analogous to medical tests, our algorithm generates false positives at most 25 percent of the time for any N.

> Some composites will pass the test and be declared prime. A composite is very unlikely to pass 20 consecutive independent random tests.

These odds do not seem very good because a 25 percent error rate generally is considered very high. However, if we independently use 20 values of A, the chances that none of them will witness a composite number is $1/4^{20}$, which is about one in a million million. Those odds are much more reasonable and can be made even better by using more trials. The routine `isPrime`, which is also shown in Figure 9.8, uses five trials.[3]

summary

In this chapter we described how random numbers are generated and used. The linear congruential generator is a good choice for simple applications, so long as care is taken in choosing the parameters A and M. Using a uniform random number generator, we can derive random numbers for other distributions, such as the Poisson and negative exponential distributions.

Random numbers have many uses, including the empirical study of algorithms, the simulation of real-life systems, and the design of algorithms that probabilistically avoid the worst case. We use random numbers in other parts of this text, notably in Section 13.2 and Exercise 21.21.

This concludes Part Two of the book. In Part Three we look at some simple applications, beginning with a discussion of games in Chapter 10 that illustrates three important problem-solving techniques.

key concepts

false positives / false negatives Mistakes randomly made (presumably with low probability) by some randomized algorithms that work in a fixed amount of time. (356)

---

3. These bounds are typically pessimistic, and the analysis involves number theory that is much too involved for this text.

Fermat's Little Theorem States that if P is prime and $0 < A < P$, then $A^{P-1} \equiv 1 (\text{mod } P)$. It is necessary but not sufficient to establish primality. (357)

full-period linear congruential generator A random number generator that has period $M - 1$. (347)

linear congruential generator A good algorithm for generating uniform distributions. (347)

negative exponential distribution A form of distribution used to model the time between occurrences of random events. Its mean equals its variance. (352)

period The length of the sequence until a number is repeated. A random number generator with period P generates the same random sequence of random numbers after P iterations. (347)

permutation A permutation of 1, 2, ..., N is a sequence of N integers that includes each of 1, 2, ..., N exactly once. (344)

Poisson distribution A distribution that models the number of occurrences of a rare event. (351)

pseudorandom numbers Numbers that have many properties of random numbers. Good generators of pseudorandom numbers are hard to find. (345)

random permutation A random arrangement of N items. Can be generated in linear time using one random number per item. (353)

randomized algorithm An algorithm that uses random numbers rather than deterministic decisions to control branching. (355)

seed The initial value of a random number generator. (347)

trial division The simplest algorithm for primality testing. It is fast for small (32-bit) numbers but cannot be used for larger numbers. (357)

uniform distribution A distribution in which all numbers in the specified range are equally likely to occur. (345)

witness to compositeness A value of A that proves that a number is not prime, using Fermat's Little Theorem. (358)

common errors

1. Using an initial seed of zero gives bad random numbers.
2. Inexperienced users occasionally reinitialize the seed prior to generating a random permutation. This action guarantees that the same permutation will be repeatedly produced, which is probably not intended.
3. Many random number generators are notoriously bad; for serious applications in which long sequences of random numbers are required, the linear congruential generator is also unsatisfactory.

4. The low-order bits of linear congruential generators are known to be somewhat nonrandom, so avoid using them. For example, `nextInt()%2` is often a bad way to flip a coin.
5. When random numbers are being generated in some interval, a common error is to be slightly off at the boundaries and either allow some number outside the interval to be generated or not allow the smallest number to be generated with fair probability.
6. Many random permutation generators do not generate all permutations with equal likelihood. As discussed in the text, our algorithm is limited by the random number generator.
7. Tinkering with a random number generator is likely to weaken its statistical properties.

on the internet

Most of the code in this chapter is available.

Random.java Contains the `Random` class implementation.
Numerical.java Contains the primality-testing routine shown in Figure 9.8 and the math routines presented in Section 7.4.

exercises

IN SHORT

9.1 For the random number generator described in the text, determine the first 10 values of `state`, assuming that it is initialized with a value of 1.

9.2 Show the result of running the primality-testing algorithm for $N = 561$ with values of A ranging from 2 to 5.

9.3 If 42,000,000 lottery tickets are sold (with 14,000,000 to 1 odds of a ticket being a winner), what is the expected number of winners? What are the odds that there will be no winners? One winner?

9.4 Why can't zero be used as a seed for the linear congruential generator?

IN THEORY

9.5 Prove that Equation 9.4 is equivalent to Equation 9.1 and that the resulting program in Figure 9.2 is correct.

9.6 Complete the proof that each permutation obtained in Figure 9.6 is equally likely.

9.7 Suppose that you have a biased coin that comes up heads with probability p and tails with probability $1 - p$. Show how to design an algorithm that uses the coin to generate a 0 or 1 with equal probability.

IN PRACTICE

9.8 Write a program that calls `nextInt` (that returns an `int` in the specified interval) 100,000 times to generate numbers between 1 and 1,000. Does it meet the stronger statistical tests given in Section 9.2?

9.9 Run the Poisson generator shown in Figure 9.4 1,000,000 times, using an expected value of 2. Does the distribution agree with Figure 9.3?

9.10 Consider a two-candidate election in which the winner received a fraction p of the vote. If the votes are counted sequentially, what is the probability that the winner was ahead (or tied) at every stage of the election? This problem is the so-called *ballot problem*. Write a program that verifies the answer, $2 - \frac{1}{p}$, assuming that $p > \frac{1}{2}$ and that large numbers of votes are the case. (*Hint*: Simulate an election of 10,000 voters. Generate random arrays of $10{,}000p$ ones and $10{,}000(1 - p)$ zeros. Then verify in a sequential scan that the difference between 1s and 0s is never negative.)

PROGRAMMING PROJECTS

9.11 An alternative permutation algorithm is to fill the array `a` from `a[0]` to `a[n-1]`, as follows. To fill `a[i]`, generate random numbers until you get one that has not been used previously. Use an array of Booleans to perform that test. Give an analysis of the expected running time (this is tricky) and then write a program that compares this running time with both your analysis and the routine shown in Figure 9.6.

9.12 Suppose that you want to generate a random permutation of N distinct items drawn from the range 1, 2, ..., M. (The case $M = N$, of course, has already been discussed.) Floyd's algorithm does the following. First, it recursively generates a permutation of $N - 1$ distinct items drawn from the range $M - 1$. It then generates a random integer in the range 1 to M. If the random integer is not already in the permutation we add it; otherwise, we add M.

a. Prove that this algorithm does not add duplicates.
b. Prove that each permutation is equally likely.
c. Give a recursive implementation of the algorithm.
d. Give an iterative implementation of the algorithm.

9.13 A *random walk* in two dimensions is the following game played on the x–y coordinate system. Starting at the origin (0, 0), each iteration consists of a random step either 1 unit left, up, right, or down. The walk terminates when the walker returns to the origin. (The probability of this happening is 1 in two dimensions but less than 1 in three dimensions.) Write a program that performs 100 independent random walks and computes the average number of steps taken in each direction.

9.14 A simple and effective statistical test is the *chi-square test*. Suppose that you generate N positive numbers that can assume one of M values (for example, we could generate numbers between 1 and M, inclusive). The number of occurrences of each number is a random variable with mean $\mu = N/M$. For the test to work, you should have $\mu > 10$. Let f_i be the number of times i is generated. Then compute the chi-square value $V = \sum(f_i - \mu)^2/\mu$. The result should be close to M. If the result is consistently more than $2\sqrt{M}$ away from M (i.e., more than once in 10 tries), then the generator has failed the test. Implement the chi-square test and run it on your implementation of the `nextInt` method (with `low` = 1 and `high` = 100).

references

A good discussion of elementary random number generators is provided in [3]. The permutation algorithm is due to R. Floyd and is presented in [1]. The randomized primality-testing algorithm is taken from [2] and [4]. More information on random numbers is available in any good book on statistics or probability.

1. J. Bentley, "Programming Pearls," *Communications of the ACM* **30** (1987), 754–757.
2. G. L. Miller, "Riemann's Hypothesis and Tests for Primality," *Journal of Computer and System Science* **13** (1976), 300–317.
3. S. K. Park and K. W. Miller, "Random Number Generators: Good Ones Are Hard to Find," *Communications of the ACM* **31** (1988) 1192–1201. (See also *Technical Correspondence* in **36** (1993) 105–110, which provides the value of `A` used in Figure 9.2.)
4. M. O. Rabin, "Probabilistic Algorithms for Testing Primality," *Journal of Number Theory* **12** (1980), 128–138.

part three

Applications

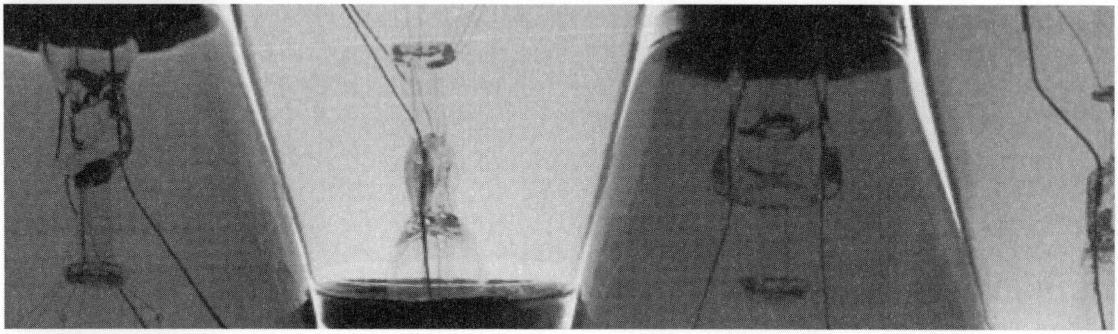

chapter 10

fun and games

In this chapter we introduce three important algorithmic techniques and show how to use them by implementing programs to solve two recreational problems. The first problem is the *word search puzzle* and involves finding words in a two-dimensional grid of characters. The second is optimal play in the game of Tic-Tac-Toe.

In this chapter, we show

- How to use the binary search algorithm to incorporate information from unsuccessful searches and to solve large instances of a word search problem in under 1 sec
- How to use the *alpha–beta pruning* algorithm to speed up the recursive algorithm presented in Section 7.7
- How to use maps to increase the speed of the Tic-Tac-Toe algorithm

10.1 word search puzzles

The input to the *word search puzzle* problem is a two-dimensional array of characters and a list of words, and the object is to find the words in the grid. These words may be horizontal, vertical, or diagonal in any direction (for a total of eight directions). As an example, the grid shown in Figure 10.1 con-

The *word search puzzle* requires searching for words in a two-dimensional grid of letters. Words may be oriented in one of eight directions.

tains the words `this`, `two`, `fat`, and `that`. The word `this` begins at row 0, column 0—the point (0, 0)—and extends to (0, 3); `two` goes from (0, 0) to (2, 0); `fat` goes from (3, 0) to (1, 2); and `that` goes from (3, 3) to (0, 0). (Additional, mostly shorter, words are not listed here.)

10.1.1 theory

The brute-force algorithm searches each word in the word list.

We can use any of several naive algorithms to solve the word search puzzle problem. The most direct is the following brute-force approach:

```
for each word W in the word list
    for each row R
        for each column C
            for each direction D
                check if W exists at row R, column C in direction D
```

An alternative algorithm searches from each point in the grid in each direction for each word length and looks for the word in the word list.

Because there are eight directions, this algorithm requires eight word/row/column ($8WRC$) checks. Typical puzzles published in magazines feature 40 or so words and a 16×16 grid, which involves roughly 80,000 checks. That number is certainly easy to compute on any modern machine. Suppose, however, that we consider the variation in which only the puzzle board is given and the word list is essentially an English dictionary. In this case, the number of words might be 40,000 instead of 40, resulting in 80,000,000 checks. Doubling the grid would require 320,000,000 checks, which is no longer a trivial calculation. We want an algorithm that can solve a puzzle of this size in a fraction of a second (not counting disk I/O time), so we must consider an alternative algorithm:

```
for each row R
    for each column C
        for each direction D
            for each word length L
                check if L chars starting at row R column C
                            in direction D form a word
```

figure 10.1

A sample word search grid

	0	1	2	3
0	t	h	i	s
1	w	a	t	s
2	o	a	h	g
3	f	g	d	t

This algorithm rearranges the loop to avoid searching for every word in the word list. If we assume that words are limited to 20 characters, the number of checks used by the algorithm is $160RC$. For a 32×32 puzzle, this number is roughly 160,000 checks. The problem, of course, is that we must now decide whether a word is in the word list. If we use a linear search, we lose. If we use a good data structure, we can expect an efficient search. If the word list is sorted, which is to be expected for an online dictionary, we can use a binary search (shown in Figure 5.12) and perform each check in roughly $\log W$ string comparisons. For 40,000 words, doing so involves perhaps 16 comparisons per check, for a total of less than 3,000,000 string comparisons. This number of comparisons can certainly be done in a few seconds and is a factor of 100 better than the previous algorithm.

The lookups can be done by a binary search.

We can further improve the algorithm based on the following observation. Suppose that we are searching in some direction and see the character sequence `qx`. An English dictionary will not contain any words beginning with `qx`. So is it worth continuing the innermost loop (over all word lengths)? The answer obviously is no: If we detect a character sequence that is not a prefix of any word in the dictionary, we can immediately look in another direction. This algorithm is given by the following pseudocode:

If a character sequence is not a prefix of any word in the dictionary, we can terminate searching in that direction.

```
for each row R
    for each column C
        for each direction D
            for each word length L
                check if L chars starting at row R column
                          C in direction D form a word
                if they do not form a prefix,
                    break;    // the innermost loop
```

The only remaining algorithmic detail is the implementation of the prefix test: Assuming that the current character sequence is not in the word list, how can we decide whether it is a prefix of some word in the word list? The answer turns out to be simple. Recall from Section 6.4.3 that the `binarySearch` method in the Collections API returns either the index of a match or the position of the smallest element that is at least as large as the target (as a negative number). The caller can easily check on whether a match is found. If a match is not found, verifying that the character sequence is a prefix of some word in the list also is easy, because, if it is, it must be a prefix of the word in the position implied in the return value (in Exercise 10.3 you are asked to prove this outcome).

Prefix testing can also be done by binary search.

10.1.2 java implementation

Our Java implementation follows the algorithm description almost verbatim. We design a `WordSearch` class to store the grid and word list, as well as the corresponding input streams. The class skeleton is shown in Figure 10.2. The public

Our implementation follows the algorithm description.

figure 10.2

The `WordSearch` class skeleton

```
import java.io.BufferedReader;
import java.io.FileReader;
import java.io.InputStreamReader;
import java.io.IOException;

import java.util.Arrays;
import java.util.ArrayList;
import java.util.Iterator;
import java.util.List;


// WordSearch class interface: solve word search puzzle
//
// CONSTRUCTION: with no initializer
// ******************PUBLIC OPERATIONS******************
// int solvePuzzle( )   --> Print all words found in the
//                          puzzle; return number of matches

public class WordSearch
{
    public WordSearch( ) throws IOException
      { /* Figure 10.3 */ }
    public int solvePuzzle( )
      { /* Figure 10.7 */ }

    private int rows;
    private int columns;
    private char theBoard[ ][ ];
    private String [ ] theWords;
    private BufferedReader puzzleStream;
    private BufferedReader wordStream;
    private BufferedReader in = new
            BufferedReader( new InputStreamReader( System.in ) );

    private static int prefixSearch( String [ ] a, String x )
      { /* Figure 10.8 */ }
    private BufferedReader openFile( String message )
      { /* Figure 10.4 */ }
    private void readWords( ) throws IOException
      { /* Figure 10.5 */ }
    private void readPuzzle( ) throws IOException
      { /* Figure 10.6 */ }
    private int solveDirection( int baseRow, int baseCol,
                                int rowDelta, int colDelta )
      { /* Figure 10.8 */ }
}
```

part of the class consists of a constructor and a single method, `solvePuzzle`. The private part includes the data members and supporting routines.

Figure 10.3 gives the code for the constructor. It merely opens and reads the two files corresponding to the grid and the word list. The supporting routine `openFile`, shown in Figure 10.4, repeatedly prompts for a file until an open is successful. The `readWords` routine, shown in Figure 10.5, reads the word list.

The constructor opens and reads the data files. We skimp on error checks for brevity.

```
/**
 * Constructor for WordSearch class.
 * Prompts for and reads puzzle and dictionary files.
 */
public WordSearch( ) throws IOException
{
    puzzleStream = openFile( "Enter puzzle file" );
    wordStream   = openFile( "Enter dictionary name" );
    System.out.println( "Reading files..." );
    readPuzzle( );
    readWords( );
}
```

figure 10.3

The `WordSearch` class constructor

```
/**
 * Print a prompt and open a file.
 * Retry until open is successful.
 * Program exits if end of file is hit.
 */
private BufferedReader openFile( String message )
{
    String fileName = "";
    FileReader theFile;
    BufferedReader fileIn = null;

    do
    {
        System.out.println( message + ": " );

        try
        {
            fileName = in.readLine( );
            if( fileName == null )
                System.exit( 0 );
            theFile = new FileReader( fileName );
            fileIn  = new BufferedReader( theFile );
        }
        catch( IOException e )
          { System.err.println( "Cannot open " + fileName ); }
    } while( fileIn == null );

    System.out.println( "Opened " + fileName );
    return fileIn;
}
```

figure 10.4

The `openFile` routine for opening either the grid or word list file

```
    /**
     * Routine to read the dictionary.
     * Error message is printed if dictionary is not sorted.
     */
    private void readWords( ) throws IOException
    {
        List<String> words = new ArrayList<String>( );

        String lastWord = null;
        String thisWord;

        while( ( thisWord = wordStream.readLine( ) ) != null )
        {
            if( lastWord != null && thisWord.compareTo( lastWord ) < 0 )
            {
                System.err.println( "Dictionary is not sorted... skipping" );
                continue;
            }
            words.add( thisWord );
            lastWord = thisWord;
        }

        theWords = new String[ words.size( ) ];
        theWords = words.toArray( theWords );
    }
```

figure 10.5

The `readWords` routine for reading the word list

The code includes an error check to ensure that the word list has been sorted. Similarly, `readPuzzle`, shown in Figure 10.6, reads the grid and is also concerned with error handling. We need to be sure that we can handle missing puzzles, and we want to warn the user if the grid is not rectangular.

We use two loops to iterate over the eight directions.

The `solvePuzzle` routine shown in Figure 10.7 nests the row, column, and direction loops and then calls the private routine `solveDirection` for each possibility. The return value is the number of matches found. We give a direction by indicating a column direction and then a row direction. For instance, south is indicated by `cd=0` and `rd=1` and northeast by `cd=1` and `rd=-1`; `cd` can range from -1 to 1 and `rd` from -1 to 1, except that both cannot be `0` simultaneously. All that remains to be done is to provide `solveDirection`, which is coded in Figure 10.8. The `solveDirection` routine constructs a string by starting at the base row and column and extending in the appropriate direction.

We also assume that one-letter matches are not allowed (because any one-letter match would be reported eight times). At lines 14 through 16, we iterate and extend the string while ensuring that we do not go past the grid's boundary. At line 18 we tack on the next character, using `+=`, and perform a binary

```
    /**
     * Routine to read the grid.
     * Checks to ensure that the grid is rectangular.
     * Checks to make sure that capacity is not exceeded is omitted.
     */
    private void readPuzzle( ) throws IOException
    {
        String oneLine;
        List<String> puzzleLines = new ArrayList<String>( );

        if( ( oneLine = puzzleStream.readLine( ) ) == null )
            throw new IOException( "No lines in puzzle file" );

        columns = oneLine.length( );
        puzzleLines.add( oneLine );

        while( ( oneLine = puzzleStream.readLine( ) ) != null )
        {
            if( oneLine.length( ) != columns )
                System.err.println( "Puzzle is not rectangular; skipping row" );
            else
                puzzleLines.add( oneLine );
        }

        rows = puzzleLines.size( );
        theBoard = new char[ rows ][ columns ];

        int r = 0;
        for( String theLine : puzzleLines )
            theBoard[ r++ ] = theLine.toCharArray( );
    }
```

figure 10.6

The `readPuzzle` routine for reading the grid

search at line 19. If we do not have a prefix, we can stop looking and return. Otherwise, we know that we have to continue after checking at line 26 for a possible exact match. Line 35 returns the number of matches found when the call to `solveDirection` can find no more words. A simple `main` program is shown in Figure 10.9.

10.2 the game of tic-tac-toe

> The *minimax strategy* examines lots of positions. We can get by with less without losing any information.

Recall from Section 7.7 a simple algorithm, known as the *minimax strategy*, allows the computer to select an optimal move in a game of Tic-Tac-Toe. This recursive strategy involves the following decisions.

figure 10.7

The `solvePuzzle` routine for searching in all directions from all starting points

```
    /**
     * Routine to solve the word search puzzle.
     * Performs checks in all eight directions.
     * @return number of matches
     */
    public int solvePuzzle( )
    {
        int matches = 0;

        for( int r = 0; r < rows; r++ )
            for( int c = 0; c < columns; c++ )
                for( int rd = -1; rd <= 1; rd++ )
                    for( int cd = -1; cd <= 1; cd++ )
                        if( rd != 0 || cd != 0 )
                            matches += solveDirection( r, c, rd, cd );

        return matches;
    }
```

1. A *terminal position* can immediately be evaluated, so if the position is terminal, return its value.
2. Otherwise, if it is the computer's turn to move, return the maximum value of all positions reachable by making one move. The reachable values are calculated recursively.
3. Otherwise, it is the human player's turn to move. Return the minimum value of all positions reachable by making one move. The reachable values are calculated recursively.

A *refutation* is a countermove that proves that a proposed move is not an improvement over moves previously considered. If we find a refutation, we do not have to examine any more moves and the recursive call can return.

10.2.1 alpha–beta pruning

Although the minimax strategy gives an optimal Tic-Tac-Toe move, it performs a lot of searching. Specifically, to choose the first move, it makes roughly a half-million recursive calls. One reason for this large number of calls is that the algorithm does more searching than necessary. Suppose that the computer is considering five moves: C_1, C_2, C_3, C_4, and C_5. Suppose also that the recursive evaluation of C_1 reveals that C_1 forces a draw. Now C_2 is evaluated. At this stage, we have a position from which it would be the human player's turn to move. Suppose that in response to C_2, the human player can consider H_{2a}, H_{2b}, H_{2c}, and H_{2d}. Further, suppose that an evaluation of H_{2a} shows a forced draw. Automatically, C_2 is at best a draw and possibly even a loss for the computer (because the human player is assumed to play optimally). Because we need to improve on C_1, we do not have to evaluate any of H_{2b}, H_{2c}, and H_{2d}. We say that H_{2a} is a *refutation,* meaning that it proves that

```
    /**
     * Search the grid from a starting point and direction.
     * @return number of matches
     */
    private int solveDirection( int baseRow, int baseCol,
                                int rowDelta, int colDelta )
    {
        String charSequence = "";
        int numMatches = 0;
        int searchResult;

        charSequence += theBoard[ baseRow ][ baseCol ];

        for( int i = baseRow + rowDelta, j = baseCol + colDelta;
                 i >= 0 && j >= 0 && i < rows && j < columns;
                 i += rowDelta, j += colDelta )
        {
            charSequence += theBoard[ i ][ j ];
            searchResult = prefixSearch( theWords, charSequence );

            if( searchResult == theWords.length )
                break;
            if( !theWords[ searchResult ].startsWith( charSequence ) )
                break;

            if( theWords[ searchResult ].equals( charSequence ) )
            {
                numMatches++;
                System.out.println( "Found " + charSequence + " at " +
                                    baseRow + " " + baseCol + " to " +
                                    i + " " + j );
            }
        }

        return numMatches;
    }

    /**
     * Performs the binary search for word search.
     * Returns the last position examined this position
     * either matches x, or x is a prefix of the mismatch, or there is
     * no word for which x is a prefix.
     */
    private static int prefixSearch( String [ ] a, String x )
    {
        int idx = Arrays.binarySearch( a, x );

        if( idx < 0 )
            return -idx - 1;
        else
            return idx;
    }
```

figure 10.8

Implementation of a single search

figure 10.9

A simple `main` routine for the word search puzzle problem

```
    // Cheap main
public static void main( String [ ] args )
{
    WordSearch p = null;

    try
    {
        p = new WordSearch( );
    }
    catch( IOException e )
    {
        System.out.println( "IO Error: " );
        e.printStackTrace( );
        return;
    }

    System.out.println( "Solving..." );
    p.solvePuzzle( );
}
```

C_2 is not a better move than what has already been seen. Thus we return that C_2 is a draw and keep C_1 as the best move seen so far, as shown in Figure 10.10. In general, then, a *refutation* is a countermove that proves that a proposed move is not an improvement over moves previously considered.

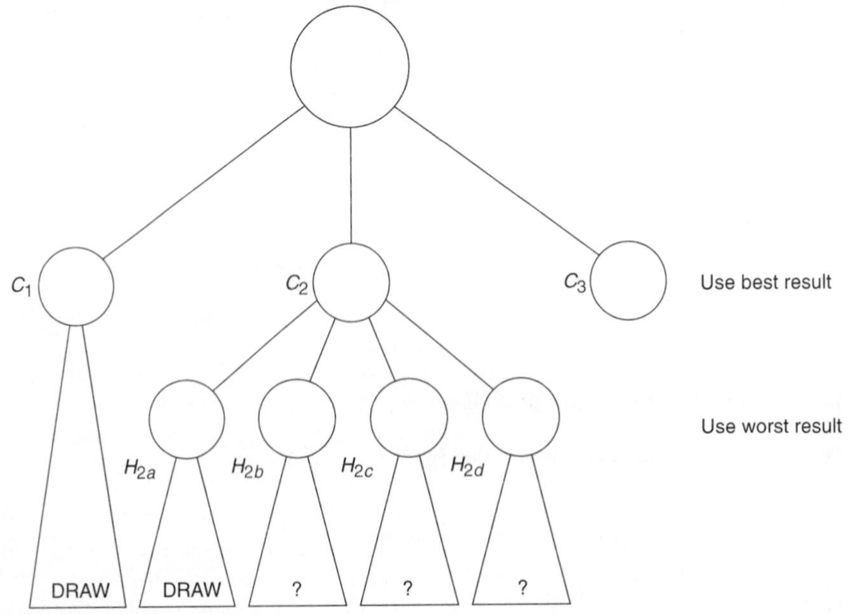

figure 10.10

Alpha–beta pruning: After H_{2a} is evaluated, C_2, which is the minimum of the H_2's, is at best a draw. Consequently, it cannot be an improvement over C_2. We therefore do not need to evaluate H_{2b}, H_{2c}, and H_{2d} and can proceed directly to C_3.

We do not need to evaluate each node completely; for some nodes, a refutation suffices and some loops can terminate early. Specifically, when the human player evaluates a position, such as C_2, a refutation, if found, is just as good as the absolute best move. The same logic applies to the computer. At any point in the search, `alpha` is the value that the human player has to refute, and `beta` is the value that the computer has to refute. When a search is done on the human player's side, any move less than `alpha` is equivalent to `alpha`; when a search is done on the computer side, any move greater than `beta` is equivalent to `beta`. This strategy of reducing the number of positions evaluated in a minimax search is commonly called *alpha–beta pruning.*

Alpha–beta pruning is used to reduce the number of positions evaluated in a minimax search. Alpha is the value that the human player has to refute, and beta is the value that the computer has to refute.

As Figure 10.11 shows, alpha–beta pruning requires only a few changes to `chooseMove`. Both `alpha` and `beta` are passed as additional parameters. Initially, `chooseMove` is started with `alpha` and `beta` representing `HUMAN_WIN` and `COMPUTER_WIN`, respectively. Lines 17 and 21 reflect a change in the initialization of `value`. The move evaluation is only slightly more complex than originally shown in Figure 7.29. The recursive call at line 30 includes the parameters `alpha` and `beta`, which are adjusted at line 37 or 39 if needed. The only other change is at line 42, which provides for an immediate return when a refutation is found.

To take full advantage of alpha–beta pruning, game programs usually try to apply heuristics to place the best moves early in the search. This approach results in even more pruning than we would expect from a random search of positions. In practice, alpha–beta pruning limits the searching to $O(\sqrt{N})$ nodes, where N is the number of nodes that would be examined without alpha–beta pruning, resulting in a huge savings. The Tic-Tac-Toe example is not ideal because there are so many identical values. Even so, the initial search is reduced to roughly 18,000 positions.

Alpha–beta pruning works best when it finds refutations early.

10.2.2 transposition tables

Another commonly employed practice is to use a table to keep track of all positions that have been evaluated. For instance, in the course of searching for the first move, the program will examine the positions shown in Figure 10.12. If the values of the positions are saved, the second occurrence of a position need not be recomputed; it essentially becomes a terminal position. The data structure that records and stores previously evaluated positions is called a *transposition table;* it is implemented as a map of positions to values.[1]

A *transposition table* stores previously evaluated positions.

1. We discussed this generic technique, which avoids repeated recursive calls by storing values in a table, in a different context in Section 7.6. This technique is also known as *memoizing*. The term *transposition table* is slightly misleading because fancier implementations of this technique recognize and avoid searching not only exactly identical positions, but also symmetrically identical positions.

```
    // Find optimal move
private Best chooseMove( int side, int alpha, int beta, int depth )
{
    int opp;              // The other side
    Best reply;           // Opponent's best reply
    int dc;               // Placeholder
    int simpleEval;       // Result of an immediate evaluation
    int bestRow = 0;
    int bestColumn = 0;
    int value;

    if( ( simpleEval = positionValue( ) ) != UNCLEAR )
        return new Best( simpleEval );

    if( side == COMPUTER )
    {
        opp = HUMAN; value = alpha;
    }
    else
    {
        opp = COMPUTER; value = beta;
    }

Outer:
    for( int row = 0; row < 3; row++ )
        for( int column = 0; column < 3; column++ )
            if( squareIsEmpty( row, column ) )
            {
                place( row, column, side );
                reply = chooseMove( opp, alpha, beta, depth + 1 );
                place( row, column, EMPTY );

                if( side == COMPUTER && reply.val > value ||
                    side == HUMAN && reply.val < value )
                {
                    if( side == COMPUTER )
                        alpha = value = reply.val;
                    else
                        beta = value = reply.val;

                    bestRow = row; bestColumn = column;
                    if( alpha >= beta )
                        break Outer;  // Refutation
                }
            }

    return new Best( value, bestRow, bestColumn );
}
```

figure 10.11

The chooseMove routine for computing an optimal Tic-Tac-Toe move, using alpha–beta pruning

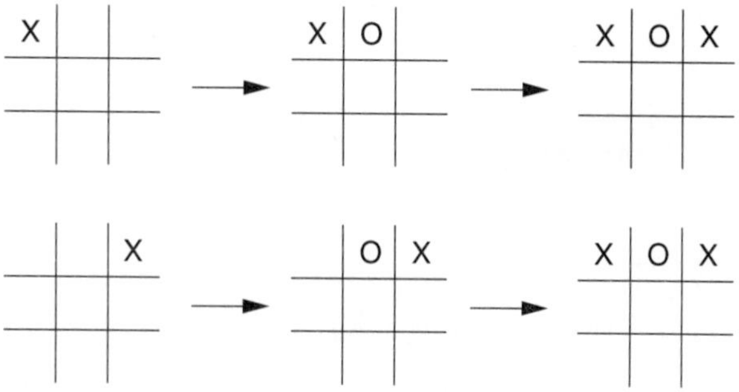

figure 10.12

Two searches that arrive at identical positions

We do not need an ordered map—so the `HashMap`—an unordered map, with a data structure called a *hash table* as the underlying implementation is used to implement the transposition table. We discuss hash tables in Chapter 20.

A map is used to implement the transposition table. Often the underlying implementation is a hash table.

To implement the transposition table we first define a `Position` class, as shown in Figure 10.13, which we use to store each position. Values in the board will be `HUMAN`, `COMPUTER`, or `EMPTY` (defined shortly in the `TicTacToe` class, as shown in Figure 10.14). The `HashMap` requires that we define `equals` and `hashCode`. Recall that if `equals` declares two `Position` objects as equal, `hashCode` must yield identical values for those objects. We also provide a constructor that can be initialized with a matrix representing the board.

An important issue concerns whether including all positions in the transposition table is worthwhile. The overhead of maintaining the table suggests that positions near the bottom of the recursion ought not be saved because

We do not store positions that are at the bottom of the recursion in the transposition table.

- There are so many
- The point of alpha–beta pruning and transposition tables is to reduce search times by avoiding recursive calls early in the game; saving a recursive call very deep in the search does not greatly reduce the number of positions examined because that recursive call would examine only a few positions anyway.

We show how this technique applies to the game of Tic-Tac-Toe when we implement the transposition table. The changes needed in the `TicTacToe` class are shown in Figure 10.14. The additions are the new data member at line 7 and the new declaration for `chooseMove` at line 14. We now pass `alpha` and `beta` (as in alpha–beta pruning) and also the `depth` of the recursion, which is zero by default. The initial call to `chooseMove` is shown at line 11.

The `chooseMove` method has additional parameters, all of which have defaults.

```
final class Position
{
    private int [ ][ ] board;

    public Position( int [ ][ ] theBoard )
    {
        board = new int[ 3 ][ 3 ];
        for( int i = 0; i < 3; i++ )
            for( int j = 0; j < 3; j++ )
                board[ i ][ j ] = theBoard[ i ][ j ];
    }

    public boolean equals( Object rhs )
    {
        if( ! (rhs instanceof Position ) )
            return false;

        Position other = (Position) rhs;

        for( int i = 0; i < 3; i++ )
            for( int j = 0; j < 3; j++ )
                if( board[ i ][ j ] != ( (Position) rhs ).board[ i ][ j ] )
                    return false;
        return true;
    }

    public int hashCode( )
    {
        int hashVal = 0;

        for( int i = 0; i < 3; i++ )
            for( int j = 0; j < 3; j++ )
                hashVal = hashVal * 4 + board[ i ][ j ];

        return hashVal;
    }
}
```

figure 10.13

The `Position` class

Figures 10.15 and 10.16 show the new `chooseMove`. At line 8, we declare a `Position` object, `thisPosition`. When the time comes it will be placed in the transposition table. `tableDepth` tells us how deep in the search to allow positions to be placed in the transposition table. By experimenting we found that depth 5 was optimal. Allowing positions at depth 6 to be saved hurt because the extra cost of maintaining the larger transposition table was not offset by the fewer examined positions.

```
// Original import directives plus:
import java.util.Map;
import java.util.HashMap;

class TicTacToe
{
    private Map<Position,Integer> transpositions
                                    = new HashMap<Position,Integer>( );

    public Best chooseMove( int side )
      { return chooseMove( side, HUMAN_WIN, COMPUTER_WIN, 0 ); }

        // Find optimal move
    private Best chooseMove( int side, int alpha, int beta, int depth )
      { /* Figures 10.15 and 10.16 */ }

      ...
}
```

figure 10.14

Changes to the TicTacToe class to incorporate transposition table and alpha–beta pruning

Lines 17 to 24 are new. If we are in the first call to chooseMove, we initialize the transposition table. Otherwise, if we are at an appropriate depth, we determine whether the current position has been evaluated; if it has, we return its value. The code has two tricks. First, we can transpose only at depth 3 or higher, as Figure 10.12 suggests. The only other difference is the addition of lines 57 and 58. Immediately before the return, we store the value of the position in the transposition table.

The code has a few little tricks but nothing major.

The use of the transposition table in this Tic-Tac-Toe algorithm removes about half the positions from consideration, with only a slight cost for the transposition table operations. The program's speed is almost doubled.

10.2.3 computer chess

In a complex game such as Chess or Go, it is infeasible to search all the way to the terminal nodes: Some estimates claim that there are roughly 10^{100} legal chess positions, and all the tricks in the world will not bring it down to a manageable level. In this case, we have to stop the search after a certain depth of recursion is reached. The nodes at which the recursion is stopped become terminal nodes. These terminal nodes are evaluated with a function that estimates the value of the position. For instance, in a chess program, the evaluation function measures such variables as the relative amount and strength of pieces and other positional factors.

Terminal positions cannot be searched in computer chess. In the best programs, considerable knowledge is built into the evaluation function.

```
    // Find optimal move
private Best chooseMove( int side, int alpha, int beta, int depth )
{
    int opp;                  // The other side
    Best reply;               // Opponent's best reply
    int dc;                   // Placeholder
    int simpleEval;           // Result of an immediate evaluation
    Position thisPosition = new Position( board );
    int tableDepth = 5;       // Max depth placed in Trans. table
    int bestRow = 0;
    int bestColumn = 0;
    int value;

    if( ( simpleEval = positionValue( ) ) != UNCLEAR )
        return new Best( simpleEval );

    if( depth == 0 )
        transpositions.clear( );
    else if( depth >= 3 && depth <= tableDepth )
    {
        Integer lookupVal = transpositions.get( thisPosition );
        if( lookupVal != null )
            return new Best( lookupVal );
    }

    if( side == COMPUTER )
    {
        opp = HUMAN; value = alpha;
    }
    else
    {
        opp = COMPUTER; value = beta;
    }
```

figure 10.15

The Tic-Tac-Toe algorithm with alpha–beta pruning and transposition table (part 1)

The best computer chess programs play at grandmaster level.

Computers are especially adept at playing moves involving deep combinations that result in exchanges of material. The reason is that the strength of pieces is easily evaluated. However, extending the search depth merely one level requires an increase in processing speed by a factor of about 6 (because the number of positions increases by about a factor of 36). Each extra level of search greatly enhances the ability of the program, up to a certain limit (which appears to have been reached by the best programs). On the other hand, computers generally are not as good at playing quiet positional games in which

```
        Outer:
            for( int row = 0; row < 3; row++ )
                for( int column = 0; column < 3; column++ )
                    if( squareIsEmpty( row, column ) )
                    {
                        place( row, column, side );
                        reply = chooseMove( opp, alpha, beta, depth + 1 );
                        place( row, column, EMPTY );

                        if( side == COMPUTER && reply.val > value ||
                            side == HUMAN && reply.val < value )
                        {
                            if( side == COMPUTER )
                                alpha = value = reply.val;
                            else
                                beta = value = reply.val;

                            bestRow = row; bestColumn = column;
                            if( alpha >= beta )
                                break Outer;  // Refutation
                        }
                    }

            if( depth <= tableDepth )
                transpositions.put( thisPosition, value );

            return new Best( value, bestRow, bestColumn );
        }
```

figure 10.16

The Tic-Tac-Toe algorithm with alpha–beta pruning and transposition table (part 2)

more subtle evaluations and knowledge of the game is required. However, this shortcoming is apparent only when the computer is playing very strong opposition. The mass-marketed computer chess programs are better than all but a small fraction of today's players.

In 1997, the computer program *Deep Blue,* using an enormous amount of computational power (evaluating as many as 200 million moves per second), was able to defeat the reigning world chess champion in a six-game match. Its evaluation function, although top secret, is known to contain a large number of factors, was aided by several chess grandmasters, and was the result of years of experimentation. Writing the top computer chess program is certainly not a trivial task.

summary

In this chapter we introduced an application of binary search and some algorithmic techniques that are commonly used in solving word search puzzles and in game-playing programs such as Chess, Checkers, and Othello. The top programs for these games are all world class. The game of Go, however, appears too complex for computer searching.

key concepts

alpha-beta pruning A technique used to reduce the number of positions that are evaluated in a minimax search. Alpha is the value that the human player has to refute, and beta is the value that the computer has to refute. (377)

minimax strategy A recursive strategy that allows the computer to select an optimal move in a game of Tic-Tac-Toe. (373)

refutation A countermove that proves that a proposed move is not an improvement over moves previously considered. If we find a refutation, we do not have to examine any more moves and the recursive call can return. (374)

terminal position A position in a game that can be evaluated immediately. (374)

transposition table A map that stores previously evaluated positions. (377)

word search puzzle A program that requires searching for words in a two-dimensional grid of letters. Words may be oriented in one of eight directions. (368)

common errors

1. When using a transposition table, you should limit the number of stored positions to avoid running out of memory.
2. Verifying your assumptions is important. For instance, in the word search puzzle, be sure that the dictionary is sorted. A common error is to forget to check your assumptions.

on the internet

Both the word search and the game Tic-Tac-Toe are completely coded, although the interface for the latter leaves a little to be desired.

WordSearch.java Contains the word search puzzle algorithm.

TicTacToe.java Contains the `TicTacToe` class; a `main` is supplied separately in **TicTacMain.java**.

exercises

IN SHORT

10.1 What error checks are missing from Figure 10.6?

10.2 For the situation in Figure 10.17
  a. Which of the responses to move C_2 is a refutation?
  b. What is the value of the position?

IN THEORY

10.3 Verify that, if `x` is a prefix of some word in the sorted array `a`, then `x` is a prefix of the word at the index that `prefixSearch` returns.

10.4 Explain how the running time of the word search algorithm changes when
  a. The number of words doubles.
  b. The number of rows and columns double (simultaneously).

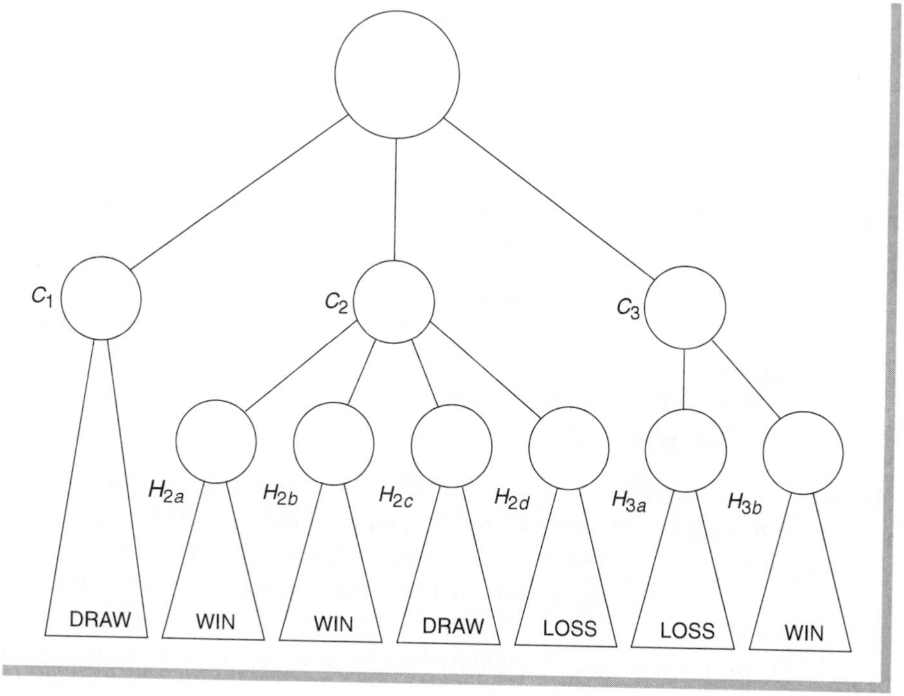

figure 10.17

Alpha–beta pruning example for Exercise 10.2

IN PRACTICE

10.5 For the word search problem, replace the binary search with a sequential search. How does that change affect performance?

10.6 Compare the performance of the word search algorithm with and without the prefix search.

10.7 Replace the `HashMap` with the `TreeMap` in the Tic-Tac-Toe program and compare the performance of the two versions.

10.8 Even if the computer has a move that gives an immediate win, it may not make it if it detects another move that is also guaranteed to win. Some early chess programs had the problem that they would get into a repetition of position when a forced win was detected, allowing the opponent to claim a draw. In the Tic-Tac-Toe program this outcome is not a problem because the program eventually will win. Modify the Tic-Tac-Toe algorithm so that when a winning position is found, the move that leads to the shortest win is always taken. You can do so by adding `9-depth` to `COMPUTER_WIN`, so that a quicker win gives the highest value.

10.9 Compare the performance of the Tic-Tac-Toe program with and without alpha–beta pruning.

10.10 Implement the Tic-Tac-Toe algorithm and measure the performance when various depths are allowed to be stored in the transposition table. Also measure the performance when no transposition table is used. How are the results affected by alpha–beta pruning?

PROGRAMMING PROJECTS

10.11 Write a program to play 5×5 Tic-Tac-Toe, where 4 in a row wins. Can you search to terminal nodes?

10.12 The game of Boggle consists of a grid of letters and a word list. The object is to find words in the grid subject to the constraint that two adjacent letters must be adjacent in the grid (i.e., north, south, east, or west of each other) and each item in the grid can be used at most once per word. Write a program to play Boggle.

10.13 Write a program to play MAXIT. The board is represented as an $N \times N$ grid of numbers randomly placed at the start of the game. One position is designated as the initial current position. Two players alternate turns. At each turn, a player must select a grid element in the current row or column. The value of the selected position is added to the player's score, and that position becomes the current position and cannot be selected again. Players alternate until all grid elements in the current row and column have been selected, at which point the game ends and the player with the highest score wins.

10.14 Othello played on a 6×6 board is a forced win for black. Prove this assertion by writing a program. What is the final score if play on both sides is optimal?

references

If you are interested in computer games, a good starting point for information is the article cited in [1]. In this special issue of the journal, devoted exclusively to the subject, you will also find plenty of information and references to other works covering Chess, Checkers, and other computer games.

1. K. Lee and S. Mahajan, "The Development of a World Class Othello Program," *Artificial Intelligence* **43** (1990), 21–36.

chapter 11

stacks and compilers

Stacks are used extensively in compilers. In this chapter we present two simple components of a compiler: a balanced symbol checker and a simple calculator. We do so to show simple algorithms that use stacks and to show how the Collections API classes described in Chapter 6 are used.

In this chapter, we show

- How to use a stack to check for balanced symbols
- How to use a *state machine* to parse symbols in a balanced symbol program
- How to use *operator precedence parsing* to evaluate infix expressions in a simple calculator program

11.1 balanced-symbol checker

As discussed in Section 6.6, compilers check your programs for syntax errors. Frequently, however, a lack of one symbol (such as a missing */ comment ender or }) can cause the compiler to produce numerous lines of diagnostics without identifying the real error. A useful tool to help debug compiler error messages is a program that checks whether symbols are balanced. In other words, every { must correspond to a }, every [to a], and so on. However, simply counting the numbers of each symbol is insufficient. For example, the sequence [()] is legal, but the sequence [(]) is wrong.

11.1.1 basic algorithm

A stack can be used to detect mismatched symbols.

A stack is useful here because we know that when a closing symbol such as) is seen, it matches the most recently seen unclosed (. Therefore, by placing an opening symbol on a stack, we can easily determine whether a closing symbol makes sense. Specifically, we have the following algorithm.

1. Make an empty stack.
2. Read symbols until the end of the file.
   a. If the symbol is an opening symbol, push it onto the stack.
   b. If it is a closing symbol, do the following.
      i. If the stack is empty, report an error.
      ii. Otherwise, pop the stack. If the symbol popped is not the corresponding opening symbol, report an error.
3. At the end of the file, if the stack is not empty, report an error.

In this algorithm, illustrated in Figure 11.1, the fourth, fifth, and sixth symbols all generate errors. The } is an error because the symbol popped from the top of the stack is a (, so a mismatch is detected. The) is an error because the stack is empty, so there is no corresponding (. The [is an error detected when the end of input is encountered and the stack is not empty.

figure 11.1

Stack operations in a balanced-symbol algorithm

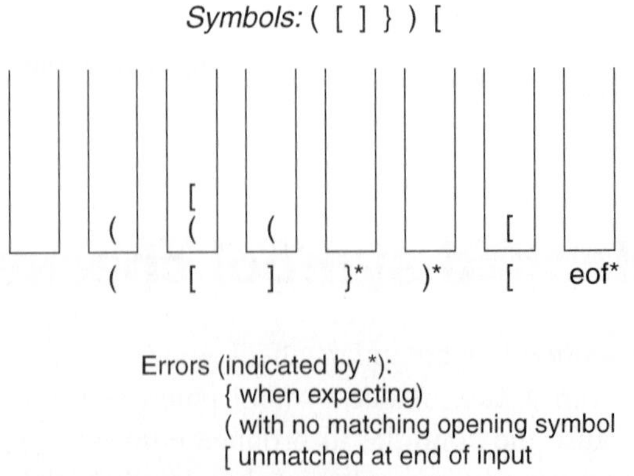

To make this technique work for Java programs, we need to consider all the contexts in which parentheses, braces, and brackets need not match. For example, we should not consider a parenthesis as a symbol if it occurs inside a comment, string constant, or character constant. We thus need routines to skip comments, string constants, and character constants. A character constant in Java can be difficult to recognize because of the many escape sequences possible, so we need to simplify things. We want to design a program that works for the bulk of inputs likely to occur.

Symbols in comments, string constants, and character constants need not be balanced.

For the program to be useful, we must not only report mismatches but also attempt to identify where the mismatches occur. Consequently, we keep track of the line numbers where the symbols are seen. When an error is encountered, obtaining an accurate message is always difficult. If there is an extra `}`, does that mean that the `}` is extraneous? Or was a `{` missing earlier? We keep the error handling as simple as possible, but once one error has been reported, the program may get confused and start flagging many errors. Thus only the first error can be considered meaningful. Even so, the program developed here is very useful.

Line numbers are needed for meaningful error messages.

11.1.2 implementation

The program has two basic components. One part, called *tokenization,* is the process of scanning an input stream for opening and closing symbols (the tokens) and generating the sequence of tokens that need to be recognized. The second part is running the balanced symbol algorithm, based on the tokens. The two basic components are represented as separate classes.

Tokenization is the process of generating the sequence of symbols (tokens) that need to be recognized.

Figure 11.2 shows the `Tokenizer` class skeleton, and Figure 11.3 shows the `Balance` class skeleton. The `Tokenizer` class provides a constructor that requires a `Reader` and then provides a set of accessors that can be used to get

- The next token (either an opening/closing symbol for the code in this chapter or an identifier for the code in Chapter 12)
- The current line number
- The number of errors (mismatched quotes and comments)

The `Tokenizer` class maintains most of this information in private data members. The `Balance` class also provides a similar constructor, but its only publicly visible routine is `checkBalance`, shown at line 24. Everything else is a supporting routine or a class data member.

We begin by describing the `Tokenizer` class. `in` is a reference to a `PushbackReader` object and is initialized at construction. Because of the I/O hierarchy (see Section 4.5.3), it may be constructed with any `Reader` object. The current character being scanned is stored in `ch`, and the current line

figure 11.2

The Tokenizer class skeleton, used to retrieve tokens from an input stream

```
import java.io.Reader;
import java.io.PushbackReader;
import java.io.IOException;

// Tokenizer class.
//
// CONSTRUCTION: with a Reader object
// ******************PUBLIC OPERATIONS***********************
// char getNextOpenClose( ) --> Get next opening/closing symbol
// int getLineNumber( )     --> Return current line number
// int getErrorCount( )     --> Return number of parsing errors
// String getNextID( )      --> Get next Java identifier
//                               (see Section 12.2)
// ******************ERRORS**********************************
// Error checking on comments and quotes is performed

public class Tokenizer
{
    public Tokenizer( Reader inStream )
      { errors = 0; ch = '\0'; currentLine = 1;
        in = new PushbackReader( inStream ); }

    public static final int SLASH_SLASH = 0;
    public static final int SLASH_STAR  = 1;

    public int getLineNumber( )
      { return currentLine; }
    public int getErrorCount( )
      { return errors; }
    public char getNextOpenClose( )
      { /* Figure 11.7 */ }
    public char getNextID( )
      { /* Figure 12.29 */ }

    private boolean nextChar( )
      { /* Figure 11.4 */ }
    private void putBackChar( )
      { /* Figure 11.4 */ }
    private void skipComment( int start )
      { /* Figure 11.5 */ }
    private void skipQuote( char quoteType )
      { /* Figure 11.6 */ }
    private void processSlash( )
      { /* Figure 11.7 */ }
    private static final boolean isIdChar( char ch )
      { /* Figure 12.27 */ }
    private String getRemainingString( )
      { /* Figure 12.28 */ }

    private PushbackReader in;    // The input stream
    private char ch;              // Current character
    private int currentLine;      // Current line
    private int errors;           // Number of errors seen
}
```

```
import java.io.Reader;
import java.io.FileReader;
import java.io.IOException;
import java.io.InputStreamReader;

import java.util.Stack;


// Balance class: check for balanced symbols
//
// CONSTRUCTION: with a Reader object
// *****************PUBLIC OPERATIONS**********************
// int checkBalance( )   --> Print mismatches
//                           return number of errors
// *****************ERRORS*********************************
// Error checking on comments and quotes is performed
// main checks for balanced symbols.

public class Balance
{
    public Balance( Reader inStream )
      { errors = 0; tok = new Tokenizer( inStream ); }

    public int checkBalance( )
      { /* Figure 11.8 */ }

    private Tokenizer tok;
    private int errors;

    /**
     * Symbol nested class;
     * represents what will be placed on the stack.
     */
    private static class Symbol
    {
        public char token;
        public int  theLine;

        public Symbol( char tok, int  line )
        {
            token   = tok;
            theLine = line;
        }
    }

    private void checkMatch( Symbol opSym, Symbol clSym )
      { /* Figure 11.9 */ }
}
```

figure 11.3

Class skeleton for a balanced-symbol program

number is stored in `currentLine`. Finally, an integer that counts the number of errors is declared at line 53. The constructor, shown at lines 19 to 21, initializes the error count to 0 and the current line number to 1 and sets the `PushbackReader` reference.

Lexical analysis is used to ignore comments and recognize symbols.

We can now implement the class methods, which as we mentioned, are concerned with keeping track of the current line and attempting to differentiate symbols that represent opening and closing tokens from those that are inside comments, character constants, and string constants. This general process of recognizing tokens in a stream of symbols is called *lexical analysis*. Figure 11.4 shows a pair of routines, `nextChar` and `putBackChar`. The `nextChar` method reads the next character from `in`, assigns it to `ch`, and updates `currentLine` if a newline is encountered. It returns `false` only if the end of the file has been reached. The complementary procedure `putBackChar`

```
/**
 * nextChar sets ch based on the next character in the input stream.
 * putBackChar puts the character back onto the stream.
 * It should be used only once after a call to nextChar.
 * Both routines adjust currentLine if necessary.
 */
private boolean nextChar( )
{
    try
    {
        int readVal = in.read( );
        if( readVal == -1 )
            return false;
        ch = (char) readVal;
        if( ch == '\n' )
            currentLine++;
        return true;
    }
    catch( IOException e )
      { return false; }
}

private void putBackChar( )
{
    if( ch == '\n' )
        currentLine--;
    try
      { in.unread( (int) ch ); }
    catch( IOException e ) { }
}
```

figure 11.4

The `nextChar` routine for reading the next character, updating `currentLine` if necessary, and returning `true` if not at the end of file; and the `putBackChar` routine for putting back `ch` and updating `currentLine` if necessary puts the current character, ch, back onto the input stream, and decrements currentLine if the character is a newline. Clearly, putBackChar should be called at most once between calls to nextChar; as it is a private routine, we do not worry about abuse on the part of the class user. Putting characters back onto the input stream is a commonly used technique in parsing. In many instances we have read one too many characters, and undoing the read is useful. In our case this occurs after processing a /. We must determine whether the next character begins the comment start token; if it does not, we cannot simply disregard it because it could be an opening or closing symbol or a quote. Thus we pretend that it is never read.

Next is the routine skipComment, shown in Figure 11.5. Its purpose is to skip over the characters in the comment and position the input stream so that the next read is the first character after the comment ends. This technique is complicated by the fact that comments can either begin with //, in which case the line ends the comment, or /*, in which case */ ends the comment.[1] In the // case, we continually get the next character until either the end of file is reached (in which

```
/**
 * Precondition: We are about to process a comment;
 *                   have already seen comment-start token
 * Postcondition: Stream will be set immediately after
 *                   comment-ending token
 */
private void skipComment( int start )
{
    if( start == SLASH_SLASH )
    {
        while( nextChar( ) && ( ch != '\n' ) )
            ;
        return;
    }

        // Look for a */ sequence
    boolean state = false;    // True if we have seen *

    while( nextChar( ) )
    {
        if( state && ch == '/' )
            return;
        state = ( ch == '*' );
    }
    errors++;
    System.out.println( "Unterminated comment!" );
}
```

figure 11.5

The skipComment routine for moving past an already started comment

1. We do not consider deviant cases involving \, nor /**/.

case, the first half of the && operator fails) or we get a newline. At that point we return. Note that the line number is updated automatically by `nextChar`. Otherwise, we have the /* case, which is processed starting at line 17.

The *state machine* is a common technique used to parse symbols; at any point, it is in some state, and each input character takes it to a new state. Eventually, the state machine reaches a state in which a symbol has been recognized.

The `skipComment` routine uses a simplified state machine. The *state machine* is a common technique used to parse symbols; at any point, it is in some state, and each input character takes it to a new state. Eventually, it reaches a state at which a symbol has been recognized.

In `skipComment`, at any point, it has matched 0, 1, or 2 characters of the */ terminator, corresponding to states 0, 1, and 2. If it matches two characters, it can return. Thus, inside the loop, it can be in only state 0 or 1 because, if it is in state 1 and sees a /, it returns immediately. Thus the state can be represented by a Boolean variable that is `true` if the state machine is in state 1. If it does not return, it either goes back to state 1 if it encounters a * or goes back to state 0 if it does not. This procedure is stated succinctly at line 23.

If we never find the comment-ending token, eventually `nextChar` returns `false` and the `while` loop terminates, resulting in an error message. The `skipQuote` method, shown in Figure 11.6, is similar. Here, the parameter is the opening quote character, which is either " or '. In either case, we need to see that character as the closing quote. However, we must be prepared to handle the \ character; otherwise, our program will report errors when it is run on its

figure 11.6

The `skipQuote` routine for moving past an already started character or string constant

```
/**
 * Precondition: We are about to process a quote;
 *                   have already seen beginning quote.
 * Postcondition: Stream will be set immediately after
 *                   matching quote
 */
private void skipQuote( char quoteType )
{
    while( nextChar( ) )
    {
        if( ch == quoteType )
            return;
        if( ch == '\n' )
        {
            errors++;
            System.out.println( "Missing closed quote at line " +
                                currentLine );
            return;
        }
        else if( ch == '\\' )
            nextChar( );
    }
}
```

own source. Thus we repeatedly digest characters. If the current character is a closing quote, we are done. If it is a newline, we have an unterminated character or string constant. And if it is a backslash, we digest an extra character without examining it.

Once we've written the skipping routine, writing `getNextOpenClose` is easier. The bulk of the logic is deferred to `processSlash`. If the current character is a /, we read a second character to see whether we have a comment. If so, we call `skipComment`; if not, we undo the second read. If we have a quote, we call `skipQuote`. If we have an opening or closing symbol, we can return. Otherwise, we keep reading until we eventually run out of input or find an opening or closing symbol. Both `getNextOpenClose` and `processSlash` are shown in Figure 11.7.

The `getLineNumber` and `getErrorCount` methods are one-liners that return the values of the corresponding data members and are shown in Figure 11.2. We discuss the `getNextID` routine in Section 12.2.2 when it is needed.

In the `Balance` class, the balanced symbol algorithm requires that we place opening symbols on a stack. In order to print diagnostics, we store a line number with each symbol, as shown previously in the `Symbol` nested class at lines 34 to 44 in Figure 11.3.

The `checkBalance` routine is implemented as shown in Figure 11.8. It follows the algorithm description almost verbatim. A stack that stores pending opening symbols is declared at line 9. Opening symbols are pushed onto the stack with the current line number. When a closing symbol is encountered and the stack is empty, the closing symbol is extraneous; otherwise, we remove the top item from the stack and verify that the opening symbol that was on the stack matches the closing symbol just read. To do so we use the `checkMatch` routine, which is shown in Figure 11.9. Once the end of input is encountered, any symbols on the stack are unmatched; they are repeatedly output in the `while` loop that begins at line 40. The total number of errors detected is then returned.

The current implementation allows multiple calls to `checkBalance`. However, if the input stream is not reset externally, all that happens is that the end of the file is immediately detected and we return immediately. We can add functionality to the `Tokenizer` class, allowing it to change the stream source, and then add functionality to the `Balance` class to change the input stream (passing on the change to the `Tokenizer` class). We leave this task for you to do as Exercise 11.9.

> The `checkBalance` routine does all the algorithmic work.

Figure 11.10 shows that we expect a `Balance` object to be created and then `checkBalance` to be invoked. In our example, if there are no command-line arguments, the associated `Reader` is attached to `System.in` (via an `InputStreamReader` bridge); otherwise, we repeatedly use `Readers` associated with the files given in the command-line argument list.

figure 11.7

The `getNextOpenClose` routine for skipping comments and quotes and returning the next opening or closing character, along with the `processSlash` routine

```
    /**
     * Get the next opening or closing symbol.
     * Return false if end of file.
     * Skip past comments and character and string constants
     */
    public char getNextOpenClose( )
    {
        while( nextChar( ) )
        {
            if( ch == '/' )
                processSlash( );
            else if( ch == '\'' || ch == '"' )
                skipQuote( ch );
            else if( ch == '(' || ch == '[' || ch == '{' ||
                     ch == ')' || ch == ']' || ch == '}' )
                return ch;
        }
        return '\0';            // End of file
    }

    /**
     * After the opening slash is seen deal with next character.
     * If it is a comment starter, process it; otherwise putback
     * the next character if it is not a newline.
     */
    private void processSlash( )
    {
        if( nextChar( ) )
        {
            if( ch == '*' )
            {
                // Javadoc comment
                if( nextChar( ) && ch != '*' )
                    putBackChar( );
                skipComment( SLASH_STAR );
            }
            else if( ch == '/' )
                skipComment( SLASH_SLASH );
            else if( ch != '\n' )
                putBackChar( );
        }
    }
```

```
/**
 * Print an error message for unbalanced symbols.
 * @return number of errors detected.
 */
public int checkBalance( )
{
    char ch;
    Symbol match = null;
    Stack<Symbol> pendingTokens = new Stack<Symbol>( );

    while( ( ch = tok.getNextOpenClose( ) ) != '\0' )
    {
        Symbol lastSymbol = new Symbol( ch, tok.getLineNumber( ) );

        switch( ch )
        {
          case '(': case '[': case '{':
            pendingTokens.push( lastSymbol );
            break;

          case ')': case ']': case '}':
            if( pendingTokens.isEmpty( ) )
            {
                errors++;
                System.out.println( "Extraneous " + ch +
                                    " at line " + tok.getLineNumber( ) );
            }
            else
            {
                match = pendingTokens.pop( );
                checkMatch( match, lastSymbol );
            }
            break;

          default: // Cannot happen
            break;
        }
    }

    while( !pendingTokens.isEmpty( ) )
    {
        match = pendingTokens.pop( );
        System.out.println( "Unmatched " + match.token +
                            " at line "  + match.theLine );
        errors++;
    }
    return errors + tok.getErrorCount( );
}
```

figure 11.8

The checkBalance algorithm

```
/**
 * Print an error message if clSym does not match opSym.
 * Update errors.
 */
private void checkMatch( Symbol opSym, Symbol clSym )
{
    if( opSym.token == '(' && clSym.token != ')' ||
        opSym.token == '[' && clSym.token != ']' ||
        opSym.token == '{' && clSym.token != '}' )
    {
        System.out.println( "Found " + clSym.token + " on line " +
              tok.getLineNumber( ) + "; does not match " + opSym.token
              + " at line " + opSym.theLine );
        errors++;
    }
}
```

figure 11.9

The `checkMatch` routine for checking that the closing symbol matches the opening symbol

11.2 a simple calculator

Some of the techniques used to implement compilers can be used on a smaller scale in the implementation of a typical pocket calculator. Typically, calculators evaluate *infix expressions,* such as 1+2, which consist of a binary operator with arguments to its left and right. This format, although often fairly easy to evaluate, can be more complex. Consider the expression

```
1 + 2 * 3
```

In an *infix expression* a binary operator has arguments to its left and right.

Mathematically, this expression evaluates to 7 because the multiplication operator has higher precedence than addition. Some calculators give the answer 9, illustrating that a simple left-to-right evaluation is not sufficient; we cannot begin by evaluating 1+2. Now consider the expressions

```
10 - 4 - 3
2 ^ 3 ^ 3
```

When there are several operators, precedence and associativity determine how the operators are processed.

in which ^ is the exponentiation operator. Which subtraction and which exponentiation get evaluated first? On the one hand, subtractions are processed left-to-right, giving the result 3. On the other hand, exponentiation is generally processed right-to-left, thereby reflecting the mathematical 2^{3^3} rather than $(2^3)^3$. Thus subtraction associates left-to-right, whereas exponentiation associates from right-to-left. All of these possibilities suggest that evaluating an expression such as

```
// main routine for balanced symbol checker.
// If no command line parameters, standard output is used.
// Otherwise, files in command line are used.
public static void main( String [ ] args )
{
    Balance p;

    if( args.length == 0 )
    {

        p = new Balance( new InputStreamReader( System.in ) );
        if( p.checkBalance( ) == 0 )
            System.out.println( "No errors!" );
        return;
    }

    for( int i = 0; i < args.length; i++ )
    {
        FileReader f = null;
        try
        {
            f = new FileReader( args[ i ] );

            System.out.println( args[ i ] + ": " );
            p = new Balance( f );
            if( p.checkBalance( ) == 0 )
                System.out.println( "   ...no errors!" );
        }
        catch( IOException e )
          { System.err.println( e + args[ i ] ); }
        finally
        {
            try
              { if( f != null ) f.close( ); }
            catch( IOException e )
              { }
        }
    }
}
```

figure 11.10

The `main` routine with command-line arguments

```
1 - 2 - 4 ^ 5 * 3 * 6 / 7 ^ 2 ^ 2
```

would be quite challenging.

If the calculations are performed in integer math (i.e., rounding down on division), the answer is `-8`. To show this result, we insert parentheses to clarify ordering of the calculations:

```
( 1 - 2 ) - ( ( ( ( 4 ^ 5 ) * 3 ) * 6 ) / ( 7 ^ ( 2 ^ 2 ) ) )
```

Although the parentheses make the order of evaluations unambiguous, they do not necessarily make the mechanism for evaluation any clearer. A different expression form, called a *postfix expression,* which can be evaluated by a postfix machine without using any precedence rules, provides a direct mechanism for evaluation. In the next several sections we explain how it works. First, we examine the postfix expression form and show how expressions can be evaluated in a simple left-to-right scan. Next, we show algorithmically how the previous expressions, which are presented as infix expressions, can be converted to postfix. Finally, we give a Java program that evaluates infix expressions containing additive, multiplicative, and exponentiation operators—as well as overriding parentheses. We use an algorithm called *operator precedence parsing* to convert an infix expression to a postfix expression in order to evaluate the infix expression.

A postfix expression can be evaluated as follows. Operands are pushed onto a single stack. An operator pops its operands and then pushes the result. At the end of the evaluation, the stack should contain only one element, which represents the result.

11.2.1 postfix machines

A postfix expression is a series of operators and operands. A *postfix machine* is used to evaluate a postfix expression as follows. When an operand is seen, it is pushed onto a stack. When an operator is seen, the appropriate number of operands are popped from the stack, the operator is evaluated, and the result is pushed back onto the stack. For binary operators, which are the most common, two operands are popped. When the complete postfix expression is evaluated, the result should be a single item on the stack that represents the answer. The postfix form represents a natural way to evaluate expressions because precedence rules are not required.

A simple example is the postfix expression

```
1 2 3 * +
```

The evaluation proceeds as follows: `1`, then `2`, and then `3` are each pushed onto the stack. To process `*`, we pop the top two items on the stack: `3` and then `2`. Note that the first item popped becomes the `rhs` parameter to the binary operator and that the second item popped is the `lhs` parameter; thus parameters are popped in reverse order. For multiplication, the order does not matter, but for subtraction and division, it does. The result of the multiplication is `6`, and that is pushed back onto the stack. At this point, the top of the stack is `6`; below it is `1`. To process the `+`, the `6` and `1` are popped, and their sum, `7`, is pushed. At this point, the expression has been read and the stack has only one item. Thus the final answer is `7`.

Every valid infix expression can be converted to postfix form. For example, the earlier long infix expression can be written in postfix notation as

```
1 2 - 4 5 ^ 3 * 6 * 7 2 2 ^ ^ / -
```

Evaluation of a postfix expression takes linear time.

Figure 11.11 shows the steps used by the postfix machine to evaluate this expression. Each step involves a single push. Consequently, as there are 9

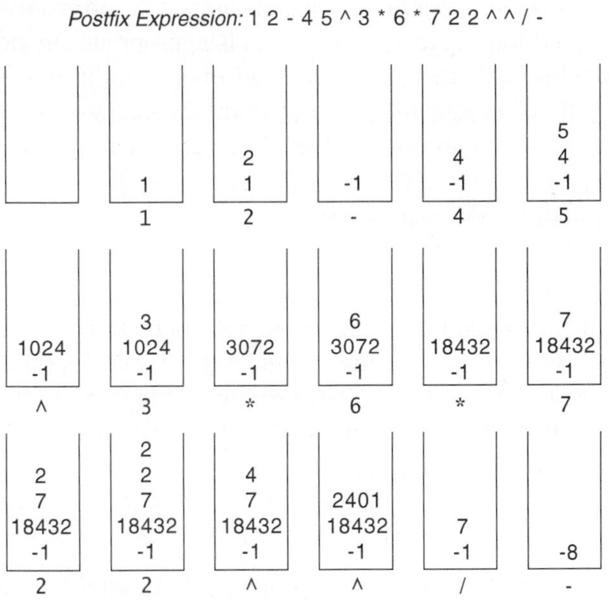

figure 11.11

Steps in the evaluation of a postfix expression

operands and 8 operators, there are 17 steps and 17 pushes. Clearly, the time required to evaluate a postfix expression is linear.

The remaining task is to write an algorithm to convert from infix notation to postfix notation. Once we have it, we also have an algorithm that evaluates an infix expression.

11.2.2 infix to postfix conversion

The operator precedence parsing algorithm converts an infix expression to a postfix expression, so we can evaluate the infix expression.

The basic principle involved in the operator precedence parsing algorithm, which converts an infix expression to a postfix expression, is the following. When an operand is seen, we can immediately output it. However, when we see an operator, we can never output it because we must wait to see the second operand, so we must save it. In an expression such as

```
1 + 2 * 3 ^ 4
```

which in postfix form is

```
1 2 3 4 ^ * +
```

a postfix expression in some cases has operators in the reverse order than they appear in an infix expression. Of course, this order can occur only if the pre-

An operator stack is used to store operators that have been seen but not yet output.

cedence of the involved operators is increasing as we go from left to right. Even so, this condition suggests that a stack is appropriate for storing operators. Following this logic, then, when we read an operator it must somehow be placed on a stack. Consequently, at some point the operator must get off the stack. The rest of the algorithm involves deciding when operators go on and come off the stack.

In another simple infix expression

```
2 ^ 5 - 1
```

When an operator is seen on the input, operators of higher priority (or left-associative operators of equal priority) are removed from the stack, signaling that they should be applied. The input operator is then placed on the stack.

when we reach the - operator, 2 and 5 have been output and ^ is on the stack. Because - has lower precedence than ^, the ^ needs to be applied to 2 and 5. Thus we must pop the ^ and any other operands of higher precedence than - from the stack. After doing so, we push the -. The resulting postfix expression is

```
2 5 ^ 1 -
```

In general, when we are processing an operator from input, we output those operators from the stack that the precedence (and associativity) rules tell us need to be processed.

A second example is the infix expression

```
3 * 2 ^ 5 - 1
```

When we reach the ^ operator, 3 and 2 have been output and * is on the stack. As ^ has higher precedence than *, nothing is popped and ^ goes on the stack. The 5 is output immediately. Then we encounter a - operator. Precedence rules tell us that ^ is popped, followed by the *. At this point, nothing is left to pop, we are done popping, and - goes onto the stack. We then output 1. When we reach the end of the infix expression, we can pop the remaining operators from the stack. The resulting postfix expression is

```
3 2 5 ^ * 1 -
```

A left parenthesis is treated as a high-precedence operator when it is an input symbol but as a low-precedence operator when it is on the stack. A left parenthesis is removed only by a right parenthesis.

Before the summarizing algorithm, we need to answer a few questions. First, if the current symbol is a + and the top of the stack is a +, should the + on the stack be popped or should it stay? The answer is determined by deciding whether the input + implies that the stack + has been completed. Because + associates from left to right, the answer is yes. However, if we are talking about the ^ operator, which associates from right to left, the answer is no. Therefore, when examining two operators of equal precedence, we look at the associativity to decide, as shown in Figure 11.12.

What about parentheses? A left parenthesis can be considered a high-precedence operator when it is an input symbol, a low-precedence operator

Infix Expression	Postfix Expression	Associativity
`2 + 3 + 4`	`2 3 + 4 +`	Left-associative: Input + is lower than stack +.
`2 ^ 3 ^ 4`	`2 3 4 ^ ^`	Right-associative: Input ^ is higher than stack ^.

figure 11.12

Examples of using associativity to break ties in precedence

when it is on the stack. Consequently, the input left parenthesis is simply placed on the stack. When a right parenthesis appears on the input, we pop the operator stack until we come to a left parenthesis. The operators are written, but the parentheses are not.

The following is a summary of the various cases in the operator precedence parsing algorithm. With the exception of parentheses, everything popped from the stack is output.

- *Operands:* Immediately output.
- *Close parenthesis:* Pop stack symbols until an open parenthesis appears.
- *Operators:* Pop all stack symbols until a symbol of lower precedence or a right-associative symbol of equal precedence appears. Then push the operator.
- *End of input:* Pop all remaining stack symbols.

As an example, Figure 11.13 shows how the algorithm processes

```
1 - 2 ^ 3 ^ 3 - ( 4 + 5 * 6 ) * 7
```

Below each stack is the symbol read. To the right of each stack, in boldface, is any output.

11.2.3 implementation

The `Evaluator` class will parse and evaluate infix expressions.

We now have the theoretical background required to implement a simple calculator. Our calculator supports addition, subtraction, multiplication, division, and exponentiation. We write an `Evaluator` class that works on `long` integers. We make a simplifying assumption: Negative numbers are not allowed. Distinguishing between the binary minus operator and the unary minus requires extra work in the scanning routine and also complicates matters because it introduces a nonbinary operator. Incorporating unary operators is not difficult, but the extra code does not illustrate any unique concepts and thus we leave it for you to do as an exercise.

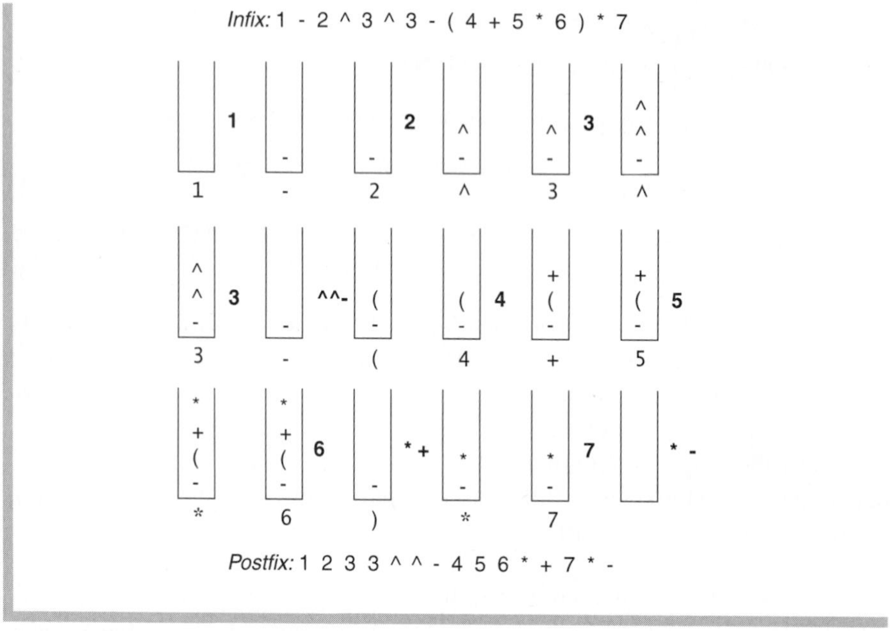
Infix: 1 - 2 ^ 3 ^ 3 - (4 + 5 * 6) * 7
Postfix: 1 2 3 3 ^ ^ - 4 5 6 * + 7 * -

figure 11.13

Infix to postfix conversion

> We need two stacks: an operator stack and a stack for the postfix machine.

Figure 11.14 shows the `Evaluator` class skeleton, which is used to process a single string of input. The basic evaluation algorithm requires two stacks. The first stack is used to evaluate the infix expression and generate the postfix expression. It is the stack of operators declared at line 34. An `int` represents different kinds of tokens, such as `PLUS`, `MINUS`, and so on. These constants are shown later. Rather than explicitly outputting the postfix expression, we send each postfix symbol to the postfix machine as it is generated. Thus we also need a stack that stores operands; the postfix machine stack is declared at line 35. The remaining data member is a `StringTokenizer` object used to step through the input line.

As was the case with the balanced symbol checker, we can write a `Tokenizer` class that can be used to give us the token sequence. Although we could reuse code, there is in fact little commonality, so we write a `Tokenizer` class for this application only. Here, however, the tokens are a little more complex because, if we read an operand, the type of token is `VALUE`, but we must also know what the value is that has been read. To avoid confusion we name the class `EvalTokenizer` and make it nested. Its placement is shown at line 22; its implementation, along with the nested `Token` class, is shown in Figure 11.15. A `Token` stores both a token type, and if the token is a `VALUE`, its numeric value. Accessors can be used to obtain information about a token. (The `getValue` method could be made more robust by signaling an error if `type` is not `VALUE`.) The `EvalTokenizer` class has one method.

```
import java.util.Stack;
import java.util.StringTokenizer;
import java.io.IOException;
import java.io.BufferedReader;
import java.io.InputStreamReader;

// Evaluator class interface: evaluate infix expressions.
//
// CONSTRUCTION: with a String
//
// ******************PUBLIC OPERATIONS***********************
// long getValue( )      --> Return value of infix expression
// ******************ERRORS**********************************
// Some error checking is performed

public class Evaluator
{
    private static class Precendence
      { /* Figure 11.20 */ }
    private static class Token
      { /* Figure 11.15 */ }
    private static class EvalTokenizer
      { /* Figure 11.15 */ }

    public Evaluator( String s )
    {
        opStack = new Stack<Integer>( ); opStack.push( EOL );
        postfixStack = new Stack<Long>( );
        str = new StringTokenizer( s, "+*-/^() ", true );
    }
    public long getValue( )
      { /* Figure 11.17 */ }

    private Stack<Integer>  opStack;      // Operator stack for conversion
    private Stack<Long>     postfixStack; // Stack for postfix machine
    private StringTokenizer str;          // StringTokenizer stream

    private void processToken( Token lastToken )
      { /* Figure 11.21 */ }
    private long getTop( )
      { /* Figure 11.18 */ }
    private void binaryOp( int topOp )
      { /* Figure 11.19 */ }
}
```

figure 11.14

The Evaluator class skeleton

figure 11.15

The `Token` and `EvalTokenizer` nested classes

```
    private static class Token
    {
        public Token( )
          { this( EOL ); }
        public Token( int t )
          { this( t, 0 ); }
        public Token( int t, long v )
          { type = t; value = v; }

        public int getType( )
          { return type; }
        public long getValue( )
          { return value; }

        private int type = EOL;
        private long value = 0;
    }

    private static class EvalTokenizer
    {
        public EvalTokenizer( StringTokenizer is )
          { str = is; }

        /**
         * Find the next token, skipping blanks, and return it.
         * For VALUE token, place the
         * processed value in currentValue.
         * Print error message if input is unrecognized.
         */
        public Token getToken( )
          { /* Figure 11.16 */ }

        private StringTokenizer str;
    }
```

Figure 11.16 shows the `getToken` routine. Line 10 checks for the end of the input line. When `getToken` gets past line 11, we know that more tokens are available. If we have not reached the end of line, we check to see whether we match any of the one-character operators. If so, we return the appropriate token. Otherwise, we expect that what remains is an operand, so we use `Long.parseLong` to get the value, and then return a `Token` object by explicitly constructing a `Token` object based on the value read.

We can now discuss the methods of the `Evaluator` class. The only publicly visible method is `getValue`. Shown in Figure 11.17, `getValue` repeatedly reads a token and processes it until the end of line is detected. At that point the item at the top of the stack is the answer.

```
    /**
     * Find the next token, skipping blanks, and return it.
     * For VALUE token, place the processed value in currentValue.
     * Print error message if input is unrecognized.
     */
    public Token getToken( )
    {
        long theValue;

        if( !str.hasMoreTokens( ) )
            return new Token( );

        String s = str.nextToken( );
        if( s.equals( " " ) ) return getToken( );
        if( s.equals( "^" ) ) return new Token( EXP );
        if( s.equals( "/" ) ) return new Token( DIV );
        if( s.equals( "*" ) ) return new Token( MULT );
        if( s.equals( "(" ) ) return new Token( OPAREN );
        if( s.equals( ")" ) ) return new Token( CPAREN );
        if( s.equals( "+" ) ) return new Token( PLUS );
        if( s.equals( "-" ) ) return new Token( MINUS );

        try
          { theValue = Long.parseLong( s ); }
        catch( NumberFormatException e )
        {
            System.err.println( "Parse error" );
            return new Token( );
        }

        return new Token( VALUE, theValue );
    }
```

figure 11.16

The `getToken` routine for returning the next token in the input stream

Figures 11.18 and 11.19 show the routines used to implement the postfix machine. The routine in Figure 11.18 is used to pop the postfix stack and print an error message if needed. The `binaryOp` routine in Figure 11.19 applies `topOp` (which is expected to be the top item in the operator stack) to the top two items on the postfix stack and replaces them with the result. It also pops the operator stack (at line 33), signifying that processing for `topOp` is complete.

A *precedence table* is used to decide what is removed from the operator stack. Left-associative operators have the operator stack precedence set at 1 higher than the input symbol precedence. Right-associative operators go the other way.

Figure 11.20 declares a *precedence table,* which stores the operator precedences and is used to decide what is removed from the operator stack. The operators are listed in the same order as the token constants.

figure 11.17

The `getValue` routine for reading and processing tokens and then returning the item at the top of the stack

```
/**
 * Public routine that performs the evaluation.
 * Examine the  postfix machine to see if a single result is
 * left and if so, return it; otherwise print error.
 * @return the result.
 */
public long getValue( )
{
    EvalTokenizer tok = new EvalTokenizer( str );
    Token lastToken;

    do
    {
        lastToken = tok.getToken( );
        processToken( lastToken );
    } while( lastToken.getType( ) != EOL );

    if( postfixStack.isEmpty( ) )
    {
        System.err.println( "Missing operand!" );
        return 0;
    }

    long theResult = postFixTopAndPop( );
    if( !postfixStack.isEmpty( ) )
        System.err.println( "Warning: missing operators!" );

    return theResult;
}
```

figure 11.18

The routines for popping the top item in the postfix stack

```
/*
 * topAndPop the postfix machine stack; return the result.
 * If the stack is empty, print an error message.
 */
private long postfixPop( )
{
    if ( postfixStack.isEmpty( ) )
    {
        System.err.println( "Missing operand" );
        return 0;
    }
    return postfixStack.pop( );
}
```

figure 11.19

The `BinaryOp` routine for applying `topOp` to the postfix stack

```
/**
 * Process an operator by taking two items off the postfix
 * stack, applying the operator, and pushing the result.
 * Print error if missing closing parenthesis or division by 0.
 */
private void binaryOp( int topOp )
{
    if( topOp == OPAREN )
    {
        System.err.println( "Unbalanced parentheses" );
        opStack.pop( );
        return;
    }
    long rhs = postfixPop( );
    long lhs = postfixPop( );

    if( topOp == EXP )
        postfixStack.push( pow( lhs, rhs ) );
    else if( topOp == PLUS )
        postfixStack.push( lhs + rhs );
    else if( topOp == MINUS )
        postfixStack.push( lhs - rhs );
    else if( topOp == MULT )
        postfixStack.push( lhs * rhs );
    else if( topOp == DIV )
        if( rhs != 0 )
            postfixStack.push( lhs / rhs );
        else
        {
            System.err.println( "Division by zero" );
            postfixStack.push( lhs );
        }
    opStack.pop( );
}
```

We want to assign a number to each level of precedence. The higher the number, the higher is the precedence. We could assign the additive operators precedence 1, multiplicative operators precedence 3, exponentiation precedence 5, and parentheses precedence 99. However, we also need to take into account associativity. To do so, we assign each operator a number that represents its precedence when it is an input symbol and a second number that represents its precedence when it is on the operator stack. A left-associative operator has the operator stack precedence set at 1 higher than the input symbol precedence, and a right-associative operator goes the other way. Thus the precedence of the + operator on the stack is 2.

figure 11.20

Table of precedences used to evaluate an infix expression

```
private static final int EOL     = 0;
private static final int VALUE   = 1;
private static final int OPAREN  = 2;
private static final int CPAREN  = 3;
private static final int EXP     = 4;
private static final int MULT    = 5;
private static final int DIV     = 6;
private static final int PLUS    = 7;
private static final int MINUS   = 8;

private static class Precedence
{
    public int inputSymbol;
    public int topOfStack;

    public Precedence( int inSymbol, int topSymbol )
    {
        inputSymbol = inSymbol;
        topOfStack  = topSymbol;
    }
}

    // precTable matches order of Token enumeration
private static Precedence [ ] precTable =
{
    new Precedence(   0, -1 ),  // EOL
    new Precedence(   0,  0 ),  // VALUE
    new Precedence( 100,  0 ),  // OPAREN
    new Precedence(   0, 99 ),  // CPAREN
    new Precedence(   6,  5 ),  // EXP
    new Precedence(   3,  4 ),  // MULT
    new Precedence(   3,  4 ),  // DIV
    new Precedence(   1,  2 ),  // PLUS
    new Precedence(   1,  2 )  // MINUS
}
```

A consequence of this rule is that any two operators that have different precedences are still correctly ordered. However, if a + is on the operator stack and is also the input symbol, the operator on the top of the stack will appear to have higher precedence and thus will be popped. This is what we want for left-associative operators.

Similarly, if a ^ is on the operator stack and is also the input symbol, the operator on the top of the stack will appear to have lower precedence and thus it will not be popped. That is what we want for right-associative operators. The token VALUE never gets placed on the stack, so its precedence is meaningless. The end-of-line token is given lowest precedence because it is placed on the stack for use as a sentinel (which is done in the constructor). If we treat it as a right-associative operator, it is covered under the operator case.

The remaining method is `processToken`, which is shown in Figure 11.21. When we see an operand, we push it onto the postfix stack. When we see a closing parenthesis, we repeatedly pop and process the top operator on the operator stack until the opening parenthesis appears (lines 18–19). The opening parenthesis is then popped at line 21. (The test at line 20 is used to avoid popping the sentinel in the event of a missing opening parenthesis.) Other-

```
1     /**
2      * After a token is read, use operator precedence parsing
3      * algorithm to process it; missing opening parentheses
4      * are detected here.
5      */
6     private void processToken( Token lastToken )
7     {
8         int topOp;
9         int lastType = lastToken.getType( );
10
11        switch( lastType )
12        {
13          case VALUE:
14            postfixStack.push( lastToken.getValue( ) );
15            return;
16
17          case CPAREN:
18            while( ( topOp = opStack.peek( ) ) != OPAREN && topOp != EOL )
19                binaryOp( topOp );
20            if( topOp == OPAREN )
21                opStack.pop( );  // Get rid of opening parenthesis
22            else
23                System.err.println( "Missing open parenthesis" );
24            break;
25
26          default:    // General operator case
27            while( precTable[ lastType ].inputSymbol <=
28                     precTable[ topOp = opStack.peek( ) ].topOfStack )
29                binaryOp( topOp );
30            if( lastType != EOL )
31                opStack.push( lastType );
32            break;
33        }
34    }
```

figure 11.21

The `processToken` routine for processing `lastToken`, using the operator precedence parsing algorithm wise, we have the general operator case, which is succinctly described by the code in lines 27–31.

A simple `main` routine is given in Figure 11.22. It repeatedly reads a line of input, instantiates an `Evaluator` object, and computes its value.

11.2.4 expression trees

In an *expression tree,* the leaves contain operands and the other nodes contain operators.

Figure 11.23 shows an example of an *expression tree,* the leaves of which are operands (e.g., constants or variable names) and the other nodes contain operators. This particular tree happens to be binary because all the operations are binary. Although it is the simplest case, nodes can have more than two children. A node also may have only one child, as is the case with the unary minus operator.

figure 11.22

A simple `main` for evaluating expressions repeatedly

```
/**
 * Simple main to exercise Evaluator class.
 */
public static void main( String [ ] args )
{
    String str;
    BufferedReader in = new BufferedReader(
                             new InputStreamReader( System.in ) );

    try
    {
        System.out.println( "Enter expressions, 1 per line:" );
        while( ( str = in.readLine( ) ) != null )
        {
            System.out.println( "Read: " + str );
            Evaluator ev = new Evaluator( str );
            System.out.println( ev.getValue( ) );
            System.out.println( "Enter next expression:" );
        }
    }
    catch( IOException e ) { e.printStackTrace( ); }
}
```

figure 11.23

Expression tree for `(a+b)*(a-b)`

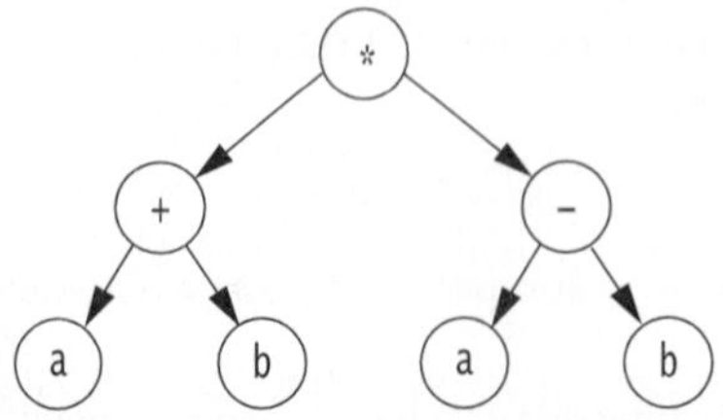

We evaluate an expression tree *T* by applying the operator at the root to the values obtained by recursively evaluating the left and right subtrees. In this example, the left subtree evaluates to `(a+b)` and the right subtree evaluates to `(a-b)`. The entire tree therefore represents `((a+b)*(a-b))`. We can produce an (overly parenthesized) infix expression by recursively producing a parenthesized left expression, printing out the operator at the root, and recursively producing a parenthesized right expression. This general strategy (left, node, right) is called an *inorder traversal.* This type of traversal is easy to remember because of the type of expression it produces.

A second strategy is to print the left subtree recursively, then the right subtree, and then the operator (without parentheses). Doing so, we obtain the postfix expression, so this strategy is called a *postorder traversal of the tree*. A third strategy for evaluating a tree results in a prefix expression. We discuss all these strategies in Chapter 18. The expression tree (and its generalizations) are useful data structures in compiler design because they allow us to see an entire expression. This capability makes code generation easier and in some cases greatly enhances optimization efforts.

Recursive printing of the expression tree can be used to obtain an infix, postfix, or prefix expression.

Of interest is the construction of an expression tree given an infix expression. As we have already shown, we can always convert an infix expression to a postfix expression, so we merely need to show how to construct an expression tree from a postfix expression. Not surprisingly, this procedure is simple. We maintain a stack of trees. When we see an operand, we create a single-node tree and push it onto our stack. When we see an operator, we pop and merge the top two trees on the stack. In the new tree, the node is the operator, the right child is the first tree popped from the stack, and the left child is the second tree popped. We then push the result back onto the stack. This algorithm is essentially the same as that used in a postfix evaluation, with tree creation replacing the binary operator computation.

Expression trees can be constructed from a postfix expression similar to postfix evaluation.

summary

In this chapter we examined two uses of stacks in programming language and compiler design. We demonstrated that, even though the stack is a simple structure, it is very powerful. Stacks can be used to decide whether a sequence of symbols is well balanced. The resulting algorithm requires linear time and, equally important, consists of a single sequential scan of the input. Operator precedence parsing is a technique that can be used to parse infix expressions. It, too, requires linear time and a single sequential scan. Two stacks are used in the operator precedence parsing algorithm. Although the stacks store different types of objects, the generic stack code allows the use of a single stack implementation for both types of objects.

key concepts

expression tree A tree in which the leaves contain operands and the other nodes contain operators. (414)

infix expression An expression in which a binary operator has arguments to its left and right. When there are several operators, precedence and associativity determine how the operators are processed. (400)

lexical analysis The process of recognizing tokens in a stream of symbols. (394)

operator precedence parsing An algorithm that converts an infix expression to a postfix expression in order to evaluate the infix expression. (403)

postfix expression An expression that can be evaluated by a postfix machine without using any precedence rules. (402)

postfix machine Machine used to evaluate a postfix expression. The algorithm it uses is as follows: Operands are pushed onto a stack and an operator pops its operands and then pushes the result. At the end of the evaluation, the stack should contain exactly one element, which represents the result. (402)

precedence table A table used to decide what is removed from the operator stack. Left-associative operators have the operator stack precedence set at 1 higher than the input symbol precedence. Right-associative operators go the other way. (409)

state machine A common technique used to parse symbols; at any point, the machine is in some state, and each input character takes it to a new state. Eventually, the state machine reaches a state at which a symbol has been recognized. (396)

tokenization The process of generating the sequence of symbols (tokens) from an input stream. (391)

common errors

1. In production code, input errors must be handled as carefully as possible. Being lax in this regard leads to programming errors.
2. For the balanced symbol routine, handling quotes incorrectly is a common error.
3. For the infix to postfix algorithm, the precedence table must reflect the correct precedence and associativity.

on the internet

Both application programs are available. You should probably download the balancing program; it may help you debug other Java programs.

Balance.java	Contains the balanced symbol program.
Tokenizer.java	Contains the `Tokenizer` class implementation for checking Java programs.
Evaluator.java	Contains the expression evaluator.

exercises

IN SHORT

11.1 Show the result of running the balanced symbol program on

a. `}`
b. `( }`
c. `[ [ [`
d. `) (`
e. `[ ) ]`

11.2 Show the postfix expression for

a. `1 + 2 - 3 ^ 4`
b. `1 ^ 2 - 3 * 4`
c. `1 + 2 * 3 - 4 ^ 5 + 6`
d. `( 1 + 2 ) * 3 - ( 4 ^ ( 5 - 6 ) )`

11.3 For the infix expression `a + b ^ c * d ^ e ^ f - g - h / ( i + j )`, do the following:

a. Show how the operator precedence parsing algorithm generates the corresponding postfix expression.
b. Show how a postfix machine evaluates the resulting postfix expression.
c. Draw the resulting expression tree.

IN THEORY

11.4 For the balanced symbol program, explain how to print out an error message that is likely to reflect the probable cause.

11.5 In general terms, explain how unary operators are incorporated into expression evaluators. Assume that the unary operators precede their operands and have high precedence. Include a description of how they are recognized by the state machine.

IN PRACTICE

11.6 Use of the ^ operator for exponentiation is likely to confuse Java programmers (because it is the bitwise exclusive-or operator). Rewrite the `Evaluator` class with ** as the exponentiation operator.

11.7 The infix evaluator accepts illegal expressions in which the operators are misplaced.

a. What will `1 2 3 + *` be evaluated as?
b. How can we detect these illegalities?
c. Modify the `Evaluator` class to do so.

PROGRAMMING PROJECTS

11.8 Modify the expression evaluator to handle negative input numbers.

11.9 For the balanced symbol checker, modify the `Tokenizer` class by adding a public method that can change the input stream. Then add a public method to `Balance` that allows `Balance` to change the source of the input stream.

11.10 Implement a complete Java expression evaluator. Handle all Java operators that can accept constants and make arithmetic sense (e.g., do not implement `[]`).

11.11 Implement a Java expression evaluator that includes variables. Assume that there are at most 26 variables—namely, `A` through `Z`—and that a variable can be assigned to by an `=` operator of low precedence.

11.12 Write a program that reads an infix expression and generates a postfix expression.

11.13 Write a program that reads a postfix expression and generates an infix expression.

references

The infix to postfix algorithm (*operator precedence parsing*) was first described in [3]. Two good books on compiler construction are [1] and [2].

1. A. V. Aho, R. Sethi, and J. D. Ullman, *Compiler Design: Principles, Techniques, and Tools,* Addison-Wesley, Reading, MA, 1986.
2. C. N. Fischer and R. J. LeBlanc, *Crafting a Compiler with C,* Benjamin Cummings, Redwood City, CA, 1991.
3. R. W. Floyd, "Syntactic Analysis and Operator Precedence," *Journal of the ACM* **10:3** (1963), 316–333.

chapter 12

utilities

In this chapter we discuss two utility applications of data structures: data compression and cross-referencing. Data compression is an important technique in computer science. It can be used to reduce the size of files stored on disk (in effect increasing the capacity of the disk) and also to increase the effective rate of transmission by modems (by transmitting less data). Virtually all newer modems perform some type of compression. Cross-referencing is a scanning and sorting technique that is done, for example, to make an index for a book.

In this chapter, we show

- An implementation of a file-compression algorithm called *Huffman's algorithm*
- An implementation of a cross-referencing program that lists, in sorted order, all identifiers in a program and gives the line numbers on which they occur

12.1 file compression

A standard encoding of C characters uses $\lceil \log C \rceil$ bits.

The ASCII character set consists of roughly 100 printable characters. To distinguish these characters, $\lceil \log 100 \rceil = 7$ bits are required. Seven bits allow the representation of 128 characters, so the ASCII character set adds some other "unprintable" characters. An eighth bit is added to allow parity checks. The important point, however, is that if the size of the character set is C, then $\lceil \log C \rceil$ bits are needed in a standard fixed-length encoding.

Suppose that you have a file that contains only the characters *a, e, i, s,* and *t,* blank spaces (*sp*), and newlines (*nl*). Suppose further that the file has 10 *a*'s, 15 *e*'s, 12 *i*'s, 3 *s*'s, 4 *t*'s, 13 blanks, and 1 newline. As Figure 12.1 shows, representing this file requires 174 bits because there are 58 characters and each character requires 3 bits.

Reducing the number of bits required for data representation is called *compression*, which actually consists of two phases: the encoding phase (compressing) and the decoding phase (uncompressing).

In real life, files can be quite large. Many very large files are the output of some program, and there is usually a big disparity between the most frequently and least frequently used characters. For instance, many large data files have an inordinately large number of digits, blanks, and newlines but few *q*'s and *x*'s.

In many situations reducing the size of a file is desirable. For instance, disk space is precious on virtually every machine, so decreasing the amount of space required for files increases the effective capacity of the disk. When data are being transmitted across phone lines by a modem, the effective rate of transmission is increased if the amount of data transmitted can be reduced. Reducing the number of bits required for data representation is called *compression,* which actually consists of two phases: the encoding phase (compression) and the decoding phase (uncompression). A simple strategy discussed in this chapter achieves 25 percent savings on some large files and as much as 50 or 60 percent savings on some large data files. Extensions provide somewhat better compression.

figure 12.1

A standard coding scheme

Character	Code	Frequency	Total Bits
a	000	10	30
e	001	15	45
i	010	12	36
s	011	3	9
t	100	4	12
sp	101	13	39
nl	110	1	3
Total			**174**

The general strategy is to allow the code length to vary from character to character and to ensure that frequently occurring characters have short codes. If all characters occur with the same or very similar frequency, you cannot expect any savings.

In a variable-length code, the most-frequent characters have the shortest representation.

12.1.1 prefix codes

The binary code presented in Figure 12.1 can be represented by the binary tree shown in Figure 12.2. In this data structure, called a *binary trie* (pronounced "try"), characters are stored only in leaf nodes; the representation of each character is found by starting at the root and recording the path, using a 0 to indicate the left branch and a 1 to indicate the right branch. For instance, *s* is reached by going left, then right, and finally right. This is encoded as 011. If character c_i is at depth d_i and occurs f_i times, the *cost* of the code is $\sum d_i f_i$.

In a *binary trie*, a left branch represents 0 and a right branch represents 1. The path to a node indicates its representation.

We can obtain a better code than the one given in Figure 12.2 by recognizing that *nl* is an only child. By placing it one level higher (replacing its parent), we obtain the new tree shown in Figure 12.3. This new tree has a cost of 173 but is still far from optimal.

Note that the tree in Figure 12.3 is a *full tree,* in which all nodes either are leaves or have two children. An optimal code always has this property; otherwise, as already shown, nodes with only one child could move up a level. If the characters are placed only at the leaves, any sequence of bits can always be decoded unambiguously.

In a *full tree*, all nodes either are leaves or have two children.

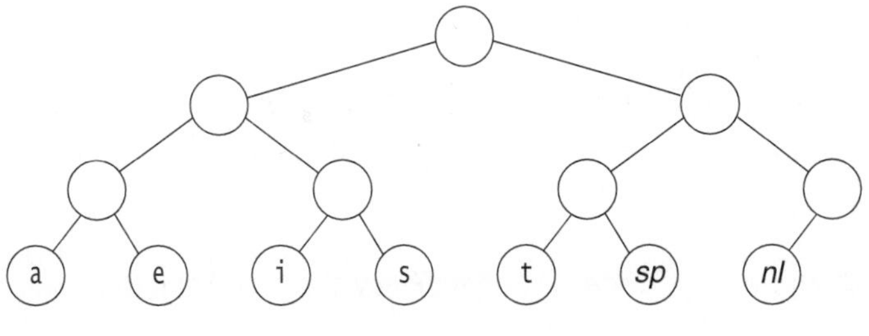

figure 12.2

Representation of the original code by a tree

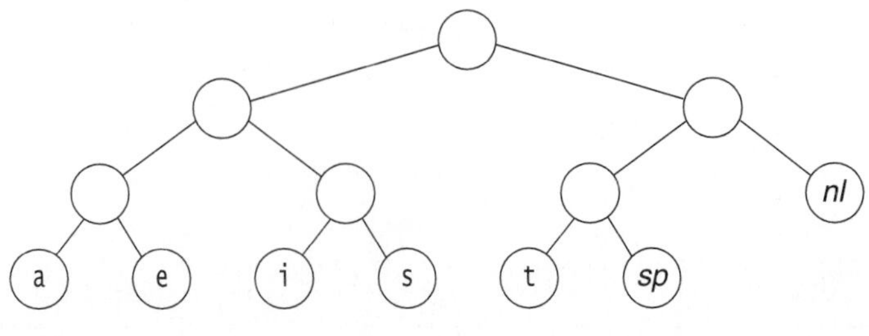

figure 12.3

A slightly better tree

For instance, suppose that the encoded string is 0100111100010110001000111. Figure 12.3 shows that 0 and 01 are not character codes but that 010 represents *i*, so the first character is *i*. Then 011 follows, which is an *s*. Then 11 follows, which is a newline (*nl*). The remainder of the code is *a, sp, t, i, e,* and *nl*.

In a *prefix code*, no character code is a prefix of another character code. This is guaranteed if the characters are only in leaves. A prefix code can be decoded unambiguously.

The character codes can be different lengths, as long as no character code is a prefix of another character code, an encoding called a *prefix code*. Conversely, if a character is contained in a nonleaf node, guaranteeing unambiguous decoding is no longer possible.

Thus our basic problem is to find the full binary tree of minimum cost (as defined previously) in which all characters are contained in the leaves. The tree shown in Figure 12.4 is optimal for our sample alphabet. As shown in Figure 12.5, this code requires only 146 bits. There are many optimal codes, which can be obtained by swapping children in the encoding tree.

figure 12.4

An optimal prefix code tree

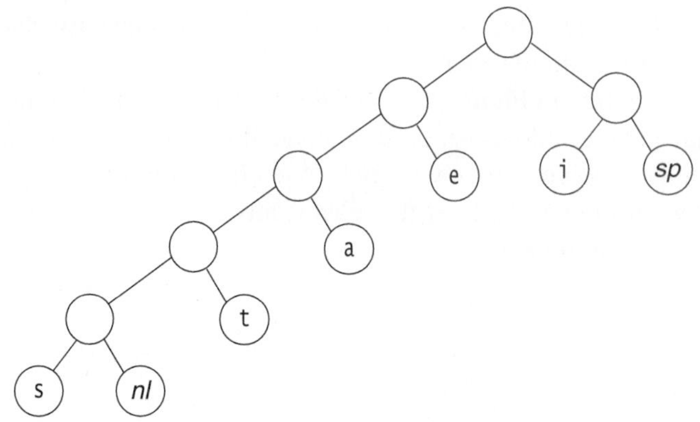

figure 12.5

Optimal prefix code

Character	Code	Frequency	Total Bits
a	001	10	30
e	01	15	30
i	10	12	24
s	00000	3	15
t	0001	4	16
sp	11	13	26
nl	00001	1	5
Total			146

12.1.2 huffman's algorithm

How is the coding tree constructed? The coding system algorithm was given by Huffman in 1952. Commonly called *Huffman's algorithm,* it constructs an optimal prefix code by repeatedly merging trees until the final tree is obtained.

Huffman's algorithm constructs an optimal prefix code. It works by repeatedly merging the two minimum-weight trees.

Throughout this section, the number of characters is C. In Huffman's algorithm we maintain a forest of trees. The *weight* of a tree is the sum of the frequencies of its leaves. $C - 1$ times, two trees, T_1 and T_2, of smallest weight are selected, breaking ties arbitrarily, and a new tree is formed with subtrees T_1 and T_2. At the beginning of the algorithm, there are C single-node trees (one for each character). At the end of the algorithm, there is one tree, giving an optimal Huffman tree. In Exercise 12.4 you are asked to prove Huffman's algorithm gives an optimal tree.

Ties are broken arbitrarily.

An example helps make operation of the algorithm clear. Figure 12.6 shows the initial forest; the weight of each tree is shown in small type at the root. The two trees of lowest weight are merged, creating the forest shown in Figure 12.7. The new root is *T1*. We made *s* the left child arbitrarily; any tie-breaking procedure can be used. The total weight of the new tree is just the sum of the weights of the old trees and can thus be easily computed.

Now there are six trees, and we again select the two trees of smallest weight, *T1* and *t*. They are merged into a new tree with root *T2* and weight 8, as shown in Figure 12.8. The third step merges *T2* and *a,* creating *T3*, with weight $10 + 8 = 18$. Figure 12.9 shows the result of this operation.

After completion of the third merge, the two trees of lowest weight are the single-node trees representing *i* and *sp.* Figure 12.10 shows how these trees are merged into the new tree with root *T4*. The fifth step is to merge the trees with roots *e* and *T3* because these trees have the two smallest weights, giving the result shown in Figure 12.11.

Finally, an optimal tree, shown previously in Figure 12.4, is obtained by merging the two remaining trees. Figure 12.12 shows the optimal tree, with root *T6*.

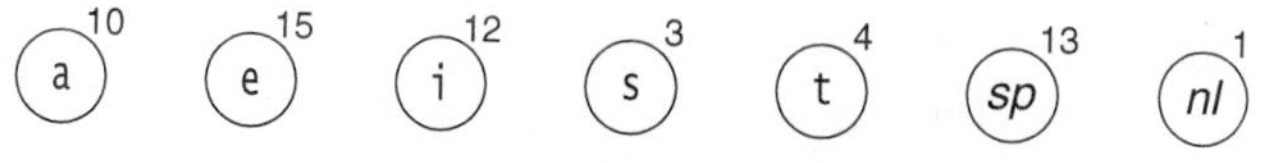

figure 12.6

Initial stage of Huffman's algorithm

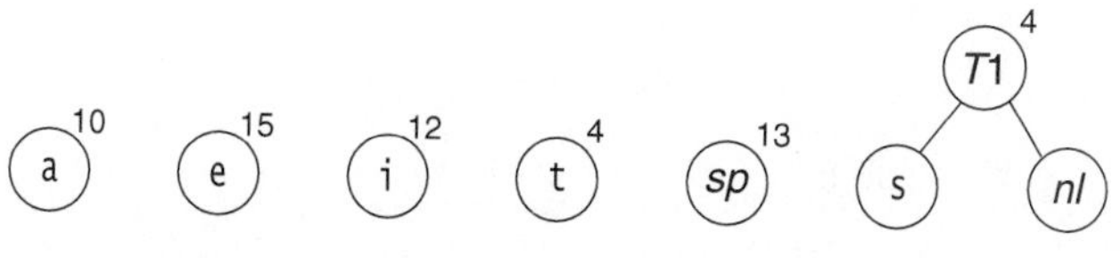

figure 12.7

Huffman's algorithm after the first merge

figure 12.8

Huffman's algorithm after the second merge

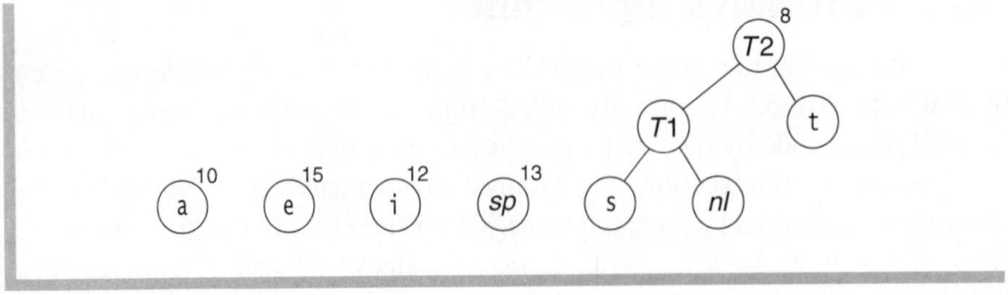

figure 12.9

Huffman's algorithm after the third merge

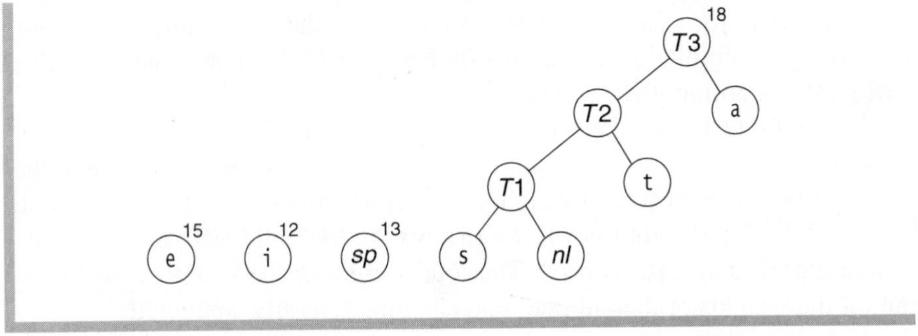

figure 12.10

Huffman's algorithm after the fourth merge

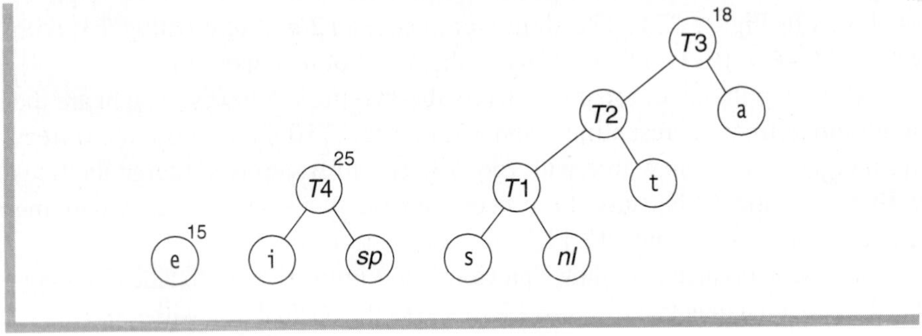

figure 12.11

Huffman's algorithm after the fifth merge

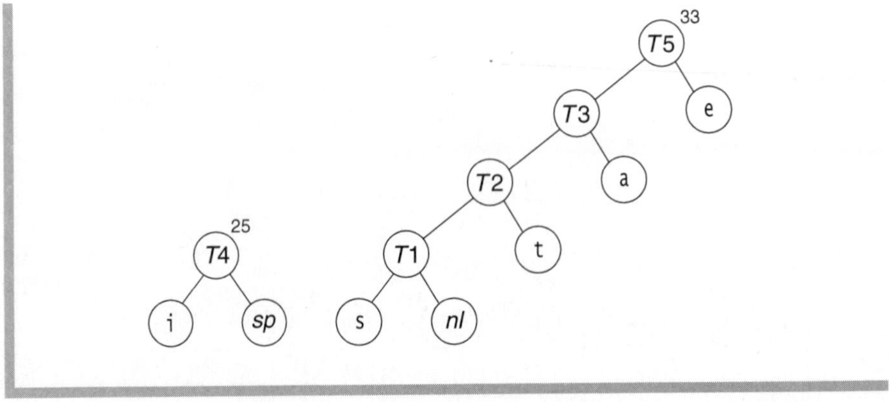

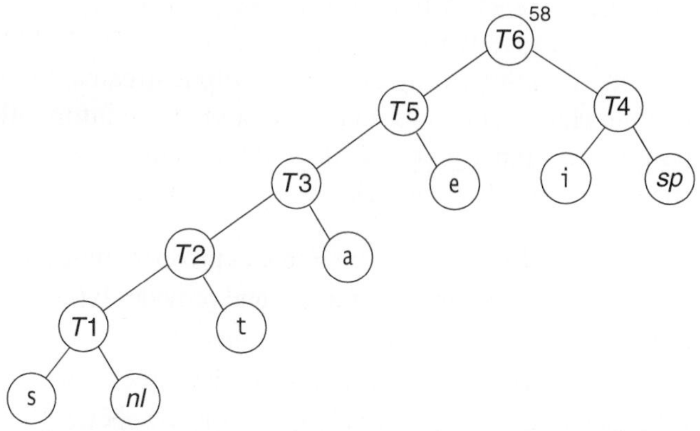

figure 12.12

Huffman's algorithm after the final merge

12.1.3 implementation

We now provide an implementation of the Huffman coding algorithm, without attempting to perform any significant optimizations; we simply want a working program that illustrates the basic algorithmic issues. After discussing the implementation we comment on possible enhancements. Although significant error checking needs to be added to the program, we have not done so because we did not want to obscure the basic ideas.

Figure 12.13 illustrates some of the I/O classes and constants to be used. We maintain a priority queue of tree nodes (recall that we are to select two trees of lowest weight).

```
import java.io.IOException;
import java.io.InputStream;
import java.io.OutputStream;
import java.io.FileInputStream;
import java.io.FileOutputStream;
import java.io.DataInputStream;
import java.io.DataOutputStream;
import java.io.BufferedInputStream;
import java.io.BufferedOutputStream;
import java.util.PriorityQueue;

interface BitUtils
{
    public static final int BITS_PER_BYTES = 8;
    public static final int DIFF_BYTES = 256;
    public static final int EOF = 256;
}
```

figure 12.13

The `import` directives and some constants used in the main compression program algorithms

In addition to the standard I/O classes, our program consists of several additional classes. Because we need to perform bit-at-a-time I/O, we write wrapper classes representing bit-input and bit-output streams. We write other classes to maintain character counts and create and return information about a Huffman coding tree. Finally, we write compression and uncompression stream wrappers. To summarize, the classes that we write are

`BitInputStream`	Wraps an `Inputstream` and provides bit-at-a-time input.
`BitOutputStream`	Wraps an `Outputstream` and provides bit-at-a-time output.
`CharCounter`	Maintains character counts.
`HuffmanTree`	Manipulates Huffman coding trees.
`HZIPInputStream`	Contains an uncompression wrapper.
`HZIPOutputStream`	Contains a compression wrapper.

bit-input and bit-output stream classes

The `BitInputStream` and `BitOutputStream` classes are similar and are shown in Figures 12.14 and 12.15, respectively. Both work by wrapping a stream. A reference to the stream is stored as a private data member. Every eighth `readBit` of the `BitInputStream` (or `writeBit` of the `BitOutputStream` classes) causes a `byte` to be read (or written) on the underlying stream. The `byte` is stored in a buffer, appropriately named `buffer`, and `bufferPos` provides an indication of how much of the buffer is unused.

The `getBit` and `setBit` methods are used to access an individual bit in an 8-bit `byte`; they work by using bit operations. (Appendix C describes the bit operators in more detail.) In `readBit`, we check at line 19 to find out whether the bits in the buffer have already been used. If so, we get 8 more bits at line 21 and reset the position indicator at line 24. Then we can call `getBit` at line 27.

The `BitOutputStream` class is similar to `BitInputStream`. One difference is that we provide a `flush` method because there may be bits left in the buffer at the end of a sequence of `writeBit` calls. The `flush` method is called when a call to `writeBit` fills the buffer and also is called by `close`.

Neither class performs error checking; instead they propagate any `IOExceptions`. Thus full error checking is available.

```
// BitInputStream class: Bit-input stream wrapper class.
//
// CONSTRUCTION: with an open InputStream.
//
// ******************PUBLIC OPERATIONS***********************
// int readBit( )              --> Read one bit as a 0 or 1
// void close( )               --> Close underlying stream

public class BitInputStream
{
    public BitInputStream( InputStream is )
    {
        in = is;
        bufferPos = BitUtils.BITS_PER_BYTES;
    }

    public int readBit( ) throws IOException
    {
        if( bufferPos == BitUtils.BITS_PER_BYTES )
        {
            buffer = in.read( );
            if( buffer == -1 )
                return -1;
            bufferPos = 0;
        }

        return getBit( buffer, bufferPos++ );
    }

    public void close( ) throws IOException
    {
        in.close( );
    }

    private static int getBit( int pack, int pos )
    {
        return ( pack & ( 1 << pos ) ) != 0 ? 1 : 0;
    }

    private InputStream in;
    private int buffer;
    private int bufferPos;
}
```

figure 12.14

The `BitInputStream` class

figure 12.15

The `BitOutputStream` class

```
// BitOutputStream class: Bit-output stream wrapper class.
//
// CONSTRUCTION: with an open OutputStream.
//
// ******************PUBLIC OPERATIONS***********************
// void writeBit( val )          --> Write one bit (0 or 1)
// void writeBits( vals )        --> Write array of bits
// void flush( )                 --> Flush buffered bits
// void close( )                 --> Close underlying stream

public class BitOutputStream
{
    public BitOutputStream( OutputStream os )
      { bufferPos = 0; buffer = 0; out = os; }

    public void writeBit( int val ) throws IOException
    {
        buffer = setBit( buffer, bufferPos++, val );
        if( bufferPos == BitUtils.BITS_PER_BYTES )
            flush( );
    }

    public void writeBits( int [ ] val ) throws IOException
    {
        for( int i = 0; i < val.length; i++ )
            writeBit( val[ i ] );
    }

    public void flush( ) throws IOException
    {
        if( bufferPos == 0 )
            return;
        out.write( buffer );
        bufferPos = 0;
        buffer = 0;
    }

    public void close( ) throws IOException
      { flush( ); out.close( ); }

    private int setBit( int pack, int pos, int val )
    {
        if( val == 1 )
            pack |= ( val << pos );
        return pack;
    }

    private OutputStream out;
    private int buffer;
    private int bufferPos;
}
```

the character-counting class

Figure 12.16 provides the `CharCounter` class, which is used to obtain the character counts in an input stream (typically a file). Alternatively, the character counts can be set manually and then obtained later. (Implicitly, we are treating eight-bit `bytes` as ASCII characters for this program.)

the huffman tree class

The tree is maintained as a collection of nodes. Each node has links to its left child, right child, and parent (in Chapter 18 we discuss the implementation of trees in detail). The node declaration is shown in Figure 12.17.

The `HuffmanTree` class skeleton is provided in Figure 12.18. We can create a `HuffmanTree` object by providing a `CharCounter` object, in which case the tree is built immediately. Alternatively, it can be created without a `CharCounter` object. In that case, the character counts are read by a subsequent call to `readEncodingTable`, and at that point the tree is built.

figure 12.16

The `CharCounter` class

```
// CharCounter class: A character counting class.
//
// CONSTRUCTION: with no parameters or an open InputStream.
//
// ******************PUBLIC OPERATIONS***********************
// int getCount( ch )          --> Return # occurrences of ch
// void setCount( ch, count )  --> Set # occurrences of ch
// ******************ERRORS**********************************
// No error checks.

class CharCounter
{
    public CharCounter( )
      { }

    public CharCounter( InputStream input ) throws IOException
    {
        int ch;
        while( ( ch = input.read( ) ) != -1 )
            theCounts[ ch ]++;
    }

    public int getCount( int ch )
      { return theCounts[ ch & 0xff ]; }

    public void setCount( int ch, int count )
      { theCounts[ ch & 0xff ] = count; }

    private int [ ] theCounts = new int[ BitUtils.DIFF_BYTES ];
}
```

figure 12.17

Node declaration for the Huffman coding tree

```
// Basic node in a Huffman coding tree.
class HuffNode implements Comparable<HuffNode>
{
    public int value;
    public int weight;

    public int compareTo( HuffNode rhs )
    {
        return weight - rhs.weight;
    }

    HuffNode left;
    HuffNode right;
    HuffNode parent;

    HuffNode( int v, int w, HuffNode lt, HuffNode rt, HuffNode pt )
      { value = v; weight = w; left = lt; right = rt; parent = pt; }
}
```

The `HuffmanTree` class provides the `writeEncodingTable` method to write the tree out to an output stream (in a form suitable for a call to `readEncodingTable`). It also provides public methods to convert from a character to a code, and vice versa.[1] Codes are represented by an `int[]` or `String`, as appropriate, in which each element is either a 0 or 1.

Internally, `root` is a reference to the root node of the tree, and `theCounts` is a `CharCounter` object that can be used to initialize the tree nodes. We also maintain an array, `theNodes`, which maps each character to the tree node that contains it.

Figure 12.19 shows the constructors and the routine (public method and private helper) to return the code for a given character. The constructors start with empty trees, and the one-parameter constructor initializes the `CharCounter` object, and immediately calls the private routine `createTree`. The `CharCounter` object is initialized to be empty in the zero-parameter constructor.

For `getCode`, by consulting `theNodes`, we obtain the tree node that stores the character whose code we are looking for. If the character is not represented, we signal an error by returning a `null` reference. Otherwise we use a straightforward loop up the tree, following parent links, until we reach the root (which has no parent). Each step prepends a 0 or 1 to a string, which is converted to an array of `int` prior to returning (of course, this creates many temporary strings; we leave it to the reader to optimize this step).

1. Technical alert: An `int` is used instead of `byte` to allow all characters and the `EOF` symbol.

```
// Huffman tree class interface: manipulate Huffman coding tree.
//
// CONSTRUCTION: with no parameters or a CharCounter object.
//
// ******************PUBLIC OPERATIONS***********************
// int [ ] getCode( ch )         --> Return code given character
// int getChar( code )           --> Return character given code
// void writeEncodingTable( out ) --> Write coding table to out
// void readEncodingTable( in ) --> Read encoding table from in
// ******************ERRORS*********************************
// Error check for illegal code.

class HuffmanTree
{
    public HuffmanTree( )
      { /* Figure 12.19 */ }
    public HuffmanTree( CharCounter cc )
      { /* Figure 12.19 */ }

    public static final int ERROR = -3;
    public static final int INCOMPLETE_CODE = -2;
    public static final int END = BitUtils.DIFF_BYTES;

    public int [ ] getCode( int ch )
      { /* Figure 12.19 */ }
    public int getChar( String code )
      { /* Figure 12.20 */ }

      // Write the encoding table using character counts
    public void writeEncodingTable( DataOutputStream out ) throws IOException
      { /* Figure 12.21 */ }
    public void readEncodingTable( DataInputStream in ) throws IOException
      { /* Figure 12.21 */ }

    private CharCounter theCounts;
    private HuffNode [ ] theNodes = new HuffNode[ BitUtils.DIFF_BYTES + 1 ];
    private HuffNode root;

    private void createTree( )
      { /* Figure 12.22 */ }
}
```

figure 12.18

The `HuffmanTree` class skeleton

figure 12.19

Some of the Huffman tree methods, including constructors and the routine for returning a code for a given character

```
public HuffmanTree( )
{
    theCounts = new CharCounter( );
    root = null;
}

public HuffmanTree( CharCounter cc )
{
    theCounts = cc;
    root = null;
    createTree( );
}

/**
 * Return the code corresponding to character ch.
 * (The parameter is an int to accommodate EOF).
 * If code is not found, return an array of length 0.
 */
public int [ ] getCode( int ch )
{
    HuffNode current = theNodes[ ch ];
    if( current == null )
        return null;

    String v = "";
    HuffNode par = current.parent;

    while ( par != null )
    {
        if( par.left == current )
            v = "0" + v;
        else
            v = "1" + v;
        current = current.parent;
        par = current.parent;
    }

    int [ ] result = new int[ v.length( ) ];
    for( int i = 0; i < result.length; i++ )
        result[ i ] = v.charAt( i ) == '0' ? 0 : 1;

    return result;
}
```

The `getChar` method shown in Figure 12.20 is simpler: We start at the root and branch left or right, as directed by the code. Reaching `null` prematurely generates an error. Otherwise, we return the value stored in the node (which for nonleaf nodes turns out to be the symbol `INCOMPLETE`).

In Figure 12.21 we have routines to read and write the encoding table. The format that we use is simple and is not necessarily the most space-efficient. For each character that has a code, we write it out (using one byte) and then write out its character count (using four bytes). We signal the end of the table by writing out an extra entry containing a null terminator character `'\0'` with a count of zero. The count of zero is the special signal.

The `readEncodingTable` method initializes all the character counts to zero and then reads the table, and updates the counts as they are read. It calls `createTree`, shown in Figure 12.22, to build the Huffman tree.

In that routine, we maintain a priority queue of tree nodes. To do so we must provide a comparison function for tree nodes. Recall from Figure 12.17 that `HuffNode` implements `Comparable<HuffNode>`, ordering `HuffNode` objects on the basis of node weight.

We then search for characters that have appeared at least once. When the test at line 9 succeeds, we have such a character. We create a new tree node at lines 11 and 12, add it to `theNodes` at line 13, and then add it to the priority queue at line 14. At lines 17 and 18 we add the end-of-file symbol. The loop that extends from lines 20 to 28 is a line-for-line translation of the tree construction algorithm. While we have two or more trees, we extract two trees from the priority queue, merge the result, and put it back in the priority queue. At the end of the loop, only one tree is left in the priority queue, and we can extract it and set `root`.

```java
    /**
     * Get the character corresponding to code.
     */
    public int getChar( String code )
    {
        HuffNode p = root;
        for( int i = 0; p != null && i < code.length( ); i++ )
            if( code.charAt( i ) == '0' )
                p = p.left;
            else
                p = p.right;

        if( p == null )
            return ERROR;

        return p.value;
    }
```

figure 12.20

A routine for decoding (generating a character, given the code)

```
/**
 * Writes an encoding table to an output stream.
 * Format is character, count (as bytes).
 * A zero count terminates the encoding table.
 */
public void writeEncodingTable( DataOutputStream out ) throws IOException
{
    for( int i = 0; i < BitUtils.DIFF_BYTES; i++ )
    {
        if( theCounts.getCount( i ) > 0 )
        {
            out.writeByte( i );
            out.writeInt( theCounts.getCount( i ) );
        }
    }
    out.writeByte( 0 );
    out.writeInt( 0 );
}

/**
 * Read the encoding table from an input stream in format
 * given and then construct the Huffman tree.
 * Stream will then be positioned to read compressed data.
 */
public void readEncodingTable( DataInputStream in ) throws IOException
{
    for( int i = 0; i < BitUtils.DIFF_BYTES; i++ )
        theCounts.setCount( i, 0 );

    int ch;
    int num;

    for( ; ; )
    {
        ch = in.readByte( );
        num = in.readInt( );
        if( num == 0 )
            break;
        theCounts.setCount( ch, num );
    }

    createTree( );
}
```

figure 12.21

Routines for reading and writing encoding tables

```java
    /**
     * Construct the Huffman coding tree.
     */
    private void createTree( )
    {
        PriorityQueue<HuffNode> pq = new PriorityQueue<HuffNode>( );

        for( int i = 0; i < BitUtils.DIFF_BYTES; i++ )
            if( theCounts.getCount( i ) > 0 )
            {
                HuffNode newNode = new HuffNode( i,
                           theCounts.getCount( i ), null, null, null );
                theNodes[ i ] =  newNode;
                pq.add( newNode );
            }

        theNodes[ END ] = new HuffNode( END, 1, null, null, null );
        pq.add( theNodes[ END ] );

        while( pq.size( ) > 1 )
        {
            HuffNode n1 = pq.remove( );
            HuffNode n2 = pq.remove( );
            HuffNode result = new HuffNode( INCOMPLETE_CODE,
                                  n1.weight + n2.weight, n1, n2, null );
            n1.parent = n2.parent = result;
            pq.add( result );
        }

        root = pq.element( );
    }
```

figure 12.22

A routine for constructing the Huffman coding tree

The tree produced by `createTree` is dependent on how the priority queue breaks ties. Unfortunately, this means that if the program is compiled on two different machines, with two different priority queue implementations, it is possible to compress a file on the first machine, and then be unable to obtain the original when attempting to uncompress on the second machine. Avoiding this problem requires some additional work.

compression stream classes

All that is left to do is to write a compression and uncompression stream wrapper and then a `main` that calls them. We repeat our earlier disclaimer about skimping on error checking so that we can illustrate the basic algorithmic ideas.

The `HZIPOutputStream` class is shown in Figure 12.23. The constructor initiates a `DataOutputStream`, on which we can write the compressed stream. We also maintain a `ByteArrayOutputStream`. Each call to `write` appends onto the `ByteArrayOutputStream`. When `close` is called, the actual compressed stream is written.

The `close` routine extracts all the `bytes` that have been stored in the `ByteArrayOutputStream` for reading at line 26. It then constructs a `CharCounter` object at line 29 and a `HuffmanTree` object at line 32. Since `CharCounter` needs an `InputStream`, we construct a `ByteArrayInputStream` from the array of bytes that were just extracted. At line 33 we write out the encoding table.

At this point we are ready to do the main encoding. We create a bit-output stream object at line 35. The rest of the algorithm repeatedly gets a character and writes its code (line 38). There is a tricky piece of code at line 38: The `int` passed to `getCode` may be confused with `EOF` if we simply use the byte because the high bit can be interpreted as a sign bit. Thus we use a bit mask. When we exit the loop, we have reached the end of file, so we write out the end-of-file code at line 39. The `BitOutputStream` `close` flushes any remaining bits to the output file, so an explicit call to `flush` is not needed.

The `HZIPInputStream` class is next, in Figure 12.24. The constructor creates a `DataInputStream` and constructs a `HuffmanTree` object by reading the encoding table (lines 15 and 16) from the compressed stream. We then create a bit-input stream at line 18. The dirty work is done in the `read` method.

The `bits` object, declared at line 23, represents the (Huffman) code that we are currently examining. Each time we read a bit at line 29, we add the bit to the end of the Huffman code (at line 33). We then look up the Huffman code at line 34. If it is incomplete, we continue the loop (lines 35 and 36). If there is an illegal Huffman code, we throw an `IOException` (lines 37 to 38). If we reach the end-of-file code, we return –1, as is standard for `read` (lines 39 and 40); otherwise, we have a match, so we return the character that matches the Huffman code (line 42).

```
import java.io.IOException;
import java.io.OutputStream;
import java.io.DataOutputStream;
import java.io.ByteArrayInputStream;
import java.io.ByteArrayOutputStream;

/**
 * Writes to HZIPOutputStream are compressed and
 * sent to the output stream being wrapped.
 * No writing is actually done until close.
 */
public class HZIPOutputStream extends OutputStream
{
    public HZIPOutputStream( OutputStream out ) throws IOException
    {
        dout = new DataOutputStream( out );
    }

    public void write( int ch ) throws IOException
    {
        byteOut.write( ch );
    }

    public void close( ) throws IOException
    {
        byte [ ] theInput = byteOut.toByteArray( );
        ByteArrayInputStream byteIn = new ByteArrayInputStream( theInput );

        CharCounter countObj = new CharCounter( byteIn );
        byteIn.close( );

        HuffmanTree codeTree = new HuffmanTree( countObj );
        codeTree.writeEncodingTable( dout );

        BitOutputStream bout = new BitOutputStream( dout );

        for( int i = 0; i < theInput.length; i++ )
            bout.writeBits( codeTree.getCode( theInput[ i ] & 0xff ) );
        bout.writeBits( codeTree.getCode( BitUtils.EOF ) );

        bout.close( );
        byteOut.close( );
    }

    private ByteArrayOutputStream byteOut = new ByteArrayOutputStream( );
    private DataOutputStream dout;
}
```

figure 12.23

The `HZIPOutputStream` class

figure 12.24

The HZIPInputStream class

```
import java.io.IOException;
import java.io.InputStream;
import java.io.DataInputStream;

/**
 * HZIPInputStream wraps an input stream. read returns an
 * uncompressed byte from the wrapped input stream.
 */
public class HZIPInputStream extends InputStream
{
    public HZIPInputStream( InputStream in ) throws IOException
    {
        DataInputStream din = new DataInputStream( in );

        codeTree = new HuffmanTree( );
        codeTree.readEncodingTable( din );

        bin = new BitInputStream( in );
    }

    public int read( ) throws IOException
    {
        String bits = "";
        int bit;
        int decode;

        while( true )
        {
            bit = bin.readBit( );
            if( bit == -1 )
                throw new IOException( "Unexpected EOF" );

            bits += bit;
            decode = codeTree.getChar( bits );
            if( decode == HuffmanTree.INCOMPLETE_CODE )
                continue;
            else if( decode == HuffmanTree.ERROR )
                throw new IOException( "Decoding error" );
            else if( decode == HuffmanTree.END )
                return -1;
            else
                return decode;
        }
    }

    public void close( ) throws IOException
      { bin.close( ); }

    private BitInputStream bin;
    private HuffmanTree codeTree;
}
```

the `main` routine

The `main` routine is shown in the online code. If invoked with the `-c` argument, it compresses; with the `-u` argument it uncompresses. Figure 12.25 illustrates the wrapping of streams for compression and uncompression. Compression adds a "`.huf`" to the filename; uncompression adds a "`.uc`" to the filename, to avoid clobbering original files.

improving the program

The program, as written, serves its main purpose of illustrating the basics of the Huffman coding algorithm. It achieves some compression, even on moderately sized files. For instance, it obtains roughly 40 percent compression when run on its own source file, `Hzip.java`. However, the program could be improved in several ways.

1. The error checking is limited. A production program should rigorously ensure that the file being decompressed is actually a compressed file. (One way to have it do so is to write extra information in the encoding table.) The internal routines should have more checks.
2. Little effort has been made to minimize the size of the encoding table. For large files this lack is of little consequence, but for smaller files a large encoding table can be unacceptable because the encoding table takes up space itself.
3. A robust program checks the size of the resulting compressed file and aborts if the size is larger than the original.
4. In many places we made little attempt to optimize for speed. Memoization could be used to avoid repeated searching of the tree for codes.

Further improvements to the program are left for you to do as Exercises 12.11–12.13.

```java
class Hzip
{
    public static void compress( String inFile ) throws IOException
    {
        String compressedFile = inFile + ".huf";
        InputStream in = new BufferedInputStream(
                         new FileInputStream( inFile ) );
        OutputStream fout = new BufferedOutputStream(
                            new FileOutputStream( compressedFile ) );
        HZIPOutputStream hzout = new HZIPOutputStream( fout );
        int ch;
        while( ( ch = in.read( ) ) != -1 )
            hzout.write( ch );
        in.close( );
        hzout.close( );
    }

    public static void uncompress( String compressedFile ) throws IOException
    {
        String inFile;
        String extension;

        inFile = compressedFile.substring( 0, compressedFile.length( ) - 4 );
        extension = compressedFile.substring( compressedFile.length( ) - 4 );

        if( !extension.equals( ".huf" ) )
        {
            System.out.println( "Not a compressed file!" );
            return;
        }

        inFile += ".uc";    // for debugging, to not clobber original
        InputStream fin = new BufferedInputStream(
                          new FileInputStream( compressedFile ) );
        DataInputStream in = new DataInputStream( fin );
        HZIPInputStream hzin = new HZIPInputStream( in );

        OutputStream fout = new BufferedOutputStream(
                            new FileOutputStream( inFile ) );
        int ch;
        while( ( ch = hzin.read( ) ) != -1 )
            fout.write( ch );

        hzin.close( );
        fout.close( );
    }
}
```

figure 12.25

A simple `main` for file compression and uncompression

12.2 a cross-reference generator

In this section, we design a program called a *cross-reference generator* that scans a Java source file, sorts the identifiers, and outputs all the identifiers, along with the line numbers on which they occur. One compiler application is to list, for each method, the names of all other methods that it directly calls.

A *cross-reference generator* lists identifiers and their line numbers. It is a common application because it is similar to creating an index.

However, this is a general problem that occurs in many other contexts. For instance, it can be used to generalize the creation of an index for a book. Another use, spell checking, is described in Exercise 12.17. As a spelling checker detects misspelled words in a document, those words are gathered, along with the lines on which they occur. This process avoids repeatedly printing out the same misspelled word and indicates where the errors are.

12.2.1 basic ideas

Our main algorithmic idea is to use a map to store each identifier and the line numbers on which it occurs. In the map, the identifier is the key, and the list of line numbers is the value. After the source file has been read and the map built, we can iterate over the collection, outputting identifiers and their corresponding line numbers.

We use a map to store identifiers and their line numbers. We store the line numbers for each identifier in a list.

12.2.2 java implementation

The `Xref` class skeleton is shown in Figure 12.26. It is similar to (but simpler than) the `Balance` class shown in Figure 11.3, which was part of a balanced symbol program. Like that class, it makes use of the `Tokenizer` class defined in Figure 11.2.

We can now discuss the implementation of the two remaining routines in the `Tokenizer` class: `getNextID` and `getRemainingString`. These new parsing routines deal with recognizing an identifier.

The routine shown in Figure 12.27 tests whether a character is part of an identifier. In the `getRemainingString` routine shown in Figure 12.28 we assume that the first character of an identifier has already been read and is stored in the `Tokenizer` class data member `ch`. It repeatedly reads characters until one that is not part of an identifier appears. At that point we put the character back (at line 12) and then return a `String`.

The parsing routines are straightforward, though as usual they require some effort.

figure 12.26

The Xref class skeleton

```
import java.io.InputStreamReader;
import java.io.IOException;
import java.io.FileReader;
import java.io.Reader;
import java.util.Set
import java.util.TreeMap;
import java.util.List;
import java.util.ArrayList;
import java.util.Iterator;
import java.util.Map;

// Xref class interface: generate cross-reference
//
// CONSTRUCTION: with a Reader object
//
// ******************PUBLIC OPERATIONS***********************
// void generateCrossReference( ) --> Name says it all ...
// ******************ERRORS**********************************
// Error checking on comments and quotes is performed

public class Xref
{
    public Xref( Reader inStream )
      { tok = new Tokenizer( inStream ); }

    public void generateCrossReference( )
      { /* Figure 12.30 */ }

    private Tokenizer tok;    // tokenizer object
}
```

figure 12.27

A routine for testing whether a character could be part of an identifier

```
    /**
     * Return true if ch can be part of a Java identifier
     */
    private static final boolean isIdChar( char ch )
    {
        return Character.isJavaIdentifierPart( ch );
    }
```

The `getNextID` routine shown in Figure 12.29 is similar to the routine shown in Figure 11.7. The difference is that here at line 17, if the first character of an identifier is encountered, we call `getRemainingString` to return the

```java
/**
 * Return an identifier read from input stream
 * First character is already read into ch
 */
private String getRemainingString( )
{
    String result = "" + ch;

    for( ; nextChar( ); result += ch )
        if( !isIdChar( ch ) )
        {
            putBackChar( );
            break;
        }

    return result;
}
```

figure 12.28

A routine for returning a `String` from input

```java
/**
 * Return next identifier, skipping comments
 * string constants, and character constants.
 * Place identifier in currentIdNode.word and return false
 * only if end of stream is reached.
 */
public String getNextID( )
{
    while( nextChar( ) )
    {
        if( ch == '/' )
            processSlash( );
        else if( ch == '\\' )
            nextChar( );
        else if( ch == '\'' || ch == '"' )
            skipQuote( ch );
        else if( !Character.isDigit( ch ) && isIdChar( ch ) )
            return getRemainingString( );
    }
    return null;       // End of file
}
```

figure 12.29

A routine for returning the next identifier

token. The fact that `getNextID` and `getNextOpenClose` are so similar suggests that it would have been worthwhile to write a private member function that performs their common tasks.

With all the supporting routines written, let us consider the only method, `generateCrossReference`, shown in Figure 12.30. Lines 6 and 7 create an empty map. We read the input and build the map at lines 11–20. At each iteration, we

```
1   /**
2    * Output the cross reference
3    */
4   public void generateCrossReference( )
5   {
6       Map<String,List<Integer>> theIdentifiers =
7                               new TreeMap<String,List<Integer>>( );
8       String current;
9
10          // Insert identifiers into the search tree
11      while( ( current = tok.getNextID( ) ) != null )
12      {
13          List<Integer> lines = theIdentifiers.get( current );
14          if( lines == null )
15          {
16              lines = new ArrayList<Integer>( );
17              theIdentifiers.put( current, lines );
18          }
19          lines.add( tok.getLineNumber( ) );
20      }
21
22          // Iterate through search tree and output
23          // identifiers and their line number
24      Set entries = theIdentifiers.entrySet( );
25      for( Map.Entry<String,List<Integer>> thisNode : entries )
26      {
27          Iterator<Integer> lineItr = thisNode.getValue( ).iterator( );
28
29              // Print identifier and first line where it occurs
30          System.out.print( thisNode.getKey( ) + ": " );
31          System.out.print( lineItr.next( ) );
32
33              // Print all other lines on which it occurs
34          while( lineItr.hasNext( ) )
35              System.out.print( ", " + lineItr.next( ) );
36          System.out.println( );
37      }
38  }
```

figure 12.30

The main cross-reference algorithm

have the current identifier. Let us see how the loop body works. There are two cases:

1. The current identifier is in the map. In this case, lines gives a reference to the List of line numbers, and the new line number is added to the end of the List.
2. The current identifier is not in the map. In this case, lines 16 and 17 add current to the map with an empty List. Thus the call to add appends the new line number to the list, and as a result, the List contains the single line number, as desired.

The output is obtained by using a map traversal and an enhanced for loop on the entry set. A list iterator is used to get the line numbers.

Once we have built the map, we merely iterate through it by using an enhanced for loop on the underlying entry set. The map is visited in key-sorted order because the map is a TreeMap. Each time a map entry appears, we need to print out information for the identifier currently being examined by the map iterator.

Recall that an entry set iterator looks at Map.Entrys; in Map.Entry, the key is given by the method getKey, and the value is given by the method getValue. Thus the identifier being scanned is given by thisNode.getKey( ), as shown at line 30. To access individual lines, we need a list iterator; the iterator at line 27 refers to the line numbers of the current entry.

We print the word and the first line number at lines 30 and 31 (we are guaranteed that the list is not empty). Then, so long as we have not reached the end of the list, we repeatedly output line numbers in the loop that extends from line 34 to 35. We print out a newline at line 36. We do not provide a main program here because it is essentially the same as that shown in Figure 11.10.

summary

In this chapter we presented implementations of two important utilities: text compression and cross-referencing. Text compression is an important technique that allows us to increase both effective disk capacity and effective modem speed. It is an area of active research. The simple method described here—namely, Huffman's algorithm—typically achieves compression of 25 percent on text files. Other algorithms and extensions of Huffman's algorithm perform better. Cross-referencing is a general approach that has many applications.

key concepts

binary trie A data structure in which a left branch represents 0 and a right branch represents 1. The path to a node indicates its representation. (421)

compression The act of reducing the number of bits required for data representation, which actually has two phases: the encoding phase (compression) and the decoding phase (uncompression). (420)

cross-reference generator A program that lists identifiers and their line numbers. It is a common application because it is similar to creating an index. (441)

full tree A tree whose nodes either are leaves or have two children. (421)

Huffman's algorithm An algorithm that constructs an optimal prefix code by repeatedly merging the two minimum weight trees. (423)

prefix code Code in which no character code is a prefix of another character code. This condition is guaranteed in a trie if the characters are only in leaves. A prefix code can be decoded unambiguously. (421)

common errors

1. When working with character I/O, you often need to use an `int` to store the characters because of the additional `EOF` symbol. There are several other tricky coding issues.
2. Using too much memory to store the compression table is a common mistake. Doing so limits the amount of compression that can be achieved.

on the internet

The compression program and cross-reference generator is available.

Hzip.java Contains the source for the Huffman coding compression and uncompression program. See also **HZIPInputStream.java**, **HZIPOutputStream.java**, and **Tokenizer.java**.

Xref.java Contains the source for the cross-reference generator.

exercises

IN SHORT

12.1 Show the Huffman tree that results from the following distribution of punctuation characters and digits: colon (100), space (605), newline (100), comma (705), 0 (431), 1 (242), 2 (176), 3 (59), 4 (185), 5 (250), 6 (174), 7 (199), 8 (205), and 9 (217).

12.2 Most systems come with a compression program. Compress several types of files to determine the typical compression rate on your system. How large do the files have to be to make compression worthwhile? Compare their performance with the Huffman coding program (`Hzip`) provided in the online source code.

12.3 What happens if a file compressed with Huffman's algorithm is used to transmit data over a phone line and a single bit is accidentally lost? What can be done in this situation?

IN THEORY

12.4 Prove the correctness of Huffman's algorithm by expanding the following steps.

a. Show that no node has only one child.
b. Show that the two least frequent characters must be the two deepest nodes in the tree.
c. Show that the characters in any two nodes at the same depth can be swapped without affecting optimality.
d. Use induction: As trees are merged, consider the new character set to be the characters in the tree roots.

12.5 Under what circumstances could a Huffman tree of ASCII characters generate a 2-bit code for some character? Under what circumstances could it generate a 20-bit code?

12.6 Show that, if the symbols have already been sorted by frequency, Huffman's algorithm can be implemented in linear time.

12.7 Huffman's algorithm occasionally generates compressed files that are not smaller than the original. Prove that all compression algorithms must have this property (i.e., no matter what compression algorithm you design, some input files must always exist for which the algorithm generates compressed files that are not smaller than the originals).

IN PRACTICE

12.8 In the cross-reference generator, store the line numbers in a `LinkedList` instead of an `ArrayList` and compare performance.

12.9 If a word occurs twice on a line, the cross-reference generator will list it twice. Modify the algorithm so that duplicates are only listed once.

12.10 Modify the algorithm so that, if a word appears on consecutive lines, a range is indicated. For example,

```
if: 2, 4, 6-9, 11
```

PROGRAMMING PROJECTS

12.11 Storing the character counts in the encoding table gives the uncompression algorithm the ability to perform extra consistency checks. Add code that verifies that the result of the uncompression has the same character counts as the encoding table claimed.

12.12 Describe and implement a method of storing the encoding table that uses less space than the trivial method of storing character counts.

12.13 Add the robust error checks for the compression program suggested at the end of Section 12.1.3.

12.14 Analyze empirically the performance of the compression program and determine whether its speed can be significantly improved. If so, make the required changes.

12.15 Split the `Tokenizer` class into three classes: an abstract base class that handles the common functionality and two separate derived classes (one that handles the tokenization for the balanced symbol program, and another that handles the tokenization for the cross-reference generator).

12.16 Generate an index for a book. The input file consists of a set of index entries. Each line consists of the string `IX:`, followed by an index entry name enclosed in braces and then by a page number enclosed in braces. Each `!` in an index entry name represents a sublevel. A `|(` represents the start of a range and a `|)` represents the end of the range. Occasionally, this range will be the same page. In that case, output only a single page number. Otherwise, do not collapse or expand ranges on your own. As an example, Figure 12.31 shows sample input and Figure 12.32 shows the corresponding output.

```
IX: {Series|(}            {2}
IX: {Series!geometric|(}  {4}
IX: {Euler's constant}    {4}
IX: {Series!geometric|)}  {4}
IX: {Series!arithmetic|(} {4}
IX: {Series!arithmetic|)} {5}
IX: {Series!harmonic|(}   {5}
IX: {Euler's constant}    {5}
IX: {Series!harmonic|)}   {5}
IX: {Series|)}            {5}
```

figure 12.31

Sample input for Exercise 12.16

```
Euler's constant: 4, 5
Series: 2-5
   arithmetic: 4-5
   geometric: 4
   harmonic: 5
```

figure 12.32

Sample output for Exercise 12.16

12.17 Use a map to implement a spelling checker. Assume that the dictionary comes from two sources: one file containing an existing large dictionary and a second file containing a personal dictionary. Output all misspelled words and the line numbers on which they occur (note that keeping track of the misspelled words and their line numbers is identical to generating a cross-reference). Also, for each misspelled word, list any words in the dictionary that are obtainable by applying any of the following rules.

a. Add one character.

b. Remove one character.

c. Exchange adjacent characters.

12.18 Two words are anagrams if they contain the same set of letters (with same frequencies). For instance, `least` and `steal` are anagrams. Use a map to implement a program that finds large groups of words (five words or more) in which each word in the group is an anagram of every other word in the group. For instance, `least`, `steal`, `tales`, `stale`, and `slate` are anagrams of each other and form a large group of anagrams. Assume that there is a large list of words in a file. For each word, compute its *representative*. The representative is the characters of the word in sorted order. For instance, the representative for the word `enraged` is `adeegnr`. Observe that words that are anagrams will have the same representative. Thus the representative for `grenade` is also `adeegnr`. You will use a `Map` in which the key is a `String` that is a representative, and the value is a `List` of all words that have the key as their representative. After constructing the `Map`, you simply need to find all values whose `List`s have size five or higher and print those `List`s. Ignore any case distinctions.

12.19 Implement a sorting algorithm using a `TreeMap`. Because a `TreeMap` does not allow duplicates, each value in the `TreeMap` is a list containing duplicates.

12.20 Assume that you have a `Map` in which the keys are names of students (`String`), and for each student, the value is a `List` of courses (each course name is a `String`). Write a routine that computes the inverse map, in which the keys are the names of the courses and the values are lists of enrolled students.

12.21 Static method `computeCounts` takes as input an array of strings and returns a map that stores the strings as keys and the number of occurrences of each string as values.

a. Implement `computeCounts` and provide the running time of your implementation.

b. Write a routine, `mostCommonStrings`, that takes the map generated in part (a) and returns a list of the strings that occur most often (i.e., if there are k strings that are tied as the most common, the return list will have size k), and provide the running time of your routine.

references

The original paper on Huffman's algorithm is [3]. Variations on the algorithm are discussed in [2] and [4]. Another popular compression scheme is *Ziv-Lempel encoding,* described in [7] and [6]. It works by generating a series of fixed-length codes. Typically, we would generate 4,096 12-bit codes that represent the most common substrings in the file. References [1] and [5] are good surveys of the common compression schemes.

1. T. Bell, I. H. Witten, and J. G. Cleary, "Modelling for Text Compression," *ACM Computing Surveys* **21** (1989), 557–591.
2. R. G. Gallager, "Variations on a Theme by Huffman," *IEEE Transactions on Information Theory* **IT-24** (1978), 668–674.
3. D. A. Huffman, "A Model for the Construction of Minimum Redundancy Codes," *Proceedings of the IRE* **40** (1952), 1098–1101.
4. D. E. Knuth, "Dynamic Huffman Coding," *Journal of Algorithms* **6** (1985), 163–180.
5. D. A. Lelewer and D. S. Hirschberg, "Data Compression," *ACM Computing Surveys* **19** (1987), 261–296.
6. T. A. Welch, "A Technique for High-Performance Data Compression," *Computer* **17** (1984), 8–19.
7. J. Ziv and A. Lempel, "Compression of Individual Sequences via Variable-Rate Coding," *IEEE Transactions on Information Theory* **IT-24** (1978), 530–536.

chapter 13

simulation

An important use of computers is for *simulation,* in which the computer is used to emulate the operation of a real system and gather statistics. For example, we might want to simulate the operation of a bank with k tellers to determine the minimum value of k that gives reasonable service time. Using a computer for this task has many advantages. First, the information would be gathered without involving real customers. Second, a simulation by computer can be faster than the actual implementation because of the speed of the computer. Third, the simulation could be easily replicated. In many cases, the proper choice of data structures can help us improve the efficiency of the simulation.

An important use of computers is *simulation,* in which the computer is used to emulate the operation of a real system and gather statistics.

In this chapter, we show

- How to simulate a game modeled on the Josephus problem
- How to simulate the operation of a computer modem bank

13.1 the josephus problem

The *Josephus problem* is the following game: N people, numbered 1 to $N,$ are sitting in a circle; starting at person 1, a hot potato is passed; after M passes, the person holding the hot potato is eliminated, the circle closes ranks, and the game continues with the person who was sitting after the eliminated person picking up the hot potato; the last remaining person wins. A common assumption is that M is a constant, although a random number generator can be used to change M after each elimination.

In the *Josephus problem,* a hot potato is repeatedly passed; when passing terminates, the player holding the potato is eliminated; the game continues, and the last remaining player wins.

The Josephus problem arose in the first century A.D. in a cave on a mountain in Israel where Jewish zealots were being besieged by Roman soldiers. The historian Josephus was among them. To Josephus's consternation, the zealots voted to enter into a suicide pact rather than surrender to the Romans. He suggested the game that now bears his name. The hot potato was the sentence of death to the person next to the one who got the potato. Josephus rigged the game to get the last lot and convinced the remaining intended victim that the two of them should surrender. That is how we know about this game; in effect, Josephus cheated.[1]

If $M = 0$, the players are eliminated in order, and the last player always wins. For other values of M, things are not so obvious. Figure 13.1 shows that if $N = 5$ and $M = 1$, the players are eliminated in the order 2, 4, 1, 5. In this case, player 3 wins. The steps are as follows.

1. At the start, the potato is at player 1. After one pass, it is at player 2.
2. Player 2 is eliminated. Player 3 picks up the potato, and after one pass, it is at player 4.
3. Player 4 is eliminated. Player 5 picks up the potato and passes it to player 1.
4. Player 1 is eliminated. Player 3 picks up the potato and passes it to player 5.
5. Player 5 is eliminated, so player 3 wins.

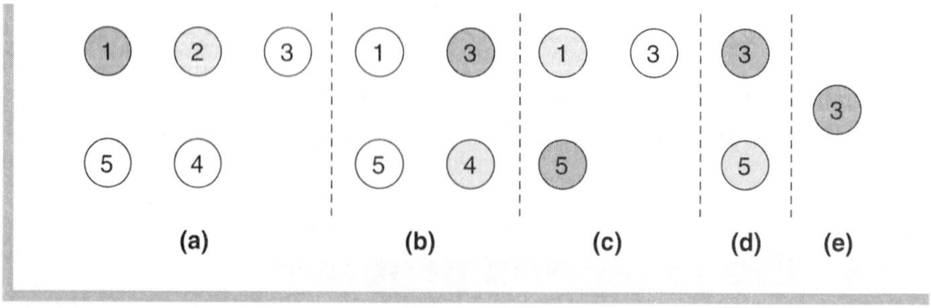

figure 13.1

The Josephus problem: At each step, the darkest circle represents the initial holder and the lightly shaded circle represents the player who receives the hot potato (and is eliminated). Passes are made clockwise.

1. Thanks to David Teague for relaying this story. The version that we solve differs from the historical description. In Exercise 13.11 you are asked to solve the historical version.

First, we write a program that simulates, pass for pass, a game for any values of N and M. The running time of the simulation is $O(MN)$, which is acceptable if the number of passes is small. Each step takes $O(M)$ time because it performs M passes. We then show how to implement each step in $O(\log N)$ time, regardless of the number of passes performed. The running time of the simulation becomes $O(N \log N)$.

13.1.1 the simple solution

We can represent the players by a linked list and use the iterator to simulate the passing.

The passing stage in the Josephus problem suggests that we represent the players in a linked list. We create a linked list in which the elements 1, 2, …, N are inserted in order. We then set an iterator to the front element. Each pass of the potato corresponds to a `next` operation on the iterator. At the last player (currently remaining) in the list we implement the pass by creating a new iterator positioned prior to the first element. This action mimics the circle. When we have finished passing, we remove the element on which the iterator has landed.

An implementation is shown in Figure 13.2. The linked list and iterator are declared at lines 8 and 15, respectively. We construct the initial list by using the loop at lines 11 and 12.

In Figure 13.2, the code at lines 18 to 25 plays one step of the algorithm by passing the potato (lines 18 to 24) and then eliminating a player (line 25). This procedure is repeated until the test at line 16 tells us that only one player remains. At that point we return the player's number at line 30.

The running time of this routine is $O(MN)$ because that is exactly the number of passes that occur during the algorithm. For small M, this running time is acceptable, although we should mention that the case $M = 0$ does not yield a running time of $O(0)$; obviously the running time is $O(N)$. We do not merely multiply by zero when trying to interpret a Big-Oh expression. Note that we can replace `LinkedList` with `ArrayList`, without affecting the running time. We can also use a `TreeSet`, but the cost of construction will not be $O(N)$.

13.1.2 a more efficient algorithm

If we implement each round of passing in a single logarithmic operation, the simulation will be faster.

A more efficient algorithm can be obtained if we use a data structure that supports accessing the kth smallest item (in logarithmic time). Doing so allows us to implement each round of passing in a single operation. Figure 13.1 shows why. Suppose that we have N players remaining and are currently at player P from the front. Initially N is the total number of players and P is 1. After M passes, a calculation tells us that we are at player $((P + M) \bmod N)$ from the front, except if that would give us player 0, in which case, we go to player N. The calculation is fairly tricky, but the concept is not.

figure 13.2

Linked list implementation of the Josephus problem

```
/**
 * Return the winner in the Josephus problem.
 * Linked list implementation.
 * (Can replace with ArrayList or TreeSet).
 */
public static int josephus( int people, int passes )
{
    Collection<Integer> theList = new LinkedList<Integer>( );

        // Construct the list
    for( int i = 1; i <= people; i++ )
        theList.add( i );

        // Play the game;
    Iterator<Integer> itr = theList.iterator( );
    while( people-- != 1 )
    {
        for( int i = 0; i <= passes; i++ )
        {
            if( !itr.hasNext( ) )
                itr = theList.iterator( );

            itr.next( );
        }
        itr.remove( );
    }

    itr = theList.iterator( );

    return itr.next( );
}
```

The calculation is tricky because of the circle.

Applying this calculation to Figure 13.1, we observe that M is 1, N is initially 5, and P is initially 1. So the new value of P is 2. After the deletion, N drops to 4, but we are still at position 2, as part (b) of the figure suggests. The next value of P is 3, also shown in part (b), so the third element in the list is deleted and N falls to 3. The next value of P is 4 mod 3, or 1, so we are back at the first player in the remaining list, as shown in part (c). This player is removed and N becomes 2. At this point, we add M to P, obtaining 2. Because 2 mod 2 is 0, we set P to player N, and thus the last player in the list is the one that is removed. This action agrees with part (d). After the removal, N is 1 and we are done.

All we need then is a data structure that efficiently supports the `findKth` operation. The `findKth` operation returns the kth (smallest) item, for any parameter k.[2] Unfortunately, no Collections API data structures support the findKth operation. However, we can use one of the generic data structures that we implement in Part Four. Recall from the discussion in Section 6.7 that the data structures we implement in Chapter 19 follow a basic protocol that uses insert, remove, and find. We can then add findKth to the implementation.

findKth can be supported by a search tree.

There are several similar alternatives. All of them use the fact that, as discussed in Section 6.7, TreeSet could have supported the ranking operation in logarithmic time on average or logarithmic time in the worst case if we had used a sophisticated binary search tree. Consequently, we can expect an $O(N \log N)$ algorithm if we exercise care.

The simplest method is to insert the items sequentially into a worst-case efficient binary search tree such as a red-black tree, an AA-tree, or a splay tree (we discuss these trees in later chapters). We can then call findKth and remove, as appropriate. It turns out that a splay tree is an excellent choice for this application because the findKth and insert operations are unusually efficient and remove is not terribly difficult to code. We use an alternative here, however, because the implementations of these data structures that we provide in the later chapters leave implementing findKth for you to do as an exercise.

We use the BinarySearchTreeWithRank class that supports the findKth operation and is completely implemented in Section 19.2. It is based on the simple binary search tree and thus does not have logarithmic worst-case performance but merely average-case performance. Consequently, we cannot merely insert the items sequentially; that would cause the search tree to exhibit its worst-case performance.

A balanced search tree will work, but it is not needed if we are careful and construct a simple binary search tree that is not unbalanced at the start.

There are several options. One is to insert a random permutation of 1, ..., N into the search tree. The other is to build a perfectly balanced binary search tree with a class method. Because a class method would have access to the inner workings of the search tree, it could be done in linear time. This routine is left for you to do as Exercise 19.18 when search trees are discussed.

A class method can be used to construct a perfectly balanced tree in linear time.

The method we use is to write a recursive routine that inserts items in a balanced order. By inserting the middle item at the root and recursively building the two subtrees in the same manner, we obtain a balanced tree. The cost of our routine is an acceptable $O(N \log N)$. Although not as efficient as the linear-time class routine, it does not adversely affect the asymptotic running time of the overall algorithm. The remove operations are then guaranteed to be logarithmic. This routine is called buildTree; it and the josephus method are then coded as shown in Figure 13.3.

We construct the same tree by recursive insertions but use $O(N \log N)$ time.

2. The parameter k for findKth ranges from 1 to N, inclusive, where N is the number of items in the data structure.

```
/**
 * Recursively construct a perfectly balanced BinarySearchTreeWithRank
 * by repeated insertions in O( N log N ) time.
 * t should be empty on the initial call.
 */
public static void buildTree( BinarySearchTreeWithRank<Integer> t,
                              int low, int high )
{
    int center = ( low + high ) / 2;

    if( low <= high )
    {
        t.insert( center );

        buildTree( t, low, center - 1 );
        buildTree( t, center + 1, high );
    }
}

/**
 * Return the winner in the Josephus problem.
 * Search tree implementation.
 */
public static int josephus( int people, int passes )
{
    BinarySearchTreeWithRank<Integer> t =
            new BinarySearchTreeWithRank<Integer>( );

    buildTree( t, 1, people );

    int rank = 1;
    while( people > 1 )
    {
        rank = ( rank + passes ) % people;
        if( rank == 0 )
            rank = people;

        t.remove( t.findKth( rank ) );
        people--;
    }

    return t.findKth( 1 );
}
```

figure 13.3

An $O(N \log N)$ solution of the Josephus problem

13.2 event-driven simulation

Let us return to the bank simulation problem described in the introduction. Here, we have a system in which customers arrive and wait in line until one of k tellers is available. Customer arrival is governed by a probability distribution function, as is the *service time* (the amount of time to be served once a teller becomes available). We are interested in statistics such as how long on average a customer has to wait and what percentage of the time tellers are actually servicing requests. (If there are too many tellers, some will not do anything for long periods.)

With certain probability distributions and values of k, we can compute these answers exactly. However, as k gets larger the analysis becomes considerably more difficult and the use of a computer to simulate the operation of the bank is extremely helpful. In this way, bank officers can determine how many tellers are needed to ensure reasonably smooth service. Most simulations require a thorough knowledge of probability, statistics, and queueing theory.

13.2.1 basic ideas

A discrete event simulation consists of processing events. Here, the two events are (1) a customer arriving and (2) a customer departing, thus freeing up a teller.

We can use a probability function to generate an input stream consisting of ordered pairs of arrival and service time for each customer, sorted by arrival time.[3] We do not need to use the exact time of day. Rather, we can use a quantum unit, referred to as a *tick*.

The *tick* is the quantum unit of time in a simulation.

In a *discrete time-driven simulation* we might start a simulation clock at zero ticks and advance the clock one tick at a time, checking to see whether an event occurs. If so, we process the event(s) and compile statistics. When no customers are left in the input stream and all the tellers are free, the simulation is over.

A *discrete time-driven simulation* processes each unit of time consecutively. It is inappropriate if the interval between successive events is large.

The problem with this simulation strategy is that its running time does not depend on the number of customers or events (there are two events per customer in this case). Rather, it depends on the number of ticks, which is not really part of the input. To show why this condition is important, let us change the clock units to microticks and multiply all the times in the input by 1,000,000. The simulation would then take 1,000,000 times longer.

3. The probability function generates *interarrival times* (times between arrivals), thus guaranteeing that arrivals are generated chronologically.

An *event-driven simulation* advances the current time to the next event.

The key to avoiding this problem is to advance the clock to the next event time at each stage, called an *event-driven simulation,* which is conceptually easy to do. At any point, the next event that can occur is either the arrival of the next customer in the input stream or the departure of one of the customers from a teller's station. All the times at which the events will happen are available, so we just need to find the event that happens soonest and process that event (setting the current time to the time that the event occurs).

If the event is a departure, processing includes gathering statistics for the departing customer and checking the line (queue) to determine whether another customer is waiting. If so, we add that customer, process whatever statistics are required, compute the time when the customer will leave, and add that departure to the set of events waiting to happen.

If the event is an arrival, we check for an available teller. If there is none, we place the arrival in the line (queue). Otherwise, we give the customer a teller, compute the customer's departure time, and add the departure to the set of events waiting to happen.

The *event set* (i.e., events waiting to happen) is organized as a priority queue.

The waiting line for customers can be implemented as a queue. Because we need to find the next soonest event, the set of events should be organized in a priority queue. The next event is thus an arrival or departure (whichever is sooner); both are easily available. An event-driven simulation is appropriate if the number of ticks between events is expected to be large.

13.2.2 example: a modem bank simulation

The main algorithmic item in a simulation is the organization of the events in a priority queue. To focus on this requirement, we write a simple simulation. The system we simulate is a *modem bank* at a university computing center.

The modem bank removes the waiting line from the simulation. Thus there is only one data structure.

A modem bank consists of a large collection of modems. For example, Florida International University (FIU) has 288 modems available for students. A modem is accessed by dialing one telephone number. If any of the 288 modems are available, the user is connected to one of them. If all the modems are in use, the phone will give a busy signal. Our simulation models the service provided by the modem bank. The variables are

- The number of modems in the bank
- The probability distribution that governs dial-in attempts
- The probability distribution that governs connect time
- The length of time the simulation is to be run

The modem bank simulation is a simplified version of the bank teller simulation because there is no waiting line. Each dial-in is an arrival, and the total time spent once a connection has been established is the service time. By removing the waiting line, we remove the need to maintain a queue. Thus we have only one data structure, the priority queue. In Exercise 13.17 you are asked to incorporate a queue; as many as L calls will be queued if all the modems are busy.

To simplify matters, we do not compute statistics. Instead, we list each event as it is processed. We also assume that attempts to connect occur at constant intervals; in an accurate simulation, we would model this interarrival time by a random process. Figure 13.4 shows the output of a simulation.

We list each event as it happens; gathering statistics is a simple extension.

The simulation class requires another class to represent events. The `Event` class is shown in Figure 13.5. The data members consist of the customer number, the time that the event will occur, and an indication of what type of event (`DIAL_IN` or `HANG_UP`) it is. If this simulation were more complex, with several types of events, we would make `Event` an abstract base class and derive subclasses from it. We do not do that here because that would complicate things and obscure the basic workings of the simulation algorithm. The `Event` class contains a constructor and a comparison function used by the priority queue. The `Event` class grants package visible status to the modem simulation class so

The `Event` class represents events. In a complex simulation, it would derive all possible types of events as subclasses. Using inheritance for the `Event` class would complicate the code.

```
User 0 dials in at time 0 and connects for 1 minute
User 0 hangs up at time 1
User 1 dials in at time 1 and connects for 5 minutes
User 2 dials in at time 2 and connects for 4 minutes
User 3 dials in at time 3 and connects for 11 minutes
User 4 dials in at time 4 but gets busy signal
User 5 dials in at time 5 but gets busy signal
User 6 dials in at time 6 but gets busy signal
User 1 hangs up at time 6
User 2 hangs up at time 6
User 7 dials in at time 7 and connects for 8 minutes
User 8 dials in at time 8 and connects for 6 minutes
User 9 dials in at time 9 but gets busy signal
User 10 dials in at time 10 but gets busy signal
User 11 dials in at time 11 but gets busy signal
User 12 dials in at time 12 but gets busy signal
User 13 dials in at time 13 but gets busy signal
User 3 hangs up at time 14
User 14 dials in at time 14 and connects for 6 minutes
User 8 hangs up at time 14
User 15 dials in at time 15 and connects for 3 minutes
User 7 hangs up at time 15
User 16 dials in at time 16 and connects for 5 minutes
User 17 dials in at time 17 but gets busy signal
User 15 hangs up at time 18
User 18 dials in at time 18 and connects for 7 minutes
```

figure 13.4

Sample output for the modem bank simulation involving three modems: A dial-in is attempted every minute; the average connect time is 5 minutes; and the simulation is run for 18 minutes

figure 13.5

The Event class used for modem simulation

```java
/**
 * The event class.
 * Implements the Comparable interface
 * to arrange events by time of occurrence.
 * (nested in ModemSim)
 */
private static class Event implements Comparable<Event>
{
    static final int DIAL_IN = 1;
    static final int HANG_UP = 2;

    public Event( )
    {
        this( 0, 0, DIAL_IN );
    }

    public Event( int name, int tm, int type )
    {
        who  = name;
        time = tm;
        what = type;
    }

    public int compareTo( Event rhs )
    {
        return time - rhs.time;
    }

    int who;         // the number of the user
    int time;        // when the event will occur
    int what;        // DIAL_IN or HANG_UP
}
```

that `Event`'s internal members can be accessed by `ModemSim` methods. The `Event` class is nested inside the `ModemSim` class.

The modem simulation class skeleton, `ModemSim`, is shown in Figure 13.6. It consists of a lot of data members, a constructor, and two methods. The data members include a random number object `r` shown at line 27. At line 28 the `eventSet` is maintained as a priority queue of `Event` objects. The remaining data members are `freeModems`, which is initially the number of modems in the simulation but changes as users connect and hang up, and `avgCallLen` and `freqOfCalls`, which are parameters of the simulation. Recall that a dial-in attempt will be made every `freqOfCalls` ticks. The constructor, declared at line 15 and implemented in Figure 13.7, initializes these members and places the first arrival in the `eventSet` priority queue.

```java
import java.util.Random;
import java.util.PriorityQueue;

// ModemSim clas interface: run a simulation
//
// CONSTRUCTION: with three parameters: the number of
//     modems, the average connect time, and the
//     interarrival time
//
// ******************PUBLIC OPERATIONS*********************
// void runSim( )        --> Run a simulation

public class ModemSim
{
    public ModemSim( int modems, double avgLen, int callIntrvl )
      { /* Figure 13.7 */ }

      // Run the simulation.
    public void runSim( long stoppingTime )
      { /* Figure 13.9 */ }

      // Add a call to eventSet at the current time,
      // and schedule one for delta in the future.
    private void nextCall( int delta )
      { /* Figure 13.8 */ }

    private Random r;                         // A random source
    private PriorityQueue<Event> eventSet;   // Pending events

        // Basic parameters of the simulation
    private int freeModems;             // Number of modems unused
    private double avgCallLen;          // Length of a call
    private int freqOfCalls;            // Interval between calls

    private static class Event implements Comparable<Event>
      { /* Figure 13.5 */ }
}
```

figure 13.6

The `ModemSim` class skeleton

The simulation class consists of only two methods. First, `nextCall`, shown in Figure 13.8, adds a dial-in request to the event set. It maintains two private variables: the number of the next user who will attempt to dial in and when that event will occur. Again, we have made the simplifying assumption that calls are made at regular intervals. In practice, we would use a random number generator to model the arrival stream.

The `nextCall` method adds a dial-in request to the event set.

figure 13.7

The `ModemSim` constructor

```
/**
 * Constructor.
 * @param modem number of modems.
 * @param avgLen averge length of a call.
 * @param callIntrvl the average time between calls.
 */
public ModemSim( int modems, double avgLen, int callIntrvl )
{
    eventSet    = new PriorityQueue<Event>( );
    freeModems  = modems;
    avgCallLen  = avgLen;
    freqOfCalls = callIntrvl;
    r           = new Random( );
    nextCall( freqOfCalls );  // Schedule first call
}
```

figure 13.8

The `nextCall` method places a new `DIAL_IN` event in the event queue and advances the time when the next `DIAL_IN` event will occur

```
private int userNum = 0;
private int nextCallTime = 0;

/**
 * Place a new DIAL_IN event into the event queue.
 * Then advance the time when next DIAL_IN event will occur.
 * In practice, we would use a random number to set the time.
 */
private void nextCall( int delta )
{
    Event ev = new Event( userNum++, nextCallTime, Event.DIAL_IN );
    eventSet.insert( ev );
    nextCallTime += delta;
}
```

The `runSim` method runs the simulation.

The other method is `runSim`, which is called to run the entire simulation. The `runSim` method does most of the work and is shown in Figure 13.9. It is called with a single parameter that indicates when the simulation should end. As long as the event set is not empty, we process events. Note that it should never be empty because at the time we arrive at line 12 there is exactly one dial-in request in the priority queue and one hang-up request for every currently connected modem. Whenever we remove an event at line 12 and it is confirmed to be a dial-in, we generate a replacement dial-in event at line 40. A hang-up event is also generated at line 35 if the dial-in succeeds. Thus the only way to finish the routine is if `nextCall` is set up not to generate an event eventually or (more likely) by executing the `break` statement at line 15.

```
/**
 * Run the simulation until stoppingTime occurs.
 * Print output as in Figure 13.4.
 */
public void runSim( long stoppingTime )
{
    Event e = null;
    int howLong;

    while( !eventSet.isEmpty( ) )
    {
        e = eventSet.remove( );

        if( e.time > stoppingTime )
            break;

        if( e.what == Event.HANG_UP )    // HANG_UP
        {
            freeModems++;
            System.out.println( "User " + e.who +
                                " hangs up at time " + e.time );
        }
        else                          // DIAL_IN
        {
            System.out.print(  "User " + e.who +
                                " dials in at time " + e.time + " " );
            if( freeModems > 0 )
            {
                freeModems--;
                howLong = r.nextPoisson( avgCallLen );
                System.out.println(  "and connects for "
                                   + howLong + " minutes" );
                e.time += howLong;
                e.what = Event.HANG_UP;
                eventSet.add( e );
            }
            else
                System.out.println( "but gets busy signal" );

            nextCall( freqOfCalls );
        }
    }
}
```

figure 13.9

The basic simulation routine

A hang-up increases `freeModems`. A dial-in checks on whether a modem is available and if so decreases `freeModems`.

Let us summarize how the various events are processed. If the event is a hang-up, we increment `freeModems` at line 19 and print a message at lines 20 and 21. If the event is a dial-in, we generate a partial line of output that records the attempt, and then, if any modems are available, we connect the user. To do so, we decrement `freeModems` at line 29, generate a connection time (using a Poisson distribution rather than a uniform distribution) at line 30, print the rest of the output at lines 31–32, and add a hang-up to the event set (lines 33–35). Otherwise, no modems are available, and we give the busy signal message. Either way, an additional dial-in event is generated. Figure 13.10 shows the state of the priority queue after each `deleteMin` for the early stages of the sample output shown in Figure 13.4. The time at which each event occurs is shown in boldface, and the number of free modems (if any) are shown to the right of the priority queue. (Note that the call length is not actually stored in an `Event` object; we include it, when appropriate, to make the figure more self-contained. A '?' for the call length signifies a dial-in event that eventually will result in a busy signal; however, that outcome is not known at the time the event is added to the priority queue.) The sequence of priority queue steps is as follows.

1. The first `DIAL_IN` request is inserted.
2. After `DIAL_IN` is removed, the request is connected, thereby resulting in a `HANG_UP` and a replacement `DIAL_IN` request.
3. A `HANG_UP` request is processed.
4. A `DIAL_IN` request is processed resulting in a connect. Thus both a `HANG_UP` event and a `DIAL_IN` event are added (three times).
5. A `DIAL_IN` request fails; a replacement `DIAL_IN` is generated (three times).
6. A `HANG_UP` request is processed (twice).
7. A `DIAL_IN` request succeeds, and `HANG_UP` and `DIAL_IN` are added.

The simulation uses a poor model. Negative exponential distributions would more accurately model the time between dial-in attempts and total connect time.

Again, if `Event` were an abstract base class, we would expect a procedure `doEvent` to be defined through the `Event` hierarchy; then we would not need long chains of `if/else` statements. However to access the priority queue, which is in the simulation class, we would need `Event` to store a reference to the simulation `ModemSim` class as a data member. We would insert it at construction time.

A minimal (in the truest sense) `main` routine is shown for completeness in Figure 13.11. Note that using a Poisson distribution to model connect time is not appropriate. A better choice would be to use a negative exponential distri-

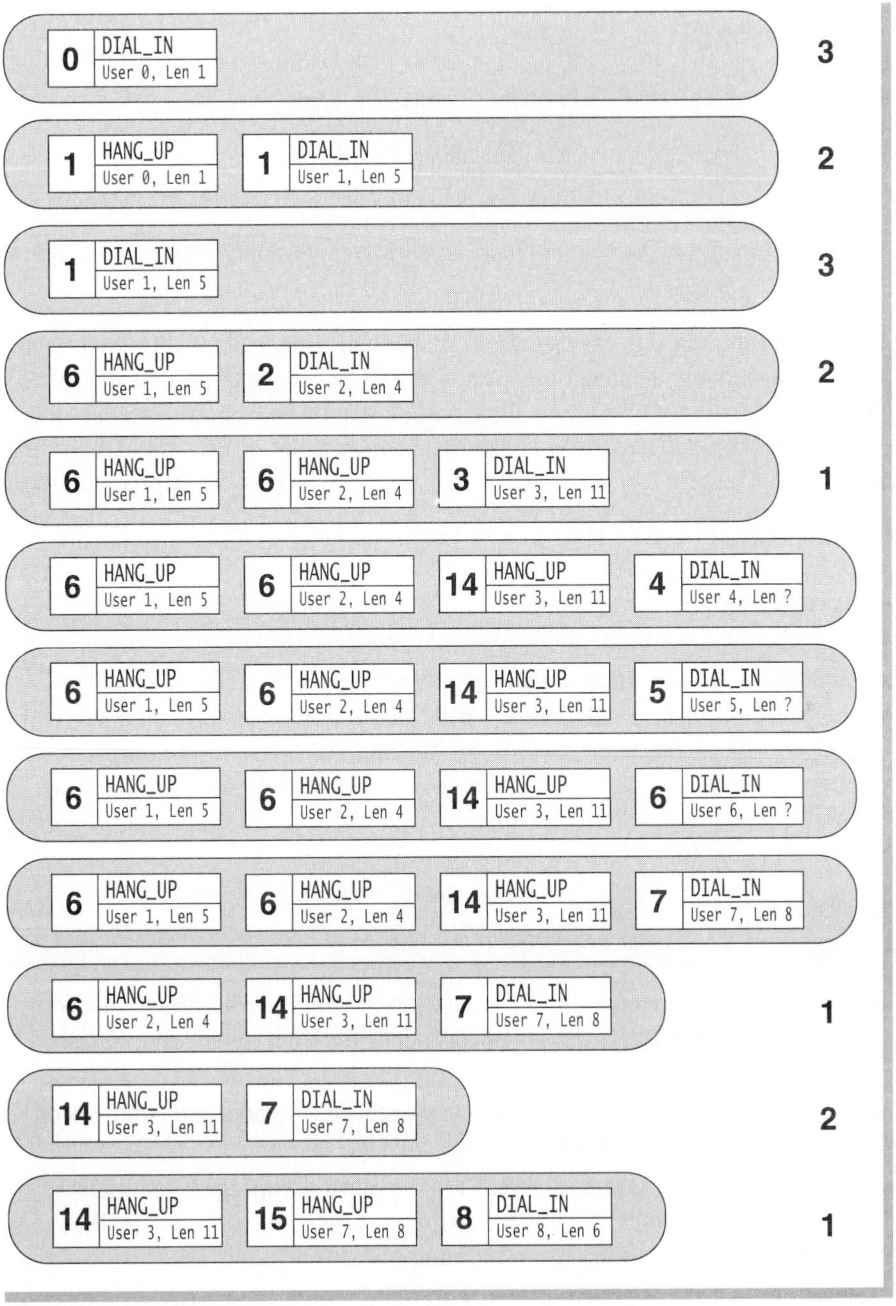

figure 13.10

The priority queue for modem bank simulation after each step

figure 13.11

A simple `main` to test the simulation

```
/**
 * Quickie main for testing purposes.
 */
public static void main( String [ ] args )
{
    ModemSim s = new ModemSim( 3, 5.0, 1 );
    s.runSim( 20 );
}
```

bution (but the reasons for doing so are beyond the scope of this text). Additionally, assuming a fixed time between dial-in attempts is also inaccurate. Again, a negative exponential distribution would be a better model. If we change the simulation to use these distributions, the clock would be represented as a `double`. In Exercise 13.13 you are asked to implement these changes.

summary

Simulation is an important area of computer science and involves many more complexities than we could discuss here. A simulation is only as good as the model of randomness, so a solid background in probability, statistics, and queueing theory is required in order for the modeler to know what types of probability distributions are reasonable to assume. Simulation is an important application area for object-oriented techniques.

key concepts

discrete time-driven simulation A simulation in which each unit of time is processed consecutively. It is inappropriate if the interval between successive events is large. (457)

event-driven simulation A simulation in which the current time is advanced to the next event. (458)

Josephus problem A game in which a hot potato is repeatedly passed; when passing terminates, the player holding the potato is eliminated; the game then continues, and the last remaining player wins. (452)

simulation An important use of computers, in which the computer is used to emulate the operation of a real system and gather statistics. (451)

tick The quantum unit of time in a simulation. (457)

common errors

1. The most common error in simulation is using a poor model. A simulation is only as good as the accuracy of its random input.

on the internet

Both examples in this chapter are available online.

Josephus.java	Contains both implementations of `josephus` and a `main` to test them.
ModemSim.java	Contains the code for the modem bank simulation.

exercises

IN SHORT

13.1 If $M = 0$, who wins the Josephus game?

13.2 Show the operation of the Josephus algorithm in Figure 13.3 for the case of seven people with three passes. Include the computation of `rank` and a picture that contains the remaining elements after each iteration.

13.3 Are there any values of M for which player 1 wins a 30-person Josephus game?

13.4 Show the state of the priority queue after each of the first 10 lines of the simulation depicted in Figure 13.4.

IN THEORY

13.5 Let $N = 2^k$ for any integer k. Prove that if M is 1, then player 1 always wins the Josephus game.

13.6 Let $J(N)$ be the winner of an N-player Josephus game with $M = 1$. Show that

a. If N is even, then $J(N) = 2J(N/2) - 1$.
b. If N is odd and $J(\lceil N/2 \rceil) \neq 1$, then $J(N) = 2J(\lceil N/2 \rceil) - 3$.
c. If N is odd and $J(\lceil N/2 \rceil) = 1$, then $J(N) = N$.

13.7 Use the results in Exercise 13.6 to write an algorithm that returns the winner of an N-player Josephus game with $M = 1$. What is the running time of your algorithm?

13.8 Give a general formula for the winner of an N-player Josephus game with $M = 2$.

13.9 Using the algorithm for $N = 20$, determine the order of insertion into the `BinarySearchTreeWithRank`.

IN PRACTICE

13.10 Suppose that the Josephus algorithm shown in Figure 13.2 is implemented with a `TreeSet` instead of a `LinkedList`. If the change worked, what would be the running time?

13.11 Write a program that solves the historical version of the Josephus problem. Give both the linked list and search tree algorithms.

13.12 Implement the Josephus algorithm with a queue. Each pass of the potato is a `dequeue`, followed by an `enqueue`.

13.13 Rework the simulation so that the clock is represented as a `double`, the time between dial-in attempts is modeled with a negative exponential distribution, and the connect time is modeled with a negative exponential distribution.

13.14 Rework the modem bank simulation so that `Event` is an abstract base class and `DialInEvent` and `HangUpEvent` are derived classes. The `Event` class should store a reference to a `ModemSim` object as an additional data member, which is initialized on construction. It should also provide an abstract method named `doEvent` that is implemented in the derived classes and that can be called from `runSim` to process the event.

PROGRAMMING PROJECTS

13.15 Implement the Josephus algorithm with splay trees (see Chapter 22) and sequential insertion. (The splay tree class is available online, but it will need a `findKth` method.) Compare the performance with that in the text and with an algorithm that uses a linear-time, balanced tree-building algorithm.

13.16 Rewrite the Josephus algorithm shown in Figure 13.3 to use a *median heap* (see Exercise 6.17). Use a simple implementation of the median heap; the elements are maintained in sorted order. Compare the running time of this algorithm with the time obtained by using the binary search tree.

13.17 Suppose that FIU has installed a system that queues phone calls when all modems are busy. Rewrite the simulation routine to allow for queues of various sizes. Make an allowance for an "infinite" queue.

13.18 Rewrite the modem bank simulation to gather statistics rather than output each event. Then compare the speed of the simulation, assuming several hundred modems and a very long simulation, with some other possible priority queues (some of which are available online)—namely, the following.

a. An asymptotically inefficient priority queue representation described in Exercise 6.12
b. An asymptotically inefficient priority queue representation described in Exercise 6.13
c. Splay trees (see Chapter 22)
d. Skew heaps (see Chapter 23)
e. Pairing heaps (see Chapter 23)

chapter 14

graphs and paths

In this chapter we examine the *graph* and show how to solve a particular kind of problem—namely, calculation of shortest paths. The computation of shortest paths is a fundamental application in computer science because many interesting situations can be modeled by a graph. Finding the fastest routes for a mass transportation system, and routing electronic mail through a network of computers are but a few examples. We examine variations of the shortest path problems that depend on an interpretation of *shortest* and the graph's properties. Shortest-path problems are interesting because, although the algorithms are fairly simple, they are slow for large graphs unless careful attention is paid to the choice of data structures.

In this chapter, we show

- Formal definitions of a graph and its components
- The data structures used to represent a graph
- Algorithms for solving several variations of the shortest-path problem, with complete Java implementations

14.1 definitions

A *graph* consists of a set of vertices and a set of edges that connect the vertices. If the edge pair is ordered, the graph is a *directed graph.*

A graph consists of a set of vertices and a set of edges that connect the vertices. That is, $G = (V, E)$, where V is the set of vertices and E is the set of edges. Each edge is a pair (v, w), where $v, w \in V$. Vertices are sometimes called *nodes,* and edges are sometimes called *arcs*. If the edge pair is ordered, the graph is called a *directed graph.* Directed graphs are sometimes called *digraphs*. In a digraph, vertex w is *adjacent* to vertex v if and only if $(v, w) \in E$. Sometimes an edge has a third component, called the *edge cost* (or *weight*) that measures the cost of traversing the edge. In this chapter, all graphs are directed.

Vertex w is *adjacent* to vertex v if there is an edge from v to w.

The graph shown in Figure 14.1 has seven vertices,

$$V = \{V_0, V_1, V_2, V_3, V_4, V_5, V_6\}$$

and 12 edges,

$$E = \left\{\begin{matrix} (V_0, V_1, 2), (V_0, V_3, 1), (V_1, V_3, 3), (V_1, V_4, 10) \\ (V_3, V_4, 2), (V_3, V_6, 4), (V_3, V_5, 8), (V_3, V_2, 2) \\ (V_2, V_0, 4), (V_2, V_5, 5), (V_4, V_6, 6), (V_6, V_5, 1) \end{matrix}\right\}$$

A *path* is a sequence of vertices connected by edges.

The following vertices are adjacent to V_3: V_2, V_4, V_5, and V_6. Note that V_0 and V_1 are not adjacent to V_3. For this graph, $|V| = 7$ and $|E| = 12$; here, $|S|$ represents the size of set S.

The *unweighted path length* measures the number of edges on a path.

A *path* in a graph is a sequence of vertices connected by edges. In other words, $w_1, w_2, \ldots, w_N$ the sequence of vertices is such that $(w_i, w_{i+1}) \in E$ for $1 \le i < N$. The *path length* is the number of edges on the path—namely, $N - 1$—also called the *unweighted path length.* The *weighted path length* is the sum of the costs of the edges on the path. For example, V_0, V_3, V_5 is a

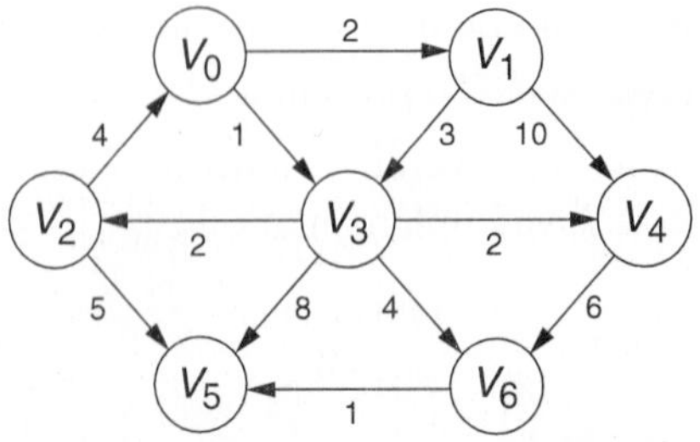

figure 14.1

A directed graph

path from vertex V_0 to V_5. The path length is two edges—the shortest path between V_0 and V_5, and the weighted path length is 9. However, if cost is important, the weighted shortest path between these vertices has cost 6 and is V_0, V_3, V_6, V_5. A path may exist from a vertex to itself. If this path contains no edges, the path length is 0, which is a convenient way to define an otherwise special case. A *simple path* is a path in which all vertices are distinct, except that the first and last vertices can be the same.

The *weighted path length* is the sum of the edge costs on a path.

A *cycle* in a directed graph is a path that begins and ends at the same vertex and contains at least one edge. That is, it has a length of at least 1 such that $w_1 = w_N$; this cycle is simple if the path is simple. A *directed acyclic graph (DAG)* is a type of directed graph having no cycles.

A *cycle* in a directed graph is a path that begins and ends at the same vertex and contains at least one edge.

An example of a real-life situation that can be modeled by a graph is the airport system. Each airport is a vertex. If there is a nonstop flight between two airports, two vertices are connected by an edge. The edge could have a weight representing time, distance, or the cost of the flight. In an undirected graph, an edge (v, w) would imply an edge (w, v). However, the costs of the edges might be different because flying in different directions might take longer (depending on prevailing winds) or cost more (depending on local taxes). Thus we use a directed graph with both edges listed, possibly with different weights. Naturally, we want to determine quickly the best flight between any two airports; *best* could mean the path with the fewest edges or one, or all, of the weight measures (distance, cost, and so on).

A *directed acyclic graph* has no cycles. Such graphs are an important class of graphs.

A second example of a real-life situation that can be modeled by a graph is the routing of electronic mail through computer networks. Vertices represent computers, the edges represent links between pairs of computers, and the edge costs represent communication costs (phone bill per megabyte), delay costs (seconds per megabyte), or combinations of these and other factors.

For most graphs, there is likely at most one edge from any vertex v to any other vertex w (allowing one edge in each direction between v and w). Consequently, $|E| \le |V|^2$. When most edges are present, we have $|E| = \Theta(|V|^2)$. Such a graph is considered to be a *dense graph*—that is, it has a large number of edges, generally quadratic.

A graph is *dense* if the number of edges is large (generally quadratic). Typical graphs are not dense. Instead, they are *sparse*.

In most applications, however, a *sparse graph* is the norm. For instance, in the airport model, we do not expect direct flights between every pair of airports. Instead, a few airports are very well connected and most others have relatively few flights. In a complex mass transportation system involving buses and trains, for any one station we have only a few other stations that are directly reachable and thus represented by an edge. Moreover, in a computer network most computers are attached to a few other local computers. So, in most cases, the graph is relatively sparse, where $|E| = \Theta(|V|)$ or perhaps slightly more (there is no standard definition of sparse). The algorithms that we develop, then, must be efficient for sparse graphs.

14.1.1 representation

An *adjacency matrix* represents a graph and uses quadratic space.

The first thing to consider is how to represent a graph internally. Assume that the vertices are sequentially numbered starting from 0, as the graph shown in Figure 14.1 suggests. One simple way to represent a graph is to use a two-dimensional array called an *adjacency matrix*. For each edge (v, w), we set `a[v][w]` equal to the edge cost; nonexistent edges can be initialized with a logical `INFINITY`. The initialization of the graph seems to require that the entire adjacency matrix be initialized to `INFINITY`. Then, as an edge is encountered, an appropriate entry is set. In this scenario, the initialization takes $O(|V|^2)$ time. Although the quadratic initialization cost can be avoided (see Exercise 14.6), the space cost is still $O(|V|^2)$, which is fine for dense graphs but completely unacceptable for sparse graphs.

An *adjacency list* represents a graph, using linear space.

For sparse graphs, a better solution is an *adjacency list,* which represents a graph by using linear space. For each vertex, we keep a list of all adjacent vertices. An adjacency list representation of the graph in Figure 14.1 using a linked list is shown in Figure 14.2. Because each edge appears in a list node, the number of list nodes equals the number of edges. Consequently, $O(|E|)$ space is used to store the list nodes. We have $|V|$ lists, so $O(|V|)$ additional space is also required. If we assume that every vertex is in some edge, the number of edges is at least $\lceil |V|/2 \rceil$. Hence we may disregard any $O(|V|)$ terms when an $O(|E|)$ term is present. Consequently, we say that the space requirement is $O(|E|)$, or linear in the size of the graph.

Adjacency lists can be constructed in linear time from a list of edges.

The adjacency list can be constructed in linear time from a list of edges. We begin by making all the lists empty. When we encounter an edge $(v, w, c_{v,w})$, we add an entry consisting of w and the cost $c_{v,w}$ to v's adjacency list. The insertion can be anywhere; inserting it at the front can be done in constant time. Each edge can be inserted in constant time, so the entire adjacency list structure can be constructed in linear time. Note that

figure 14.2

Adjacency list representation of the graph shown in Figure 14.1; the nodes in list i represent vertices adjacent to i and the cost of the connecting edge.

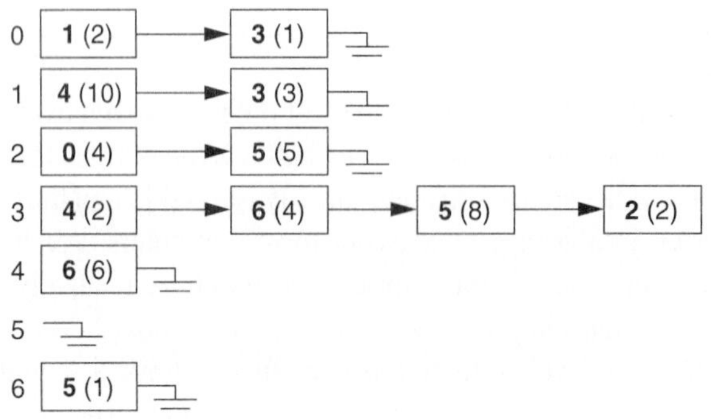

when inserting an edge, we do not check whether it is already present. That cannot be done in constant time (using a simple linked list), and doing the check would destroy the linear-time bound for construction. In most cases, ignoring this check is unimportant. If there are two or more edges of different cost connecting a pair of vertices, any shortest-path algorithm will choose the lower cost edge without resorting to any special processing. Note also that `ArrayLists` can be used instead of linked lists, with the constant-time `add` operation replacing insertions at the front.

A map can be used to map vertex names to internal numbers.

In most real-life applications the vertices have names, which are unknown at compile time, instead of numbers. Consequently, we must provide a way to transform names to numbers. The easiest way to do so is to provide a *map* by which we map a vertex name to an internal number ranging from 0 to $|V| - 1$ (the number of vertices is determined as the program runs). The internal numbers are assigned as the graph is read. The first number assigned is 0. As each edge is input, we check whether each of the two vertices has been assigned a number, by looking in the map. If it has been assigned an internal number, we use it. Otherwise, we assign to the vertex the next available number and insert the vertex name and number in the map. With this transformation, all the graph algorithms use only the internal numbers. Eventually, we have to output the real vertex names, not the internal numbers, so for each internal number we must also record the corresponding vertex name. One way to do so is to keep a string for each vertex. We use this technique to implement a `Graph` class. The class and the shortest-path algorithms require several data structures—namely, a list, a queue, a map, and a priority queue. The `import` directives are shown in Figure 14.3. The queue (implemented with a linked list) and priority queue are used in various shortest-path calculations. The adjacency list is represented with `LinkedList`. A `HashMap` is also used to represent the graph.

```
import java.io.FileReader;
import java.io.InputStreamReader;
import java.io.BufferedReader;
import java.io.IOException;
import java.util.StringTokenizer;

import java.util.Collection;
import java.util.List;
import java.util.LinkedList;
import java.util.Map;
import java.util.HashMap;
import java.util.Iterator;
import java.util.Queue;
import java.util.PriorityQueue;
import java.util.NoSuchElementException;
```

figure 14.3

The `import` directives for the `Graph` class

When we write an actual Java implementation, we do not need internal vertex numbers. Instead, each vertex is stored in a `Vertex` object, and instead of using a number, we can use a reference to the `Vertex` object as its (uniquely identifying) number. However, when describing the algorithms, assuming that vertices are numbered is often convenient, and we occasionally do so.

Before we show the `Graph` class skeleton, let us examine Figures 14.4 and 14.5, which show how our graph is to be represented. Figure 14.4 shows the representation in which we use internal numbers. Figure 14.5 replaces the internal numbers with `Vertex` variables, as we do in our code. Although this simplifies the code, it greatly complicates the picture. Because the two figures represent identical inputs, Figure 14.4 can be used to follow the complications in Figure 14.5.

As indicated in the part labeled *Input,* we can expect the user to provide a list of edges, one per line. At the start of the algorithm, we do not know the names of any of the vertices, how many vertices there are, or how many edges there are. We use two basic data structures to represent the graph. As we mentioned in the preceding paragraph, for each vertex we maintain a `Vertex` object that stores some information. We describe the details of `Vertex` (in particular, how different `Vertex` objects interact with each other) last.

As mentioned earlier, the first major data structure is a map that allows us to find, for any vertex name, the `Vertex` object that represents it. This map is shown in Figure 14.5 as `vertexMap` (Figure 14.4 maps the name to an `int` in the component labeled *Dictionary*).

figure 14.4

An abstract scenario of the data structures used in a shortest-path calculation, with an input graph taken from a file. The shortest weighted path from `A` to `C` is `A` to `B` to `E` to `D` to `C` (cost is 76).

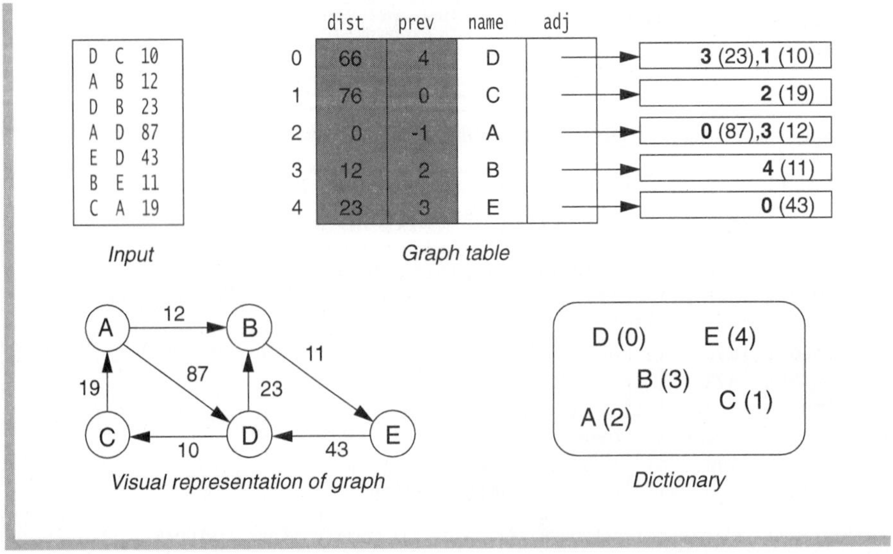

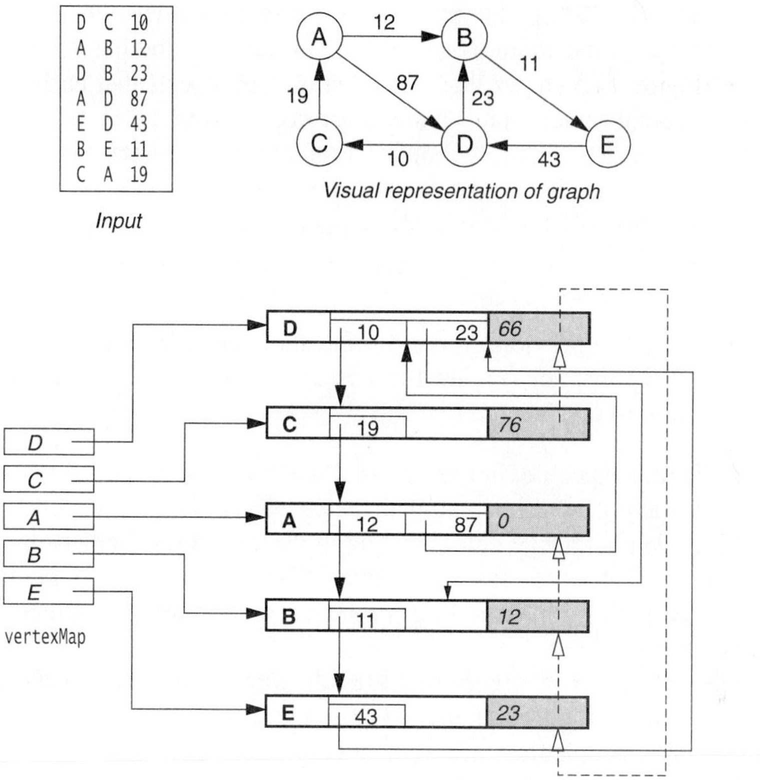

figure 14.5

Data structures used in a shortest-path calculation, with an input graph taken from a file; the shortest weighted path from `A` to `C` is `A` to `B` to `E` to `D` to `C` (cost is 76).

Legend: Dark-bordered boxes are `Vertex` objects. The unshaded portion in each box contains the name and adjacency list and does not change when shortest-path computation is performed. Each adjacency list entry contains an `Edge` that stores a reference to another `Vertex` object and the edge cost. Shaded portion is `dist` and `prev`, filled in after shortest path computation runs.

Dark arrows emanate from `vertexMap`. Light arrows are adjacency list entries. Dashed arrows are the `prev` data member that results from a shortest-path computation.

The second major data structure is the `Vertex` object that stores information about all the vertices. Of particular interest is how it interacts with other `Vertex` objects. Figures 14.4 and 14.5 show that a `Vertex` object maintains four pieces of information for each vertex.

- `name`: The name corresponding to this vertex is established when the vertex is placed in the map and never changes. None of the shortest-path algorithms examines this member. It is used only to print a final path.

- adj: This list of adjacent vertices is established when the graph is read. None of the shortest-path algorithms changes the list. In the abstract, Figure 14.4 shows that it is a list of Edge objects that each contain an internal vertex number and edge cost. In reality, Figure 14.5 shows that each Edge object contains a reference to a Vertex and an edge cost and that the list is actually stored by using an ArrayList or LinkedList.
- dist: The length of the shortest path (either weighted or unweighted, depending on the algorithm) from the starting vertex to this vertex as computed by the shortest-path algorithm.
- prev: The previous vertex on the shortest path to this vertex, which in the abstract (Figure 14.4) is an int but in reality (the code and Figure 14.5) is a reference to a Vertex.

To be more specific, in Figures 14.4 and 14.5 the unshaded items are not altered by any of the shortest-path calculations. They represent the input graph and do not change unless the graph itself changes (perhaps by addition or deletion of edges at some later point). The shaded items are computed by the shortest-path algorithms. Prior to the calculation we can assume that they are uninitialized.[1]

The shortest-path algorithms are *single-source* algorithms that compute the shortest paths from some starting point to all vertices.

The shortest-path algorithms are all *single-source algorithms,* which begin at some starting point and compute the shortest paths from it to all vertices. In this example the starting point is A, and by consulting the map we can find its Vertex object. Note that the shortest-path algorithm declares that the shortest path to A is 0.

The prev member can be used to extract the actual path.

The prev data member allows us to print out the shortest path, not just its length. For instance, by consulting the Vertex object for C, we see that the shortest path from the starting vertex to C has a total cost of 76. Obviously, the last vertex on this path is C. The vertex before C on this path is D, before D is E, before E is B, and before B is A—the starting vertex. Thus, by tracing back through the prev data member, we can construct the shortest path. Although this trace gives the path in reverse order, unreversing it is a simple matter. In the remainder of this section we describe how the unshaded parts of all the Vertex objects are constructed and give the method that prints out a shortest path, assuming that the dist and prev data members have been computed. We discuss individually the algorithms used to fill in the shortest path.

The item in an adjacency list is a reference to the Vertex object of the adjacent vertex and the edge cost.

Figure 14.6 shows the Edge class that represents the basic item placed in the adjacency list. The Edge consists of a reference to a Vertex and the edge cost. The Vertex class is shown in Figure 14.7. An additional member named scratch is provided and has different uses in the various algorithms.

1. The computed information (shaded) could be separated into a separate class, with Vertex maintaining a reference to it, making the code more reusable but more complex.

```
// Represents an edge in the graph.
class Edge
{
    public Vertex dest;         // Second vertex in Edge
    public double cost;         // Edge cost

    public Edge( Vertex d, double c )
    {
        dest = d;
        cost = c;
    }
}
```

figure 14.6

The basic item stored in an adjacency list

```
// Represents a vertex in the graph.
class Vertex
{
    public String     name;   // Vertex name
    public List<Edge> adj;    // Adjacent vertices
    public double     dist;   // Cost
    public Vertex     prev;   // Previous vertex on shortest path
    public int        scratch;// Extra variable used in algorithm

    public Vertex( String nm )
      { name = nm; adj = new LinkedList<Edge>( ); reset( ); }

    public void reset( )
      { dist = Graph.INFINITY; prev = null; pos = null; scratch = 0; }
}
```

figure 14.7

The `Vertex` class stores information for each vertex

Everything else follows from our preceding description. The `reset` method is used to initialize the (shaded) data members that are computed by the shortest-path algorithms; it is called when a shortest-path computation is restarted.

We are now ready to examine the `Graph` class skeleton, which is shown in Figure 14.8. The `vertexMap` field stores the map. The rest of the class provides methods that perform initialization, add vertices and edges, print the shortest path, and perform various shortest-path calculations. We discuss each routine when we examine its implementation.

First, we consider the constructor. The default creates an empty map via field initialization; that works, so we accept it.

```
// Graph class: evaluate shortest paths.
//
// CONSTRUCTION: with no parameters.
//
// ******************PUBLIC OPERATIONS**********************
// void addEdge( String v, String w, double cvw )
//                                --> Add additional edge
// void printPath( String w )     --> Print path after alg is run
// void unweighted( String s )    --> Single-source unweighted
// void dijkstra( String s )      --> Single-source weighted
// void negative( String s )      --> Single-source negative weighted
// void acyclic( String s )       --> Single-source acyclic
// ******************ERRORS*********************************
// Some error checking is performed to make sure that graph is ok
// and that graph satisfies properties needed by each
// algorithm.  Exceptions are thrown if errors are detected.

public class Graph
{
    public static final double INFINITY = Double.MAX_VALUE;

    public void addEdge( String sourceName, String destName, double cost )
      { /* Figure 14.10 */ }
    public void printPath( String destName )
      { /* Figure 14.13 */ }
    public void unweighted( String startName )
      { /* Figure 14.22 */ }
    public void dijkstra( String startName )
      { /* Figure 14.27 */ }
    public void negative( String startName )
      { /* Figure 14.29 */ }
    public void acyclic( String startName )
      { /* Figure 14.32 */ }

    private Vertex getVertex( String vertexName )
      { /* Figure 14.9 */ }
    private void printPath( Vertex dest )
      { /* Figure 14.12 */ }
    private void clearAll( )
      { /* Figure 14.11 */ }

    private Map<String,Vertex> vertexMap = new HashMap<String,Vertex>( );
}

// Used to signal violations of preconditions for
// various shortest path algorithms.
class GraphException extends RuntimeException
{
    public GraphException( String name )
      { super( name ); }
}
```

figure 14.8

The Graph class skeleton

We can now look at the main methods. The getVertex method is shown in Figure 14.9. We consult the map to get the Vertex entry. If the Vertex does not exist, we create a new Vertex and update the map. The addEdge method, shown in Figure 14.10 is short. We get the corresponding Vertex entries and then update an adjacency list.

Edges are added by insertions in the appropriate adjacency list.

The members that are eventually computed by the shortest-path algorithm are initialized by the routine clearAll, shown in Figure 14.11. The next routine, printPath, prints a shortest path after the computation has been performed. As we mentioned earlier, we can use the prev member to trace back the path, but doing so gives the path in reverse order. This order is not a problem if we use recursion: The vertices on the path to dest are the same as those on the path to dest's previous vertex (on the path), followed by dest. This strategy translates directly into the short recursive routine shown in Figure 14.12, assuming of course that a path actually exists. The printPath routine, shown in Figure 14.13, performs this check first and then prints a message if the path does not exist. Otherwise, it calls the recursive routine and outputs the cost of the path.

The clearAll routine clears out the data members so that the shortest path algorithms can begin.

The printPath routine prints the shortest path after the algorithm has run.

```
/**
 * If vertexName is not present, add it to vertexMap.
 * In either case, return the Vertex.
 */
private Vertex getVertex( String vertexName )
{
    Vertex v = vertexMap.get( vertexName );
    if( v == null )
    {
        v = new Vertex( vertexName );
        vertexMap.put( vertexName, v );
    }
    return v;
}
```

figure 14.9

The getVertex routine returns the Vertex object that represents vertexName, creating the object if it needs to do so

```
/**
 * Add a new edge to the graph.
 */
public void addEdge( String sourceName, String destName, double cost )
{
    Vertex v = getVertex( sourceName );
    Vertex w = getVertex( destName );
    v.adj.add( new Edge( w, cost ) );
}
```

figure 14.10

Add an edge to the graph

figure 14.11

Private routine for initializing the output members for use by the shortest-path algorithms

```
/**
 * Initializes the vertex output info prior to running
 * any shortest path algorithm.
 */
private void clearAll( )
{
    for( Vertex v : vertexMap.values( ) )
        v.reset( );
}
```

figure 14.12

A recursive routine for printing the shortest path

```
/**
 * Recursive routine to print shortest path to dest
 * after running shortest path algorithm. The path
 * is known to exist.
 */
private void printPath( Vertex dest )
{
    if( dest.prev != null )
    {
        printPath( dest.prev );
        System.out.print( " to " );
    }
    System.out.print( dest.name );
}
```

figure 14.13

A routine for printing the shortest path by consulting the graph table (see Figure 14.5)

```
/**
 * Driver routine to handle unreachables and print total cost.
 * It calls recursive routine to print shortest path to
 * destNode after a shortest path algorithm has run.
 */
public void printPath( String destName )
{
    Vertex w = vertexMap.get( destName );
    if( w == null )
        throw new NoSuchElementException( );
    else if( w.dist == INFINITY )
        System.out.println( destName + " is unreachable" );
    else
    {
        System.out.print( "(Cost is: " + w.dist + ") " );
        printPath( w );
        System.out.println( );
    }
}
```

We provide a simple test program that reads a graph from an input file, prompts for a start vertex and a destination vertex, and then runs one of the shortest-path algorithms. Figure 14.14 illustrates that to construct the `Graph` object, we repeatedly read one line of input, assign the line to a `StringTokenizer` object, parse that line, and call `addEdge`. Using a `StringTokenizer` allows us to verify that every line has the three pieces corresponding to an edge.

The `Graph` class is easy to use.

Once the graph has been read, we repeatedly call `processRequest`, shown in Figure 14.15. This version prompts for a starting and ending vertex and then calls one of the shortest-path algorithms. This algorithm throws a `GraphException` if, for instance, it is asked for a path between vertices that are not in the graph. Thus `processRequest` catches any `GraphException` that might be generated and prints an appropriate error message.

14.2 unweighted shortest-path problem

Recall that the unweighted path length measures the number of edges. In this section we consider the problem of finding the shortest unweighted path length between specified vertices.

The *unweighted path length* measures the number of edges on a path.

unweighted single-source, shortest-path problem
Find the shortest path (measured by number of edges) from a designated vertex S to every vertex.

The unweighted shortest-path problem is a special case of the weighted shortest-path problem (in which all weights are 1). Hence it should have a more efficient solution than the weighted shortest-path problem. That turns out to be true, although the algorithms for all the path problems are similar.

All variations of the shortest-path problem have similar solutions.

14.2.1 theory

To solve the unweighted shortest-path problem, we use the graph previously shown in Figure 14.1, with V_2 as the starting vertex S. For now, we are concerned with finding the length of all shortest paths. Later, we maintain the corresponding paths.

We can see immediately that the shortest path from S to V_2 is a path of length 0. This information yields the graph shown in Figure 14.16. Now we can start looking for all vertices that are distance 1 from S. We can find them by looking at the vertices adjacent to S. If we do so, we see that V_0 and V_5 are one edge away from S, as shown in Figure 14.17.

```
    /**
     * A main routine that
     * 1. Reads a file (supplied as a command-line parameter)
     *    containing edges.
     * 2. Forms the graph.
     * 3. Repeatedly prompts for two vertices and
     *    runs the shortest path algorithm.
     * The data file is a sequence of lines of the format
     *    source destination.
     */
    public static void main( String [ ] args )
    {
        Graph g = new Graph( );
        try
        {
            FileReader fin = new FileReader( args[0] );
            BufferedReader graphFile = new BufferedReader( fin );

            // Read the edges and insert
            String line;
            while( ( line = graphFile.readLine( ) ) != null )
            {
                StringTokenizer st = new StringTokenizer( line );

                try
                {
                    if( st.countTokens( ) != 3 )
                    {
                        System.err.println( "Skipping bad line " + line );
                        continue;
                    }
                    String source  = st.nextToken( );
                    String dest    = st.nextToken( );
                    int    cost    = Integer.parseInt( st.nextToken( ) );
                    g.addEdge( source, dest, cost );
                }
                catch( NumberFormatException e )
                  { System.err.println( "Skipping bad line " + line ); }
            }
        }
        catch( IOException e )
          { System.err.println( e ); }

        System.out.println( "File read..." );
        System.out.println( g.vertexMap.size( ) + " vertices" );

        BufferedReader in = new BufferedReader(
                            new InputStreamReader( System.in ) );
        while( processRequest( in, g ) )
            ;
    }
```

figure 14.14

A simple `main`

```
    /**
     * Process a request; return false if end of file.
     */
    public static boolean processRequest( BufferedReader in, Graph g )
    {
        String startName = null;
        String destName = null;
        String alg = null;

        try
        {
            System.out.print( "Enter start node:" );
            if( ( startName = in.readLine( ) ) == null )
                return false;
            System.out.print( "Enter destination node:" );
            if( ( destName = in.readLine( ) ) == null )
                return false;
            System.out.print( " Enter algorithm (u, d, n, a ): " );
            if( ( alg = in.readLine( ) ) == null )
                return false;

            if( alg.equals( "u" ) )
                g.unweighted( startName );
            else if( alg.equals( "d" ) )
                g.dijkstra( startName );
            else if( alg.equals( "n" ) )
                g.negative( startName );
            else if( alg.equals( "a" ) )
                g.acyclic( startName );

            g.printPath( destName );
        }
        catch( IOException e )
          { System.err.println( e ); }
        catch( NoSuchElementException e )
          { System.err.println( e ); }
        catch( GraphException e )
          { System.err.println( e ); }
        return true;
    }
```

figure 14.15

For testing purposes, `processRequest` calls one of the shortest-path algorithms

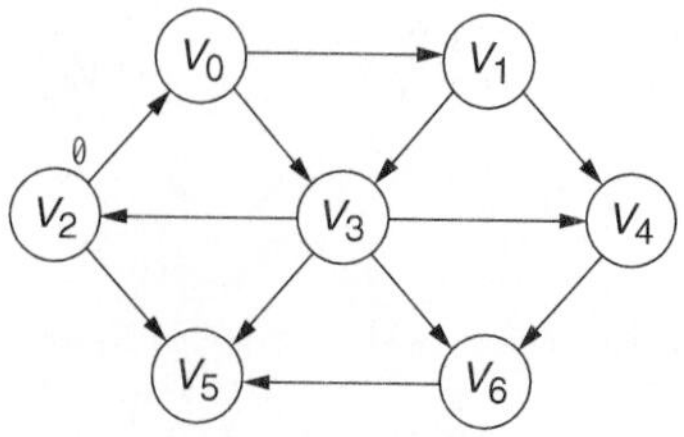

figure 14.16

The graph after the starting vertex has been marked as reachable in zero edges

figure 14.17

The graph after all the vertices whose path length from the starting vertex is 1 have been found

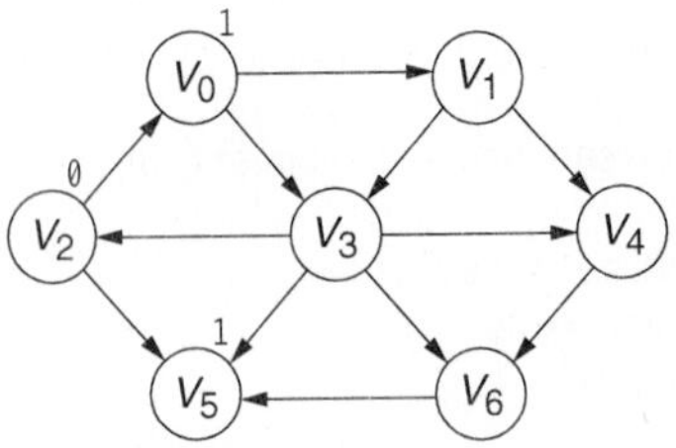

Next, we find each vertex whose shortest path from S is exactly 2. We do so by finding all the vertices adjacent to V_0 or V_5 (the vertices at distance 1) whose shortest paths are not already known. This search tells us that the shortest path to V_1 and V_3 is 2. Figure 14.18 shows our progress so far.

Breadth-first search processes vertices in layers: Those closest to the start are evaluated first.

Finally, by examining the vertices adjacent to the recently evaluated V_1 and V_3 ,we find that V_4 and V_6 have a shortest path of 3 edges. All vertices have now been calculated. Figure 14.19 shows the final result of the algorithm.

This strategy for searching a graph is called *breadth-first search,* which operates by processing vertices in layers: Those closest to the start are evaluated first, and those most distant are evaluated last.

figure 14.18

The graph after all the vertices whose shortest path from the starting vertex is 2 have been found

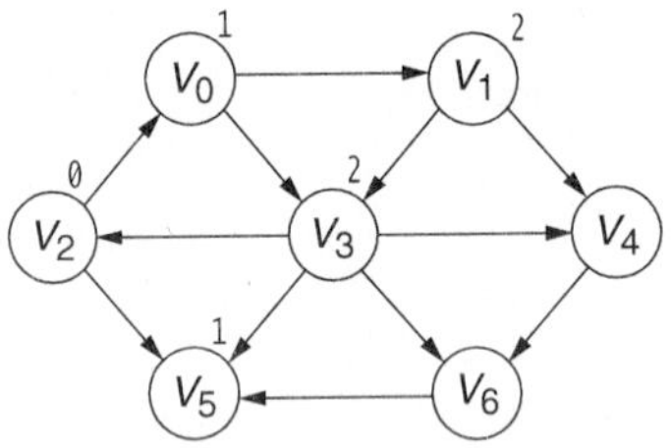

figure 14.19

The final shortest paths

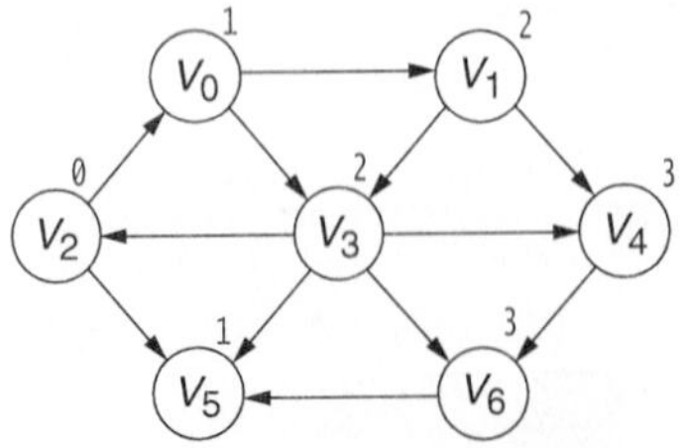

Figure 14.20 illustrates a fundamental principle: If a path to vertex v has cost D_v and w is adjacent to v, then there exists a path to w of cost $D_w = D_v + 1$. All the shortest-path algorithms work by starting with $D_w = \infty$ and reducing its value when an appropriate v is scanned. To do this task efficiently, we must scan vertices v systematically. When a given v is scanned, we update the vertices w adjacent to v by scanning through v's adjacency list.

The *roving eyeball* moves from vertex to vertex and updates distances for adjacent vertices.

From the preceding discussion, we conclude that an algorithm for solving the unweighted shortest-path problem is as follows. Let D_i be the length of the shortest path from S to i. We know that $D_S = 0$ and that $D_i = \infty$ initially for all $i \neq S$. We maintain a *roving eyeball* that hops from vertex to vertex and is initially at S. If v is the vertex that the eyeball is currently on, then, for all w that are adjacent to v, we set $D_w = D_v + 1$ if $D_w = \infty$. This reflects the fact that we can get to w by following a path to v and extending the path by the edge (v, w)—again, illustrated in Figure 14.20. So we update vertices w as they are seen from the vantage point of the eyeball. Because the eyeball processes each vertex in order of its distance from the starting vertex and the edge adds exactly 1 to the length of the path to w, we are guaranteed that the first time D_w is lowered from ∞, it is lowered to the value of the length of the shortest path to w. These actions also tell us that the next-to-last vertex on the path to w is v, so one extra line of code allows us to store the actual path.

After we have processed all of v's adjacent vertices, we move the eyeball to another vertex u (that has not been visited by the eyeball) such that $D_u \equiv D_v$. If that is not possible, we move to a u that satisfies $D_u = D_v + 1$. If that is not possible, we are done. Figure 14.21 shows how the eyeball visits vertices and updates distances. The lightly shaded node at each stage represents the position of the eyeball. In this picture and those that follow, the stages are shown top to bottom, left to right.

All vertices adjacent to v are found by scanning v's adjacency list.

The remaining detail is the data structure, and there are two basic actions to take. First, we repeatedly have to find the vertex at which to place the eyeball. Second, we need to check all w's adjacent to v (the current vertex) throughout the algorithm. The second action is easily implemented by iterating through v's adjacency list. Indeed, as each edge is processed only once,

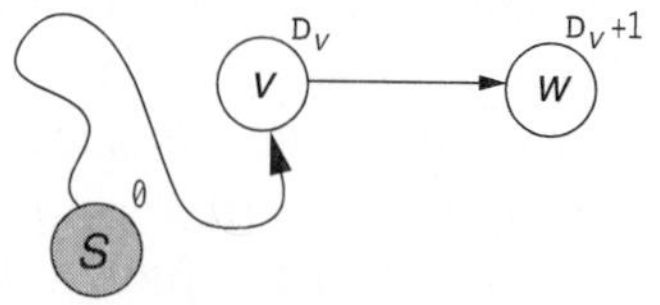

figure 14.20

If w is adjacent to v and there is a path to v, there also is a path to w.

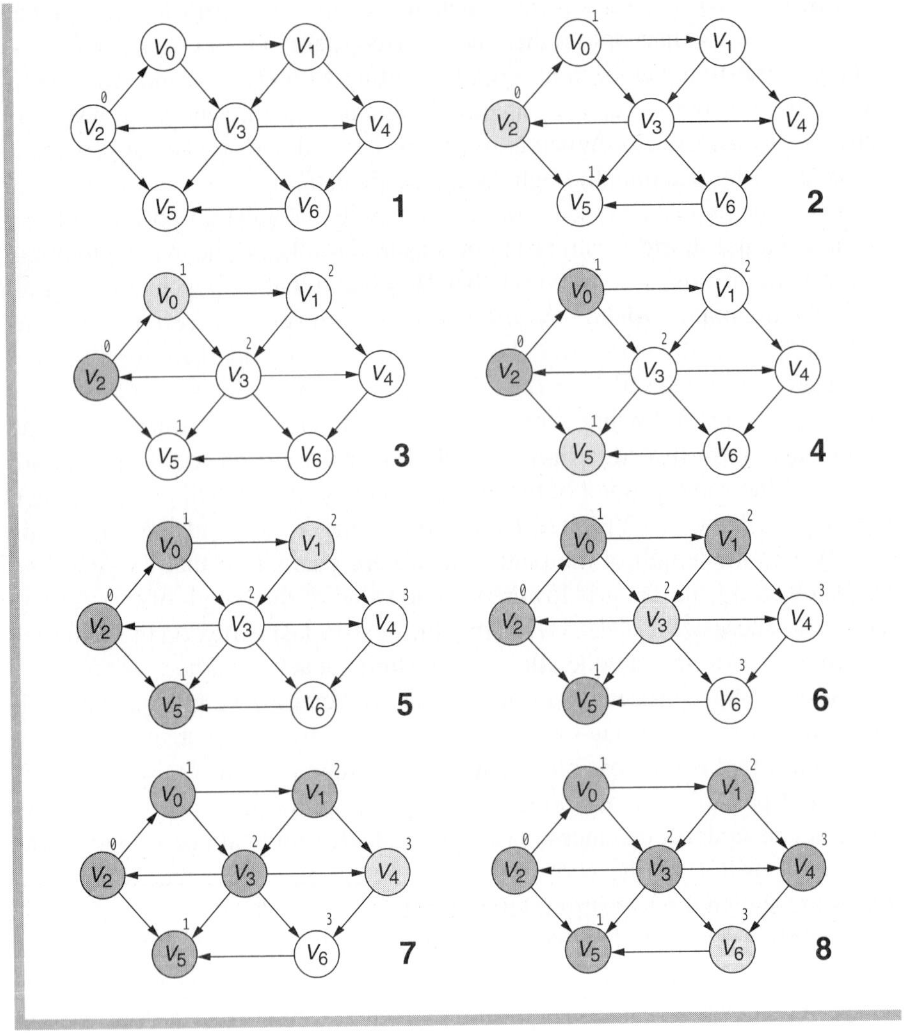

figure 14.21

Searching the graph in the unweighted shortest-path computation. The darkest-shaded vertices have already been completely processed, the lightest vertices have not yet been used as v, and the medium-shaded vertex is the current vertex, v. The stages proceed left to right, top to bottom, as numbered.

the total cost of all the iterations is $O(|E|)$. The first action is more challenging: We cannot simply scan through the graph table (see Figure 14.4) looking for an appropriate vertex because each scan could take $O(|V|)$ time and we need to perform it $|V|$ times. Thus the total cost would be $O(|V|^2)$, which is unacceptable for sparse graphs. Fortunately, this technique is not needed.

When a vertex w has its D_w lowered from ∞, it becomes a candidate for an eyeball visitation at some point in the future. That is, after the eyeball visits vertices in the current distance group D_v, it visits the next distance group $D_v + 1$, which is the group containing w. Thus w just needs to wait in line for its turn. Also, as it clearly does not need to go before any other vertices that have already had their distances lowered, w needs to be placed at the end of a queue of vertices waiting for an eyeball visitation.

To select a vertex v for the eyeball, we merely choose the front vertex from the queue. We start with an empty queue and then we enqueue the starting vertex S. A vertex is enqueued and dequeued at most once per shortest-path calculation, and queue operations are constant time, so the cost of choosing the vertex to select is only $O(|V|)$ *for the entire algorithm*. Thus the cost of the breadth-first search is dominated by the scans of the adjacency list and is $O(|E|)$, or linear, in the size of the graph.

When a vertex has its distance lowered (which can happen only once), it is placed on the queue so that the eyeball can visit it in the future. The starting vertex is placed on the queue when its distance is initialized to zero.

14.2.2 java implementation

The unweighted shortest-path algorithm is implemented by the method `unweighted`, as shown in Figure 14.22. The code is a line-for-line translation of the algorithm described previously. The initialization at lines 6–13 makes all the distances infinity, sets D_S to 0, and then enqueues the start vertex. The queue is declared at line 12. While the queue is not empty, there are vertices to visit. Thus at line 17 we move to the vertex v that is at the front of the queue. Line 19 iterates over the adjacency list and produces all the w's that are adjacent to v. The test $D_w = \infty$ is performed at line 23. If it returns `true`, the update $D_w = D_v + 1$ is performed at line 25 along with the update of w's `prev` data member and enqueueing of w at lines 26 and 27, respectively.

Implementation is much simpler than it sounds. It follows the algorithm description verbatim.

14.3 positive-weighted, shortest-path problem

Recall that the weighted path length of a path is the sum of the edge costs on the path. In this section we consider the problem of finding the weighted shortest path, in a graph whose edges have nonnegative cost. We want to find the shortest weighted path from some starting vertex to all vertices. As we show shortly, the assumption that edge costs are nonnegative is important because it allows a relatively efficient algorithm. The method used to solve the positive-weighted, shortest-path problem is known as *Dijkstra's algorithm*. In the next section we examine a slower algorithm that works even if there are negative edge costs.

The *weighted path length* is the sum of the edge costs on a path.

positive-weighted, single-source, shortest-path problem
Find the shortest path (measured by total cost) from a designated vertex S to every vertex. All edge costs are nonnegative.

```
/**
 * Single-source unweighted shortest-path algorithm.
 */
public void unweighted( String startName )
{
    clearAll( );

    Vertex start = vertexMap.get( startName );
    if( start == null )
        throw new NoSuchElementException( "Start vertex not found" );

    Queue<Vertex> q = new LinkedList<Vertex>( );
    q.add( start ); start.dist = 0;

    while( !q.isEmpty( ) )
    {
        Vertex v = q.remove( );

        for( Edge e : v.adj )
        {
            Vertex w = e.dest;

            if( w.dist == INFINITY )
            {
                w.dist = v.dist + 1;
                w.prev = v;
                q.add( w );
            }
        }
    }
}
```

figure 14.22

The unweighted shortest-path algorithm, using breadth-first search

14.3.1 theory: dijkstra's algorithm

Dijkstra's algorithm is used to solve the positive-weighted shortest-path problem.

The positive-weighted, shortest-path problem is solved in much the same way as the unweighted problem. However, because of the edge costs, a few things change. The following issues must be examined:

1. How do we adjust D_w?
2. How do we find the vertex v for the eyeball to visit?

We begin by examining how to alter D_w. In solving the unweighted shortest-path problem, if $D_w = \infty$, we set $D_w = D_v + 1$ because we lower the value of D_w if vertex v offers a shorter path to w. The dynamics of the algorithm ensure that we need alter D_w only once. We add 1 to D_v because the length of the path to w is 1 more than the length of the path to v. If we apply this logic to the weighted case, we should set $D_w = D_v + c_{v,w}$ if this new value of D_w is better than the original value. However, we are no longer guaranteed that D_w is altered only once. Consequently, D_w should be altered if its current value is larger than $D_v + c_{v,w}$ (rather than merely testing against ∞). Put simply, the algorithm decides whether v should be used on the path to w. The original cost D_w is the cost without using v; the cost $D_v + c_{v,w}$ is the cheapest path using v (so far).

We use $D_v + c_{v,w}$ as the new distance and to decide whether the distance should be updated.

Figure 14.23 shows a typical situation. Earlier in the algorithm, w had its distance lowered to 8 when the eyeball visited vertex u. However, when the eyeball visits vertex v, vertex w needs to have its distance lowered to 6 because we have a new shortest path. This result never occurs in the unweighted algorithm because all edges add 1 to the path length, so $D_u \le D_v$ implies $D_u + 1 \le D_v + 1$ and thus $D_w \le D_v + 1$. Here, even though $D_u \le D_v$, we can still improve the path to w by considering v.

A queue is no longer appropriate for storing vertices awaiting an eyeball visit.

Figure 14.23 illustrates another important point. When w has its distance lowered, it does so only because it is adjacent to some vertex that has been visited by the eyeball. For instance, after the eyeball visits v and processing has been completed, the value of D_w is 6 and the last vertex on the path is a vertex that has been visited by the eyeball. Similarly, the vertex prior to v must also have been visited by the eyeball, and so on. Thus at any point the value of D_w represents *a path from S to w using only vertices that have been visited by the eyeball as intermediate nodes.* This crucial fact gives us Theorem 14.1.

The distance for unvisited vertices represents a path with only visited vertices as intermediate nodes.

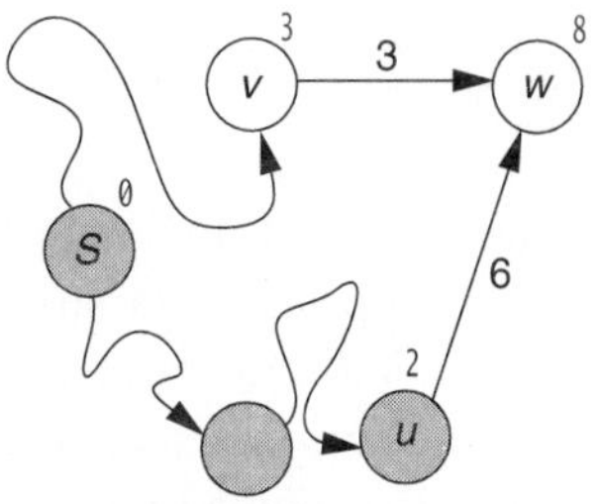

figure 14.23

The eyeball is at v and w is adjacent, so D_w should be lowered to 6.

Theorem 14.1 If we move the eyeball to the unseen vertex with minimum D_i, the algorithm correctly produces the shortest paths if there are no negative edge costs.

Proof Call each eyeball visit a "stage." We prove by induction that, after any stage, the values of D_i for vertices visited by the eyeball form the shortest path and that the values of D_i for the other vertices form the shortest path using only vertices visited by the eyeball as intermediates. Because the first vertex visited is the starting vertex, this statement is correct through the first stage. Assume that it is correct for the first k stages. Let v be the vertex chosen by the eyeball in stage $k + 1$. Suppose, for the purpose of showing a contradiction, that there is a path from S to v of length less than D_v.

This path must go through an intermediate vertex that has not yet been visited by the eyeball. Call the first intermediate vertex on the path not visited by the eyeball u. This situation is shown in Figure 14.24. The path to u uses only vertices visited by the eyeball as intermediates, so by induction, D_u represents the optimal distance to u. Moreover, $D_u < D_v$, because u is on the supposed shorter path to v. This inequality is a contradiction because then we would have moved the eyeball to u instead of v. The proof is completed by showing that all the D_i values remain correct for nonvisited nodes, which is clear by the update rule.

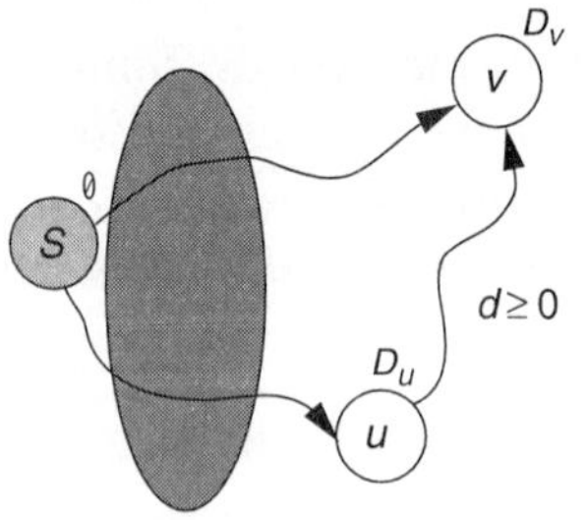

figure 14.24

If D_v is minimal among all unseen vertices and if all edge costs are nonnegative, D_v represents the shortest path.

Figure 14.25 shows the stages of Dijkstra's algorithm. The remaining issue is the selection of an appropriate data structure. For dense graphs, we can scan down the graph table looking for the appropriate vertex. As with the unweighted shortest-path algorithm, this scan will take $O(|V|^2)$ time, which is optimal for a dense graph. For a sparse graph, we want to do better.

Certainly, a queue does not work. The fact that we need to find the vertex v with minimum D_v suggests that a priority queue is the method of choice. There are two ways to use the priority queue. One is to store each vertex in the

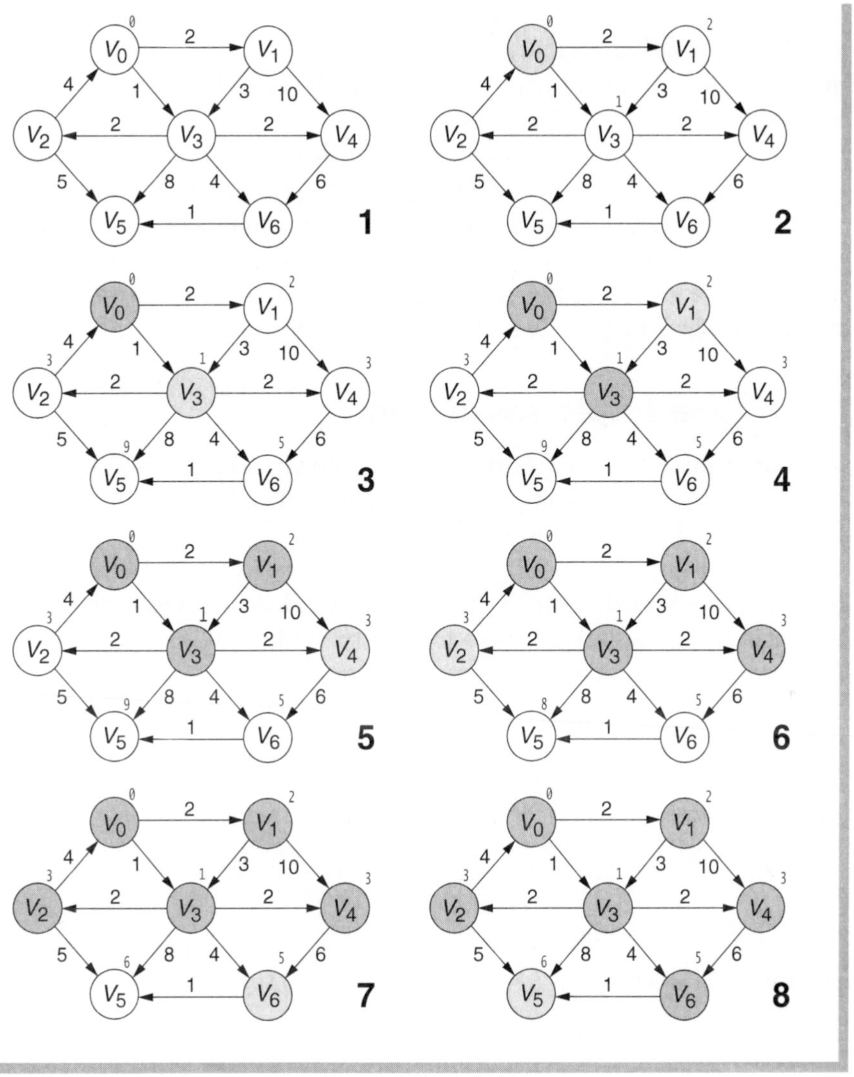

figure 14.25

Stages of Dijkstra's algorithm. The conventions are the same as those in Figure 14.21.

priority queue and use the distance (obtained by consulting the graph table) as the ordering function. When we alter any D_w, we must update the priority queue by reestablishing the ordering property. This action amounts to a `decreaseKey` operation. To take it we need to be able to find the location of w in the priority queue. Many implementations of the priority queue do not support `decreaseKey`. One that does is the *pairing heap;* we discuss use of the pairing heap for this application in Chapter 23.

The priority queue is an appropriate data structure. The easiest method is to add a new entry, consisting of a vertex and a distance, to the priority queue every time a vertex has its distance lowered. We can find the new vertex to move to by repeatedly removing the minimum distance vertex from the priority queue until an unvisited vertex emerges.

Rather than use a fancy priority queue, we use a method that works with a simple priority queue, such as the binary heap, to be discussed in Chapter 21. Our method involves inserting an object consisting of w and D_w in the priority queue whenever we lower D_w. To select a new vertex v for visitation, we repeatedly remove the minimum item (based on distance) from the priority queue until an unvisited vertex emerges. Because the size of the priority queue could be as large as $|E|$ and there are at most $|E|$ priority queue insertions and deletions, the running time is $O(|E|\log|E|)$. Because $|E| \le |V|^2$ implies $\log|E| \le 2\log|V|$, we have the same $O(|E|\log|V|)$ algorithm that we would have if we used the first method (in which the priority queue size is at most $|V|$).

14.3.2 java implementation

Again, the implementation follows the description fairly closely.

The object placed on the priority queue is shown in Figure 14.26. It consists of w and D_w and a comparison function defined on the basis of D_w. Figure 14.27 shows the routine `dijkstra` that calculates the shortest paths.

Line 6 declares the priority queue `pq`. We declare `vrec` at line 18 to store the result of each `deleteMin`. As with the unweighted shortest-path algorithm, we begin by setting all distances to infinity, setting $D_S = 0$, and placing the starting vertex in our data structure.

```java
// Represents an entry in the priority queue for Dijkstra's algorithm.
class Path implements Comparable<Path>
{
    public Vertex     dest;   // w
    public double     cost;   // d(w)

    public Path( Vertex d, double c )
    {
        dest = d;
        cost = c;
    }

    public int compareTo( Path rhs )
    {
        double otherCost = rhs.cost;

        return cost < otherCost ? -1 : cost > otherCost ? 1 : 0;
    }
}
```

figure 14.26

Basic item stored in the priority queue

```
1 /**
2  * Single-source weighted shortest-path algorithm.
3  */
4 public void dijkstra( String startName )
5 {
6     PriorityQueue<Path> pq = new PriorityQueue<Path>( );
7 
8     Vertex start = vertexMap.get( startName );
9     if( start == null )
10        throw new NoSuchElementException( "Start vertex not found" );
11
12    clearAll( );
13    pq.add( new Path( start, 0 ) ); start.dist = 0;
14
15    int nodesSeen = 0;
16    while( !pq.isEmpty( ) && nodesSeen < vertexMap.size( ) )
17    {
18        Path vrec = pq.remove( );
19        Vertex v = vrec.dest;
20        if( v.scratch != 0 )  // already processed v
21            continue;
22
23        v.scratch = 1;
24        nodesSeen++;
25
26        for( Edge e : v.adj )
27        {
28            Vertex w = e.dest;
29            double cvw = e.cost;
30
31            if( cvw < 0 )
32                throw new GraphException( "Graph has negative edges" );
33
34            if( w.dist > v.dist + cvw )
35            {
36                w.dist = v.dist + cvw;
37                w.prev = v;
38                pq.add( new Path( w, w.dist ) );
39            }
40        }
41    }
42 }
```

figure 14.27

A positive-weighted, shortest-path algorithm: Dijkstra's algorithm

Each iteration of the `while` loop that begins at line 16 puts the eyeball at a vertex *v* and processes it by examining adjacent vertices *w*. *v* is chosen by repeatedly removing entries from the priority queue (at line 18) until we encounter a vertex that has not been processed. We use the scratch variable to record it. Initially, scratch is 0. Thus, if the vertex is unprocessed, the test fails at line 20, and we reach line 23. Then, when the vertex is processed, scratch is set to 1 (at line 23). The priority queue might be empty if, for instance, some of the vertices are unreachable. In that case, we can return immediately. The loop at lines 26–40 is much like the loop in the unweighted algorithm. The difference is that at line 29, we must extract cvw from the adjacency list entry, ensure that the edge is nonnegative (otherwise, our algorithm could produce incorrect answers), add cvw instead of 1 at lines 34 and 36, and add to the priority queue at line 38.

14.4 negative-weighted, shortest-path problem

Negative edges cause Dijkstra's algorithm not to work. An alternative algorithm is needed.

Dijkstra's algorithm requires that edge costs be nonnegative. This requirement is reasonable for most graph applications, but sometimes it is too restrictive. In this section we briefly discuss the most general case: the negative-weighted, shortest-path algorithm.

negative-weighted, single-source, shortest-path problem
Find the shortest path (measured by total cost) from a designated vertex S to every vertex. Edge costs may be negative.

14.4.1 theory

A *negative-cost cycle* makes most, if not all, paths undefined because we can stay in the cycle arbitrarily long and obtain an arbitrarily small weighted path length.

The proof of Dijkstra's algorithm required the condition that edge costs, and thus paths, be nonnegative. Indeed, if the graph has negative edge costs, Dijkstra's algorithm does not work. The problem is that, once a vertex v has been processed, there may be, from some other unprocessed vertex u, a negative path back to v. In such a case, taking a path from S to u to v is better than going from S to v without using u. If the latter were to happen, we would be in trouble. Not only would the path to v be wrong, but we also would have to revisit v because the distances of vertices reachable from v may be affected. (In Exercise 14.10 you are asked to construct an explicit example; four vertices suffice.)

We have an additional problem to worry about. Consider the graph shown in Figure 14.28. The path from V_3 to V_4 has a cost of 2. However, a shorter path exists by following the loop V_3, V_4, V_1, V_3, V_4, which has a cost of –3. This path is still not the shortest because we could stay in the loop arbitrarily long. Thus the shortest path between these two points is undefined.

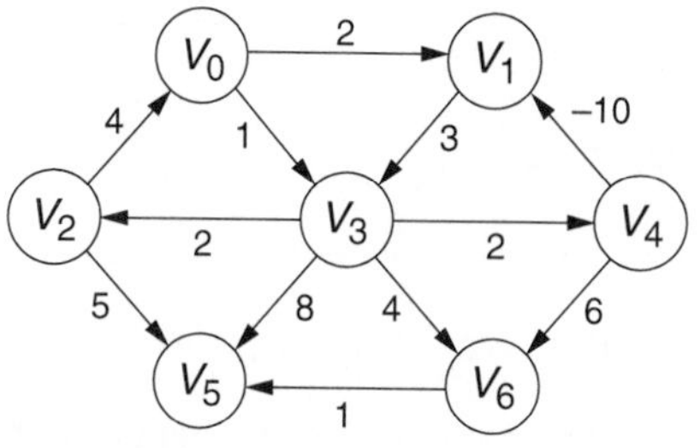

figure 14.28

A graph with a negative-cost cycle

This problem is not restricted to nodes in the cycle. The shortest path from V_2 to V_5 is also undefined because there is a way to get into and out of the loop. This loop is called a *negative-cost cycle,* which when present in a graph makes most, if not all, the shortest paths undefined. Negative-cost edges by themselves are not necessarily bad; it is the cycles that are. Our algorithm either finds the shortest paths or reports the existence of a negative-cost cycle.

A combination of the weighted and unweighted algorithms will solve the problem, but at the cost of a potentially drastic increase in running time. As suggested previously, when D_w is altered, we must revisit it at some point in the future. Consequently, we use the queue as in the unweighted algorithm, but we use $D_v + c_{v,w}$ as the distance measure (as in Dijkstra's algorithm). The algorithm that is used to solve the negative-weighted, shortest-path problem is known as the *Bellman–Ford algorithm.*

Whenever a vertex has its distance lowered, it must be placed on a queue. This may happen repeatedly for each vertex.

When the eyeball visits vertex v for the ith time, the value of D_v is the length of the shortest weighted path consisting of i or fewer edges. We leave the proof for you to do as Exercise 14.12. Consequently, if there are no negative-cost cycles, a vertex can dequeue at most $|V|$ times and the algorithm takes at most $O(|E||V|)$ time. Further, if a vertex dequeues more than $|V|$ times, we have detected a negative-cost cycle.

The running time can be large, especially if there is a negative-cost cycle.

14.4.2 java implementation

Implementation of the negative-weighted, shortest-path algorithm is given in Figure 14.29. We make one small change to the algorithm description—namely, we do not enqueue a vertex if it is already on the queue. This change involves use of the `scratch` data member. When a vertex is enqueued, we increment `scratch` (at line 31). When it is dequeued, we increment it again (at line 18). Thus `scratch` is odd if the vertex is on the queue, and `scratch/2` tells us how many times it has left the queue (which explains the test at line 18). When some w has its distance changed, but it is already on the queue (because `scratch` is odd), we do not

The tricky part of the implementation is the manipulation of the `scratch` variable. We attempt to avoid having any vertex appear on the queue twice at any instant.

```
1  /**
2   * Single-source negative-weighted shortest-path algorithm.
3   */
4  public void negative( String startName )
5  {
6      clearAll( );
7
8      Vertex start = vertexMap.get( startName );
9      if( start == null )
10         throw new NoSuchElementException( "Start vertex not found" );
11
12     Queue<Vertex> q = new LinkedList<Vertex>( );
13     q.add( start ); start.dist = 0; start.scratch++;
14
15     while( !q.isEmpty( ) )
16     {
17         Vertex v = q.removeFirst( );
18         if( v.scratch++ > 2 * vertexMap.size( ) )
19             throw new GraphException( "Negative cycle detected" );
20
21         for( Edge e : v.adj )
22         {
23             Vertex w = e.dest;
24             double cvw = e.cost;
25
26             if( w.dist > v.dist + cvw )
27             {
28                 w.dist = v.dist + cvw;
29                 w.prev = v;
30                   // Enqueue only if not already on the queue
31                 if( w.scratch++ % 2 == 0 )
32                     q.add( w );
33                 else
34                     w.scratch--;  // undo the enqueue increment
35             }
36         }
37     }
38 }
```

figure 14.29

A negative-weighted, shortest-path algorithm: Negative edges are allowed.

enqueue it. However, we do not add 2 to it to indicate that it has gone on (and off) the queue; this is done by offsetting of lines 31 and 34. The rest of the algorithm uses code that has already been introduced in both the unweighted shortest-path algorithm (Figure 14.22) and Dijkstra's algorithm (Figure 14.27).

14.5 path problems in acyclic graphs

Recall that a directed acyclic graph has no cycles. This important class of graphs simplifies the solution to the shortest-path problem. For instance, we do not have to worry about negative-cost cycles because there are no cycles. Thus we consider the following problem.

weighted single-source, shortest-path problem for acyclic graphs
Find the shortest path (measured by total cost) from a designated vertex S to every vertex in an acyclic graph. Edge costs are unrestricted.

14.5.1 topological sorting

Before considering the shortest-path problem, let us examine a related problem: a topological sort. A *topological sort* orders vertices in a directed acyclic graph such that if there is a path from u to v, then v appears after u in the ordering. For instance, a graph is typically used to represent the prerequisite requirement for courses at universities. An edge (v, w) indicates that course v must be completed before course w may be attempted. A topological order of the courses is any sequence that does not violate the prerequisite requirements.

A *topological sort* orders vertices in a directed acyclic graph such that if there is a path from u to v, then v appears *after* u in the ordering. A graph that has a cycle cannot have a topological order.

Clearly, a topological sort is not possible if a graph has a cycle because, for two vertices v and w on the cycle, there is a path from v to w and w to v. Thus any ordering of v and w would contradict one of the two paths. A graph may have several topological orders, and in most cases, any legal ordering will do.

In a simple algorithm for performing a topological sort we first find any vertex v that has no incoming edges. Then we print the vertex and logically remove it, along with its edges, from the graph. Finally, we apply the same strategy to the rest of the graph. More formally, we say that the *indegree* of a vertex v is the number of incoming edges (u, v).

We compute the indegrees of all vertices in the graph. In practice, *logically remove* means that we lower the count of incoming edges for each vertex adjacent to v. Figure 14.30 shows the algorithm applied to an acyclic graph. The indegree is computed for each vertex. Vertex V_2 has indegree 0, so it is first in the topological order. If there were several vertices of indegree 0, we could choose any one of them. When V_2 and its edges are removed from the graph, the indegrees of V_0, V_3, and V_5 are all decremented by 1. Now V_0 has indegree 0, so it is next in the topological order, and V_1 and V_3 have their indegrees lowered. The algorithm continues, and the remaining vertices are examined in the order V_1, V_3, V_4, V_6, and V_5. To reiterate, we do not physically delete edges from the graph; removing edges just makes it easier to see how the indegree count is lowered.

The *indegree* of a vertex is the number of incoming edges. A topological sort can be performed in linear time by repeatedly and logically removing vertices that have no incoming edges.

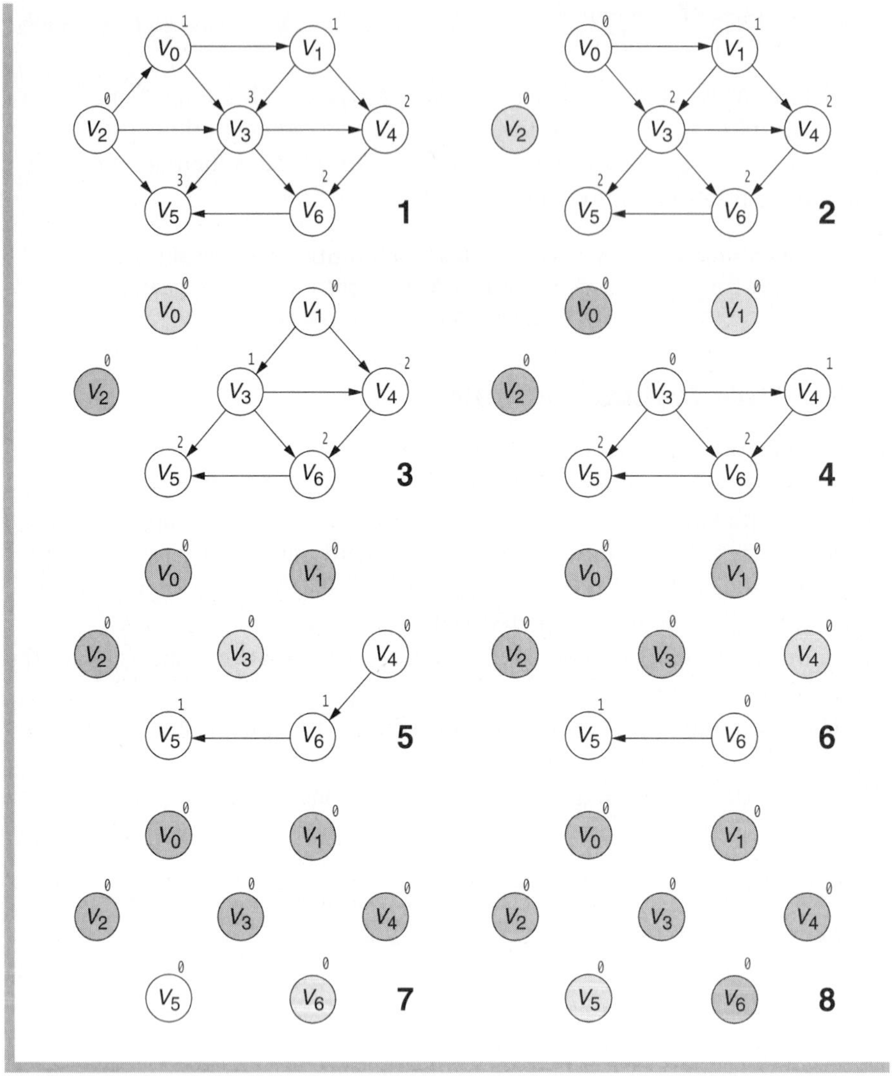

figure 14.30

A topological sort. The conventions are the same as those in Figure 14.21.

> The algorithm produces the correct answer and detects cycles if the graph is not acyclic.

Two important issues to consider are *correctness* and *efficiency*. Clearly, any ordering produced by the algorithm is a topological order. The question is whether every acyclic graph has a topological order, and if so, whether our algorithm is guaranteed to find one. The answer is yes to both questions.

If at any point there are unseen vertices but none of them have an indegree of 0, we are guaranteed that a cycle exists. To illustrate we can pick any vertex A_0. Because A_0 has an incoming edge, let A_1 be the vertex connected to it. And as A_1 has an incoming edge, let A_2 be the vertex connected to it. We repeat this process N times, where N is the number of unprocessed vertices left in the graph. Among $A_0, A_1, \ldots, A_N$, there must be two identical vertices (because there are N vertices but $N + 1$ A_i's). Tracing backward between those identical A_i and A_j exhibits a cycle.

We can implement the algorithm in linear time by placing all unprocessed indegree 0 vertices on a queue. Initially, all vertices of indegree 0 are placed on the queue. To find the next vertex in the topological order, we merely get and remove the front item from the queue. When a vertex has its indegree lowered to 0, it is placed on the queue. If the queue empties before all the vertices have been topologically sorted, the graph has a cycle. The running time is clearly linear, by the same reasoning used in the unweighted shortest-path algorithm.

The running time is linear if a queue is used.

14.5.2 theory of the acyclic shortest-path algorithm

An important application of topological sorting is its use in solving the shortest-path problem for acyclic graphs. The idea is to have the eyeball visit vertices in topological order.

In an acyclic graph, the eyeball merely visits vertices in topological order.

This idea works because, when the eyeball visits vertex v, we are guaranteed that D_v can no longer be lowered; by the topological ordering rule, it has no incoming edges emanating from unvisited nodes. Figure 14.31 shows the stages of the shortest-path algorithm, using topological ordering to guide the vertex visitations. Note that the sequence of vertices visited is not the same as in Dijkstra's algorithm. Also note that vertices visited by the eyeball prior to its reaching the starting vertex are unreachable from the starting vertex and have no influence on the distances of any vertex.

We do not need a priority queue. Instead, we need only to incorporate the topological sort into the shortest-path computation. Thus we find that the algorithm runs in linear time and works even with negative edge weights.

The result is a linear-time algorithm even with negative edge weights.

14.5.3 java implementation

The implementation of the shortest-path algorithm for acyclic graphs is shown in Figure 14.32. We use a queue to perform the topological sort and maintain the indegree information in the `scratch` data member. Lines 15–18 compute the indegrees, and at lines 21–23 we place any indegree 0 vertices on the queue.

The implementation combines a topological sort calculation and a shortest-path calculation. The indegree information is stored in the `scratch` data member.

We then repeatedly remove a vertex from the queue at line 28. Note that, if the queue is empty, the `for` loop is terminated by the test at line 26. If the loop terminates because of a cycle, this fact is reported at line 50. Otherwise, the loop at line 30 steps through the adjacency list and a value of w is obtained

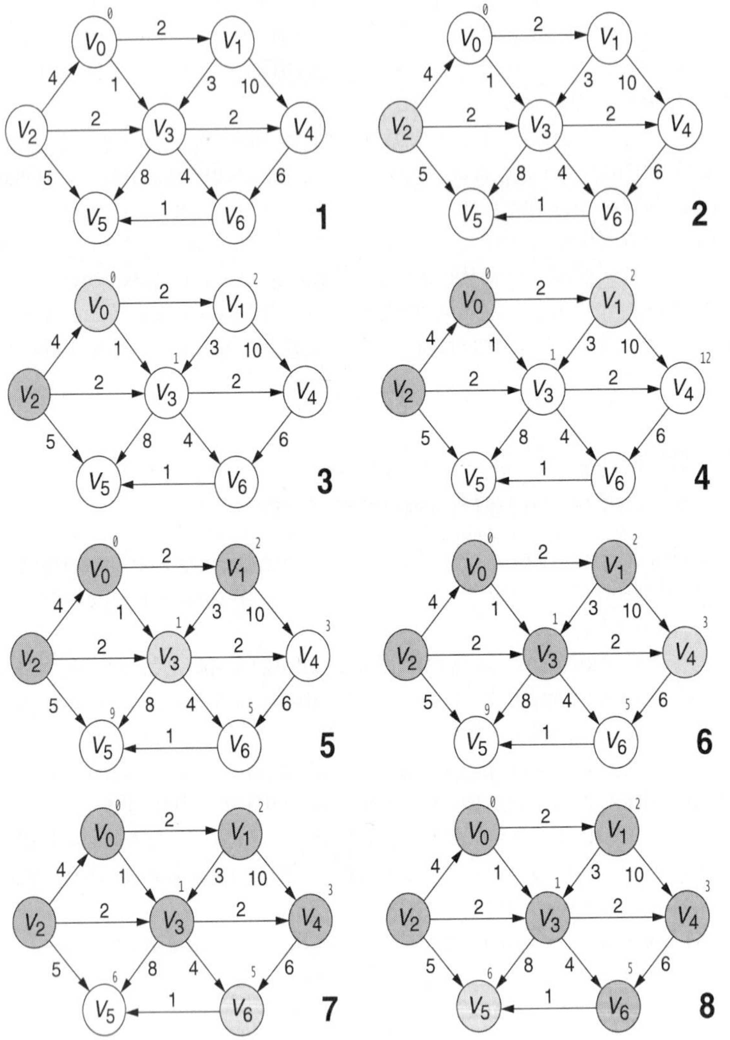

figure 14.31

The stages of acyclic graph algorithm. The conventions are the same as those in Figure 14.21.

at line 32. Immediately we lower w's indegree at line 35 and, if it has fallen to 0, we place it on the queue at line 36.

Vertices that appear before S in the topological order are unreachable.

Recall that if the current vertex v appears prior to S in topological order, v must be unreachable from S. Consequently, it still has $D_v \equiv \infty$ and thus cannot hope to provide a path to any adjacent vertex w. We perform a test at line 38, and if a path cannot be provided, we do not attempt any distance calculations. Otherwise, at lines 41 to 45, we use the same calculations as in Dijkstra's algorithm to update D_w if necessary.

```
/**
 * Single-source negative-weighted acyclic-graph shortest-path algorithm.
 */
public void acyclic( String startName )
{
    Vertex start = vertexMap.get( startName );
    if( start == null )
        throw new NoSuchElementException( "Start vertex not found" );

    clearAll( );
    Queue<Vertex> q = new LinkedList<Vertex>( );
    start.dist = 0;

      // Compute the indegrees
    Collection<Vertex> vertexSet = vertexMap.values( );
    for( Vertex v : vertexSet )
        for( Edge e : v.adj )
            e.dest.scratch++;

      // Enqueue vertices of indegree zero
    for( Vertex v : vertexSet )
        if( v.scratch == 0 )
            q.add( v );

    int iterations;
    for( iterations = 0; !q.isEmpty( ); iterations++ )
    {
        Vertex v = q.remove( );

        for( Edge e : v.adj )
        {
            Vertex w = e.dest;
            double cvw = e.cost;

            if( --w.scratch == 0 )
                q.add( w );

            if( v.dist == INFINITY )
                continue;

            if( w.dist > v.dist + cvw )
            {
                w.dist = v.dist + cvw;
                w.prev = v;
            }
        }
    }

    if( iterations != vertexMap.size( ) )
        throw new GraphException( "Graph has a cycle!" );
}
```

figure 14.32

A shortest-path algorithm for acyclic graphs

14.5.4 an application: critical-path analysis

Critical-path analysis is used to schedule tasks associated with a project.

An important use of acyclic graphs is *critical-path analysis,* a form of analysis used to schedule tasks associated with a project. The graph shown in Figure 14.33 provides an example. Each vertex represents an activity that must be completed, along with the time needed to complete it. The graph is thus called an *activity-node graph,* in which vertices represent activities and edges represent precedence relationships. An edge (v, w) indicates that activity v must be completed before activity w may begin, which implies that the graph must be acyclic. We assume that any activities that do not depend (either directly or indirectly) on each other can be performed in parallel by different servers.

An *activity-node graph* represents activities as vertices and precedence relationships as edges.

This type of graph could be (and frequently is) used to model construction projects. Two important questions must be answered. First, what is the earliest completion time for the project? The answer, as the graph shows, is 10 time units—required along path *A, C, F, H.* Second, which activities can be delayed, and by how long, without affecting the minimum completion time? For instance, delaying any of *A, C, F,* or *H* would push the completion time past 10 time units. However, activity *B* is less critical and can be delayed up to 2 time units without affecting the final completion time.

The *event-node graph* consists of event vertices that correspond to the completion of an activity and all its dependent activities.

To perform these calculations, we convert the activity-node graph to an *event-node graph,* in which each event corresponds to the completion of an activity and all its dependent activities. Events reachable from a node v in the event-node graph may not commence until after the event v is completed. This graph can be constructed automatically or by hand (from the activity-node graph). Dummy edges and vertices may need to be inserted to avoid introducing false dependencies (or false lack of dependencies). The event-node graph corresponding to the activity-node graph in Figure 14.33 is shown in Figure 14.34.

To find the earliest completion time of the project, we merely need to find the length of the *longest* path from the first event to the last event. For general graphs, the longest-path problem generally does not make sense because of

figure 14.33

An activity-node graph

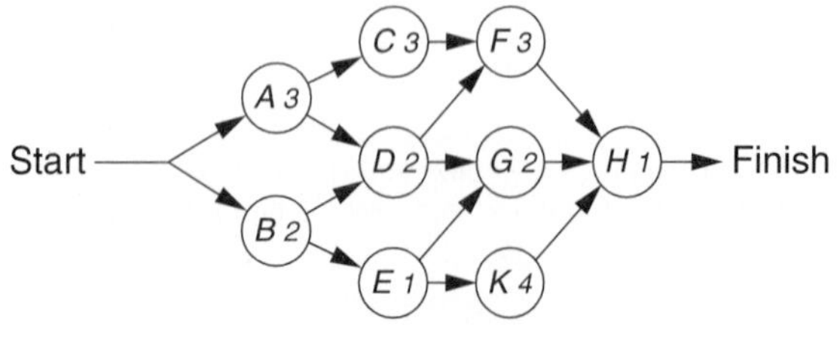

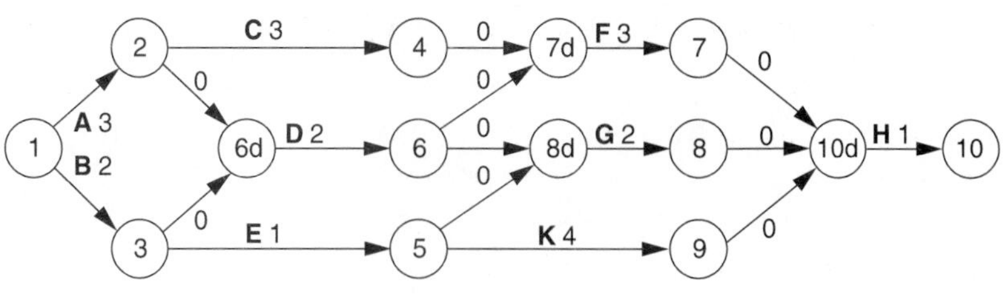

figure 14.34

An event-node graph

the possibility of a *positive-cost cycle,* which is equivalent to a negative-cost cycle in shortest-path problems. If any positive-cost cycles are present, we could ask for the longest simple path. However, no satisfactory solution is known for this problem. Fortunately, the event-node graph is acyclic; thus we need not worry about cycles. We can easily adapt the shortest-path algorithm to compute the earliest completion time for all nodes in the graph. If EC_i is the earliest completion time for node *i,* the applicable rules are

Edges show which activity must be completed to advance from one vertex to the next. The earliest completion time is the longest path.

$$EC_1 = 0 \quad \text{and} \quad EC_w = \text{Max}_{(v,\, w) \in E}(EC_v + c_{v,\, w})$$

Figure 14.35 shows the earliest completion time for each event in our example event-node graph. We can also compute the latest time, LC_i, that each event can finish without affecting final completion time. The formulas to do this are

The latest time an event can finish without delaying the project is also easily computable.

$$LC_N = EC_N \quad \text{and} \quad LC_v = \text{Min}_{(v,\, w) \in E}(LC_w - c_{v,\, w})$$

These values can be computed in linear time by maintaining for each vertex a list of all adjacent and preceding vertices. The earliest completion times are computed for vertices by their topological order, and the latest completion times are computed by reverse topological order. The latest completion times are shown in Figure 14.36.

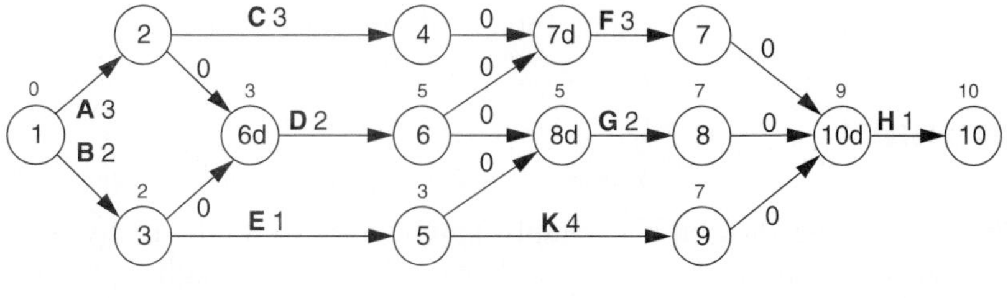

figure 14.35

Earliest completion times

figure 14.36

Latest completion times

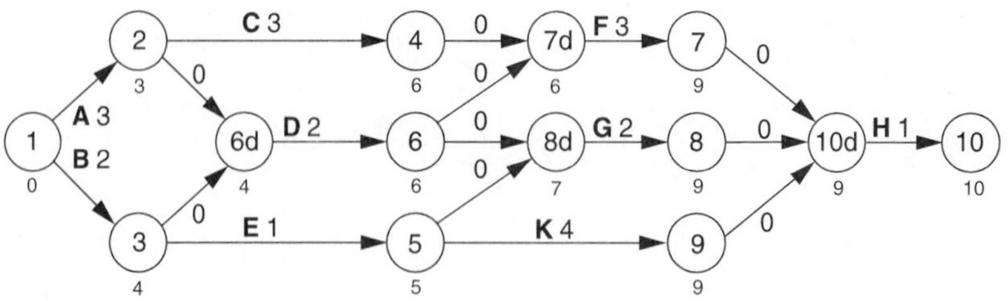

figure 14.37

Earliest completion time, latest completion time, and slack (additional edge item)

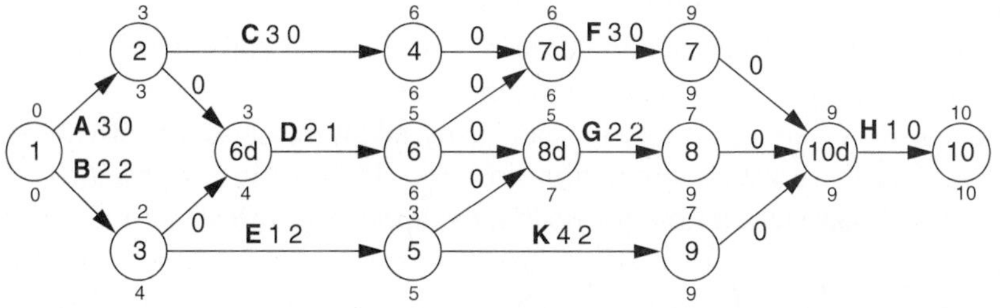

Slack time is the amount of time that an activity can be delayed without delaying overall completion.

The *slack time* for each edge in the event-node graph is the amount of time that the completion of the corresponding activity can be delayed without delaying the overall completion, or

$$\text{Slack}_{(v,\ w)} = LC_w - EC_v - c_{v,\ w}$$

Figure 14.37 shows the slack (as the third entry) for each activity in the event-node graph. For each node, the top number is the earliest completion time and the bottom number is the latest completion time.

Zero-slack activities are critical and cannot be delayed. A path of zero-slack edges is a critical path.

Some activities have zero slack. These are critical activities that must be finished on schedule. A path consisting entirely of zero-slack edges is a *critical path.*

summary

In this chapter we showed how graphs can be used to model many real-life problems and in particular how to calculate the shortest path under a wide variety of circumstances. Many of the graphs that occur are typically very

Type of Graph Problem	Running Time	Comments
Unweighted	$O(\|E\|)$	Breadth-first search
Weighted, no negative edges	$O(\|E\| \log \|V\|)$	Dijkstra's algorithm
Weighted, negative edges	$O(\|E\| \cdot \|V\|)$	Bellman–Ford algorithm
Weighted, acyclic	$O(\|E\|)$	Uses topological sort

figure 14.38

Worst-case running times of various graph algorithms

sparse, so choosing appropriate data structures to implement them is important.

For unweighted graphs, the shortest path can be computed in linear time, using breadth-first search. For positive-weighted graphs, slightly more time is needed, using Dijkstra's algorithm and an efficient priority queue. For negative-weighted graphs, the problem becomes more difficult. Finally, for acyclic graphs, the running time reverts to linear time with the aid of a topological sort.

Figure 14.38 summarizes those characteristics for these algorithms.

key concepts

activity-node graph A graph of vertices as activities and edges as precedence relationships. (504)

adjacency lists An array of lists used to represent a graph, using linear space. (474)

adjacency matrix A matrix representation of a graph that uses quadratic space. (474)

adjacent vertices Vertex w is adjacent to vertex v if there is an edge from v to w. (472)

Bellman–Ford algorithm An algorithm that is used to solve the negative-weighted, shortest-path problem. (497)

breadth-first search A search procedure that processes vertices in layers: Those closest to the start are evaluated first, and those most distant are evaluated last. (486)

critical-path analysis A form of analysis used to schedule tasks associated with a project. (504)

cycle In a directed graph, a path that begins and ends at the same vertex and contains at least one edge. (473)

dense and sparse graphs A dense graph has a large number of edges (generally quadratic). Typical graphs are not dense but are sparse. (473)

Dijkstra's algorithm An algorithm that is used to solve the positive-weighted, shortest-path problem. (490)

directed acyclic graph (DAG) A type of directed graph having no cycles. (473)

directed graph A graph in which edges are ordered pairs of vertices. (472)

edge cost (weight) The third component of an edge that measures the cost of traversing the edge. (472)

event-node graph A graph that consists of event vertices that correspond to the completion of an activity and all its dependent activities. Edges show what activity must be completed to advance from one vertex to the next. The earliest completion time is the longest path. (504)

graph A set of vertices and a set of edges that connect the vertices. (472)

indegree The number of incoming edges of a vertex. (499)

negative-cost cycle A cycle whose cost is less than zero and makes most, if not all, paths undefined because we can loop around the cycle arbitrarily many times and obtain an arbitrarily small weighted path length. (496)

path A sequence of vertices connected by edges. (472)

path length The number of edges on a path. (472)

positive-cost cycle In a longest-path problem, the equivalent of a negative-cost cycle in a shortest-path problem. (505)

simple path A path in which all vertices are distinct, except that the first and last vertices can be the same. (473)

single-source algorithms Algorithms that compute the shortest paths from some starting point to all vertices in a graph. (478)

slack time The amount of time that an activity can be delayed without delaying overall completion. (506)

topological sort A process that orders vertices in a directed acyclic graph such that if there is a path from *u* to *v*, then *v* appears after *u* in the ordering. A graph that has a cycle cannot have a topological order. (499)

unweighted path length The number of edges on a path. (483)

weighted path length The sum of the edge costs on a path. (489)

common errors

1. A common error is failing to ensure that the input graph satisfies the requisite conditions for the algorithm being used (i.e., acyclic or positive weighted).

2. For `Path`, the comparison function compares the `cost` data member only. If the `dest` data member is used to drive the comparison function, the algorithm may appear to work for small graphs, but for larger graphs, it is incorrect and gives slightly suboptimal answers. It never produces a path that does not exist, however. Thus this error is difficult to track down.
3. The shortest-path algorithm for negative-weighted graphs must have a test for negative cycles; otherwise, it potentially runs forever.

on the internet

All the algorithms in this chapter are online in one file. The `Vertex` class has an additional data member that is used in the alternative implementation of Dijkstra's algorithm shown in Section 23.2.3.

Graph.java Contains everything in one file with the simple `main` shown in Figure 14.14.

exercises

IN SHORT

14.1 Find the shortest unweighted path from V_3 to all others in the graph shown in Figure 14.1.

14.2 Find the shortest weighted path from V_2 to all others in the graph shown in Figure 14.1.

14.3 Which algorithms in this chapter can be used to solve Figure 14.2?

14.4 In Figure 14.5, reverse the direction of edges (D, C) and (E, D). Show the changes that result in the figure and the result of running the topological sorting algorithm.

14.5 Suppose that edges (C, B) with a cost of 11 and (B, F) with a cost of 10 are added to the end of the input in Figure 14.5. Show the changes that result in the figure and recompute the shortest path emanating from vertex A.

IN THEORY

14.6 Show how to avoid quadratic initialization inherent in adjacency matrices while maintaining constant-time access of any edge.

14.7 Explain how to modify the unweighted shortest-path algorithm so that, if there is more than one minimum path (in terms of number of edges), the tie is broken in favor of the smallest total weight.

14.8 Explain how to modify Dijkstra's algorithm to produce a count of the number of different minimum paths from v to w.

14.9 Explain how to modify Dijkstra's algorithm so that, if there is more than one minimum path from v to w, a path with the fewest edges is chosen.

14.10 Give an example of when Dijkstra's algorithm gives the wrong answer in the presence of a negative edge but no negative-cost cycle.

14.11 Consider the following algorithm to solve the negative-weighted, shortest-path problem: Add a constant c to each edge cost, thus removing negative edges; calculate the shortest path on the new graph; and then use that result on the original. What is wrong with this algorithm?

14.12 Prove the correctness of the negative-weighted, shortest-path algorithm. To do so, show that when the eyeball visits vertex v for the ith time, the value of D_v is the length of the shortest weighted path consisting of i or fewer edges.

14.13 Give a linear-time algorithm to find the longest weighted path in an acyclic graph. Does your algorithm extend to graphs that have cycles?

14.14 Show that if edge weights are 0 or 1, exclusively, Dijkstra's algorithm can be implemented in linear time by using a *deque* (Section 16.5).

14.15 For any path in a graph, the *bottleneck cost* is given by the weight of the shortest edge on the path. For example, in Figure 14.4, the bottleneck cost of the path *E, D, B* is 23 and the bottleneck cost of the path *E, D, C, A, B* is 10. The *maximum bottleneck problem* is to find the path between two specified vertices with the maximum bottleneck cost. Thus the maximum bottleneck path between *E* and *B* is the path *E, D, B*. Give an efficient algorithm to solve the maximum bottleneck problem.

14.16 Let G be a (directed) graph and u and v be any two distinct vertices in G. Prove or disprove each of the following.

a. If G is acyclic, at least one of (u, v) or (v, u) can be added to the graph without creating a cycle.

b. If adding one of either (u, v) or (v, u) to G without creating a cycle is impossible, then G already has a cycle.

IN PRACTICE

14.17 In this chapter we claim that, for the implementation of graph algorithms that run on large input, data structures are crucial to ensure reasonable performance. For each of the following instances in which a poor data structure or algorithm is used, provide a Big-Oh analysis of the result and compare the actual performance with the algorithms and data structures presented in the text. Implement only one change at a time. You should run your tests on a reasonably large and somewhat sparse random graph. Then do the following.

a. When an edge is read, determine whether it is already in the graph.
b. Implement the "dictionary" by using a sequential scan of the vertex table.
c. Implement the queue by using the algorithm in Exercise 6.10 (which should affect the unweighted shortest-path algorithm).
d. In the unweighted shortest-path algorithm, implement the search for the minimum-cost vertex as a sequential scan of the vertex table.
e. Implement the priority queue by using the algorithm in Exercise 6.12 (which should affect the weighted shortest-path algorithm).
f. Implement the priority queue by using the algorithm in Exercise 6.13 (which should affect the weighted shortest-path algorithm).
g. In the weighted shortest-path algorithm, implement the search for the minimum-cost vertex as a sequential scan of the vertex table.
h. In the acyclic shortest-path algorithm, implement the search for a vertex with indegree 0 as a sequential scan of the vertex table.
i. Implement any of the graph algorithms by using an adjacency matrix instead of adjacency lists.

PROGRAMMING PROJECTS

14.18 A directed graph is strongly connected if there is a path from every vertex to every other vertex. Do the following.

a. Pick any vertex *S*. Show that, if the graph is strongly connected, a shortest-path algorithm will declare that all nodes are reachable from *S*.
b. Show that, if the graph is strongly connected and then the directions of all edges are reversed and a shortest-path algorithm is run from *S*, all nodes will be reachable from *S*.

c. Show that the tests in parts (a) and (b) are sufficient to decide whether a graph is strongly connected (i.e., a graph that passes both tests must be strongly connected).

d. Write a program that checks whether a graph is strongly connected. What is the running time of your algorithm?

Explain how each of the following problems can be solved by applying a shortest-path algorithm. Then design a mechanism for representing an input and write a program that solves the problem.

14.19 The input is a list of league game scores (and there are no ties). If all teams have at least one win and a loss, we can generally "prove," by a silly transitivity argument, that any team is better than any other. For instance, in the six-team league where everyone plays three games, suppose that we have the following results: *A* beat *B* and *C*; *B* beat *C* and *F*; *C* beat *D*; *D* beat *E*; *E* beat *A*; and *F* beat *D* and *E*. Then we can prove that *A* is better than *F* because *A* beat *B* who in turn beat *F*. Similarly, we can prove that *F* is better than *A* because *F* beat *E* and *E* beat *A*. Given a list of game scores and two teams *X* and *Y*, either find a proof (if one exists) that *X* is better than *Y* or indicate that no proof of this form can be found.

14.20 A word can be changed to another word by a one-character substitution. Assume that a dictionary of five-letter words exists. Give an algorithm to determine whether a word *A* can be transformed to a word *B* by a series of one-character substitutions, and if so, outputs the corresponding sequence of words. For example, `bleed` converts to `blood` by the sequence `bleed`, `blend`, `blond`, `blood`.

14.21 The input is a collection of currencies and their exchange rates. Is there a sequence of exchanges that makes money instantly? For instance, if the currencies are *X*, *Y*, and *Z* and the exchange rate is 1 *X* equals 2 *Y*s, 1 *Y* equals 2 *Z*s, and 1 *X* equals 3 *Z*s, then 300 *Z*s will buy 100 *X*s, which in turn will buy 200 *Y*s, which in turn will buy 400 *Z*s. We have thus made a profit of 33 percent.

14.22 A student needs to take a certain number of courses to graduate, and these courses have prerequisites that must be followed. Assume that all courses are offered every semester and that the student can take an unlimited number of courses. Given a list of courses and their prerequisites, compute a schedule that requires the minimum number of semesters.

14.23 The object of the *Kevin Bacon Game* is to link a movie actor to Kevin Bacon via shared movie roles. The minimum number of links is an actor's *Bacon number.* For instance, Tom Hanks has a Bacon number of 1. He was in *Apollo 13* with Kevin Bacon. Sally Field has a Bacon number of 2 because she was in *Forest Gump* with Tom Hanks, who was in *Apollo 13* with Kevin Bacon. Almost all well-known actors have a Bacon number of 1 or 2. Assume that you have a comprehensive list of actors, with roles, and do the following.

a. Explain how to find an actor's Bacon number.
b. Explain how to find the actor with the highest Bacon number.
c. Explain how to find the minimum number of links between two arbitrary actors.

14.24 The input is a two-dimensional maze with walls, and the problem is to traverse the maze, using the shortest route, from the upper left-hand corner to the lower right-hand corner. You may knock down walls, but each wall you knock down incurs a penalty p (that is specified as part of the input).

references

The use of adjacency lists to represent graphs was first advocated in [3]. Dijkstra's shortest-path algorithm was originally described in [2]. The algorithm for negative edge costs is taken from [1]. A more efficient test for termination is described in [6], which also shows how data structures play an important role in a wide range of graph theory algorithms. The topological sorting algorithm is from [4]. Many real-life applications of graph algorithms are presented in [5], along with references for further reading.

1. R. E. Bellman, "On a Routing Problem," *Quarterly of Applied Mathematics* **16** (1958), 87–90.
2. E. W. Dijkstra, "A Note on Two Problems in Connexion with Graphs," *Numerische Mathematik* **1** (1959), 269–271.
3. J. E. Hopcroft and R. E. Tarjan, "Algorithm 447: Efficient Algorithms for Graph Manipulation," *Communications of the ACM* **16** (1973), 372–378.
4. A. B. Kahn, "Topological Sorting of Large Networks," *Communications of the ACM* **5** (1962), 558–562.
5. D. E. Knuth, *The Stanford GraphBase*, Addison-Wesley, Reading, MA, 1993.
6. R. E. Tarjan, *Data Structures and Network Algorithms*, Society for Industrial and Applied Mathematics, Philadelphia, PA, 1985.

part four Implementations

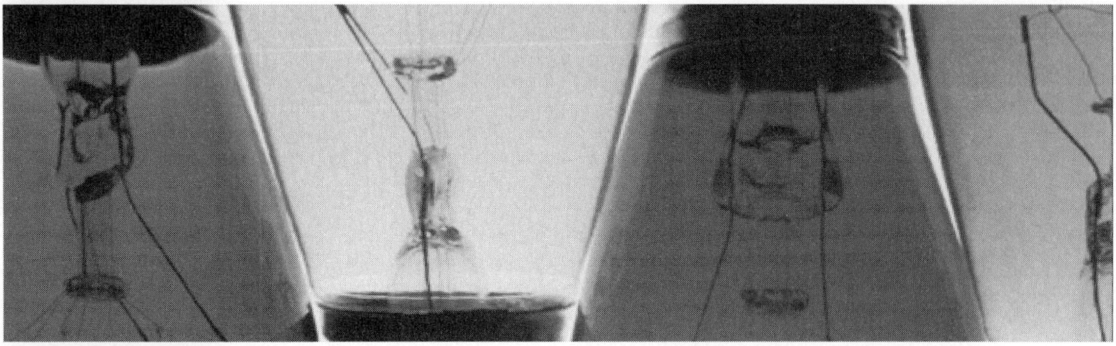

chapter 15

inner classes and implementation of `ArrayList`

This chapter begins our discussion of the implementation of standard data structures. One of the simplest data structures is the `ArrayList` that is part of the Collections API. In Part One (specifically Figure 3.11 and Figure 4.23) we have already seen skeletons of the implementation, so in this chapter we concentrate on the details of implementing the complete class, with the associated iterators. In doing so, we make use of an interesting Java syntactic creation, the *inner class*. We discuss the inner class in this chapter, rather than in Part One (where other syntactic elements are introduced) because we view the inner class as a Java implementation technique, rather than a core language feature.

In this chapter, we will see

- The uses and syntax of the inner class
- An implementation of a new class called the `AbstractCollection`
- An implementation of the `ArrayList` class

15.1 iterators and nested classes

We begin by reviewing the simple iterator implementation first described in Section 6.2. Recall that we defined a simple iterator interface, which mimics the standard (nongeneric) Collections API `Iterator`, and this interface is shown in Figure 15.1.

We then defined two classes: the container and its iterator. Each container class is responsible for providing an implementation of the iterator interface. In our case, the implementation of the iterator interface is provided by the `MyContainerIterator` class, shown in Figure 15.2. The `MyContainer` class shown in Figure 15.3 provides a factory method that creates an instance of `MyContainerIterator` and returns this instance using the interface type `Iterator`. Figure 15.4 provides a `main` that illustrates the use of the container/iterator combination. Figures 15.1 to 15.4 simply replicate Figures 6.5 to 6.8 in the original iterator discussion from Section 6.2.

figure 15.1

The `Iterator` interface from Section 6.2

```
package weiss.ds;

public interface Iterator
{
    boolean hasNext( );
    Object next( );
}
```

figure 15.2

Implementation of the `MyContainerIterator` from Section 6.2

```
// An iterator class that steps through a MyContainer.

package weiss.ds;

class MyContainerIterator implements Iterator
{
    private int current = 0;
    private MyContainer container;

    MyContainerIterator( MyContainer c )
      { container = c; }

    public boolean hasNext( )
      { return current < container.size; }

    public Object next( )
      { return container.items[ current++ ]; }
}
```

```
package weiss.ds;

public class MyContainer
{
    Object [ ] items;
    int size;

    public Iterator iterator( )
      { return new MyContainerIterator( this ); }

    // Other methods not shown.
}
```

figure 15.3

The MyContainer class from Section 6.2

```
    public static void main( String [ ] args )
    {
        MyContainer v = new MyContainer( );

        v.add( "3" );
        v.add( "2" );

        System.out.println( "Container contents: " );
        Iterator itr = v.iterator( );
        while( itr.hasNext( ) )
            System.out.println( itr.next( ) );
    }
```

figure 15.4

main method to illustrate iterator design from Section 6.2

This design hides the iterator class implementation because MyContainerIterator is not a public class. Thus the user is forced to program to the Iterator interface and does not have access to the details of how the iterator was implemented—the user cannot even declare objects of type weiss.ds.MyContainerIterator. However, it still exposes more details than we usually like. In the MyContainer class, the data are not private, and the corresponding iterator class, while not public, is still package visible. We can solve both problems by using nested classes: We simply move the iterator class inside of the container class. At that point the iterator class is a member of the container class, and thus it can be declared as a private class and its methods can access private data from MyContainer. The revised code is illustrated in Figure 15.5, with only a stylistic change of renaming MyContainerIterator as LocalIterator. No other changes are required; however the LocalIterator constructor can be made private and still be callable from MyContainer, since LocalIterator is part of MyContainer.

figure 15.5

Iterator design using nested class

```
package weiss.ds;

public class MyContainer
{
    private Object [ ] items;
    private int size = 0;
    // Other methods for MyContainer not shown

    public Iterator iterator( )
      { return new LocalIterator( this ); }

    // The iterator class as a nested class
    private static class LocalIterator implements Iterator
    {
        private int current = 0;
        private MyContainer container;

        private LocalIterator( MyContainer c )
          { container = c; }

        public boolean hasNext( )
          { return current < container.size; }

        public Object next( )
          { return container.items[ current++ ]; }
    }
}
```

15.2 iterators and inner classes

An *inner class* is similar to a nested class in that it is a class inside another class and is declared using the same syntax as a nested class, except that it is not a `static` class. An inner class always contains an implicit reference to the outer object that created it.

In Section 15.1, we used a nested class to further hide details. In addition to nested classes, Java provides inner classes. An *inner class* is similar to a nested class in that it is a class inside another class and is treated as a member of the outer class for visibility purposes. An inner class is declared using the same syntax as a nested class, except that it is not a static class. In other words, the `static` qualifier is missing in the inner class declaration.

Before getting into the inner class specifics, let us look at the problem that they are designed to solve. Figure 15.6 illustrates the relationship between the iterator and container classes that were written in the previous section. Each instance of the `LocalIterator` maintains a reference to the container over which it is iterating and a notion of the iterator's current position. The relationship that we have is that each `LocalIterator` must be associated with exactly one instance of `MyContainer`. It is impossible for the `container` reference in any iterator to be `null`, and the iterator's existence makes no sense without knowing which `MyContainer` object caused its creation.

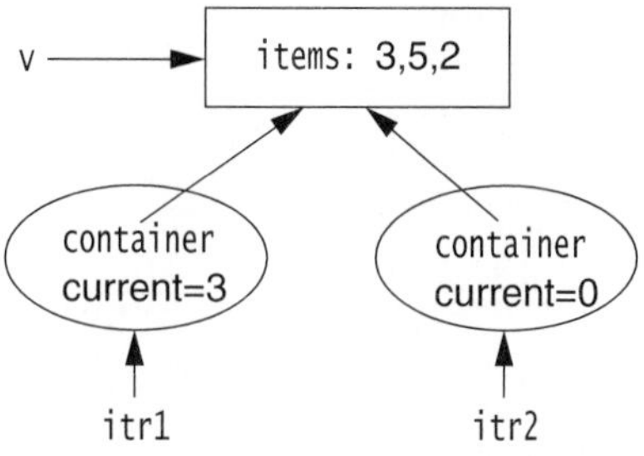

figure 15.6

Iterator/container relationship

Since we know that `itr1` must be tied to one and only one iterator, it seems that the expression `container.items` is redundant: If the iterator could only remember the container that constructed it, we wouldn't have to keep track of it ourselves. And if it remembered it, we might expect that if inside of the `LocalIterator` we referred to `items`, then since the `LocalIterator` does not have an `items` field, the compiler (and run-time system) would be smart enough to deduce that we are talking about the `items` field of the `MyContainer` object that caused the construction of this particular `LocalIterator`. This is exactly what an inner class does, and what distinguishes it from a nested class.

The big difference between an inner class and a nested class is that when an instance of an inner class object is constructed, there is an implicit reference to the outer class object that caused its construction. This implies that an inner class object cannot exist without an outer class object for it to be attached to, with an exception being if it is declared in a static method (because local and anonymous classes are technically inner classes), a detail we will discuss later.

The big difference between an inner class and a nested class is that when an instance of an inner class object is constructed, there is an implicit reference to the outer class object that caused its construction.

If the name of the outer class is `Outer`, then the implicit reference is `Outer.this`. Thus, if `LocalIterator` was declared as an instance inner class (i.e., the `static` keyword was removed), then the `MyContainer.this` reference could be used to replace the `container` reference that the iterator is storing. The picture in Figure 15.7 illustrates that the structure would be identical. A revised class is shown in Figure 15.8.

If the name of the outer class is `Outer`, then the implicit reference is `Outer.this`.

In the revised implementation, observe that `LocalIterator` no longer has an explicit reference to a `MyContainer`, and also observe that its constructor is no longer necessary, since it only initialized the `MyContainer` reference. Finally, Figure 15.9 illustrates that just as using `this` is optional in an instance method, the `Outer.this` reference is also optional if there is no name clash. Thus, `MyContainer.this.size` can be shortened to `size`, as long as there is no other variable named `size` that is in a closer scope.

figure 15.7

Iterator/container with inner classes

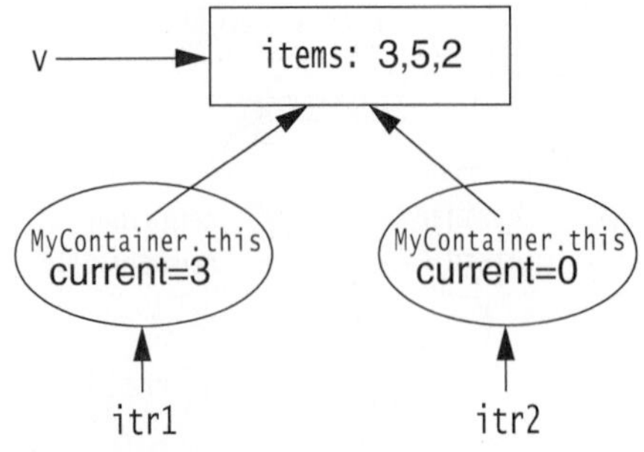

figure 15.8

Iterator design using inner class

```
package weiss.ds;

public class MyContainer
{
    private Object [ ] items;
    private int size = 0;

    // Other methods for MyContainer not shown

    public Iterator iterator( )
      { return new LocalIterator( ); }

    // The iterator class as an inner class
    private class LocalIterator implements Iterator
    {
        private int current = 0;

        public boolean hasNext( )
          { return current < MyContainer.this.size; }

        public Object next( )
          { return MyContainer.this.items[ current++ ]; }
    }
}
```

Local classes and anonymous classes do not specify whether they are `static`, and they are always technically considered inner classes. However, if such a class is declared in a static method, it has no implicit outer reference (and thus behaves like a nested class), whereas if it is declared inside an instance method, its implicit outer reference is the invoker of the method.

The addition of inner classes requires a significant set of rules, many of which attempt to deal with language corner cases and dubious coding prac-

```
// The iterator class as an inner class
private class LocalIterator implements Iterator
{
    private int current = 0;

    public boolean hasNext( )
      { return current < size; }

    public Object next( )
      { return items[ current++ ]; }
}
```

figure 15.9

Inner class; `Outer.this` may be optional.

tices. For instance, suppose we suspend belief for a minute and imagine that `LocalIterator` is public. We do so only to illustrate the complications that the language designers face when adding a new language feature. Under this assumption the iterator's type is `MyContainer.LocalIterator`, and since it is visible, one might expect that

```
MyContainer.LocalIterator itr = new MyContainer.LocalIterator( );
```

is legal, since like all classes, it has a public default zero-parameter constructor. However, this cannot possibly work, since there is no way to initialize the implicit reference. Which `MyContainer` is `itr` referring to? We need some syntax that won't conflict with any other language rules. Here's the rule: If there is a container `c`, then `itr` could be constructed using a bizarre syntax invented for just this case, in which the outer object in effect invokes `new`:

```
MyContainer.LocalIterator itr = c.new LocalIterator( );
```

Notice that this implies that in an instance factory method, `this.new` is legal, and shorthands to the more conventional `new` seen in a factory method. If you find yourself using the bizarre syntax, you probably have a bad design. In our example, once `LocalIterator` is private, this entire issue goes away, and if `LocalIterator` is not private, there is little reason to use an inner class in the first place.

There are also other rules, some of which are arbitrary. Private members of the inner or nested class are public to the outer class. To access any member of an inner class, the outer class only needs to provide a reference to an inner class instance and use the dot operator, as is normal for other classes. Thus inner and nested classes are considered part of the outer class.

Both inner and nested classes can be final, or they can be abstract, or they can be interfaces (but interfaces are always static, because they cannot have any data, including an implicit reference), or they can be none of these. Inner classes may not have static fields or methods, except for static final fields. Inner classes may have nested classes or interfaces. Finally, when you compile the above example, you will see that the compiler generates a class file named `MyContainer$LocalIterator.class`, which would have to be included in any distribution to clients. In other words, each inner and nested class is a class and has a corresponding class file. Anonymous classes use numbers instead of names.

15.3 the `AbstractCollection` class

The `AbstractCollection` implements some of the methods in the `Collection` interface.

Before we implement the `ArrayList` class, observe that some of the methods in the `Collection` interface can be easily implemented in terms of others. For instance, `isEmpty` is easily implemented by checking if the size is 0. Rather than doing so in `ArrayList`, `LinkedList`, and all the other concrete implementations, it would be preferable to do this once and use inheritance to obtain `isEmpty`. We could even override `isEmpty` if it turns out that for some collections there is a faster way of performing `isEmpty` than computing the current size. However, we cannot implement `isEmpty` in the `Collection` interface; this can only be done in an abstract class. This will be the `AbstractCollection` class. To simplify implementations, programmers designing new `Collections` classes can extend the `AbstractCollection` class rather than implementing the `Collection` interface. A sample implementation of `AbstractCollection` is shown in Figures 15.10 to 15.12.

The Collections API also defines additional classes such as `AbstractList`, `AbstractSequentialList`, and `AbstractSet`. We have chosen not to implement those, in keeping with our intention of providing a simplified subset of the Collections API. If, for some reason, you are implementing your own collections and extending the Java Collections API, you should extend the most specific abstract class.

In Figure 15.10, we see implementations of `isEmpty`, `clear`, and `add`. The first two methods have straightforward implementations. Certainly the implementation of `clear` is usable, since it removes all items in the collection, but there might be more efficient ways of performing the `clear`, depending on the type of collection being manipulated. Thus this implementation of `clear` serves as a default, but it is likely to be overridden. There is no sensible way of providing a usable implementation for `add`. So the two alternatives are to make `add` abstract (which is clearly doable, since `AbstractCollection` is abstract) or to provide an implementation that throws a runtime exception. We have done the latter, which matches the behavior in `java.util`. (Farther down the road, this decision also makes it easier to create the class needed to express the values of a map). Figure 15.11 provides default implementations

```
package weiss.util;

/**
 * AbstractCollection provides default implementations for
 * some of the easy methods in the Collection interface.
 */
public abstract class AbstractCollection<AnyType> implements Collection<AnyType>
{
    /**
     * Tests if this collection is empty.
     * @return true if the size of this collection is zero.
     */
    public boolean isEmpty( )
    {
        return size( ) == 0;
    }

    /**
     * Change the size of this collection to zero.
     */
    public void clear( )
    {
        Iterator<AnyType> itr = iterator( );
        while( itr.hasNext( ) )
        {
            itr.next( );
            itr.remove( );
        }
    }

    /**
     * Adds x to this collections.
     * This default implementation always throws an exception.
     * @param x the item to add.
     * @throws UnsupportedOperationException always.
     */
    public boolean add( AnyType x )
    {
        throw new UnsupportedOperationException( );
    }
```

figure 15.10

Sample implementation of AbstractCollection (part 1)

of contains and remove. Both implementations use a sequential search, so they are not efficient, and need to be overridden by respectable implementations of the Set interface.

figure 15.11

Sample implementation of `AbstractCollection` (part 2)

```
    /**
     * Returns true if this collection contains x.
     * If x is null, returns false.
     * (This behavior may not always be appropriate.)
     * @param x the item to search for.
     * @return true if x is not null and is found in
     * this collection.
     */
    public boolean contains( Object x )
    {
        if( x == null )
            return false;

        for( AnyType val : this )
            if( x.equals( val ) )
                return true;

        return false;
    }

    /**
     * Removes non-null x from this collection.
     * (This behavior may not always be appropriate.)
     * @param x the item to remove.
     * @return true if remove succeeds.
     */
    public boolean remove( Object x )
    {
        if( x == null )
            return false;

        Iterator itr = iterator( );
        while( itr.hasNext( ) )
            if( x.equals( itr.next( ) ) )
            {
                itr.remove( );
                return true;
            }

        return false;
    }
```

Figure 15.12 contains the implementations of the two `toArray` methods. The zero-parameter `toArray` is fairly simple to implement. The one-parameter `toArray` makes use of a feature of Java known as reflection to create an array object that matches the parameter type in the case that the parameter is not large enough to store the underlying collection.

```
    /**
     * Obtains a primitive array view of the collection.
     * @return the primitive array view.
     */
    public Object [ ] toArray( )
    {
        Object [ ] copy = new Object[ size( ) ];
        int i = 0;

        for( AnyType val : this )
            copy[ i++ ] = val;

        return copy;
    }

    public <OtherType> OtherType [ ] toArray( OtherType [ ] arr )
    {
        int theSize = size( );

        if( arr.length < theSize )
            arr = ( OtherType [ ] ) java.lang.reflect.Array.newInstance(
                            arr.getClass( ).getComponentType( ), theSize );
        else if( theSize < arr.length )
            arr[ theSize ] = null;

        Object [ ] copy = arr;
        int i = 0;

        for( AnyType val : this )
            copy[ i++ ] = val;

        return copy;
    }

    /**
     * Return a string representation of this collection.
     */
    public String toString( )
    {
        StringBuilder result = new StringBuilder( "[ " );

        for( AnyType obj : this )
            result.append( obj + " " );

        result.append( "]" );

        return result.toString( );
    }
}
```

figure 15.12

Sample implementation of AbstractCollection (part 3)

15.4 StringBuilder

Figure 15.12 also shows a respectable linear-time implementation of toString, using a StringBuilder to avoid quadratic running time. (StringBuilder was added in Java 5 and is slightly faster than StringBuffer; it is preferable for single-threaded applications). To see why StringBuilder is needed, consider the following code fragment that builds a String with *N* A's:

```
String result = "";
for( int i = 0; i < N; i++ )
    result += 'A';
```

While there is no doubt that this fragment works correctly because String objects are immutable, each call to result += 'A' is rewritten as result = result + 'A', and once we see that, it is apparent that each String concatenation creates a new String object. As we get farther into the loop, these String objects become more expensive to create. We can estimate the cost of the *i*th String concatenation to be *i*, so the total cost is $1 + 2 + 3 + \ldots + N$, or $O(N^2)$. If *N* is 100,000, it is simple to write the code and see that the running time is significant. Yet a simple rewrite

```
char [ ] theChars = new char[ N ];
for( int i = 0; i < N; i++ )
    theChars[ i ] = 'A';
String result = new String( theChars );
```

results in a linear-time algorithm that executes in the blink of the eye.

The use of an array of characters works only if we know the final size of the String. Otherwise, we have to use something like ArrayList<char>. A StringBuilder is similar in concept to an ArrayList<char>, with array doubling but with method names that are specific for String operations. Using a StringBuilder, the code looks like

```
StringBuilder sb = new StringBuilder( );
for( int i = 0; i < N; i++ )
    sb.append( 'A' );
String result = new String( sb );
```

This code is linear-time and runs quickly. Some String concatenations, such as those in a single expression, are optimized by the compiler to avoid repeated creations of Strings. But if your concatenations are intermingled with other statements, as is the case here, then you often can use a StringBuilder for more efficient code.

15.5 implementation of ArrayList with an iterator

The various ArrayList classes shown in Part One were not iterator-aware. This section provides an implementation of ArrayList that we will place in weiss.util and includes support for bidirectional iterators. In order to keep the amount of code somewhat manageable, we have stripped out the bulk of the javadoc comments. They can be found in the online code.

The implementation is found in Figures 15.13 to 15.16. At line 3 we see that ArrayList extends the AbstractCollection abstract class, and at line 4 ArrayList declares that it implements the List interface.

The internal array, theItems, and collection size, theSize, are declared at lines 9 and 10, respectively. More interesting is modCount, which is declared at line 11. modCount represents the number of structural modifications (adds, removes) made to the ArrayList. The idea is that when an iterator is constructed, the iterator saves this value in its data member expectedModCount. When any iterator operation is performed, the iterator's expectedModCount member is compared with the ArrayList's modCount, and if they disagree, a ConcurrentModificationException can be thrown.

Line 16 illustrates the typical constructor that performs a shallow copy of the members in another collection, simply by stepping through the collection and calling add. The clear method, started at line 26, initializes the ArrayList and can be called from the constructor. It also resets theItems, which allows the garbage collector to reclaim all the otherwise unreferenced objects that were in the ArrayList. The remaining routines in Figure 15.13 are relatively straightforward.

Figure 15.14 implements the remaining methods that do not depend on iterators. findPos is a private helper that returns the position of an object that is either being removed or subjected to a contains call. Extra code is present because it is legal to add null to the ArrayList, and if we were not careful, the call to equals at line 60 could have generated a NullPointerException. Observe that both add and remove will result in a change to modCount.

In Figure 15.15 we see the two factory methods that return iterators, and we see the beginning of the implementation of the ListIterator interface. Observe that ArrayListIterator *IS-A* ListIterator and ListIterator *IS-A* Iterator. So ArrayListIterator can be returned at lines 103 and 106.

In the implementation of ArrayListIterator, done as a private inner class, we maintain the current position at line 111. The current position represents the index of the element that would be returned by calling next. At line 112 we declare the expectedModCount member. Like all class members, it is initialized

figure 15.13

ArrayList implementation (part 1)

```
package weiss.util;

public class ArrayList<AnyType> extends AbstractCollection<AnyType>
                                implements List<AnyType>
{
    private static final int DEFAULT_CAPACITY = 10;
    private static final int NOT_FOUND = -1;

    private AnyType [ ] theItems;
    private int theSize;
    private int modCount = 0;

    public ArrayList( )
      { clear( ); }

    public ArrayList( Collection<AnyType> other )
    {
        clear( );
        for( AnyType obj : other )
            add( obj );
    }

    public int size( )
      { return theSize; }

    public void clear( )
    {
        theSize = 0;
        theItems = (AnyType []) new Object[ DEFAULT_CAPACITY ];
        modCount++;
    }

    public AnyType get( int idx )
    {
        if( idx < 0 || idx >= size( ) )
            throw new ArrayIndexOutOfBoundsException( );
        return theItems[ idx ];
    }

    public AnyType set( int idx, AnyType newVal )
    {
        if( idx < 0 || idx >= size( ) )
            throw new ArrayIndexOutOfBoundsException( );
        AnyType old = theItems[ idx ];
        theItems[ idx ] = newVal;

        return old;
    }

    public boolean contains( Object x )
      { return findPos( x ) != NOT_FOUND; }
```

```
    private int findPos( Object x )
    {
        for( int i = 0; i < size( ); i++ )
            if( x == null )
            {
                if( theItems[ i ] == null )
                    return i;
            }
            else if( x.equals( theItems[ i ] ) )
                return i;

        return NOT_FOUND;
    }

    public boolean add( AnyType x )
    {
        if( theItems.length == size( ) )
        {
            AnyType [ ] old = theItems;
            theItems = (AnyType []) new Object[ theItems.length * 2 + 1 ];
            for( int i = 0; i < size( ); i++ )
                theItems[ i ] = old[ i ];
        }
        theItems[ theSize++ ] = x;
        modCount++;
        return true;
    }

    public boolean remove( Object x )
    {
        int pos = findPos( x );

        if( pos == NOT_FOUND )
            return false;
        else
        {
            remove( pos );
            return true;
        }
    }

    public AnyType remove( int idx )
    {
        AnyType removedItem = theItems[ idx ];
        for( int i = idx; i < size( ) - 1; i++ )
            theItems[ i ] = theItems[ i + 1 ];
        theSize--;
        modCount++;
        return removedItem;
    }
```

figure 15.14

ArrayList implementation (part 2)

figure 15.15

ArrayList implementation (part 3)

```
    public Iterator<AnyType> iterator( )
      { return new ArrayListIterator( 0 ); }

    public ListIterator<AnyType> listIterator( int idx )
      { return new ArrayListIterator( idx ); }

    // This is the implementation of the ArrayListIterator
    private class ArrayListIterator implements ListIterator<AnyType>
    {
        private int current;
        private int expectedModCount = modCount;
        private boolean nextCompleted = false;
        private boolean prevCompleted = false;

        ArrayListIterator( int pos )
        {
            if( pos < 0 || pos > size( ) )
                throw new IndexOutOfBoundsException( );
            current = pos;
        }

        public boolean hasNext( )
        {
            if( expectedModCount != modCount )
                throw new ConcurrentModificationException( );
            return current < size( );
        }

        public boolean hasPrevious( )
        {
            if( expectedModCount != modCount )
                throw new ConcurrentModificationException( );
            return current > 0;
        }
```

when an instance of the iterator is created (immediately prior to calling the constructor); `modCount` is a shorthand for `ArrayList.this.modCount`. The two Boolean instance members that follow are flags used to verify that a call to `remove` is legal.

The `ArrayListIterator` constructor is declared package visible; thus it is usable by the `ArrayList`. Of course it could be declared public, but there is no reason to do so and even if it were private, it would still be usable by `ArrayList`. Package visible, however, seems most natural in this situation. Both `hasNext` and `hasPrevious` verify that there have been no external structural modifications since the iterator was created, throwing an exception if the `ArrayList` `modCount` does not match the `ArrayListIterator` `expectedModCount`.

```
136         public AnyType next( )
137         {
138             if( !hasNext( ) )
139                 throw new NoSuchElementException( );
140             nextCompleted = true;
141             prevCompleted = false;
142             return theItems[ current++ ];
143         }
144
145         public AnyType previous( )
146         {
147             if( !hasPrevious( ) )
148                 throw new NoSuchElementException( );
149             prevCompleted = true;
150             nextCompleted = false;
151             return theItems[ --current ];
152         }
153
154         public void remove( )
155         {
156             if( expectedModCount != modCount )
157                 throw new ConcurrentModificationException( );
158
159             if( nextCompleted )
160                 ArrayList.this.remove( --current );
161             else if( prevCompleted )
162                 ArrayList.this.remove( current );
163             else
164                 throw new IllegalStateException( );
165
166             prevCompleted = nextCompleted = false;
167             expectedModCount++;
168         }
169     }
170 }
```

figure 15.16
ArrayList implementation (part 4)

The ArrayListIterator class is completed in Figure 15.16. next and previous are mirror image symmetries. Examining next, we see first a test at line 138 to make sure we have not exhausted the iteration (implicitly this tests for structural modifications also). We then set nextCompleted to true to allow remove to succeed, and then we return the array item that current is examining, advancing current after its value has been used.

The previous method is similar, except that we must lower current's value first. This is because when traversing in reverse, if current equals the container size, we have not yet started the iteration, and when current equals zero, we have completed the iteration (but can remove the item in this position if the prior operation was previous). Observe that next followed by previous yields identical items.

Finally, we come to remove, which is extremely tricky because the semantics of remove depend on which direction the traversal is proceeding. In fact, this probably suggests a bad design in the Collections API: Method semantics should not depend so strongly on which methods have been called prior to it. But remove is what it is, so we have to implement it.

The implementation of remove begins with the test for structural modification at line 156. If the prior iterator state change operation was a next, as evidenced by the test at line 159 showing that nextCompleted is true, then we call the ArrayList remove method (started at line 93 in Figure 15.14) that takes an index as a parameter. The use of ArrayList.this.remove is required because the local version of remove hides the outer class version. Because we have already advanced past the item to be removed, we must remove the item in position current-1. This slides the next item from current to current-1 (since the old current-1 position has now been removed), so we use the expression --current in line 160.

When traversing the other direction, we are sitting on the last item that was returned, so we simply pass current as a parameter to the outer remove. After it returns, the elements in higher indices are slid one index lower, so current is sitting on the correct element and can be used in the expression at line 162.

In either case, we cannot do another remove until we do a next or previous, so at line 166 we clear both flags. Finally, at line 167, we increase the value of expectedModCount to match the container's. Observe that this is increased only for this iterator, so any other iterators are now invalidated.

This class, which is perhaps the simplest of the Collections API classes that contains iterators, illustrates why in Part Four we elect to begin with a simple protocol and then provide more complete implementations at the end of the chapter.

summary

This chapter introduced the inner class, which is a Java technique that is commonly used to implement iterator classes. Each instance of an inner class corresponds to exactly one instance of an outer class and automatically maintains a reference to the outer class object that caused its construction. A nested class relates two types to each other, while an inner class relates two objects to each other. The inner class is used in this chapter to implement the ArrayList.

The next chapter illustrates implementations of stacks and queues.

key concepts

AbstractCollection Implements some of the methods in the `Collection` interface. (524)

inner class A class inside a class, which is useful for implementing the iterator pattern. The inner class always contains an implicit reference to the outer object that created it. (520)

StringBuilder Used to construct `String`s without repeatedly creating a large number of intermediate `String`s. (528)

common errors

1. An instance inner class cannot be constructed without an outer object. This is most easily done with a factory method in the outer class. It is common to forget the word `static` when declaring a nested class, and this will often generate a difficult-to-understand error related to this rule.
2. Excessive `String` concatenations can turn a linear-time program into a quadratic-time program.

on the internet

The following files are available:

MyContainerTest.java	The test program for the final iterator example that uses inner classes, as shown in Section 15.2. **Iterator.java** and **MyContainer.java** are both found in the `weiss.ds` package online.
AbstractCollection.java	Contains the code in Figures 15.10 to 15.12.
ArrayList.java	Contains the code in Figures 15.13 to 15.16.

exercises

IN SHORT

15.1 What is the difference between a nested class and an inner class?

15.2 Are private members of an inner (or nested) class visible to methods in the outer class?

15.3 In Figure 15.17, are the declarations of `a` and `b` legal? Why or why not?

figure 15.17

Code for Exercises 15.3 and 15.4

```
class Outer
{
    private int x = 0;
    private static int y = 37;

    private class Inner1 implements SomeInterface
    {
        private int a = x + y;
    }

    private static class Inner2 implements SomeInterface
    {
        private int b = x + y;
    }
}
```

15.4 In Figure 15.17 (assuming illegal code is fixed), how are objects of type `Inner1` and `Inner2` created (you may suggest additional members)?

15.5 What is a `StringBuilder`?

IN THEORY

15.6 Suppose an inner class *I* is declared public in its outer class *O*. Why might unusual syntax be required to declare a class *E* that extends *I* but is declared as a top-level class? (The required syntax is even more bizarre than what was seen for `new`, but often requires bad design to be needed.)

15.7 What is the running time of `clear`, as implemented for `ArrayList`? What would be the running time if the inherited version from `AbstractCollection` was used instead?

IN PRACTICE

15.8 Add both the `previous` and `hasPrevious` methods to the final version of the `MyContainer` class.

15.9 Assume that we would like an iterator that implements the `isValid`, `advance`, and `retrieve` set of methods, but all we have is the standard `java.util.Iterator` interface.

a. What pattern describes the problem we are trying to solve?

b. Design a `BetterIterator` class, and then implement it in terms of `java.util.Iterator`.

```
public void clear( )    // Version #1
{
    Iterator<AnyType> itr = iterator( );
    while( !isEmpty( ) )
        remove( itr.next( ) );
}

public void clear( )    // Version #2
{
    while( !isEmpty( ) )
        remove( iterator( ).next(  );
}
```

figure 15.18

Proposed implementations of `clear` for `AbstractCollection`

15.10 Figure 15.18 contains two proposed implementations of `clear` for `AbstractCollection`. Does either work?

PROGRAMMING PROJECTS

15.11 The `Collection` interface in the Java Collections API defines methods `removeAll`, `addAll`, and `containsAll`. Add these methods to the `Collection` interface and provide implementations in `AbstractCollection`.

15.12 `Collections.unmodifiableCollection` takes a `Collection` and returns an immutable `Collection`. Implement this method. To do so, you will need to use a local class (a class inside a method). The class implements the `Collection` interface and throws an `UnsupportedOperationException` for all mutating methods. For other methods, it forwards the request to the `Collection` being wrapped. You will also have to hide an unmodifiable iterator.

15.13 Two `Collection` objects are equal if either both implement the `List` interface and contain the same items in the same order or both implement the `Set` interface and contain the same items in any order. Otherwise, the `Collection` objects are not equal. Provide, in `AbstractCollection`, an implementation of `equals` that follows this general contract. Additionally, provide a `hashCode` method in `AbstractCollection` that follows the general contract of `hashCode`. (Do this by using an iterator and adding the `hashCodes` of all the entries. Watch out for `null` entries.)

chapter 16

stacks and queues

In this chapter we discuss implementation of the stack and queue data structures. Recall from Chapter 6 that the basic operations are expected to take constant time. For both the stack and queue, there are two basic ways to arrange for constant-time operations. The first is to store the items contiguously in an array, and the second is to store items noncontiguously in a linked list. We present implementations for both data structures, using both methods, in this chapter.

In this chapter, we show

- An array-based implementation of the stack and queue
- A linked list–based implementation of the stack and queue
- A brief comparison of the two methods
- An illustration of Collections API stack implementation

16.1 dynamic array implementations

In this section we use a simple array to implement the stack and queue. The resulting algorithms are extremely efficient and also are simple to code. Recall that we have been using `ArrayList` instead of arrays. The `add` method of ArrayList is, in effect, the same as push. However, because we are interested in a general discussion of the algorithms, we implement the array-based stack using basic arrays, duplicating some of the code seen earlier in the ArrayList implementations.

16.1.1 stacks

A stack can be implemented with an array and an integer that indicates the index of the top element.

As Figure 16.1 shows, a stack can be implemented with an array and an integer. The integer tos (*top of stack*) provides the array index of the top element of the stack. Thus when tos is –1, the stack is empty. To push, we increment tos and place the new element in the array position tos. Accessing the top element is thus trivial, and we can perform the pop by decrementing tos. In Figure 16.1, we begin with an empty stack. Then we show the stack after three operations: push(a), push(b), and pop.

Figure 16.2 shows the skeleton for the array-based Stack class. It specifies two data members: theArray, which is expanded as needed, stores the items in the stack; and topOfStack gives the index of the current top of the stack. For an empty stack, this index is –1. The constructor is shown in Figure 16.3.

Most of the stack routines are applications of previously discussed ideas.

The public methods are listed in lines 22–33 of the skeleton. Most of these routines have simple implementations. The isEmpty and makeEmpty routines are one-liners, as shown in Figure 16.4. The push method is shown in Figure 16.5. If it were not for the array doubling, the push routine would be only the single line of code shown at line 9. Recall that the use of the prefix ++ operator means that topOfStack is incremented and that its new value is used to index theArray. The remaining routines are equally short, as shown in Figures 16.6 and 16.7. The postfix -- operator used in Figure 16.7 indicates that, although topOfStack is decremented, its prior value is used to index theArray.

Recall that array doubling does not affect performance in the long run.

If there is no array doubling, every operation takes constant time. A push that involves array doubling will take $O(N)$ time. If this were a frequent occurrence, we would need to worry. However, it is infrequent because an

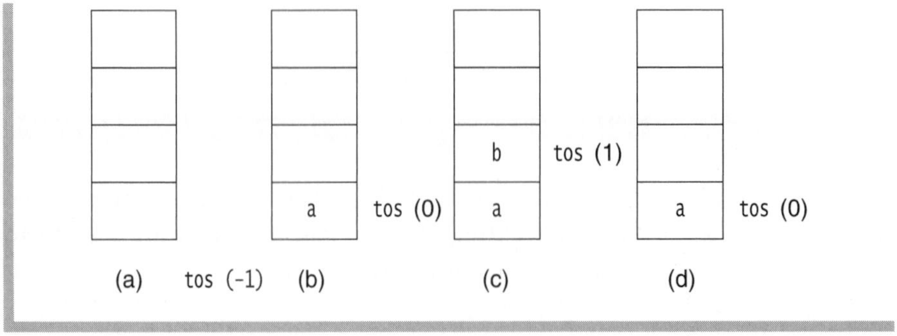

figure 16.1

How the stack routines work: (a) empty stack; (b) push(a); (c) push(b); (d) pop( )

```
package weiss.nonstandard;

// ArrayStack class
//
// CONSTRUCTION: with no initializer
//
// ******************PUBLIC OPERATIONS*********************
// void push( x )          --> Insert x
// void pop( )             --> Remove most recently inserted item
// AnyType top( )          --> Return most recently inserted item
// AnyType topAndPop( )    --> Return and remove most recent item
// boolean isEmpty( )      --> Return true if empty; else false
// void makeEmpty( )       --> Remove all items
// ******************ERRORS********************************
// top, pop, or topAndPop on empty stack

public class ArrayStack<AnyType> implements Stack<AnyType>
{
    public ArrayStack( )
      { /* Figure 16.3 */ }

    public boolean isEmpty( )
      { /* Figure 16.4 */ }
    public void makeEmpty( )
      { /* Figure 16.4 */ }
    public Object top( )
      { /* Figure 16.6 */ }
    public void pop( )
      { /* Figure 16.6 */ }
    public AnyType topAndPop( )
      { /* Figure 16.7 */ }
    public void push( AnyType x )
      { /* Figure 16.5 */ }

    private void doubleArray( )
      { /* Implementation in online code  */ }

    private AnyType [ ] theArray;
    private int         topOfStack;

    private static final int DEFAULT_CAPACITY = 10;
}
```

figure 16.2

Skeleton for the array-based stack class

array doubling that involves N elements must be preceded by at least $N/2$ pushes that do not involve an array doubling. Consequently, we can charge the $O(N)$ cost of the doubling over these $N/2$ easy pushes, thereby effectively raising the cost of each push by only a small constant. This technique is known as *amortization*.

figure 16.3

The zero-parameter constructor for the ArrayStack class

```
/**
 * Construct the stack.
 */
public ArrayStack( )
{
    theArray = (AnyType []) new Object[ DEFAULT_CAPACITY ];
    topOfStack = -1;
}
```

figure 16.4

The isEmpty and makeEmpty routines for the ArrayStack class

```
/**
 * Test if the stack is logically empty.
 * @return true if empty, false otherwise.
 */
public boolean isEmpty( )
{
    return topOfStack == -1;
}

/**
 * Make the stack logically empty.
 */
public void makeEmpty( )
{
    topOfStack = -1;
}
```

figure 16.5

The push method for the ArrayStack class

```
/**
 * Insert a new item into the stack.
 * @param x the item to insert.
 */
public void push( AnyType x )
{
    if( topOfStack + 1 == theArray.length )
        doubleArray( );
    theArray[ ++topOfStack ] = x;
}
```

A real-life example of amortization is payment of income taxes. Rather than pay your entire bill on April 15, the government requires that you pay most of your taxes through withholding. The total tax bill is always the same;

```
    /**
     * Get the most recently inserted item in the stack.
     * Does not alter the stack.
     * @return the most recently inserted item in the stack.
     * @throws UnderflowException if the stack is empty.
     */
    public AnyType top( )
    {
        if( isEmpty( ) )
            throw new UnderflowException( "ArrayStack top" );
        return theArray[ topOfStack ];
    }

    /**
     * Remove the most recently inserted item from the stack.
     * @throws UnderflowException if the stack is empty.
     */
    public void pop( )
    {
        if( isEmpty( ) )
            throw new UnderflowException( "ArrayStack pop" );
        topOfStack--;
    }
```

figure 16.6

The top and pop methods for the ArrayStack class

```
    /**
     * Return and remove the most recently inserted item
     * from the stack.
     * @return the most recently inserted item in the stack.
     * @throws Underflow if the stack is empty.
     */
    public AnyType topAndPop( )
    {
        if( isEmpty( ) )
            throw new UnderflowException( "ArrayStack topAndPop" );
        return theArray[ topOfStack-- ];
    }
```

figure 16.7

The topAndPop method for the ArrayStack class

it is *when* the tax is paid that varies. The same is true for the time spent in the push operations. We can charge for the array doubling at the time it occurs, or we can bill each push operation equally. An amortized bound requires that we bill each operation in a sequence for its fair share of the total cost. In our example, the cost of array doubling therefore is not excessive.

16.1.2 queues

Storing the queue items beginning at the start of any array makes dequeueing expensive.

A `dequeue` is implemented by incrementing the `front` position.

The easiest way to implement the queue is to store the items in an array with the front item in the front position (i.e., array index 0). If `back` represents the position of the last item in the queue, then to `enqueue` we merely increment `back` and place the item there. The problem is that the `dequeue` operation is very expensive. The reason is that, by requiring that the items be placed at the start of the array, we force the `dequeue` to shift all the items one position after we remove the front item.

Figure 16.8 shows that we can overcome this problem when performing a `dequeue` by incrementing `front` rather than shifting all the elements. When the queue has one element, both `front` and `back` represent the array index of that element. Thus, for an empty queue, `back` must be initialized to `front-1`.

This implementation ensures that both `enqueue` and `dequeue` can be performed in constant time. The fundamental problem with this approach is shown in the first line of Figure 16.9. After three more `enqueue` operations, we cannot add any more items, even though the queue is not really full. Array

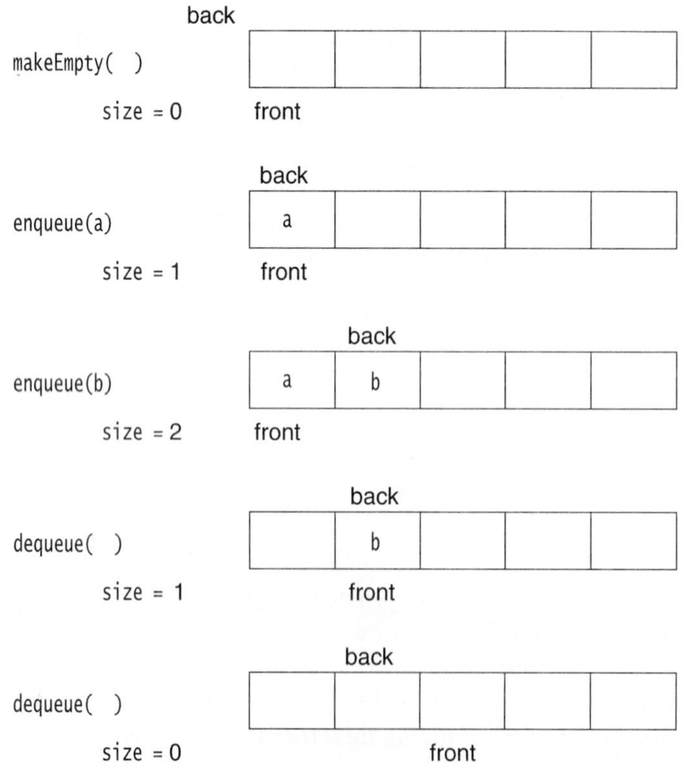

figure 16.8

Basic array implementation of the queue

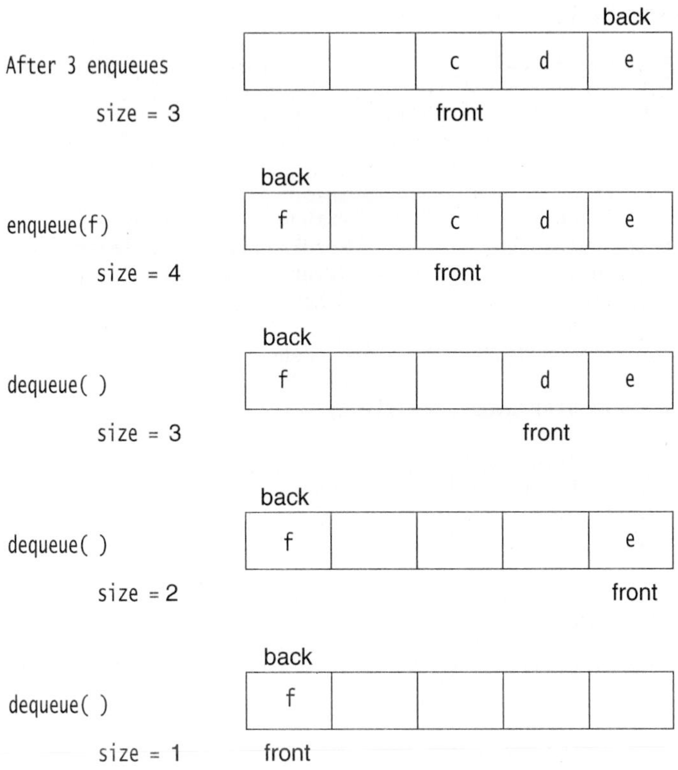

figure 16.9

Array implementation of the queue with wraparound

doubling does not solve the problem because, even if the size of the array is 1,000, after 1,000 `enqueue` operations there is no room in the queue, regardless of its actual size. Even if 1,000 `dequeue` operations have been performed, thus abstractly making the queue empty, we cannot add to it.

As Figure 16.9 shows, however, there is plenty of extra space: All the positions before `front` are unused and can thus be recycled. Hence we use *wraparound;* that is, when either `back` or `front` reaches the end of the array, we reset it to the beginning. This operation implementing a queue is called a *circular array implementation.* We need to double the array only when the number of elements in the queue equals the number of array positions. To `enqueue(f)`, we therefore reset `back` to the start of the array and place `f` there. After three `dequeue` operations, `front` is also reset to the start of the array.

Wraparound returns `front` or `back` to the beginning of the array when either reaches the end. Using wraparound to implement the queue is called a *circular array implementation.*

The skeleton for the `ArrayQueue` class is shown in Figure 16.10. The `ArrayQueue` class has four data members: a dynamically expanding array, the number of items currently in the queue, the array index of the front item, and the array index of the back item.

figure 16.10

Skeleton for the array-based queue class

```
package weiss.nonstandard;

// ArrayQueue class
//
// CONSTRUCTION: with no initializer
//
// ******************PUBLIC OPERATIONS*********************
// void enqueue( x )      --> Insert x
// AnyType getFront( )    --> Return least recently inserted item
// AnyType dequeue( )     --> Return and remove least recent item
// boolean isEmpty( )     --> Return true if empty; else false
// void makeEmpty( )      --> Remove all items
// ******************ERRORS********************************
// getFront or dequeue on empty queue

public class ArrayQueue<AnyType>
{
    public ArrayQueue( )
      { /* Figure 16.12 */ }

    public boolean isEmpty( )
      { /* Figure 16.13 */ }
    public void makeEmpty( )
      { /* Figure 16.17 */ }
    public AnyType dequeue( )
      { /* Figure 16.16 */ }
    public AnyType getFront( )
      { /* Figure 16.16 */ }
    public void enqueue( AnyType x )
      { /* Figure 16.14 */ }

    private int increment( int x )
      { /* Figure 16.11 */ }
    private void doubleQueue( )
      { /* Figure 16.15 */ }

    private AnyType [ ] theArray;
    private int         currentSize;
    private int         front;
    private int         back;

    private static final int DEFAULT_CAPACITY = 10;
}
```

If the queue is full, we must implement array doubling carefully.

We declare two methods in the private section. These methods are used internally by the `ArrayQueue` methods but are not made available to the user of the class. One of these methods is the `increment` routine, which adds 1 to its parameter and returns the new value. Because this method implements wraparound, if the result would equal the array size it is wrapped around to zero. This routine is shown in Figure 16.11. The other routine is `doubleQueue`, which is called if an `enqueue` requires a doubling of the array. It is slightly more complex than the usual expansion because the queue items are not necessarily stored in an array starting at location 0. Thus items must be copied carefully. We discuss `doubleQueue` along with `enqueue`.

Many of the public methods resemble their stack counterparts, including the constructor shown in Figure 16.12 and `isEmpty`, shown in Figure 16.13. This constructor is not particularly special, except that we must be sure that we have the correct initial values for both `front` and `back`. This is done by calling `makeEmpty`.

The `enqueue` routine is shown in Figure 16.14. The basic strategy is simple enough, as illustrated by lines 9–11 in the `enqueue` routine. The `doubleQueue` routine, shown in Figure 16.15, begins by resizing the array. We must move items starting at position `front`, rather than 0.

When we double the queue array, we cannot simply copy the entire array directly.

```java
/**
 * Internal method to increment with wraparound.
 * @param x any index in theArray's range.
 * @return x+1, or 0 if x is at the end of theArray.
 */
private int increment( int x )
{
    if( ++x == theArray.length )
        x = 0;
    return x;
}
```

figure 16.11

The wraparound routine

```java
/**
 * Construct the queue.
 */
public ArrayQueue( )
{
    theArray = (AnyType []) new Object[ DEFAULT_CAPACITY ];
    makeEmpty( );
}
```

figure 16.12

The constructor for the `ArrayQueue` class

```java
/**
 * Test if the queue is logically empty.
 * @return true if empty, false otherwise.
 */
public boolean isEmpty( )
{
    return currentSize == 0;
}
```

figure 16.13

The `isEmpty` routine for the `ArrayQueue` class

Thus doubleQueue steps through the old array and copies each item to the new part of the array at lines 11–12. Then we reset back at line 16. The dequeue and getFront routines are shown in Figure 16.16; both are short. Finally, the makeEmpty routine is shown in Figure 16.17. The queue routines clearly are constant-time operations, so the cost of array doubling can be amortized over the sequence of enqueue operations, as for the stack.

The circular array implementation of the queue can easily be done incorrectly when attempts to shorten the code are made. For instance, if you attempt to avoid using the size member by using front and back to infer the size, the array must be resized when the number of items in the queue is 1 less than the array's size.

figure 16.14

The enqueue routine for the ArrayQueue class

```
    /**
     * Insert a new item into the queue.
     * @param x the item to insert.
     */
    public void enqueue( AnyType x )
    {
        if( currentSize == theArray.length )
            doubleQueue( );
        back = increment( back );
        theArray[ back ] = x;
        currentSize++;
    }
```

```
1       /**
2        * Internal method to expand theArray.
3        */
4       private void doubleQueue( )
5       {
6           AnyType [ ] newArray;
7
8           newArray = (AnyType []) new Object[ theArray.length * 2 ];
9
10              // Copy elements that are logically in the queue
11          for( int i = 0; i < currentSize; i++, front = increment( front ) )
12              newArray[ i ] = theArray[ front ];
13
14          theArray = newArray;
15          front = 0;
16          back = currentSize - 1;
17      }
```

figure 16.15

Dynamic expansion for the ArrayQueue class

```java
/**
 * Return and remove the least recently inserted item
 * from the queue.
 * @return the least recently inserted item in the queue.
 * @throws UnderflowException if the queue is empty.
 */
public AnyType dequeue( )
{
    if( isEmpty( ) )
        throw new UnderflowException( "ArrayQueue dequeue" );
    currentSize--;

    AnyType returnValue = theArray[ front ];
    front = increment( front );
    return returnValue;
}

/**
 * Get the least recently inserted item in the queue.
 * Does not alter the queue.
 * @return the least recently inserted item in the queue.
 * @throws UnderflowException if the queue is empty.
 */
public AnyType getFront( )
{
    if( isEmpty( ) )
        throw new UnderflowException( "ArrayQueue getFront" );
    return theArray[ front ];
}
```

figure 16.16

The dequeue and getFront routines for the ArrayQueue class

```java
/**
 * Make the queue logically empty.
 */
public void makeEmpty( )
{
    currentSize = 0;
    front = 0;
    back = -1;
}
```

figure 16.17

The makeEmpty routine for the ArrayQueue class

16.2 linked list implementations

An alternative to the contiguous array implementation is a linked list. Recall from Section 6.5 that in a linked list, we store each item in a separate object that also contains a reference to the next object in the list.

The advantage of the linked list is that the excess memory is only one reference per item. In contrast, a contiguous array implementation uses excess space equal to the number of vacant array items (plus some additional memory during the doubling phase). The linked list advantage can be significant in other languages if the vacant array items store uninitialized instances of objects that consume significant space. In Java this advantage is minimal. Even so, we discuss the linked list implementations for three reasons.

The advantage of a linked list implementation is that the excess memory is only one reference per item. The disadvantage is that the memory management could be time consuming.

1. An understanding of implementations that might be useful in other languages is important.
2. Implementations that use linked lists can be shorter for the queue than the comparable array versions.
3. These implementations illustrate the principles behind the more general linked list operations given in Chapter 17.

For the implementation to be competitive with contiguous array implementations, we must be able to perform the basic linked list operations in constant time. Doing so is easy because the changes in the linked list are restricted to the elements at the two ends (front and back) of the list.

16.2.1 stacks

In implementing the stack class, the top of the stack is represented by the first item in a linked list.

The stack class can be implemented as a linked list in which the top of the stack is represented by the first item in the list, as shown in Figure 16.18. To implement a `push`, we create a new node in the list and attach it as the new first element. To implement a `pop`, we merely advance the top of the stack to the second item in the list (if there is one). An empty stack is represented by an empty linked list. Clearly, each operation is performed in constant time because, by restricting operations to the first node, we have made all calculations independent of the size of the list. All that remains is the Java implementation.

Figure 16.19 provides the class skeleton. Lines 39 to 49 give the type declaration for the nodes in the list. A `ListNode` consists of two data members:

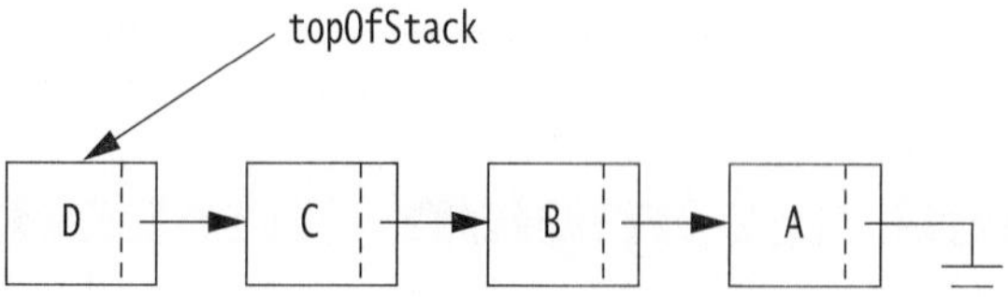

figure 16.18

Linked list implementation of the `Stack` class

```java
package weiss.nonstandard;

// ListStack class
//
// CONSTRUCTION: with no initializer
//
// ******************PUBLIC OPERATIONS*********************
// void push( x )          --> Insert x
// void pop( )             --> Remove most recently inserted item
// AnyType top( )          --> Return most recently inserted item
// AnyType topAndPop( )    --> Return and remove most recent item
// boolean isEmpty( )      --> Return true if empty; else false
// void makeEmpty( )       --> Remove all items
// ******************ERRORS********************************
// top, pop, or topAndPop on empty stack

public class ListStack<AnyType> implements Stack<AnyType>
{
    public boolean isEmpty( )
      { return topOfStack == null; }
    public void makeEmpty( )
      { topOfStack = null; }

    public void push( AnyType x )
      { /* Figure 16.20 */ }
    public void pop( )
      { /* Figure 16.20 */ }
    public AnyType top( )
      { /* Figure 16.21 */ }
    public AnyType topAndPop( )
      { /* Figure 16.21 */ }

    private ListNode<AnyType> topOfStack = null;
}

// Basic node stored in a linked list.
// Note that this class is not accessible outside
// of package weiss.nonstandard
class ListNode<AnyType>
{
    public ListNode( AnyType theElement )
      { this( theElement, null ); }

    public ListNode( AnyType theElement, ListNode<AnyType> n )
      { element = theElement; next = n; }

    public AnyType   element;
    public ListNode next;
}
```

figure 16.19

Skeleton for linked list-based stack class

element stores the item and next stores a reference to the next ListNode in the linked list. We provide constructors for ListNode that can be used to execute both

```
ListNode<AnyType> p1 = new ListNode<AnyType>( x );
```

and

```
ListNode<AnyType> p2 = new ListNode<AnyType>( x, ptr2 );
```

The ListNode declaration is package-visible but can be used by the queue implementation in the same package.

One option is to nest ListNode in the Stack class. We use the slightly inferior alternative of making it a top-level class that is only package-visible, thus enabling reuse of the class for the queue implementation. The stack itself is represented by a single data member, topOfStack, which is a reference to the first ListNode in the linked list.

The constructor is not explicitly written, since by default we obtain an empty stack by setting topOfStack to NULL. makeEmpty and isEmpty are thus trivial and are shown at lines 19–22.

The stack routines are essentially one-liners.

Two routines are shown in Figure 16.20. The push operation is essentially one line of code, in which we allocate a new ListNode whose data member contains the item x to be pushed. The next reference for this new node is the original topOfStack. This node then becomes the new topOfStack. We do all this at line 7.

The pop operation also is simple. After the obligatory test for emptiness, we reset topOfStack to the second node in the list.

figure 16.20

The push and pop routines for the ListStack class

```
 1     /**
 2      * Insert a new item into the stack.
 3      * @param x the item to insert.
 4      */
 5     public void push( AnyType x )
 6     {
 7         topOfStack = new ListNode<AnyType>( x, topOfStack );
 8     }
 9
10     /**
11      * Remove the most recently inserted item from the stack.
12      * @throws UnderflowException if the stack is empty.
13      */
14     public void pop( )
15     {
16         if( isEmpty( ) )
17             throw new UnderflowException( "ListStack pop" );
18         topOfStack = topOfStack.next;
19     }
```

```
/**
 * Get the most recently inserted item in the stack.
 * Does not alter the stack.
 * @return the most recently inserted item in the stack.
 * @throws UnderflowException if the stack is empty.
 */
public AnyType top( )
{
    if( isEmpty( ) )
        throw new UnderflowException( "ListStack top" );
    return topOfStack.element;
}

/**
 * Return and remove the most recently inserted item
 * from the stack.
 * @return the most recently inserted item in the stack.
 * @throws UnderflowException if the stack is empty.
 */
public AnyType topAndPop( )
{
    if( isEmpty( ) )
        throw new UnderflowException( "ListStack topAndPop" );

    AnyType topItem = topOfStack.element;
    topOfStack = topOfStack.next;
    return topItem;
}
```

figure 16.21

The top and topAndPop routines for the ListStack class

Finally, top and topAndPop are straightforward routines and are implemented as shown in Figure 16.21.

16.2.2 queues

A linked list in which we maintain a reference to the first and last item can be used to implement the queue in constant time per operation.

The queue can be implemented by a linked list, provided we keep references to both the front and back of the list. Figure 16.22 shows the general idea.

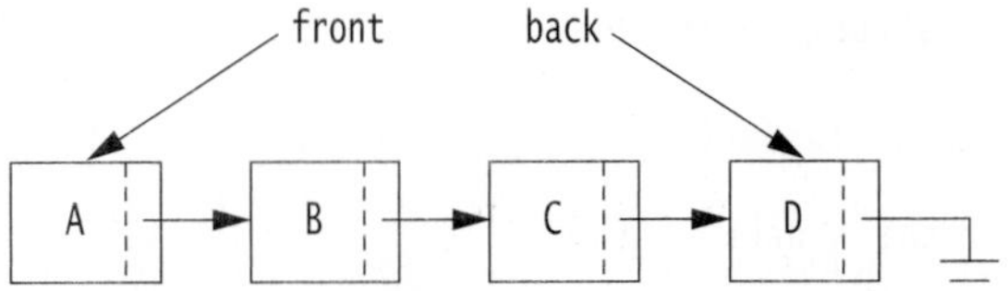

figure 16.22

Linked list implementation of the queue class

The ListQueue class is similar to the ListStack class. The ListQueue class skeleton is given in Figure 16.23. The only new thing here is that we maintain two references instead of one. Figure 16.24 shows the constructors for the ListQueue class.

figure 16.23

Skeleton for the linked list-based queue class

```
package weiss.nonstandard;

// ListQueue class
//
// CONSTRUCTION: with no initializer
//
// ******************PUBLIC OPERATIONS*********************
// void enqueue( x )       --> Insert x
// AnyType getFront( )     --> Return least recently inserted item
// AnyType dequeue( )      --> Return and remove least recent item
// boolean isEmpty( )      --> Return true if empty; else false
// void makeEmpty( )       --> Remove all items
// ******************ERRORS********************************
// getFront or dequeue on empty queue

public class ListQueue<AnyType>
{
    public ListQueue( )
      { /* Figure 16.24 */ }
    public boolean isEmpty( )
      { /* Figure 16.27 */ }
    public void enqueue( AnyType x )
      { /* Figure 16.25 */ }
    public AnyType dequeue( )
      { /* Figure 16.25 */ }
    public AnyType getFront( )
      { /* Figure 16.27 */ }
    public void makeEmpty( )
      { /* Figure 16.27 */ }

    private ListNode<AnyType> front;
    private ListNode<AnyType> back;
}
```

figure 16.24

Constructor for the linked list-based ListQueue class

```
    /**
     * Construct the queue.
     */
    public ListQueue( )
    {
        front = back = null;
    }
```

Figure 16.25 implements both enqueue and dequeue. The dequeue routine is logically identical to a stack pop (actually popAndTop). The enqueue routine has two cases. If the queue is empty, we create a one-element queue by calling new and having both front and back reference the single node. Otherwise, we create a new node with data value x, attach it at the end of the list, and then reset the end of the list to this new node, as illustrated in Figure 16.26. Note that enqueueing the first element is a special case because there is no next reference to which a new node can be attached. We do all this at line 10 in Figure 16.25.

Enqueueing the first element is a special case because there is no next reference to which a new node can be attached.

The remaining methods for the ListQueue class are identical to the corresponding ListStack routines. They are shown in Figure 16.27.

```
1      /**
2       * Insert a new item into the queue.
3       * @param x the item to insert.
4       */
5      public void enqueue( AnyType x )
6      {
7          if( isEmpty( ) )    // Make a queue of one element
8              back = front = new ListNode<AnyType>( x );
9          else                // Regular case
10             back = back.next = new ListNode<AnyType>( x );
11     }
12
13     /**
14      * Return and remove the least recently inserted item
15      * from the queue.
16      * @return the least recently inserted item in the queue.
17      * @throws UnderflowException if the queue is empty.
18      */
19     public AnyType dequeue( )
20     {
21         if( isEmpty( ) )
22             throw new UnderflowException( "ListQueue dequeue" );
23
24         AnyType returnValue = front.element;
25         front = front.next;
26         return returnValue;
27     }
```

figure 16.25

The enqueue and dequeue routines for the ListQueue class

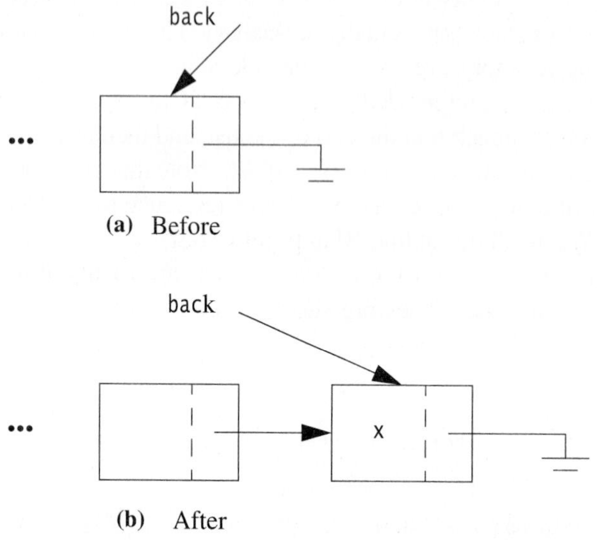

figure 16.26

The enqueue operation for the linked list-based implementation

figure 16.27

Supporting routines for the ListQueue class

```
/**
 * Get the least recently inserted item in the queue.
 * Does not alter the queue.
 * @return the least recently inserted item in the queue.
 * @throws UnderflowException if the queue is empty.
 */
public AnyType getFront( )
{
    if( isEmpty( ) )
        throw new UnderflowException( "ListQueue getFront" );
    return front.element;
}

/**
 * Make the queue logically empty.
 */
public void makeEmpty( )
{
    front = null;
    back = null;
}

/**
 * Test if the queue is logically empty.
 */
public boolean isEmpty( )
{
    return front == null;
}
```

16.3 comparison of the two methods

Both the array and linked list versions run in constant time per operation. Thus they are so fast that they are unlikely to be the bottleneck of any algorithm and, in that regard, which version is used rarely matters.

The array versus linked list implementations represent a classic time–space trade-off.

The array versions of these data structures are likely to be faster than their linked list counterparts, especially if an accurate estimation of capacity is available. If an additional constructor is provided to specify the initial capacity (see Exercise 16.2) and the estimate is correct, no doubling is performed. Also, the sequential access provided by an array is typically faster than the potential nonsequential access offered by dynamic memory allocation.

The array implementation does have two drawbacks, however. First, for queues, the array implementation is arguably more complex than the linked list implementation, owing to the combined code for wraparound and array doubling. Our implementation of array doubling was not as efficient as possible (see Exercise 16.8), thus a faster implementation of the queue would require a few additional lines of code. Even the array implementation of the stack uses a few more lines of code than its linked list counterpart.

The second drawback affects other languages, but not Java. When doubling, we temporarily require three times as much space as the number of data items suggests. The reason is that, when the array is doubled, we need to have memory to store both the old and the new (double-sized) array. Further, at the queue's peak size, the array is between 50 percent and 100 percent full; on average it is 75 percent full, so for every three items in the array, one spot is empty. The wasted space is thus 33 percent on average and 100 percent when the table is only half full. As discussed earlier, in Java, each element in the array is simply a reference. In other languages, such as C++, objects are stored directly, rather than referenced. In these languages, the wasted space could be significant when compared to the linked list–based version that uses only an extra reference per item.

16.4 the `java.util.Stack` class

The Collections API provides a `Stack` class. The `Stack` class in `java.util` is considered a legacy class and is not widely used. Figure 16.28 provides an implementation.

figure 16.28

A simplified Collections-style Stack class, based on the ArrayList class

```
package weiss.util;

/**
 * Stack class. Unlike java.util.Stack, this is not extended from
 * Vector. This is the minimum respectable set of operations.
 */
public class Stack<AnyType> implements java.io.Serializable
{
    public Stack( )
    {
        items = new ArrayList<AnyType>( );
    }

    public AnyType push( AnyType x )
    {
        items.add( x );
        return x;
    }

    public AnyType pop( )
    {
        if( isEmpty( ) )
            throw new EmptyStackException( );
        return items.remove( items.size( ) - 1 );
    }

    public AnyType peek( )
    {
        if( isEmpty( ) )
            throw new EmptyStackException( );
        return items.get( items.size( ) - 1 );
    }

    public boolean isEmpty( )
    {
        return size( ) == 0;
    }

    public int size( )
    {
        return items.size( );
    }

    public void clear( )
    {
        items.clear( );
    }

    private ArrayList<AnyType> items;
}
```

16.5 double-ended queues

A *double-ended queue* (*deque*) is like a queue, except that access is allowed at both ends. Exercise 14.14 describes an application of the deque. Rather than the terms `enqueue` and `dequeue`, the terms used are `addFront`, `addRear`, `removeFront`, and `removeRear`.

A *double-ended queue* (*deque*) allows access at both ends.

A deque can be implemented using an array in much the same way as a queue. The implementation is left as Exercise 16.5. However, using a singly linked list does not work cleanly because it is difficult to remove the last item in a singly linked list. However, `java.util.LinkedList` efficiently supports the deque operations.

summary

In this chapter we described implementation of the stack and queue classes. Both classes can be implemented by using a contiguous array or a linked list. In each case, all operations use constant time; thus all operations are fast.

key concepts

circular array implementation The use of wraparound to implement a queue. (545)

double-ended queue (deque) A queue that allows access at both ends. (559)

wraparound Occurs when `front` or `back` returns to the beginning of the array when it reaches the end. (545)

common errors

1. Using an implementation that does not provide constant-time access is a bad error. There is no justification for this inefficiency.

on the internet

The files listed are available.

ArrayStack.java Contains the implementation of an array-based stack.

ArrayQueue.java Contains the implementation of an array-based queue.

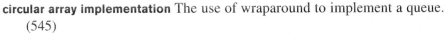

ListStack.java	Contains the implementation of a linked list-based stack.
ListQueue.java	Contains the implementation of a linked list-based queue.
Stack.java	Contains the implementation of a Collections API stack.

exercises

IN SHORT

16.1 Draw the stack and queue data structures (for both the array and linked list implementations) for each step in the following sequence: *add*(1), *add*(2), *remove*, *add*(3), *add*(4), *remove*, *remove*, *add*(5). Assume an initial size of 3 for the array implementation.

IN PRACTICE

16.2 Add constructors to the `ArrayStack` and `ArrayQueue` classes that allow the user to specify an initial capacity.

16.3 Compare the running times for the array and linked list versions of the stack class. Use `Integer` objects.

16.4 Write a `main` that declares and uses a stack of `Integer` and a stack of `Double` simultaneously.

16.5 Implement a `Deque` class.

16.6 Implement the array-based stack class with an `ArrayList`. What are the advantages and disadvantages of this approach?

16.7 Implement the array-based queue class with an `ArrayList`. What are the advantages and disadvantages of this approach?

16.8 For the queue implementation presented in Section 16.1.2, show how to copy the queue elements in the `doubleQueue` operation without making calls to `increment`.

PROGRAMMING PROJECTS

16.9 An output-restricted double-ended queue supports insertions from both ends but accesses and deletions only from the front. Implement this data structure with a singly linked list.

16.10 Suppose that you want to add the `findMin` (but not `deleteMin`) operation to the stack repertoire. Implement this class as two stacks, as described in Exercise 6.5.

16.11 Suppose that you want to add the `findMin` (but not `deleteMin`) operation to the `Deque` repertoire. Implement this class using four stacks. If a deletion empties a stack, you will need to reorganize the remaining items evenly.

chapter 17

linked lists

In Chapter 16 we demonstrated that linked lists can be used to store items noncontiguously. The linked lists used in that chapter were simplified, with all the accesses performed at one of the list's two ends.

In this chapter, we show

- How to allow access to any item by using a general linked list
- The general algorithms for the linked list operations
- How the iterator class provides a safe mechanism for traversing and accessing linked lists
- List variations, such as doubly linked lists and circularly linked lists
- How to use inheritance to derive a sorted linked list class
- How to implement the Collections API `LinkedList` class

17.1 basic ideas

In this chapter we implement the linked list and allow general access (arbitrary insertion, deletion, and find operations) through the list. The basic linked list consists of a collection of connected, dynamically allocated nodes. In a *singly linked list,* each node consists of the data element and a link to the next node in the list. The last node in the list has a `null` `next` link. In this section we assume that the node is given by the following `ListNode` declaration, which does not use generics:

```
class ListNode
{
    Object element;
    ListNode   next;
}
```

The first node in the linked list is accessible by a reference, as shown in Figure 17.1. We can print or search in the linked list by starting at the first item and following the chain of `next` links. The two basic operations that must be performed are insertion and deletion of an arbitrary item `x`.

Insertion consists of splicing a node into the list and can be accomplished with one statement.

For insertion we must define where the insertion is to take place. If we have a reference to some node in the list, the easiest place to insert is immediately after that item. As an example, Figure 17.2 shows how we insert `x` after item `a` in a linked list. We must perform the following steps:

```
tmp = new ListNode( );          // Create a new node
tmp.element = x;                // Place x in the element member
tmp.next = current.next;        // x's next node is b
current.next = tmp;             // a's next node is x
```

As a result of these statements, the old list ... `a, b,` ... now appears as ... `a, x, b,` ... . We can simplify the code if the `ListNode` has a constructor that initializes the data members directly. In that case, we obtain

figure 17.1

Basic linked list

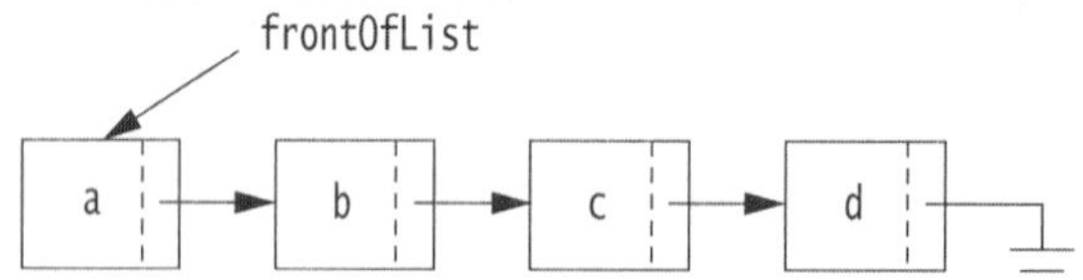

figure 17.2

Insertion in a linked list: Create new node (`tmp`), copy in `x`, set `tmp`'s next link, and set `current`'s next link.

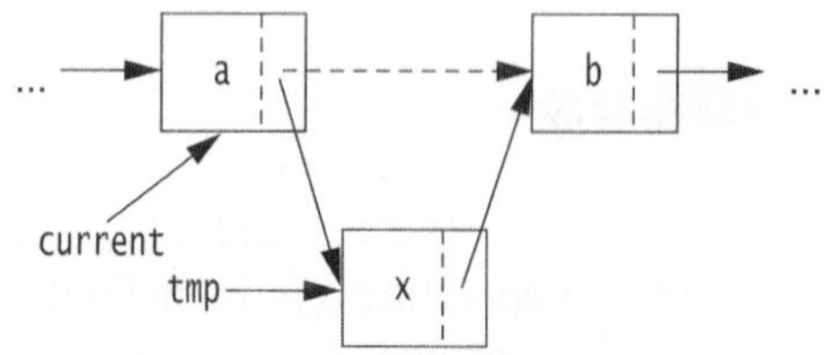

```
tmp = new ListNode( x, current.next ); // Create new node
current.next = tmp;                    // a's next node is x
```

We now see that tmp is no longer necessary. Thus we have the one-liner

```
current.next = new ListNode( x, current.next );
```

The remove command can be executed in one link change. Figure 17.3 shows that to remove item x from the linked list, we set current to be the node prior to x and then have current's next link bypass x. This operation is expressed by the statement

Removal can be accomplished by bypassing the node. We need a reference to the node prior to the one we want to remove.

```
current.next = current.next.next;
```

The list ... a, x, b, ... now appears as ... a, b, ...

The preceding discussion summarizes the basics of inserting and removing items at arbitrary places in a linked list. The fundamental property of a linked list is that changes to it can be made by using only a constant number of data movements, which is a great improvement over an array implementation. Maintaining contiguousness in an array means that whenever an item is added or deleted, all items that follow it in the list must move.

Linked list operations use only a constant number of data movements.

17.1.1 header nodes

There is one problem with the basic description: It assumes that whenever an item x is removed, some previous item is always present to allow a bypass. Consequently, removal of the first item in the linked list becomes a special case. Similarly, the insert routine does not allow us to insert an item to be the new first element in the list. The reason is that insertions must follow some existing item. So, although the basic algorithm works fine, some annoying special cases must be dealt with.

Special cases are always problematic in algorithm design and frequently lead to bugs in the code. Consequently, writing code that avoids special cases is generally preferable. One way to do that is to introduce a header node.

A *header node* is an extra node in a linked list that holds no data but serves to satisfy the requirement that every node containing an item have a

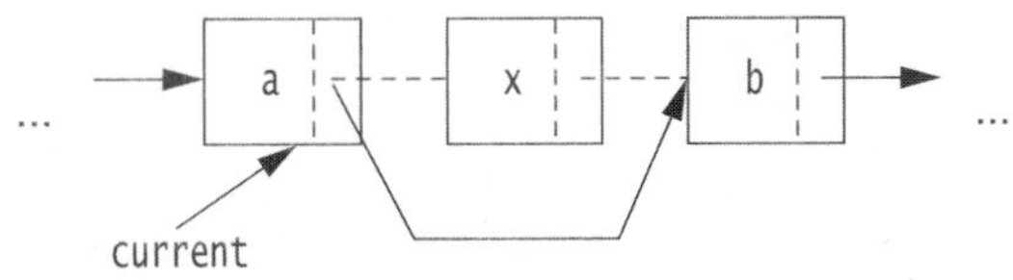

figure 17.3

Deletion from a linked list

A *header node* holds no data but serves to satisfy the requirement that every node have a previous node. A header node allows us to avoid special cases such as insertion of a new first element and removal of the first element.

previous node in the list. The header node for the list `a`, `b`, `c` is shown in Figure 17.4. Note that `a` is no longer a special case. It can be deleted just like any other node by having `current` reference the node before it. We can also add a new first element to the list by setting `current` equal to the header node and calling the insertion routine. By using the header node, we greatly simplify the code—with a negligible space penalty. In more complex applications, header nodes not only simplify the code but also improve speed because, after all, fewer tests mean less time.

The use of a header node is somewhat controversial. Some argue that avoiding special cases is not sufficient justification for adding fictitious cells; they view the use of header nodes as little more than old-style hacking. Even so, we use them here precisely because they allow us to demonstrate the basic link manipulations without obscuring the code with special cases. Whether a header should be used is a matter of personal preference. Furthermore, in a class implementation, its use would be completely transparent to the user. However, we must be careful: The printing routine must skip over the header node, as must all searching routines. Moving to the front now means setting the current position to `header.next`, and so on. Furthermore, as Figure 17.5 shows, with a dummy header node, a list is empty if `header.next` is `null`.

17.1.2 iterator classes

The typical primitive strategy identifies a linked list by a reference to the header node. Each individual item in the list can then be accessed by providing a reference to the node that stores it. The problem with that strategy is that

figure 17.4

Using a header node for the linked list

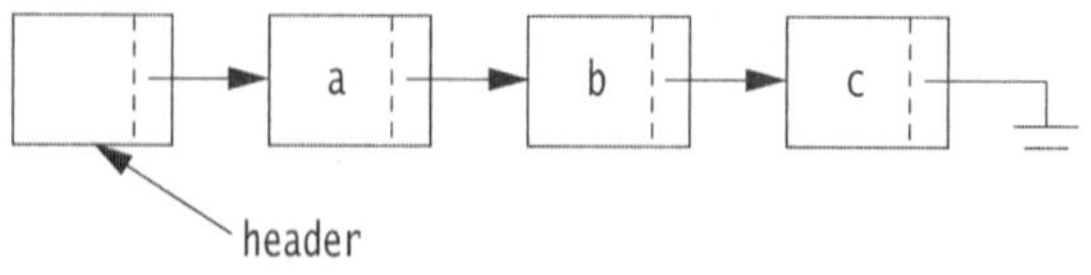

figure 17.5

Empty list when a header node is used

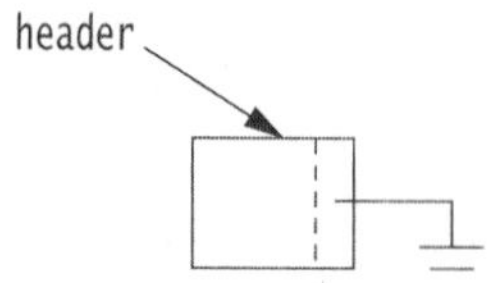

checking for errors is difficult. For example, a user could pass a reference to something that is a node in a different list. One way to guarantee that this cannot happen is to store a current position as part of a list class. To do so, we add a second data member, `current`. Then, as all access to the list goes through the class methods, we can be certain that `current` always represents a node in the list, the header node, or `null`.

By storing a current position in a list class, we ensure that access is controlled.

This scheme has a problem: With only one position, the case of two iterators needing to access the list independently is left unsupported. One way to avoid this problem is to define a separate *iterator class,* which maintains a notion of its current position. A list class would then not maintain any notion of a current position and would only have methods that treat the list as a unit, such as `isEmpty` and `makeEmpty`, or that accept an iterator as a parameter, such as `insert`. Routines that depend only on an iterator itself, such as the `advance` routine that advances the iterator to the next position, would reside in the iterator class. Access to the list is granted by making the iterator class either package-visible or an inner class. We can view each instance of an iterator class as one in which only legal list operations, such as advancing in the list, are allowed.

An *iterator class* maintains a current position and typically is package-visible or an inner class of a list (or other container) class.

In Section 17.2 we define a generic list class `LinkedList` and an iterator class `LinkedListIterator`. The `LinkedList` class does not have the same semantics as `java.util.LinkedList`. However, later in the chapter we define a version that does. To show how the nonstandard version works, let us look at a static method that returns the size of a linked list, as shown in Figure 17.6. We declare `itr` as an iterator that can access the linked list `theList`.

We initialize `itr` to the first element in `theList` (skipping over the header, of course) by referencing the iterator given by `theList.first()`.

The test `itr.isValid()` attempts to mimic the test `p!=null` that would be conducted if `p` were a visible reference to a node. Finally, the expression `itr.advance()` mimics the conventional idiom `p=p.next`.

```
// In this routine, LinkedList and LinkedListIterator are the
// classes written in Section 17.2.
public static <AnyType> int listSize( LinkedList<AnyType> theList )
{
    LinkedListIterator<AnyType> itr;
    int size = 0;

    for( itr = theList.first(); itr.isValid(); itr.advance() )
        size++;

    return size;
}
```

figure 17.6

A static method that returns the size of a list

Thus, as long as the iterator class defines a few simple operations, we can iterate over the list naturally. In Section 17.2 we provide its implementation in Java. The routines are surprisingly simple.

There is a natural parallel between the methods defined in the `LinkedList` and `LinkedListIterator` classes and those in the Collections API `LinkedList` class. For instance, the `LinkedListIterator advance` method is roughly equivalent to `hasNext` in the Collections API iterators. The list class in Section 17.2 is simpler than the Collections API `LinkedList` class; as such it illustrates many basic points and is worth examining. In Section 17.5 we implement most of the Collections API `LinkedList` class.

17.2 java implementation

As suggested in the preceding description, a list is implemented as three separate generic classes: one class is the list itself (`LinkedList`), another represents the node (`ListNode`), and the third represents the position (`LinkedListIterator`).

`ListNode` was shown in Chapter 16. Next, Figure 17.7 presents the class that implements the concept of position—namely, `LinkedListIterator`. The class stores a reference to a `ListNode`, representing the current position of the iterator. The `isValid` method returns `true` if the position is not past the end of the list, `retrieve` returns the element stored in the current position, and `advance` advances the current position to the next position. The constructor for `LinkedListIterator` requires a reference to a node that is to be the current node. Note that this constructor is package-visible and thus cannot be used by client methods. Instead, the general idea is that the `LinkedList` class returns preconstructed `LinkedListIterator` objects, as appropriate; `LinkedList` is in the same package as `LinkedListIterator`, so it can invoke the `LinkedList` constructor.

The `LinkedList` class skeleton is shown in Figure 17.8. The single data member is a reference to the header node allocated by the constructor. `isEmpty` is an easily implemented short one-liner. The methods `zeroth` and `first` return iterators corresponding to the header and first element, respectively, as shown in Figure 17.9. Other routines either search the list for some item or change the list via insertion or deletion, and are shown later.

Figure 17.10 illustrates how the `LinkedList` and `LinkedListIterator` classes interact. The `printList` method outputs the contents of a list. `printList` uses only public methods and a typical iteration sequence of obtaining a starting point (via `first`), testing that it has not gone past the ending point (via `isValid`), and advancing in each iteration (via `advance`).

```
package weiss.nonstandard;

// LinkedListIterator class; maintains "current position"
//
// CONSTRUCTION: Package visible only, with a ListNode
//
// ******************PUBLIC OPERATIONS*********************
// void advance( )          --> Advance
// boolean isValid( )       --> True if at valid position in list
// AnyType retrieve         --> Return item in current position

public class LinkedListIterator<AnyType>
{
    /**
     * Construct the list iterator
     * @param theNode any node in the linked list.
     */
    LinkedListIterator( ListNode<AnyType> theNode )
      { current = theNode; }

    /**
     * Test if the current position is a valid position in the list.
     * @return true if the current position is valid.
     */
    public boolean isValid( )
      { return current != null; }

    /**
     * Return the item stored in the current position.
     * @return the stored item or null if the current position
     * is not in the list.
     */
    public AnyType retrieve( )
      { return isValid( ) ? current.element : null; }

    /**
     * Advance the current position to the next node in the list.
     * If the current position is null, then do nothing.
     */
    public void advance( )
    {
        if( isValid( ) )
            current = current.next;
    }

    ListNode<AnyType> current;    // Current position
}
```

figure 17.7

The `LinkedListIterator` class

```
package weiss.nonstandard;

// LinkedList class
//
// CONSTRUCTION: with no initializer
// Access is via LinkedListIterator class
//
// ******************PUBLIC OPERATIONS*********************
// boolean isEmpty( )     --> Return true if empty; else false
// void makeEmpty( )      --> Remove all items
// LinkedListIterator zeroth( )
//                        --> Return position to prior to first
// LinkedListIterator first( )
//                        --> Return first position
// void insert( x, p )    --> Insert x after current iterator position p
// void remove( x )       --> Remove x
// LinkedListIterator find( x )
//                        --> Return position that views x
// LinkedListIterator findPrevious( x )
//                        --> Return position prior to x
// ******************ERRORS********************************
// No special errors

public class LinkedList<AnyType>
{
    public LinkedList( )
      { /* Figure 17.9 */ }

    public boolean isEmpty( )
      { /* Figure 17.9 */ }
    public void makeEmpty( )
      { /* Figure 17.9 */ }
    public LinkedListIterator<AnyType> zeroth( )
      { /* Figure 17.9 */ }
    public LinkedListIterator<AnyType> first( )
      { /* Figure 17.9 */ }
    public void insert( AnyType x, LinkedListIterator<AnyType> p )
      { /* Figure 17.14 */ }
    public LinkedListIterator<AnyType> find( AnyType x )
      { /* Figure 17.11 */ }
    public LinkedListIterator<AnyType> findPrevious( AnyType x )
      { /* Figure 17.13 */ }
    public void remove( Object x )
      { /* Figure 17.12 */ }

    private ListNode<AnyType> header;
}
```

figure 17.8

The LinkedList class skeleton

```java
/**
 * Construct the list
 */
public LinkedList( )
{
    header = new ListNode<AnyType>( null );
}

/**
 * Test if the list is logically empty.
 * @return true if empty, false otherwise.
 */
public boolean isEmpty( )
{
    return header.next == null;
}

/**
 * Make the list logically empty.
 */
public void makeEmpty( )
{
    header.next = null;
}

/**
 * Return an iterator representing the header node.
 */
public LinkedListIterator<AnyType> zeroth( )
{
    return new LinkedListIterator<AnyType>( header );
}

/**
 * Return an iterator representing the first node in the list.
 * This operation is valid for empty lists.
 */
public LinkedListIterator<AnyType> first( )
{
    return new LinkedListIterator<AnyType>( header.next );
}
```

figure 17.9

Some `LinkedList` class one-liners

Let us revisit the issue of whether all three classes are necessary. For instance, couldn't we just have the `LinkedList` class maintain a notion of a current position? Although this option is feasible and works for many applications, using a separate iterator class expresses the abstraction that the

```
// Simple print method
public static <AnyType> void printList( LinkedList<AnyType> theList )
{
    if( theList.isEmpty( ) )
        System.out.print( "Empty list" );
    else
    {
        LinkedListIterator<AnyType> itr = theList.first( );
        for( ; itr.isValid( ); itr.advance( ) )
            System.out.print( itr.retrieve( ) + " " );
    }

    System.out.println( );
}
```

figure 17.10

A method for printing the contents of a `LinkedList`

position and list actually are separate objects. Moreover, it allows for a list to be accessed in several places simultaneously. For instance, to remove a sublist from a list, we can easily add a `remove` operation to the list class that uses two iterators to specify the starting and ending points of the sublist to be removed. Without the iterator class, this action would be more difficult to express.

Short-circuiting is used in the `find` routine at line 10 and in the similar part of the `remove` routine.

We can now implement the remaining `LinkedList` methods. First is `find`, shown in Figure 17.11, which returns the position in the list of some element. Line 10 takes advantage of the fact that the *and* (`&&`) operation is short-cir-

```
1   /**
2    * Return iterator corresponding to the first node containing x.
3    * @param x the item to search for.
4    * @return an iterator; iterator isPastEnd if item is not found.
5    */
6   public LinkedListIterator<AnyType> find( AnyType x )
7   {
8       ListNode<AnyType> itr = header.next;
9
10      while( itr != null && !itr.element.equals( x ) )
11          itr = itr.next;
12
13      return new LinkedListIterator<AnyType>( itr );
14  }
```

figure 17.11

The `find` routine for the `LinkedList` class

```
/**
 * Remove the first occurrence of an item.
 * @param x the item to remove.
 */
public void remove( AnyType x )
{
    LinkedListIterator<AnyType> p = findPrevious( x );

    if( p.current.next != null )
        p.current.next = p.current.next.next;  // Bypass deleted node
}
```

figure 17.12

The `remove` routine for the `LinkedList` class

cuited: If the first half of the *and* is false, the result is automatically false and the second half is not evaluated.

Our next routine removes some element `x` from the list. We need to decide what to do if `x` occurs more than once or not at all. Our routine removes the first occurrence of `x` and does nothing if `x` is not in the list. To make that happen, we find `p`, which is the cell prior to the one containing `x`, via a call to `findPrevious`. The code for implementing the `remove` routine is shown in Figure 17.12. This code is not foolproof: There may be two iterators, and one can be left logically in limbo if the other removes a node. The `findPrevious` routine is similar to the `find` routine and is shown in Figure 17.13.

This code is not foolproof: There may be two iterators, and one can be left dangling if the other removes a node.

```
/**
 * Return iterator prior to the first node containing an item.
 * @param x the item to search for.
 * @return appropriate iterator if the item is found. Otherwise, the
 * iterator corresponding to the last element in the list is returned.
 */
public LinkedListIterator<AnyType> findPrevious( AnyType x )
{
    ListNode<AnyType> itr = header;

    while( itr.next != null && !itr.next.element.equals( x ) )
        itr = itr.next;

    return new LinkedListIterator<AnyType>( itr );
}
```

figure 17.13

The `findPrevious` routine—similar to the `find` routine—for use with `remove`

The insert routine takes constant time.

The last routine we write here is an insertion routine. We pass an element to be inserted and a position `p`. This particular insertion routine inserts an element after position `p`, as shown in Figure 17.14. Note that the `insert` routine makes no use of the list it is in; it depends only on `p`.

The find and findPrevious routines take $O(N)$ time.

With the exception of the `find` and `findPrevious` routines (and `remove`, which calls `findPrevious`), all the operations that we have coded so far take $O(1)$ time. The `find` and `findPrevious` routines take $O(N)$ time in the worst case because the entire list might need to be traversed if the element either is not found or is last in the list. On average, the running time is $O(N)$, because on average half the list must be traversed.

The retreat method is not efficiently supported. A doubly linked list is used if that is a liability.

We certainly could have added more operations, but this basic set is quite powerful. Some operations, such as `retreat`, are not efficiently supported by this version of the linked list; variations on the linked list that allow constant-time implementation of that and other operators are discussed later in this chapter.

17.3 doubly linked lists and circularly linked lists

A *doubly linked list* allows bidirectional traversal by storing two links per node.

As we mentioned in Section 17.2, the singly linked list does not efficiently support some important operations. For instance, although it is easy to go to the front of the list, it is time consuming to go to the end. Although we can easily advance via `advance`, implementing `retreat` cannot be done efficiently with only a `next` link. In some applications that might be crucial. For instance,

```java
/**
 * Insert after p.
 * @param x the item to insert.
 * @param p the position prior to the newly inserted item.
 */
public void insert( AnyType x, LinkedListIterator<AnyType> p )
{
    if( p != null && p.current != null )
        p.current.next = new ListNode<AnyType>( x, p.current.next );
}
```

figure 17.14

The insertion routine for the `LinkedList` class

when designing a text editor, we can maintain the internal image of the file as a linked list of lines. We want to be able to move up just as easily as down in the list, to insert both before and after a line rather than just after, and to be able to get to the last line quickly. A moment's thought suggests that to implement this procedure efficiently we should have each node maintain two links: one to the next node in the list and one to the previous node. Then, to make everything symmetric, we should have not only a header but also a tail. A linked list that allows bidirectional traversal by storing two links per node is called a *doubly linked list.* Figure 17.15 shows the doubly linked list representing `a` and `b`. Each node now has two links (`next` and `prev`), and searching and moving can easily be performed in both directions. Obviously, there are some important changes from the singly linked list.

First, an empty list now consists of a `head` and `tail`, connected as shown in Figure 17.16. Note that `head.prev` and `tail.next` are not needed in the algorithms and are not even initialized. The test for emptiness is now

Symmetry demands that we use both a `head` and a `tail` and that we support roughly twice as many operations.

```
head.next == tail
```

or

```
tail.prev == head
```

We no longer use `null` to decide whether an advance has taken us past the end of the list. Instead, we have gone past the end if `current` is either `head` or `tail` (recall that we can go in either direction). The `retreat` operation can be implemented by

When we advance past the end of the list, we now hit the `tail` node instead of `null`.

```
current = current.prev;
```

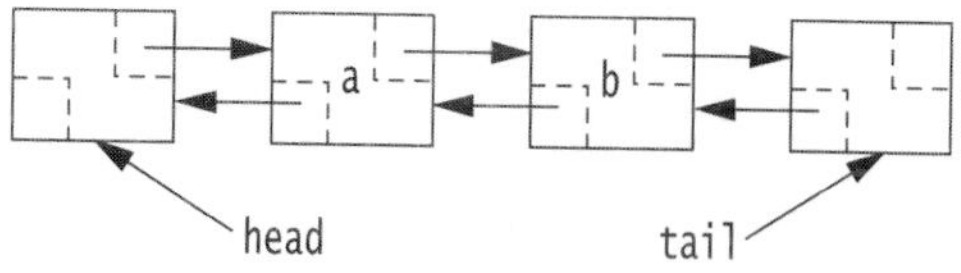

figure 17.15

A doubly linked list

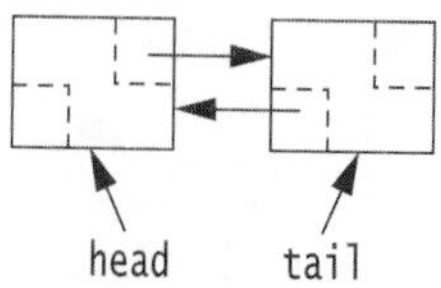

figure 17.16

An empty doubly linked list

Insertion and removal involve twice as many link changes as for a singly linked list.

Before describing some of the additional operations that are available, let us consider how the insertion and removal operations change. Naturally, we can now do both `insertBefore` and `insertAfter`. Twice as many link moves are involved for `insertAfter` with doubly linked lists as with singly linked lists. If we write each statement explicitly, we obtain

```
newNode = new DoublyLinkedListNode( x );
newNode.prev = current;                    // Set x's prev link
newNode.next = current.next;               // Set x's next link
newNode.prev.next = newNode;               // Set a's next link
newNode.next.prev = newNode;               // Set b's prev link
current = newNode;
```

As we showed earlier, the first two link moves can be collapsed into the `DoublyLinkedListNode` construction that is done by `new`. The changes (in order *1*, *2*, *3*, *4*) are illustrated in Figure 17.17.

The `remove` operation can proceed from the current node because we can obtain the previous node instantly.

Figure 17.17 can also be used as a guide in the removal algorithm. Unlike the singly linked list, we can remove the current node because the previous node is available to us automatically. Thus to `remove x` we have to change a's `next` link and b's `prev` link. The basic moves are

```
current.prev.next = current.next;       // Set a's next link
current.next.prev = current.prev;       // Set b's prev link
current = head;                         // So current is not stale
```

To do a complete doubly linked list implementation, we need to decide which operations to support. We can reasonably expect twice as many operations as in the singly linked list. Each individual procedure is similar to the linked list routines; only the dynamic operations involve additional link moves. Moreover, for many of the routines, the code is dominated by error checks. Although some of the checks will change (e.g., we do not test against `null`), they certainly do not become any more complex. In Section 17.5, we use a

figure 17.17

Insertion in a doubly linked list by getting new node and then changing pointers in the order indicated

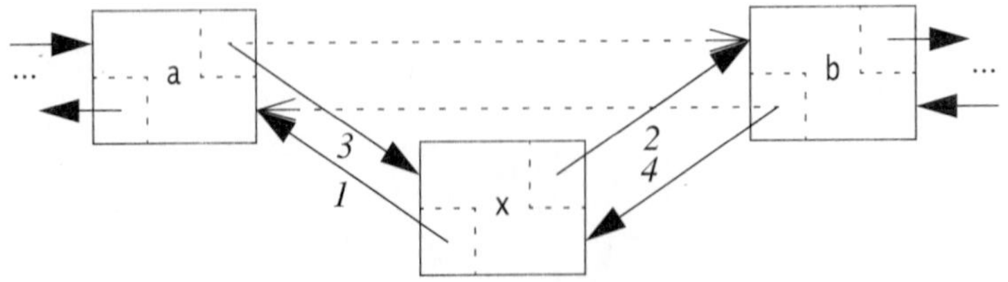

doubly linked list to implement the Collections API linked list class, along with its associated iterators. There are lots of routines, but most are short.

A popular convention is to create a *circularly linked list,* in which the last cell's `next` link references `first`, which can be done with or without a header. Typically, it is done without a header because the header's main purpose is to ensure that every node has a previous node, which is already true for a nonempty circularly linked list. Without a header, we have only the empty list as a special case. We maintain a reference to the first node, but that is not the same as a header node. We can use circularly linked lists and doubly linked lists simultaneously, as shown in Figure 17.18. The circular list is useful when we want searching to allow wraparound, as is the case for some text editors. In Exercise 17.16 you are asked to implement a circularly and doubly linked list.

In a *circularly linked list,* the last cell's `next` link references `first`. This action is useful when wraparound matters.

17.4 sorted linked lists

Sometimes we want to keep the items in a linked list in sorted order, which we can do with a *sorted linked list.* The fundamental difference between a sorted linked list and an unsorted linked list is the insertion routine. Indeed, we can obtain a sorted list class by simply altering the insertion routine from our already written list class. Because the `insert` routine is part of the `LinkedList` class, we should be able to base a new derived class, `SortedLinkedList`, from `LinkedList`. We can, and it is shown in Figure 17.19.

We can maintain items in sorted order by deriving a `SortedLinkedList` class from `LinkedList`.

The new class has two versions of `insert`. One version takes a position and then ignores it; the insertion point is determined solely by the sorted order. The other version of `insert` requires more code.

The one-parameter `insert` uses two `LinkedListIterator` objects to traverse down the corresponding list until the correct insertion point is found. At that point we can apply the base class `insert` routine.

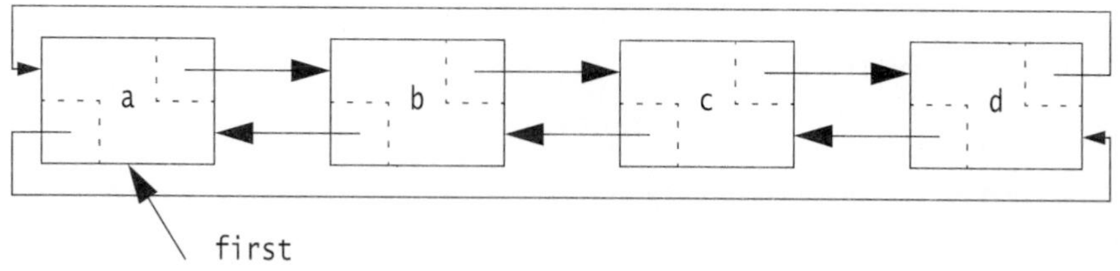

figure 17.18

A circularly and doubly linked list

```java
package weiss.nonstandard;

// SortedLinkedList class
//
// CONSTRUCTION: with no initializer
// Access is via LinkedListIterator class
//
// ******************PUBLIC OPERATIONS*********************
// void insert( x )         --> Insert x
// void insert( x, p )      --> Insert x (ignore p)
// All other LinkedList operations
// ******************ERRORS********************************
// No special errors

public class SortedLinkedList<AnyType extends Comparable<? super AnyType>>
                              extends LinkedList<AnyType>
{
    /**
     * Insert after p.
     * @param x the item to insert.
     * @param p this parameter is ignored.
     */
    public void insert( AnyType x, LinkedListIterator<AnyType> p )
    {
        insert( x );
    }

    /**
     * Insert in sorted order.
     * @param x the item to insert.
     */
    public void insert( AnyType x )
    {
        LinkedListIterator<AnyType> prev = zeroth( );
        LinkedListIterator<AnyType> curr = first( );

        while( curr.isValid( ) && x.compareTo( curr.retrieve( ) ) > 0 )
        {
            prev.advance( );
            curr.advance( );
        }

        super.insert( x, prev );
    }
}
```

figure 17.19

The `SortedLinkedList` class, in which insertions are restricted to sorted order

17.5 implementing the collections api LinkedList class

In this section we implement the Collections API LinkedList class discussed in Section 6.5. Although we present lots of code, we described most of the techniques earlier in this chapter.

As we indicated previously, we need a class to store the basic list node, a class for the iterator, and a class for the list itself. The skeleton for the LinkedList class is shown in Figure 17.20. LinkedList implements the List and Queue interfaces and, as usual, it extends AbstractCollection. Line 5 begins the declaration for the Node class, which is nested and private. Line 7 begins the declaration for the LinkedListIterator, which is a private inner

```
1  package weiss.util;
2  public class LinkedList<AnyType> extends AbstractCollection<AnyType>
3                                   implements List<AnyType>, Queue<AnyType>
4  {
5      private static class Node<AnyType>
6        { /* Figure 17.21 */ }
7      private class LinkedListIterator<AnyType> implements ListIterator<AnyType>
8        { /* Figure 17.30 */ }
9
10     public LinkedList( )
11       { /* Figure 17.22 */ }
12     public LinkedList( Collection<AnyType> other )
13       { /* Figure 17.22 */ }
14
15     public int size( )
16       { /* Figure 17.23 */ }
17     public boolean contains( Object x )
18       { /* Figure 17.23 */ }
19     public boolean add( AnyType x )
20       { /* Figure 17.24 */ }
21     public void add( int idx, AnyType x )
22       { /* Figure 17.24 */ }
23     public void addFirst( AnyType x )
24       { /* Figure 17.24 */ }
25     public void addLast( AnyType x )
26       { /* Figure 17.24 */ }
27     public AnyType element( )
28       { /* Added in Java 5; same as getFirst */ }
29     public AnyType getFirst( )
30       { /* Figure 17.25 */ }
31     public AnyType getLast( )
32       { /* Figure 17.25 */ }
```

figure 17.20a

Class skeleton for standard LinkedList class (*continues*)

figure 17.20b

Class skeleton for standard `LinkedList` class (*continued*)

```
33      public AnyType remove( )
34        { /* Added in Java 5; same as removeFirst */ }
35      public AnyType removeFirst( )
36        { /* Figure 17.27 */ }
37      public AnyType removeLast( )
38        { /* Figure 17.27 */ }
39      public boolean remove( Object x )
40        { /* Figure 17.28 */ }
41      public AnyType get( int idx )
42        { /* Figure 17.25 */ }
43      public AnyType set( int idx, AnyType newVal )
44        { /* Figure 17.25 */ }
45      public AnyType remove( int idx )
46        { /* Figure 17.27 */ }
47      public void clear( )
48        { /* Figure 17.22 */ }
49      public Iterator<AnyType> iterator( )
50        { /* Figure 17.29 */ }
51      public ListIterator<AnyType> listIterator( int idx )
52        { /* Figure 17.29 */ }
53
54      private int theSize;
55      private Node<AnyType> beginMarker;
56      private Node<AnyType> endMarker;
57      private int modCount = 0;
58
59      private static final Node<AnyType> NOT_FOUND = null;
60      private Node<AnyType> findPos( Object x )
61        { /* Figure 17.23 */ }
62      private AnyType remove( Node<AnyType> p )
63        { /* Figure 17.27 */ }
64      private Node<AnyType> getNode( int idx )
65        { /* Figure 17.26 */}
66  }
```

class. The iterator pattern was described in Chapter 6. The same pattern was used in the `ArrayList` implementation with inner classes in Chapter 15.

The list class keeps track of its size in a data member declared at line 54. We use this approach so that the `size` method can be performed in constant time. `modCount` is used by the iterators to determine if the list has changed while an iteration is in progress; the same idea was used in `ArrayList`. `beginMarker` and `endMarker` correspond to `head` and `tail` in Section 17.3. All the methods use signatures that we have shown before.

Figure 17.21 shows the `Node` class, which is similar to the `ListNode` class. The main difference is that, because we use a doubly linked list, we have both `prev` and `next` links.

The implementation of `LinkedList` begins in Figure 17.22, where we have the constructors and `clear`. All in all, little is new here; we combined a lot of the nonstandard `LinkedList` code with the concepts presented in Section 17.3.

```
/**
 * This is the doubly linked list node.
 */
private static class Node<AnyType>
{
    public Node( AnyType d, Node<AnyType> p, Node<AnyType> n )
    {
        data = d; prev = p; next = n;
    }

    public AnyType       data;
    public Node<AnyType> prev;
    public Node<AnyType> next;
}
```

figure 17.21

Node nested class for standard `LinkedList` class

Figure 17.23 shows `size`, which is trivial, and `contains`, which is also trivial because it calls the private `findPos` routine that does all the work. `findPos` deals with `null` values at lines 30–34; otherwise, it would be four lines of code.

```
/**
 * Construct an empty LinkedList.
 */
public LinkedList( )
{
    clear( );
}

/**
 * Construct a LinkedList with same items as another Collection.
 */
public LinkedList( Collection<AnyType> other )
{
    clear( );
    for( AnyType val : other )
        add( val );
}

/**
 * Change the size of this collection to zero.
 */
public void clear( )
{
    beginMarker = new Node<AnyType>( null, null, null );
    endMarker = new Node<AnyType>( null, beginMarker, null );
    beginMarker.next = endMarker;

    theSize = 0;
    modCount++;
}
```

figure 17.22

Constructors and `clear` method for standard `LinkedList` class

Figure 17.24 shows the various add methods. All of these eventually funnel into the last add method at lines 39–47, which splices into the doubly linked list as was done in Section 17.3. It requires a private routine, getNode, whose implementation we will discuss shortly. getNode returns a reference to the node at index idx. In order for this to be suitable for addLast, getNode will start its search from the end closest to the target node.

```
/**
 * Returns the number of items in this collection.
 * @return the number of items in this collection.
 */
public int size( )
{
    return theSize;
}

/**
 * Tests if some item is in this collection.
 * @param x any object.
 * @return true if this collection contains an item equal to x.
 */
public boolean contains( Object x )
{
    return findPos( x ) != NOT_FOUND;
}

/**
 * Returns the position of first item matching x
 * in this collection, or NOT_FOUND if not found.
 * @param x any object.
 * @return the position of first item matching x
 * in this collection, or NOT_FOUND if not found.
 */
private Node<AnyType> findPos( Object x )
{
    for( Node<AnyType> p = beginMarker.next; p != endMarker; p = p.next )
        if( x == null )
        {
            if( p.data == null )
                return p;
        }
        else if( x.equals( p.data ) )
            return p;

    return NOT_FOUND;
}
```

figure 17.23

size and contains for standard LinkedList class

```java
    /**
     * Adds an item to this collection, at the end.
     * @param x any object.
     * @return true.
     */
    public boolean add( AnyType x )
    {
        addLast( x );
        return true;
    }

    /**
     * Adds an item to this collection, at the front.
     * Other items are slid one position higher.
     * @param x any object.
     */
    public void addFirst( AnyType x )
    {
        add( 0, x );
    }

    /**
     * Adds an item to this collection, at the end.
     * @param x any object.
     */
    public void addLast( AnyType x )
    {
        add( size( ), x );
    }

    /**
     * Adds an item to this collection, at a specified position.
     * Items at or after that position are slid one position higher.
     * @param x any object.
     * @param idx position to add at.
     * @throws IndexOutOfBoundsException if idx is not
     *         between 0 and size(), inclusive.
     */
    public void add( int idx, AnyType x )
    {
        Node<AnyType> p = getNode( idx );
        Node<AnyType> newNode = new Node<AnyType>( x, p.prev, p );
        newNode.prev.next = newNode;
        p.prev = newNode;
        theSize++;
        modCount++;
    }
```

figure 17.24

add methods for standard LinkedList class

Figure 17.25 details the various get methods, plus a set method. There is little special in any of those routines. The element method from the Queue interface is not shown. Figure 17.26 has the previously mentioned private getNode method. If the index represents a node in the first half of the list, then

figure 17.25

get and set methods for standard LinkedList class

```
    /**
     * Returns the first item in the list.
     * @throws NoSuchElementException if the list is empty.
     */
    public AnyType getFirst( )
    {
        if( isEmpty( ) )
            throw new NoSuchElementException( );
        return getNode( 0 ).data;
    }

    /**
     * Returns the last item in the list.
     * @throws NoSuchElementException if the list is empty.
     */
    public AnyType getLast( )
    {
        if( isEmpty( ) )
            throw new NoSuchElementException( );
        return getNode( size( ) - 1 ).data;
    }

    /**
     * Returns the item at position idx.
     * @param idx the index to search in.
     * @throws IndexOutOfBoundsException if index is out of range.
     */
    public AnyType get( int idx )
    {
        return getNode( idx ).data;
    }

    /**
     * Changes the item at position idx.
     * @param idx the index to change.
     * @param newVal the new value.
     * @return the old value.
     * @throws IndexOutOfBoundsException if index is out of range.
     */
    public AnyType set( int idx, AnyType newVal )
    {
        Node<AnyType> p = getNode( idx );
        AnyType oldVal = p.data;

        p.data = newVal;
        return oldVal;
    }
```

at lines 17–19 we step through the linked list, in the forward direction. Otherwise, we go backwards, starting at the end, as shown on lines 23–25.

The `remove` methods are shown in Figures 17.27 and 17.28, and those funnel through a private `remove` method, shown at lines 40–48 (in Figure 17.27), that mimics the algorithm in Section 17.3.

The iterator factories are shown in Figure 17.29. Both return a freshly constructed `LinkedListIterator` object. Finally, the `LinkedListIterator`, which is perhaps the trickiest part of the whole implementation, is shown in Figure 17.30.

The iterator maintains a current position, shown at line 8. `current` represents the node containing the item that is to be returned by a call to `next`. Observe that when `current` is positioned at the endmarker, a call to `next` is illegal, but the call to `previous` should give the first item, going backwards. As in the `ArrayList`, the iterator also maintains the `modCount` of the list it is iterating over, initialized at the time the iterator was constructed. This variable,

```
 1     /**
 2      * Gets the Node at position idx, which must range from 0 to size( ).
 3      * @param idx index to search at.
 4      * @return internal node corresponding to idx.
 5      * @throws IndexOutOfBoundsException if idx is not
 6      *         between 0 and size(), inclusive.
 7      */
 8     private Node<AnyType> getNode( int idx )
 9     {
10         Node<AnyType> p;
11 
12         if( idx < 0 || idx > size( ) )
13             throw new IndexOutOfBoundsException( );
14 
15         if( idx < size( ) / 2 )
16         {
17             p = beginMarker.next;
18             for( int i = 0; i < idx; i++ )
19                 p = p.next;
20         }
21         else
22         {
23             p = endMarker;
24             for( int i = size( ); i > idx; i-- )
25                 p = p.prev;
26         }
27 
28         return p;
29     }
```

figure 17.26

Private `getNode` for standard `LinkedList` class

figure 17.27

remove methods for standard LinkedList class

```
/**
 * Removes the first item in the list.
 * @return the item was removed from the collection.
 * @throws NoSuchElementException if the list is empty.
 */
public AnyType removeFirst( )
{
    if( isEmpty( ) )
        throw new NoSuchElementException( );
    return remove( getNode( 0 ) );
}

/**
 * Removes the last item in the list.
 * @return the item was removed from the collection.
 * @throws NoSuchElementException if the list is empty.
 */
public AnyType removeLast( )
{
    if( isEmpty( ) )
        throw new NoSuchElementException( );
    return remove( getNode( size( ) - 1 ) );
}

/**
 * Removes an item from this collection.
 * @param idx the index of the object.
 * @return the item that was removed from the collection.
 */
public AnyType remove( int idx )
{
    return remove( getNode( idx ) );
}

/**
 * Removes the object contained in Node p.
 * @param p the Node containing the object.
 * @return the item that was removed from the collection.
 */
private AnyType remove( Node<AnyType> p )
{
    p.next.prev = p.prev;
    p.prev.next = p.next;
    theSize--;
    modCount++;

    return p.data;
}
```

```java
/**
 * Removes an item from this collection.
 * @param x any object.
 * @return true if this item was removed from the collection.
 */
public boolean remove( Object x )
{
    Node<AnyType> pos = findPos( x );

    if( pos == NOT_FOUND )
        return false;
    else
    {
        remove( pos );
        return true;
    }
}
```

figure 17.28

Additional remove method for standard LinkedList class

```java
/**
 * Obtains an Iterator object used to traverse the collection.
 * @return an iterator positioned prior to the first element.
 */
public Iterator<AnyType> iterator( )
{
    return new LinkedListIterator( 0 );
}

/**
 * Obtains a ListIterator object used to traverse the
 * collection bidirectionally.
 * @return an iterator positioned prior to the requested element.
 * @param idx the index to start the iterator. Use size() to do
 * complete reverse traversal. Use 0 to do complete forward traversal.
 * @throws IndexOutOfBoundsException if idx is not
 *          between 0 and size(), inclusive.
 */
public ListIterator<AnyType> listIterator( int idx )
{
    return new LinkedListIterator( idx );
}
```

figure 17.29

Iterator factory methods for standard LinkedList class

```
/**
 * This is the implementation of the LinkedListIterator.
 * It maintains a notion of a current position and of
 * course the implicit reference to the LinkedList.
 */
private class LinkedListIterator implements ListIterator<AnyType>
{
    private Node<AnyType> current;
    private Node<AnyType> lastVisited = null;
    private boolean lastMoveWasPrev = false;
    private int expectedModCount = modCount;

    public LinkedListIterator( int idx )
    {
        current = getNode( idx );
    }

    public boolean hasNext( )
    {
        if( expectedModCount != modCount )
            throw new ConcurrentModificationException( );
        return current != endMarker;
    }

    public AnyType next( )
    {
        if( !hasNext( ) )
            throw new NoSuchElementException( );

        AnyType nextItem = current.data;
        lastVisited = current;
        current = current.next;
        lastMoveWasPrev = false;
        return nextItem;
    }
```

figure 17.30a

Iterator inner class implementation for standard `LinkedList` class (*continues*)

`expectedModCount`, can change only if the iterator performs a `remove`. `lastVisited` is used to represent the last node that was visited; this is used by `remove`. If `lastVisited` is `null`, the `remove` is illegal. Finally, `lastMoveWasPrev` is `true` if the last movement of the iterator prior to `remove` was via `previous`; it is `false` if the last movement was via `next`.

The `hasNext` and `hasPrevious` methods are fairly routine. Both throw an exception if an external modification to the list has been detected.

```
36         public void remove( )
37         {
38             if( expectedModCount != modCount )
39                 throw new ConcurrentModificationException( );
40             if( lastVisited == null )
41                 throw new IllegalStateException( );
42 
43             LinkedList.this.remove( lastVisited );
44             lastVisited = null;
45             if( lastMoveWasPrev )
46                 current = current.next;
47             expectedModCount++;
48         }
49 
50         public boolean hasPrevious( )
51         {
52             if( expectedModCount != modCount )
53                 throw new ConcurrentModificationException( );
54             return current != beginMarker.next;
55         }
56 
57         public AnyType previous( )
58         {
59             if( expectedModCount != modCount )
60                 throw new ConcurrentModificationException( );
61             if( !hasPrevious( ) )
62                 throw new NoSuchElementException( );
63 
64             current = current.prev;
65             lastVisited = current;
66             lastMoveWasPrev = true;
67             return current.data;
68         }
69     }
```

figure 17.30b

Iterator inner class implementation for standard `LinkedList` class (*continued*)

The `next` method advances `current` (line 32) after getting the value in the node (line 30) that is to be returned (line 34). Data fields `lastVisited` and `lastMoveWasPrev` are updated at lines 31 and 33, respectively. The implementation of `previous` is not exactly symmetric, because for `previous`, we advance `current` prior to obtaining the value. This is evident when one considers that the initial state for backwards iteration is that `current` is at the endmarker.

Finally, remove is shown at lines 36–48. After the obligatory error checks, we use the LinkedList remove method to remove the lastVisited node. The explicit reference to the outer class is required because the iterator remove hides the list remove. After making lastVisited null, to disallow a second remove, we check whether the last operation was a next or previous. In the latter case, we adjust current, as shown on line 46, to its state prior to the previous/remove combination.

All in all, there is a large amount of code, but it simply embellishes the basics presented in the original implementation of the nonstandard LinkedList class in Section 17.2.

summary

In this chapter we described why and how linked lists are implemented, illustrating the interactions among the list, iterator, and node classes. We examined variations of the linked list including doubly linked lists. The doubly linked list allows bidirectional traversal of the list. We also showed how a sorted linked list class can easily be derived from the basic linked list class. Finally, we provided an implementation of most of the Collections API LinkedList class.

key concepts

circularly linked list A linked list in which the last cell's next link references first. This action is useful when wraparound matters. (577)

doubly linked list A linked list that allows bidirectional traversal by storing two links per node. (574)

header node An extra node in a linked list that holds no data but serves to satisfy the requirement that every node have a previous node. A header node allows us to avoid special cases such as the insertion of a new first element and the removal of the first element. (565)

iterator class A class that maintains a current position in a container, such as a list. An iterator class is usually in the same package as, or an inner class of, a list class. (567)

sorted linked list A list in which items are in sorted order. A sorted linked list class can be derived from a list class. (577)

common errors

1. The most common linked list error is splicing in nodes incorrectly when performing an insertion. This procedure is especially tricky with doubly linked lists.
2. Methods should not be allowed to access fields via a `null` reference. We perform error checks to catch this mistake and throw exceptions as warranted.
3. When several iterators access a list simultaneously, problems can result. For instance, what if one iterator deletes the node that the other iterator is about to access? Solving these types of problems requires additional work, such as the use of a concurrent modification counter.

on the internet

The singly linked list class, including the sorted linked list, is available, as is our Collections API list implementation.

LinkedList.java	Contains the implementation for `weiss.nonstandard.LinkedList`.
LinkedListIterator.java	Contains the implementation for `LinkedListIterator`.
SortLinkedList.java	Contains the implementation for `SortedLinkedList`.
LinkedList.java	Contains the implementation of the Collections API `LinkedList` class and iterator.

exercises

IN SHORT

17.1 Draw an empty linked list with header implementation.

17.2 Draw an empty doubly linked list that uses both a header and a tail.

IN THEORY

17.3 Write an algorithm for printing a singly linked list in reverse, using only constant extra space. This instruction implies that you cannot use recursion but you may assume that your algorithm is a list method.

17.4 A linked list contains a cycle if, starting from some node *p*, following a sufficient number of `next` links brings us back to node *p*. Node *p* does not have to be the first node in the list. Assume that you have a linked list that contains *N* nodes. However, the value of *N* is unknown.

a. Design an $O(N)$ algorithm to determine whether the list contains a cycle. You may use $O(N)$ extra space.
b. Repeat part (a), but use only $O(1)$ extra space. (*Hint:* Use two iterators that are initially at the start of the list, but advance at different speeds.)

17.5 One way to implement a queue is to use a circularly linked list. Assume that the list does not contain a header and that you can maintain one iterator for the list. For which of the following representations can all basic queue operations be performed in constant worst-case time? Justify your answers.

a. Maintain an iterator that corresponds to the first item in the list.
b. Maintain an iterator that corresponds to the last item in the list.

17.6 Suppose that you have a reference to a node in a singly linked list that is guaranteed *not to be the last node* in the list. You do not have references to any other nodes (except by following links). Describe an $O(1)$ algorithm that logically removes the value stored in such a node from the linked list, maintaining the integrity of the linked list. (*Hint:* Involve the next node.)

17.7 Suppose that a singly linked list is implemented with both a header and a tail node. Using the ideas discussed in Exercise 17.6, describe constant-time algorithms to

a. Insert item `x` before position `p`.
b. Remove the item stored at position `p`.

IN PRACTICE

17.8 Modify the `find` routine in the nonstandard `LinkedList` class to return the last occurrence of item `x`.

17.9 Modify `remove` in the nonstandard `LinkedList` class to remove all occurrences of `x`.

17.10 Suppose that you want to splice part of one linked list into another (a so-called *cut and paste* operation). Assume that three `LinkedListIterator` parameters represent the starting point of the *cut*, the ending point of the *cut*, and the point at which the *paste* is to be attached. Assume that all iterators are valid and that the number of items cut is not zero.

a. Write a method to cut and paste that is not a part of `weiss.nonstandard`. What is the running time of the algorithm?

b. Write a method in the `LinkedList` class to do the cut and paste. What is the running time of the algorithm?

17.11 The `SortedLinkedList` `insert` method uses only public iterator methods. Can it access private members of the iterator?

17.12 Implement an efficient `Stack` class by using a `LinkedList` (either standard or nonstandard) as a data member. You need to use an iterator, but it can be either a data member or a local variable for any routine that needs it.

17.13 Implement an efficient `Queue` class by using (as in Exercise 17.12) a singly linked list and appropriate iterators. How many of these iterators must be data members in order to achieve an efficient implementation?

17.14 Implement `retreat` for singly linked lists. Note that it will take linear time.

17.15 Implement the nonstandard `LinkedList` class without the header node.

PROGRAMMING PROJECTS

17.16 Implement a circularly and doubly linked list.

17.17 If the order that items in a list are stored is not important, you can frequently speed searching with the heuristic known as *move to front:* Whenever an item is accessed, move it to the front of the list. This action usually results in an improvement because frequently accessed items tend to migrate toward the front of the list, whereas less frequently accessed items tend to migrate toward the end of the list. Consequently, the most frequently accessed items tend to require the least searching. Implement the move-to-front heuristic for linked lists.

17.18 Write routines `makeUnion` and `intersect` that return the union and intersection of two sorted linked lists.

17.19 Write a line-based text editor. The command syntax is similar to the Unix line editor *ed*. The internal copy of the file is maintained as a linked list of lines. To be able to go up and down in the file, you have to maintain a doubly linked list. Most commands are represented by a one-character string. Some are two characters and require an argument (or two). Support the commands shown in Figure 17.31.

figure 17.31

Commands for editor in Exercise 17.19

Command	Function
`1`	Go to the top.
`a`	Add text after current line until **.** on its own line
`d`	Delete current line.
`dr num num`	Delete several lines.
`f name`	Change name of the current file (for next write).
`g num`	Go to a numbered line.
`h`	Get help.
`i`	Like append, but add lines before current line.
`m num`	Move current line after some other line.
`mr num num num`	Move several lines as a unit after some other line.
`n`	Toggle whether line numbers are displayed.
`p`	Print current line.
`pr num num`	Print several lines.
`q!`	Abort without write.
`r name`	Read and paste another file into the current file.
`s text text`	Substitute text with other text.
`t num`	Copy current line to after some other line.
`tr num num num`	Copy several lines to after some other line.
`w`	Write file to disk.
`x!`	Exit with write.
`$`	Go to the last line.
`-`	Go up one line.
`+`	Go down one line.
`=`	Print current line number.
`/ text`	Search forward for a pattern.
`? text`	Search backward for a pattern.
`#`	Print number of lines and characters in file.

17.20 Provide an `add` method for the `ListIterator` consistent with the Collections API specification.

17.21 Provide a `set` method for the `ListIterator` consistent with the Collections API specification.

17.22 Reimplement the standard `LinkedList` class

a. with a header but no tail.
b. with a tail but no header.

chapter 18

trees

The *tree* is a fundamental structure in computer science. Almost all operating systems store files in trees or treelike structures. Trees are also used in compiler design, text processing, and searching algorithms. We discuss the latter application in Chapter 19.

In this chapter, we show

- A definition of a general tree and discuss how it is used in a file system
- An examination of the binary tree
- Implementation of tree operations, using recursion
- Nonrecursive traversal of a tree

18.1 general trees

Trees can be defined in two ways: nonrecursively and recursively. The nonrecursive definition is the more direct technique, so we begin with it. The recursive formulation allows us to write simple algorithms to manipulate trees.

18.1.1 definitions

A *tree* can be defined nonrecursively as a set of nodes and a set of directed edges that connect them.

Nonrecursively, a *tree* consists of a set of nodes and a set of directed edges that connect pairs of nodes. Throughout this text we consider only rooted trees. A rooted tree has the following properties.

- One node is distinguished as the root.
- Every node *c*, except the root, is connected by an edge from exactly one other node *p*. Node *p* is *c*'s *parent*, and *c* is one of *p*'s *children*.
- A unique path traverses from the root to each node. The number of edges that must be followed is the *path length*.

Parents and children are naturally defined. A directed edge connects the *parent* to the *child*.

Parents and children are naturally defined. A directed edge connects the *parent* to the *child.*

A *leaf* has no children.

Figure 18.1 illustrates a tree. The root node is *A; A*'s children are *B, C, D,* and *E*. Because *A* is the root, it has no parent; all other nodes have parents. For instance, *B*'s parent is *A*. A node that has no children is called a *leaf.* The leaves in this tree are *C, F, G, H, I,* and *K*. The length of the path from *A* to *K* is 3 (edges); the length of the path from *A* to *A* is 0 (edges).

The *depth of a node* is the length of the path from the root to the node. The *height of a node* is the length of the path from the node to the deepest leaf.

A tree with *N* nodes must have *N* – 1 edges because every node except the parent has an incoming edge. The *depth of a node* in a tree is the length of the path from the root to the node. Thus the depth of the root is always 0, and the depth of any node is 1 more than the depth of its parent. The *height of a node* in a tree is the length of the path from the node to the deepest leaf. Thus the height of *E* is 2. The height of any node is 1 more than the height of its maximum-height child. Thus the height of a tree is the height of the root.

figure 18.1

A tree, with height and depth information

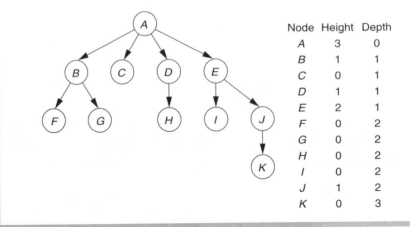

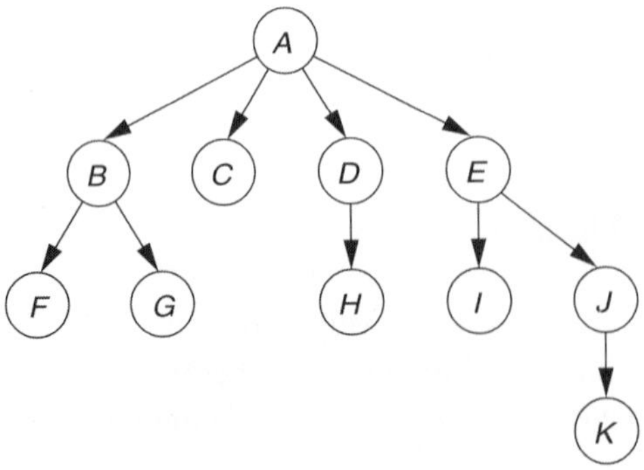

Node	Height	Depth
A	3	0
B	1	1
C	0	1
D	1	1
E	2	1
F	0	2
G	0	2
H	0	2
I	0	2
J	1	2
K	0	3

Nodes with the same parent are called *siblings;* thus *B, C, D,* and *E* are all siblings. If there is a path from node *u* to node *v,* then *u* is an *ancestor* of *v* and *v* is a *descendant* of *u*. If $u \neq v$, then *u* is a *proper ancestor* of *v* and *v* is a *proper descendant* of *u*. The *size of a node* is the number of descendants the node has (including the node itself). Thus the size of *B* is 3, and the size of *C* is 1. The size of a tree is the size of the root. Thus the size of the tree shown in Figure 18.1 is the size of its root *A,* or 11.

The *size of a node* is the number of descendants the node has (including the node itself).

An alternative definition of the tree is recursive: Either a tree is empty or it consists of a root and zero or more nonempty subtrees $T_1, T_2, \ldots, T_k$, each of whose roots are connected by an edge from the root, as illustrated in Figure 18.2. In certain instances (most notably, the *binary trees* discussed later in the chapter), we may allow some of the subtrees to be empty.

18.1.2 **implementation**

One way to implement a tree would be to have in each node a link to each child of the node in addition to its data. However, as the number of children per node can vary greatly and is not known in advance, making the children direct links in the data structure might not be feasible—there would be too much wasted space. The solution—called the *first child/next sibling method*—is simple: Keep the children of each node in a linked list of tree nodes, with each node keeping two links, one to its leftmost child (if it is not a leaf) and one to its right sibling (if it is not the rightmost sibling). This type of implementation is illustrated in Figure 18.3. Arrows that point downward are `firstChild` links, and arrows that point left to right are `nextSibling` links. We did not draw `null` links because there are too many of them. In this tree, node *B* has both a link to a sibling (*C*) and a link to a leftmost child (*F*); some nodes have only one of these links and some have neither. Given this representation, implementing a tree class is straightforward.

General trees can be implemented by using the *first child/next sibling method,* which requires two links per item.

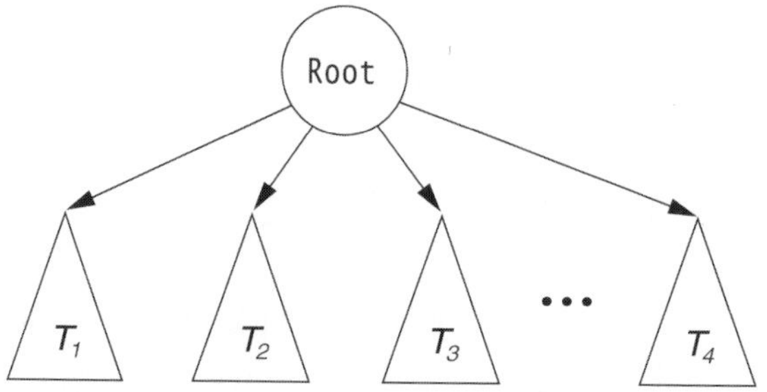

figure 18.2

A tree viewed recursively

figure 18.3

First child/next sibling representation of the tree in Figure 18.1

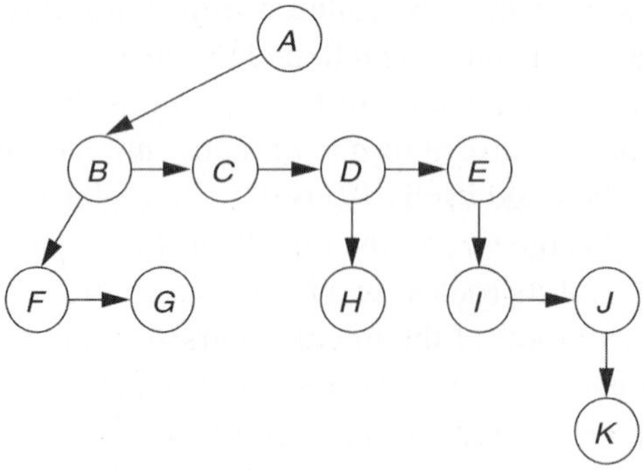

18.1.3 an application: file systems

File systems use treelike structures.

Trees have many applications. One of their popular uses is the directory structure in many operating systems, including Unix, VAX/VMS, and Windows/DOS. Figure 18.4 shows a typical directory in the Unix file system. The root of this directory is `mark`. (The asterisk next to the name indicates that `mark` is itself a directory.) Note that `mark` has three children: `books`, `courses`, and `.login`, two of which are themselves directories. Thus `mark` contains two directories and one regular file. The filename `mark/books/dsaa/ch1` is obtained by following the leftmost child three times. Each / after the first name indicates an edge; the result is a pathname. If the path begins at the root of the entire file system, rather than at an arbitrary directory inside the file system, it is a full pathname; otherwise, it is a relative pathname (to the current directory).

This hierarchical file system is popular because it allows users to organize their data logically. Furthermore, two files in different directories can share the same name because they have different paths from the root and thus have

figure 18.4

A Unix directory

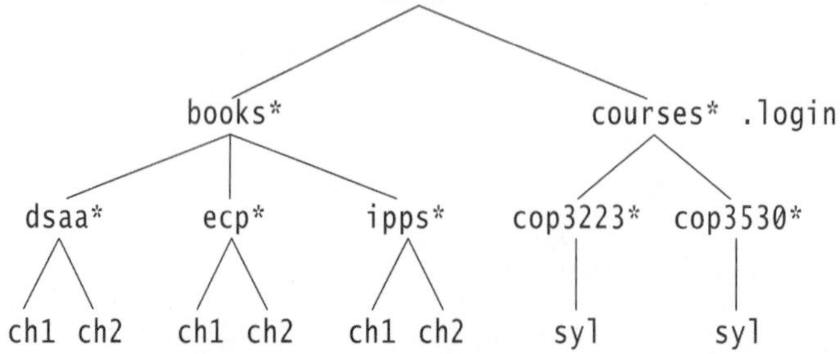

different full pathnames. A directory in the Unix file system is just a file with a list of all its children,[1] so the directories can be traversed with an iteration scheme; that is, we can sequentially iterate over each child. Indeed, on some systems, if the normal command to print a file is applied to a directory, the filenames in the directory appear in the output (along with other non-ASCII information).

Suppose that we want to list the names of all the files in a directory (including its subdirectories), and in our output format files of depth *d* have their names indented by *d* tab characters. A short algorithm to do this task is given in Figure 18.5. Output for the directory presented in Figure 18.4 is shown in Figure 18.6.

The directory structure is most easily traversed by using recursion.

```
void listAll( int depth = 0 ) // depth is initially 0
{
    printName( depth );       // Print the name of the object
    if( isDirectory( ) )
        for each file c in this directory (for each child)
            c.listAll( depth + 1 );
}
```

figure 18.5

A routine for listing a directory and its subdirectories in a hierarchical file system

```
mark
    books
        dsaa
            ch1
            ch2
        ecp
            ch1
            ch2
        ipps
            ch1
            ch2
    courses
        cop3223
            syl
        cop3530
            syl
    .login
```

figure 18.6

The directory listing for the tree shown in Figure 18.4

1. Each directory in the Unix file system also has one entry (`.`) that points to itself and another entry (`..`) that points to the parent of the directory, which introduces a cycle. Thus, technically, the Unix file system is not a tree but is treelike. The same is true for Windows/DOS.

We assume the existence of the class `FileSystem` and two methods, `printName` and `isDirectory`. `printName` outputs the current `FileSystem` object indented by `depth` tab stops; `isDirectory` tests whether the current `FileSystem` object is a directory, returning `true` if it is. Then we can write the recursive routine `listAll`. We need to pass it the parameter `depth`, indicating the current level in the directory relative to the root. The `listAll` routine is started with `depth` 0 to signify no indenting for the root. This depth is an internal bookkeeping variable and is hardly a parameter about which a calling routine should be expected to know. Thus the pseudocode specifies a default value of 0 for `depth` (specification of a default value is not legal Java).

The logic of the algorithm is simple to follow. The current object is printed out, with appropriate indentation. If the entry is a directory, we process all the children recursively, one by one. These children are one level deeper in the tree and thus must be indented an extra tab stop. We make the recursive call with `depth+1`. It is hard to imagine a shorter piece of code that performs what appears to be a very difficult task.

In a *preorder tree traversal,* work at a node is performed before its children are processed. The traversal takes constant time per node.

In this algorithmic technique, known as a *preorder tree traversal,* work at a node is performed before (*pre*) its children are processed. In addition to being a compact algorithm, the preorder traversal is efficient because it takes constant time per node. We discuss why later in this chapter.

In a *postorder tree traversal,* work at a node is performed after its children are evaluated. The traversal takes constant time per node.

Another common method of traversing a tree is the *postorder tree traversal,* in which the work at a node is performed after (*post*) its children are evaluated. It also takes constant time per node. As an example, Figure 18.7 represents the same directory structure as that shown in Figure 18.4. The numbers in parentheses represent the number of disk blocks taken up by each file. The directories themselves are files, so they also use disk blocks (to store the names and information about their children).

Suppose that we want to compute the total number of blocks used by all files in our example tree. The most natural way to do so is to find the total

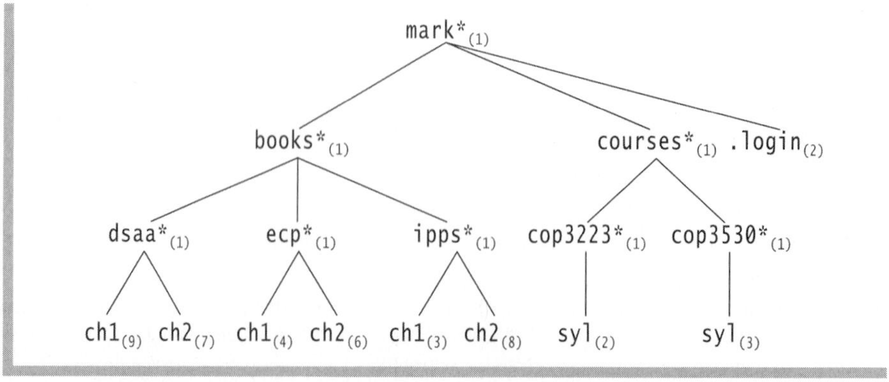

figure 18.7

The Unix directory with file sizes

number of blocks contained in all the children (which may be directories that must be evaluated recursively): `books` (41), `courses` (8), and `.login` (2). The total number of blocks is then the total in all the children plus the blocks used at the root (1), or 52. The `size` routine shown in Figure 18.8 implements this strategy. If the current `FileSystem` object is not a directory, `size` merely returns the number of blocks it uses. Otherwise, the number of blocks in the current directory is added to the number of blocks (recursively) found in all the children. To illustrate the difference between postorder traversal and preorder traversal, in Figure 18.9 we show how the size of each directory (or file) is produced by the algorithm. We get a classic postorder signature because the total size of an entry is not computable until the information for its children has been computed. As indicated previously, the running time is linear. We have much more to say about tree traversals in Section 18.4.

```
int size( )
{
    int totalSize = sizeOfThisFile( );

    if( isDirectory( ) )
        for each file c in this directory (for each child)
            totalSize += c.size( );

    return totalSize;
}
```

figure 18.8

A routine for calculating the total size of all files in a directory

```
                    ch1                    9
                    ch2                    7
            dsaa                          17
                    ch1                    4
                    ch2                    6
            ecp                           11
                    ch1                    3
                    ch2                    8
            ipps                          12
    books                                 41
                    syl                    2
            cop3223                        3
                    syl                    3
            cop3530                        4
    courses                                8
    .login                                 2
mark                                      52
```

figure 18.9

A trace of the `size` method

java implementation

Java provides a class named `File` in package `java.io` that can be used to traverse directory hierarchies. We can use it to implement the pseudocode in Figure 18.8. The `size` method can also be implemented; this is done in the online code. The class `File` provides several useful methods.

A `File` can be constructed by providing a filename. `getName` provides the name of a `File` object. It does not include the directory part of the path; this can be obtained by `getPath`. `isDirectory` returns `true` if the `File` is a directory, and its size in bytes can be obtained by a call to `length`. If the file is a directory, the `list` method returns an array of `String` that represents the filenames in the directory (not including `.` and `..`).

To implement the `FileSystem` object described in the pseudocode, we simply extend `File` and provide a constructor, `printName`, and `listAll`. This is shown in Figure 18.10. The only tricky part is lines 36 and 37, where we must construct the `child` `FileSystem` object. The filename consists of the name of the directory, followed by a separator (/ on Unix; \ on DOS), followed by the filename. A simple `main` is also provided.

18.2 binary trees

A *binary tree* has no node with more than two children.

A *binary tree* is a tree in which no node can have more than two children. Because there are only two children, we can name them `left` and `right`. Recursively, a binary tree is either empty or consists of a root, a left tree, and a right tree. The left and right trees may themselves be empty; thus a node with one child could have either a left or right child. We use the recursive definition several times in the design of binary tree algorithms. Binary trees have many important uses, two of which are illustrated in Figure 18.11.

An expression tree is one example of the use of binary trees. Such trees are central data structures in compiler design.

One use of the binary tree is in the *expression tree,* which is a central data structure in compiler design. The leaves of an expression tree are operands, such as constants or variable names; the other nodes contain operators. This particular tree is binary because all the operations are binary. Although this case is the simplest, nodes can have more than two children (and in the case of unary operators, only one child). We can evaluate an expression tree T by applying the operator at the root to the values obtained by recursively evaluating the left and right subtrees. Doing so yields the expression `(a+((b-c)*d))`. (See Section 11.2 for a discussion of the construction of expression trees and their evaluation.)

A second use of the binary tree is the *Huffman coding tree,* which is used to implement a simple but relatively effective data compression algorithm.

```
import java.io.File;

public class FileSystem extends File
{
        // Constructor
    public FileSystem( String name )
    {
        super( name );
    }

        // Output file name with indentation
    public void printName( int depth )
    {
        for( int i = 0; i < depth; i++ )
            System.out.print( "\t" );
        System.out.println( getName( ) );
    }

        // Public driver to list all files in directory
    public void listAll( )
    {
        listAll( 0 );
    }

        // Recursive method to list all files in directory
    private void listAll( int depth )
    {
        printName( depth );

        if( isDirectory( ) )
        {
            String [ ] entries = list( );

            for( String entry : entries)
            {
                FileSystem child = new FileSystem( getPath( )
                             + separatorChar + entry );
                child.listAll( depth + 1 );
            }
        }
    }

        // Simple main to list all files in current directory
    public static void main( String [ ] args )
    {
        FileSystem f = new FileSystem( "." );
        f.ListAll( );
    }
}
```

figure 18.10

Java implementation for a directory listing

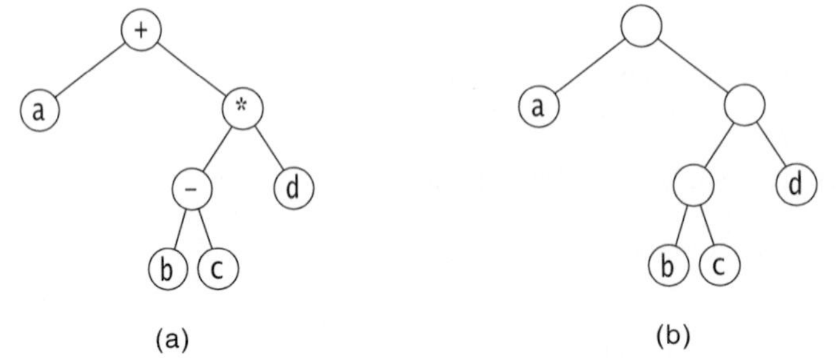

figure 18.11

Uses of binary trees: (a) an expression tree and (b) a Huffman coding tree

Each symbol in the alphabet is stored at a leaf. Its code is obtained by following the path to it from the root. A left link corresponds to a 0 and a right link to a 1. Thus `b` is coded as 100. (See Section 12.1 for a discussion of the construction of the optimal tree, that is, the best code.)

An important use of binary trees is in other data structures, notably the binary search tree and the priority queue.

Other uses of the binary tree are in binary search trees (discussed in Chapter 19), which allow logarithmic time insertions and accessing of items, and priority queues, which support the access and deletion of the minimum in a collection of items. Several efficient implementations of priority queues use trees (discussed in Chapters 21–23).

Figure 18.12 gives the skeleton for the `BinaryNode` class. Lines 49–51 indicate that each node consists of a data item plus two links. The constructor, shown at lines 18 to 20, initializes all the data members of the `BinaryNode` class. Lines 22–33 provide accessors and mutators for each of the data members.

Many of the `BinaryNode` routines are recursive. The `BinaryTree` methods use the `BinaryNode` routines on the `root`.

The `duplicate` method, declared at line 39, is used to replicate a copy of the tree rooted at the current node. The routines' `size` and `height`, declared at lines 35 and 37, compute the named properties for the node referenced by parameter `t`. We implement these routines in Section 18.3. (Recall that static methods do not require a controlling object.) We also provide, at lines 42–47, routines that print out the contents of a tree rooted at the current node, using various recursive traversal strategies. We discuss tree traversals in Section 18.4. Why do we pass a parameter for `size` and `height` and make them `static` but use the current object for the traversals and `duplicate`? There is no particular reason; it is a matter of style, and we show both styles here. The implementations show that the difference between them occurs when the required test for an empty tree (given by a `null` reference) is performed.

The `BinaryNode` class is implemented separately from the `BinaryTree` class. The only data member in the `BinaryTree` class is a reference to the root node.

In this section we describe implementation of the `BinaryTree` class. The `BinaryNode` class is implemented separately, instead of as a nested class. The `BinaryTree` class skeleton is shown in Figure 18.13. For the most part, the routines are short because they call `BinaryNode` methods. Line 44 declares the only data member—a reference to the `root` node.

```
// BinaryNode class; stores a node in a tree.
//
// CONSTRUCTION: with no parameters, or an Object,
//     left child, and right child.
//
// *******************PUBLIC OPERATIONS**********************
// int size( )            --> Return size of subtree at node
// int height( )          --> Return height of subtree at node
// void printPostOrder( ) --> Print a postorder tree traversal
// void printInOrder( )   --> Print an inorder tree traversal
// void printPreOrder( )  --> Print a preorder tree traversal
// BinaryNode duplicate( )--> Return a duplicate tree

class BinaryNode<AnyType>
{
    public BinaryNode( )
      { this( null, null, null ); }
    public BinaryNode( AnyType theElement,
                       BinaryNode<AnyType> lt, BinaryNode<AnyType> rt )
      { element = theElement; left = lt; right = rt; }

    public AnyType getElement( )
      { return element; }
    public BinaryNode<AnyType> getLeft( )
      { return left; }
    public BinaryNode<AnyType> getRight( )
      { return right; }
    public void setElement( AnyType x )
      { element = x; }
    public void setLeft( BinaryNode<AnyType> t )
      { left = t; }
    public void setRight( BinaryNode<AnyType> t )
      { right = t; }

    public static <AnyType> int size( BinaryNode<AnyType> t )
      { /* Figure 18.19 */ }
    public static <AnyType> int height( BinaryNode<AnyType> t )
      { /* Figure 18.21 */ }
    public BinaryNode<AnyType> duplicate( )
      { /* Figure 18.17 */ }

    public void printPreOrder( )
      { /* Figure 18.22 */ }
    public void printPostOrder( )
      { /* Figure 18.22 */ }
    public void printInOrder( )
      { /* Figure 18.22 */ }

    private AnyType             element;
    private BinaryNode<AnyType> left;
    private BinaryNode<AnyType> right;
}
```

figure 18.12

The BinaryNode class skeleton

figure 18.13

The `BinaryTree` class, except for `merge`

```
 1 // BinaryTree class; stores a binary tree.
 2 //
 3 // CONSTRUCTION: with (a) no parameters or (b) an object to
 4 //    be placed in the root of a one-element tree.
 5 //
 6 // ******************PUBLIC OPERATIONS**********************
 7 // Various tree traversals, size, height, isEmpty, makeEmpty.
 8 // Also, the following tricky method:
 9 // void merge( Object root, BinaryTree t1, BinaryTree t2 )
10 //                         --> Construct a new tree
11 // ******************ERRORS*********************************
12 // Error message printed for illegal merges.
13
14 public class BinaryTree<AnyType>
15 {
16     public BinaryTree( )
17       { root = null; }
18     public BinaryTree( AnyType rootItem )
19       { root = new BinaryNode<AnyType>( rootItem, null, null ); }
20
21     public BinaryNode<AnyType> getRoot( )
22       { return root; }
23     public int size( )
24       { return BinaryNode.size( root ); }
25     public int height( )
26       { return BinaryNode.height( root ); }
27
28     public void printPreOrder( )
29       { if( root != null ) root.printPreOrder( ); }
30     public void printInOrder( )
31       { if( root != null ) root.printInOrder( ); }
32     public void printPostOrder( )
33       { if( root != null ) root.printPostOrder( ); }
34
35     public void makeEmpty( )
36       { root = null; }
37     public boolean isEmpty( )
38       { return root == null; }
39
40     public void merge( AnyType rootItem,
41                        BinaryTree<AnyType> t1, BinaryTree<AnyType> t2 )
42       { /* Figure 18.16 */ }
43
44     private BinaryNode<AnyType> root;
45 }
```

Two basic constructors are provided. The one at lines 16 and 17 creates an empty tree, and the one at lines 18 and 19 creates a one-node tree. Routines to traverse the tree are written at lines 28–33. They apply a `BinaryNode` method to

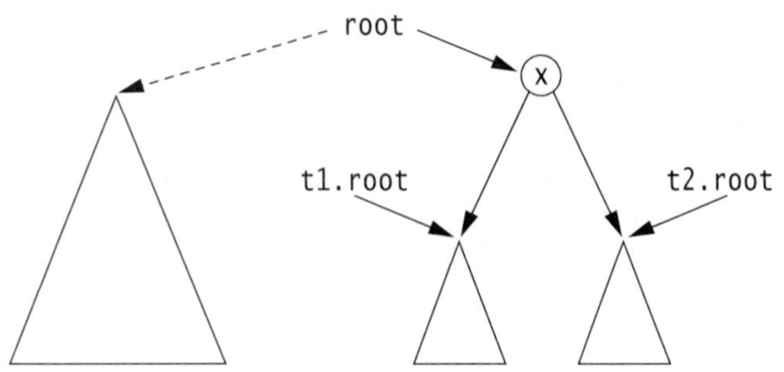

figure 18.14

Result of a naive merge operation: Subtrees are shared.

the root, after verifying that the tree is not empty. An alternative traversal strategy that can be implemented is level-order traversal. We discuss these traversal routines in Section 18.4. Routines to make an empty tree and test for emptiness are given, with their inline implementations, at lines 35 to 38, as are routines to compute the tree's size and height. Note that, as size and height are static methods in BinaryNode, we can call them by simply using BinaryNode.size and BinaryNode.height.

The merge routine is a one-liner in principle. However, we must also handle aliasing, ensure that a node is not in two trees, and check for errors.

The last method in the class is the merge routine, which uses two trees—t1 and t2—and an element to create a new tree, with the element at the root and the two existing trees as left and right subtrees. In principle, it is a one-liner:

We set the original trees' root to null so that each node is in one tree.

```
root = new BinaryNode<AnyType>( rootItem, t1.root, t2.root );
```

If things were always this simple, programmers would be unemployed. Fortunately for our careers, there are a host of complications. Figure 18.14 shows the result of the simple one-line merge. A problem becomes apparent: Nodes in t1 and t2's trees are now in two trees (their original trees and the merged result). This sharing is a problem if we want to remove or otherwise alter subtrees (because multiple subtrees may be removed or altered unintentionally).

If the two input trees are aliases, we should disallow the operation unless the trees are empty.

The solution is simple in principle. We can ensure that nodes do not appear in two trees by setting t1.root and t2.root to null after the merge.

Complications ensue when we consider some possible calls that contain aliasing:

```
t1.merge( x, t1, t2 );
t2.merge( x, t1, t2 );
t1.merge( x, t3, t3 );
```

The first two cases are similar, so we consider only the first one. A diagram of the situation is shown in Figure 18.15. Because t1 is an alias for the current object, t1.root and root are aliases. Thus, after the call to new, if we execute t1.root=null, we change root to the null reference, too. Consequently, we need to be very careful with the aliases for these cases.

figure 18.15

Aliasing problems in the `merge` operation; `t1` is also the current object.

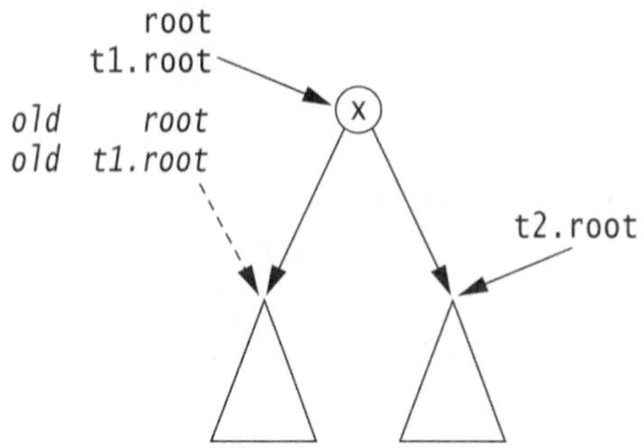

If an input tree is aliased to the output tree, we must avoid having the resultant `root` reference being set to `null`.

The third case must be disallowed because it would place all the nodes that are in tree `t3` in two places in `t1`. However, if `t3` represents an empty tree, the third case should be allowed. All in all, we got a lot more than we bargained for. The resulting code is shown in Figure 18.16. What used to be a one-line routine has gotten quite large.

```
/**
 * Merge routine for BinaryTree class.
 * Forms a new tree from rootItem, t1 and t2.
 * Does not allow t1 and t2 to be the same.
 * Correctly handles other aliasing conditions.
 */
public void merge( AnyType rootItem,
                   BinaryTree<AnyType> t1, BinaryTree<AnyType> t2 )
{
    if( t1.root == t2.root && t1.root != null )
        throw new IllegalArgumentException( );

        // Allocate new node
    root = new BinaryNode<AnyType>( rootItem, t1.root, t2.root );

        // Ensure that every node is in one tree
    if( this != t1 )
        t1.root = null;
    if( this != t2 )
        t2.root = null;
}
```

figure 18.16

The `merge` routine for the `BinaryTree` class

18.3 recursion and trees

Because trees can be defined recursively, many tree routines, not surprisingly, are most easily implemented by using recursion. Recursive implementations for almost all the remaining `BinaryNode` and `BinaryTree` methods are provided here. The resulting routines are amazingly compact.

Recursive routines are used for `size` and `duplicate`.

We begin with the `duplicate` method of the `BinaryNode` class. Because it is a `BinaryNode` method, we are assured that the tree we are duplicating is not empty. The recursive algorithm is then simple. First, we create a new node with the same data field as the current root. Then we attach a left tree by calling `duplicate` recursively and attach a right tree by calling `duplicate` recursively. In both cases, we make the recursive call after verifying that there is a tree to copy. This description is coded verbatim in Figure 18.17.

Because `duplicate` is a `BinaryNode` method, we make recursive calls only after verifying that the subtrees are not `null`.

The next method we write is the `size` routine in the `BinaryNode` class. It returns the size of the tree rooted at a node referenced by `t`, which is passed as a parameter. If we draw the tree recursively, as shown in Figure 18.18, we see that the size of a tree is the size of the left subtree plus the size of the right

The `size` routine is easily implemented recursively after a drawing is made.

```
/**
 * Return a reference to a node that is the root of a
 * duplicate of the binary tree rooted at the current node.
 */
public BinaryNode<AnyType> duplicate( )
{
    BinaryNode<AnyType> root =
            new BinaryNode<AnyType>( element, null, null );

    if( left != null )            // If there's a left subtree
        root.left = left.duplicate( );    // Duplicate; attach
    if( right != null )          // If there's a right subtree
        root.right = right.duplicate( );  // Duplicate; attach
    return root;                       // Return resulting tree
}
```

figure 18.17

A routine for returning a copy of the tree rooted at the current node

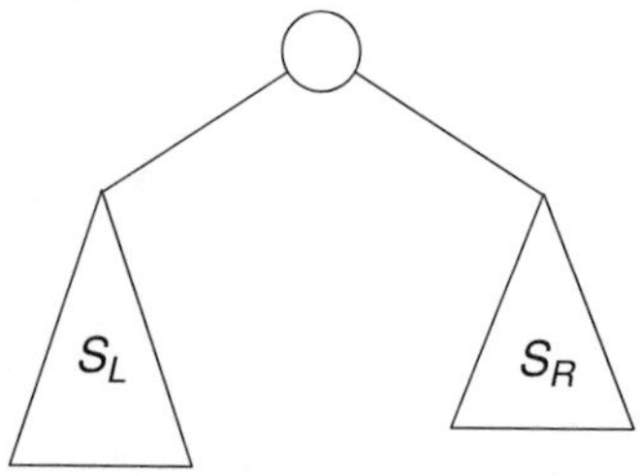

figure 18.18

Recursive view used to calculate the size of a tree: $S_T = S_L + S_R + 1$.

figure 18.19

A routine for computing the size of a node

```java
/**
 * Return the size of the binary tree rooted at t.
 */
public static <AnyType> int size( BinaryNode<AnyType> t )
{
    if( t == null )
        return 0;
    else
        return 1 + size( t.left ) + size( t.right );
}
```

subtree plus 1 (because the root counts as a node). A recursive routine requires a base case that can be solved without recursion. The smallest tree that `size` might have to handle is the empty tree (if `t` is `null`), and the size of an empty tree is clearly 0. We should verify that the recursion produces the correct answer for a tree of size 1. Doing so is easy, and the recursive routine is implemented as shown in Figure 18.19.

The `height` routine is also easily implemented recursively. The height of an empty tree is −1.

The final recursive routine presented in this section calculates the height of a node. Implementing this routine is difficult to do nonrecursively but is trivial recursively, once we have made a drawing. Figure 18.20 shows a tree viewed recursively. Suppose that the left subtree has height H_L and the right subtree has height H_R. Any node that is d levels deep with respect to the root of the left subtree is $d + 1$ levels deep with respect to the root of the entire tree. The same holds for the right subtree. Thus the path length of the deepest node in the original tree is 1 more than its path length with respect to the root of its subtree. If we compute this value for both subtrees, the maximum of these two values plus 1 is the answer we want. The code for doing so is shown in Figure 18.21.

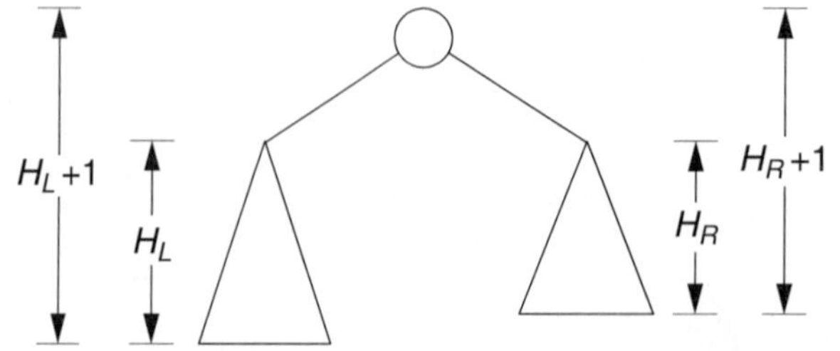

figure 18.20

Recursive view of the node height calculation: $H_T = \text{Max}\ (H_L + 1, H_R + 1)$

```
/**
 * Return the height of the binary tree rooted at t.
 */
public static <AnyType> int height( BinaryNode<AnyType> t )
{
    if( t == null )
        return -1;
    else
        return 1 + Math.max( height( t.left ), height( t.right ) );
}
```

figure 18.21

A routine for computing the height of a node

18.4 tree traversal: iterator classes

In this chapter we have shown how recursion can be used to implement the binary tree methods. When recursion is applied, we compute information about not only a node but also about all its descendants. We say then that we are *traversing the tree*. Two popular traversals that we have already mentioned are the preorder and postorder traversals.

In a preorder traversal, the node is processed and then its children are processed recursively. The `duplicate` routine is an example of a preorder traversal because the root is created first. Then a left subtree is copied recursively, followed by copying the right subtree.

In a postorder traversal, the node is processed after both children are processed recursively. Two examples are the methods `size` and `height`. In both cases, information about a node (e.g., its size or height) can be obtained only after the corresponding information is known for its children.

In an *inorder traversal*, the current node is processed between recursive calls.

A third common recursive traversal is the *inorder traversal,* in which the left child is recursively processed, the current node is processed, and the right child is recursively processed. This mechanism is used to generate an algebraic expression corresponding to an expression tree. For example, in Figure 18.11 the inorder traversal yields `(a+((b-c)*d))`.

Simple traversal using any of these strategies takes linear time.

Figure 18.22 illustrates routines that print the nodes in a binary tree using each of the three recursive tree traversal algorithms. Figure 18.23 shows the order in which nodes are visited for each of the three strategies. The running time of each algorithm is linear. In every case, each node is output only once. Consequently, the total cost of an output statement over any traversal is $O(N)$. As a result, each `if` statement is also executed at most once per node, for a total cost of $O(N)$. The total number of method calls made (which involves the constant work of the internal run-time stack pushes and pops) is likewise once per node, or $O(N)$. Thus the total running time is $O(N)$.

figure 18.22

Routines for printing nodes in preorder, postorder, and inorder

```
// Print tree rooted at current node using preorder traversal.
public void printPreOrder( )
{
    System.out.println( element );      // Node
    if( left != null )
        left.printPreOrder( );          // Left
    if( right != null )
        right.printPreOrder( );         // Right
}

// Print tree rooted at current node using postorder traversal.
public void printPostOrder( )
{
    if( left != null )                  // Left
        left.printPostOrder( );
    if( right != null )                 // Right
        right.printPostOrder( );
    System.out.println( element );      // Node
}

// Print tree rooted at current node using inorder traversal.
public void printInOrder( )
{
    if( left != null )                  // Left
        left.printInOrder( );
    System.out.println( element );      // Node
    if( right != null )
        right.printInOrder( );          // Right
}
```

figure 18.23

(a) Preorder, (b) postorder, and (c) inorder visitation routes

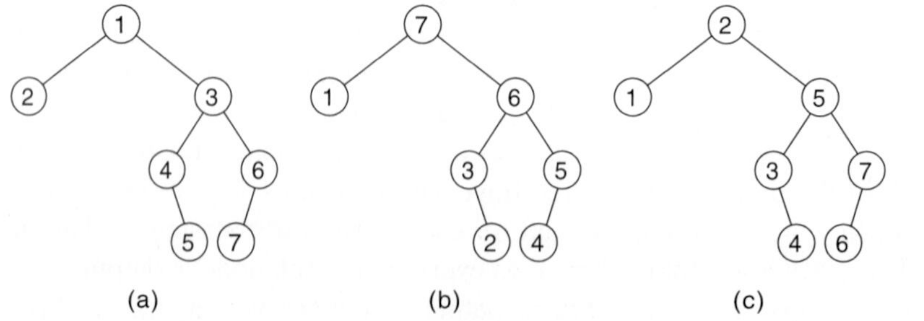

Must we use recursion to implement the traversals? The answer is clearly no because, as discussed in Section 7.3, recursion is implemented by using a stack. Thus we could keep our own stack.[2] We might expect that a somewhat faster program could result because we can place only the essentials on the stack rather than have the compiler place an entire activation record on the stack. The difference in speed between a recursive and nonrecursive algorithm is very dependent on the platform, and on modern computers may well be negligible. It is possible for instance, that if an array-based stack is used, the bounds checks that must be performed for all array access could be significant; the run-time stack might not be subjected to such tests if an aggressive optimizing compiler proves that a stack underflow is impossible. Thus in many cases, the speed improvement does not justify the effort involved in removing recursion. Even so, knowing how to do so is worthwhile, in case your platform is one that would benefit from recursion removal and also because seeing how a program is implemented nonrecursively can sometimes make the recursion clearer.

> We can traverse nonrecursively by maintaining the stack ourselves.

We write three iterator classes, each in the spirit of the linked list. Each allows us to go to the first node, advance to the next node, test whether we have gone past the last node, and access the current node. The order in which nodes are accessed is determined by the type of traversal. We also implement a level-order traversal, which is inherently nonrecursive and in fact uses a queue instead of a stack and is similar to the preorder traversal.

> An iterator class allows step-by-step traversal.

Figure 18.24 provides an abstract class for tree iteration. Each iterator stores a reference to the tree root and an indication of the current node.[3] These are declared at lines 47 and 48, respectively, and initialized in the constructor. They are `protected` to allow the derived classes to access them. Four methods are declared at lines 22–42. The `isValid` and `retrieve` methods are invariant over the hierarchy, so an implementation is provided and they are declared `final`. The abstract methods `first` and `advance` must be provided by each type of iterator. This iterator is similar to the linked list iterator (`LinkedListIterator`, in Section 17.2), except that here the `first` method is part of the tree iterator, whereas in the linked list the `first` method was part of the list class itself.

> The abstract tree iterator class has methods similar to those of the linked list iterator. Each type of traversal is represented by a derived class.

---

2. We can also add parent links to each tree node to avoid both recursion and stacks. In this chapter we demonstrate the relation between recursion and stacks, so we do not use parent links.
3. In these implementations, once the iterators have been constructed, structurally modifying the tree during an iteration is unsafe because references may become stale.

```
import java.util.NoSuchElementException;

// TreeIterator class; maintains "current position"
//
// CONSTRUCTION: with tree to which iterator is bound
//
// ******************PUBLIC OPERATIONS**********************
//     first and advance are abstract; others are final
// boolean isValid( )    --> True if at valid position in tree
// AnyType retrieve( )   --> Return item in current position
// void first( )         --> Set current position to first
// void advance( )       --> Advance (prefix)
// ******************ERRORS*********************************
// Exceptions thrown for illegal access or advance

abstract class TreeIterator<AnyType>
{
    /**
     * Construct the iterator. The current position is set to null.
     * @param theTree the tree to which the iterator is bound.
     */
    public TreeIterator( BinaryTree<AnyType> theTree )
      { t = theTree; current = null; }

    /**
     * Test if current position references a valid tree item.
     * @return true if the current position is not null; false otherwise.
     */
    final public boolean isValid( )
      { return current != null; }

    /**
     * Return the item stored in the current position.
     * @return the stored item.
     * @exception NoSuchElementException if the current position is invalid.
     */
    final public AnyType retrieve( )
    {
        if( current == null )
            throw new NoSuchElementException( );
        return current.getElement( );
    }

    abstract public void first( );
    abstract public void advance( );

    protected BinaryTree<AnyType> t;          // The tree root
    protected BinaryNode<AnyType> current;    // The current position
}
```

figure 18.24

The tree iterator abstract base class

18.4.1 postorder traversal

The postorder traversal is implemented by using a stack to store the current state. The top of the stack will represent the node that we are visiting at some instant in the postorder traversal. However, we may be at one of three places in the algorithm:

Postorder traversal maintains a stack that stores nodes that have been visited but whose recursive calls are not yet complete.

1. About to make a recursive call to the left subtree
2. About to make a recursive call to the right subtree
3. About to process the current node

Consequently, each node is placed on the stack three times during the course of the traversal. If a node is popped from the stack a third time, we can mark it as the current node to be visited.

Otherwise, the node is being popped for either the first time or the second time. In this case, it is not yet ready to be visited, so we push it back onto the stack and simulate a recursive call. If the node was popped for a first time, we need to push the left child (if it exists) onto the stack. Otherwise, the node was popped for a second time, and we push the right child (if it exists) onto the stack. In any event, we then pop the stack, applying the same test. Note that, when we pop the stack, we are simulating the recursive call to the appropriate child. If the child does not exist and thus was never pushed onto the stack, when we pop the stack we pop the original node again.

Each node is placed on the stack three times. The third time off, the node is declared visited. The other times, we simulate a recursive call.

Eventually, either the process pops a node for the third time or the stack empties. In the latter case, we have iterated over the entire tree. We initialize the algorithm by pushing a reference to the root onto the stack. An example of how the stack is manipulated is shown in Figure 18.25.

When the stack is empty, every node has been visited.

A quick summary: The stack contains nodes that we have traversed but not yet completed. When a node is pushed onto the stack, the counter is 1, 2, or 3 as follows:

1. If we are about to process the node's left subtree
2. If we are about to process the node's right subtree
3. If we are about to process the node itself

Let us trace through the postorder traversal. We initialize the traversal by pushing root `a` onto the stack. The first pop visits `a`. This is `a`'s first pop, so it is placed back on the stack, and we push its left child, `b`, onto the stack. Next `b` is popped. It is `b`'s first pop, so it is placed back on the stack. Normally, `b`'s left child would then be pushed, but `b` has no left child, so nothing is pushed. Thus the next pop reveals `b` for the second time, `b` is placed back on the stack, and its right child, `d`, is pushed onto the stack. The next pop produces `d` for the first

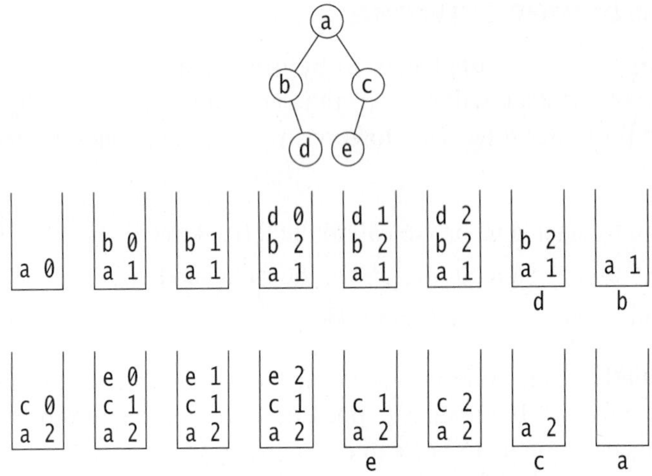

figure 18.25
Stack states during postorder traversal

time, and d is pushed back onto the stack. No other push is performed because d has no left child. Thus d is popped for the second time and is pushed back, but as it has no right child, nothing else is pushed. Therefore the next pop yields d for the third time, and d is marked as a visited node. The next node popped is b, and as this pop is b's third, it is marked visited.

Then a is popped for the second time, and it is pushed back onto the stack along with its right child, c. Next, c is popped for the first time, so it is pushed back, along with its left child, e. Now e is popped, pushed, popped, pushed, and finally popped for the third time (typical for leaf nodes). Thus e is marked as a visited node. Next, c is popped for the second time and is pushed back onto the stack. However, it has no right child, so it is immediately popped for the third time and marked as visited. Finally, a is popped for the third time and marked as visited. At this point, the stack is empty and the postorder traversal terminates.

An `StNode` stores a reference to a node and a count that tells how many times it has already been popped.

The `PostOrder` class is implemented directly from the algorithm described previously and is shown, minus the `advance` method, in Figure 18.26. The `StNode` nested class represents the objects placed on the stack. It contains a reference to a node and an integer that stores the number of times the item has been popped from the stack. An `StNode` object is always initialized to reflect the fact that it has not yet been popped from the stack. (We use a nonstandard `Stack` class from Chapter 16.)

The `PostOrder` class is derived from `TreeIterator` and adds an internal stack to the inherited data members. The `PostOrder` class is initialized by initializing the `TreeIterator` data members and then pushing the root onto the

```
import weiss.nonstandard.Stack;
import weiss.nonstandard.ArrayStack;

// PostOrder class; maintains "current position"
//     according to a postorder traversal
//
// CONSTRUCTION: with tree to which iterator is bound
//
// ******************PUBLIC OPERATIONS**********************
// boolean isValid( )   --> True if at valid position in tree
// AnyType retrieve( )  --> Return item in current position
// void first( )        --> Set current position to first
// void advance( )      --> Advance (prefix)
// ******************ERRORS*********************************
// Exceptions thrown for illegal access or advance

class PostOrder<AnyType> extends TreeIterator<AnyType>
{
    protected static class StNode<AnyType>
    {
        StNode( BinaryNode<AnyType> n )
          { node = n; timesPopped = 0; }
        BinaryNode<AnyType> node;
        int timesPopped;
    }

    /**
     * Construct the iterator. The current position is set to null.
     */
    public PostOrder( BinaryTree<AnyType> theTree )
    {
        super( theTree );
        s = new ArrayStack<StNode<AnyType>>( );
        s.push( new StNode<AnyType>( t.getRoot( ) ) );
    }

    /**
     * Set the current position to the first item.
     */
    public void first( )
    {
        s.makeEmpty( );
        if( t.getRoot( ) != null )
        {
            s.push( new StNode<AnyType>( t.getRoot( ) ) );
            advance( );
        }
    }

    protected Stack<StNode<AnyType>> s; // The stack of StNode objects
}
```

figure 18.26

The `PostOrder` class (complete class except for `advance`)

The advance routine is complicated. Its code follows the earlier description almost verbatim.

stack. This process is illustrated in the constructor at lines 30 to 35. Then `first` is implemented by clearing the stack, pushing the root, and calling `advance`.

Figure 18.27 implements `advance`. It follows the outline almost verbatim. Line 8 tests for an empty stack. If the stack is empty, we have completed the

```
 1     /**
 2      * Advance the current position to the next node in the tree,
 3      *     according to the postorder traversal scheme.
 4      * @throws NoSuchElementException if the current position is null.
 5      */
 6     public void advance( )
 7     {
 8         if( s.isEmpty( ) )
 9         {
10             if( current == null )
11                 throw new NoSuchElementException( );
12             current = null;
13             return;
14         }
15
16         StNode<AnyType> cnode;
17
18         for( ; ; )
19         {
20             cnode = s.topAndPop( );
21
22             if( ++cnode.timesPopped == 3 )
23             {
24                 current = cnode.node;
25                 return;
26             }
27
28             s.push( cnode );
29             if( cnode.timesPopped == 1 )
30             {
31                 if( cnode.node.getLeft( ) != null )
32                     s.push( new StNode<AnyType>( cnode.node.getLeft( ) ) );
33             }
34             else  // cnode.timesPopped == 2
35             {
36                 if( cnode.node.getRight( ) != null )
37                     s.push( new StNode<AnyType>( cnode.node.getRight( ) ) );
38             }
39         }
40     }
```

figure 18.27

The `advance` routine for the `PostOrder` iterator class

iteration and can set `current` to `null` and return. (If `current` is already `null`, we have advanced past the end, and an exception is thrown.) Otherwise, we repeatedly perform stack pushes and pops until an item emerges from the stack for a third time. When this happens, the test at line 22 is successful and we can return. Otherwise, at line 24 we push the node back onto the stack (note that the `timesPopped` component has already been incremented at line 22). We then implement the recursive call. If the node was popped for the first time and it has a left child, its left child is pushed onto the stack. Likewise, if the node was popped for a second time and it has a right child, its right child is pushed onto the stack. Note that, in either case, the construction of the `StNode` object implies that the pushed node goes on the stack with zero pops.

Eventually, the `for` loop terminates because some node will be popped for the third time. Over the entire iteration sequence, there can be at most $3N$ stack pushes and pops, which is another way of establishing the linearity of a postorder traversal.

18.4.2 inorder traversal

The inorder traversal is the same as the postorder traversal, except that a node is declared visited after it is popped a second time. Prior to returning, the iterator pushes the right child (if it exists) onto the stack so that the next call to `advance` can continue by traversing the right child. Because this action is so similar to a postorder traversal, we derive the `InOrder` class from the `PostOrder` class (even though an *IS-A* relationship does not exist). The only change is the minor alteration to `advance`. The new class is shown in Figure 18.28.

Inorder traversal is similar to postorder, except that a node is declared visited when it is popped for the second time.

18.4.3 preorder traversal

The preorder traversal is the same as the inorder traversal, except that a node is declared visited after it has been popped the first time. Prior to returning, the iterator pushes the right child onto the stack and then pushes the left child. Note the order: We want the left child to be processed before the right child, so we must push the right child first and the left child second.

We could derive the `PreOrder` class from the `InOrder` or `PostOrder` class, but doing so would be wasteful because the stack no longer needs to maintain a count of the number of times an object has been popped. Consequently, the `PreOrder` class is derived directly from `TreeIterator`. The resulting class with implementations of the constructor and `first` method is shown in Figure 18.29.

Preorder is the same as postorder, except that a node is declared visited the first time it is popped. The right and then left children are pushed prior to the return.

```
// InOrder class; maintains "current position"
//     according to an inorder traversal
//
// CONSTRUCTION: with tree to which iterator is bound
//
// ******************PUBLIC OPERATIONS**********************
// Same as TreeIterator
// ******************ERRORS*********************************
// Exceptions thrown for illegal access or advance

class InOrder<AnyType> extends PostOrder<AnyType>
{
    public InOrder( BinaryTree<AnyType> theTree )
      { super( theTree ); }

    /**
     * Advance the current position to the next node in the tree,
     *     according to the inorder traversal scheme.
     * @throws NoSuchElementException if iteration has
     *     been exhausted prior to the call.
     */
    public void advance( )
    {
        if( s.isEmpty( ) )
        {
            if( current == null )
                throw new NoSuchElementException( );
            current = null;
            return;
        }

        StNode<AnyType> cnode;
        for( ; ; )
        {
            cnode = s.topAndPop( );

            if( ++cnode.timesPopped == 2 )
            {
                current = cnode.node;
                if( cnode.node.getRight( ) != null )
                    s.push( new StNode<AnyType>( cnode.node.getRight( ) ) );
                return;
            }
                // First time through
            s.push( cnode );
            if( cnode.node.getLeft( ) != null )
                s.push( new StNode<AnyType>( cnode.node.getLeft( ) ) );
        }
    }
}
```

figure 18.28

The complete `InOrder` iterator class

```
1 // PreOrder class; maintains "current position"
2 //
3 // CONSTRUCTION: with tree to which iterator is bound
4 //
5 // ******************PUBLIC OPERATIONS**********************
6 // boolean isValid( )   --> True if at valid position in tree
7 // AnyType retrieve( )  --> Return item in current position
8 // void first( )        --> Set current position to first
9 // void advance( )      --> Advance (prefix)
10 // ******************ERRORS*********************************
11 // Exceptions thrown for illegal access or advance
12 
13 class PreOrder<AnyType> extends TreeIterator<AnyType>
14 {
15     /**
16      * Construct the iterator. The current position is set to null.
17      */
18     public PreOrder( BinaryTree<AnyType> theTree )
19     {
20         super( theTree );
21         s = new ArrayStack<BinaryNode<AnyType>>( );
22         s.push( t.getRoot( ) );
23     }
24 
25     /**
26      * Set the current position to the first item, according
27      * to the preorder traversal scheme.
28      */
29     public void first( )
30     {
31         s.makeEmpty( );
32         if( t.getRoot( ) != null )
33         {
34             s.push( t.getRoot( ) );
35             advance( );
36         }
37     }
38 
39     public void advance( )
40       { /* Figure 18.30 */ }
41 
42     private Stack<BinaryNode<AnyType>> s; // Stack of BinaryNode objects
43 }
```

figure 18.29

The `PreOrder` class skeleton and all members except `advance`

At line 42, we added a stack of tree nodes to the `TreeIterator` data fields. The constructor and `first` methods are similar to those already presented. As illustrated by Figure 18.30, `advance` is simpler: We no longer need a `for` loop. As soon as a node is popped at line 17, it becomes the current node. We then push the right child and the left child, if they exist.

Popping only once allows some simplification.

figure 18.30

The PreOrder iterator class advance routine

```
/**
 * Advance the current position to the next node in the tree,
 *     according to the preorder traversal scheme.
 * @throws NoSuchElementException if iteration has
 *     been exhausted prior to the call.
 */
public void advance( )
{
    if( s.isEmpty( ) )
    {
        if( current == null )
            throw new NoSuchElementException( );
        current = null;
        return;
    }

    current = s.topAndPop( );

    if( current.getRight( ) != null )
        s.push( current.getRight( ) );
    if( current.getLeft( ) != null )
        s.push( current.getLeft( ) );
}
```

18.4.4 level-order traversals

In a *level-order traversal,* nodes are visited top to bottom, left to right. Level-order traversal is implemented via a queue. The traversal is a breadth-first search.

We close by implementing a *level-order traversal,* which processes nodes starting at the root and going from top to bottom, left to right. The name is derived from the fact that we output level 0 nodes (the root), level 1 nodes (root's children), level 2 nodes (grandchildren of the root), and so on. A level-order traversal is implemented by using a queue instead of a stack. The queue stores nodes that are yet to be visited. When a node is visited, its children are placed at the end of the queue where they are visited after the nodes that are already in the queue have been visited. This procedure guarantees that nodes are visited in level order. The LevelOrder class shown in Figures 18.31 and 18.32 looks very much like the PreOrder class. The only differences are that we use a queue instead of a stack and that we enqueue the left child and then the right child, rather than vice versa. Note that the queue can get very large. In the worst case, all the nodes on the last level (possibly $N/2$) could be in the queue simultaneously.

The level-order traversal implements a more general technique known as *breadth-first search*. We illustrated an example of this in a more general setting in Section 14.2.

```
// LevelOrder class; maintains "current position"
//     according to a level-order traversal
//
// CONSTRUCTION: with tree to which iterator is bound
//
// ******************PUBLIC OPERATIONS**********************
// boolean isValid( )   --> True if at valid position in tree
// AnyType retrieve( )  --> Return item in current position
// void first( )        --> Set current position to first
// void advance( )      --> Advance (prefix)
// ******************ERRORS*********************************
// Exceptions thrown for illegal access or advance

class LevelOrder<AnyType> extends TreeIterator<AnyType>
{
    /**
     * Construct the iterator.
     */
    public LevelOrder( BinaryTree<AnyType> theTree )
    {
        super( theTree );
        q = new ArrayQueue<BinaryNode<AnyType>>( );
        q.enqueue( t.getRoot( ) );
    }

    public void first( )
      { /* Figure 18.32 */ }

    public void advance( )
      { /* Figure 18.32 */ }

    private Queue<BinaryNode<AnyType>> q; // Queue of BinaryNode objects
}
```

figure 18.31

The LevelOrder iterator class skeleton

summary

In this chapter we discussed the tree and, in particular, the binary tree. We demonstrated the use of trees to implement file systems on many computers and also some other applications, such as expression trees and coding, that we more fully explored in Part Three. Algorithms that work on trees make heavy use of recursion. We examined three recursive traversal algorithms—preorder, postorder, and inorder—and showed how they can be implemented nonrecursively. We also examined the level-order traversal, which forms the basis for an important searching technique known as breadth-first search. In Chapter 19 we examine another fundamental type of tree—the *binary search tree*.

figure 18.32

The `first` and `advance` routines for the `LevelOrder` iterator class

```
/**
 * Set the current position to the first item, according
 * to the level-order traversal scheme.
 */
public void first( )
{
    q.makeEmpty( );
    if( t.getRoot( ) != null )
    {
        q.enqueue( t.getRoot( ) );
        advance( );
    }
}

/**
 * Advance the current position to the next node in the tree,
 *     according to the level-order traversal scheme.
 * @throws NoSuchElementException if iteration has
 *     been exhausted prior to the call.
 */
public void advance( )
{
    if( q.isEmpty( ) )
    {
        if( current == null )
            throw new NoSuchElementException( );
        current = null;
        return;
    }

    current = q.dequeue( );

    if( current.getLeft( ) != null )
        q.enqueue( current.getLeft( ) );
    if( current.getRight( ) != null )
        q.enqueue( current.getRight( ) );
}
```

key concepts

ancestor and **descendant** If there is a path from node *u* to node *v*, then *u* is an ancestor of *v* and *v* is a descendant of *u*. (597)

binary tree A tree in which no node can have more than two children. A convenient definition is recursive. (602)

depth of a node The length of the path from the root to a node in a tree. (596)

first child/next sibling method A general tree implementation in which each node keeps two links per item: one to the leftmost child (if it is not a leaf) and one to its right sibling (if it is not the rightmost sibling). (597)

height of a node The length of the path from a node to the deepest leaf in a tree. (596)

inorder traversal The current node is processed between recursive calls. (611)

leaf A tree node that has no children. (596)

level-order traversal Nodes are visited top to bottom, left to right. Level-order traversal is implemented by using a queue. The traversal is breadth first. (622)

parent and **child** Parents and children are naturally defined. A directed edge connects the parent to the child. (596)

postorder tree traversal Work at a node is performed after its children are evaluated. The traversal takes constant time per node. (600)

preorder tree traversal Work at a node is performed before its children are processed. The traversal takes constant time per node. (600)

proper ancestor and **proper descendant** On a path from node u to node v, if $u \neq v$, then u is a proper ancestor of v and v is a proper descendant of u. (597)

siblings Nodes with the same parents. (597)

size of a node The number of descendants a node has (including the node itself). (597)

tree Defined nonrecursively, a set of nodes and the directed edges that connect them. Defined recursively, a tree is either empty or consists of a root and zero or more subtrees. (596)

common errors

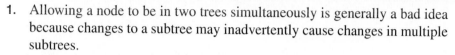

1. Allowing a node to be in two trees simultaneously is generally a bad idea because changes to a subtree may inadvertently cause changes in multiple subtrees.
2. Failing to check for empty trees is a common error. If this failure is part of a recursive algorithm, the program will likely crash.
3. A common error when working with trees is thinking iteratively instead of recursively. Design algorithms recursively first. Then convert them to iterative algorithms, if appropriate.

on the internet

Many of the examples discussed in this chapter are explored in Chapter 19, where we discuss binary search trees. Consequently, the only code available is for the iterator classes.

BinaryNode.java	Contains the `BinaryNode` class.
BinaryTree.java	Contains the implementation of `BinaryTree`.
TestTreeIterators.java	Contains the implementation of the `TreeIterator` hierarchy.

exercises

IN SHORT

18.1 For the tree shown in Figure 18.33, determine
  a. Which node is the root
  b. Which nodes are leaves
  c. The tree's depth
  d. The result of preorder, postorder, inorder, and level-order traversals

18.2 For each node in the tree shown in Figure 18.33
  a. Name the parent node
  b. List the children
  c. List the siblings
  d. Compute the height
  e. Compute the depth
  f. Compute the size

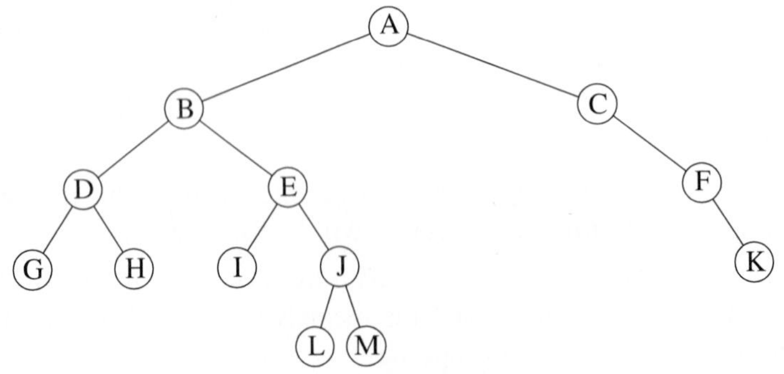

figure 18.33
Tree for Exercises 18.1 and 18.2

18.3 What is the output of the method presented in Figure 18.34 for the tree shown in Figure 18.25?

18.4 Show the stack operations when an inorder and preorder traversal is applied to the tree shown in Figure 18.25.

IN THEORY

18.5 Show that the maximum number of nodes in a binary tree of height H is $2^{H+1} - 1$.

18.6 A *full node* is a node with two children. Prove that in a binary tree the number of full nodes plus 1 equals the number of leaves.

18.7 How many `null` links are there in a binary tree of N nodes? How many are in an M-ary tree of N nodes?

18.8 Suppose that a binary tree has leaves $l_1, l_2, \ldots, l_M$ at depths $d_1, d_2, \ldots, d_M$, respectively. Prove that $\sum_{i=1}^{M} 2^{-d_i} \le 1$ and determine when equality is true (known as *Kraft's inequality*).

IN PRACTICE

18.9 Write efficient methods (and give their Big-Oh running times) that take a reference to a binary tree root T and compute

a. The number of leaves in T
b. The number of nodes in T that contain one non-`null` child
c. The number of nodes in T that contain two non-`null` children

18.10 Implement some of the recursive routines with tests that ensure that a recursive call is not made on a `null` subtree. Compare the running time with identical routines that defer the test until the first line of the recursive routine.

```
public static <AnyType> void mysteryPrint( BinaryNode<AnyType> t )
{
    if( t != null )
    {
        System.out.println( t.getElement( ) );
        mysteryPrint( t.getLeft( ) );
        System.out.println( t.getElement( ) );
        mysteryPrint( t.getRight( ) );
        System.out.println( t.getElement( ) );
    }
}
```

figure 18.34
Mystery program for Exercise 18.3

18.11 Rewrite the iterator class to throw an exception when `first` is applied to an empty tree. Why might this be a bad idea?

PROGRAMMING PROJECTS

18.12 A binary tree can be generated automatically for desktop publishing by a program. You can write this program by assigning an *x*-*y* coordinate to each tree node, drawing a circle around each coordinate, and connecting each nonroot node to its parent. Assume that you have a binary tree stored in memory and that each node has two extra data members for storing the coordinates. Assume that (0, 0) is the top-left corner. Do the following.

a. The *x*-coordinate can be computed by assigning the inorder traversal number. Write a routine to do so for each node in the tree.

b. The *y*-coordinate can be computed by using the negative of the depth of the node. Write a routine to do so for each node in the tree.

c. In terms of some imaginary unit, what will be the dimensions of the picture? Also determine how you can adjust the units so that the tree is always roughly two-thirds as high as it is wide.

d. Prove that when this system is used, no lines cross and that for any node *X*, all elements in *X*'s left subtree appear to the left of *X*, and all elements in *X*'s right subtree appear to the right of *X*.

e. Determine whether both coordinates can be computed in one recursive method.

f. Write a general-purpose tree-drawing program to convert a tree into the following graph-assembler instructions (circles are numbered in the order in which they are drawn):

```
circle( x, y );    // Draw circle with center (x, y)
drawLine( i, j ); // Connect circle i to circle j
```

g. Write a program that reads graph-assembler instructions and outputs the tree to your favorite device.

18.13 If you are running on a Unix system, implement the *du* command.

chapter 19

binary search trees

For large amounts of input, the linear access time of linked lists is prohibitive. In this chapter we look at an alternative to the linked list: the *binary search tree,* a simple data structure that can be viewed as extending the binary search algorithm to allow insertions and deletions. The running time for most operations is $O(\log N)$ on average. Unfortunately, the worst-case time is $O(N)$ per operation.

In this chapter, we show

- The basic binary search tree
- A method for adding order statistics (i.e., the `findKth` operation)
- Three different ways to eliminate the $O(N)$ worst case (namely, the *AVL tree, red-black tree,* and *AA-tree*)
- Implementation of the Collections API `TreeSet` and `TreeMap`
- Use of the *B-tree* to search a large database quickly

19.1 basic ideas

In the general case, we search for an item (or element) by using its *key.* For instance, a student transcript could be searched on the basis of a student ID number. In this case, the ID number is referred to as the item's key.

For any node in the *binary search tree*, all smaller keyed nodes are in the left subtree and all larger keyed nodes are in the right subtree. Duplicates are not allowed.

The *binary search tree* satisfies the search order property; that is, for every node *X* in the tree, the values of all the keys in the left subtree are smaller than the key in *X* and the values of all the keys in the right subtree are larger than the key in *X*. The tree shown in Figure 19.1(a) is a binary search tree, but the tree shown in Figure 19.1(b) is not because key 8 does not belong in the left subtree of key 7. The binary search tree property implies that all the items in the tree can be ordered consistently (indeed, an inorder traversal yields the items in sorted order). This property also does not allow duplicate items. We could easily allow duplicate keys; storing different items having identical keys in a secondary structure is generally better. If these items are exact duplicates, having one item and keeping a count of the number of duplicates is best.

binary search tree order property
In a binary search tree, for every node *X*, all keys in *X*'s left subtree have smaller values than the key in *X*, and all keys in *X*'s right subtree have larger values than the key in *X*.

19.1.1 the operations

A `find` operation is performed by repeatedly branching either left or right, depending on the result of a comparison.

For the most part, the operations on a binary search tree are simple to visualize. We can perform a `find` operation by starting at the root and then repeatedly branching either left or right, depending on the result of a comparison. For instance, to find 5 in the binary search tree shown in Figure 19.1(a), we start at 7 and go left. This takes us to 2, so we go right, which takes us to 5. To look for 6, we follow the same path. At 5, we would go right and encounter a `null` link and thus not find 6, as shown in Figure 19.2(a). Figure 19.2(b) shows that 6 can be inserted at the point at which the unsuccessful search terminated.

The binary search tree efficiently supports the `findMin` and `findMax` operations. To perform a `findMin`, we start at the root and repeatedly branch left as long as there is a left child. The stopping point is the smallest element. The

figure 19.1

Two binary trees: (a) a search tree; (b) not a search tree

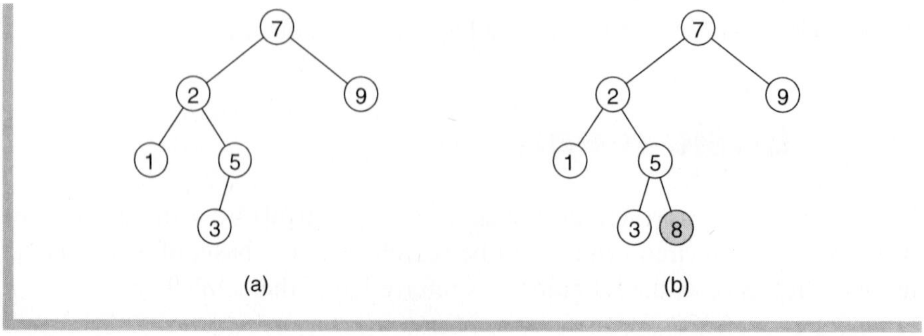

findMax operation is similar, except that branching is to the right. Note that the cost of all the operations is proportional to the number of nodes on the search path. The cost tends to be logarithmic, but it can be linear in the worst case. We establish this result later in the chapter.

The findMin operation is performed by following left nodes as long as there is a left child. The findMax operation is similar.

The hardest operation is remove. Once we have found the node to be removed, we need to consider several possibilities. The problem is that the removal of a node may disconnect parts of the tree. If that happens, we must carefully reattach the tree and maintain the binary search tree property. We also want to avoid making the tree unnecessarily deep because the depth of the tree affects the running time of the tree algorithms.

The remove operation is difficult because nonleaf nodes hold the tree together and we do not want to disconnect the tree.

When we are designing a complex algorithm, solving the simplest case first is often easiest, leaving the most complicated case until last. Thus, in examining the various cases, we start with the easiest. If the node is a leaf, its removal does not disconnect the tree, so we can delete it immediately. If the node has only one child, we can remove the node after adjusting its parent's child link to bypass the node. This is illustrated in Figure 19.3, with the removal of node 5. Note that removeMin and removeMax are not complex because the affected nodes are either leaves or have only one child. Note also that the root is a special case because it does not have a parent. How-

If a node has one child, it can be removed by having its parent bypass it. The root is a special case because it does not have a parent.

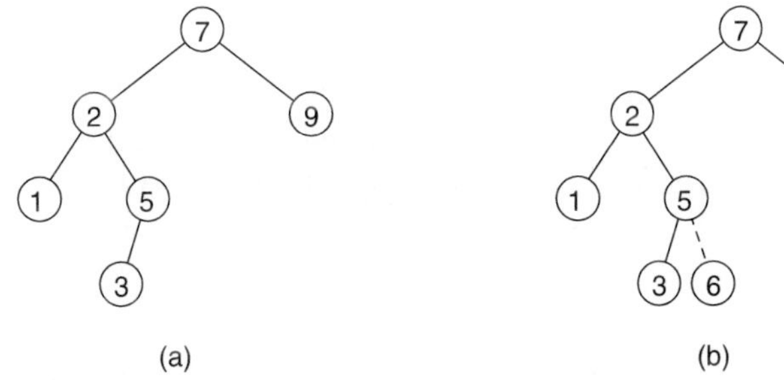

figure 19.2

Binary search trees (a) before and (b) after the insertion of 6

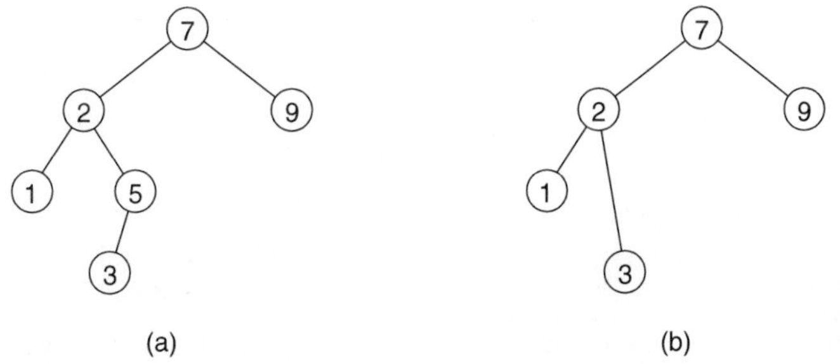

figure 19.3

Deletion of node 5 with one child: (a) before and (b) after

ever, when the `remove` method is implemented, the special case is handled automatically.

A node with two children is replaced by using the smallest item in the right subtree. Then another node is removed.

The complicated case deals with a node having two children. The general strategy is to replace the item in this node with the smallest item in the right subtree (which is easily found, as mentioned earlier) and then remove that node (which is now logically empty). The second `remove` is easy to do because, as just indicated, the minimum node in a tree does not have a left child. Figure 19.4 shows an initial tree and the result of removing node 2. We replace the node with the smallest node (3) in its right subtree and then remove 3 from the right subtree. Note that in all cases removing a node does not make the tree deeper.[1] Many alternatives do make the tree deeper; thus these alternatives are poor options.

19.1.2 java implementation

In principle, the binary search tree is easy to implement. To keep the Java features from clogging up the code, we introduce a few simplifications. First, Figure 19.5 shows the `BinaryNode` class. In the new `BinaryNode` class, we make everything package-visible. More typically, `BinaryNode` would be a nested class. The `BinaryNode` class contains the usual list of data members (the item and two links).

The `root` references at the root of the tree, which is `null` if the tree is empty.

The `BinarySearchTree` class skeleton is shown in Figure 19.6. The only data member is the reference to the root of the tree, `root`. If the tree is empty, `root` is `null`.

The public class functions call hidden private routines.

The public `BinarySearchTree` class methods have implementations that call the hidden methods. The constructor, declared at line 21, merely sets `root` to `null`. The publicly visible methods are listed at lines 24–39.

figure 19.4

Deletion of node 2 with two children: (a) before and (b) after

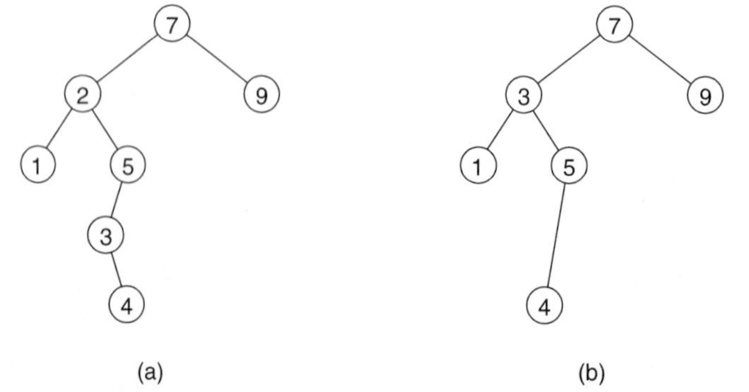

1. The deletion can, however, increase the average node depth if a shallow node is removed.

```
package weiss.nonstandard;

// Basic node stored in unbalanced binary search trees
// Note that this class is not accessible outside
// this package.

class BinaryNode<AnyType>
{
        // Constructor
    BinaryNode( AnyType theElement )
    {
        element = theElement;
        left = right = null;
    }

      // Data; accessible by other package routines
    AnyType             element;  // The data in the node
    BinaryNode<AnyType> left;     // Left child
    BinaryNode<AnyType> right;    // Right child
}
```

figure 19.5

The BinaryNode class for the binary search tree

```
package weiss.nonstandard;

// BinarySearchTree class
//
// CONSTRUCTION: with no initializer
//
// ******************PUBLIC OPERATIONS*********************
// void insert( x )       --> Insert x
// void remove( x )       --> Remove x
// void removeMin( )      --> Remove minimum item
// Comparable find( x )   --> Return item that matches x
// Comparable findMin( )  --> Return smallest item
// Comparable findMax( )  --> Return largest item
// boolean isEmpty( )     --> Return true if empty; else false
// void makeEmpty( )      --> Remove all items
// ******************ERRORS********************************
// Exceptions are thrown by insert, remove, and removeMin if warranted

public class BinarySearchTree<AnyType extends Comparable<? super AnyType>>
{
    public BinarySearchTree( )
      {  root = null; }

    public void insert( AnyType x )
      { root = insert( x, root ); }
```

figure 19.6a

The BinarySearchTree class skeleton (*continues*)

```
    public void remove( AnyType x )
      { root = remove( x, root ); }
    public void removeMin( )
      { root = removeMin( root ); }
    public AnyType findMin( )
      { return elementAt( findMin( root ) ); }
    public AnyType findMax( )
      { return elementAt( findMax( root ) ); }
    public AnyType find( AnyType x )
      { return elementAt( find( x, root ) ); }
    public void makeEmpty( )
      { root = null; }
    public boolean isEmpty( )
      { return root == null; }

    private AnyType elementAt( BinaryNode<AnyType> t )
      { /* Figure 19.7 */ }
    private BinaryNode<AnyType> find( AnyType x, BinaryNode<AnyType> t )
      { /* Figure 19.8 */ }
    protected BinaryNode<AnyType> findMin( BinaryNode<AnyType> t )
      { /* Figure 19.9 */ }
    private BinaryNode<AnyType> findMax( BinaryNode<AnyType> t )
      { /* Figure 19.9 */ }
    protected BinaryNode<AnyType> insert( AnyType x, BinaryNode<AnyType> t )
      { /* Figure 19.10 */ }
    protected BinaryNode<AnyType> removeMin( BinaryNode<AnyType> t )
      { /* Figure 19.11 */ }
    protected BinaryNode<AnyType> remove( AnyType x, BinaryNode<AnyType> t )
      { /* Figure 19.12 */ }

    protected BinaryNode<AnyType> root;
}
```

figure 19.6b

The BinarySearchTree class skeleton (*continued*)

Next, we have several methods that operate on a node passed as a parameter, a general technique that we used in Chapter 18. The idea is that the publicly visible class routines call these hidden routines and pass root as a parameter. These hidden routines do all the work. In a few places, we use protected rather than private because we derive another class from BinarySearchTree in Section 19.2.

The insert method adds x to the current tree by calling the hidden insert with root as an additional parameter. This action fails if x is already in the tree; in that case, a DuplicateItemException would be thrown. The findMin, findMax, and find operations return the minimum, maximum, or named item (respectively) from the tree. If the item is not found because the tree is empty or the named item is not present, then `null` is returned. Figure 19.7 shows the private `elementAt` method that implements the `elementAt` logic.

The `removeMin` operation removes the minimum item from the tree; it throws an exception if the tree is empty. The `remove` operation removes a named item `x` from the tree; it throws an exception if warranted. The `makeEmpty` and `isEmpty` methods are the usual fare.

As is typical of most data structures, the `find` operation is easier than `insert`, and `insert` is easier than `remove`. Figure 19.8 illustrates the `find` routine. So long as a `null` link has not been reached, we either have a match or need to branch left or right. The code implements this algorithm quite succinctly.

```java
/**
 * Internal method to get element field.
 * @param t the node.
 * @return the element field or null if t is null.
 */
private AnyType elementAt( BinaryNode<AnyType> t )
{
    return t == null ? null : t.element;
}
```

figure 19.7

The `elementAt` method

```java
/**
 * Internal method to find an item in a subtree.
 * @param x is item to search for.
 * @param t the node that roots the tree.
 * @return node containing the matched item.
 */
private BinaryNode<AnyType> find( AnyType x, BinaryNode<AnyType> t )
{
    while( t != null )
    {
        if( x.compareTo( t.element ) < 0 )
            t = t.left;
        else if( x.compareTo( t.element ) > 0 )
            t = t.right;
        else
            return t;    // Match
    }

    return null;         // Not found
}
```

figure 19.8

The `find` operation for binary search trees

Note the order of the tests. The test against `null` must be performed first; otherwise, the access `t.element` would be illegal. The remaining tests are arranged with the least likely case last. A recursive implementaion is possible, but we use a loop instead; we use recursion in the `insert` and `remove` methods. In Exercise 19.15 you are asked to write the searching algorithms recursively.

Because of call by value, the actual argument (`root`) is not changed.

At first glance, statements such as `t=t.left` may seem to change the root of the tree. That is not the case, however, because `t` is passed by value. In the initial call, `t` is simply a *copy* of `root`. Although `t` changes, `root` does not. The calls to `findMin` and `findMax` are even simpler because branching is unconditionally in one direction. These routines are shown in Figure 19.9. Note how the case of an empty tree is handled.

For `insert`, we must return the new tree root and reconnect the tree.

The `insert` routine is shown in Figure 19.10. Here we use recursion to simplify the code. A nonrecursive implementation is also possible; we apply this technique when we discuss red–black trees later in this chapter. The basic algorithm is simple. If the tree is empty, we can create a one-node tree. The test is performed at line 10, and the new node is created at line 11. Notice carefully that, as before, local changes to `t` are lost. Thus we return the new root, `t`, at line 18.

figure 19.9

The `findMin` and `findMax` methods for binary search trees

```
    /**
     * Internal method to find the smallest item in a subtree.
     * @param t the node that roots the tree.
     * @return node containing the smallest item.
     */
    protected BinaryNode<AnyType> findMin( BinaryNode<AnyType> t )
    {
        if( t != null )
            while( t.left != null )
                t = t.left;

        return t;
    }

    /**
     * Internal method to find the largest item in a subtree.
     * @param t the node that roots the tree.
     * @return node containing the largest item.
     */
    private BinaryNode<AnyType> findMax( BinaryNode<AnyType> t )
    {
        if( t != null )
            while( t.right != null )
                t = t.right;

        return t;
    }
```

If the tree is not already empty, we have three possibilities. First, if the item to be inserted is smaller than the item in node `t`, we call `insert` recursively on the left subtree. Second, if the item is larger than the item in node `t`, we call `insert` recursively on the right subtree (these two cases are coded at lines 12 to 15). Third, if the item to insert matches the item in `t`, we throw an exception.

The remaining routines concern deletion. As described earlier, the `removeMin` operation is simple because the minimum node has no left child. Thus the removed node merely needs to be bypassed, which appears to require us to keep track of the parent of the current node as we descend the tree. But, again, we can avoid the explicit use of a parent link by using recursion. The code is shown in Figure 19.11.

If the tree `t` is empty, `removeMin` fails. Otherwise, if `t` has a left child, we recursively remove the minimum item in the left subtree via the recursive call at line 13. If we reach line 17, we know that we are currently at the minimum node, and thus `t` is the root of a subtree that has no left child. If we set `t` to `t.right`, `t` is now the root of a subtree that is missing its former minimum element. As before, we return the root of the resulting subtree. That is what we do at line 17. But doesn't that disconnect the tree? The answer again is no. If `t` was `root`, the new `t` is returned and assigned to `root` in the public method. If `t` was not `root`, it is `p.left`, where `p` is `t`'s parent at the time of the recursive call.

The root of the new subtree must be returned in the `remove` routines. In effect we maintain the parent in the recursion stack.

```
1       /**
2        * Internal method to insert into a subtree.
3        * @param x the item to insert.
4        * @param t the node that roots the tree.
5        * @return the new root.
6        * @throws DuplicateItemException if x is already present.
7        */
8       protected BinaryNode<AnyType> insert( AnyType x, BinaryNode<AnyType> t )
9       {
10          if( t == null )
11              t = new BinaryNode<AnyType>( x );
12          else if( x.compareTo( t.element ) < 0 )
13              t.left = insert( x, t.left );
14          else if( x.compareTo( t.element ) > 0 )
15              t.right = insert( x, t.right );
16          else
17              throw new DuplicateItemException( x.toString( ) );  // Duplicate
18          return t;
19      }
```

figure 19.10

The recursive `insert` for the `BinarySearchTree` class

figure 19.11

The `removeMin` method for the `BinarySearchTree` class

```
/**
 * Internal method to remove minimum item from a subtree.
 * @param t the node that roots the tree.
 * @return the new root.
 * @throws ItemNotFoundException if t is empty.
 */
protected BinaryNode<AnyType> removeMin( BinaryNode<AnyType> t )
{
    if( t == null )
        throw new ItemNotFoundException( );
    else if( t.left != null )
    {
        t.left = removeMin( t.left );
        return t;
    }
    else
        return t.right;
}
```

The method that has `p` as a parameter (in other words, the method that called the current method) changes `p.left` to the new `t`. Thus the parent's `left` link references `t`, and the tree is connected. All in all, it is a nifty maneuver—we have maintained the parent in the recursion stack rather than explicitly kept track of it in an iterative loop.

Having used this trick for the simple case, we can then adapt it for the general `remove` routine shown in Figure 19.12. If the tree is empty, the `remove` is unsuccessful and we can throw an exception at line 11. If we do not have a match, we can recursively call `remove` for either the left or right subtree, as appropriate. Otherwise, we reach line 16, indicating that we have found the node that needs to be removed.

The `remove` routine involves tricky coding but is not too bad if recursion is used. The case for one child, root with one child, and zero children are all handled together at line 22.

Recall (as illustrated in Figure 19.4) that, if there are two children, we replace the node with the minimum element in the right subtree and then remove the right subtree's minimum (coded at lines 18–19). Otherwise, we have either one or zero children. If there is a left child, we set `t` equal to its left child, as we would do in `removeMax`. Otherwise, we know that there is no left child and that we can set `t` equal to its right child. This procedure is succinctly coded in line 22, which also covers the leaf case.

Two points need to be made about this implementation. First, during the basic `insert`, `find`, or `remove` operation, we use two three-way comparisons per node accessed to distinguish among the cases <, =, and >. Obviously we can compute `x.compareTo(t.element)` once per loop iteration, and reduce the cost to one three-way comparison per node. Actually, however, we can get by with

```
/**
 * Internal method to remove from a subtree.
 * @param x the item to remove.
 * @param t the node that roots the tree.
 * @return the new root.
 * @throws ItemNotFoundException if x is not found.
 */
protected BinaryNode<AnyType> remove( AnyType x, BinaryNode<AnyType> t )
{
    if( t == null )
        throw new ItemNotFoundException( x.toString( ) );
    if( x.compareTo( t.element ) < 0 )
        t.left = remove( x, t.left );
    else if( x.compareTo( t.element ) > 0 )
        t.right = remove( x, t.right );
    else if( t.left != null && t.right != null ) // Two children
    {
        t.element = findMin( t.right ).element;
        t.right = removeMin( t.right );
    }
    else
        t = ( t.left != null ) ? t.left : t.right;
    return t;
}
```

figure 19.12

The `remove` method for the `BinarySearchTree` class

only one two-way comparison per node. The strategy is similar to what we did in the binary search algorithm in Section 5.6. We discuss the technique for binary search trees in Section 19.6.2 when we illustrate the deletion algorithm for AA-trees.

Second, we do not have to use recursion to perform the insertion. In fact, a recursive implementation is probably slower than a nonrecursive implementation. We discuss an iterative implementation of `insert` in Section 19.5.3 in the context of red–black trees.

19.2 order statistics

The binary search tree allows us to find either the minimum or maximum item in time that is equivalent to an arbitrarily named `find`. Sometimes, we also have to be able to access the *K*th smallest element, for an arbitrary *K* provided as a parameter. We can do so if we keep track of the size of each node in the tree.

We can implement `findKth` by maintaining the size of each node as we update the tree.

Recall from Section 18.1 that the size of a node is the number of its descendants (including itself). Suppose that we want to find the Kth smallest element and that K is at least 1 and at most the number of nodes in the tree. Figure 19.13 shows three possible cases, depending on the relation of K and the size of the left subtree, denoted S_L. If K equals $S_L + 1$, the root is the Kth smallest element and we can stop. If K is smaller than $S_L + 1$ (i.e., smaller than or equal to S_L), the Kth smallest element must be in the left subtree and we can find it recursively. (The recursion can be avoided; we use it to simplify the algorithm description.) Otherwise, the Kth smallest element is the $(K - S_L - 1)$th smallest element in the right subtree and can be found recursively.

The main effort is maintaining the node sizes during tree changes. These changes occur in the `insert`, `remove`, and `removeMin` operations. In principle, this maintenance is simple enough. During an `insert`, each node on the path to the insertion point gains one node in its subtree. Thus the size of each node increases by 1, and the inserted node has size 1. In `removeMin`, each node on the path to the minimum loses one node in its subtree; thus the size of each node decreases by 1. During a `remove`, all nodes on the path to the node that is physically removed also lose one node in their subtrees. Consequently, we can maintain the sizes at the cost of only a slight amount of overhead.

19.2.1 java implementation

We derive a new class that supports the order statistic.

Logically, the only changes required are the adding of `findKth` and the maintenance of a `size` data member in `insert`, `remove`, and `removeMin`. We derive a new class from `BinarySearchTree`, the skeleton for which is shown in Figure 19.14. We provide a nested class that extends `BinaryNode` and adds a `size` data member.

`BinarySearchTreeWithRank` adds only one public method, namely `findKth`, shown at lines 31 and 32. All other public methods are inherited unchanged. We must override some of the `protected` recursive routines (lines 36–41).

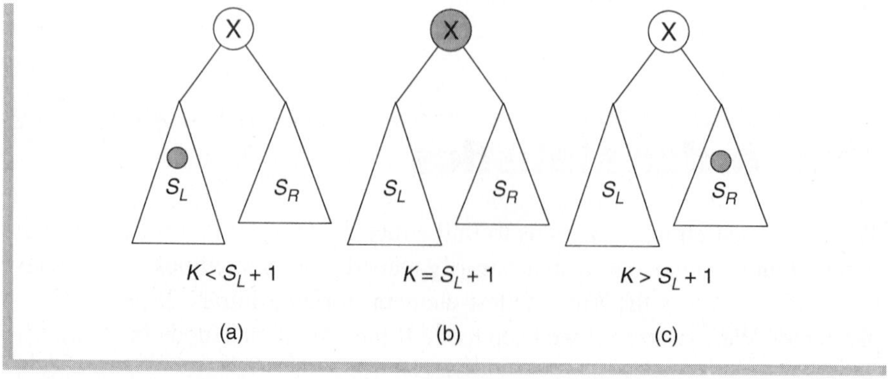

figure 19.13

Using the `size` data member to implement `findKth`

```
package weiss.nonstandard;

// BinarySearchTreeWithRank class
//
// CONSTRUCTION: with no initializer
//
// ******************PUBLIC OPERATIONS*********************
// Comparable findKth( k )--> Return kth smallest item
// All other operations are inherited
// ******************ERRORS*******************************
// IllegalArgumentException thrown if k is out of bounds

public class BinarySearchTreeWithRank<AnyType extends Comparable<? super AnyType>>
                     extends BinarySearchTree<AnyType>
{
    private static class BinaryNodeWithSize<AnyType> extends BinaryNode<AnyType>
    {
        BinaryNodeWithSize( AnyType x )
          { super( x ); size = 0; }

        int size;
    }

    /**
     * Find the kth smallest item in the tree.
     * @param k the desired rank (1 is the smallest item).
     * @return the kth smallest item in the tree.
     * @throws IllegalArgumentException if k is less
     *     than 1 or more than the size of the subtree.
     */
    public AnyType findKth( int k )
      { return findKth( k, root ).element; }

    protected BinaryNode<AnyType> findKth( int k, BinaryNode<AnyType> t )
      { /* Figure 19.15 */ }
    protected BinaryNode<AnyType> insert( AnyType x, BinaryNode<AnyType> tt )
      { /* Figure 19.16 */ }
    protected BinaryNode<AnyType> remove( AnyType x, BinaryNode<AnyType> tt )
      { /* Figure 19.18 */ }
    protected BinaryNode<AnyType> removeMin( BinaryNode<AnyType> tt )
      { /* Figure 19.17 */ }
}
```

figure 19.14

The `BinarySearchTreeWithRank` class skeleton

The `findKth` operation shown in Figure 19.15 is written recursively, although clearly it need not be. It follows the algorithmic description line for line. The test against `null` at line 10 is necessary because `k` could be invalid.

```
1  /**
2   * Internal method to find kth smallest item in a subtree.
3   * @param k the desired rank (1 is the smallest item).
4   * @return the node containing the kth smallest item in the subtree.
5   * @throws IllegalArgumentException if k is less
6   *     than 1 or more than the size of the subtree.
7   */
8  protected BinaryNode<AnyType> findKth( int k, BinaryNode<AnyType> t )
9  {
10     if( t == null )
11         throw new IllegalArgumentException( );
12     int leftSize = ( t.left != null ) ?
13                    ((BinaryNodeWithSize<AnyType>) t.left).size : 0;
14
15     if( k <= leftSize )
16         return findKth( k, t.left );
17     if( k == leftSize + 1 )
18         return t;
19     return findKth( k - leftSize - 1, t.right );
20 }
```

figure 19.15

The `findKth` operation for a search tree with order statistics

The `findKth` operation is easily implemented once the size members are known.

Lines 12 and 13 compute the size of the left subtree. If the left subtree exists, accessing its `size` member gives the required answer. If the left subtree does not exist, its size can be taken to be 0. Note that this test is performed after we are sure that `t` is not `null`.

The `insert` and `remove` operations are potentially tricky because we do not update the size information if the operation is unsuccessful.

The `insert` operation is shown in Figure 19.16. The potentially tricky part is that, if the insertion call succeeds, we want to increment `t`'s `size` member. If the recursive call fails, `t`'s `size` member is unchanged and an exception should be thrown. In an unsuccessful insertion, can some sizes change? The answer is no; `size` is updated only if the recursive call succeeds without an exception. Note that when a new node is allocated by a call to `new`, the `size` member is set to 0 by the `BinaryNodeWithSize` constructor, and then incremented at line 20.

Figure 19.17 shows that the same trick can be used for `removeMin`. If the recursive call succeeds, the `size` member is decremented; if the recursive call fails, `size` is unchanged. The `remove` operation is similar and is shown in Figure 19.18.

```
/**
 * Internal method to insert into a subtree.
 * @param x the item to insert.
 * @param tt the node that roots the tree.
 * @return the new root.
 * @throws DuplicateItemException if x is already present.
 */
protected BinaryNode<AnyType> insert( AnyType x, BinaryNode<AnyType> tt )
{
    BinaryNodeWithSize<AnyType> t = (BinaryNodeWithSize<AnyType>) tt;

    if( t == null )
        t = new BinaryNodeWithSize<AnyType>( x );
    else if( x.compareTo( t.element ) < 0 )
        t.left = insert( x, t.left );
    else if( x.compareTo( t.element ) > 0 )
        t.right = insert( x, t.right );
    else
        throw new DuplicateItemException( x.toString( ) );
    t.size++;
    return t;
}
```

figure 19.16

The `insert` operation for a search tree with order statistics

```
/**
 * Internal method to remove the smallest item from a subtree,
 *     adjusting size fields as appropriate.
 * @param t the node that roots the tree.
 * @return the new root.
 * @throws ItemNotFoundException if the subtree is empty.
 */
protected BinaryNode<AnyType> removeMin( BinaryNode<AnyType> tt )
{
    BinaryNodeWithSize<AnyType> t = (BinaryNodeWithSize<AnyType>) tt;

    if( t == null )
        throw new ItemNotFoundException( );
    if( t.left == null )
        return t.right;

    t.left = removeMin( t.left );
    t.size--;
    return t;
}
```

figure 19.17

The `removeMin` operation for a search tree with order statistics

```
/**
 * Internal method to remove from a subtree.
 * @param x the item to remove.
 * @param t the node that roots the tree.
 * @return the new root.
 * @throws ItemNotFoundException if x is not found.
 */
protected BinaryNode<AnyType> remove( AnyType x, BinaryNode<AnyType> tt )
{
    BinaryNodeWithSize<AnyType> t = (BinaryNodeWithSize<AnyType>) tt;

    if( t == null )
        throw new ItemNotFoundException( x.toString( ) );
    if( x.compareTo( t.element ) < 0 )
        t.left = remove( x, t.left );
    else if( x.compareTo( t.element ) > 0 )
        t.right = remove( x, t.right );
    else if( t.left != null && t.right != null ) // Two children
    {
        t.element = findMin( t.right ).element;
        t.right = removeMin( t.right );
    }
    else
        return ( t.left != null ) ? t.left : t.right;

    t.size--;
    return t;
}
```

figure 19.18

The `remove` operation for a search tree with order statistics

19.3 analysis of binary search tree operations

The cost of an operation is proportional to the depth of the last accessed node. The cost is logarithmic for a well-balanced tree, but it could be as bad as linear for a degenerate tree.

The cost of each binary search tree operation (`insert`, `find`, and `remove`) is proportional to the number of nodes accessed during the operation. We can thus charge the access of any node in the tree a cost of 1 plus its depth (recall that the depth measures the number of edges on a path rather than the number of nodes), which gives the cost of a successful search.

Figure 19.19 shows two trees. Figure 19.19(a) shows a balanced tree of 15 nodes. The cost to access any node is at most 4 units, and some nodes require fewer accesses. This situation is analogous to the one that occurs in the binary search algorithm. If the tree is perfectly balanced, the access cost is logarithmic.

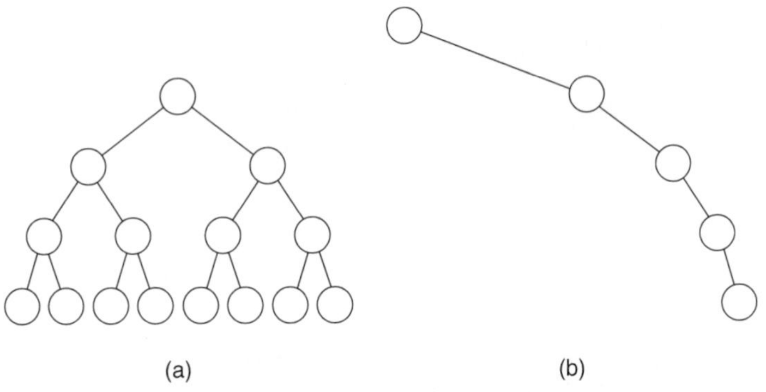

figure 19.19

(a) The balanced tree has a depth of $\lfloor \log N \rfloor$; (b) the unbalanced tree has a depth of $N - 1$.

Unfortunately, we have no guarantee that the tree is perfectly balanced. The tree shown in Figure 19.19(b) is the classic example of an unbalanced tree. Here, all N nodes are on the path to the deepest node, so the worst-case search time is $O(N)$. Because the search tree has degenerated to a linked list, the average time required to search in *this particular instance* is half the cost of the worst case and is also $O(N)$. So we have two extremes: In the best case, we have logarithmic access cost, and in the worst case we have linear access cost. What, then, is the average? Do most binary search trees tend toward the balanced or unbalanced case, or is there some middle ground, such as $\sqrt{N}$? The answer is identical to that for quicksort: The average is 38 percent worse than the best case.

On average, the depth is 38 percent worse than the best case. This result is identical to that obtained using quicksort.

We prove in this section that the average depth over all nodes in a binary search tree is logarithmic, under the assumption that each tree is created as a result of random insertion sequences (with no `remove` operations). To see what that means, consider the result of inserting three items in an empty binary search tree. Only their relative ordering is important, so we can assume without loss of generality that the three items are 1, 2, and 3. Then there are six possible insertion orders: (1, 2, 3), (1, 3, 2), (2, 1, 3), (2, 3, 1), (3, 1, 2), and (3, 2, 1). We assume in our proof that each insertion order is equally likely. The binary search trees that can result from these insertions are shown in Figure 19.20. Note that the tree with root 2, shown in Figure 19.20(c), is formed from either the insertion sequence (2, 3, 1) or the sequence (2, 1, 3). Thus some trees are more likely to result than others, and as we show, balanced trees are more likely to occur than unbalanced trees (although this result is not evident from the three-element case).

We begin with the following definition.

definition: The *internal path length* of a binary tree is the sum of the depths of its nodes.

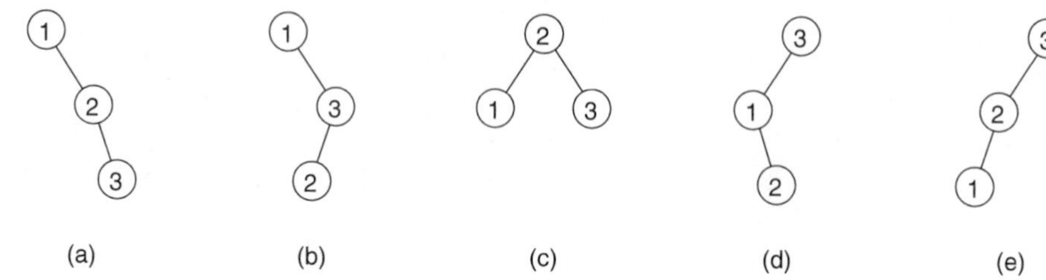

figure 19.20

Binary search trees that can result from inserting a permutation 1, 2, and 3; the balanced tree shown in part (c) is twice as likely to result as any of the others.

The *internal path length* is used to measure the cost of a successful search.

When we divide the internal path length of a tree by the number of nodes in the tree, we obtain the average node depth. Adding 1 to this average gives the average cost of a successful search in the tree. Thus we want to compute the average internal path length for a binary search tree, where the average is taken over all (equally probable) input permutations. We can easily do so by viewing the tree recursively and by using techniques from the analysis of quicksort given in Section 8.6. The average internal path length is established in Theorem 19.1.

Theorem 19.1

The internal path length of a binary search tree is approximately $1.38 N \log N$ on average, under the assumption that all permutations are equally likely.

Proof

Let $D(N)$ be the average internal path length for trees of N nodes, so $D(1) = 0$. An N-node tree T consists of an i-node left subtree and an $(N - i - 1)$-node right subtree, plus a root at depth 0 for $0 \le i < N$. By assumption, each value of i is equally likely. For a given i, $D(i)$ is the average internal path length of the left subtree with respect to its root. In T, all these nodes are one level deeper. Thus the average contribution of the nodes in the left subtree to the internal path length of T is $(1/N)\sum_{i=0}^{N-1} D(i)$, plus 1 for each node in the left subtree. The same holds for the right subtree. We thus obtain the recurrence formula $D(N) = (2/N)(\sum_{i=0}^{N-1} D(i)) + N - 1$, which is identical to the quicksort recurrence solved in Section 8.6. The result is an average internal path length of $O(N \log N)$.

The *external path length* is used to measure the cost of an unsuccessful search.

The insertion algorithm implies that the cost of an insert equals the cost of an unsuccessful search, which is measured by using the external path length. In an insertion or unsuccessful search, we eventually reach the test `t==null`.

Recall that in a tree of N nodes there are $N + 1$ `null` links. The external path length measures the total number of nodes that are accessed, including the `null` node for each of these $N + 1$ `null` links. The `null` node is sometimes called an *external tree node,* which explains the term *external path length.* As we show later in the chapter, replacing the `null` node with a sentinel may be convenient.

> **definition:** The *external path length* of a binary search tree is the sum of the depths of the $N + 1$ `null` links. The terminating `null` node is considered a node for these purposes.

One plus the result of dividing the average external path length by $N + 1$ yields the average cost of an unsuccessful search or insertion. As with the binary search algorithm, the average cost of an unsuccessful search is only slightly more than the cost of a successful search, which follows from Theorem 19.2.

Theorem 19.2

For any tree T, let $IPL(T)$ be the internal path length of T and let $EPL(T)$ be its external path length. Then, if T has N nodes, $EPL(T) = IPL(T) + 2N$.

Proof

This theorem is proved by induction and is left as Exercise 19.7.

Random `remove` operations do not preserve the randomness of a tree. The effects are not completely understood theoretically, but they apparently are negligible in practice.

It is tempting to say immediately that these results imply that the average running time of all operations is $O(\log N)$. This implication is true in practice, but it has not been established analytically because the assumption used to prove the previous results do not take into account the deletion algorithm. In fact, close examination suggests that we might be in trouble with our deletion algorithm because the `remove` operation always replaces a two-child deleted node with a node from the right subtree. This result would seem to have the effect of eventually unbalancing the tree and tending to make it left-heavy. It has been shown that if we build a random binary search tree and then perform roughly N^2 pairs of random `insert`/`remove` combinations, the binary search trees will have an expected depth of $O(\sqrt{N})$. However, a reasonable number of random `insert` and `remove` operations (in which the order of `insert` and `remove` is also random) does not unbalance the tree in any observable way. In fact, for small search trees, the `remove` algorithm seems to balance the tree. Consequently, we can reasonably assume that for random input all operations behave in logarithmic average time, although this result has not been proved mathematically. In Exercise 19.25 we describe some alternative deletion strategies.

The most important problem is not the potential imbalance caused by the `remove` algorithm. Rather, it is that, if the input sequence is sorted, the worst-case tree occurs. When that happens, we are in deep trouble: We have linear time per operation (for a series of N operations) rather than logarithmic cost per operation. This case is analogous to passing items to quicksort but having an insertion sort executed instead. The resulting running time is completely unacceptable. Moreover, it is not just sorted input that is problematic, but also any input that contains long sequences of nonrandomness. One solution to this problem is to insist on an extra structural condition called *balance:* No node is allowed to get too deep.

A *balanced binary search tree* has an added structure property to guarantee logarithmic depth in the worst case. Updates are slower, but accesses are faster.

Any of several algorithms can be used to implement a *balanced binary search tree,* which has an added structure property that guarantees logarithmic depth in the worst case. Most of these algorithms are much more complicated than those for the standard binary search trees, and all take longer on average for insertion and deletion. They do, however, provide protection against the embarrassingly simple cases that lead to poor performance for (unbalanced) binary search trees. Also, because they are balanced, they tend to give faster access time than those for the standard trees. Typically, their internal path lengths are very close to the optimal $N \log N$ rather than $1.38N \log N$, so searching time is roughly 25 percent faster.

19.4 avl trees

The *AVL tree* was the first balanced binary search tree. It has historical significance and also illustrates most of the ideas that are used in other schemes.

The first balanced binary search tree was the *AVL tree* (named after its discoverers, Adelson-Velskii and Landis), which illustrates the ideas that are thematic for a wide class of balanced binary search trees. It is a binary search tree that has an additional balance condition. Any balance condition must be easy to maintain and ensures that the depth of the tree is $O(\log N)$. The simplest idea is to require that the left and right subtrees have the same height. Recursion dictates that this idea apply to all nodes in the tree because each node is itself a root of some subtree. This balance condition ensures that the depth of the tree is logarithmic. However, it is too restrictive because inserting new items while maintaining balance is too difficult. Thus the definition of an AVL tree uses a notion of balance that is somewhat weaker but still strong enough to guarantee logarithmic depth.

> **definition:** An *AVL tree* is a binary search tree with the additional balance property that, for any node in the tree, the height of the left and right subtrees can differ by at most 1. As usual, the height of an empty subtree is -1.

19.4.1 properties

Every node in an AVL tree has subtrees whose heights differ by at most 1. An empty subtree has height −1.

Figure 19.21 shows two binary search trees. The tree shown in Figure 19.21(a) satisfies the AVL balance condition and is thus an AVL tree. The tree shown in Figure 19.21(b), which results from inserting 1, using the usual algorithm, is not an AVL tree because the darkened nodes have left subtrees whose heights are 2 larger than their right subtrees. If 13 were inserted, using the usual binary search tree insertion algorithm, node 16 would also be in violation. The reason is that the left subtree would have height 1, while the right subtree would have height −1.

The AVL tree has height at most roughly 44 percent greater than the minimum.

The AVL balance condition implies that the tree has only logarithmic depth. To prove this assertion we need to show that a tree of height H must have at least C^H nodes for some constant $C > 1$. In other words, the minimum number of nodes in a tree is exponential in its height. Then the maximum depth of an N-item tree is given by $\log_C N$. Theorem 19.3 shows that every AVL tree of height H has many nodes.

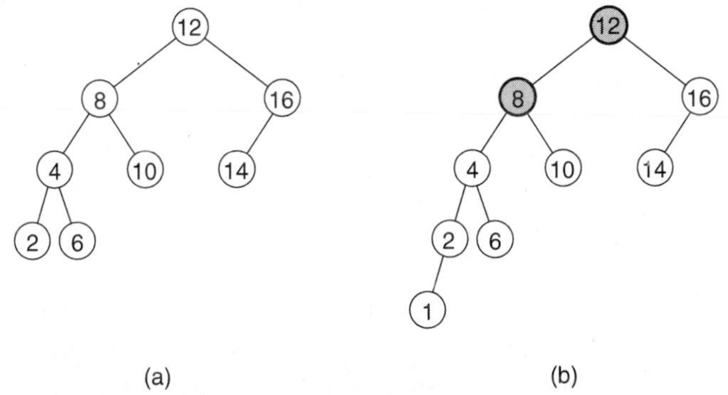

figure 19.21

Two binary search trees: (a) an AVL tree; (b) not an AVL tree (unbalanced nodes are darkened)

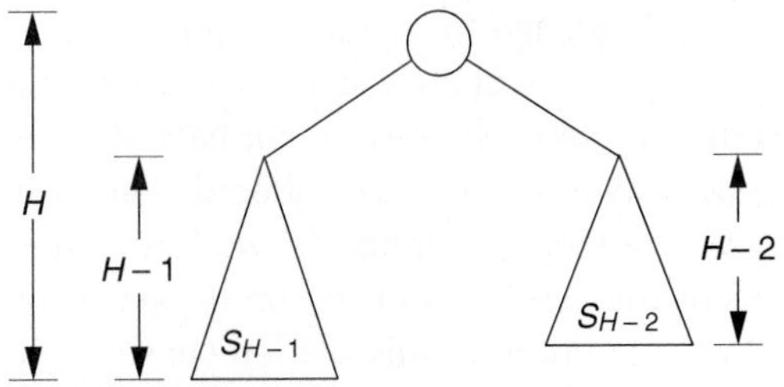

figure 19.22

Minimum tree of height H

Theorem 19.3

An AVL tree of height H has at least $F_{H+3} - 1$ nodes, where F_i is the ith Fibonacci number (see Section 7.3.4).

Proof

Let S_H be the size of the smallest AVL tree of height H. Clearly, $S_0 = 1$ and $S_1 = 2$. Figure 19.22 shows that the smallest AVL tree of height H must have subtrees of height $H - 1$ and $H - 2$. The reason is that at least one subtree has height $H - 1$ and the balance condition implies that subtree heights can differ by at most 1. These subtrees must themselves have the fewest number of nodes for their heights, so $S_H = S_{H-1} + S_{H-2} + 1$. The proof can be completed by using an induction argument.

From Exercise 7.8, $F_i \approx \phi^i/\sqrt{5}$, where $\phi = (1 + \sqrt{5})/2 \approx 1.618$. Consequently, an AVL tree of height H has at least (roughly) $\phi^{H+3}/\sqrt{5}$ nodes. Hence its depth is at most logarithmic. The height of an AVL tree satisfies

$$H < 1.44 \log (N + 2) - 1.328 \qquad \textbf{(19.1)}$$

so the worst-case height is at most roughly 44 percent more than the minimum possible for binary trees.

The depth of a typical node in an AVL tree is very close to the optimal $\log N$.

The depth of an average node in a randomly constructed AVL tree tends to be very close to $\log N$. The exact answer has not yet been established analytically. We do not even know whether the form is $\log N + C$ or $(1 + \varepsilon) \log N + C$, for some ε that would be approximately 0.01. Simulations have been unable to demonstrate convincingly that one form is more plausible than the other.

An update in an AVL tree could destroy the balance. It must then be rebalanced before the operation can be considered complete.

A consequence of these arguments is that all searching operations in an AVL tree have logarithmic worst-case bounds. The difficulty is that operations that change the tree, such as `insert` and `remove`, are not quite as simple as before. The reason is that an insertion (or deletion) can destroy the balance of several nodes in the tree, as shown in Figure 19.21. The balance must then be restored before the operation can be considered complete. The insertion algorithm is described here, and the deletion algorithm is left for Exercise 19.9.

Only nodes on the path from the root to the insertion point can have their balances altered.

A key observation is that after an insertion, only nodes that are on the path from the insertion point to the root might have their balances altered because only those nodes have their subtrees altered. This result applies to almost all the balanced search tree algorithms. As we follow the path up to the root and update the balancing information, we may find a node whose new balance violates the AVL condition. In this section we show how to rebalance the tree at the first (i.e., the deepest) such node and prove that this rebalancing guarantees that the entire tree satisfies the AVL property.

The node to be rebalanced is X. Because any node has at most two children and a height imbalance requires that the heights of X's two subtrees differ by 2, a violation might occur in any of four cases:

1. An insertion in the left subtree of the left child of X
2. An insertion in the right subtree of the left child of X
3. An insertion in the left subtree of the right child of X
4. An insertion in the right subtree of the right child of X

If we fix the balance at the deepest unbalanced node, we rebalance the entire tree. There are four cases that we might have to fix; two are mirror images of the other two.

Cases 1 and 4 are mirror-image symmetries with respect to X, as are cases 2 and 3. Consequently, there theoretically are two basic cases. From a programming perspective, of course, there are still four cases and numerous special cases.

The first case, in which the insertion occurs on the *outside* (i.e., left–left or right–right), is fixed by a single rotation of the tree. A *single rotation* switches the roles of the parent and child while maintaining search order. The second case, in which the insertion occurs on the *inside* (i.e., left–right or right–left), is handled by the slightly more complex *double rotation.* These fundamental operations on the tree are used several times in balanced tree algorithms. In the remainder of this section we describe these rotations and prove that they suffice to maintain the balance condition.

Balance is restored by tree rotations. A *single rotation* switches the roles of the parent and child while maintaining the search order.

19.4.2 single rotation

Figure 19.23 shows the single rotation that fixes case 1. In Figure 19.23(a), node k_2 violates the AVL balance property because its left subtree is two levels deeper than its right subtree (the dashed lines mark the levels in this section). The situation depicted is the only possible case 1 scenario that allows k_2 to satisfy the AVL property before the insertion but violate it afterward. Subtree A has grown to an extra level, causing it to be two levels deeper than C. Subtree B cannot be at the same level as the new A because then k_2 would have been out of balance *before* the insertion. Subtree B cannot be at the same level as C because then k_1 would have been the first node on the path that was in violation of the AVL balancing condition (and we are claiming that k_2 is).

A single rotation handles the outside cases (1 and 4). We rotate between a node and its child. The result is a binary search tree that satisfies the AVL property.

Ideally, to rebalance the tree, we want to move A up one level and C down one level. Note that these actions are more than the AVL property requires. To do so we rearrange nodes into an equivalent search tree, as shown in Figure 19.23(b). Here is an abstract scenario: Visualize the tree as being flexible, grab the child node k_1, close your eyes, and shake the tree, letting gravity take hold. The result is that k_1 will be the new root. The binary search tree property tells us that in the original tree, $k_2 > k_1$, so k_2 becomes the right child of k_1 in the new tree. Subtrees A and C remain as the left child of k_1 and the right child of k_2, respectively. Sub-

figure 19.23

Single rotation to fix case 1

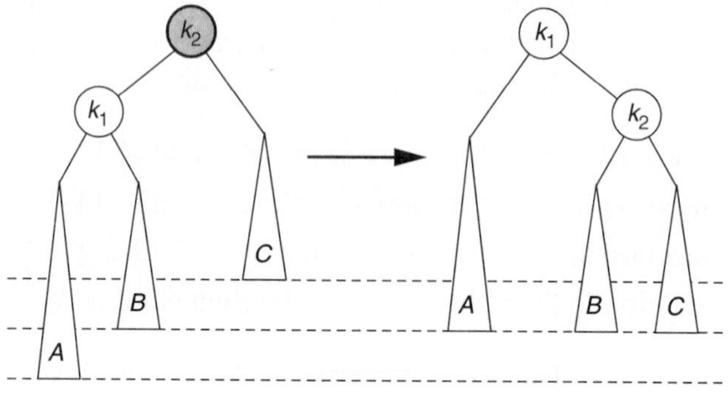

(a) Before rotation (b) After rotation

tree B, which holds items between k_1 and k_2 in the original tree, can be placed as k_2's left child in the new tree and satisfy all the ordering requirements.

One rotation suffices to fix cases 1 and 4 in an AVL tree.

This work requires only the few child link changes shown as pseudocode in Figure 19.24 and results in another binary tree that is an AVL tree. This outcome occurs because A moves up one level, B stays at the same level, and C moves down one level. Thus k_1 and k_2 not only satisfy the AVL requirements, but they also have subtrees that are the same height. Furthermore, the new height of the entire subtree is *exactly the same* as the height of the original subtree before the insertion that caused A to grow. Thus no further updating of the heights on the path to the root is needed, and consequently, *no further rotations are needed.* We use this single rotation often in other balanced tree algorithms in this chapter.

Figure 19.25(a) shows that after the insertion of 1 into an AVL tree, node 8 becomes unbalanced. This is clearly a case 1 problem because 1 is in 8's left–left subtree. Thus we do a single rotation between 8 and 4, thereby obtaining the tree shown in Figure 19.25(b). As mentioned earlier in this section, case 4 represents a symmetric case. The required rotation is shown in

figure 19.24

Pseudocode for a single rotation (case 1)

```
/**
 * Rotate binary tree node with left child.
 * For AVL trees, this is a single rotation for case 1.
 */
static BinaryNode rotateWithLeftChild( BinaryNode k2 )
{
    BinaryNode k1 = k2.left;
    k2.left = k1.right;
    k1.right = k2;
    return k1;
}
```

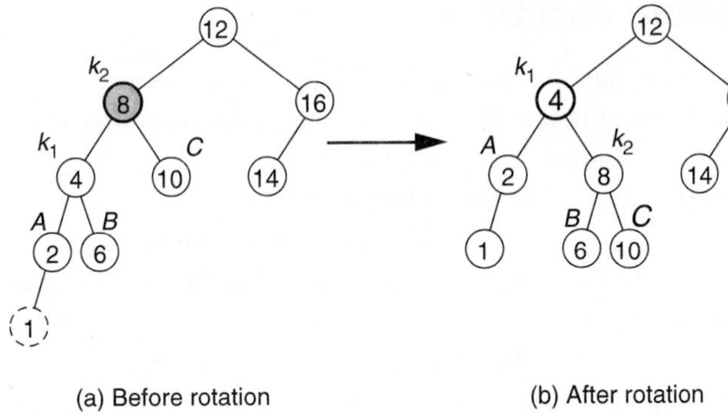

figure 19.25

Single rotation fixes an AVL tree after insertion of 1.

Figure 19.26, and the pseudocode that implements it is shown in Figure 19.27. This routine, along with other rotations in this section, is replicated in various balanced search trees later in this text. These rotation routines appear in the online code for several balanced search tree implementations.

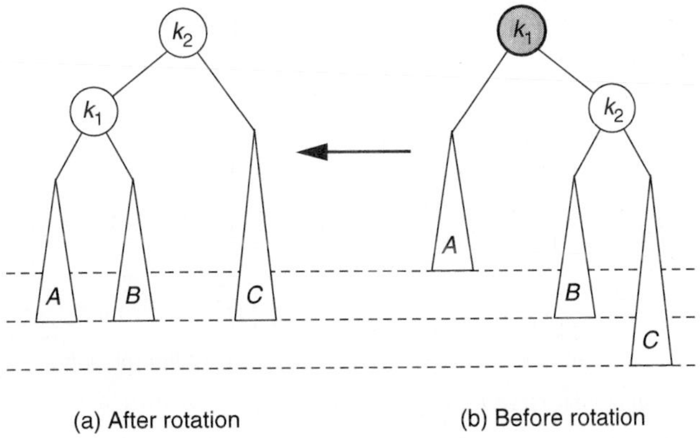

figure 19.26

Symmetric single rotation to fix case 4

```
/**
 * Rotate binary tree node with right child.
 * For AVL trees, this is a single rotation for case 4.
 */
static BinaryNode rotateWithRightChild( BinaryNode k1 )
{
    BinaryNode k2 = k1.right;
    k1.right = k2.left;
    k2.left = k1;
    return k2;
}
```

figure 19.27

Pseudocode for a single rotation (case 4)

19.4.3 double rotation

The single rotation does not fix the inside cases (2 and 3). These cases require a double rotation, involving three nodes and four subtrees.

The single rotation has a problem: As Figure 19.28 shows, it does not work for case 2 (or, by symmetry, for case 3). The problem is that subtree Q is too deep, and a single rotation does not make it any less deep. The double rotation that solves the problem is shown in Figure 19.29.

The fact that subtree Q in Figure 19.28 has had an item inserted into it guarantees that it is not empty. We may assume that it has a root and two (possibly empty) subtrees, so we may view the tree as four subtrees connected by three nodes. We therefore rename the four trees A, B, C, and D. As Figure 19.29 suggests, either subtree B or subtree C is two levels deeper than subtree D (unless both are empty, in which case both are), but we cannot be sure which one. Actually it does not matter; here, both B and C are drawn at 1.5 levels below D.

To rebalance, we cannot leave k_3 as the root. In Figure 19.28 we showed that a rotation between k_3 and k_1 does not work, so the only alternative is to

figure 19.28

Single rotation does not fix case 2.

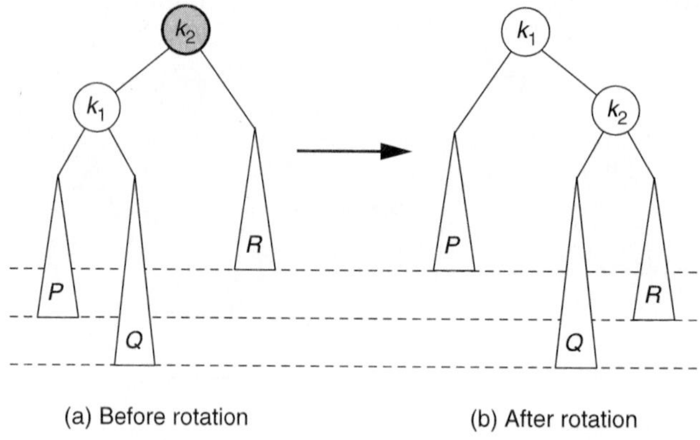

figure 19.29

Left–right double rotation to fix case 2

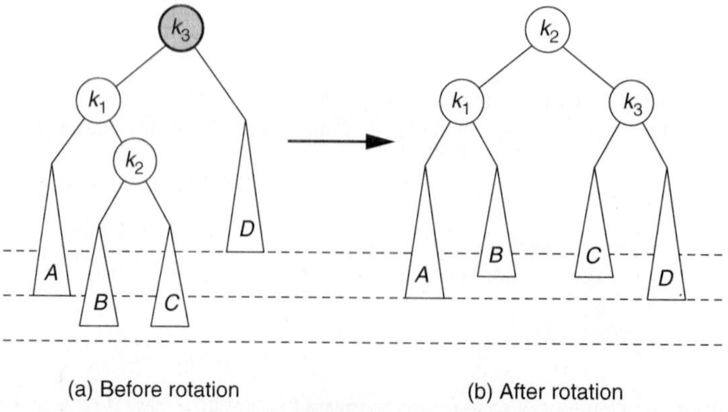

place k_2 as the new root. Doing so forces k_1 to be k_2's left child and k_3 to be k_2's right child. It also determines the resulting locations of the four subtrees, and the resulting tree satisfies the AVL property. Also, as was the case with the single rotation, it restores the height to the height before the insertion, thus guaranteeing that all rebalancing and height updating are complete.

As an example, Figure 19.30(a) shows the result of inserting 5 into an AVL tree. A height imbalance is caused at node 8, resulting in a case 2 problem. We perform a double rotation at that node, thereby producing the tree shown in Figure 19.30(b).

A *double rotation* is equivalent to two single rotations.

Figure 19.31 shows that the symmetric case 3 can also be fixed by a double rotation. Finally, note that, although a double rotation appears complex, it turns out to be equivalent to the following sequence:

- A rotation between *X*'s child and grandchild
- A rotation between *X* and its new child

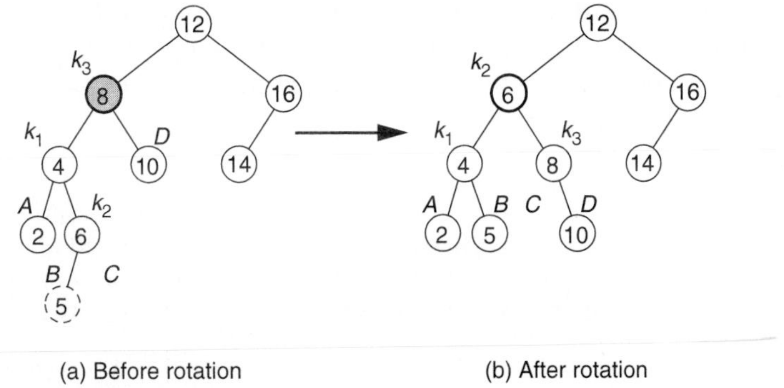

figure 19.30

Double rotation fixes AVL tree after the insertion of 5.

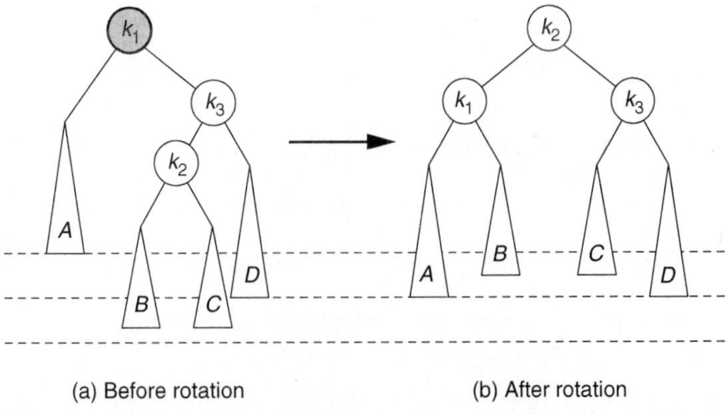

figure 19.31

Right–Left double rotation to fix case 3.

The pseudocode to implement the case 2 double rotation is compact and is shown in Figure 19.32. The mirror-image pseudocode for case 3 is shown in Figure 19.33.

19.4.4 summary of avl insertion

A casual AVL implementation is not excessively complex, but it is not efficient. Better balanced search trees have since been discovered, so implementing an AVL tree is not worthwhile.

Here is a brief summary how an AVL insertion is implemented. A recursive algorithm turns out to be the simplest method of implementing an AVL insertion. To insert a new node with key X in an AVL tree T, we recursively insert it in the appropriate subtree of T (denoted T_{LR}). If the height of T_{LR} does not change, we are done. Otherwise, if a height imbalance appears in T, we do the appropriate single or double rotation (rooted at T), depending on X and the keys in T and T_{LR}, and then we are done (because the old height is the same as the postrotation height). This recursive description is best described as a *casual implementation.* For instance, at each node we compare the subtree's heights. In general, storing the result of the comparison in the node is more efficient than maintaining the height information. This approach avoids the repetitive calculation of balance factors. Furthermore, recursion incurs substantially more overhead than does an iterative version. The reason is that, in effect, we go down the tree and completely back up instead of stopping as soon as a rotation has been performed. Consequently, in practice, other balanced search tree schemes are used.

figure 19.32

Pseudocode for a double rotation (case 2)

```
/**
 * Double rotate binary tree node: first left child
 * with its right child; then node k3 with new left child.
 * For AVL trees, this is a double rotation for case 2.
 */
static BinaryNode doubleRotateWithLeftChild( BinaryNode k3 )
{
    k3.left = rotateWithRightChild( k3.left );
    return rotateWithLeftChild( k3 );
}
```

figure 19.33

Pseudocode for a double rotation (case 3)

```
/**
 * Double rotate binary tree node: first right child
 * with its left child; then node k1 with new right child.
 * For AVL trees, this is a double rotation for case 3.
 */
static BinaryNode doubleRotateWithRightChild( BinaryNode k1 )
{
    k1.right = rotateWithLeftChild( k1.right );
    return rotateWithRightChild( k1 );
}
```

19.5 red–black trees

A historically popular alternative to the AVL tree is the *red–black tree*, in which a single top-down pass can be used during the insertion and deletion routines. This approach contrasts with an AVL tree, in which a pass down the tree is used to establish the insertion point and a second pass up the tree is used to update heights and possibly rebalance. As a result, a careful nonrecursive implementation of the red–black tree is simpler and faster than an AVL tree implementation. As on AVL trees, operations on red–black trees take logarithmic worst-case time.

A *red–black tree* is a good alternative to the AVL tree. The coding details tend to give a faster implementation because a single top-down pass can be used during the insertion and deletion routines.

A red–black tree is a binary search tree having the following ordering properties:

1. Every node is colored either red or black.
2. The root is black.
3. If a node is red, its children must be black.
4. Every path from a node to a `null` link must contain the same number of black nodes.

Consecutive red nodes are disallowed, and all paths have the same number of black nodes.

In this discussion of red–black trees, shaded nodes represent red nodes. Figure 19.34 shows a red–black tree. Every path from the root to a `null` node contains three black nodes.

Shaded nodes are red throughout this discussion.

We can show by induction that, if every path from the root to a `null` node contains B black nodes, the tree must contain at least $2^B - 1$ black nodes. Furthermore, as the root is black and there cannot be two consecutive red nodes on a path, the height of a red–black tree is at most $2\log(N + 1)$. Consequently, searching is guaranteed to be a logarithmic operation.

The depth of a red–black tree is guaranteed to be logarithmic. Typically, the depth is the same as for an AVL tree.

The difficulty, as usual, is that operations can change the tree and possibly destroy the coloring properties. This possibility makes insertion difficult and removal especially so. First, we implement the insertion, and then we examine the deletion algorithm.

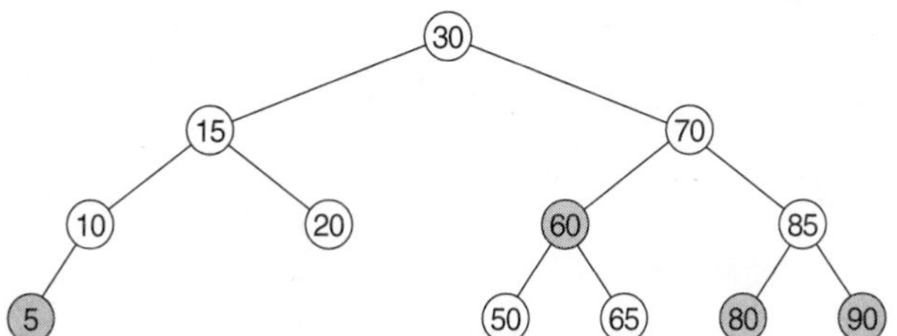

figure 19.34

A red–black tree: The insertion sequence is 10, 85, 15, 70, 20, 60, 30, 50, 65, 80, 90, 40, 5, and 55 (shaded nodes are red).

19.5.1 bottom-up insertion

Recall that a new item is always inserted as a leaf in the tree. If we color a new item black, we violate property 4 because we create a longer path of black nodes. Thus a new item must be colored red. If the parent is black, we are done; thus the insertion of 25 into the tree shown in Figure 19.34 is trivial. If the parent is already red, we violate property 3 by having consecutive red nodes. In this case, we have to adjust the tree to ensure that property 3 is enforced and do so without introducing a violation of property 4. The basic operations used are color changes and tree rotations.

New items must be colored red. If the parent is already red, we must recolor and/or rotate to remove consecutive red nodes.

We have to consider several cases (each with mirror-image symmetry) if the parent is red. First, suppose that the sibling of the parent is black (we adopt the convention that `null` nodes are black), which would apply for the insertions of 3 or 8 but not for the insertion of 99. Let *X* be the newly added leaf, *P* be its parent, *S* be the sibling of the parent (if it exists), and *G* be the grandparent. Only *X* and *P* are red in this case; *G* is black because otherwise there would be two consecutive red nodes *prior* to the insertion—a violation of property 3. Adopting the AVL tree terminology, we say that relative to *G*, *X* can be either an outside or inside node.[2] If *X* is an outside grandchild, a single rotation of its parent and grandparent along with some color changes will restore property 3. If *X* is an inside grandchild, a double rotation along with some color changes are needed. The single rotation is shown in Figure 19.35, and the double rotation is shown in Figure 19.36. Even though *X* is a leaf, we have drawn a more general case that allows *X* to be in the middle of the tree. We use this more general rotation later in the algorithm.

If the parent's sibling is black, a single or double rotation fixes things, as in an AVL tree.

Before continuing, consider why these rotations are correct. We need to be sure that there are never two consecutive red nodes. As shown in Figure 19.36, for instance, the only possible instances of consecutive red nodes would be between *P* and one of its children or between *G* and *C*. But

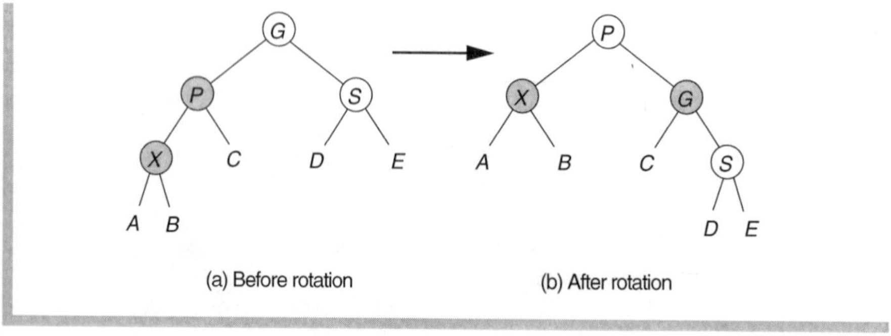

figure 19.35

If *S* is black, a single rotation between parent and grandparent, with appropriate color changes, restores property 3 if *X* is an outside grandchild.

2. See Section 19.4.1, page 651.

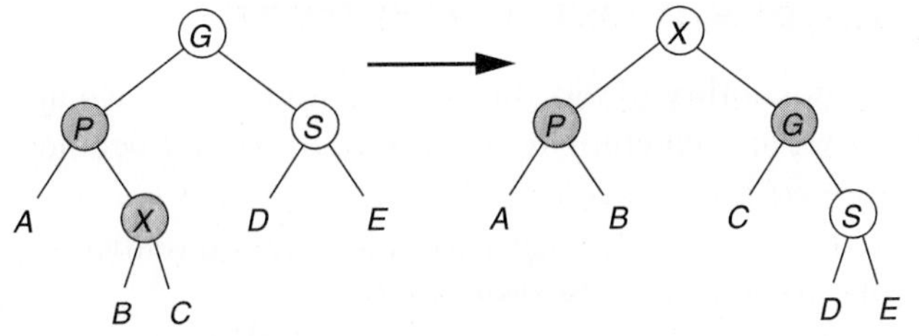

(a) Before rotation (b) After rotation

figure 19.36

If S is black, a double rotation involving X, the parent, and the grandparent, with appropriate color changes, restores property 3 if X is an inside grandchild.

the roots of A, B, and C must be black; otherwise, there would have been additional property 3 violations in the original tree. In the original tree, there is one black node on the path from the subtree root to A, B, and C and two black nodes on the paths to D and E. We can verify that this pattern holds after rotation and recoloring.

So far so good. But what happens if S is red, as when we attempt to insert 79 in the tree shown in Figure 19.34? Then neither the single nor the double rotation works because both result in consecutive red nodes. In fact, in this case three nodes must be on the path to D and E and only one can be black. Hence both S and the subtree's new root must be colored red. For instance, the single rotation case that occurs when X is an outside grandchild is shown in Figure 19.37. Although this rotation seems to work, there is a problem: What happens if the parent of the subtree root (i.e., X's original great grandparent) is also red? We could percolate this procedure up toward the root until we no longer have two consecutive red nodes or we reach the root (which would be recolored black). But then we would be back to making a pass up the tree, as in the AVL tree.

If the parent's sibling is red, then after we fix things, we induce consecutive red nodes at a higher level. We need to iterate up the tree to fix things.

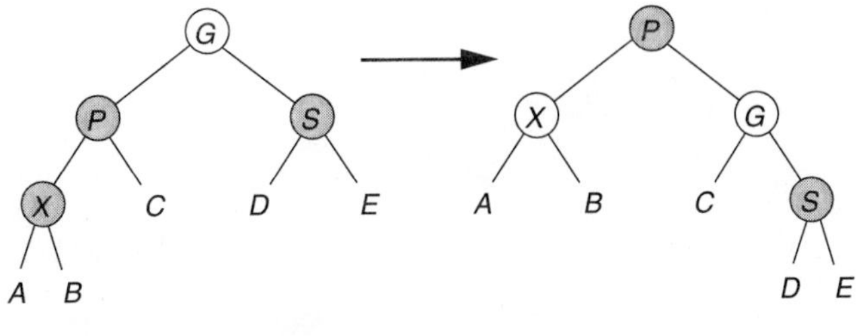

(a) Before rotation (b) After rotation

figure 19.37

If S is red, a single rotation between parent and grandparent, with appropriate color changes, restores property 3 between X and P.

19.5.2 top-down red–black trees

To avoid iterating back up the tree, we ensure as we descend the tree that the sibling's parent is not red. We can do so with color flips and/or rotations.

To avoid the possibility of having to rotate up the tree, we apply a top-down procedure as we are searching for the insertion point. Specifically, we guarantee that, when we arrive at a leaf and insert a node, *S* is not red. Then we can just add a red leaf and if necessary use one rotation (either single or double). The procedure is conceptually easy.

On the way down, when we see a node *X* that has two red children, we make *X* red and its two children black. Figure 19.38 shows this color flip. (If *X* is the root, it will be made red by this process. We could then recolor it back to black, without violating any red–black tree properties.) The number of black nodes on paths below *X* remains unchanged. However, if *X*'s parent is red, we would introduce two consecutive red nodes. But in this case, we can apply either the single rotation in Figure 19.35 or the double rotation in Figure 19.36. But what if *X*'s parent's sibling is also red? *This situation cannot happen.* If on the way down the tree, we see a node *Y* that has two red children, we know that *Y*'s grandchildren must be black. And as *Y*'s children are also made black via the color flip—even after the rotation that may occur—we would not see another red node for two levels. Thus when we see *X*, if *X*'s parent is red, *X*'s parent's sibling cannot also be red.

For example, suppose that we want to insert 45 in the tree shown in Figure 19.34. On the way down the tree we see node 50, which has two red children. Thus we perform a color flip, making 50 red and 40 and 55 black. The result is shown in Figure 19.39. However, now 50 and 60 are both red.

figure 19.38

Color flip: Only if *X* 's parent is red do we continue with a rotation.

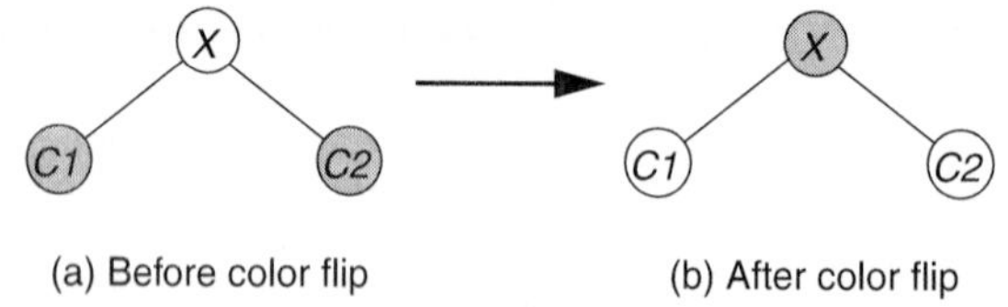

figure 19.39

A color flip at 50 induces a violation; because the violation is outside, a single rotation fixes it.

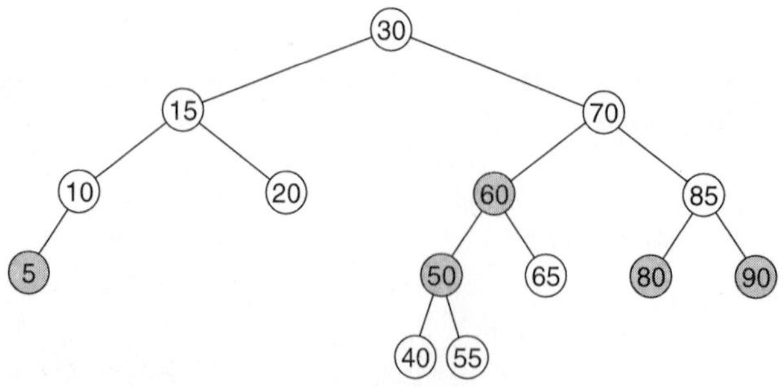

We perform a single rotation (because 50 is an outside node) between 60 and 70, thus making 60 the black root of 30's right subtree and making 70 red, as shown in Figure 19.40. We then continue, performing an identical action if we see other nodes on the path that contain two red children. It happens that there are none.

When we get to the leaf, we insert 45 as a red node, and as the parent is black, we are done. The resulting tree is shown in Figure 19.41. Had the parent been red, we would have needed to perform one rotation.

As Figure 19.41 shows, the red–black tree that results is frequently well balanced. Experiments suggest that the number of nodes traversed during an average red–black tree search is almost identical to the average for AVL trees, even though the red–black tree's balancing properties are slightly weaker. The advantage of a red–black tree is the relatively low overhead required to perform insertion and the fact that, in practice, rotations occur relatively infrequently.

19.5.3 java implementation

An actual implementation is complicated, not only by many possible rotations, but also by the possibility that some subtrees (such as the right subtree of the node containing 10 in Figure 19.41) might be empty and by the special

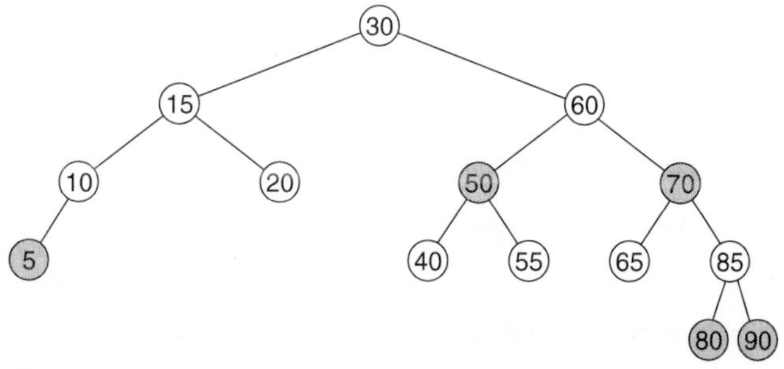

figure 19.40

Result of single rotation that fixes the violation at node 50

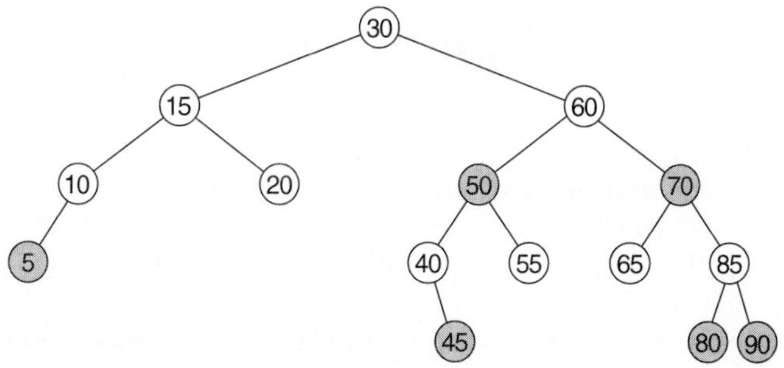

figure 19.41

Insertion of 45 as a red node

We remove special cases by using a sentinel for the `null` node and a pseudoroot. Doing so requires minor modifications of almost every routine.

case of dealing with the root (which, among other things, has no parent). To remove special cases, we use two sentinels.

- We use `nullNode` in place of a `null` link; `nullNode` will always be colored black.
- We use `header` as a pseudoroot; it has a key value of $-\infty$ and a right link to the real root.

On the way down, we maintain references to the current, parent, grandparent, and great-grandparent nodes.

Therefore even basic routines such as `isEmpty` need to be altered. Consequently, inheriting from `BinarySearchTree` does not make sense, and we write the class from scratch. The `RedBlackNode` class, which is nested in `RedBlackTree`, is shown in Figure 19.42 and is straightforward. The `RedBlackTree` class skeleton is shown in Figure 19.43. Lines 55 and 56 declare the sentinels that we discussed previously. Four references—`current`, `parent`, `grand`, and `great`—are used in the `insert` routine. Their placement at lines 62–65 allows them to be shared by `insert` and the `handleReorient` routine. The `remove` method is unimplemented.

The remaining routines are similar to their `BinarySearchTree` counterparts, except that they have different implementations because of the sentinel nodes. The constructor could be provided with the value of $-\infty$, to initialize the header node. We do not do that. The alternative is to use the `compare` method,

figure 19.42

The `RedBlackNode` class

```
private static class RedBlackNode<AnyType>
{
        // Constructors
    RedBlackNode( AnyType theElement )
    {
        this( theElement, null, null );
    }

    RedBlackNode( AnyType theElement, RedBlackNode<AnyType> lt,
                                      RedBlackNode<AnyType> rt )
    {
        element  = theElement;
        left     = lt;
        right    = rt;
        color    = RedBlackTree.BLACK;
    }

    AnyType               element;     // The data in the node
    RedBlackNode<AnyType> left;        // Left child
    RedBlackNode<AnyType> right;       // Right child
    int                   color;       // Color
}
```

```
package weiss.nonstandard;

// RedBlackTree class
//
// CONSTRUCTION: with no parameters
//
// ******************PUBLIC OPERATIONS*********************
// Same as BinarySearchTree; omitted for brevity
// ******************ERRORS********************************
// Exceptions are thrown by insert if warranted and remove.

public class RedBlackTree<AnyType extends Comparable<? super AnyType>>
{
    public RedBlackTree( )
      { /* Figure 19.44 */ }

    public void insert( AnyType item )
      { /* Figure 19.47 */ }
    public void remove( AnyType x )
      { /* Not implemented */ }

    public AnyType findMin( )
      { /* See online code */ }
    public AnyType findMax( )
      { /* Similar to findMin */ }
    public AnyType find( AnyType x )
      { /* Figure 19.46 */ }

    public void makeEmpty( )
      { header.right = nullNode; }
    public boolean isEmpty( )
      { return header.right == nullNode; }
    public void printTree( )
      { printTree( header.right ); }

    private void printTree( RedBlackNode<AnyType> t )
      { /* Figure 19.45 */ }
    private final int compare( AnyType item, RedBlackNode<AnyType> t )
      { /* Figure 19.47 */ }
    private void handleReorient( AnyType item )
      { /* Figure 19.48 */ }
    private RedBlackNode<AnyType>
    rotate( AnyType item, RedBlackNode<AnyType> parent )
      { /* Figure 19.49 */ }

    private static <AnyType>
    RedBlackNode<AnyType> rotateWithLeftChild( RedBlackNode<AnyType> k2 )
      { /* Implementation is as usual; see online code */ }
    private static <AnyType>
    RedBlackNode<AnyType> rotateWithRightChild( RedBlackNode<AnyType> k1 )
      { /* Implementation is as usual; see online code */ }
```

figure 19.43a

The `RedBlackTree` class skeleton (*continues*)

figure 19.43b
The RedBlackTree class skeleton (*continued*)

```
    private static class RedBlackNode<AnyType>
      { /* Figure 19.42 */ }

    private RedBlackNode<AnyType> header;
    private RedBlackNode<AnyType> nullNode;

    private static final int BLACK = 1;    // BLACK must be 1
    private static final int RED   = 0;

        // Used in insert routine and its helpers
    private RedBlackNode<AnyType> current;
    private RedBlackNode<AnyType> parent;
    private RedBlackNode<AnyType> grand;
    private RedBlackNode<AnyType> great;
}
```

defined at lines 38 and 39, where appropriate. A constructor is shown in Figure 19.44. The constructor allocates `nullNode` and then the header and sets the header's `left` and `right` links to `nullNode`.

> Tests against `null` are replaced by tests against `nullNode`.

Figure 19.45 shows the simplest change that results from the use of the sentinels. The test against `null` needs to be replaced with a test against `nullNode`.

For the `find` routine shown in Figure 19.46 we use a common trick. Before we begin the search, we place `x` in the `nullNode` sentinel. Thus we are guaranteed to match `x` eventually, even if `x` is not found. If the match occurs at `nullNode`, we can tell that the item was not found. We use this trick in the `insert` procedure.

> When performing a `find` operation, we copy `x` into the `nullNode` sentinel to avoid extra tests.

The `insert` method follows directly from our description and is shown in Figure 19.47. The `while` loop encompassing lines 11 to 20 descends the tree and fixes nodes that have two red children by calling `handleReorient`, as shown in Figure 19.48. To do so, it keeps track of not only the current node but also the parent, grandparent, and great-grandparent. Note that after a rotation the

figure 19.44
The RedBlackTree constructor

```
    /**
     * Construct the tree.
     */
    public RedBlackTree( )
    {
        nullNode = new RedBlackNode<AnyType>( null );
        nullNode.left = nullNode.right = nullNode;
        header      = new RedBlackNode<AnyType>( null );
        header.left = header.right = nullNode;
    }
```

```
/**
 * Internal method to print a subtree in sorted order.
 * @param t the node that roots the tree.
 */
private void printTree( RedBlackNode<AnyType> t )
{
    if( t != nullNode )
    {
        printTree( t.left );
        System.out.println( t.element );
        printTree( t.right );
    }
}
```

figure 19.45

The `printTree` method for the `RedBlackTree` class

```
/**
 * Find an item in the tree.
 * @param x the item to search for.
 * @return the matching item or null if not found.
 */
public AnyType find( AnyType x )
{
    nullNode.element = x;
    current = header.right;

    for( ; ; )
    {
        if( x.compareTo( current.element ) < 0 )
            current = current.left;
        else if( x.compareTo( current.element ) > 0 )
            current = current.right;
        else if( current != nullNode )
            return current.element;
        else
            return null;
    }
}
```

figure 19.46

The `RedBlackTree` `find` routine. Note the use of `header` and `nullNode`.

values stored in the grandparent and great-grandparent are no longer correct. However, they will be restored by the time they are next needed. When the loop ends, either `x` is found (as indicated by `current!=nullNode`) or `x` is not found (as indicated by `current==nullNode`). If `x` is found, we throw an exception at line 24. Otherwise, `x` is not already in the tree, and it needs to be made a child of `parent`. We allocate a new node (as the new `current` node), attach it to the parent, and call `handleReorient` at lines 25–32.

The code is relatively compact for the number of cases involved and the fact that the implementation is nonrecursive. For these reasons the red–black tree performs well.

```
    /**
     * Insert into the tree.
     * @param item the item to insert.
     * @throws DuplicateItemException if item is already present.
     */
    public void insert( AnyType item )
    {
        current = parent = grand = header;
        nullNode.element = item;

        while( compare( item, current ) != 0 )
        {
            great = grand; grand = parent; parent = current;
            current = compare( item, current ) < 0 ?
                         current.left : current.right;

                // Check if two red children; fix if so
            if( current.left.color == RED && current.right.color == RED )
                 handleReorient( item );
        }

            // Insertion fails if already present
        if( current != nullNode )
            throw new DuplicateItemException( item.toString( ) );
        current = new RedBlackNode<AnyType>( item, nullNode, nullNode );

            // Attach to parent
        if( compare( item, parent ) < 0 )
            parent.left = current;
        else
            parent.right = current;
        handleReorient( item );
    }

    /**
     * Compare item and t.element, using compareTo, with
     * caveat that if t is header, then item is always larger.
     * This routine is called if it is possible that t is a header.
     * If it is not possible for t to be a header, use compareTo directly.
     */
    private final int compare( AnyType item, RedBlackNode<AnyType> t )
    {
        if( t == header )
            return 1;
        else
            return item.compareTo( t.element );
    }
```

figure 19.47
The insert and compare routines for the RedBlackTree class

```
1      /**
2       * Internal routine that is called during an insertion
3       * if a node has two red children. Performs flip and rotations.
4       * @param item the item being inserted.
5       */
6      private void handleReorient( AnyType item )
7      {
8              // Do the color flip
9          current.color = RED;
10         current.left.color = BLACK;
11         current.right.color = BLACK;
12
13         if( parent.color == RED )   // Have to rotate
14         {
15             grand.color = RED;
16             if( ( compare( item, grand ) < 0 ) != ( compare( item, parent ) < 0 ) )
17                 parent = rotate( item, grand );  // Start dbl rotate
18             current = rotate( item, great );
19
20             current.color = BLACK;
21         }
22         header.right.color = BLACK; // Make root black
23     }
```

figure 19.48

The `handleReorient` routine, which is called if a node has two red children or when a new node is inserted

At lines 11 and 14 we see the call to `compare`, which is used since the header might be one of the nodes involved in the comparison. The value in the header is logically $-\infty$, but is actually `null`. The implementation of `compare` ensures that the value in the header `compares` as less than any other value. `compare` is also shown in Figure 19.47.

The code used to perform a single rotation is shown in the `rotate` method in Figure 19.49. Because the resultant tree must be attached to a parent, `rotate` takes the parent node as a parameter. Rather than keep track of the type of rotation (left or right) as we descend the tree, we pass `item` as a parameter. We expect very few rotations during the insertion, so doing it this way is not only simple but is actually faster.

The `rotate` method has four possibilities. The `?:` operator collapses the code but is logically equivalent to an `if/else` test.

The `handleReorient` routine calls `rotate` as necessary to perform either a single or double rotation. As a double rotation is just two single rotations, we can test whether we have an inside case, and if so, do an extra rotation between the current node and its parent (bypassing the grandparent to `rotate`). In either case we rotate between the parent and grandparent (by passing the great-grandparent to `rotate`). This action is succinctly coded in lines 16–17 of Figure 19.48.

```java
/**
 * Internal routine that performs a single or double rotation.
 * Because the result is attached to the parent, there are 4 cases.
 * Called by handleReorient.
 * @param item the item in handleReorient.
 * @param parent the parent of the root of the rotated subtree.
 * @return the root of the rotated subtree.
 */
private RedBlackNode<AnyType>
rotate( AnyType item, RedBlackNode<AnyType> parent )
{
    if( compare( item, parent ) < 0 )
        return parent.left = compare( item, parent.left ) < 0 ?
            rotateWithLeftChild( parent.left )  :  // LL
            rotateWithRightChild( parent.left ) ;  // LR
    else
        return parent.right = compare( item, parent.right ) < 0 ?
            rotateWithLeftChild( parent.right ) :  // RL
            rotateWithRightChild( parent.right );  // RR
}
```

figure 19.49

A routine for performing an appropriate rotation

19.5.4 top-down deletion

Deletion in red–black trees can also be performed top-down. Needless to say, an actual implementation is fairly complicated because the `remove` algorithm for unbalanced search trees is nontrivial in the first place. The normal binary search tree deletion algorithm removes nodes that are leaves or have one child. Recall that nodes with two children are never removed; their contents are simply replaced.

Deletion is fairly complex. The basic idea is to ensure that the deleted node is red.

If the node to be deleted is red, there is no problem. However, if the node to be deleted is black, its removal will violate property 4. The solution to the problem is to ensure that any node we are about to delete is red.

Throughout this discussion, we let X be the current node, T be its sibling, and P be their parent. We begin by coloring the sentinel root red. As we traverse down the tree, we attempt to ensure that X is red. When we arrive at a new node, we are certain that P is red (inductively, by the invariant that we are trying to maintain) and that X and T are black (because we cannot have two consecutive red nodes). There are two main cases, along with the usual symmetric variants (which are omitted).

First, suppose that X has two black children. There are three subcases, which depend on T's children.

1. *T* has two black children: Flip colors (Figure 19.50).
2. *T* has an outer red child: Perform a single rotation (Figure 19.51).
3. *T* has an inner red child: Perform a double rotation (Figure 19.52).

Examination of the rotations shows that if *T* has two red children, either a single rotation or double rotation will work (so it makes sense to do the single rotation). Note that, if *X* is a leaf, its two children are black, so we can always apply one of these three mechanisms to make *X* red.

Second, suppose that one of *X*'s children is red. Because the rotations in the first main case always color *X* red, if *X* has a red child, consecutive red nodes would be introduced. Thus we need an alternative solution. In this case, we fall through to the next level, obtaining a new *X*, *T*, and *P*. If we are lucky, we will fall onto a red node (we have at least a 50 percent chance that this will

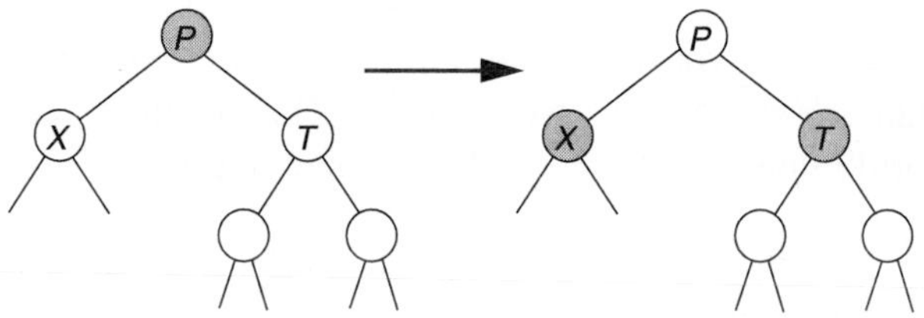

figure 19.50

X has two black children, and both of its sibling's children are black; do a color flip.

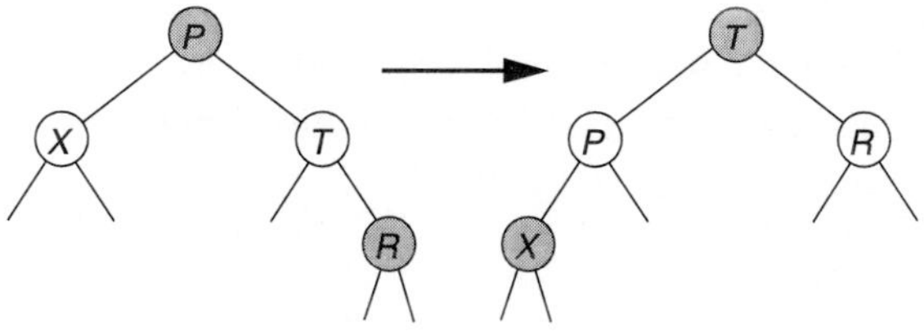

figure 19.51

X has two black children, and the outer child of its sibling is red; do a single rotation.

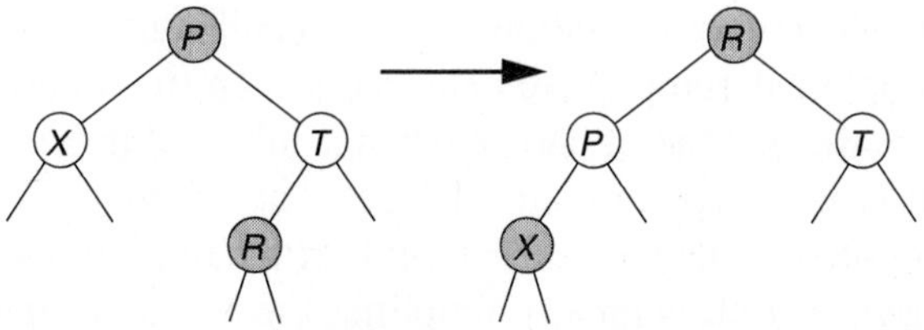

figure 19.52

X has two black children, and the inner child of its sibling is red; do a double rotation.

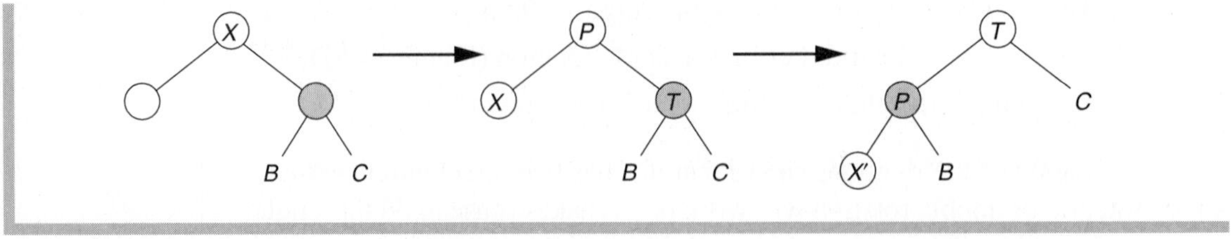

figure 19.53

X is black, and at least one child is red; if we fall through to the next level and land on a red child, fine; if not, we rotate a sibling and parent.

happen), thereby making the new current node red. Otherwise, we have the situation shown in Figure 19.53. That is, the current X is black, the current T is red, and the current P is black. We can then rotate T and P, thereby making X's new parent red; X and its new grandparent are black. Now X is not yet red, but we are back to the starting point (although one level deeper). This outcome is good enough because it shows that we can iteratively descend the tree. Thus, so long as we eventually either reach a node that has two black children or land on a red node, we are okay. This result is guaranteed for the deletion algorithm because the two eventual states are

- X is a leaf, which is always handled by the main case since X has two black children.
- X has only one child, for which the main case applies if the child is black, and if it is red, we can delete X, if necessary, and make the child black.

Lazy deletion is the marking of items as deleted.

Lazy deletion, in which items are marked as deleted but not actually deleted, is sometimes used. However, lazy deletion wastes space and complicates other routines (see Exercise 19.23).

19.6 aa-trees

The *AA-tree* is the method of choice when a balanced tree is needed, a casual implementation is acceptable, and deletions are needed.

Because of many possible rotations, the red–black tree is fairly tricky to code. In particular, the `remove` operation is quite challenging. In this section we describe a simple but competitive balanced search tree known as an *AA-tree.* The AA-tree is the method of choice when a balanced tree is needed, a casual implementation is acceptable, and deletions are needed. The AA-tree adds one extra condition to the red–black tree: Left children may not be red.

This simple restriction greatly simplifies the red–black tree algorithms for two reasons: First, it eliminates about half of the restructuring cases; second, it simplifies the `remove` algorithm by removing an annoying case. That is, if an internal node has only one child, the child must be a red right child because red left children are now illegal, whereas a single black child would violate property 4 for red–black trees. Thus we can always replace an internal node with the smallest node in its right subtree. That smallest node is either a leaf or has a red child and can be easily bypassed and removed.

To simplify the implementation further, we represent balance information in a more direct way. Instead of storing a color with each node, we store the node's level. The *level of a node* represents the number of left links on the path to the `nullNode` sentinel and is

The *level of a node* in an AA-tree represents the number of left links on the path to the `nullNode` sentinel.

- Level 1, if the node is a leaf
- The level of its parent, if the node is red
- One less than the level of its parent, if the node is black

The result is an AA-tree. If we translate the structure requirement from colors to levels, we know that the left child must be one level lower than its parent and that the right child may be zero or one level lower than its parent (but not more). A *horizontal link* is a connection between a node and a child of equal levels. The coloring properties imply

A *horizontal link* in an AA-tree is a connection between a node and a child of equal levels. A horizontal link should go only to the right, and there should not be two consecutive horizontal links.

1. Horizontal links are right links (because only right children may be red)
2. There may not be two consecutive horizontal links (because there cannot be consecutive red nodes)
3. Nodes at level 2 or higher must have two children
4. If a node does not have a right horizontal link, its two children are at the same level

Figure 19.54 shows a sample AA-tree. The root of this tree is the node with key 30. Searching is done with the usual algorithm. And as usual, `insert` and `remove` are more difficult because the natural binary search tree algorithms may induce a violation of the horizontal link properties. Not surprisingly, tree rotations can fix all the problems encountered.

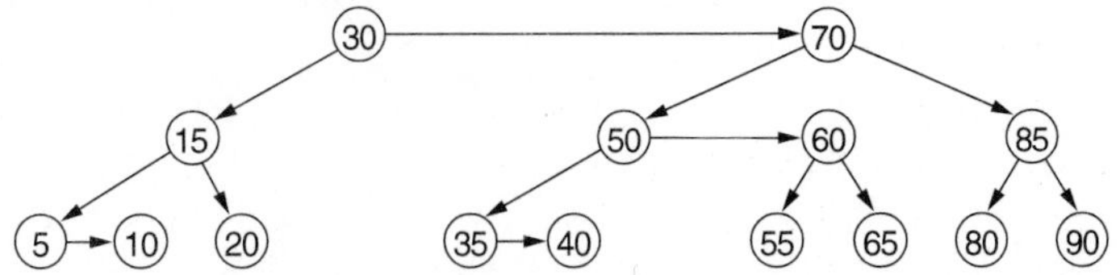

figure 19.54

AA-tree resulting from the insertion of 10, 85, 15, 70, 20, 60, 30, 50, 65, 80, 90, 40, 5, 55, and 35

19.6.1 insertion

Insertion is done by using the usual recursive algorithm and two method calls.

Insertion of a new item is always done at the bottom level. As usual, that may create problems. In the tree shown in Figure 19.54, insertion of 2 would create a horizontal left link, whereas insertion of 45 would generate consecutive right links. Consequently, after a node has been added at the bottom level, we may need to perform some rotations to restore the horizontal link properties.

Left horizontal links are removed by a skew (rotation between a node and its left child). Consecutive right horizontal links are fixed by a split (rotation between a node and its right child). A skew precedes a split.

In both cases, a single rotation fixes the problem. We remove left horizontal links by rotating between the node and its left child, a procedure called `skew`. We fix consecutive right horizontal links by rotating between the first and second (of the three) nodes joined by the two links, a procedure called `split`.

The `skew` procedure is illustrated in Figure 19.55, and the `split` procedure is illustrated in Figure 19.56. Although a `skew` removes a left horizontal link, it might create consecutive right horizontal links because *X*'s right child might also be horizontal. Thus we would process a `skew` first and then a `split`. After a `split`, the middle node increases in level. That may cause problems for the original parent of *X* by creating either a left horizontal link or consecutive right horizontal links: Both problems can be fixed by applying the `skew/split` strategy on the path up toward the root. It can be done automatically if we use recursion, and a recursive implementation of `insert` is only two method calls longer than the corresponding unbalanced search tree routine.

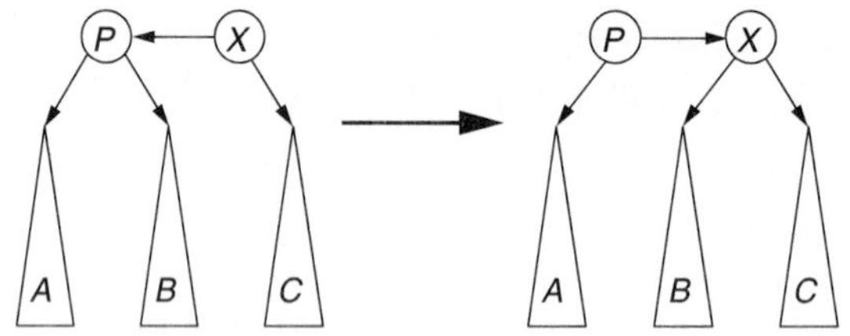

figure 19.55
The `skew` procedure is a simple rotation between *X* and *P*.

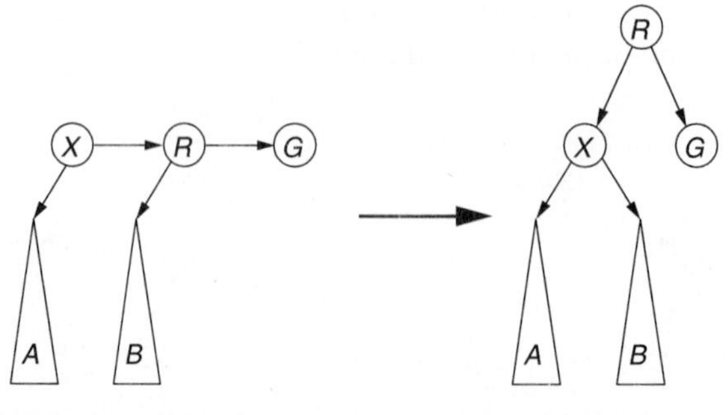

figure 19.56
The `split` procedure is a simple rotation between *X* and *R*; note that *R*'s level increases.

To show the algorithm in action, we insert 45 in the AA-tree shown in Figure 19.54. In Figure 19.57, when 45 is added at the bottom level, consecutive horizontal links form. Then skew/split pairs are applied as necessary from the bottom up toward the root. Thus, at node 35 a split is needed because of the consecutive horizontal right links. The result of the split is shown in Figure 19.58. When the recursion backs up to node 50, we encounter a horizontal left link. Thus we perform a skew at 50 to remove the horizontal left link (the result is shown in Figure 19.59) and then a split at 40 to remove the consecutive horizontal right links. The result after the split is shown in Figure 19.60. The result of the split is that 50 is on level 3 and is a

This is a rare algorithm in that it is harder to simulate on paper than implement on a computer.

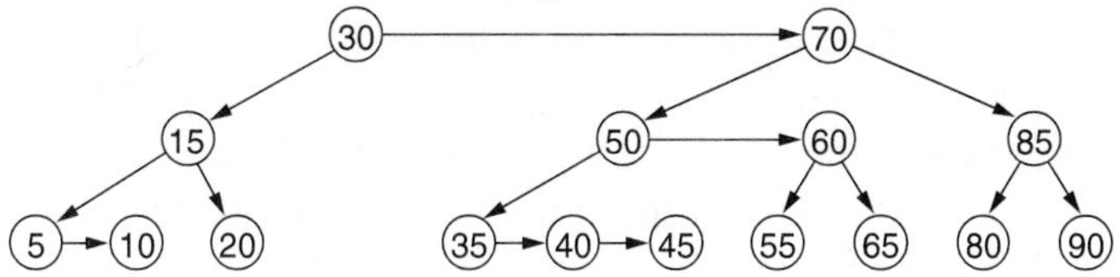

figure 19.57

After insertion of 45 in the sample tree; consecutive horizontal links are introduced, starting at 35.

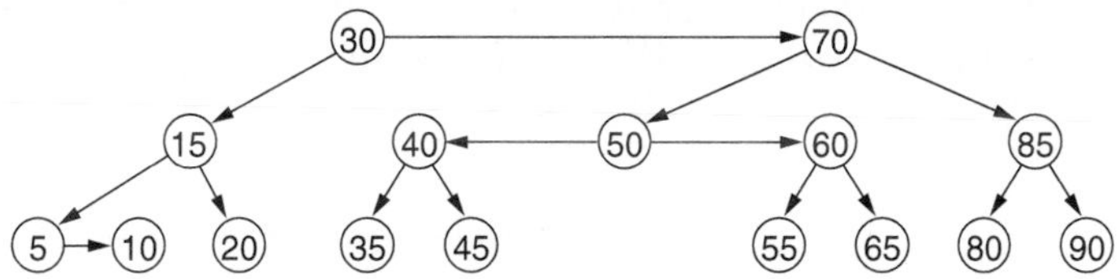

figure 19.58

After split at 35; a left horizontal link at 50 is introduced.

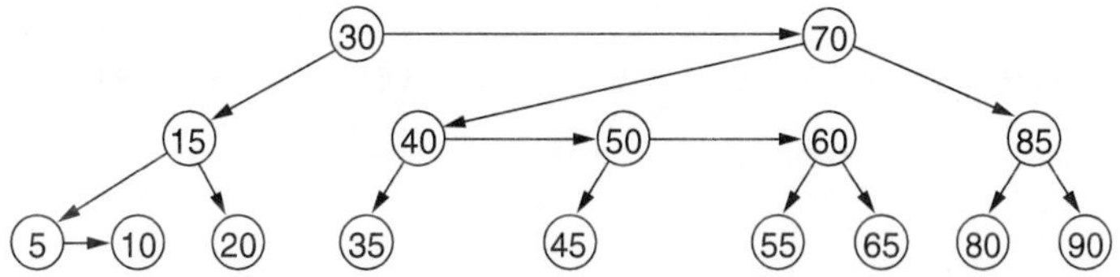

figure 19.59

After skew at 50; consecutive horizontal nodes are introduced starting at 40.

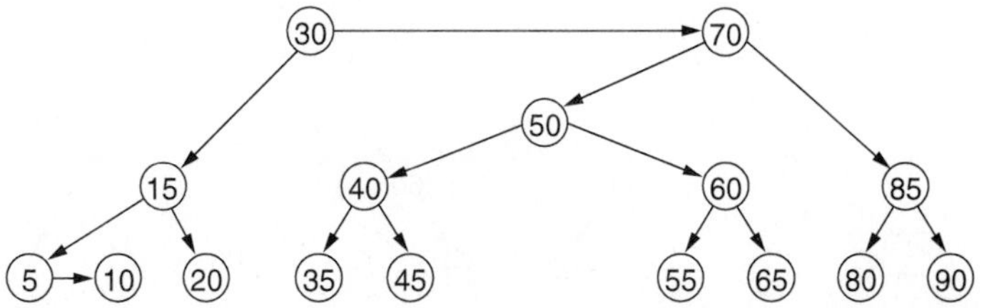

figure 19.60

After split at 40; 50 is now on the same level as 70, inducing an illegal left horizontal link.

left horizontal child of 70. Therefore we need to perform another `skew/split` pair. The `skew` at 70 removes the left horizontal link at the top level but creates consecutive right horizontal nodes, as shown in Figure 19.61. When the final `split` is applied, the consecutive horizontal nodes are removed and 50 becomes the new root of the tree. The result is shown in Figure 19.62.

19.6.2 deletion

Deletion is made easier because the one-child case can occur only at level 1 and we are willing to use recursion.

For general binary search trees, the `remove` algorithm is broken into three cases: The item to be removed is a leaf, has one child, or has two children. For AA-trees, we treat the one-child case the same way as the two-child case because the one-child case can occur only at level 1. Moreover, the two-child case is also easy because the node used as the replacement value is guaranteed to be at level 1 and at worst has only a right horizontal link. Thus everything boils down to being able to `remove` a level-1 node. Clearly, this action might affect the balance (consider, for instance, the removal of 20 in Figure 19.62).

We let *T* be the current node and use recursion. If the deletion has altered one of *T*'s children to two less than *T*'s level, *T*'s level needs to be lowered also (only the child entered by the recursive call could actually be affected, but for simplicity we do not keep track of it). Furthermore, if *T* has a horizontal right link, its right child's level must also be lowered. At this point, we

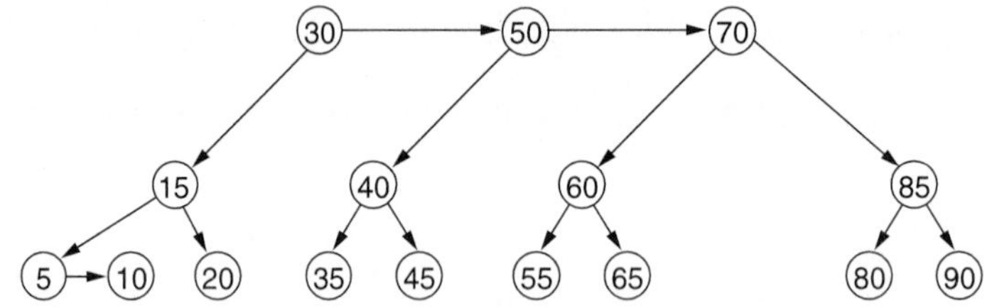

figure 19.61
After `skew` at 70; consecutive horizontal links are introduced, starting at 30.

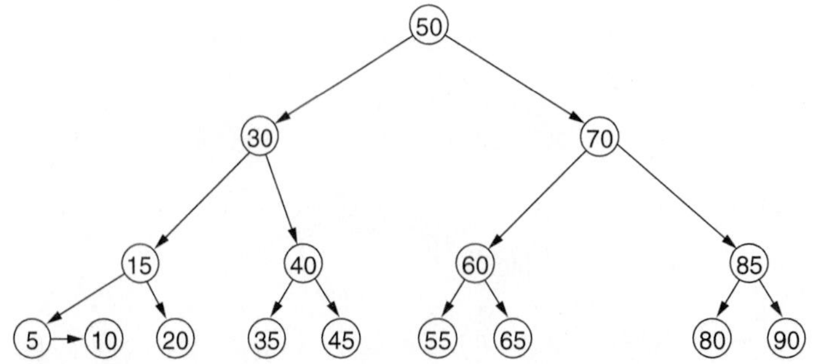

figure 19.62
After `split` at 30; the insertion is complete.

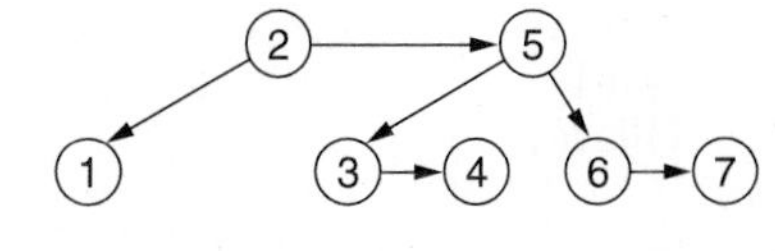

figure 19.63

When 1 is deleted, all nodes become level 1, thereby introducing horizontal left links.

could have six nodes on the same level: *T*, *T*'s horizontal right child *R*, *R*'s two children, and those children's horizontal right children. Figure 19.63 shows the simplest possible scenario.

After a recursive removal, three skews and two splits guarantee rebalancing.

After node 1 has been removed, node 2 and thus node 5 become level-1 nodes. First, we must fix the left horizontal link that is now introduced between nodes 5 and 3. Doing so essentially requires two rotations: one between nodes 5 and 3 and then one between nodes 5 and 4. In this case, the current node *T* is not involved. However, if a deletion came from the right side, *T*'s left node could suddenly become horizontal; that would require a similar double rotation (starting at *T*). To avoid testing all these cases, we merely call `skew` three times. Once we have done that, two calls to `split` suffice to rearrange the horizontal edges.

19.6.3 java implementation

The implementation is relatively simple (compared to those of the red–black tree).

The class skeleton for the AA-tree is shown in Figure 19.64 and includes a nested node class. Much of it duplicates previous tree code. Again, we use a `nullNode` sentinel; however, we do not need a pseudoroot. The constructor allocates `nullNode`, as for red–black trees, and has `root` reference at it. The `nullNode` is at level 0. The routines use private helpers.

```
package weiss.nonstandard;

// AATree class
//
// CONSTRUCTION: with no initializer
//
// ******************PUBLIC OPERATIONS*********************
// Same as BinarySearchTree; omitted for brevity
// ******************ERRORS*********************************
// Exceptions are thrown by insert and remove if warranted

public class AATree<AnyType extends Comparable<? super AnyType>>
{
    public AATree( )
    {
        nullNode = new AANode<AnyType>( null, null, null );
```

Figure 19.64a

The class skeleton for AA-trees (*continues*)

figure 19.64b

The class skeleton for AA-trees (*continues*)

```
        nullNode.left = nullNode.right = nullNode;
        nullNode.level = 0;
        root = nullNode;
    }

    public void insert( AnyType x )
      { root = insert( x, root ); }

    public void remove( AnyType x )
      { deletedNode = nullNode; root = remove( x, root ); }
    public AnyType findMin( )
      { /* Implementation is as usual; see online code */ }
    public AnyType findMax( )
      { /* Implementation is as usual; see online code */ }
    public AnyType find( AnyType x )
      { /* Implementation is as usual; see online code */ }
    public void makeEmpty( )
      { root = nullNode; }
    public boolean isEmpty( )
      { return root == nullNode; }

    private AANode<AnyType> insert( AnyType x, AANode<AnyType> t )
      { /* Figure 19.65 */ }
    private AANode<AnyType> remove( AnyType x, AANode<AnyType> t )
      { /* Figure 19.67 */ }
    private AANode<AnyType> skew( AANode<AnyType> t )
      { /* Figure 19.66 */ }
    private AANode<AnyType> split( AANode<AnyType> t )
      { /* Figure 19.66 */ }

    private static <AnyType>
    AANode<AnyType> rotateWithLeftChild( AANode<AnyType> k2 )
      { /* Implementation is as usual; see online code */ }
    private static <AnyType>
    AANode<AnyType> rotateWithRightChild( AANode<AnyType> k1 )
      { /* Implementation is as usual; see online code */ }

    private static class AANode<AnyType>
    {
            // Constructors
        AANode( AnyType theElement )
        {
            element = theElement;
            left    = right = nullNode;
            level   = 1;
        }

        AnyType         element;   // The data in the node
        AANode<AnyType> left;      // Left child
        AANode<AnyType> right;     // Right child
        int             level;     // Level
    }

```

```
    private AANode<AnyType> root;
    private AANode<AnyType> nullNode;

    private AANode<AnyType> deletedNode;
    private AANode<AnyType> lastNode;
}
```

figure 19.64c

The class skeleton for AA-trees (*continued*)

The `insert` method is shown in Figure 19.65. As mentioned earlier in this section, it is nearly identical to the recursive binary search tree `insert`. The only difference is that it adds a call to `skew` followed by a call to `split`. In Figure 19.66 `skew` and `split` are easily implemented, using the already existing tree rotations. Finally, `remove` is shown in Figure 19.67.

To help us out, we keep two instance variables, `deletedNode` and `lastNode`. When we traverse a right child, we adjust `deletedNode`. Because we call `remove` recursively until we reach the bottom (we do not test for equality on the way down), we are guaranteed that, if the item to be removed is in the tree, `deletedNode` will reference the node that contains it. Note that this technique can be used in the `find` procedure to replace the three-way comparisons done at each node with two-way comparisons at each node plus one

```
    /**
     * Internal method to insert into a subtree.
     * @param x the item to insert.
     * @param t the node that roots the tree.
     * @return the new root.
     * @throws DuplicateItemException if x is already present.
     */
    private AANode<AnyType> insert( AnyType x, AANode<AnyType> t )
    {
        if( t == nullNode )
            t = new AANode<AnyType>( x, nullNode, nullNode );
        else if( x.compareTo( t.element ) < 0 )
            t.left = insert( x, t.left );
        else if( x.compareTo( t.element ) > 0 )
            t.right = insert( x, t.right );
        else
            throw new DuplicateItemException( x.toString( ) );

        t = skew( t );
        t = split( t );
        return t;
    }
```

figure 19.65

The `insert` routine for the `AATree` class

```
/**
 * Skew primitive for AA-trees.
 * @param t the node that roots the tree.
 * @return the new root after the rotation.
 */
private static <AnyType> AANode<AnyType> skew( AANode<AnyType> t )
{
    if( t.left.level == t.level )
        t = rotateWithLeftChild( t );
    return t;
}

/**
 * Split primitive for AA-trees.
 * @param t the node that roots the tree.
 * @return the new root after the rotation.
 */
private static <AnyType> AANode<AnyType> split( AANode<AnyType> t )
{
    if( t.right.right.level == t.level )
    {
        t = rotateWithRightChild( t );
        t.level++;
    }
    return t;
}
```

figure 19.66

The `skew` and `split` procedures for the `AATree` class

The `deletedNode` variable references the node containing x (if x is found) or `nullNode` if x is not found. The `lastNode` variable references the replacement node. We use two-way comparisons instead of three-way comparisons.

extra equality test at the bottom. `lastNode` points at the level-1 node at which this search terminates. Because we do not stop until we reach the bottom, if the item is in the tree, `lastNode` will reference the level-1 node that contains the replacement value and must be removed from the tree.

After a given recursive call terminates, we are either at level 1 or we are not. If we are at level 1, we can copy the node's value into the internal node that is to be replaced; we can then bypass the level-1 node. Otherwise, we are at a higher level, and we need to determine whether the balance condition has been violated. If so, we restore the balance and then make three calls to `skew` and two calls to `split`. As discussed previously, these actions guarantee that the AA-tree properties will be restored.

```
/**
 * Internal method to remove from a subtree.
 * @param x the item to remove.
 * @param t the node that roots the tree.
 * @return the new root.
 * @throws ItemNotFoundException if x is not found.
 */
private AANode<AnyType> remove( AnyType x, AANode<AnyType> t )
{
    if( t != nullNode )
    {
        // Step 1: Search down the tree and
        //         set lastNode and deletedNode
        lastNode = t;
        if( x.compareTo( t.element ) < 0 )
            t.left = remove( x, t.left );
        else
        {
            deletedNode = t;
            t.right = remove( x, t.right );
        }

        // Step 2: If at the bottom of the tree and
        //         x is present, remove it
        if( t == lastNode )
        {
            if( deletedNode == nullNode ||
                        x.compareTo( deletedNode.element ) != 0 )
                throw new ItemNotFoundException( x.toString( ) );
            deletedNode.element = t.element;
            t = t.right;
        }

        // Step 3: Otherwise, we are not at the bottom; rebalance
        else
            if( t.left.level < t.level - 1 || t.right.level < t.level - 1 )
            {
                if( t.right.level > --t.level )
                    t.right.level = t.level;
                t = skew( t );
                t.right = skew( t.right );
                t.right.right = skew( t.right.right );
                t = split( t );
                t.right = split( t.right );
            }
    }
    return t;
}
```

figure 19.67

The remove method for AA-trees

19.7 implementing the collections api TreeSet and TreeMap classes

In this section we provide a reasonably efficient implementation of the Collections API TreeSet and TreeMap classes. The code is a blend of the Collections API linked list implementation presented in Section 17.5 and the AA-tree implementation in Section 19.6. Some AA-tree details are not reproduced here because the core private routines, such as the tree rotations, are essentially unchanged. Those routines are contained in the online code. Other routines, such as the private insert and remove, are only slightly different than those in Section 19.6, but we rewrite them to show the similarity and for completeness.

The basic implementation resembles that of the standard LinkedList class with its node, set, and iterator classes. However, there are two main differences between the classes.

1. The TreeSet class can be constructed with a Comparator, and the Comparator is saved as a data member.
2. The TreeSet iteration routines are more complex than those of the LinkedList class.

Iteration is the trickiest part. We must decide how to perform the traversal. Several alternatives are available:

1. Use parent links
2. Have the iterator maintain a stack that represents the nodes on the path to the current position
3. Have each node maintain a link to its inorder successor, a technique known as a *threaded tree*

To make the code look as much as possible like the AA-tree code in Section 19.6, we use the option of having the iterator maintain a stack. We leave using parent links for you to do as Exercise 19.30.

Figure 19.68 shows the TreeSet class skeleton. The node declaration is shown at lines 12 and 13; the body of the declaration is identical to the AANode in Section 19.6. At line 18 is the data member that stores the comparison function object. The routines and fields in lines 54–55, 57–58, 62–63, and 70–77 are essentially identical to their AA-tree counterparts. For instance, the differences between the insert method at lines 54–55 and the one in the AATree class is that the AAtree version throws an exception if a duplicate is

```
package weiss.util;

import java.io.Serializable;
import java.io.IOException;

public class TreeSet<AnyType> extends AbstractCollection<AnyType>
                              implements SortedSet<AnyType>
{
    private class TreeSetIterator implements Iterator<AnyType>
      { /* Figure 19.74 */ }

    private static class AANode<AnyType> implements Serializable
      { /* Same as in Figure 19.64 */ }

    private int modCount = 0;
    private int theSize = 0;
    private AANode<AnyType> root = null;
    private Comparator<? super AnyType> cmp;
    private AANode<AnyType> nullNode;

    public TreeSet( )
      { /* Figure 19.69 */ }
    public TreeSet( Comparator<? super AnyType> c )
      { /* Figure 19.69 */ }
    public TreeSet( SortedSet<AnyType> other )
      { /* Figure 19.69 */ }
    public TreeSet( Collection<? extends AnyType> other )
      { /* Figure 19.69 */ }

    public Comparator<? super AnyType> comparator( )
      { /* Figure 19.69 */ }
    private void copyFrom( Collection<? extends AnyType> other )
      { /* Figure 19.69 */ }

    public int size( )
      { return theSize; }

    public AnyType first( )
      { /* Similar to findMin; see online code. */ }
    public AnyType last( )
      { /* Similar to findMax; see online code. */ }

    public AnyType getMatch( AnyType x )
      { /* Figure 19.70 */ }

    private AANode<AnyType> find( AnyType x )
      { /* Figure 19.69 */ }
    private int compare( AnyType lhs, AnyType rhs )
      { /* Figure 19.69 */ }
    public boolean contains( Object x )
      { /* Figure 19.69 */ }
```

figure 19.68a

TreeSet class skeleton (*continues*)

```
    public boolean add( AnyType x )
      { /* Figure 19.71 */ }
    private AANode<AnyType> insert( AnyType x, AANode<AnyType> t )
      { /* Figure 19.71 */ }

    private AANode<AnyType> deletedNode;
    private AANode<AnyType> lastNode;

    public boolean remove( Object x )
      { /* Figure 19.72 */ }
    private AANode<AnyType> remove( AnyType x, AANode<AnyType> t )
      { /* Figure 19.73 */ }
    public void clear( )
      { /* Figure 19.72 */ }

    public Iterator<AnyType> iterator( )
      { return new TreeSetIterator( ); }

    private static <AnyType> AANode<AnyType> skew( AANode<AnyType> t )
      { /* Same as in Figure 19.66 */ }
    private static <AnyType> AANode<AnyType> split( AANode<AnyType> t )
      { /* Same as in Figure 19.66 */ }
    private static <AnyType> AANode<AnyType> rotateWithLeftChild( AANode<AnyType> k2 )
      { /* Same as usual */ }
    private static <AnyType> AANode<AnyType> rotateWithRightChild( AANode<AnyType> k1 )
      { /* Same as usual */ }
}
```

Figure 19.68b

TreeSet class skeleton (*continued*)

inserted, whereas this insert returns immediately, this version of insert maintains the size and modCount data members, and this new version uses a comparator.

The constructors and comparator accessor for the TreeSet class are shown in Figure 19.69. The private helper, copyFrom, is also shown. Figure 19.70 implements the public getMatch, which is a nonstandard method (that is used to help out with TreeMap later on). The private find method is identical to the one in Section 19.6. The compare method uses the comparator if one was provided; otherwise it assumes that the parameters are Comparable and uses their compareTo method.

The public add method is shown in Figure 19.71. It simply calls the private insert method, which is similar to the previously seen code in Section 19.6. Observe that add succeeds if and only if the size of the set changes.

```
    /**
     * Construct an empty TreeSet.
     */
    public TreeSet( )
    {
        nullNode = new AANode<AnyType>( null, null, null );
        nullNode.left = nullNode.right = nullNode;
        nullNode.level = 0;
        root = nullNode;
        cmp = null;
    }

    /**
     * Construct an empty TreeSet with a specified comparator.
     */
    public TreeSet( Comparator<? super AnyType> c )
      { this( ); cmp = c; }

    /**
     * Construct a TreeSet from another SortedSet.
     */
    public TreeSet( SortedSet<AnyType> other )
      { this( other.comparator( ) ); copyFrom( other ); }

    /**
     * Construct a TreeSet from any collection.
     * Uses an O( N log N ) algorithm, but could be improved.
     */
    public TreeSet( Collection<? extends AnyType> other )
      { this( ); copyFrom( other ); }

    /**
     * Return the comparator used by this TreeSet.
     * @return the comparator or null if the default comparator is used.
     */
    public Comparator<? super AnyType> comparator( )
      { return cmp; }

    /**
     * Copy any collection into a new TreeSet.
     */
    private void copyFrom( Collection<? extends AnyType> other )
    {
        clear( );
        for( AnyType x : other )
            add( x );
    }
```

figure 19.69

Constructors and comparator method for TreeSet

figure 19.70

Search methods for `TreeSet`

```
    /**
     * This method is not part of standard Java.
     * Like contains, it checks if x is in the set.
     * If it is, it returns the reference to the matching
     * object; otherwise it returns null.
     * @param x the object to search for.
     * @return if contains(x) is false, the return value is null;
     * otherwise, the return value is the object that causes
     * contains(x) to return true.
     */
    public AnyType getMatch( AnyType x )
    {
        AANode<AnyType> p = find( x );
        if( p == null )
            return null;
        else
            return p.element;
    }

    /**
     * Find an item in the tree.
     * @param x the item to search for.
     * @return the matching item or null if not found.
     */
    private AANode<AnyType> find( AnyType x )
    {
        AANode<AnyType> current = root;
        nullNode.element = x;

        for( ; ; )
        {
            int result = compare( x, current.element );

            if( result < 0 )
                current = current.left;
            else if( result > 0 )
                current = current.right;
            else if( current != nullNode )
                return current;
            else
                return null;
        }
    }

    private int compare( AnyType lhs, AnyType rhs )
    {
        if( cmp == null )
            return ((Comparable) lhs).compareTo( rhs );
        else
            return cmp.compare( lhs, rhs );
    }
```

```java
    /**
     * Adds an item to this collection.
     * @param x any object.
     * @return true if this item was added to the collection.
     */
    public boolean add( AnyType x )
    {
        int oldSize = size( );

        root = insert( x, root );
        return size( ) != oldSize;
    }

    /**
     * Internal method to insert into a subtree.
     * @param x the item to insert.
     * @param t the node that roots the tree.
     * @return the new root.
     */
    private AANode<AnyType> insert( AnyType x, AANode<AnyType> t )
    {
        if( t == nullNode )
        {
            t = new AANode<AnyType>( x, nullNode, nullNode );
            modCount++;
            theSize++;
        }
        else
        {
            int result = compare( x, t.element );

            if( result < 0 )
                t.left = insert( x, t.left );
            else if( result > 0 )
                t.right = insert( x, t.right );
            else
                return t;
        }

        t = skew( t );
        t = split( t );
        return t;
    }
```

figure 19.71

Insertion methods for TreeSet

Figure 19.72 shows the public remove and clear methods. The public remove calls a private remove, shown in Figure 19.73, which is very similar to the code in Section 19.6. The main changes are the use of a comparator (via method compare), and the additional code at lines 31 and 32.

figure 19.72

Public deletion methods for `TreeSet`

```
    /**
     * Removes an item from this collection.
     * @param x any object.
     * @return true if this item was removed from the collection.
     */
    public boolean remove( Object x )
    {
        int oldSize = size( );

        deletedNode = nullNode;
        root = remove( (AnyType) x, root );

        return size( ) != oldSize;
    }

    /**
     * Change the size of this collection to zero.
     */
    public void clear( )
    {
        theSize = 0;
        modCount++;
        root = nullNode;
    }
```

The iterator class is shown in Figure 19.74; `current` is positioned at the node containing the next unseen item. The tricky part is maintaining the stack, `path`, which includes all nodes on the path to the current node, but not the current node itself. The constructor simply follows all the left links, pushing all but the last node on the path onto the stack. We also maintain the number of items visited, thus making the `hasNext` test easy.

The core routine is the private method `next`, shown in Figure 19.75. After we record the value in the current node, and set `lastVisited` (for `remove`), we need to advance `current`. If the current node has a right child, we go right once and then left as far as possible (lines 11–17). Otherwise, as lines 21–32 illustrate, we need to go back up the path toward the root until we find the node from which we turned left. That node, which must exist because otherwise an exception would have been thrown at line 4, is the next node in the iteration.

Figure 19.76 shows the remarkably tricky `remove`. The relatively easy part is shown at lines 3–15, where after some error checks, we remove the item from the tree at line 11. At line 13, we fix the `expectedModCount`, so as to not get a subsequent `ConcurrentModificationException` for this iterator (only). At line 14, we lower `visited` (so `hasNext` will work), and at line 15, we set `lastVisited` to `null`, so a consecutive `remove` will be disallowed.

```
    /**
     * Internal method to remove from a subtree.
     * @param x the item to remove.
     * @param t the node that roots the tree.
     * @return the new root.
     */
    private AANode<AnyType> remove( AnyType x, AANode<AnyType> t )
    {
        if( t != nullNode )
        {
            // Step 1: Search down the tree and
            //         set lastNode and deletedNode
            lastNode = t;
            if( compare( x, t.element ) < 0 )
                t.left = remove( x, t.left );
            else
            {
                deletedNode = t;
                t.right = remove( x, t.right );
            }

            // Step 2: If at the bottom of the tree and
            //         x is present, we remove it
            if( t == lastNode )
            {
                if( deletedNode == nullNode ||
                            compare( x, deletedNode.element ) != 0 )
                    return t;   // Item not found; do nothing
                deletedNode.element = t.element;
                t = t.right;
                theSize--;
                modCount++;
            }

            // Step 3: Otherwise, we are not at the bottom; rebalance
            else
                if( t.left.level < t.level - 1 || t.right.level < t.level - 1 )
                {
                    if( t.right.level > --t.level )
                        t.right.level = t.level;
                    t = skew( t );
                    t.right = skew( t.right );
                    t.right.right = skew( t.right.right );
                    t = split( t );
                    t.right = split( t.right );
                }
        }
        return t;
    }
```

figure 19.73

Private remove method for TreeSet

```
/**
 * This is the implementation of the TreeSetIterator.
 * It maintains a notion of a current position and of
 * course the implicit reference to the TreeSet.
 */
private class TreeSetIterator implements Iterator<AnyType>
{
    private int expectedModCount = modCount;
    private int visited = 0;
    private Stack<AANode<AnyType>> path = new Stack<AANode<AnyType>>( );
    private AANode<AnyType> current = null;
    private AANode<AnyType> lastVisited = null;

    public TreeSetIterator( )
    {
        if( isEmpty( ) )
            return;

        AANode<AnyType> p = null;
        for( p = root; p.left != nullNode; p = p.left )
            path.push( p );

        current = p;
    }

    public boolean hasNext( )
    {
        if( expectedModCount != modCount )
            throw new ConcurrentModificationException( );

        return visited < size( );
    }

    public AnyType next( )
      { /* Figure 19.75 */ }

    public void remove( )
      { /* Figure 19.76 */ }
}
```

figure 19.74

`TreeSetIterator` inner class skeleton

If we have not removed the last item in the iteration, then we have to reset the stack, because rotations may have rearranged the tree. This is done at lines 20–36. Line 35 is needed because we do not want `current` to be on the stack.

We finish by providing an implementation of the `TreeMap` class. A `TreeMap` is simply a `TreeSet` in which we store key/value pairs; in fact, a similar obser-

```
    public AnyType next( )
    {
        if( !hasNext( ) )
            throw new NoSuchElementException( );

        AnyType value = current.element;
        lastVisited = current;

        if( current.right != nullNode )
        {
            path.push( current );
            current = current.right;
            while( current.left != nullNode )
            {
                path.push( current );
                current = current.left;
            }
        }
        else
        {
            AANode<AnyType> parent;

            for( ; !path.isEmpty( ); current = parent )
            {
                parent = path.pop( );

                if( parent.left == current )
                {
                    current = parent;
                    break;
                }
            }
        }

        visited++;
        return value;
    }
```

figure 19.75

next method for TreeSetIterator

vation will hold for HashMap, relative to HashSet. Thus we implement the package-visible abstract class MapImpl, which can be constructed from any Set (or Map). TreeMap and HashMap will extend MapImpl, providing implementations of the abstract methods. The class skeleton for MapImpl is shown in Figures 19.77 and 19.78.

One data member, the underlying set theSet, is declared at line 10. The key/value pairs are represented by a concrete implementation of the Map.Entry class; this implementation is partially supplied by the abstract Pair class that extends MapImpl (at lines 52–72). In TreeMap this Pair class is extended further

```
        public void remove( )
        {
            if( expectedModCount != modCount )
                throw new ConcurrentModificationException( );

            if( lastVisited == null )
                throw new IllegalStateException( );

            AnyType valueToRemove = lastVisited.element;

            TreeSet.this.remove( valueToRemove );

            expectedModCount++;
            visited--;
            lastVisited = null;

            if( !hasNext( ) )
                return;

              // Remaining code reinstates the stack, in case of rotations
            AnyType nextValue = current.element;
            path.clear( );
            AANode<AnyType> p = root;
            for( ; ; )
            {
                path.push( p );
                int result = compare( nextValue, p.element );
                if( result < 0 )
                    p = p.left;
                else if( result > 0 )
                    p = p.right;
                else
                    break;
            }
            path.pop( );
            current = p;
        }
```

figure 19.76

remove method for `TreeSetIterator`

by providing `compareTo`, while in `HashMap` it is extended by providing `equals` and `hashCode`.

Lines 17–21 declare the three abstract methods. These are factories that create the appropriate concrete object and return it through the interface type. For instance, in `TreeMap`, `makeEmptyKeySet` returns a newly constructed `TreeSet`, whereas in `HashMap`, `makeEmptyKeySet` returns a newly constructed `HashSet`. Most important, `makePair` creates an object of type `Map.Entry` that represents the key/

```
package weiss.util;

/**
 * MapImpl implements the Map on top of a set.
 * It should be extended by TreeMap and HashMap, with
 * chained calls to the constructor.
 */
abstract class MapImpl<KeyType,ValueType> implements Map<KeyType,ValueType>
{
    private Set<Map.Entry<KeyType,ValueType>> theSet;

    protected MapImpl( Set<Map.Entry<KeyType,ValueType>> s )
      { theSet = s; }
    protected MapImpl( Map<KeyType,ValueType> m )
      { theSet = clonePairSet( m.entrySet( ) ); }

    protected abstract Map.Entry<KeyType,ValueType>
                       makePair( KeyType key, ValueType value );
    protected abstract Set<KeyType> makeEmptyKeySet( );
    protected abstract Set<Map.Entry<KeyType,ValueType>>
                       clonePairSet( Set<Map.Entry<KeyType,ValueType>> pairSet );

    private Map.Entry<KeyType,ValueType> makePair( KeyType key )
      { return makePair( (KeyType) key, null ); }
    protected Set<Map.Entry<KeyType,ValueType>> getSet( )
      { return theSet; }

    public int size( )
      { return theSet.size( ); }
    public boolean isEmpty( )
      { return theSet.isEmpty( ); }
    public boolean containsKey( KeyType key )
      { return theSet.contains( makePair( key ) ); }
    public void clear( )
      { theSet.clear( ); }
    public String toString( )
    {
        StringBuilder result = new StringBuilder( "{" );
        for( Map.Entry e : entrySet( ) )
            result.append( e + ", " );
        result.replace( result.length() - 2, result.length(), "}" );
        return result.toString( );
    }

    public ValueType get( KeyType key )
      { /* Figure 19.79 */ }
    public ValueType put( KeyType key, ValueType value )
      { /* Figure 19.79 */ }
    public ValueType remove( KeyType key )
      { /* Figure 19.79 */ }
```

figure 19.77

Abstract MapImpl helper class skeleton (part 1)

```
    // Pair class
    protected static abstract class Pair<KeyType,ValueType>
                      implements Map.Entry<KeyType,ValueType>
    {
        public Pair( KeyType k, ValueType v )
          { key = k; value = v; }

        final public KeyType getKey( )
          { return key; }

        final public ValueType getValue( )
          { return value; }

        final public ValueType setValue( ValueType newValue )
          { ValueType oldValue = value; value = newValue; return oldValue; }

        final public String toString( )
          { return key + "=" + value; }

        private KeyType key;
        private ValueType value;
    }

    // Views
    public Set<KeyType> keySet( )
      { return new KeySetClass( ); }
    public Collection<ValueType> values( )
      { return new ValueCollectionClass( ); }
    public Set<Map.Entry<KeyType,ValueType>> entrySet( )
      {  return getSet( ); }

    private abstract class ViewClass<AnyType> extends AbstractCollection<AnyType>
      { /* Figure 19.80 */ }
    private class KeySetClass extends ViewClass<KeyType> implements Set<KeyType>
      { /* Figure 19.80 */ }
    private class ValueCollectionClass extends ViewClass<ValueType>
      { /* Figure 19.80 */ }

    private class ValueCollectionIterator implements Iterator<ValueType>
      { /* Figure 19.81 */ }
    private class KeySetIterator implements Iterator<KeyType>
      { /* Figure 19.81 */ }
}
```

figure 19.78

Abstract MapImpl helper class skeleton (part 2)

value pair. For a TreeSet, the object turns out to be Comparable, and applies the TreeSet comparator to the key. Details of this will be discussed later.

Many of the map routines translate into operations on the underlying set, as shown at lines 28–35. The basic routines get, put, and remove, are shown in Figure 19.79. These simply translate into operations on the set. All require a call to makePair to create an object of the same type as those in theSet; put is representative of the strategy.

The tricky part of the MapImpl class is providing the ability to obtain the views of the keys and values. In the MapImpl class declaration in Figure 19.78, we see that keySet, implemented at lines 75 and 76, returns a reference to an instance of an inner class named KeySetClass, and values, implemented at lines 77 and 78, returns a reference to an instance of an inner class named ValueCollectionClass. KeySetClass and ValueCollectionClass have some commonality, so they extend the generic inner class named ViewClass. These three classes appear in lines 82 to 87 of the class declaration, and their implementation is shown in Figure 19.80.

In Figure 19.80, we see that in the generic ViewClass, calls to clear and size are delegated to the underlying map. This class is abstract because AbstractCollection does not provide the iterator method specified in Collection, and neither does ViewClass. The ValueCollectionClass extends ViewClass<ValueType> and provides an iterator method; this method returns a newly constructed instance of the inner class ValueCollectionIterator (which of course implements the Iterator interface). ValueCollectionIterator delegates calls to next and hasNext and is shown in Figure 19.81; we discuss it shortly. KeySetClass extends ViewClass<KeyType>, but since it is a Set, it must provide the (nonstandard) getMatch method in addition to the iterator method. Because the KeySet class will not itself be used to represent a Map, this method is not needed, so the implementation simply throws an exception. We also provide a remove method to remove the associated key/value pair from the underlying map. If this method is not provided, the default that is inherited from AbstractCollection uses a sequential search, which is grossly inefficient.

Figure 19.81 completes the MapImpl class by providing implementations of KeySetIterator and ValueCollectionIterator. Both maintain an iterator that views the underlying map, and both delegate calls to next, hasNext, and remove to the underlying map. In the case of next, the appropriate part of the Map.Entry object being viewed by the map's iterator is returned.

With MapImpl written, TreeMap turns out to be simple, as shown in Figure 19.82. Most of the code centers around the definition of the private inner class Pair, which implements the Map.Entry interface by extending MapImpl.Pair. Pair implements Comparable, using the comparator on the key if one is provided, or downcasting to Comparable.

```java
/**
 * Returns the value in the map associated with the key.
 * @param key the key to search for.
 * @return the value that matches the key or null
 * if the key is not found. Since null values are allowed,
 * checking if the return value is null may not
 * be a safe way to ascertain if the key is present in the map.
 */
public ValueType get( KeyType key )
{
    Map.Entry<KeyType,ValueType> match = theSet.getMatch( makePair( key ) );

    if( match == null )
        return null;
    else
        return match.getValue( );
}

/**
 * Adds the key value pair to the map, overriding the
 * original value if the key was already present.
 * @param key the key to insert.
 * @param value the value to insert.
 * @return the old value associated with the key, or
 * null if the key was not present prior to this call.
 */
public ValueType put( KeyType key, ValueType value )
{
    Map.Entry<KeyType,ValueType> match = theSet.getMatch( makePair( key ) );

    if( match != null )
        return match.setValue( value );

    theSet.add( makePair( key, value ) );
    return null;
}

/**
 * Remove the key and its value from the map.
 * @param key the key to remove.
 * @return the previous value associated with the key,
 * or null if the key was not present prior to this call.
 */
public ValueType remove( KeyType key )
{
    ValueType oldValue = get( key );
    if( oldValue != null )
        theSet.remove( makePair( key ) );

    return oldValue;
}
```

figure 19.79

Implementations of basic `MapImpl` methods

```
/**
 * Abstract class to model a view (either key or value view).
 * Implements size and clear methods, but not iterator method.
 * View delegates to underlying map.
 */
private abstract class ViewClass<AnyType> extends AbstractCollection<AnyType>
{
    public int size( )
      {  return MapImpl.this.size( ); }

    public void clear( )
      { MapImpl.this.clear( ); }
}

/**
 * Class to model the key set view.
 * remove is overridden (otherwise a sequential search is used).
 * iterator gives a KeySetIterator (see Figure 19.81).
 * getMatch, the nonstandard part of weiss.util.Set is not needed.
 */
private class KeySetClass extends ViewClass<KeyType> implements Set<KeyType>
{
    public boolean remove( Object key )
      { return MapImpl.this.remove( (KeyType) key ) != null; }

    public Iterator<KeyType> iterator( )
      { return new KeySetIterator( ); }

    public KeyType getMatch( KeyType key )
      { throw new UnsupportedOperationException( ); }
}

/**
 * Class to model the value collection view.
 * Default remove which is a sequential search is used.
 * iterator gives a ValueCollectionIterator (see Figure 19.81).
 */
private class ValueCollectionClass extends ViewClass<ValueType>
{
    public Iterator<ValueType> iterator( )
      { return new ValueCollectionIterator( ); }
}
```

figure 19.80

View classes for MapImpl

```
/**
 * Class used to iterate through key set view.
 * Delegates to an underlying entry set iterator.
 */
private class KeySetIterator implements Iterator<KeyType>
{
    private Iterator<Map.Entry<KeyType,ValueType>> itr = theSet.iterator( );

    public boolean hasNext( )
      { return itr.hasNext( ); }

    public void remove( )
      { itr.remove( ); }

    public KeyType next( )
      { return itr.next( ).getKey( ); }
}

/**
 * Class used to iterate through value collection view.
 * Delegates to an underlying entry set iterator.
 */
private class ValueCollectionIterator implements Iterator<ValueType>
{
    private Iterator<Map.Entry<KeyType,ValueType>> itr = theSet.iterator( );

    public boolean hasNext( )
      { return itr.hasNext( ); }

    public void remove( )
      { itr.remove( ); }

    public ValueType next( )
      { return itr.next( ).getValue( ); }
}
```

figure 19.81

View iterator classes

```
package weiss.util;

public class TreeMap<KeyType,ValueType> extends MapImpl<KeyType,ValueType>
{
    public TreeMap( )
      { super( new TreeSet<Map.Entry<KeyType,ValueType>>( ) ); }
    public TreeMap( Map<KeyType,ValueType> other )
      { super( other ); }
    public TreeMap( Comparator<? super KeyType> comparator )
    {
        super( new TreeSet<Map.Entry<KeyType,ValueType>>( ) );
        keyCmp = comparator;
    }

    public Comparator<? super KeyType> comparator( )
      { return keyCmp; }

    protected Map.Entry<KeyType,ValueType> makePair( KeyType key, ValueType value )
      { return new Pair( key, value ); }

    protected Set<KeyType> makeEmptyKeySet( )
      { return new TreeSet<KeyType>( keyCmp ); }

    protected Set<Map.Entry<KeyType,ValueType>>
          clonePairSet( Set<Map.Entry<KeyType,ValueType>> pairSet )
      { return new TreeSet<Map.Entry<KeyType,ValueType>>( pairSet ); }

    private final class Pair extends MapImpl.Pair<KeyType,ValueType>
                             implements Comparable<Map.Entry<KeyType,ValueType>>
    {
        public Pair( KeyType k, ValueType v )
          { super( k ,v ); }

        public int compareTo( Map.Entry<KeyType,ValueType> other )
        {
            if( keyCmp != null )
                return keyCmp.compare( getKey( ), other.getKey( ) );
            else
                return (( Comparable) getKey( ) ).compareTo( other.getKey( ) );
        }
    }

    private Comparator<? super KeyType> keyCmp;
}
```

figure 19.82

TreeMap implementation

19.8 b-trees

So far, we have assumed that we can store an entire data structure in the main memory of a computer. Suppose, however, that we have more data than can fit in main memory, and, as a result, we must have the data structure reside on disk. When that happens, the rules of the game change, because the Big-Oh model is no longer meaningful.

The problem is that a Big-Oh analysis assumes that all operations are equal. However, that is not true, especially when disk I/O is involved. On the one hand, a 500-MIPS machine supposedly executes 500 million instructions per second. That is fairly fast, mainly because the speed depends largely on electrical properties. On the other hand, a disk is mechanical. Its speed depends largely on the time required to spin the disk and move a disk head. Many disks spin at 7,200 RPM. Thus in 1 minute, it makes 7,200 revolutions; hence one revolution occurs in 1/120 of a second, or 8.3 ms. On average we might expect that we have to spin a disk halfway to find what we are looking for, but this is compensated by the time to move the disk head, so we get an access time of 8.3 ms. (This estimate is very charitable; 9 to 11 ms. access times are more common.) Consequently, we can do approximately 120 disk accesses per second. This number of accesses sounds good, until we compare it with the processor speed: We have 500 million instructions versus 120 disk accesses. Put another way, one disk access is worth about 4,000,000 instructions. Of course, everything here is a rough calculation, but the relative speeds are rather clear: Disk accesses are incredibly expensive. Furthermore, processor speeds are increasing at a much faster rate than disk speeds (it is disk *sizes* that are increasing quite quickly). Thus, we are willing to do lots of calculations just to save a disk access. In almost all cases, the number of disk accesses dominates the running time. By halving the number of disk accesses, we can halve the running time.

When data are too large to fit in memory, the number of disk accesses becomes important. A disk access is unbelievably expensive compared to a typical computer instruction.

Here is how the typical search tree performs on disk. Suppose that we want to access the driving records for citizens in the State of Florida. We assume that we have 10,000,000 items, that each key is 32 bytes (representing a name), and that a record is 256 bytes. We assume that this data set does not fit in main memory and that we are 1 of 20 users on a system (so we have 1/20 of the resources). Thus in 1 sec. we can execute 25 million instructions or perform six disk accesses.

Even logarithmic performance is unacceptable. We need to perform searches in three or four accesses. Updates can take slightly longer.

The unbalanced binary search tree is a disaster. In the worst case, it has linear depth and thus could require 10,000,000 disk accesses. On average a successful search would require $1.38 \log N$ disk accesses, and as log 10,000,000 is approximately 24, an average search would require 32 disk accesses, or 5 sec. In a typical randomly constructed tree, we would expect that a few nodes are three times deeper; they would require about 100 disk accesses, or 16 sec. A red–black tree is somewhat better: The worst case of $1.44 \log N$ is unlikely to occur, and the typical case is very close to log N. Thus a red–black tree would use about 25 disk accesses on average, requiring 4 sec.

An *M-ary search tree* allows *M*-way branching. As branching increases, the depth decreases.

We want to reduce disk accesses to a very small constant number, such as three or four. We are willing to write complicated code to do so because machine instructions are essentially free, so long as we are not ridiculously unreasonable. A binary search tree does not work because the typical red–black tree is close to optimal height, and we cannot go below log N with a binary search tree. The solution is intuitively simple: If we have more branching, we have less height. Thus, whereas a perfect binary tree of 31 nodes has five levels, a 5-ary tree of 31 nodes has only three levels, as shown in Figure 19.83. An *M-ary search tree* allows M-way branching, and as branching increases, the depth decreases. Whereas a complete binary tree has height that is roughly $\log_2 N$, a complete M-ary tree has height that is roughly $\log_M N$.

We can create an M-ary search tree in much the same way we created a binary search tree. In a binary search tree, we need one key to decide which of two branches to take. In an M-ary search tree, we need $M - 1$ keys to decide which branch to take. To make this scheme efficient in the worst case, we need to ensure that the M-ary search tree is balanced in some way. Otherwise, like a binary search tree, it could degenerate into a linked list. Actually, we want an even more restrictive balancing condition. That is, we do not want an M-ary search tree to degenerate to even a binary search tree because then we would be stuck with log N accesses.

The *B-tree* is the most popular data structure for disk-bound searching.

One way to implement this is to use a *B-tree,* which is the most popular data structure for disk-bound searching. Here, we describe the basic B-tree;[3] many variations and improvements exist, and an implementation is somewhat complex because quite a few cases must be addressed. However, in principle this technique guarantees only a few disk accesses.

The B-tree has a host of structure properties.

A B-tree of order M is an M-ary tree with the following properties.[4]

1. The data items are stored at leaves.
2. The nonleaf nodes store as many as $M - 1$ keys to guide the searching; key i represents the smallest key in subtree $i + 1$.
3. The root is either a leaf or has between 2 and M children.

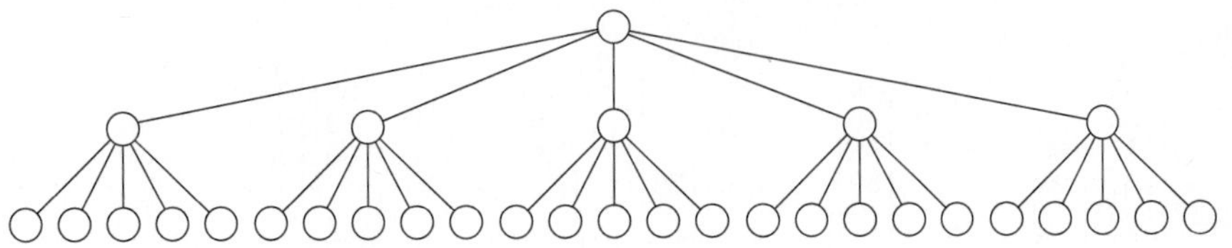

figure 19.83

A 5-ary tree of 31 nodes has only three levels

3. What we describe is popularly known as a B^+-tree.
4. Properties 3 and 5 must be relaxed for the first L insertions. (L is a parameter used in property 5.)

4. All nonleaf nodes (except the root) have between $\lceil M/2 \rceil$ and M children.
5. All leaves are at the same depth and have between $\lceil L/2 \rceil$ and L data items, for some L (the determination of L is described shortly).

Nodes must be half full to guarantee that the tree does not degenerate into a simple binary tree.

An example of a B-tree of order 5 is shown in Figure 19.84. Note that all nonleaf nodes have between three and five children (and thus between two and four keys); the root could possibly have only two children. Here, $L = 5$, which means that L and M are the same in this example, but this condition is not necessary. Because L is 5, each leaf has between three and five data items. Requiring nodes to be half full guarantees that the B-tree does not degenerate into a simple binary tree. Various definitions of B-trees change this structure, mostly in minor ways, but the definition presented here is one of the most commonly used.

We choose the maximum M and L that allow a node to fit in one disk block.

Each node represents a disk block, so we choose M and L on the basis of the size of the items being stored. Suppose that one block holds 8,192 bytes. In our Florida example, each key uses 32 bytes, so in a B-tree of order M, we would have $M - 1$ keys, for a total of $32M - 32$ bytes plus M branches. Because each branch is essentially a number of another disk block, we can assume that a branch is 4 bytes. Thus the branches use $4M$ bytes, and the total memory requirement for a nonleaf node is $36M - 32$. The largest value of M for which $36M - 32$ is no more than 8,192 is 228, so we would choose $M = 228$. As each data record is 256 bytes, we would be able to fit 32 records in a block. Thus we would choose $L = 32$. Each leaf has between 16 and 32 data records, and each internal node (except the root) branches in at least 114 ways. For the 10,000,000 records, there are at most 625,000 leaves. Consequently, in the worst case, leaves would be on level 4. In more concrete terms, the worst-case number of accesses is given by approximately $\log_{M/2} N$, give or take 1.

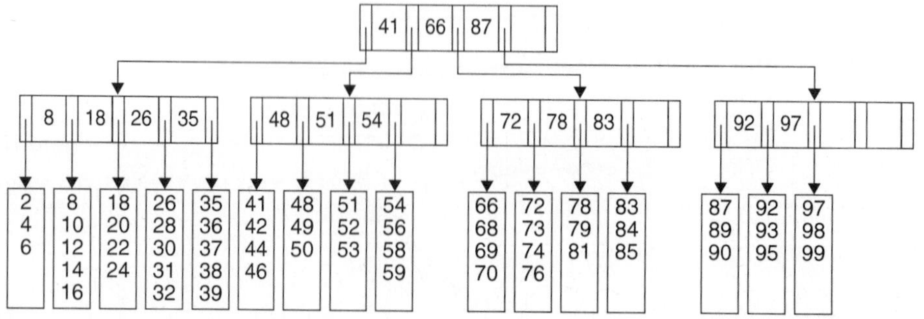

figure 19.84

A B-tree of order 5

The remaining issue is how to add and remove items from the B-tree. In the ideas sketched, note that many themes presented earlier recur.

We begin by examining insertion. Suppose that we want to insert 57 into the B-tree shown in Figure 19.84. A search down the tree reveals that 57 is not already in the tree. We can add 57 to the leaf as a fifth child, but we may have to reorganize all the data in the leaf to do so. However, the cost is negligible compared to that of the disk access, which in this case also includes a disk write.

If the leaf contains room for a new item, we insert it and are done.

That procedure was relatively painless because the leaf was not already full. Suppose that we now want to insert 55. Figure 19.85 shows a problem: The leaf where 55 should go is already full. The solution is simple: We now have $L + 1$ items, so we split them into two leaves, both guaranteed to have the minimum number of data records needed. Hence we form two leaves with three items each. Two disk accesses are required to write these leaves and a third disk access is required to update the parent. Note that in the parent, both keys and branches change, but they do so in a controlled way that can easily be calculated. The resulting B-tree is shown in Figure 19.86. Although splitting nodes is time consuming because it requires at least two additional disk writes, it is a relatively rare occurrence. If L is 32, for example, when a node is split two leaves with 16 and 17 items, respectively, are created. For the leaf with 17 items, we can perform 15 more insertions without another split. Put another way, for every split, there are roughly $L/2$ nonsplits.

If the leaf is full, we can insert a new item by splitting the leaf and forming two half-empty nodes.

The node splitting in the preceding example worked because the parent did not have its full complement of children. But what would happen if it did? Suppose that we insert 40 into the B-tree shown in Figure 19.86. We must split the leaf containing the keys 35 through 39 and now 40 into two leaves. But doing so would give the parent six children, and it is allowed only five. The solution is to split the parent, the result of which is shown in Figure 19.87. When the parent is split, we must update the values of the keys

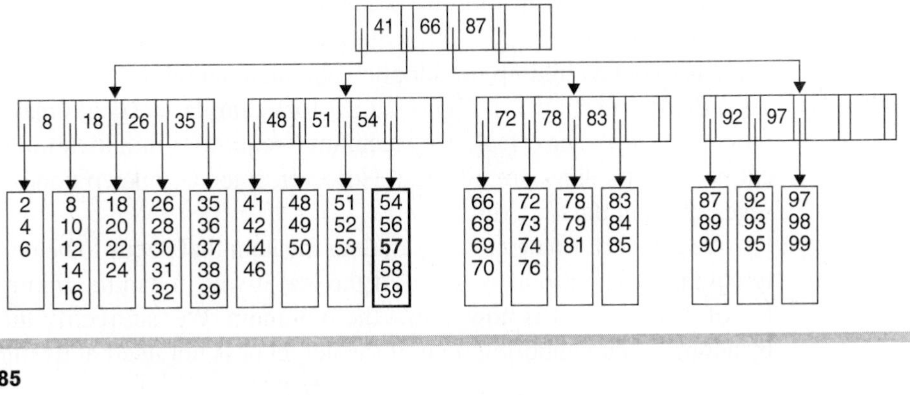

figure 19.85

The B-tree after insertion of 57 in the tree shown in Figure 19.84.

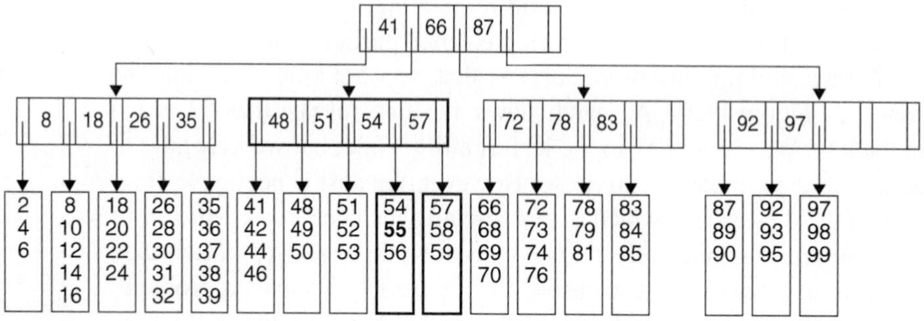

figure 19.86

Insertion of 55 in the B-tree shown in Figure 19.85 causes a split into two leaves.

Node splitting creates an extra child for the leaf's parent. If the parent already has a full number of children, we split the parent.

We may have to continue splitting all the way up the tree (though this possibility is unlikely). In the worst case, we split the root, creating a new root with two children.

and also the parent's parent, incurring an additional two disk writes (so this insertion costs five disk writes). Again, however, the keys change in a very controlled manner, although the code is certainly not simple because of the number of cases involved.

When a nonleaf node is split, as here, its parent gains a child. What if the parent already has reached its limit of children? Then we continue splitting nodes up the tree until we find a parent that does not need to be split or we reach the root. Note that we introduced this idea in bottom-up red–black trees and AA-trees. If we split the root, we have two roots, but obviously, this outcome is unacceptable. However, we can create a new root that has the split roots as its two children, which is why the root is granted the special two-child minimum exemption. It is also the only way that a B-tree gains height. Needless to say, splitting all the way up to the root is an exceptionally rare event because a tree with four levels indicates that the root has been split two times throughout the entire sequence of insertions (assuming that no deletions have occurred). In fact, splitting of any nonleaf node is also quite rare.

There are other ways to handle the overflowing of children. One technique is to put a child up for adoption should a neighbor have room. To insert 29 in the B-tree shown in Figure 19.87, for example, we could make room by moving 32 to the next leaf. This technique requires a modification of the parent because the keys are affected. However, it tends to keep nodes fuller and saves space in the long run.

We can perform deletion by finding the item that needs to be removed and removing it. The problem is that, if the leaf it was in had the minimum number of data items, it is now below the minimum. We can rectify the situation by adopting a neighboring item, if the neighbor is not itself at its minimum. If

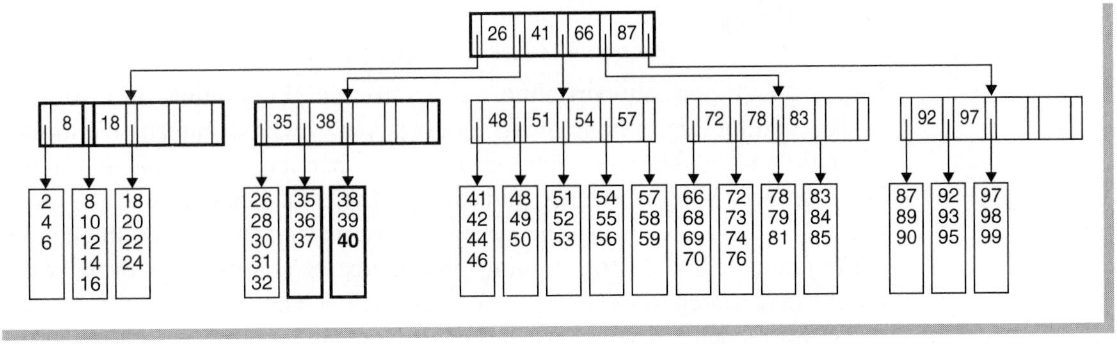

figure 19.87

Insertion of 40 in the B-tree shown in Figure 19.86 causes a split into two leaves and then a split of the parent node.

it is, we can combine with the neighbor to form a full leaf. Unfortunately, in this case the parent has lost a child. If that causes the parent to fall below its minimum, we follow the same strategy. This process could percolate up all the way up to the root. The root cannot have just one child (and even if it were allowed, it would be silly). If a root is left with one child as a result of the adoption process, we remove the root, making its child the new root of the tree—the only way for a B-tree to lose height. Suppose that we want to remove 99 from the B-tree shown in Figure 19.87. The leaf has only two items and its neighbor is already at its minimum of three, so we combine the items into a new leaf of five items. As a result, the parent has only two children. However, it can adopt from a neighbor because the neighbor has four children. As a result of the adoption, both end up with three children, as shown in Figure 19.88.

Deletion works in reverse: If a leaf loses a child, it may need to combine with another leaf. Combining of nodes may continue all the way up the tree, though this possibility is unlikely. In the worst case, the root loses one of its two children. Then we delete the root and use the other child as the new root.

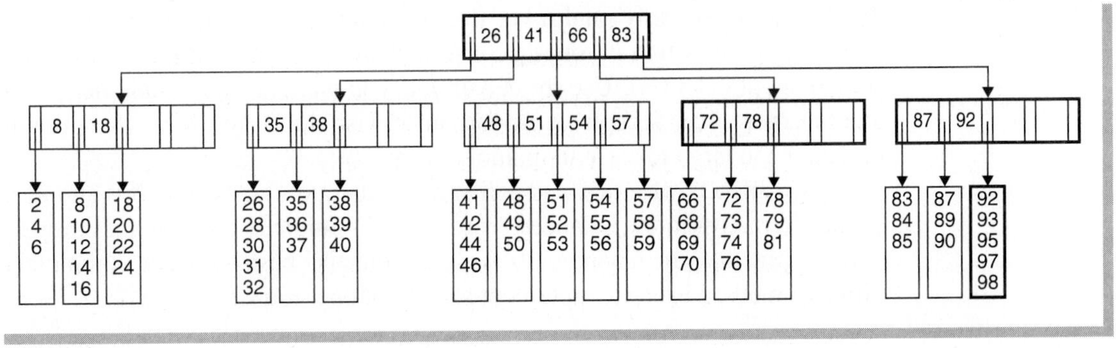

figure 19.88

The B-tree after deletion of 99 from the tree shown in Figure 19.87.

summary

Binary search trees support almost all of the useful operations in algorithm design, and the logarithmic average cost is very small. Nonrecursive implementations of search trees are somewhat faster than recursive versions, but the latter are sleeker, more elegant, and easier to understand and debug. The problem with search trees is that their performance depends heavily on the input's being random. If it is not, running time increases significantly, even to the point where search trees become expensive linked lists.

Ways of dealing with this problem all involve restructuring the tree to ensure some sort of balance at each node. Restructuring is achieved through tree rotations that preserve the binary search tree property. The cost of a search is typically less than for an unbalanced binary search tree because the average node tends to be closer to the root. Insertion and deletion costs, however, are usually higher. The balanced variations differ in the amount of coding effort involved in implementing operations that change the tree.

The classic scheme is the AVL tree in which, for every node, the heights of its left and right subtrees can differ by at most 1. The practical problem with AVL trees is that they involve large numbers of different cases, making the overhead of each insertion and deletion relatively high. We examined two alternatives in the chapter. The first was the top-down red–black tree. Its primary advantage is that rebalancing can be implemented in a single pass down the tree, rather than the traditional pass down and back up. This technique leads to simpler code and faster performance than the AVL tree allows. The second is the AA-tree, which is similar to the bottom-up red–black tree. Its primary advantage is a relatively simple recursive implementation of both insertion and deletion. Both structures use sentinel nodes to eliminate annoying special cases.

You should use an unbalanced binary search tree only if you are sure that the data are reasonably random or that the amount of data is relatively small. Use the red–black tree if you are concerned about speed (and are not too concerned about deletion). Use the AA-tree if you want an easy implementation that has more than acceptable performance. Use the B-tree when the amount of data is too large to store in main memory.

In Chapter 22 we examine another alternative: the splay tree. It is an interesting alternative to the balanced search tree, is simple to code, and is competitive in practice. In Chapter 20 we examine the hash table, a completely different method used to implement searching operations.

key concepts

AA-tree A balanced search tree that is the tree of choice when an $O(\log N)$ worst case is needed, a casual implementation is acceptable, and deletions are needed. (670)

AVL tree A binary search tree with the additional balance property that, for any node in the tree, the height of the left and right subtrees can differ by at most 1. As the first balanced search tree, it has historical significance. It also illustrates most of the ideas that are used in other search tree schemes. (648)

balanced binary search tree A tree that has an added structure property to guarantee logarithmic depth in the worst case. Updates are slower than with the binary search tree, but accesses are faster. (648)

binary search tree A data structure that supports insertion, searching, and deletion in $O(\log N)$ average time. For any node in the binary search tree, all smaller keyed nodes are in the left subtree and all larger keyed nodes are in the right subtree. Duplicates are not allowed. (630)

B-tree The most popular data structure for disk-bound searching. There are many variations of the same idea. (699)

double rotation Equivalent to two single rotations. (654)

external path length The sum of the cost of accessing all external tree nodes in a binary tree, which measures the cost of an unsuccessful search. (646)

external tree node The `null` node. (647)

horizontal link In an AA-tree, a connection between a node and a child of equal levels. A horizontal link should go only to the right, and there should not be two consecutive horizontal links. (671)

internal path length The sum of the depths of the nodes in a binary tree, which measures the cost of a successful search. (646)

lazy deletion A method that marks items as deleted but does not actually delete them. (670)

level of a node In an AA-tree, the number of left links on the path to the `nullNode` sentinel. (671)

M-ary tree A tree that allows M-way branching, and as branching increases, the depth decreases. (699)

red-black tree A balanced search tree that is a good alternative to the AVL tree because a single top-down pass can be used during the insertion and deletion routines. Nodes are colored red and black in a restricted way that guarantees logarithmic depth. The coding details tend to give a faster implementation. (657)

single rotation Switches the roles of the parent and child while maintaining search order. Balance is restored by tree rotations. (651)

skew Removal of left horizontal links by performing a rotation between a node and its left child. (672)

split Fixing consecutive right horizontal links by performing a rotation between a node and its right child. (672)

common errors

1. Using an unbalanced search tree when the input sequence is not random will give poor performance.
2. The `remove` operation is very tricky to code correctly, especially for a balanced search tree.
3. Lazy deletion is a good alternative to the standard `remove`, but you must then change other routines, such as `findMin`.
4. Code for balanced search trees is almost always error-prone.
5. Forgetting to return a reference to the new subtree root is wrong for the private helper methods `insert` and `remove`. The return value should be assigned to `root`.
6. Using sentinels and then writing code that forgets about the sentinels can lead to infinite loops. A common case is testing against `null` when a `nullNode` sentinel is used.

on the internet

All of the code in this chapter is available online.

BinarySearchTree.java	Contains the implementation of `BinarySearchTree`; **BinaryNode.java** has the node declaration.
BinarySearchTreeWithRank.java	Adds order statistics.
Rotations.java	Contains the basic rotations, as static methods.
RedBlackTree.java	Contains the implementation of the `RedBlackTree` class.
AATree.java	Contains the implementation of the `AATree` class.
TreeSet.java	Contains the implementation of the `TreeSet` class.
MapImpl.java	Contains the abstract `MapImpl` class.
TreeMap.java	Contains the implementation of the `TreeMap` class.

exercises

IN SHORT

19.1 Show the result of inserting 3, 1, 4, 6, 9, 2, 5, and 7 in an initially empty binary search tree. Then show the result of deleting the root.

19.2 Draw all binary search trees that can result from inserting permutations of 1, 2, 3, and 4. How many trees are there? What are the probabilities of each tree's occurring if all permutations are equally likely?

19.3 Draw all AVL trees that can result from inserting permutations of 1, 2, and 3. How many trees are there? What are the probabilities of each tree's occurring if all permutations are equally likely?

19.4 Repeat Exercise 19.3 for four elements.

19.5 Show the result of inserting 2, 1, 4, 5, 9, 3, 6, and 7 into an initially empty AVL tree. Then show the result for a top-down red–black tree.

19.6 Repeat Exercises 19.3 and 19.4 for a red–black tree.

IN THEORY

19.7 Prove Theorem 19.2.

19.8 Show the result of inserting items 1 through 15 in order in an initially empty AVL tree. Generalize this result (with proof) to show what happens when items 1 through $2^k - 1$ are inserted into an initially empty AVL tree.

19.9 Give an algorithm to perform `remove` in an AVL tree.

19.10 Prove that the height of a red–black tree is at most approximately $2 \log N$ and give an insertion sequence that achieves this bound.

19.11 Show that every AVL tree can be colored as a red–black tree. Do all red–black trees satisfy the AVL tree property?

19.12 Prove that the algorithm for deletion in an AA-tree is correct.

19.13 Suppose that the `level` data member in an AA-tree is represented by an 8-bit `byte`. What is the smallest AA-tree that would overflow the `level` data member at the root?

19.14 A B*-tree of order M is a B-tree in which each interior node has between $2M/3$ and M children. Leaves are similarly filled. Describe a method that can be used to perform insertion in a B*-tree.

IN PRACTICE

19.15 Implement `find`, `findMin`, and `findMax` recursively.

19.16 Implement `findKth` nonrecursively, using the same technique used for a nonrecursive `find`.

19.17 An alternative representation that allows the `findKth` operation is to store in each node the value of 1 plus the size of the left subtree. Why might this approach be advantageous? Rewrite the search tree class to use this representation.

19.18 Write a binary search tree method that takes two keys, `low` and `high`, and prints all elements X that are in the range specified by `low` and `high`. Your program should run in $O(K + \log N)$ average time, where K is the number of keys printed. Thus if K is small, you should be examining only a small part of the tree. Use a hidden recursive method and do not use an inorder iterator. Bound the running time of your algorithm.

19.19 Write a binary search tree method that takes two integers, `low` and `high`, and constructs an optimally balanced `BinarySearchTreeWithRank` that contains all the integers between `low` and `high`, inclusive. All leaves should be at the same level (if the tree size is 1 less than a power of 2) or on two consecutive levels. *Your routine should take linear time.* Test your routine by using it to solve the Josephus problem presented in Section 13.1.

19.20 The routines for performing double rotations are inefficient because they perform unnecessary changes to children links. Rewrite them to avoid calls to the single rotation routine.

19.21 Give a nonrecursive top-down implementation of an AA-tree. Compare the implementation with the text's for simplicity and efficiency.

19.22 Write the `skew` and `split` procedures recursively so that only one call of each is needed for `remove`.

PROGRAMMING PROJECTS

19.23 Redo the `BinarySearchTree` class to implement lazy deletion. Note that doing so affects all the routines. Especially challenging are `findMin` and `findMax`, which must now be done recursively.

19.24 Implement the binary search tree to use only one two-way comparison per level for `find`, `insert`, and `remove`.

19.25 Write a program to evaluate empirically the following strategies for removing nodes with two children. Recall that a strategy involves replacing the value in a deleted node with some other value. Which strategy gives the best balance? Which takes the least CPU time to process an entire sequence of operations?

a. Replace with the value in the largest node, X, in T_L and recursively remove X.

b. Alternatively replace with the value in the largest node in T_L or the value in the smallest node in T_R and recursively remove the appropriate node.

c. Replace with the value in the largest node in T_L or the value in the smallest node in T_R (recursively remove the appropriate node), making the choice randomly.

19.26 Implement a binary search tree to allow duplicates. Have each node store a linked list of items that are considered duplicates (using the first item in the linked list) to control branching.

19.27 Implement a `toString` method for class `BinarySearchTree`. Make sure your method runs in linear time. *Hint:* Use a private recursive method that has a `Node` and a `StringBuilder` as its parameters.

19.28 Write the `remove` method for red–black trees.

19.29 Implement the search tree operations with order statistics for the balanced search tree of your choice.

19.30 Reimplement the `TreeSet` class by using parent links.

19.31 Modify the `TreeSet` and `TreeMap` classes so that their iterators are bidirectional.

19.32 Add the `headSet`, `subSet`, and `tailSet` methods to the `TreeSet` class. The behavior of these methods is specified in the Java API documentation.

19.33 Implement a B-tree that works in main memory.

19.34 Implement a B-tree that works for disk files.

references

More information on binary search trees, and in particular the mathematical properties of trees, is available in [18] and [19].

Several papers deal with the theoretical lack of balance caused by biased deletion algorithms in binary search trees. Hibbard [16] proposed the original deletion algorithm and established that one deletion preserves the randomness of the trees. A complete analysis has been performed only for trees with three nodes [17] and four nodes [3]. Eppinger [10] provided early empirical evidence of nonrandomness, and Culberson and Munro [7] and [8] provide some analytical evidence (but not a complete proof for the general case of intermixed insertions and deletions). The claim that the deepest node in a random binary search tree is three times deeper than the average node is proved in [11]; the result is by no means simple.

AVL trees were proposed by Adelson-Velskii and Landis [1]. A deletion algorithm is presented in [19]. Analysis of the average costs of searching an AVL tree is incomplete, but some results are contained in [20]. The top-down red–black tree algorithm is from [15]; a more accessible description is presented in [21]. An implementation of top-down red–black trees without sentinel nodes is given in [12]; it provides a convincing demonstration of the usefulness of `nullNode`. The AA-tree is based on the symmetric binary B-tree discussed in [4]. The implementation shown in the text is adapted from the description in [2]. Many other balanced search trees are described in [13].

B-trees first appeared in [5]. The implementation described in the original paper allows data to be stored in internal nodes as well as in leaves. The data structure described here is sometimes called a B^+-tree. Information on the B*-tree, described in Exercise 19.14, is available in [9]. A survey of the different types of B-trees is presented in [6]. Empirical results of the various schemes are reported in [14]. A C++ implementation is contained in [12].

1. G. M. Adelson-Velskii and E. M. Landis, "An Algorithm for the Organization of Information," *Soviet Math. Doklady* **3** (1962), 1259–1263.
2. A. Andersson, "Balanced Search Trees Made Simple," *Proceedings of the Third Workshop on Algorithms and Data Structures* (1993), 61–71.
3. R. A. Baeza-Yates, "A Trivial Algorithm Whose Analysis Isn't: A Continuation," *BIT* **29** (1989), 88–113.
4. R. Bayer, "Symmetric Binary B-Trees: Data Structure and Maintenance Algorithms," *Acta Informatica* **1** (1972), 290–306.
5. R. Bayer and E. M. McCreight, "Organization and Maintenance of Large Ordered Indices," *Acta Informatica* **1** (1972), 173–189.
6. D. Comer, "The Ubiquitous B-tree," *Computing Surveys* **11** (1979), 121–137.
7. J. Culberson and J. I. Munro, "Explaining the Behavior of Binary Search Trees Under Prolonged Updates: A Model and Simulations," *Computer Journal* **32** (1989), 68–75.
8. J. Culberson and J. I. Munro, "Analysis of the Standard Deletion Algorithm in Exact Fit Domain Binary Search Trees," *Algorithmica* **5** (1990), 295–311.

9. K. Culik, T. Ottman, and D. Wood, "Dense Multiway Trees," *ACM Transactions on Database Systems* **6** (1981), 486–512.
10. J. L. Eppinger, "An Empirical Study of Insertion and Deletion in Binary Search Trees," *Communications of the ACM* **26** (1983), 663–669.
11. P. Flajolet and A. Odlyzko, "The Average Height of Binary Search Trees and Other Simple Trees," *Journal of Computer and System Sciences* **25** (1982), 171–213.
12. B. Flamig, *Practical Data Structures in C++*, John Wiley & Sons, New York, NY, 1994.
13. G. H. Gonnet and R. Baeza-Yates, *Handbook of Algorithms and Data Structures,* 2d ed., Addison-Wesley, Reading, MA, 1991.
14. E. Gudes and S. Tsur, "Experiments with B-tree Reorganization," *Proceedings of ACM SIGMOD Symposium on Management of Data* (1980), 200–206.
15. L. J. Guibas and R. Sedgewick, "A Dichromatic Framework for Balanced Trees," *Proceedings of the Nineteenth Annual IEEE Symposium on Foundations of Computer Science* (1978), 8–21.
16. T. H. Hibbard, "Some Combinatorial Properties of Certain Trees with Applications to Searching and Sorting," *Journal of the ACM* **9** (1962), 13–28.
17. A. T. Jonassen and D. E. Knuth, "A Trivial Algorithm Whose Analysis Isn't," *Journal of Computer and System Sciences* **16** (1978), 301–322.
18. D. E. Knuth, *The Art of Computer Programming: Vol. 1: Fundamental Algorithms*, 3d ed., Addison-Wesley, Reading, MA, 1997.
19. D. E. Knuth, *The Art of Computer Programming: Vol. 3: Sorting and Searching*, 2d ed., Addison-Wesley, Reading, MA, 1998.
20. K. Melhorn, "A Partial Analysis of Height-Balanced Trees Under Random Insertions and Deletions," *SIAM Journal on Computing* **11** (1982), 748–760.
21. R. Sedgewick, *Algorithms in C++*, Addison-Wesley, Reading, MA, 1992.

chapter 20

hash tables

In Chapter 19 we discussed the binary search tree, which allows various operations on a set of elements. In this chapter we discuss the hash table, which supports only a subset of the operations allowed by binary search trees. The implementation of hash tables is frequently called *hashing,* and it performs insertions, deletions, and finds in constant average time.

Unlike with the binary search tree, the average-case running time of hash table operations is based on statistical properties rather than the expectation of random-looking input. This improvement is obtained at the expense of a loss of ordering information among the elements: Operations such as `findMin` and `findMax` and the printing of an entire table in sorted order in linear time are not supported. Consequently, the hash table and binary search tree have somewhat different uses and performance properties.

In this chapter, we show

- Several methods of implementing the hash table
- Analytical comparisons of these methods
- Some applications of hashing
- Comparisons of hash tables and binary search trees

20.1 basic ideas

The *hash table* is used to implement a set in constant time per operation.

The *hash table* supports the retrieval or deletion of any named item. We want to be able to support the basic operations in constant time, as for the stack and queue. Because the accesses are much less restricted, this support seems like an impossible goal. That is, surely when the size of the set increases, searches in the set should take longer. However, that is not necessarily the case.

Suppose that all the items we are dealing with are small nonnegative integers, ranging from 0 to 65,535. We can use a simple array to implement each operation as follows. First, we initialize an array `a` that is indexed from 0 to 65,535 with all 0s. To perform `insert(i)`, we execute `a[i]++`. Note that `a[i]` represents the number of times that `i` has been inserted. To perform `find(i)`, we verify that `a[i]` is not 0. To perform `remove(i)`, we make sure that `a[i]` is positive and then execute `a[i]--`. The time for each operation is clearly constant; even the overhead of the array initialization is a constant amount of work (65,536 assignments).

There are two problems with this solution. First, suppose that we have 32-bit integers instead of 16-bit integers. Then the array `a` must hold 4 billion items, which is impractical. Second, if the items are not integers but instead are strings (or something even more generic), they cannot be used to index an array.

The second problem is not really a problem at all. Just as a number `1234` is a collection of digits `1`, `2`, `3`, and `4`, the string `"junk"` is a collection of characters `'j'`, `'u'`, `'n'`, and `'k'`. Note that the number `1234` is just $1 \cdot 10^3 + 2 \cdot 10^2 + 3 \cdot 10^1 + 4 \cdot 10^0$. Recall from Section 12.1 that an ASCII character can typically be represented in 7 bits as a number between 0 and 127. Because a character is basically a small integer, we can interpret a string as an integer. One possible representation is `'j'` $\cdot\ 128^3 +$ `'u'` $\cdot\ 128^2 +$ `'n'` $\cdot\ 128^1 +$ `'k'` $\cdot\ 128^0$. This approach allows the simple array implementation discussed previously.

The problem with this strategy is that the integer representation described generates huge integers: The representation for `"junk"` yields 224,229,227, and longer strings generate much larger representations. This result brings us back to the first problem: How do we avoid using an absurdly large array?

A *hash function* converts the item into an integer suitable to index an array where the item is stored. If the hash function were one to one, we could access the item by its array index.

We do so by using a function that maps large numbers (or strings interpreted as numbers) into smaller, more manageable numbers. A function that maps an item into a small index is known as a *hash function.* If `x` is an arbitrary (nonnegative) integer, then `x%tableSize` generates a number between `0` and `tableSize-1` suitable for indexing into an array of size `tableSize`. If `s` is a string, we can convert `s` to a large integer `x` by using the method suggested previously and then apply the mod operator (`%`) to get a suitable index. Thus, if `tableSize` is 10,000, `"junk"` would be indexed to 9,227. In Section 20.2 we discuss implementation of the hash function for strings in detail.

The use of the hash function introduces a complication: Two or more different items can hash out to the same position, causing a *collision.* This situation can never be avoided because there are many more items than positions. However, many methods are available for quickly resolving a collision. We investigate three of the simplest: linear probing, quadratic probing, and separate chaining. Each method is simple to implement, but each yields a different performance, depending on how full the array is.

Because the hash function is not one to one, several items collide at the same index and cause a *collision.*

20.2 hash function

Computing the hash function for strings has a subtle complication: The conversion of the `String` `s` to `x` generates an integer that is almost certainly larger than the machine can store conveniently—because $128^4 = 2^{28}$. This integer size is only a factor of 8 from the largest `int`. Consequently, we cannot expect to compute the hash function by directly computing powers of 128. Instead, we use the following observation. A general polynomial

$$A_3X^3 + A_2X^2 + A_1X^1 + A_0X^0 \qquad \textbf{(20.1)}$$

can be evaluated as

$$(((A_3)X + A_2)X + A_1)X + A_0 \qquad \textbf{(20.2)}$$

Note that in Equation 20.2, we avoid computation of the polynomial directly, which is good for three reasons. First, it avoids a large intermediate result, which, as we have shown, overflows. Second, the calculation in the equation involves only three multiplications and three additions; an N-degree polynomial is computed in N multiplications and additions. These operations compare favorably with the computation in Equation 20.1. Third, the calculation proceeds left to right (A_3 corresponds to `'j'`, A_2 to `'u'`, and so on, and X is 128).

By using a trick, we can evaluate the hash function efficiently and without overflow.

However, an overflow problem persists: The result of the calculation is still the same and is likely to be too large. But, we need only the result taken mod `tableSize`. By applying the `%` operator after each multiplication (or addition), we can ensure that the intermediate results remain small.[1] The resulting hash function is shown in Figure 20.1. An annoying feature of this hash function is that the mod computation is expensive. Because overflow is allowed (and its results are consistent on a given platform), we can make the hash

1. Section 7.4 contains the properties of the mod operation.

figure 20.1

A first attempt at a hash function implementation

```
// Acceptable hash function
public static int hash( String key, int tableSize )
{
    int hashVal = 0;

    for( int i = 0; i < key.length( ); i++ )
        hashVal = ( hashVal * 128 + key.charAt( i ) )
                                              % tableSize;
    return hashVal;
}
```

function somewhat faster by performing a single mod operation immediately prior to the return. Unfortunately, the repeated multiplication by 128 would tend to shift the early characters to the left—out of the answer. To alleviate this situation, we multiply by 37 instead of 128, which slows the shifting of early characters.

The hash function must be simple to compute but also distribute the keys equitably. If there are too many collisions, the performance of the hash table will suffer dramatically.

The result is shown in Figure 20.2. It is not necessarily the best function possible. Also, in some applications (e.g., if long strings are involved), we may want to tinker with it. Generally speaking, however, the function is quite good. Note that overflow could introduce negative numbers. Thus if the mod generates a negative value, we make it positive (lines 15 and 16). Also note that the result obtained by allowing overflow and doing a final mod is not the same as performing the mod after every step. Thus we have slightly altered the hash function—which is not a problem.

figure 20.2

A faster hash function that takes advantage of overflow

```
 1  /**
 2   * A hash routine for String objects.
 3   * @param key the String to hash.
 4   * @param tableSize the size of the hash table.
 5   * @return the hash value.
 6   */
 7  public static int hash( String key, int tableSize )
 8  {
 9      int hashVal = 0;
10
11      for( int i = 0; i < key.length( ); i++ )
12          hashVal = 37 * hashVal + key.charAt( i );
13
14      hashVal %= tableSize;
15      if( hashVal < 0 )
16          hashVal += tableSize;
17
18      return hashVal;
19  }
```

```
// A poor hash function when tableSize is large
public static int hash( String key, int tableSize )
{
    int hashVal = 0;

    for( int i = 0; i < key.length( ); i++ )
       hashVal += key.charAt( i );

    return hashVal % tableSize;
}
```

figure 20.3

A bad hash function if `tableSize` is large

Although speed is an important consideration in designing a hash function, we also want to be sure that it distributes the keys equitably. Consequently, we must not take our optimizations too far. An example is the hash function shown in Figure 20.3. It simply adds the characters in the keys and returns the result mod `tableSize`. What could be simpler? The answer is that little could be simpler. The function is easy to implement and computes a hash value very quickly. However, if `tableSize` is large, the function does not distribute the keys well. For instance, suppose that `tableSize` is 10,000. Also suppose that all keys are 8 or fewer characters long. Because an ASCII `char` is an integer between 0 and 127, the hash function can assume values only between 0 and 1,016 (127×8). This restriction certainly does not permit an equitable distribution. Any speed gained by the quickness of the hash function calculation is more than offset by the effort taken to resolve a larger than expected number of collisions. However, a reasonable alternative is described in Exercise 20.14.

Finally, note that 0 is a possible result of the hash function, so hash tables are indexed starting at 0.

The table runs from `0` to `tableSize-1`.

20.3 linear probing

In *linear probing*, collisions are resolved by sequentially scanning an array (with wraparound) until an empty cell is found.

Now that we have a hash function, we need to decide what to do when a collision occurs. Specifically, if X hashes out to a position that is already occupied, where do we place it? The simplest possible strategy is *linear probing*, or searching sequentially in the array until we find an empty cell. The search wraps around from the last position to the first, if necessary. Figure 20.4 shows the result of inserting the keys 89, 18, 49, 58, and 9 in a hash table when linear probing is used. We assume a hash function that returns the key X mod the size of the table. Figure 20.4 includes the result of the hash function.

The first collision occurs when 49 is inserted; the 49 is put in the next available spot—namely, spot 0, which is open. Then 58 collides with 18, 89, and 49 before an empty spot is found three slots away in position 1. The colli-

figure 20.4

Linear probing hash table after each insertion

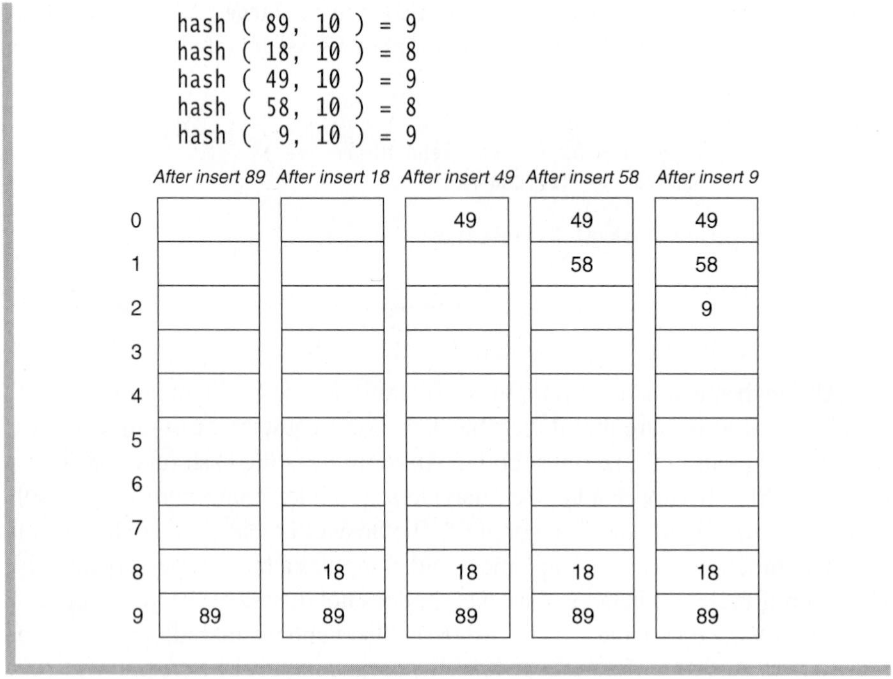
hash (89, 10) = 9
hash (18, 10) = 8
hash (49, 10) = 9
hash (58, 10) = 8
hash (9, 10) = 9
After insert 89
After insert 18
After insert 49
After insert 58
After insert 9
0
1
2
3
4
5
6
7
8
9
49
58
9
18
89

sion for element 9 is resolved similarly. So long as the table is large enough, a free cell can always be found. However, the time needed to find a free cell can get to be quite long. For example, if there is only one free cell left in the table, we may have to search the entire table to find it. On average we would expect to have to search half the table to find it, which is far from the constant time per access that we are hoping for. But, if the table is kept relatively empty, insertions should not be so costly. We discuss this approach shortly.

The `find` algorithm follows the same probe sequence as the `insert` algorithm.

The `find` algorithm merely follows the same path as the `insert` algorithm. If it reaches an empty slot, the item we are searching for is not found; otherwise, it finds the match eventually. For example, to find 58, we start at slot 8 (as indicated by the hash function). We see an item, but it is the wrong one, so we try slot 9. Again, we have an item, but it is the wrong one, so we try slot 0 and then slot 1 until we find a match. A `find` for 19 would involve trying slots 9, 0, 1, and 2 before finding the empty cell in slot 3. Thus 19 is not found.

We must use *lazy deletion.*

Standard deletion cannot be performed because, as with a binary search tree, an item in the hash table not only represents itself, but it also connects other items by serving as a placeholder during collision resolution. Thus, if we removed 89 from the hash table, virtually all the remaining `find` operations would fail. Consequently, we implement *lazy deletion,* or marking items as deleted rather than physically removing them from the table. This information is recorded in an extra data member. Each item is either *active* or *deleted.*

20.3.1 naive analysis of linear probing

To estimate the performance of linear probing, we make two assumptions:

1. The hash table is large
2. Each probe in the hash table is independent of the previous probe.

The simplistic analysis of linear probing is based on the assumption that successive probes are independent. This assumption is not true and thus the analysis underestimates the costs of searching and insertion.

Assumption 1 is reasonable; otherwise, we would not be bothering with a hash table. Assumption 2 says that, if the fraction of the table that is full is λ, each time we examine a cell the probability that it is occupied is also λ, independent of any previous probes. Independence is an important statistical property that greatly simplifies the analysis of random events. Unfortunately, as discussed in Section 20.3.2, the assumption of independence is not only unjustified, but it also is erroneous. Thus the naive analysis that we perform is incorrect. Even so, it is helpful because it tells us what we can hope to achieve if we are more careful about how collisions are resolved. As mentioned earlier in the chapter, the performance of the hash table depends on how full the table is. Its fullness is given by the load factor.

The *load factor* of a probing hash table is the fraction of the table that is full. It ranges from 0 (empty) to 1 (full).

definition: The *load factor,* λ,of a probing hash table is the fraction of the table that is full. The load factor ranges from 0 (empty) to 1 (completely full).

We can now give a simple but incorrect analysis of linear probing in Theorem 20.1.

Theorem 20.1

If independence of probes is assumed, the average number of cells examined in an insertion using linear probing is $1/(1-\lambda)$.

Proof

For a table with a load factor of λ, the probability of any cell's being empty is $1-\lambda$. Consequently, the expected number of independent trials required to find an empty cell is $1/(1-\lambda)$.

In the proof of Theorem 20.1 we use the fact that, if the probability of some event's occurring is *p,* then on average $1/p$ trials are required until the event occurs, provided that the trials are independent. For example, the expected number of coin flips until a heads occurs is two, and the expected number of rolls of a single six-sided die until a 4 occurs is six, assuming independence.

20.3.2 what really happens: primary clustering

The effect of *primary clustering* is the formation of large clusters of occupied cells, making insertions into the cluster expensive (and then the insertion makes the cluster even larger).

Unfortunately, independence does not hold, as shown in Figure 20.5. Part (a) shows the result of filling a hash table to 70 percent capacity, if all successive probes are independent. Part (b) shows the result of linear probing. Note the group of clusters: the phenomenon known as *primary clustering*.

In *primary clustering,* large blocks of occupied cells are formed. Any key that hashes into this cluster requires excessive attempts to resolve the collision, and then it adds to the size of the cluster. Not only do items that collide because of identical hash functions cause degenerate performance, but also an item that collides with an alternative location for another item causes poor performance. The mathematical analysis required to take this phenomenon into account is complex but has been solved, yielding Theorem 20.2.

Theorem 20.2 The average number of cells examined in an insertion using linear probing is roughly $(1 + 1/(1 - \lambda)^2)/2$.

Proof The proof is beyond the scope of this text. See reference [6].

For a half-full table, we obtain 2.5 as the average number of cells examined during an insertion. This outcome is almost the same as what the naive

(a) (b) (c)

figure 20.5

Illustration of primary clustering in linear probing (b) versus no clustering (a) and the less significant secondary clustering in quadratic probing (c). Long lines represent occupied cells, and the load factor is 0.7.

analysis indicated. The main difference occurs as λ gets close to 1. For instance, if the table is 90 percent full, $\lambda = 0.9$. The naive analysis suggests that 10 cells would have to be examined—a lot but not completely out of the question. However, by Theorem 20.2, the real answer is that some 50 cells need to be examined. That is excessive (especially as this number is only an average and thus some insertions must be worse).

Primary clustering is a problem at high load factors. For half-empty tables, the effect is not disastrous.

20.3.3 analysis of the `find` operation

The cost of an insertion can be used to bound the cost of a `find`. There are two types of `find` operations: unsuccessful and successful. An unsuccessful `find` is easy to analyze. The sequence of slots examined for an unsuccessful search of X is the same as the sequence examined to `insert` X. Thus we have an immediate answer for the cost of an unsuccessful `find`.

An unsuccessful `find` costs the same as an insertion.

For successful `finds`, things are slightly more complicated. Figure 20.4 shows a table with $\lambda = 0.5$. Thus the average cost of an insertion is 2.5. The average cost to `find` the newly inserted item would then be 2.5, no matter how many insertions follow. The average cost to find the first item inserted in the table is always 1.0 probe. Thus, in a table with $\lambda = 0.5$, some searches are easy and some are hard. In particular, the cost of a successful search of X is equal to the cost of inserting *X at the time X was inserted.* To find the average time to perform a successful search in a table with load factor λ, we must compute the average insertion cost by averaging over all the load factors leading to λ. With this groundwork, we can compute the average search times for linear probing, as asserted and proved in Theorem 20.3.

The cost of a successful `find` is an average of the insertion costs over all smaller load factors.

Theorem 20.3

The average number of cells examined in an unsuccessful search using linear probing is roughly $(1 + 1/(1-\lambda)^2)/2$. The average number of cells examined in a successful search is approximately $(1 + 1/(1-\lambda))/2$.

Proof

The cost of an unsuccessful search is the same as the cost of an insertion. For a successful search, we compute the average insertion cost over the sequence of insertions. Because the table is large, we can compute this average by evaluating

$$S(\lambda) = \frac{1}{\lambda}\int_{x=0}^{\lambda} I(x)dx$$

(*continued on next page*)

Proof of Theorem 20.3

(continued from previous page)

In other words, the average cost of a successful search for a table with a load factor of λ equals the cost of an insertion in a table of load factor x, averaged from load factors 0 through λ. From Theorem 20.2, we can derive the following equation:

$$\begin{aligned} S(\lambda) &= \frac{1}{\lambda}\int_{x=0}^{\lambda}\frac{1}{2}\left(1+\frac{1}{(1-x)^2}\right)dx \\ &= \frac{1}{2\lambda}\left(x+\frac{1}{(1-x)}\right)\Bigg|_{x=0}^{\lambda} \\ &= \frac{1}{2\lambda}\left(\left(\lambda+\frac{1}{(1-\lambda)}\right)-1\right) \\ &= \frac{1}{2}\left(\frac{2-\lambda}{1-\lambda}\right) \\ &= \frac{1}{2}\left(1+\frac{1}{(1-\lambda)}\right) \end{aligned}$$

We can apply the same technique to obtain the cost of a successful `find` under the assumption of independence (by using $I(x) = 1/(1-x)$ in Theorem 20.3). If there is no clustering, the average cost of a successful `find` for linear probing is $-\ln(1-\lambda)/\lambda$. If the load factor is 0.5, the average number of probes for a successful search using linear probing is 1.5, whereas the nonclustering analysis suggests 1.4 probes. Note that this average does not depend on any ordering of the input keys; it depends only on the fairness of the hash function. Note also that, even when we have good hash functions, both longer and shorter probe sequences are bound to contribute to the average. For instance, there are certain to be some sequences of length 4, 5, and 6, even in a hash table that is half empty. (Determining the expected longest probe sequence is a challenging calculation.) Primary clustering not only makes the average probe sequence longer, but it also makes a long probe sequence more likely. The main problem with primary clustering therefore is that performance degrades severely for insertion at high load factors. Also, some of the longer probe sequences typically encountered (those at the high end of the average) are made more likely to occur.

To reduce the number of probes, we need a collision resolution scheme that avoids primary clustering. Note, however, that, if the table is half empty, removing the effects of primary clustering would save only half a probe on average for an insertion or unsuccessful search and one-tenth a probe on average for a successful search. Even though we might expect to reduce the probability of getting a somewhat lengthier probe sequence, *linear probing is not a terrible strategy.* Because it is so easy to implement, any method we use to remove primary clustering must be of comparable complexity. Otherwise, we expend too much time in saving only a fraction of a probe. One such method is *quadratic probing*.

20.4 quadratic probing

Quadratic probing examines cells 1, 4, 9, and so on, away from the original probe point.

Quadratic probing is a collision resolution method that eliminates the primary clustering problem of linear probing by examining certain cells away from the original probe point. Its name is derived from the use of the formula $F(i) = i^2$ to resolve collisions. Specifically, if the hash function evaluates to H and a search in cell H is inconclusive, we try cells $H + 1^2$, $H + 2^2$, $H + 3^2$, …, $H + i^2$ (employing wraparound) in sequence. This strategy differs from the linear probing strategy of searching $H + 1$, $H + 2$, $H + 3$, …, $H + i$.

Remember that subsequent probe points are a quadratic number of positions from the *original probe point.*

Figure 20.6 shows the table that results when quadratic probing is used instead of linear probing for the insertion sequence shown in Figure 20.4. When 49 collides with 89, the first alternative attempted is one cell away. This cell is empty, so 49 is placed there. Next, 58 collides at position 8. The cell at position 9 (which is one away) is tried, but another collision occurs. A vacant cell is found at the next cell tried, which is $2^2 = 4$ positions away *from the original hash position*. Thus 58 is placed in cell 2. The same thing happens for 9. Note that the alternative locations for items that hash to position 8 and

```
hash ( 89, 10 ) = 9
hash ( 18, 10 ) = 8
hash ( 49, 10 ) = 9
hash ( 58, 10 ) = 8
hash (  9, 10 ) = 9
```

	After insert 89	After insert 18	After insert 49	After insert 58	After insert 9
0			49	49	49
1					
2				58	58
3					9
4					
5					
6					
7					
8		18	18	18	18
9	89	89	89	89	89

figure 20.6

A quadratic probing hash table after each insertion (note that the table size was poorly chosen because it is not a prime number).

the alternative locations for the items that hash to position 9 are not the same. The long probe sequence to insert 58 did not affect the subsequent insertion of 9, which contrasts with what happened with linear probing.

We need to consider a few details before we write code.

- In linear probing, each probe tries a different cell. Does quadratic probing guarantee that, when a cell is tried, we have not already tried it during the course of the current access? Does quadratic probing guarantee that, when we are inserting X and the table is not full, X will be inserted?
- Linear probing is easily implemented. Quadratic probing appears to require multiplication and mod operations. Does this apparent added complexity make quadratic probing impractical?
- What happens (in both linear probing and quadratic probing) if the load factor gets too high? Can we dynamically expand the table, as is typically done with other array-based data structures?

If the table size is prime and the load factor is no larger than 0.5, all probes will be to different locations and an item can always be inserted.

Fortunately, the news is relatively good on all cases. If the table size is prime and the load factor never exceeds 0.5, we can always place a new item X and no cell is probed twice during an access. However, for these guarantees to hold, we need to ensure that the table size is a prime number. We prove this case in Theorem 20.4.

Theorem 20.4

If quadratic probing is used and the table size is prime, then a new element can always be inserted if the table is at least half empty. Furthermore, in the course of the insertion, no cell is probed twice.

Proof

Let M be the size of the table. Assume that M is an odd prime greater than 3. We show that the first $\lceil M/2 \rceil$ alternative locations (including the original) are distinct. Two of these locations are $H + i^2 (\text{mod } M)$ and $H + j^2 (\text{mod } M)$, where $0 \le i, j \le \lfloor M/2 \rfloor$. Suppose, for the sake of contradiction, that these two locations are the same but that $i \ne j$. Then

$$H + i^2 \equiv H + j^2 (\text{mod } M)$$
$$i^2 \equiv j^2 (\text{mod } M)$$
$$i^2 - j^2 \equiv 0 (\text{mod } M)$$
$$(i - j)(i + j) \equiv 0 (\text{mod } M)$$

Because M is prime, it follows that either $i - j$ or $i + j$ is divisible by M. As i and j are distinct and their sum is smaller than M, neither of these possibilities can occur. Thus we obtain a contradiction. It follows that the first $\lceil M/2 \rceil$ alternatives (including the original location) are all distinct and guarantee that an insertion must succeed if the table is at least half empty.

```java
/**
 * Method to find a prime number at least as large as n.
 * @param n the starting number (must be positive).
 * @return a prime number larger than or equal to n.
 */
private static int nextPrime( int n )
{
    if( n % 2 == 0 )
        n++;

    for( ; !isPrime( n ); n += 2 )
        ;

    return n;
}
```

figure 20.7

A routine used in quadratic probing to find a prime greater than or equal to N

For completeness, Figure 20.7 shows a routine that generates prime numbers, using the algorithm shown in Figure 9.7 (a more complex algorithm is not warranted).

If the table is even 1 more than half full, the insertion could fail (although failure is extremely unlikely). If we keep the table size prime and the load factor below 0.5, we have a guarantee of success for the insertion. If the table size is not prime, the number of alternative locations can be severely reduced. For example, if the table size was 16, the only alternative locations would be at distances 1, 4, or 9 from the original probe point. Again, size is not really an issue: Although we would not have a guarantee of $\lfloor M/2 \rfloor$ alternatives, we would usually have more than we need. However, it is best to play it safe and use the theory to guide us in selecting parameters. Furthermore, it has been shown empirically that prime numbers tend to be good for hash tables because they tend to remove some of the nonrandomness that is occasionally introduced by the hash function.

Quadratic probing can be implemented without multiplications and mod operations. Because it does not suffer from primary clustering, it outperforms linear probing in practice.

The second important consideration is efficiency. Recall that, for a load factor of 0.5, removing primary clustering saves only 0.5 probe for an average insertion and 0.1 probe for an average successful search. We do get some additional benefits: Encountering a long probe sequence is significantly less likely. However, if performing a probe using quadratic probing takes twice as long, doing so is hardly worth the effort. Linear probing is implemented with a simple addition (by 1), a test to determine whether wraparound is needed, and a very rare subtraction (if we need to do the wraparound). The formula for quadratic probing suggests that we need to do an addition by 1 (to go from $i-1$ to i), a multiplication (to compute i^2), another addition, and then a mod operation. Certainly this calculation appears to be much too expensive to be practical. However, we can use the following trick, as explained in Theorem 20.5.

Theorem 20.5

Quadratic probing can be implemented without expensive multiplications and divisions.

Proof

Let H_{i-1} be the most recently computed probe (H_0 is the original hash position) and H_i be the probe we are trying to compute. Then we have

$$\begin{aligned} H_i &= H_0 + i^2 (\text{mod } M) \\ H_{i-1} &= H_0 + (i-1)^2 (\text{mod } M) \end{aligned} \tag{20.3}$$

If we subtract these two equations, we obtain

$$H_i = H_{i-1} + 2i - 1 (\text{mod } M) \tag{20.4}$$

Equation 20.4 tells us that we compute the new value H_i from the previous value H_{i-1} without squaring i. Although we still have a multiplication, the multiplication is by 2, which is a trivially implemented bit shift on most computers. What about the mod operation? That, too, is not really needed because the expression $2i - 1$ must be smaller than M. Therefore, if we add it to H_{i-1}, the result will be either still smaller than M (in which case, we do not need the mod) or just a little larger than M (in which case, we can compute the mod equivalent by subtracting M).

Expand the table as soon as the load factor reaches 0.5, which is called *rehashing*. Always double to a prime number. Prime numbers are easy to find.

Theorem 20.5 shows that we can compute the next position to probe by using an addition (to increment i), a bit shift (to evaluate $2i$), a subtraction by 1 (to evaluate $2i - 1$), another addition (to increment the old position by $2i - 1$), a test to determine whether wraparound is needed, and a very rare subtraction to implement the mod operation. The difference is thus a bit shift, a subtraction by 1, and an addition per probe. The cost of this operation is likely to be less than the cost of doing an extra probe if complex keys (such as strings) are involved.

The final detail to consider is dynamic expansion. If the load factor exceeds 0.5, we want to double the size of the hash table. This approach raises a few issues. First, how hard will it be to find another prime number? The answer is that prime numbers are easy to find. We expect to have to test only $O(\log N)$ numbers until we find a number that is prime. Consequently, the routine shown in Figure 20.7 is very fast. The primality test takes at most $O(N^{1/2})$ time, so the search for a prime number takes at most $O(N^{1/2} \log N)$ time.[2] This cost is much less than the $O(N)$ cost of transferring the contents of the old table to the new.

2. This routine is also required if we add a constructor that allows the user to specify an approximate initial size for the hash table. The hash table implementation must ensure that a prime number is used.

Once we have allocated a larger array, do we just copy everything over? The answer is most definitely no. The new array implies a new hash function, so we cannot use the old array positions. Thus we have to examine each element in the old table, compute its new hash value, and insert it in the new hash table. This process is called *rehashing*. Rehashing is easily implemented in Java.

When expanding a hash table, reinsert in the new table by using the new hash function.

20.4.1 **java implementation**

We are now ready to give a complete Java implementation of a quadratic probing hash table. We will do so by implementing most of `HashSet` and `HashMap` from the Collections API. Recall that `HashSet` and `HashMap` both require a `hashCode` method. `hashCode` has no `tableSize` parameter; the hash table algorithms perform a final mod operation internally after using the user-supplied hash function. The version for `String` is similar to Figure 20.2, with 31 replacing 37. The class skeleton for `HashSet` is shown in Figure 20.8. For the algorithms to work correctly, `equals` and `hashCode` must be consistent. That is, if two objects are equal, their hash values must be equal.

The user must provide an appropriate `hashCode` method for objects.

The hash table consists of an array of `HashEntry` references. Each `HashEntry` reference is either `null` or an object that stores an item and a data member that tells us that the entry is either active or deleted. Because arrays of generic types are illegal, `HashEntry` is not generic. The `HashEntry` nested class is shown in Figure 20.9. The array is declared at line 49. We need to keep track of both the logical size of the `HashSet` and the number of items in the hash table (including elements marked as deleted); these values are stored in `currentSize` and `occupied`, respectively, which are declared at lines 46 and 47.

The rest of the class contains declarations for the hash table routines and iterator. The general layout is similar to that for `TreeSet`.

The general layout is similar to that for `TreeSet`.

Three private methods are declared; we describe them when they are used in the class implementation. We can now discuss the implementation of the `HashSet` class.

The hash table constructors are shown in Figure 20.10; nothing special is going on here. The searching routine, `contains`, and the nonstandard `getMatch` are shown in Figure 20.11. `contains` uses the private method `isActive`, shown in Figure 20.12. Both `contains` and `getMatch` also call `findPos`, shown later, to implement quadratic probing. The `findPos` method is the only place in the entire code that depends on quadratic probing. Then `contains` and `getMatch` are easy to implement: An element is found if the result of `findPos` is an active cell (if `findPos` stops on an active cell, there must be a match). Similarly, the `remove` routine shown in Figure 20.13 is short. We check whether `findPos` takes us to an active cell; if so, the cell is marked deleted. Otherwise,

Most routines are just a few lines of code because they call `findPos` to perform quadratic probing.

figure 20.8

The class skeleton for a quadratic probing hash table

```
package weiss.util;

public class HashSet<AnyType> extends AbstractCollection<AnyType>
                              implements Set<AnyType>
{
    private class HashSetIterator implements Iterator<AnyType>
      { /* Figure 20.17 */ }
    private static class HashEntry implements java.io.Serializable
      { /* Figure 20.9 */ }

    public HashSet( )
      { /* Figure 20.10 */ }
    public HashSet( Collection<? extends AnyType> other )
      { /* Figure 20.10 */ }

    public int size( )
      { return currentSize; }
    public Iterator iterator( )
      { return new HashSetIterator( ); }

    public boolean contains( Object x )
      { /* Figure 20.11 */ }
    private static boolean isActive( HashEntry [ ] arr, int pos )
      { /* Figure 20.12 */ }
    public AnyType getMatch( AnyType x )
      { /* Figure 20.11 */ }

    public boolean remove( Object x )
      { /* Figure 20.13 */ }
    public void clear( )
      { /* Figure 20.13 */ }
    public boolean add( AnyType x )
      { /* Figure 20.14 */ }
    private void rehash( )
      { /* Figure 20.15 */ }
    private int findPos( Object x )
      { /* Figure 20.16 */ }

    private void allocateArray( int arraySize )
      { array = new HashEntry[ arraySize ]; }
    private static int nextPrime( int n )
      { /* Figure 20.7 */ }
    private static boolean isPrime( int n )
      { See online code  */ }

    private int currentSize = 0;
    private int occupied = 0;
    private int modCount = 0;
    private HashEntry [ ] array;
}
```

```
private static class HashEntry implements java.io.Serializable
{
    public Object  element;   // the element
    public boolean isActive;  // false if marked deleted

    public HashEntry( Object e )
    {
        this( e, true );
    }

    public HashEntry( Object e, boolean i )
    {
        element  = e;
        isActive = i;
    }
}
```

figure 20.9

The `HashEntry` nested class

```
private static final int DEFAULT_TABLE_SIZE = 101;

/**
 * Construct an empty HashSet.
 */
public HashSet( )
{
    allocateArray( DEFAULT_TABLE_SIZE );
    clear( );
}

/**
 * Construct a HashSet from any collection.
 */
public HashSet( Collection<? extends AnyType> other )
{
    allocateArray( nextPrime( other.size( ) * 2 ) );
    clear( );

    for( AnyType val : other )
        add( val );
}
```

figure 20.10

Hash table initialization

`false` is returned immediately. Note that this lowers `currentSize`, but not `occupied`. Also, if there are many deleted items, the hash table is resized, at lines 16–17. The maintenance of `modCount` is identical to the other Collections API components previously implemented. `clear` removes all items from the `HashSet`.

figure 20.11

The searching routines for a quadratic probing hash table

```
/**
 * This method is not part of standard Java.
 * Like contains, it checks if x is in the set.
 * If it is, it returns the reference to the matching
 * object; otherwise it returns null.
 * @param x the object to search for.
 * @return if contains(x) is false, the return value is null;
 * otherwise, the return value is the object that causes
 * contains(x) to return true.
 */
public AnyType getMatch( AnyType x )
{
    int currentPos = findPos( x );

    if( isActive( array, currentPos ) )
        return (AnyType) array[ currentPos ].element;
    return null;
}

/**
 * Tests if some item is in this collection.
 * @param x any object.
 * @return true if this collection contains an item equal to x.
 */
public boolean contains( Object x )
{
    return isActive( array, findPos( x ) );
}
```

```
/**
 * Tests if item in pos is active.
 * @param pos a position in the hash table.
 * @param arr the HashEntry array (can be oldArray during rehash).
 * @return true if this position is active.
 */
private static boolean isActive( HashEntry [ ] arr, int pos )
{
    return arr[ pos ] != null && arr[ pos ].isActive;
}
```

figure 20.12

The `isActive` method for a quadratic probing hash table

The `add` routine is shown in Figure 20.14. At line 8 we call `findPos`. If `x` is found, we return `false` at line 10 because duplicates are not allowed. Otherwise, `findPos` gives the place to insert `x`. The insertion is performed at line 12. We adjust `currentSize`, `occupied`, and `modCount` at lines 13–15 and return unless a rehash is in order; otherwise, we call the private method `rehash`.

```
/**
 * Removes an item from this collection.
 * @param x any object.
 * @return true if this item was removed from the collection.
 */
public boolean remove( Object x )
{
    int currentPos = findPos( x );
    if( !isActive( array, currentPos ) )
        return false;

    array[ currentPos ].isActive = false;
    currentSize--;
    modCount++;

    if( currentSize < array.length / 8 )
        rehash( );

    return true;
}

/**
 * Change the size of this collection to zero.
 */
public void clear( )
{
    currentSize = occupied = 0;
    modCount++;
    for( int i = 0; i < array.length; i++ )
        array[ i ] = null;
}
```

figure 20.13

The `remove` and `clear` routines for a quadratic probing hash table

The code that implements rehashing is shown in Figure 20.15. Line 7 saves a reference to the original table. We create a new, empty hash table at lines 10–12 that will have a 0.25 load factor when `rehash` terminates. Then we scan through the original array and `add` any active elements in the new table. The `add` routine uses the new hash function (as it is logically based on the size of `array`, which has changed) and automatically resolves all collisions. We can be sure that the recursive call to `add` (at line 17) does not force another rehash. Alternatively, we could replace line 17 with two lines of code surrounded by braces (see Exercise 20.13).

The `add` routine performs rehashing if the table is (half) full.

So far, nothing that we have done depends on quadratic probing. Figure 20.16 implements `findPos`, which finally deals with the quadratic probing algorithm. We keep searching the table until we find an empty cell or a match. Lines 22–25 directly implement the methodology described in Theorem 20.5, using two additions. There are additional complications because `null` is a valid item in the `HashSet`; the code illustrates why it is preferable to assume that `null` is invalid.

figure 20.14

The add routine for a quadratic probing hash table

```
/**
 * Adds an item to this collection.
 * @param x any object.
 * @return true if this item was added to the collection.
 */
public boolean add( AnyType x )
{
    int currentPos = findPos( x );
    if( isActive( array, currentPos ) )
        return false;

    array[ currentPos ] = new HashEntry( x, true );
    currentSize++;
    occupied++;
    modCount++;

    if( occupied > array.length / 2 )
        rehash( );

    return true;
}
```

figure 20.15

The rehash method for a quadratic probing hash table

```
/**
 * Private routine to perform rehashing.
 * Can be called by both add and remove.
 */
private void rehash( )
{
    HashEntry [ ] oldArray = array;

        // Create a new, empty table
    allocateArray( nextPrime( 4 * size( ) ) );
    currentSize = 0;
    occupied = 0;

        // Copy table over
    for( int i = 0; i < oldArray.length; i++ )
        if( isActive( oldArray, i ) )
            add( (AnyType) oldArray[ i ].element );
}
```

Figure 20.17 gives the implementation of the iterator inner class. It is relatively standard fare, though quite tricky. `visited` represents the number of calls to `next`, while `currentPos` represents the index of the last object returned by `next`.

Finally, Figure 20.18 implements `HashMap`. It is much like `TreeMap`, except that `Pair` is a nested class rather than an inner class (it does not need access to

```
/**
 * Method that performs quadratic probing resolution.
 * @param x the item to search for.
 * @return the position where the search terminates.
 */
private int findPos( Object x )
{
    int offset = 1;
    int currentPos = ( x == null ) ?
                     0 : Math.abs( x.hashCode( ) % array.length );

    while( array[ currentPos ] != null )
    {
        if( x == null )
        {
            if( array[ currentPos ].element == null )
                break;
        }
        else if( x.equals( array[ currentPos ].element ) )
            break;

        currentPos += offset;                 // Compute ith probe
        offset += 2;
        if( currentPos >= array.length )      // Implement the mod
            currentPos -= array.length;
    }

    return currentPos;
}
```

figure 20.16

The routine that finally deals with quadratic probing

an outer object), and implements both `equals` and `hashCode` methods instead of the `Comparable` interface.

Quadratic probing is implemented in `findPos`. It uses the previously described trick to avoid multiplications and mods.

20.4.2 analysis of quadratic probing

Quadratic probing has not yet been mathematically analyzed, although we know that it eliminates primary clustering. In quadratic probing, elements that hash to the same position probe the same alternative cells, which is known as *secondary clustering*. Again, the independence of successive probes cannot be assumed. Secondary clustering is a slight theoretical blemish. Simulation results suggest that it generally causes less than an extra one-half probe per search and that this increase is true only for high load factors. Figure 20.5 illustrates the difference between linear probing and quadratic probing and

figure 20.17

The `HashSetIterator` inner class

```
/**
 * This is the implementation of the HashSetIterator.
 * It maintains a notion of a current position and of
 * course the implicit reference to the HashSet.
 */
private class HashSetIterator implements Iterator<AnyType>
{
    private int expectedModCount = modCount;
    private int currentPos = -1;
    private int visited = 0;

    public boolean hasNext( )
    {
        if( expectedModCount != modCount )
            throw new ConcurrentModificationException( );

        return visited != size( );
    }

    public AnyType next( )
    {
        if( !hasNext( ) )
            throw new NoSuchElementException( );

        do
        {
            currentPos++;
        } while( currentPos < array.length &&
                               !isActive( array, currentPos ) );

        visited++;
        return (AnyType) array[ currentPos ].element;
    }

    public void remove( )
    {
        if( expectedModCount != modCount )
          throw new ConcurrentModificationException( );
        if( currentPos == -1 || !isActive( array, currentPos ) )
            throw new IllegalStateException( );

        array[ currentPos ].isActive = false;
        currentSize--;
        visited--;
        modCount++;
        expectedModCount++;
    }
}
```

```java
package weiss.util;

public class HashMap<KeyType,ValueType> extends MapImpl<KeyType,ValueType>
{
    public HashMap( )
      { super( new HashSet<Map.Entry<KeyType,ValueType>>( ) ); }

    public HashMap( Map<KeyType,ValueType> other )
      { super( other ); }

    protected Map.Entry<KeyType,ValueType> makePair( KeyType key, ValueType value )
      { return new Pair<KeyType,ValueType>( key, value ); }

    protected Set<KeyType> makeEmptyKeySet( )
      { return new HashSet<KeyType>( ); }

    protected Set<Map.Entry<KeyType,ValueType>>
    clonePairSet( Set<Map.Entry<KeyType,ValueType>> pairSet )
    {
        return new HashSet<Map.Entry<KeyType,ValueType>>( pairSet );
    }

    private static final class Pair<KeyType,ValueType>
                                  extends MapImpl.Pair<KeyType,ValueType>
    {
        public Pair( KeyType k, ValueType v )
          { super( k, v ); }

        public int hashCode( )
        {
            KeyType k = getKey( );
            return k == null ? 0 : k.hashCode( );
        }

        public boolean equals( Object other )
        {
            if( other instanceof Map.Entry )
            {
                KeyType thisKey = getKey( );
                KeyType otherKey = ((Map.Entry<KeyType,ValueType>) other).getKey( );

                if( thisKey == null )
                    return thisKey == otherKey;
                return thisKey.equals( otherKey );
            }
            else
                return false;
        }
    }
}
```

figure 20.18

The HashMap class

In *secondary clustering,* elements that hash to the same position probe the same alternative cells. Secondary clustering is a minor theoretical blemish.

Double hashing is a hashing technique that does not suffer from secondary clustering. A second hash function is used to drive the collision resolution.

shows that quadratic probing does not suffer from as much clustering as does linear probing.

Techniques that eliminate secondary clustering are available. The most popular is *double hashing,* in which a second hash function is used to drive the collision resolution. Specifically, we probe at a distance $Hash_2(X)$, $2Hash_2(X)$, and so on. The second hash function must be carefully chosen (e.g., it should *never* evaluate to 0), and all cells must be capable of being probed. A function such as $Hash_2(X) = R - (X \bmod R)$, with R a prime smaller than M, generally works well. Double hashing is theoretically interesting because it can be shown to use essentially the same number of probes as the purely random analysis of linear probing would imply. However, it is somewhat more complicated than quadratic probing to implement and requires careful attention to some details.

There seems to be no good reason not to use a quadratic probing strategy, unless the overhead of maintaining a half-empty table is burdensome. That would be the case in other programming languages if the items being stored were very large.

20.5 separate chaining hashing

Separate chaining hashing is a space-efficient alternative to quadratic probing in which an array of linked lists is maintained. It is less sensitive to high load factors.

A popular and space-efficient alternative to quadratic probing is *separate chaining hashing* in which an array of linked lists is maintained. For an array of linked lists, L_0, L_1, ..., L_{M-1}, the hash function tells us in which list to insert an item X and then, during a `find`, which list contains X. The idea is that, although searching a linked list is a linear operation, if the lists are sufficiently short, the search time will be very fast. In particular, suppose that the load factor, N/M, is λ, which is not bounded by 1.0. Thus the average list has length λ, making the expected number of probes for an insertion or unsuccessful search λ and the expected number of probes for a successful search $1 + \lambda/2$. The reason is that a successful search must occur in a nonempty list, and in such a list we expect to have to traverse halfway down the list. The relative cost of a successful search versus an unsuccessful search is unusual in that, if $\lambda < 2$, the successful search is more expensive than the unsuccessful search. This condition makes sense, however, because many unsuccessful searches encounter an empty linked list.

A typical load factor is 1.0; a lower load factor does not significantly enhance performance, but it costs extra space. The appeal of separate chaining hashing is that performance is not affected by a moderately increasing load factor; thus rehashing can be avoided. For languages that do not allow dynamic array expansion, this consideration is significant. Furthermore, the expected number of probes for a search is less than in quadratic probing, particularly for unsuccessful searches.

For separate chaining hashing, a reasonable load factor is 1.0. A lower load factor does not significantly improve performance; a moderately higher load factor is acceptable and can save space.

We can implement separate chaining hashing by using our existing linked list classes. However, because the header node adds space overhead and is not really needed, if space were at a premium we could elect not to reuse components and instead implement a simple stacklike list. The coding effort turns out to be remarkably light. Also, the space overhead is essentially one reference per node, plus an additional reference per list; for example, when the load factor is 1.0, it is two references per item. This feature could be important in other programming languages if the size of an item is large. In that case, we have the same trade-offs as with the array and linked list implementations of stacks. The Java Collections API uses seperate chaining hashing, with a default load factor of 0.75.

20.6 hash tables versus binary search trees

Use a hash table instead of a binary search tree if you do not need order statistics and are worried about nonrandom inputs.

We can also use binary search trees to implement `insert` and `find` operations. Although the resulting average time bounds are $O(\log N)$, binary search trees also support routines that require order and thus are more powerful. Using a hash table, we cannot efficiently find the minimum element or extend the table to allow computation of an order statistic. We cannot search efficiently for a string unless the exact string is known. A binary search tree could quickly find all items in a certain range, but this capability is not supported by a hash table. Furthermore, the $O(\log N)$ bound is not necessarily that much more than $O(1)$, especially since no multiplications or divisions are required by search trees.

The worst case for hashing generally results from an implementation error, whereas sorted input can make binary search trees perform poorly. Balanced search trees are quite expensive to implement. Hence, if no ordering information is required and there is any suspicion that the input might be sorted, hashing is the data structure of choice.

20.7 hashing applications

Hashing applications are abundant.

Hashing applications are abundant. Compilers use hash tables to keep track of declared variables in source code. The data structure is called a *symbol table*. Hash tables are the ideal application for this problem because only `insert` and `find` operations are performed. Identifiers are typically short, so the hash function can be computed quickly. In this application, most searches are successful.

Another common use of hash tables is in game programs. As the program searches through different lines of play, it keeps track of positions that it has encountered by computing a hash function based on the position (and storing its move for that position). If the same position recurs, usually by a simple transposition of moves, the program can avoid expensive recomputation. This general feature of all game-playing programs is called the *transposition table*. We discussed this feature in Section 10.2, where we implemented the tic-tac-toe algorithm.

A third use of hashing is in online spelling checkers. If misspelling detection (as opposed to correction) is important, an entire dictionary can be prehashed and words can be checked in constant time. Hash tables are well suited for this purpose because the words do not have to be alphabetized. Printing out misspellings in the order they occurred in the document is acceptable.

summary

Hash tables can be used to implement the `insert` and `find` operations in constant average time. Paying attention to details such as load factor is especially important in the use of hash tables; otherwise, the constant time bounds are not meaningful. Choosing the hash function carefully is also important when the key is not a short string or integer. You should pick an easily computable function that distributes well.

For separate chaining hashing, the load factor is typically close to 1, although performance does not significantly degrade unless the load factor becomes very large. For quadratic probing, the table size should be prime and the load factor should not exceed 0.5. Rehashing should be used for quadratic probing to allow the table to grow and maintain the correct load factor. This approach is important if space is tight and it is not possible just to declare a huge hash table.

This completes the discussion of basic searching algorithms. In Chapter 21 we examine the binary heap, which implements the priority queue and thus supports efficient access of the minimum item in a collection of items.

key concepts

collision The result when two or more items in a hash table hash out to the same position. This problem is unavoidable because there are more items than positions. (715)

double hashing A hashing technique that does not suffer from secondary clustering. A second hash function is used to drive the collision resolution. (736)

hash function A function that converts the item into an integer suitable to index an array where the item is stored. If the hash function were one to one, we could access the item by its array index. Since the hash function is not one to one, several items will collide at the same index. (714)

hash table A table used to implement a dictionary in constant time per operation. (714)

hashing The implementation of hash tables to perform insertions, deletions, and finds. (713)

linear probing A way to avoid collisions by sequentially scanning an array until an empty cell is found. (717)

load factor The number of elements in a hash table divided by the size of the hash table array, or the fraction of the table that is full. In a probing hash table, the load factor ranges from 0 (empty) to 1 (full). In separate chaining hashing, it can be greater than 1. (719)

lazy deletion The technique of marking elements as deleted instead of physically removing them from a hash table. It is required in probing hash tables. (718)

primary clustering Large clusters of occupied cells form during linear probing, making insertions in the cluster expensive (and then the insertion makes the cluster even larger) and affecting performance. (720)

quadratic probing A collision resolution method that examines cells 1, 4, 9, and so on, away from the original probe point. (723)

secondary clustering Clustering that occurs when elements that hash to the same position probe the same alternative cells. It is a minor theoretical blemish. (733)

separate chaining A space-efficient alternative to quadratic probing in which an array of linked lists is maintained. It is less sensitive to high load factors and exhibits some of the trade-offs considered in the array versus linked list stack implementations. (736)

common errors

1. The hash function returns an `int`. Because intermediate calculations allow overflow, the local variable should check that the result of the mod operation is nonnegative to avoid risking an out-of-bounds return value.

2. The performance of a probing table degrades severely as the load factor approaches 1.0. Do not let this happen. Rehash when the load factor reaches 0.5.
3. The performance of all hashing methods depends on using a good hash function. A common error is providing a poor function.

on the internet

The quadratic probing hash table is available for your perusal.

HashSet.java Contains the implementation of the `HashSet` class.
HashMap.java Contains the implementation of the `HashMap` class.

exercises

IN SHORT

20.1 What are the array indices for a hash table of size 11?

20.2 What is the appropriate probing table size if the number of items in the hash table is 10?

20.3 Explain how deletion is performed in both probing and separate chaining hash tables.

20.4 What is the expected number of probes for both successful and unsuccessful searches in a linear probing table with load factor 0.25?

20.5 Given the input {4371, 1323, 6173, 4199, 4344, 9679, 1989}, a fixed table size of 10, and a hash function $H(X) = X \bmod 10$, show the resulting
a. Linear probing hash table
b. Quadratic probing hash table
c. Separate chaining hash table

20.6 Show the result of rehashing the probing tables in Exercise 20.5. Rehash to a prime table size.

IN THEORY

20.7 An alternative collision resolution strategy is to define a sequence, $F(i) = R_i$, where $R_0 = 0$ and $R_1, R_2, \ldots, R_{M-1}$ is a random permutation of the first $M - 1$ integers (recall that the table size is M).
a. Prove that under this strategy, if the table is not full, the collision can always be resolved.
b. Would this strategy be expected to eliminate primary clustering?

c. Would this strategy be expected to eliminate secondary clustering?
d. If the load factor of the table is λ, what is the expected time to perform an insertion?
e. Generating a random permutation using the algorithm in Section 9.4 involves a large number of (expensive) calls to a random number generator. Give an efficient algorithm to generate a random-looking permutation that avoids calling a random number generator.

20.8 If rehashing is implemented as soon as the load factor reaches 0.5, when the last element is inserted the load factor is at least 0.25 and at most 0.5. What is the expected load factor? In other words, is it true or false that the load factor is 0.375 on average?

20.9 When the rehashing step is implemented, you must use $O(N)$ probes to reinsert the N elements. Give an estimate for the number of probes (i.e., N or $2N$ or something else). (*Hint:* Compute the average cost of inserting in the new table. These insertions vary from load factor 0 to load factor 0.25.)

20.10 Under certain assumptions, the expected cost of an insertion in a hash table with secondary clustering is given by $1/(1 - \lambda) - \lambda - \ln(1 - \lambda)$. Unfortunately, this formula is not accurate for quadratic probing. However, assuming that it is,

a. What is the expected cost of an unsuccessful search?
b. What is the expected cost of a successful search?

20.11 A quadratic probing hash table is used to store 10,000 `String` objects. Assume that the load factor is 0.4 and that the average string length is 8. Determine

a. The hash table size
b. The amount of memory used to store the 10,000 `String` objects
c. The amount of additional memory used by the hash table
d. The total memory used by the hash table
e. The space overhead

IN PRACTICE

20.12 Implement linear probing.

20.13 For the probing hash table, implement the rehashing code without making a recursive call to `add`.

20.14 Experiment with a hash function that examines every other character in a string. Is this a better choice than the one in the text? Explain.

20.15 Experiment with the following alternative for line 12 in Figure 20.2:

```
hashVal = ( hashVal << 5 ) ^ hashVal ^ key.charAt( i );
```

PROGRAMMING PROBLEMS

20.16 Find yourself a large online dictionary. Choose a table size that is twice as large as the dictionary. Apply the hash function described in the text to each word, and store a count of the number of times each position is hashed to. You will get a distribution: Some percentage of the positions will not be hashed to, some will be hashed to once, some twice, and so on. Compare this distribution with what would occur for theoretical random numbers (discussed in Section 9.3).

20.17 Perform simulations to compare the observed performance of hashing with the theoretical results. Declare a probing hash table, insert 10,000 randomly generated integers into the table, and count the average number of probes used. This number is the average cost of a successful search. Repeat the test several times for a good average. Run it for both linear probing and quadratic probing, and do it for final load factors 0.1, 0.2, ..., 0.9. Always declare the table so that no rehashing is needed. Thus the test for load factor 0.4 would declare a table of size approximately 25,000 (adjusted to be prime).

20.18 Compare the time required to perform successful searches and insertions in a separate chaining table with load factor 1 and a quadratic probing table with load factor 0.5. Run it for simple integers, strings, and complex records in which the search key is a string.

20.19 A BASIC program consists of a series of statements, each of which is numbered in ascending order. Control is passed by use of a *goto* or *gosub* and a statement number. Write a program that reads a legal BASIC program and renumbers the statements so that the first starts at number F and each statement has a number D higher than the previous statement. The statement numbers in the input might be as large as a 32-bit integer, and you may assume that the renumbered statement numbers fit in a 32-bit integer. Your program must run in linear time.

references

Despite the apparent simplicity of hashing, much of the analysis is quite difficult and many questions remain unresolved. Also there are many interesting ideas that generally attempt to make it unlikely that worst-case possibilities of hashing arise.

An early paper on hashing is [11]. A wealth of information on the subject, including an analysis of hashing with linear probing, is presented in [6]. Double hashing is analyzed in [5] and [7]. Yet another collision resolution scheme, *coalesced hashing,* is described in [12]. An excellent survey on the subject is [8], and [9] contains suggestions for and pitfalls in choosing hash functions. Precise analytic and simulation results for all the methods described in this chapter are available in [4]. Uniform hashing, in which no clustering exists, is optimal with respect to the cost of a successful search [13].

If the input keys are known in advance, perfect hash functions, which do not allow collisions, exist [1]. Some more complicated hashing schemes, for which the worst case depends not on the particular input but on random numbers chosen by the algorithm, appear in [2] and [3]. These schemes guarantee that only a constant number of collisions occur in the worst case (although construction of a hash function can take a long time in the unlikely case of bad random numbers). They are useful for implementing tables in hardware.

One method of implementing Exercise 20.7 is described in [10].

1. J. L. Carter and M. N. Wegman, "Universal Classes of Hash Functions," *Journal of Computer and System Sciences* **18** (1979), 143–154.
2. M. Dietzfelbinger, A. R. Karlin, K. Melhorn, F. Meyer auf def Heide, H. Rohnert, and R. E. Tarjan, "Dynamic Perfect Hashing: Upper and Lower Bounds," *SIAM Journal on Computing* **23** (1994), 738–761.
3. R. J. Enbody and H. C. Du, "Dynamic Hashing Schemes," *Computing Surveys* **20** (1988), 85–113.
4. G. H. Gonnet and R. Baeza-Yates, *Handbook of Algorithms and Data Structures,* 2d ed., Addison-Wesley, Reading, MA, 1991.
5. L. J. Guibas and E. Szemeredi, "The Analysis of Double Hashing," *Journal of Computer and System Sciences* **16** (1978), 226–274.
6. D. E. Knuth, *The Art of Computer Programming, Vol 3: Sorting and Searching,* 2d ed., Addison-Wesley, Reading, MA, 1998.
7. G. Lueker and M. Molodowitch, "More Analysis of Double Hashing," *Combinatorica* **13** (1993), 83–96.
8. W. D. Maurer and T. G. Lewis, "Hash Table Methods," *Computing Surveys* **7** (1975), 5–20.
9. B. J. McKenzie, R. Harries, and T. Bell, "Selecting a Hashing Algorithm," *Software-Practice and Experience* **20** (1990), 209–224.
10. R. Morris, "Scatter Storage Techniques," *Communications of the ACM* **11** (1968), 38–44.

11. W. W. Peterson, "Addressing for Random Access Storage," *IBM Journal of Research and Development* **1** (1957), 130–146.
12. J. S. Vitter, "Implementations for Coalesced Hashing," *Information Processing Letters* **11** (1980), 84–86.
13. A. C. Yao, "Uniform Hashing Is Optimal," *Journal of the ACM* **32** (1985), 687–693.

chapter 21

a priority queue: the binary heap

The priority queue is a fundamental data structure that allows access only to the minimum item. In this chapter we discuss one implementation of the priority queue data structure, the elegant *binary heap*. The binary heap supports the insertion of new items and the deletion of the minimum item in logarithmic worst-case time. It uses only an array and is easy to implement.

In this chapter, we show

- The basic properties of the binary heap
- How the `insert` and `deleteMin` operations can be performed in logarithmic time
- A linear-time heap construction algorithm
- A Java 5 implementation of class `PriorityQueue`
- An easily implemented sorting algorithm, *heapsort*, that runs in $O(N \log N)$ time but uses no extra memory
- The use of heaps to implement external sorting

21.1 basic ideas

A linked list or array requires that some operation use linear time.

As discussed in Section 6.9, the priority queue supports the access and deletion of the minimum item with `findMin` and `deleteMin`, respectively. We could use a simple linked list, performing insertions at the front in constant time, but then finding and/or deleting the minimum would require a linear scan of the list. Alternatively, we could insist that the list always be kept sorted. This condition makes the access and deletion of the minimum cheap, but then insertions would be linear.

An unbalanced binary search tree does not have a good worst case. A balanced search tree requires lots of work.

Another way of implementing priority queues is to use a binary search tree, which gives an $O(\log N)$ average running time for both operations. However, a binary search tree is a poor choice because the input is typically not sufficiently random. We could use a balanced search tree, but the structures shown in Chapter 19 are cumbersome to implement and lead to sluggish performance in practice. (In Chapter 22, however, we cover a data structure, the *splay tree,* that has been shown empirically to be a good alternative in some situations.)

The priority queue has properties that are a compromise between a queue and a binary search tree.

On the one hand, because the priority queue supports only some of the search tree operations, it should not be more expensive to implement than a search tree. On the other hand, the priority queue is more powerful than a simple queue because we can use a priority queue to implement a queue as follows. First, we insert each item with an indication of its insertion time. Then, a `deleteMin` on the basis of minimum insertion time implements a `dequeue`. Consequently, we can expect to obtain an implementation with properties that are a compromise between a queue and a search tree. This compromise is realized by the binary heap, which

- Can be implemented by using a simple array (like the queue)
- Supports `insert` and `deleteMin` in $O(\log N)$ worst-case time (a compromise between the binary search tree and the queue)
- Supports `insert` in constant average time and `findMin` in constant worst-case time (like the queue)

The *binary heap* is the classic method used to implement priority queues.

The *binary heap* is the classic method used to implement priority queues and—like the balanced search tree structures in Chapter 19—has two properties: a structure property and an ordering property. And as with balanced search trees, an operation on a binary heap can destroy one of the properties, so a binary heap operation must not terminate until both properties are in order. This outcome is simple to achieve. (In this chapter, we use the word *heap* to refer to the binary heap.)

21.1.1 structure property

The only structure that gives dynamic logarithmic time bounds is the tree, so it seems natural to organize the heap's data as a tree. Because we want the logarithmic bound to be a worst-case guarantee, the tree should be balanced.

> The heap is a *complete binary tree,* allowing representation by a simple array and guaranteeing logarithmic depth.

A *complete binary tree* is a tree that is completely filled, with the possible exception of the bottom level, which is filled from left to right and has no missing nodes. An example of a complete binary tree of 10 items is shown in Figure 21.1. Had the node J been a right child of E, the tree would not be complete because a node would be missing.

The complete tree has a number of useful properties. First, the height (longest path length) of a complete binary tree of N nodes is at most $\lfloor \log N \rfloor$. The reason is that a complete tree of height H has between 2^H and $2^{H+1} - 1$ nodes. This characteristic implies that we can expect logarithmic worst-case behavior if we restrict changes in the structure to one path from the root to a leaf.

> The parent is in position $\lfloor i/2 \rfloor$, the left child is in position $2i$, and the right child is in position $2i + 1$.

Second and equally important, in a complete binary tree, `left` and `right` links are not needed. As shown in Figure 21.1, we can represent a complete binary tree by storing its level-order traversal in an array. We place the root in position 1 (position 0 is often left vacant, for a reason discussed shortly). We also need to maintain an integer that tells us the number of nodes currently in the tree. Then for any element in array position i, its left child can be found in position $2i$. If this position extends past the number of nodes in the tree, we know that the left child does not exist. Similarly, the right child is located immediately after the left child; thus it resides in position $2i + 1$. We again test against the actual tree size to be sure that the child exists. Finally, the parent is in position $\lfloor i/2 \rfloor$.

Note that every node except the root has a parent. If the root were to have a parent, the calculation would place it in position 0. Thus we reserve position 0 for a dummy item that can serve as the root's parent. Doing so can simplify one of the operations. If instead we choose to place the root in position 0, the locations of the children and parent of the node in position i change slightly (in Exercise 21.15 you are asked to determine the new locations).

> Using an array to store a tree is called *implicit representation.*

Using an array to store a tree is called *implicit representation.* As a result of this representation, not only are child links not required, but also the opera-

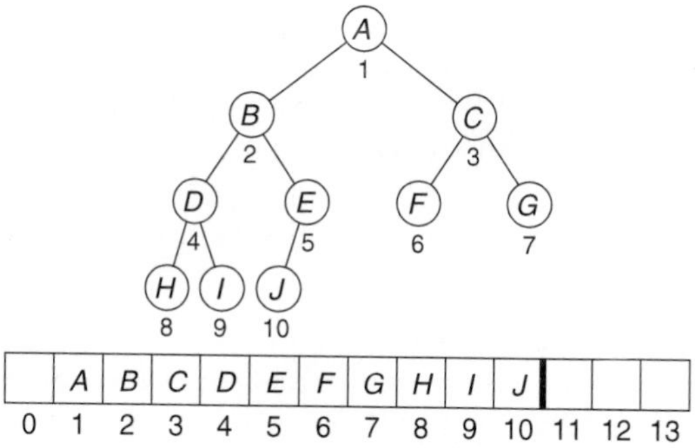

figure 21.1

A complete binary tree and its array representation

tions required to traverse the tree are extremely simple and likely to be very fast on most computers. The heap entity consists of an array of objects and an integer representing the current heap size.

In this chapter, heaps are drawn as trees to make the algorithms easier to visualize. In the implementation of these trees we use an array. We do not use the implicit representation for all search trees. Some of the problems with doing so are covered in Exercise 21.8.

21.1.2 heap-order property

The *heap-order property* states that, in a heap, the item in the parent is never larger than the item in a node.

The property that allows operations to be performed quickly is the *heap-order property*. We want to be able to find the minimum quickly, so it makes sense that the smallest element should be at the root. If we consider that any subtree should also (recursively) be a heap, any node should be smaller than all of its descendants. Applying this logic, we arrive at the heap-order property.

The root's parent can be stored in position 0 and given a value of negative infinity.

heap-order property
In a heap, for every node X with parent P, the key in P is smaller than or equal to the key in X.

The heap-order property is illustrated in Figure 21.2. In Figure 21.3(a), the tree is a heap, but in Figure 21.3(b), the tree is not (the dashed line

figure 21.2
Heap-order property

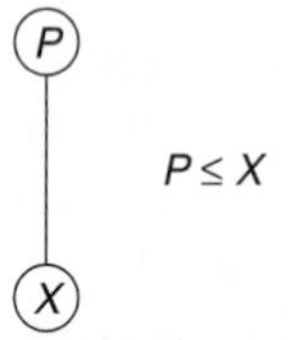

figure 21.3
Two complete trees: (a) a heap; (b) not a heap

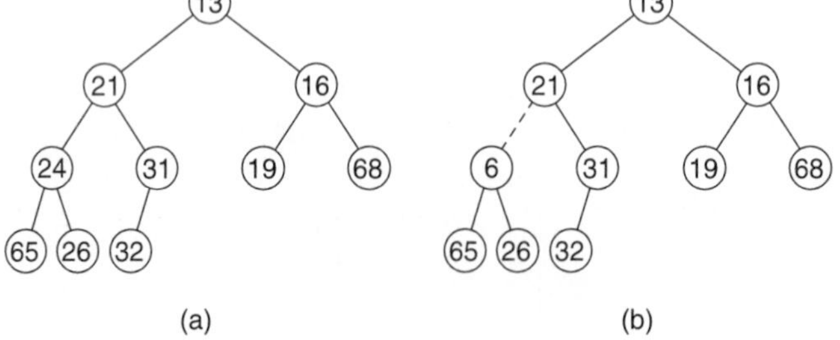

shows the violation of heap order). Note that the root does not have a parent. In the implicit representation, we could place the value $-\infty$ in position 0 to remove this special case when we implement the heap. By the heap-order property, we see that the minimum element can always be found at the root. Thus `findMin` is a constant time operation. A *max heap* supports access of the maximum *instead* of the minimum. Minor changes can be used to implement max heaps.

21.1.3 **allowed operations**

Now that we have settled on the representation, we can start writing code for our implementation of `java.util.PriorityQueue`. We already know that our heap supports the basic `insert`, `findMin`, and `deleteMin` operations and the usual `isEmpty` and `makeEmpty` routines. Figure 21.4 shows the class skeleton using the naming conventions in `java.util.PriorityQueue`. We will refer to the operations using both the historic names and their `java.util` equivalents.

We provide a constructor that accepts a collection containing an initial set of items and calls `buildHeap`.

We begin by examining the public methods. A trio of constructors are declared at lines 9 to 14. The third constructor accepts a collection of items that should initially be in the priority queue. Why not just insert the items one at a time?

The reason is that in numerous applications we can add many items before the next `deleteMin` occurs. In those cases, we do not need to have heap order in effect until the `deleteMin` occurs. The `buildHeap` operation, declared at line 32, reinstates the heap order—no matter how messed up the heap is—and we will see that it works in linear time. Thus, if we need to place N items in the heap before the first `deleteMin`, placing them in the array sloppily and then doing one `buildHeap` is more efficient than doing N insertions.

The `add` method is declared at line 25. It adds a new item `x` into the heap, performing the necessary operations to maintain the heap-order property.

The remaining operations are as expected. The `element` routine is declared at line 23 and returns the minimum item in the heap. `remove` is declared at line 27 and removes and then returns the minimum item. The usual `size`, `clear`, and `iterator` routines are declared at lines 16 to 21.

The constructors are shown in Figure 21.5. All initialize the array, the size, and the comparator; the third constructor additionally copies in the collection passed as a parameter and then calls `buildHeap`. Figure 21.6 shows `element`.

```java
package weiss.util;

/**
 * PriorityQueue class implemented via the binary heap.
 */
public class PriorityQueue<AnyType> extends AbstractCollection<AnyType>
                                    implements Queue<AnyType>
{
    public PriorityQueue( )
      { /* Figure 21.5 */ }
    public PriorityQueue( Comparator<? super AnyType> c )
      { /* Figure 21.5 */ }
    public PriorityQueue( Collection<? extends AnyType> coll )
      { /* Figure 21.5 */ }

    public int size( )
      { /* return currentSize; */ }
    public void clear( )
      { /* currentSize = 0; */ }
    public Iterator<AnyType> iterator( )
      { /* See online code */ }

    public AnyType element( )
      { /* Figure 21.6 */ }
    public boolean add( AnyType x )
      { /* Figure 21.9 */ }
    public AnyType remove( )
      { /* Figure 21.13 */ }

    private void percolateDown( int hole )
      { /* Figure 21.14 */ }
    private void buildHeap( )
      { /* Figure 21.16 */ }

    private int currentSize;   // Number of elements in heap
    private AnyType [ ] array; // The heap array
    private Comparator<? super AnyType> cmp;

    private void doubleArray( )
      { /* See online code */ }
    private int compare( AnyType lhs, AnyType rhs )
      { /* Same code as in TreeSet; see Figure 19.70 */ }
}
```

figure 21.4

The PriorityQueue class skeleton

```java
    private static final int DEFAULT_CAPACITY = 100;

    /**
     * Construct an empty PriorityQueue.
     */
    public PriorityQueue( )
    {
        currentSize = 0;
        cmp = null;
        array = (AnyType[]) new Object[ DEFAULT_CAPACITY + 1 ];
    }

    /**
     * Construct an empty PriorityQueue with a specified comparator.
     */
    public PriorityQueue( Comparator<? super AnyType> c )
    {
        currentSize = 0;
        cmp = c;
        array = (AnyType[]) new Object[ DEFAULT_CAPACITY + 1 ];
    }


    /**
     * Construct a PriorityQueue from another Collection.
     */
    public PriorityQueue( Collection<? extends AnyType> coll )
    {
        cmp = null;
        currentSize = coll.size( );
        array = (AnyType[]) new Object[ ( currentSize + 2 ) * 11 / 10 ];

        int i = 1;
        for( AnyType item : coll )
            array[ i++ ] = item;
        buildHeap( );
    }
```

figure 21.5

Constructors for the PriorityQueue class

```java
    /**
     * Returns the smallest item in the priority queue.
     * @return the smallest item.
     * @throws NoSuchElementException if empty.
     */
    public AnyType element( )
    {
        if( isEmpty( ) )
            throw new NoSuchElementException( );
        return array[ 1 ];
    }
```

figure 21.6

The element routine

21.2 implementation of the basic operations

The heap-order property looks promising so far because easy access to the minimum is provided. We must now show that we can efficiently support insertion and `deleteMin` in logarithmic time. Performing the two required operations is easy (both conceptually and practically): The work merely involves ensuring that the heap-order property is maintained.

21.2.1 insertion

Insertion is implemented by creating a hole at the next available location and then *percolating* it up until the new item can be placed in it without introducing a heap-order violation with the hole's parent.

To insert an element X in the heap, we must first add a node to the tree. The only option is to create a hole in the next available location; otherwise, the tree is not complete and we would violate the structure property. If X can be placed in the hole without violating heap order, we do so and are done. Otherwise, we slide the element that is in the hole's parent node into the node, bubbling the hole up toward the root. We continue this process until X can be placed in the hole. Figure 21.7 shows that to insert 14, we create a hole in the next available heap location. Inserting 14 into the hole would violate the heap-order property, so 31 is slid down into the hole. This strategy is continued in Figure 21.8 until the correct location for 14 is found.

This general strategy is called *percolate up,* in which insertion is implemented by creating a hole at the next available location and bubbling it up the heap until the correct location is found. Figure 21.9 shows the `add` method, which implements the percolate up strategy by using a very tight loop. At line 13, we place `x` as the $-\infty$ sentinel in position 0. The statement at line 12 increments the current size and sets the hole to the newly added node. We iterate the loop at line 15 as long as the item in the parent node is larger than `x`. Line

figure 21.7

Attempt to insert 14, creating the hole and bubbling the hole up

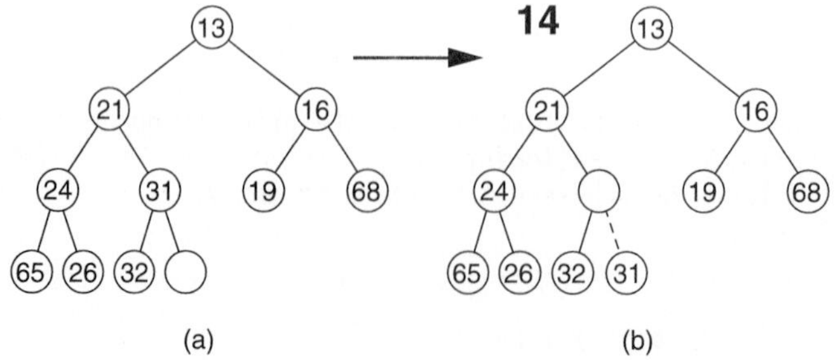

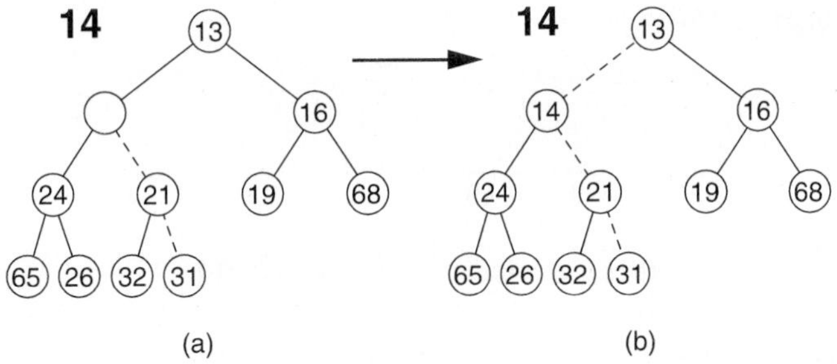

figure 21.8

The remaining two steps required to insert 14 in the original heap shown in Figure 21.7

```
1   /**
2    * Adds an item to this PriorityQueue.
3    * @param x any object.
4    * @return true.
5    */
6   public boolean add( AnyType x )
7   {
8       if( currentSize + 1 == array.length )
9           doubleArray( );
10
11          // Percolate up
12      int hole = ++currentSize;
13      array[ 0 ] = x;
14
15      for( ; compare( x, array[ hole / 2 ] ) < 0; hole /= 2 )
16          array[ hole ] = array[ hole / 2 ];
17      array[ hole ] = x;
18
19      return true;
20  }
```

figure 21.9

The add method

16 moves the item in the parent down into the hole, and then the third expression in the for loop moves the hole up to the parent. When the loop terminates, line 17 places x in the hole.

Insertion takes constant time on average but logarithmic time in the worst case.

The time required to do the insertion could be as much as $O(\log N)$ if the element to be inserted is the new minimum. The reason is that it will be percolated up all the way to the root. On average the percolation terminates early: It has been shown that 2.6 comparisons are required on average to perform the add, so the average add moves an element up 1.6 levels.

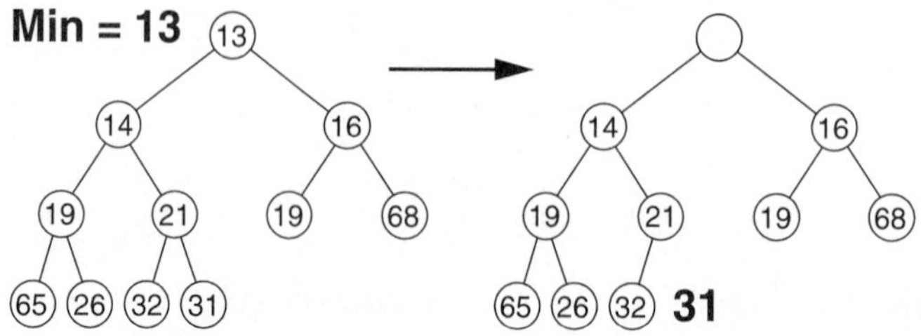

figure 21.10
Creation of the hole at the root

Deletion of the minimum involves placing the former last item in a hole that is created at the root. The hole is *percolated down* the tree through minimum children until the item can be placed without violating the heap-order property.

The `deleteMin` operation is logarithmic in both the worst and average cases.

21.2.2 **the `deleteMin` operation**

The `deleteMin` operation is handled in a similar manner to the insertion operation. As shown already, finding the minimum is easy; the hard part is removing it. When the minimum is removed, a hole is created at the root. The heap now becomes one size smaller, and the structure property tells us that the last node must be eliminated. Figure 21.10 shows the situation: The minimum item is 13, the root has a hole, and the former last item needs to be placed in the heap somewhere.

If the last item could be placed in the hole, we would be done. That is impossible, however, unless the size of the heap is two or three, because elements at the bottom are expected to be larger than elements on the second level. We must play the same game as for insertion: We put some item in the hole and then move the hole. The only difference is that for the `deleteMin` we move down the tree. To do so, we find the smaller child of the hole, and if that child is smaller than the item that we are trying to place, we move the child into the hole, pushing the hole down one level and repeating these actions until the item can be correctly placed—a process called *percolate down.* In Figure 21.11, we place the smaller child (14) in the hole, sliding the hole down one level. We repeat this action, placing 19 in the hole and creating a new hole one level deeper. We then place 26 in the hole and create a new

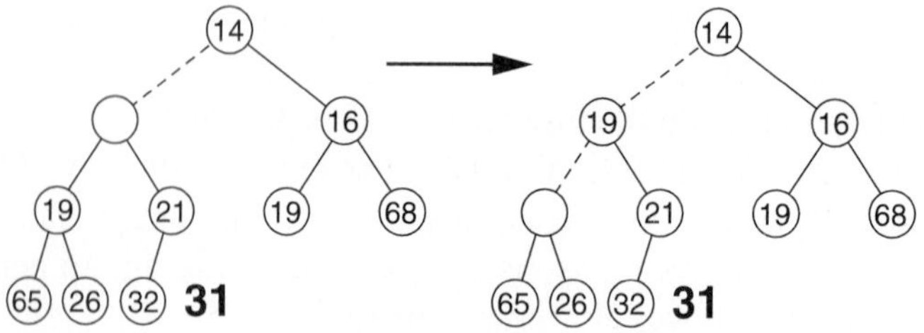

figure 21.11
The next two steps in the `deleteMin` operation

hole on the bottom level. Finally, we are able to place 31 in the hole, as shown in Figure 21.12. Because the tree has logarithmic depth, `deleteMin` is a logarithmic operation in the worst case. Not surprisingly, percolation rarely terminates more than one or two levels early, so `deleteMin` is logarithmic on average, too.

Figure 21.13 shows this method, which is named `remove` in the standard library. The test for emptiness in `remove` is automatically done by the call to `element`, which is named `remove` in the standard library, at line 8. The real work is done in `percolateDown`, shown in Figure 21.14. The code shown there is similar in spirit to the percolation up code in the `add` routine. However, because there are two children rather than one parent, the code is a bit more complicated. The `percolateDown` method takes a single parameter that indicates where the hole is to be placed. The item in the hole is then moved out, and the percolation begins. For `remove`, `hole` will be position 1. The `for` loop at line 10 terminates when there is no left child. The third expression moves the hole to the child. The smaller child is found at lines 13–15. We have to be careful because the last node in an even-sized heap is an only child; we cannot always assume that there are two children, which is why we have the first test at line 13.

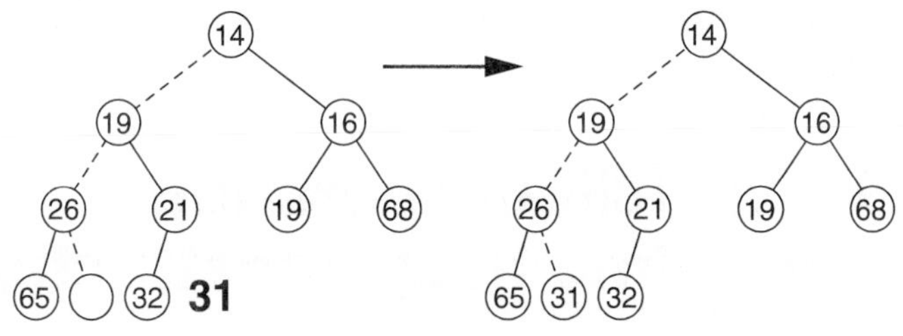

figure 21.12

The last two steps in the `deleteMin` operation

```
1   /**
2    * Removes the smallest item in the priority queue.
3    * @return the smallest item.
4    * @throws NoSuchElementException if empty.
5    */
6   public AnyType remove( )
7   {
8       AnyType minItem = element( );
9       array[ 1 ] = array[ currentSize-- ];
10      percolateDown( 1 );
11
12      return minItem;
13  }
```

figure 21.13

The `remove` method

```
/**
 * Internal method to percolate down in the heap.
 * @param hole the index at which the percolate begins.
 */
private void percolateDown( int hole )
{
    int child;
    AnyType tmp = array[ hole ];

    for( ; hole * 2 <= currentSize; hole = child )
    {
        child = hole * 2;
        if( child != currentSize &&
                compare( array[ child + 1 ], array[ child ] ) < 0 )
            child++;
        if( compare( array[ child ], tmp ) < 0 )
            array[ hole ] = array[ child ];
        else
            break;
    }
    array[ hole ] = tmp;
}
```

figure 21.14

The `percolateDown` method used for `remove` and `buildHeap`

21.3 the `buildHeap` operation: linear-time heap construction

The `buildHeap` operation can be done in linear time by applying a percolate down routine to nodes in reverse level order.

The `buildHeap` *operation* takes a complete tree that does not have heap order and reinstates it. We want it to be a linear-time operation, since N insertions could be done in $O(N \log N)$ time. We expect that $O(N)$ is attainable because N successive insertions take a total of $O(N)$ time on average, based on the result stated at the end of Section 21.2.1. The N successive insertions do more work than we require because they maintain heap order after every insertion and we need heap order only at one instant.

The easiest abstract solution is obtained by viewing the heap as a recursively defined structure, as shown in Figure 21.15: We recursively call `buildHeap` on the left and right subheaps. At that point, we are guaranteed that heap order has been established everywhere except at the root. We can establish heap order everywhere by calling `percolateDown` for the root. The recursive routine works by guaranteeing that when we apply `percolateDown(i)`, all descendants of `i` have been processed recursively by their own calls to `percolateDown`. The recursion, however, is not necessary, for the following reason. If we call `percolateDown` on nodes in reverse level order, then at the point `percolateDown(i)` is processed, all descendants of node `i` will have been processed by a prior call to `percolateDown`. This process leads to an incredibly simple algorithm for `buildHeap`, which is shown in Figure 21.16. Note that `percolateDown` need not be performed on a leaf. Thus we start at the highest numbered nonleaf node.

The tree in Figure 21.17(a) is the unordered tree. The seven remaining trees in Figures 21.17(b) through 21.20 show the result of each of the seven `percolateDown` operations. Each dashed line corresponds to two comparisons: one to find the smaller child and one to compare the smaller child with the node. Notice that the ten dashed lines in the algorithm correspond to 20 comparisons. (There could have been an eleventh line.)

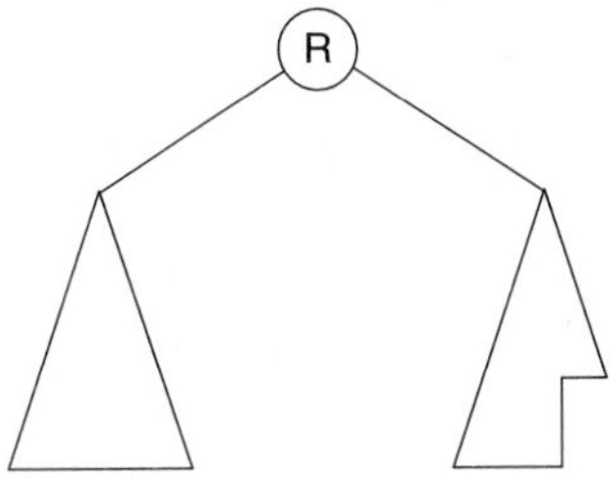

figure 21.15

Recursive view of the heap

```java
/**
 * Establish heap order property from an arbitrary
 * arrangement of items. Runs in linear time.
 */
private void buildHeap( )
{
    for( int i = currentSize / 2; i > 0; i-- )
        percolateDown( i );
}
```

figure 21.16

Implementation of the linear-time `buildHeap` method

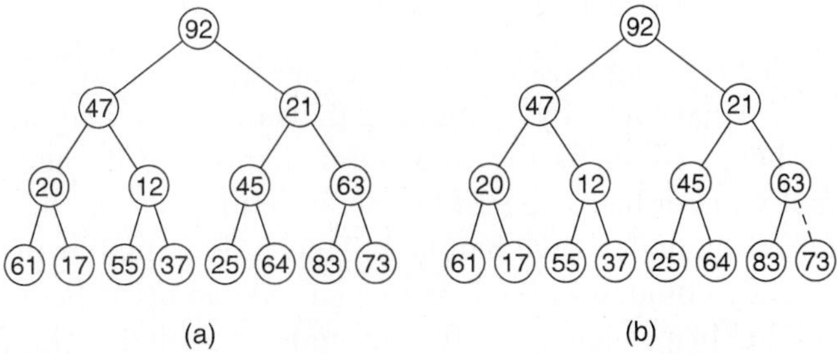

figure 21.17

(a) Initial heap;
(b) after `percolateDown(7)`

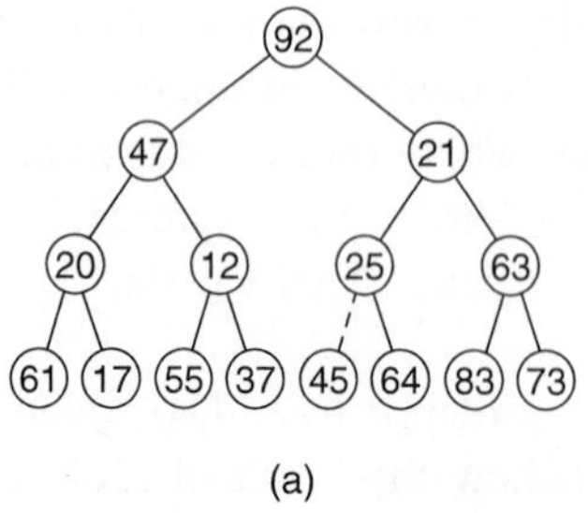

figure 21.18
(a) After `percolateDown(6)`; (b) after `percolateDown(5)`

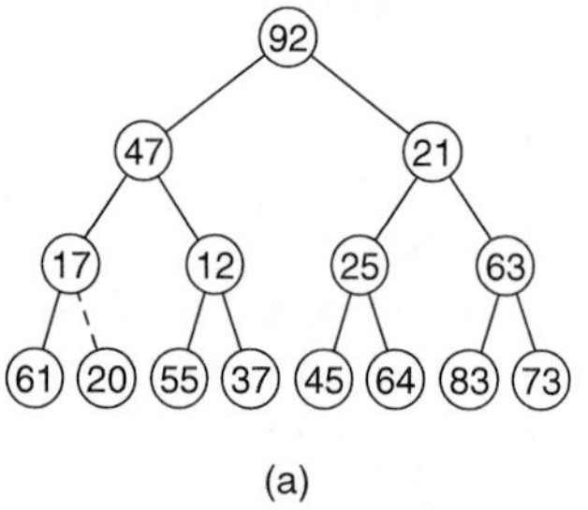

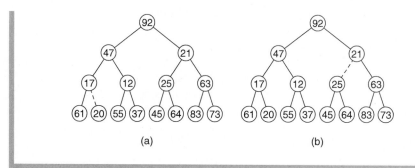

figure 21.19
(a) After `percolateDown(4)`; (b) after `percolateDown(3)`

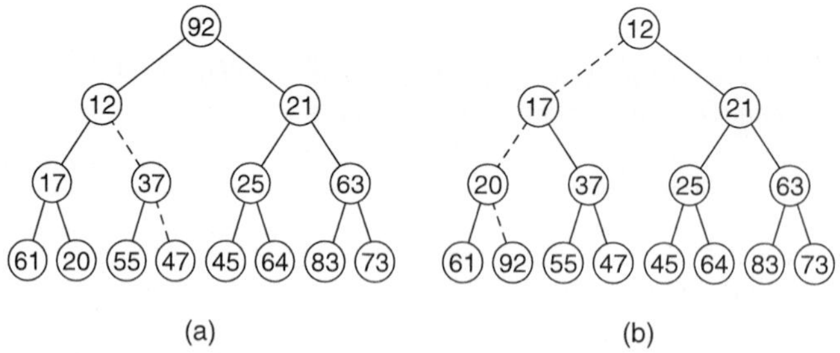

figure 21.20
(a) After `percolateDown(2)`; (b) after `percolateDown(1)` and `buildHeap` terminates

The linear-time bound can be shown by computing the sum of the heights of all the nodes in the heap.

To bound the running time of `buildHeap`, we must bound the number of dashed lines. We can do so by computing the sum of the heights of all the nodes in the heap, which is the maximum number of dashed lines. We expect a small number because half the nodes are leaves and have height 0 and a quarter of the nodes have height 1. Thus only a quarter of the nodes (those not already counted in the first two cases) can contribute more than 1 unit of height. In particular, only one node contributes the maximum height of $\lfloor \log N \rfloor$.

To obtain a linear-time bound for `buildHeap`, we need to establish that the sum of the heights of the nodes of a complete binary tree is $O(N)$. We do so in Theorem 21.1, proving the bound for perfect trees by using a marking argument.

We prove the bound for perfect trees by using a marking argument.

Theorem 21.1

For the perfect binary tree of height H containing $N = 2^{H+1} - 1$ nodes, the sum of the heights of the nodes is $N - H - 1$.

Proof

We use a tree-marking argument. (A more direct brute-force calculation could also be done, as in Exercise 21.10.) For any node in the tree that has some height h, we darken h tree edges as follows. We go down the tree by traversing the left edge and then only right edges. Each edge traversed is darkened. An example is a perfect tree of height 4. Nodes that have height 1 have their left edge darkened, as shown in Figure 21.21. Next, nodes of height 2 have a left edge and then a right edge darkened on the path from the node to the bottom, as shown in Figure 21.22. In Figure 21.23, three edges are darkened for each node of height 3: the first left edge leading out of the node and then the two right edges on the path to the bottom. Finally, in Figure 21.24 four edges are darkened: the left edge leading out of the root and the three right edges on the path to the bottom. Note that no edge is ever darkened twice and that every edge except those on the right path is darkened. As there are $(N - 1)$ tree edges (every node has an edge coming into it except the root) and H edges on the right path, the number of darkened edges is $N - H - 1$. This proves the theorem.

A complete binary tree is not a perfect binary tree, but the result we have obtained is an upper bound on the sum of the heights of the nodes in a complete binary tree. A complete binary tree has between 2^H and $2^{H+1} - 1$ nodes,

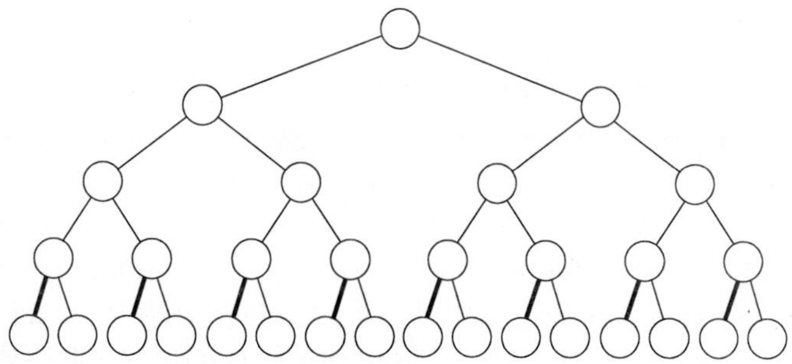

figure 21.21

Marking the left edges for height 1 nodes

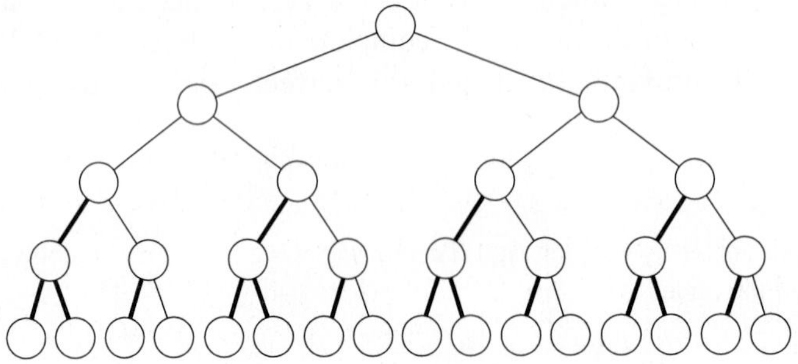

figure 21.22

Marking the first left edge and the subsequent right edge for height 2 nodes

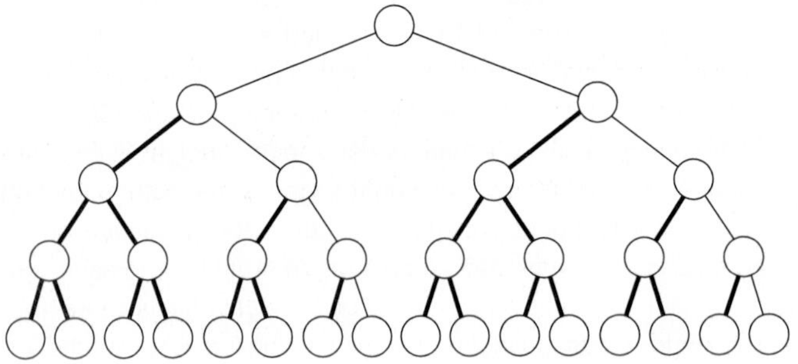

figure 21.23

Marking the first left edge and the subsequent two right edges for height 3 nodes

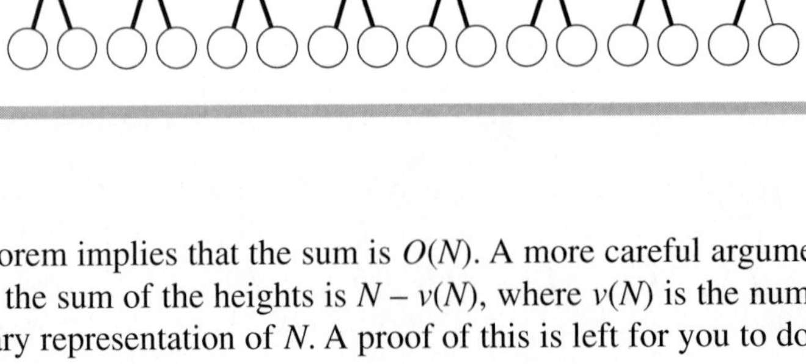

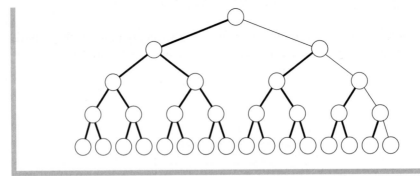

figure 21.24

Marking the first left edge and the subsequent two right edges for the height 4 node

so this theorem implies that the sum is $O(N)$. A more careful argument establishes that the sum of the heights is $N - \nu(N)$, where $\nu(N)$ is the number of 1s in the binary representation of N. A proof of this is left for you to do as Exercise 21.12.

21.4 advanced operations: `decreaseKey` and `merge`

In Chapter 23 we examine priority queues that support two additional operations. The `decreaseKey` operation lowers the value of an item in the priority queue. The item's position is presumed known. In a binary heap this operation is easily implemented by percolating up until heap order is reestablished. However, we must be careful because by assumption each item's position is being stored separately, and all items involved in the percolation have their positions altered. It is possible to incorporate `decreaseKey` into the `PriorityQueue` class. This is left as Exercise 21.30. The `decreaseKey` operation is useful in implementing graph algorithms (e.g., Dijkstra's algorithm presented in Section 14.3).

The `merge` routine combines two priority queues. Because the heap is array-based, the best we can hope to achieve with a merge is to copy the items from the smaller heap to the larger heap and do some rearranging. Doing so takes at least linear time per operation. If we use general trees with nodes connected by links, we can reduce the bound to logarithmic cost per operation. Merging has uses in advanced algorithm design.

21.5 internal sorting: heapsort

The priority queue can be used to sort N items by the following:

A priority queue can be used to sort in $O(N \log N)$ time. An algorithm based on this idea is *heapsort.*

1. Inserting every item into a binary heap
2. Extracting every item by calling `deleteMin` N times, thus sorting the result

Using the observation in Section 21.4, we can more efficiently implement this procedure by

1. Tossing each item into a binary heap
2. Applying `buildHeap`
3. Calling `deleteMin` N times, with the items exiting the heap in sorted order

Step 1 takes linear time total, and step 2 takes linear time. In step 3, each call to `deleteMin` takes logarithmic time, so N calls take $O(N \log N)$ time. Consequently, we have an $O(N \log N)$ worst-case sorting algorithm, called *heapsort,* which is as good as can be achieved by a comparison-based algorithm (see Section 8.8). One problem with the algorithm as it stands now is that sorting an array requires the use of the binary heap data structure, which itself carries the overhead of an array. Emulating the heap data structure on the array that is input—rather than going through the heap class apparatus—would be preferable. We assume for the rest of this discussion that this is done.

Even though we do not use the heap class directly, we still seem to need a second array. The reason is that we have to record the order in which items exit the heap equivalent in a second array and then copy that ordering back into the original array. The memory requirement is doubled, which could be crucial in some applications. Note that the extra time spent copying the second array back to the first is only $O(N)$, so, unlike mergesort, the extra array does not affect the running *time* significantly. The problem is *space*.

By using empty parts of the array, we can perform the sort in place.

A clever way to avoid using a second array makes use of the fact that, after each `deleteMin`, the heap shrinks by 1. Thus the cell that was last in the heap can be used to store the element just deleted. As an example, suppose that we have a heap with six elements. The first `deleteMin` produces A_1. Now the heap has only five elements, so we can place A_1 in position 6. The next `deleteMin` produces A_2. As the heap now has only four elements, we can place A_2 in position 5.

If we use a max heap, we obtain items in increasing order.

When we use this strategy, after the last `deleteMin` the array will contain the elements in *decreasing* sorted order. If we want the array to be in the more typical *increasing* sorted order, we can change the ordering property so that the parent has a larger key than the child does. Thus we have a max heap. For example, let us say that we want to sort the input sequence 59, 36, 58, 21, 41, 97, 31, 16, 26, and 53. After tossing the items into the max heap and applying `buildHeap`, we obtain the arrangement shown in Figure 21.25. (Note that there is no sentinel; we presume the data starts in position 0, as is typical for the other sorts described in Chapter 8.)

Figure 21.26 shows the heap that results after the first deleteMax. The last element in the heap is 21; 97 has been placed in a part of the heap array that is technically no longer part of the heap.

figure 21.25

Max heap after the `buildHeap` phase

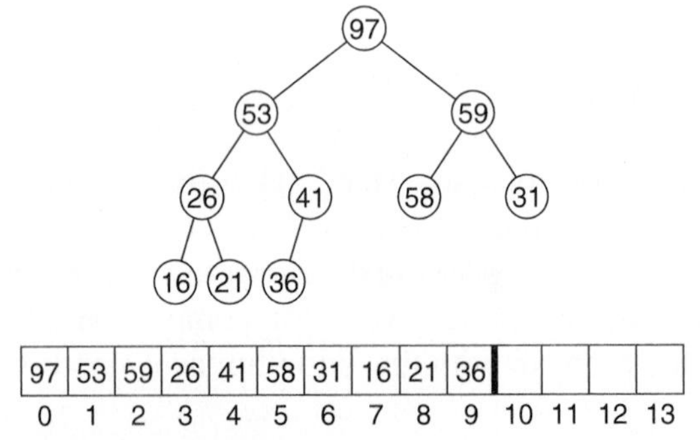

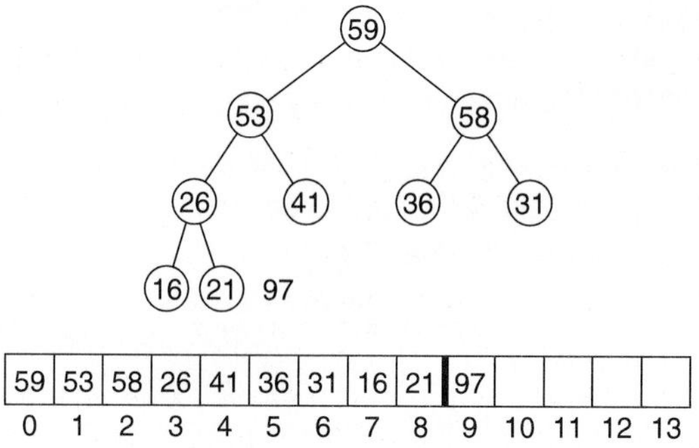

figure 21.26

Heap after the first deleteMax operation

Figure 21.27 shows that after a second deleteMax, 16 becomes the last element. Now only eight items remain in the heap. The maximum element removed, 59, is placed in the dead spot of the array. After seven more deleteMax operations, the heap represents only one element, but the elements left in the array will be sorted in increasing order.

Minor changes are required for heapsort because the root is stored in position 0.

Implementation of the heapsort operation is simple because it basically follows the heap operation. There are three minor differences between the two operations. First, because we are using a max heap, we need to reverse the logic of the comparisons from > to <. Second, we can no longer assume that there is a sentinel position 0. The reason is that all our other sorting algorithms store data at position 0, and we must assume that `heapSort` is no different. Although the sentinel is not needed anyway (there are no percolate up operations), its absence affects calculations of the child and parent. That is, for a node in position i, the parent is in position $(i-1)/2$, the left child is in position $2i+1$, and the right child is next to the left child. Third, `percDown` needs to be informed of the current heap size (which is lowered by 1 in each iteration of deleteMax). The implementation of `percDown` is left for you to do as

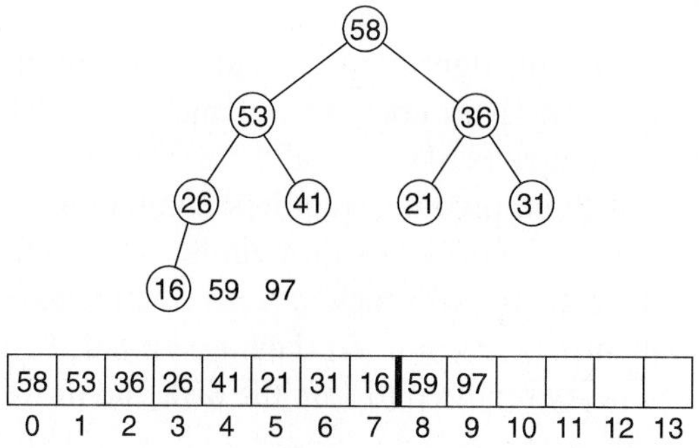

figure 21.27

Heap after the second deleteMax operation

figure 21.28

The heapSort routine

```
// Standard heapsort.
public static <AnyType extends Comparable<? super AnyType>>
void heapsort( AnyType [ ] a )
{
    for( int i = a.length / 2; i >= 0; i-- )  // Build heap
        percDown( a, i, a.length );
    for( int i = a.length - 1; i > 0; i-- )
    {
        swapReferences( a, 0, i );            // deleteMax
        percDown( a, 0, i );
    }
}
```

Exercise 21.23. Assuming that we have written percDown, we can easily express heapSort as shown in Figure 21.28.

Although heapsort is not as fast as quicksort, it can still be useful. As discussed in Section 8.6 (and detailed in Exercise 8.18), in quicksort we can keep track of each recursive call's depth, and switch to an $O(N \log N)$ worst-case sort for any recursive call that is too deep (roughly $2 \log N$ nested calls). Exercise 8.18 suggested mergesort, but actually heapsort is the better candidate.

21.6 external sorting

External sorting is used when the amount of data is too large to fit in main memory.

So far, all the sorting algorithms examined require that the input fit in main memory. However, the input for some applications is much too large to fit in main memory. In this section we discuss *external sorting,* which is used to handle such very large inputs. Some of the external sorting algorithms involve the use of heaps.

21.6.1 why we need new algorithms

Most of the internal sorting algorithms take advantage of the fact that memory is directly accessible. Shellsort compares elements `a[i]` and `a[i-gap]` in one time unit. Heapsort compares `a[i]` and `a[child=i*2]` in one time unit. Quicksort, with median-of-three pivoting, requires comparing `a[first]`, `a[center]`, and `a[last]` in a constant number of time units. If the input is on a tape, all these operations lose their efficiency because elements on a tape can be accessed only sequentially. Even if the data are on a disk, efficiency still suffers because of the delay required to spin the disk and move the disk head.

To demonstrate how slow external accesses really are, we could create a random file that is large but not too big to fit in main memory. When we read in the file and sort it by using an efficient algorithm, the time needed to read the input is likely to be significant compared to the time required to sort the input, even though sorting is an $O(N \log N)$ operation (or worse for Shellsort) and reading the input is only $O(N)$.

21.6.2 model for external sorting

The wide variety of mass storage devices makes external sorting much more device-dependent than internal sorting. The algorithms considered here work on tapes, which are probably the most restrictive storage medium. Access to an element on tape is gained by winding the tape to the correct location, so tapes can be efficiently accessed only in sequential order (in either direction).

We assume that sorts are performed on tape. Only sequential access of the input is allowed.

Let us assume that we have at least three tape drives for performing the sort. We need two drives to do an efficient sort; the third drive simplifies matters. If only one tape drive is present, we are in trouble: Any algorithm will require $\Omega(N^2)$ tape accesses.

21.6.3 the simple algorithm

The basic external sorting algorithm involves the use of the merge routine from mergesort. Suppose that we have four tapes A1, A2, B1, and B2, which are two input and two output tapes. Depending on the point in the algorithm, the A tapes are used for input and the B tapes for output, or vice versa. Suppose further that the data are initially on A1 and that the internal memory can hold (and sort) M records at a time. The natural first step is to read M records at a time from the input tape, sort the records internally, and then write the sorted records alternately to B1 and B2. Each group of sorted records is called a *run*. When done, we rewind all the tapes. If we have the same input as in our example for Shellsort, the initial configuration is as shown in Figure 21.29. If

The basic external sort uses repeated two-way merging. Each group of sorted records is a *run*. As a result of a pass, the length of the runs doubles and eventually only a single run remains.

A1	81	94	11	96	12	35	17	99	28	58	41	75	15
A2													
B1													
B2													

figure 21.29

Initial tape configuration

$M = 3$, after the runs have been constructed, the tapes contain the data, as shown in Figure 21.30.

Now B1 and B2 contain a group of runs. We take the first runs from each tape, merge them, and write the result—which is a run twice as long—to A1. Then we take the next runs from each tape, merge them, and write the result to A2. We continue this process, alternating output to A1 and A2 until either B1 or B2 is empty. At this point, either both are empty or one (possibly short) run is left. In the latter case, we copy this run to the appropriate tape. We rewind all four tapes and repeat the same steps, this time using the A tapes as input and the B tapes as output. This process gives runs of length $4M$. We continue this process until we get one run of length N, at which point the run represents the sorted arrangement of the input. Figures 21.31–21.33 show how this process works for our sample input.

We need $\lceil \log(N/M) \rceil$ passes over the input before we have one giant run.

The algorithm will require $\lceil \log(N/M) \rceil$ passes, plus the initial run-constructing pass. For instance, if we have 10,000,000 records of 6,400 bytes each and 200 MB of internal memory, the first pass creates 320 runs. We

figure 21.30

Distribution of length 3 runs to two tapes

A1							
A2							
B1	11 81 94	17 28 99	15				
B2	12 35 96	41 58 75					

figure 21.31

Tapes after the first round of merging (run length = 6)

A1	11 12 35 81 94 96	15	
A2	17 28 41 58 75 99		
B1			
B2			

figure 21.32

Tapes after the second round of merging (run length = 12)

A1		
A2		
B1	11 12 17 28 35 41 58 75 81 94 96 99	
B2	15	

A1	11	12	15	17	28	35	41	58	75	81	94	96	99
A2													
B1													
B2													

figure 21.33

Tapes after the third round of merging

would then need nine more passes to complete the sort. This formula also correctly tells us that our example in Figure 21.30 requires $\lceil \log(13/3) \rceil$, or three more passes.

21.6.4 multiway merge

K-way merging reduces the number of passes. The obvious implementation uses 2*K* tapes.

If we have extra tapes, we can reduce the number of passes required to sort our input with a *multiway* (or *K*-way) *merge*. We do so by extending the basic (two-way) merge to a *K*-way merge and use 2*K* tapes.

Merging two runs is done by winding each input tape to the beginning of each run. Then the smaller element is found and placed on an output tape, and the appropriate input tape is advanced. If there are *K* input tapes, this strategy works in the same way; the only difference is that finding the smallest of the *K* elements is slightly more complicated. We can do so by using a priority queue. To obtain the next element to write on the output tape, we perform a `deleteMin` operation. The appropriate input tape is advanced, and if the run on that input tape has not yet been completed, we insert the new element in the priority queue. Figure 21.34 shows how the input from the previous example is distributed onto three tapes. Figures 21.35 and 21.36 show the two passes of three-way merging that complete the sort.

A1						
A2						
A3						
B1	11	81	94	41	58	75
B2	12	35	96	15		
B3	17	28	99			

figure 21.34

Initial distribution of length 3 runs to three tapes

figure 21.35

After one round of three-way merging (run length = 9)

A1	11	12	17	28	35	81	94	96	99
A2	15	41	58	75					
A3									
B1									
B2									
B3									

figure 21.36

After two rounds of three-way merging

A1													
A2													
A3													
B1	11	12	15	17	28	35	41	58	75	81	94	96	99
B2													
B3													

After the initial run-construction phase, the number of passes required using K-way merging is $\lceil \log_K(N/M) \rceil$ because the length of the runs gets K times larger in each pass. For our example, the formula is verified because $\lceil \log_3 13/3 \rceil = 2$. If we have 10 tapes, $K = 5$. For the large example in Section 21.6.3, 320 runs would require $\log_5 320 = 4$ passes.

21.6.5 polyphase merge

The *polyphase merge* implements a K-way merge with $K + 1$ tapes

The K-way merging strategy requires the use of $2K$ tapes, which could be prohibitive for some applications. We can get by with only $K + 1$ tapes, called a *polyphase merge.* An example is performing two-way merging with only three tapes.

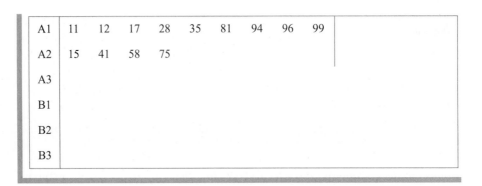

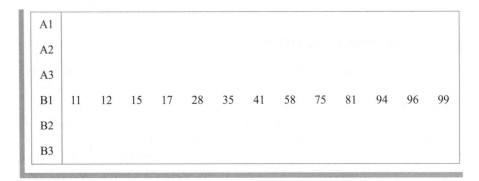

Suppose that we have three tapes—T1, T2, and T3—and an input file on T1 that can produce 34 runs. One option is to put 17 runs each on T2 and T3. We could then merge this result onto T1, thereby obtaining one tape with 17 runs. The problem is that, as all the runs are on one tape, we must now put some of these runs on T2 to perform another merge. The logical way to do that is to copy the first eight runs from T1 to T2 and then perform the merge. This approach adds an extra half pass for every pass that we make. The question is, can we do better?

An alternative method is to split the original 34 runs unevenly. If we put 21 runs on T2 and 13 runs on T3, we could merge 13 runs on T1 before T3 was empty. We could then rewind T1 and T3 and merge T1, with 13 runs, and T2, with 8 runs, on T3. Next, we could merge 8 runs until T2 was empty, leaving 5 runs on T1 and 8 runs on T3. We could then merge T1 and T3, and so on. Figure 21.37 shows the number of runs on each tape after each pass.

The distribution of runs affects performance. The best distribution is related to the Fibonacci numbers.

The original distribution of runs makes a great deal of difference. For instance, if 22 runs are placed on T2, with 12 on T3, after the first merge we obtain 12 runs on T1 and 10 runs on T2. After another merge, there are 10 runs on T1 and 2 runs on T3. At this point, the going gets slow because we can merge only two sets of runs before T3 is exhausted. Then T1 has 8 runs and T2 has 2 runs. Again we can merge only two sets of runs, obtaining T1 with 6 runs and T3 with 2 runs. After three more passes, T2 has 2 runs and the other tapes are empty. We must copy 1 run to another tape. Then we can finish the merge.

Our first distribution turns out to be optimal. If the number of runs is a Fibonacci number, F_N, the best way to distribute them is to split them into two Fibonacci numbers, F_{N-1} and F_{N-2}. Otherwise, the tape must be padded with dummy runs in order to increase the number of runs to a Fibonacci number. We leave the details of how to place the initial set of runs on the tapes for you to handle as Exercise 21.22. We can extend this technique to a K-way merge, in which we need Kth-order Fibonacci numbers for the distribution. The Kth-order Fibonacci number is defined as the sum of the K previous Kth-order Fibonacci numbers:

$$F^{(K)}(N) = F^{(K)}(N-1) + F^{(K)}(N-2) + \cdots + F^{(K)}(N-K)$$
$$F^{(K)}(0 \le N \le K-2) = 0$$
$$F^{(K)}(K-1) = 1$$

		After						
	Run Const.	**T3 + T2**	**T1 + T2**	**T1 + T3**	**T2 + T3**	**T1 + T2**	**T1 + T3**	**T2 + T3**
T1	0	13	5	0	3	1	0	1
T2	21	8	0	5	2	0	1	0
T3	13	0	8	3	0	2	1	0

figure 21.37

The number of runs for a polyphase merge

21.6.6 replacement selection

The last topic we consider in this chapter is construction of the runs. The strategy used so far is the simplest: We read as many elements as possible and sort them, writing the result to a tape. This seems like the best approach possible, until we realize that as soon as the first element is written to the output tape, the memory it used becomes available for another element. If the next element on the input tape is larger than the element just output, it can be included in the run.

If we are clever, we can make the length of the runs that we initially construct larger than the amount of available main memory. This technique is called *replacement selection*.

Using this observation, we can write an algorithm for producing runs, commonly called *replacement selection.* Initially, M elements are read into memory and placed in a priority queue efficiently with a single `buildHeap`. We perform a `deleteMin`, writing the smallest element to the output tape. We read the next element from the input tape. If it is larger than the element just written, we can add it to the priority queue; otherwise, it cannot go into the current run. Because the priority queue is smaller by one element, this element is stored in the dead space of the priority queue until the run has been completed and is then used for the next run. Storing an element in the dead space is exactly what is done in heapsort. We continue doing this process until the size of the priority queue is 0, at which point the run is over. We start a new run by rebuilding a new priority queue with a `buildHeap` operation, in the process using all of the elements in the dead space.

Figure 21.38 shows the run construction for the small example we have been using, with $M = 3$. Elements that are reserved for the next run are shaded. Elements 11, 94, and 81 are placed with `buildHeap`. Element 11 is output, and then 96 is placed in the heap by an insertion because it is larger than 11. Element 81 is output next, and then 12 is read. As 12 is smaller than the 81 just output, it cannot be included in the current run. Thus it is placed in the heap dead space. The heap now logically contains only 94 and 96. After they are output, we have only dead space elements, so we construct a heap and begin run 2.

In this example, replacement selection produces only 3 runs, compared to the 5 runs obtained by sorting. As a result, a three-way merge finishes in one pass instead of two. If the input is randomly distributed, replacement selection produces runs of average length $2M$. For our large example, we would expect 160 runs instead of 320 runs, so a five-way merge would still require four passes. In this case, we have not saved a pass, although we might if we get lucky and have 125 runs or fewer. Because external sorts take so long, every pass saved can make a significant difference in the running time.

As we have shown, replacement selection may do no better than the standard algorithm. However, the input is frequently nearly sorted to start with, in

figure 21.38

Example of run construction

	Three Elements in Heap Array				
	`array[1]`	`array[2]`	`array[3]`	**Output**	**Next Item Read**
Run 1	11	94	81	11	96
	81	94	96	81	12
	94	96	12	94	35
	96	35	12	96	17
	17	35	12	End of Run	Rebuild
Run 2	12	35	17	12	99
	17	35	99	17	28
	28	99	35	28	58
	35	99	58	35	41
	41	99	58	41	75
	58	99	75	58	15
	75	99	15	75	End of Tape
	99		15	99	
			15	End of Run	Rebuild
Run 3	15			15	

which case replacement selection produces only a few abnormally long runs. This kind of input is common for external sorts and makes replacement selection extremely valuable.

summary

In this chapter we showed an elegant implementation of the priority queue. The binary heap uses only an array, yet it supports the basic operations in logarithmic worst-case time. The heap leads to a popular sorting algorithm, heapsort. In Exercises 21.26 and 21.27 you are asked to compare the performance of heapsort with that of quicksort. Generally speaking, heapsort is slower than quicksort but it is certainly easier to implement. Finally, we showed that priority queues are important data structures for external sorting.

This completes implementation of the fundamental and classic data structures. In Part Five we examine more sophisticated data structures, beginning with the splay tree, a binary search tree that has some remarkable properties.

key concepts

binary heap The classic method used to implement priority queues. The binary heap has two properties: structure and ordering. (746)

`buildHeap` operation The process of reinstating heap order in a complete tree, which can be done in linear time by applying a percolate down routine to nodes in reverse level order. (756)

complete binary tree A tree that is completely filled and has no missing nodes. The heap is a complete binary tree, which allows representation by a simple array and guarantees logarithmic depth. (747)

external sorting A form of sorting used when the amount of data is too large to fit in main memory. (764)

heap-order property States that in a (min) heap, the item in the parent is never larger than the item in a node. (748)

heapsort An algorithm based on the idea that a priority queue can be used to sort in $O(N \log N)$ time. (761)

implicit representation Using an array to store a tree. (747)

max heap Supports access of the maximum instead of the minimum. (749)

multiway merge K-way merging that reduces the number of passes. The obvious implementation uses $2K$ tapes. (767)

percolate down Deletion of the minimum involves placing the former last item in a hole that is created at the root. The hole is pushed down the tree through minimum children until the item can be placed without violating the heap-order property. (754)

percolate up Implements insertion by creating a hole at the next available location and then bubbling it up until the new item can be placed in it without introducing a heap-order violation with the hole's parent. (752)

polyphase merge Implements a K-way merge with $K + 1$ tapes. (768)

replacement selection The length of the runs initially constructed can be larger than the amount of available main memory. If we can store M objects in main memory, then we can expect runs of length $2M$. (770)

run A sorted group in the external sort. At the end of the sort, a single run remains. (765)

common errors

1. The trickiest part of the binary heap is the percolate down case in which only one child is present. This case occurs rarely, so spotting an incorrect implementation is difficult.

2. For heapsort, the data begins in position 0, so the children of node i are in positions $2i + 1$ and $2i + 2$.

on the internet

The code to implement the `PriorityQueue` is available in one file.

PriorityQueue.java Contains the implementation of the `PriorityQueue` class.

exercises

IN SHORT

21.1 Describe the structure and ordering properties of the binary heap.

21.2 In a binary heap, for an item in position i where are the parent, left child, and right child located?

21.3 Show the result of inserting 10, 12, 1, 14, 6, 5, 8, 15, 3, 9, 7, 4, 11, 13, and 2, one at a time, in an initially empty heap. Then show the result of using the linear-time `buildHeap` algorithm instead.

21.4 Where could the 11th dashed line in Figures 21.17–21.20 have been?

21.5 A max heap supports `insert`, `deleteMax`, and `findMax` (but not `deleteMin` or `findMin`). Describe in detail how max heaps can be implemented.

21.6 Show the result of the heapsort algorithm after the initial construction and then two `deleteMax` operations on the input in Exercise 21.3.

21.7 Is heapsort a stable sort (i.e., if there are duplicates, do the duplicate items retain their initial ordering among themselves)?

IN THEORY

21.8 A complete binary tree of N elements uses array positions 1 through N. Determine how large the array must be for

a. A binary tree that has two extra levels (i.e., is slightly unbalanced)
b. A binary tree that has a deepest node at depth $2 \log N$
c. A binary tree that has a deepest node at depth $4.1 \log N$
d. The worst-case binary tree

21.9 Show the following regarding the maximum item in the heap.

a. It must be at one of the leaves

b. There are exactly $\lceil N/2 \rceil$ leaves

c. Every leaf must be examined to find it

21.10 Prove Theorem 21.1 by using a direct summation. Do the following.

a. Show that there are 2^i nodes of height $H - i$

b. Write the equation for the sum of the heights using part (a)

c. Evaluate the sum in part (b)

21.11 Verify that the sum of the heights of all the nodes in a perfect binary tree satisfies $N - \nu(N)$, where $\nu(N)$ is the number of 1s in N's binary representation.

21.12 Prove the bound in Exercise 21.11 by using an induction argument.

21.13 For heapsort, $O(N \log N)$ comparisons are used in the worst case. Derive the leading term (i.e., decide whether it is $N \log N$, $2N \log N$, $3N \log N$, and so on).

21.14 Show that there are inputs that force every `percDown` in heapsort to go all the way to a leaf. (*Hint:* Work backward.)

21.15 Suppose that the binary heap is stored with the root at position r. Give formulas for the locations of the children and parent of the node in position i.

21.16 Suppose that binary heaps are represented by explicit links. Give a simple algorithm to find the tree node that is at implicit position i.

21.17 Suppose that binary heaps are represented by explicit links. Consider the problem of merging binary heap `lhs` with `rhs`. Assume that both heaps are full complete binary trees, containing $2^l - 1$ and $2^r - 1$ nodes, respectively.

a. Give an $O(\log N)$ algorithm to merge the two heaps if $l = r$.

b. Give an $O(\log N)$ algorithm to merge the two heaps if $|l - r| = 1$.

c. Give an $O(\log^2 N)$ algorithm to merge the two heaps regardless of l and r.

21.18 A *d-heap* is an implicit data structure that is like a binary heap, except that nodes have d children. A d-heap is thus shallower than a binary heap, but finding the minimum child requires examining d children instead of two children. Determine the running time (in terms of d and N) of the insertion and `deleteMin` operations for a d-heap.

21.19 A *min–max heap* is a data structure that supports both `deleteMin` and `deleteMax` at logarithmic cost. The structure is identical to the binary heap. The min–max heap-order property is that for any node *X* at even depth, the key stored at *X* is the smallest in its subtree, whereas for any node *X* at odd depth, the key stored at *X* is the largest in its subtree. The root is at even depth. Do the following.

a. Draw a possible min–max heap for the items 1, 2, 3, 4, 5, 6, 7, 8, 9, and 10. Note that there are many possible heaps.
b. Determine how to find the minimum and maximum elements.
c. Give an algorithm to insert a new node into the min–max heap.
d. Give an algorithm to perform `deleteMin` and `deleteMax`.
e. Give an algorithm to perform `buildHeap` in linear time.

21.20 The *2-D heap* is a data structure that allows each item to have two individual keys. The `deleteMin` operation can be performed with respect to either of these keys. The 2-D heap-order property is that for any node *X* at even depth, the item stored at *X* has the smallest key #1 in its subtree, and for any node *X* at odd depth, the item stored at *X* has the smallest key #2 in its subtree. Do the following.

a. Draw a possible 2-D heap for the items (1, 10), (2, 9), (3, 8), (4, 7), and (5, 6).
b. Explain how to find the item with minimum key #1.
c. Explain how to find the item with minimum key #2.
d. Give an algorithm to insert a new item in the 2-D heap.
e. Give an algorithm to perform `deleteMin` with respect to either key.
f. Give an algorithm to perform `buildHeap` in linear time.

21.21 A *treap* is a binary search tree in which each node stores an item, two children, and a randomly assigned priority generated when the node is constructed. The nodes in the tree obey the usual binary search tree order, but they must also maintain heap order with respect to the priorities. The treap is a good alternative to the balanced search tree because balance is based on the random priorities, rather than on the items. Thus the average case results for binary search trees apply. Do the following.

a. Prove that a collection of distinct items, each of which has a distinct priority, can be represented by only one treap.
b. Show how to perform insertion in a treap by using a bottom-up algorithm.
c. Show how to perform insertion in a treap by using a top-down algorithm.
d. Show how to perform deletion from a treap.

21.22 Explain how to place the initial set of runs on two tapes when the number of runs is not a Fibonacci number.

IN PRACTICE

21.23 Write the `percDown` routine with the declaration

```
static void percDown( AnyType [ ] a, int index, int size )
```

Recall that the max heap starts at position 0, not position 1.

PROGRAMMING PROJECTS

21.24 Write a program to compare the running time of using the `PriorityQueue`'s one-parameter constructor to initialize the heap with N items versus starting with an empty `PriorityQueue` and performing N separate insertions. Run your program for sorted, reverse sorted, and random inputs.

21.25 Suppose that you have a number of boxes, each of which can hold total weight 1.0 and items i_1, i_2, i_3, ..., i_N, which weigh w_1, w_2, w_3, ..., w_N, respectively. The object is to pack all the items, using as few boxes as possible, without placing more weight in any box than its capacity. For instance, if the items have weights 0.4, 0.4, 0.6, and 0.6, you can solve the problem with two boxes. This problem is difficult, and no efficient algorithm is known. Several strategies give good, but not optimal, packings. Write programs to implement efficiently the following approximation strategies.

a. Scan the items in the order given; place each new item in the most-filled box that can accept it without overflowing. Use a priority queue to determine the box that an item goes in.
b. Sort the items, placing the heaviest item first; then use the strategy in part (a).

21.26 Implement both heapsort and quicksort and compare their performances on both sorted inputs and random inputs. Use different types of data for the tests.

21.27 Suppose that you have a hole at node X. The normal `percDown` routine is to compare X's children and then move the child up to X if it is larger (in the case of a max heap) than the element to be placed, thereby pushing the hole down. Stop when placing the new element in the hole is safe. Consider the following alternative strategy for `percDown`. Move elements up and the hole down as far as possible without testing whether the new cell can be inserted. These actions would place the new cell in a leaf and probably violate heap order. To fix the heap order, percolate the new cell up in the normal manner. The expectation is that the percolation up will be only one or two levels on average. Write a routine to include this idea. Compare the running time with that of a standard implementation of heapsort.

21.28 Redo Exercise 8.18, using heapsort instead of mergesort.

21.29 Implement an external sort.

21.30 Have the `PriorityQueue` support `decreaseKey` as follows: Define a nested class that implements `PriorityQueue.Position`. The binary heap will be represented by an array of objects, in which each object stores a data item and its index. Each `PriorityQueue.Position` object stores a reference back to the corresponding object in the array.

references

The binary heap was first described in the context of heapsort in [8]. The linear-time `buildHeap` algorithm is from [4]. Precise results on the number of comparisons and data movements used by heapsort in the best, worst, and average case are given in [7]. External sorting is discussed in detail in [6]. Exercise 21.18 is solved in [5]. Exercise 21.19 is solved in [2]. Exercise 21.20 is solved in [3]. Treaps are described in [1].

1. C. Aragon and R. Seidel, "Randomized Search Trees," *Algorithmica* **16** (1996), 464–497.
2. M. D. Atkinson, J. R. Sack, N. Santoro, and T. Strothotte, "Min-Max Heaps and Generalized Priority Queues," *Communications of the ACM* **29** (1986), 996–1000.
3. Y. Ding and M. A. Weiss, "The k-d Heap: An Efficient Multi-dimensional Priority Queue," *Proceedings of the Third Workshop on Algorithms and Data Structures* (1993), 302–313.
4. R. W. Floyd, "Algorithm 245: Treesort 3," *Communications of the ACM* **7** (1964), 701.
5. D. B. Johnson, "Priority Queues with Update and Finding Minimum Spanning Trees," *Information Processing Letters* **4** (1975), 53–57.
6. D. E. Knuth, *The Art of Computer Programming. Vol. 3: Sorting and Searching*, 2d ed., Addison-Wesley, Reading, MA, 1998.
7. R. Schaffer and R. Sedgewick, "The Analysis of Heapsort," *Journal of Algorithms* **14** (1993), 76–100.
8. J. W. J. Williams, "Algorithm 232: Heapsort," *Communications of the ACM* **7** (1964), 347–348.

part five

Advanced Data Structures

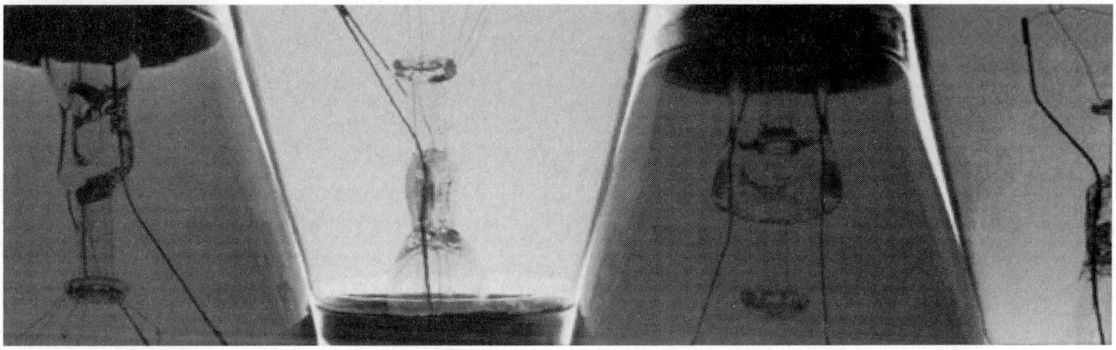

chapter 22

splay trees

In this chapter we describe a remarkable data structure called the *splay tree,* which supports all the binary search tree operations but does not guarantee $O(\log N)$ worst-case performance. Instead, its bounds are *amortized,* meaning that, although individual operations can be expensive, any sequence of operations is guaranteed to behave as though each operation in the sequence exhibited logarithmic behavior. Because this guarantee is weaker than that provided by balanced search trees, only the data and two links per node are required for each item and the operations are somewhat simpler to code. The splay tree has some other interesting properties, which we reveal in this chapter.

In this chapter, we show

- The concepts of amortization and self-adjustment
- The basic bottom-up splay tree algorithm and a proof that it has logarithmic amortized cost per operation
- Implementation of splay trees with a top-down algorithm, using a complete splay tree implementation (including a deletion algorithm)
- Comparisons of splay trees with other data structures

22.1 self-adjustment and amortized analysis

Although balanced search trees provide logarithmic worst-case running time per operation, they have several limitations.

- They require storing an extra piece of balancing information per node.
- They are complicated to implement. As a result, insertions and deletions are expensive and potentially error-prone.
- They do not provide a win when easy inputs occur.

The real problem is that the extra data members add complications.

Let us examine the consequences of each of these deficiencies. First, balanced search trees require an extra data member. Although in theory this member can be as small as a single bit (as in a red–black tree), in practice the extra data member uses an entire integer for storage in order to satisfy hardware restrictions. Because computer memories are becoming huge, we must ask whether worrying about memory is a large issue. The answer in most cases is probably not, except that maintaining the extra data members requires more complex code and tends to lead to longer running times and more errors. Indeed, identifying whether the balancing information for a search tree is correct is difficult because errors lead only to an unbalanced tree. If one case is slightly wrong, spotting the errors might be difficult. Thus, as a practical matter, algorithms that allow us to remove some complications without sacrificing performance deserve serious consideration.

The *90–10 rule* states that 90 percent of the accesses are to 10 percent of the data items. However, balanced search trees do not take advantage of this rule.

Second, the worst-case, average-case, and best-case performances of a balanced search are essentially identical. An example is a `find` operation for some item *X*. We could reasonably expect that, not only the cost of the `find` will be logarithmic, but also that if we perform an immediate second `find` for *X*, the second access will be cheaper than the first. However, in a red–black tree, this condition is not true. We would also expect that, if we perform an access of *X*, *Y*, and *Z* in that order, a second set of accesses for the same sequence would be easy. This assumption is important because of the *90–10 rule*. As suggested by empirical studies, the *90–10 rule* states that in practice 90 percent of the accesses are to 10 percent of the data items. Thus we want easy wins for the 90 percent case, but balanced search trees do not take advantage of this rule.

The 90–10 rule has been used for many years in disk I/O systems. A *cache* stores in main memory the contents of some of the disk blocks. The hope is that when a disk access is requested, the block can be found in the main memory cache and thus save the cost of an expensive disk access. Of course, only relatively few disk blocks can be stored in memory. Even so, storing the most recently accessed disk blocks in the cache enables large improvements in performance because many of the same disk blocks are accessed repeatedly. Browsers make use of the same idea: A cache stores locally the previously visited Web pages.

22.1.1 amortized time bounds

We are asking for a lot: We want to avoid balancing information and, at the same time, we want to take advantage of the 90–10 rule. Naturally, we should expect to have to give up some feature of the balanced search tree.

We choose to sacrifice the logarithmic worst-case performance. We are hoping that we do not have to maintain balance information, so this sacrifice seems inevitable. However, we cannot accept the typical performance of an unbalanced binary search tree. But there is a reasonable compromise: $O(N)$ time for a single access may be acceptable so long as it does not happen too often. In particular, if any M operations (starting with the first operation) take a total of $O(M \log N)$ worst-case time, the fact that some operations are expensive might be inconsequential. When we can show that a worst-case bound for a sequence of operations is better than the corresponding bound obtained by considering each operation separately and can be spread evenly to each operation in the sequence, we have performed an *amortized analysis* and the running time is said to be *amortized*. In the preceding example, we have logarithmic amortized cost. That is, some single operations may take more than logarithmic time, but we are guaranteed compensation by some cheaper operations that occur earlier in the sequence.

Amortized analysis bounds the cost of a sequence of operations and distributes this cost evenly to each operation in the sequence.

However, amortized bounds are not always acceptable. Specifically, if a single bad operation is too time consuming, we really do need worst-case bounds rather than amortized bounds. Even so, in many cases a data structure is used as part of an algorithm and only the total amount of time used by the data structure in the course of running an algorithm is important.

We have already presented one example of an amortized bound. When we implement array doubling in a stack or queue, the cost of a single operation can be either constant, if no doubling is needed, or $O(N)$, if doubling is needed. However, for any sequence of M stack or queue operations, the total cost is guaranteed to be $O(M)$, yielding constant amortized cost per operation. The fact that the array doubling step is expensive is inconsequential because its cost can be distributed to many earlier inexpensive operations.

22.1.2 a simple self-adjusting strategy (that does not work)

In a binary search tree, we cannot expect to store the frequently accessed items in a simple table. The reason is that the caching technique benefits from the great discrepancy between main memory and disk access times. Recall that the cost of an access in a binary search tree is proportional to the depth of the accessed node. Thus we can attempt to restructure the tree by moving frequently accessed items toward the root. Although this process costs extra time during the first `find` operation, it could be worthwhile in the long run.

The *rotate-to-root strategy* rearranges a binary search tree after each access so as to move frequently accessed items closer to the root.

The easiest way to move a frequently accessed item toward the root is to rotate it continually with its parent, moving the item closer to the root, a process called the *rotate-to-root strategy.* Then, if the item is accessed a second time, the second access is cheap, and so on. Even if a few other operations intervene before the item is reaccessed, that item will remain close to the root and thus will be quickly found. An application of the rotate-to-root strategy to node 3 is shown in Figure 22.1.[1]

The rotate-to-root strategy is good if the 90–10 rule applies. It can be a bad strategy when the rule does not apply.

As a result of the rotation, future accesses of node 3 are cheap (for a while). Unfortunately, in the process of moving node 3 up two levels, nodes 4 and 5 each move down a level. Thus, if access patterns do not follow the 90–10 rule, a long sequence of bad accesses can occur. As a result, the rotate-to-root rule does not exhibit logarithmic amortized behavior, which is likely unacceptable. A bad case is illustrated in Theorem 22.1.

Theorem 22.1

There are arbitrarily long sequences for which M rotate-to-root accesses use $\Theta(MN)$ time.

Proof

Consider the tree formed by the insertion of $1, 2, 3, \ldots, N$ in an initially empty tree. The result is a tree consisting of only left children. This outcome is not bad, as the time to construct the tree is only $O(N)$ total.

As illustrated in Figure 22.2, each newly added item is made a child of the root. Then, only one rotation is needed to place the new item at the root. The bad part, as shown in Figure 22.3, is that accessing the node with key 1 takes N units of time. After the rotations have been completed, access of the node with key 2 takes N units of time and access of key 3 takes $N-1$ units of time. The total for accessing the N keys in order is $N + \sum_{i=2}^{N} i = \Theta(N^2)$. After they have been accessed, the tree reverts to its original state and we can repeat the sequence. Thus we have an amortized bound of only $\Theta(N)$.

1. An insertion counts as an access. Thus an item would always be inserted as a leaf and then immediately rotated to the root. An unsuccessful search counts as an access on the leaf at which the search terminates.

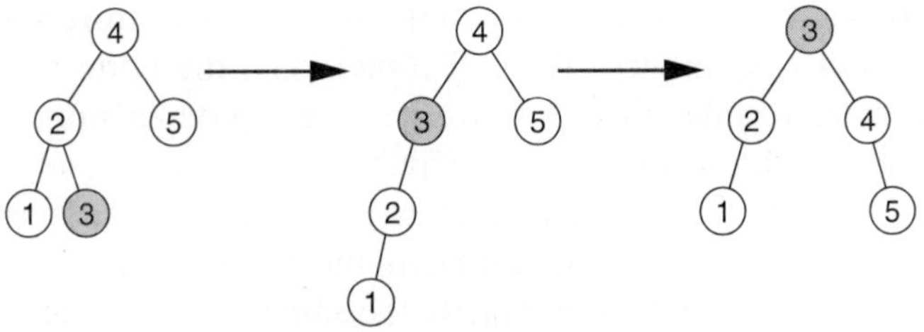

figure 22.1

Rotate-to-root strategy applied when node 3 is accessed

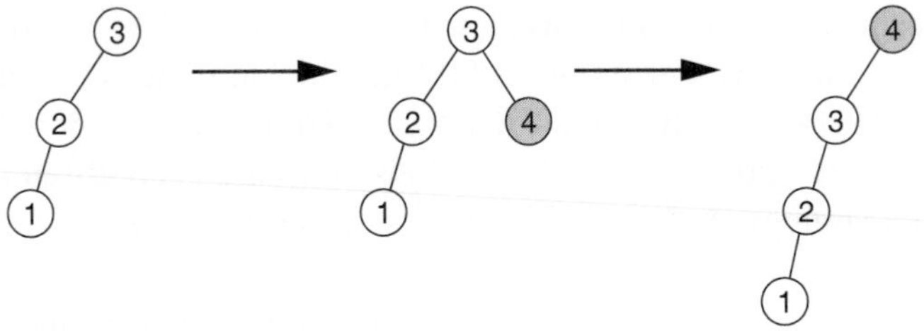

figure 22.2

Insertion of 4 using the rotate-to-root strategy

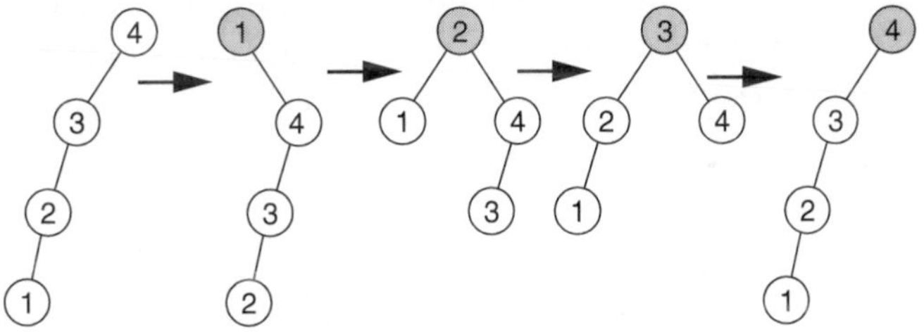

figure 22.3

Sequential access of items takes quadratic time

22.2 the basic bottom-up splay tree

Achieving logarithmic amortized cost seems impossible because, when we move an item to the root via rotations, other items are pushed deeper. Seemingly, that would always result in some very deep nodes if no balancing information is maintained. Amazingly, we can apply a simple fix to the rotate-to-root strategy that allows the logarithmic amortized bound to be obtained. Implementation of this slightly more complicated rotate-to-root method called *splaying* leads to the basic *bottom-up splay tree*.

In a basic *bottom-up splay tree*, items are rotated to the root by using a slightly more complicated method than that used for a simple rotate-to-root strategy.

The splaying strategy is similar to the simple rotate-to-root strategy, but it has one subtle difference. We still rotate from the bottom up along the access path (later in the chapter we describe a top-down strategy). If X is a nonroot node on the access path on which we are rotating and the parent of X is the root of the tree, we merely rotate X and the root, as shown in Figure 22.4. This rotation is the last along the access path, and it places X at the root. Note that this action is exactly the same as that in the rotate-to-root algorithm and is referred to as the *zig* case.

The *zig* and *zig-zag* cases are identical to rotate-to-root.

Otherwise, X has both a parent P and a grandparent G, and we must consider two cases and symmetries. The first case is the so called *zig-zag* case, which corresponds to the inside case for AVL trees. Here X is a right child and P is a left child (or vice versa). We perform a double rotation exactly like an AVL double rotation, as shown in Figure 22.5. Note that, as a double rotation is the same as two bottom-up single rotations, this case is no different than the rotate-to-root strategy. In Figure 22.1, the splay at node 3 is a single zig-zag rotation.

The *zig-zig* case is unique to the splay tree.

The final case, the *zig-zig* case, is unique to the splay tree and is the outside case for AVL trees. Here, X and P are either both left children or both right children. In this case, we transform the left-hand tree of Figure 22.6 to the right-hand tree. Note that this method differs from the rotate-to-root strategy. The zig-zig splay rotates between P and G and then X and P, whereas the rotate-to-root strategy rotates between X and P and then between X and G.

figure 22.4

The zig case (normal single rotation)

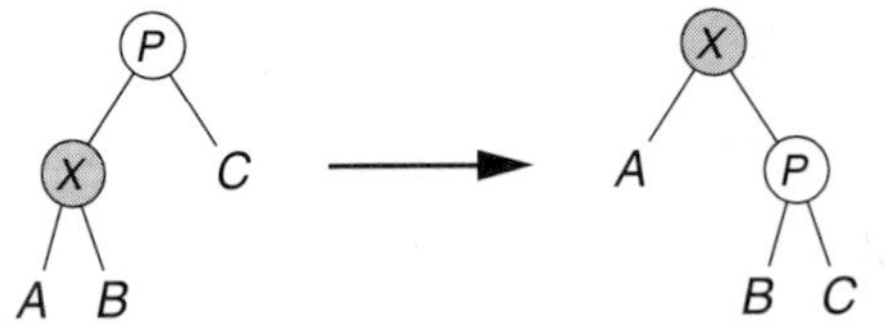

figure 22.5

The zig-zag case (same as a double rotation); the symmetric case has been omitted

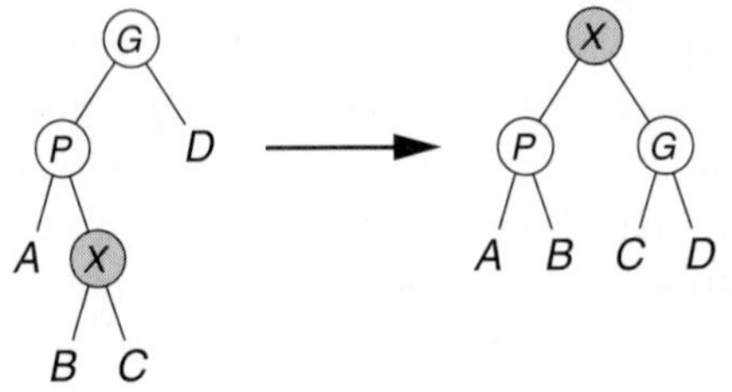

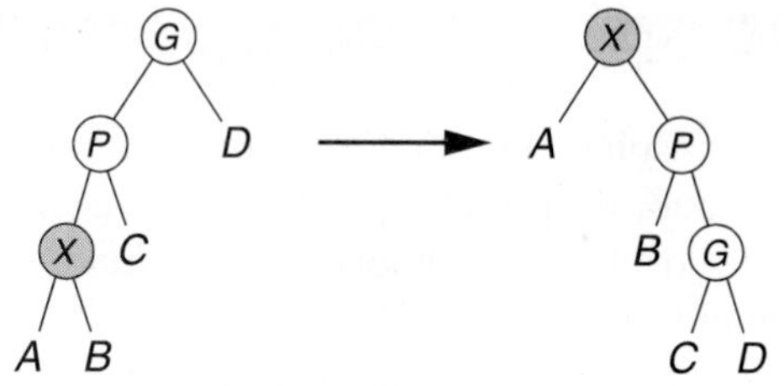

figure 22.6

Zig-zig case (unique to the splay tree); the symmetric case has been omitted

The difference seems quite minor, and the fact that it matters is somewhat surprising. To see this difference consider the sequence that gave the poor results in Theorem 22.1. Again, we insert keys 1, 2, 3, ..., N in an initially empty tree in linear total time and obtain an unbalanced left-child-only tree. However, the result of a splay is somewhat better, as shown in Figure 22.7. After the splay at node 1, which takes N node accesses, a splay at node 2 takes only roughly $N/2$ accesses, rather than $N - 1$ accesses. Splaying not only moves the accessed node to the root, but it also roughly halves the depth of most nodes on the access path (some shallow nodes are pushed down at most two levels). A subsequent splay at node 2 brings nodes to within $N/4$ of the root. Splaying is repeated until the depth becomes roughly log N. In fact, a complicated analysis shows that what used to be a bad case for the rotate-to-root algorithm is a good case for splaying: Sequential access of the N items in the splay tree takes a total of only $O(N)$ time. Thus we win on easy input. In Section 22.4 we show, by subtle accounting, that there are no bad access sequences.

Splaying has the effect of roughly halving the depth of most nodes on the access path and increasing by at most two levels the depth of a few other nodes.

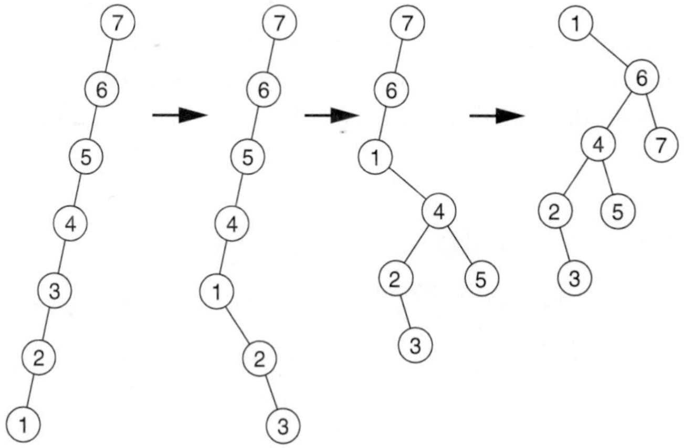

figure 22.7

Result of splaying at node 1 (three zig-zigs)

22.3 basic splay tree operations

After an item has been inserted as a leaf, it is splayed to the root.

As mentioned earlier, a splay operation is performed after each access. When an insertion is performed, we perform a splay. As a result, the newly inserted item becomes the root of the tree. Otherwise, we could spend quadratic time constructing an N item tree.

All searching operations incorporate a splay.

For the `find`, we splay at the last node accessed during the search. If the search is successful, the node found is splayed and becomes the new root. If the search is unsuccessful, the last node accessed prior to reaching the `null` reference is splayed and becomes the new root. This behavior is necessary because, otherwise, we could repeatedly perform a `find` for 0 in the initial tree in Figure 22.7 and use linear time per operation. Likewise, operations such as `findMin` and `findMax` perform a splay after the access.

The interesting operations are the deletions. Recall that the `deleteMin` and `deleteMax` are important priority queue operations. With splay trees, these operations become simple. We can implement `deleteMin` as follows. First, we perform a `findMin`. This brings the minimum item to the root, and by the binary search tree property, there is no left child. We can use the right child as the new root. Similarly, `deleteMax` can be implemented by calling `findMax` and setting the root to the post-splay root's left child.

Deletion operations are much simpler than usual. They also contain a splaying step (sometimes two).

Even the `remove` operation is simple. To perform deletion, we access the node to be deleted, which puts the node at the root. If it is deleted, we get two subtrees, L and R (left and right). If we find the largest element in L, using a `findMax` operation, its largest element is rotated to L's root and L's root has no right child. We finish the `remove` operation by making R the right child of L's root. An example of the `remove` operation is shown in Figure 22.8.

The cost of the `remove` operation is two splays. All other operations cost one splay. Thus we need to analyze the cost of a series of splay steps. The next section shows that the amortized cost of a splay is at most $3 \log N + 1$ single rotations. Among other things, this means we do not have to worry that the remove algorithm described previously is biased. The splay tree's amortized

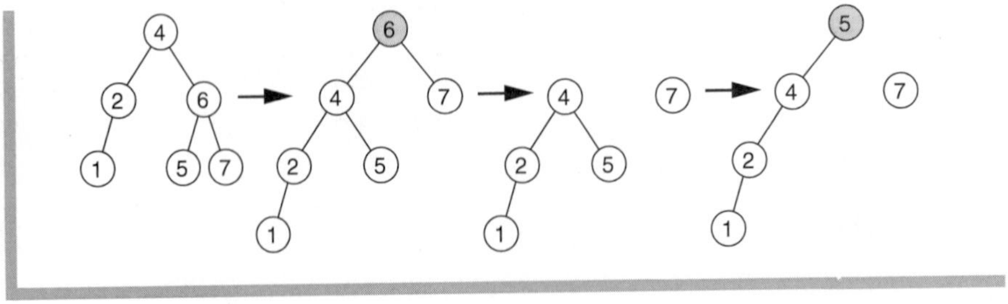

figure 22.8

The `remove` operation applied to node 6: First, 6 is splayed to the root, leaving two subtrees; a `findMax` is performed on the left subtree, raising 5 to the root of the left subtree; then the right subtree can be attached (not shown).

bound guarantees that any sequence of M splays will use at most $3M \log N + M$ tree rotations. Consequently, any sequence of M operations starting from an empty tree will take a total of at most $O(M \log N)$ time.

22.4 analysis of bottom-up splaying

The analysis of the splay tree algorithm is complicated because each splay can vary from a few rotations to $O(N)$ rotations. Each splay can drastically change the structure of the tree. In this section we prove that the amortized cost of a splay is at most $3 \log N + 1$ single rotations. The splay tree's amortized bound guarantees that any sequence of M splays use at most $3M \log N + M$ tree rotations, and consequently any sequence of M operations starting from an empty tree take a total of at most $O(M \log N)$ time.

> The analysis of the splay tree is complicated and is part of a much larger theory of amortized analysis.

To prove this bound, we introduce an accounting function called the *potential function*. Not maintained by the algorithm, the *potential function* is merely an accounting device used to establish the required time bound. Its choice is not obvious and is the result of a large amount of trial and error.

> The *potential function* is an accounting device used to establish the required time bound.

For any node i in the splay tree, let $S(i)$ be the number of descendants of i (including i itself). The potential function is the sum, over all nodes i in the tree T, of the logarithm of $S(i)$. Specifically,

$$\Phi(T) = \sum_{i \in T} \log S(i)$$

> The *rank* of a node is the logarithm of its size. Ranks and sizes are not maintained but are merely accounting tools for the proof. Only nodes on the splay path have their ranks changed.

To simplify the notation, we let $R(i) = \log S(i)$, which gives

$$\Phi(T) = \sum R(i)$$

The term $R(i)$ represents the *rank* of node i, or the logarithm of its size. Note that the rank of the root is $\log N$. Recall that neither ranks nor sizes are maintained by splay tree algorithms (unless, of course, order statistics are needed). When a zig rotation is performed, only the ranks of the two nodes involved in the rotation change. When a zig-zig or a zig-zag rotation is performed, only the ranks of the three nodes involved in the rotation change. And finally, a single splay consists of some number of zig-zig or zig-zag rotations followed by perhaps one zig rotation. Each zig-zig or zig-zag rotation can be counted as two single rotations.

For Theorem 22.2 we let Φ_i be the potential function of the tree immediately after the ith splay and Φ_0 be the potential prior to the first splay.

Theorem 22.2 If the ith splay operation uses r_i rotations, $\Phi_i - \Phi_{i-1} + r_i \leq 3 \log N + 1$.

In all the proofs in this section we use the concept of telescoping sums.

Before proving Theorem 22.2, let us determine what it means. The cost of M splays can be taken as $\sum_{i=1}^{M} r_i$ rotations. If the M splays are consecutive (i.e., no insertions or deletions intervene), the potential of the tree after the ith splay is the same as prior to the $(i + 1)$th splay. Thus we can use Theorem 22.2 M times to obtain the following sequence of equations:

$$
\begin{aligned}
\Phi_1 - \Phi_0 + r_1 &\leq 3 \log N + 1 \\
\Phi_2 - \Phi_1 + r_2 &\leq 3 \log N + 1 \\
\Phi_3 - \Phi_2 + r_3 &\leq 3 \log N + 1 \\
&\cdots \\
\Phi_M - \Phi_{M-1} + r_M &\leq 3 \log N + 1
\end{aligned}
\tag{22.1}
$$

These equations telescope, so if we add them, we obtain

$$\Phi_M - \Phi_0 + \sum_{i=1}^{M} r_i \leq (3 \log N + 1)M \tag{22.2}$$

which bounds the total number of rotations as

$$\sum_{i=1}^{M} r_i \leq (3 \log N + 1)M - (\Phi_M - \Phi_0)$$

Now consider what happens when insertions are intermingled with find operations. The potential of an empty tree is 0, so when a node is inserted in the tree as a leaf, prior to the splay the potential of the tree increases by at most $\log N$ (which we prove shortly). Suppose that r_i rotations are used for an insertion and that the potential prior to the insertion is Φ_{i-1}. After the insertion, the potential is at most $\Phi_{i-1} + \log N$. After the splay that moves the inserted node to the root, the new potential will satisfy

$$
\begin{aligned}
\Phi_i - (\Phi_{i-1} + \log N) + r_i &\leq 3 \log N + 1 \\
\Phi_i - \Phi_{i-1} + r_i &\leq 4 \log N + 1
\end{aligned}
\tag{22.3}
$$

Suppose further that there are F finds and I insertions and that Φ_i represents the potential after the ith operation. Then, because each `find` is governed by Theorem 22.2 and each insertion is governed by Equation 22.3, the telescoping logic indicates that

$$\sum_{i=1}^{M} r_i \leq (3 \log N + 1)F + (4 \log N + 1)I - (\Phi_M - \Phi_0) \tag{22.4}$$

Moreover, before the first operation the potential is 0, and since it can never be negative, $\Phi_M - \Phi_0 \geq 0$. Consequently, we obtain

$$\sum_{i=1}^{M} r_i \leq (3 \log N + 1)F + (4 \log N + 1)I \qquad \textbf{(22.5)}$$

showing that the cost of any sequence of finds and insertions is at most logarithmic per operation. A deletion is equivalent to two splays, so it too is logarithmic. Thus we must prove the two dangling claims—namely, Theorem 22.2 and the fact that an insertion of a node adds at most log N to the potential. We prove both theorems by using telescoping arguments. We take care of the insertion claim first, as Theorem 22.3.

Theorem 22.3

Insertion of the Nth node in a tree as a leaf adds at most $\log N$ to the potential of the tree.

Proof

The only nodes whose ranks are affected are those on the path from the inserted leaf to the root. Let $S_1, S_2, \ldots, S_k$ be their sizes prior to the insertion and note that $S_k = N - 1$ and $S_1 < S_2 < \cdots < S_k$. Let $S_1', S_2', \ldots, S_k'$ be the sizes after the insertion. Clearly, $S_i' \leq S_{i+1}$ for $i < k$, since $S_i' = S_i + 1$. Consequently, $R_i' \leq R_{i+1}$. The change in potential is thus

$$\sum_{i=1}^{k}(R_i' - R_i) \leq R_k' - R_k + \sum_{i=1}^{k-1}(R_{i+1} - R_i) \leq \log N - R_1 \leq \log N.$$

To prove Theorem 22.2, we break each splay step into its constituent zig, zig-zag, and zig-zig parts and establish a bound for the cost of each type of rotation. By telescoping these bounds, we obtain a bound for the splay. Before continuing, we need a technical theorem, Theorem 22.4.

Theorem 22.4

If $a + b \leq c$ and a and b are both positive integers, then $\log a + \log b \leq 2 \log c - 2$.

Proof

By the arithmetic–geometric mean inequality, $\sqrt{ab} \leq (a+b)/2$. Thus $\sqrt{ab} \leq c/2$. Squaring both sides gives $ab \leq c^2/4$. Then taking logarithms of both sides proves the theorem.

We are now ready to prove Theorem 22.2.

22.4.1 proof of the splaying bound

First, if the node to splay is already at the root, there are no rotations and no potential change. Thus the theorem is trivially true, and we may assume at least one rotation. We let X be the node involved in the splay. We need to show that, if r rotations are performed (a zig-zig or zig-zag counts as two rotations), r plus the change in potential is at most $3 \log N + 1$. Next, we let Δ be the change in potential caused by any of the splay steps zig, zig-zag, or zig-zig. Finally, we let $R_i(X)$ and $S_i(X)$ be the rank and size of any node X immediately before a splay step and $R_f(X)$ and $S_f(X)$ be the rank and size of any node X immediately after a splay step. Following are the bounds that are to be proven.

For a zig step that promotes node X, $\Delta \le 3(R_f(X) - R_i(X))$; for the other two steps, $\Delta \le 3(R_f(X) - R_i(X)) - 2$. When we add these bounds over all the steps that comprise a splay, the sum telescopes to the desired bound. We prove each bound separately in Theorems 22.5–22.7. Then we can complete the proof of Theorem 22.2 by applying a telescoping sum.

Theorem 22.5 For a zig step, $\Delta \le 3(R_f(X) - R_i(X))$.

Proof As mentioned earlier in this section, the only nodes whose ranks change in a zig step are X and P. Consequently, the potential change is $R_f(X) - R_i(X) + R_f(P) - R_i(P)$. From Figure 22.4, $S_f(P) < S_i(P)$; thus it follows that $R_f(P) - R_i(P) < 0$. Consequently, the potential change satisfies $\Delta \le R_f(X) - R_i(X)$. As $S_f(X) > S_i(X)$, it follows that $R_f(X) - R_i(X) > 0$; hence $\Delta \le 3(R_f(X) - R_i(X))$.

The zig-zag and zig-zig steps are more complicated because the ranks of three nodes are affected. First, we prove the zig-zag case.

Theorem 22.6 For a zig-zag step, $\Delta \le 3(R_f(X) - R_i(X)) - 2$.

Proof As before, we have three changes, so the potential change is given by

$$\Delta = R_f(X) - R_i(X) + R_f(P) - R_i(P) + R_f(G) - R_i(G)$$

From Figure 22.5, $S_f(X) = S_i(G)$, so their ranks must be equal. Thus we obtain

$$\Delta = -R_i(X) + R_f(P) - R_i(P) + R_f(G)$$

(continues next page)

(continued from previous page)

Proof of Theorem 22.6

Also, $S_i(P) \geq S_i(X)$. Consequently, $R_i(P) \geq R_i(X)$. Making this substitution and rearranging terms gives

$$\Delta \leq R_f(P) + R_f(G) - 2R_i(X) \quad \textbf{(22.6)}$$

From Figure 22.5, $S_f(P) + S_f(G) \leq S_f(X)$. Applying Theorem 22.4, we obtain $\log S_f(P) + \log S_f(G) \leq 2 \log S_f(X) - 2$, which by the definition of rank, becomes

$$R_f(P) + R_f(G) \leq 2R_f(X) - 2 \quad \textbf{(22.7)}$$

Substituting Equation 22.7 into Equation 22.6 yields

$$\Delta \leq 2R_f(X) - 2R_i(X) - 2 \quad \textbf{(22.8)}$$

As for the zig rotation, $R_f(X) - R_i(X) > 0$, so we can add it to the right side of Equation 22.8, factor, and obtain the desired

$$\Delta \leq 3(R_f(X) - R_i(X)) - 2$$

Finally, we prove the bound for the zig-zig case.

Theorem 22.7

For a zig-zig step, $\Delta \leq 3(R_f(X) - R_i(X)) - 2$.

Proof

As before, we have three changes, so the potential change is given by

$$\Delta = R_f(X) - R_i(X) + R_f(P) - R_i(P) + R_f(G) - R_i(G)$$

From Figure 22.6, $S_f(X) = S_i(G)$; their ranks must be equal, so we obtain

$$\Delta = -R_i(X) + R_f(P) - R_i(P) + R_f(G)$$

We also can obtain $R_i(P) > R_i(X)$ and $R_f(P) < R_f(X)$. Making this substitution and rearranging gives

$$\Delta < R_f(X) + R_f(G) - 2R_i(X) \quad \textbf{(22.9)}$$

(continues next page)

Proof of Theorem 22.7

(*continued from previous page*)

From Figure 22.6, $S_i(X) + S_f(G) \le S_f(X)$, so applying Theorem 22.4 yields

$$R_i(X) + R_f(G) \le 2R_f(X) - 2 \quad (22.10)$$

Rearranging Equation 22.10, we obtain

$$R_f(G) \le 2R_f(X) - R_i(X) - 2 \quad (22.11)$$

When we substitute Equation 22.11 into Equation 22.9, we get

$$\Delta \le 3(R_f(X) - R_i(X)) - 2$$

Now that we have established bounds for each splaying step, we can finally complete the proof of Theorem 22.2.

Proof of Theorem 22.2

Let $R_0(X)$ be the rank of X prior to the splay. Let $R_i(X)$ be X's rank after the ith splaying step. Prior to the last splaying step, all splaying steps must be zig-zags or zig-zigs. Suppose that there are k such steps. Then the total number of rotations performed at that point is $2k$. The total potential change is $\sum_{i=1}^{k} (3(R_i(X) - R_{i-1}(X)) - 2$. This sum telescopes to $3(R_k(X) - R_0(X)) - 2k$. At this point, the total number of rotations plus the total potential change is bounded by $3R_k(X)$ because the $2k$ term cancels and the initial rank of X is not negative. If the last rotation is a zig-zig or a zig-zag, then a continuation of the telescoping sum gives a total of $3R(root)$. Note that here, on the one hand, the -2 in the potential increase cancels the cost of two rotations. On the other hand, this cancellation does not happen in the zig, so we would get a total of $3R(root) + 1$. The rank of the root is $\log N$, so then—in the worst case—the total number of rotations plus the change in potential during a splay is at most $3 \log N + 1$.

Although it is complex, the proof of the splay tree bound illustrates several interesting points. First, the zig-zig case is apparently the most expensive: It contributes a leading constant of 3, whereas the zig-zag contributes 2. The proof would fall apart if we tried to adapt it to the rotate-to-root algorithm because, in the zig case, the number of rotations plus the potential change is $R_f(X) - R_i(X) + 1$. The 1 at the end does not telescope out, so we would not be able to show a logarithmic bound. This is fortunate because we already know that a logarithmic bound would be incorrect.

The technique of amortized analysis is very interesting, and some general principles have been developed to formalize the framework. Check the references for more details.

22.5 top-down splay trees

A direct implementation of the bottom-up splay strategy requires a pass down the tree to perform an access and then a second pass back up the tree. These passes can be made by maintaining parent links, by storing the access path on a stack, or by using a clever trick to store the path (using the available links in the accessed nodes). Unfortunately, all these methods require expending a substantial amount of overhead and handling many special cases. Recall from Section 19.5 that implementing search tree algorithms with a single top-down pass is a better approach and we can use dummy nodes to avoid special cases. In this section we describe a *top-down splay tree* that maintains the logarithmic amortized bound, is faster in practice, and uses only constant extra space. It is the method recommended by the inventors of the splay tree.

As for red–black trees, *top-down splay trees* are more efficient in practice than their bottom-up counterparts.

The basic idea behind the top-down splay tree is that, as we descend the tree searching for some node *X,* we must take the nodes that are on the access path and move them and their subtrees out of the way. We must also perform some tree rotations to guarantee the amortized time bound.

At any point in the middle of the splay, a current node *X* is the root of its subtree; it is represented in the diagrams as the middle tree. Tree *L* stores nodes that are less than *X;* similarly, tree *R* stores nodes that are larger than *X.* Initially, *X* is the root of *T,* and *L* and *R* are empty. Descending the tree two levels at a time, we encounter a pair of nodes. Depending on whether these nodes are smaller or larger than *X,* we place them in *L* or *R,* along with subtrees that are not on the access path to *X.* Thus the current node on the search path is *always* the root of the middle tree. When we finally reach *X,* we can then attach *L* and *R* to the bottom of the middle tree. As a result, *X* has been moved to the root. The remaining tasks then are to place nodes in *L* and *R* and to perform the reattachment at the end, as illustrated in the trees shown in Figure 22.9. As is customary, three symmetric cases are omitted.

We maintain three trees during the top-down pass.

In all the diagrams, *X* is the current node, *Y* is its child, and *Z* is a grandchild (should an applicable node exist). (The precise meaning of the term *applicable* is made clear during the discussion of the zig case.)

If the rotation should be a zig, the tree rooted at *Y* becomes the new root of the middle tree. Node *X* and subtree *B* are attached as a left child of the small-

figure 22.9

Top-down splay rotations: (a) zig, (b) zig-zig, and (c) zig-zag

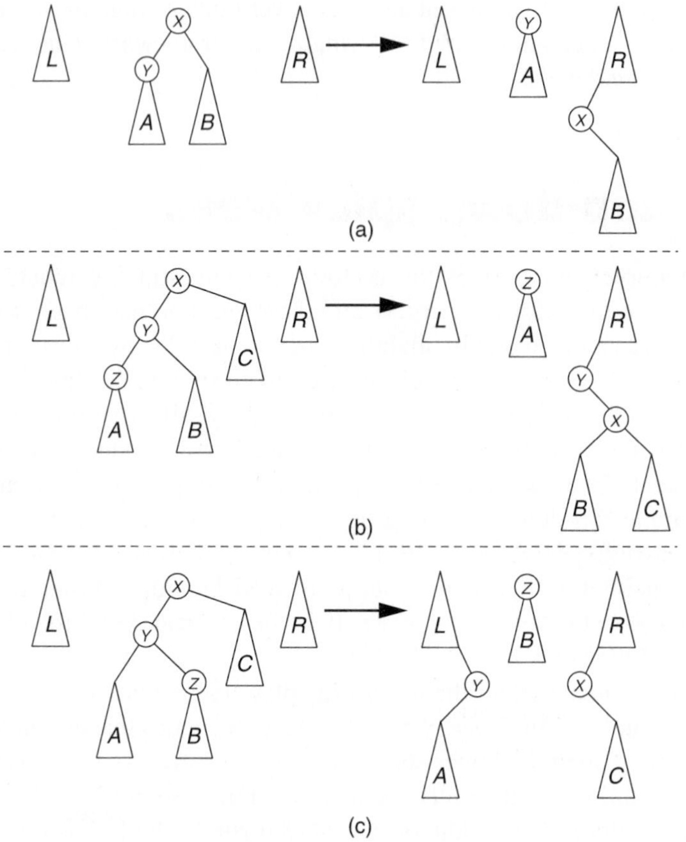

est item in *R;* *X*'s left child is logically made `null`.[2] As a result, *X* is the new smallest element in *R,* making future attachments easy.

Note that *Y* does not have to be a leaf for the zig case to apply. If the item sought is found in *Y,* a zig case will apply even if *Y* has children. A zig case also applies if the item sought is smaller than *Y* and *Y* has no left child, even if *Y* has a right child, and also for the symmetric case.

A similar dissection applies to the zig-zig case. The crucial point is that a rotation between *X* and *Y* is performed. The zig-zag case brings the bottom node *Z* to the top of the middle tree and attaches subtrees *X* and *Y* to *R* and *L,* respectively. Note that *Y* is attached to, and then becomes, the largest item in *L.*

2. In the code written here, the smallest node in *R* does not have a `null` left link because it is not needed.

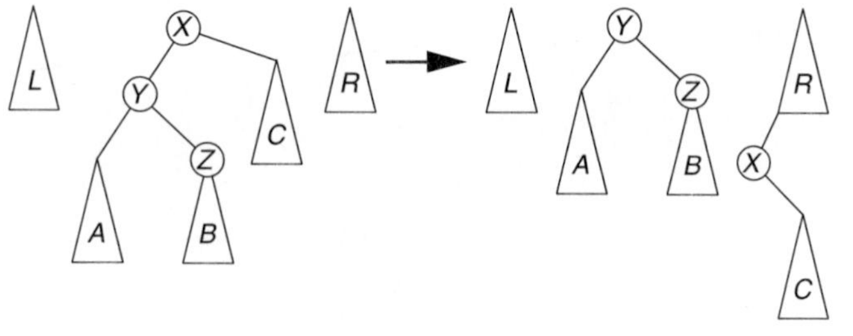

figure 22.10

Simplified top-down zig-zag

The zig-zag step can be simplified somewhat because no rotations are performed. Instead of making *Z* the root of the middle tree, we make *Y* the root, as shown in Figure 22.10. This action simplifies the coding because the action for the zig-zag case becomes identical to the zig case and would seem advantageous, as testing for a host of cases is time-consuming. The disadvantage is that a descent of only one level results in more iterations in the splaying procedure.

Eventually, the three trees are reassembled into one.

Once we have performed the final splaying step, *L, R,* and the middle tree are arranged to form a single tree, as shown in Figure 22.11. Note that the result is different from that obtained with bottom–up splaying. The crucial fact is that the $O(\log N)$ amortized bound is preserved (see Exercise 22.3).

An example of the simplified top-down splaying algorithm is shown in Figure 22.12. When we attempt to access 19, the first step is a zig-zag. In accordance with a symmetric version of Figure 22.10, we bring the subtree rooted at 25 to the root of the middle tree and attach 12 and its left subtree to *L*.

Next, we have a zig-zig: 15 is elevated to the root of the middle tree, and a rotation between 20 and 25 is performed, with the resulting subtree being attached to *R*. The search for 19 then results in a terminal zig. The middle's new root is 18, and 15 and its left subtree are attached as a right child of *L*'s largest node. The reassembly, in accordance with Figure 22.11, terminates the splay step.

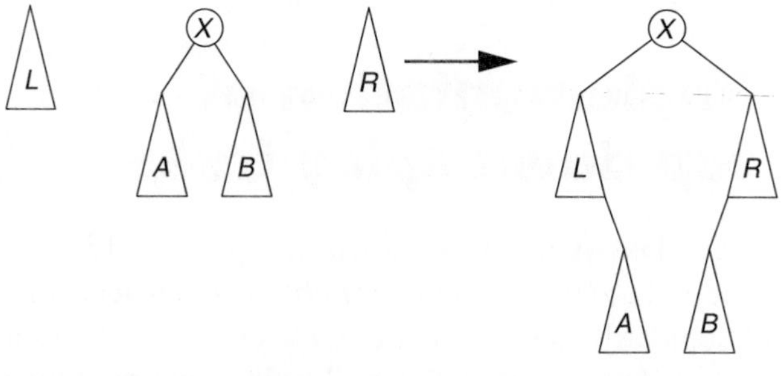

figure 22.11

Final arrangement for top-down splaying

figure 22.12

Steps in a top-down splay (accessing 19 in the top tree)

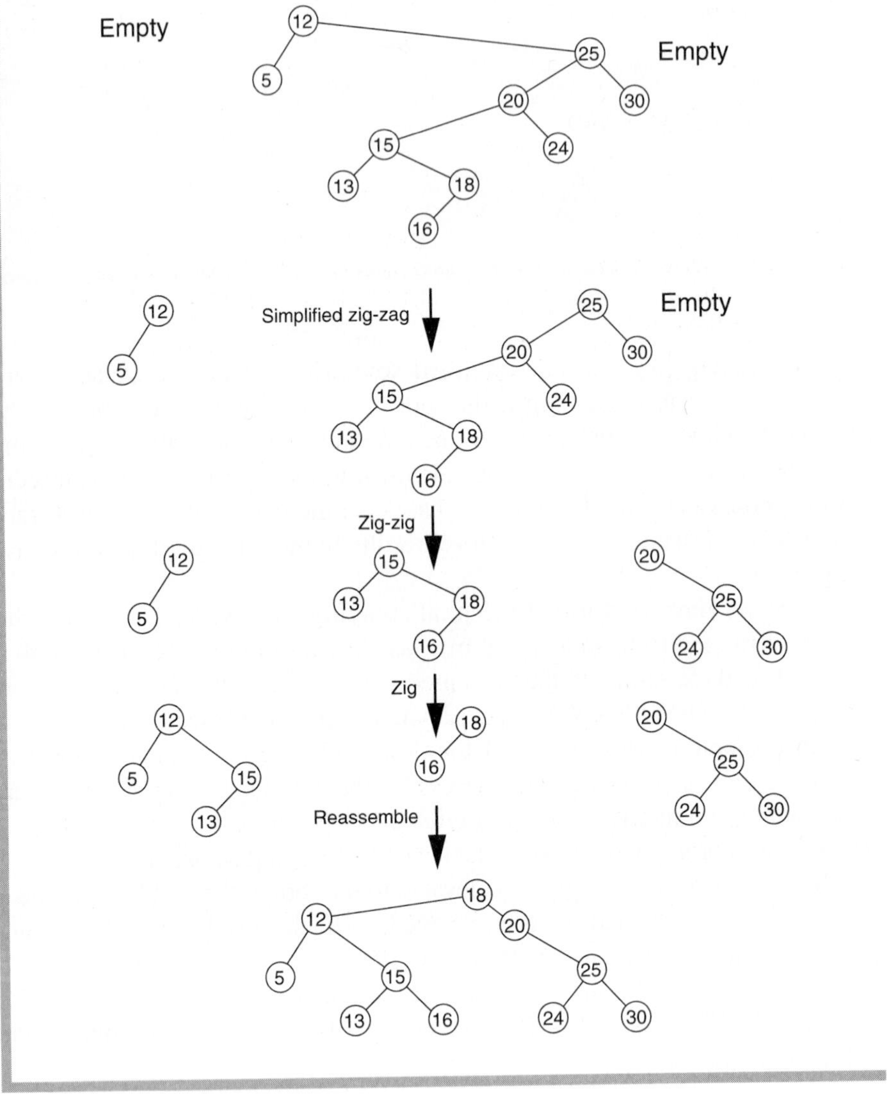

22.6 implementation of top-down splay trees

The splay tree class skeleton is shown in Figure 22.13. We have the usual methods, except that `find` is a mutator rather than an accessor. The `BinaryNode` class is our standard package-visible node class that contains data and two child references, but it is not shown. To eliminate annoying special cases,

```
package weiss.nonstandard;

// SplayTree class
//
// CONSTRUCTION: with no initializer
//
// ******************PUBLIC OPERATIONS*********************
// void insert( x )       --> Insert x
// void remove( x )       --> Remove x
// Comparable find( x )   --> Return item that matches x
// boolean isEmpty( )     --> Return true if empty; else false
// void makeEmpty( )      --> Remove all items
// ******************ERRORS********************************
// Exceptions are thrown by insert and remove if warranted

public class SplayTree<AnyType extends Comparable<? super AnyType>>
{
    public SplayTree( )
      { /* Figure 22.14 */ }

    public void insert( AnyType x )
      { /* Figure 22.15 */ }
    public void remove( AnyType x )
      { /* Figure 22.16 */ }
    public AnyType find( AnyType x )
      { /* Figure 22.18 */ }

    public void makeEmpty( )
      { root = nullNode; }
    public boolean isEmpty( )
      { return root == nullNode; }

    private BinaryNode<AnyType> splay( AnyType x, BinaryNode<AnyType> t )
      { /* Figure 22.17 */ }

    private BinaryNode<AnyType> root;
    private BinaryNode<AnyType> nullNode;
}
```

figure 22.13

The top-down SplayTree class skeleton

we maintain a nullNode sentinel. We allocate and initialize the sentinel in the constructor, as shown in Figure 22.14.

Figure 22.15 shows the method for insertion of an item x. A new node (newNode) is allocated, and if the tree is empty, a one-node tree is created. Otherwise, we splay around x. If the data in the tree's new root equal x, we have a duplicate. In this case, we do not want to insert x; we throw an exception instead at line 39. We use an instance variable so that the next call to insert

figure 22.14

The SplayTree class constructor

```
/**
 * Construct the tree.
 */
public SplayTree( )
{
    nullNode = new BinaryNode<AnyType>( null );
    nullNode.left = nullNode.right = nullNode;
    root = nullNode;
}
```

figure 22.15

The top-down SplayTree class insertion routine

```
  // Used between different inserts
private BinaryNode<AnyType> newNode = null;

/**
 * Insert into the tree.
 * @param x the item to insert.
 * @throws DuplicateItemException if x is already present.
 */
public void insert( AnyType x )
{
    if( newNode == null )
        newNode = new BinaryNode<AnyType>( null );
    newNode.element = x;

    if( root == nullNode )
    {
        newNode.left = newNode.right = nullNode;
        root = newNode;
    }
    else
    {
        root = splay( x, root );
        if( x.compareTo( root.element ) < 0 )
        {
            newNode.left = root.left;
            newNode.right = root;
            root.left = nullNode;
            root = newNode;
        }
        else
        if( x.compareTo( root.element ) > 0 )
        {
            newNode.right = root.right;
            newNode.left = root;
            root.right = nullNode;
            root = newNode;
        }
        else
            throw new DuplicateItemException( x.toString( ) );
    }
    newNode = null;    // So next insert will call new
}
```

can avoid calling `new`, in the case that the `insert` fails because of a duplicate item. (Normally, we would not be so concerned with this exceptional case; however, a reasonable alternative is to use a Boolean return value rather than using exceptions.)

If the new root contains a value larger than `x`, the new root and its right subtree become a right subtree of `newNode`, and the root's left subtree becomes a left subtree of `newNode`. Similar logic applies if the new root contains a value smaller than `x`. In either case, `newNode` is assigned to `root` to indicate that it is the new root. Then we make `newNode` `null` at line 41 so that the next call to `insert` will call `new`.

Figure 22.16 shows the deletion routine for splay trees. A deletion procedure rarely is shorter than the corresponding insertion procedure. Next, is the top-down splaying routine.

Our implementation, shown in Figure 22.17, uses a header with left and right links to contain eventually the roots of the left and right trees. These trees are initially empty; a header is used to correspond to the min or max node of the right or left tree, respectively, in this initial state. In this way we can avoid checking for empty trees. The first time the left tree becomes nonempty, the header's right link is initialized and does not change in the future.

```
/**
 * Remove from the tree.
 * @param x the item to remove.
 * @throws ItemNotFoundException if x is not found.
 */
public void remove( AnyType x )
{
    BinaryNode<AnyType> newTree;

        // If x is found, it will be at the root
    root = splay( x, root );
    if( root.element.compareTo( x ) != 0 )
        throw new ItemNotFoundException( x.toString( ) );

    if( root.left == nullNode )
        newTree = root.right;
    else
    {
        // Find the maximum in the left subtree
        // Splay it to the root; and then attach right child
        newTree = root.left;
        newTree = splay( x, newTree );
        newTree.right = root.right;
    }
    root = newTree;
}
```

figure 22.16

The top-down `SplayTree` class deletion routine

```
private BinaryNode<AnyType> header = new BinaryNode<AnyType>( null );

/**
 * Internal method to perform a top-down splay.
 * The last accessed node becomes the new root.
 * @param x the target item to splay around.
 * @param t the root of the subtree to splay.
 * @return the subtree after the splay.
 */
private BinaryNode<AnyType> splay( AnyType x, BinaryNode<AnyType> t )
{
    BinaryNode<AnyType> leftTreeMax, rightTreeMin;

    header.left = header.right = nullNode;
    leftTreeMax = rightTreeMin = header;

    nullNode.element = x;   // Guarantee a match

    for( ; ; )
        if( x.compareTo( t.element ) < 0 )
        {
            if( x.compareTo( t.left.element ) < 0 )
                t = Rotations.rotateWithLeftChild( t );
            if( t.left == nullNode )
                break;
            // Link Right
            rightTreeMin.left = t;
            rightTreeMin = t;
            t = t.left;
        }
        else if( x.compareTo( t.element ) > 0 )
        {
            if( x.compareTo( t.right.element ) > 0 )
                t = Rotations.rotateWithRightChild( t );
            if( t.right == nullNode )
                break;
            // Link Left
            leftTreeMax.right = t;
            leftTreeMax = t;
            t = t.right;
        }
        else
            break;

    leftTreeMax.right = t.left;
    rightTreeMin.left = t.right;
    t.left = header.right;
    t.right = header.left;
    return t;
}
```

figure 22.17

A top-down splay algorithm

Thus it contains the root of the left tree at the end of the top-down search. Similarly, the header's left link eventually contains the root of the right tree. The `header` variable is not local because we want to allocate it only once over the entire sequence of splays.

Before the reassembly at the end of the splay, `header.left` and `header.right` reference *R* and *L*, respectively (this is not a typo—follow the links). Note that we are using the simplified top-down splay. The `find` method, shown in Figure 22.18, completes the implementation of the splay tree.

22.7 comparison of the splay tree with other search trees

The implementation just presented suggests that splay trees are not as complicated as red–black trees and almost as simple as AA-trees. Are they worth using? The answer has yet to be resolved completely, but if the access patterns are nonrandom, splay trees seem to perform well in practice. Some properties relating to their performances also can be proved analytically. Nonrandom accesses include those that follow the 90–10 rule, as well as several special cases such as sequential access, double-ended access, and apparently access patterns that are typical of priority queues during some types of event simulations. In the exercises you are asked to examine this question in more detail.

Splay trees are not perfect. One problem with them is that the `find` operation is expensive because of the splay. Hence when access sequences are random and uniform, splay trees do not perform as well as other balanced trees.

```
/**
 * Find an item in the tree.
 * @param x the item to search for.
 * @return the matching item or null if not found.
 */
public AnyType find( AnyType x )
{
    root = splay( x, root );

    if( isEmpty( ) || root.element.compareTo( x ) != 0 )
        return null;

    return root.element;
}
```

figure 22.18

The `find` routine, for top-down splay trees

summary

In this chapter we described the splay tree, which is a recent alternative to the balanced search tree. Splay trees have several remarkable properties that can be proved, including their logarithmic cost per operation. Other properties are suggested in the exercises. Some studies have suggested that splay trees can be used for a wide range of applications because of their apparent ability to adapt to easy access sequences.

In Chapter 23 we describe two priority queues that, like the splay tree, have poor worst-case performance but good amortized performance. One of these, the pairing heap, seems to be an excellent choice for some applications.

key concepts

90–10 rule States 90 percent of the accesses are to 10 percent of the data items. However, balanced search trees do not take advantage of this rule. (782)

amortized analysis Bounds the cost of a sequence of operations and distributes the cost evenly to each operation in the sequence. (783)

bottom-up splay tree A tree in which items are rotated to the root by using a slightly more complicated method than that used for a simple rotate-to-root strategy. (785)

potential function An accounting device used to establish an amortized time bound. (789)

rank In the splay tree analysis, the logarithm of a node's size. (789)

rotate-to-root strategy Rearranges a binary search tree after each access so as to move frequently accessed items closer to the root. (784)

splaying A rotate-to-root strategy that allows the logarithmic amortized bound to be obtained. (786)

top-down splay tree A type of splay tree that is more efficient in practice than its bottom-up counterpart, as was the case for red–black trees. (795)

zig and **zig-zag** Cases that are identical to the rotate-to-root cases. Zig is used when X is a child of the root, and zig-zag is used when X is an inside (grandchild) node. (786)

zig-zig A case unique to the splay tree, which is used when X is an outside (grandchild) node. (786)

common errors

1. A splay must be performed after every access, even an unsuccessful one, or the performance bounds are not valid.
2. The code is still tricky.
3. Recursive private methods cannot be used safely in the `SplayTree` class because the tree depth may be large, even while performance is otherwise acceptable.

on the internet

The `SplayTree` class is available online. The code includes versions of `findMin` and `findMax` that are efficient in an amortized sense but not completely optimized.

SplayTree.java Contains the implementation for the `SplayTree` class.

exercises

IN SHORT

22.1 Show the result of inserting 3, 1, 4, 5, 2, 9, 6, and 8 into a
  a. Bottom-up splay tree
  b. Top-down splay tree

22.2 Show the result of deleting 3 from the splay tree shown in Exercise 22.1 for both the bottom-up and top-down versions.

IN THEORY

22.3 Prove that the amortized cost of a top-down splay is $O(\log N)$.

22.4 Prove that if all nodes in a splay tree are accessed in sequential order, the resulting tree consists of a chain of left children.

22.5 Suppose that, in an attempt to save time, we splay on every second tree operation. Does the amortized cost remain logarithmic?

22.6 Nodes 1 through $N = 1024$ form a splay tree of left children.
  a. What is the internal path length of the tree (exactly)?
  b. Calculate the internal path length after each of `find(1)`, `find(2)`, and `find(3)` when a bottom-up splay is performed.

22.7 By changing the potential function, you can prove different bounds for splaying. Let the weight function $W(i)$ be some function assigned to each node in the tree and $S(i)$ be the sum of the weights of all nodes in the subtree rooted at i, including i itself. The special case $W(i) = 1$ for all nodes corresponds to the function used in the proof of the splaying bound. Let N be the number of nodes in the tree and M be the number of accesses. Prove the following two theorems.

a. The total access time is $O(M + (M + N) \log N)$.

b. If q_i is the total number of times that item i is accessed and $q_i > 0$ for all i, then the total access time is $O(M + \sum_{i=1}^{N} q_i \log(M/q_i))$.

IN PRACTICE

22.8 Use the splay tree to implement a priority queue class.

22.9 Modify the splay tree to support order statistics.

PROGRAMMING PROJECTS

22.10 Compare empirically the simplified top-down splay implemented in Section 22.6 with the original top-down splay discussed in Section 22.5.

22.11 Unlike balanced search trees, splay trees incur overhead during a `find` operation that can be undesirable if the access sequence is sufficiently random. Experiment with a strategy that splays on a `find` operation only after a certain depth d is traversed in the top-down search. The splay does not move the accessed item all the way to the root, but rather to the point at depth d where the splaying is started.

22.12 Compare empirically a top-down splay tree priority queue implementation with a binary heap by using

a. Random `insert` and `deleteMin` operations

b. `insert` and `deleteMin` operations corresponding to an event-driven simulation

c. `insert` and `deleteMin` operations corresponding to Dijkstra's algorithm

references

The splay tree is described in the paper [3]. The concept of amortized analysis is discussed in the survey paper [4] and also in greater detail in [5]. A comparison of splay trees and AVL trees is given in [1], and [2] shows that splay trees perform well in some types of event-driven simulations.

1. J. Bell and G. Gupta, "An Evaluation of Self-Adjusting Binary Search Tree Techniques," *Software-Practice and Experience* **23** (1993), 369–382.
2. D. W. Jones, "An Empirical Comparison of Priority-Queue and Event-Set Implementations," *Communications of the ACM* **29** (1986), 300–311.
3. D. D. Sleator and R. E. Tarjan, "Self-adjusting Binary Search Trees," *Journal of the ACM* **32** (1985), 652–686.
4. R. E. Tarjan, "Amortized Computational Complexity," *SIAM Journal on Algebraic and Discrete Methods* **6** (1985), 306–318.
5. M. A. Weiss, *Data Structures and Algorithm Analysis in Java*, Addison-Wesley, Reading, MA, 1999.

chapter 23

merging priority queues

In this chapter we examine priority queues that support an additional operation: The `merge` operation, which is important in advanced algorithm design, combines two priority queues into one (and logically destroys the originals). We represent the priority queues as general trees, which simplifies somewhat the `decreaseKey` operation and is important in some applications.

In this chapter, we show

- How the *skew heap*—a mergeable priority queue implemented with binary trees—works.
- How the *pairing heap*—a mergeable priority queue based on the *M*-ary tree—works. The pairing heap appears to be a practical alternative to the binary heap even if the `merge` operation is not needed.

23.1 the skew heap

The *skew heap* is a heap-ordered binary tree without a balancing condition and supports all operations in logarithmic amortized time.

The *skew heap* is a heap-ordered binary tree without a balancing condition. Without this structural constraint on the tree—unlike with the heap or the balanced binary search trees—there is no guarantee that the depth of the tree is logarithmic. However, it supports all operations in logarithmic amortized time. The skew heap is thus somewhat similar to the splay tree.

23.1.1 merging is fundamental

If a heap-ordered, structurally unconstrained binary tree is used to represent a priority queue, merging becomes the fundamental operation. This is because we can perform other operations as follows:

- `h.insert( x )`: Create a one-node tree containing `x` and merge that tree into the priority queue.
- `h.findMin( )`: Return the item at the root.
- `h.deleteMin( )`: Delete the root and merge its left and right subtrees.
- `h.decreaseKey( p, newVal )`: Assuming that `p` is a reference to a node in the priority queue, we can lower `p`'s key value appropriately and then detach `p` from its parent. Doing so yields two priority queues that can be merged. Note that `p` (meaning the position) does not change as a result of this operation (in contrast to the equivalent operation in a binary heap).

The `decreaseKey` operation is implemented by detaching a subtree from its parent and then using `merge`.

We need show only how to implement merging; the other operations become trivial. The `decreaseKey` operation is important in some advanced applications. We presented one illustration in Section 14.3—Dijkstra's algorithm for shortest paths in a graph. We did not use the `decreaseKey` operation in our implementation because of the complications of maintaining the position of each item in the binary heap. In a merging heap, the position can be maintained as a reference to the tree node, and unlike in the binary heap, the position never changes.

In this section we discuss one implementation of a mergeable priority queue that uses a binary tree: the skew heap. First, we show that, if we are not concerned with efficiency, merging two heap-ordered trees is easy. Next, we cover a simple modification (the skew heap) that avoids the obvious inefficiencies in the original algorithm. Finally, we give a proof that the `merge` operation for skew heaps is logarithmic in an amortized sense and comment on the practical significance of this result.

23.1.2 simplistic merging of heap-ordered trees

Two trees are easily merged recursively.

Let us assume that we have two heap-ordered trees, H_1 and H_2, that need to be merged. Clearly, if either of the two trees is empty, the other tree is the result of the merge. Otherwise, to merge the two trees, we compare their roots. We recursively merge the tree with the larger root into the right subtree of the tree with the smaller root.[1]

Figure 23.1 shows the effect of this recursive strategy: The right paths of the two priority queues are merged to form the new priority queue. Each node on the right path retains its original left subtree, and only the nodes on the right path are touched. The outcome shown in Figure 23.1 is unattainable by using only insertions and merges because, as just mentioned, left children cannot be added by a merge. The practical effect is that what seems to be a heap-ordered binary tree is in fact an ordered arrangement consisting only of a single right path. Thus all operations take linear time. Fortunately, a simple modification ensures that the right path is not always long.

The result is that right paths are merged. We must be careful not to create unduly long right paths.

23.1.3 the skew heap: a simple modification

The merge shown in Figure 23.1 creates a temporary merged tree. We can make a simple modification in the operation as follows. Prior to the completion of a merge, we swap the left and right children for every node in the resulting right path of the temporary tree. Again, only those nodes on the original right paths are on the right path in the temporary tree. As a result of the swap, shown in Figure 23.2, these nodes then form the left path of the resulting tree. When a merge is performed in this way, the heap-ordered tree is also called a *skew heap*.

To avoid the problem of unduly long right paths, we make the resulting right path after a `merge` a left path. Such a merge results in a *skew heap*.

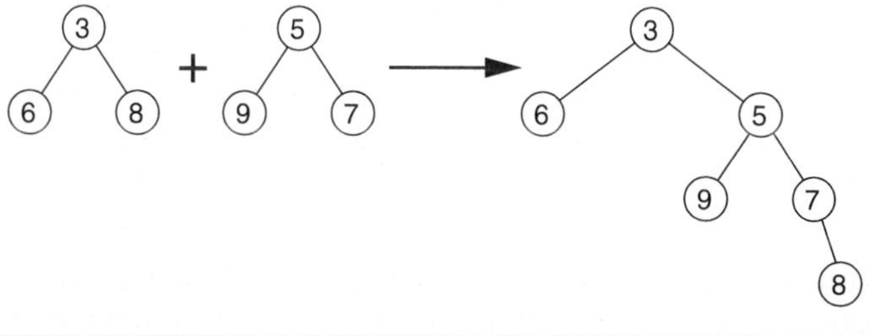

figure 23.1

Simplistic merging of heap-ordered trees: Right paths are merged.

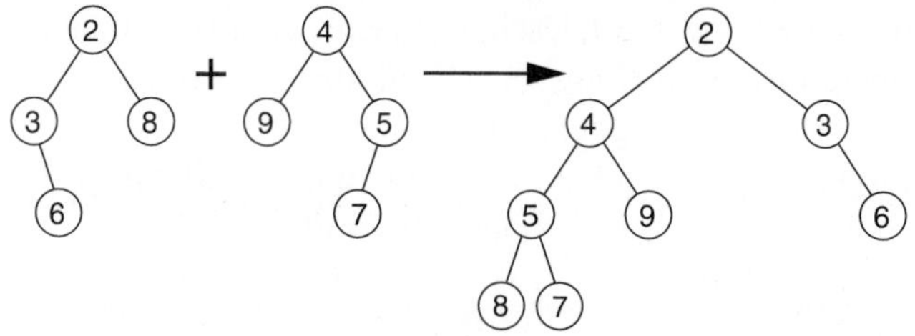

figure 23.2

Merging of skew heap; right paths are merged, and the result is made a left path.

1. Clearly, either subtree could be used. We arbitrarily use the right subtree.

A recursive viewpoint is as follows. If we let L be the tree with the smaller root and R be the other tree, the following is true.

1. If one tree is empty, the other can be used as the merged result.
2. Otherwise, let *Temp* be the right subtree of L.
3. Make L's left subtree its new right subtree.
4. Make the result of the recursive merge of *Temp* and R the new left subtree of L.

A long right path is still possible. However, it rarely occurs and must be preceded by many merges involving short right paths.

We expect the result of the child swapping to be that the length of the right path will not be unduly large all the time. For instance, if we merge a pair of long right-path trees, the nodes involved in the path do not reappear on a right path for quite some time in the future. Obtaining trees that have the property that every node appears on a right path is still possible, but that can be done only as a result of a large number of relatively inexpensive merges. In Section 23.1.4, we prove this assertion rigorously by establishing that the amortized cost of a merge operation is only logarithmic.

23.1.4 analysis of the skew heap

The actual cost of a merge is the number of nodes on the right paths of the two trees that are merged.

Suppose that we have two heaps, H_1 and H_2, and that there are r_1 and r_2 nodes on their respective right paths. Then the time required to perform the merge is proportional to $r_1 + r_2$. When we charge 1 unit for each node on the right paths, the cost of the merge is proportional to the number of charges. Because the trees have no structure, all the nodes in both trees may lie on the right path. This condition would give a $\Theta(N)$ worst-case bound for merging the trees (in Exercise 23.4 you are asked to construct such a tree). As we demonstrate shortly, the amortized time needed to merge two skew heaps is $O(\log N)$.

As with the splay tree, we introduce a potential function that cancels the varying costs of skew heap operations. We want the potential function to increase by a total of $O(\log N) - (r_1 + r_2)$ so that the total of the merge cost and potential change is only $O(\log N)$. If the potential is minimal prior to the first operation, applying the telescoping sum guarantees that the total spent for any M operations is $O(M \log N)$, as with the splay tree.

What we need is some potential function that captures the effect of skew heap operations. Finding such a function is quite challenging. Once we have found one, however, the proof is relatively short.

definition: A node is a *heavy node* if the size of its right subtree is larger than the size of its left subtree. Otherwise, it is a *light node*; a node is light if its subtrees are of equal size.

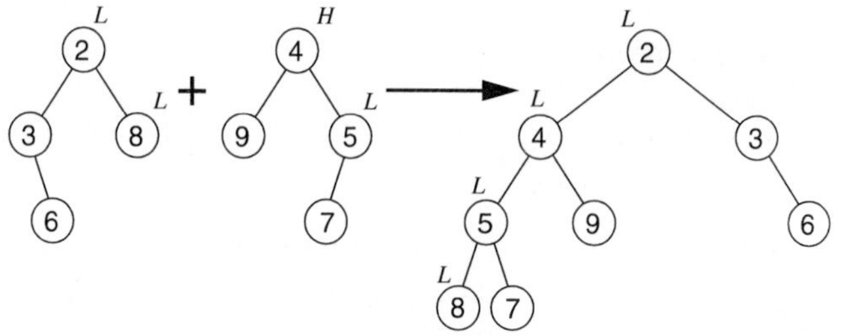

figure 23.3

Change in the heavy or light status of nodes after a merge

In Figure 23.3, prior to the merge, nodes 3 and 4 are heavy. After the merge, only node 3 is heavy. Three facts are easily shown. First, as a result of a merge, only nodes on the right path can have their heavy or light status changed because no other nodes have their subtrees altered. Second, a leaf is light. Third, the number of light nodes on the right path of an N node tree is at most $\lfloor \log N \rfloor + 1$. The reason is that the right child of a light node is less than half the size of the light node itself, and the halving principle applies. The additional +1 is a result of the leaf's being light. With these preliminaries, we can now state and prove Theorems 23.1 and 23.2.

The potential function is the number of heavy nodes. Only nodes on the merged path have their heavy or light status changed. The number of light nodes on a right path is logarithmic.

Theorem 23.1

Let H_1 and H_2 be two skew heaps with N_1 and N_2 nodes, respectively, and let N be their combined size (that is, $N_1 + N_2$). Suppose that the right path of H_1 has l_1 light nodes and h_1 heavy nodes, for a total of $l_1 + h_1$, whereas the right path of H_2 has l_2 light nodes and h_2 heavy nodes, for a total of $l_2 + h_2$. If the potential is defined as the total number of heavy nodes in the collection of skew heaps, then the merge costs at most $2 \log N + (h_1 + h_2)$, but the change in potential is at most $2 \log N - (h_1 + h_2)$.

Proof

The cost of the merge is merely the total number of nodes on the right paths, $l_1 + l_2 + h_1 + h_2$. The number of light nodes is logarithmic, so $l_1 \le \lfloor \log N_1 \rfloor + 1$ and $l_2 \le \lfloor \log N_2 \rfloor + 1$. Thus $l_1 + l_2 \le \log N_1 + \log N_2 + 2 \le 2 \log N$, where the last inequality follows from Theorem 22.4. The merge cost is thus at most $2 \log N + (h_1 + h_2)$. The bound on the potential change follows from the fact that only the nodes involved in the merge can have their heavy/light status changed and from the fact that any heavy node on the path must become light because its children are swapped. Even if all the light nodes became heavy, the potential change would still be limited to $l_1 + l_2 - (h_1 + h_2)$. Based on the same argument as before, that is at most $2 \log N - (h_1 + h_2)$.

Theorem 23.2

The amortized cost of the skew heap is at most $4 \log N$ for the `merge`, `insert`, and `deleteMin` operations.

Proof

Let Φ_i be the potential in the collection of skew heaps immediately following the ith operation. Note that $\Phi_0 = 0$ and $\Phi_i \geq 0$. An insertion creates a single node tree whose root is by definition light and thus does not alter the potential prior to the resulting merge. A `deleteMin` operation discards the root prior to the merge, so it cannot raise the potential (it may, in fact, lower it). We need to consider only the merging costs. Let c_i be the cost of the merge that occurs as a result of the ith operation. Then $c_i + \Phi_i - \Phi_{i-1} \leq 4 \log N$. Telescoping over any M operations yields $\sum_{i=1}^{M} c_i \leq 4M \log N$ because $\Phi_M - \Phi_0$ is not negative.

Finding a useful potential function is the most difficult part of the analysis.

The skew heap is a remarkable example of a simple algorithm with an analysis that is not obvious. The analysis, however, is easy to perform once we have identified the appropriate potential function. Unfortunately, there is still no general theory that allows us to decide on a potential function. Typically, many different functions have to be tried before a usable one is found.

A nonrecursive algorithm should be used because of the possibility that we could run out of stack space.

One comment is in order: Although the initial description of the algorithm uses recursion and recursion provides the simplest code, it cannot be used in practice. The reason is that the linear worst-case time for an operation could cause an overflow of the runtime stack when the recursion is implemented. Consequently, a nonrecursive algorithm must be used. Rather than explore those possibilities, we discuss an alternative data structure that is slightly more complicated: the pairing heap. This data structure has not been completely analyzed, but it seems to perform well in practice.

23.2 the pairing heap

The *pairing heap* is a heap-ordered *M*-ary tree with no structural constraints. Its analysis is incomplete, but it appears to perform well in practice.

The *pairing heap* is a structurally unconstrained heap-ordered M-ary tree for which all operations except deletion take constant worst-case time. Although `deleteMin` could take linear worst-case time, any *sequence* of pairing heap operations has logarithmic amortized performance. It has been conjectured—but not proved—that even better performance is guaranteed. However, the best possible scenario—namely, that all operations except for `deleteMin` have constant amortized cost, while `deleteMin` has logarithmic amortized cost—has recently been shown to be untrue.

Figure 23.4 shows an abstract pairing heap. The actual implementation uses a left child/right sibling representation (see Chapter 18). The `decreaseKey` method, as we discuss shortly, requires that each node contain an additional link. A node that is a leftmost child contains a link to its parent; otherwise, the node is a right sibling and contains a link to its left sibling. This representation is shown in Figure 23.5, where the darkened line indicates that two links (one in each direction) connect pairs of nodes.

The pairing heap is stored by using a left child/right sibling representation. A third link is used for `decreaseKey`.

23.2.1 pairing heap operations

In principle, the basic pairing heap operations are simple, which is why the pairing heap performs well in practice. To merge two pairing heaps, we make the heap with the larger root the new first child of the heap with the smaller root. Insertion is a special case of merging. To perform a `decreaseKey` operation, we lower the value of the requested node. Because we are not maintaining parent links for all nodes, we do not know if this action violates the heap order. Thus we detach the adjusted node from its parent and complete `decreaseKey` by merging the two pairing heaps that result. Figure 23.5 shows that detaching a node from its parent means removing it from what is essentially a linked list of children. So far we are in great shape: Every operation described takes constant time. However, we are not so lucky with the `deleteMin` operation.

Merging is simple: Attach the larger root tree as a left child of the smaller root tree. Insertion and decreasing are also simple.

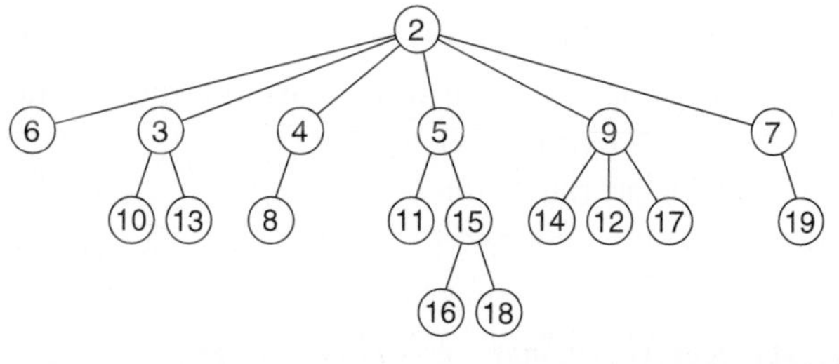

figure 23.4

Abstract representation of a sample pairing heap

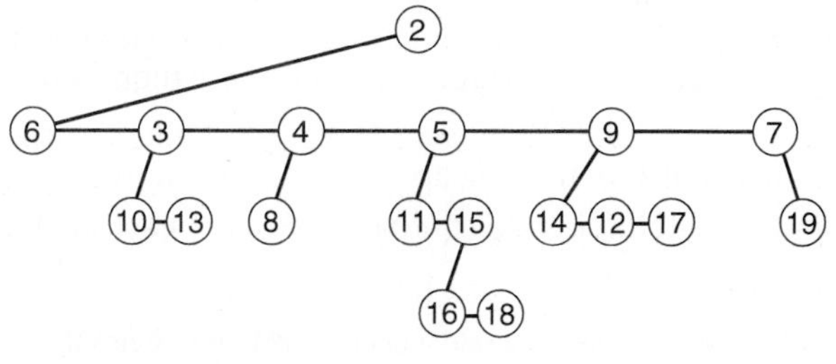

figure 23.5

Actual representation of the pairing heap shown in Figure 23.4; the dark lines represent a pair of links that connect nodes in both directions.

The deleteMin operation is expensive because the new root could be any of the c children of the old root. We need $c - 1$ merges.

To perform a deleteMin, we must remove the root of the tree, creating a collection of heaps. If there are c children of the root, combining these heaps into one heap requires $c - 1$ merges. Hence, if there are lots of children of the root, the deleteMin operation costs lots of time. If the insertion sequence is 1, 2, …, N, then 1 is at the root and all the other items are in nodes that are children of the root. Consequently, deleteMin is $O(N)$ time. The best that we can hope to do is to arrange the merges so that we do not have repeatedly expensive deleteMin operations.

The order in which pairing heap subtrees are merged is important. The simplest algorithm is *two-pass merging.*

The order in which pairing heap subtrees are merged is important. The simplest and most practical of the many variants of doing so that have been proposed is *two-pass merging,* in which a first scan merges pairs of children from left to right[2] and then a second scan, right to left, is performed to complete the merging. After the first scan, we have half as many trees to merge. In the second scan, at each step, we merge the rightmost tree that remains from the first scan with the current merged result. For example, if we have children c_1 through c_8, the first scan performs the merges c_1 and c_2, c_3 and c_4, c_5 and c_6, and c_7 and c_8. The result is d_1, d_2, d_3, and d_4. We perform the second pass by merging d_3 and d_4; d_2 is then merged with that result, and d_1 is then merged with the result of that merge, completing the deleteMin operation. Figure 23.6 shows the result of using deleteMin on the pairing heap shown in Figure 23.5.

Several alternatives have been proposed. Most are indistinguishable, but using a single left-to-right pass is a bad idea.

Other merging strategies are possible. For instance, we can place each subtree (corresponding to a child) on a queue, repeatedly dequeue two trees, and then enqueue the result of merging them. After $c - 1$ merges, only one tree remains on the queue, which is the result of the deleteMin. However, using a stack instead of a queue is a disaster because the root of the resulting tree may possibly have $c - 1$ children. If that occurs in a sequence, the deleteMin operation will have linear, rather than logarithmic, amortized cost per operation. In Exercise 23.8 you are asked to construct such a sequence.

23.2.2 implementation of the pairing heap

The prev data member links to either a left sibling or a parent.

The PairingHeap class skeleton is shown in Figure 23.7. The nested class PairNode implements the nested Position interface that is declared at lines 16 and 17.

In the pairing heap, insert returns a Position which is the newly created PairNode.

The basic node of a pairing heap, PairNode, is shown in Figure 23.8 and consists of an item and three links. Two of these links are the left child and the

2. Care must be exercised if there is an odd number of children. When that happens, we merge the last child with the result of the rightmost merge to complete the first scan.

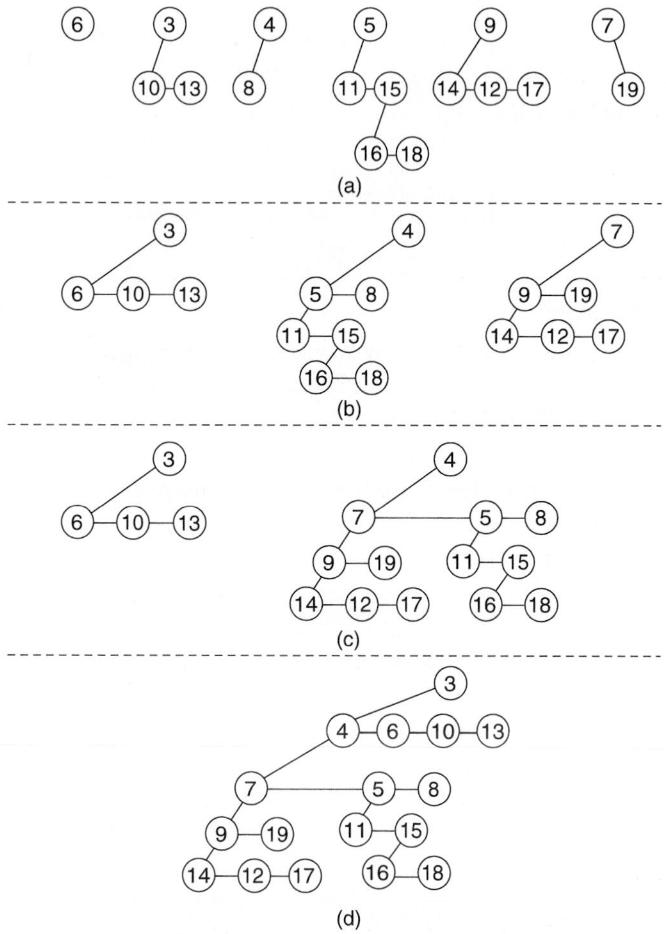

figure 23.6

Recombination of siblings after a `deleteMin`. In each merge, the larger root tree is made the left child of the smaller root tree: (a) the resulting trees; (b) after the first pass; (c) after the first merge of the second pass; (d) after the second merge of the second pass

next sibling. The third link is `prev`, which references the parent if the node is a first child or to a left sibling otherwise.

The `findMin` routine is coded in Figure 23.9. The minimum is at the root, so this routine is easily implemented. The `insert` routine, shown in Figure 23.10, creates a one-node tree and merges it with the `root` to obtain a new tree. As mentioned earlier in the section, `insert` returns a reference to the newly allocated node. Note that we must handle the special case of an insertion in an empty tree.

```
package weiss.nonstandard;

// PairingHeap class
//
// CONSTRUCTION: with no initializer
//
// ******************PUBLIC OPERATIONS*********************
// General methods for priority queues and also:
// void decreaseKey( Position p, newVal )
//                        --> Decrease value in node p
// ******************ERRORS********************************
// Exceptions thrown as warranted

public class PairingHeap<AnyType extends Comparable<? super AnyType>>
{
    public interface Position<AnyType>
      { AnyType getValue( ); }

    private static class PairNode<AnyType> implements Position<AnyType>
      { /* Figure 23.8 */ }

    private PairNode<AnyType> root;
    private int      theSize;

    public PairingHeap( )
      { root = null; theSize = 0; }

    public boolean isEmpty( )
      { return root == null; }
    public int size( )
      { return theSize; }
    public void makeEmpty( )
      { root = null; theSize = 0; }

    public Position<AnyType> insert( AnyType x )
      { /* Figure 23.10 */ }
    public AnyType findMin( )
      { /* Figure 23.9 */ }
    public AnyType deleteMin( )
      { /* Figure 23.11 */ }
    public void decreaseKey( Position<AnyType> pos, AnyType newVal )
      { /* Figure 23.12 */ }

    private PairNode<AnyType> compareAndLink( PairNode<AnyType> first,
                                              PairNode<AnyType> second )
      { /* Figure 23.14 */ }
    private PairNode [ ] doubleIfFull( PairNode [ ] array, int index )
      { /* Implementation is as usual; see online code */ }
    private PairNode<AnyType> combineSiblings( PairNode<AnyType> firstSibling )
      { /* Figure 23.15 */ }
}
```

figure 23.7

The PairingHeap class skeleton

```
/**
 * Private static class for use with PairingHeap.
 */
private static class PairNode<AnyType> implements Position<AnyType>
{
    /**
     * Construct the PairNode.
     * @param theElement the value stored in the node.
     */
    public PairNode( AnyType theElement )
    {
        element     = theElement;
        leftChild   = null;
        nextSibling = null;
        prev        = null;
    }

    /**
     * Returns the value stored at this position.
     */
    public AnyType getValue( )
    {
        return element;
    }

    public AnyType           element;
    public PairNode<AnyType> leftChild;
    public PairNode<AnyType> nextSibling;
    public PairNode<AnyType> prev;
}
```

figure 23.8
The `PairNode` nested class

```
/**
 * Find the smallest item in the priority queue.
 * @return the smallest item.
 * @throws UnderflowException if pairing heap is empty.
 */
public AnyType findMin( )
{
    if( isEmpty( ) )
        throw new UnderflowException( );
    return root.element;
}
```

figure 23.9
The `findMin` method for the `PairingHeap` class

figure 23.10

The insert routine for the PairingHeap class

```
/**
 * Insert into the priority queue, and return a Position
 * that can be used by decreaseKey.
 * Duplicates are allowed.
 * @param x the item to insert.
 * @return the node containing the newly inserted item.
 */
public Position<AnyType> insert( AnyType x )
{
    PairNode<AnyType> newNode = new PairNode<AnyType>( x );

    if( root == null )
        root = newNode;
    else
        root = compareAndLink( root, newNode );

    theSize++;
    return newNode;
}
```

The deleteMin operation is implemented as a call to combineSiblings.

Figure 23.11 implements the deleteMin routine. If the pairing heap is empty, we have an error. After saving the value found in the root (at line 11) and clearing the value at line 12, we make a call to combineSiblings at line 16 to merge the root's subtrees and set the result to the new root. If there are no subtrees, we merely set root to null at line 14.

```
1     /**
2      * Remove the smallest item from the priority queue.
3      * @return the smallest item.
4      * @throws UnderflowException if pairing heap is empty.
5      */
6     public AnyType deleteMin( )
7     {
8         if( isEmpty( ) )
9             throw new UnderflowException( );
10
11        AnyType x = findMin( );
12        root.element = null; // So decreaseKey can detect stale Position
13        if( root.leftChild == null )
14            root = null;
15        else
16            root = combineSiblings( root.leftChild );
17
18        theSize--;
19        return x;
20    }
```

figure 23.11

The deleteMin method for the PairingHeap class

The `decreaseKey` method is implemented in Figure 23.12. If the new value is larger than the original, we might destroy the heap order. We have no way of knowing that without examining all the children. Because many children may exist, doing so would be inefficient. Thus we assume that it is always an error to attempt to increase the key by using the `decreaseKey`. (In Exercise 23.9 you are asked to describe an algorithm for `increaseKey`.) After performing this test, we lower the value in the node. If the node is the root, we are done. Otherwise, we splice the node out of the list of children that it is in, using the code in lines 21 to 28. After doing that, we merely merge the resulting tree with the root.

The two remaining routines are `compareAndLink`, which combines two trees, and `combineSiblings`, which combines all the siblings, when given the first sibling. Figure 23.13 shows how two subheaps are combined. The procedure is generalized to allow the second subheap to have siblings (which is needed for the second pass in the two-pass merge). As mentioned earlier in the chapter,

```
 1     /**
 2      * Change the value of the item stored in the pairing heap.
 3      * @param pos any Position returned by insert.
 4      * @param newVal the new value, which must be smaller
 5      *    than the currently stored value.
 6      * @throws IllegalArgumentException if pos is null.
 7      * @throws IllegalValueException if new value is larger than old.
 8      */
 9     public void decreaseKey( Position<AnyType> pos, AnyType newVal )
10     {
11         if( pos == null )
12             throw new IllegalArgumentException( );
13
14         PairNode<AnyType> p = (PairNode<AnyType>) pos;
15
16         if( p.element == null || p.element.compareTo( newVal ) < 0 )
17             throw new IllegalValueException( );
18         p.element = newVal;
19         if( p != root )
20         {
21             if( p.nextSibling != null )
22                 p.nextSibling.prev = p.prev;
23             if( p.prev.leftChild == p )
24                 p.prev.leftChild = p.nextSibling;
25             else
26                 p.prev.nextSibling = p.nextSibling;
27
28             p.nextSibling = null;
29             root = compareAndLink( root, p );
30         }
31     }
```

figure 23.12

The `decreaseKey` method for the `PairingHeap` class

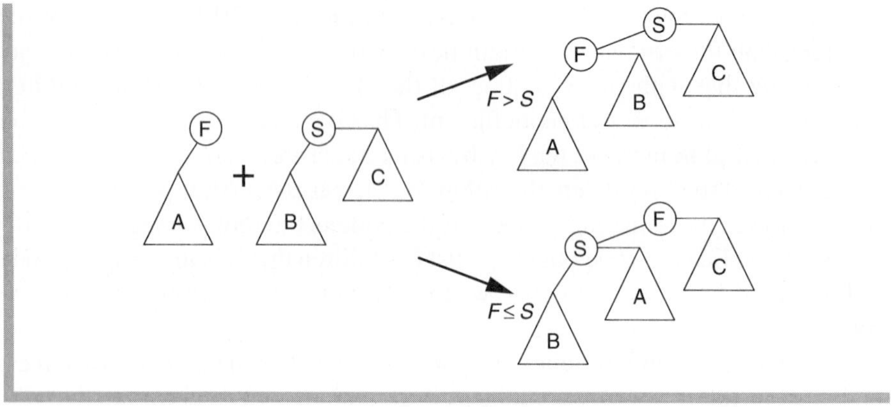

figure 23.13
The compareAndLink method merges two trees

the subheap with the larger root is made a leftmost child of the other subheap, the code for which is shown in Figure 23.14. Note that in several instances a link reference is tested against `null` before it accesses its `prev` data member. This action suggests that having a `nullNode` sentinel—as was customary in the advanced search tree implementations—might be useful. This possibility is left for you to explore as Exercise 23.12.

Finally, Figure 23.15 implements `combineSiblings`. We use the array `treeArray` to store the subtrees. We begin by separating the subtrees and storing them in `treeArray`, using the loop at lines 16 to 22. Assuming that we have more than one sibling to merge, we make a left-to-right pass at lines 28 and 29. The special case of an odd number of trees is handled at lines 31–36. We finish the merging with a right-to-left pass at lines 40 and 41. Once we have finished, the result appears in array position 0 and can be returned.

23.2.3 application: dijkstra's shortest weighted path algorithm

The `decreaseKey` operation is an improvement for Dijkstra's algorithm in instances for which there are many calls to it.

As an example of how the `decreaseKey` operation is used, we rewrite Dijkstra's algorithm (see Section 14.3). Recall that at any point we are maintaining a priority queue of `Path` objects, ordered by the `dist` data member. For each vertex in the graph, we needed only one `Path` object in the priority queue at any instant, but for convenience we had many. In this section, we rework the code so that if a vertex *w*'s distance is lowered, its position in the priority queue is found, and a `decreaseKey` operation is performed for its corresponding `Path` object.

The new code is shown in Figure 23.16, and all the changes are relatively minor. First, at line 6 we declare that `pq` is a pairing heap rather than a binary heap. Note that the `Vertex` object has an additional data member `pos` that rep-

```java
/**
 * Internal method that is the basic operation to maintain order.
 * Links first and second together to satisfy heap order.
 * @param first root of tree 1, which may not be null.
 *    first.nextSibling MUST be null on entry.
 * @param second root of tree 2, which may be null.
 * @return result of the tree merge.
 */
private PairNode<AnyType> compareAndLink( PairNode<AnyType> first,
                                          PairNode<AnyType> second )
{
    if( second == null )
        return first;

    if( second.element.compareTo( first.element ) < 0 )
    {
        // Attach first as leftmost child of second
        second.prev = first.prev;
        first.prev = second;
        first.nextSibling = second.leftChild;
        if( first.nextSibling != null )
            first.nextSibling.prev = first;
        second.leftChild = first;
        return second;
    }
    else
    {
        // Attach second as leftmost child of first
        second.prev = first;
        first.nextSibling = second.nextSibling;
        if( first.nextSibling != null )
            first.nextSibling.prev = first;
        second.nextSibling = first.leftChild;
        if( second.nextSibling != null )
            second.nextSibling.prev = second;
        first.leftChild = second;
        return first;
    }
}
```

figure 23.14

The `compareAndLink` routine

resents its position in the priority queue (and is `null` if the `Vertex` is not in the priority queue). Initially, all the positions are `null` (which is done in `clearAll`). Whenever a vertex is inserted in the pairing heap, we adjust its `pos` data member—at lines 13 and 35. The algorithm itself is simplified. Now we merely call `deleteMin` so long as the pairing heap is not empty, rather than

```
    // The tree array for combineSiblings
private PairNode [ ] treeArray =  new PairNode[ 5 ];

/**
 * Internal method that implements two-pass merging.
 * @param firstSibling the root of the conglomerate;
 *     assumed not null.
 */
private PairNode<AnyType> combineSiblings( PairNode<AnyType> firstSibling )
{
    if( firstSibling.nextSibling == null )
        return firstSibling;

        // Store the subtrees in an array
    int numSiblings = 0;
    for( ; firstSibling != null; numSiblings++ )
    {
        treeArray = doubleIfFull( treeArray, numSiblings );
        treeArray[ numSiblings ] = firstSibling;
        firstSibling.prev.nextSibling = null;  // break links
        firstSibling = firstSibling.nextSibling;
    }
    treeArray = doubleIfFull( treeArray, numSiblings );
    treeArray[ numSiblings ] = null;

        // Combine subtrees two at a time, going left to right
    int i = 0;
    for( ; i + 1 < numSiblings; i += 2 )
        treeArray[ i ] = compareAndLink( treeArray[ i ], treeArray[ i + 1 ] );

    int j = i - 2;

        // j has the result of last compareAndLink.
        // If an odd number of trees, get the last one.
    if( j == numSiblings - 3 )
        treeArray[ j ] = compareAndLink( treeArray[ j ], treeArray[ j + 2 ] );

        // Now go right to left, merging last tree with
        // next to last. The result becomes the new last.
    for( ; j >= 2; j -= 2 )
        treeArray[ j - 2 ] = compareAndLink( treeArray[ j - 2 ], treeArray[ j ] );

    return (PairNode<AnyType>) treeArray[ 0 ];
}
```

figure 23.15

The heart of the pairing heap algorithm: implementing a two-pass merge to combine all the siblings, given the first sibling

```
1  /**
2   * Single-source weighted shortest-path algorithm using pairing heaps.
3   */
4  public void dijkstra( String startName )
5  {
6      PairingHeap<Path> pq = new PairingHeap<Path>( );
7
8      Vertex start = vertexMap.get( startName );
9      if( start == null )
10         throw new NoSuchElementException( "Start vertex not found" );
11
12     clearAll( );
13     start.pos = pq.insert( new Path( start, 0 ) ); start.dist = 0;
14
15     while ( !pq.isEmpty( ) )
16     {
17         Path vrec = pq.deleteMin( );
18         Vertex v = vrec.dest;
19
20         for( Edge e : v.adj )
21         {
22             Vertex w = e.dest;
23             double cvw = e.cost;
24
25             if( cvw < 0 )
26                 throw new GraphException( "Graph has negative edges" );
27
28             if( w.dist > v.dist + cvw )
29             {
30                 w.dist = v.dist + cvw;
31                 w.prev = v;
32
33                 Path newVal = new Path( w, w.dist );
34                 if( w.pos == null )
35                     w.pos = pq.insert( newVal );
36                 else
37                     pq.decreaseKey( w.pos, newVal );
38             }
39         }
40     }
41 }
```

figure 23.16

Dijkstra's algorithm, using the pairing heap and the `decreaseKey` operation

repeatedly calling `deleteMin` until an unseen vertex emerges. Consequently, we no longer need the `scratch` data member. Compare lines 15–18 to the corresponding code presented in Figure 14.27. All that remains to be done are the updates after line 28 that indicate a change is in order. If the vertex has never been placed in the priority queue, we insert it for the first time, updating its `pos` data member. Otherwise, we merely call `decreaseKey` at line 37.

Whether the binary heap implementation of Dijkstra's algorithm is faster than the pairing heap implementation depends on several factors. One study (see the Reference section), suggests that the pairing heap is slightly better than the binary heap when both are carefully implemented. The results depend heavily on the coding details and the frequency of the `decreaseKey` operations. More study is needed to decide when the pairing heap is suitable in practice.

summary

In this chapter we described two data structures that support merging and that are efficient in the amortized sense: the skew heap and the pairing heap. Both are easy to implement because they lack a rigid structure property. The pairing heap seems to have practical utility, but its complete analysis remains an intriguing open problem.

In Chapter 24, which is the last chapter, we describe a data structure that is used to maintain disjoint sets and that also has a remarkable amortized analysis.

key concepts

pairing heap A structurally unconstrained heap-ordered M-ary tree for which all operations except deletion take constant worst-case time. Its analysis is not complete, but it appears to perform well in practice. (814)

skew heap A heap-ordered binary tree without a balancing condition that supports all operations in logarithmic amortized time. (809)

two-pass merging The order in which the pairing heap subtrees are merged is important. The simplest algorithm is two-pass merging, in which subtrees are merged in pairs in a left-to-right scan and then a right-to-left scan is performed to finish the merging. (816)

common errors

1. A recursive implementation of the skew heap cannot be used in practice because the depth of the recursion could be linear.
2. Be careful not to lose track of the `prev` links in the skew heap.

3. Tests to ensure that references are not `null` must be made throughout the pairing heap code.
4. When a merge is performed, a node should not reside in two pairing heaps.

on the internet

The pairing heap class is available, with a test program. Figure 23.16 is part of the `Graph` class shown in Chapter 14 **(Graph.java).**

PairingHeap.java Contains the implementation for the `PairingHeap` class.

exercises

IN SHORT

23.1 Show the result of a skew heap built from the insertion sequence
 a. 1, 2, 3, 4, 5, 6, 7
 b. 4, 3, 5, 2, 6, 7, 1

23.2 Show the result of a pairing heap built from the insertion sequence
 a. 1, 2, 3, 4, 5, 6, 7
 b. 4, 3, 5, 2, 6, 7, 1

23.3 For each heap in Exercises 23.1 and 23.2, show the result of two `deleteMin` operations.

IN THEORY

23.4 Show that the logarithmic amortized bound for skew heap operations is not a worst-case bound by giving a sequence of operations that lead to a `merge` that requires linear time.

23.5 Show that both the `decreaseKey` and `increaseKey` operations can be supported by skew heaps in logarithmic amortized time.

23.6 Describe a linear-time `buildHeap` algorithm for the skew heap.

23.7 Show that storing the length of the right path for each node in the tree enables you to impose a balancing condition that yields logarithmic worst-case time per operation. Such a structure is called a *leftist heap*.

23.8 Show that using a stack to implement the `combineSiblings` operation for pairing heaps is bad. Do so by constructing a sequence that has linear amortized cost per operation.

23.9 Describe how to implement `increaseKey` for pairing heaps.

IN PRACTICE

23.10 Add the public `merge` method to the `PairingHeap` class. Be sure that a node appears in only one tree.

PROGRAMMING PROBLEMS

23.11 Implement a nonrecursive version of the skew heap algorithm.

23.12 Implement the pairing heap algorithm with a `nullNode` sentinel.

23.13 Implement the queue algorithm for `combineSiblings` and compare its performance with the two-pass algorithm code shown in Figure 23.15.

23.14 If the `decreaseKey` operation is not supported, parent links are not necessary. Implement the pairing heap algorithm without parent links and compare its performance with the binary heap and/or skew heap and/or splay tree algorithm.

references

The *leftist heap* [1] was the first efficient mergeable priority queue. It is the worst-case variant of the skew heap suggested in Exercise 23.7. Skew heaps are described in [6], which also contains solutions to Exercises 23.4 and 23.5.

[3] describes the pairing heap and proves that, when two-pass merging is used, the amortized cost of all operations is logarithmic. It was long conjectured that the amortized cost of all operations except `deleteMin` is actually constant and that the amortized cost of the `deleteMin` is logarithmic, so that any sequence of D `deleteMin` and I other operations takes $O(I + D \log N)$ time. However, this conjecture was recently shown to be false [2]. A data structure that does achieve this bound, but is too complicated to be practical, is the *Fibonacci heap* [4]. The hope is that the pairing heap is a practical alternative to the theoretically interesting Fibonacci heap, even though its worst case is slightly worse. Leftist heaps and Fibonacci heaps are discussed in [7].

In [5] is a comparison of various priority queues in the setting of solving the minimum spanning tree problem (discussed in Section 24.2.2) using a method very similar to Dijkstra's algorithm.

1. C. A. Crane, "Linear Lists and Priority Queues as Balanced Binary Trees," *Technical Report STAN-CS-72-259,* Computer Science Department, Stanford University, Palo Alto, CA, 1972.
2. M. L. Fredman, "On the Efficiency of Pairing Heaps and Related Data Structures," *Journal of the ACM* **46** (1999), 473–501.

3. M. L. Fredman, R. Sedgewick, D. D. Sleator, and R. E. Tarjan, "The Pairing Heap: A New Form of Self-adjusting Heap," *Algorithmica* **1** (1986), 111–129.

4. M. L. Fredman and R. E. Tarjan, "Fibonacci Heaps and Their Uses in Improved Network Optimization Algorithms," *Journal of the ACM* **34** (1987), 596–615.

5. B. M. E. Moret and H. D. Shapiro, "An Empirical Analysis of Algorithms for Constructing a Minimum Spanning Tree," *Proceedings of the Second Workshop on Algorithms and Data Structures* (1991), 400–411.

6. D. D. Sleator and R. E. Tarjan, "Self-adjusting Heaps," *SIAM Journal on Computing* **15** (1986), 52–69.

7. M. A. Weiss, *Data Structures and Algorithm Analysis in Java*, Addison-Wesley, Reading, MA, 1999.

chapter 24

the disjoint set class

In this chapter we describe an efficient data structure for solving the equivalence problem: the disjoint set class. This data structure is simple to implement, with each routine requiring only a few lines of code. Its implementation is also extremely fast, requiring constant average time per operation. This data structure is also very interesting from a theoretical point of view because its analysis is extremely difficult; the functional form of the worst case is unlike any discussed so far in this text.

In this chapter, we show

- Three simple applications of the disjoint set class
- A way to implement the disjoint set class with minimal coding effort
- A method for increasing the speed of the disjoint set class, using two simple observations
- An analysis of the running time of a fast implementation of the disjoint set class

24.1 equivalence relations

A *relation* is defined on a set if every pair of elements either is related or is not. An *equivalence relation* is reflexive, symmetric, and transitive.

A *relation R* is defined on a set *S* if for every pair of elements (a, b), $a, b \in S$, $a\ R\ b$ is either true or false. If $a\ R\ b$ is true, we say that *a* is related to *b*.

An *equivalence relation* is a relation *R* that satisfies three properties.

1. *Reflexive:* $a\ R\ a$ is true for all $a \in S$.
2. *Symmetric:* $a\ R\ b$ if and only if $b\ R\ a$.
3. *Transitive:* $a\ R\ b$ and $b\ R\ c$ implies that $a\ R\ c$.

Electrical connectivity, where all connections are by metal wires, is an equivalence relation. The relation is clearly reflexive, as any component is connected to itself. If *a* is electrically connected to *b,* then *b* must be electrically connected to *a,* so the relation is symmetric. Finally, if *a* is connected to *b* and *b* is connected to *c,* then *a* is connected to *c*.

Likewise, connectivity through a bidirectional network forms equivalence classes of connected components. However, if the connections in the network are directed (i.e., a connection from *v* to *w* does not imply one from *w* to *v*), we do not have an equivalence relation because the symmetric property does not hold. An example is a relation in which town *a* is related to town *b* if traveling from *a* to *b* by road is possible. This relationship is an equivalence relation if the roads are two-way.

24.2 dynamic equivalence and applications

For any equivalence relation, denoted ~, the natural problem is to decide for any *a* and *b* whether $a \sim b$. If the relation is stored as a two-dimensional array of Boolean variables, equivalence can be tested in constant time. The problem is that the relation is usually implicitly, rather than explicitly, defined.

The *equivalence class* of an element *x* in set *S* is the subset of *S* that contains all the elements related to *x*. The equivalence classes form *disjoint sets.*

For example, an equivalence relation is defined over the five-element set $\{a_1, a_2, a_3, a_4, a_5\}$. This set yields 25 pairs of elements, each of which either is or is not related. However, the information that $a_1 \sim a_2$, $a_3 \sim a_4$, $a_1 \sim a_5$, and $a_4 \sim a_2$ are all related implies that all pairs are related. We want to be able to infer this condition quickly.

The *equivalence class* of an element $x \in S$ is the subset of *S* that contains all the elements related to *x*. Note that the equivalence classes form a partition of *S:* Every member of *S* appears in exactly one equivalence class. To decide whether $a \sim b$, we need only check whether *a* and *b* are in the same equivalence class. This information provides the strategy to solve the equivalence problem.

The input is initially a collection of N sets, each with one element. In this initial representation all relations (except reflexive relations) are false. Each set has a different element, so $S_i \cap S_j = \varnothing$ and such sets (in which any two sets contain no common elements) are called *disjoint sets.*

The two basic *disjoint set class* operations are `find`, which returns the name of the set (i.e., the equivalence class) containing a given element, and the `union`, which adds relations. If we want to add the pair (a, b) to the list of relations, we first determine whether a and b are already related. We do so by performing `find` operations on both a and b and finding out whether they are in the same equivalence class; if they are not, we apply `union`. This operation merges the two equivalence classes containing a and b into a new equivalence class. In terms of sets the result is a new set $S_k = S_i \cup S_j$, which we create by simultaneously destroying the originals and preserving the disjointedness of all the sets. The data structure to do this is often called the disjoint set *union/find data structure.* The *union/find algorithm* is executed by processing union/find requests within the disjoint set data structure.

The two basic *disjoint set class* operations are `union` and `find`.

The algorithm is *dynamic* because, during the course of algorithm execution, the sets can change via the `union` operation. The algorithm must also operate as an *online algorithm* so that, when a `find` is performed, an answer must be given before the next query can be viewed. Another possibility is an *offline algorithm* in which the entire sequence of `union` and `find` requests are made visible. The answer it provides for each `find` must still be consistent with all the `union`s performed before the `find`. However, the algorithm can give all its answers after it has dealt with *all* the questions. This distinction is similar to the difference between taking a written exam (which is generally offline because you only have to give the answers before time expires) and taking an oral exam (which is online because you must answer the current question before proceeding to the next question).

In an *online algorithm*, an answer must be provided for each query before the next query can be viewed.

Note that we do not perform any operations to compare the relative values of elements but merely require knowledge of their location. For this reason, we can assume that all elements have been numbered sequentially, starting from 0, and that the numbering can be determined easily by some hashing scheme.

The set elements are numbered sequentially, starting from 0.

Before describing how to implement the `union` and `find` operations, we provide three applications of the data structure.

24.2.1 application: generating mazes

An example of the use of the union/find data structure is to generate mazes, such as the one shown in Figure 24.1. The starting point is the top-left corner,

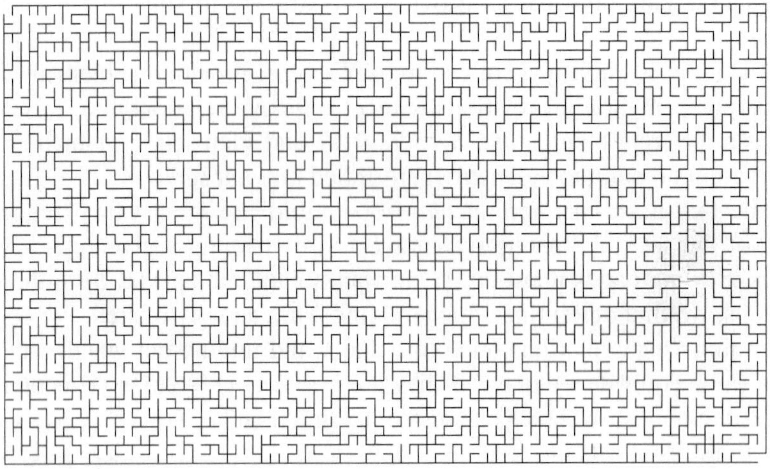

figure 24.1
A 50 × 88 maze

and the ending point is the bottom-right corner. We can view the maze as a 50×88 rectangle of cells in which the top-left cell is connected to the bottom-right cell, and cells are separated from their neighboring cells via walls.

A simple algorithm to generate the maze is to start with walls everywhere (except for the entrance and exit). We then continually choose a wall randomly and knock it down if the cells that the wall separates are not already connected to each other. If we repeat this process until the starting and ending cells are connected, we have a maze. Continuing to knock down walls until every cell is reachable from every other cell is actually better because doing so generates more false leads in the maze.

We illustrate the algorithm with a 5×5 maze, and Figure 24.2 shows the initial configuration. We use the union/find data structure to represent sets of cells that are connected to each other. Initially, walls are everywhere, and each cell is in its own equivalence class.

Figure 24.3 shows a later stage of the algorithm, after a few walls have been knocked down. Suppose, at this stage, that we randomly target the wall that connects cells 8 and 13. Because 8 and 13 are already connected (they are in the same set), we would not remove the wall because to do so would simply trivialize the maze. Suppose that we randomly target cells 18 and 13 next. By performing two `find` operations, we determine that these cells are in different sets; thus 18 and 13 are not already connected. Therefore we knock down the wall that separates them, as shown in Figure 24.4. As a

{0} {1} {2} {3} {4} {5} {6} {7} {8} {9} {10} {11} {12} {13} {14}
{15} {16} {17} {18} {19} {20} {21} {22} {23} {24}

figure 24.2

Initial state: All walls are up, and all cells are in their own sets.

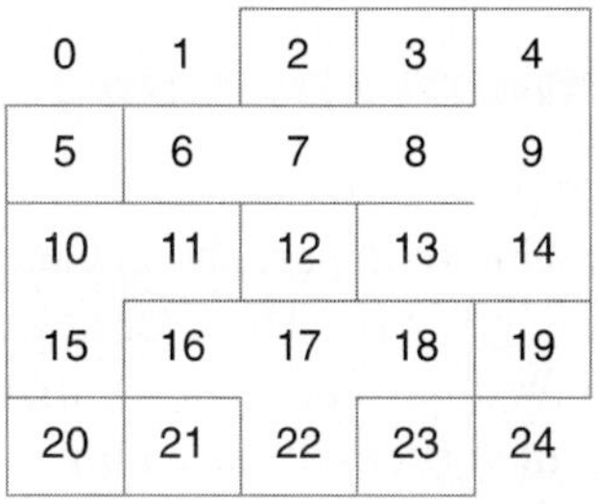

{0, 1} {2} {3} {4, 6, 7, 8, 9, 13, 14} {5} {10, 11, 15} {12}
{16, 17, 18, 22} {19} {20} {21} {23} {24}

figure 24.3

At some point in the algorithm, several walls have been knocked down and sets have been merged. At this point, if we randomly select the wall between 8 and 13, this wall is not knocked down because 8 and 13 are already connected.

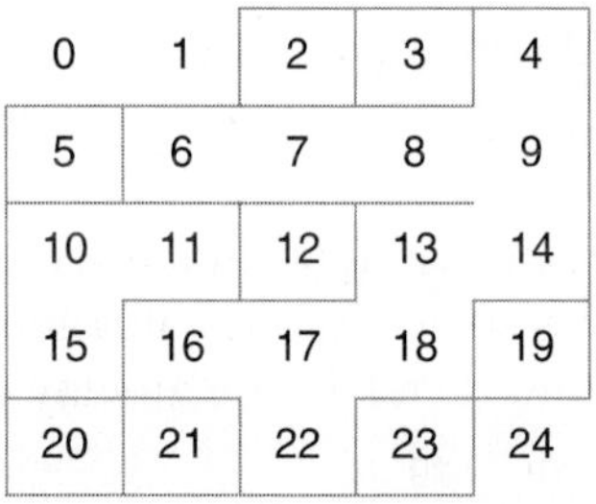

{0, 1} {2} {3} {5} {10, 11, 15} {12}
{4, 6, 7, 8, 9, 13, 14, 16, 17, 18, 22} {19} {20} {21} {23} {24}

figure 24.4

We randomly select the wall between squares 18 and 13 in Figure 24.3; this wall has been knocked down because 18 and 13 were not already connected, and their sets have been merged.

result of this operation, the sets containing cells 18 and 13 are combined by a `union` operation. The reason is that all the cells previously connected to 18 are now connected to all the cells previously connected to 13. At the end of the algorithm, as depicted in Figure 24.5, all the cells are connected, and we are done.

The running time of the algorithm is dominated by the union/find costs. The size of the union/find universe is the number of cells. The number of `find` operations is proportional to the number of cells because the number of removed walls is 1 less than the number of cells. If we look carefully, however, we can see that there are only about twice as many walls as cells in the first place. Thus, if N is the number of cells and as there are two `find`s per randomly targeted wall, we get an estimate of between (roughly) $2N$ and $4N$ `find` operations throughout the algorithm. Therefore the algorithm's running time depends on the cost of $O(N)$ `union` and $O(N)$ `find` operations.

24.2.2 application: minimum spanning trees

The *minimum spanning tree* is a connected subgraph of G that spans all vertices at minimum total cost.

A *spanning tree* of an undirected graph is a tree formed by graph edges that connect all the vertices of the graph. Unlike the graphs in Chapter 14, an edge (u, v) in a graph G is identical to an edge (v, u). The cost of a spanning tree is the sum of the costs of the edges in the tree. The *minimum spanning tree* is a connected subgraph of G that spans all vertices at minimum cost. A minimum spanning tree exists only if the subgraph of G is connected. As we show shortly, testing a graph's connectivity can be done as part of the minimum spanning tree computation.

In Figure 24.6(b), the graph is a minimum spanning tree of the graph in Figure 24.6(a) (it happens to be unique, which is unusual if the graph has many edges of equal cost). Note that the number of edges in the minimum spanning tree is $|V| - 1$. The minimum spanning tree is a *tree* because it is

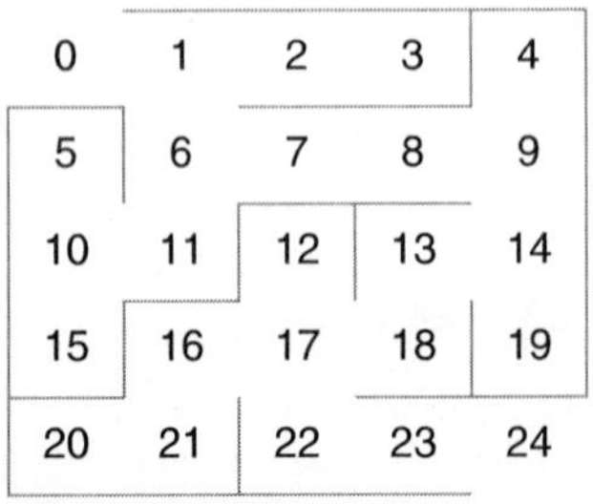

{0, 1, 2, 3, 4, 5, 6, 7, 8, 9, 10, 11, 12, 13, 14, 15, 16, 17, 18, 19, 20, 21, 22, 23, 24}

figure 24.5

Eventually, 24 walls have been knocked down, and all the elements are in the same set.

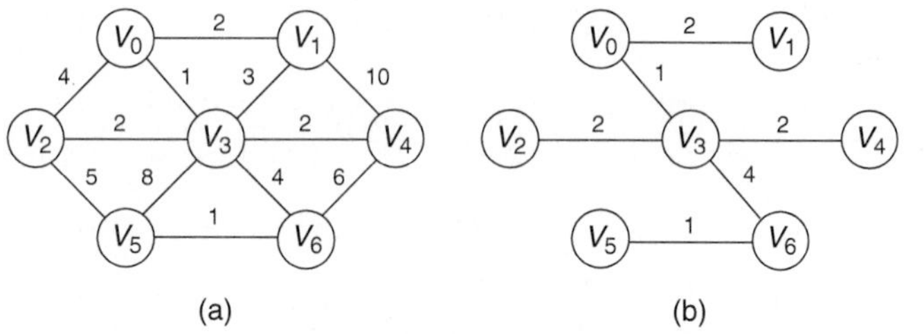

figure 24.6

(a) A graph G and (b) its minimum spanning tree

acyclic, it is *spanning* because it covers every vertex, and it is *minimum* for the obvious reason. Suppose that we need to connect several towns with roads, minimizing the total construction cost, with the provision that we can transfer to another road only at a town (in other words, no extra junctions are allowed). Then we need to solve a minimum spanning tree problem, where each vertex is a town, and each edge is the cost of building a road between the two cities it connects.

A related problem is the *minimum Steiner tree problem,* which is like the minimum spanning tree problem, except that junctions can be created as part of the solution. The minimum Steiner tree problem is much more difficult to solve. However, it can be shown that if the cost of a connection is proportional to the Euclidean distance, the minimum spanning tree is at most 15 percent more expensive than the minimum Steiner tree. Thus a minimum spanning tree, which is easy to compute, provides a good approximation for the minimum Steiner tree, which is hard to compute.

Kruskal's algorithm is used to select edges in order of increasing cost and adds an edge to the tree if it does not create a cycle.

A simple algorithm, commonly called *Kruskal's algorithm,* is used to select edges continually in order of smallest weight and to add an edge to the tree if it does not cause a cycle. Formally, Kruskal's algorithm maintains a forest—a collection of trees. Initially, there are $|V|$ single-node trees. Adding an edge merges two trees into one. When the algorithm terminates, there is only one tree, which is the minimum spanning tree.[1] By counting the number of accepted edges, we can determine when the algorithm should terminate.

Figure 24.7 shows the action of Kruskal's algorithm on the graph shown in Figure 24.6. The first five edges are all accepted because they do not create cycles. The next two edges, (v_1, v_3) (of cost 3) and then (v_0, v_2) (of cost 4), are rejected because each would create a cycle in the tree. The next edge considered is accepted, and because it is the sixth edge in a seven-vertex graph, we can terminate the algorithm.

1. If the graph is not connected, the algorithm will terminate with more than one tree. Each tree then represents a minimum spanning tree for each connected component of the graph.

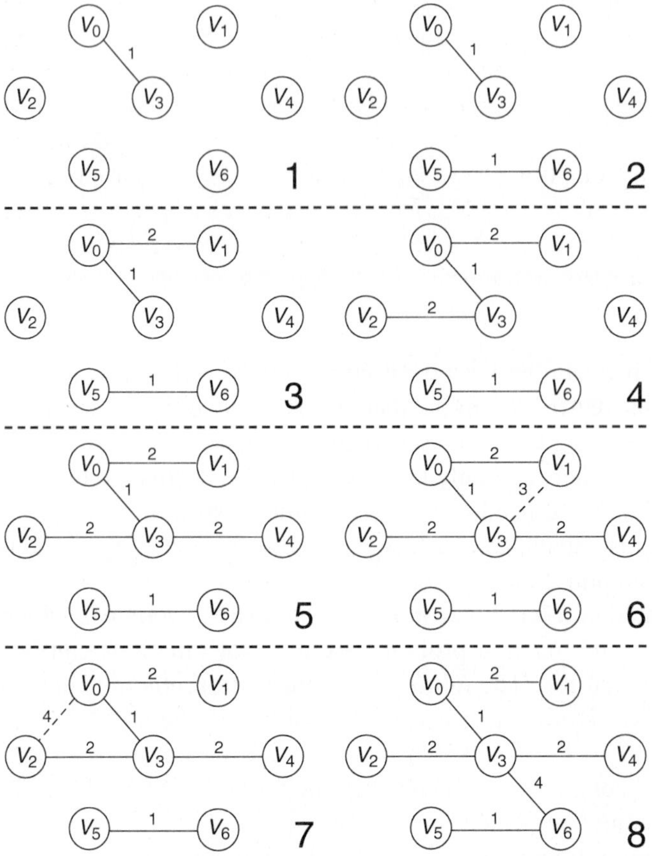

figure 24.7

Kruskal's algorithm after each edge has been considered. The stages proceed left-to-right, top-to-bottom, as numbered.

The edges can be sorted, or a priority queue can be used.

Ordering the edges for testing is simple enough to do. We can sort them at a cost of $|E| \log |E|$ and then step through the ordered array of edges. Alternatively, we can construct a priority queue of $|E|$ edges and repeatedly obtain edges by calling `deleteMin`. Although the worst-case bound is unchanged, using a priority queue is sometimes better because Kruskal's algorithm tends to test only a small fraction of the edges on random graphs. Of course, in the worst case, all the edges may have to be tried. For instance, if there were an extra vertex v_8 and edge (v_5, v_8) of cost 100, all the edges would have to be examined. In this case, a quicksort at the start would be faster. In effect, the choice between a priority queue and an initial sort is a gamble on how many edges are likely to have to be examined.

More interesting is the issue of how we decide whether an edge (u, v) should be accepted or rejected. Clearly, adding the edge (u, v) causes a cycle if (and only if) u and v are already connected in the current spanning *forest,* which is a collection of trees. Thus we merely maintain each connected component in the spanning forest as a disjoint set. Initially, each vertex is in its own disjoint set. If *u* and *v* are in the same disjoint set, as determined by two `find` operations, the edge is rejected because *u* and *v* are already connected. Otherwise, the edge is accepted and a `union` operation is performed on the two disjoint sets containing *u* and *v*, in effect, combining the connected components. This result is what we want because once edge (*u*, *v*) has been added to the spanning forest, if *w* was connected to *u* and *x* was connected to *v*, *x* and *w* must be connected and thus belong in the same set.

The test for cycles is done by using a union/find data structure.

24.2.3 application: the nearest common ancestor problem

Another illustration of the union/find data structure is the offline *nearest common ancestor* (NCA) *problem.*

offline nearest common ancestor problem
Given a tree and a list of pairs of nodes in the tree, find the nearest common ancestor for each pair of nodes.

As an example, Figure 24.8 shows a tree with a pair list containing five requests. For the pair of nodes *u* and *z*, node *C* is the nearest ancestor of both. (*A* and *B* are also ancestors, but they are not the closest.) The problem is offline because we can see the entire request sequence prior to providing the first answer. Solution of this problem is important in graph theory applications and computational biology (where the tree represents evolution) applications.

Solution of the NCA is important in graph algorithm and computational biology applications.

The algorithm works by performing a postorder tree traversal. When we are about to return from processing a node, we examine the pair list to determine whether any ancestor calculations are to be performed. If *u* is the current

A postorder traversal can be used to solve the problem.

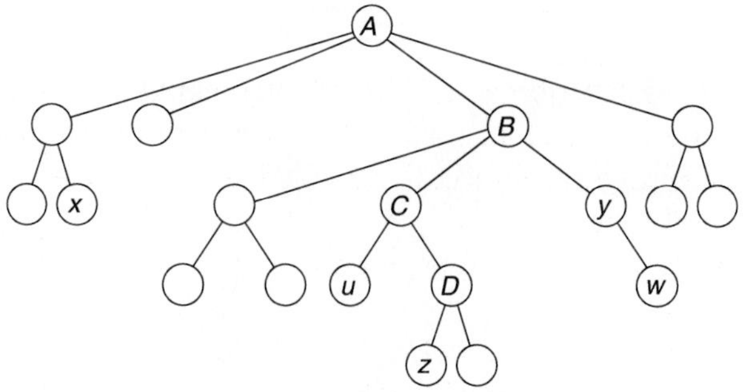

figure 24.8
The nearest common ancestor for each request in the pair sequence (*x*, *y*), (*u*, *z*), (*w*, *x*), (*z*, *w*), and (*w*, *y*) is *A*, *C*, *A*, *B*, and *y*, respectively.

node, (u, v) is in the pair list and we have already finished the recursive call to v, we have enough information to determine NCA(u, v).

The *anchor* of a visited (but not necessarily marked) node v is the node on the current access path that is closest to v.

Figure 24.9 helps in understanding how this algorithm works. Here, we are about to finish the recursive call to D. All shaded nodes have been visited by a recursive call, and except for the nodes on the path to D, all the recursive calls have already finished. We mark a node after its recursive call has been completed. If v is marked, then NCA(D, v) is some node on the path to D. The *anchor* of a visited (but not necessarily marked) node v is the node on the current access path that is closest to v. In Figure 24.9, p's anchor is A, q's anchor is B, and r is unanchored because it has yet to be visited; we can argue that r's anchor is r at the point that r is first visited. Each node on the current access path is an anchor (of at least itself). Furthermore, the visited nodes form equivalence classes: Two nodes are related if they have the same anchor, and we can regard each unvisited node as being in its own class. Now suppose once again that (D, v) is in the pair list. Then we have three cases.

1. v is unmarked, so we have no information to compute NCA(D, v). However, when v is marked, we are able to determine NCA(v, D).
2. v is marked but not in D's subtree, so NCA(D, v) is v's anchor.
3. v is in D's subtree, so NCA$(D, v) = D$. Note that this is not a special case because v's anchor is D.

The union/find algorithm is used to maintain the sets of nodes with common anchors.

All that remains to be done is to ensure that, at any instant, we can determine the anchor of any visited node. We can easily do so with the union/find algorithm. After a recursive call returns, we call `union`. For instance, after the recursive call to D in Figure 24.9 returns, all nodes in D have their anchor

figure 24.9

The sets immediately prior to the return from the recursive call to D; D is marked as visited and NCA(D, v) is v's anchor to the current path.

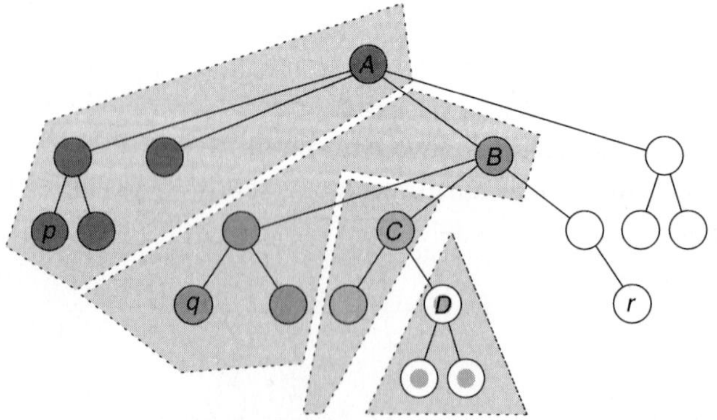

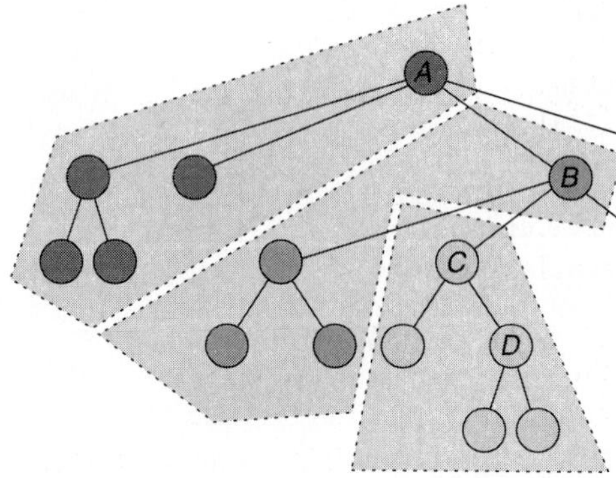

figure 24.10

After the recursive call from D returns, we merge the set anchored by D into the set anchored by C and then compute all NCA(C, v) for nodes v marked prior to completing C's recursive call.

changed from D to C. The new situation is shown in Figure 24.10. Thus we need to merge the two equivalence classes into one. At any point, we can obtain the anchor for a vertex v by a call to a disjoint set `find`. Because `find` returns a set number, we use an array `anchor` to store the anchor node corresponding to a particular set.

The pseudocode is compact.

A pseudocode implementation of the NCA algorithm is shown in Figure 24.11. As mentioned earlier in the chapter, the `find` operation generally is based on the assumption that elements of the set are 0, 1, ..., $N-1$, so we store a preorder number in each tree node in a preprocessing step that computes the size of the tree. An object-oriented approach might attempt to incorporate a mapping into the `find`, but we do not do so. We also assume that we have an array of lists in which to store the NCA requests; that is, list i stores the requests for tree node i. With those details taken care of, the code is remarkably short.

When a node u is first visited, it becomes the anchor of itself, as in line 18 of Figure 24.11. It then recursively processes its children v by making the call at line 23. After each recursive call returns, the subtree is combined into u's current equivalence class and we ensure that the anchor is updated at lines 24 and 25. When all the children have been processed recursively, we can mark u as processed at line 29 and finish by checking all NCA requests involving u at lines 30 to 33.[2]

2. Strictly speaking, u should be marked at the last statement, but marking it earlier handles the annoying request NCA(u, u).

```
// Nearest Common Ancestors algorithm
//
// Preconditions (and global objects):
//  1. union/find structure is initialized
//  2. All nodes are initially unmarked
//  3. Preorder numbers are already assigned in num field
//  4. Each node can store its marked status
//  5. List of pairs is globally available

DisjSets s = new DisjSets( treeSize );  // union/find
Node [ ] anchor = new Node[ treeSize ]; // Anchor node for each set

// main makes the call NCA( root )
// after required initializations

void NCA( Node u )
{
    anchor[ s.find( u.num ) ] = u;

    // Do postorder calls
    for( each child v of u )
    {
        NCA( v );
        s.union( s.find( u.num ), s.find( v.num ) );
        anchor[ s.find( u.num ) ] = u;
    }

    // Do nca calculation for pairs involving u
    u.marked = true;
    for( each v such that NCA( u, v ) is required )
        if( v.marked )
            System.out.println( "NCA( " + u + ", " + v +
                    " ) is " + anchor[ s.find( v.num ) ] );
}
```

figure 24.11

Pseudocode for the nearest common ancestors problem

24.3 the quick-find algorithm

In this section and Section 24.4 we lay the groundwork for the efficient implementation of the union/find data structure. There are two basic strategies for solving the union/find problem. The first approach, the *quick-find algorithm,* ensures that the `find` instruction can be executed in constant worst-case time. The other approach, the *quick-union algorithm,* ensures that the `union` operation can be executed in constant worst-case time. It has been shown that both cannot be done simultaneously in constant worst-case (or even amortized) time.

For the `find` operation to be fast, in an array we could maintain the name of the equivalence class for each element. Then `find` is a simple constant-time lookup. Suppose that we want to perform `union`(a, b). Suppose, too, that a is in equivalence class i and that b is in equivalence class j. Then we can scan down the array, changing all i's to j's. Unfortunately, this scan takes linear time. Thus a sequence of $N - 1$ `union` operations (the maximum because then everything is in one set) would take quadratic time. In the typical case in which the number of `find`s is subquadratic, this time is clearly unacceptable.

One possibility is to keep all the elements that are in the same equivalence class in a linked list. This approach saves time when we are updating because we do not have to search the entire array. By itself that does not reduce the asymptotic running time, as performing $\Theta(N^2)$ equivalence class updates over the course of the algorithm is still possible.

If we also keep track of the size of the equivalence classes—and when performing a `union` change the name of the smaller class to the larger—the total time spent for N `union`s is $O(N \log N)$. The reason is that each element can have its equivalence class changed at most $\log N$ times because every time its class is changed, its new equivalence class is at least twice as large as its old class (so the repeated doubling principle applies).

The argument that an equivalence class can change at most $\log N$ times per item is also used in the quick-union algorithm. Quick-find is a simple algorithm, but quick-union is better.

This strategy provides that any sequence of at most M `find` and $N - 1$ `union` operations take at most $O(M + N \log N)$ time. If M is linear (or slightly nonlinear), this solution is still expensive. It also is a bit messy because we must maintain linked lists. In Section 24.4 we examine a solution to the union/find problem that makes `union` easy but `find` hard—the quick-union algorithm. Even so, the running time for any sequence of at most M `find` and $N - 1$ `union` operations is only negligibly more than $O(M + N)$ time and, moreover, only a single array of integers is used.

24.4 the quick-union algorithm

Recall that the union/find problem does not require a `find` operation to return any specific name; it requires just that `find`s on two elements return the same answer if and only if they are in the same set. One possibility might be to use a tree to represent a set, as each element in a tree has the same root and the root can be used to name the set.

A tree is represented by an array of integers representing parent nodes. The set name of any node in a tree is the root of a tree.

The `union` operation is constant time.

The cost of a `find` depends on the depth of the accessed node and could be linear.

Each set is represented by a tree (recall that a collection of trees is called a *forest*). The name of a set is given by the node at the root. Our trees are not necessarily binary trees, but their representation is easy because the only information we need is the parent. Thus we need only an array of integers: Each entry `p[i]` in the array represents the parent of element `i`, and we can use –1 as a parent to indicate a root. Figure 24.12 shows a forest and the array that represents it.

To perform a `union` of two sets, we merge the two trees by making the root of one tree a child of the root of the other. This operation clearly takes constant time. Figures 24.13–24.15 represent the forest after each of `union(4, 5)`, `union(6, 7)`, and `union(4, 6)`, where we have adopted the convention that the new root after `union`(x, y) is x.

A `find` operation on element x is performed by returning the root of the tree containing x. The time for performing this operation is proportional to the number of nodes on the path from x to the root. The `union` strategy outlined previously enables us to create a tree whose every node is on the path to x, resulting in a worst-case running time of $\Theta(N)$ per `find`. Typically (as shown in the preceding

figure 24.12

A forest and its eight elements, initially in different sets

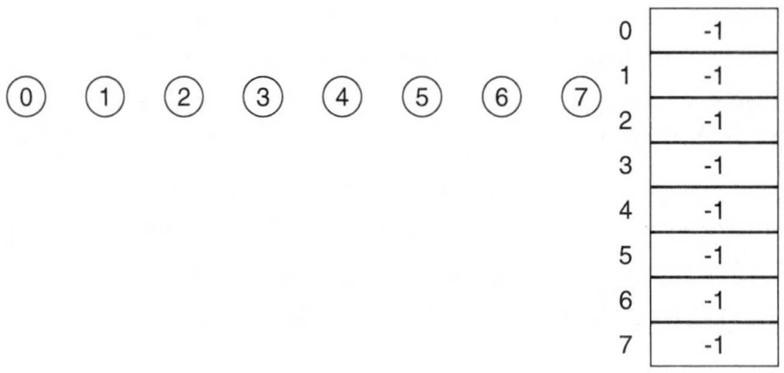

figure 24.13

The forest after the `union` of trees with roots 4 and 5

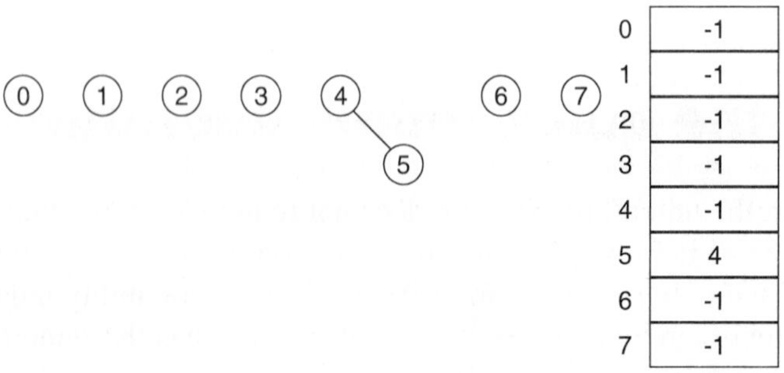

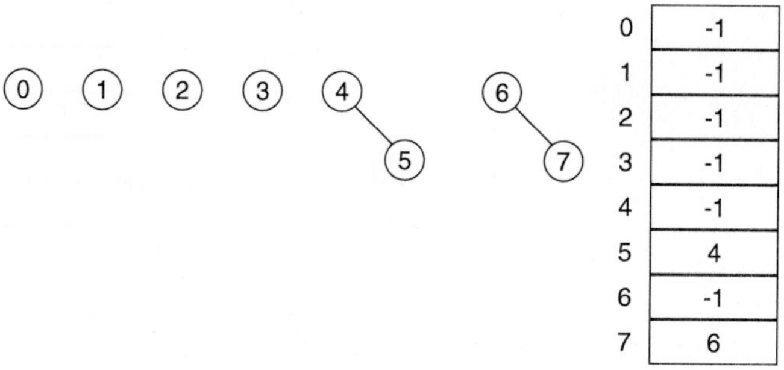

figure 24.14

The forest after the `union` of trees with roots 6 and 7

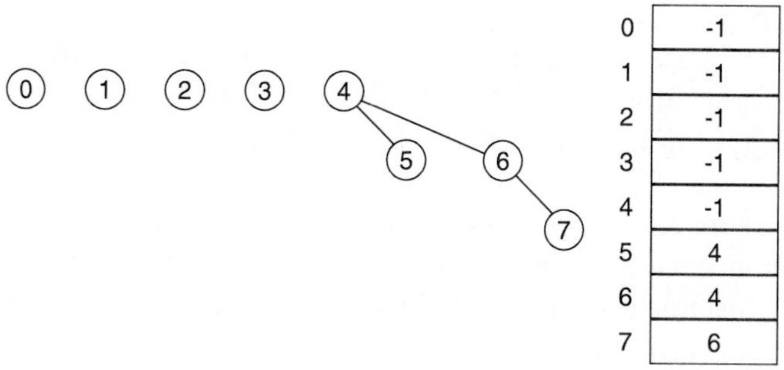

figure 24.15

The forest after the `union` of trees with roots 4 and 6

applications), the running time is computed for a sequence of M intermixed instructions. In the worst case, M consecutive operations could take $\Theta(MN)$ time.

Quadratic running time for a sequence of operations is generally unacceptable. Fortunately, there are several ways to easily ensure that this running time does not occur.

24.4.1 smart union algorithms

We performed the previous `unions` rather arbitrarily by making the second tree a subtree of the first. A simple improvement is always to make the smaller tree a subtree of the larger, breaking ties by any method, an approach called *union-by-size.* The preceding three `union` operations were all ties, so we can consider that they were performed by size. If the next operation is `union`(3, 4), the forest shown in Figure 24.16 forms. Had the size heuristic not been used, a deeper forest would have been formed (three nodes rather than one would have been one level deeper).

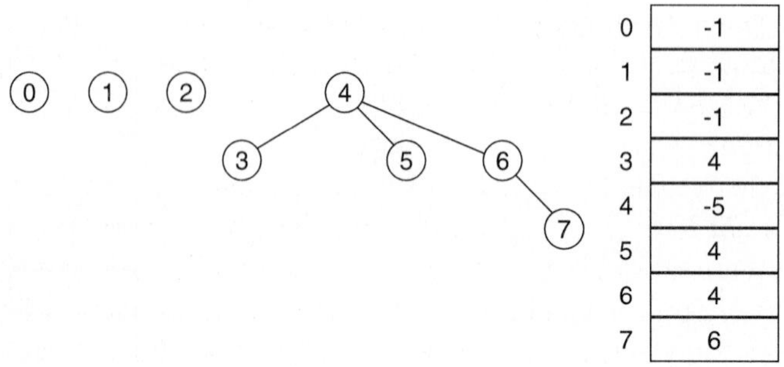

figure 24.16

The forest formed by union-by-size, with the sizes encoded as negative numbers

Union-by-size guarantees logarithmic finds.

If the `union` operation is done by size, the depth of any node is never more than log N. A node is initially at depth 0, and when its depth increases as a result of a `union`, it is placed in a tree that is at least twice as large as before. Thus its depth can be increased at most log N times. (We used this argument in the quick-find algorithm in Section 24.3.) This outcome implies that the running time for a `find` operation is $O(\log N)$ and that a sequence of M operations takes at most $O(M \log N)$ time. The tree shown in Figure 24.17 illustrates the worst tree possible after 15 `union` operations and is obtained if all the `unions` are between trees of equal size. (The worst-case tree is called a *binomial tree*. Binomial trees have other applications in advanced data structures.)

Instead of −1 being stored for roots, the negative of the size is stored.

To implement this strategy, we need to keep track of the size of each tree. Since we are just using an array, we can have the array entry of the root contain the *negative* of the size of the tree, as shown in Figure 24.16. Thus the initial representation of the tree with all −1s is reasonable. When a `union` operation is performed, we check the sizes; the new size is the sum of the old. Thus union-by-size is not at all difficult to implement and requires no extra space. It is also fast on average because, when random `union` operations are

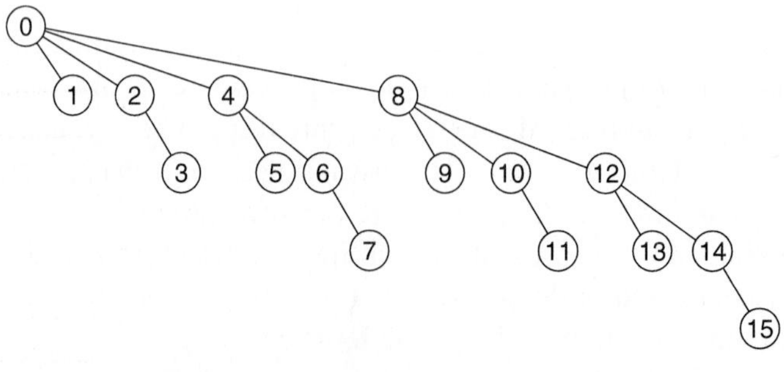

figure 24.17

Worst-case tree for $N = 16$

performed, generally very small (usually one-element) sets are merged with large sets throughout the algorithm. Mathematical analysis of this process is quite complex; the references at the end of the chapter provide some pointers to the literature.

Union-by-height also guarantees logarithmic `find` operations.

An alternative implementation that also guarantees logarithmic depth is *union-by-height* in which we keep track of the height of the trees instead of the size and perform `union` operations by making a shallower tree a subtree of the deeper tree. This algorithm is easy to write and use because the height of a tree increases only when two equally deep trees are joined (and then the height goes up by 1). Thus union-by-height is a trivial modification of union-by-size. As heights start at 0, we store the negative of the number of nodes rather than the height on the deepest path, as shown in Figure 24.18.

24.4.2 **path compression**

The union/find algorithm, as described so far, is quite acceptable for most cases. It is very simple and linear on average for a sequence of M instructions. However, the worst case is still unappealing. The reason is that a sequence of `union` operations occurring in some particular application (such as the NCA problem) is not obviously random (in fact, for certain trees, it is far from random). Hence we have to seek a better bound for the worst case of a sequence of M operations. Seemingly, no more improvements to the union algorithm are possible because the worst case is achievable when identical trees are merged. The only way to speed up the algorithm then, without reworking the data structure entirely, is to do something clever with the `find` operation.

Path compression makes every accessed node a child of the root until another `union` occurs.

That something clever is *path compression.* Clearly, after we perform a `find` on x, changing x's parent to the root would make sense. In that way, a second `find` on x or any item in x's subtree becomes easier. There is no need to stop there, however. We might as well change the parents for all the nodes on the access path. In path compression *every* node on the path from x to the root

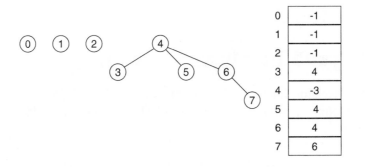

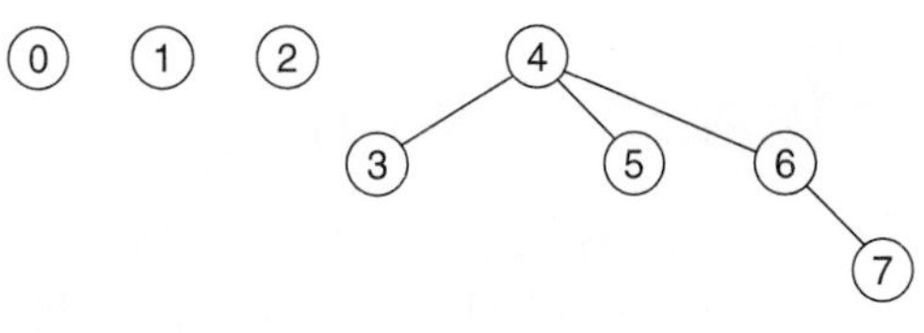

0	-1
1	-1
2	-1
3	4
4	-3
5	4
6	4
7	6

figure 24.18

A forest formed by union-by-height, with the height encoded as a negative number

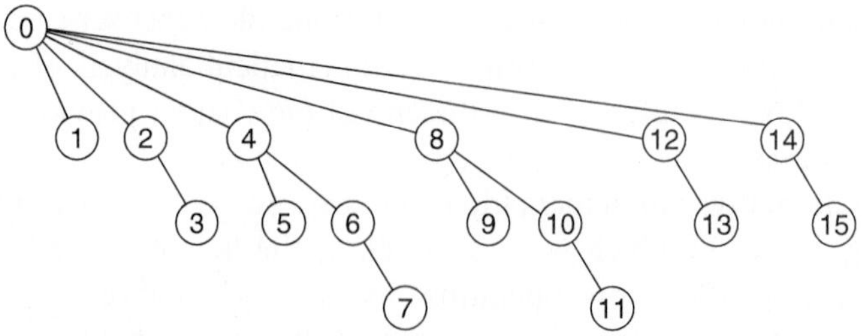

figure 24.19

Path compression resulting from a `find(14)` on the tree shown in Figure 24.17

has its parent changed to the root. Figure 24.19 shows the effect of path compression after `find(14)` on the generic worst tree shown in Figure 24.17. With an extra two parent changes, nodes 12 and 13 are now one position closer to the root and nodes 14 and 15 are now two positions closer. The fast future accesses on the nodes pay (we hope) for the extra work to do the path compression. Note that subsequent `union`s push the nodes deeper.

Path compression guarantees logarithmic amortized cost for the `find` operation.

When `union`s are done arbitrarily, path compression is a good idea because of the abundance of deep nodes; they are brought near the root by path compression. It has been proved that when path compression is done in this case, a sequence of M operations requires at most $O(M \log N)$ time, so path compression by itself guarantees logarithmic amortized cost for the `find` operation.

Path compression and a smart union rule guarantee essentially constant amortized cost per operation (i.e., a long sequence can be executed in almost linear time).

Path compression is perfectly compatible with union-by-size. Thus both routines can be implemented at the same time. However, path compression is not entirely compatible with union-by-height because path compression can change the heights of the trees. We do not know how to recompute them efficiently, so we do not attempt to do so. Then the heights stored for each tree become estimated heights, called *ranks,* which is not a problem. The resulting algorithm, *union-by-rank,* is thus obtained from union-by-height when compression is performed. As we show in Section 24.6, the combination of a smart union rule and path compression gives an almost linear guarantee on the running time for a sequence of M operations.

24.5 java implementation

Disjoint sets are relatively simple to implement.

The class skeleton for a disjoint sets class is given in Figure 24.20, and the implementation is completed in Figure 24.21. The entire algorithm is amazingly short.

```java
package weiss.nonstandard;

// DisjointSets class
//
// CONSTRUCTION: with int representing initial number of sets
//
// ******************PUBLIC OPERATIONS*********************
// void union( root1, root2 ) --> Merge two sets
// int find( x )              --> Return set containing x
// ******************ERRORS********************************
// Error checking or parameters is performed

public class DisjointSets
{
    public DisjointSets( int numElements )
      { /* Figure 24.21 */ }

    public void union( int root1, int root2 )
      { /* Figure 24.21 */ }

    public int find( int x )
      { /* Figure 24.21 */ }

    private int [ ] s;


    private void assertIsRoot( int root )
    {
        assertIsItem( root );
        if( s[ root ] >= 0 )
            throw new IllegalArgumentException( );
    }

    private void assertIsItem( int x )
    {
        if( x < 0 || x >= s.length )
            throw new IllegalArgumentException( );
    }
}
```

figure 24.20

The disjoint sets class skeleton

In our routine, `union` is performed on the roots of the trees. Sometimes the operation is implemented by passing any two elements and having `union` perform the `find` operation to determine the roots.

The interesting procedure is `find`. After the `find` has been performed recursively, `array[x]` is set to the root and then is returned. Because this procedure is recursive, all nodes on the path have their entries set to the root.

figure 24.21

Implementation of a disjoint sets class

```java
    /**
     * Construct the disjoint sets object.
     * @param numElements the initial number of disjoint sets.
     */
    public DisjointSets( int numElements )
    {
        s = new int[ numElements ];
        for( int i = 0; i < s.length; i++ )
            s[ i ] = -1;
    }

    /**
     * Union two disjoint sets using the height heuristic.
     * root1 and root2 are distinct and represent set names.
     * @param root1 the root of set 1.
     * @param root2 the root of set 2.
     * @throws IllegalArgumentException if root1 or root2
     * are not distinct roots.
     */
    public void union( int root1, int root2 )
    {
        assertIsRoot( root1 );
        assertIsRoot( root2 );
        if( root1 == root2 )
            throw new IllegalArgumentException( );

        if( s[ root2 ] < s[ root1 ] )  // root2 is deeper
            s[ root1 ] = root2;        // Make root2 new root
        else
        {
            if( s[ root1 ] == s[ root2 ] )
                s[ root1 ]--;          // Update height if same
            s[ root2 ] = root1;        // Make root1 new root
        }
    }

    /**
     * Perform a find with path compression.
     * @param x the element being searched for.
     * @return the set containing x.
     * @throws IllegalArgumentException if x is not valid.
     */
    public int find( int x )
    {
        assertIsItem( x );
        if( s[ x ] < 0 )
            return x;
        else
            return s[ x ] = find( s[ x ] );
    }
```

24.6 worst case for union-by-rank and path compression

When both heuristics are used, the algorithm is almost linear in the worst case. Specifically, the time required to process a sequence of at most $N - 1$ `union` operations and M `find` operations in the worst case is $\Theta(M\alpha(M, N))$ (provided that $M \geq N$), where $\alpha(M, N)$ is a functional inverse of *Ackermann's function,* which grows very quickly and is defined as follows:[3]

$$
\begin{aligned}
A(1,j) &= 2^j & j \geq 1 \\
A(i,1) &= A(i-1,2) & i \geq 2 \\
A(i,j) &= A(i-1, A(i,j-1)) & i,j \geq 2
\end{aligned}
$$

From the preceding, we define

$$\alpha(M, N) = \min\{i \geq 1 \mid (A(i, \lfloor M/N \rfloor) > \log N)\}$$

Ackermann's function grows very quickly, and its inverse is essentially at most 4.

You might want to compute some values, but for all practical purposes, $\alpha(M, N) \leq 4$, which is all that really matters here. For instance, for any $j > 1$, we have

$$
\begin{aligned}
A(2,j) &= A(1, A(2,j-1)) \\
&= 2^{A(2,j-1)} \\
&= 2^{2^{2^{2\cdots}}}
\end{aligned}
$$

where the number of 2s in the exponent is j. The function $F(N) = A(2, N)$ is commonly called a *single-variable Ackermann's function*. The single-variable inverse of Ackermann's function, sometimes written as $\log^*N$, is the number of times the logarithm of N needs to be applied until $N \leq 1$. Thus $\log^*65536 = 4$, because $\log\log\log\log 65536 = 1$, and $\log^*2^{65536} = 5$. However, keep in mind that 2^{65536} has more than 20,000 digits. The function $\alpha(M, N)$ grows even slower than $\log^*N$. For instance, $A(3, 1) = A(2, 2) = 2^{2^2} = 16$. Thus for $N < 2^{16}$, $\alpha(M, N) \leq 3$. Further, because $A(4, 1) = A(3, 2) = A(2, A(3, 1)) = A(2, 16)$, which is 2 raised to a power of 16 stacked 2s, in practice, $\alpha(M, N) \leq 4$. However, $\alpha(M, N)$ is not a constant when M is slightly more than N, so the running time is not linear.[4]

3. Ackermann's function is frequently defined with $A(1, j) = j + 1$ for $j \geq 1$. The form we use in this text grows faster; thus the inverse grows more slowly.
4. Note, however, that if $M = N\log^*N$, then $\alpha(M, N)$ is at most 2. Thus, so long as M is slightly more than linear, the running time is linear in M.

In the remainder of this section, we prove a slightly weaker result. We show that any sequence of $M = \Omega(N)$ `union` and `find` operations takes a total of $O(M \log^* N)$ time. The same bound holds if we replace union-by-rank with union-by-size. This analysis is probably the most complex in this text and is one of the first truly complex analyses ever performed for an algorithm that is essentially trivial to implement. By extending this technique, we can show the stronger bound claimed previously.

24.6.1 analysis of the union/find algorithm

In this section, we establish a fairly tight bound on the running time of a sequence of $M = \Omega(N)$ `union` and `find` operations. The `union` and `find` operations may occur in any order, but `union` is done by rank and `find` is done with path compression.

We begin with some theorems concerning the number of nodes of rank r. Intuitively, because of the union-by-rank rule, there are many more nodes of small rank than of large rank. In particular, there can be at most one node of rank $\log N$. What we want to do is to produce as precise a bound as possible on the number of nodes of any particular rank r. Because ranks change only when `union` operations are performed (and then only when the two trees have the same rank), we can prove this bound by ignoring path compression. We do so in Theorem 24.1.

Theorem 24.1

In the absence of path compression, when a sequence of `union` instructions is being executed, a node of rank r must have 2^r descendants (including itself).

Proof

The proof is by induction. The basis $r = 0$ is clearly true. Let T be the tree of rank r with the fewest number of descendants and x be T's root. Suppose that the last `union` with which x was involved was between T_1 and T_2. Suppose that T_1's root was x. If T_1 had rank r, then T_1 would be a tree of rank r with fewer descendants than T. This condition contradicts the assumption that T is the tree with the smallest number of descendants. Hence the rank of T_1 is at most $r - 1$. The rank of T_2 is at most the rank of T_1 because of union-by-rank. As T has rank r and the rank could only increase because of T_2, it follows that the rank of T_2 is $r - 1$. Then the rank of T_1 is also $r - 1$. By the induction hypothesis, each tree has at least 2^{r-1} descendants, giving a total of 2^r and establishing the theorem.

Theorem 24.1 says that if no path compression is performed, any node of rank r must have at least 2^r descendants. Path compression can change this condition, of course, because it can remove descendants from a node. However, when `union` operations are performed—even with path compression—we are using ranks, or estimated heights. These ranks behave as if there is no path compression. Thus when the number of nodes of rank r are being bounded, path compression can be ignored, as in Theorem 24.2.

Theorem 24.2

The number of nodes of rank r is at most $N/2^r$.

Proof

Without path compression, each node of rank r is the root of a subtree of at least 2^r nodes. No other node in the subtree can have rank r. Thus all subtrees of nodes of rank r are disjoint. Therefore there are at most $N/2^r$ disjoint subtrees and hence $N/2^r$ nodes of rank r.

Theorem 24.3 seems somewhat obvious, but it is crucial to the analysis.

Theorem 24.3

At any point in the union/find algorithm, the ranks of the nodes on a path from a leaf to a root increase monotonically.

Proof

The theorem is obvious if there is no path compression. If after path compression, some node v is a descendant of w, then clearly v must have been a descendant of w when only `union` operations were considered. Hence the rank of v is strictly less than the rank of w.

There are not too many nodes of large rank, and the ranks increase on any path up toward a root.

The following is a summary of the preliminary results. Theorem 24.2 describes the number of nodes that can be assigned rank r. Because ranks are assigned only by `union` operations, which do not rely on path compression, Theorem 24.2 is valid at any stage of the union/find algorithm—even in the midst of path compression. Theorem 24.2 is tight in the sense that there can be $N/2^r$ nodes for any rank r. It also is slightly loose because the bound cannot hold for all ranks r simultaneously. While Theorem 24.2 describes the number of nodes in a rank r, Theorem 24.3 indicates the distribution of nodes in a rank r. As expected, the rank of nodes strictly increases along the path from a leaf to the root.

We are now ready to prove the main theorem, and our basic plan is as follows. A `find` operation on any node v costs time proportional to the number of nodes on the path from v to the root. We charge 1 unit of cost for every node on the path from v to the root during each `find`. To help count the charges, we

Pennies are used like a potential function. The total number of pennies is the total time.

deposit an imaginary penny in each node on the path. This is strictly an accounting gimmick that is not part of the program. It is somewhat equivalent to the use of a potential function in the amortized analysis for splay trees and skew heaps. When the algorithm has finished, we collect all the coins that have been deposited to determine the total time.

We have both U.S. and Canadian pennies. Canadian pennies account for the first few times a node is compressed; U.S. pennies account for later compressions or noncompressions.

As a further accounting gimmick, we deposit both U.S. and Canadian pennies. We show that, during execution of the algorithm, we can deposit only a certain number of U.S. pennies during each `find` operation (regardless of how many nodes there are). We will also show that we can deposit only a certain number of Canadian pennies to each node (regardless of how many `find`s there are). Adding these two totals gives a bound on the total number of pennies that can be deposited.

We now sketch our accounting scheme in more detail. We begin by dividing the nodes by their ranks. We then divide the ranks into rank groups. On each `find`, we deposit some U.S. pennies in a general kitty and some Canadian pennies in specific nodes. To compute the total number of Canadian pennies deposited, we compute the deposits per node. By summing all the deposits for each node in rank r, we get the total deposits per rank r. Then we sum all the deposits for each rank r in group g and thereby obtain the total deposits for each rank group g. Finally, we sum all the deposits for each rank group g to obtain the total number of Canadian pennies deposited in the forest. Adding that total to the number of U.S. pennies in the kitty gives us the answer.

Ranks are partitioned into groups. The actual groups are determined at the end of the proof. Group 0 has only rank 0.

As mentioned previously, we partition the ranks into groups. Rank r goes into group $G(r)$, and G is to be determined later (to balance the U.S. and Canadian deposits). The largest rank in any rank group g is $F(g)$, where $F = G^{-1}$ is the *inverse* of G. The number of ranks in any rank group, $g > 0$, is thus $F(g) - F(g - 1)$. Clearly, $G(N)$ is a very loose upper bound on the largest rank group. Suppose that we partitioned the ranks as shown in Figure 24.22. In this case, $G(r) = \lceil \sqrt{r} \rceil$. The largest rank in group g is $F(g) = g^2$. Also, observe that group $g > 0$ contains ranks $F(g - 1) + 1$ through $F(g)$. This formula does not apply for rank group 0, so for convenience we ensure that rank group 0 contains only elements of rank 0. Note that the groups comprise consecutive ranks.

As mentioned earlier in the chapter, each `union` instruction takes constant time, so long as each root keeps track of its rank. Thus `union` operations are essentially free, as far as this proof goes.

When a node is compressed, its new parent will have a higher rank than its old parent.

Each `find` operation takes time proportional to the number of nodes on the path from the node representing the accessed item i to the root. We thus deposit one penny for each vertex on the path. If that is all we do, however, we cannot expect much of a bound because we are not taking advantage of path

Group	Rank
0	0
1	1
2	2,3,4
3	5 through 9
4	10 through 16
i	$(i-1)^2$ through i^2

figure 24.22

Possible partitioning of ranks into groups

compression. Thus we must use some fact about path compression in our analysis. The key observation is that, as a result of path compression, a node obtains a new parent and the new parent is guaranteed to have a higher rank than the old parent.

Rules for U.S. and Canadian deposits.

To incorporate this fact into the proof, we use the following fancy accounting: For each node v on the path from the accessed node i to the root, we deposit one penny in one of two accounts.

1. If v is the root or if the parent of v is the root or if the parent of v is in a different rank group from v, then charge 1 unit under this rule and deposit a U.S. penny in the kitty.
2. Otherwise, deposit a Canadian penny in the node.

Theorem 24.4 states that the accounting is accurate.

Theorem 24.4

For any `find` operation, the total number of pennies deposited, either in the kitty or in a node, is exactly equal to the number of nodes accessed during the `find`.

Proof

Obvious.

Thus we need only sum all the U.S. pennies deposited under rule 1 and all the Canadian pennies deposited under rule 2. Before we go on with the proof, let us sketch the ideas. Canadian pennies are deposited in a node when it is compressed and its parent is in the same rank group as the node. Because the

U.S. charges are limited by the number of different groups. Canadian charges are limited by the size of the groups. We eventually need to balance these costs.

node gets a parent of higher rank after each path compression and because the size of a rank group is finite, eventually the node obtains a parent that is not in its rank group. Consequently, on the one hand, only a limited number of Canadian pennies can be placed in any node. This number is roughly the size of the node's rank group. On the other hand, the U.S. charges are also limited, essentially by the number of rank groups. Thus we want to choose both small rank groups (to limit the Canadian charges) and few rank groups (to limit the U.S. charges). We are now ready to fill in the details with a rapid-fire series of theorems, Theorems 24.5–24.10.

Theorem 24.5

Over the entire algorithm, the total deposits of U.S. pennies under rule 1 amount to $M(G(N) + 2)$.

Proof

For any `find` operation, at most two U.S. pennies are deposited because of the root and its child. By Theorem 24.3, the vertices going up the path are monotonically increasing in rank, and thus the rank group never decreases as we go up the path. Because there are at most $G(N)$ rank groups (besides group 0), only $G(N)$ other vertices can qualify as a rule 1 deposit for any particular `find`. Thus, during any `find`, at most $G(N) + 2$ U.S. pennies can be placed in the kitty. Thus at most $M(G(N) + 2)$ U.S. pennies can be deposited under rule 1 for a sequence of M `find`s.

Theorem 24.6

For any single node in rank group g, the total number of Canadian pennies deposited is at most $F(g)$.

Proof

If a Canadian penny is deposited in a vertex v under rule 2, v will be moved by path compression and get a new parent of rank higher than its old parent. As the largest rank in its group is $F(g)$, we are guaranteed that after $F(g)$ coins are deposited, v's parent will no longer be in v's rank group.

The bound in Theorem 24.6 can be improved by using only the size of the rank group rather than its largest member. However, this modification does not improve the bound obtained for the union/find algorithm.

Theorem 24.7

The number of nodes, $N(g)$, in rank group $g > 0$ is at most $N/2^{F(g-1)}$.

Proof

By Theorem 24.2, there are at most $N/2^r$ nodes of rank r. Summing over the ranks in group g, we obtain

$$
\begin{aligned}
N(g) &\le \sum_{r=F(g-1)+1}^{F(g)} \frac{N}{2^r} \\
&\le \sum_{r=F(g-1)+1}^{\infty} \frac{N}{2^r} \\
&\le N \sum_{r=F(g-1)+1}^{\infty} \frac{1}{2^r} \\
&\le \frac{N}{2^{F(g-1)+1}} \sum_{s=0}^{\infty} \frac{1}{2^s} \\
&\le \frac{2N}{2^{F(g-1)+1}} \\
&\le \frac{N}{2^{F(g-1)}}
\end{aligned}
$$

Theorem 24.8

The maximum number of Canadian pennies deposited in all vertices in rank group g is at most $NF(g)/2^{F(g-1)}$.

Proof

The result follows from a simple multiplication of the quantities obtained in Theorems 24.6 and 24.7.

Theorem 24.9

The total deposit under rule 2 is at most $N\Sigma_{g=1}^{G(N)} F(g)/2^{F(g-1)}$ Canadian pennies.

Proof

Because rank group 0 contains only elements of rank 0, it cannot contribute to rule 2 charges (it cannot have a parent in the same rank group). The bound is obtained by summing the other rank groups.

Thus we have the deposits under rules 1 and 2. The total is

$$M(G(N) + 2) + N \sum_{g=1}^{G(N)} \frac{F(g)}{2^{F(g-1)}} \tag{24.1}$$

Now we can specify the rank groups to minimize the bound. Our choice is not quite minimal, but it is close.

We still have not specified $G(N)$ or its inverse $F(N)$. Obviously, we are free to choose virtually anything we want, but choosing $G(N)$ to minimize the bound in Equation 24.1 makes sense. However, if $G(N)$ is too small, $F(N)$ will be large, thus hurting the bound. An apparently good choice is $F(i)$ to be the function recursively defined by $F(0)$ and $F(i) = 2^{F(i-1)}$, which gives $G(N) = 1 + \lfloor \log^* N \rfloor$. Figure 24.23 shows how this choice partitions the ranks. Note that group 0 contains only rank 0, which we required in the proof of Theorem 24.9. Note also that F is very similar to the single-variable Ackermann's function, differing only in the definition of the base case. With this choice of F and G, we can complete the analysis in Theorem 24.10.

Theorem 24.10

The running time of the union/find algorithm with $M = \Omega(N)$ `find` operations is $O(M \log^* N)$.

Proof

Insert the definitions of F and G in Equation 24.1. The total number of U.S. pennies is $O(MG(N)) = O(M \log^* N)$. Because $F(g) = 2^{F(g-1)}$, the total number of Canadian pennies is $NG(N) = O(N \log^* N)$, and because $M = \Omega(N)$, the bound follows.

figure 24.23

Actual partitioning of ranks into groups used in the proof

Group	Rank
0	0
1	1
2	2
3	3, 4
4	5 through 6
5	17 through 65,536
6	65,537 through $2^{65,536}$
7	Truly huge ranks

Note that we have more U.S. pennies than Canadian pennies. The function $\alpha(M, N)$ balances things out, which is why it gives a better bound.

summary

In this chapter we discussed a simple data structure for maintaining disjoint sets. When the `union` operation is performed, it does not matter, as far as correctness is concerned, which set retains its name. A valuable lesson that should be learned here is that considering the alternatives when a particular step is not totally specified can be very important. The `union` step is flexible. By taking advantage of this flexibility, we can get a much more efficient algorithm.

Path compression is one of the earliest forms of self-adjustment, which we have used elsewhere (splay trees and skew heaps). Its use here is extremely interesting from a theoretical point of view because it was one of the first examples of a simple algorithm with a not-so-simple worst-case analysis.

key concepts

Ackermann's function A function that grows very quickly. Its inverse is essentially at most 4. (851)

disjoint set class operations The two basic operations needed for disjoint set manipulation: They are `union` and `find`. (833)

disjoint sets Sets having the property that each element appears in only one set. (833)

equivalence class The equivalence class of an element x in set S is the subset of S that contains all the elements related to x. (832)

equivalence relation A relation that is reflexive, symmetric, and transitive. (832)

forest A collection of trees. (838)

Kruskal's algorithm An algorithm used to select edges in increasing cost and that adds an edge to the tree if it does not create a cycle. (837)

minimum spanning tree A connected subgraph of G that spans all vertices at minimum total cost. It is a fundamental graph theory problem. (836)

nearest common ancestor problem Given a tree and a list of pairs of nodes in the tree, find the nearest common ancestor for each pair of nodes. Solution of this problem is important in graph algorithm and computational biology applications. (839)

offline algorithm An algorithm in which the entire sequence of queries are made visible before the first answer is required. (833)

online algorithm An algorithm in which an answer must be provided for each query before the next query can be viewed. (833)

path compression Makes every accessed node a child of the root until another `union` occurs. (847)

quick-find algorithm The union/find implementation in which `find` is a constant-time operation. (842)

quick-union algorithm The union/find implementation in which `union` is a constant-time operation. (843)

ranks In the disjoint set algorithm, the estimated heights of nodes. (848)

relation Defined on a set if every pair of elements either is related or is not. (832)

spanning tree A tree formed by graph edges that connect all the vertices of an undirected graph. (836)

union-by-height Makes a shallower tree a child of the root of a deeper tree during a `union` operation. (847)

union-by-rank Union-by-height when path compression is performed. (848)

union-by-size Makes a smaller tree a child of the root of a larger tree during a `union` operation. (846)

union/find algorithm An algorithm that is executed by processing `union` and `find` operations within a union/find data structure. (833)

union/find data structure A method used to manipulate disjoint sets. (833)

common errors

1. In using `union` we often assume that its parameters are tree roots. Havoc can result in code if we call such a `union` with non-roots as parameters.

on the internet

The disjoint sets class is available online. The following is the filename.

DisjointSets.java Contains the disjoint sets class.

exercises

IN SHORT

24.1 Show the result of the following sequence of instructions: *union* (1, 2), *union* (3, 4), *union* (3, 5), *union* (1, 7), *union* (3, 6), *union* (8, 9), *union* (1, 8), *union* (3, 10), *union* (3, 11), *union* (3, 12), *union* (3, 13), *union* (14, 15), *union* (16, 0), *union* (14, 16), *union* (1, 3), and *union* (1, 14) when the `union` operations are performed

a. Arbitrarily
b. By height
c. By size

24.2 For each of the trees in Exercise 24.1, perform a `find` operation with path compression on the deepest node.

24.3 Find the minimum spanning tree for the graph shown in Figure 24.24.

24.4 Show the operation of the NCA algorithm for the data given in Figure 24.8.

IN THEORY

24.5 Prove that for the mazes generated by the algorithm in Section 24.2.1 the path from the starting to ending points is unique.

24.6 Design an algorithm that generates a maze that contains no path from start to finish but has the property that the removal of a *prespecified* wall creates a unique path.

24.7 Prove that Kruskal's algorithm is correct. In your proof do you assume that the edge costs are nonnegative?

24.8 Show that, if a `union` operation is performed by height, the depth of any tree is logarithmic.

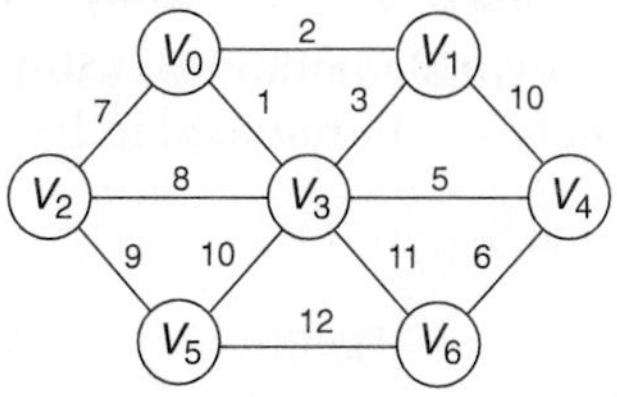

figure 24.24
A graph G for Exercise 24.3

24.9 Show that, if all the `union` operations precede the `find` operations, then the disjoint set algorithm with path compression is linear, even if the `unions` are done arbitrarily. Note that the algorithm does not change; only the performance changes.

24.10 Suppose that you want to add an extra operation, `remove(x)`, which removes `x` from its current set and places it in its own. Show how to modify the union/find algorithm so that the running time of a sequence of M `union`, `find`, and `remove` operations is still $O(M\alpha(M, N))$.

24.11 Prove that, if `union` operations are done by size and path compression is performed, the worst-case running time is still $O(M \log^* N)$.

24.12 Suppose that you implement partial path compression on `find(i)` by changing the parent of every other node on the path from `i` to the root to its grandparent (where doing so makes sense). This process is called *path halving*. Prove that, if path halving is performed on the `finds` and either `union` heuristic is used, the worst-case running time is still $O(M \log^* N)$.

IN PRACTICE

24.13 Implement the `find` operation nonrecursively. Is there a noticeable difference in running time?

24.14 Suppose that you want to add an extra operation, `deunion`, which undoes the last `union` operation not already undone. One way to do so is to use union-by-rank—but a compressionless `find`—and use a stack to store the old state prior to a `union`. A `deunion` can be implemented by popping the stack to retrieve an old state.

d. Why can't we use path compression?
e. Implement the union/find/deunion algorithm.

PROGRAMMING PROBLEMS

24.15 Write a program to determine the effects of path compression and the various union strategies. Your program should process a long sequence of equivalence operations, using all the strategies discussed (including path halving, introduced in Exercise 24.12).

24.16 Implement Kruskal's algorithm.

24.17 An alternative minimum spanning tree algorithm is due to Prim [12]. It works by growing a single tree in successive stages. Start by picking any node as the root. At the start of a stage, some nodes are part of the tree and the rest are not. In each stage, add the minimum-cost edge that connects a tree node with a nontree node. An implementation of Prim's algorithm is essentially identical to Dijkstra's shortest-path algorithm given in Section 14.3, with an update rule:

$$d_w = \min(d_w, c_{v,w})$$

(instead of $d_w = \min(d_w, d_v + c_{v,w})$). Also, as the graph is undirected, each edge appears in two adjacency lists. Implement Prim's algorithm and compare its performance to that of Kruskal's algorithm.

24.18 Write a program to solve the offline NCA problem for binary trees. Test its efficiency by constructing a random binary search tree of 10,000 elements and performing 10,000 ancestor queries.

references

Representation of each set by a tree was proposed in [8]. [1] attributes path compression to McIlroy and Morris and contains several applications of the union/find data structure. Kruskal's algorithm is presented in [11], and the alternative discussed in Exercise 24.17 is from [12]. The NCA algorithm is described in [2]. Other applications are described in [15].

The $O(M \log^* N)$ bound for the union/find problem is from [9]. Tarjan [13] obtained the $O(M\alpha(M, N))$ bound and showed that the bound is tight. That the bound is intrinsic to the general problem and cannot be improved by an alternative algorithm is demonstrated in [14]. A more precise bound for $M < N$ appears in [3] and [16]. Various other strategies for path compression and `union` achieve the same bounds; see [16] for details. If the sequence of `union` operations is known in advance, the union/find problem can be solved in $O(M)$ time [7]. This result can be used to show that the offline NCA problem is solvable in linear time.

Average-case results for the union/find problem appear in [6], [10], [17], and [5]. Results bounding the running time of any single operation (as opposed to the entire sequence) are given in [4].

1. A. V. Aho, J. E. Hopcroft, and J. D. Ullman, *The Design and Analysis of Computer Algorithms,* Addison-Wesley, Reading, MA, 1974.
2. A. V. Aho, J. E. Hopcroft, and J. D. Ullman, "On Finding Lowest Common Ancestors in Trees," *SIAM Journal on Computing* **5** (1976), 115–132.
3. L. Banachowski, "A Complement to Tarjan's Result about the Lower Bound on the Set Union Problem," *Information Processing Letters* **11** (1980), 59–65.

4. N. Blum, "On the Single-Operation Worst-Case Time Complexity of the Disjoint Set Union Problem," *SIAM Journal on Computing* **15** (1986), 1021–1024.

5. B. Bollobas and I. Simon, "Probabilistic Analysis of Disjoint Set Union Algorithms," *SIAM Journal on Computing* **22** (1993), 1053–1086.

6. J. Doyle and R. L. Rivest, "Linear Expected Time of a Simple Union Find Algorithm," *Information Processing Letters* **5** (1976), 146–148.

7. H. N. Gabow and R. E. Tarjan, "A Linear-Time Algorithm for a Special Case of Disjoint Set Union," *Journal of Computer and System Sciences* **30** (1985), 209–221.

8. B. A. Galler and M. J. Fischer, "An Improved Equivalence Algorithm," *Communications of the ACM* **7** (1964), 301–303.

9. J. E. Hopcroft and J. D. Ullman, "Set Merging Algorithms," *SIAM Journal on Computing* **2** (1973), 294–303.

10. D. E. Knuth and A. Schonage, "The Expected Linearity of a Simple Equivalence Algorithm," *Theoretical Computer Science* **6** (1978), 281–315.

11. J. B. Kruskal, Jr., "On the Shortest Spanning Subtree of a Graph and the Traveling Salesman Problem," *Proceedings of the American Mathematical Society* **7** (1956), 48–50.

12. R. C. Prim, "Shortest Connection Networks and Some Generalizations," *Bell System Technical Journal* **36** (1957), 1389–1401.

13. R. E. Tarjan, "Efficiency of a Good but Not Linear Set Union Algorithm," *Journal of the ACM* **22** (1975), 215–225.

14. R. E. Tarjan, "A Class of Algorithms Which Require Nonlinear Time to Maintain Disjoint Sets," *Journal of Computer and System Sciences* **18** (1979), 110–127.

15. R. E. Tarjan, "Applications of Path Compression on Balanced Trees," *Journal of the ACM* **26** (1979), 690–715.

16. R. E. Tarjan and J. van Leeuwen, "Worst Case Analysis of Set Union Algorithms," *Journal of the ACM* **31** (1984), 245–281.

17. A. C. Yao, "On the Average Behavior of Set Merging Algorithms," *Proceedings of the Eighth Annual ACM Symposium on the Theory of Computation* (1976), 192–195.

appendix A

operators

Figure A.1 shows the precedence and associativity of the common Java operators discussed. The bitwise operators are discussed in Appendix C.

Category	Examples	Associativity
Operations on References	`. []`	Left to right
Unary	`++ -- ! - (type)`	Right to left
Multiplicative	`* / %`	Left to right
Additive	`+ -`	Left to right
Shift (bitwise)	`<< >>`	Left to right
Relational	`< <= > >= instanceof`	Left to right
Equality	`== !=`	Left to right
Boolean (or bitwise) AND	`&`	Left to right
Boolean (or bitwise) XOR	`^`	Left to right
Boolean (or bitwise) OR	`|`	Left to right
Logical AND	`&&`	Left to right
Logical OR	`||`	Left to right
Conditional	`?:`	Right to left
Assignment	`= *= /= %= += -=`	Right to left

figure A.1

Java operators listed from highest to lowest precedence

appendix B

graphical user interfaces

A *graphical user interface (GUI)* is the modern alternative to terminal I/O that allows a program to communicate with its user. In a GUI, a window application is created. Some of the ways to perform input include selection from a list of alternatives, pressing buttons, checking boxes, typing in text fields, and using the mouse. Output can be performed by writing into text fields as well as drawing graphics. In Java 1.2 or higher, GUI programming is performed by using the *Swing* package.

In this appendix, we will see

- The basic GUI components in Swing
- How these components communicate information
- How these components can be arranged in a window
- How to draw graphics

A *graphical user interface* (*GUI*) is the modern alternative to terminal I/O that allows a program to communicate with its user.

B.1 the abstract window toolkit and swing

The *Abstract Window Toolkit (AWT)* is a GUI toolkit that is supplied with all Java systems.

The *Abstract Window Toolkit* (*AWT*) is a GUI toolkit that is supplied with all Java systems. It provides the basic classes to allow user interfaces. These classes can be found in the package `java.awt`.[1] The AWT is designed to be portable and work across multiple platforms. For relatively simple interfaces, the AWT is easy to use. GUIs can be written without resorting to visual development aids and provide a significant improvement over basic terminal interfaces.

GUI programming is event-driven.

In a program that uses terminal I/O, the program typically prompts the user for input and then executes a statement that reads a line from the terminal. When the line is read, it is processed. The flow of control in this situation is easy to follow. GUI programming is different. In GUI programming, the input components are arranged in a window. After the window is displayed, the program waits for an event, such as a button push, at which point an event handler is called. This means that the flow of control is less obvious in a GUI program. The programmer must supply the event handler to execute some piece of code.

The event model changed in incompatible ways from Java 1.0 to Java 1.1. The latter version is described here.

Java 1.0 provided an event model that was cumbersome to use. It was replaced in Java 1.1 by a more robust event model. Not surprisingly, these models are not entirely compatible. Specifically, a Java 1.0 compiler will not successfully compile code that uses the new event model. Java 1.1 compilers will give diagnostics about Java 1.0 constructs. However, already compiled Java 1.0 code can be run by a Java 1.1 Virtual Machine. This appendix describes the newer event model only. Many of the classes required by the new event model are found in the `java.awt.event` package.

Swing is a GUI package provided in Java 1.2 that is built on top of the AWT and provides slicker components.

The AWT provided a simple GUI but was criticized for its lack of flair, as well as poor performance. In Java 1.2, an improved set of components was added in a new package called `javax.swing`. These components are known as *Swing*. Components in Swing look much better than their AWT counterparts; there are new Swing components that did not exist in AWT (such as sliders and progress bars) and have many more options (such as easy tooltips and mnemonics). Additionally, Swing provides the notion of look-and-feel, in which a programmer can display the GUI in Windows, X-Motif, Macintosh, platform independent (metal), or even customized style, regardless of the underlying platform (although, because of copyright issues and perhaps bad blood between Sun and Microsoft, Windows look-and-feel works only on Windows systems).

1. Code in this appendix uses the wild-card import directive to save space.

Swing is built on top of the AWT, and as a result, the event-handling model is unchanged. Programming in Swing is very similar to the programming in Java 1.1 AWT, except that many names have changed. In this appendix we describe Swing programming only. Swing is a large library; it is not unusual to see entire books devoted to the topic, so our presentation greatly understates the issues that are involved in user interface design.

Figure B.1 illustrates some of the basic components provided by Swing. These include the `JComboBox` (currently *Circle* is selected), a `JList` (currently *blue* is selected), basic `JTextFields` for input, three `JRadioButtons` and a `JCheckBox`, and a `JButton` (named *Draw*). Next to the button is a `JTextField` that is used for output only (hence, it is darker than the input `JTextFields` above it). In the top left-hand corner is a `JPanel` object that can be used for drawing pictures and handling mouse input.

This appendix describes the basic organization of the Swing API. It covers the different types of objects, how they can be used to perform input and output, how these objects are arranged in a window, and how events are handled.

B.2 basic objects in swing

The AWT and Swing are organized using a class inheritance hierarchy. A compressed version of this hierarchy is shown in Figure B.2. This is compressed because some intermediate classes are not shown. In the full hierarchy, `JTextField` and `JTextArea`, for instance, are extended from `JTextComponent`, while many classes that deal with fonts, colors, and other objects and are not in the `Component` hierarchy are not shown at all. The classes `Font` and `Color`, which are defined in the `java.awt` package, are extended from `Object`.

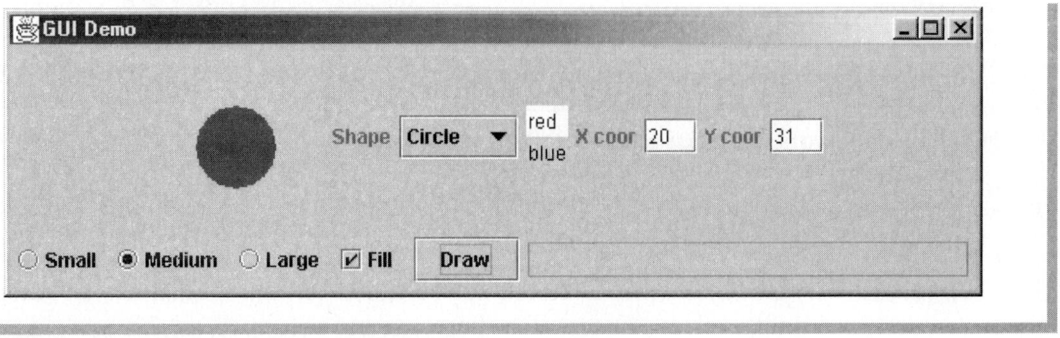

figure B.1

A GUI that illustrates some of the basic Swing components

figure B.2

Compressed hierarchy of Swing

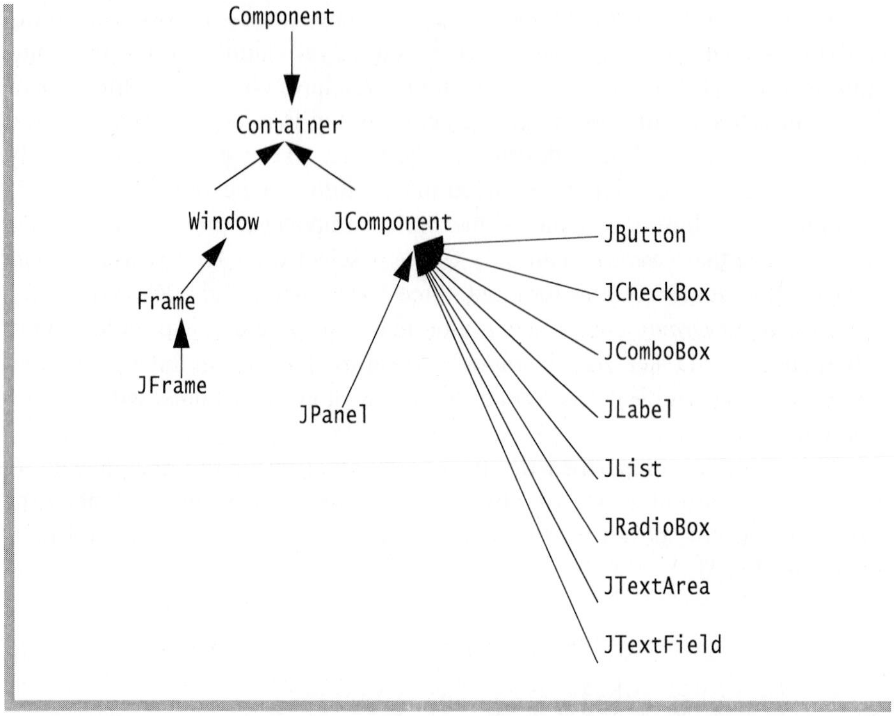

B.2.1 Component

The *Component* class is an abstract class that is the superclass of many AWT objects, and thus Swing objects. Because it is abstract, it cannot be instantiated. A `Component` represents something that has a position and a size and can be painted on the screen as well as receive input events. Some examples of the `Component` are evident from Figure B.2.

The *Component* class is an abstract class that is the superclass of many AWT objects. It represents something that has a position and a size and can be painted on the screen as well as receive input events.

The `Component` class contains many methods. Some of these can be used to specify the color or font; others are used to handle events. Some of the important methods are

```
void setSize( int width, int height );
void setBackground( Color c );
void setFont( Font f );
void show( );
```

The `setSize` method is used to change the size of an object. It works with `JFrame` objects, but it should not be called for objects that use an automatic layout, such as `JButtons`. For those, use `setPreferredSize`; this method takes a `Dimension` object that itself is constructed with a length and width (and is defined in JComponent). The setBackground and setFont methods are used to change the background color and font associated with a Component. They require a Color and Font object, respectively. Finally, the show method makes a component visible. Its typical use is for a JFrame.

B.2.2 Container

In the AWT, a Container is the abstract superclass representing all components that can hold other components. An example of an AWT Container is the Window class, which represents a top-level window. As the inheritance hierarchy shows, a Container IS-A Component. A particular instance of a Container object will store a collection of Components as well as other Containers.

A Container is the abstract superclass representing all components that can hold other components.

The container has a useful helper object called a LayoutManager, which is a class that positions components inside the container. Some useful methods are

```
void setLayout( LayoutManager mgr );
void add( Component comp );
void add( Component comp, Object where );
```

Layout managers are described in Section B.3.1. A container must first define how objects in the container should be arranged. This is done by using setLayout. It then adds the objects into the container one-by-one by using add. Think of the container as a suitcase, in which you can add clothes. Think of the layout manager as the packing expert who will explain how clothes are to be added to the suitcase.

B.2.3 top-level containers

As Figure B.2 shows, there are two types of Container objects, namely

The basic containers are the top-level Window and JComponent. The typical heavyweight components are JWindow, JFrame, and JDialog.

1. The top-level windows, which eventually reaches JFrame
2. The JComponent, which eventually reaches most other Swing components

JFrame is an example of a "heavyweight component," while all Swing components in the JComponent hierarchy are "lightweight." The basic difference between heavyweight and lightweight components is that lightweight components are drawn on a canvas entirely by Swing whereas heavyweight components interact with the native windowing system. As a result, lightweight components can add other lightweight components (for instance, you can use add to place several JButton objects in a JPanel), but you should not add directly into a heavyweight component. Instead you obtain a Container representing its "content pane" and add into the content pane, thus allowing

Swing to update the content pane. Thus the native windowing system is not involved in the update (you will get a run-time exception if you attempt to add into a heavyweight component), increasing update performance.

There are only a few basic top-level windows, including

1. `JWindow`: A top-level window that has no border
2. `JFrame`: A top-level window that has a border and can also have an associated `JMenuBar`[2]
3. `JDialog`: A top-level window used to create dialogs

An application that uses a Swing interface should have a `JFrame` (or a class extended from `JFrame`) as the outermost container.

B.2.4 JPanel

The `JPanel` is used to store a collection of objects but does not create borders. As such, it is the simplest of the `Container` classes.

The other `Container` subclass is the `JComponent`. One such `JComponent` is the `JPanel`, which is used to store a collection of objects but does not create borders, so it is the simplest of the container classes.

The primary use of the `JPanel` is to organize objects into a unit. For instance, consider a registration form that requires a name, address, social security number, and home and work telephone numbers. All of these form components might produce a `PersonPanel`. Then the registration form could contain several `PersonPanel` entities to allow the possibility of multiple registrants.

As an example, Figure B.3 shows how the components shown in Figure B.1 are grouped into a `JPanel` class and illustrates the general technique of creating a subclass of `JPanel`. It remains to construct the objects, lay them out nicely, and handle the button push event.

Note that `GUI` implements the `ActionListener` interface. This means that it understands how to handle an *action event* (in this case, a button push). To implement the `ActionListener` interface, a class must provide an `actionPerformed` method. Also, when the button generates an action event, it must know which component is to receive the event. In this case, by making the call at 11 (in Figure B.3), the `GUI` object that contains the `JButton` tells the `Button` to send it the event. These event-handling details are discussed in Section B.3.3.

A second use of the `JPanel` is the grouping of objects into a unit for the purpose of simplifying layouts. This is discussed in Section B.3.5.

---

2. Menus are not discussed in this appendix.

```
import java.awt.*;
import java.awt.event.*;
import javax.swing.*;

class GUI extends JPanel implements ActionListener
{
    public GUI( )
    {
        makeTheObjects( );
        doTheLayout( );
        theDrawButton.addActionListener( this );
    }
        // Make all the objects
    private void makeTheObjects( )
      { /* Implementation in Figure B.4*/ }

        // Lay out all the objects
    private void doTheLayout( )
      { /* Implementation in Figure B.7 */ }

        // Handle the draw button push
    public void actionPerformed( ActionEvent evt )
      { /* Implementation in Figure B.9 */ }

    private GUICanvas    theCanvas;
    private JComboBox    theShape;
    private JList        theColor;
    private JTextField   theXCoor;
    private JTextField   theYCoor;
    private JRadioButton smallPic;
    private JRadioButton mediumPic;
    private JRadioButton largePic;
    private JCheckBox    theFillBox;
    private JButton      theDrawButton;
    private JTextField   theMessage;
}
```

figure B.3

Basic GUI class shown in Figure B.1

Almost all of the `JPanel` functionality is in fact inherited from `JComponent`. This includes routines for painting, sizing, and event handling and the method to set tooltips:

```
void setToolTipText( String txt );
void setPreferredSize( Dimension d );
```

B.2.5 important i/o components

Swing provides a set of components that can be used to perform input and output. These components are easy to set up and use. The code in Figure B.4 illustrates how each of the basic components that are shown in Figure B.1 are constructed. Generally, this involves calling a constructor and applying a method to customize a component. This code does not specify how items are arranged in the `JPanel` or how the states of the components are examined. Recall that GUI programming consists of drawing the interface and then waiting for events to occur. Component layout and event handling is discussed in Section B.3.

figure B.4

Code that constructs the objects in Figure B.1

```
    // Make all the objects
    private void makeTheObjects( )
    {
        theCanvas = new GUICanvas( );
        theCanvas.setBackground( Color.green );
        theCanvas.setPreferredSize( new Dimension( 99, 99 ) );

        theShape = new JComboBox( new String [ ]
                                  { "Circle", "Square" } );

        theColor = new JList( new String [ ] { "red", "blue" } );
        theColor.setSelectionMode(
                        ListSelectionModel.SINGLE_SELECTION );
        theColor.setSelectedIndex( 0 ); // make red default

        theXCoor = new JTextField( 3 );
        theYCoor = new JTextField( 3 );

        ButtonGroup theSize = new ButtonGroup( );
        smallPic = new JRadioButton( "Small", false );
        mediumPic = new JRadioButton( "Medium", true );
        largePic = new JRadioButton( "Large", false );
        theSize.add( smallPic );
        theSize.add( mediumPic );
        theSize.add( largePic );

        theFillBox = new JCheckBox( "Fill" );
        theFillBox.setSelected( false );

        theDrawButton = new JButton( "Draw" );

        theMessage = new JTextField( 25 );
        theMessage.setEditable( false );
    }
```

JLabel

A JLabel is a component for placing text in a container. Its primary use is to label other components such as a JComboBox, JList, JTextField, or JPanel (many other components already have their names displayed in some way). In Figure B.1, the phrases *Shape*, *X Coor*, and *Y Coor* are labels. A JLabel is constructed with an optional String and can be changed with the method setText. These methods are

A JLabel is a component for placing text in a container. Its primary use is to label other components.

```
JLabel( );
JLabel( String theLabel );
void setText( String theLabel );
```

JButton

The JButton is used to create a labeled button. Figure B.1 contains a JButton with the label *Draw*. When the JButton is pushed, an *action event* is generated. Section B.3.3 describes how action events are handled. The JButton is similar to the JLabel in that a JButton is constructed with an optional String. The JButton label can be changed with the method setText. These methods are

The JButton is used to create a labeled button. When it is pushed, an *action event* is generated.

```
JButton( );
JButton( String theLabel );
void setText( String theLabel );
void setMnemonic( char c );
```

JComboBox

The JComboBox is used to select a single object (typically a string) via a pop-up list of choices. Only one choice can be selected at any time, and by default only an object that is one of the choices can be selected. If the JComboBox is made editable, the user can type in an entry that is not one of the choices. In Figure B.1, the type of shape is a JComboBox object; *Circle* is currently selected. Some of the JComboBox methods are

The JComboBox is used to select a single string via a pop-up list of choices.

```
JComboBox( );
JComboBox( Object [ ] choices );
void   addItem( Object item );
Object getSelectedItem( );
int    getSelectedIndex( );
void   setEditable( boolean edit );
void   setSelectedIndex( int index );
```

A JComboxBox is constructed with no parameters or with an array of options. Objects (typically strings) can then be added to (or removed from) the list of JComboxBox options. When getSelectedItem is called, an Object representing the current selected item (or null, if no choice is selected) is returned.

Instead of returning the actual Object, its index (as computed by the order of calls to addItem) can be returned by calling getSelectedIndex. The first item added has index 0, and so on. This can be useful because if an array stores information corresponding to each of the choices, getSelectedIndex can be used to index this array. The setSelectedIndex method is used to specify a default selection.

JList

The JList component allows the selection from a scrolling list of Objects. It can be set up to allow for either one selected item or multiple selected items.

The JList component allows the selection from a scrolling list of Objects. In Figure B.1, the choice of colors is presented as a JList. The JList differs from the JComboBox in three fundamental ways:

1. The JList can be set up to allow either one selected item or multiple selected items (the default is multiple selection).
2. The JList allows the user to see more than one choice at a time.
3. The JList will take up more screen real estate than the Choice.

The basic JList methods are

```
JList( );
JList( Object [ ] items );
void       setListData( Object [ ] items );
int        getSelectedIndex( );
int [ ]    getSelectedIndices( );
Object     getSelectedValue( );
Object [ ] getSelectedValues( );
void       setSelectedIndex( int index );
void       setSelectedValue( Object value );
void       setSelectionMode( int mode );
```

A JList is constructed with either no parameters or an array of items (there are other constructors that are more sophisticated). Most of the listed methods have the same behavior (with possibly different names) as the corresponding methods in JComboxBox. getSelectedValue returns null if no items are selected. getSelectedValues is used to handle multiple selection; it returns an array of Objects (possibly length 0) corresponding to the selected items. As with the JComboxBox, indices instead of Objects can be obtained by other public methods.

setSelectionMode is used to allow only single-item selection. The boilerplate code is

```
lst.setSelectionMode( ListSelectionModel.SINGLE_SELECTION );
```

JCheckBox and JRadioButton

A JCheckBox is a GUI component that has an *on* state and an *off* state. The *on* state is true and the *off* state is false. It is considered a button (a class AbstractButton is defined in the Swing API from which JButton, JCheckBox, and JRadioButton are all derived). A JRadioButton is similar to a check box, except that JRadioButtons are round; we use *check box* as a generic term to describe both. Figure B.1 contains four check box objects. In this figure, the *Fill* check box is currently true and the three other check boxes are in a ButtonGroup: Only one check box in the group of three may be true. When a check box in a group is selected, all the others in the group are deselected. A ButtonGroup is constructed with zero parameters. Note that it is not a Component; it is simply a helper class that extends Object.

A *check box* is a GUI component that has an *on* state and an *off* state. A ButtonGroup can contain a set of buttons in which only one may be true at a time.

The common methods for JCheckBox are similar to JRadioButton and are:

```
JCheckBox( );
JCheckBox( String theLabel );
JCheckBox( String theLabel, boolean state );
boolean isSelected( );
void    setLabel( String theLabel );
void    setSelected( boolean state );
```

A stand-alone JCheckBox is constructed with an optional label. If a label is not provided, it can be added later with setLabel. setLabel can also be used to change the existing JCheckBox label. setSelected is most commonly used to set a default for a stand-alone JCheckBox. isSelected returns the state of a JCheckBox.

A JCheckBox that is part of a ButtonGroup is constructed as usual and is then added to the ButtonGroup object by use of the ButtonGroup add method. The ButtonGroup methods are

```
ButtonGroup( );
void add( AbstractButton b );
```

canvases

In the AWT, a Canvas component represents a blank rectangular area of the screen onto which the application can draw. Primitive graphics are described in Section B.3.2. A Canvas could also receive input from the user in the form of mouse and keyboard events. The Canvas was never used directly: Instead, the programmer defined a subclass of Canvas with appropriate functionality. The subclass overrode the public method

A canvas component represents a blank rectangular area of the screen onto which the application can draw or receive input events.

```
void paint( Graphics g );
```

In Swing, this is no longer in vogue. The same effect is obtained by extending `JPanel` and overriding the public method

```
void paintComponent( Graphics g );
```

Although this works for any component, by using a `JPanel` of a preferred size, one can avoid having any painting run over the boundary of the "canvasing area."

JTextField and JTextAreas

A `JTextField` is a component that presents the user with a single line of text. A `JTextArea` allows multiple lines and has similar functionality.

A `JTextField` is a component that presents the user with a single line of text. A `JTextArea` allows multiple lines and has similar functionality. Thus only `JTextField` is considered here. By default, the text can be edited by the user, but it is possible to make the text uneditable. In Figure B.1, there are three `JTextField` objects: two for the coordinates and one, which is not editable by the user, that is used to communicate error messages. The background color of an uneditable text field differs from that of an editable text field. Some of the common methods associated with `JTextField` are

```
JTextField( );
JTextField( int cols );
JTextField( String text, int cols );
String  getText( );
boolean isEditable( );
void    setEditable( boolean editable );
void    setText( String text );
```

A `JTextField` is constructed either with no parameters or by specifying initial optional text and the number of columns. The `setEditable` method can be used to disallow input into the `JTextField`. `setText` can be used to print messages into the `JTextField`, and `getText` can be used to read from the `JTextField`.

B.3 basic principles

This section examines three important facets of AWT programming: first, how objects are arranged inside a container, followed by how events, such as button pushing, are handled. Finally, it describes how graphics are drawn inside canvas objects.

B.3.1 layout managers

A *layout manager* automatically arranges components of the container. It is associated with a container by issuing the setLayout command. An example of using setLayout is the call

```
setLayout( new FlowLayout( ) );
```

Notice that a reference to the layout manager need not be saved. The container in which the setLayout command is applied stores it as a private data member. When a layout manager is used, requests to resize many of the components, such as buttons, do not work because the layout manager will choose its own sizes for the components, as it deems appropriate. The idea is that the layout manager will determine the best sizes that allow the layout to meet the specifications.

Think of the layout manager as an expert packer hired by the container to make the final decisions about how to pack items that are added to the container.

The *layout manager* automatically arranges components of the container. A layout manager is associated with a container by the setLayout method.

FlowLayout

The simplest of the layouts is the FlowLayout. When a container is arranged using the FlowLayout, its components are added in a row from left to right. When there is no room left in a row, a new row is formed. By default, each row is centered. This can be changed by providing an additional parameter in the constructor with the value FlowLayout.LEFT or FlowLayout.RIGHT.

The problem with using a FlowLayout is that a row may break in an awkward place. For instance, if a row is too short, a break may occur between a JLabel and a JTextField, even though logically they should always remain adjacent. One way to avoid this is to create a separate JPanel with those two elements and then add the JPanel into the container. Another problem with the FlowLayout is that it is difficult to line up things vertically.

The FlowLayout is the default for a JPanel.

The simplest of the layouts is the FlowLayout, which adds components in a row from left to right.

BorderLayout

A BorderLayout is the default for objects in the Window hierarchy, such as JFrame. It lays out a container by placing components in one of five locations. For this to happen, the add method must provide as a second parameter one of the strings "North", "South", "East", "West", and "Center"; the second parameter defaults to "Center" if not provided (so one single-parameter add will work, but several adds place items on top of each other). Figure B.5 shows five buttons added to a Frame using a BorderLayout. The code to generate this layout is

BorderLayout is the default for objects in the Window hierarchy, such as JFrame and JDialog. It lays out a container by placing components in one of five locations.

figure B.5

Five buttons arranged using `BorderLayout`

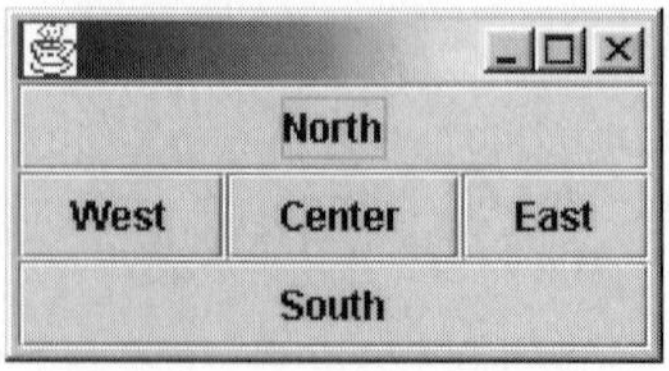

shown in Figure B.6. Observe that we use the typical idiom of adding into a lightweight `JPanel` and then adding the `JPanel` into the top-level `JFrame`'s content pane. Typically, some of the five locations may be unused. Also, the component placed in a location is typically a `JPanel` that contains other components using some other layout.

As an example, the code in Figure B.7 shows how the objects in Figure B.1 are arranged. Here, we have two rows, but we want to ensure that the check boxes, buttons, and output text field are placed below the rest of the GUI. The idea is to create a `JPanel` that stores the items that should be in the top half and another `JPanel` that stores the items in the bottom half. These two `JPanels` can be placed on top of each other by arranging them using a `BorderLayout`.

figure B.6

Code that illustrates `BorderLayout`

```
import java.awt.*;
import javax.swing.*;

    // Generate Figure B.5
public class BorderTest extends JFrame
{
    public static void main( String [ ] args )
    {
        JFrame f = new BorderTest( );
        JPanel p = new JPanel( );

        p.setLayout( new BorderLayout( ) );
        p.add( new JButton( "North" ), "North" );
        p.add( new JButton( "East" ), "East" );
        p.add( new JButton( "South" ), "South" );
        p.add( new JButton( "West" ), "West" );
        p.add( new JButton( "Center" ), "Center" );

        Container c = f.getContentPane( );
        c.add( p );
        f.pack( );    // Resize frame to minimum size
        f.show( );    // Display the frame
    }
}
```

```
1        // Lay out all the objects
2     private void doTheLayout( )
3     {
4         JPanel topHalf    = new JPanel( );
5         JPanel bottomHalf = new JPanel( );
6
7             // Lay out the top half
8         topHalf.setLayout( new FlowLayout( ) );
9         topHalf.add( theCanvas );
10        topHalf.add( new JLabel( "Shape" ) );
11        topHalf.add( theShape );
12        topHalf.add( theColor );
13        topHalf.add( new JLabel( "X coor" ) );
14        topHalf.add( theXCoor );
15        topHalf.add( new JLabel( "Y coor" ) );
16        topHalf.add( theYCoor );
17
18            // Lay out the bottom half
19        bottomHalf.setLayout( new FlowLayout( ) );
20        bottomHalf.add( smallPic );
21        bottomHalf.add( mediumPic );
22        bottomHalf.add( largePic );
23        bottomHalf.add( theFillBox );
24        bottomHalf.add( theDrawButton );
25        bottomHalf.add( theMessage );
26
27            // Now lay out GUI
28        setLayout( new BorderLayout( ) );
29        add( topHalf, "North" );
30        add( bottomHalf, "South" );
31    }
```

figure B.7

Code that lays out the objects in Figure B.1

Lines 4 and 5 create the two `JPanel` objects `topHalf` and `bottomHalf`. Each of the `JPanel` objects are then separately arranged using a `FlowLayout`. Notice that the `setLayout` and `add` methods are applied to the appropriate `JPanel`. Because the `JPanels` are arranged with the `FlowLayout`, they may consume more than one row if there is not enough horizontal real estate available. This could cause a bad break between a `JLabel` and a `JTextField`. It is left as an exercise for the reader to create additional `JPanels` to ensure that any breaks do not disconnect a `JLabel` and the component it labels. Once the `JPanels` are done, we use a `BorderLayout` to line them up. This is done at lines 28 to 30. Notice also that the contents of both `JPanels` are centered. This is a result of the `FlowLayout`. To have the contents of the `JPanels` left-aligned, lines 8 and 19 would construct the `FlowLayout` with the additional parameter `FlowLayout.LEFT`.

When the BorderLayout is used, an add command that is issued without a String defaults to "Center".

When the BorderLayout is used, any add commands that are issued without a String use "Center" as the default. If a String is provided but is not one of the acceptable five (including having correct case), then a run-time exception is thrown.[3]

null layout

The null layout is used to perform precise positioning.

The null layout is used to perform precise positioning. In the null layout, each object is added to the container by add. Its position and size may then be set by calling the setBounds method:

```
void setBounds( int x, int y, int width, int height );
```

Here x and y represent the location of the upper left-hand corner of the object, relative to the upper left-hand corner of its container. And width and height represent the size of the object. All units are pixels.

The null layout is platform dependent; typically, this is a significant liability.

fancier layouts

Other layouts simulate tabbed index cards and allow arranging over an arbitrary grid.

Java also provides the CardLayout, GridLayout, and GridBagLayout. The CardLayout simulates the tabbed index cards popular in Windows applications. The GridLayout adds components into a grid but will make each grid entry the same size. This means that components are stretched in sometimes unnatural ways. It is useful for when this is not a problem, such as a calculator keypad that consists of a two-dimensional grid of buttons. The GridBagLayout adds components into a grid but allows components to cover several grid cells. It is more complicated than the other layouts.

visual tools

Commercial products include tools that allow the programmer to draw the layout using a CAD-like system. The tool then produces the Java code to construct the objects and provide a layout. Even with this system, the programmer must still write most of the code, including the handling of events, but is relieved of the dirty work involved in calculating precise object positions.

3. Note that in Java 1.0, the arguments to add were reversed, and missing or incorrect Strings were quietly ignored, thus leading to difficult debugging. The old style is still allowed, but it is officially discouraged.

B.3.2 graphics

As mentioned in Section B.2.5, graphics are drawn by using a JPanel object. Specifically, to generate graphics, the programmer must define a new class that extends JPanel. This new class provides a constructor (if a default is unacceptable), overrides a method named paintComponent, and provides a public method that can be called from the canvas's container. The paintComponent method is

Graphics are drawn by defining a class that extends JPanel. The new class overrides the paintComponent method and provides a public method that can be called from the canvas's container.

```
void paintComponent( Graphics g );
```

Graphics is an abstract class that defines several methods. Some of these are

```
void drawOval( int x, int y, int width, int height );
void drawRect( int x, int y, int width, int height );
void fillOval( int x, int y, int width, int height );
void fillRect( int x, int y, int width, int height );
void drawLine( int x1, int y1, int x2, int y2 );
void drawString( String str, int x, int y );
void setColor( Color c );
```

Graphics is an abstract class that defines several drawing methods.

In Java, coordinates are measured relative to the upper left-hand corner of the component. drawOval, drawRect, fillOval, and fillRect all draw an object of specified width and height with the upper left-hand corner at coordinates given by x and y. drawLine and drawString draw lines and text, respectively. setColor is used to change the current color; the new color is used by all drawing routines until it is changed.

In Java, coordinates are measured relative to the upper left-hand corner of the component.

It is important that the first line of paintComponent calls the superclass's paintComponent.

It is important that the first line of paintComponent calls the superclass's paintComponent.

Figure B.8 illustrates how the canvas in Figure B.1 is implemented. The new class GUICanvas extends JPanel. It provides various private data members that describe the current state of the canvas. The default GUICanvas constructor is reasonable, so we accept it.

The data members are set by the public method setParams, which is provided so that the container (that is, the GUI class that stores the GUICanvas) can communicate the state of its various input components to the GUICanvas. setParams is shown at lines 3 to 13. The last line of setParams calls the method repaint.

The repaint method schedules a component clearing and subsequent call to paintComponent. Thus all we need to do is to write a paintComponent method that draws the canvas as specified in the class data members. As can be seen by its implementation in lines 15 to 35, after chaining up to the superclass, paintComponent simply calls the Graphics methods described previously in this appendix.

The repaint method schedules a component clearing and then calls paintComponent.

figure B.8

Basic canvas shown in top left-hand corner of Figure B.1

```
class GUICanvas extends JPanel
{
    public void setParams( String aShape, String aColor, int x,
                           int y, int size, boolean fill )
    {
        theShape = aShape;
        theColor = aColor;
        xcoor = x;
        ycoor = y;
        theSize = size;
        fillOn = fill;
        repaint( );
    }

    public void paintComponent( Graphics g )
    {
        super.paintComponent( g );
        if( theColor.equals( "red" ) )
            g.setColor( Color.red );
        else if( theColor.equals( "blue" ) )
            g.setColor( Color.blue );

        theWidth = 25 * ( theSize + 1 );

        if( theShape.equals( "Square" ) )
            if( fillOn )
                g.fillRect( xcoor, ycoor, theWidth, theWidth );
            else
                g.drawRect( xcoor, ycoor, theWidth, theWidth );
        else if( theShape.equals( "Circle" ) )
            if( fillOn )
                g.fillOval( xcoor, ycoor, theWidth, theWidth );
            else
                g.drawOval( xcoor, ycoor, theWidth, theWidth );
    }

    private String theShape = "";
    private String theColor = "";
    private int xcoor;
    private int ycoor;
    private int theSize;  // 0 = small, 1 = med, 2 = large
    private boolean fillOn;
    private int theWidth;
}
```

B.3.3 events

When the user types on the keyboard or uses the mouse, the operating system produces an event. Java's original event-handling system was cumbersome and has been completely redone. The new model, in place since Java 1.1, is much simpler to program than the old. Note that the two models are incompatible: Java 1.1 events are not understood by Java 1.0 compilers. The basic rules are as follows:

Java's original event-handling system was cumbersome and has been completely redone.

1. Any class that is willing to provide code to handle an event must `implement` a *listener* interface. Examples of listener interfaces are `ActionListener`, `WindowListener`, and `MouseListener`. As usual, implementing an interface means that all methods of the interface must be defined by the class.
2. An object that is willing to handle the event generated by a component must register its willingness with an *addListener* message sent to the event-generating component. When a component generates an event, the event will be sent to the object that has registered to receive it. If no object has registered to receive it, then it is ignored.

For an example, consider the action event, which is generated when the user presses a `JButton`, hits *Return* while in a `JTextField`, or selects from a `JList` or `JMenuItem`. The simplest way to handle the `JButton` click is to have its container implement `ActionListener` by providing an `actionPerformed` method and registering itself with the `JButton` as its event handler.

An action event is generated when the user presses a `JButton`; it is handled by an `actionListener`.

This is shown for our running example in Figure B.1 as follows. Recall that in Figure B.3, we already have done two things. At line 5, `GUI` declares that it implements the `ActionListener`, and at line 11, an instance of `GUI` registers itself as its `JButton`'s action event handler. In Figure B.9, we implement the listener by having `actionPerformed` call `setParam` in the `GUICanvas` class. This example is simplified by the fact that there is only one `JButton`, so when `actionPerformed` is called, we know what to do. If `GUI` contained several `JButtons` and it registered to receive events from all of these `JButtons`, then `actionPerformed` would have to examine the `evt` parameter to determine which `JButton` event was to be processed: This might involve a sequence of `if/else` tests.[4] The `evt` parameter, which in this case is an `ActionEvent` reference, is always passed to an event handler. The event will be specific to the type of handler (`ActionEvent`, `WindowEvent`, and so on), but it will always be a subclass of `AWTEvent`.

4. One way to do this is to use `evt.getSource( )`, which returns a reference to the object that generated the event.

figure B.9

Code to handle the draw button push for Figure B.1

```
   // Handle the draw button push
public void actionPerformed( ActionEvent evt )
{
    try
    {
        theCanvas.setParams(
            (String) theShape.getSelectedItem( ),
            (String) theColor.getSelectedValue( ),
            Integer.parseInt( theXCoor.getText( ) ),
            Integer.parseInt( theYCoor.getText( ) ),
            smallPic.isSelected( ) ? 0 :
                    mediumPic.isSelected( ) ? 1 : 2,
            theFillBox.isSelected( ) );

        theMessage.setText( "" );
    }
    catch( NumberFormatException e )
      { theMessage.setText( "Incomplete input" ); }
}
```

A window-closing event is generated when an application is closed.

An important event that needs to be processed is the window-closing event. This event is generated when an application is closed by pressing on the ☒ that is at the top right-hand corner of the application window. Unfortunately, by default, this event is ignored, so if an event handler is not provided, the normal mechanism for closing an application will not work.

The window-closing event is handled by implementing the `WindowListener` interface.

Window closing is one of several events that is associated with a `WindowListener` interface. Because implementing the interface requires us to provide implementations for many methods (which are likely to be empty bodies), the most reasonable course of action is to define a class that extends `JFrame` and implements the `WindowListener` interface. This class, `CloseableFrame`, is shown in Figure B.10. The window-closing event handler is simple to write — it just calls `System.exit`. The other methods remain without a special implementation. The constructor registers that it is willing to accept the window-closing event. Now we can use `CloseableFrame` instead of `JFrame` throughout.

`CloseableFrame` extends `JFrame` and implements `WindowListener`.

Notice that the code for `CloseableFrame` is cumbersome; we will revisit it shortly and see a use for anonymous inner classes.

The `pack` method simply makes the `JFrame` as tight as possible, given its constituent components. The `show` method displays the `JFrame`.

Figure B.11 provides a `main` that can be used to start the application in Figure B.1. We place this in a separate class, which we call `BasicGUI`. `BasicGUI` extends the class `CloseableFrame`. `main` simply creates a `JFrame` into which we place a `GUI` object. We then add an unnamed `GUI` object into the `JFrame`'s content pane and `pack` the `JFrame`. The `pack` method simply makes the `JFrame` as tight as possible, given its constituent components. The `show` method displays the `JFrame`.

```java
// Frame that closes on a window-close event

public class CloseableFrame extends JFrame
                            implements WindowListener
{
    public CloseableFrame( )
      { addWindowListener( this ); }

    public void windowClosing( WindowEvent event )
      { System.exit( 0 ); }
    public void windowClosed( WindowEvent event )
      { }
    public void windowDeiconified( WindowEvent event )
      { }
    public void windowIconified( WindowEvent event )
      { }
    public void windowActivated( WindowEvent event )
      { }
    public void windowDeactivated( WindowEvent event )
      { }
    public void windowOpened( WindowEvent event )
      { }
}
```

figure B.10

CloseableFrame class: same as JFrame but handles the window-closing event

```java
class BasicGUI extends CloseableFrame
{
    public static void main( String [ ] args )
    {
        JFrame f = new BasicGUI( );
        f.setTitle( "GUI Demo" );

        Container contentPane = f.getContentPane( );
        contentPane.add( new GUI( ) );
        f.pack( );
        f.show( );
    }
}
```

figure B.11

main routine for Figure B.1

B.3.4 event handling: adapters and anonymous inner classes

The CloseableFrame class is a mess. To listen for a WindowEvent, we must declare a class that implements the WindowListener interface, instantiate the class, and then register that object with the CloseableFrame. Since the Window-

Listener interface has seven methods, we must implement all seven methods, even though we are interested in only one of the seven methods.

One can imagine the messy code that will ensue when a large program handles numerous events. The problem is that every event-handling strategy corresponds to a new class, and it would be bizarre to have many classes with lots of methods that simply declare { }.

The *listener adapter classes* provide default implementations of all the listener methods.

As a result, the java.awt.event package defines a set of *listener adapter classes*. Each listener interface that has more than one method is implemented by a corresponding listener adapter class, with empty bodies. Thus instead of providing the empty bodies ourselves, we can simply extend the adapter class and override the methods we are interested in. In our case, we need to extend WindowAdapter. This gives the (flawed) implementation for CloseableFrame, shown in Figure B.12.

The code in Figure B.12 fails because multiple implementation inheritance is illegal in Java. This is not a serious problem, however, because we do not need the CloseableFrame to be the object that handles its own events. Instead, it can be delegated to a function object.

Figure B.13 illustrates this approach. The ExitOnClose class implements the WindowListener interface by extending WindowAdapter. An instance of that class is created and registered as the frame's window listener. ExitOnClose is declared as an inner class instead of a nested class. This would give it access to any of the CloseableFrame's instance members, should it need it. The event-handling model is a classic example of the use of function objects and is the reason that inner classes were deemed an essential addition to the language (recall that inner classes and the new event model appeared simultaneously in Java 1.1).

Figure B.14 shows the logical continuation, using anonymous inner classes. Here we are adding a WindowListener and explaining, on pretty much the next line of code, what the WindowListener does. This is a classic use of the anonymous inner classes. The pollution of braces, parentheses, and semico-

figure B.12

CloseableFrame class using WindowAdapter. This does not work because there is no multiple inheritance in Java.

```
// Frame that closes on a window-close event: (flawed)
public class CloseableFrame extends JFrame, WindowAdapter
{
    public CloseableFrame( )
      { addWindowListener( this ); }

    public void windowClosing( WindowEvent event )
      { System.exit( 0 ); }
}
```

```
// Frame that closes on a window-close event: (works!)
public class CloseableFrame extends JFrame
{
    public CloseableFrame( )
      { addWindowListener( new ExitOnClose( ) ); }

    private class ExitOnClose extends WindowAdapter
    {
        public void windowClosing( WindowEvent event )
          { System.exit( 0 ); }
    }
}
```

figure B.13
`CloseableFrame` class using `WindowAdapter` and inner class

```
// Frame that closes on a window-close event: (works!)
public class CloseableFrame extends JFrame
{
    public CloseableFrame( )
    {
        addWindowListener( new WindowAdapter( )
            {
              public void windowClosing( WindowEvent event )
                { System.exit( 0 ); }
            }
        );
    }
}
```

figure B.14
`CloseableFrame` class using `WindowAdapter` and anonymous inner class

lons is horrific, but experienced readers of Java code skip over those syntactic details and easily see what the event-handling code does. The main benefit here is that if there are lots of small event-handling methods, they need not be scattered in top-level classes but instead can be placed near the objects that these events are coming from.

B.3.5 summary: putting the pieces together

Here is a summary of how to create a GUI application. Place the GUI functionality in a class that extends `JPanel`. For that class, do the following:

1. Decide on the basic input elements and text output elements. If the same elements are used twice, make an extra class to store the common functionality and apply these principles on that class.

2. If graphics are used, make an extra class that extends `JPanel`. That class must provide a `paintComponent` method and a public method that can be used by the container to communicate to it. It may also need to provide a constructor.
3. Pick a layout and issue a `setLayout` command.
4. Add components to the GUI using `add`.
5. Handle events. The simplest way to do this is to use a `JButton` and trap the button push with `actionPerformed`.

Once a GUI class is written, an application defines a class that extends `CloseableFrame` with a `main` routine. The `main` routine simply creates an instance of this extended frame class, places the GUI panel inside the frame's content pane, and issues a `pack` command and a `show` command for the frame.

B.3.6 is this everything i need to know about swing?

What we have described so far will work well for toy user interfaces and is an improvement over console-based applications. But there are significant complications that a professional applications programmer would have to deal with.

It is rare that the layout manager will make you happy. Often you need to tinker by adding additional subpanels. To help out, Swing defines elements such as spacers, struts, and so on that allow you to position elements more precisely, along with elaborate layout managers. Using these elements is quite challenging.

Other Swing components include sliders, progress bars, scrolling (which can be added to any `JComponent`), password textfields, file choosers, option panes and dialog boxes, tree structures (such as what you see in File Manager on Windows systems), tables, and on and on. Image acquisition and display is also supported by Swing. Additionally, one often needs to know about fonts, colors, and the screen environment that one is working in.

Additionally, there is the important issue of what happens if an event occurs while you are in an event handler. It turns out that events are queued. However, if you get trapped in an event handler for a long time, your application can appear unresponsive; we've all seen this in application code. For instance, if the button-handling code has an infinite loop, you will not be able to close a window. To solve this problem, typically programmers use a technique known as *multithreading*, which opens up a whole new can of worms.

summary

This appendix examined the basics of the Swing package, which allows the programming of GUIs. This makes the program look much more professional than simple terminal I/O.

GUI applications differ from terminal I/O applications in that they are event-driven. To design a GUI, we write a class. We must decide on the basic input elements and output elements, pick a layout and issue a `setLayout` command, add components to the GUI using `add`, and handle events. All this is part of the class. Starting with Java 1.1, event-handling is done with event listeners.

Once this class is written, an application defines a class that extends `JFrame` with a `main` routine and an event handler. The event handler processes the window-closing event. The simplest way to do this is to use the `CloseableFrame` class in Figure B.14. The `main` routine simply creates an instance of this extended frame class, places an instance of the class (whose constructor likely creates a GUI panel) inside the frame's content pane, and issues a `pack` command and a `show` command for the frame.

Only the basics of Swing have been discussed here. Swing is the topic of entire books.

key concepts

Abstract Window Toolkit (AWT) A GUI toolkit that is supplied with all Java systems. Provides the basic classes to allow user interfaces. (868)

`ActionEvent` An event generated when a user presses a `JButton`, hits *Return* in a `JTextField`, or selects from a `JList` or `JMenuItem`. Should be handled by the `actionPerformed` method in a class that implements the `ActionListener` interface. (885)

`ActionListener` interface An interface used to handle action events. Contains the abstract method `actionPerformed`. (885)

`actionPerformed` A method used to handle action events. (885)

`AWTEvent` An object that stores information about an event. (885)

`BorderLayout` The default for objects in the `Window` hierarchy. Used to lay out a container by placing components in one of five locations (`"North"`, `"South"`, `"East"`, `"West"`, `"Center"`). (879)

`ButtonGroup` An object used to group a collection of button objects and guarantee that only one may be *on* at any time. (877)

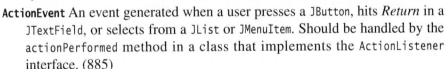

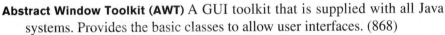

canvas A blank rectangular area of the screen onto which an application can draw and receive input from the user in the form of keyboard and mouse events. In Swing, this is implemented by extending `JPanel`. (883)

`Component` An abstract class that is the superclass of many AWT objects. Represents something that has a position and a size and that can be painted on the screen as well as receive input events. (870)

`Container` The abstract superclass representing all components that can hold other components. Typically has an associated layout manager. (871)

event Produced by the operating system for various occurrences, such as input operations, and passed to Java. (885)

`FlowLayout` A layout that is the default for `JPanel`. Used to lay out a container by adding components in a row from left to right. When there is no room left in a row, a new row is formed. (879)

graphical user interface (GUI) The modern alternative to terminal I/O that allows a program to communicate with its user via buttons, check boxes, text fields, choice lists, menus, and the mouse. (867)

`Graphics` An abstract class that defines several methods that can be used to draw shapes. (883)

`JButton` A component used to create a labeled button. When the button is pushed, an action event is generated. (875)

`JCheckBox` A component that has an *on* state and an *off* state. (877)

`JComboBox` A component used to select a single string via a pop-up list of choices. (875)

`JComponent` An abstract class that is the superclass of lightweight Swing objects. (871)

`JDialog` A top-level window used to create dialogs. (872)

`JFrame` A top-level window that has a border and can also have an associated `JMenuBar`. (872)

`JLabel` A component that is used to label other components such as a `JComboBox`, `JList`, `JTextField`, or `JPanel`. (875)

`JList` A component that allows the selection from a scrolling list of strings. Can allow one or multiple selected items but uses more screen real estate than `JComboBox`. (876)

`JPanel` A container used to store a collection of objects but does not create borders. Also used for canvases. (872)

`JTextArea` A component that presents the user with several lines of text. (878)

`JTextField` A component that presents the user with a single line of text. (878)

`JWindow` A top-level window that has no border. (872)

layout manager A helper object that automatically arranges components of a container. (879)

listener adapter class Provides default implementations for a listener interface that has more than one method. (888)

`null` layout A layout used to perform precise positioning. (882)

`pack` A method used to pack a `JFrame` into its smallest size given its constituent components. (886)

`paintComponent` A method used to draw onto a component. Typically overridden by classes that extend `JPanel`. (883)

`repaint` A method used to clear and repaint a component. (883)

`setLayout` A method that associates a layout with a container. (879)

`show` A method that makes a component visible. (886)

`WindowAdapter` A class that provides default implementations of the `WindowListener` interface. (872)

`WindowListener` interface An interface used to specify the handling of window events, such as window closing. (886)

common errors

1. Forgetting to set a layout manager is a common mistake. If you forget it, you'll get a default. However, it may not be the one you want.
2. The layout manager must appear prior to the calls to `add`.
3. Applying `add` or setting a layout manager to the wrong container is a common mistake. For instance, in a container that contains panels, applying the `add` method without specifying the panel means that the `add` is applied to the main container.
4. A missing `String` argument to `add` for `BorderLayout` uses `"Center"` as the default. A common mistake is to specify it in the wrong case, as in `"north"`. The five valid arguments are `"North"`, `"South"`, `"East"`, `"West"`, and `"Center"`. In Java 1.1, if the `String` is the second parameter, a run-time exception will catch the error. If you use the old style, in which the `String` comes first, the error might not be detected.
5. Special code is needed to process the window-closing event.

on the internet

All code found in this Appendix is available:

BorderTest.java Simple illustration of the `BorderLayout`, shown in Figure B.6.

BasicGUI.java The main example for the GUI application used in this chapter, with `CloseableFrame` from Figure B.14.

exercises

IN SHORT

B.1 What is a GUI?

B.2 List the various `JComponent` classes that can be used for GUI input.

B.3 Describe the difference between heavyweight components and lightweight components and give examples of each.

B.4 What are the differences between the `JList` and `JComboBox` components?

B.5 What is a `ButtonGroup` used for?

B.6 Explain the steps taken to design a GUI.

B.7 Explain how the `FlowLayout`, `BorderLayout`, and `null` layouts arrange components.

B.8 Describe the steps taken to include a graphical component inside a `JPanel`.

B.9 What is the default behavior when an event occurs? How is the default changed?

B.10 What events generate an `ActionEvent`?

B.11 How is the window-closing event handled?

IN PRACTICE

B.12 `paintComponent` can be written for any component. Show what happens when a circle is painted in the `GUI` class instead of its own canvas.

B.13 Handle the pressing of the *Enter* key in the *y*-coordinate text field in class `GUI`.

B.14 Add a default of (0, 0) for the coordinates of a shape in class `GUI`.

PROGRAMMING PROJECTS

B.15 Write a program that can be used to input two dates and output the number of days between them. Use the `Date` class from Exercise 3.16.

B.16 Write a program that allows you to draw lines inside a canvas using the mouse. A click starts the line draw; a second click ends the line. Multiple lines can be drawn on the canvas. To do this, extend the `JPanel` class and handle mouse events by implementing `MouseListener`. You should keep an `ArrayList` that maintains the set of lines that have been drawn, and use it to guide `paintComponent`. Add a button to clear the canvas.

B.17 Write an application that contains two `GUI` objects. When actions occur in one of the `GUI` objects, the other `GUI` object saves its old state. You will need to add a `copyState` method to the `GUI` class that will copy the states of all of the `GUI` fields and redraw the canvas.

B.18 Write a program that contains a single canvas and a set of ten GUI input components that each specify a shape, color, coordinates, and size, and a check box that indicates the component is active. Then draw the union of the input components onto a canvas. Represent the GUI input component by using a class with accessor functions. The main program should have an array of these input components plus the canvas.

references

In addition to the standard set of references in Chapter 1, a complete Swing tutorial is provided in the 950-page book [1].

1. K. Walrath and M. Campione, *The JFC Swing Tutorial*, Addison-Wesley, Reading, MA, 1999.

appendix C

bitwise operators

Java provides *bitwise operators* for the bit-by-bit manipulation of integers. This process allows the packing of several Boolean objects into an integral type. The operators ~ (unary complement), << and >> (left and right shift), & (bitwise AND), ^ (bitwise exclusive OR), | (bitwise OR), and assignment operators corresponding to all these operators except unary complement. Figure C.1 illustrates the result of applying these operators.

Java provides *bitwise operators* for the bit-by-bit manipulation of integers. This process allows the packing of several Boolean objects into an integral type.

The precedence and associativity of the bitwise operators are somewhat arbitrary. When working with them, you should use parentheses.

Figure C.2 shows how the bitwise operators are used to pack information into a 16-bit integer. Such information is maintained by a typical university

```
//Pretend ints are 16 bits
int a = 3737;      // 0000111010011001
int b = a << 1;    // 0001110100110010
int c = a >> 2;    // 0000001110100110
int d = 1 << 15;   // 1000000000000000
int e = a | b;     // 0001111110111011
int f = a & b;     // 0000110000010000
int g = a ^ b;     // 0001001110101011
int h = ~g;        // 1110110001010100
```

figure C.1

Examples of bitwise operators

for a wide variety of reasons, including state and federal mandates. Many of the items require simple yes/no answers and are thus logically representable by a single bit. As Figure C.2 shows, 10 bits are used to represent 10 categories. A faculty member can have one of four possible ranks (assistant, associate, and full professor, as well as nontenure earning), and thus two bits are required. The remaining 4 bits are used to represent one of 16 possible colleges in the university.

Lines 24 and 25 show how `tim` is represented. Tim is a tenured associate professor in the College of Arts and Science. He holds a Ph.D., is a U.S. citizen, and works on the university's main campus. He is not a member of a minority group, disabled, or a veteran. He is on a 12-month contract. Thus `tim`'s bit pattern is given by

```
0011 10 1 0 1 1 1 1 0 0 0 0
```

or `0x3af0`. This bit pattern is formed by applying the OR operator on the appropriate fields.

Lines 28 and 29 show the logic used when Tim is deservedly promoted to the rank of full professor. The `RANK` category has the two rank bits set to 1 and all other bits set to 0; or

```
0000 11 0 0 0 0 0 0 0 0 0 0
```

The complement, `~RANK`, is thus

```
1111 00 1 1 1 1 1 1 1 1 1 1
```

Applying a bitwise AND of this pattern and `tim`'s current setting turns off `tim`'s rank bits, giving

```
0011 00 1 0 1 1 1 1 0 0 0 0
```

The result of the bitwise OR operator at line 29 thus makes `tim` a full professor without altering any other bits, yielding

```
0011 11 1 0 1 1 1 1 0 0 0 0
```

We learn that Tim is tenured because `tim&TENURED` is a nonzero result. We can also find out that Tim is in College #3 by shifting to the right 12 bits and then looking at the resulting low 4 bits. Note that parentheses are required. The expression is `(tim>>12)&0xf`.

```
    // Faculty Profile Fields
  static int SEX          = 0x0001; // On if female
  static int MINORITY     = 0x0002; // On if in a minority group
  static int VETERAN      = 0x0004; // On if veteran
  static int DISABLED     = 0x0008; // On if disabled
  static int US_CITIZEN   = 0x0010; // On if citizen
  static int DOCTORATE    = 0x0020; // On if holds a doctorate
  static int TENURED      = 0x0040; // On if tenured
  static int TWELVE_MON   = 0x0080; // On if 12 month contract
  static int VISITOR      = 0x0100; // On if visiting faculty
  static int CAMPUS       = 0x0200; // On if at main campus

  static int RANK         = 0x0c00; // 2 bits to represent rank
  static int ASSISTANT    = 0x0400; // Assistant Professor
  static int ASSOCIATE    = 0x0800; // Associate Professor
  static int FULL         = 0x0c00; // Full Professor

  static int COLLEGE      = 0xf000; // Represents 16 colleges
       ...
  static int ART_SCIENCE  = 0x3000; // Arts & Science: College 3
       ...

      // Later in a method initialize appropriate fields
    tim = ART_SCIENCE | ASSOCIATE | CAMPUS | TENURED |
            TWELVE_MON | DOCTORATE | US_CITIZEN;

      // Promote tim To Full Professor
    tim &= ~RANK;        // Turn all rank fields off
    tim |= FULL;         // Turn rank fields on
```

figure C.2

Packing bits for faculty profiles

index

Numeric

Symbols

A

B

C

D

E

F

G

J

K

L

M

N

P

S

T

U

V

W

X

Z